MEDIA FREEDOM UNDER THE HUMAN RIGHTS ACT

H. FENWICK

AND

G. PHILLIPSON

OXFORD
UNIVERSITY PRESS

OXFORD

UNIVERSITY PRESS

Great Clarendon Street, Oxford OX2 6DP

Oxford University Press is a department of the University of Oxford.
It furthers the University's objective of excellence in research, scholarship,
and education by publishing worldwide in

Oxford New York

Auckland   Cape Town Dar es Salaam   Hong Kong   Karachi
Kuala Lumpur Madrid Melbourne Mexico City   Nairobi
New Delhi Shanghai Taipei Toronto
With offices in
Argentina Austria Brazil Chile Czech Republic France Greece
Guatemala Hungary Italy Japan South Korea Poland Portugal
Singapore Switzerland Thailand Turkey Ukraine Vietnam

Oxford is a registered trade mark of Oxford University Press
in the UK and in certain other countries

Published in the United States
by Oxford University Press Inc., New York

ISBN 978-040-694289-0

Printed in the United Kingdom by
Lightning Source UK Ltd., Milton Keynes

CONTENTS

PART IV   MEDIA FREEDOM AND THE PROTECTION
OF PRIVACY

PART V   COPYRIGHT AND MEDIA FREEDOM

PART VI   MEDIA FREEDOM AND POLITICAL SPEECH

PREFACE

This book on media freedom goes to press at a time when freedom of expression appears to be more under threat than it has been for some years, and certainly more than was the case at the time of the inception of the Human Rights Act in 2000. The idea that there is a right not to be offended, or at least that religious sensibilities require special protection at the expense of free speech—whether on pragmatic or principled grounds—seems to be gaining currency in the post-9/11 era. This year the Blair Government pushed statues through Parliament outlawing incitement to religious hatred and creating a new offence of glorifying terrorism. As this book goes to press, the Council of Europe is holding a parliamentary hearing on freedom of expression and respect for religious beliefs,[1] with many groups lobbying for a Europe-wide blasphemy law, according to reports in British newspapers.[2] In May of this year, the Asia Gallery in London closed an exhibition portraying Hindu deities by the Indian artist P. F. Husain, after threats and complaints from Hindus and the destruction of two paintings; following the murder of the Dutch film-maker Van Gogh by a Muslim extremist in 2004 over his film on Islam and women, *Submission*, the closure in the same year of the play *Behzti*, after protests by hundreds of Sikhs, the unprecedented protests by Christians following the BBC's broadcast of the satirical *Jerry Springer: The Opera* in 2005, and, of course, the notorious worldwide protests over the publication in 2006 of cartoons depicting the Islamic prophet Mohammed, tensions and controversies surrounding speech offensive to religious feelings seem to be at a greater height than at any time since the Rushdie affair.[3] The Human Rights Act itself is under threat[3a] due to the effects of a grossly ill-informed media campaign and a governmental preparedness to use the Act as a scapegoat for executive incompetence, despite the fact that it is a Labour project.

These remarks give some indications of the duality that animates this book and which it seeks to capture. The book is about media freedom rather than freedom of expression: although the two often coincide, they can stand in conflict with each other, and the UK media themselves often oppose those liberal values associated with the defence of free speech. The fact that most free expression cases these days are media cases, and the ability thus afforded to the media to hide their true concerns behind free speech claims, sometimes goes unrecognized in judicial reasoning and elsewhere. It is no coincidence that it is the media that are the driving force behind the current attack on the Human Rights Act, despite the fact that it contains a modern

[1] See www.coe.int/T/DC/Press/NoteRedac2006/20060516_ap_en.asp

[2] See, e.g., N. Cohen, *Observer*, 14 May 2006: the article stated that Keith Porteous Wood, of the National Secular Society, who is to attend the hearing at the Council of Europe 'has files full of policy papers from religious groups agitating for the EU or UN to impose a universal blasphemy law'.

[3] See Chapter 9 for full discussion.

[3a] David Cameron, in a speech to the Centre for Policy Studies, London, on 26.6.06, committed the Conservative Party to the repeal of the HRA and its replacement with a British Bill of Rights.

free speech clause in Article 10, confirming the status of freedom of expression as a positive right rather than a negative liberty. The anti-liberal tendency of parts of the UK media, especially the tabloids *The Sun* and *The Daily Mail*, is becoming more strongly marked.[4] The Fox Channel, now received in the UK via Sky, is of course a US import, but is a strongly right-wing, partisan influence in news broadcasting. Taking account of such current illiberal trends, this book sets out to examine the divergence between media freedom and freedom of expression in the Human Rights Act era. It does not seek to defend media freedom as an unqualified good without examining the true connections between the claims of free speech and those of the media. In so doing, it acknowledges the ascendancy of the Internet as a strongly *participatory* medium, and its role in giving a voice to minority groups excluded from the mainstream media.

In this enterprise an intellectual debt must be acknowledged to Eric Barendt's seminal work, *Freedom of Speech*,[6] which takes a similar stance. However, the two books differ in aim: ours concentrates principally on domestic media freedom law, looking especially at the use of Strasbourg principles under the Human Rights Act in English courts, while Barendt's is a comparative work. This book also differs from the canon of literature on media regulation[7]—it is not concerned with regulation in terms of ownership and structure, but in relation to *content*. The book seeks above all to capture the constantly shifting and multi-faceted landscape of domestic media freedom law at the beginning of the 21st century, and in particular to analyse closely the complex and patchy impact that the Human Rights Act is having.

Part I of this book covers Article 10 of the European Convention on Human Rights and relevant aspects of the Human Rights Act, laying the foundations for the treatment of substantive topics of media law in the remainder of the book. In particular, it seeks in Chapter 2 to explore in detail the crucial, but somewhat elusive, concept of proportionality as understood at Strasbourg, and its relationship with the 'margin of appreciation' doctrine, in a critical analysis that seeks to pin down the criteria that really guide Strasbourg in considering claims of freedom of speech.

Part II covers restraints on trial-related reporting and the protection of journalistic sources, giving particular consideration to the important decision in *Ashworth*.[8] Both topics are somewhat neglected in recent academic literature. It seeks in particular to examine how far something akin to a 'shield' law for journalists can now be said to exist in this area, and also how far the law has been successful in balancing free speech and fair trial concerns in contempt cases, arguing that the balance is unsatisfactory in its drift away from Strasbourg principles, something that is particularly evident in the House of Lords' decision in *A-G v Punch*.[9]

---

[4] *The Sun* is currently—in May 2006—running a petition for the repeal of the Human Rights Act: see www.thesun.co.uk/article/0,,2-2006220181,00.html.

[5] Rupert Murdoch's just-completed purchase of the Community site MySpace for $580m may be noted in this context.

[6] Cambridge: CUP: 2nd edn., 2005.

[7] For the most recent contribution to this area, see M. Feintuck and M. Varney, *Media Regulation, Public Interest and the Law*, Edinburgh: Edinburgh University Press, 2nd edn., 2006.

[8] *Ashworth Hospital Authority v MGN Ltd* [2002] 1 WLR 2033.

[9] (2003) 1 AC 1046.

Part III examines offence, morality, and 'hate speech'. It considers the theoretical issues raised by the attempt of the law to place curbs on sexually explicit and religiously offensive speech: in particular, it examines in some detail feminist arguments against pornography, their partial adoption by Canadian courts, and the possibility and desirability of their transplantation into English law. Chapters 8 and 9, on sexually explicit and religiously offensive speech respectively, subject both English and Convention law in these areas to sustained criticism, in terms of both legal doctrine and underlying values. Chapter 9 notably provides the first sustained academic analysis of the new offences of religious hatred and of glorifying terrorism. Having evaluated the basic criminal offences that set the boundaries of explicit and offensive expression, Part III proceeds to consider their reflection in the regulation of the visual media under the Communications Act 2003. The new regime represented by that Act, and the approach of the new media regulator, Ofcom, to content regulation, is also a topic that has not received any extensive consideration so far in academic literature. Our highly critical analysis of the House of Lords' disappointing decision in *BBC v Prolife Alliance*[10] is central to these chapters on the regulation of broadcasters, films, videoworks, and the Internet.

Part IV covers the recent and dramatic post-HRA developments in the protection of privacy against the media, and the means by which the conflict with media freedom thereby raised should be resolved. Strasbourg case law in this area, in particular the recent, expansive, and controversial decision in *Von Hannover v Germany,*[11] is subject to sustained critical analysis in a separate chapter; the implications of the House of Lords' decision in *Campbell v MGN*[12] is considered in detail in Chapters 14 and 15, with particular reference to the question of whether these two decisions are reconcilable. We give separate treatment to the issue of the protection from the press of the privacy of children, particularly when caught up in the criminal justice system, in Chapter 16, as recently expounded in the House of Lords' decision in *Re S;*[13] Chapter 17 offers the first detailed analysis of the new regime for protecting privacy through broadcasting regulation, under the Communications Act 2003.

Part V explores the relationship between copyright law and freedom of expression, through a close analysis of the post-HRA case law in this area, which, Chapter 18 argues, exhibits a particularly tokenistic engagement with Strasbourg expression principles.

Part VI examines curbs on political speech, in terms of both substantive law and regulation of the broadcast media. Chapter 19 considers the still-restrictive laws on state secrets, and the limited impact upon them of the decision in *Shayler,*[14] while also considering in detail the Freedom of Information Act 2000, and the early signs of its practical effect, taking a somewhat less dismissive view of that Act's potentially liberalizing effect than other recent commentaries. Chapter 20 examines the position of the ban on political advertising in the broadcast media under the HRA, and the due

---

[10] *ProLife Alliance v BBC* [2004] 1 AC 185.   [11] [2005] 40 EHRR 1.
[12] [2004] 2 AC 457.   [13] [2005] 1 AC 593.   [14] [2003] 1 AC 247.

impartiality provisions binding on broadcasters, taking account of the fall-out from the incidents leading to the Hutton Report. It considers the case for preserving the special position of the BBC in the run-up to the renewal of its Charter at the end of this year. Chapter 21 looks in detail at developments in defamation law since *Reynolds* in comparative perspective: it centres around a substantial new analysis of the extensive Strasbourg case law in this area in the context of re-evaluating the *Reynolds* approach.

The last chapter attempts the difficult task of reaching some interim and tentative conclusions as to the impact of the Human Rights Act on media freedom. It finds that an ongoing constitutionalization of media freedom is apparent. It ends by offering the following finding: despite the weak and disappointing nature of some of the post-HRA media decisions, it is possible to see the emergent beginnings of a more sophisticated and theoretically informed media freedom jurisprudence in the post-HRA era — one that does not accept media free speech claims uncritically, but also one that is prepared to accept arguments for special media privileges where they are firmly situated in the free speech rationales.

We would like to acknowledge with gratitude the contribution of a number of people. Jonathan Griffiths, Senior Lecturer at Queen Mary, London, wrote Chapter 18 on copyright law with Ronan Deazley, Reader in Law at Birmingham University; Claire O'Brien, doctoral candidate at the European Institute, Florence, and former research fellow at the LSE, co-wrote Chapter 21 on Defamation and Political Speech with Gavin Phillipson. Kate Whetter and Lisa Schnellmann of Oxford University Press have been invariably patient, understanding, and of invaluable assistance during the various stages of the production of this book. We would also like to acknowledge most warmly the enormous levels of support and encouragement we have received from our partners, family, and friends during the long evolution of this lengthy book. Finally, we have drawn on certain of our articles in writing Chapters 13–16, and we acknowledge their original place of publication as follows:

G. PHILLIPSON, 'The Human Rights Act, "Horizontal Effect" and the Common Law: A Bang or a Whimper?' (1999) 62(6) MLR 824.

G. PHILLIPSON and H. FENWICK, 'Breach of Confidence as a Privacy Remedy in the Human Rights Act Era' [2000] 63(5) MLR 660–93.

G. PHILLIPSON, 'Transforming Breach of Confidence? Towards a Common Law Right of Privacy under the Human Rights Act', (2003) 66(5) MLR 726.

G. PHILLIPSON, 'Judicial Reasoning in Breach of Confidence Cases under the Human Rights Act: Not Taking Privacy Seriously' [2003] EHRLR (*Privacy Special*) 53.

H. FENWICK 'Clashing Rights, the Welfare of the Child and the HRA' [2004] 67(6) MLR 889.

The main body of the text was completed by January 2006, but it was possible to add some later material in March and May 2006.

Helen Fenwick and Gavin Phillipson
University of Durham and King's College London
June 2006

For Paul and for Serife

TABLE OF CASES

TABLE OF LEGISLATION

Page numbers in **bold** indicate that the text is reproduced in full. See also general index for references to Human Rights Act 1998.

1

INTRODUCTION

INTRODUCTION

In 2000 the Human Rights Act (HRA) came into force, affording the European Convention on Human Rights further effect in domestic law. Britain had ratified the Convention almost fifty years earlier, in 1951, and thereafter adhered to it at the international level. Completed in early 2006, this book represents an interim attempt to evaluate the impact of the HRA, and especially of the free expression guarantee under Article 10 of the Convention, on media freedom. A number of commentators have pointed out that the inception of Bills of Rights tends to have the effect, as in Canada, of requiring courts to grapple with justifications for free expression and its limitation, taking a more philosophical approach to legal reasoning as they attempt to resolve conflicts between media speech rights and competing societal and individual interests. This book, as the title states, examines media freedom under the Human Rights Act. It is thus concerned quite specifically with what we term 'the domestic Article 10 endeavour'—the multiplicity of issues thrown up by the attempt to interweave into a mass of existing statutory and common law provisions and restrictions governing media freedom, the uneven and often flawed jurisprudence of the European Court of Human Rights, and in so doing to adopt a more theorized approach to media freedom. We should make clear from the outset that whilst there are issues of critical importance to the overall position of the media in terms of diversity and treatment by the state in matters of taxation,[1] for example, this book is exclusively concerned with the law governing the *output* of the media. It does not therefore deal with issues of media regulation such as governance within the BBC and cross-media ownership (and readers are referred to the extensive literature on that subject),[2] but it does include comprehensive and substantial analysis of the new regime for the regulation of the broadcast media in terms of content, under the Communications Act 2003.[3]

---

[1] On which, see E. Barendt, *Freedom of Speech*, 2nd edn., Oxford: OUP, 2005, at 427–8.

[2] See T. Gibbons, *Media Regulation*, 2nd edn., London: Sweet and Maxwell, 1998; Goldberg, Prosser and Verhulst, *Regulating the Changing Media*, 1st edn., Oxford: OUP, 1998; M. Feintuck, *Media Regulation, Public Interest and the Law*, Edinburgh: Edinburgh University Press, 1998.

[3] See Chapters 10–12 (broadly on standards aimed at protecting against offensive speech in Broadcasting); Chapter 17 (on measures aimed at avoiding undue interference with privacy); and Chapter 19—broadly on 'due impartiality' requirements and the ban on political advertising.

This book is about *media* freedom under the Human Rights Act 1998. Thus it is not about freedom of expression *per se*, although, clearly, almost all free expression jurisprudence is, today, media jurisprudence. This Introduction—and the book as a whole—challenges the assumptions quite often made about the harmony between the rationales underpinning freedom of expression and the claims of the media for freedom from various forms of interference. It questions the unthinking assumption that media freedom is an unqualified good, and argues that the relationship between the two interests is often of a deeply complex and problematic nature, when looked at under closer analysis. The media often appear Janus-faced: on the one hand, they can be characterized as the fearless guardians of the people, acting as watch-dogs and safeguarding democracy. There continue to be notable instances of the media carrying out this enormously important role, in relation in particular to the decision of the Blair Government to join the United States in overthrowing the Saddam regime in Iraq and its support for the US 'War on Terror' generally. As this book went to press, the media were hard at work uncovering the denied Government connivance in US 'extraordinary rendition' missions, taking suspected terrorists to places in which they could be questioned under torture.[4] Only the media have the resources to carry out such investigations and the capacity to put their findings before a mass audience, and it is no part of this book's purpose to question or devalue their vital function in so doing. On the other hand, the media are prepared on occasions to tear lives apart by invading privacy, or destroying reputations,[5] and (more rarely) to render fair criminal trials impossible, through prejudicial coverage, often largely or wholly motivated by commercial concerns.[6] Moreover, as argued more fully in Chapter 15, such stories in themselves cheapen and impoverish journalistic culture. As one strong defender of media freedom, which was wholly opposed to the victories for privacy in the *Campbell* case, concedes:

The fact that public debate is increasingly concentrated on private life is problematic. The rise of personally orientated and confessional styles of journalism undermines broad-ranging and journalistic public debate—the foundation of a progressive, open democratic culture.[7]

Before turning to consider the interface between media freedom and free speech values, and considering the stance that this book will take towards it, it is necessary to point out that even to speak of the 'media' as though the term could sensibly encompass all the bodies or persons covered by it, necessitates a conscious over-simplification. The term covers a spectrum of bodies, from, on the one hand,

---

[4] See, for example: 'Torture Flights: What No 10 knew and tried to cover up', *The Guardian*, 19 January 2006.

[5] See Chapters 14, 16, and 21.   [6] See Chapter 6.

[7] 'Press Freedom: it's not trivial', http://www.spiked-online.com/Articles/00000006D8E3.htm. For discussion of the *Campbell* case, see Chapter 14.

powerful international corporate players, such as News Corporation, run by Rupert Murdoch, 'a global broadcasting empire, worth £30 billion',[8] to, on the other, individuals using the internet to set up a 'blog', or small groups of people running a magazine with a tiny circulation on a meagre budget. The interests of such bodies should not be assumed *a priori* to be the same. Further, within one media body a wide range of interests may be at work, sometimes in opposition to each other; to take an obvious example, a reporter's free expression may be stifled due to editorial interference.[9] So when the term 'the media' is used below, it is accepted that it in itself is highly problematic.

At this point something more must be said about the position of the internet. It is the first democratic mass communications media, allowing individual speakers to reach audiences that may run into hundreds of thousands with relative ease: it takes very little time or effort or resources to set up a Live Journal on the internet—that is, to obtain web space in which to post thoughts on political, cultural, or personal events. Some websites steadily acquire a following and have viewing figures in excess of the circulation figures of small magazines. The rise of Google and other search engines has enabled this. The importance of this change can hardly be over-estimated: it means that the public do not have to rely solely upon the mass communications media in order to obtain information and engage in debate, thereby putting themselves in the hands of powerful groups with a particular agenda, although such media still represent the most important means by which people obtain such information.[10] The internet also has a globalizing effect—in other words, a range of perspectives may be encountered from around the world. The internet empowers the individual to use expression in a meaningful and effective way rather than merely in the pub to a couple of friends. It also places the 'blogger' with a website in something close to the position of the mass media in terms of communication.

Thus when this book speaks of the media and challenges its position in relation to the individual speaker, it must be borne in mind that the remarks tend to be most relevant to large commercial media concerns. The position of the individual artist or

---

[8] 'Rupert Murdoch: Bigger than Kane', BBC news report, 22 July 2002: http://news.bbc.co.uk/1/hi/uk/2162658.stm.

[9] For a case that arose in Germany on this point, see *Spiegel*, 20 BVerfGE 162 (1966), discussed by Barendt, op cit, at 443–4.

[10] One survey in the US found as follows: 'The number of Americans relying on political news from the Internet grew six-fold between the 1996 and 2004 presidential campaigns. This growth was achieved by a sharp drop in the influence of newspapers. The *Chicago Sun-Times* reported that 18% of American adults cited the Internet as one of their two main sources of news about the presidential races, compared with only 3% in 1996. The reliance on TV grew only slightly to 78 percent, up from 72 percent. Meanwhile, the influence of newspapers dropped sharply to 39% last year, from 60 percent in 1996, according to the joint, telephone-based survey from the Pew Research Center for the People and the Press and the Pew Internet and American Life Project. Twenty-eight percent said they primarily used news pages of AOL, Yahoo, Google News and other online services, which carry dispatches from traditional news sources like the AP and Reuters.' Source: IT Manager's Journal, 7 March 2005: http://eyeonit.itmanagersjournal.com/article.pl?sid=05/03/07/1628248&tid=105&tid=112.

the freelance journalist will be distinguished from that of such concerns at certain pertinent points.[11] It will also be recognized that in certain instances, an individual journalist, albeit one working for a large organization, may be pursuing a story of great significance to that individual personally, as well as to the wider audience. In such a case, she can readily be equated with an individual speaker, in terms of her free speech rights.

This Introduction begins by considering the changing position of the law of media freedom in the UK constitutional order. It traces the process of change that has occurred by means of the development of common law principle, the influence of Article 10 of the European Convention on Human Rights, and now of the Human Rights Act. It seeks to sketch some of the layers of complexity that the apparently simple task of applying Strasbourg jurisprudence under the HRA actually entails—a theme returned to repeatedly throughout this book. It also indicates why we believe that any straightforward notion that a new era of media freedom is dawning under the HRA is a naïve and even potentially damaging one. It moves on to consider the classic free speech rationales and then examines their interface with media freedom, identifying four models for that interface that are recognized in free speech jurisprudence and Bills of Rights from around the world. The perspective that will be adopted throughout this book is outlined, to lay the basis for the discussion in the substantive chapters that follow.

CONSTITUTIONALIZING MEDIA FREEDOM

In broad terms, this book is about the constitutionalization of areas of media law directly affecting the freedom to broadcast or publish. Historically, in English law, there was no such thing as 'media freedom' as a constitutional or legal concept: Dicey said, ' "Freedom of discussion" is in England little else than the right to write or say anything which a jury, consisting of twelve shopkeepers, think it expedient should be said or written.'[12] It was indeed crucial to the Diceyan paradigm that, insofar as press freedom was protected, it was a result of ordinary court judgments determining the rights of private citizens. In some areas of law affecting the media, where the media sought to make claims that could not be made by individual speakers, they were denied completely—perhaps the most notorious example is Lord Wilberforce's trenchant assertion in a major case on protection of journalists' sources: 'This case does not touch upon the freedom of the press even at its periphery'.[13] More typically, under the traditional English view, freedom of the press was simply the absence of a

---

[11] See e.g. Chapter 2 at 106–7.

[12] A. V. Dicey, *Introduction to the Study of the Law of the Constitution*, 10th edn. London: Macmillan, 1959, Chapter VI.

[13] *British Steel Corp v Granada Television Ltd* [1981] AC 1096, 116, see further Chapter 7.

prior system of censorship, but other than that, simply a negative liberty. As Lord Wilberforce observed in the same case:

Freedom of the press imports, generally, freedom to publish without pre-censorship, subject always to the laws relating to libel, official secrets, sedition and other recognised inhibitions.[14]

As the above passage suggests, 'the law of media freedom' consisted merely of a mechanical application of the law deriving from statute and common law precedents; and media freedom, like any other negative liberty, was simply what was left over after the scope of the restrictions had been determined. Often there was an application of common law precedents or a mechanistic approach to statutory interpretation, which was devoid of principle in the sense of recognizing that any important issues were at stake requiring a departure from such normal judicial technique. Numerous examples of such an approach are instanced in Chapter 8, when discussing cases concerning obscenity law and in Chapter 9 on blasphemy; it may also be perceived in pre-HRA cases on disclosure of journalist sources, discussed in Chapter 7.

The various free expression justifications put forward by various commentators[15]— a number of which have found widespread acceptance—found little recognition in common law free expression jurisprudence until the period immediately prior to the inception of the Human Rights Act—the late 1990s. This can be illustrated by consideration of a number of significant and well-known decisions mainly from the 1970s and 1980s, considered in Chapters 8 and 19, including *Knuller v DPP*,[16] *Lemon*,[17] *Ponting*,[18] and the *Spycatcher* cases.[19] The historical tendency of UK courts, exemplified in these decisions, has been to treat problems relating to the legal limits of media freedom without an awareness of the deeper human rights issues that they raise. The focus has been on the restriction in question, rather than on the freedom of expression issues.

Indeed, when one examined UK law in this area in the pre-HRA era, one confronted a mass of common law and statutory restrictions on freedom of expression and on expressive activities associated with it, such as marches or demonstrations. Traditionally, as explored in Civil Liberties texts of the 1980s or early 1990s, in order to determine how far freedom of expression was protected, it was necessary to consider the width of these restrictions in order to determine how much of an area of freedom was left within which expression could be exercised.[20]

However, in the period immediately preceding the inception of the HRA, a

[14] Ibid.   [15] Discussed below at 12 *et seq.*

[16] [1973] AC 435; [1972] 3 WLR 143; (1972) 56 Cr App R 633, HL.

[17] [1979] AC 617; [1979] 2 WLR 281; [1979] 1 All ER 898, HL.   [18] [1985] Crim LR 318.

[19] Particularly *A-G v Times Newspapers* [1992] 7 AC 191; *A-G v Guardian Newspapers Ltd* [1987] 3 All ER 316.

[20] See C. Gearty and K. Ewing, *Freedom under Thatcher*, Oxford: Oxford Paperbacks, 1990; H. Fenwick, *Civil Liberties*, 1st edn. London: Cavendesh, 1993; D. Feldman, *Civil Liberties*, 1st edn. Oxford: OUP, 1993. See also C. Gearty and K. Ewing, *The Struggle for Civil Liberties*, Oxford: Clarendon, 2000, for a perspective on the preceding era.

common law right of free expression was recognized in a group of cases which showed common tendencies: *Derbyshire*[21] was a forerunner of such decisions, as was *R v Central Independent Television plc.*[22] Just before the HRA came into force, the even more significant decisions in *ex parte Simms*[23] and *Reynolds*[24] were handed down by the House of Lords. Freedom of expression appeared to be acquiring the status of a positive right as opposed to a residual liberty, with consequent changes in the structure and nature of judicial reasoning.[25] In these decisions it will be argued that the judiciary sought to theorize domestic free expression jurisprudence and showed an awareness of the issues with which judges in other jurisdictions, including the US and Canada, had been grappling for much longer. It is readily arguable that the imminence of the HRA provided the impetus for this change.

However, the position of the UK in relation to the European Convention on Human Rights (ECHR) under the HRA does not parallel the position in jurisdictions such as Canada, for a number of reasons. Firstly, the domestic courts and legislation had already been influenced by the Convention jurisprudence, either as a result of successful applications to Strasbourg or indirectly, as a result of a reliance on Convention jurisprudence in domestic decision-making.[26] Thus the position was that two bodies of expression jurisprudence ran parallel to each other prior to the inception of the HRA, the one influencing the other. Secondly, the HRA brought to bear on domestic law an established body of jurisprudence, itself problematic. Thirdly, the Convention cannot be seen as the equivalent of a domestic Bill of Rights—the judges have to construct one out of it, if so minded. These points are developed more fully in what follows.

It is important to understand, therefore, that what might be seen as the 'cure' for the situation of media freedom law prior to 2000, namely the application, via the Human Rights Act, of a modern free speech guarantee, Article 10 ECHR, is itself deeply problematic on a number of levels. Strasbourg's speech jurisprudence under Article 10 is often notably under-theorized.[27] The reasoning is frequently brief, and lacking in rigour. In particular, the effects of the doctrine of the margin of appreciation result in some decisions in an almost complete failure to examine in any meaningful way the proportionality of restrictions upon expression adopted by states.[28] Sometimes, indeed, the main thrust of the judgment is devoted to explaining why the Court should *not* use Article 10 to interfere with the decision of the national authorities in the particular case. Great variation in the intensity of review may be discerned; no single coherent account of proportionality can be derived from the Strasbourg jurisprudence. These points are explored in detail in Chapter 2, which is strongly critical of aspects of the Court's Article 10 jurisprudence.

It is important to note, however, that as just indicated, the Strasbourg Court *cannot* be equated with a national Constitutional Court: it is an international court of

---

[21] [1993] AC 534.   [22] [1994] 3 All ER 641.

[23] *R v Secretary of State for the Home Department ex parte Simms* [2000] 2 AC 115.

[24] *Reynolds v Times Newspapers* [1999] 4 All ER 609.   [25] See Chapter 3 at 109.

[26] Ibid.   [27] See generally Chapter 2.

[28] See e.g. Chapter 2 at 56–60 and Chapter 8 at 416–19.

review—and the only successful international court of human rights in existence. Its jurisprudence cannot therefore be expected to serve the purpose of that of a constitutional court in terms of detail, rigour, or comprehensiveness. This is in part due to the origins, institutional underpinnings, and *raison d'être* of the Strasbourg system. Its purpose is to provide a basic level of protection for human rights—a 'floor' not a 'ceiling' of rights—across a vast and disparate area, an area with hugely differing cultural sensitivities, and one which has grown dramatically recently, to include moreover states that are deeply problematic in human rights terms, such as Turkey and Russia. This may explain why, for example, its jurisprudence is so weak in relation to what may be termed 'offensive speech' relating to sexuality and religious beliefs, discussed in Chapters 2, 8, 9, and 10. The sexual and religious instincts are simply not susceptible to rationality: there may be an attachment in particular communities to certain standards, beliefs, or customs that is founded in instinct and tradition rather than any rational process.[29] The Court may at some level recognize this—that if it merely imposed rationally based standards in such sensitive and highly charged areas[30] it could incur disproportionate opprobrium, damaging its capacity to intervene successfully and effectively in other areas. Pragmatically speaking, the view may be taken that defending the rights of pornographers, or even of film makers, to produce films satirizing religion,[31] has to take second place to its key enterprise of controlling state abuse of power.

Strasbourg has also been disappointing at times in relation to national security concerns, although there are notable exceptions.[32] In this case, this may be due to the origins and underpinnings of the Convention system. The Convention system, operating as it does at an inter-governmental level, can only subsist by holding on to the allegiance of governments, rather than peoples. Its origins are completely different from those of Bills of Rights adopted in a particular country, over which the people feel a certain ownership.[33] The ECHR owes its origins to decisions of states to sign up to it. In the UK, for example, the decision to accede to the Convention was never even approved by Parliament, let alone by referendum.[34] Therefore the Court has above all to retain the loyalty of *governments*, rather than of the peoples of Europe. Governments who object to a decision of the Court have various options open to them. They can respond to an adverse judgment by furious public denunciation of it—as the UK Government did, following *McCann v UK*;[35] this may well weaken the legitimacy of the

---

[29] See the Court's statements on this matter, discussed in Chapter 2 at 73 and Chapter 9 at 493.

[30] Consider, for example, the reaction of the worldwide Muslim community to the publication of Salman Rushdie's *Satanic Verses*, discussed in Chapter 1, R. Abel, *Speech and Respect*, London: Sweet and Maxwell, 1994.

[31] See Chapter 8 at 488–94.

[32] E.g. in *McCann v UK* (1995) 21 EHRR 97. See the discussion in Chapter 20 at 954–5.

[33] See below in relation to the Canadian Charter.

[34] For an account, see A. Lester, 'UK Acceptance of the Strasbourg jurisprudence: what really went on in Whitehall in 1965' (1998) *PL* 237.

[35] (1995) 21 EHRR 97. This was the decision in which the Court found a breach of Article 2 in relation to the notorious 'Death on the Rock' incident, in which members of the SAS shot dead four IRA members on Gibraltar.

Court in the eyes of members of the public. Following such a judgment, they can withdraw from some of the rights via derogation, as in the *Brogan* case.[36] There is also the possibility of withdrawal, followed by re-entry, but with a reservation in relation to a right or an aspect of it: the UK Government has actively floated this as a possibility in relation to the *Chahal*[37] principle deriving from Article 3, which the Government claims is hindering its fight against international terrorism.[38] Finally, of course, there is the 'nuclear option' of complete withdrawal—exercised so far only by the Greek Colonel's regime in the 1960s. Given the relatively fragile position of the Convention, Strasbourg no doubt feels that it has to tread cautiously at times, to avoid wholly alienating the loyalty of governments, upon which its continuing existence hangs.

It is important, therefore, to be realistic about the limitations of the Strasbourg speech jurisprudence, lest it be thought that its 'application' in English law can cure all our current speech ills. Indeed, application of the case-law without a keen awareness of its limitations can actually have the effect of *legitimizing* areas of law that were previously seen as increasingly untenable. For example, the finding by Strasbourg that the UK law of blasphemy does not violate the Convention, despite its openly discriminatory nature and its lack of either a public good defence, or requirement of specific intent,[39] gives an appearance of human rights respectability to the offence, allowing the government to claim that it is Convention-compliant, and does not therefore require reform or abolition. Much the same may be said of findings in relation to other countries that have used very broadly drafted obscenity laws against artists:[40] they appear to lend respectability to the UK's outdated obscenity laws.[41]

For all the reasons canvassed above, we are not confronted under the HRA with an era in which the judges can straightforwardly set about the task of interpreting and applying the Strasbourg jurisprudence, thus *by itself* creating a new era of media freedom reform. The position of the UK under the HRA is indeed very different from that of countries such as Canada, which adopted a Charter of Rights, in the run-up to which there was a genuine popular debate. The Charter enjoys consistently high levels of support amongst the Canadian people, and commentators remark upon a genuine sense of 'ownership' by Canadians of 'their' Charter. As Peter Hogg notes:

---

[36] *Brogan and Others v UK* (1988), Series A no. 145–B.

[37] (1996) 23 EHRR 413. That is, the principle that a signatory to the ECHR is not only prohibited from directly inflicting treatment contrary to Article 3, but may not deport a person to a country where there is a real risk of such treatment.

[38] The Government has floated at various points the idea of either denouncing the Convention and re-entering it while entering a reservation to Article 3, so that it can deport suspects to countries despite a risk of torture; it also suggested introducing legislation directing judges how to interpret Article 3 so that they would prioritize national security over individual rights in this context: see 'There is no justification for this: Blair is showing the arrogance of Charles I', *The Guardian*, 12 August 2005. For an analysis, see A. Lester and K. Beattie, 'Risking Torture' (2005) 6 *EHRLR* 265.

[39] *Wingrove v UK* (1996) 24 EHRR 1. The offence only covers the Christian religion: see generally Chapter 9.

[40] See e.g. *Müller v Switzerland* (1991) 13 EHRR 212.   [41] As argued generally in Chapter 8.

[The Charter's] adoption in 1982 was the product of a widespread public debate, in which the inevitable risks of judicial review played a prominent role. Admittedly, the Charter was never put to and approved by a popular referendum, but it has always commanded widespread popular support. A poll taken in 1999, on the heels of two controversial Charter decisions by the Supreme Court of Canada, showed 82 per cent of those polled saying that the Charter was 'a good thing', and 61 per cent saying that the courts, not the legislatures, should have the last word when the courts decide that a law is unconstitutional.[42]

The same can be said of the US Constitution, which is accorded almost religious reverence by the American people.[43] The position of the HRA in the UK is far more precarious: the main opposition party, the Conservative Party, has regularly floated the possibility of repealing it, if it cannot be made to work more satisfactorily—that is, watered down. In 2005, the then Conservative Leader, Michael Howard, strongly endorsed the notorious prediction of Lord McCluskey, arguing that the HRA had established 'a field day for crackpots, a pain in the neck for judges and legislators and a gold mine for lawyers'.[44] The modification or repeal of the HRA was indeed a manifesto pledge of the Conservative Party at the 2005 election. Moreover, the very Government that introduced the HRA exhibits at times at best a lukewarm attachment to its own project.[45] The attitude of many of the judiciary to it remains deeply ambivalent; it can not only be seen as an unwelcome foreign import, but also as an intrusion into—in the judicial view—the impressive common law tradition of free speech protection.[46] In this respect it appears to be no coincidence that there was a brief burst of strong free speech judgments in 1999–2000, in particular *ex parte Simms*:[47] it might appear that the judiciary were determined that the common law should not be found to uphold lesser standards than the Convention, at the moment of incorporation.[48]

It is also the case that, in addition to the difficulties inherent in the Strasbourg jurisprudence, and the lack of solidly based political and popular support for the HRA, that instrument itself is highly problematic. As discussed in Chapter 3, not only is it analytically and doctrinally ambiguous in some key areas—those of horizontal effect, the ambit of section 3(1), and the public authority definition[49]—but it is also hotly contested at a normative level. There is doubt not only as to the basic desirability of incorporation of the Convention,[50] but more importantly as to the approach that should be taken to its interpretation, in terms of the balance to be struck between the

---

[42] P. Hogg, 'The Charter Revolution: Is It Undemocratic?' (2002) 12 *Constitutional Forum* 1 (footnotes omitted). For a more sceptical view, see F. L. Morton and R. Knopff, *Charter Revolution and the Court Party*, Peterborough: Broadview Press, 2000.

[43] See e.g. 'Americans Proud of U.S. and Constitution, but Want Children Taught the Bad with the Good'—findings of a comprehensive survey of the attitudes of American citizens to their country and constitution: see http://www.publicagenda.org/press/press_release_detail.cfm?list=48.

[44] *The Telegraph*, 10 August 2005.   [45] See above, note 38.   [46] See e.g. Chapter 3.

[47] *R v Secretary of State for the Home Department ex parte Simms* [2000] 2 AC 115.

[48] See Chapter 3 at 109.   [49] See Chapter 3 for discussion of these issues.

[50] See e.g. C. Gearty and K. Ewing, 'Rocky Foundations for Labour's New Rights' (1997) 2 *EHRLR* 146. Gearty has since modified his position to one which endorses the HRA, provided it is read in the way he suggests in note 51 below; Ewing, in contrast remains an unrepentant critique: see 'The Futility of the Human Rights Act' (2004) *PL* 829.

power of the judiciary and that of Parliament and the Executive.[51] These points are explored in detail in Chapter 3, but, briefly, the HRA, as an incorporating instrument, gives rise to ambiguity at a number of levels. First of all, there is the need to interpret the Strasbourg jurisprudence itself, to draw out the principles to be applied, by no means an easy task in many instances, given the characteristics of that jurisprudence described above. Second, there is sometimes a question whether to apply the case law in domestic law at all—it is non-binding and there may be arguments in particular cases that it should not be followed.[52] In particular, this may be argued where a Strasbourg decision follows and appears to contradict a decision of an appellate court on the same point of interpretation of Convention articles.[53] As discussed in Chapter 14, precisely this problem is raised in relation to the crucial decision on privacy in *Von Hannover v Germany*,[54] which immediately followed, and appears inconsistent in some respects with, the decision of the House of Lords in *Campbell v MGN Ltd*.[55] (In another field, an even clearer clash is evident in relation to the House of Lords decision in *Qazi*,[56] on the scope of Article 8, which was rapidly contradicted on point by the decision of the Strasbourg court in *Connors v United Kingdom*:[57] it was held by the Court of Appeal that courts below the House of Lords were bound to follow the decision of that House.)[58] Third, even if agreement can be reached as to the principles to be applied from the Strasbourg jurisprudence, there is still the vexed question as to the extent that the courts should defer to a 'discretionary area of judgment', enjoyed by the executive and/or Parliament, and as to its relation (if any) with the international law doctrine of the margin of appreciation.[59] Finally, if dealing with a statute, there is the question whether its wording and overall scheme allows the courts to change its interpretation to achieve compliance, or whether instead a declaration of incompatibility should be made. This involves determining the scope of section 3(1) HRA, the crucial duty to interpret legislation compatibly with the Convention rights, if possible. As discussed in Chapter 3, the proper approach to this provision has given rise to a great deal of academic and judicial disagreement.[60] Even where the judges agree in deciding that existing domestic law is incompatible as it stands, there still remains the question of the extent to which it needs to change in order to become compatible.[61]

We suggest in Chapter 3 that the HRA, through these layers of complexity, allows the judges plenty of scope to adopt either an 'activist' or 'minimalist' approach to judicial reform of domestic law:[62] broadly speaking, the latter would seek merely to achieve

---

[51] Thus Professor Gearty has argued for an approach to the HRA which maximizes those aspects of it which preserve both the unfettered sovereignty of Parliament and a measure of discretion of the executive in relation to human rights issues: see his *Principles of Human Rights Adjudication*, Oxford: OUP, 2003.

[52] Under section 2(1) HRA it must be taken into account, but is not binding. This issue is discussed further in Chapter 3; see also R. Masterman, 'Taking the Strasbourg Jurisprudence into Account: Developing a "Municipal Law of Human Rights" Under the Human Rights Act' (2005) 54 *ICLQ* 907.

[53] See dicta in Chapter 3 at note 230.   [54] [2004] EMLR 21.

[55] [2004] 2 AC 457; See Chapter 8 at 763–9.

[56] *Harrow London Borough Council v Qazi* [2004] 1 AC 983, HL(E).   [57] (2004) 40 EHRR 189.

[58] *Leeds City Council v Price and Others* [2005] 1 WLR 1825.   [59] See Chapter 3 at 145–51.

[60] See 157–63.   [61] See e.g. Chapter 8 at 763–79.   [62] See Chapter 3 at 141–51.

minimal compliance with the Strasbourg case law; the former would seek to build upon it, and deploy more general Convention principles, in order to construct something much more like a Bill of Rights approach. We also, in Chapter 2,[63] suggest reasons why domestic courts may appropriately employ a more consistent and rigorous standard of proportionality than has Strasbourg. The issue of judicial activism can raise profound issues of political philosophy which we do not seek to address in this work.[64] Rather, we confine ourselves to a more practical observation. Unlike in the fields, say, of family or discrimination law, in which a pretty comprehensive legislative code has been laid down by Parliament, the area of media freedom is one in which Parliament has tended to leave the hard choices to the judiciary. The most striking example considered in this book is the whole issue of the horizontal effect of the Convention rights under the HRA,[65] a critical issue for media law, which, we argue, was left almost deliberately ambiguous by the Government and Parliament, forcing its resolution upon the judges. In particular, the HRA left the immensely controversial issue of the development of privacy rights against the press in the hands of the courts, primarily through its refusal to resolve the horizontal effect issue, fobbing off a worried press with section 12 of the Act.[66] But this example is not the only one, although it is the most significant. The imprecise wording of parts of the Contempt of Court Act 1981[67] and of the Obscene Publications Act 1959[68] are further, notable examples of this tendency. The strong presence of the common law in media free expression law is further evidence of this tendency. The common law has—in effect—nothing now to say in relation to discrimination or family and child law. In contrast, statutory incursion into media freedom issues has frequently either been based on common law powers, as under provisions of the Contempt of Court Act,[69] or has left them intact, as did certain provisions of the Obscene Publications Act.[70] The most striking example, however, is the Copyright, Designs and Patents Act 1988, which contains a statutory concession to the effect that the rights granted under the Act do not affect 'any rule of law preventing or restricting the enforcement of copyright, on grounds of public interest or otherwise'.[71] The Act therefore preserved, but did not clarify or strengthen, the pre-existing public interest defence to infringement of copyright. There remain archaic common law offences, in the fields of obscenity, indecency, and blasphemy, which Parliament has persistently refused to reform or repeal.[72] Given the above, the judiciary has no option but to shoulder a very significant degree of responsibility in relation to the future development of the law of media freedom under the HRA—that job has indeed in many areas been given or left to them (expressly or impliedly) by Parliament.

---

[63] At 40.   [64] For a recent view sceptical of judicial activism under the HRA, see Gearty, op cit.

[65] That is, the extent to which the rights would have effect as between private parties, in the absence of any relevant statute. See Chapter 3.

[66] See Chapter 3 at 123–6.   [67] In particular, s 2(2) and s 10: see Chapter 5.

[68] See Chapter 8.   [69] s 10, CCA 1981.   [70] s 6(a) and s 1 OPA 1959.

[71] s 171(3) CDPA: see Chapter 18.

[72] These are discussed in Chapter 8 and Chapter 9.

In the UK the judiciary are slowly (and with difficulty) taking on this task, building a post-HRA jurisprudential framework for the use of the HRA itself and for the acceptance of the Strasbourg jurisprudence into domestic law. As it develops, it is possible to discern in it resistance at times to the HRA mechanisms and to the jurisprudence;[73] at others they are embraced with seeming enthusiasm.[74] Where there is a clash between a domestic jurisprudential stance and a Strasbourg one, the domestic courts have at times shown a tendency to avoid confronting the implications of the conflict.[75]

Thus a major theme of this book concerns the uncovering of the sheer complexity of what we term the domestic Article 10 endeavour. At present, the attempt is being made by applicants under the HRA to use the Convention as a liberalizing mechanism acting on domestic law, in order to achieve greater media freedom. This means using highly problematic case law which at times fails the basic tenets of constitutional review, especially in terms of proportionality[76] in order to reform a whole mass of common law and statutory restrictions formulated at a time when, as discussed above, there was no conception of media freedom as a positive right. Our positive aim is to point out some of the main pitfalls in this endeavour in order to render the process as fruitful as possible.

FREE EXPRESSION JUSTIFICATIONS

All countries which have a Bill of Rights protect freedom of expression because it is perceived as one of the most fundamental rights. But why should this particular freedom be viewed as so worthy of protection? Four main justifications for offering protection to free speech have been offered and will be considered in this section in turn. In each case, an indication will be given as to the kinds of expression the various justifications will support, because all the theories will not be relevant to all forms of expression. We would stress at the outset that our aim in this section is a modest one. We are not seeking to provide fresh insights into the justifications themselves, at the level of political philosophy. There is a rich theoretical literature on this subject, including prominent works by Dworkin,[77] Schauer,[78] Greenwalt,[79] and, in this country, Raz[80] and Barendt.[81] What we are seeking to do in this book as a whole is to provide original insights in terms of the *application* of these justifications to the domestic

---

[73] This has been particularly evident in the field of copyright law: see Chapter 18.

[74] As is apparent, we argue, in Chapter 14, in the decision in *Campbell v MGN* [2004] 2 AC 457.

[75] See e.g. Chapter 6 at 291–301. See also the discussion of *Shayler* [2003] 1 AC 247 in Chapter 19 at 939–45.

[76] See above notes 27 and 28.

[77] In particular, 'Do we have a right to pornography?' in *A Matter of Principle*, Cambridge, Mass.: Harvard University Press (hereafter HUP), 1985; see also *Freedom's Law*, New York: OUP, 1996.

[78] *Free Speech: A Philosophical Enquiry*, Cambridge: CUP, 1982.

[79] K. Greenwalt, 'Free speech justifications' (1989) 89 *Columbia L Rev* 119.

[80] 'Free Expression and Personal Identification' (1991) 11 *OJLS* 303.   [81] Op cit, Chapter 1.

Article 10 endeavour: the gradualist judicial reform of UK media freedom law through the interweaving into it of principles derived from the Strasbourg case law. This section is therefore intended merely as a brief introduction to the key principles underlying the various rationales.

Initially, it should be noted that three of the justifications are inherently more contingent and therefore more precarious than the first. These three justifications—the arguments for the opportunity to arrive at the truth through free discussion, for the necessity of free speech to enable meaningful participation in democracy, and for individual self-fulfilment—all ultimately argue that speech is to be valued not for its own sake, but because it will lead to some other outcome we think desirable; thus, they may be characterized as teleological or instrumental justifications. If, therefore, when considering a particular form of speech, a persuasive argument can be made out that permitting the speech is likely to achieve a result antithetical to the desired outcome, protection will no longer be justifiable. By contrast, as will be seen below, it is inherent in the first main justification for free speech—the argument from moral autonomy—that arguments about the likely effects of permitting the particular speech are not relevant to the question whether the justification applies—although clearly, such arguments may still be relevant in deciding whether the speech should nonetheless be abrogated. The discussion below is meant to provide only a brief overview of the main rationales; their concrete implication for the weighting of speech as against other interests, and particularly against other individual rights, such as privacy, are considered in the substantive chapters of this work.

THE ARGUMENT FROM MORAL AUTONOMY

This argument is well known as one of the key liberal deontological justifications for human rights in general and so will only briefly be rehearsed here. Ultimately, whether the particular argument used is Rawls's hypothetical social contract[82] or Dworkin's basic postulate of the State's duty to treat its citizens with equal concern and respect,[83] this justification for free expression is centred around the liberal conviction that matters of moral choice must be left to the individual. In either case, the conclusion reached is that the State offends against human dignity,[84] or treats certain citizens with contempt, if the coercive power of the law is used to force the moral convictions of some upon others. The argument perhaps has a more common and conspicuous application with regard to sexual autonomy and so is often disregarded in arguments about free speech.[85] The justification is less contingent than the others,

---

[82] As postulated in *A Theory of Justice*, Harvard University Press, 1971.

[83] First put forward in *Taking Rights Seriously*, Harvard University Press, 1977. The relevant chapter 'Rights as Trumps' is reprinted in J. Waldron (ed.), *Theories of Rights*, Oxford: OUP, 1984.

[84] Barendt makes the point, however, that unlimited speech may also assault human dignity; see below note 110.

[85] Barendt, for example, finds that the general freedom to moral autonomy is 'of little help' in relation to supporting free speech claims, op cit, at 15.

as mentioned above, because any restriction on what an individual is allowed to read, see, or hear clearly amounts to an interference with her right to judge such matters for herself. Thus, the argument consistently defends virtually all kinds of speech and other forms of expression,[86] whereas the arguments from truth and democracy will tend to have a somewhat less comprehensive range of application. Since the argument also sets up freedom of speech as a strong 'trump' right,[87] or as part of the individual's claim to inviolability,[88] the right in both cases overrides normal utilitarian arguments about the benefit or detriment to society of the particular form of speech under consideration.[89] By contrast, the justifications from democracy and truth both set out goals for society as a whole and, therefore, would seem reasonably to allow abrogation of speech in the interests of other public concerns which may be immediately and directly damaged by the exercise of speech. As Barendt puts it, in discussing the argument from truth: 'a government worried that inflammatory speech may provoke disorder is surely entitled to elevate immediate public order considerations over the long term intellectual development of the man on the Clapham omnibus'.[90]

THE ARGUMENT FROM TRUTH

The most famous exposition of this argument is to be found in J. S. Mill's *On Liberty*.[91] The basic thesis is that truth is most likely to emerge from free and uninhibited discussion and debate. It is worth noting that this is a proposition about a causal relationship between two phenomena—discussion and truth—which of course has never been conclusively verified. However, its general truth is taken as virtually axiomatic in the Western democracies and forms the basic assumption underpinning the whole approach of reasoned, sceptical debate which is the particular hallmark of Western civilization. Such a stance may be contrasted with that taken in societies which consider that there already exists and is known a total system of values, which need only be consistently expounded and enforced for society to reach its optimum state. Islamic theocracies currently provide the most obvious example. Previously, the Communist dictatorships of the Eastern bloc would have come most readily to mind. Nonetheless, the crude assumption that more free speech will always lead to more truth has been attacked by certain feminist writers, who consider that the free availability of pornography leads not to the revelation of truth, but to the creation of false and damaging images of women or, more controversially, that pornography actually

---

[86] It also covers material which could only doubtfully be classified as speech, e.g., photographic pornography.

[87] In Ronald Dworkin's well-known phrase; see note 83 above.

[88] The idea is Rawls's; see note 82 above.

[89] See Dworkin, op cit, for a discussion of justifications for allowing strong rights to be overridden.

[90] Op cit, at 9.

[91] J. S. Mill, *On Liberty*, in M. Cowling (ed.), *Selected Writings of John Stuart Mill*, London: Everyman, 1972.

'constructs the [sexist] social reality of gender'[92]—a claim that will be examined in detail in Chapter 8.[93]

It appears that Mill envisaged his argument as applicable mainly to the expression of opinion and debate, but it can equally well be used to support claims for freedom of information, since the possession of pertinent information about a subject will nearly always be a prerequisite to the formation of a well-worked-out opinion on the matter. However, *prima facie*, it may be thought that the theory does not immediately make it clear *when* we need to know the truth about a given subject. Thus, it could be argued that a delay in receiving certain information (owing, for example, to government restrictions) would not greatly matter, as long as the truth eventually emerged. In response to this, it may be argued that if truth is valued substantively—a position most would assent to[94]—then any period of time during which citizens are kept in ignorance of the truth or form erroneous opinions because of such ignorance, amounts to an evil, thus giving rise to a presumption against secrecy. If, alternatively or in addition, knowledge of the truth is valued because of its importance for political participation, then clearly it will be most important to know the information at the time that the issue it concerns is most likely to affect the political climate. This rationale would thus provide a strong argument against the propensity of UK governments to attempt to conceal political secrets until revelation would no longer have a damaging effect on their interests.[95]

Clearly, whether truth is valued instrumentally—for example, as essential to self-development—or as a good in itself, some kinds of truths must be regarded as more important than others.[96] Thus, in the context of a collision between free speech and privacy rights, the small intrinsic value of knowing the facts about (say) a film star's sexual life, juxtaposed with the implausibility of the notion that such information would enable more effective political participation or individual growth, provides reasonable grounds for favouring the privacy interest in such a case. By contrast, revelations about corruption amongst prominent politicians will arguably not only have a more important part to play in the formation and development of individuals' general opinions, they will also play a vital role in enabling informed contribution to be made to the political process. Thus, a compelling argument for favouring free speech in this situation is readily made out. We will return to this argument in Chapter 14: the point to be made here is simply that this justification for free speech,

---

[92] C. MacKinnon, *Feminism Unmodified*, Cambridge: Harvard University Press, 1987, p 166.

[93] See in particular 309–407.

[94] Mill, as a utilitarian, would probably not see truth as inherently valuable, but rather as a very important means of ensuring the overall welfare of society.

[95] See e.g. the discussion of attempts by governments to use the law of confidence to prevent discussion of allegations about the security services in the *Spycatcher* litigation and the long delays on the expiry of exemptions under the Freedom of Information Act 2000 in Chapter 19.

[96] It is outside the scope of this work to attempt a normative inquiry into the relative value of different truths. A commonsensical consensus approach is all that is employed in the text, where it is suggested only that the mere satisfaction of curiosity without more is of a relatively low value compared to the ending of a deception.

like two of the others, provides sharply differentiated support for different classes of speech. It is largely for this reason that throughout this book we argue for a sensitive and nuanced weighting of speech claims against other interests; we do not consider that this undermines, overall, the claims of free speech; rather, it serves to preserve and uphold a genuine defence of free speech, as opposed to a reified one, that can, when such claims are plainly misused, actually undermine respect for a free media and engender cynicism about its importance.

THE ARGUMENT FROM PARTICIPATION IN A DEMOCRACY

Barendt describes this theory as 'the most fashionable free speech theory in modern Western democracies', and concludes that 'it has been much the most influential theory in the development of 20th century free speech law'.[97] The argument, which is associated primarily with the American writer Meiklejohn,[98] is simply that citizens cannot participate fully in a democracy unless they have a reasonable understanding of political issues; therefore, open debate on such matters is essential. In so far as democracy rests upon ideas both of participation and accountability, the argument from democracy may be seen to encompass also the function which a free press performs in exposing abuses of power,[99] thereby allowing for their remedy and also providing a deterrent effect for those contemplating such wrong-doing.[100] The influence of this argument can be seen in the fact that directly political speech has a special protected status in most Western democracies. As we argue in Chapter 2, it is this justification that is particularly marked in the Strasbourg jurisprudence. This justification is also the one which has for some time been predominant in English judicial reasoning in free speech cases; when the British judiciary consider the claims of free speech, they seem in general to be particularly concerned to protect free criticism of the political authorities. Thus, in the seminal House of Lords decision in *Derbyshire v Times Newspapers*,[101] Lord Keith, in holding that neither local nor central government could sustain an action in defamation, said: 'It is of the highest importance that a democratically elected governmental body should be open to uninhibited public criticism.' The fact that he based his decision on *this* justification for free speech and not on, for example, the individual right of journalists to express themselves freely, is evidence of judicial endorsement of the argument from democracy—and also, possibly, of their failure to give much consideration to other, rights-based justifications.

The fact that the judiciary have mainly, or even only, this interest in mind when considering threats to free speech, helps to explain why they are so often prepared to allow speech to be overridden by other considerations. This is because this argument sees speech as a public interest and as justified instrumentally by reference to its

---

[97] *Freedom of Speech*, op cit, at 18 and 20 respectively.
[98] See, e.g., his 'The First Amendment is an absolute' (1961) *Sup Ct Rev* 245.
[99] See V. Blasi, 'The checking value in First Amendment theory' (1977) *Am B Found Res J*, p 521.
[100] See K. Greenwalt, 'Free speech justifications' (1989) 89 *Columbia L Rev* 119, p 143.
[101] [1993] AC 534; [1993] 1 All ER 1011; [1992] 3 WLR 28, HL.

beneficial effects on democracy, rather than seeing it as an individual right of inherent value. Therefore, clearly, it can render speech vulnerable to arguments that it should be overridden by competing public interests which are also claimed to be essential to the maintenance of democracy. Hence Margaret Thatcher's well-known justification for the media ban challenged unsuccessfully in the *Brind* case:[102] 'We do sometimes have to sacrifice a little of the freedom we cherish in order to defend ourselves from those whose aim is to destroy that freedom altogether.' Clearly, to a judge who sees the value of free speech only in terms of its contribution to the political process, an argument that allowing the speech in question will do more harm than good to the maintenance of democracy will always seem compelling. This is not to suggest that the argument from democracy is fundamentally flawed—clearly its basic premiss is correct and offers an important reason to protect speech—but rather that one should be wary of using it as the sole justification even for directly political speech.

There is, however, an argument which does see the justification as fundamentally flawed because it would appear to allow suppression of free speech by the democracy acting through its elected representatives. However, this objection may be answered by the argument that certain values, such as protection for minorities and fundamental freedoms generally, are implicit in any mature conception of a democracy.[103] Therefore, the term 'democracy' or the furtherance of democracy should not be narrowly defined to include only the decisions of the particular government in power, acting through Parliament, but should also encompass the general principles mentioned; by affording respect to such principles, democracy will ultimately be preserved. This argument would suggest that the justification would appear to have little direct relevance to sexually explicit forms of expression or blasphemous speech but, on the other hand, since freedom of expression is arguably one of the freedoms the suppression of which would undermine democracy, protection for these forms of speech can also be argued for by the justification. It should be borne in mind, however, that as this argument depends on a separate and somewhat controversial contention about the nature of democracy, it offers only an indirect defence of non-political speech.[104] Nevertheless, if the above contention is accepted, one may then conclude that the argument from democracy is actually concerned to further two values: maintenance of the democracy and effective participation in it. The two values are distinct in that, although effective as opposed to passive or inert participation may help to

---

[102] *Secretary of State for the Home Department ex parte Brind* [1991] 1 AC 696; [1991] 1 All ER 720; [1991] 2 WLR 588, HL. The decision is discussed in Chapter 20.

[103] Such a view is in fact endorsed by a number of legal philosophers and civil libertarians, and amounts to the most satisfactory reply to the charge that an entrenched Bill of Rights is undemocratic. See Dworkin, *A Bill of Rights for Britain*, 1990; the view also clearly underpins his general political philosophy, see, e.g., 'Liberalism', in *A Matter of Principle*, 1985. See also H. L. A. Hart, *Law, Liberty and Morality*, 1963 and A. Lester, *Democracy and Individual Rights*, 1968.

[104] Most commentators seem to assume that the argument from democracy has little, if any, application to pornographic material. See, e.g., A. Dworkin, 'Do we have a right to pornography?' in op cit, p 335. Similarly, the Williams Committee did not regard the argument as pertinent to their deliberations (*Report of the Committee on Obscenity and Film Censorship*, Cmnd 7772, 1979); see further Chapter 8.

secure maintenance of the democracy, nevertheless, some of its members, while wishing to see its continuance, might not wish to participate actively in it. Thus, political speech would contribute to the maintenance of both the values, while other forms of speech would contribute only to the first, confirming what was suggested at the outset, namely that this justification argues for special protection of political speech.

THE ARGUMENT FROM HUMAN DEVELOPMENT

Finally, we may turn to the thesis that freedom of speech is necessary in order to enable individual self-fulfilment. It is argued that individuals will not be able to develop morally and intellectually unless they are free to air views and ideas in free debate with each other. However, as Barendt notes,[105] it may be objected that free speech should not be singled out as especially necessary for individual fulfilment; the individual might also claim that, for example, foreign travel or a certain kind of education was equally necessary. On the other hand, freedom of speech represents a means of furthering individual growth which it is possible to uphold as a 'negative freedom'; other methods of furthering individual freedom would require positive action on the part of the government. Moreover, the right to education is also seen as sufficiently fundamental to human development as to be protected by numerous constitutional and international instruments. It is often overlooked that this right is included in the founding statement of modern international human rights law, the Universal Declaration of Human Rights. Article 26(1) states:

Everyone has the right to education. Education shall be free, at least in the elementary and fundamental stages. Elementary education shall be compulsory. Technical and professional education shall be made generally available and higher education shall be equally accessible to all on the basis of merit.[106]

The right to education is protected by Article 2 of Protocol 1 ECHR;[107] it is also given comprehensive protection by Article 29 of the South African Constitution.[108] Similarly, the right to freedom of movement is seen as a fundamental right, guaranteed again by the Universal Declaration, Article 13 of which states:

Everyone has the right to freedom of movement and residence within the borders of each State. Everyone has the right to leave any country, including his own, and return to his country.

This right is also protected by Article 12 of the International Covenant on Civil and

---

[105] Op cit, at 14.

[106] This right is given force in the International Covenant on Economic, Social and Cultural Rights (1966), Articles 13 and 14 of which provides comprehensive protection for this right.

[107] 'No person shall be denied the right to education.'

[108] Article 29(1) provides: 29 (1) Everyone has the right (a) to a basic education, including adult basic education; and (b) to further education, which the state, through reasonable measures, must make progressively available and accessible.

Political Rights, and by Article 2 of the Fourth Protocol to the ECHR.[109] Therefore the objection that self-development does not provide a distinctive rationale for freedom of speech, because the right to education and to travel are also fundamental, loses some of its force. If, indeed, these two other fundamental preconditions for self-development are also seen as basic rights, this simply suggests that where certain interests *are* genuine preconditions to the individual's development, they are given protection as human rights. Freedom of speech may therefore be seen as one amongst some other fundamental rights that are necessary for self-development.

This justification is clearly rights-based and, as such, in theory at least, is less vulnerable to competing societal claims; however, it does not value speech in itself, but rather, instrumentally, as a means to individual growth. Therefore, in situations where it seems that allowing free expression of the particular material will be likely to retard or hinder the growth of others or of the 'speaker', the justification does not offer a strong defence of speech.[110] Precisely this argument has been used by feminist commentators to justify the censorship of pornography. Thus, MacKinnon asserts that far from aiding in the growth of anyone, 'Pornography strips and devastates women of credibility'[111] through the images of women it constructs in its readers' minds. The thesis which forms the basis of the UK law on obscenity—that certain kinds of pornography actually damage the moral development of those who read it by depraving and corrupting them, similarly fastens onto the argument that this kind of material achieves the opposite of the outcome which allowing freedom of expression is designed to ensure.[112] The apparent vulnerability of the argument from self-development when used to justify the protection of material which is arguably degrading[113] leads Barendt to suggest[114] that a sounder formulation of the theory is one which frames it in terms of the individual's right to moral autonomy. It is submitted that moral autonomy does provide the most persuasive defence of sexually explicit 'speech' and this argument will be developed in Chapter 8 when theoretical approaches to obscenity law are discussed. However, it will also be argued that autonomy is conceptually distinct from the notion of self-fulfilment and that nothing is to be gained by conflating the two concepts.

---

[109] It is also, of course, one of the four fundamental freedoms under the Treaty Establishing the European Union, as amended—Article 39.

[110] Barendt argues (op cit, at 33) that justifications for suppressing some forms of speech could be advanced on the basis that human dignity (the value promoted by allowing self-development) would thereby receive protection. He instances the displays of pictures of the recently dead and the scrawling of racist graffiti in areas of racial tension.

[111] MacKinnon, op cit, at 193.

[112] It should be noted first that pro-censorship feminists deny that their arguments have anything in common with conservative objections to pornography, e.g. MacKinnon, op cit, at 175, and secondly that the feminist thesis on pornography is far more complex than this. It will be explored in more detail in Chapter 8.

[113] Dworkin also concludes that the argument from self-fulfilment fails to defend pornographic speech: 'Do we have a right to pornography?' in *A Matter of Principle*; he founds his defence on moral autonomy and, like the present writer, clearly regards this concept as offering a separate head of justification.

[114] Op cit, at 16.

UNPACKING MEDIA FREE SPEECH CLAIMS

THE INTERRELATIONSHIP BETWEEN MEDIA FREEDOM AND FREE EXPRESSION CLAIMS

How then do these free speech justifications relate to the media, as opposed to the individual speaker? One of the key arguments of this book is that an uncritical acceptance of media claims to free speech rights, and the assumption that the speech rationales discussed are always at stake in support of such claims, tends to lead ultimately to detriment to the free speech interests of the audience and, on occasions, of other individual actors, whose interests might be directly opposed to the unfettered freedom to speak of the media. Rather than make such an assumption, the following section focuses closely on the interrelationship between such rationales and media free expression claims.

Clearly, when the media claims free speech rights, and these are evaluated by courts, the rights of both the audience and the speaker may be in question. A particular media demand to publish material may have very little clear link with the free speech rationales in terms of speaker's rights, but may readily benefit the audience in terms that fall within those rationales. As Barendt argues, it is often difficult to view media bodies as 'speakers' exercising rights to, for example, autonomy or self-fulfilment, due to the nature of the process that occurs when a large commercial concern produces a publication or broadcast.[115] It may well be hard to attribute responsibility for it to a particular reporter, broadcaster, or writer. Speakers' rights *may* be engaged in some instances of exercises of 'media freedom' but it cannot be assumed that this is the case. So this section of the chapter asks two main questions. First, how satisfactory is it to assume that a media body can be viewed as broadly the equivalent of an individual speaker? Second, how far can it be assumed that the exercise of media freedom without interference will benefit the audience in terms of the free speech rationales?

We propose four models, which encapsulate the way that constitutional and international courts and legislatures around the world have dealt with this interaction: in so doing we acknowledge our heavy indebtedness to Eric Barendt's analysis of this issue in his seminal work *Freedom of Speech*, now in its second edition.[116]

THE 'EQUIVALENCE' MODEL

Courts in a number of jurisdictions appear to have accepted that free speech claims of the mass media are indistinguishable from those of speakers generally.[117] This has

---

[115] Op cit, at 417.

[116] As will appear below, our suggestion of four models is largely based on Barendt.

[117] The prime example is the US: see Barendt, op cit, at 419. He cites D. Lange, 'The Speech and Press Clauses' (1975) 23 *UCLA Law Rev* 77; W. W. Van Alstyne, 'The Hazards to the Press of Claiming a "Preferred Position" ' (1977) 28 *Hastings Law Jo* 761.

been said in UK cases a number of times.[118] This model has benefits for the media in a number of respects. They can take advantage of the sympathy that may be extended to the lone protester, or individual pamphleteer: they are treated as if they were the powerless speaker facing the might of the state, or the censoriousness of her fellow citizens. All the jurisprudence that has built up around individual speakers struggling to be heard can be taken advantage of by powerful media corporations, which themselves sometimes have the ability to cow or influence individual governments directly, as is said to be the case in relation to Rupert Murdoch's relationship with the Blair Government.[119]

The very language classically associated with free speech claims creates associations that can be problematic when used in support of the claims of powerful corporate players. The term 'press freedom' is a powerful trope, strongly associated with a range of liberal ideas. Conversely, 'interference' with media free speech claims is almost automatically assumed to be *prima facie* an evil. The term 'media freedom' brings with it a set of associations—in particular it is associated with anti-totalitarianism; as Lord Bridge said in his powerful dissent in *Spycatcher*, 'free speech is the first casualty of a totalitarian regime'.[120] His remarks were highly pertinent in that context, but very doubtfully so when applied to enhance what are essentially commercial claims. Some free speech claims are almost indistinguishable from commercial ones—for example, the mass-production of mainstream pornography[121] or the publication of stories about the private lives of celebrities in order to sell newspapers.[122] In that context, ringing endorsements of free speech culled from struggles with repressive regimes or from democratic regimes acting repressively represent a perversion of their original purpose. But they still retain a certain rhetorical power—when it can be said that victories for privacy claimants are 'a blow to press freedom'—as indeed they are, if that term is used in a merely literal sense—it sounds as if something unequivocally damaging has occurred. *Our* position, as put forward in Chapter 15, is the exact converse: that a nuanced law of privacy has the potential to *enhance* the output of the media as it serves the public interest.

In particular, this book will argue that courts should be challenged to problematize the argument from democracy in its application to the media—it should not be unthinkingly applied to the media since exercises of media freedom may actually hinder the participation of the individual speaker in the democracy—a point we

---

[118] This was the traditional approach, as encapsulated in the Diceyean view, discussed above, text to note 12; a recent example was the comment of Sir John Donaldson MR in the *Spycatcher* case to the effect that the right of the media to know and to publish "is neither more nor less than that of the general public": *A-G v Guardian Newspapers Ltd (No. 2)* [1990] 1 AC 109, 183, CA.

[119] For a fiercely critical view of Murdoch's use of his media empire to coerce governments and thereby subvert the democratic process, see the following report by the Center for American Progress: 'Who is Rupert Murdoch?' www.americanprogress.org/site/pp.asp?c=biJRJ8OVF&b=122948.

[120] *A-G v Guardian Newspapers* [1987] 1 WLR 1248, 1287.

[121] We argue in Chapter 8 that different considerations may apply to pornography produced by, and aimed at, minority sexual groups.

[122] See further Chapter 13 at 683–8.

return to below. Courts should also be alert to recognize instances in which unhindered free speech in the media cuts sharply across the other underlying rationales for speech, such as self-development and autonomy.[123] We have already noted the feminist argument that the mass-distribution of pornography may attack the ability of women to flourish and be treated with dignity, a point considered at length in Chapter 8.

A further problem with the 'equivalence' model is that, if treated simply as if it were an individual speaker, the media player can be mis-characterized as being in an equivalent position to the individual whose rights it may have invaded. The prime example is the instance of the privacy-invading newspaper—formally speaking the situation is a 'horizontal one', involving two private parties. If they are treated as substantively equal—if the gross power imbalance between them is not recognized— then judicial reasoning can become divorced from reality. Possibly the most telling example of such a case is the *Re S*[124] decision in the House of Lords, discussed at length in Chapter 16: the interests of a five-year-old child, in an intensely vulnerable situation,[125] were pitted against those of several national newspapers, as though the two were on an equal footing.[126] Interestingly, one of the most ringing defences of freedom of expression prior to the HRA—in which it was referred to as 'a trump card, that always wins'—occurred in a similar case, one therefore in which such endorsement was *least* apt. *R v Central Independent Television Plc*[127] concerned an attempt by a mother to restrain a broadcast in order to protect a child from having his father identified as a paedophile. In other words, the application was made, broadly, to protect the child's privacy. This, again, was not an instance in which media freedom was pitted against a state interest, or one to which the common law has long attached great weight, such as reputation. In this respect, Lord Hoffman's dicta below are remarkably prescient, in forecasting the approach that was taken in *Re S*, as well as in a cluster of other cases prior to the House of Lords' decision in *Campbell*,[128] in which the courts were content to let substantively flimsy claims of press freedom override privacy interests:

publication may cause needless pain, distress and damage to individuals or harm to other aspects of the public interest. But a freedom which is restricted to what judges think to be responsible or in the public interest is no freedom. Freedom means the right to publish things which government and judges, however well motivated, think should not be published. It means the right to say things which 'right thinking people' regard as dangerous or

---

[123] See Chapter 13, at 684–7.   [124] [2005] 1 AC 593.

[125] The child's brother had been murdered by his mother; the application was for the child not to be identified in coverage of the mother's trial; despite evidence that the child would almost certainly suffer measurable psychological damage by such revelations, as well as bullying at school and possible damage to the placement with his father, the application was denied.

[126] See Chapter 16 at 826–30.   [127] [1994] 3 All ER 641.

[128] [2004] 2 WLR 1232. *Campbell* concerned an application by the fashion model for damages in respect of an article in the *Mirror* newspaper giving details of her treatment for drug addiction.

irresponsible. This freedom is subject only to clearly defined exceptions laid down by common law or statute . . . the principle that the press is free from both government and judicial control is more important than the particular case.

This principle, of course, has resoundingly *not* been applied in the area of the protection of national security, in which the courts have fallen over themselves to prevent the publication of information which the government claims is 'dangerous or irresponsible', often on rather flimsy grounds.[129] In other words, prior to the HRA at least, there were some strong defences of freedom of expression, but the inability of the courts to recognize the potentially oppressive position of the media in relation to other individuals meant that such defences often came precisely when they were most inapt—as well as being absent when they were.

Barendt comments that 'a lot of nonsense is written about media speech claims'.[130] It is also fair to find that a lot of nonsensical assumptions underlie the acceptance of such claims. It is contended that finding an equivalence between the speech claim of, say, the lone black protester entering a whites-only library, and the current Murdoch media empire, falls into that category. There are very clear advantages for the media in presenting themselves in victim-like garb and seeking to take advantage of a speech jurisprudence that developed when there was a strong consciousness of the serious jeopardizing of speech rights by Western totalitarian states. It was a jurisprudence, moreover, that relied on common law principles developed prior to the modern rise of the mass communications media.

The notion of presumptive priority for Article 10 as against Article 8, until quite recently a notable feature of domestic speech jurisprudence,[131] becomes even more problematic when examined from this perspective. Although the equivalence model might appear to lend itself to acceptance of granting presumptive equality to two 'individuals', one claiming speech, the other privacy rights, in fact it was precisely thinking within this paradigm that led to resistance to such equality for some time, until Lady Hale's seminal judgment in the Court of Appeal in *Re S*.[132] One might have expected that if the two persons claiming rights are in an equivalent position—as two individual rights-holders—then the notion of placing them in a presumptively equal position would follow fairly readily. But since the classic free speech situation tended to concern the victim-speaker who was facing the full weight of the state, it took some time for the judges to appreciate that the accordance of presumptive priority for speech in the face of competing *societal or state* concerns was appropriate—indeed required by the Convention[133]—but *not* in the face of another competing right.

---

[129] See Chapter 20.   [130] Op cit, at 449.

[131] This is the notion that privacy rights should be seen as only an exception to the primary right for freedom of expression, the onus lying upon the person seeking to interfere with press freedom to justify this: See Chapter 13 and Chapter 15.

[132] See Chapter 16 at 828–9.

[133] See the classic exposition in the *Sunday Times* case: a clash between Article 10 and a competing societal interest is not 'a choice between two conflicting principles but . . . a principle. . . . that is subject to a number of exceptions which must be narrowly interpreted' ((1979) 2 EHRR 245, at [65]).

Their thinking had been formed within a particular conception of the free speech arena.

Our argument on the 'equivalence model' has so far been that its acceptance can in certain situations lead to an unreal and unfair privileging of media interests over those of other individuals. But there are also *detriments* for the media in employing this model. As Barendt puts it: 'the traditional perspective does not meet the powerful argument that the press is entitled to some legal privileges because it performs a vital constitutional role'.[134] It seems readily arguable that this role justifies the granting of such privileges to the media, such as protection for journalistic sources, discussed in Chapter 7, special access rights to information, including in particular rights of access to court rooms,[135] special exemptions from Data Protection rules,[136] and privileges in relation to police search and seizure powers under the Police and Criminal Evidence Act.[137] However, if a media body is presenting itself merely as, in effect, an individual speaker, such privileges cannot readily be justified or claimed. However, as Chapter 16 points out, there is some UK jurisprudence on the special position of reporters in relation to the Article 6 guarantee,[138] and, as discussed in Chapter 4, some on the equivalent common law principle of open justice.[139] In other jurisdictions, notably the US, this has also been recognized as an issue worth addressing.[140] These privileges can be justified primarily on the basis that if they are not granted, the flow of valuable information to the public is likely to be impeded. For example, most people are unlikely to visit courts regularly; thus, they rely on the media to report on the work-ings of the criminal justice system, a crucial issue in a democracy. Therefore, if special privileges are denied to reporters, some reporting will never occur and consequent impoverishment of the free speech environment will follow. It is in this way that such media reporting also plays a part in the safeguarding of the quality of the justice system, as Chapters 4, 5, and 6 on the free speech/fair trial balance point out. That is why the open justice principle is so jealously guarded by the courts, as discussed in Chapter 16—even to the point of refusing to accept compelling reasons for anonym-ity.[141] Thus the granting of certain special privileges for the media readily accords with the free speech rationales, especially the arguments from democracy and truth. As discussed below, however, the notion of granting such privileges can and should be problematized—there should not be an unthinking acceptance of them either as primary or fundamental media rights, or as a means of enhancing the speech rights of individuals.

---

[134] Op cit, at 420.

[135] That right is encapsulated in Article 6(1) ECHR, although it is not expressed to apply to the media more than to ordinary speakers: see Chapter 5 at 201–2.

[136] Via Section 32 of the Data Protection Act 1998; see Chapter 14 at 721.

[137] This issue is discussed in Chapter 7: essentially there are greater procedural safeguards in obtaining a warrant to search for and seize journalistic material, as defined, and it may only be produced if it is in the public interest to do so.

[138] See p 828.   [139] See pp 168–9.   [140] See Chapter 5 at 199, 201.

[141] As in *Re S*, op cit, note 124 above.

To summarize, if special privileges are *denied* to the media, as they logically should be under the equivalence model, then audience rights may not be most effectively served in relation to the free speech rationales. On the other hand, we have seen that in some cases, the effect of treating the media simply as the equivalent of an individual speaker can create unfairness to other rights-holders, thus *over*-privileging the media. Such over-privileging often also fails to serve the broader public interest, by, for example, encouraging a climate of public discourse which is obsessed with the reportage of private life, to the detriment of a focus upon matters of real public concern. Ultimately, therefore, the 'equivalence' model both under- and over-privileges the media. It allows for legal oscillation between the two positions, and produces unsatisfactory results in relation to both. Is a better position, therefore, one which recognizes and grants to the media special privileges?

THE SPECIAL PRIVILEGES MODEL

Under this model, the media obtains special rights, of the kind just instanced. They also, in some jurisdictions, acquire distinctive constitutional protection, as under the German Constitution,[142] in which the position of the media is given separate and distinct recognition. The US First Amendment on its face protects press freedom, in addition to free speech generally,[143] although the US Supreme Court has made little of the explicit mention of 'freedom of the press' in the Constitution. The lack of recognition of the special place of the media is the traditional position under English common law and no such recognition appears in the text of Article 10 ECHR, although an important argument of this book, expounded in Chapter 2, is that the Strasbourg Court has at times come close to this model, by giving *de facto* higher protection to media speech than to the expression of individuals. It has also been very ready to accept certain *de facto* special privileges for journalists, viewed as expression rights, most notably that of source protection, discussed in Chapter 7.

The key problem with this approach is that in certain instances the special privileges for the media may be in strong tension with the general free speech guarantees, or even run directly counter to them. The exercise by the media of their privileges may create interferences with free expression that tend to go unrecognized. As Barendt puts it:

For example, one likely implication of a distinct press freedom is that the owner of a newspaper has an absolute right to determine its contents. He could exploit that right to damage the readers' interests in pluralism of information—a value underlying freedom of speech—by, say, dictating the political line of the newspaper irrespective of the editor's views, or by arbitrarily refusing to publish readers' letters in reply to what they considered

---

[142] See Barendt, op cit, at 423.

[143] 'Congress shall make no law respecting an establishment of religion, or prohibiting the free exercise thereof; or abridging the freedom of speech, or of the press; or the right of the people peaceably to assemble, and to petition the Government for a redress of grievances.'

inaccurate allegations printed in the paper. A similar clash might occur if press barons resisted the application of competition and anti-concentration laws with the argument that it would violate their free press rights. In these circumstances, it can be argued, the owner is really exercising a freedom to determine the use of his property, the newspaper, or a commercial freedom, although of course he may claim to be exercising freedom of speech. It would be unfortunate if recognition of an institutional freedom of the press were to be treated as strengthening these claims.[144]

Barendt argues therefore that the media should be not afforded any blanket privileges in comparison with individual speakers, but rather that any claim of privilege should be thoroughly scrutinized against the underlying rationales for free speech that justify the value we attach to a free media in the first place. It is to this third model that we now turn.

THE 'DIFFERENTIATED PRIVILEGES' MODEL

Under this third perspective, the possibility of affording special privileges to the media is accepted only where directly justified by the general free speech rationales. In other words, claims for such privileges are rigorously assessed against the basic reasons for valuing freedom of expression generally in the first place, and only conceded if they are seen to answer to and enhance the fulfilment of those values. As Barendt puts it:

Free press clauses and other provisions guaranteeing media freedom should, therefore, be understood to confer on all communications media—a term not confined to the established press and broadcasting media—some constitutional rights and immunities which are not conferred on individuals under freedom of expression or speech clauses. But they should be interpreted in conformity with the values of free speech, since it is the importance of that basic right which justifies the further protection of the institutional media.[145]

This is therefore a more sophisticated and satisfactory model than the first two. The fourth model put forward below is in most instances indistinguishable from this one and we do not suggest that the arguments it puts forward are not accepted by Barendt: he asserts them very positively.[146] However, we think it preferable, for the sake of analytical clarity, to separate out his third category into two. This is because it is logically possible to have two positions: under the first, claims for media *privileges* would always be subject to rigorous scrutiny by reference to the free speech justifications. Under the second, this would also be the case, but in addition, *all* claims for free speech by the media would be so assessed. It would be logically possible to embrace the third position without embracing the additional aspect imported by the fourth.

---

[144] Op cit, at 421.   [145] Ibid, at 424.

[146] See e.g. his conclusion to his chapter on media freedom in *Freedom of Speech*: 'On that perspective, press and media freedom is, as we have argued in this chapter, protected because it promotes the values which underlie freedom of speech. But on that perspective it seems legitimate to ensure that the press, as well as the broadcasting media, serves freedom of speech by enriching public discourse.' (op cit, at 450).

Of course, Constitutional Courts would no doubt contend that they *do* always assess media speech claims by reference to such underpinning values;[147] however, our contention is that both English and US courts in particular have not always done so. Chapters 13 and 15 explore this matter in relation to the issue of privacy. We therefore suggest this additional distinction precisely to underline the critical importance of making such an assessment in all cases.

THE FOURTH MODEL: A 'VARIABLE GEOMETRY' OF MEDIA FREEDOM

The aim of the fourth model, then, is broadly to ensure the best possible expressive environment for the *audience* by subjecting all media speech claims to rigorous assessment under the free speech rationales. The claim of the media as *speaker* can be tested against those rationales under this model, but only where it is realistic to do so: it may not be in relation to the speech that emerges as the output of a large media corporate body. We would stress that this model upholds media freedom just as strongly as the others when it is genuinely directed at the public interest, in terms of both truth-promotion and democracy, or where a genuine argument from autonomy or self-development exists in relation to either the media 'speaker' or the audience.[148] As J. White argued in relation to regulations constraining the editorial freedom of terrestrial radio broadcasting stations in the *Red Lion* case in the US: '[i]t is the right of viewers and listeners, not the right of the broadcasters which is paramount'.[149]

Acceptance of this model tends, therefore, to allow for the imposition of specific regulation of the media with the aim of perfecting or enhancing speech from an audience perspective. Such regulation may include duties upon the media that might be termed 'anti-privileges', that is, particular burdens that would not be acceptable (or simply nonsensical) if imposed upon individuals. Obvious examples are 'right to reply' provisions, in which newspapers are obliged to carry apologies and corrections if they are found to have published defamatory and/or privacy-invading material, and 'must carry' regulations, obliging broadcasters to provide a plurality of cultural and

---

[147] Barendt contends that the German Constitutional Court accepts what we would term the fourth model: '[The Court] takes account of the underlying rationale of press freedom when it decides whether the limits imposed on its exercise by legislation or to respect other basic rights are constitutional. For example, although press freedom covers both the serious and the tabloid press, the Court is more willing to countenance limits on a fabricated interview in the latter in order to protect personal privacy; a tabloid paper cannot claim free speech or free press rights when its story is made up and contributes nothing of value to public discourse': op cit, at 424.

[148] We instance such an interest in Chapter 8 in relation to the freedom to produce sexually explicit literature aimed at minorities, which may have the effect of preserving and enhancing their sense of identity and solidarity; the autonomy argument in this context generally argues for freedom from government restrictions in favour of the individuals' right, in Dworkin's phrase, to 'moral independence'.

[149] *Red Lion Broadcasting v FCC* 395 US 367 (1969). As Barendt notes, the case is in fact out of line with the dominant strand of US jurisprudence in this field: 'The First Amendment and the Media', in I. Loveland (ed.) *Importing the First Amendment*, Oxford: Hart, 1998, at 34.

political material as part of their output. Requirements to observe due impartiality in news broadcasting represent a further similar constraint. Plainly, such provisions infringe unfettered editorial freedom, with the aim of enhancing the benefits to the audience by enriching the expressive environment, as well as protecting particular individuals whose rights or interests have been invaded by media bodies. Barendt notes that the US Supreme Court has consistently invalidated 'right of reply' provisions and must carry requirements,[150] as an invasion of editorial freedom. In contrast, as discussed in Chapters 10 and 19, the UK has a tradition of imposing quite substantial due impartiality or 'must carry' requirements upon broadcasting,[151] together with a ban on political advertising, while the Strasbourg Commission has found 'right of reply' provisions to be compatible with Article 10.[152]

This book supports the imposition of such burdens—although an interference with editorial freedom, they are justified partly by reference to the record of the print media. That is, in certain areas it may be argued that the unfettered political output of the press can produce effects which run directly counter to certain classical free speech aims, in particular the arguments from truth and from participation in democracy. Such effects can be enhanced in the UK by the marked concentration of cross-media ownership, mainly, although not exclusively, in relation to Rupert Murdoch,[153] which allows for the running of concerted campaigns on particular issues. The obvious example at present is the stance of the Murdoch newspapers on the Euro: Murdoch has said publicly that he will deploy the full weight of his newspaper empire against any attempt to join the Euro system.[154] Moreover, it is not hard to find more sinister aspects of the effects of unregulated political speech in the print media. A notorious example is the stance of British newspapers, particularly, but not exclusively, most of the tabloids, on the issue of asylum seekers. The evidence as to the public's perception of the number of asylum seekers in the UK not only reveals the capacity of the media to sow disinformation and fear, but also that even more objective news sources, perceived as more reliable, such as the BBC, can be and are drowned out by the more hysterical and emotive reportage of the newspapers. It should be noted that in relation to many issues, such as that of asylum seekers, the general public is heavily dependent on the information they receive from the media; in most cases, aside from anecdotal or personal experiences, they cannot ascertain the facts for themselves from their own experience. What then is the evidence? Opinion polls in fact consistently show that the public enormously over-estimates the number of asylum seekers in the UK and also the number of ethnic minority people living in the UK. A Mori Poll conducted for Refugee Week in 2002[155] showed gross distortions in people's knowledge about the

---

[150] See e.g. op cit, at 425, instancing *Miami Herald v Tornillo* 418 US 241 (1974).

[151] See Chapters 10 and 19.   [152] *Ediciones Tiempo v Spain* (1989) 62 D & R 247.

[153] Murdoch's company, News Corp, owns *The Sun*, *The Times*, *The Sunday Times*, and *The News of the World* in the UK; it also owns the *Sky* group.

[154] See 'Murdoch's Euro Snub to Blair' BBC report, 11 June 2002: http://news.bbc.co.uk/1/hi/business/2039237.stm.

[155] http://www.mori.com/polls/2002/refugee.shtml.

asylum issue, which can only have come about as a result of relentless media coverage. The public over-estimated the proportion of total world refugees taken by the UK by a staggering 1000 per cent. That is, the proportion named by the public as being taken by the UK—23 per cent—was more than ten times higher than the actual figure of 1.98 per cent. Evidence of the media *tone* towards asylum seekers came in the part of the poll in which the public was asked whether they primarily associated positive or negative words with media coverage of asylum seekers. The results were as follows:

Overall, 85% of respondents associated negative words with media reporting. Two-thirds (64%) said that the media most use the term 'illegal immigrant' when referring to refugees and asylum seekers, yet refugees and asylum seekers are not in the UK illegally. Other words commonly associated with media coverage were 'desperate', 'foreigners', 'bogus' and 'scroungers'.

At the other end of the scale, words not readily associated with media coverage and chosen by just 1–2 per cent of respondents were: 'skilled', 'talented', 'intelligent', 'hard working', and 'welcome'.[156] The Refugee Council became so concerned at the constant reiteration of 'myths and scare stories' in the media, particularly in the run-up to the 2005 General Election, in which the Conservative Party promised withdrawal from the Refugee Convention in order to be able to impose an annual 'quota' on the number of asylum seekers that the UK would take, that it published a guide to responsible and accurate discussion of the issue.[157]

To take another example, The Kings Fund, in a major report on media coverage of health scares, such as the bogus MMR scare, found that the level of media reportage of health risks was in fact inverse to the actual risk in question.[158] Instances of such distortion in risk perception by press coverage come readily to mind—they would include: the media's relentless focus on the relatively small number of deaths which come about through ecstasy use, as compared to alcohol and tobacco consumption,[159] and its reportage of deaths or accidents on the railways, as compared to the vastly greater number occurring on the roads.[160] Aside from the fact that such media campaigns actively mislead, they also distort the democratic process, and hamper people's participation in it—approaching a political issue with a profoundly mistaken set of perceptions is not likely to engender constructive participation.

We are not using these examples to argue for contents-based regulation of the print media in relation to coverage of controversial issues, but simply to give some concrete examples to underpin the contention that it is naïve to assume that unrestrained free

---

[156] Ibid.   [157] www.refugeecouncil.org.uk/news/myths/myth001.htm.

[158] See http://www.kingsfund.org.uk/resources/publications/health_in_the.html and Polly Toynbee's discussion in the *Guardian*: 'The BBC must not be led by the shock tactics of the Mail' (11 August 2004).

[159] Official figures show that ecstasy causes between 10 and 20 deaths a year, alcohol around 4,000, and tobacco over 100,000. Source: ww.urban75.com/Drugs/drugdeath.html.

[160] Between 1990 and 1998, there was an average of between 5 and 10 deaths a year on the trains; around 3,600 die each year on the roads: see 'Is Rail Travel Becoming Less Safe?' http://news.bbc.co.uk/1/hi/uk/465594.stm.

speech in the press will consistently promote the values underlying freedom of speech itself. This point also has a practical application; it highlights the importance of *retaining* such regulation of the broadcast media, at a time when many of the commercial satellite broadcasters, such as Fox News, and certain of the domestic licensed services are pushing for changes in the UK regulatory framework to allow for partisan news reporting in broadcasting.[161]

Examples such as those given above highlight the importance, under this fourth model, of testing media claims instrumentally under the arguments from democracy and truth, just as an individual speaker's rights would be. This is uncontentious. If the type of speech in question would either be irrelevant to such goals, or actively damage them, then its claim for protection by reference to the rationales can be minimized or denied. Examples outside the media field could include the speech of organizations engaged in the promotion of terrorist activity which are proscribed under the Terrorism Act 2000,[162] and the use of Article 17 ECHR[163] to deny protection to racist speech, as for example in *Norwood v UK*,[164] in which a claim of breach of Article 10 by a BNP member convicted of a public order offence after putting up a racially inflammatory poster in his window was rejected by the Court. In the mainstream media context, less extreme cases may arise, in which a careful assessment of the speech claim by the media reveals it to have little or nothing to do with the promotion of genuine values underlying that claim. A welcome recent example of such an approach was Lady Hale's caustic analysis in *Naomi Campbell v MGN*[165] of the free speech claim of the *Daily Mirror*:

The political and social life of the community, and the intellectual, artistic or personal development of individuals, are not obviously assisted by poring over the intimate details of a fashion model's private life.[166]

What we have argued so far is relatively unproblematic and has been rehearsed many times by free speech theorists. However, let us suppose that the media claims that the arguments from democracy or truth *are* engaged by the exercise of speech rights *but* the audience interests might be detrimentally affected. The two rationales should be considered in combination since their aims, if considered in isolation, may eventually come into conflict with each other. *Two* stages in the causal argument arise for the media, but not for individual speakers in relation to the speech rationales. First, would the exercise of speech further the aims of those rationales in the sense that the media speaker is seeking to engage in a debate on matters of political significance from which the truth might eventually emerge? *Second*, would the speech enhance audience participation in democracy as well as the search for truth from an audience perspective

---

[161] See the discussion in Chapter 19.   [162] Per ss 3 and 11 of the Act of 2000.

[163] This provides: 'Nothing in [the] Convention may be interpreted as implying for any State, group or person any right to engage in any activity or perform any act aimed at the destruction of any of the rights and freedoms set forth herein or at their limitation to a greater extent than is provided for in the Convention.'

[164] (2005) 40 EHRR SE11. For discussion, see Chapter 9.

[165] [2004] 2 WLR 1232. See above note 128 for the facts.   [166] Ibid, at [149].

or, for example, could it sow misinformation and mistrust? The exercise of speech rights on this rationale could mean participation in the democracy from a flawed perspective for the individuals who make up the audience, as discussed above, because they are acting on false information and may not have access to a trusted source. The truth might be unlikely ever to emerge, permanently damaging their democratic participation. This analysis appears to require a weighing up of the harm caused by reference to the rationales engaged, and it might be found that the harm caused in terms of the audience outweighed that in relation to the media. If so, the media speech right would be placed in a more precarious position. This argument could be said to involve dual instrumentality in relation to the media; in other words, these rationales are of their nature instrumental, but a further level of instrumentality is introduced since the overriding concern is with the causal connection between media speech and audience benefit, in terms of the rationales.

It follows that we are not 'agnostic' on due impartiality and 'must carry' require-ments—[167] we warmly embrace them in principle even though the practice may be clumsy and may on occasion in fact interfere with media freedom even from this perspective.[168] Such content-based controls, designed to ensure plurality, impartiality, and diversity, are in accord with the free speech rationales, since they enhance broad-cast speech in comparison with that of individual speakers and also have instrumental value in enabling and enhancing the speech of such speakers. They allow the public to be informed on matters of strong public interest in an effective fashion.

In conclusion, therefore, under what we term the fourth model, we are strongly supportive of media freedom, where the free speech rationales are engaged, but we would argue that courts and citizens must be prepared to assess media claims for free expression rigorously and sceptically. We are therefore advocating in this book a morally differentiated approach to media freedom, what might be termed a functional approach, in enquiring as to the purpose and value of the expressive act in question. The Strasbourg decision in *Von Hannover v Germany*,[169] discussed in detail in Chapter 13, may be seen as an exemplar of such an approach, albeit a relatively crude one. In that decision, concerned with a complaint by Princess Caroline of Monaco, the Court took a rigorously analytical view towards the claim of free expression by the media bodies in Germany who were demanding the right to publish relentless coverage of the Princess's daily life, shown in photographs taken without her consent, on the grounds that she was a 'public figure', whose doings were of great interest to the public. The Court said, in a passage of great significance for its overall speech jurisprudence:

---

[167] As Barendt expressed himself to be in his essay in *Importing the First Amendment*, although he also said they should be 'approached sympathetically, if critically': op cit, at 46. However, in the second edition of *Freedom of Speech*, published in 2005, he states: 'The arguments from pluralism, however, remain persuasive for the principal private terrestrial channels and networks, and, of course, for public broadcasters': op cit, at 448.

[168] There is an argument that the difficulty in having to broadcast a 'balancing programme' for one expressing a controversial point of view may 'steer' broadcasters towards bland output. For discussion, see Chapters 10 and 19.

[169] [2004] EMLR 21.

the decisive factor in balancing the protection of private life against freedom of expression should lie in the contribution that the published photos and articles make to a debate of general interest. It is clear in the instant case that they made no such contribution since the applicant exercises no official function and the photos and articles related exclusively to details of her private life.[170]

The Court thus refused to take claims of media freedom at face value; instead they were assessed by the *function* they carried out, and found to be wanting in force.

CONCLUSIONS

This chapter has argued that the traditional UK stance towards claims of media freedom largely reflected the first perspective discussed above, in which such claims were treated as if they were made by individual speakers.[171] In contrast, the ECHR jurisprudence, as the discussion in this book will reveal, largely reflects the fourth one, although we will note in the next chapter a tendency unfairly to privilege speech claims from the media in comparison to those of individual speakers. English media freedom law thus appears to be in the process of moving from one model to the other as the Strasbourg jurisprudence is absorbed more rapidly into domestic law. This book argues that this process is largely to be welcomed, but that the Strasbourg jurisprudence must be applied in a way that recognizes its limitations in particular areas.

This work will therefore consistently argue for strong protection for the media, when it is carrying out its role of a watchdog acting in the public interest, or promoting artistic or other forms of speech that challenge prevailing norms and enrich our cultural environment. It will argue for the ever-present need to protect the media from oppressive legislation, governmental interference, or wealthy, powerful individuals using libel or privacy actions to stifle legitimate, important public debate.[172] But we are not media freedom fundamentalists, seeing media freedom as an unqualified good. We therefore advocate a preparedness to strip away Article 10 protection from the media, or to minimize it, where there is no substantive claim that the free speech rationales are being furthered. We view what we have termed the fourth model as a useful analytical tool from which to view Article 10 jurisprudence, existing domestic media law and media free speech claims. The treatment of substantive topics of law throughout this book will reflect this model.

What, above all, then that this book seeks to do is to bring to light unspoken or

---

[170] Ibid, at [76].

[171] This may be seen particularly clearly in relation to the issue of protection of journalists sources. See Chapter 7.

[172] See, for example, our critical discussion of the Strasbourg decision in *Plon (Société) v France* (No. 58148/00, 18 May 2004) in Chapter 13 at 696–9.

unexplicated assumptions that are prevalent in this area of law and which might hinder the attempt to transform it. We fully support the movement from a negative liberty to speak to recognition of positive media expression rights under the HRA. But this enterprise will not be furthered by a failure to recognize the defects of the Convention and the HRA as the means to be employed. An unsophisticated, under-theorized application of the ECHR case law could damage or destroy the nascent reformative process.

PART I

ARTICLE 10 OF THE EUROPEAN CONVENTION ON HUMAN RIGHTS AND THE HUMAN RIGHTS ACT

This Part lays the foundations for the treatment of substantive topics of media law in the remainder of this book by considering in Chapter 2 the general principles as to the protection of media freedom that may be derived from the Strasbourg case law on Article 10 ECHR. It focuses in particular upon the notion of a 'hierarchy of speech' and the linked notions of the margin of appreciation and proportionality. Chapter 3 analyses particular aspects of the Human Rights Act that are of particular relevance to the media.

2

STRASBOURG, MEDIA FREEDOM, AND PROPORTIONALITY: ARTICLE 10 OF THE EUROPEAN CONVENTION ON HUMAN RIGHTS

INTRODUCTION

Article 10 ECHR

1. *Everyone has the right to freedom of expression. This right shall include freedom to hold opinions and to receive and impart information and ideas without interference by public authority and regardless of frontiers. This Article shall not prevent States from requiring the licensing of broadcasting, television or cinema enterprises.*

2. *The exercise of these freedoms, since it carries with it duties and responsibilities, may be subject to such formalities, conditions, restrictions or penalties as are prescribed by law and are necessary in a democratic society, in the interests of national security, territorial integrity or public safety, for the prevention of disorder or crime, for the protection of health or morals, for the protection of the reputation or rights of others, for preventing the disclosure of information received in confidence, or for maintaining the authority and impartiality of the judiciary*

PARAMETERS AND THEMES: STRASBOURG AND VALUES UNDERLYING ARTICLE 10[1]

This chapter considers broad themes in the jurisprudence of the European Court of Human Rights on Article 10, the right to freedom of expression. The following chapter goes on to examine some of the issues that have arisen through the introduction into

---

[1] The rationales for expression referred to in this chapter are considered in the Introduction to this book.

domestic law of Article 10, and the other Convention rights, via the Human Rights Act.[2] The relevant Article 10 jurisprudence for each discrete area of law considered in this book (privacy, contempt of court, sexually explicit speech, hate speech, media regulation, copyright, and political deformation) will be analysed closely in the particular chapters that deal with those areas. The purpose of this chapter is therefore not to expound what may be termed 'the law of freedom of expression' as decided by Strasbourg, something that emerges from the book considered as a totality. It is instead to look for cross-cutting themes in the interpretation of Article 10 in the Court's jurisprudence. Clearly, since this involves touching upon themes such as the well-known hierarchy of speech the Court has outlined,[3] which are also relevant to particular chapters, there will be a limited amount of thematic overlap with those chapters: we here inevitably consider Article 10 cases that deal with particular areas of law, and are therefore examined in detail in the relevant chapter. But the emphasis in this chapter is different: it is concerned ultimately with two main questions. First, what, in the Court's view, is Article 10 for? What are the broad values in political philosophy that underpin it? Second, what kind of standard does Article 10, as the Court has interpreted it, impose on national authorities seeking to justify a restriction on expression? The answer to this question, while inevitably touching upon the issues of legality and legitimate aim, will primarily focus upon the difficult and complex issue of proportionality, together with the linked doctrine of the margin of appreciation.[4] Indeed, part of our exposition of the relationship between the proportionality enquiry and the margin of appreciation will involve explaining why we choose to present discussion of these issues in a somewhat novel way.

One of the best-known Strasbourg expositions of the values underlying freedom of expression came in the early case of *Handyside v UK.*[5]

Freedom of expression constitutes one of the essential foundations of . . . a [democratic] society, one of the basic conditions for its progress and for the development of every man. Subject to paragraph 2 of Article 10, it is applicable not only to 'information' or 'ideas' that are favourably received or regarded as inoffensive or as a matter of indifference, but also to those that offend, shock or disturb the State or any sector of the population. Such are the demands of that pluralism, tolerance and broadmindedness without which there is no 'democratic society'.[6]

These findings have been strongly echoed in recent times by the English courts. In some now well-known dicta, Lord Steyn recognized three main justifications for freedom of speech: 'First it promotes the self-fulfilment of individuals in society. Secondly, in the famous words of Holmes J (echoing John Stuart Mill), the best test of

---

[2] This includes the complex and difficult issue of the judicial deference to the executive and/or Parliament. This topic is clearly related to that of the notion of a margin of appreciation, considered in this chapter, but the two are considered separately as they belong, formally, to different legal systems.

[3] Political speech, artistic speech, and commercial speech.

[4] The use of proportionality is not, of course, unique to the Article 10; the same test is used within Articles 8–11.

[5] *Handyside v UK* A 24 para 48 (1976).   [6] Ibid, at [49].

truth is the power of the thought to get itself accepted in the competition of the market . . . Thirdly, freedom of speech is the lifeblood of democracy.'[7] It will be seen that the rationales enumerated here closely echo those described in *Handyside*. Both refer to the 'individual development' rationale expressly. The reference to the 'progress' of such a society by the Strasbourg Court in *Handyside* can plausibly be taken to refer to the 'discovery of truth' rationale, in one of its variants. Clearly, progress in scientific and social understanding, and to a large extent in relation to politics and policy, is heavily dependent upon the free exchange of research, and of ideas and arguments. The 'truth' and 'democracy' rationales are thus linked and the Court does not here sharply differentiate between the two. Both courts refer explicitly to the foundational importance of freedom of expression for the establishment and healthy workings of a democratic society, the rationale, which, as will be seen, has had by far the most influence upon the Strasbourg Court. The Court has referred to 'freedom of political debate' as lying 'at the very core of the concept of a democratic society which prevails throughout the Convention'.[8]

It should be recalled that paragraph 2 of Article 10 requires the Court to assess the lawfulness of restrictions upon expression by reference to what is 'necessary in a democratic society'; the Court is bound therefore to afford particular protection to speech that can most readily be justified as contributing to the maintenance of such a society. Since democracy rests upon ideas both of popular participation *and* accountability, the argument from democracy may be seen to encompass in particular the function that a free press performs in exposing abuses of power[9] and failures of government policy, thereby allowing for their remedy, providing a deterrent effect for those contemplating such wrongdoing, and allowing voters to assess the actual record of the government.[10] The 'democracy' rationale, in which the importance of informing and educating the voters has such prominence, therefore *inherently* gives particular weight to the role of the *media*, as opposed to individual expression, since it is only 'the fourth estate'[11] which has the ability to disseminate information and political discussion on a large scale. As we shall see, this particular privileging of the role of the mass media is reflected strongly in the Strasbourg case law; indeed, it will be argued, too strongly. It should also be noted that as an instrumental, or goal-based, justification, the 'democracy' rationale provides support for freedom of expression which is qualified in a number of ways. Most obviously, it does not provide a justification for speech that runs counter to the basic goal of upholding democracy, such as pro-Nazi

---

[7] *R v Secretary of State for the Home Department ex parte Simms* [1999] 3 All ER 400, 408.

[8] *Lingens v Austria* (1986) A 103, para 42.

[9] The argument has most powerfully been put by V. Blasi, 'The Checking Value in First Amendment Theory' (1977) *Am. B. Found. Res. J* 521.

[10] As Greenwalt puts it, 'what people do is partly dependent on what they think will become known. Most particularly, persons are less likely to perform acts that are widely regarded as wrong and that commonly trigger some sanction unless they are confident that they can keep the acts secret.' 'Free Speech Justifications', 89 *Columbia Law Review* 119, 143.

[11] As the media has been referred to.

propaganda, intended to garner support for the ending of democracy itself. The European Court of Human Rights has indeed held that pro-Nazi speech may fall outside the protection of Article 10 altogether,[12] since it is directed against the Convention's underlying values.[13]

It was argued in the Introduction to this book that, upon examination, particular types of speech are often unsupported by one or more of the key rationales underlying free speech theory,[14] an insight which unfortunately often goes unrealized, so that, as Gavison puts it, 'we often find a tendency to assume that all speech performs all the many functions of free speech, so that any limitation on any speech endangers all these functions'.[15] However, the European Court has shown clear awareness of this consideration; at times, as we shall see in this and subsequent chapters, it has, perhaps sometimes rather bluntly and crudely, afforded different kinds of speech a 'high' or 'low' value in assessing the proportionality of an interference with Article 10 rights. As we shall see also, it attributes substantially greater or lesser weight to the different state aims enumerated in paragraph 2 of Article 10. The result is that justifying interference with freedom of expression can, from the state's point of view, vary from being a highly exacting task to one that consists largely of simply stating its view of the matter and successfully inviting the Court to defer to it.

It should also be pointed out at the outset that the guarantee of freedom of expression in Article 10 is, relatively, a heavily qualified one, particularly when compared to the absolute text of the First Amendment: 'Congress shall make no law abridging freedom of speech or of the press'.[16] As Barendt puts it,

The most obvious feature of [Article 10] is the extensive list of circumstances in which limitations to the freedom of expression may be upheld. On a superficial view it appears that Article 10(2) virtually removes the right granted by the first paragraph.[17]

In fact, the Convention generally, and particularly as regards Articles 8–11, seeks to give rights only *presumptive* priority over other societal interests. Thus, these rights exhibit what Mullender has termed 'qualified deontology';[18] whilst they purport to uphold a set of human rights established regardless of consequences, they allow for their restriction by reference to sufficiently weighty consequentialist considerations,

---

[12] In other words, it is not counted as 'expression' within the meaning of Article 10, paragraph 1, and therefore interference with it does not require justification under paragraph 2.

[13] *Lehideux v France* (1998) 5 BHRC 548 para 53. In *Socialist Party and Others v Turkey* (1999) 27 EHRR 51, it was held that the Convention required toleration of diverse political programmes *other than* those which call for 'the use of violence, an uprising or any other form of rejection of democratic principles' (paras 46–47). See the similar reasoning employed in *Kuhnen v FRG* 56 DR 205 (1988).

[14] See pp 12–32.

[15] R. Gavison, 'Too Early for a Requiem: Warren and Brandeis were right on privacy *vs* free speech' (1992) 43(3) *South Carolina Law Review* 437, at 463.

[16] For extended comparison between the US First Amendment jurisprudence and that of the English courts and Strasbourg, see I. Loveland (ed.) *Importing the First Amendment*, 2nd edn., Oxford: Hart Publishing, 1998.

[17] E. Barendt, *Freedom of Speech*, 2nd edn., Oxford: OUP, 2005 at 65.

[18] See R. Mullender, 'Theorising the Third Way: Qualified Consequentialism, the Proportionality Principle and the New Social Democracy', 27(4), *Journal of Law and Society*, 493–516.

in pursuance of a legitimate aim and in a manner proportionate in the circumstances. Moreover, since Articles 10, 9,[19] and 8[20] are each qualified in favour of each other (each recognize 'the rights of others' as a legitimate aim for limiting the primary right), they also provide a method of resolving competing individual *rights*. As the authors have argued elsewhere, such resolution may be found through recognition of the rights' mutual supportiveness as upholding certain, more basic values,[21] and then through giving consideration to which of those values are more strongly engaged by which right in the particular case.[22]

In a recent, important critique,[23] Conor Gearty has argued that the Convention represents not an absolutist statements of rights that vest in persons by very nature of the holders' common humanity, but a mixture of civil libertarian building blocks towards a democratic society[24] (expression, assembly, the right to vote, the right to liberty, and so on) recognition of individual dignity (manifested in the rights to life, to privacy, freedom from torture and from slavery) and respect for the democratic process, tempered by a commitment to the rule of law. He summarizes his view of the Convention conception of rights as a:

Nexus of a devotion to human dignity (the basic rights) which is on the one hand qualified by a realistic sensitivity to the democratic status quo (the pro-majoritarian qualifications in most of the rights) and on the other fortified by a commitment to legality (the requirement that restrictions on rights must be in accordance with the law).[25]

Gearty arguably overstates his case considerably, like any scholar constructing a tendentious thesis, he can be prone to omitting evidence that contradicts its thrust. For example, he states that:

Respect for parliamentary sovereignty shown by the [Human Rights Act], for example, is not foreign to the framework of rights adopted in the . . . Convention, with its derogations and public interest opt-outs but is . . . integral to it.'[26]

This assertion is *partly* true. But Gearty reaches this conclusion simply by citing the derogability of most of the rights and the qualified nature of most;[27] and by omitting real acknowledgement of the fact that some rights are unqualified and therefore absolute,[28] that others have no broad 'public interest opt-outs' but only narrowly

---

[19] The right to freedom of conscience, thought, and belief and to express religious beliefs peacefully.

[20] The right to respect for private and family life. Article 11 also of course protects the right to freedom of assembly and association but there are no instances of a clash between this right and freedom of expression.

[21] These include autonomy and self-development, both of which are recognized as underlying justifications for both freedom of expression and privacy; moreover, the right to privacy to develop one's thoughts can be seen as an essential precursor to expression. On this, see E. Bloustein, 'Privacy as an Aspect of Human Behaviour: an answer to Dean Prosser' (1964) 39 *NUULR* 962; A. Westin, *Privacy and Freedom*, Atheneum: New York, 1970, esp at 34.

[22] This issue is explored in detail in Chapters 13 and 15.

[23] *Principles of Human Rights Adjudication*, Oxford: OUP, 2003.

[24] His views on this matter are considered in more detail below at p 69.

[25] Op cit, at 20.   [26] Ibid, at 25.   [27] Ibid, at 8–12.

[28] Those in Article 3 (the anti-torture and degrading treatment guarantee), Article 4 (1) (prohibition of slavery), Article 6 (right to fair trial), Article 7 (prohibition on retroactive criminal law).

defined ones[29] and that others *cannot* be derogated from[30] even 'in time of war or other public emergency threatening the life of the nation'[31]—the trigger for a derogation to become lawful. For the Human Rights Act specifically to provide that Acts of Parliament that violate Convention rights remain lawful and of full effect,[32] thus allowing, for example, the UK Government to introduce powers to hold people in slavery, torture them,[33] or subject them to retroactive criminal law, *is* foreign to the scheme of the Convention, and *not* 'integral to it'. The HRA allows on its face for a crude override of each and every right in the Convention, at the behest of a bare majority in the House of Commons, which very rarely represents even a majority of the electorate;[34] the Convention itself carefully distinguishes between rights that are absolute, rights with narrow qualifications, and rights with broader ones, providing even for the latter that intrusion into the rights must be 'necessary in a democratic society'.

Gearty also misstates the nature of the qualifications of these rights. He is apt to characterize *all* the qualified rights in Articles 8–11 as recognizing a general majoritarian override; this is not the case. It is clearly evident that, despite the broad exceptions in, say, Article 10, a number of measures would remain unlawful under it, whatever the broad popular support for them: for example, measures wholly proscribing the ability of unpopular, minority groups to express their views in public. At one point, indeed, Gearty's eagerness to stress the pro-majoritarian characteristics of the Convention led him into more obvious error—he states that: '*each* of the freedoms of thought, conscience, religion, expression, assembly and association set out in Articles 9–11 is subject to a wide variety of exceptions'.[35] This statement is erroneous: Article 9 has an *absolute* right contained in it—the right to freedom of conscience, thought, and religion. It is only the freedom to *manifest* such beliefs that is

---

[29] Article 2 (right to life), Article 4(2), Article 5.

[30] Article 2 (except re deaths resulting from war), Articles 3, 4(1), and 7.

[31] The wording of Article 15, which governs derogations.   [32] Sections 3(2) and 6(2).

[33] In comparison, it is probably not possible for the UK to avoid its Article 3 obligations at all (save by wholesale withdrawal from the ECHR). Theoretically, the UK could denounce the ECHR and then re-enter it, with a reservation to Article 3. There is no explicit exclusion of the right to make reservations to Article 3, but, as a matter of international law, reservations may not be made that are incompatible with the object and purpose of a treaty (Vienna Convention Article 19(c)). There is little doubt that the European Court of HR would claim the right to determine this question under the ECHR (see Van Dijk and Van Hoof, *The European Convention on Human Rights: Theory and Practice*, 2nd edn., Kluwer, 1998, pp 774–5 and cf p 776 for the non-derogable provisions). It has not yet had to do so. The UN Human Rights Committee (HRC) has taken a strong position against the power of States to make reservations with respect to the non-derogable provisions of the Covenant (General Comment 24) and, in the case of torture, an absolute one, since the HRC says torture is contrary to a peremptory norm of international law. Thus, even if the UK could avoid the Article 3 duty under the ECHR by reservation, it could not do so under the ICCPR, Article 7. Obviously the UK would not be permitted to enter a reservation to the UN Convention Against Torture. It may be noted that the UN Committee Against Torture made a statement directly communicating with the State Parties (22.11.2001, 27th session) reminding them, in the light of the September 11 atrocities, that obligations under the Convention against Torture in Articles 2, 15, and 16 are non-derogable and 'must be observed in all circumstances'.

[34] At present, the Labour Government represents only 35.3 per cent of the electorate.

[35] Op cit, at 42 (emphasis added).

qualified.[36] This demonstrates a classically liberal concern with the absolute liberty of the individual to his or her own thoughts and thus his or her own self-development, and it is perhaps not surprising that Gearty, in his eagerness to stress the communitarian aspects of the Convention, misses this point.

Nevertheless, while Gearty's case is overstated and flawed in places, its broad thrust deserves recognition: the Convention is very much a compromise between rights-based liberalism and communitarianism,[37] both in the trade-offs it recognizes between individual and collective interests and in the necessity for rights claims to be proportionate to the claims of rights by other individuals. Lord Steyn brings out these points in a passage that is worth quoting in full:

> The framers of the Convention recognised that it was not only morally right to promote the observance of human rights but that it was also the best way of achieving pluralistic and just societies in which all can peaceably go about their lives. The second aim was to foster effective political democracy. This aim necessarily involves the creation of conditions of stability and order under the rule of law, not for its own sake, but as the best way to ensuring the well being of the inhabitants of the European countries. After all, democratic government has only one raison d'etre, namely to serve the interests of all the people. The inspirers of the European Convention realised that from time to time the fundamental right of one individual may conflict with the human right of another . . . They also realised only too well that a single-minded concentration on the pursuit of fundamental rights of individuals to the exclusion of the interests of the wider public might be subversive of the ideal of tolerant European liberal democracies. The fundamental rights of individuals are of supreme importance but those rights are not unlimited: we live in communities of individuals who also have rights. The direct lineage of this ancient idea is clear: the European Convention (1950) is the descendant of the Universal Declaration of Human Rights (1948) which in article 29 expressly recognised the duties of everyone to the community and the limitation on rights in order to secure and protect respect for the rights of others. It is also noteworthy that article 17 of the European Convention prohibits, among others, individuals from abusing their rights to the detriment of others . . . The European Convention requires that where difficult questions arise a balance must be struck. Subject to a limited number of absolute guarantees, the scheme and structure of the Convention reflects this balanced approach.[38]

As we shall see below, the themes of balance between rights and societal concerns, and of the rights themselves being conceptualized above all as basic building blocks of a democratic society, continue in relation to the *interpretation* of Article 10 by the European Court. It has tended to stress the vital *function* of Article 10 within a democratic society, rather than its status as a moral individual entitlement. This approach manifests itself in the value it attaches to different types of speech, the extent of the margin of appreciation it affords to states when limiting speech, and the proportionality tests applied in different situations to assess the legality of such

---

[36] See the wording of para 2.

[37] On this theme, see generally, D. Feldman, 'The Human Rights Act 1998 and constitutional principles' (1999) 19 *LS* 165.

[38] *Brown v Stott* [2001] 2 WLR 817 at 839, 840.

limitations. In other words, this underlying approach of the Court has a decisive effect upon *all* of the key interpretative tasks it performs.

The remainder of this chapter will proceed as follows: we will first look briefly at the interpretation of the first paragraph of Article 10—in other words, at what counts as 'expression' for the purposes of this right; we will then consider what we term the 'foundational rules' for justifying interferences with expression, namely the requirement of a 'legitimate aim' and that any interference be 'prescribed by law'. *Within* that section, we explain why, in order to maximize analytical clarity, we take a different approach to analysing the other foundational rules—proportionality and pressing social need, and the linked doctrine of margin of appreciation, from that often taken, so that we consider the margin of appreciation *before* the doctrine of proportionality. We then go on, in the remainder of the chapter, to consider, first, the key factors that the width of the margin of appreciation granted, devoting a whole main section to the most important of those factors—the nature of the expression in question—and then, in the final main part of the chapter, consider the different proportionality tests that can be used, pointing out the radical effects that use of the different tests can have upon the type and intensity of scrutiny undertaken by Strasbourg.

ARTICLE 10(1): THE SCOPE OF THE PRIMARY RIGHT[39]

It is a well-known characteristic of the Strasbourg Court's jurisprudence that it has defined the scope of Article 10 very generously. Broadly speaking, nearly anything counting as 'expression'—a broader term in itself than 'speech', the term used in the US First Amendment—has been counted as falling within Article 10(1). The real work of the Court has been done in relation to 10(2)—in analysing the requirements for the lawful *restrictions* upon freedom of expression, not in defining what counts as expression in the first place. This is in sharp contrast to First Amendment jurisprudence, which, because of the absolute wording of that guarantee, has had to limit it by excluding certain types of expressive activities from its ambit altogether.[40] Thus hardcore pornography has been found to be 'expression' under Article 10,[41] as has direct action protest, such as physical interference with hunting and road-building.[42] However, whilst Article 10 refers to the right to 'receive information', this guarantee has not been interpreted by the Court as a freedom of information guarantee, that is, a positive obligation on States to release government information.[43] Rather, it indicates

---

[39] We do not consider some aspects of Article 10 that are not relevant to media law, such as 'the right to hold opinions'; the provisions in Article 10 relevant to the licensing of broadcasting are considered in Chapter 10.

[40] Thus, for example, 'obscene speech' is excluded from the protection of Article 10, leaving its regulation to the States (*Miller v California* (1973) 413 US 15, as is defamatory speech known by the 'speaker' to be false: *New York Times v Sullivan* (1964) 376 US 354).

[41] *Hoare v UK* [1997] EHRLR 678.   [42] *Steel v UK* (1998) 28 EHRR 603.

[43] *Leander v Sweden* (1987) A 116; *Guerra v Italy* (1998) 26 EHRR 357, esp at [53].

that where a willing speaker is prevented from expressing him- or herself, both the speaker's *and* his or her potential audience's rights have been (*prima facie*) violated.[44]

Perhaps the most striking exclusion from the ambit of Article 10 that Strasbourg has formulated relates to 'hate speech'—there is some political speech that falls outside the protection of Article 10 altogether on the basis of its extreme message. The Court here has clearly *not* followed the doctrine of content neutrality, under which speech may not be proscribed because of its objectionable content, in terms of political claims or values. Under this approach, the State may no more forbid someone from disseminating pro-Nazi ideology, on the basis that it considers Nazi ideas evil or mistaken, than it may prohibit the dissemination of socialist ideas on the basis that many consider them false and (if followed) damaging to economic prosperity. The US courts have, controversially, followed the doctrine of content neutrality further than most constitutional courts, including Strasbourg, generally holding that the proscription of speech because of its objectionable content is unconstitutional, even in the case of racist speech. Thus they have, for example, invalidated a relatively narrowly drawn prohibition upon the placing of burning crosses and the like on public or private property[45] and upheld the right of a pro-Nazi group to demonstrate in a town with a large Jewish population in the famous 'Nazis at Skokie' cases.[46] Feldman has suggested a four-fold classification of the different types of content neutrality as an analytical tool:[47] firstly, the state may not discriminate between speakers on the basis of the *topic* that the speaker wishes to address[48] by, for example, forbidding discussion of possible differences between the races. Secondly, there must not be discrimination in relation to the content of speech, insofar as that is made up of the 'factual claims and narrative content' of the speech; thus speakers may not be forbidden from claiming, for example, that men are inherently more inclined to promiscuity than women; nor may expression which consists almost entirely of sexually explicit images, by way of narrative, be treated differently from non-explicit speech. Thirdly, states should be neutral as between the different forms or modes of expression, and fourthly, states should not discriminate on the basis of the viewpoint or perspective taken by the speaker on the subject in question (for example, the opinion that immigration threatens to destroy national identity). While it is fairly common for some discrimination to occur in relation to the third category (for example, by having particular regulation of expression that takes the form of public demonstrations, on public order and traffic management grounds), the Strasbourg Court has more controversially, in some eyes, also *declined* to be neutral in relation to types two and four also (narrative and factual claims, and viewpoint or perspective). Thus the Strasbourg

---

[44] See e.g. *Autronic AG v Switzerland* (1990) 12 EHRR 485.

[45] *RAV v City of St Paul, Minnesota* (1992) 120 L.Ed. 2d. 305.

[46] *Collin v Smith* (1978) 578 F 2d 1197, 7th Cir, (1978) 436 US 953, (1978) 439 US 916; *Skokie v Nat Socialist Party* (1978) 373 NE 2d 21. For general discussion of the Supreme Court's stance in this area, see R. Abel, *Speech and Respect*, London: Sweet & Maxwell, 1994, chapter 1.

[47] D. Feldman, 'Content Neutrality', in I. Loveland (ed.) *Importing the First Amendment*, 2nd edn., Oxford: Hart Publishing, 1998, at 147.

[48] Ibid.

Court—and most European countries—broadly hold that the prohibition of the direct incitement of hatred based on race and other discriminatory grounds is *not* contrary to free speech guarantees, even though this involves taking a view based on the content of the speech. Thus, the crudely racist sentiments of the far-right 'Greenjackets' group, in *Jersild v Denmark*,[49] in which members referred to immigrant workers as 'animals' did not, the majority and minority of the Court agreed, attract even the *prima facie* protection of Article 10; however, the documentary, which included interviews with the 'Greenjackets' in which those views were expounded *was* protected. In *Lehideux and Isorni v France*[50] the Court held:

There is no doubt that, like any other remark directed against the Convention's underlying values . . . the justification of pro-Nazi policy could not be allowed to enjoy the protection afforded by Article 10.[51]

These dicta, on their face, allow for a very wide exception to the protection afforded by Article 10—they could mean that *any* 'intolerant' speech was unprotected, since, as seen above, tolerance and pluralism have been identified as key Convention values. However, certainly at present, and bearing in mind some of the Turkish cases, in which quite extreme speech has been afforded protection,[52] it appears that the only kind of speech which falls outside the scope of Article 10 altogether is intentionally racist speech and speech that amounts to pro-Nazi propaganda, which would presumably include speech which denies the existence of historical events such as the Holocaust.[53] It should be noted that this stance is broadly in line with Articles 19 and 20 of the International Covenant on Civil and Political Rights: the former guarantees the right to freedom of expression, but the latter *requires* states to prohibit by law 'any advocacy of national, racial or religious hatred that constitutes incitement to discrimination, hostility or violence . . .'.

JUSTIFYING INTERFERENCE WITH EXPRESSION: THE FOUNDATIONAL RULES

As is well known, to be justified, state interference with Article 10 expression rights must be prescribed by law, have a legitimate aim (one of those specified in paragraph 2 of Article 10),[54] be applied in a non-discriminatory fashion,[55] and be necessary in a

---

[49] Op cit. The case concerned a documentary in which members of the Greenjackets, a far-right organization, were interviewed about their views.

[50] (1998–VII).   [51] Op cit, at [53].

[52] See, e.g., *Karata v Turkey* (8 July 1999) discussed below, at 68.

[53] Strasbourg's stance on these matters is discussed in detail in Chapter 9.

[54] The exceptions likely to be relevant in public protest cases, specified in both Articles, are actions necessary for the protection of 'public safety [or] public health, the prevention of disorder or crime . . . [or] the protection of the rights and freedoms of others.'

[55] Under Article 14 of the Convention.

democratic society. The Court has interpreted this last and most significant requirement as connoting the twin requirements that 'an interference [must] correspond to a
pressing social need and, in particular . . . [be] proportionate to the legitimate aim
pursued'.[56] While this chapter will touch in places upon the requirement of legitimate
aim, it is extremely rare for it to be found that state interference fails this test, principally because the prescribed aims are very wide-ranging in terms, and have been given
a generous interpretation by the Court. The Court has also been fairly lenient in
assessing what is meant by 'prescribed by law'; however, this requirement is not an
empty one and is briefly considered below.

'PRESCRIBED BY LAW': THE PRINCIPLE OF LEGALITY

At its simplest, this requirement is that the interference with Article 10 must be
authorized by the law of the relevant state. The Court has, however, gone further than
this formal requirement, in holding that such 'law' must have certain qualities, a
matter addressed by the European Court in a famous passage in *Sunday Times v
United Kingdom*:[57]

. . . a norm cannot be regarded as a 'law' unless it is formulated with sufficient precision to
enable the citizen to regulate his conduct; he must be able, if need be with appropriate
advice, to foresee to a degree that is reasonable in all the circumstances, the consequences
which a given action may entail . . . [However] those consequences need not be attainable
with absolute certainty: experience shows this to be unattainable . . . whilst certainly is
highly desirable, it may bring in its train excessive rigidity and the law must be able to keep
pace with changing circumstances. Accordingly many laws are inevitably couched in terms
which, to a greater or lesser extent, are vague and whose interpretation and application are
questions of practice.[58]

Thus, the requirement that interferences be prescribed by law is not only a *formal*
requirement, it says something about the qualities which that law must have. One of
the relatively rare cases in which an interference with a Convention right was found
to be unlawful on this basis[59] was an Article 10 case, although not one involving the
media, *Hashman and Harrup v UK*.[60] The application to the European Court was
made by hunt saboteurs, complaining of a violation of their right of freedom of
expression. They had blown a horn and engaged in hallooing with the intention of
disrupting a hunt. They succeeded in drawing some of the hounds away from the
hunt, and one was killed when it ran across a road. Following a complaint to the local
magistrates, they were bound over to keep the peace and be of good behaviour,[61]

---

[56] *Olsson v Sweden*, A 130 para 67 (1988).   [57] (1979) 2 EHRR 245.   [58] Ibid, at [49].

[59] A complaint as to telephone tapping (as opposed to metering) was found in *Malone v United Kingdom*
(1985) 7 EHRR 14 to disclose a violation of Article 8 on this basis, since the applicable law, together with
Government statements explaining its practice in relation to telephone tapping, was found to be so vague and
complex as not to fulfil the above requirements.

[60] (2000) EHRR 24.

[61] In the sum of £100 for 12 months under the Justices of the Peace Act 1361.

something that, *inter alia*, prevented them engaging in further such protests. The binding over was based on the finding that their behaviour had been '*contra bonos mores*' ('contrary to a good way of life'). The applicants' argument at Strasbourg was that the binding over orders, which interfered with their right to freedom of expression under Article 10, could not be said to be 'prescribed by law', since the relevant domestic law was too vague and unclear.

The Court noted first of all that 'conduct *contra bonos mores* is defined as behaviour which is "wrong rather than right in the judgment of the majority of contemporary fellow citizens" '. It found that such a definition lacked a sufficiently objective basis; it did not, as did other laws that the Court had found to be sufficiently precise, proscribe conduct by reference to its likely effects; in fact, it 'is conduct which is not described at all, but merely expressed to be "wrong" in the opinion of a majority of citizens'.[62] Thus, 'with specific reference to the facts of the present case, the Court does not accept that it must have been evident to the applicants what they were being ordered not to do for the period of their binding over'.[63] Therefore, the interference with their expression rights was not 'prescribed by law' of sufficient clarity to satisfy the Convention standard. This is, however, a rare finding: even in areas of relatively vague common law offences, such as blasphemy, the Court has been prepared to find that the law is sufficiently clear to pass the Convention test.[64]

The final requirement in Article 10 is that interferences with expression rights, if prescribed by law and in pursuit of a legitimate aim, must be undertaken only where there is a pressing social need and must be limited, so that the interference is proportionate to the legitimate aim pursued.

THE RELATIONSHIP BETWEEN THE MARGIN OF APPRECIATION AND PROPORTIONALITY

It is a significant feature of Convention case law that, in determining this key issue of proportionality, the standard of review varies markedly. In justifying applying such a varying standard, the Court often refers to what is known as the margin of appreciation doctrine. This doctrine reflects Strasbourg's view that the role of the Convention in protecting human rights is subsidiary to the role of the national legal system[65] and that since the domestic authorities are in many cases better placed than the international judge to balance individual rights against general societal interests, Strasbourg will in such cases operate only a restrained review of the balance struck. The Court expresses the basic idea thus:

By reason of their direct and continuous contact with the vital forces of their countries, State

---

[62] Op cit, at [38].   [63] Ibid, at [40].   [64] See Chapter 9.

[65] *Handyside v UK* A 24 para 48 (1976). The rationale of the margin of appreciation doctrine is considered in more detail below, at pp 82–4. For a recent, detailed discussion, although not, unfortunately, one we have been able to consider here, see Y. Arai-Takahati, *The Margin of Appreciation Doctrine and the Principle of Proportionality in the Jurisprudence of the ECHR*, Antwerp: Intersentia, 2004.

authorities are in principle in a better position than the international judge to give an opinion on the exact content of [the requirement of morals] as well as on the 'necessity' of a 'restriction' or 'penalty' intended to meet them." Consequently, Article 10 para. 2 leaves to the Contracting States a margin of appreciation. This margin is given both to the domestic legislator ('prescribed by law') and to the bodies, judicial amongst others, that are called upon to interpret and apply the laws in force.[66]

In other words, the doctrine allows the Court to defer, to a greater or lesser extent, to the views of the relevant national authorities, both that it was *necessary* to interfere with freedom of expression to protect another interest (for example, the protection of morals), and as regards the choice of *means* to afford that protection (such as criminal prosecutions, injunctions, awards of damages, etc.). In so doing, the Court is able to allow for a certain amount of diversity amongst the various signatory States to the Convention in the way that they deal with controversial and culturally sensitive issues, such as pornography, blasphemy, hate speech, and the like. The discussion that follows teases out some of the implications of the doctrine.

The type of speech that Strasbourg is dealing with directly influences the width of the margin of appreciation it concedes and hence the intensity of scrutiny. It is for this reason that we, perhaps unusually, deal with the topic of proportionality *after* examining the margin of appreciation doctrine. It is common for examination of the Convention to deal with proportionality first, with consideration of the margin of appreciation doctrine tacked on the end—as if the Court somehow performs a proportionality enquiry, and *then* affords a margin of appreciation. In a few cases, as we shall see, this may be the case, as where the Court engages in a straightforward balancing act between the right that has been infringed and the importance of the social interest justifying the infringement.[67] In such a case, if the Court, on weighing the matter up, considers that no clear answer as to which interest is more important emerges, it may be tempted to defer to the decision of the national authorities. But the crucial point is that by choosing such a method, it has *already chosen* a relatively soft-edged form of review, ruling out more rigorous alternatives, such as requiring the State to show that the infringing measures taken were the least restrictive possible in the circumstances.[68]

We think it therefore preferable first to indicate the factors, including in particular the type of speech under consideration, that motivate the Court to grant a narrow or a wide margin of appreciation, that is, to conduct a rigorous or light-touch method of review. Once it has determined the intensity of review it wishes to undertake, the Court then selects the proportionality test that will achieve this aim.[69] In other words, it is not in itself the 'margin of appreciation' that determines the intensity of review. Rather, the *factors underlying* the margin of appreciation doctrine guide the Court towards selecting a more or less rigorous form of proportionality enquiry, and it is the type of

---

[66] Ibid.   [67] For examples, see below at pp 101–4.   [68] See further below at pp 98–100.

[69] We are not claiming that this method occurs consciously, it may well be that the presence of factors minding the Court's judges to perform a light-touch review unconsciously led it to deploying a soft-edged proportionality test.

proportionality test used that actually determines how intense the scrutiny is. In other words, the Court identifies certain factors, including, crucially, the nature of the speech, and the legitimate aim for interference adduced, which guide it towards adopting a form of scrutiny, varying from an 'absolutely necessary' to interfere test on the one hand to a 'not unreasonable' to interfere test, on the other. As we shall in the next major section, in some cases, in which the Court is minded to subject a decision only to light touch review, critical stages in the proportionality enquiry are simply omitted, effectively relieving the State from its obligation of defending its actions in detail. If it adopts a light touch review, then looking back on the decision (as it were), it can be characterized as one in which a wide margin of appreciation was granted to the State. But it is misleading and tautologous to say that the review was 'light touch' *because* the State was granted a wide margin of appreciation—these are just two ways of saying the same thing.[70] It is the factors that determine the Court's sense of how rigorous the scrutiny should be, which in turn lead to the adoption of a more or less strict form of proportionality test being used, that are crucial. In this section, therefore we sketch the most important of these factors and consider some criticisms of the margin of appreciation doctrine. Bosma comments that, 'the Court has not been inclined to provide clarity as to the role played by the margin of appreciation in the reasoning which leads to the decision, or to indicate what "principles or standards" determine the scope of the margin of appreciation.'[71] It has simply said: 'the scope of the margin of appreciation will vary according to the circumstances, the subject matter and the background'.[72] Nevertheless, a number of commentators have succeeded in identifying a number of factors, *other* than the nature of the expression in question, that go to the width of the margin granted, and these are explored in the subsequent section.

FACTORS AFFECTING THE INTENSITY OF STRASBOURG REVIEW

THE HIERARCHY OF EXPRESSION

Of the factors affecting the intensity of review, one of the most important, though as we will argue, not always decisive, is the type of speech in question, and it to this issue that we first turn. While Strasbourg's *rhetorical* attachment to free speech is always strong, it is by now a familiar commentary upon Article 10 jurisprudence to observe that clearly political speech, which more directly engages the self-government rationale, receives a much more robust degree of protection than other types of expression, such as artistic speech. Thus the leading 'political' speech cases of *Sunday Times v*

---

[70] See the similar critique of Singh *et al.*, below text to note 235.

[71] H. Bosma, *Freedom of Expression in England an under the ECHR: In Search of a Common Ground,* Oxford: Hart, 2000, at 178.

[72] Op cit, at 178.

UK,[73] *Jersild v Denmark*,[74] *Lingens v Austria*[75] and *Thorgeirson v Iceland*[76] all resulted in findings that Article 10 had been violated, and all were marked by an intensive review of the restriction in question, in which the margin of appreciation was narrowed almost to vanishing point. By contrast, in cases involving artistic speech, supported by the values of autonomy and self-development rather than self-government,[77] an exactly converse pattern emerges: applicants have tended to be unsuccessful and a very deferential approach to the judgments of the national authorities as to its obscene or blasphemous nature has been adopted.[78] As one of the leading works on the Convention concludes: 'It is clear that the Court ascribes a hierarchy of value' to different classes of speech, attaching 'the highest importance to the protection of political expression . . . widely understood'; artistic expression is firmly in the second rank.[79] In *Wingrove v UK*,[80] the Court defended this normative variation expressly:

Whereas there is little scope under Article 10(2) of the Convention for restrictions on political speech or on debate of questions of public interest . . . a wider margin of appreciation is generally available to the Contracting States when regulating freedom of expression in relation to matters liable to offend intimate personal convictions within the sphere of morals or, especially, religion.

We may now take a closer look at some of the cases that illustrate the effect of this variation in the standard and intensity of scrutiny.

Some illustrative cases: Protection for 'political' and 'artistic' speech contrasted

There is no doubt that, as Feldman puts it, 'the Court closely scrutinizes any interference with speech and associated activities (particularly those of the press and broadcasters) which may advance democratic participation or accountability or the free market of ideas.'[81] In *Hertel v Switzerland*,[82] for example, the Court said that it

---

[73] A 30 (1979). The case concerned a contempt of court action brought against the newspaper in respect of revelations it published concerning the dangers of the drug thalidomide.

[74] (1994) 19 EHRR 1. The case concerned an application by a Danish journalist who had been convicted of a racially offensive offence after preparing and broadcasting a programme about racism which included overtly racist speech by the subjects of the documentary.

[75] (1986) 8 EHRR 407. The case concerned the defamation of a political figure. The finding of a violation rested partly upon the fact that the journalist had been asked, by the Austrian courts, in effect to prove the truth, not only of the defamatory facts he alleged but of the value judgments his articles contained also. As the Strasbourg Court observed, this was to place an impossible burden on him.

[76] (1992) 14 EHRR 843. The case concerned newspaper articles reporting allegations of brutality against the Reykjavik police.

[77] See Introduction, at pp 12–14 and 18–20.

[78] The following cases all concerned artistic speech which was restricted by the national authorities on the basis either of protection of public morals or religious feelings, or both: *Müller v Switzerland* (1991) 13 EHRR 212; *Gibson v UK* no. 17634 (declared inadmissible by Commission); *Otto Preminger*, op cit; *Gay News v UK* (1989) 12 EHRR 123; *Wingrove v UK* (1997) 24 EHRR 1, esp para 58.

[79] Harris O'Boyle and Warbrick, *Law of the European Convention on Human Rights*, London: Butterworths, 1995, pp 397 and 414. The third rank is commercial speech, e.g. advertising.

[80] (1997) 24 EHRR 1. For discussion, see Harris *et al.*, op cit., 397 and 414.

[81] D. Feldman, 'Content Neutrality', op cit, at 157.   [82] (1998) 28 EHRR 534 at [47].

was 'necessary to reduce the extent of the margin of appreciation when what is at stake is . . . an individual's participation in a debate affecting the general interest, for example, over public health.' This case in fact indicates that to speak of the Court as affording a high level of protection to 'political' speech is not strictly accurate. *Hertel* clearly concerned what we might term 'legitimate public concern' speech (relating to public health), rather than directly political expression. The same can be said of the famous *Sunday Times* decision, discussed below, which concerned discussion of the civil justice system, in the context of the alleged negligence of a major drug company, not 'politics' in the narrower sense. Indeed, in *Thorgeison*, the Court said that there was 'no warrant' in its case law for distinguishing between political and other 'public concern' speech. However, these dicta are not perhaps as radical as at first they appear; they need to be understood in the context in which they were utttered. The Court made this remark in the context of the consideration of the conviction of journalists of the offence of criminal defamation after they had published an article containing allegations of police brutality. In particular, the Court was responding to a specific government claim that the speech in question deserved less protection than that given in other cases such as *Lingens, because* it was not 'political' speech. It would have been very surprising had the Court acceded to the notion that discussion of an allegation of serious abuse of power by a primary state institution such as the police was not as important as 'political speech'. Acceptance of such a notion would have meant accepting that revelations of police brutality were, *categorically*, of less importance in Article 10 terms than reportage of some obviously 'political matter', such as some minor error of judgment by an MP. In any event, many people would call the issue of police brutality a 'political' issue, even in a narrow sense—it is certainly an issue which tends to divide left-wing parties, generally concerned with civil rights, from those on the right, which are generally pro-'law and order' and therefore pro-police. Thus the finding by the Court that the expression at issue in this case was as worthy of protection as political speech was scarcely a surprising one. Given the weighty and serious nature of the reportage in this case, however, the Court's endorsement of such 'public concern' speech as being of equal importance to overtly 'political speech' does *not* mean that the Court in *Thorgeirson* was coming even close to endorsing the kind of flimsy claims of 'public interest' made recently by English courts in the context of celebrity gossip—we have in mind claims of public interest notoriously made by the Court of Appeal in relation to revelations about the private lives of footballers[83] based on some vague notion of the impact of 'role models' on public perceptions. The Court in *Thorgeirson* may have asserted that speech about matters of public concern was of equal importance to overtly political speech, but the type of speech it had in mind—abuse of power by a state institution—was plainly of a serious, weighty and indisputably 'public' character.

Properly understood, however, the basic principle enunciated in *Thorgeirson* is a sound one. As Barendt puts it:

---

[83] *A v B plc*, op cit: for discussion, see Chapter 15 at 794–7.

The public is entitled to discuss a wide range of topics, irrespective of whether they are taken up by government and political parties. 'Political speech' refers to all speech relevant to the development of public opinion on the whole range of issues which an intelligent citizen should think about, [a] ... proposition ... approved by the High Court of Australia in 1994.[84]

The unsatisfactory later jurisprudence of the Australian High Court, seeking to distinguish directly political speech (i.e., clearly linked to the electoral choice of the people) from other speech of general public concern, illustrates the point.[85]

Having made these general observations, it is useful next to turn to look for a moment at the *Sunday Times*[86] decision in some detail as an illustrative case on the Court's approach to 'political speech', partly because it was one of the most significant early Article 10 decisions on such speech, but also because it was in its judgment in that case that the Court split directly on the question of how great a margin of appreciation should be afforded to the national authorities. The facts of the case are well known, but in brief, the applicant was the *Sunday Times* newspaper, which had been prevented by an injunction from publishing any further stories on the Thalidomide tragedy, in which a sedative drug was found to cause severe harm to the foetus, when taken by pregnant women. Hundreds of legal actions in negligence against Distillers, the producers of the drug, resulted. Protracted negotiations as to the settling of these case were still in process when the *Sunday Times* published an article which was generally critical of the law relating to compensation by drug companies and which called upon Distillers, to 'think again' about the level of compensation it had offered to the women concerned. After complaints by Distillers that this article was prejudicial, the *Sunday Times* sent the draft of a further article, which contained an argument with some supporting evidence to the effect that Distillers had not taken proper care when testing the safety of Thalidomide, to the Attorney General, seeking reassurance that it would not be punished for contempt of court, if the article were published. The Attorney General sought and obtained an injunction preventing the publication of the article and any other article that prejudged the issue of negligence or dealt with the evidence relating to any of the issues arising in the litigation between the parties. On appeal, the injunction was ultimately confirmed by the House of Lords. It should be noted that none of the cases against Distillers had been set down for trial at this point, and negotiations had been continuing for years.

The *Sunday Times* complained of a breach of Article 10. The Court found that the injunction served a legitimate aim—upholding the authority of the judiciary—and were prescribed by law, but by the narrowest of majorities, found that it was not 'necessary in a democratic society'.[87] Of particular note for our purposes is the fact that the minority, who found no violation, argued that the Court's review should be

---

[84] Barendt, *Freedom of Speech*, at 161–2; the Australian case referred to is the judgment of Mason, CJ. Toohey and Gaudron JJ. in *Theophanous v Herald & Weekly Times Ltd* (1994) 182 CLR 104, 124, HC of A.

[85] *Lange v Australian Broadcasting Corporation* (1997) 189 CLR 520, 558.   [86] (1979) 2 EHRR 245.

[87] The case is considered in detail in relation to contempt of court specifically in Chapter 4, at 183–5.

confined to asking whether the state had 'exercised its discretion reasonably, carefully and in good faith'.[88] In other words, the Court should not ask itself whether the injunction was necessary in a democratic society, but whether the UK Courts reasonably and honestly *thought* it was. The majority of the Court, however, rejected this approach, finding instead that it had a duty to decide *itself* on the question of necessity. Clearly, one of the principal factors that led the Court to undertake this more intensive form of review was the nature of the speech, which the Court assessed as being of the highest importance.

The thalidomide disaster was a matter of undisputed public concern. It posed the question whether the powerful company which had marketed the drug bore legal or moral responsibility towards hundreds of individuals experiencing an appalling personal tragedy or whether the victims could demand or hope for indemnification only from the community as a whole; fundamental issues concerning protection against and compensation for injuries resulting from scientific developments were raised and many facets of the existing law on these subjects were called in question.

As the Court has already observed, Article 10 guarantees not only the freedom of the press to inform the public but also the right of the public to be properly informed . . . In the present case, the families of numerous victims of the tragedy, who were unaware of the legal difficulties involved, had a vital interest in knowing all the underlying facts and the various possible solutions. They could be deprived of this information, which was crucially important for them, only if it appeared absolutely certain that its diffusion would have presented a threat to the 'authority of the judiciary.[89]

The last sentence is highly significant: The Court sets the remarkably strict test that only if it was 'absolutely certain' that the proposed publications would have damaged the authority of the judiciary could the injunction have been justified. Bosma comments that, given the full review undertaken by the Court in this case, 'there seemed not much left of the margin of appreciation.'[90]

The intensive review of the case by the Court involved a number of features—notably it was prepared to second-guess the findings of the national courts on the relevant *facts*, including the claim that the article would be likely to prejudice future proceedings or put pressure on Distiller to settle. This involved the Court assessing for itself the nature and likely effect of the article:

. . . the proposed *Sunday Times* article was couched in moderate terms and did not present just one side of the evidence or claim that there was only one possible result at which a court could arrive; although it analysed in detail evidence against Distillers, it also summarised arguments in their favour and closed with the words: 'There appears to be no neat set of answers . . .'. In the Court's opinion, the effect of the article, if published, would therefore have varied from reader to reader.[91]

---

[88] Op cit, at [48].   [89] Op cit, at [66].

[90] H. Bosma, *Freedom of Expression in England and under the ECHR: In Search of a Common Ground*, Oxford: Hart, 2000, at 177.

[91] Op cit, at [63].

The Court also made its own assessment of the whole factual background:

One of the reasons relied on was the pressure which the article would have brought to bear on Distillers to settle the actions out of court on better terms. However, even in 1972, publication of the article would probably not have added much to the pressure already on Distillers . . . This applies with greater force to the position obtaining in July 1973, when the House of Lords gave its decision: by that date, the thalidomide case had been debated in Parliament and had been the subject not only of further press comment but also of a nationwide campaign.[92]

Essentially, the Court here undertakes its own evaluation and assessment of the whole situation, and substitutes its own view of the matter for that of the English courts. Its conclusion was as follows:

. . . the Court concludes that the interference complained of did not correspond to a social need sufficiently pressing to outweigh the public interest in freedom of expression within the meaning of the Convention.[93]

A more recent example of such a robust approach in the context of political speech is the less well-known decision in *Vereniging Weekblad Bluf! v Netherlands*.[94] The applicants published a weekly left-wing journal; an edition published in 1987 included a report dating from 1981—an internal review of the Dutch internal security service (the BVD)—which showed that it was interested in the activities of the Communist Party and the anti-nuclear movement. Before distribution, a judge ordered the seizure of the entire print-run. The Government decided not to attempt to stop distribution on the streets, for fear of public disorder, and 2,500 copies were sold. Withdrawal and seizure orders were then carried out. The Court found that the aim was a legitimate one—the protection of national security. However, in terms of necessity, the Court doubted the need to prohibit the distribution of a 6 year old report. It also noted that it had ruled in its previous *Observer and Guardian*[95] judgment that it could not be considered necessary to prohibit the disclosure of information that had already been made public. In this case it noted that the information:

had been made accessible to large numbers of people, who were able in turn to communicate it to others. Furthermore, the events were commented on by the media. That being so, the protection of the information as a State secret was no longer justified.

As a result, the withdrawal and seizure of the issue of the journal dealing with the matter could not be seen as 'necessary', the Court noting that it would, alternatively, have been possible to prosecute the offenders. As Mowbray comments, the judgment 'reveals the Court making its own assessment of whether national security interests, even in the sensitive field of security service operations, require the limitation of freedom of expression concerning such activities'.[96]

---

[92] Ibid.   [93] Op cit, at [67].   [94] (1995) 20 EHRR 189.
[95] *Observer and Guardian v UK* (1991) 14 EHRR 153.
[96] A. Mowbray, *Cases and Materials on the European Convention on Human Rights*, London: Butterworths, 2001, at 521.

It is instructive to contrast the intensive review undertaken in the above two cases with that adopted in *Müller v Switzerland*,[97] one of the leading decisions on 'artistic speech'. The facts were as follows. Müller, an artist with an international reputation, produced three large paintings for an exhibition. The catalogue contained a photographic reproduction of the paintings. The paintings amounted to explicit portrayals of a variety of sexual acts, including between men, women and animals. He was prosecuted for obscenity. It seemed that the prosecutor had acted following a complaint 'by a man whose daughter, a minor, had reacted violently to the paintings on show; some days earlier another visitor to the exhibition had apparently thrown down one of the paintings, trampled on it and crumpled it.'[98] The artist and others were convicted of obscenity under the Swiss Criminal Code and the paintings seized by the authorities.

The Swiss Courts observed of the paintings:

The overall impression is of persons giving free rein to licentiousness and even perversion. The subjects—sodomy, fellatio, bestiality, the erect penis—are obviously morally offensive to the vast majority of the population. Although allowance has to be made for changes in the moral climate, even for the worse, what we have here would revolutionise it. Comment on the confiscated works is superfluous; their vulgarity is plain to see and needs no elaborating upon.[99]

As to the relevant Swiss Law, the Federal Court found:

The decided cases show that for the purposes of Article 204 of the Criminal Code, any item is obscene which offends, in a manner that is difficult to accept, the sense of sexual propriety; the effect of the obscenity may be to arouse a normal person sexually or to disgust or repel him.[100]

The Court found that the paintings clearly fell within this definition. The applicants argued for a more contextual approach to the definition of obscenity, and for greater weight to be given to the need for freedom of expression with the arts:

Visitors to an exhibition of contemporary art like 'Fri-Art 81' should expect to be faced with modern works that might be incomprehensible. If they did not like the paintings in issue, they were free to look away from them and pass them by; there was no need for the protection of the criminal law. It was not for the court to undertake indirect censorship of the arts.[101]

This submission goes to the *seriousness* of the harm perceived by the Government; it queries what harm was actually being done by the paintings, especially in the context of a serious art exhibition. On the particular point of the *confiscation* of the paintings, the applicants argued that:

---

[97] (1998) 13 EHRR 212.
[98] Op cit, at [12].   [99] Ibid, at [14].
[100] Ibid, at [18].   [101] Ibid, at [17].

Confiscation of the disputed paintings ... could only be ordered if they represented a danger to public order such that returning them could not be justified—and that was a matter the Court of Cassation had not considered. Since the pictures had been openly on display for ten days without giving rise to any protests, it was difficult to see how such a danger was made out. Josef Felix Müller would certainly not show his paintings in Fribourg [where the complained of exhibition was held] in the near future. On the other hand, they could be shown without any difficulty elsewhere, as was proved by his exhibition in Basle in February 1982. It was consequently out of all proportion to deprive him of them.[102]

This submission goes to the issue of means/end balancing—in other words, to the question whether, even if it was accepted that *some* action was needed to prevent the paintings causing further offence, the actual measure taken—confiscation—went further than necessary.[103] The paintings, it should be noted, in fact remained confiscated for some 8 years.

The first question for the Court to determine was the importance of the speech in a democratic society. As to this, the applicants submitted as follows:

In the applicants' view, freedom of artistic expression was of such fundamental importance that banning a work or convicting the artist of an offence struck at the very essence of the right guaranteed in Article 10 and had damaging consequences for a democratic society. No doubt the impugned paintings reflected a conception of sexuality that was at odds with the currently prevailing social morality, but, the applicants argued, their symbolical meaning had to be considered, since these were works of art. Freedom of artistic expression would become devoid of substance if paintings like those of Müller could not be shown to people interested in the arts as part of an exhibition of experimental contemporary art.[104]

In response, the Court did affirm the vital role of the artist in a democratic society:

Those who create, perform, distribute or exhibit works of art contribute to the exchange of ideas and opinions which is essential for a democratic society. Hence the obligation on the State not to encroach unduly on their freedom of expression.[105]

However, it is when we examine the actual approach used by the Court in determining whether the interference was lawful that the strong contrast with the approach adopted in the *Sunday Times* and *Vereniging* cases becomes apparent:

having inspected the original paintings, the Court does not find unreasonable the view taken by the Swiss courts that those paintings, with their emphasis on sexuality in some of its crudest forms, were 'liable grossly to offend the sense of sexual propriety of persons of ordinary sensitivity' ... the Swiss courts were entitled to consider it 'necessary' for the protection of morals to impose a fine on the applicants for publishing obscene material.[106]

---

[102] Ibid.   [103] This method of protection is explored further at pp 100–1.
[104] Ibid, at [31].   [105] Ibid, at [33].   [106] Op cit, at [36].

It will be recalled that in the *Sunday Times* case, the Court asked itself whether the interference was 'absolutely necessary', and, taking its own view of the facts of the case, decided that it was not. Here, in contrast, the Court asks itself, not whether the punishment visited on *Müller* was necessary, but whether the Swiss Courts were 'entitled to think it necessary'—a very different question. Moreover, no real reasoning is given to support the conclusion that they were so entitled. The first sentence in the above paragraph, it will be noted, goes not to the question of whether the punishment was 'necessary' in Article 10 terms, but whether Swiss law had been violated or not, and so is not strictly relevant. It will be recalled that there is supposed to be a 'pressing social need' to interfere with freedom of expression and that Article 10 includes protection for speech that 'shocks, offends or disturbs'.[107] In the two 'political speech' cases above, it was noted that the Court rigorously examined the *evidence* of the necessity of interference—the possibility of harm to the security services in *Vereniging Weekblad Bluf!*, and in the *Sunday Times* case of prejudice to the eventual trial in the *Distillers* case, and in each case, concluded that the national authorities had wrongly evaluated it. Here, one might expect the Court to be looking for evidence of widespread offence or outrage to justify such a draconian interference with expression. In fact, the evidence was rather the other way: There had been no public outcry and Müller had exhibited elsewhere in Switzerland without complaint. The Court noted this evidence, but simply observed:

It does not, however, follow that the applicants' conviction in Fribourg did not, in all the circumstances of the case, respond to a genuine social need as was affirmed in substance by all three of the Swiss courts which dealt with the case.[108]

The fact was that the evidence of a need to censor the pictures on grounds of wide-spread offence was extremely weak—only 3 people appeared to have been seriously offended by the pictures[109] and it was on this basis that the Swiss Courts had made orders prohibiting everyone in Switzerland from seeing them. In the absence of any real evidence, the Court relied on the views of the Swiss courts which had dealt with the case. This however is disingenuous: the view of the Swiss courts was *not* that there was a 'pressing social need' to punish the artist, a question they evidently did not consider; their view was simply that the pictures fell within the definition of 'obscene' in the Swiss Criminal Code. No doubt they did, on the facts; what is remarkable, however, is that the Strasbourg Court at no point asked whether that law was *itself* compatible with the Convention. Instead it took the view of the Swiss courts that the paintings fell foul of Swiss law as proof that there was a pressing social need to punish the artist, an extraordinarily flawed mode of analysis. Given in fact that the Swiss courts made no finding on pressing social need, the sole evidence before the Court was the reaction of three people—the fact that far more people were

---

[107] *Handyside*, op cit, at [49].

[108] Ibid.

[109] The man who complained, whose daughter was upset by them, and the visitor who trampled a painting to the floor.

presumably not offended, and the generally high reputation of the artist is simply dismissed. The reality is that this judgment simply amounts to acceptance of the Swiss Court's view. Far from challenging it, the Court preferred simply to dismiss possible objections to it.

The remarkable second aspect of the judgment is its rank failure to deal with the proportionality point. As well as asking whether there was a pressing social need to protect morals, justifying taking *some* action against the artist, the Court is required to consider whether the particular action was 'proportionate', which, particularly where there was more than one course of action available to the authorities, involves[110] asking whether the actual measures taken went further than was necessary. The paintings, having been seized by the authorities, could not be shown anywhere else by the artist. In effect, the Swiss courts banned them from being shown anywhere in the world. This was, by any standards, a grave interference with freedom of expression. However, under Swiss law, having been seized as obscene items, they would normally have been destroyed; thus the authorities had not taken the most drastic action available to them. Moreover, the applicant, albeit some eight years later, successfully applied for the return of his paintings. This may have been one of the matters that persuaded the Court that the actions of the Swiss authorities were not disproportionate. The applicants specifically argued:

the relevant courts could have chosen a less draconian measure or, in the interests of protecting human rights, could have decided to take no action at all . . . by confiscating the paintings the Fribourg authorities in reality imposed their view of morals on the country as a whole and . . . this was unacceptable, contradictory and contrary to the Convention, having regard to the well-known diversity of opinions on the subject.[111]

The Court's response to this argument was to ignore it. Noting that the paintings could have been destroyed, it simply remarked:

The applicants' conviction responded to a genuine social need under Article 10 § 2 of the Convention . . . The same reasons which justified that measure also apply in the view of the Court to the confiscation order made at the same time.

This quite plainly sidesteps the issue of the proportionality of the *seizure* order. Punishing the artist by a fine is one matter—confiscating the paintings themselves for eight years, thus preventing them being shown even outside Switzerland, is very much another. A bland assertion that the reasons justifying one justify the other simply fails to deal with the point at hand and is intellectually dishonest. The only other point the Court made is that the artist was entitled to apply to regain confiscated works, and that, although he was deprived of them for eight years, he could have applied earlier, and there was nothing to show that the application would have failed.[112] In fact, there *was* evidence that he might have failed—the reluctance with

---

[110] See further below for discussion of different formulations of proportionality.
[111] Ibid, at [40].   [112] Ibid, at [43].

which, even after eight years, the Swiss courts allowed him to have his paintings back.[113] Thus, rather than examining whether lesser means could have achieved the same effect, the Court pointed to the fact that more drastic measures could have been imposed (destruction of the paintings) as proof that the actual measures taken were proportionate. This is the least intrusive means test in reverse. As Warbrick comments tersely:

> It is hard to accept that [the acceptance of the confiscation order] comports with any notion of proportionality, whatever the margin of appreciation, given the importance of factors particular to the exhibition as the justification for interfering with the paintings at all ... The result was that the application of the standards prevailing in a small part of Switzerland had an *erga omnes* effect of universal proportion.[114]

As we shall see, strikingly similar tendencies appear in the other leading 'artistic expression' decision, *Otto Preminger v Austria*,[115] a case which has strong factual parallels with *Müller*. As examined below, the seizure and forfeiture of a film found offensive on religious grounds was again accepted by the Court with no examination of whether the interefence went further than necessary, even though in that case, the reason for punishing the makers of the film relied heavily upon local conditions (the very high proportion of Catholics in the area in which the film was to have been shown) that were plainly logically incapable of justifying a measure that made it impossible to show the film anywhere in Austria.[116]

Thus the contrast between the approach taken by the Court in relation to different types of speech seems clear: 'political speech' attracts a high level of protection, in which the state's justifications for interference are subjected to sustained and critical scrutiny; interference with 'artistic speech', in contrast, is very readily justified, even on the basis of virtually no real evidence, while key issues of proportionality are all but ignored.

Finally, we turn briefly to commercial speech, that is, primarily, speech that has the purpose of forwarding the commercial interests of an organization by promoting its products or services. As one might expect, commercial speech is afforded the lowest weight by the Court, thus giving states a wide area of discretion in regulating it. It was found in *X and Church of Scientology v Sweden*[117] that commercial speech is protected by Article 10, but that the level of protection should be less than that accorded to the expression of political ideas. In *Markt Intern Verlag v FRG*,[118] a commercial speech case, the Court found: 'The European Court of Human Rights should not substitute its own evaluation for that of the national courts in the instant case, where those

---

[113] 'The court considers, *admittedly with some hesitation*, that the [confiscation] order may now be discharged.' ibid, at [19] (emphasis added).

[114] Op cit, at 187.   [115] (1995) 19 EHRR 34.

[116] The case is examined further below in relation to legitimate aim (at 77–8) and proportionality (at 99).

[117] Appl No 7805/77 (1979); YB XXII.

[118] In *Markt Intern Verlag v FRG*, A165 (1989), at [47].

courts, on reasonable grounds, had considered the restrictions to be necessary', an extreme statement of the extent to which Strasbourg should defer to the national decision.[119]

Unpacking the Court's stance on political speech

In this next section, we seek to unpack the notion that the Court affords a specially high level of protection to 'political speech' and demonstrate the simplistic nature of the claim. To do so, it is necessary to probe the apparent dichotomy between 'political' and 'artistic' speech a little deeper. Our aim will be to show that, in reality, some forms of 'political speech' are given as little protection as 'artistic speech' and explain why we consider this to be the case. First of all, the difference in treatment between the two types of cases does depend solely upon the type of speech in question. It also relates to the nature of the interest the state was seeking to further. In *Müller*, that interest was the protection of morals; in the *Sunday Times* case, it was the protection of the authority of the judiciary. The Court itself has made clear that this factor directly affects the intensity of the scrutiny applied. In *Sunday Times* itself, the Court observed that the view taken by the Contracting States of the 'requirements of morals varies from time to time and from place to place, especially in our era', and that, 'State authorities are in principle in a better position than the international judge to give an opinion on the exact content of these requirements'. It went on to say:

Precisely the same cannot be said of the far more objective notion of the 'authority' of the judiciary. The domestic law and practice of the Contracting States reveal a fairly substantial measure of common ground in this area. This is reflected in a number of provisions of the Convention, including Article 6 [protecting the right to fair trial] which have no equivalent as far as 'morals' are concerned. Accordingly, here a more extensive European supervision corresponds to a less discretionary power of appreciation.[120]

The type of speech, then, is not the sole factor affecting the margin of appreciation—the grounds for interfering with it are also important. In the *Müller* case, not only was the speech 'artistic' rather than political, but the state's objective, the protection of morality, was, as appears above, one that the Court finds so variable and subjective that judgments upon it are better left to the national authorities.

The famous *Handyside*[121] decision, another 'protection of morals' case, reveals a further complicating tendency—where protection of morals is the aim, this may affect the Court's assessment of the character and value of 'speech' in question.[122] Our contention is that the speech in this case was afforded a low weight despite the fact

---

[119] The issue of commercial speech is considered in more detail in relation to the UK regulation of advertising—perhaps the most important form of such speech—in Chapter 10 at 545–9. See also K. R. Randall, 'Commercial Speech under the European Convention on Human Rights' (2006) 6 Human Rights Law Review, 53.

[120] Op cit, at [59].

[121] *Handyside v UK* A 24 (1976). The case is considered further in the context of obscenity law in Chapter 8.

[122] The lax approach of the Court towards the proportionality enquiry in that case will be considered below.

that it was, in some sense, political. The applicant author complained to the Court that the forfeiture of a book—an act of censorship—was incompatible with Article 10. 'The Little Red Schoolbook' was aimed at teenage school children, and contained practical advice on sex, masturbation, and drug-taking, from a liberal, anti-authoritarian perspective. As such, it was clearly arguable that the book in question expressed ideas, in the purest sense—and that it was for these 'ideas' that it was punished. This was not an instance in which the contested work was 'obscene' or 'indecent', in the sense of consisting merely of gratuitous sexual imagery, with no aim other than sexual arousal. Nor was it alleged that the book's contents would tend to inculcate a degrading view of women. The book simply took a liberal, anti-authoritarian viewpoint to sexuality and self-exploration generally. The national courts made these comments when looking at the work:

For example, looking at the book as a whole, marriage was very largely ignored. Mixing a very one-sided opinion with fact and purporting to be a book of reference, it would tend to undermine, for a very considerable proportion of children, many of the influences, such as those of parents, the Churches and youth organisations, which might otherwise provide the restraint and sense of responsibility for oneself which found inadequate expression in the book.[123]

This is pure ideological criticism of the book, mixed with a concern that the control over children of authority figures could be weakened by it. But the view that children should be less subject to the influence of teachers and the churches with respect to the issue of sexual morality is, of course, itself a political one. The points made on the book's treatment of homosexuality are particularly illuminating in this respect. The English courts found this:

. . . a factual, very compassionate, understanding and valuable statement. But again, no matter how good one assessed the value of this section, it was hopelessly damned by its setting and context, and the fact that it, only, contained any suggestion of a stable relationship in relation to sex and that marriage received no such treatment at all. Moreover, there was a very real danger that this passage would create in the minds of children a conclusion that that kind of relationship was something permanent.[124]

In other words, the treatment of homosexuality was one that gave a message that homosexual relations could be permanent. This, then, was pure contents-based censorship: the book, it was thought, would tend to undermine influences from the Church and other figures, whose views were more in favour with the authorities.

The Court did find that:

the anti-authoritarian aspects of the Schoolbook as such were not held in the judgment of 29 October 1971 to fall foul of the [obscenity] Acts. Those aspects were taken into account only insofar as the appeal court considered that, by undermining the moderating influence

---

[123] Op cit, at [31].
[124] Ibid, at [34].

of parents, teachers, the Churches and youth organisations, they aggravated the tendency to 'deprave and corrupt' which in its opinion resulted from other parts of the work.[125]

Whether this token nod to the fact that the book did have a 'message' is taken seriously or not, it remains the case, however, that the perception of the English authorities that the book had a tendency to 'deprave and corrupt', that is, render morally worse its readers, proceeded purely from the fact that the book's content was *not* one devoid of intellectual content and designed purely to arouse, but simply contained a 'message' that the authorities ideologically disagreed with. That message was one that in time, of course, led to what we now term the 'sexual revolution', a cultural change with enormous social and political implications. But the Court simply refused to treat the speech as political in content, arguably because the case had been characterized as one to do with the protection of morality by the national authorities. In consequence, as we shall see below, its method of protection was extremely weak— not only did it require little or nothing in the way of evidence to satisfy itself that there was a 'pressing social need' to seize and destroy the book, but it also failed to apply any of the more rigorous proportionality tests that might have led it to the conclusion that the authorities' actions had been plainly disproportionate.

In short, no simple thesis to the effect that 'political speech demands a high level of protection' can be accepted. One further important, but, we believe, generally overlooked point, is that such a thesis does not in fact accord with the Court's jurisprudence on public protest and assembly, in which it has been extraordinarily deferential to state judgments as to what 'the prevention of disorder' demands, despite the fact that public protest nearly always involves the exercise of directly political speech by the protestors arrested or punished.[126] Article 10 has been recently relied upon in important cases[127] concerning public protest that have reached Strasbourg. But despite the importance of free public protest to a democracy, and the fact that many of the cases involved clearly political speech, the strong tendency under Articles 10 (and 11) in such cases has been to concede a wide margin of appreciation[128] to the state. In other words, the interferences in question have not been rigorously scrutinized. In particular, no enquiry has been made as to whether less intrusive means of dealing with the threatened disorder (as it usually is) could have been employed. This tendency also typically results in a terse and scantily reasoned judgment in which the key determination as to proportionality is dealt with in very short order, sometimes in a single sentence, just as we saw in *Müller*.

---

[125] Op cit, at [52].

[126] See further on this, the authors' 'Public Protest, The Human Rights Act and Judicial Response to Political Expression' [2000] *PL* 527; 'Direct Action, Convention Values and the Human Rights Act' (2001) 21(4) *Legal Studies* 535.

[127] In *Steel v UK* (note 131 below) and *Hashman v UK*, although the general tendency has been to treat Article 11 as *lex specialis* in such cases, it being found that Article 10 required no separate consideration *per se*, but that it nevertheless provided relevant principles to assist in the consideration of the Article 11 claim: see e.g. *Ezelin v France* A 202 (1991) at [35].

[128] *Ezelin* is probably the only exception. Indeed, three dissenting judges complained that it had improperly played little or no part in the Court's judgment.

Choherr v Austria[129] is a good example. In this case, a peaceful anti-militarist protester, whose only offence appeared to be that he had briefly obscured the view of those watching a military parade with his large placard, was arrested and convicted of disturbing the peace. In this case, the Court did nothing more than accept the Government's assessment, which itself was merely that disorder 'might' have resulted (no concrete evidence of this was adduced). As Bosma comments, 'the aim brought forward by the national authorities seems decisive for the Court, not the effect of the restriction . . . [or] the nature of the expression.'[130] This was, after all, directly political speech, which should surely have been afforded a high value in a democracy. Nevertheless, the very weak argument of the national authorities was very readily accepted by Strasbourg. The same pattern may be seen in other cases.

In *Steel v UK*,[131] which concerned interferences with the freedom of expression of five applicants, the proportionality of the arrest and 17-hour detention of the second applicant and her subsequent imprisonment for seven days on refusing to be bound over was airily determined by the Court in a mere two sentences. The applicant was physically impeding digging equipment by sitting on the ground, and the Court found that her arrest and detention were justified as necessary to prevent disorder and protect the rights of others. But these grounds had scant substantiation—it was accepted that no violent incidents or damage to property had been caused by the road protesters[132] and the conduct of the second applicant had been entirely peaceful, she had never resisted being removed from the area by security guards—so it is hard to see wherein lay the 'risk of disorder',[133] still less why it was sufficient to justify such comparatively drastic action. As for 'the rights of others', the court, rather extraordinarily, nowhere said what these 'rights' were, although presumably the judges had in mind the fact that the road-builders were engaged in a lawful activity—building a road—which the protesters were disrupting. The issue of the *gravity* of the interference with these 'rights' was not touched upon—the road-builders did have security guards, and were apparently able to carry on with their work, albeit at the cost of some inconvenience. In neither case was the question of alternative means of protecting the road-builders even adverted to, much less subjected to any analysis. In other words, one of the justificatory grounds for the interference with Article 10 rights was unsubstantiated by any real evidence; the other was subject to no analysis.

In *Pendragon*[134] and *Chappell*,[135] Commission cases on challenges to blanket bans[136] on assemblies at and around Stonehenge, these tendencies are even more marked.

---

[129] (1993) 17 EHRR 358.   [130] Op cit, at 188 and 191.   [131] (1998) 28 EHRR 603, at [109].
[132] Op cit, at [15].

[133] The court referred to its reasoning in relation in to the first applicant, who it had found, 'had created a danger of serious physical injury to herself and others and had formed part of a protest which risked culminating in disorder and violence' (para 105). Neither of these factors was present in relation to the second applicant, so the reference was unhelpful and positively misleading (as the Court itself seemed partly to recognize (at para 109)).

[134] No. 31416/96 (1998).   [135] No. 12587/86 (1987).

[136] In *Chappell*, these were made under the National Heritage Act 1983, and the Ancient Monuments and Archaeological Areas Act 1979, in *Pendragon*, under s 14A itself.

In both cases, the bans under challenge prevented Druids from holding *bona fide* religious ceremonies, which had been held for over 80 years during the summer solstice period. Since such bans constitute prior restraint, and in both cases resulted in the criminalization of those engaged in purely peaceful gatherings, it might have been expected that they would have been subjected to that 'most careful scrutiny' which prior restraints on expression demand in other contexts.[137] In *Pendragon*, the ban caught a group of Druids conducting a ceremony *near* Stonehenge; the justification for it put forward by the Chief Constable was that in the previous year about 40 people had tried to gain access to the monument itself, during the solstice period. The Commission cited no evidence whatever to justify the assertion that the use of a blanket order—the most serious interference possible—was *the only way* of protecting Stonehenge, an assertion which must be seriously open to question, given the plethora of other powers available.[138] In fact, the Commission made no enquiry at all as to whether less intrusive means could have been used, it merely asserted blandly: 'it cannot be considered to be an unreasonable response to prohibit assemblies at Stonehenge for a given period'. In *Chappell*, the Commission simply asserted that the decision to enforce a total ban 'was . . . necessary . . . in the interests of public safety, for the protection of public order or for the protection of the rights and freedoms of others'.[139] As in *Steel*, there was no mention of what these rights might be, still less any analysis of why they should outweigh the primary Convention rights of freedom of religion and assembly, exercised in a wholly peaceful manner. Both cases were dismissed as 'manifestly ill-founded'. In other words, they were considered not to be seriously arguable in favour of the applicants. Strasbourg asked merely whether the interference could be deemed 'unreasonable', rather than *requiring* the State, as in the *Sunday Times* case, to show that the interference was 'absolutely necessary'—a strikingly different approach.

Perhaps more noteworthy still, in some ways, is the decision in *Janowski v Poland*.[140] A journalist intervened when two municipal guards were trying to move on a stallholder, informing them that they had no legal authority to do so. But in the course of an argument with the guards, he also insulted them, calling them 'oafs' and 'dumb'. He was convicted of an offence aimed at preventing civil servants being hindered in carrying out their duties. The Court, on Janowski's application alleging a violation of Article 10, found that the relevant part of his speech did not form part of 'an open discussion of matters of public concern', since he was convicted for insulting the guards, not criticizing them. Press freedom was also not involved. The aim served by

---

[137] *Observer and Guardian v UK* (1991) 14 EHRR 153, at para 60.

[138] Namely powers to arrest for: actual or apprehended breach of the peace; attempted or actual criminal damage; breach of conditions (e.g. to keep clear of Stonehenge) imposed under s 14 POA 1986 on specific assemblies; breaches of s 5 POA 1986 and possibly s 69 CJPOA; breach of an order imposed under the powers used in *Chappell*.

[139] The ban had *prima facie* interfered with the Druids' rights under both Article 11 and Article 9, which protects freedom of religion.

[140] (1999) (21 January) Applic no 25716/94.

his conviction, the Court found, was the prevention of offensive and abusive verbal attacks on civil servants; this was found to fall within the legitimate aim of preventing 'disorder'. It must be noted that this is a somewhat questionable finding—given that Article 10 is perhaps most critically concerned with guaranteeing to the press and the individual the freedom to make robust, even vitriolic criticism of the state, including its personnel (in relation to the performance of their duties),[141] this decision, in which a journalist who intervened to criticize heavy-handed, and seemingly unlawful, police action, was punished for insulting the policemen in question is disturbing. One is left with the impression of the police punishing Janowski for his impudence. It is very hard to point to any real harm to the guards involved: it is not generally a criminal offence, in free societies, to insult someone by calling them an oaf. To give special protection to state agents seems very difficult to justify.

While the Court, rather artificially, isolated only the particular insulting words used, it would surely have been preferable to look at the incident as a whole, and cite the regrettable comments within the context. The Court did recognize that, 'the applicant resorted to abusive language out of genuine concern for the well-being of fellow citizens in the course of a heated discussion', but this did not appear to affect the judgment. Moreover, 'the language was directed at law-enforcement officers who were trained how to respond to it'—in other words, there was in fact little or no risk of disorder breaking out. What, then, was the actual threat to the interests of the state represented by these insults? The best the Court could come up with was to point out that the guards were insulted 'in a public place, in front of a group of bystanders, while they were carrying out their duties'. It did add that, 'civil servants must enjoy public confidence in conditions free of undue perturbation if they are to be successful in performing their tasks and it may therefore prove necessary to protect them from offensive and verbal attacks when on duty'.[142] This, while it may justify having some protection for civil servants from harassment, does nothing to establish why these officers required protection from being mildly insulted in the particular circumstances. The Court's conclusion, however, does not address the specific situation any further, it simply states that: 'sufficient grounds existed for the decision . . . arrived at by the national authorities'.

It may well be said that this was an extremely generous, state-friendly interpretation of the notion of preventing 'disorder'. Public disorder is generally taken to mean a situation in which the orderly and lawful regulation of the movement and behaviour of people in public has broken down, examples may be: streets or roads being blocked, mobs roaming the streets intimidating others, mass acts of trespass, and so on. A single journalist calling two policeman abusing their powers 'oafs' is scarcely a situation in which law and order is under threat. This may be an instance in which Strasbourg allowed a very doubtful claim of legitimate aim to be admitted by it, with far too little critical scrutiny.

Now, while it is common to claim that the discrepancies between the 'public order'

---

[141] See e.g. *Lingens v Austria*, op cit.   [142] Op cit, at [33].

cases and the other political speech cases we have mentioned are explicable by reference to the greater discretion granted to the member state in the context of public order, there is an alternative explanation, of great significance to the media. Bosma points out that in several cases, restriction of the *press*, as opposed merely to an individual, is seen as a matter that enhances the gravity of the interference with Article 10; an example is the *Janowski* case just referred to.[143] This is a significant point. In *Lingens* the Court said:

Freedom of the press furthermore affords the public one of the best means of discovering and forming an opinion of the ideas and attitudes of political leaders. More generally, freedom of political debate is at the very core of the concept of a democratic society which prevails throughout the Convention.[144]

Jones emphatically agrees as to the importance that the Court attaches to press freedom in particular:

One area where the Court has set narrow parameters to state discretion to restrict a right or freedom is where a special function in a democratic society is being served. In particular, the Court has often stressed that freedom of expression 'constitutes one of the essential foundations of a democratic society and one of the basic conditions for its progress' (*Castells v Spain* (1992) 14 EHRR 445, 476). The Court has also emphasized 'the pre-eminent role of the press in a State governed by the rule of law', describing it as 'incumbent on [the press] to impart information and ideas on political questions and on other matters of public interest' (ibid).[145]

Taking this into account, our alternative explanation notes that one thing that the individual protest and the artistic speech cases have in common is that *both concern individual speakers rather than the mass media.* We can hypothesize perhaps that the Court is concerned not primarily with the symbolic value of the freedom of speech, or even with the moral autonomy of the speaker to give voice to her thoughts, nor, despite what it has said, with the individual development of the speaker. It is concerned instead with the beneficial *effects* of speech upon society as a whole. Thus, broadly speaking, what most raises its concern is interference with the wide-spread dissemination of information relevant to public, particularly political debate. Thus, in the *Sunday Times* case, it was the fact that 'the injunction more or less blocked any form of comment on a matter of great public concern that contributed to a narrow margin of appreciation.'[146] In *Hertel v Switzerland*,[147] the infringement complained of was an attempt by the Swiss authorities to silence the applicant's concern about the health risk of microwave ovens; in *Lingens* it was the punishment of speech, given great publicity about the character of the Chancellor; in *Thorgeirson*, it concerned sanctions against a newspaper article revealing police malpractice; and in *Goodwin v*

---

[143] Bosma also instances *Gerger v Turkey* (1999), *Ergodgdu and Ince v Turkey* (1999).

[144] *Lingens v Austria* (1986) A.103 at [42].

[145] T. H. Jones, 'The Devaluation of Human Rights under the European Convention' [1997] *PL* 430, 442–3.

[146] Ibid, at 189.   [147] [1999] EHRLR 116.

UK,[148] an order to reveal journalistic sources, which posed a general threat to the ability of the press to perform its function. It is no coincidence that, as Jones notes, the burden on the state to justify limitations on political expression 'is even [greater] where the expression which the state purports to restrict is that of an elected representative (or comments about him or her)'.[149]

Another important point to note is the way that the Court often talks about information that 'the public has a right to receive'. If this is the case—that the values the Strasbourg Court are concerned with are *audience*-based, rather than speaker-based—it would follow naturally that the Court would be principally concerned with *media* freedom, *not* individual freedom of expression. This follows logically from the pragmatic stance of the Court—expression is valued for its contribution to the democratic process, both in watchdog and educational terms. The right of the individual artist to cry aloud from her soul—perhaps to only a few onlookers—is, under this perspective, inevitably afforded much less protection because, *in terms of practical consequences*, it doesn't matter as much. It may be said that the political speech cases *tend* to be concerned with the media and the artistic cases with the individual, and that the discrepancy can therefore alternatively be explained by the Court's view of the subjectivity and variability of moral standards, and therefore of the wide margin of appreciation that should be granted to the national authorities in respect of measures necessary to protect them. However, the evidence of the protest cases just considered, however, also involving political speech, and *not* offence or harm to moral standards, seems to suggest that this is not the case.

The exception to the rule that individual, in this case, artistic speech attracts only a low level of expression, is *Karata v Turkey*.[150] The case is an interesting one, in that it concerned political speech expressed in artistic form. A Kurdish poet was convicted of disseminating propaganda against the unity of the state and sentenced to 20 months' imprisonment and a fine. His poetry seemed to call for violent resistance ('we will sacrifice our heads, drunk on the fire of rebellion') and referred to the State as 'preparing genocide'. The Court found that the fact that these violent sentiments were expressed in poetry was relevant, meaning that they could be taken less literally. It was also influenced in favour of the applicant because of the fact that the poems had not been distributed through the mass media: the dangers to national security, public order, and so on, were less, because of this.[151] A violation of Article 10 was found. The decision can perhaps be explained by a number of very particular factors: the punishment—a 20-month prison sentence—was draconian, especially compared to the other individual speech cases we have considered. Moreover, there was a history of serious repression of the Kurds by the Turkish state, and the poetry was very

---

[148] (1996) Reports 1996–II. The facts appear below at note 321.

[149] Jones, op cit, at 442–3, citing (*Oberschlick v Austria* (1995) 19 EHRR 389 and *Lingens v Austria* (1986) 8 EHRR 103).

[150] 8 July 1999.

[151] Op cit, at [52].

directly political in a way that the works in question in *Müller* and *Otto Preminger* were not.[152]

The case may therefore be seen as an exception, explicable by its particular facts, to the general rule that Strasbourg is not principally concerned with freedom of expression as an *individual right*, but as a vital *interest*, buttressing a healthy democratic society. Hence, individuals, whether they be protesters or artists (artists of course, *being* protesters, in a sense) receive short shrift, precisely because the Court is not strongly concerned with their self-development, nor with their moral autonomy to express themselves, nor with the autonomy of the citizen denied the ability to watch, for example, the play banned in *Otto Preminger*, or to see the artistic works seized in *Müller*.

Interestingly, this hypothesis links up neatly with Conor Gearty's recent exposition[153] of the Convention as being concerned primarily with civil liberties, rather than absolutist human rights. Gearty defines the former as 'those freedoms which are essential to the maintenance and fostering of our system of representative government':[154] freedom of thought, of speech, of the press, of assembly and association; the right to vote and to stand for Parliament; access to information; to be free from arbitrary arrest, detention, torture, and killing by the state. Gearty's thesis is controversial, and some of its problematic aspects are touched on above[155] and elsewhere,[156] but for present purposes it suffices to note that his exposition of the concern of the Convention for civil liberties is strongly in harmony with the authors' thesis, put forward above, as to the primary interpretative principle underlying the Court's approach to Article 10.

Gearty explains the conceptual difference between notions of civil liberties as opposed to human rights:

a consequence of thinking about liberty, expression and so on . . . as *civil liberties* rather than *human rights*[157] is to focus attention away from the possibility of these being absolute entitlements vested in human beings as such and to divert the analytical spotlight instead onto their utility as part of the essential fabric that goes into the making of our democratic tapestry.[158]

This analysis seems to fit the Court's expression jurisprudence very well. The fact that the Court tends to regard interference with media freedom as a more serious matter than restrictions on individual expression suggests that Strasbourg is concerned primarily with pragmatic, consequentialist-based protection of the media's role in a democracy, rather than a deontological, principled protection of the

---

[152] There was, moreover, a substantial dissent, which found that incitement to violence was the antithesis of democracy and free speech, since it amounted to 'the denial of dialogue, the rejection of the testing of different thoughts and theories in favour of a clash of might and power' (op cit).

[153] *Principles of Human Rights Adjudication*, Oxford: OUP, 2003.

[154] Op cit, at 34.   [155] See pp 41–3.

[156] See G. Phillipson, 'Deference, Discretion and Democracy: Judicial Reasoning under the Human Rights Act', *Current Legal Problems*, 2007.

[157] The contrast is not the Hohfeldian one between liberties and rights, but between civil liberties as an essential part of democratic society and human rights as individual, deontological entitlements.

[158] Op cit, at 35.

individual right to free speech. From this point of view, it matters far more if the whole of the British public are prevented from discussing the thalidomide affair in an informed manner, as in the *Sunday Times* case, than it does if an individual protester (or a handful of them) are unable to carry out their demonstrations as planned. This hypothesis may also account for the Court's reluctance to uphold the freedom of artists whose work gives offence, since their work would probably only have a small audience and would not directly contribute to public-political debate, the Court is not concerned with a scenario of a large number of people being deprived of useful information and political comment and therefore provides only a low level of protection. It is possible, therefore, that the Court's thoroughly pragmatic approach, and the very high value it places upon the role of speech in a functioning democracy, accounts for its clear preference for media freedom[159] over freedom of expression generally, and thus its (flawed) adoption of the fourth model discussed in the Introduction.

Since, as discussed above, it is the argument from democracy that has most influenced the Court this is, perhaps, not surprising: as Feldman puts it, 'Meiklejohn's freedom of speech theory is designed to safeguard the collective decision-making process, rather than individual autonomy.'[160] The rationale is thus very much reader-, rather than speaker-based. As Mowbray remarks:

'the Court equates democracy with societies where there is a vigorous public debate about matters of public policy and constitutional arrangements conducted by the public themselves and through their representatives in the forms of political parties and elected politicians' and that furthermore '[n]ational governments are under Convention duties to safeguard these components of democracy by, *inter alia*, facilitating diversity in the media, respecting protected forms of free expression . . .'[161]

This would also account for its recent stance in *Von Hannover*,[162] in which the Court emphatically upheld the Article 8 rights of Princess Caroline of Monaco not to be photographed when going about her everyday life, over the freedom of the media to report on her.[163] Such was the bland, gossipy nature of the contested photographs, revealing nothing more than the details of the Princess's everyday life, that it was not possible to mount even a colourable argument that they contributed to any discussion of legitimate public concern. This may account for the Court's unanimous decision in the case that the failure to give a remedy in respect of the publication of the photographs was a clear breach of Article 8, and the evident narrowness of the margin of

---

[159] It may be noted that in both the *Jacubowski* and *Casado Coca* cases (op cit), the Court was particularly influenced by the fact that the public, as it saw it, had other ways of gaining access to the information in question: the violation of the speaker's autonomy was therefore of little moment.

[160] D. Feldman, 'Content Neutrality', in I. Loveland (ed.) *Importing the First Amendment*, 2nd edn., Oxford: Hart Publishing, 1998, at 144. Feldman attributes this analysis of Meiklejohn to R. Post, *Constitutional Domains: Democracy, Community, Management*, Cambridge, Mass, 1995, Chapter 6.

[161] A. Mowbray, 'The Role of the European Court of Human Rights in the Promotion of Democracy' [1999] *PL* 703, 704.

[162] (2004), [2004] EMLR 21—for a summary and comment, see (2004) 5, EHRLR 593–6.

[163] The case is discussed in detail in Chapter 13.

appreciation afforded—the type of media activity that the Court was concerned to protect was simply not engaged here. As the Court said:

... a fundamental distinction needs to be made between reporting facts—even controversial ones—capable of contributing to a debate in a democratic society relating to politicians in the exercise of their functions, for example, and reporting details of the private life of an individual who, moreover, as in this case, does not exercise official functions. While in the former case the press exercises its vital role of 'watchdog' in a democracy by contributing to 'impart[ing] information and ideas on matters of public interest (*Observer and Guardian v UK*) it does not do so in the latter case.[164]

In conclusion then, Strasbourg's reasoning is firmly consequentialist, practical, and concerned above all with ensuring the free flow of widely disseminated information relevant to legitimate public debate. Freedom of expression is valued not really as an aspect of individual autonomy or for the contribution it makes to the flourishing of individuals, but for the part it plays in maintaining a democratic society. In practice, it is the media that provides for the mass dissemination of information and arguments vital to the democratic process—it is therefore primarily with *media freedom* to carry out this function—not with 'political speech' as such—that the Court is concerned.

Ronald Dworkin, one of the most doughty defenders of a deontological view of rights,[165] has expressed caution in relation to instrumentalist speech justifications, precisely because they are vulnerable to situations in which the evidence shows little or no harm in relation to suppression of such speech; perhaps indeed, positive benefit. He instances, for example, the way that the argument that freedom of expression is vital for self-development has been turned on its head by feminist campaigners against pornography, who have argued that if in fact pornography stunts and hampers the development of its (male) consumers, by constructing an unhealthy and destructive attitude towards women (and thus in turn severely damages women's own flourishing), there is no good reason for the freedom to produce or consume it to be upheld.[166] Clearly, his anxieties, for one wanting to establish a strong, deontological protection for speech, are well founded. There are of course dangers either way: under the consequentialist path, there must be continuous 'attempts to identify that which is *truly* valuable with that which is not, with the risk that the latter will reduce the range and eventually diminish the status of speech' and equally with the 'libertarian' or 'autonomy'-based rationale, in which speech is 'valuable simply because the speaker wishes to speak, which ... reduces speech to "noise" '.[167] What

---

[164] Ibid, at [63].

[165] See also Thomas Scanlon's influential approach, set out in 'A Theory of Freedom of Expression' (1972) 1 *Phil. & Pub. Aff.* 216.

[166] See in particular, 'Do We Have a Right to Pornography?' in *A Matter of Principle*, Cambridge, Mass: Harvard University Press, 1985.

[167] C. Warbrick, 'Federalism and Free Speech' in I. Loveland (ed.) *Importing the First Amendment*, 2nd edn., Oxford: Hart Publishing, 1998, at 179, summarizing the argument of G. White, 'The First Amendment Comes of Age' (1996) *Michigan LR* 299, 390–2.

will be clear by now is that the European Court has put itself very firmly indeed in the consequentialist, functionalist camp.

As noted above, the type of speech at issue is one of the factors—albeit perhaps the most important, that leads the Court to vary the margin of appreciation it affords to the State. It is time to turn to the remainder of the factors that cause it to grant a wider or narrower margin, and at the criticisms that have been levelled at the doctrine.

THE TEXTUAL PROVISIONS OF THE CONVENTION RIGHTS

A commonsensical factor may be initially briefly referred to: the textual provisions of the Convention are relevant in this context—the more precise the terms, the less leeway there is for states in interpreting them, and thus the less scope for granting them a wide margin of appreciation.[168] For example, as Mahoney has pointed out, Article 5 sets out the lawful exceptions to the right to liberty in exhaustive detail, leaving little room for state discretion.[169] Schokkenbroek has pointed out that conversely, the margin may be greatest where the relevant Convention article involves vague or broad expressions.[170] Four main others factors have been identified by scholars: The nature of expression at issue, dealt with above; the 'consensus factor' or 'common European standards' doctrine; the legitimate aim justifying interference and the seriousness of the interference.[171] These factors will be considered in turn.

THE EXISTENCE OF COMMON GROUND BETWEEN DIFFERENT EUROPEAN STATES

This factor is fairly straightforward in conception, if not in practical operation. The Court will look (generally not very systematically) for the existence of a common stance in European states as to the necessity or otherwise of limiting or controlling the right in question. Where such common ground is found, for example, *against* such necessity, such that the State in question seems isolated in its restrictive practices, the Court is likely to review its decisions more strictly. Some of the reasoning in the *Goodwin v UK*[172] decision, in which the Court changed its position on whether state refusal to recognize transgendered sexual identities was a breach of Article 8, was directly influenced by the Court's perception of 'an emerging consensus' within Europe on the importance of such recognition and 'a continuing international trend towards legal recognition [of transsexual people]'. As Warbrick observes:

---

[168] T. O'Donnell (1982) 4 *HRQ* 474, at 496.   [169] Note 221 below.

[170] 'The Basis, Nature and Application of the Margin of Appreciation Doctrine in the Case-Law of the European Court of Human Rights' (1998) 19 *HRLJ* 30 at 36.

[171] Also relevant will be two further issues, dealt with in subsequent chapters: where there is the necessity for balancing conflicting Convention rights, and where the State's obligation is a positive, rather than a negative, one (see Mahoney, 'Marvellous Richness', op cit). In relation to freedom of expression, the State's duty is generally only a negative one, so this factor rarely applies in Article 10 cases.

[172] (2002) 35 EHRR 447.

The Court can find objective support for its judgments which drag along the reluctant State, where for reasons of local prejudice, inertia, or even for conscious cost allocation reasons, the State has not kept up with the European understanding of the fundamental right.[173]

Conversely, in the absence of any consensus, the Court is minded to grant more discretion to the State, in recognition, presumably of the notion that the subject is a difficult one, about which reasonable people disagree. This is apparent most strongly in the cases involving restrictions upon speech on grounds of morality. The court has taken the view that this is one of the most fluid and hard-to-assess of the exceptions to Article 10. As it observed in the crucial *Handyside* decision, which firmly set the tone for subsequent decisions based upon the protection of morality:

In particular, it is not possible to find in the domestic law of the various Contracting States a uniform European conception of morals. The view taken by their respective laws of the requirements of morals varies from time to time and from place to place, especially in our era which is characterised by a rapid and far-reaching evolution of opinions on the subject.[174]

This then, besides the 'artistic' nature of the speech, is another reason why the margin of appreciation conceded was so wide in cases such as *Müller* and *Otto Preminger*. As Warbrick puts it:

[The Court] has singled out the protection of morals as being a criterion with respect to which a state enjoys a wide margin of appreciation. The reason for this is that the Court has been unable to detect a 'European consensus', which would fill out the subjective notion of 'morals' and, therefore, provide the Court with some guidance about how it should discharge is subsidiary supervisory role.[175]

While the notion of varying the intensity of review on the basis of the degree of consensus over the necessity of restrictions seems on its face both commonsensical and likely to maintain loyalty towards the Convention, it raises two difficulties, one practical, the other principled. As to the former, Jones has observed that the Court in fact has no particular methodology for deciding whether there is or is not a common European standard in a particular area. As he points out:

This difficulty was most apparent in the *Sunday Times* case, where the Court divided eleven to nine on the issue of the uniformity of European laws in respect of the necessary restrictions on freedom of expression to protect the authority of the judiciary. (The conclusions on both sides were reached without citing a single national law.) The majority took the view that: 'The domestic law and practice of the Contracting States reveals a fairly substantial measure of common ground in this area.' By way of contrast, the minority maintained that, 'contrary to what the majority of the court holds, the notion of the authority of the judiciary is by no means divorced from the national circumstances and cannot be determined in a uniform way'.[176]

---

[173] C. Warbrick, ' "Federal" Aspects of the European Convention on Human Rights' (1989) 10 *Michigan Jnl. of Int'l Law* 698, at 719.

[174] Op cit, at [48].   [175] Warbrick, op cit, at 185.

[176] T. H. Jones, 'The Devaluation of Human Rights under the European Convention' [1997] *PL* 430, 440–1.

In other cases, the Court has applied such evidence as there is in a rather haphazard fashion. A good example is *Handyside* itself, discussed above. The Court stated that it found little consensus on moral issues in Europe. It did not explain this, nor—as in *Sunday Times*—give examples of diverging standards, but used this finding as a major reason for conceding to the UK a wide margin of appreciation which resulted in no violation being found, despite a clear instance of censorship. However, as Bosma points out, one piece of objective evidence as to moral standards *was* before the Court: The fact that the *Schoolbook* was freely circulating in most other European states,[177] something, we would suggest, that could have been taken as indicating that there *was* in fact a European consensus—of tolerance on moral matters. Thus in this case the 'consensus' factor, objectively evidenced, could have been used to argue for an intensive review of the UK Government's relatively *intolerant* attitude. Instead, the *un*-evidenced assertion of lack of consensus was used to justify a very light touch review.[178] It is disturbing both that a factual claim was used with no attempt to substantiate it, and that the Court appears to select arbitrarily which factors as to 'consensus' it uses to help it set the standard of appropriate review. Such haphazard methodology clearly carries the danger of arbitrary and poorly-evidenced findings.

There is also an objection of principle. The danger of the 'consensus' principle is clear—it means that the Court of Human Rights, rather than *setting* the standards for Europe, *follows* them. Thus, if applied literally, the principle would mean that the Court would be powerless to arrest a drift towards authoritarianism in Europe, or even a drift by some states, which, by breaking up an existing consensus, might logically lead to a wider margin of appreciation being applied to the issue in question. The same, as a number of commentators have pointed out, can be said about the effect of the accession of states that do not have the same standard of protection for media freedom as Western Europe; Russia is a crucial example.[179]

It might be argued that recognition and protection of human rights should not be dependent upon such factors. Indeed, looking at *state practice* in relation to a controversial human rights issue might strike one as being precisely the *wrong* exercise. Of course the fact that other states have recognized a human right is a useful argument for an applicant disputing a particular government's argument that it would be too costly, impractical or divisive to follow suit. However, for state practice to *determine* the content of rights is surely to allow the cart to drive the horses. Rights are claimed *against* states; rights are there at least in part for the protection of dissenting and often deeply unpopular individuals or minority groups. To say that the citizens' rights depend upon what governments have been prepared to concede to them in practice is a strange doctrine indeed, from a liberal-normativist stance. It also, at least in theory, opens up a frightening prospect—if new content for a right (such as

---

[177] Op cit, at [57].

[178] The non-intensive nature of review engaged in *Handyside* is considered more fully below at note 281 *et seq.*

[179] See e.g. A. Lester, 'Universality versus subsidiarity: a reply' (1998) 1 *EHRLR* 73, 74. See also P. Mahoney, 'Speculating on the future of the reformed European Court of Human Rights (1999) 20 *HRLJ* 1,3.

recognition of a new gender identity) can come about because of increasing protection for it in signatory states, presumably it could later be taken away, due to *decreasing* protection, or the breakdown of a previous consensus on the need for it. To give an example, it is likely that the so-called 'war on terror' may lead to more and more European states adopting draconian, anti-civil-libertarian stances in terms of due process, deportation and administrative detention:[180] will the rights granted under Articles 3, 5 and 6 be seen by the European Court as having therefore diminished in scope or weight as a consequence? Logically, the answer might be yes. As Gearty points out, in relation to the *Goodwin* decision, above:

Perhaps the decision would have gone the other way [against the applicant] in the *Goodwin* case had the UK Parliament consciously voted down a proposal for change rather than merely, through executive inertia, not had such a proposal put to it.[181]

He asks rhetorically:

Is it not theoretically the job of the court to detect the breach of human rights in the abstract by a process of moral reasoning, and then to apply that insight to the facts before it, whatever the reaction of the domestic legislature or the position in the rest of Europe?[182]

The Court's stance on this matter, perhaps more than anything else, reveals it not as a Constitutional Court, fearlessly protecting the rights it believes citizens should have against the state, but a pragmatic organ, which will protect rights where it believes states will acquiesce in its decisions, not prone to push its fragile position too far, and led very much by consensus amongst states. Overall, whilst acknowledging the practical utility of the consensus doctrine, as a useful means of showing a state to be putting forward arguments for restricting rights that experience in other states have shown to be unpersuasive, it is suggested that the principle should be used with three caveats in mind. First, it should not be used against an applicant in the absence of clear evidence: to put it another way, states wishing to rely upon an absence of consensus should have to adduce proper evidence. Second, it should be used consistently, rather

---

[180] The UK has led the way in this respect, with its derogation from Article 5 in 2001 in order to allow it to detain non-British international terrorist suspects without trial under Part IV of the Anti-Terrorism Crime and Security Act 2001; it has recently replaced those powers with new provisions, under the Prevention of Terrorism Act 2005, which are far broader, in applying to *all* suspected terrorists, and in giving a much broader range of powers to the authorities, including, at their most draconian, the power of house arrest, which will require a further derogation from Article 5 of the Convention. Following the terrorist attacks in London in July 2005, the UK Government requested action from the EU on retention for one year of all mobile phone, text, and email records (showing who contacted whom, though not the content of the message)—a significant extension of data-retention powers, with obvious implications for the protection of privacy; at the time of writing, there are further proposals before Parliament to increase dramatically the length of time that suspects may be held for questioning by police without charge, introduce a new offence of 'glorifying terrorism'. The UK Government is also seeking to circumvent the rule, deriving from Article 3 ECHR, that suspect foreign nationals may not be deported to states where they will face torture or the death penalty.

[181] Op cit ('*Principles*'), at 201.

[182] Ibid. Gearty recognizes that this is only theoretically the case, however and would not support such an approach, which, in his view, would do nothing more than unfairly privilege the moral intuitions of a small elite over what he likes to term 'the wisdom of the crowd'.

than opportunistically: where objective consideration of state practice shows the respondent state to be unduly repressive (as in the *Handyside* case), the Court should be prepared to say so. Thirdly, it should not be used so as to *diminish* levels of protection under the Convention from levels previously employed.[183]

THE LEGITIMATE AIM FOR INTERFERENCE ADVANCED BY THE STATE

In the *Sunday Times* case, the Court found that 'the scope of the margin of appreciation is not identical in respect of each of the aims justifying restrictions.'[184] As with the 'consensus' factor, the obvious example is the protection of morals, in relation to which the Court has taken the view that national authorities are better able to assess the necessity of restrictions on speech than it is.[185] In contrast, the Court regards the demands of protecting the authority of the judiciary as an aim that is subject to more objective determination and assessment.[186] To an extent, this difference in treatment results simply from the Court's perception of the presence or absence of a European consensus on protecting the state aim in question, the issue just considered. But the matter goes somewhat wider than this. The assessment of different state needs differs for other reasons. The needs of national security tend to weigh in on the 'wider margin' side of the scales.[187] So does the notion of prevention of disorder: this in part accounts for decisions such as *Choherr v Austria*,[188] in which the Court appeared to do little more than accept the Government's assessment of the case.

In relation to both national security and public order concerns, the Court's willingness to grant the state more leeway flows *not* from the presence or absence of European consensus but from the *fact-sensitivity* of the matter. Actions taken to protect national security sometimes rely upon the assessment of intelligence information, something which Governments are often simply unwilling to see publicly analysed and which is often also a question of expert judgment which courts are arguably ill-equipped to second-guess. In relation to public order situations, it is the on-the-spot decisions (usually of police officers) to take particular measures to avoid disorder that are at issue. Here, the European Court is evidently unwilling to question too closely the decisions made, often in the heat of the moment. Where, however, the facts are fairly clear and indisputable, in terms of the risk to national security, the Court has been prepared to be firm. For example, in both the *Observer and Guardian*[189] and *Vereniging*

---

[183] That is not to say that a genuine increase in a serious threat to the peoples of Europe from terrorism, for example, should not be taken into account in assessing against Convention standards the lawfulness of new restrictions upon Convention rights designed to counter that threat, but given the propensity of governments to use terrorist incidents to justify draconian new measures, the mere fact that such measures have been taken in a number of states should not be used as an argument that they are justified, under the common standards doctrine.

[184] Ibid, at [59].   [185] *Handyside v UK*, op cit.   [186] *Sunday Times v UK*, op cit.
[187] See e.g. the cautious judgment of the Court in *Observer and Guardian v UK*, op cit.
[188] Op cit, discussed above.
[189] *Observer and Guardian v UK* (1991) 14 EHRR 153.

Weekblad Bluf![190] decisions, the Court was prepared to find that injunctions or other measures designed to stop the publication of sensitive material were disproportionate, because ineffectual, once it was clear that the information at issue was already effectively in the public domain, so that any damage to security interests had already been done. The latter case has been discussed already: In the former, the Court was prepared to find a violation of Article 10 by reference to the wide-ranging injunction granted by the UK Courts against the publication of *Spycatcher*, a book by a former security service agent, revealing alleged misconduct by MI5 on the basis that continuation of the injunction once the book had been extensively published abroad was futile. This was arguably because the factual assessment that little or no further damage to national security could be done by publication in the UK was a straightforward one by that point. A very similar approach and result was attained in the *Vereniging* case.[191]

The Court's greater deference to the state when it is acting in pursuit of certain categories of 'legitimate aim' has extended, on occasion, to finding such aims to be present on arguably very tenuous grounds. Perhaps the most controversial finding of a 'legitimate aim' to interfere with expression was made in the *Otto Preminger*[192] decision already alluded to. The facts, briefly, were as follows: the Otto Preminger institute ran an art-house cinema. It planned to put on a film called *Das Liebeskonzil* (Council in Heaven) which contained a production of a 19th century play of the same name amounting to a savage satire of the Christian religion. The play depicted God as a senile old man, Christ as a low grade mental defective, and Mary as sexually attracted to the devil. The Institute publicized the proposed showing of the film, giving a clear idea of its contents and prohibiting under 17s from attending. Following complaints from the local Catholic Church, criminal proceedings were brought against the Institute, and the film was seized and forfeited. The applicants applied to Strasbourg alleging a breach of Article 10. The case is notable in a number of respects, and will be returned to below, and in Chapter 9.[193] For present purposes, it is the characterization by the Court of the legitimate aim pursued by the Austrian authorities in taking the action they did that is of interest. This point is discussed in full in Chapter 9, to which it is of most direct relevance; for present purposes it need be noted only that the Court accepted that the aim in question was not just the protection of morals, but a far weightier one, finding Article 9, the right to religious freedom to be involved:

. . . the manner in which religious beliefs and doctrines are opposed or denied is a matter which may engage the responsibility of the State, notably its responsibility to ensure the peaceful enjoyment of the right guaranteed under Article 9 to the holders of those beliefs and doctrines.[194]

This finding, that the seizure of the film had the purpose not merely of preventing a *social* evil—outrage and offence—but of preventing interference with a fundamental right—freedom of religious belief—had a decisive *structural* effect upon the judgment.

---

[190] (1995) 20 EHRR 189.   [191] See discussion above at note 54.   [192] (1995) 19 EHRR 34.
[193] See also Chapter 2.   [194] Op cit, at [57].

Rather than the case taking the usual form, in which the State had to prove that the measures taken were necessary restrictions upon speech, *two* competing Convention rights were seen as in play. Thus the issue became one of balancing conflicting rights. As the Court put it,

The issue before the Court involves weighing up the conflicting interests of the exercise of two fundamental freedoms guaranteed under the Convention, namely the right of the applicant association to impart to the public controversial views and, by implication, the right of interested persons to take cognisance of such views, on the one hand, and the right of other persons to proper respect for their freedom of thought, conscience and religion, on the other hand. In so doing, regard must be had to the margin of appreciation left to the national authorities, whose duty it is in a democratic society also to consider, within the limits of their jurisdiction, the interests of society as a whole. (at [55])

Cases in which conflicting rights must be balanced are generally regarded by the Court as instances in which a wide margin of appreciation should be afforded, allowing the national authorities to strike the balance by reference to their detailed knowledge of local standards and needs.[195] Once the case had been characterized as one involving a clash of rights, the degree of offence to religious feeling likely to be caused by the film in this case was seen as something much better evaluated by the national authorities. For example, the area in which the film was to be shown had a very high level of Roman Catholic believers. It is noteworthy that the Court chose to interpret the case as concerning clashing rights,[196] thus justifying it in affording a wider margin of appreciation than in an ordinary rights *vs* social interest case. It may be doubted whether quite such an accommodating finding would have been made had the issue not concerned the protection of morals.

SERIOUSNESS OF THE INTERFERENCE

The final factor affecting the width of the margin of appreciation is relatively straight-forward: The more serious the interference with Convention rights, the more closely the decision will be scrutinized. Thus, as Bosma points out, in *Open Door Dublin Well Woman v Ireland*,[197] it was precisely the seriousness of the interference with expression, coupled perhaps perversely with its ineffectiveness, which led to the finding of the violation.[198] The case concerned an injunction granted by the Irish Supreme Court preventing various organizations from giving counselling services to pregnant women, which included giving information about the availability of abortion services abroad (abortion is banned as unconstitutional in Ireland). One of the reasons for the Court's finding of a violation of Article 10 was the restriction's blanket nature—it was 'struck by the absolute nature of the . . . injunction'[199]—no account was taken of the

---

[195] See further the discussion of clashing rights in Chapter 13 and Chapter 16.
[196] It reasoning in respect of this matter is analysed in detail in Chapter 8.
[197] (1992) A.246.   [198] The case is considered further below.   [199] Op cit, at [73].

women's health or reasons for seeking a termination. The Court pointed out that it was not an offence under Irish law for a woman to travel abroad for an abortion and that abortion itself was of course legal in most of the Contracting States. The injunction therefore restrained the giving of information about lawful activities relevant to health—a serious interference with freedom of expression.[200] The outcome of the case might thus be explained by the fact that this was an instance of wholesale denial of information to the public at large on a matter that was clearly of legitimate, serious concern—the availability of abortion abroad.

However, the Court has not been consistent in applying the factor of the seriousness of the interference. We have already seen that instances of prior restraint of expression—the bans on meetings near Stonehenge[201]—received the most cursory scrutiny by the Commission. The facts in *Handyside* itself amounted to prior restraint, in that the book was seized and destroyed—but was a case in which a wide margin was granted, as were the 'artistic speech' cases of *Müller* and *Otto-Preminger*. In the *Observer and Guardian* case,[202] there was again a serious interference (prior restraint, preventing the British public from obtaining the book *Spycatcher*, or extracts from it, within the jurisdiction), but this factor did not seem to affect the margin of appreciation granted, which was wide, *until* the availability of the book in the US undermined the national security argument. In other words, the nature of the legitimate aim (national security) kept the margin wide, and review therefore light, despite the gravity of the interference. 'Close scrutiny on the part of the Court only took place after the information was freely available in the United States' and the national security concern was therefore 'reduced.[203] In other words, this factor, whilst clearly relevant to the intensity of scrutiny, is sometimes disregarded where other factors push the Court in the direction of light touch review.

THE *EFFECT* OF THE VARIATION IN THE WIDTH OF THE MARGIN OF APPRECIATION

In the previous section, we examined the factors influencing the scope of the margin of appreciation. In this section, we look briefly at what the consequences are, in concrete terms, of the Court deciding how wide a margin should be granted and thus how intense its scrutiny should be. As Bosma puts it:

When the margin . . . is wide, the national authorities are left a significant amount of room to decide on the necessity of a restriction. Under such circumstances, the Court merely formulates the outer boundaries of the necessity of a restriction. When the margin of appreciation is narrow [in contrast] the Court itself formulates the required protection.[204]

---

[200] Ibid, at [72].   [201] Above notes 134–9.   [202] Op cit.
[203] Bosma, op cit, at 189.   [204] Ibid, at 173.

As argued above, the key effect of the Court's assessment of how wide or narrow margin should be granted is in terms of the type of proportionality test applied. The various tests available under the Court's jurisprudence are considered in detail in the next section. However, in order to indicate in general terms the importance of the Court's assessment of the margin, it is worth making some broad observations at this point. The crucial point is that the standard of review undertaken by the Court can vary dramatically. As Bosma points out, the two extremes are represented by the Court asking, on the one hand, whether 'it was absolutely certain' that the measures taken were necessary (as in the *Sunday Times* case) to, on the other hand, asking only whether it was 'not unreasonable' for the authorities to consider them necessary (as in *Otto Preminger*). The variation is thus from an intensively strict proportionality standard, on the one hand, to a form of *Wednesbury* review, on the other, that is, that the Court will not interfere save where the decision-maker has acted perversely or in a manner that no reasonable person *could* have acted. Singh *et al.* have suggested that the standard of review, even under a wide margin of appreciation,[205] does *not* equate to the *Wednesbury* doctrine. However, the cases cited by the authors in support of this proposition are *Dugdeon*[206] and *Sunday Times,*[207] and these are decisions in which it is well known that the Court applied a relatively strict test. In contrast, Van Dijk and Van Hoof argue that three broad classes of review standard are applied by the Court: the narrow approach (full review); the 'reasonable' approach (was the state reasonable to conclude that its interference was necessary); and the 'not unreasonable' approach (the applicant must show that the state's action was *un*reasonable). This also affects the burden of proof lying on those before the Court. Formally speaking, of course, once it has been found that the expression fell within Article 10(1) and that there was some interference with it, the burden *always* passes to the state to justify the interference. But that is not, practically, how the matter lies at the extreme end of the deference/margin of appreciation scale. For example, in *Otto Preminger*, in which a 'not unreasonable' standard of review was used, the Court noted the reasoning of the Austrian courts to the effect that neither the artistic merit of the play nor its contribution to public debate were enough to outweigh the offence it had caused. It then went on to say simply: 'The content of the film cannot be said to be incapable of grounding the conclusion arrived at by the Austrian courts.' Thus it appeared that the burden lay on the applicant to show, in effect, that no reasonable courts could have come to this conclusion after seeing the film. In other words, for the applicant to succeed, the content of the film had to be shown to be *incapable* of supporting the findings made. This was, in effect, *Wednesbury* review: the Austrian courts had made their decision, and it was for the applicant to show that the evidence could not support it.[208] This approach can also be expressed as asking merely whether the state was 'entitled

---

[205] Below, note 230.   [206] (1981) 4 EHRR 149.   [207] Ibid, at 17.
[208] Bosma considers that the 'not unreasonable' approach is roughly comparable with Wednesbury: op cit, at 206.

to think' that the interference could be justified, as in *Müller v Switzerland*.[209] Such a standard was also evidently used in *Choherr v Austria, Markt Intern Verlag v Germany*,[210] and the *Pendragon*[211] and *Chappell*[212] decisions, while Bosma notes that in one decision, *Casado Coca v Spain*,[213] the Court was satisfied by finding only that the measures were not 'unreasonable and disproportionate' to the aim pursued.

Methodologically, this is a world away from requiring that the state adduce reasons that are 'relevant and sufficient', still less from testing its actions against a strict standard that they must have been the least intrusive or restrictive possible. Controversially, Bosma also suggests that the 'reasonable approach' at Strasbourg, in which the Court asks whether the national authorities 'could reasonably' have thought the restriction in question necessary, may be equated to heightened, or anxious, scrutiny of *Wednesbury* review,[214] in which the restriction of the right will only be *Wednesbury* reasonable when it has been sufficiently justified by a weighty competing public interest. If this is correct, it means, as Bosma points out, that the HRA requires a change in approach only in the narrow band of cases in which Strasbourg would, it is thought, have applied a 'full review' approach,[215] an issue examined further in the succeeding chapter.

This point demonstrates the danger of seeing compliance with Article 10 as, itself, guaranteeing freedom of expression—the danger, in other words, of substituting unthinking legalism for first principle arguments about the legitimate role of the media in a democracy. Gardner refers to: 'the widespread but mistaken belief that accommodating international human rights jurisprudence is the same thing as respecting human rights'. He goes on to argue that, 'There could come a point where it would be better to have no Convention of Human Rights at all than one that can be used to legitimate and congratulate any decision under the sun.'[216] The key to avoiding this danger is full awareness of the outright failure of the Strasbourg Court to apply 'proportionality' scrutiny in any meaningful sense at all to a wide range of speech situations due to a deference that at times shades into a simple refusal to subject national decisions to any kind of critical analysis. This matter will be looked at more closely in the next section, but before turning to examine the different proportionality tests in detail, we conclude this section by noting briefly some of the criticisms of the margin of appreciation doctrine.

---

[209] Op cit, at [36].   [210] A165 (1989), at [47].   [211] Op cit.   [212] Op cit.
[213] (1994) A.285A.   [214] See Chapter 3, at note 225.   [215] Op cit, at 206.
[216] J. Gardner, 'Freedom of Expression' in C. McCrudden and G. Chambers (eds) *Individual Rights and the Law in Britain*, Oxford: OUP, 1994, at 236.

THE RAISON D'ÊTRE OF THE MARGIN OF APPRECIATION DOCTRINE AND CRITIQUE

THE RAISON D'ÊTRE

The Court has found direct textual support for the doctrine in the wording and basic principles of the Convention, in particular the key notion that the role of the Strasbourg institutions is seen as subsidiary to that of the national authorities. Thus, in *Handyside* it remarked:

The Convention leaves to each Contracting State, in the first place, the task of securing the rights and liberties it enshrines [via Article 1].[217] The institutions created by it 'make their own contribution to this task but they become involved only through contentious proceedings and once all domestic remedies have been exhausted' (Article 26).[218]

The Court has added that 'it is for the national authorities to make the *initial* assessment of the reality of the pressing social need implied by the notion of "necessity" in this context' (emphasis added).[219] Strasbourg of course makes the secondary, or reviewing, assessment. There is thus a system of dual responsibility for protection of the Convention rights, which raises the question of the respective competencies of the states and the Strasbourg organs. This dual system leaves the Court with two possible extreme approaches to steer between. As Bosma puts it:

. . . on the one hand, the interpretation of the Convention could not be left entirely to the States party to the Convention; on the other hand [Strasbourg] could not impose their own views on the meaning of the provisions in the Convention, completely disregarding the assessment of the national authorities on a matter.[220]

Thus, 'responsibility to protect the [Convention] rights . . . is shared between [Strasbourg] and the states party to the Convention'. Bosma sees the margin of appreciation as a 'translation' of this shared responsibility, since it allows for a variable standard of review, allowing the importance of the roles of Strasbourg and the national authorities to vary according to the context.

Others see a more grandiose purpose for the doctrine. Paul Mahoney sees it as stemming from the basic values underlying the Convention system, including subsidiarity, enshrined in Article 1, democracy, as recognized in the preambles, and cultural diversity. It encapsulates, he argues, some deference to sovereignty in the sense of 'the freedom of different societies to disagree, to choose different solutions according to their own notions and needs . . . in relation to the regulation of the vast range of

---

[217] Article 1 requires the State parties to 'secure to everyone in their jurisdiction the rights and freedoms' set out in the Convention.
[218] *Handyside*, at [48].   [219] Ibid.   [220] Bosma, op cit, at 12–13.

human activity covered by the Convention.[221] For Yourow, it encapsulates deference to state discretion in several linked categories:

to the will of the democratic legislature, to state executive and judicial fact-finding in individual cases, to state interpretation of the Convention, and to choice of means in carrying out responsibility for enforcement under the subsidiarity principle.[222]

Others see a more prosaic purpose. One scholar refers to it as 'the necessary juris-prudential grease in the enforcement mechanisms provided by the Convention'.[223] A former President of the Commission is frank about this pragmatic importance of the doctrine. Because of the broad terms of many of the rights and the effect of the evolution of concepts such as 'morality':

the so-called supervisory function [of the Strasbourg courts] has in it a creative, legislative element comparable to that of the judiciary in common law countries; so that in certain cases its exercise might strain the enthusiasm of the Member States for the Convention. The doctrine ... is ... one of the more important safeguards developed by [Strasbourg] to reconcile the effective operation of the Convention with the sovereign powers and responsibilities of governments in a democracy.[224]

This is a part pragmatic, part principled justification for the Convention. It is prag-matic because, by allowing Strasbourg to respect strongly held local beliefs relating to, for example, the portrayal of sexuality,[225] or religious doctrines,[226] and to defer to the protection of state interests that are seen as of vital concern, such as national security,[227] the Court is able to avoid putting too great a strain on the loyalty to the Convention of the diverse peoples and governments of the states in the Council of Europe and thus retain their allegiance to it.[228] But as some of the comments above suggest, the margin can also be seen as serving a more principled purpose—to respect both democratic decision-making and a certain degree of cultural diversity. Thus, specifically in relation to freedom of expression, Mahoney sees the margin of appreciation and Article 10 together as affording:

priority to the *universality* of the standard of freedom of expression ... in regard to political and public-concern speech, but much more scope for *subsidiarity*—that is the exercise of democratic discretion at local level—in regard to cultural or artistic speech. Between those two clear poles exists a vast territory of human expression ... whether the pull is in the

---

[221] 'Marvellous Richness of Diversity or Invidious Cultural Relativism?' (1998) 19 *HRLJ* 3.

[222] *The Margin of Appreciation Doctrine in the Dynamics of European Human Rights Jurisprudence*, London: Kluwer, 1996, 195–6.

[223] Ibid.   [224] H. Waldock (1980) 1 *HRLJ* 1, at 9.   [225] As in *Müller v Switzerland*, op cit.

[226] As in *Otto Preminger*, op cit.

[227] As in *Observer and Guardian v UK* (1991) 14 EHRR 153 ('the *Spycatcher*' case).

[228] The furious reaction of the British Government to the finding in *McCann v UK* ((1995) 21 EHRR 97) of a violation of the right to life of three IRA suspects shot dead by the SAS in Gibraltar is an example of the hos-tility to the Convention that can be produced by adverse findings in particularly sensitive areas. Public statements by Ministers suggested the possibility of withdrawal from the Convention. For a more measured criticism of the judgment, see the remarks of the then Attorney General in Parliament: HC Deb 265 (1994–95) col 14. See Introduction pp 6–8.

direction of universality or the direction of subsidiarity will depend on the context and on the mix of interests at stake.[229]

Whether this is a realistic defence of the way the variability of the margin operates in practice may be doubted, given that deference to the local *judiciary* rather than to 'democratic' decision-making will often be the actual result of affording a wide margin, as in both *Müller* and *Otto Preminger*.

Singh, Hunt, and Demetriou,[230] in a recent significant article, argue that a number of features of the margin of appreciation doctrine can be identified. One point, they suggest, is that the Court makes 'clear that it regards the concept . . . as defining the relationship between a supranational court and national authorities (including national courts).' The authors comment:

It is understandable that a court with many nationalities represented on it, and which is far removed from the conditions in a given . . . state may feel that certain questions are best left primarily to national authorities (including courts).[231]

This suggests a criterion of deference to *judgment and expertise*, rather than to democratic decision-making, in other words, to what may be referred to as greater 'institutional competence', rather than to superior political legitimacy.[232] Third, Singh *et al.* note that the Court has stressed the special place of the legislature in certain areas, such as taxation. This is really a version of the deference to democracy point noted earlier. In fact, however, as Gearty has pointed out, the Court's use of the margin of appreciation doctrine does not always correspond very well to any realistic assessment of how much democratic input there was into the decision under challenge.[233] We have already seen that the very high degree of deference paid to the decision of state authorities in the *Müller* case[234] could not be attributed to any such explanation.

CRITIQUE OF THE DOCTRINE

Singh *et al.* argue that, although the notion of the margin has been described as a 'doctrine', 'concept', or 'principle' that can be 'applied' in different circumstances, and talked of in terms of 'discovering its width', in fact 'it is a conclusory label which only serves to obscure the true basis on which a reviewing court decides whether or not intervention in a particular case is justifiable'.[235] In other words, prior, often unarticulated factors lead the Court to apply a more or less intensive standard of

---

[229] 'Universality versus Subsidiarity in the Strasbourg Case Laws on Free Speech: Explaining Some Recent Judgments' [1997] *EHRLR* 364, 379. For a critical response, see A. Lester, 'Universality versus Subsidiarity: A Reply' (1998) 1 *EHRLR*, 73.

[230] M. Hunt, R. Singh and M. Demetriou, 'Is there a role for the "margin of appreciation" in national law after the Human Rights Act?' (1999) 1 *EHRLR* 15

[231] Ibid.

[232] These matters are discussed more fully in the succeeding chapter: see pp 152–3 and J. Jowell, 'Judicial deference: servility, civility or institutional capacity?' [2003] *PL* 592.

[233] Gearty, op cit.   [234] (1991) 13 EHRR 212.

[235] Op cit, at 20–1.

review—which often involves using quite different tests, as explored below—and once it has done so, the Court announces that is applying a wide or a narrow margin of appreciation. But it is not the 'doctrine' of the margin that dictates the intensity of review, but the other way around. In Singh *et al.*'s view, the notion of a margin prevents a proper articulation of the reasons for more or less deferential standards of review, and therefore 'operates as a substitute for a principled and transparent approach to the proper scope of review'.[236]

They give the following example:

Where a court whose supervisory jurisdiction has been invoked declines to grant a remedy, giving as its 'reason' that the matter is within the authority's margin of appreciation, it may be saying one of two things. First it may be saying that is not appropriate for the court to substitute its judgment on a particular matter for the judgment of the challenged authority. Or secondly it may be saying that it has reviewed the decision and finds it to be justifiable. In the first case, the court is declining to exercise its review jurisdiction; in the second, it has carried out its review, and only declined to intervene because it finds there to be no unjustifiable breach.[237]

While this argument points up a possible area of confusion it is, in our view, partially overstated. Strasbourg can never 'decline' to exercise jurisdiction (unless it finds that it is not engaged at all, e.g., for territorial reasons). And whenever it exercises jurisdiction, whilst it may find that it is not appropriate for it to substitute its judgment for that of the domestic court, this must be because it has reviewed the decision and found it to fall within a range of responses, all of which can be viewed as giving sufficient respect to the Convention right in question. In other words, it does engage in a review of the decision—and its conclusion then is that the state's action, having been reviewed, is sufficiently respectful of the right in question to fall within its area of discretionary judgment. Now of course what 'sufficiently respectful' means will depend both upon the nature of the right in question (for example, is it political speech?) and upon the nature of the purpose for which the right is restricted (is it something that the Court considers itself not competent to second guess, such as the needs of national security or of morality?). But in a sense, the Court is *always* engaging in the second of the two possibilities—even in cases in which it engages in very light touch review, it has considered the decision and found it to be justifiable, with the caveat that 'justifiable' may well mean a decision that the Court itself would not have taken.

A more limited criticism of the doctrine would be that it produces such huge variations in the strictness of review as to make it misleading to think that the same tests are being carried out at all. In this way, the notion of a 'margin of appreciation' serves simply to obscure that, in fact, the Court carries out widely varying standards of review. The authors' view is that *no* margin should prevent a state from having to answer certain basic questions as to proportionality, and that the factors that lead the

236 Ibid, at 21.
237 Ibid.

Court to vary the standard of review should be much more openly articulated.[238] As Judge McDonald puts it:

perhaps the Convention system is now sufficiently mature to move beyond the margin of appreciation and grapple more openly with the questions of appropriateness which that device obscures . . . [it] should not permit the Court's evasion of its responsibility to articulate the reasons why its intervention in particular cases may nor may not be appropriate.[239]

The factors identified above by academics amount to a start in this articulation process, but the Court must be prepared to make a much more decisive contribution than hitherto.

PROPORTIONALITY: THEORY AND STRASBOURG PRACTICE[240]

INTRODUCTION

It is easy to take the notion that interferences with expression rights are permissible only if 'necessary' as being a straightforward test. Unfortunately, however, this is not the case. It is well accepted that the notion of 'necessity' in fact breaks down into two tests: that there must be a pressing social need to interfere with the Convention right and that the interference must be proportionate to the legitimate aim pursued. The pressing social need test acts—once a legitimate aim has been found—as a threshold test; it ensures that the state interest pursued (say, preserving national security) must be of a weighty or important character in the context, ruling out trivial grounds for interfering with Convention rights. The proportionality test then examines whether the actual measures taken were proportionate to the aim pursued; however, some of the factors relevant to establishing a pressing social need will again be relevant when examining the proportionality of the measures taken, because a key concern of proportionality is often the balancing of the seriousness of the interference with the right against the importance of the aim pursued. In assessing the latter, the Court will be bound to consider matters it has already considered under the 'pressing social

---

[238] Singh *et al.* suggest seven possible factors, at least some of which are used at times by the Court, albeit often without acknowledgment. They are: (1) importance of the right; (2) seriousness of the interference; (3) the relative specialist knowledge of experience of the body under review; (4) whether that body is elected or otherwise accountable; (5) whether the aim of the measure under review is to promote other human rights (e.g. does it have a rights-friendly aim, such as positive action); (6) whether the applicants are likely to be particularly vulnerable or unpopular thus requiring special vigilance; (7) whether the context is one in which there are fairly consistent standards.

[239] 'The Margin of Appreciation' in McDonald *et al.* (eds), *The European System of the Protection of Human Rights*, Dordrecht: Nijhoff, 1993, at 124.

[240] The analysis in this section is particularly indebted to the insights in Bosma's excellent study: op cit, esp chapters IV and VII. See further J. Rivers, 'Proportionality and Variable Intensity of Review' (2006) 65(1) CLJ 174.

need' test, a matter explored further below. But having set out this basic construct, a host of questions remain. The notion of a 'pressing social need' seems relatively unproblematic, but in fact, as suggested above, and explored further below, in application it demands widely varying standards. At its highest, the state is required to prove that the restriction of expression is 'absolutely necessary'; at its lowest, merely that it was 'not unreasonable' of the state to perceive a pressing social need to take action; in some cases, indeed, there is no positive reasoning at all to sustain the finding of a pressing social need,[241] or minimal critical scrutiny of the 'evidence' of such a need advanced.[242] Meanwhile, the notion of proportionality can be—and is, particularly by the Strasbourg Court—used to mean a wide variety of different things.

In this section, we look first at the concept of proportionality as explained by scholars and used by different constitutional courts, teasing out the various strands within what is actually a broad church concept; we then examine the way in which the Strasbourg Court applies different proportionality tests in different cases, guided, as argued above, by the factors that lead it to apply a more or less intensive standard of review (or margin of appreciation); finally, the implications of the different tests applied are considered.

PROPORTIONALITY IN COMPARATIVE PERSPECTIVE

Proportionality, when put under the analytical spotlight, proves to be a surprisingly protean concept and one in relation to which it is difficult to generalize accurately. A useful starting point in considering the application of the test both by other constitutional courts and by Strasbourg is Paul Craig's exhaustive definition of the various stages in proportionality. Craig notes first of all that 'to talk of proportionality at all assumes that the public body was entitled to pursue its desired objective. The presumption is, therefore, that the general objective was a legitimate one.'[243] In Convention terms, this equates to a stage prior to proportionality—that of deciding whether the state is acting in pursuit of a legitimate aim, as defined in paragraph 2 of the relevant article. Craig goes on:

There are [five][244] steps in any application of proportionality:

(i)   The relevant interests must be identified.

(ii) There must be some ascription of weight or value to those interests, since this is a necessary condition precedent to any balancing operation.

(iii) Some view must be taken as to whether certain interests can be traded off to achieve other goals at all. Should we, for example, trade off a fundamental right in order to enhance the general economic good? Certain respected theories would answer

---

[241] An example is the *Open Door* case, above.

[242] As, e.g., in *Handyside* and *Müller*, see above, at pp 52–9 and below, at 95–6.

[243] P. Craig, *Administrative Law*, 4th edn., Oxford: OUP, 1999, p 590.

[244] Craig states that there are six steps but only goes on to enumerate five, so we assume that this is his meaning at this point.

no [e.g. modern theories of liberalism espoused by writers such as Rawls and Dworkin].[245]

It may be said that the Convention, as it were, pre-answers these questions, at least when dealing with a conflict between a Convention right and a societal interest, rather than between two Convention rights. In the former situation, the interests are already identified and weighed (in the sense that the primary right is given *prima facie* priority) and the different Convention articles themselves answer Craig's question three— in some cases no grounds for infringing Convention rights (in the case of Article 3), or strictly limited ones (in the case of Articles 2 and 5) are identified. In others, (Articles 8–11), much broader and wide-ranging grounds are specified. Thus the philosophical question Craig poses is largely answered by the Convention system itself. But it is not fully answered. The phrase 'the rights of others' leaves open a very significant question: what 'rights' may count as reasons for infringing Convention rights, and when will the need to enforce those rights amount to a 'pressing social need'? As seen above, the Court has sometimes been remarkably vague on this subject, failing even to specify what rights it has in mind when using this aim as a reason for finding a legitimate interference with a Convention right. For example, we saw above that in *Steel v UK*, supposedly fundamental rights of peaceful protest were overridden by 'rights of others' which were not even identified, still less demonstrated to be more weighty in the particular context.[246] This is in spite of the fact that the Court has said in *Chassagnou v France*[247] that when dealing with 'rights of others' that are not themselves competing Convention rights, 'only *indisputable imperatives* can justify interference with enjoyment of a Convention right'.[248] It is very doubtful whether this robust statement of principle in fact represents the reality.

Craig then goes on to the remaining two steps:

(iv) . . . is the disputed measure the least restrictive which could be adopted in the circumstances; is the challenged act suitable and necessary for the achievement of its objective, and one which does not impose excessive burdens on the individual; what are the relative costs and benefits of the disputed measure? It will be seen that different formulations tend to be used in different types of case. For example, the first version will commonly be used in cases where the disputed measure is in conflict with a fundamental right. The most common version of the test is, however, the second. This requires the court to go through three stages and ask whether the measure was necessary to achieve the desired objective, whether it was suitable for this end, and whether it none the less imposed excessive burdens on the individual. The last part of this inquiry is often termed proportionality *stricto sensu* [in a strict sense]

(v) The court will have to decide how intensively it is going to apply any one of the tests mentioned above. It is important to realise that the tests can be applied more or less intensively . . .[249]

---

[245] The remaining two tests are considered below.   [246] See text to note 131 above.
[247] (2000) 29 EHRR 615.   [248] Ibid, at [113] (emphasis added).   [249] Ibid.

Here, step (v) corresponds to the notion of the margin of appreciation; depending upon both the importance of the particular aspect of the right at stake and upon the nature of the competing societal considerations, a more or less rigorous insistence upon justification in relation to each of the different tests will be applied. We have, as argued above, identified a more expansive role for the margin of appreciation doctrine; not only does it determine how intensively the tests are applied, it also determines which proportionality test is used. It is notable that Craig identifies the first, strict method (least intrusive means) as one commonly used where fundamental rights are at stake (it should be recalled that, in other jurisdictions, the proportionality principle is used in a number of contexts outside fundamental rights). That might lead us to believe that this test would be consistently used by the European Court of Human Rights; however, as we have already seen above and will be explored further below, this is far from the case. The Court uses a number of other, less strict approaches when the factors underlying the margin of appreciation so guide it.

Harris, O'Boyle, and Warbrick distinguish three different uses of the notion of proportionality.[250] First, a measure is disproportionate if is not necessary—in other words, if the seriousness of the measure outweighs the goal the state is pursuing (the legitimate aim). This may be referred to as 'means/ends analysis' and corresponds to the first stage of the 'most common' version of proportionality outlined at (iv) above by Craig. Since 'necessary' in the Convention system means 'pressing social need', this at its simplest means that a measure *cannot* be considered proportionate if there is not a pressing social need for it. Used in this way, the test would therefore suggest simply that the threshold test for legitimate interference with a Convention right has not been passed. However, given that this test involves balancing the *seriousness* of the measure in question with the importance of the state goal, the latter could be deemed to have been weighty enough to cross the initial 'pressing social need' test, but not important enough to justify the particular measure in question. This, then, is an instance in which the importance of the state aim, although having been deemed sufficiently pressing to justify *in principle* an interference with a Convention right, might not be deemed sufficiently weighty to justify the particular measure the state had adopted. In the context of media freedom, for example, a particular state aim— protection of the reputation of others, say—might be deemed to justify some measure of interference with apparently defamatory speech (for example, the availability of damages), but not prior restraint.

Harris *et al.*'s second version of proportionality is much more specific: interference is not proportionate if a less intrusive means of serving the legitimate aim exists, but was not pursued (this corresponds to the 'strict' first version).[251] Their third version is that a measure is not proportionate where the object of the interference cannot be achieved by the interference—the 'ineffective' or 'unsuitableness' test (this corres- ponds, broadly, to the second stage of Craig's 'most common version'). The definition

---

[250] Op cit, at 300.
[251] Specifically, to the test set out in the first sentence of Craig's stage (iv) above.

put forward by Emilou, it will be evident, corresponds to the second of the Harris *et al.* formulation:

where there is a choice between several appropriate measures, recourse should be made to the least onerous and the disadvantages caused [to the individual] should not be disproportionate to the aim pursued.[252]

The second part of this sentence is merely tautologous (something is proportionate if it is not disproportionate); the first captures the 'least intrusive measure' principle, which, as seen, is the most rigorous type of proportionality enquiry and one which is often not in fact pursued by the Court.

It is useful to compare the attempts to elucidate the general approach of the Strasbourg Court with the standards laid down by other constitutional courts. Clayton, having examined proportionality as a test applied in EC law, and by courts in South Africa, Canada, and New Zealand, suggests an international standard of proportionality:

A number of threads can be drawn together. There is universal acknowledgment that the court is exercising a review function and is not substituting its own judgment for that of the original decision-maker. However, the decision in question is to be subject to an intense standard of review. The necessity of the interference is closely scrutinised and a public authority must usually show it has used the least restrictive means available to it to accomplish its objective.[253]

He then takes a closer look at the proportionality standard applied by the Canadian Supreme Court to test the lawfulness of actions that *prima facie* infringe rights under the Canadian Charter of Rights, but which rely upon the general exception clause in section 1 of the Charter, which states:

The Canadian Charter of Rights and Freedoms guarantees the rights and freedoms set out in it subject only to such reasonable limits prescribed by law as can be demonstrably justified in a free and democratic society.

Clayton cites the 'classical standard' approach to assessing the lawfulness of actions taken in reliance on section 1 as set out in *R v Oakes*,[254] the first part of which is as follows:

First, the objective, which the measures responsible for a limit on a Charter right or freedom are designed to serve, must be of 'sufficient importance to warrant overriding a consti-tutionally protected right or freedom' ... The standard must be high in order to ensure that objectives which are trivial or discordant with the principles integral to a free and democratic society do not gain ... protection. It is necessary, at a minimum, that the objective relate to concerns which are pressing and substantial in a free and democratic society before it can be characterised as sufficiently important.

---

[252] *The Principle of Proportionality in the case-law of the European Convention on Human Rights*, Dordrecht: Kluwer, 1995, p 2.

[253] Op cit, at 512.   [254] [1986] 1 SCR 103 at 137, 138.

It is evident that this part of the proportionality test, which is not actually the proportionality test *strictu sensu*, corresponds to the 'pressing social need' part of the Convention test, as the very similar words makes plain. In other words, this part of the test sets out the importance that a competing aim must have, before it can be used to justify any interference with Charter rights. Of course, under section 1 of the Canadian Charter, the Courts have the additional burden of deciding whether the aim pursued is a legitimate one at all, since such aims are not set out in section 1, as they are in paragraph (2) of Articles 8–11. In other words, this part of the test is a threshold one—to ensure that the aim is both sufficiently legitimate (not 'trivial' or 'discordant' with democratic principles) and sufficiently weighty ('pressing and substantial') to justify infringing a fundamental right at all. It is further evident that this part of the *Oakes* test mirrors stage one of the so-called *de Freitas*[255] three-stage test, which was adopted by the House of Lords for use in Convention cases in the leading case of *Daly*.[256] Under the *de Freitas* test, the reviewing court must ask itself three questions, of which the first is: 'whether . . . the legislative objective is sufficiently important to justify limiting a fundamental right'. Here then we have a remarkable degree of consensus at least on the establishment of the threshold criterion for interference.

We then come to the strict proportionality part of the *Oakes* test, which—just as with Craig's formulation[257]—is put in a number of different possible ways:

Second [the state] . . . must show that the means chosen are reasonable and demonstrably justified. This involves a form of proportionality test . . . Although the nature of the proportionality test will vary depending on the circumstances, in each case courts will be required to balance the interests of society with those of individuals and groups. There are, in my view, three important components of a proportionality test. First, the measures adopted must be carefully designed to meet the objective in question. They must not be arbitrary, unfair or based on irrational considerations. In short, they must be rationally connected to the objective. Second, the means, even if rationally connected to the objective in the first sense, should impair 'as little as possible' the rights or freedoms in question . . . Third, there must be a proportionality between the effects of the measures which are responsible for limiting the Charter's right or freedom and the objective which has been identified as of 'sufficient importance'.[258]

This formulation may be compared with the *de Freitas* test:

(ii) the measures designed to meet the legislative objective are rationally connected to it; and

(iii) the means used to impair the right or freedom are no more than is necessary to accomplish the objective.[259]

---

[255] From the decision of the Privy Council in *de Freitas v Permanent Secretary of Ministry of Agriculture, Fisheries, Lands and Housing* [1999] 1 AC 69, 80.

[256] *R v Secretary of State for the Home Department ex parte Daly* [2001] 2 WLR 1622. The UK Court's approach to proportionality is examined in detail in the subsequent chapter.

[257] Above, at 88.

[258] *R v Oakes*, op cit.

[259] Op cit.

It will be seen that the two tests largely correlate: both insist upon rational connection between the measures taken by the state to restrict the right in question and the end that the state is seeking to achieve; both also require that those measures should be no more than necessary to achieve the objective, which means that they should impair the freedom as little as possible. The *Oakes* test adds that there must be a 'proportion-ality' between the measures taken and the objective of the state; however, it is difficult to see how a measure that was rationally connected to its objective and went no further than necessary in bringing about that objective could yet still be regarded as lacking in 'proportionality'. In other words, it is questionable whether this third part of the *Oakes* formulation actually adds anything. What is of more significance is the fact that both formulations use the strict 'least restrictive' test. As explored further in the next chapter, the House of Lords may have here imported into English law a proportionality test that is in fact stricter than that used by the Strasbourg Court on a number of occasions.

The leading decision on proportionality in South Africa indicates again a broad international consensus on proportionality:

In the balancing process, the relevant considerations will include the nature of the right that is limited, and its importance to an open and democratic society based on freedom and equality, the purpose for which the right is limited and the importance of that purpose to such a society, the extent of the limitation, its efficacy, and particularly, where the limitation has to be necessary, whether its desired end could be reasonably achieved through other means less damaging to the right in question.[260]

The first two factors essentially call for a balancing between the right and the competing societal interest. The third and fourth call for a means/ends balancing exercise (the extent of the limitation and its efficacy); the final is the well-known 'least onerous test'.

However, the Court also commented, frankly:

there is no absolute standard which can be laid down for determining the reasonableness and necessity. Principles can be established, but the application of those principles to par-ticular circumstances can only be done on a case by case basis. This is inherent to the requirement of proportionality.[261]

The final South African Constitution defined proportionality in some detail in section 35(1):

The rights in the Bill of Rights may be limited only in terms of laws of general application to the extent that the limitation is reasonable and justifiable in an open and democratic society based on human dignity, equality and freedom, having regard to all relevant factors including—

(a) the nature of the right;

(b) the importance of the purpose of the limitation;

---

[260] *S v Makwanyane* [1995] 3 SA 391.   [261] Ibid.

(c) the nature and extent of the limitation;

(d) the relationship between the limitation and its purpose; and

(e) less restrictive means to achieve the purpose.

Note that this requires an assessment of the importance of the right (in the particular context) and of the importance of the purpose of the limitation—the latter corresponding to the 'pressing social need' part of the ECHR test. Thus we have expressly set out in the Constitution the 'means/ends' assessment and the 'least restrictive means' test.

THE PROPORTIONALITY TEST AS USED BY STRASBOURG

A 'rigorous approach in the context of freedom of expression'?[262]

All of the tests discussed above are used at different times by the Strasbourg Court. However, as Bosma demonstrates,[263] they are not consistently used in a cumulative manner, and sometimes, as with the 'balancing' cases,[264] none of them are used. Clayton concedes that, 'the European Court of Human Rights has not identified a consistent or uniform set of principles when considering the doctrine of proportionality',[265] noting that it sometimes asks whether there was 'a reasonable relationship between the interference and the legitimate aim pursued'[266] (a means/ends analysis). However, he asserts: 'More frequently . . . the Court has applied a more rigorous approach, particularly in the context of freedom of expression',[267] and cites the approach taken in the *Sunday Times* case,[268] a three-fold test:

- whether the interference complained of corresponded to a 'pressing social need';

- whether it was 'proportionate to the legitimate aim pursued'; and

- whether the reasons given by the national authority to justify it were 'relevant and sufficient'.

He comments that 'this stricter formulation is appropriate where fundamental rights are at stake' (such as freedom of expression, citing *Handyside* and *Lingens v Austria*).

The difficulty here is that the test of there being a pressing social need is not, strictly, a test of whether the action taken was *proportionate*, but of whether

---

[262] The phrase is taken from R. Clayton, 'Regaining a sense of proportion: the Human Rights Act and the Proportionality Principle' (2001) 5 *EHRLR* 504, 510.

[263] Op cit, Chapter IV.

[264] That is, those in which the seriousness of the interference is balanced directly against the importance of the right in question.

[265] Clayton, op cit.

[266] Ibid, citing e.g. *Hadjianastassiou v Greece* (1992) 16 EHRR 219, at para. 19; *Chorherr v Austria* (1993) 17 EHRR 358, at [37].

[267] Clayton, ibid: citing *Sunday Times v United Kingdom* (1979) 2 EHRR 245; *Lingens v Austria* (1986) 8 EHRR 407.

[268] Ibid.

sufficiently serious grounds existed for abridging Convention rights in the first place; it will then be asked whether the particular measures taken were proportionate to that pressing need. Moreover, the requirement that the 'reasons' given be 'relevant and sufficient' is largely meaningless. It is self-evident that they must be 'relevant'; what counts as 'sufficient' evidence will depend upon how closely the Court is minded to scrutinize the factual matrix, which really depends upon how intensely it is applying the proportionality test. Clearly, the word 'sufficient' has no particular meaning; we have already seen that the Court has in some cases found a state's evidence of a necessity to act sufficient if it is 'not unreasonable' for it to hold this view, while in other cases it has insisted on clear evidence of necessity. Finally, in using the word 'proportionate', the Court in the *Sunday Times* case does not tell us what this word means—as we have seen, it can apparently signify a number of quite different tests. In other words, the so-called 'three-stage test' in *Sunday Times* does not itself signify a 'more rigorous approach' since the definition given begs a number of questions.

What does emerge from it, however, is that there should indeed be two separate enquiries: one as to pressing social need, and one as to proportionality. Bosma refers to these as 'two different substantive methods of protection',[269] but notes that the Court does not always distinguish clearly between them. She finds that there are cases in which the Court has only looked at pressing social need (*Müller*), those in which it has clearly looked at both (*Jersild*),[270] those in which neither requirement was expressly mentioned (*Otto Preminger, Autronic v Switzerland*),[271] those in which it claimed to be reviewing whether the restriction served a pressing social need but concluded that the measure was proportionate (*Informationsverein Lentia v Austria*),[272] and those in which it has looked at both, but concluded only on the proportionality of a restriction (*Open Door, Wingrove*[273], *Barthold*).[274]

This, it is suggested, is a basic flaw in the Court's reasoning: the two tests of pressing social need and proportionality are not *alternatives* but must go together as part of a necessary logical sequence. As seen, *both* tests are used in sequence in both the *Oakes* and *de Freitas* formulations. This is because they play different roles: the first step looks at whether there exists sufficient cause to justify curtailing a Convention right *in some way*—that is, in principle. In other words, the task of the Court at this point is to assess the gravity of the situation the national authorities were trying to tackle through the disputed measure. As examples, in *Handyside* this meant looking at the content of the book in question and its likely effect on children; in *Observer and Guardian* at how damaging to national security the revelations in the book would be; in *Sunday Times*, at the risk of prejudice to the possible future legal proceedings of the injuncted article. Once it is established that the threat to national security, or the

---

[269] Op cit, at 136.

[270] Op cit. The case concerned a documentary in which members of the Greenjackets, a far-right organization, were interviewed about their views.

[271] (1990) A 178, at [61].   [272] (1993) A 276.   [273] (1997) 24 EHRR 1.   [274] Bosma, ibid.

morals of children, or the rights of others (as the case may be) was sufficiently grave to justify interference with expression *in principle*, the Court goes on to ask whether the *particular measures taken* were proportionate to the risk, threat, or damage that the state was seeking to avert. The second question would make no sense without the first, while to satisfy oneself of the first alone would amount to deciding only that there was a need to take *some* action that curtailed a Convention right, without going on to ask whether the *actual action taken* was justified.

It may be fairly commented, however, that if the Court finds that there is no pressing social need, it is legitimate for it to cease the analysis at that point. For, as Feldman points out, and as we saw in relation to the first version of proportionality put forward by Harris *et al.*,[275] a measure *cannot* be considered proportionate if it does not correspond to a pressing social need.[276] In other words, if the pressing social need test is failed, the state, logically has lost the argument at that point, without the need to go into issues of proportionality proper. In that sense, the pressing social need test is, as suggested above, a threshold one: showing it to be satisfied is a necessary but not a sufficient condition of justifying interference with a Convention right. That these two parts of the enquiry are indeed separate was recognized by what is still probably the leading judgment on proportionality under the HRA: *Daly*.[277] There, Lord Steyn spoke of the 'twin requirements' that 'the limitation of the right was necessary in a democratic society, in the sense of meeting a pressing social need, and the question whether the interference was really proportionate to the legitimate aim being pursued'.[278] Bosma concludes that the Strasbourg Court does not distinguish clearly between the two enquiries.[279] On this basis, she goes on to conclude that, 'these classifications are not appropriate to distinguish different substantive methods of protection in its case law'.[280] We would respectfully disagree—the two are conceptually different enquires; as suggested above, they are both logically necessary (although interconnected to an extent); both are present in the *Oakes* and in the *de Freitas* formulations.

There can never, therefore, be any justification for omitting consideration of the pressing social need issue. It was, however, omitted in *Handyside*, in the sense that the Court at no point formally stated why there was a 'pressing social need' to prohibit distribution of the book. Rather, the Court seemed to *assume* the existence of such a need, and concentrate instead upon dismissing arguments that cast doubt upon it. There were two such arguments. The first was that other British authorities—those in Scotland, Northern Ireland, and the Isle of Man—had taken no action at all against the book. As to this, the Court said:

Their failure to act—into which the Court does not have to enquire and which did not prevent the measures taken in England from leading to revision of the Schoolbook—does

---

[275] Above, note 250.

[276] D. Feldman, *Civil Liberties and Human Rights in England and Wales*, 2nd edn., Oxford: OUP, 2001, p 337.

[277] [2001] 2 AC 532.   [278] Ibid, at [27].   [279] Ibid, at 137.   [280] Ibid.

not prove that the judgment of 29 October 1971 was not a response to a real necessity, bearing in mind the national authorities' margin of appreciation.[281]

The second argument was the fact that the book was circulating freely in other European states also:

> The applicant and the minority of the Commission laid stress on the further point that, in addition to the original Danish edition, translations of the 'Little Book' appeared and circulated freely in the majority of the member States of the Council of Europe ... Here again, the national margin of appreciation and the optional nature of the 'restrictions' and 'penalties' referred to in Article 10 para. 2 prevent the Court from accepting the argument. The Contracting States have each fashioned their approach in the light of the situation obtaining in their respective territories; they have had regard, inter alia, to the different views prevailing there about the demands of the protection of morals in a democratic society. The fact that most of them decided to allow the work to be distributed does not mean that the contrary decision of the Inner London Quarter Sessions was a breach of Article 10.

In fact, these matters *did* go to the question of whether the confiscation answered to a pressing social need, and in an area as difficult to assess as the protection of morals, they provided some objective evidence that there was no such need. For surely, if the book presented a grave danger to the morals of children, how could this need not be perceived by the authorities so nearby in Scotland or in Northern Ireland? While it is true that Article 10 *allows* for restrictions on speech rather than mandating them, the fact that state authorities so close to the English ones evidently saw no need to take action against the book *does* amount to evidence that there was no real need to do so. In short, in this case, there was no positive reasoning to show that there was a pressing social need, merely an unconvincing dismissal of the arguments *against* there being such a need. In this respect, the remarks of the Canadian Supreme Court are apposite:

> Where the contextual factors indicate that the government has not established that the harm which it is seeking to prevent is widespread or significant, a deferential approach to the particular means chosen by the legislature to implement the legislative purpose is not warranted.[282]

As Clayton comments:

> The approach taken by the Canadian courts to judicial deference is highly instructive to an English lawyer. A close analysis of the factual justification for the decisions of public author-ities is the only practical method of achieving a proper balance between respect for the democratic will and the protection of human rights.[283]

This was an instance in which the refusal of the Court to engage in such analysis meant that *in effect* a key stage of the analysis was not undertaken.

Bosma goes on to ask what tests Strasbourg uses *other than* the 'pressing social need' enquiry and finds three: suitability, least restrictive alternative, and a balancing

---

[281] Op cit, at [54].   [282] *Thompson Newspapers v Canada (Attorney-General)* [1998] 1 SCR 877.
[283] Op cit, at 524.

exercise—of means against ends.[284] She points out that a fourth is also sometimes used: a balancing of interests test that does *not* ask any of the above classic proportionality questions, but straightforwardly balances the importance of the aim served by restricting expression (i.e., how 'pressing' the 'social need' is) with the importance of the expression itself, a method that may be referred to as 'speech/harm balancing'. Under such a test there is no consideration as such of whether the specific measures taken were proportionate.[285] We now turn to some examples of the use of these four approaches, which we will refer to throughout this book.

Suitability of the means of interference

For Schokkenbroek, the notion of assessing whether the means chosen to restrict the right are suitable to achieve the state's legitimate aim is incompatible with the doctrine of the margin of appreciation, since it interferes with the national authority's discretion as to what restrictions are necessary in a democratic society.[286] Bosma notes that perhaps because of this factor, the Court is cautious about using this test, and 'never applie[s] [it] separately' from other methods.[287] Such a comment, however, serves only to illustrate the misleading nature of the margin of appreciation doctrine. The doctrine does not preclude the Court from assessing the suitability of the means chosen to protect legitimate state aims. Indeed, as we have argued above, and as Singh *et al.* point out,[288] the 'margin of appreciation doctrine' is simply a shorthand for the fact that the Court will use a variable standard of review depending on the circumstances. All the concept of a margin of appreciation indicates is that it may *sometimes* be inappropriate for the Court to ask whether the restriction was suitable. In any event, Schokkenbroek's comment is arguably wrong as a matter of principle: if a measure is evidently not suitable for attaining the aim (because, for example, it is ineffective), then it is impossible for it be 'necessary' in pursuit of a legitimate aim. If the legitimate aim is not in fact served by the measure, then the measure is not linked to it and is therefore not capable of falling within paragraph 2 of Article 10. Of course, this should not involve the Court in intricate discussion of whether in fact other measures might work slightly better than the one impugned; but in a case in which the measure is manifestly unsuitable or ineffective (as, for example, in the *Observer and Guardian* case), the Court would be failing in its duty not to find it so.

Bosma identifies the *Open Door Dublin Well Woman v Ireland*[289] decision as one in which the Court did, however, use this method. It will be recalled[290] that the case concerned the issuing of a blanket prohibition upon the provision of information in Ireland to woman as to the availability of abortion services abroad. Aside from the seriousness of the interference (discussed above), one of the grounds for finding the injunction disproportionate to the aim pursued (discouraging abortion) was that it was in fact ineffective—the information was otherwise obtainable elsewhere, through normal means such as telephone directories and contacts with people in Britain, but

---

[284] Op cit, at 138.   [285] Ibid.   [286] Op cit, at 198.   [287] Op cit, at 139.
[288] Above, text to note 235.   [289] (1992) A.246.
[290] The facts appear above—text to note 198.

without proper supervision and therefore in ways that were less protective of a woman's health.[291] The injunction might also have led to women seeking abortion later, since they had not had proper counselling and information.[292] It was also noted that the injunction did not stop a large number of Irish women travelling to Britain for abortions.[293] In other words, the measure was not suitable because it was both relatively ineffective in protecting the life of the foetus and in some ways counter-productive. It also applied in an unfair way—it might mean that less educated women, with less access to resources, would be likely to end up having later abortions, with greater risk to mental and physical health.[294] Bosma points out that a similar approach was taken in *Observer and Guardian v UK*,[295] the efficacy of the injunction against the publication of the book *Spycatcher* to protect national security was doubted, given that copies of the book were freely available outside the UK. The measure was both excessive and ineffective.

In contrast, *Handyside* is a case in which the suitability of the measure itself—the forfeiture of the book—received no real examination by the Court at all, which appeared to satisfy itself with dismissing arguments against there being a real need to take action against the book.[296] This type of review was in fact carried out by a dissentient, with revealing consequences. Justice Mosler stated: 'it is beyond question that the measure [interfering with expression] must be appropriate for achieving the aim'[297] and then went on to engage in a fairly rigorous analysis of the suitability of the measure in question:

The greater part of the first edition of the book circulated without impediment. The measures taken by the competent authorities and confirmed by the Inner London Quarter Sessions prevented merely the distribution of under 10 per cent of the impression. The remainder, that is about 90 per cent, reached the public including probably, to a large extent, the adolescents meant to be protected . . . The measures in respect of the applicant thus had so little success that they must be taken as ineffectual in relation to the aim pursued . . .

Thus, for Justice Mosler, the fatal blow to the government's case was the 'clear lack of proportion between that part of the impression [of the book] subjected to the said measures and that part whose circulation was not impeded'.

In conclusion, the 'suitability' test is internationally endorsed, and provides a means of subjecting measures interfering with human rights to a test that no government should object to: demonstrating that the measures in question will be likely to achieve the aims in view. Any measure failing such a test cannot possibly be deemed a 'necessary' restriction on a fundamental right.

Less restrictive measures available

As noted above, this is one of the more rigorous tests that can be applied. It amounts to the most rigorous forms of means/ends balancing, by holding that if any less

---

[291] Op cit, at [76].   [292] Ibid, at [77].   [293] Ibid, at [76].   [294] Ibid, at [77].
[295] Op cit; see above at text to 189 and, see further Chapter 19.   [296] Above at pp 95–6.
[297] Op cit at, at para 2 of his judgment.

restrictive means of achieving the same end was available, the measures actually taken will for that reason be found to be disproportionate to the aim in view. As Bosma points out, there are 'many cases'[298] in which the Court has employed neither this test nor the 'suitability' principle just outlined. In *Müller*, in fact, we witness a species of *reversal* of this test, as touched on above.[299] The state's action (confiscating allegedly obscene paintings) was held to be justified partly because it did not take the more draconian action of destroying them. This is surely a perverse approach—states will nearly always being able to imagine *more* punitive action that they *could* have taken. There are always more severe infringements on expression that may be imagined: injunctions instead of damages; final injunctions instead of interim ones; criminal sanctions instead of civil ones; prison sentences instead of fines.[300] Thus, this argument should not be accepted and the Court should instead ask the *legitimate* question: would a lesser measure than that taken have dealt satisfactorily with the problem the state perceived? States should not be allowed to turn this enquiry on its head. The reasoning of the Court in *Müller*, in accepting a kind of 'reverse' least restrictive means argument, meant that it wholly failed to consider the question whether lesser measures than outright confiscation of the paintings could have achieved the aim sought. Exactly the same phenomenon occurred in *Otto Preminger*, which also involved both conviction *and* forfeiture of the film in question, as discussed in Chapter 9.[301]

Of course, the 'least intrusive' means test is not unproblematic. As the Canadian Supreme Court has recognized:

It is established that the deference accorded to Parliament or the legislatures may vary with the social context in which the limitation on rights is imposed . . . A limit prescribed by law should not be struck out merely because the Court can conceive of an alternative which seems to it to be less restrictive . . . If the law falls within a range of reasonable alternatives, the courts will not find it overbroad merely because they can conceive of an alternative which might better tailor objective to infringement.[302]

This is because, given human ingenuity, it will very often be possible to conjure up possible alternative measures that might have been less intrusive, and also because assessing whether those measures would have been just as effective may often be a matter of conjecture: detailed research, or simply the lessons of experience, might be needed to establish the point, but may not be present. The point, however, is that the test should be used at least to put the state to proof as to *obvious* alternatives: 'if the government fails to explain why a significantly less intrusive and equally effective measure was not chosen, the law may fail'.[303] Quite plainly, no such explanation was demanded in *Otto Preminger*.

---

[298] Op cit, at 142.   [299] Above, at 59–60.
[300] The Court, for example, noted that Janowski's initial prison sentence was quashed on appeal.
[301] See 488–94.
[302] *RJR-McDonald v Canada (Attorney-General)* [1993] 3 SCR 199 at [133] to [137].
[303] Ibid, at [160].

Means / ends balancing

As Harris *et al.* put it, this test involves an assessment of whether the seriousness of the restriction outweighs the interest in realization of the legitimate aim.[304] Of course, in asking this question, the question whether there was a less restrictive measure available is highly relevant: the latter is not a conceptually separate enquiry, but simply one means of assessing whether the restriction *does* go further than necessary. Exactly the same can be said for the 'suitability' enquiry, as Bosma acknowledges.[305] Under this method, then, in a media freedom case, the exercise would balance the gravity of the particular interference (an injunction, say) against the importance of the aim to be achieved: did it go further than was necessary? This on its face omits any assessment of the importance of the speech in question. However, first of all, that question will be considered in relation to whether there was a pressing social need to restrict the speech in the first place,[306] and secondly, it arguably enters the equation in terms of assessing the gravity of the interference—the more important the speech in question is in Convention terms, the more serious any interference with it is. In other words, as Shokkenbroek would have it, the importance of the right is considered as part of the 'gravity of the means' part of the assessment.[307]

Bosma points out that *Fressoz and Roire v France*[308] is a good example both of means /ends balancing and of the manner in which the importance of the speech in question can enter into the means /ends equation, in the manner just discussed. The applicants in *Fressoz* were journalists. During a period of industrial unrest within the Peugeot motor car company, caused by the refusal of the management, led by M. Calvet, to award pay increases to the workforce, they published an article revealing the very large pay rises awarded during that period to M. Calvet himself. They proved the truth of this story by quoting figures from, and reproducing part of, M. Calvert's tax return, which had been sent to them anonymously. The applicants were convicted of the offence of handling confidential information obtained through a breach of professional confidence by an unidentified tax official and of handling stolen photocopies of M. Calvert's tax assessment; they were fined around £1,000 and £500 respectively. They applied to Strasbourg, alleging a breach of Article 10. There were two main factors that led the Court to find a violation. The first was the fact that the information in question was publicly obtainable elsewhere and therefore could not be said to be confidential.[309] Therefore, the importance of the aim in view—the protection of information that was not in fact confidential—could not outweigh the seriousness of the interference: criminal sanctions. However, in assessing the gravity of the interference, the Court was clearly heavily influenced by the nature of the speech in question. The Court commented:

The article was published during an industrial dispute—widely reported in the press—at

---

[304] Op cit, at 300.   [305] Ibid, at 142.

[306] As in the *Sunday Times* case, in which the Court considered that a very strong overriding interest was needed to justify the interference, given the importance of the speech.

[307] See Bosma, op cit, at 143–4.   [308] (1999) 5 BHRC 654.   [309] Ibid, at [54].

one of the major French car manufacturers . . . The article showed that the company chairman had received large pay increases during the period under consideration while at the same time opposing his employees' claims for a rise. By making such a comparison against that background, the article . . . was not intended to damage Mr Calvet's reputation but to contribute to the more general debate on a topic that interested the public (see, for example, *Thorgeir Thorgeirson v Iceland* (1992) A 239, p 28).[310]

The Court continued:

Not only does the press have the task of imparting information and ideas on matters of public interest: the public also has a right to receive them . . . That is particularly true in the instant case, as issues concerning employment and pay generally attract considerable attention. Consequently, an interference with the exercise of press freedom cannot be compatible with Article 10 of the Convention unless it is justified by an overriding requirement in the public interest.[311]

Of course, this can be read another way: as straight balancing between the speech, which was of high importance, and the reasons for the interference, which were weak, because the information was not confidential and did not, moreover, fall within M. Calvet's private life[312] so that Article 8 was not engaged as a countervailing consideration. But the importance of the speech also directly contributed to the assessment of the gravity of the interference when balanced against its effectiveness. The case nicely illustrates the complexity of the proportionality enquiry—not only were there arguably two different methods used—means/ends balancing and balancing between the seriousness of the interference and the importance of the right, but, as discussed above, the importance of the right contributed strongly to the finding that the means employed were disproportionate to the aim in view.

Balancing the seriousness of the interference against the importance of the right

We have used the term 'speech / harm balancing' as a shorthand for this test. While it has been argued that, on one interpretation the approach of the Court in the *Sunday Times* case was simply to find the absence of a pressing social need, it could also be interpreted as engaging in a straightforward balancing act:

Having regard to all the circumstances of the case . . . the Court concludes that the interference complained of did not correspond to a social need sufficiently pressing to outweigh the public interest in freedom of expression within the meaning of the Convention.[313]

Such balancing does not look at proportionality in the *de Freitas* and *Oakes* sense, in that there is no assessment of the suitability of the measures taken. Its dangers lie in the fact that it is a purely normative exercise; furthermore, particularly if undertaken without clear acknowledgement of the basic principle that the Court in deciding whether a given interference with free expression was necessary in a democratic society 'is faced not with a choice between two conflicting principles, but with a

---

[310] Ibid, at [50].   [311] Ibid, at [52].
[312] Ibid, at [50]. Because it concerned the financial affairs of a public figure.   [313] Op cit, at [67].

principle of freedom of expression that is subject to a number of exceptions which must be narrowly interpreted',[314] the test runs the risk of becoming a mere *ad hoc* exercise of rationalizing judicial preferences. Bosma[315] notes that in *Barfold*,[316] the Court said: 'In the present case, proportionality implies that the pursuit of the aims mentioned in Article 10, para 2 has to be weighed against the value of open discussion of topics of public concern.' As Bosma comments, 'the Court subsequently referred to this review as "striking a fair balance between these interests".'[317] The problem with such a technique is that a simple weighing exercise creates the risk of the courts simply deciding themselves which interest is most important in the given situation, without any more structured reasoning process. In particular, the notion of 'fair balance' does not itself bring in the presumptive priority of the primary Convention guarantee. In *Janowski v Poland*,[318] as Bosma points out, no means / ends analysis was undertaken: the court simply weighed up the different interests (the freedom of expression of the journalist against the interest in civil servants being free from harassment in carrying out their duties) and 'declared one interest to be of greater weight than the other'.[319] The problem is the seeming arbitrariness and subjectivity of such findings. A means / ends enquiry, examining, for example, whether there were possible lesser measures that could have been adopted, is more structured and less open to charges of subjectivism. Showing, as could have been done in *Otto Preminger*, that the measures used by the state factually speaking went further than necessary to protect the Catholics of Tyrol, or were not actually suitable for attaining the aim sought (as in the *Open Door* case) is plainly a more objective and rational exercise. As the Canadian Supreme Court has put it:

In determining proportionality, [the Court] must determine the actual connection between the objective and what the law will in fact achieve; [and] the actual degree to which it impairs the right . . .[320]

In contrast, abjuring these more hard-edged questions, and simply deciding, as in *Janowski*, that the aim of protecting police officers from being insulted in the course of their duties is more important than the aim of protecting political though offensive expression, is a purely evaluative exercise and will always be controversial.

It is important therefore both that this test is not deployed in isolation and that, when carried out, it is firmly rooted in a principled argument for the value of the speech in question. A good example of both these tendencies is *Goodwin v UK*.[321] Goodwin, a journalist, obtained information from a source (probably an employee) about the financial difficulties of a company, Tetra. The company, having obtained an injunction preventing Goodwin and all relevant media publications from disclosing the information, then applied for, and obtained, an order forcing Goodwin to reveal

---

[314] Chapter 1, note 133.   [315] Op cit, at 146.   [316] (1989) 13 EHRR 493.
[317] Op cit, at 147.   [318] Op cit, the case is discussed in more detail above at pp 65–6.
[319] Op cit, at 147.   [320] *RJR-McDonald v Canada (Attorney General)* [1993] 3 SCR 199, at [133].
[321] (1996) Reports 1996–II. The report is considered in detail in the context of discussion of the law relating to protection of journalistic sources in Chapter 7.

the identity of this source; the order was ultimately upheld by the House of Lords. Goodwin refused to obey the order, was convicted of contempt of court and fined. He applied to Strasbourg, alleging a breach of Article 10. The Government stated that the purposes served by the disclosure order were: to enable Tetra to achieve the unmasking of the disloyal employee who had leaked the information; to allow the company to bring proceedings against him for recovery of the stolen document; to enable them to apply for an injunction preventing further disclosures by him; and to enable the company to obtain compensation (by suing the employee). The Court responded with a mixture of 'least intrusive means' and 'balancing' reasoning. In terms of the former, it noted that if the aim was to neutralize the damage to Tetra's reputation, a less intrusive means than forcing a journalist to disclose his source was available, and had in fact been used—namely, the injunction already granted, which restrained publication about Tetra's financial difficulties. Thus this information would not become known to its creditors, customers, suppliers, and competitors.[322] Therefore, as the Court put it,

The purpose of the disclosure order was to a very large extent the same as that already being achieved by the injunction, namely to prevent dissemination of the confidential information contained in the plan.[323]

This is a classic example of means / ends balancing. Since the principal end in view— the prevention of further financial damage to Tetra—was already being largely met, it was disproportionate to use such a grave measure as a disclosure order, to achieve that same end. However, the Court acknowledged that Tetra had other interests in the disclosure order. It was in relation to these interests that the Court engaged in a straightforward balancing exercise between the ends sought and the importance of the expression principal at stake—the protection of journalistic sources. In this respect, the Court had already found that the necessity of affording such protection was a crucial aspect of Article 10:

Protection of journalistic sources is one of the basic conditions for press freedom, as is reflected in the laws and the professional codes of conduct in a number of Contracting States and is affirmed in several international instruments on journalistic freedoms. Without such protection, sources may be deterred from assisting the press in informing the public on matters of public interest. As a result the vital public-watchdog role of the press may be undermined and the ability of the press to provide accurate and reliable information may be adversely affected. Having regard to the importance of the protection of journalistic sources for press freedom in a democratic society and the potentially chilling effect an order of source disclosure has on the exercise of that freedom, such a measure cannot be compatible with Article 10 (art. 10) of the Convention unless it is justified by an overriding requirement in the public interest.[324]

Thus, having assigned considerable weight to the particular expression interest in

---

[322] We are indebted to Bosma for the discussion of this case: ibid, at 144.   [323] Op cit, at [42].
[324] Op cit, at [39].

question, the Court proceeded to weigh it against the interests that the disclosure order sought to advance:

On the facts of the present case, the Court cannot find that Tetra's interests in eliminating, by proceedings against the source, the residual threat of damage through dissemination of the confidential information otherwise than by the press, in obtaining compensation and unmasking a disloyal employee or collaborator were, even if considered cumulatively, sufficient to outweigh the vital public interest in the protection of the applicant journalist's source.[325]

The interests 'did not . . . amount to an overriding requirement in the public interest'. Bosma concludes: 'In other words, the weight awarded to the aim was not as great as that awarded to freedom of expression.'[326] It must be said that the Court does not provide any real reasoning for this finding; however, *unlike* the approach taken in *Janowski*, the value assigned to the expression interest was at least carefully and soundly rooted in underlying Convention principles.[327]

    Bosma speculates that the use of the balancing of interests test:

could be explained by the fact that the Court in principle maintains a reserved attitude towards the review of legislation . . . If a balancing of interests results in the conclusion that there has been a violation of the Convention, this will usually not require the national authorities to adjust their restrictive regulations . . . [merely] adjust the application of the legislation in cases that are similar as to the circumstances and . . . pay damages.[328]

We are unpersuaded by this distinction. It is equally the case that a finding that the particular method chosen by the authorities to restrict or punish the speech in question was disproportionate would often not require the state to change its regulations. For example, a state could prosecute for a lesser criminal offence, or could refrain from prosecuting such cases in future, leaving the matter to civil remedies; courts could award damages instead of injunctions, where the latter had been found to be disproportionate. These matters of means are likely to be within the state's discretion and therefore inherently also unlikely to require the modification of legislation. It is clearly not possible to do anything more than speculate as to why the Court employs different methods—it may be nothing more than mere sloppiness, inadvertence, or an instinctive adjustment of methodology to justify the decision reached. Bosma's explanation is not really plausible, but it is impossible to arrive at a definitive alternative.

Concluding comments on proportionality

The above discussion has been a critical one. It has revealed that the Strasbourg Court uses a wide variety of tests under the rubric of 'proportionality', which vary widely in intensity and rigour. In some cases, vital stages of the proportionality enquiry, as understood by other Constitutional courts, are simply omitted, so that states are

---

[325] Ibid, at [45].   [326] Op cit, at 145.   [327] See above, at pp 65–6.
[328] Ibid, at 149–50.

almost entirely relieved of the burden of justifying particular aspects of their interference with Convention rights.[329] In others, as we have seen, only an imprecise and vague balancing act is used, with an outcome that is often supported by little or no reasoning—as in the public order expression cases we looked at earlier. In this way, under the banner of the bland notion of granting a 'margin of appreciation' to states, the Strasbourg Court retains to itself a high degree of discretion as to how rigorously it wishes to scrutinize the decisions of respondent states. The contrast, for example, with the more rigorous approach of the Canadian Supreme Court is strong. The latter has remarked that:

... while the impugned law must be considered in its social and economic context, nothing in the jurisprudence suggests that the contextual approach reduces the obligation on the state to meet the burden of demonstrating that the limitation on rights imposed by the law is reasonable and justified.[330]

We have singled out in particular the failure of the Court to apply *consistently* a 'least intrusive means' test, which, as Clayton puts it, 'has become the heart and soul of proving that interferences with rights are justified under [the Canadian proportionality test]'.[331]

It is thus clear that the European Court often applies a test significantly less rigorous than at least some of its international cousins. It must, however, be noted, that there is an obvious explanation for this. The Canadian Supreme Court is made up of Canadian judges, interpreting and applying a Constitution applying only to Canada and enacted by the Canadian Parliament. In contrast, the Strasbourg Court is an international court, policing adherence to an international treaty, often entered into by states without popular endorsement,[332] and required to adjudicate upon claims arising from a bewildering variety of societies and legal systems. It is not surprising that it uses at times a much more restrained form of review than a national Constitutional court. What *is* important is that this difference is not overlooked or glossed over. As suggested in the Introduction to this book, success in domestically implementing the Convention depends in part upon a keen awareness of the limitation of much of its associated jurisprudence, particularly as compared to the kind of standards that a *national* court might be expected to apply.

Domestic courts, it is suggested, should apply a standard more akin to that of the Canadian Supreme Court. This would involve ensuring that the 'pressing social need' test is *always* applied as a preliminary threshold, with the government having to adduce evidence as to the importance of the aim to be pursued. In *all* cases, the courts should insist upon ensuring that the measure taken was rationally connected to this aim and therefore 'suitable' for its attainment. As discussed above, if it is not, it *cannot*

---

[329] Prime examples are the forfeiture orders made in *Müller* and *Otto Preminger*.

[330] *RJR-McDonald v Canada (Attorney General)* [1993] 3 SCR 199 at [134].

[331] Clayton note 362 above.

[332] In the case of the UK, without any approval being necessary by Parliament, still less 'the people'. See further Chapter 1, at 6–9.

be considered a proportionate response. As to the further tests to be applied, much depends upon the circumstances of the case. In some instances, there will clearly have been a range of different measures open to the state in the particular situation. In such a case, it is necessary to engage in a fairly structured means / ends balancing test, using the 'least intrusive means' test as an important part of this enquiry, albeit with the proviso that the test does not involve the judiciary in reaching conclusions as to the suitability of other measures that are beyond their ability to assess. But where the measures taken plainly go beyond achieving the stated aim—as in *Otto Preminger*—courts should not be afraid to so find. Where it does not appear that there was a range of possible response, as, for example, where the state either prosecutes the only relevant offence or does not,[333] then the more appropriate test is what we have referred to as 'speech/harm balancing', as in *Goodwin* and *Sunday Times*. As discussed above, when carried out, this test should be rooted as firmly and specifically as possible in the values underlying the speech in question. In such a way, the domestic courts can provide a more systematic and rigorous proportionality auditing than Strasbourg, as an international court of review, has felt itself able to do. The inapplicability of the margin of appreciation doctrine to the domestic context, a matter discussed further in the next chapter, provides clear justification for such a course of action.

CONCLUSION

Eric Barendt has remarked:

at the end of the twentieth century, virtually all significant speech is mass speech. The soapbox orator, the pamphleteer and individual canvassers now play little part in forming public opinion.[334]

This practical, if perhaps rather dispiriting, observation probably, we have suggested, holds the key to understanding the pragmatic civil libertarian approach to Article 10 of the European Court. As such, and if one accepts that the primary value lying behind Article 10 is the maintenance of a democracy, it is a sensible, if not an inspiring, one. It also accounts for the wide variation we have seen in the standard of review applied by the Court and its sometimes eccentric manipulation of 'proportionality' as a test for determining the legitimacy of state interference with the Convention rights: where expression does not engage the functionalist virtues of directly contributing to general debate on public-political matters, the Court employs a style and method of review that largely fails to insist upon any proper justification for the interference in question.

But there are wider implications flowing from the combination of the increasing

---

[333] As, for example, in contempt cases or those concerning obscenity or indecency.

[334] E. Barendt, 'The First Amendment and the Media' in I. Loveland (ed), *Importing the First Amendment*, 2nd edn., Oxford: Hart Publishing, 1998, at 30. The only possible exception to this is the new phenomenon of the 'blogger', see p 3 above.

dominance of the mass media and the heavy bias in Strasbourg's expression juris-prudence in their favour, at the expense of the individual speaker's rights. Barendt goes on:

Moreover, subversive opinion and the voices of minority groups are not suppressed because they are dangerous to the State. Rather, they are not suppressed at all . . . they find no space on television schedules, the tabloids or even in much of the broadsheet press, because they do not attract large audiences and are unattractive to the advertisers who finance the mass media.[335]

The consequence of this quiet exclusion of minority voices from the media is clear: dissenting individuals may chose to express themselves through art, through public protest, and indeed by direct action. But, given Barendt's comments about the domin-ance of contemporary discourse by the mass media, and the corresponding decline in the importance of the lone pamphleteer, it can be argued that the Court's stance discussed above is profoundly flawed as a matter of principle: it grants the maximum level of human rights protection, with all the rhetorical as well as legal protection that such protection entails, to those speech players that arguably need it least—the mass media, in reality, powerful corporate organizations. It largely withholds protection from those who most need it: individual protesters, dissident artists, and lone voices generally. Not only is this, as just asserted, wrong in principle, it is also clearly mis-judged in consequentialist terms: if one of the key principles underlying speech protection is the market place of ideas, and the maintenance of diversity and plurality in public discourse, the Court's approach risks actively undermining it. While dove-tailing nicely with a pragmatic concern for the maintenance of efficient democracy, such an approach arguably shows little concern for the *quality* of that democracy, and for the very importance of the values of plurality and tolerance that the Court, in some of its most famous dicta, has expressed to be founding principles underlying the Convention. As the next chapter will explore, very similar concerns may be expressed about at least the dominant strands in English free speech jurisprudence.

[335] Op cit, at 31.

3

THE HUMAN RIGHTS ACT IN THE CONTEXT OF MEDIA FREEDOM

INTRODUCTION

The media might have been expected to be the prime beneficiaries of the introduction via the Human Rights Act of Article 10 ECHR, providing for the right to freedom of expression. Indeed, as is well known, the media were designed to be the specific beneficiaries of one of the more meaningful late amendments to the HRA, section 12.[1] However, as this chapter—and the book as a whole—will make clear, the picture is not quite so clear-cut as this. First, at least some of the protection perhaps intended to be given to the media by section 12 has been removed by judicial interpretation, as will be explored further below.[2] Second, due in part to the influence of early decisions at Strasbourg on Article 10 concerning the UK,[3] a number of provisions in UK statutes, and a number of specific common law doctrines, already provided specific protection for media freedom. Examples include: sections 5[4] and

---

[1] Section 12 contains a number of provisions: it applies (per ss (1)) if: 'a court is considering whether to grant any relief which, if granted, might affect the exercise of the Convention right to freedom of expression.' Subsections (2) and (3) raise the threshold for the granting of interlocutory injunctions and give certain procedural protections, and are considered in detail below at 153–7. The other main provision is as follows:

(4) The court must have particular regard to the importance of the Convention right to freedom of expression and, where the proceedings relate to material which the respondent claims, or which appears to the court, to be journalistic, literary or artistic material (or to conduct connected with such material), to—
   (a) the extent to which—
      (i) the material has, or is about to, become available to the public; or
      (ii) it is, or would be, in the public interest for the material to be published;
   (b) any relevant privacy code.
   S 12 does not apply in criminal proceedings (s 12(5)).

[2] *Douglas and Zeta Jones v Hello!* [2001] QB 967; see further below at p 126.

[3] Most importantly, of course, *Sunday Times v UK* (1979) A 30.

[4] S 5 protects publications which are *prima facie* in contempt as producing a substantial risk of serious prejudice to imminent ('active') legal proceedings. It states that a statement made 'as or as part of a discussion in good faith of public affairs or other matters of general public interest is not to be treated as a contempt of court under the strict liability rule if the risk of impediment or prejudice to particular legal proceedings is merely incidental to the discussion.' For interpretation of this section, see *A-G v English* (1983) 1 AC 116, (1982) 2 All ER 903. This area of law is considered in detail in Chapter 6.

10^5 of the Contempt of Court Act; section 4 of the Obscene Publications Act;[6] the defence of 'public interest' to the action in breach of confidence,[7] and of 'qualified privilege' to libel;[8] provisions of the Broadcasting Acts upholding the importance of media freedom, and the statutory retention of a common law public interest defence to infringement of copyright.[9] However, there are, of course, some notorious exceptions to this general tendency: the common law offences of blasphemy,[10] indecency,[11] and contempt of court[12] have no defences of 'public good' or 'public interest'. In a number of areas, therefore, it is doubtful whether the advent of the HRA is likely appreciably to enhance protection for media freedom beyond those given by the protection afforded by the existing law (we use the future tense because the effects of the Act are untested in relation to many areas of media law). Moreover, by the time the HRA came into force, the House of Lords had elevated freedom of expression from being a mere residual liberty—an aspect of the general freedom to do that which the law does not forbid[13]—into a constitutional right: an entitlement that is not to be displaced except by clear terms in primary legislation.[14] Importantly also, the courts had, prior to the HRA, been as ready to recognize media freedom in private law[15] as in the public arena. In other words, the media were already the beneficiaries, before the HRA, of a substantial measure of protection for their freedom of expression.

Finally, one of the most significant developments in the media field so far wrought by the HRA has been the strong impetus it has given to the development of a common

---

[5] Section 10 gives the court power to order a journalist to reveal a source—a serious threat to media freedom. However s 10 provides that 'No court may require a person to disclose, nor is any person guilty of contempt of court for refusing to disclose, the source of information contained in a publication for which he is responsible, unless it be established to the satisfaction of the court that disclosure is necessary in the interests of justice or national security or for the prevention of disorder or crime.' This test of necessity echoes the 'necessary in a democratic society' test for restrictions on expression in Article 10(2). For discussion, see Chapter 7.

[6] Under s 4 it is a defence to a finding that a publication is obscene if it can be shown that 'the publication of the article in question is justified as for the public good in that it is in the interests of science, literature, art, learning or of other objects of general concern'. Similar defences apply to films and theatre productions under Acts of 1977 and 1968.

[7] It was confirmed by *Lion Laboratories v Evans* [1985] QB 526 that information may be published or otherwise disclosed in admitted breach of confidence if it is in the public interest.

[8] The leading case on *Reynolds v Times Newspapers* [1999] 4 All ER 609, discussed in detail in Chapter 21.

[9] Per s 171 Copyright, Designs and Patents Act 1988; the 'fair dealing' defences in s 30 also afford some recognition to media freedom. See Chapter 18.

[10] *R v Lemon* [1979] AC 617, discussed in Chapter 9.

[11] *Shaw v DPP* (1962) AC 220; *Knuller v DPP* (1973) AC 435. See Chapter 8.

[12] *A-G v Hislop and Pressdram Ltd* (1991) 1 QB 514; *A-G v Sport Newspapers Ltd* (1992) 1 All ER 503. See Chapter 6.

[13] Its status in English law (persons were free to speak provided the law had not provided otherwise) led Dicey to remark, famously, that 'Freedom of discussion is in England little else than the right to write or say anything which a jury, consisting of twelve shopkeepers, think it expedient should be said or written.' A. V. Dicey, *Introduction to the Study of the Law of the Constitution*, 10th edn. London: Macmillan, 1959, Chapter VI.

[14] *R v Secretary of State for the Home Department ex parte Simms* [2000] 2 AC 115.

[15] As in the breach of confidence and libel cases (above).

law right to privacy,[16] something that *threatens* media freedom; further, the interpretation of Article 9 ECHR by Strasbourg as including a right not to be subject to the offensive or provocative portrayal of sacred subjects[17] threatens to bolster *restrictions* upon media discussion of religious matters.[18]

Thus, the HRA provides both less of a step change in *enhancing* protection for media freedom than might have been anticipated *and* gives effect to certain Convention principles that conflict with that freedom. Nevertheless, the Act remains crucial to contemporary protection of media freedom,[19] although, in some areas, its effects remain wholly untested.[20] The purpose of this chapter is to analyse particular aspects of the Act that are relevant to the law of media freedom. It does not purport to provide a full analysis of the Act, which would be both beyond the scope of this book, and impracticable for reasons of space.[21] Upon examination, certain aspects of the Act are of no real relevance to the media: for example the intense debate about the standard of judicial review as applied against the Secretary of State taking sensitive decisions about immigration and national security is only of marginal relevance to this book. Furthermore the only media bodies likely to be judicially reviewed are Ofcom, the broadcast regulator, and, possibly the BBC, the decisions of which carry neither the democratic imprimatur of elected Ministers nor approach the acute sensitivity of those made in relation to national security and anti-terrorism law. Therefore, the complex and ideologically charged debate as to the proper role of

---

[16] A development consolidated and radicalized by the recent House of Lords' decision in *Campbell v MGN* [2004] 2 WLR 1232; for detailed discussion, see Chapter 14.

[17] *Otto Preminger Institute v Austria* (1995) 19 EHRR 34: 'The respect for the religious feelings of believers as guaranteed in Article 9 can legitimately be thought to have been violated by provocative portrayals of objects of religious veneration'. See further Chapter 9.

[18] This jurisprudence will both influence the interpretation of the offence of incitement to religious hatred introduced via the Racial and Religious Hatred Act 2006, and may ensure the retention by the Courts of the common law offence of blasphemy, which it might otherwise have been thought would have come under strong challenge via Article 10 and the HRA; the Strasbourg Court in *Wingrove v UK* (1997) 24 EHRR 1 specifically found that the English law of blasphemy was compatible with Article 10 of the Convention. For detailed discussion, see Chapter 9.

[19] Which is not to say that common law protection is irrelevant: for example, the decision of the Court of Appeal in *ProLife Alliance v BBC* [2002] 3 WLR 1080 was based primarily on common law principle.

[20] Examples include its impact upon the offences of prejudicing proceedings at common law and under the Contempt of Court Act 1981, on the full range of offences of indecency and obscenity, and on the offences of blasphemy and incitement to racial hatred.

[21] Readers are referred to Clayton and Tomlinson's magisterial *The Law of Human Rights*, Oxford: OUP, 2000; Lester and Pannick's *Human Rights Law and Practice*, 2nd edn., London: Butterworths, 2004; and Grosz, Beatson, and Duffy's *Human Rights: The 1998 Act and the European Convention on Human Rights*, London: Sweet & Maxwell, 1999. Professor Gearty's *Principles of Human Rights Adjudication*, Oxford: OUP, 2004 is a notable scholarly work devoted to the HRA, representing very much an application of the particular political philosophy of the author to the task of reading the HRA and decisions made under it. Books that also provide good accounts of the Act include David Feldman's *Civil Liberties and Human Rights in England Wales* 2nd edn., 2002 and Helen Fenwick's *Civil Liberties and Human Rights*, 3rd edn., 2002. For a useful survey of recent developments, see F. Klug and K. Starmer, 'Standing Back from the Human Rights Act: How Effective is it Five Years On?' (2005) *PL* 716.

judicial deference[22] under the HRA will also not require extensive examination, although, as will be seen, the notion of deference has been very influential in relation to judicial review of the decisions of media regulators, an issue that will be considered primarily in the chapters dedicated to issues of media regulation.[23] For the same reason, the issue of the damages that may be awarded against public authorities[24] is largely irrelevant—damages are most unlikely to be claimed against either of those bodies. Similarly, there have been no declarations of incompatibility in relation to laws governing media freedom and none are likely save in one specific instance,[25] which will be considered in the relevant chapter.[26] Section 4 of the Act will not therefore be considered in any detail. We also do not envisage the test for standing under section 7 of the Act giving rise to any issues in relation to the media, although it is considered briefly below.[27]

However, a number of aspects of the Act *are* of clear importance to this book. The interpretation by the courts of the definition of 'public authority'[28]–those bodies bound under s 6 HRA to act compatibly with the Convention rights[29] is of importance to one major question of media law: will the BBC—and possibly Channel 4—be deemed to fall within it? The linked issue of the 'horizontal effect' of the HRA—its effect on private law—is clearly crucial to the media, for obvious reasons.[30] The treatment by the courts of the apparently 'media-friendly' section 12(4) HRA is also significant and will be considered both here and in subsequent chapters. The stance taken by the UK courts to interpretation and application of the Strasbourg jurisprudence under section 2(1) of the HRA is also of critical importance to this book, and will be addressed both in this chapter and in relation to particular areas of law considered in other chapters. The modified test for the granting of interim

---

[22] Otherwise known as the notion of respect for a 'discretionary area of judgement', a phrase coined by D. Pannick, 'Principles of interpretation of Convention rights under the Human Rights Act and the discretionary area of judgement' (1998) *PL* 545. See also, P. Craig, 'The Courts, the Human Rights Act and Judicial Review' (2001) 117 *LQR* 589; R. Edwards, 'Judicial Review under the Human Rights Act' (2002) 65 *CLJ*. See further R. Edwards, 'Judicial Deference under the Human Rights Act' 65(6) *MLR* 859; F. Klug, 'Judicial Deference under the Human Rights Act' (2003) 2 *EHRLR* 125;', Judicial Deference: Servility, civility or institutional capacity?' [2004] *PL* 592, 600; J. Jowell, Lord Steyn, 'Deference: A Tangled Story' [2005] *PL* 346; T. Hickman, 'Constitutional Dialogue, Constitutional Theories and the Human Rights Act 1998' [2005] *PL* 306; C. O'Cinneide, 'Democracy and Rights: New Directions in the Human Rights Era' [2004] 57 *Current Legal Problems* 175.

[23] See Chapters 11 and 17.

[24] See J. Hartshorne, 'The Human Rights Act and Damages for Non-Pecuniary Loss' (2004) 6 *EHRLR* 660; R. Clayton, 'Damage Limitation: the Courts and Human Rights Act Damages' [2005] *PL* 429.

[25] Namely the outright ban on political advertising contained in the Communications Act 2003, s 321, in relation to which the Government declined to make a declaration of compatibility with the Convention rights, under section 19 of the HRA.

[26] See Chapter 19.   [27] See text to note 46 below.

[28] As partially defined by section 6(3) HRA.   [29] *Per* section 6(1) HRA.

[30] This issue has previously been considered in detail by one of the authors: see G. Phillipson, 'The Human Rights Act, the Common Law and "Horizontal Effect": A Bang or a Whimper?' (1999) 62(6) *Modern Law Review* 824 (hereafter Phillipson (*MLR*, 1999)); 'Judicial Reasoning in Breach of Confidence Cases under the Human Rights Act: not taking privacy seriously?' [2003] *European Human Rights Law Review* (Privacy—Special Issue) 54, at 56 et seq; 'Transforming confidence? Towards a common law right to privacy under the Human Rights Act' (2003) 66(5) *Modern Law Review* 726 (hereafter Phillipson (*MLR*, 2003)).

injunctions—section 12(3)—is critical to the media, and its recent interpretation by the House of Lords in *Cream Holdings*[31] will be given full consideration, alongside relevant Strasbourg jurisprudence. Finally, section 3(1) HRA, the obligation to interpret legislation compatibly with the Convention rights 'so far as possible' to do so, is clearly of importance to an area with numerous statutory provisions and will be discussed in detail.

THE DEFINITION OF 'PUBLIC AUTHORITY' UNDER THE ACT[32]

THE STRUCTURE OF SECTION 6

Section 6(1) makes it unlawful for a 'public authority' to act in a way which is incompatible with a Convention right, and gives a cause of action under section 7(1)(a) against such a body that has acted, or proposes to act, incompatibly. The term 'public authority' is not defined exhaustively: section 6(3) states that it *includes* 'a court or tribunal, and any person *certain* of whose functions are functions of a public nature' (emphasis added).

Clayton and Tomlinson[33] have suggested that there is a three-part classification of bodies under the HRA, as a result of section 6, an analysis that has been accepted judicially.[34] First, there are public bodies that are obviously public authorities, such as government departments, local authorities, the police, and so on; these may be referred to as 'standard' public authorities. Second, there are what are variously known as 'hybrid' or 'functional' public authorities; these are bodies which have some private and some public functions ('certain of whose functions are . . . of a public nature'). Examples are bodies that are non-statutory, and which carry on ordinary business activities, but which also carry out certain governmental functions, often as a result of 'contracting out'. Group 4, a security service, which has numerous government contracts providing for it to make arrangements for the transport of prisoners to and from court, but which also carries out much private security work, is one obvious example: it would be a public authority in relation to the former work, but not the latter. Subsection (5) of the Act provides:

---

[31] *Cream Holdings Limited and others v Banerjee and others* [2005] 1 AC 253.

[32] See generally D. Oliver, 'The frontiers of the State: public authorities and public functions under the HRA' [2000] *PL* 476; M. McDermont, 'The Elusive Nature of the "Public Function": *Poplar Housing and Regeneration Community Association Ltd v Donoghue*' (2003) 66(1) *MLR* 113; J. Morgan, 'The Alchemist's Search for the Philosopher's Stone: the Status of Registered Social Landlords under the Human Rights Act (2003) 66(5) *MLR* 700; P. Cane, (2004) 120(Jan) *LQR*, 41–48.

[33] *The Law of Human Rights*, Oxford: Clarendon, 2000, para 5.08.

[34] See e.g. *Parochial Church Council of the Parish of Aston Cantlow and Wilmcote v Wallbank* [2004] 1 AC 546 [2003] 3 WLR 283.

In relation to a particular act, a person is not a public authority by virtue only of subsection (3)(b) if the nature of the act is private.

In other words, where a body is a functional public authority, with only *some* public functions, it is *not* bound by the Act when engaged in private acts, such as, for example, hiring and firing staff or making ordinary commercial contracts. In contrast, a standard public authority is obliged to act in accordance with Convention rights in relation to *all* of its activities, be they public or private in nature. In the third category are organizations with no public functions at all: these are private bodies, which fall outside the Act altogether.[35]

When seeking to determine whether a particular body may be bound in respect of a particular decision, the question will therefore be first, whether it is a standard public authority, in which case one will know that it must act compatibly with relevant Convention rights in all activities, including the decision in question. If it is not a standard public authority, then two further questions must be asked: first, does the authority have *some* public functions; second, if it does, then is the particular act in question one of its public functions? Only if the answer to both questions is 'yes' will the body be bound by the Convention rights. In terms of the law governing media freedom, this issue is of some importance, although it will often not be a really 'live' one. In relation to all the areas of *criminal* liability affecting the media, namely contempt of court, official secrecy, obscenity, indecency, racial hatred, and blasphemy, since both the courts and the prosecuting authorities are clearly public authorities, they will be bound to act compatibly with relevant Convention rights in prosecuting and trying these cases. Equally clearly, in relation to actions brought by individuals against newspapers in defamation or privacy/breach of confidence, there will be *no* public authorities involved,[36] and the matter will fall to be considered under the horizontal effect heading. In one area, copyright, the matter concerns private law, but is regulated by statute, which under section 3(1) HRA must be interpreted and applied in a manner compatible with the Convention rights.

BROADCASTERS AND REGULATORS

The only area in which a significant degree of ambiguity arises is in relation to broadcasting and media regulation generally. It seems plain beyond doubt that Ofcom, the super-regulator of all broadcasters, a creature of statute, given coercive powers and duties that are clearly governmental in nature, will be a public authority for the purposes of the HRA. It is likely to be deemed a standard public authority, as it is a statutory government regulator; even if it is not, there is no doubt that its regulatory functions will be caught by the Act, by virtue of section 6(3)(b). The same is almost certainly the case in relation to the regulators of the press and the film

---

[35] Though the law governing such bodies may be influenced indirectly via the 'horizontal effect' doctrine. See below at 123 et seq.

[36] Save for the courts themselves—a situation that raises a different issue—see ibid.

industry, the Press Complaints Commission,[37] and British Board of Film Classification, even though these bodies have no statutory basis.

Equally clearly, the private broadcasters, such as ITV, Channel 5, and Sky will *not* be even functional public authorities. The interesting question is whether the BBC—and possibly Channel 4—will be considered to be functional public authorities and therefore bound in at least some of their actions to respect Convention rights. The BBC might be so considered because it is a 'state broadcaster': it is fully funded through public monies (via the licence fee), and brought into being by a Royal Charter—directly through an act of government, in other words. In addition, as a 'public service' broadcaster it has various duties relating to the contents of its programmes designed to ensure that it serves the public interest, rather than merely entertaining the public.[38] Channel 4 is a private broadcaster, solely funded by commercial revenues, but it receives free spectrum in return for fulfilling its statutory public service obligations: it has a particular remit in relation to broadcasting innovative, creative, or educative programmes, which appeal to culturally diverse tastes.[39] It is also a creature of statute, unusually for a commercial body.[40] Both the BBC and Channel 4 are therefore possible candidates for being deemed public authorities, although the BBC is a much more likely one.

The issue of whether either have any public functions would be of relevance in two key areas. The first would arise where it was alleged that either of these broadcasters had breached the right of privacy of a person in a broadcast, for example by showing him or her engaged in some private activity.[41] The second possibility would arise where, as in the *ProLife Alliance* case,[42] the BBC, acting as its own self-regulator, refuses to broadcast an item (in that case a party election broadcast) on the grounds that it believed it to breach its own binding duties under its Charter and Agreement, and thus, in effect, acted as a government censor. In such an instance, the question would be whether Article 10 could be pleaded directly against the BBC on judicial review of the decision.

The first question to be asked, therefore, is whether the BBC[43] can be regarded as a 'standard' public authority. The leading decision on the approach to defining standard public authorities is that of the House of Lords in *Parochial Church Council of the Parish of Aston Cantlow and Wilmcote v Wallbank*.[44] One of the key points made by their Lordships was that a standard—or 'core'[45]—public authority, by virtue of being

---

[37] This point appears to have been all but conceded in *R (on the Application of Ford) v Press Complaints Commission* [2002] EMLR 5, discussed in Chapter 17.

[38] See Chapters 10 and 11.   [39] See section 265(3) of the 2003 Act.

[40] By the Broadcasting Act 1990.

[41] This scenario is considered in detail in Chapter 17 at 869–71.

[42] [2002] 2 All ER 756 CA; [2004] 1 AC 185, HL.

[43] It seems clear that Channel 4, as a commercial broadcaster, could not possibly be considered a standard public authority.

[44] [2004] 1 AC 546 [2003] 3 WLR 283.

[45] The term used by some of their Lordships in that decision.

part of the government, could logically *not* be a body that could itself claim to enjoy Convention rights. Lord Nicholls put it thus:

One consequence of being a 'core' public authority, namely, an authority falling within section 6 without reference to section 6(3), is that the body in question does not itself enjoy Convention rights. It is difficult to see how a core public authority could ever claim to be a victim of an infringement of a Convention rights. A core public authority seems inherently incapable of satisfying the Convention description of a victim: 'any person, non-governmental organisation or group of individuals' (article 34 [ECHR] . . .). Only victims of an unlawful act may bring proceedings under section 7 of the Human Rights Act 1998, and the Convention description of a victim has been incorporated into the Act, by section 7(7).[46]

The House of Lords thus strove to achieve symmetry between the obligations of bodies under the HRA and the obligations of the UK Government under the Convention as a matter of international law. As Lord Roger put it:

The essential characteristic of a public authority is that it carries out a function of government which would engage the responsibility of the United Kingdom before the Strasbourg organs.[47]

A very clear consequence flows from this in relation to the status of the BBC and Channel 4. The argument runs thus. Public authorities making up the state do not have human rights—they cannot claim Convention rights at Strasbourg, or under section 7(7) HRA. If therefore the BBC *can* claim Convention rights at Strasbourg, it cannot be a standard public authority under the HRA. The difficulty is that we do not know whether or not the BBC can so claim. In fact, on both occasions that the BBC has claimed a violation of its rights at Strasbourg, the Commission has left open the question of whether the BBC can be a 'non-governmental organization' within the terms of Article 34.[48] If it could not, then the BBC would be a standard or core public authority for the purposes of the HRA—effectively, part of the government. This, however, seems implausible; were the BBC plainly to have its freedom of expression interfered with by the government, by means, for example, of an injunction to prevent a threatened contempt of court,[49] it would seem absurd to disallow it from claiming that its freedom of expression had been interfered with. It therefore seems unlikely that the BBC is a standard public authority.

Assuming this is the case, there is the possibility that the BBC (and possibly Channel 4) may be considered 'functional public authorities'. There is now a fair amount of case law on this issue. However, since it is concerned primarily with the consequences of the 'contracting out' of governmental functions to charitable or commercial organizations, it is not directly analogous to the position of the broadcasters. One of the early leading decisions was *Poplar Housing & Regeneration*

---

[46] Ibid, at [8].   [47] Ibid, at [160].
[48] In *BBC Scotland v UK*, no. 34324/96 (1997); *BBC v UK*, no. 25798/94 (1996). In both instances, the cases were found to be inadmissible on other grounds; therefore it was not found necessary to decide the point.
[49] As in *BBC Scotland* itself.

Community Association Ltd v Donoghue.[50] A local authority, Tower Hamlets, was under a statutory duty under section 188 of the Housing Act 1996 to provide or secure the provision of housing to certain homeless people. Donoghue was provided with a flat by Tower Hamlets pending the Council's decision in relation to her application as a homeless person under the Housing Act 1996. The flat was transferred, before the determination of her application, to Poplar Housing, along with a substantial portion of its housing stock. By the transfer, the tenancy became an assured shorthold. Poplar had been set up by Tower Hamlets as a registered social landlord specifically for the purpose of receiving its housing stock. Five members of Tower Hamlets were on the board of Poplar and it was subject to the guidance of the Council as to the manner in which it acted towards its tenants. Poplar sought vacant possession of accommodation let to the claimant tenant, Donoghue. Donoghue claimed that this would violate her right to a home under Article 8 ECHR, and that Poplar Housing was bound under section 6 HRA to respect her Article 8 right because it was a public authority under the Act. Poplar claimed, *inter alia*, that it was neither a standard public authority (which the Court of Appeal accepted) nor a body performing a function of a public nature. As to this latter point, Lord Woolf said:

What can make an act, which would otherwise be private, public, is a feature or a combination of features which impose a public character or stamp on the act. Statutory authority for what is done can at least help to mark the act as being public; so can the extent of control over the function exercised by another body which is a public authority. The more closely the acts that could be of a private nature are enmeshed in the activities of a public body, the more likely they are to be public. However, the fact that the acts are supervised by a public regulatory body does not necessarily indicate that they are of a public nature. This is analogous to the position in judicial review, where a regulatory body may be deemed public but the activities of the body which is regulated may be categorised private.[51]

The Court found that Poplar *was* exercising a public function in relation to the management of the social housing it had taken over from Tower Hamlets:

. . . in providing accommodation for the defendant and then seeking possession, the association's role was so closely assimilated to that of the authority that it was acting as a public authority.[52]

However, the court was clear that only certain limited functions of social landlords, such as Poplar, were 'public functions'; it was clearly only a functional public authority. For example, the court specifically said: 'the raising of finance by Poplar could well be a private function'.[53] One of the key points in the judgment was the holding to the effect that where a function (such as managing social housing) had been transferred to a private body, the simple fact that it had previously been carried out by a public authority did not make it a public function in the hands of the private body. Thus, 'providing accommodation for rent is not, without more, a public function',[54] even

---

50 [2002] QB 48.   51 Ibid, at 69.   52 Ibid, at 70.   53 Ibid.   54 Ibid, at 69.

where the accommodation being provided had been previously the responsibility of a Local Authority.

Thus, the finding of a public function in the particular case was not made on the simple basis of whether this function was intrinsically 'public' in nature—seemingly the statutory test. Instead, the Court of Appeal managed, as appears in the above quotation, to bring in a series of wider factors, partly on the basis, as it found that:

While section 6 of the Human Rights Act 1998 requires a generous interpretation of who is a public authority, it is clearly inspired by the approach developed by the courts in identifying the bodies and activities subject to judicial review.[55]

Thus, the finding that Poplar Housing was carrying out a public function in relation to Donoghue was made not simply because it was providing social housing—a duty that the Council itself would otherwise have had under the legislation. The fact that it was carrying out a function that the Council would otherwise have had to carry out was not in itself sufficient. Instead, the finding as to public function was made for a number of reasons, including the fact that the tenant had been a tenant of the council at the time of the transfer and should not be disadvantaged, and also because of the close relationship between Poplar and the Council. Members of the Council sat on its Board and it was subject to guidance from the Council. However, as Dawn Oliver points out:

The problem here is that not all of the considerations and criteria identified by Lord Woolf relate to the nature of the functions or acts in question, which is what s.6 is about, but are institutional (the institutional arrangements of the housing association) and relational (the relationship of the local authority with the housing association and the prior relationship between the local authority and the tenant.[56]

In other words, while section 6 HRA appears to set up a single test for determining the 'public authority' issue, the courts, by bringing into the frame the additional criteria traditionally used to determine amenability to judicial review (the source of power of the body, and its status generally) have both muddied the relatively clear waters of section 6(3) *and* given themselves greater discretion in determining the issue in future—for the more criteria there are to be applied, the more complex and malleable becomes the reasoning on the matter.

---

[55] This will mean that a wider range of factors than merely function are brought into the equation. Typically, the starting point used in judicial review cases is the finding that the body is statutory or is acting under prerogative powers. But the source of a body's power is now viewed as less significant than the public element in its functions: *R v Panel of Take-Overs and Mergers ex parte Datafin* [1987] QB 815. Where a body is non-statutory, a further determining factor concerns the question whether there is evidence of government support or control for the body: *R v Disciplinary Committee of the Jockey Club ex parte Aga Khan* [1993] 1 WLR 909, while a relevant, although not a conclusive factor will be whether it has monopoly power: *R v Football Assoc ex parte Football League* [1993] 2 All ER 833; a further factor concerns the question whether, had the body not existed, the government would have set up an equivalent body: *Aga Khan*, ibid, though even if this is case, if the source of the body's power is contractual, this will be a strong indication that it is a private body: *Aga Khan*, ibid.

[56] 'Functions of a Public Nature under the Human Rights Act' [2004] *PL*, 329–351.

A question of more direct relevance to the BBC is the question whether a duty to act in the public interest in carrying out its functions, as opposed to merely seeking, as a private body would, to maximize its own interests, is a strong indicator that the function in question is a public one. The court in *Donoghue* thought that acting in the public interest was *not* necessarily indicative of being a public authority, pointing out that certain other bodies, for example charities, have duties to act in the public interest and yet remain indisputably private bodies. In *R (on the application of Heather and others) v Leonard Cheshire Foundation and another*,[57] the Foundation was a large charitable trust providing residential care homes for those with disabilities. The claimants had lived in a particular home for over 17 years and had been promised it would be their home for life. It was decided to close the home and move the residents. The claimants applied for judicial review under Article 8 ECHR. They had been placed in the home by social services and were funded by social services or (in some cases) the health authority. Lord Woolf found that the provision of the care home was *not* a public function—Article 8 was not therefore binding. The fact that it was publicly funded was not on its own enough. There were no other factors indicating that it was a public function. As McDermont notes, this 'reject[ed] by implication any "public interest" arguments'.[58]

Further guidance on this matter has now been provided by the House of Lords in the *Aston Cantlowe*[59] decision discussed above. The issue in that case was whether the action of a parochial church council seeking to enforce liability to repair a church was the action of a public authority. Lord Nicholls had this to say generally on the test for 'public authority' under the HRA:

What, then, is the touchstone to be used in deciding whether a function is public for [the purpose of s 6(3)?] Clearly there is no single test of universal application. There cannot be, given the diverse nature of governmental functions and the variety of means by which these functions are discharged today. Factors to be taken into account include the extent to which in carrying out the relevant function the body is publicly funded, or is exercising statutory powers, or is taking the place of central government or local authorities, or is providing a public service.[60]

He also said:

Behind the instinctive classification of these organisations as bodies whose nature is governmental lie factors such as the possession of special powers, democratic accountability, public funding in whole or in part, an obligation to act only in the public interest, and a statutory constitution.[61]

Their Lordships found that the parochial church council (PCC) was neither a 'core' public authority, nor was it carrying out a public function in the particular case. Lord Hope said:

---

[57] [2002] 2 All ER 936.   [58] Op cit, at 121.   [59] [2004] 1 AC 546 [2003] 3 WLR 283.
[60] Ibid, at [12].   [61] Ibid, at [8].

The nature of the act is to be found in the nature of the obligation which the PCC is seeking to enforce . . . [namely] a civil debt. The function it is performing has nothing to do with the responsibilities which are owed to the public by the state.[62]

The Court of Appeal had seen the liability as a tax and therefore as pertaining to a public function because it was enforced on people who were not necessarily church members, and because it was imposed by a public authority (a somewhat circular mode of reasoning). The House of Lords saw it as a civil liability that arose from occupation of a particular type of land. It was stressed in particular that the liability was taken on with notice—and therefore voluntarily—when purchasing the land. This distinguished it from a tax,[63] which would apply generally.

On the more general issue, the House of Lords' approach to the public authority question was to focus much more upon whether the *function* in question could be seen as public, and less upon the institutional factors relied upon by Lord Woolf in both the Court of Appeal decisions. As the Joint Committee on Human Rights has noted,[64] Lord Nicholls said that the definition of 'public function' in the HRA should be given a 'generously wide' interpretation,[65] while Lord Hope stressed that: 'It is the *function* that the person is performing that is determinative of the question whether it is, for the purposes of the case, a "hybrid" public authority.'[66] Nevertheless, as the Committee goes on to find, this approach has not been followed by the lower courts, notably so in the Court of Appeal decision in *R v Hampshire Farmers Market ex parte Beer*,[67] which post-dated that of their Lordships in *Wallbank*, but which, as the Joint Committee puts it, 'appears to restrict the "generous" functional approach'[68] of the latter. The Court of Appeal in that case noted that neither *Poplar* nor *Leonard Cheshire* had been overruled or expressly disapproved by the House of Lords,[69] and went on to apply an approach in which institutional factors played an important part, holding that the question under the HRA would remain the same as that under judicial review unless the Strasbourg case law required otherwise. The Joint Committee has concluded that, absent a situation in which the body in question is exercising coercive powers or powers of a public nature directly assigned to it by statute, its institutional connection with government is likely to remain a significant factor in determining whether any of its functions are public.[70]

The above case law is not particularly analogous to the position of the BBC but provides some indirect guidance. Clearly, insofar as institutional factors are still taken into account, as the above discussion indicates, the fact that the BBC is a creature of the state, rather than having a private status, will increase the chances of its being found to have some public functions, as will its public funding. Channel 4, a private and commercial broadcaster, is much less likely, under these criteria, to be found to have such functions. Although it was created by statute, it is entirely privately funded.

---

[62] Ibid, at [64].   [63] Ibid, at [66], per Lord Hobhouse.
[64] 'The Meaning of Public Authority under the Human Rights Act' HC 382, HL 39 (2003–04) 12.
[65] *Wallbank*, op cit, at [11].   [66] Ibid, at [41].   [67] [2003] EWCA Civ 1056.
[68] Op cit, at 15.   [69] *Hampshire*, op cit, at [15].   [70] Op cit, at 16.

If the BBC *is* a functional public authority, it must have some functions that can be labelled as public, and others that cannot. Doubtless, when the BBC hires a new member of staff, or makes a contract to buy equipment, it is not carrying out a public function. At first sight, it could be argued that it is equally carrying out a private function when it makes and broadcasts a programme. When it does so, it is bound by the same duties as the commercial broadcasters in relation to fairness, privacy and offence-avoidance standards, and regulated by OFCOM.[71] It is acting simply as a media body, albeit in the public interest, but carrying out the function of media expression, quintessentially a non-state function. Moreover, both the Channel 3 services (Granada, ITV, etc.) *and* Channel 5 (as well as C4) have 'a public service remit' in relation to their broadcasting: they have a statutory duty to provide 'a range of high quality and diverse programme'.[72] They are also covered by statutory due impartiality requirements in relation to their programme content.[73] Both obligations are policed by Ofcom. This arguably brings *all* the broadcasters[74] under the dicta of Lord Woolf in *Donoghue* noted above:

However, the fact that the acts are supervised by a public regulatory body does not necessarily indicate that they are of a public nature. This is analogous to the position in judicial review, where a regulatory body may be deemed public but the activities of the body which is regulated may be categorised private.[75]

Moreover, it would clearly be anomalous in relation to a particular programme that (say) arguably invaded the privacy of one of its participants, if Article 8 could be invoked to claim damages against the broadcaster if the programme was broadcast on a BBC channel, but not on, say, Channel 5. In such a case, their functions and their relationship with Ofcom appear identical.

On the other hand, we *know* from *ProLife*[76] that that the BBC *is* acting as a public authority when it acts, effectively, as a regulator. The BBC in that case stood in what would now be Ofcom's shoes and decided that the broadcast of the disputed ProLife Alliance party election broadcast would violate the standards binding on it by virtue of its Agreement with the Secretary of State. As such, it was clearly carrying out a governmental function: the effect of it, indeed, was to deny access to a publicly-controlled resource (the airwaves) because to do so would violate government policy, as set out in the Broadcasting Act and the BBC's Agreement. This conclusion—that in carrying out this function, it was acting as a public authority—indeed appears to have been implicitly conceded by the BBC; no-one in either the Court of Appeal or House of Lords appeared to question the amenability of the BBC to judicial review. Indeed,

---

[71] Although not in relation to the 'due impartiality' requirements— or its public service remit.

[72] Communications Act 2003, s 265(2).   [73] Communications Act 2003, ss 319 and 320.

[74] The position of the BBC is a little different: not all the statutory duties under the CA 2003 apply to it, although the Codes drawn up by OFCOM under the Act do: see further Chapters 11 at 599–607 and 17 at 858–62.

[75] Ibid, at 69.

[76] [2004] 1 AC 185. The case is further discussed in detail below, and in Chapters 11 and 17.

the whole argument proceeded on the basis that it *was* so amenable: had this not been the case, it would have been unnecessary to consider the substantive arguments that it had acted unlawfully. The amenability of the BBC to review under the HRA when acting as a censor in this way is therefore clearly established as a matter of authority. However, when this point is considered further, considerable complications emerge.

Let us take an example by changing the facts of the *ProLife* case: the election broadcast in question, instead of being likely to shock or disturb, was one that arguably invaded a person's privacy, and the BBC decided in *favour* of broadcasting it. Presumably, under this scenario, the BBC would also, in taking that decision, have been acting as a public authority (meaning that Article 8 ECHR could be directly pleaded against, under section 7(1) HRA). For if the BBC is performing a public function when it decides whether to broadcast a programme submitted by an outside body, such as the ProLife Alliance, it must remain a public function whether the decision taken is a positive or a negative one—it cannot be a public function to say 'no' to the person requesting the broadcast of their programme, but a private one to say 'yes'. The difficulty, however, is that the BBC also carries out such decisions in relation to programmes made by its own employees, in-house. This being so, can it be the case that the BBC would be performing a public function when it decides whether to broadcast a programme made by a third party, but not when it decides whether to broadcast a programme made in-house? Seemingly, the answer is no. In both cases, the same decision—to broadcast or not (or to require certain cuts or not) is being made. If this is right, however, it would mean that the BBC is acting as a public authority *whenever* it broadcasts a programme, because, before broadcasting, there has always been a decision that the broadcast would not violate any of the obligations (as to privacy and offence- avoidance) that bind the BBC. Such a conclusion, however, would leave us with a clear anomaly: when (say) Channel 5 broadcasts a programme, having made exactly the same determination as to whether broadcasting is compatible with its (identical) obligations,[77] it is plainly *not* carrying out a public function. When the BBC does so, it is. Either this anomaly simply has to be accepted, or it could be avoided by drawing the line differently and holding that the BBC only acts as a public authority when it refuses to broadcast a programme made by a third party. Such an argument could be based on the argument that self-censorship is a private act (or function), whereas the censorship of another would generally be thought of as a public—a state—function.[78]

Perhaps the least unsatisfactory resolution is to accept the apparent anomaly and

---

[77] Identical, that is, in terms of standards, under Ofcom's Programme Code. See further Chapter 11.

[78] It could be argued, contrary to this point, that where a newspaper editor received a draft article from a freelance writer, and refused to publish it, because he thought that it would violate the criminal law (say) of incitement to racial hatred, the editor is surely performing a very similar function to that of the BBC in the *ProLife* case. And yet, no-one thinks that a newspaper would be carrying out a public function in such an instance. This would suggest that the censorship/self-censorship distinction is not a strong one. The difference

hold that whenever the BBC decides to broadcast a programme, it is performing a public function, whilst the commercial broadcasters are not. While this *is* anomalous, it might be suggested that the basic scheme of the HRA, in differentiating between the obligations of public authorities and private bodies, is bound to throw up at least *some* such anomalies. For example, it might be seen as anomalous that a person being treated by a consultant engaged in private practice has no claim against him or her for any breach of her Convention rights but does have such a claim when that doctor is engaged in his or her NHS practice. Further, it could be argued that since the BBC is a state broadcaster, and benefits from full public funding, it is fair for it to accept obligations that lie upon other organs of the state.[79]

One final argument should be mentioned. We suggested above that where the BBC is prevented from broadcasting a programme by injunction,[80] it would be absurd to hold that it cannot claim that its freedom of expression has been interfered with. The difficulty is that we have just reached the tentative conclusion that its decision to broadcast a programme is one that engages its duties as public authority under the HRA. This would leave us with the problem that the same matter—the broadcasting of a programme—could figure either as a state act that could violate a Convention right, or as an act that could make the BBC the *victim* of a violation of Convention rights, were the broadcasting to be interfered with by the state. This janus-faced position appears unsatisfactory in principle. Indeed, in *Aston Cantlow*, Lord Nicholls appeared to make the clear assumption that a functional public authority could only exercise Convention rights in relation to its private functions.[81] When a body is acting as part of the government (performing a public function), it surely cannot claim human rights *against* the government. This argument would strongly suggest that the decision by the BBC to broadcast its own programmes *cannot* be a public function.

The discussion above reveals, we would submit, that there is *no* satisfactory answer to this conundrum. We believe it clearly right in principle that the BBC should be able to rely upon Article 10 if its broadcast freedom were interfered with.[82] This makes the argument that its decision to broadcast a programme is a public function, as discussed above, very doubtful. Finally, it may be observed that, as the next section reveals, whatever anomalies are thrown up by the courts' decisions in this area may in any event be softened by reliance on the doctrine of horizontal effect, a matter to which we now turn.

---

between the two cases, however (aside from the different institutional positions of the two bodies), is surely that the BBC, in the *ProLife* case, was barring access to a scarce resource, access to which is controlled by statute, whereas, in theory at least, any person may start a newspaper at any point, without the say-so of the government.

[79] Although it must be conceded that this has nothing to do with whether broadcasting is a 'public function', the test used in the HRA.

[80] As in the *BBC v Scotland* case, op cit.   [81] Op cit, at [11].

[82] Courts would have to interpret the word 'non-governmental organisation' in Art 34 ECHR (the test for standing adopted in s 7(7) HRA) to include the BBC.

HORIZONTAL EFFECT

RELEVANCE TO THE MEDIA

The issue of whether the HRA imports Convention rights—or even Convention principles—into private law is of great importance to the media. It was on this issue that
Lord Wakeham, former Chair of the Press Complaints Commission, lobbied the
Government on behalf of the press, and introduced amendments specifically designed
to protect them. It was in response to this campaign that section 12 of the Act was
introduced, largely to allay media fears. What then are the consequences to the media
of the Convention rights having some 'horizontal effect'? The key rights are clearly
Articles 10 and 8.[83] It was the fear of the media being exposed to the development of a
common law right to privacy that led to the 'outburst' in the press—as one peer
described it—[84] in response to the introduction of the (then) Human Rights Bill, which
the Government went to some lengths to soothe.[85] However, what Wakeham and
others overlooked at the time was the simple fact that that it is not only Article 8 that
is brought into the frame by the horizontal effect of the Convention, but Article 10 also.
Were the Convention freedom of expression guarantee to be effective in private, as
well as public law, the effect would self-evidently be media-*friendly*—to bolster the
protection the common law or statute law already offered for media freedom. Obvious examples are the (largely) common law of defamation[86] and the statutory regime
of copyright law,[87] in which the media rely upon Article 10 as a *defence* against
liability. Thus, had Lord Wakeham succeeded in his attempt to amend the HRA so as
to *exclude* any effect of the Convention rights in private law adjudication,[88] the
amendment would probably have at least hindered the development of a common law
right to privacy; but it would also have prevented the press from relying on Article 10
under the HRA to protect their freedom of expression when defending themselves
against claims, for example, in defamation.[89]

The other important initial point is that the notion of 'horizontal effect' signifies
effects in the private sphere both upon the common law *and* upon the interpretation

---

[83] Article 8 provides a right to respect for private and family life, the home, and correspondence. Article 9
may also be relevant; see text to notes 17 and 18 above.

[84] Lord Ackner, HL Deb col 473 (18 November 1997).

[85] The same peer remarked that 'a very large part of [the Lord Chancellor's] speech was devoted to trying
to pour oil on ruffled waters' (ibid).

[86] The detailed impact of Article 10 on the law of defamation is considered in Chapter 21.

[87] See Chapter 18. Of the other major areas covered in this book, contempt of court is a public law matter,
as is the criminal law of obscenity, indecency, and racial (and religious) hatred.

[88] The amendment put forward by Lord Wakeham, then chair of the Press Complaints Commission,
would have had the effect of excluding the courts from the definition of 'public authority' when 'the parties to
the proceedings before it [did] not include any public authority' (HL Deb Vol. 583 col 771 24 November 1997,
Amendment no 32). It was decisively rejected by Parliament.

[89] Would, that is, apart from the amendment introduced as a result of Wakeham's campaign: s 12(4), which
specifically makes Article 10 relevant in any civil proceedings.

of statutes, a number of which affect the media in a private law context. Examples include the Protection from Harassment Act, the Data Protection Act[90] and the Copyright, Designs and Patent Act 1988. To a large extent, this latter point was overlooked at the time. However, it has since been accepted by the Courts, without any hesitation, that *all* statutes should be interpreted compatibly with Convention rights, regardless of whether they regulate the behaviour of public authorities or private persons.[91] As the Court of Appeal said in *X v Y*,[92] 'Section 3 draws no distinction between legislation governing public authorities and legislation governing private individuals.' The discussion below therefore deals with the much more difficult issue of private common law.

The issue of horizontal effect also of course affects the broadcasters. The regime by which they are regulated is entirely statutory,[93] and so the horizontal effect point is straightforward: the relevant statues must be interpreted and applied compatibly with the relevant Convention rights. However, as just discussed, the fact that the BBC may be treated as a public authority when engaged in at least some of its activities—such as self-regulation—and thus be bound by Convention rights such as Article 8, throws up apparent sharp anomalies with the position of the private, commercial broadcasters, such as Granada and Sky, which would not be bound. It could lead to the BBC being sued directly under section 7 HRA[94] for invasion of private life during the making or broadcast of a programme, say, whereas no such action would be available if the broadcaster was (say) Channel 5.[95] In this area, the possibility of the Courts satisfying the requirements of Article 8 by developing a common law privacy remedy, which could be used against both private and public bodies, could have the effect of equalizing the position of the broadcasters and thus removing or at least softening this anomaly.

HORIZONTAL EFFECT: GENERAL ISSUES

It is, by now, a trite observation that the question of the effect that the HRA gives to the Convention rights in relation to private common law has been one of its most

---

[90] Both are considered in Chapter 14 at 716–21.

[91] A recent significant example is the decision in *Ghaidan v Godin-Mendoza* [2004] 2 AC 557, in which a statute governing rights as between landlord and tenant was re-interpreted quite radically using section 3(1), in order to ensure compatibly with the Convention: see below, at 162–3 for discussion of the decision. For discussion of this aspect of the Act's horizontal effect, see N. Bamforth, 'The True "Horizontal Effect" of the Human Rights Act' (2001) 117 *LQR* 34.

[92] [2004] ICR 1634 at [57(2)], in which the Court of Appeal accepted that employment law legislation had, in principle, to be interpreted and applied in a way that was compatible with any relevant Convention rights, though on the facts it was found that the claimed right (Article 8) was not engaged.

[93] The key statute being the Communications Act 2003. See generally Chapters 10, 11, and 17.

[94] Section 7 provides a cause of action against public authorities for breach of Convention rights. Section 8 allows for the award of damages in such an action.

[95] The other consequence, as explored above, would be that judicial review could be sought against the BBC under the HRA for refusal to broadcast a programme made by another, in reliance upon Article 10—as in the *ProLife Alliance* case (op cit), discussed above—whereas no such action would lie against a private broadcaster.

controversial and contested aspects. This is partly because of its complexity and nor-mative implications—the courts of virtually every country with a Bill of Rights have had to face this question, giving varying answers, depending only partly upon the text of the Bills of Rights themselves.[96] But it is also, as the author has pointed out elsewhere,[97] because Parliament contrived to omit from the HRA any mention either of its effect upon private law, or of the common law generally. All these questions were left to be dealt with by the bald provisions of sections 6(1)[98] and 6(3).[99] Section 6(1), which lays obligations only upon 'public authorities' to act compatibly with the Convention rights, on its face therefore rules out horizontal effect: private bodies, such as newspapers, and the commercial broadcasters are not bound by the Act to respect Convention rights. It is also the case that the Act does not, as such, incorporate the rights into UK law—rather, as is well known—it gives the rights particular effects in particular contexts: the two most important[100] are as interpretative aids where statutes apply[101] and as a duty binding upon public authorities. However, the courts, as 'public authorities' themselves,[102] have a duty not to act incompatibly with the Convention rights; if this duty applies even when dealing with private common law, it is bound to create *some* role for the rights even in common law litigation between private parties,[103] thus giving rise to a form of 'horizontal effect,' though the text of HRA left it unclear what this role should be. Other Bills of Rights offer at least more guidance,[104] whilst the Constitution of South Africa deals with the matter explicitly, by making plain that private persons *are* in principle bound by the constitutional rights and that the courts must develop the common law to give effect to these obligations.[105] That the Government chose not to deal with the matter expressly in the

---

[96] See e.g. the decision of the Canadian Supreme Court in *Retail Wholesale and Department Store Union Local 580 et al v Dolphin Delivery Ltd* (1985) 33 DLR (4th) 174; of the South African Constitutional Court case on the horizontal effect of human rights under the Interim Constitution: *Du Plessis and Others v De Klerk and Another* 1996 (3) SA 850, 900; discussion of the stance of the German Supreme Court in B. Markesenis, 'Privacy, Freedom of Expression, and the Horizontal Effect of the Human Rights Bill: Lessons from Germany' (1999) 115 *LQR* 47. For a more general comparative survey, see S. Gardbaum, 'The "Horizontal Effect" of Constitutional Rights' (2003) 102 *Michigan Law Review* 387.

[97] Phillipson, op cit (*MLR*, 1999) at 825.

[98] S 6(1) provides: 'It is unlawful for a public authority to act in a way which is incompatible with a Convention right.'

[99] S 6(3) provides that: 'public authority includes a court or tribunal'.

[100] The other key provision is s 7, which gives a cause of action against a public authority that has acted incompatibly with a Convention right and section 8, which gives a power to award damages where such an action succeeds.

[101] HRA, s 3.   [102] S 6(3)(a).

[103] S 3(1) HRA, *all* statutes will also have to be interpreted 'so far as possible' in accordance with Convention rights.

[104] The Canadian Constitution, s 52 states that: '*any law* that is inconsistent with the provisions of the Constitution is, to the extent of the inconsistency, of no force or effect'.

[105] Section 8 of the South African Bill of Rights states:

(2) A provision of the Bill of Rights binds a natural or a juristic person [i.e. a private person or a company] if, and to the extent that, it is applicable, taking into account the nature of the right and the nature of any duty imposed by the right.

HRA might well have a political explanation: that it wanted to pass the issue of the Act's horizontal effect into the hands of the judiciary so that any development of a right to privacy based upon the Act would be seen as a judicial creation, rather than a clear result of the Government's introduction of the HRA itself. Lord Wakeham's amendment, explicitly ruling out horizontal effect, was decisively rejected by Parliament;[106] nevertheless, the Government managed to fob off Wakeham and the press with section 12, which did probably make it a little harder to obtain interim injunctions[107] against the media, but other than that contained the, as it turns out, misleading injunction to courts to have 'particular regard' to freedom of expression.[108] We use the word 'misleading' in that, as was predictable, this provision did not result in the courts building in extra weight for expression in a way that would have distorted the Convention scheme. In fact, as is by now well known, by a wonderful stroke of irony, in which Lord Justice Sedley doubtless took great satisfaction, the very provision designed to ensure that Article 8[109] was minimized in common law adjudication, if not excluded from it, was used by his Lordship as the vehicle for smuggling it back in. Article 10 contains the exceptions it is subject to, including Article 8, under the 'rights of others' exception. Therefore, as his Lordship put it in *Douglas v Hello*:[110] 'you cannot have particular regard to Article 10 without having equally particular regard at the very least to Article 8.'[111] As we shall see below, section 12(4) is not without significance in this area, although it has not had the effect that its media sponsors hoped for.

So Parliament fudged the issue of horizontal effect; the Government fobbed off the press with section 12. But then the academics turned their attention to it. It is by now well known what happened next: comprehensive polarization of opinion. Before turning to survey briefly the academic debate, however, it is necessary to look a little more closely at the notion of horizontal effect and the terms of the HRA itself.

It is important to note at the outset that this issue raises questions at two levels, which are logically and legally distinct: first at the Convention level, as a matter of interpretation of the Convention and the Strasbourg Court's jurisprudence; second at the local, domestic level, as a matter of interpretation of the particular instrument giving effect to the Convention—the Human Rights Act. Clearly a domestic court needs to look at both levels. It is obvious that it must correctly construe the HRA itself, but if it is to act compatibly with 'Convention rights' as section 6(1) HRA demands, then, in a particular case, it must also arrive at some position as to the scope

---

(3) When applying a provision of the Bill of Rights to a natural or juristic person in terms of subsection (2), a court in order to give effect to a right in the Bill, must:
    (a) apply, or if necessary develop, the common law to the extent that legislation does not give effect to that right; and
    (b) may develop rules of the common law to limit the right.

[106] See note 88 above.   [107] Section 12(3).   [108] See above, note 1.
[109] Article 8 ECHR provides that: 'Everyone has the right to respect for . . . private life', subject to the various exceptions in para 2.
[110] [2001] QB 967.   [111] Ibid, at 1003.

and meaning which the particular right in question has in the Convention system. Moreover, section 2(1) of the Act provides that a court, 'in determining any question relating to a Convention right, must take into account' any relevant Strasbourg jurisprudence. Plainly, the issue of the horizontal effect of the Convention under the HRA is a question 'in connection with a Convention right'. Thus, when considering whether to treat the Convention right as having any relevance at all to the particular situation, the court should examine whether Strasbourg has found the right to require positive state intervention between private parties.[112] In other words, is there an obligation on the UK to provide a measure of protection for Convention rights in situations such as the one that has arisen in the litigation before the Court, which it *could* discharge in this case? The Court of Appeal accepted in *X v Y*,[113] that section 2(1) HRA required them to examine relevant Strasbourg jurisprudence in deciding the horizontal effect point,[114] in that case whether the dismissal of the applicant, based on the concealment by him of his caution for an act of gross indecency with another male, engaged his right to private life. In terms of the issue which has caused most controversy so far under the HRA—the issue of protection for privacy against the press—the question therefore is whether the Strasbourg Court has interpreted Article 8 as requiring states to provide a remedy in the hands of private persons to use against the press when the latter publish private information without consent or proper justification.[115] It is important to note that this first level must be investigated in *all* cases, including those involving statutes, since the question here is whether there are any Convention obligations in play at all.

What then as to our second level of argument as to the horizontal application of particular Convention articles? This second level is local and specific, and it derives from the particular instrument incorporating the Convention into UK law—the Human Rights Act. This second level is logically distinct from the first, because a court *might* decide that, whilst it appeared that Strasbourg had interpreted a particular right as imposing a positive obligation to intervene between private parties, the particular provisions of the HRA—in particular, section 6(1)—precluded this. Lord Hoffman, as discussed below,[116] has made precisely this distinction. It is also suggested, however, that, when deciding the issue as to the interpretation of the HRA, the courts should take account of the Strasbourg jurisprudence on whether and when the Convention requires a horizontal application.[117] In other words, the answer given at the first level is relevant to that given at the second, though not determinative of it.

At this second level, in deciding how to give effect to any horizontal effect required by the Convention, a basic distinction may be drawn between what is often termed 'direct' and 'indirect' horizontal effect. A measure has 'direct' horizontal effect if it

---

[112] As it did, for example, in *A v United Kingdom* (1998), 27 EHRR 611, in which an obligation to provide protection for a child against its parents in respect of physical discipline was found, under Article 3 of the Convention.

[113] [2004] ICR 1634   [114] Ibid at [39–42].

[115] This particular question is discussed in Chapter 13.   [116] See note 191.

[117] This is required by section 2(1) HRA—see below at 145.

lays duties directly upon a private body to abide by its provisions and makes breach of these duties directly actionable at the instance of an aggrieved party. As Lewan puts it, such a scheme creates 'absolute rights, which run against all persons'.[118] In contrast, in jurisdictions where it is clear that the rights in question were not intended to be directly binding on private bodies, courts have usually deployed some form of *indirect* horizontal effect; this means that whilst the rights cannot be applied directly to the law governing private relations or at least are not actionable *per se* in such a context, they may be relied upon indirectly, to influence the interpretation and application of pre-existing law.[119] As we will note later, there are stronger and weaker versions of the indirect horizontal effect model. But we may first seek to establish which of these broad camps the horizontal effect of the HRA falls into and the implications this has for how private litigants may invoke their Convention rights in court.

Despite the Act's silence as to its possible impact on private law, a superficial examination makes clear that its basic scheme precludes direct horizontal effect.[120] As discussed above, section 6(1) states that, 'It is unlawful for a *public authority* to act in a way which is incompatible with one or more of the Convention rights' (emphasis added). That the Act is intended to bind public authorities only appears to be confirmed by sections 7 and 8, which deal with proceedings and remedies only in relation to actions against such bodies. This basic intention was also made clear by the Lord Chancellor in a number of *Pepper v Hart*[121] statements during the Bill's passage through the House of Lords. For example, during the Second Reading of the Bill, he said:

We decided first of all that a provision of this kind [making it unlawful to contravene a Convention right] should apply only to public authorities . . . and not to private individuals . . . The Convention had its origins in a desire to protect people from the misuse of power by the state, rather than from the actions of private individuals.[122]

The Home Secretary made remarks to similar effect in the Commons' debate.[123]

The HRA will not therefore give rise to direct horizontal effect. But may a degree of *indirect* horizontal effect arise? As mentioned above, a number of commentators have argued that *some* measure of horizontal effect must arise because the courts—

---

[118] K. Lewan, 'The Significance of Constitutional Rights for Private Law: Theory and Practice in West Germany', 17 (1968) *ICLQ* 571, 572.

[119] In the German 'drittwirkung' terminology, this type of indirect horizontality would be referred to as 'mittelbare drittwirkung'; direct horizontal effect as 'unmittelbare'; for a brief explanation, see A. Dremczewski, *European Human Rights Convention in Domestic Law* Oxford: Clarendon, 1997, 200, and the articles cited therein at note 2.

[120] M. Hunt, ('The Horizontal Effect of the Human Rights Act' (1998) *PL* 423, 438) asserts that this is 'clear beyond argument'.

[121] *Pepper (Inspector of Taxes) v Hart* [1993] AC 593.

[122] HL Deb Vol. 582 col 1232, 3 November 1997.

[123] For example: 'We decided that Convention rights should be available in proceedings involving what might be very broadly described as "the state", but that they would not be directly justiciable in actions between private individuals' (HC Deb Vol. 314 col 406, 17 June 1998).

and tribunals—are stated to be public authorities for the purposes of the Act[124] and, it is argued, are therefore themselves bound to apply Convention standards in giving judgement even in cases involving only private individuals. Buxton LJ,[125] however, rejected even this argument and contended trenchantly for the Convention rights to be given no horizontal effect at all within the common law, although that was plainly opposed to the intention of Parliament in rejecting the Wakeham amendment and, as suggested below, with section 12 (4) of the Act itself. In contrast, Wade contended for a form of full horizontal effect. His view was that in practice it should make no difference whether the defendant is a public or private body, since the courts in giving judgment would have a duty to uphold Convention rights regardless under section 6. The duty, he suggested, gave the courts 'sufficient warrant to award remedies in accordance with Strasbourg principles'. He concluded that if his argument is correct, 'the definition [of public authority] . . . will not matter'.[126]

Such an outcome—the effective collapsing of the distinction between public and private applicants—would be startling indeed. It would mean that the apparent basic scheme of the HRA—to bind public authorities only and to provide procedures and remedies for this purpose—would be radically undercut. The carefully worded definition of 'public authority' in section 6 would become largely redundant and the HRA would instead effectively bind *both* public and private bodies to follow the Convention but—with no apparent justification for the distinction—make provision for proceedings and remedies in relation to the former only. In other words, Wade's view seems to cut clearly across the enacted intention of Parliament as seen in the basic scheme of the HRA.

It is also wholly unclear how the Wade reading of the HRA could possibly work in practice. The example of the privacy-invading newspaper may clarify this point. We will assume for now that the court, in adjudicating upon the plaintiff's case, has to act compatibly with the Convention. So it must hand down a judgment in the case which respects any rights the individual has under Article 8. But the difficulty lies here: how does the individual get his case to court in the first place? Indeed, what *is* his case? A litigant cannot go to court simply saying 'the newspaper has violated Article 8' because (assuming that a newspaper is not a 'public authority'), Article 8 will not be binding on it. A litigant has a cause of action against another party only if she can allege that they have acted, or are threatening to act, unlawfully. A newspaper will not have done so, solely by violating or threatening to violate Article 8. The individual's case can't therefore be *based* on violation of Article 8, at least not by a newspaper. She must have some other cause of action—some other alleged unlawful act—for the

---

[124] S 6(3)(a); Hunt describes this provision as 'of great significance for the horizontality [of the Act]' (Hunt, op cit); see also Wade, 'The United Kingdom's Bill of Rights' in *Constitutional Reform in the United Kingdom: Practice and Principles*; Beatson, Forsyth, and Hare (eds) Oxford: Hart Publishing, 1998, 62–4; Markesenis, op cit, 73.

[125] 'The Human Rights Act and Private Law' (2000) 116 *LQR* 48.

[126] Op cit, 62–3; see also his 'Horizons of Horizontality' (2000) 116 LQR 224 and, with C. F. Forsyth, *Administrative Law*, 8th edn. Oxford, 2000, Appendix 2.

court to adjudicate upon in order to get Article 8 into play at all. As the Court of Appeal said bluntly in *X v Y*,[127] which concerned an action by a former employee against his employer relying on Article 8:

The applicant did not assert any cause of action against the employer under the HRA. He does not have an HRA cause of action. The employer is not a public authority within section 6 of the HRA. It was not unlawful under section 6 of the HRA for the employer, as a private sector employer, to act in a way which was incompatible with Article 8.[128]

It went on to say specifically that the fact that the Employment Tribunal, like a court, is itself a public authority under section 6(3) HRA and so must act compatibly with the Convention rights under section 6(1), '[does] not, however, give the applicant any cause of action under the HRA against an employer which is not a public authority'.[129] Contrary to Wade's view, then, section 6(1) gives the Convention rights no purchase in private law adjudication except upon existing causes of action.

Thus the Courts have now more or less ruled out Wade's view—without full explanation, but doubtless motivated in part by a desire to protect private law from full scale take-over by the Convention. In contrast, a view that has received some support from the judiciary—and perhaps more than any other from commentators— is that put forward by Murray Hunt, in perhaps one of the most influential articles written on the HRA.[130] He argued for what he termed 'strong indirect horizontal effect': that the judges have an *absolute duty* under section 6 to interpret and apply *existing law* to render it compatible with the Convention rights; once there was reliance by either party upon an existing cause of action the judicial duty was activated. In an article published in 1999, one of the authors argued, on a number of grounds, that the HRA does not impose this absolute duty, but rather the obligation to *take account* of Convention principles or values when engaging in common law adjudication, affording them a variable weight, depending on the context. A number of other commentators, including Lester and Pannick[131] and Grosz and Beatson,[132] appeared to back Hunt's view in favour of strong horizontal effect, and at one point it looked as if there was at least a clear academic consensus building around indirect horizontal effect—in either its weaker or stronger forms. However, it is important to note that in fact this proved not to be the case. Jonathan Morgan[133] has argued for the Wade position of full or direct horizontal effect, though his article did not take account of a number of the arguments put forward against the Wade position.[134] Moreover, in a full length article published in the *Law Quarterly Review*,[135] Professor

---

[127] Op cit: the facts appear above at note 114.   [128] Ibid, at [54(2)].

[129] Ibid at [58(3)].   [130] M. Hunt, op cit.

[131] A. Lester and D. Pannick, 'The Impact of the Human Rights Act on Private Law: The Knight's Move', (2000) 116 *LQR* 380.

[132] J. Beatson and S. Grosz, 'Horizontality: A Footnote', (2000) 116 *LQR* 385.

[133] 'Questioning the True Effect of the HRA', (2002) 22(2) *Legal Studies*, 259; see also his 'Privacy, Confidence and Horizontal Effect: 'Hello' Trouble', (2003) *CLJ* 443.

[134] He did not deal with those put forward in Phillipson, op cit ('Bang or Whimper').

[135] 'Horizontality applicability and horizontal effect' (2002) 118 *LQR*, 623.

Beyleveld and Shaun Pattinson have put forward a complex and sophisticated argument in favour of full or direct horizontal effect, engaging in a full critique and analysis of the arguments of Buxton, Hunt, and Phillipson against such a position. We do not seek here to refute the arguments put forward in this article, for reasons of space and because it now appears tolerably clear that there is very little possibility of their being judicially adopted. Rather, we confine ourselves to noting that by the time the House of Lords decided *Campbell v MGN*,[136] there was a very rich and sophisticated academic literature on this subject, in which, whilst there was perhaps a consensus that the Buxton anti-horizontalist position was wrong, there was little agreement aside from that.

Before turning to examine the case law, it is worth noting a couple of provisions of the HRA *other than* sections 6 and 3 that have some bearing on this issue. First, and most straightforwardly, we have noted above that section 2(1) requires courts to 'have regard' to Strasbourg jurisprudence when 'determining a question which has arisen in connection with a Convention right'. This plainly requires courts to have regard to the substantive principles deriving from any relevant Strasbourg jurisprudence in deciding the case before it. In using the term 'have regard to', section 2(1), then, requires at least weak indirect horizontal effect—courts must, as a minimum, take into account the Convention rights in interpreting and applying the common law. Section 2(1) itself therefore arguably rules out the Buxton position.

The second provision of relevance is section 12(4), the inclusion of which means that Parliament *did* settle the relevance to common law adjudication of at least one Convention right—freedom of expression. Section 12(4), as is well known, abjures courts to have 'particular regard to the importance of the Convention right to freedom of expression'. It applies whenever 'a court is considering whether to grant *any relief* which, if granted, might affect the exercise of the Convention right to freedom of expression' (emphasis added). This provision, which therefore applies, seemingly, to all form of civil proceedings[137] ('any relief'), plainly makes at least Article 10 relevant in common law actions between private parties. As Sedley LJ put it in *Douglas v Hello!*:[138]

subsection (4) . . . puts beyond question the direct applicability of at least one article of the Convention as between one private party to litigation and another—in the jargon, its horizontal effect.

Whatever the intention behind section 12(4), it has not been accepted as building in extra weight on the side of freedom of expression at the expense of other Convention rights. This, as Sedley LJ observed, would be incompatible with the Convention itself, which does not afford Article 10 a special status in relation to the other Convention rights.[139] Therefore, even if section 12(4) might have been intended to give it such a

---

[136] [2004] 2 WLR 1232.

[137] *Per* section 12(5), s 12 does not apply to criminal proceedings.   [138] [2001] QB 967, 1003.

[139] Ibid, at 1004: 'The European Court of Human Rights has always recognised the high importance of free media of communication in a democracy, but its jurisprudence does not—and could not consistently with the Convention itself—give Article 10(1) the presumptive priority which is given, for example, to the First Amendment in the jurisprudence of the United States' courts.'

status, section 12(4) HRA itself must be interpreted compatibly with the Convention rights using section 3(1) HRA.[140] That section 12(4) confers no special status upon freedom of expression viz a viz other Convention rights was emphatically confirmed by the decision of the House of Lords in *Campbell*.[141] However, it is notable that the provision does not, strictly speaking, decide the strong/weak indirect horizontal effect point. It does not in terms, instruct the courts to 'act compatibly with the Convention right to freedom of expression' (strong indirect effect), but rather to have 'particular regard' to the right's importance (weak indirect effect). This wording was of course chosen because the intention was to bolster Article 10 against a possible future privacy right and it might have been thought that enacting a section 12 that simply instructed the courts to act compatibly with Article 10 would have done nothing but reiterate section 6, which instructs courts to act compatibly with Convention rights generally, but which was not thought to make the rights directly effective in private law.[142] But, paradoxically, the very fact that Parliament attempted to emphasize the *importance* of Article 10 led it to enact a provision which left Article 10's status in private law ambiguous. This outcome is ironic; Sedley LJ's use of section 12(4) to smuggle *Article 8* into private law adjudication, thus *threatening* media freedom, piled irony upon irony.

THE PRE-*CAMPBELL* CASE LAW ON HORIZONTAL EFFECT

It is suggested there that the case law to date—in particular, *Campbell* and *Douglas III*[143]—has meant that we can at present lay aside Wade's contentious reading of section 6 HRA as giving rise to a form of direct, or full horizontal, effect,[144] while Buxton LJ's anti-horizontalist reading[145] has been ruled out fairly conclusively.[146] The courts appear to have settled instead upon a version of 'indirect horizontal effect', whereby the Convention rights are relevant to common law adjudication; however, what has not been settled is whether the 'strong' or 'weak' version should be judicially adopted.

In *Douglas v Hello!*,[147] this matter appeared to divide the court: Brooke LJ spoke of

---

[140] Sedley LJ refers to 'the court's own obligation under section 3 of the Act to construe all legislation so far as possible compatibly with the Convention rights, an obligation which must include the interpretation of the Human Rights Act itself.' (ibid).

[141] See the detailed discussion in Chapters 13 and 15.

[142] Parliament probably took the view of the Lord Chancellor and the Home Secretary on the effect of section 6(1) generally: see notes 122 and 123 above.

[143] [2005] 3 WLR 881. This is the decision of the Court of Appeal on the appeal from the decision to award damages at final trial made by Lindsay J: [2003] 3 All ER 996 (*Douglas II*), the Court of Appeal having in 2001 declined to uphold an injunction in the case: [2001] QB 967.

[144] Op cit.   [145] Buxton LJ, 'The Human Rights Act and Private Law' (2000) 116 *LQR* 48.

[146] Most clearly by Butler Sloss in *Venables and another v News Group Newspapers* [2001] 1 All ER 908. 916: 'The decisions of the European Court in *Glaser v UK* [2000] 3 FCR 193, ECt HR and *X and Y v Netherlands* (1985) 8 EHRR 235, seem to dispose of any argument that a court is not to have regard to the Convention in private law cases.' *Douglas* and *A v B plc* also implicitly rejected this view (below).

[147] *Douglas and Zeta Jones and ors v Hello!* [2001] QB 967.

the judges' obligation of '*taking into account* the positive duties identified by the court at Strasbourg when they develop the common law,[148] while Keene LJ similarly stated that the courts' approach must now be '*informed* by the jurisprudence of the Convention in respect of article 8'.[149] Sedley LJ, in contrast, appeared explicitly to approve Hunt's stronger approach.[150] His view was that, 'by virtue of s 6 of the Act, the courts of this country *must themselves act compatibly* with . . . the . . . Convention rights'.[151] *Venables*[152] also expressly endorsed the 'strong' version: 'The duty on the court, in my view, is to act compatibly with Convention rights in adjudicating upon existing common law causes of action, and that includes a positive as well as a negative obligation.'[153] The Court of Appeal in *Campbell*,[154] on the other hand, expressed the duty in the weaker form: Phillips MR, giving the judgment of the court, held that 'the courts must *have regard* to' Articles 8 and 10[155] in a common law context; he did not speak of a duty to act compatibly with them. *A v B plc*,[156] while endorsing a clear role for the Convention rights in private law cases, does not resolve the matter: Woolf CJ, giving the judgment of the court, simply stated, without more:

Under section 6 of the [HRA], the court, as a public authority, is required not to act 'in a way which is incompatible with a Convention right.' The court is able to achieve this by absorbing the rights which Articles 8 and 10 protect into the long-established action for breach of confidence.[157]

That sounds fairly clear, but given the fact that, as appears below, these dicta were cited by two of their Lordships in *Campbell v MGN*, one of whom thought he was not deciding the question of horizontality at all,[158] while the other thought these dicta had already decided it,[159] it is evidently not without ambiguity. Purportedly following this and the other Court of Appeal decisions, Lindsay J in *Douglas II* found that the 'scope' of breach of confidence now 'needs to be evaluated in the light of' the courts' obligations under section 6 (1).[160] Moreover, Sedley LJ has remarked in a different context, 'it is probable, though as yet undecided' that the section 6(1) duty lying on courts, 'governs remedies and procedures, rather than doctrines of substantive law'.[161]

Thus, taken together, these cases do *not* disclose what one commentator[162] ascribed to the judgment in *Douglas*—'a complete acceptance of the judicial duty to act compatibly with Convention rights', although they do amount to a clear rejection of the Buxton view. The question of whether the court's duty is to 'take into account' Convention rights or to act compatibly with them is left unresolved. Thus, by the time their Lordships came to decide *Campbell*, it was unclear whether the common law,

---

[148] Ibid, at 993–4.   [149] Ibid, at 1012.   [150] Ibid, at 1002.

[151] Ibid, at 998. Sedley LJ's approach was followed in *Theakston v MGN* [2002] EMLR 22.

[152] *Venables and another v News Group Newspapers* [2001] 1 All ER 908.   [153] Op cit, at 917.

[154] [2003] QB 633, CA.   [155] Op cit, at 658.   [156] [2002] 3 WLR 542.   [157] Ibid, at 546.

[158] Lord Nicholls, op cit, at [17].   [159] Ibid, *per* Lord Hope, at [86].

[160] [2003] 3 All ER 996, at [186(i)].

[161] *R (on the application of Wooder) v Feggetter* [2002] EWCA Civ 554, at[48].

[162] I. Hare, 'Vertically Challenged: Private Parties, Privacy and the Human Rights Act' (2001) 5 *EHRLR*, 526, 533.

if found to be in conflict with the Convention, *must* or only *may* be changed in response. Indeed, the dicta of Sedley LJ just cited suggested that the Convention rights might be irrelevant in such a context. We may finally mention again *X v Y*.[163] Since the case was not concerned with common law, but with a statute, it is not of direct relevance to our focus here, but certain remarks made by the Court of Appeal are of interest. Noting the academic debate, the Court said, disarmingly:

The general question of horizontality has not yet been resolved by a court. Indeed, it may never be resolved judicially at the same high level of abstraction on which the debate has been conducted for the most part in the law books and legal periodicals. The facts of particular cases and the legal contexts in which they fall to be decided tend to put very general propositions into a more limited and manageable perspective.[164]

This then was the backdrop to the House of Lords' decision in *Campbell*—an issue that is of crucial importance to the interpretation and the impact of the HRA left largely ambiguous by Parliament; fiercely contested in leading academic articles; substantially—almost deliberately!—unresolved by the lower courts. All this uncertainty of course existed four years after the HRA came into force and six years after it was passed. One might have thought that legal certainty, if nothing else, required that the question be given a definitive answer. This backdrop, we would suggest, makes how the Law Lords actually handled the horizontal effect point in *Campbell* all the more surprising.

CAMPBELL AND HORIZONTAL EFFECT

Turning now to look at the case itself, the facts should very briefly be noted, in order to indicate the context in which the case was decided. Naomi Campbell complained of the publication of details of her treatment at Narcotics Anonymous for drug addiction, including a photograph of her taken outside the clinic. She relied upon an existing cause of action—breach of confidence; however, to provide her with a remedy required a substantial extension of the law as it stood, in reliance on Article 8;[165] therefore the application of the Convention to the case was a highly significant issue. We will consider their Lordships' approach to the issue in two ways: first, by looking at their formal dicta on the matter, and second, by looking briefly at their actual approach to Convention jurisprudence and principle.

We will start with Lady Hale, who took a clear and unambiguous position on the matter:[166]

Neither party to this appeal has challenged the basic principles which have emerged from the Court of Appeal in the wake of the Human Rights Act 1998. The 1998 Act does not create any new cause of action between private persons. But if there is a relevant cause of action applicable, the court as a public authority must act compatibly with both parties'

---

[163] Op cit.   [164] Ibid, at [45].   [165] As argued in Chapter 14.
[166] Op cit, at [132].

Convention rights. In a case such as this, the relevant vehicle will usually be the action for breach of confidence, as Lord Woolf CJ held in *A v B plc*, para 4.[167]

These dicta appear both to rule out the Wade position, *and* endorse that of Hunt: the court must act compatibly with the rights themselves—there is no talk of having regard to the values underlying the rights. Having taken this position, Lady Hale then very much proceeds to put it into practice—her judgment amounts to a very careful analysis of relevant Convention jurisprudence and principles and a reformulation of the law to reflect them, in particular in relation to the correct approach to balancing Articles 8 and 10.[168]

Next we come to Lord Hope (Lord Carswell simply agreed with Lords Hope and Hale, and so his speech adds nothing to the analysis of this point). Lord Hope is by no means as clear as Lady Hale; indeed, he takes up no explicit position on this matter. Rather, his Lordship first of all makes a somewhat ambiguous reference to the dicta of Lord Woolf already cited: 'As Lord Woolf CJ said in *A v B plc*, para 4, new breadth and strength is given to the action for breach of confidence by [Articles 8 and 10].'[169] Lord Hope then goes on to make his own comment:

In the present case it is convenient to begin by looking at the matter from the standpoint of the respondents' assertion of the Article 10 right and the court's duty as a public authority under section 6(1) of the Human Rights Act 1998, which section 12(4) reinforces, not to act in a way which is incompatible with *that* Convention right (emphasis added).[170]

This second paragraph is notable in being specifically confined in application to Article 10; it does suggest a reading of it whereby Courts must act compatibly with it in private law cases, rather than merely have particular regard to its importance, but it does not seek to resolve the horizontal effect conundrum generally. As to the other dicta, since paragraph 4 of *A v B* also contains Lord Woolf's dicta about acting compatibly with the Convention rights cited with approval by Lady Hale (above), and since Lord Hope voices no criticism or dissent from them, his Lordship *seems* at this point to be endorsing Lady Hale's view. But it is rather striking that in pronouncing upon such an important point, his Lordship does not make himself clearer. What is the more strange, especially in contrast to the view of Lord Hoffman, discussed below, is that, having seemingly decided that Articles 8 and 10 must be applied in this context, Lord Hope goes on to deny that this makes any difference, save in terms of semantics:

The language has changed following the coming into operation of the Human Rights Act 1998 and the incorporation into domestic law of Article 8 and Article 10 of the Convention. We now talk about the right to respect for private life and the countervailing right to

---

[167] That paragraph reads: 'Under section 6 of the 1998 Act, the court, as a public authority, is required not to "act in a way which is incompatible with a Convention right". The court is able to achieve this by absorbing the rights which Articles 8 and 10 protect into the long-established action for breach of confidence.'

[168] Here she builds upon the approach she had sketched out in the Court of Appeal decision in *Re S* [2003] 2 FCR 577.

[169] Op cit, at [86].   [170] Ibid, at [114].

freedom of expression. The jurisprudence of the European Court offers important guidance as to how these competing rights ought to be approached and analysed. I doubt whether the result is that the centre of gravity, as my noble and learned friend Lord Hoffmann says, has shifted. It seems to me that the balancing exercise to which that guidance is directed is essentially the same exercise, although it is plainly now more carefully focussed and more penetrating (emphasis added).[171]

However, having said that the difference between the common law and the Convention in this area is more or less semantic, Lord Hope then goes on, like Lady Hale, to engage in a detailed analysis of Convention jurisprudence: he does so in relation to the existence of a privacy interest—decided partly by reference to *Z v Finland*[172]—its strength, and the manner in which that interest should be weighed up against the competing speech interest. Thus his principal objection to the Court of Appeal decision which he, as part of the majority overturned, is that 'they do not appear to have attempted to balance the competing Convention rights against each other'. He goes on:

In my opinion the Court of Appeal's approach is open to the criticism that, because they wrongly held that [the] details [of Campbell's drug treatment] were not entitled to protection under the law of confidence, they failed to carry out the required balancing exercise.[173]

In working out how to do this, Lord Hope then quotes extensively from *Bladet Tromso v Norway*,[174] *Jersild v Denmark*,[175] *Observer and Guardian v United Kingdom*,[176] and *Fressoz and Roire v France*.[177] He concludes that the weight of both rights must be subject to searching scrutiny, as must the necessity for their restriction and the need to ensure that such restriction goes no further than is necessary. In doing so, he observes:

The jurisprudence of the European Court of Human Rights explains how these principles are to be understood and applied in the context of the facts of each case.

In carrying out the balancing act, Lord Hope uses decisions such as *Dudgeon v United Kingdom*[178] in order to establish that interference with more intimate areas of private life require a weightier justification—an important decision that had notably been omitted from consideration in earlier privacy decisions to which it had clear relevance, such as *A v B, Theakston*,[179] and the Court of Appeal decision in *Campbell*.[180] He also uses cases on 'low value speech' such as *Tammer v Estonia*,[181] to find that there were no political or democratic values at stake in the case and that no pressing social need to interfere with Campbell's privacy rights been identified, contrasting Campbell's case with *Goodwin v United Kingdom*.[182] In scrutinizing the privacy value at stake in the decision, he relied on *PG v JH v United Kingdom*[183] and *Peck v United Kingdom*.[184]

In short, both Lord Hope and Lady Hale appear to engage in what can be termed strong indirect horizontal effect reasoning. The difference between the two is that

---

[171] Ibid, at [86].   [172] 25 EHRR 371.   [173] Op cit, at [104].   [174] (2000) 29 EHRR 125.
[175] (1994) 19 EHRR 1.   [176] (1992) 14 EHRR 153.   [177] (2001) 31 EHRR 28.
[178] (1981) 4 EHRR 149.   [179] *Theakston v MGN* [2002] EMLR 22.   [180] Op cit.
[181] (2001) 37 EHRR 857 at [59].   [182] (1996) 22 EHRR 123.   [183] App no. 44787/98, para 57.
[184] [2003] 36 EHRR 719.

while Lady Hale expressly accepted the application of strong horizontal effect as a duty that must be carried out in each case involving common law actions that are in the sphere of Convention rights, Lord Hope did not.

Turning now to the minority, we may consider the comments of Lord Nicholls first. Lord Nicholls at first struck a note that sounded very much in harmony with the speech of Lady Hale:

The time has come to recognise that the values enshrined in articles 8 and 10 are now part of the cause of action for breach of confidence. As Lord Woolf CJ has said, the courts have been able to achieve this result by absorbing the rights protected by Articles 8 and 10 into this cause of action: *A v B plc*, para 4. Further, it should now be recognised that for this purpose these values are of general application. The values embodied in Articles 8 and 10 are as much applicable in disputes between individuals or between an individual and a non-governmental body such as a newspaper as they are in disputes between individuals and a public authority.[185]

Two things are noteworthy about these dicta: first, it is the *values underlying the rights* that are to be applicable in resolving disputes between private individuals; this is very different from pronouncing that there is a duty to act compatibly with the rights themselves. Second, his Lordship, like Lady Hale, cites the same dicta of Lord Woolf, but draws from them a different conclusion.

It seems, then, that Lord Nicholls has decided the question of horizontal effect. However, a surprise lies in wait when one moves to the next paragraph of his speech:

In reaching this conclusion it is not necessary to pursue the controversial question whether the European Convention itself has this wider effect. Nor is it necessary to decide whether the duty imposed on courts by section 6 of the Human Rights Act 1998 extends to questions of substantive law as distinct from questions of practice and procedure. It is sufficient to recognise that the values underlying Articles 8 and 10 are not confined to disputes between individuals and public authorities. This approach has been adopted by the courts in several recent decisions, reported and unreported, where individuals have complained of press intrusion.[186]

In other words, Lord Nicholls asserts that neither of the two questions raised by horizontal effect—whether Article 8 is applicable horizontally or whether s 6(1) requires or precludes domestic courts from giving it this effect—are relevant. The question that these dicta wholly avoid is, *why* values underlying Articles 8 and 10 should have any application in private law if it is not for the Human Rights Act?

The remainder of his Lordship's speech is all the more surprising. Having found it unnecessary to decide the applicability of the Convention, Lord Nicholls then proceeds to apply the Convention, in some detail:

In applying this approach, and giving effect to the values protected by Article 8, courts will *often* be aided by adopting the structure of Article 8 in the same way as they now habitually apply the Strasbourg court's approach to Article 10 when resolving questions concerning

---

[185] Op cit, at [17].   [186] Ibid, at [18].

freedom of expression.[187] When both [Articles 8 and 10] are engaged a difficult question of proportionality may arise. This question is distinct from the initial question of whether the published information engaged Article 8 at all by being within the sphere of the complainant's private or family life.

Accordingly, in deciding what was the ambit of an individual's 'private life' in particular circumstances courts need to be on guard against using as a touchstone a test which brings into account considerations which should more properly be considered at the later stage of proportionality. *Essentially the touchstone of private life is whether in respect of the disclosed facts the person in question had a reasonable expectation of privacy.*[188]

His Lordship thus adopts a quite specific approach based on proportionality to balancing the two articles, and also carefully distinguishes those factors which go to proportionality and those which go to the scope of the right—to whether there is a *prima facie* cause of action in privacy. He, like Lady Hale and Lord Hope, also adopts a specific doctrinal test to be used in the common law—the reasonable expectation of privacy test—something which comes, in fact, from Strasbourg jurisprudence.[189] In other words, Lord Nicholl's speech is something of an enigma on this point. He appears to back a particular view of horizontal effect (weak indirect effect), but then states that it is unnecessary to decide the issue; he then goes on to apply, if anything, strong indirect effect, by changing the common law so as to make it compatible with the relevant Convention rights.

Lord Hoffman, in contrast to Lord Nicholl's view that it was unnecessary to decide the horizontal effect point, does decide it. He seemingly does so in favour of the view of the view of Buxton LJ,[190] which, it had been generally thought, had been ruled out some time ago:

Even now that the equivalent of Article 8 has been enacted as part of English law, it is not directly concerned with the protection of privacy against private persons or corporations. It is, by virtue of section 6 of the 1998 Act, a guarantee of privacy only against public authorities. Although the Convention, as an international instrument, may impose upon the United Kingdom an obligation to take some steps (whether by statute or otherwise) to protect rights of privacy against invasion by private individuals, it does not follow that such an obligation would have any counterpart in domestic law.[191]

Note that this last sentence explicitly draws a distinction between the matter as it may stand at Strasbourg and the position under domestic law, what we referred to as the first and second levels. This passage overall seems flatly opposed to the views of Lady Hale, who accepted a clear obligation *on the domestic courts* to give effect to a right of

---

[187] Ibid, at [19].   [188] Ibid, at [20] and [21]—emphasis added.

[189] *P.G. and J.H. v the United Kingdom*, ECHR 2001–IX at [57]: 'a person's reasonable expectations as to privacy may be a significant, though not necessarily conclusive factor'; applied in *Peck v UK*, op cit, at [62]: 'As a result, the relevant moment was viewed to an extent which far exceeded any exposure to a passer-by or to security observation . . . and to a degree surpassing that which the applicant could possibly have foreseen when he walked in Brentwood on 20 August 1995.'

[190] Note 125 above.   [191] *Campbell*, op cit, at [49].

privacy against private bodies. However, having seemingly ruled out any form of horizontal effect, the next part of Lord Hoffman's speech is rather surprising:

What human rights law has done is to identify private information as something worth protecting as an aspect of human autonomy and dignity. And this recognition has raised inescapably the question of why it should be worth protecting against the state but not against a private person. I can see no logical ground for saying that a person should have less protection against a private individual than he would have against the state for the publication of personal information for which there is no justification.[192]

While it may be the case in principle that there is no reason to make such a statement, as a matter of law, there are two very obvious reasons for doing so. First, the Convention binds state parties only; second, the HRA binds only 'public authorities'. These surely provide the 'logical ground' that his Lordship cannot see. Lord Hoffman here seems to be almost wilfully missing the point. We appear to have an acceptance of horizontal effect without its being attributed to either the HRA or indeed the ECHR. And indeed this acceptance is, oddly, manifest in Lord Hoffman's speech, in which the influence of the Convention appears to be just as strong as in the speeches of his brethren:

As Sedley LJ observed in . . . *Douglas v Hello! Ltd* [2001] QB 967, 1001, the new approach takes a different view of the underlying value which the law protects. Instead of the cause of action being based upon the duty of good faith applicable to confidential personal information and trade secrets alike, it focuses upon the protection of human autonomy and dignity—the right to control the dissemination of information about one's private life and the right to the esteem and respect of other people.[193]

. . . As for human autonomy and dignity, I should have thought that the extent to which information about one's state of health, including drug dependency, should be communicated to other people was plainly something which an individual was entitled to decide for herself: compare *Z v Finland* . . .[194]

In deciding the matter, he, as well as *Z v Finland*,[195] cited *Fressoz and Roire v France*[196] and *Peck v UK*;[197] in particular, he founded upon *Fressoz* to decide that Article 10 requires a margin of latitude to be granted to journalists as to the manner in which they present their stories and that the conduct of the *Mirror* in the instant case was within that margin. In other words, despite Lord Hoffman's apparent invocation of a view similar to that of Buxton LJ, he proceeds to do precisely what that view precludes—namely, give effect to Convention principles in private law.[198]

Finally, having seen above the apparent strong disagreement amongst their Lordships on this issue in *Campbell*, it is worth noting Lord Hoffman's assertion that there is in fact no difference of significance between them:

---

[192] Ibid, at [50].   [193] Ibid, at [51].   [194] Ibid, at [53].
[195] 25 EHRR 371, at 95.   [196] (1999) 5 BHRC 654.   [197] Op cit.
[198] Buxton LJ argued that the HRA would have no effect on private common law, not even as a set of values, since the Convention rights 'remain, stubbornly, values whose content lives in public law' (op cit, 59).

But the importance of this case lies in the statements of general principle on the way in which the law should strike a balance between the right to privacy and the right to freedom of expression, on which the House is unanimous. The principles are expressed in varying language but speaking for myself I can see no significant differences.[199]

This myth of unanimity is also echoed by Lady Hale:

This case raises some big questions. How is the balance to be struck between everyone's right to respect for their private and family life under Article 8 of the European Convention on Human Rights and everyone's right to freedom of expression, including the freedom to receive and impart information and ideas under Article 10? *How do those rights come into play in a dispute between two private persons?* But the parties are *largely agreed* about the answers to these. They disagree [only] about where that balance is to be struck in the individual case.[200]

Note that her Ladyship, in the italicized sentence, specifically claims agreement upon the horizontal effect issue. How this claim is to be taken is uncertain. It could be that reference is being made to the fact that in the particular case, all of their Lordships accepted a strong degree of influence from the Convention case law. All also were plainly averse to the Wade view—with Lady Hale expressly ruling it out. But it seems odd to ignore wholly the clear differences that remained in the formal answer that their Lordships give to the question of horizontal effect.

POST-*CAMPBELL* CASE LAW ON HORIZONTAL EFFECT

The House of Lords appeared to reconsider the horizontal effect issue in a decision taken soon after *Campbell*, namely the appeal of *Re S (a child)*.[201] The facts are not material; the decision concerned what is known as the 'inherent jurisdiction' of the High Court to restrain reporting on matters relating to children.[202] The limits of this jurisdiction, and the different categories of case in which it would arise were considered in the leading pre-HRA case of *Re Z*.[203] In the course of giving the unanimous judgment of the House in *Re S*, Lord Steyn said this:

The House unanimously takes the view that since the 1998 Act came into force in October 2000, the earlier case law about the existence and scope of inherent jurisdiction need not be considered in this case or in similar cases. The foundation of the jurisdiction to restrain publicity in a case such as the present is now derived from Convention rights under the ECHR. This is the simple and direct way to approach such cases. In this case the jurisdiction is not in doubt.[204]

This is a remarkable passage. First of all, it is plain from the words, 'since the 1998 Act came into force', that Lord Steyn regards the change in approach he outlines *as*

---

[199] Ibid, at [36].   [200] Ibid, at [126] (emphasis added).
[201] [2005] 1 AC 593. The decision is analysed in detail in Chapter 16.
[202] *Re X (A Minor) (Wardship: Restriction on Publication)* [1975] Fam 47 esp at 57.
[203] *Re Z (A Minor) (Identification: Restrictions on Publication)* [1996] 2 WLR 88.
[204] Op cit, at [23].

brought about by the HRA. There is thus no ambiguity, as there is in some of the speeches in *Campbell,* as to the *reason* for applying Convention principles. Second, the dicta above, rather than referring to the Convention rights being 'absorbed into' an existing cause of action, or being 'taken into account' in deciding the result of such a case, appear rather to conceptualize the Convention rights as giving rise to a new jurisdiction—the previous basis for the jurisdiction, Lord Steyn declares, no longer needs to be considered. This sounds very much like the Convention rights not influencing but *replacing* the old cause of action, and thus very much like direct horizontal effect: The jurisdiction derives directly from the Convention rights themselves, as Lord Steyn puts it. The equivalent would have been for their Lordships in *Campbell* to say that there was no longer any need, in privacy cases like Campbell's, to bother about the common law of confidence, as the action could found directly on Article 8. Such an approach (if that is what his Lordship meant) would plainly run directly counter to that taken by the House in *Campbell* and to other dicta ruling out the direct application of the Convention rights.[205] It would be remarkable if the House of Lords had in *Re S* announced such a radical and controversial development without full discussion of their reasons for doing so or the limitations on the courts' new role. More implausible still is the notion that the House intended to overrule a key aspect of its decision in *Campbell,* handed down only a few months before *Re S,* to the effect that breach of confidence was the primary vehicle for protecting privacy—in other words, that *indirect* horizontal effect, of some form, was to be the key to developing privacy rights. Whilst the House of Lords has the power to overrule its previous decisions, it exercises it very sparingly; it would be astonishing if it were to overrule a decision taken so recently and without any acknowledgement of what it was doing.[206]

The better reading of *Re S,* therefore, is that it is dealing only with the application of the Convention rights in a particular setting. That setting is that such cases are not in reality a purely private dispute between two private parties. Rather, the court is taking the place of the state in terms of protecting the child from damaging reporting. Under the inherent jurisdiction it had the undoubted power to do so, and a duty in this respect, in appropriate cases. Therefore, the House was not, as such, asserting a new jurisdiction, based solely on Convention rights. Rather, because the duty under the Convention rights is, as Lord Steyn observes, broadly commensurate with its duties under the inherent jurisdiction,[207] the House was *not* using the Convention rights to assert powers that it did not have before, but rather simply taking the more 'simple and direct' route of relying on the Convention rights directly to assert what is in

---

[205] For example, *Venables,* op cit, at 917; *X v Y,* above, notes 127 to 129.

[206] See, for example, the decision of the House of Lords in *Murphy v Brentwood District Council* [1991] 1 AC 398, in which it overruled its previous decision in *Anns v Merton* [1978] AC 728: not only was there full analysis of why this step was taken, but their Lordships expressly stated that they were overruling *Anns.*

[207] 'I would observe on a historical note that a study of the case law revealed that the approach adopted in the past under the inherent jurisdiction was remarkably similar to that to be adopted under the ECHR' (op cit, at [23]).

substance the same jurisdiction as previously. It is simply implausible to read this passage in *Re S* as determining anything more than that.

The 2005 decision of the Court of Appeal in *Douglas III*,[208] the most recent judgment at the time of writing to deal with this issue, on its face contains rather more clarity than either of the House of Lords' decisions just considered. The case was again concerned with privacy—specifically whether *Hello!* magazine could be held liable to Michael Douglas and Catherine Zeta-Jones in respect of the publication of unauthorized photographs of their wedding.[209] The Court first of all addressed itself to the neglected first level of horizontal effect—the Strasbourg dimension:

[It has been observed] that the Strasbourg jurisprudence provides no definite answer to the question of whether the Convention *requires* states to provide a privacy remedy against private actors. That is no longer the case. In *Von Hannover v Germany* (24 June 2004) the Strasbourg Court gave judgment in respect of a series of complaints by Princess Caroline of Monaco.[210]

After quoting from the judgment, the Court said:

The ECtHR has recognised an obligation on member states to protect one individual from an unjustified invasion of private life by another individual and an obligation on the courts of a member state to interpret legislation in a way which will achieve that result.[211]

It may be that the Court of Appeal dealt with this matter, when others had not, simply because the judgment in *Von Hannover* had been so recently delivered, and provided such a clear and unambiguous answer to the question of the interpretation of Article 8. Nevertheless, it is welcome to have the matter addressed at all.

The Court of Appeal then turned to the question of the interpretation of the HRA itself, as an incorporating instrument and made what is perhaps the clearest statement so far, by a unanimous appellate court, on the horizontal effect issue. Lord Phillips MR, speaking for the court, said:

Some, such as the late Professor Sir William Wade, in Wade and Forsyth *Administrative Law* (8th Ed.) p 983, and Jonathan Morgan, in *Privacy, Confidence and Horizontal Effect: 'Hello' Trouble* (2003) CLJ 443, contend that the Human Rights Act should be given full, direct, horizontal effect. The courts have not been prepared to go this far.[212]

Interestingly, the judgment does not even cite Lord Steyn's comments in *Re S*, presumably indicating judicial acceptance of the view that they are confined to the specific context of the (former) inherent jurisdiction, and do not have wider application. Lord Phillips cites Lord Hoffman's rejection in *Wainwright v Home Office*[213] of 'some high level principle of privacy', and Lord Nicholl's confirmation at paragraph 11 of *Campbell v MGN* that: 'In this country, unlike the United States of America, there is no over-arching, all-embracing, cause of action for "invasion of privacy".'

---

[208] [2005] 3 WLR 881.   [209] The decision is fully discussed in Chapter 14.
[210] Op cit, at [74].   [211] Ibid, at [79].   [212] Ibid, at [50].
[213] [2003] UKHL 53; [2004] 2 AC 406.

Crucially, his Lordship then takes Lord Nicholl's dicta in *Campbell*,[214] together with those of Lady Hale,[215] as indicating a clear acceptance by the House of Lords of indirect horizontal effect. Lord Phillips in fact summarizes Lady Hale's comments on the matter:

Baroness Hale said that the Human Rights Act did not create any new cause of action between private persons. Nor could the courts invent a new cause of action to cover types of activity not previously covered. But where there is a cause of action, the court, as a public authority, must act compatibly with both parties' Convention rights.[216]

This is an accurate summary. Two points should be noted, however. First, the Court of Appeal continues the fiction promulgated by the House of Lords itself that there was no disagreement on this matter, when as we have seen, their Lordships expressed markedly divergent views. Second, Lord Phillips, whilst citing both Lord Nicholls and Lady Hale, in fact plumps for the view of the latter:

The court should, insofar as it can, develop the action for breach of confidence in such a manner as will give effect to both Article 8 and Article 10 rights.[217]

This quite clearly does *not* capture Lord Nicholls' stated approach. Lord Nicholls spoke of giving effect to 'the values underlying Articles 8 and 10'[218]—an approach which lays a much less precise obligation upon courts and so leaves them much more room for manoeuvre. The Court of Appeal, in blurring the distinction between the different approaches, thereby fails to distinguish between 'weak' indirect effect—acting in accordance with 'values' underlying an action, and 'strong' effect—acting compatibly with the rights themselves. As one of the authors has pointed out previously,[219] the latter suggests that only legal interests recognized as coming within paragraph 2 of the Convention rights could lawfully constitute reasons for overriding those articles, whereas under the weak model, a value, being only a reason for deciding a case in a particular way,[220] may be overridden by any other interest that the court finds compelling in a particular case.

CONCLUSIONS ON HORIZONTAL EFFECT

In short, then, we know that the courts *can* and have given the Convention rights a strong influence in the common law. However, by avoiding proper engagement with the academic debate, save for more or less ruling out the two extreme positions of zero and full horizontal effect, the courts have left themselves the *ability* to bring Convention principles into private law, but have not fully accepted a position in which they are bound to act compatibly with them. The dicta of the unanimous Court of Appeal in *Douglas III* cited above come closest to accepting such a clear duty, but their

---

[214] Above text to note 185.   [215] Above text to notes 166 and 167.   [216] Op cit, at [52].

[217] Ibid, at [53].   [218] Op cit, at [17].   [219] Phillipson, op cit (*MLR* 1999) at 831–2.

[220] The parallel with Dworkin's concept of principles, rather than rules, is clear at this point: Dworkin, *Taking Rights Seriously* (2nd impression, London: Duckworth, 1978).

force is undercut by the fact they are based partly on a false assessment of the speeches of Lady Hale and Lord Nicholls as espousing the same position on the matter, when they plainly did not. In terms of the media, the result has been that they have not, as they hoped, escaped from the effects of Article 8: a common law privacy right, which restricts the freedom to report *has* been developed. The judges have at least partially filled the perceived gap in protection caused by the historic failure of English law to recognize a right to privacy, but have done so through incremental development, and without reaching a clear stance on horizontal effect.

THE MARGIN OF APPRECIATION IN DOMESTIC COURTS, PROPORTIONALITY AND JUDICIAL DEFERENCE

THE GENERAL ISSUES

The major debate about deference and the standard of review under the HRA implied by section 6(1) has been in relation to judicial review of the decisions of government ministers in the sensitive contexts of national security, immigration, and asylum policy[221] and lies outside the scope of this book. We agree with Ian Leigh, however, that section 6(1) plainly makes compliance with Convention rights a matter of law to be determined by the courts.[222] Such a determination, in relation to Article 10, will generally turn on the issue of proportionality. We noted in the previous chapter that the tests applied by Strasbourg to determine proportionality can vary greatly, and suggested that UK courts should not themselves adopt some of the weaker versions of 'proportionality' sometimes used by Strasbourg, which are in fact closer to *Wednesbury* or 'heightened' *Wednesbury* review.[223] As is well known, however, some domestic decisions have precisely sought (in effect) to water down proportionality with *Wednesbury*,[224] even producing bastardised versions of the two.[225] We argued in the

---

[221] See the analysis of I. Leigh, 'Taking Rights Proportionality: Judicial Review, the Human Rights Act and Strasbourg' [1997] *PL* 265.

[222] Ibid.   [223] Ibid 282 et seq.

[224] A well-known example, which Lord Steyn felt obliged to correct ('clarify') in *Daly* (below) was the approach taken in *R (on the application of Mahmood) v Secretary of State for the Home Department* [2001] 1 WLR 840.

[225] For probably the worst example, see the judgment of Moses J in *Ismet Ala v Secretary of State for the Home Department* [2003] EWHC 521 at [44]: 'It is the Convention itself and, in particular, the concept of proportionality which confers upon the decision maker a margin of discretion in deciding where the balance should be struck between the interests of an individual and the interests of the community. A decision-maker may fairly reach one of two opposite conclusions, one in favour of a claimant the other [against him]. Of neither could it be said that the balance had been struck unfairly. In such circumstances, the mere fact that an alternative but favourable decision could reasonably have been reached will not lead to the conclusion that the decision maker has acted in breach of the claimant's human rights. Such a breach will only occur where the

previous chapter that UK courts should apply a robust version of proportionality, insisting as a minimum upon assessing whether the 'pressing social need' threshold had been crossed, and then applying a properly structured proportionality enquiry, tailored to the particular circumstances of the case.[226] In this respect, the adoption by the House of Lords in *ex p. Daly*[227] of the relatively rigorous proportionality test from *de Freitas*,[228] discussed in detail in the previous chapter, is to be welcomed. On its face, it represents the adoption by domestic courts of a more rigorous form of proportionality than that often used by the Strasbourg Court under the influence of the margin of appreciation doctrine. The chapters in this book dealing with particular subject areas consider how far the *de Freitas* test, and those used in the Strasbourg case law, are in fact being applied by domestic courts, and what the results would be were that to be done.[229]

The other issue to be discussed here concerns the application of Strasbourg case law and is related to the vexed issue of the margin of appreciation, discussed in detail in the preceding chapter. It should first of all be noted, that, whilst section 2(1) only requires the courts to 'take into account' relevant Strasbourg jurisprudence, the courts have read this section as imposing a rather more stringent obligation. As Lord Slynn suggested in *Alconbury:*[230]

In the absence of special circumstances it seems to me that the court should follow any clear and constant jurisprudence of the European Court of Human Rights. If it does not do so there is at least a possibility that the case will go to that court which is likely in the ordinary case to follow its own constant jurisprudence.

The question, however, is what 'following' Strasbourg jurisprudence means. As commentators have agreed[231] and as the House of Lords confirmed early on in

decision is outwith the range of reasonable responses to the question as to where a fair balance lies between the conflicting interests.' This plainly amounts to the kind of 'heightened' *Wednesbury* review adopted by the Court of Appeal in the pre-HRA case of *R v Ministry of Defence, ex parte Smith* [1996] 1 All ER 257, subsequently found to be inadequate as a means of protecting human rights in *Smith and Grady v UK* (2000) 29 EHRR 493.

[226] See pp 105–6.   [227] *R (Daly) v Secretary of State for the Home Department* [2001] 2 WLR 1622.

[228] *de Freitas v Permanent Secretary of Ministry of Agriculture, Fisheries, Lands and Housing* [1999] 1 AC 69, 80.

[229] The particular issue of balancing conflicting Convention rights is considered in Chapters 13 and 16.

[230] *R (on the application of Alconbury Developments Ltd) v Secretary of State for the Environment, Transport and the Regions* [2003] 2 AC 295, at [26]. This has been reinforced by other dicta: in *R v Special Adjudicator, ex parte Ullah,* [2004] UKHL 26, Lord Bingham said that 'a national court subject to a duty such as that imposed by section 2 should not without strong reason dilute or weaken the effect of the Strasbourg case law.' He also went on to make the suggestion that 'the duty of national courts is to keep pace with the Strasbourg jurisprudence as it evolves over time [but] no more.' This was a controversial suggestion that has not been echoed by other members of the judiciary, and which his Lordship arguably has not followed himself: in *R v Secretary of State for the Home Department, ex parte Razgar,* [2004] UKHL 27, decided the same day as *Ullah,* his Lordship found Article 8 to be engaged in circumstances where no Strasbourg precedent required the finding. See further, R. Masterman, 'Taking the Strasbourg Jurisprudence into Account: Developing a "Municipal Law of Human Rights" Under the Human Rights Act' (2005) 54 *ICLQ* 907.

[231] See L.J., Laws 'The Limitations of Human Rights' (1999) *PL* 254, at 258; D. Feldman, 'The Human Rights Act and Constitutional Principles' [1999] 19(2) *LS* 165 at 192; D. Pannick, 'Principles of interpretation

Kebeline,[232] and then again in *Brown v Stott*,[233] it would be clearly inappropriate for domestic courts themselves to apply the margin of appreciation doctrine developed by the ECtHR. But aside from the separate issue of developing a domestic equivalent—'the area of discretionary judgement'[234]—the judges have so far largely missed the point that disapplying the margin of appreciation needs to have *two* aspects. The first and obvious one is that the judges should refuse to import the doctrine into domestic decision-making on the Convention where no Strasbourg decision is in point; this was recognized from the outset in the decisions just mentioned. The second aspect, however, is that where the courts *are* applying Strasbourg decisions under section 2(1) HRA, they should seek to disentangle the margin of appreciation aspects from them, or at least make some allowance for the fact that the judgments they are applying are to a greater or lesser extent determined by the margin of appreciation doctrine. If judges simply apply decisions of the Strasbourg organs almost as if they are decisions of domestic appellate courts, then a doctrine intended to answer to the principled distance between an international court and a particular domestic context will be smuggled into a situation for which it was never intended—domestic judicial decision-making. Seeking to disapply the margin of appreciation might, for example, mean giving consideration to the likely outcome of the case at Strasbourg had the doctrine been disregarded. However, since, as discussed in the preceding chapter, the reasoning in much of the case law is quite sparse and tokenistic, 'stripping away' the effects of the doctrine might in practice merely mean treating certain judgments as non-determinative of the points raised at the domestic level.[235] Where it is clear that the outcome was determined by the doctrine, as in, say, *Otto Preminger*[236] or *Müller v Switzerland*,[237] where the issue hung on the necessity of taking action to protect the religious feelings of others and public morals, such decisions arguably tell us little about how a domestic court, unconstrained by the doctrine, should proceed.

So far, however, this point has gone largely unrecognized. In numerous appellate decisions under the HRA, the courts have paid lip service to the notion that the margin of appreciation has no role to play in domestic decision-making. In nearly every case—the few exceptions are discussed below—the courts have then gone on to apply Strasbourg case law heavily determined by that doctrine, thus precisely applying the margin of appreciation. On occasions, courts have then gone on to pile on top of it a further layer of deference—the discretionary area of judgment.[238]

What does this mean for judicial reasoning in media freedom cases? First, it should be recognized, when considering any doctrine of deference, that the courts, in

of Convention rights under the Human Rights Act and the discretionary area of judgement' (1998) *PL* 545; M. Hunt, R. Singh and M. Demetriou, 'Is there a Role for the "Margin of Appreciation" in National Law after the Human Rights Act?' (1999) 1 EHRLR 15, esp at 17.

[232] *R v DPP, ex parte Kebilene* [2000] 2 AC 326.
[233] *Brown v Stott (Procurator Fiscal)* [2001] 2 WLR 817.   [234] Discussed below at 149–53.
[235] See e.g. Chapter 9, at 498.   [236] (1995) 19 EHRR 34.   [237] (1991) 13 EHRR 212.
[238] The latter issue is discussed below.

applying jurisprudence already watered down by the margin of appreciation doctrine—as they nearly always do, are *already* applying a deferential standard. Second, because, while it seems clear in principle that the margin of appreciation should not be applied, but the point about its strong indirect influence through the Strasbourg case law has not generally been picked up, the application of that case law has become very discretionary. A series of choices open up for the courts.[239] Under the first of these, which may be referred to as 'minimalist', the courts, while pronouncing the margin of appreciation doctrine inapplicable, do not take the further step of recognizing and making due allowance for its influence on the Strasbourg decisions considered. Judges rely simplistically and solely on the *outcomes* of decisions at Strasbourg, without adverting to the influence of the margin of appreciation doctrine. Thus when judges are minded to carry out a minimalist audit of UK law against the Convention, they merely examine the outcomes of particular cases—even when those decisions were heavily influenced by the doctrine and, comparing the two, declare that because UK law cannot be seen clearly to breach findings of law made in the Strasbourg jurisprudence, there is no breach of the Convention. This, it is suggested, was the approach taken, for example, in *Alconbury*[240] and in *Brown v Stott*.[241] Indeed, in some cases, decisions of the Strasbourg Court under Convention Articles which that Court has itself found to call for a greater margin of appreciation have been applied to domestic decisions under a different Article altogether. Edwards[242] points out that in *Kebeline*, Lord Hope justified his contention that an area of discretionary judgment should be granted to the executive by citing the decision in *Sporrong & Lonnroth v Sweden*,[243] but that that decision concerned limitations on property rights under Article 1, Protocol 1, an Article that raises complex socio-economic considerations, which the Court has long recognized to attract a particularly wide margin of appreciation. In contrast, Lord Hope was dealing with the effects of anti-terrorist legislation raising issues under Articles 5 and 6, which have no general limitations for societal interests at all.

A second possible approach, which may be referred to as activist, would start from the premise that the reception of the Convention into UK law represents a decisive break with the past. Under this approach, judges would regard themselves as required to go *beyond* the minimal standards applied in the Strasbourg jurisprudence,[244] given

---

[239] Here we draw upon our article 'Public Protest, the Human Rights Act, and Judicial Reponses to Political Expression' [2000] *PL* 627, 644–5.

[240] *R v Secretary of State for the Environment, Transport and the Regions, ex parte Holding & Barnes Plc (Alconbury)* [2001] 2 WLR 1389, HL.

[241] Op cit.

[242] R. Edwards, 'Judicial Deference under the Human Rights Act' 65(6) *MLR* 859, 865–66. He points out that Lord Bingham made a similar category mistake in relying in *Brown v Stott* (concerning Article 6) on a decision concerning recognition of transsexuality—*Sheffield and Horsham v UK* (1998) 27 EHRR 163, which was made under Article 8 ECHR.

[243] (1982) 5 EHRR 35.

[244] In the words of Judge Martens, '[the task of domestic courts] goes further than seeing that the minimum standards laid down in the ECHR are maintained' ('Opinion: Incorporating the Convention: The Role of the Judiciary' [1998] 1 EHRLR 3).

that Strasbourg's view of itself as a system of protection firmly subsidiary to that afforded by national courts has led it in certain types of speech cases, to intervene only where clear and unequivocal transgressions have occurred. Such a stance would recognize that, as a consequence, most of the Strasbourg decisions on, for example, artistic speech, have *not* in fact required national authorities to demonstrate convincingly that the test of 'pressing social need' has been met, or conducted any meaningful analysis of the proportionality of the particular measures taken to restrict the expression in question.[245] Furthermore, significantly, a court taking such an approach would look for assistance to the general principles developed by Strasbourg. Decisions in which such a stance has been taken are considered below.

So in cases where the courts wish to adopt a minimalist stance, they can do so simply through the application *simpliciter* of the Strasbourg case law, thus introducing the margin of appreciation into domestic adjudication. On the other hand, where the courts have reasons of their own for wishing to use the Convention to engineer a change in the law, they can treat Strasbourg cases which appear *not* to demand any particular change as being non-determinative of the point; in doing so, they can rely upon the different position of the Strasbourg Court, as an international tribunal, from their own situation as domestic courts. This appears to have been the approach taken in a few notable decisions to date. For example, in *Starrs v Ruxton*,[246] the temporary sheriffs case, the judge reasoned his way skilfully past certain Strasbourg decisions that on their face implied that the arrangements for temporary sheriffs would not violate Article 6, arguing that such decisions had to be seen in context and could not be treated as decisive of the point.[247] One does not often see this sensitive and nuanced application of the Convention case law. Similarly, a Court of Appeal decision,[248] involving a challenge by the ProLife Alliance to the refusal of certain television companies[249] to broadcast its graphic and shocking election video on taste and decency grounds, entailed an explicit recognition of the different roles of the Strasbourg and domestic courts: 'The English court', Laws LJ said, 'is not a Strasbourg surrogate'. Relying on their different roles, his Lordship dismissed out of hand the relevance of a decision of the Strasbourg Court which on very similar facts—the banning of the ProLife's election video in 1997—had declared the application inadmissible on its merits, theoretically therefore, unarguable.[250] Similarly, his Lordship remarked in *Runa Begum v Tower Hamlets London*:[251]

---

[245]   As argued in Chapter 2.

[246]   [2000] HRLR 191. The case concerned a challenge to the system of appointing temporary sheriffs; the argument was that they had insufficient institutional security of tenure to render them 'independent and impartial' tribunals for the purposes of Article 6(1).

[247]   Ibid, at [21]–[23] and [33]–[35].   [248]   *R (ProLife Alliance) v BBC* [2002] 2 All ER 756.

[249]   These were imposed on the independent television companies by the Broadcasting Act 1990, s 6(1). The equivalent provision was binding on the BBC by virtue of its Agreement with the Secretary of State.

[250]   The decision is unreported: see the extract from the decision in *ProLife*, op cit, at [20].

[251]   [2002] 2 All ER 668 at [17].

. . . the court's task under the HRA . . . is not simply to add on the Strasbourg learning to the corpus of English law, as if it were a compulsory adjunct taken from an alien source, but to develop a municipal law of human rights by the incremental method of the common law, case by case, taking account of the Strasbourg jurisprudence as HRA s.2 enjoins us to do.

This choice before the court in public law cases—simply to apply Strasbourg case law—or on sound, principled grounds explicitly to recognize a different constitutional role for the domestic court and apply, in effect, a more rigorous standard of review, is a confusion which needs to be cleared up. It allows for a choice that should not be open to the judiciary. In a sense, it represents in concrete form the academic debate as to whether the HRA should properly be seen merely as a vehicle for giving easier access to Strasbourg standards via the domestic courts, or whether it should be seen as, in effect, a domestic Bill of Rights,[252] allowing for the creation of what Lord Justice Laws called in the ProLife case, 'an autonomous human rights jurisprudence'.[253]

But this is not the only stage in reasoning that occurs—the application of the Strasbourg case law, and thus the stealthy importation of the margin of appreciation doctrine. It should be recalled that the courts, once they have ascertained what the law *is* according to the Strasbourg jurisprudence, then have to *apply* it to a particular factual situation, and decide whether there was a breach of the applicable Convention right. At this point, the courts have the option of adding in a distinct extra element— the domestic notion of an area of discretionary judgment belonging to decision-making bodies that the courts should respect when reviewing their decisions under the HRA.[254] Thus, in the media regulation field, for example, courts can continue to apply traditional notions of deference to the expert assessments of media regulators in respect of the interpretation of broadcasting standards and the requirements of taste and decency, interfering only if grossly disproportionate action has been taken.[255] This entails the type of low intensity enquiry into the existence of a 'pressing social need' to restrict expression rights typified by some strands of the Strasbourg case law,[256] albeit adopted for partially different reasons. The issue of whether less intrusive means could have been adopted is either ignored or treated as an issue of regulatory expertise, to which the courts should likewise defer. As discussed below, the area of discretion to be respected can be very wide or very narrow. But the point is that, if such an approach is adopted then, in effect, a double dose of deference has been applied, twice watering down the Convention standards.

In fact, however, it can be argued that what is being added here is not a double, but a triple dose of deference: as commentators have pointed out the HRA *itself* has a strong principle of deference engineered into it. This requires further explanation. In adding in

---

[252] See further, Masterman, op cit.   [253] Op cit, at [34].

[254] This notion was first judicially formulated in *R v DPP ex parte Kebilene* [2000] 2 AC 326, 327; see also the discussion in *Secretary of State for the Home Department v International Transport Roth GmbH and Others* [2002] 1 CMLR 52.

[255] See *ProLife Alliance* [2004] 1 AC 185.

[256] E.g. *Otto-Preminger* (1995) 19 EHRR 34; *Müller v Switzerland* (1991) 13 EHRR 212. See discussion in Chapter 2.

this second layer of deference—the area of discretionary judgment—it sounds correct, at first sight, to say that particular deference should be afforded to decisions of Parliament expressed in legislation, as opposed to executive decisions. This indeed was the stance taken by the Court of Appeal in *Roth*[257]—and subsequently approved by the House of Lords in *ProLife Alliance*.[258] *Roth* involved a challenge to the draconian powers in a recent statute,[259] which made lorry drivers strictly liable for the offence of allowing illegal immigrants to use their lorries to gain entry to the UK and provided for the confiscation of their lorries if unable to pay the fine, with strictly limited powers of judicial oversight. In this case, two Court of Appeal judges agreed that greater deference should be given to Parliament than to the Executive, on democratic grounds.[260] While this sounds instinctively correct, it misses, it is suggested, an important point: the structure and design of the HRA itself *already* builds in far greater deference to Parliament than to the executive. Indeed, the design of the HRA is such as ultimately to subordinate the courts to unequivocally-expressed policy decisions of Parliament. Unlike decisions of the executive, which can simply be annulled by the courts under section 6(1),[261] statutes are protected against strike-down: section 3(2)(b) HRA tells us that the duty of the courts to interpret legislation compatibly with Convention rights 'so far as possible', set out in section 3(1), 'does not affect the validity, continuing operation or enforcement of any incompatible primary legislation'. Ultimately, under s 4 HRA,[262] the courts are confined merely to alerting Parliament to the fact that they have found an incompatibility. A declaration of incompatibility under section 4 'does not affect the validity, continuing operation or enforcement of the provision in respect of which it is given'.[263] The Act therefore itself *embodies*, through its preclusion of a strike-down power and the novel notion of the declaration of incompatibility, the notion of deference to the legislature and thus to majoritarianism. As Lord Steyn has put it, 'It is crystal clear that the carefully and subtly drafted [HRA] preserves the principle of parliamentary sovereignty.'[264] Therefore, to add in a further layer of deference on top of that which the Act itself provides is superfluous and a misreading of the Act. Klug concludes:[265]

'The issue of judicial deference to the legislature was settled through the intersection of [ss 3 and 4]. If they are applied as intended, no further doctrine of judicial deference to the legislature . . . is required.'[266]

In particular, 'deference' should not be used to water down the proportionality exercise, as use of the margin of appreciation has done at Strasbourg.

---

[257] *Secretary of State for the Home Department v International Transport Roth GmbH and Others* [2002] 1 CMLR 52.
[258] [2003] 2 WLR 1403 at [74].   [259] The Asylum and Immigration Act 1999.
[260] Op cit at [83] (Laws LJ) and [28] (Simon Browne LJ).
[261] Unless protected by incompatible legislation: s 6(2).
[262] Under which a declaration of incompatibility may be made if a provision of primary legislation is incompatible with the Convention rights (s 4(1) and (2)) or if a provision of subordinate legislation is incompatible and the primary legislation it is made under prevents the removal of the incompatibility (s 4(3) and (4)).
[263] S (4)(6)(a).   [264] *R v DPP ex parte Kebilene* [2000] 2 AC 326, 327.
[265] 'Judicial Deference under the Human Rights Act' (2003) 2 EHRLR 125.   [266] Ibid, at 128.

As indicated in the introduction to this chapter, the notion of deference to the executive in reviewing its decisions for compatibility for Convention rights rarely arises in relation to media law, since most of the media consists of private bodies. The issue that *is* of relevance to this book is the predisposition of the courts to afford regulators a very wide area of 'discretionary judgement,' an issue to which we now turn.

DEFERENCE AND MEDIA LAW

The decisions concerning judicial review of the regulators decision on privacy are examined in detail in Chapter 17, which deals with that specific area. However, it is appropriate to make a few observations about the leading post-HRA decision in the area of media regulation, the decision of the House of Lords in *R (on the application of ProLife Alliance) v BBC*,[267] now the leading post-HRA decision on judicial review of regulatory decisions relating to the broadcasters.

This decision gives strong endorsement at the highest level to the notion of heavy, and arguably unprincipled, judicial deference to media regulators.[268] The decision is considered in detail in Chapter 11,[269] but, in brief, the House of Lords had to consider a challenge to the decision of the BBC and other independent broadcasters[270] to refuse to broadcast, uncut, a Party Election Broadcast by the ProLife Party, which contained shocking and explicit footage of abortions being carried out. The relevant statutory provision governing the regulator, the ITC—but *not* the BBC[271]—was section 6(1)(a) of the Broadcasting Act 1990,[272] by which the ITC was bound to ensure that every licensed television service included *nothing* in its programmes 'which offends against good taste and decency or is likely . . . to be offensive to public feeling'. Despite the fact that their Lordships were dealing with censorship of directly political speech, they decided that, as Barendt puts it, 'it would be wrong for the courts to question the assessment of [the BBC] that the broadcast would be offensive'.[273] Jeffrey Jowell describes certain dicta of Lord Hoffman as 'heavy with deference.'[274] That deference was paid both to the individual decision made by the BBC, and also to the decision of Parliament to subject broadcasting to a taste and decency regime. Indeed, as Chapter 11 points out, their Lordships were so intent upon finding reasons *not* to

---

[267] [2003] 2 WLR 1403.

[268] In this case the BBC Governors, in deciding not to broadcast a PEB as submitted by the ProLife Alliance Party.

[269] And in Chapter 17.

[270] The independent broadcasters were not directly involved in the case, but their obligations were the same as those of the BBC, though, in their case, coming from statute. See further Chapter 11 at 577–80.

[271] The BBC's Agreement mirrored the wording of the statutory provision, but the statute itself did not apply to the BBC.

[272] Now superseded by similar but more extensive provisions under s 319, Part 3 Communications Act 2003; for discussion, see Chapter 11.

[273] E. Barendt, 'Free Speech and Abortion' [2004] *PL* 580, 584.

[274] 'Judicial Deference: servility, civility or institutional capacity?' [2004] *PL* 592, 600.

interfere with the broadcaster's decision that they, remarkably, omitted to give any consideration to the question whether section 3(1) HRA could be used to narrow down the very general words used in section 6(1)(a). Clearly, as the Court of Appeal had found, what is 'good taste and decency' and what is 'offensive' depends very much upon the context, and the general public, as citizens of a mature democracy, might well be prepared to accept more shocking images in the context of a political broadcast than in, say, an entertainment programme.[275] However, ignoring this point altogether, Lord Nicholls and Lord Hoffman instead treated section 6(1)(a) of the Broadcasting Act as pre-determining the outcome of this particular case, despite its extremely general wording, in that they insisted upon regarding any questioning of the particular *decision* of the BBC as in effect taking the view that the statutory provision 'should be disregarded or not taken seriously'.[276] In fact, as pointed out in Chapter 11, the challenge to the particular decision made in the case involved merely using the HRA to *re-interpret* that provision, as it was applied to Election Broadcasts.[277] This almost wilful characterization of the applicant's argument, and of the nature of the statutory provision, is striking; it indicates a judicial desire to defer so heavily to the judgement of broadcasters in this area that the judicial function under the HRA is arguably abnegated altogether. The same may be said, *a fortiori*, of the almost inexplicable failure of the House of Lords to take the point that the statute *did not in any event apply to the BBC*, which was bound only by its non-statutory Agreement.[278]

In short, judicial decisions on media regulators indicate that even where fundamental rights are at stake, the courts are strongly reluctant to overturn the decisions of regulators exercising their statutory powers and duties.[279] What is notable about the judicial approach is that it fails to differentiate between two different stages of the decision-making process. Part of the decision-making process of regulators or broadcasters in cases like *ProLife* consists of working out what exactly would be the likely (or actual) level of offence caused by a particular broadcast. This is a matter of fact or, more accurately, of expert opinion, based presumably upon detailed knowledge of the numbers of complaints received in relation to the broadcast in question, or in relation to previous, similar broadcasts, and of the results of any polling or research on the subject, and so on. In other words, this part of the determination is one that the regulator has particular, indeed, unique expertise and experience to make. Thus where a regulator makes a decision that a given part of a programme had caused (say) a high level of offence, that is a determination which, on the ground of deference based upon institutional competence, should properly be deferred to by the courts. As Jeffrey Jowell puts it:

---

[275] See [2002] 3 WLR 1080, at [37].   [276] Op cit, at [52].   [277] See pp 586–7.

[278] This aspect of the decision is discussed further at ibid.

[279] The exception, of course, is the decision of the Court of Appeal in the *ProLife* case, which robustly found the BBC's decision to be a wholly unjustifiable interference with the right to freedom of expression: [2002] 3 WLR 1080.

Although the courts have no need to defer (in any sense of that term) to Parliament or its agents on the basis of their legitimacy as bodies which command 'majority approval', it is quite appropriate for courts modestly to acknowledge a practical appreciation of their own institutional limitations. There will be occasions where other bodies, whether Parliament, the executive or a non-departmental public body containing specialist expertise, will be better equipped to decide certain questions. The extent and degree of concession of course depends upon context and the right and interest involved.[280]

In contrast, the second stage in the determination—deciding whether the level of offence likely to be caused justifies a restriction upon the broadcaster's Article 10 rights—is a *normative* question of proportionality; as such it is one that in terms of both competency and function falls squarely within the remit of the courts.[281] Courts are expressly instructed by section 6(1) HRA to decide such questions. Whilst the Court of Appeal in *ProLife* recognized that it was their constitutional responsibility to so do—albeit by reference primarily to common law principles—the House of Lords refused to take this point. The Lords' position was that Parliament had already decided the issue at hand (the balance between freedom of expression and offence avoidance); this not only clearly failed to appreciate that the very broad terms of section 6(1)(a) could not with any plausibility be said to have decided anything as specific as the balance to be struck in a particular case; it also wilfully refused to acknowledge that Parliament had also given to the courts the final responsibility of ensuring compatibly with Convention rights, and the duty to reinterpret statutes to achieve this goal, in the HRA. In short, the approach of the Law Lords to deference in *ProLife* is both analytically unsophisticated and comes close to abnegation of the courts' constitutional responsibilities to protect fundamental rights.

INTERIM INJUNCTIONS

This is an are a of particular concern to the media. The injunction is not only the most drastic interference with media freedom, it is also of greatest concern for the public— if an article is injuncted, the flow of information it represents is stopped dead; in contrast, if damages are awarded after the fact, or even a criminal sanction imposed, then the public has at least been able to benefit from receiving the speech in question.

The test for injunctive relief in cases affecting freedom of expression is now governed by section 12(1)–(3) HRA, which provides:

12(1) This section applies if a court is considering whether to grant any relief which, if granted, might affect the exercise of the Convention right to freedom of expression.

  (3) No such relief is to be granted so as to restrain publication before trial unless the

---

[280] 'Judicial Deference, Servility, Civility or Institutional Capacity?' [2003] *PL* 592, at 599.
[281] Ibid.

court is satisfied that the applicant is likely to establish that publication should not be allowed.[282]

Section 12(3) applies in all *civil law* cases.[283] Clearly, therefore, as well as cases between private parties, such as privacy claims, it would apply to injunctions sought by the Government to restrain a threatened breach of confidence, on national security grounds;[284] it would also, probably, apply to injunctions sought by the Attorney General in reliance on the strict liability rule in the Contempt of Court Act to prevent a threatened criminal contempt of court,[285] since the injunction would not be *granted* in criminal proceedings, although its breach could lead to them.

The leading case on the interpretation of section 12(3) is *Cream Holdings Limited and others v Banerjee and others*.[286] Banerjee was a senior accountant for Cream Holdings. She was dismissed and took with her copies of documents that appeared to show illegal and improper financial activities by the company, which she then passed to the *Echo* newspaper. The *Echo* published articles allegedly showing corruption involving a director of Cream and a council official. Cream sought injunctions to prevent further publication. The question was: what was the test to be applied in deciding whether to grant such an injunction? The old test was that the applicant had, as a threshold test, to show that he or she had a 'real prospect of success' at final trial. If so, the court would consider where the 'balance of convenience' lay[287] between the case for granting an injunction and that of leaving the applicant to his or her remedy in damages. The question was how this test should be modified, given the terms of section 12(3) HRA. Lord Nicholls examined first the reasons for the enactment of that provision, namely, press concern that under the old 'balance of convenience' test:

Orders imposing prior restraint on newspapers might readily be granted by the courts to preserve the status quo until trial whenever applicants claimed that a threatened publication would infringe their rights under Article 8. Section 12(3) was enacted to allay these fears. Its principal purpose was to buttress the protection afforded to freedom of speech at the interlocutory stage.[288]

The reference to 'preserving the status quo' means that, once the applicant has made

---

[282] Ss (2) provides some procedural protection against interim injunctions. It provides: 'If the person against whom the application for relief is made ("the respondent") is neither present nor represented, no such relief is to be granted unless the court is satisfied—

(a) that the applicant has taken all practicable steps to notify the respondent; or
(b) that there are compelling reasons why the respondent should not be notified.'

Essentially this sharply limits the circumstances in which *ex parte* injunctions against publication can be granted. The respondent media body must be present, absent the limited circumstances set out in (a) and (b).

[283] S 12 (5) provides: ' "relief" includes any remedy or order (*other* than in criminal proceedings)' (emphasis added).

[284] As in the notorious *Spycatcher* litigation: *A-G v Guardian Newspapers Ltd* [1987] 1 WLR 1248.

[285] See *A-G v MGN* [1987] 1 QB 1, on which, see further Chapter 5.

[286] [2004] 3 WLR 918. For comment see Smith, ATH [2005] 64(1) *CLJ* 4.

[287] *American Cyanamid Co v Ethicon Ltd* [1975] AC 396.   [288] Op cit, at [15].

out an arguable case for confidentiality, the court will be inclined to grant an interim injunction on the basis that if the story were to be published, the information would lose its confidential character, and there would be nothing to have a final trial about.[289] This consideration could be outweighed by the public interest defence at this stage, provided that the defence were supported by evidence and had a credible chance of success at final trial.[290] However, the pre-HRA test was potentially unfavourable to the media because, in balancing the rights of the two parties, courts tended to take the view that while the plaintiff's right to confidentiality would be wholly defeated by publication, the press could always still publish the story if they won at final trial; they were thus inclined toward protecting the more fragile right of the plaintiff.[291]

The leading speech was delivered by Lord Nicholls, with whom all their Lordships agreed. His Lordship said:

'Likely' in section 12(3) cannot have been intended to mean 'more likely than not' in *all* situations [emphasis added] . . . [Section 12(3)] makes the likelihood of success at the trial an essential element in the court's consideration of whether to make an interim order. But . . . there can be no single, rigid standard governing all applications for interim restraint orders. Rather, on its proper construction, the effect of section 12(3) is that the court is not to make an interim restraint order unless satisfied that the applicant's prospects of success at the trial are sufficiently favourable to justify such an order being made in the particular circumstances of the case. As to what degree of likelihood makes the prospects of success 'sufficiently favourable', the general approach should be that courts will be exceedingly slow to make interim restraint orders where the applicant has not satisfied the court he will probably ('more likely than not') succeed at the trial. In general, that should be the threshold an applicant must cross before the court embarks on exercising its discretion, duly taking into account the relevant jurisprudence on article 10 and any countervailing Convention rights. But there will be cases where it is necessary for a court to depart from this general approach and a lesser degree of likelihood will suffice as a prerequisite.[292]

Lord Nicholls said that he had in mind, as instances in which a lesser degree of likelihood would suffice, two categories of case. One would be where an injunction of short duration (days or hours) was required in order to give a judge time to consider the case properly:

an application [may be] made to the court for an interlocutory injunction to restrain publication of allegedly confidential or private information until trial. The judge needs an opportunity to read and consider the evidence and submissions of both parties. Until then the judge will often not be in a position to decide whether on balance of probability the applicant will succeed in obtaining a permanent injunction at the trial. In the nature of things this will take time, however speedily the proceedings are arranged and conducted.

---

[289] See *Attorney General v Guardian Newspapers (No 2)* [1990] 1 AC 109; *Francome v Mirror Group Newspapers* [1984] 1 WLR 892, 900; *Lion Laboratories v Evans and Express Newspapers* [1984] 1 QB 530, 551.

[290] *See Lion Laboratories*, op cit, 538, 548, 553; similarly in *Hellewell v Chief Constable of Derbyshire* [1995] 1 WLR 804, where the public interest argument prevented the award of an injunction.

[291] See *A-G v Guardian Newspapers Ltd* [1987] 1 WLR 1248, 1292 and 1305.   [292] Op cit, at [22]

The courts are remarkably adept at hearing urgent applications very speedily, but inevitably there will often be a lapse of some time in resolving such an application, whether measured in hours or longer in a complex case. What is to happen meanwhile? Confidentiality, once breached, is lost for ever. Parliament cannot have intended that, whatever the circumstances, section 12(3) would preclude a judge from making a restraining order for the period needed for him to form a view on whether on balance of probability the claim would succeed at trial. That would be absurd . . . Similarly, if a judge refuses to grant an interlocutory injunc-tion preserving confidentiality until trial the court ought not to be powerless to grant interim relief pending the hearing of an interlocutory appeal against the judge's order.[293]

In other words, short-term injunctions might be required simply in order to allow a judge sufficient time to make a reasoned finding as to whether an applicant *was* likely to succeed at final trial. This must be right—the courts cannot operate on guess-work.

The other category of cases which Lord Nicholls had in mind as requiring a lower standard for the granting of an injunction than 'more likely than not' was as follows:

Cases may arise where the adverse consequences of disclosure of information would be extremely serious, such as a grave risk of personal injury to a particular person. Threats may have been made against a person accused or convicted of a crime or a person who gave evidence at a trial. Disclosure of his current whereabouts might have extremely serious consequences. Despite the potential seriousness of the adverse consequences of disclosure, the applicant's claim to confidentiality may be weak. The applicant's case may depend, for instance, on a disputed question of fact on which the applicant has an arguable but distinctly poor case. It would be extraordinary if in such a case the court were compelled to apply a 'probability of success' test and therefore, regardless of the seriousness of the possible adverse consequences, refuse to restrain publication until the disputed issue of fact can be resolved at the trial.[294]

Clearly, his Lordship has mind cases such as *Venables and Thompson*,[295] in which the key claim of the applicants was that revelations in the press of their whereabouts and identity as the notorious killers of Jamie Bulger would be likely to put their lives at risk.[296]

Thus, in essence, in most cases, an injunction will be awarded only if the judge considers it more likely than not that the applicant will succeed at final trial.[297] So if the scales appear to be so evenly balanced between the parties that it is not possible to say who is more likely to win at final trial, interim relief will be refused, as set out in *A v B*.[298] Courts will of course have to take account of Article 10 jurisprudence on interim injunctions; indeed, section 12 instructs them to have 'particular regard' to Article 10. The leading case on prior restraints is *Observer and Guardian v UK*,[299] in which the Strasbourg Court considered the compatibility with Article 10 of interim

---

[293] Ibid, at [17]–[18].   [294] Ibid, at [19].

[295] *Venables and another v News Group Newspapers* [2001] 1 All ER 908.

[296] A decision with very similar facts is *X (A woman formerly known as Mary Bell) v SO* [2003] EWHC 1101.

[297] As discussed above.   [298] [2002] 3 WLR 542, at [12].

[299] (1991) 14 EHRR 153.

injunctions preventing those newspapers from publishing *Spycatcher* material.[300] The Court laid down a basic principle:

> while Article 10 does not in terms prohibit the imposition of prior restraints on publication . . . the dangers inherent in [them] are such that they call for the most careful scrutiny on the part of the Court . . . news is a perishable commodity and delay of its publication, even for a short period, may well deprive it of all its value and interest.[301]

While the Court's actual decision in the case seemed to suggest that the need to preserve the applicant's rights will in itself point strongly towards the imposition of an interim injunction,[302] the relatively cautious approach adopted may have been influenced by the fact that the very sensitive issue of national security was at stake. It is suggested that the domestic judiciary should look rather to the general principle laid down in the case—that the granting of interim injunctions is a particularly significant *prima facie* infringement of Article 10. This factor would then have to be weighed against the strength of the privacy claim, in the manner suggested earlier, and, in accordance with section 12(3), a court should grant an interim injunction only if it considers that the privacy argument is the stronger one.

SECTION 3(1) HRA AND MEDIA LAW

Here we consider the ambiguity surrounding section 3(1) HRA—perhaps its most important provision, since it makes the HRA into a kind of meta-statute, whose provisions affect the interpretation of all other statutes, past and future, unless and until s 3(1) is itself repealed. As this book will reveal, the field of media freedom examined here does *not* disclose numerous instances of statutory provisions which, on their face throw up sharp apparent incompatibilities with the Convention rights, thus requiring a stiff dose of section 3(1). The Contempt of Court Act, the various statutes dealing with obscenity and indecency, the Copyright Act, the Public Order Act dealing with incitement to racial hatred are all, on their face, broadly compatible with Article 10, as interpreted by Strasbourg.[303] The only statute that really raises a difficult question of compatibility with Article 10, bringing section 3(1) strongly into play, is the Official Secrets Act, and the House of Lords has already answered the question—in the negative—whether that provision can be used to liberalize substantially

---

[300] The case is discussed in more detail in Chapter 19.   [301] Ibid, [60].

[302] The initial injunctions, which prevented publication for over a year, were found not to violate Article 10, they were held to be justified on the basis that they had the aim of maintaining the A-G's ability to bring a case claiming permanent injunctions: see I. Leigh, (1992) *PL* 200.

[303] One provision of the Communications Act has already been noted to be flatly *in*compatible with Article 10; the provisions relating to taste and decency are phrased in sufficiently broad terms to be readily read compatibly: see further Chapter 11.

the protection for media revelations under section 1 of that Act.[304] Meanwhile, the Communications Act 2003 does contain one provision—the ban on political advertising[305]—which led the Government to decline to make a statement under s 19 of the HRA that the 2003 Act was compatible with the Convention rights. However, it appears to be virtually impossible for any radical re-reading of that provision to render it Convention-compliant to be attempted by the courts, such are its terms.

Thus, our consideration of section 3(1) does not need to go into the intricacies of the debate surrounding the outer limits of permissible judicial reinterpretation of statutes, as represented, for example, by the lively debate surrounding the House of Lords' decision in R v A.[306] Instead, we wish to make a more general point. It is clear that the attempt to preserve parliamentary sovereignty by allowing the courts only to interpret statutes compatibly with Convention rights 'if possible' has had the further, perhaps unforeseen consequence, of adding further ambiguity to the whole scheme of rights protection introduced by the HRA. Had section 3(1) amounted to a straightforward 'strike-down' power, or even an application of the normal doctrine of implied repeal whereby at least pre-HRA statutes would be deemed impliedly repealed if found to be incompatible, then the courts would only have had to determine two things: what the Convention required, and whether the statute was compatible or not with that. But because of the balancing act with sovereignty represented by section 3(1), having gone through these two stages in reasoning, the courts then have to go on to decide a third issue: would the change in the meaning of the statute required to bring it into line with the Convention be a 'possible' reading of it under section 3(1), given both the wording of that section and (now) the considerable appellate jurisprudence on what section 3(1) means, some of it arguably contradictory in spirit, if not in letter.

It is clear that the word 'possible' has no fixed meaning and that the decisions so far have not resolved the ambiguity inherent in section 3. The majority decision in R v A, (the rape shield case),[307] is now well known for its suggestion that only if a clear incompatibility is stated in terms will section 3(1) be unable to furnish a Convention-friendly meaning; notoriously also, the decision effectively rewrote the provision in question. As Lord Hope pointed out, the whole point of the provision was to *exclude* judicial discretion to admit evidence of the complainant's precious sexual history,

---

[304] *R v Shayler* [2003] 1 AC 247. Issues remain about the compatibility of remaining provisions of the Act, an issue considered in Chapter 19.

[305] *Per* s 321.

[306] *R v A (Complainant's Sexual History)*; [2002] 1 AC 45 (HL). For the latest word in this debate, and a spirited defence of that decision, see A. Kavanagh, 'Unlocking the Human Rights Act: the "radical approach" to section 3(1) revisited' (2005) 3 *EHRLR* 259. On s 3(1) generally, see A. Lester, 'The Art of the Possible—Interpreting Statutes under the Human Rights Act' [1009] *EHRLR* 665; F. Bennion, 'What Interpretation is "Possible" under Section 3(1) of the Human Rights Act' [2000] *PL* 77; R. Edwards, 'Reading down Legislation under the Human Rights Act' (2000) 20 *LS* 353; C. Gearty, 'Reconciling Parliamentary Democracy and Human Rights' (2002) 118 *LQR* 248; G. Phillipson, '(Mis)Reading Section 3(1) of the Human Rights Act' (2003) *LQR* 000; A. Young, 'Judicial Sovereignty and the Human Rights Act 1998' [2002] *CLJ* 53.

[307] Op cit.

unless the specified and very narrow conditions set out by Parliament in the provision in question were met.[308] The effect of Lord Steyn's reinterpretation of that provision was to restore that discretion, subject only to the broader qualification that it should be exercised positively where that was necessary to achieve a fair trial, in compliance with Article 6 EHCR.

The more recent *ProLife Alliance* case in the Court of Appeal[309] was also, we would suggest, rather cavalier in relation to the governing statute, but in a different way. Laws LJ, having concluded that both common law and Article 10 protection for freedom of expression forbade censorship of the ProLife video, did not even bother to explain how the governing statute, the Broadcasting Act 1990, could be read compatibly with this view. Section 6(1)(a) of that Act[310] requires the Regulators to ensure that '*nothing is included in broadcasts which offends against good taste or decency.*' However, perhaps surprisingly, Laws LJ did not expressly deal with the application of section 3 HRA to the statute. He simply said, 'the Broadcasting Act 1990 . . . must be read conformably with this principle'.[311]

The House of Lords also more or less ignored section 3 when the case came to it, but for very different reasons. As discussed above, the House seemed so anxious to defer to the views of the broadcasters that it appeared to forget its duty as a court to interpret the legislation in issue—the Broadcasting Act—compatibly with the Convention rights if possible. There was clearly a route to it reinterpretation that could have been taken up. Since the provision in question, forbidding the broadcast of anything offensive to 'good taste and decency', was particularly vague and open-ended ('good taste' and 'decency' are clearly terms that have no fixed meaning), it would clearly have been possible to reinterpret them so that much more robust standards were applicable to PEBs than, say, to entertainment programmes. As Barendt points out,[312] Simon-Browne LJ in the Court of Appeal made the point that precisely this approach has been adopted by the BBC itself in relation to the transmission of shocking and upsetting images, for example of dead children and cruelty to animals, in the context of serious news or analysis programmes. In other words, the taste and decency provisions were context-sensitive, and viewers in a mature democracy may rightly be expected to tolerate shocking or disturbing images in the context of a broadcast with a serious political or public interest intent.[313] This seems an instance in which the duty under section 3(1) was not so much given a limited scope, as ignored altogether.

Re W and B[314] contains a much more considered decision not to use section 3(1) to bring about radical changes to a statute, and its dicta endorse a restrained reading of that provision. Lord Nicholls observed that a reading of legislation under section 3(1) should not 'depart substantially from a fundamental feature of an Act of Parliament.'

---

[308] Ibid, at 87.   [309] [2002] 2 All ER 756.
[310] It has now been replaced by the more extensive provisions of s 319 of the Communications Act 2003.
[311] Ibid, at [44].   [312] E. Barendt, 'Free Speech and Abortion' [2003] *PL* 580.
[313] See Barendt, ibid, at 586 and the judgment of Simon Browne LJ (note 309 above) at [61]–[62].
[314] *Re W and B (Children) (Care Plan), Re W (Children) (Care Plan)* [2002] 2 WLR 720.

There are now well-known dicta to like effect from C.J. Woolf in *Poplar Housing*[315] and of Lord Hope in *R v Lambert*.[316] Lord Hope's observation in that case that section 3 'did not authorise the judges to overrule decisions which the language of the statute shows have been taken on the very point at issue by the legislator' is particularly worthy of note because that, clearly, was precisely what the majority did do in *R v A*.

However, one can take this point—the inconsistency between judicial *statements* as to the proper limits to the use of section 3(1) and their actual use of it—a stage further. It may be argued that the ambiguity inherent in section 3(1)—and the failure of the higher courts' attempts to cut that ambiguity down through interpretation—may be seen in *Lambert* itself. Our suggestion would be that the re-reading of the legislation in that case (The Misuse of Drugs Act) *did* effectively overrule a parliamentary decision, precisely what Lord Hope in that case said should not be done. The statute in question concerned a reverse onus clause which arguably violated Article 6(2) ECHR. As drafted, it clearly placed a *legal* burden on the accused: if he could not prove that he was ignorant of the fact that the substance he had in his possession was a controlled drug, he would be convicted. This could obviously happen in the case of reasonable doubt as to his innocence, since he might raise some doubt as to his state of knowledge based on certain facts, but be unable to prove his ignorance outright and thus his innocence. Their Lordships felt themselves able to reinterpret this provision, using section 3(1), into merely an *evidential* burden. Under this different type of clause, the accused merely has to *lead evidence* pointing to his ignorance so as to raise a triable issue; the burden then passes to the prosecution to prove that he was actually ignorant. In other words, the House of Lords read the words, 'proves that he neither believed or suspected that the substance in question was a controlled drug' as meaning, 'leads evidence such as to raise an issue as to whether he knew that the substance in question was a controlled drug'.

Now while such a rereading of persuasive reverse burden clauses into evidential ones has been endorsed previously by the House of Lords,[317] it is strongly arguable that it crosses into the forbidden territory articulated in *Lambert* itself, because it clearly 'overrules a decision which the language of the statute shows has been taken on the very point at issue by the legislator'.[318] As was pointed out in *Lambert*, Parliament responded to the decision in *Kebeline* on a similar clause by using only evidential reverse onus clauses in the Terrorism Act 2000. Clearly, a different choice was made in the Misuse of Drugs Act. In other words, their Lordships accepted that there were two options for Parliament when devising reverse onus clauses—whether to impose a legal or only an evidential legal burden—and that in some instances Parliament had chosen one, and in some the other. In the Act they were considering, Parliament had

---

[315] *Poplar Housing and Regeneration Community Association Limited v Secretary of State for the Environment, Transport and the Regions* [2002] QB 48.

[316] *R v Lambert* [2001] 3 All ER 577.

[317] In *R v DPP, ex p Kebilene* [2000] 2 AC 326; see also G. Williams, 'The Logic of "Exceptions" ' [1988] *CLJ* 261.

[318] As Dr Kavanagh has also recently pointed out: op cit ('Unlocking'), at 264–5.

clearly chosen to place a *legal* burden—in contrast to its choice in the Terrorism Act. The effect of converting this into an *evidential* burden was precisely then to overrule the decision made on the point by Parliament. *Lambert* therefore, we would suggest, crossed the very boundary separating interpretation from legislation which it set out. In so doing, it demonstrates, we would argue, that section 3(1) has irretrievably added a highly significant locus of judicial choice over and above those which adhere in both analysing and applying the Convention case law and that judicial attempts to clarify its scope and restrict that discretion have so far largely failed.

In terms of *academic* attempts, the authors find Dr Kavanagh's analysis of the section 3(1) cases[319] the most persuasive, at least in analytical terms,[320] in that it highlights the wide variety of factors that the courts in fact use in deciding how radical an approach to take to the reinterpretation of statutes under section 3. The breath and number of factors used by the courts and the uncertainty of the interplay between them, means that the courts retain a great deal of discretion in their application of the interpretive obligation. Effectively, as Kavanagh points out, the courts will interpret statutes compatibly, not where it is 'possible' to do so, but where they think it *appropriate*, all things considered, to do so.[321]

A number of factors are relevant. Clearly of importance is the court's concern not to cross the line between interpretation and legislation. Thus the decision in *Re S and Re W*,[322] Kavanagh argues, indicates that, whilst the courts are prepared to 'read words into' statutes, as in *R v A*, they will not do so, 'as a way of radically reforming a whole statute or writing a quasi-legislative code granting new powers and setting out new procedures to replace that statute'[323]—one reason for the refusal of the House of Lords to use section 3(1) in *Re S and Re W*.[324] This factor also applied in *Anderson*,[325] in which the incompatibility lay in the involvement of the Secretary of State in sentencing adult life prisoners. Whilst it might conceivably have been linguistically possible to have read the Secretary of State's role out of the legislation, his role was a feature that was a pervasive one: unlike *R v A*, or even *Lambert*, where the problem

---

[319] See A. Kavanagh, op cit ('Unlocking') and 'Statutory interpretation and human rights after Anderson: a more contextual approach', [2004] *PL* 537, which is a response, in part to D. Nicol, 'Statutory interpretation and human rights after Anderson', [2004] *PL* 273.

[320] That is, it seems the most accurate analysis of the current judicial approach: we are not persuaded however, that the courts *should* use such a wide variety of factors, including in particular the likely future actions of Parliament, as Dr Kavanagh argues for.

[321] Op cit ('Contextual'), at 544–5.

[322] [2002] 2 AC 291. 'The Court of Appeal had read into the Children Act 1989 a range of new powers and procedures by which courts could supervise and monitor the implementation of care orders by local authorities, so as to protect children against violations of their rights under Art.8 ECHR.' (Kavanagh ('Contextual') at 538). This decision was reversed unanimously by the House of Lords.

[323] Op cit ('Contextual'), at 540.   [324] Op cit.

[325] *R (on the application of Anderson) v Secretary of State for the Home Department* [2003] 1 AC 837. The House of Lords instead issued a declaration of incompatibility on the ground that a power conferred on the Home Secretary by s 29 of the Crime (Sentencing) Act 1997 to control the release of mandatory life sentence prisoners was inconsistent with the right to have sentence imposed by 'an independent and impartial tribunal', *per* Article 6 ECHR.

lay only in a particular sub-section of the statute, the role of the Secretary of State was embedded in the statute as a whole.

The subject matter of the statute is also of relevance. Where it relates to an aspect of the criminal or civil justice system, such as sentencing, or admissibility of evidence, a robust line is to be expected from the courts; the judges consider that the regulation of such matters lies within the sphere of their own constitutional responsibility. Hence the 'activist' uses of section 3(1) in both *R v A* and *R v Offen*.[326] Where by contrast the case involves issues of social policy or resource allocation, the courts are much less likely to be bold. Thus another reason for the decision in *Re S* is that the proposed 'interpretation' of the statute would also have had: 'far-reaching practical ramifications for local authorities and their care of children, including the authority's allocation of scarce financial and other resources.'[327]

Such contextual factors also explain the decision in *Bellinger v Bellinger*,[328] according to Kavanagh's persuasive analysis. Clearly in this case it would have been more than possible, as a matter of linguistics, to interpret the single word 'female' as including a 'female' who had arrived at that gender as a result of human intervention (i.e. post-operative transsexuals); nevertheless, the House of Lords refused to reinterpret the word in the way suggested. This case clearly demonstrates that the judges do not regard the word 'possible' in section 3(1) as connoting only linguistic possibility— nothing could have been easier, linguistically, than the reinterpretation of a single word. Their Lordships were persuaded not to do so because of a range of what essentially are policy matters; as Kavanagh puts it:

the resulting change in the law would have [had] far-reaching practical ramifications, raising issues whose solution calls for extensive inquiry and the widest public consultation and discussion which was more appropriate for Parliament than the courts.[329]

In contrast, in *Ghaidan v Godin-Mendoza*,[330] the interpretive task required not merely changing the meaning given to certain words, but the implication of (a few) words that were not there. On the death of a protected tenant of a dwelling-house, his or her surviving spouse, if then living in the house, becomes a statutory tenant by succession. But a person who was living with the original tenant 'as his or her wife or husband' is

---

[326] [2001] 1 WLR 253. The case concerned the 'reading down' of provisions governing draconian mandatory sentences for repeat offenders.

[327] Kavanagh, op cit ('Contextual'), at 540.

[328] [2003] 2 AC 467 (HL). W, a post-operative transsexual, appealed against a decision under the Matrimonial Causes Act 1973 that she was not lawfully married to her husband, H, because she, W, was in fact a man. Section 11 of the 1973 Act states: 'A marriage . . . shall be void on the following grounds only, that is to say . . . that the parties are not respectively male and female . . .'. W argued that the word 'female' should be interpreted as including her and other post-operative transsexuals, relying on her right to private and family life under Article 8 ECHR.

[329] Op cit, ("Contextual") at 541.

[330] [2004] 2 AC 557 (HL). The case concerned the reinterpretation of a statute so as to give members of homosexual couples the same rights to succeed to tenancies upon the death of their partner as were enjoyed by heterosexual couples.

treated as the spouse of the original tenant and so also succeeds to the tenancy.[331] The House of Lords, confronted with a claim that the inapplicability of this inheritance right to stable homosexual couples violated Article 8 read with Article 14,[332] managed to hold that the words living with the tenant 'as his or her wife or husband' could be interpreted as meaning: 'living with the tenant, as *if they were* his or her wife or husband'. Thus, in this case, the change, much more difficult linguistically from that required in *Bellinger*, was carried out. This appears to have been because, unlike in *Bellinger v Bellinger*, the change in meaning to the law was a straightforward one, affected only one provision of the statute, and did not (their Lordships evidently felt) have wide-ranging policy ramifications that should be left to Parliament to decide. Moreover, as Klug and Starmer put it,[333] the reinterpretation was 'fairly viewed as compatible with the thrust of the statute, which was intended to include cohabiting as well as married couples, but on its face discriminated against homosexuals'. A final factor that influenced the House in *Bellinger* was the fact that the Government had conceded that the area of law in question was now incompatible with the Convention and had announced its intention to bring legislation before Parliament to remedy the matter. In the circumstances, the courts preferred to leave reform of the law to that more systematic method, a factor which also appeared to apply in *Anderson*.[334]

As far as this book is concerned, the conclusion is that statutes restricting media freedom therefore *may* be subject to radical reinterpretation, on *Mendoza* or *R v A* lines; whether they *will* be is a complex question, to which answers can only be given in concrete cases, having examined the range of contextual matters explained by Kavanagh.

CONCLUSIONS

This chapter has not sought to present or argue for a 'theory of the Human Rights Act'; its more modest and pragmatic aim has been to highlight those aspects of the court's interpretation of the Act that have particular relevance for the media. It *has* sought to argue that, from a purely partisan pro-media viewpoint, the HRA has been something of a mixed blessing. In importing into the common law the principle of the protection of privacy, in doing little (probably) to change the interpretation of a number of statutes that restrict the media, in providing, at some levels, no more protection than the common law had already furnished,[335] in affording to Ofcom a

---

[331] Rent Act 1977, Schedule 1, para 2(2).
[332] The right to non-discrimination in the exercise of Convention rights.
[333] 'Standing Back from the Human Rights Act: How Effective is it Five Years On?' (2005) *PL* 716, at 720.
[334] See Kavangagh, op cit ("Contextual"), at 542.   [335] In e.g. *Simms* (op cit), as discussed above.

large measure of discretion in respect of its adjudications on media regulation,[336] and in watering down protections specifically written into the HRA to protect the media, the courts have imposed obligations as well as rights upon the media, and avoided being bullied into providing unqualified support for 'the fourth estate'. However, a doubtful and contentious notion of indirect, negative deference to Parliament *has* prevented the courts from outright declaration of a general tort of privacy—perhaps the development that would have most troubled the press in particular. Further, judicial interpretation of the restrictions upon prior restraint built into the HRA,[337] after initial vacillation, have given the press an appreciably greater level of protection against interim injunctions than they enjoyed previously.[338] Overall, and given the strength of the Article 10 protection for media expression that legitimately contributes to public debate, the media are plainly net beneficiaries of the HRA; moreover, the differentially robust approach taken to the use of section 3(1) of the Act means that statutes as yet untested for compatibility with the Convention are readily capable of being read sharply against their *prima facie* meaning where that is necessary to afford the requisite protection. The remainder of this book puts together the detailed narrative of the interplay between Convention principles and the domestic law of media freedom.

[336] In itself a mixed blessing, as this will sometimes allow Ofcom to dismiss complaints against the media more easily, but will also mean that attempts to challenge its decisions finding media bodies in breach of relevant Codes may be difficult to challenge—as in the pre-Ofcom decision in *R v BSC, ex parte BBC* [2000] 3 WLR 1327.

[337] That is, s 12(3).   [338] See above, at 153–7.

PART II

THE ADMINISTRATION OF JUSTICE AND MEDIA FREEDOM; FAIRNESS OF PROCEEDINGS; THE OPEN JUSTICE PRINCIPLE

Part II is about the complex relationship between media freedom and the administration of justice. It evaluates the underlying values at stake in that relationship, and the use of the law in the UK as a means of intervening in it and regulating it. Chapter 4 considers the underlying harmony between free speech and the administration of justice and examines the balance created between the two values under the European Convention on Human Rights at Strasbourg. Chapter 5 considers a range of reporting restrictions—prior restraints on the reporting of court proceedings or on issues relating to them, while Chapter 6 examines post-publication sanctions arising from the law of contempt of court. Chapter 7 examines the role of journalistic sources and the balance struck between the interests of the administration of justice and the legal protection of such sources. Essentially, this Part considers and evaluates the 'balance' the law currently seeks to strike between media freedom and the administration of justice in the Human Rights Act era.

4

FREE SPEECH AND FAIR
TRIAL VALUES

INTRODUCTION[1]

The notion of creating a balance between media freedom and the interests of the justice system is frequently a starting point for discussions of this topic, and it is sometimes assumed by commentators and by courts that media commentating is highly likely to undermine the fairness of trials. It may well do so, and this chapter and the next will consider the role of the law in such instances. At the present time, concern about the impact of the media on the administration of justice is very marked and has led to the introduction of a range of further restraints on reporting.[2] But it is argued that speaking of creating a balance, as though the exercise of the freedom of the media to report on or comment on court actions came inevitably into conflict with the fair administration of justice, is misleading. A conception of this relationship based only on the notion of conflict is an impoverished and simplistic one.

The underlying aims of the exercise of media freedom and of the administration of justice are in many respects in harmony. Chapter 16 argues that the conflict between speech and privacy is more apparent than real since, as Emerson puts it, the rights are 'mutually supportive in that both are vital features of the basic system of individual rights'.[3] Equally, this may be said of media freedom and fair hearings. But the harmony between the two interests is much more specific than that. Free speech serves

---

[1] See in general: A.L. Goodhart, 'Newspapers and contempt of court in England' (1935) 48 *Harv LR* 885; B. Sufrin and N. Lowe, *The Law of Contempt*, 3rd edn., Butterworths, 1996; C.J. Miller, *Contempt of Court*, Clarendon Press, 1999; E. Barendt, *Freedom of Speech*, 2nd edn, OUP, 2005, Chapter 9; G. Robertson, *Media Law*, Penguin, 1999, Chapter 6; A. Arlidge and A.T.H. Smith, *Arlidge, Eady and Smith on Contempt*, 2nd edn., London: Sweet and Maxwell, 1999; E. Barendt and L. Hitchens, *Media Law: Cases and Materials*, London: Longman, 2000, Chapters 12, 13, 14; R. Clayton and H. Tomlinson, *The Law of Human Rights*, Oxford: OUP, 2000, Chapter 15; I. Cram, *A Virtue Less Cloistered: Courts, Speech and Constitutions* Oxford: Hart, 2002; G. Marshall, 'Press freedom and free speech theory' [1992] *PL* 40; Laws LJ, 'Current Problems in the law of contempt' (1990) *CLP* 99; B. Naylor, 'Fair Trial or Free Press: legal responses to media reports of criminal trials' [1994] *CLJ* 492; Laws LJ (2000) 116 *LQR* 157; C. Walker, 'Fundamental Rights, Fair Trials and the New Audio-Visual Sector' [1996] 59 *MLR* 517; D. Corker and M. Levi, 'Pre-trial Publicity and its Treatment in the English Courts' [1996] *Crim LR* 622.

[2] See Chapter 5 at 209.

[3] C. Emerson, 'The right to privacy and the freedom of the press' (1979) 14(2), *Harvard Civil Rights-Civil Liberties L Rev* 329, p 331.

the ends of justice since it plays an informing and scrutinizing role. The exercise of both roles by the media is generally viewed as enhancing the moral authority of the justice system.[4] Restrictions on reporting aimed at ensuring the fairness of court hearings are intended to secure the integrity of the criminal or civil justice system, but the legal significance attached to the principle of open justice is also aimed at ensuring such integrity, and a key reason for insisting upon open justice is to allow for media scrutiny of the workings of the justice system.

The principle of open justice is clearly served by securing the freedom of the media to report fairly, accurately, and contemporaneously on proceedings, since in practice such reporting aids in maintaining public trust and confidence in the justice system.[5] Most members of the public have never or rarely attended a criminal trial or any other proceedings. If the public is to have an awareness of the workings of this significant aspect of civic life, it must rely on the media for information.[6] As the European Court of Human Rights put it in *Sunday Times v UK*, 'not only do the media have the task of imparting such information and ideas [relating to the settlement of disputes in court]: the public also has a right to receive them'.[7]

Where a failure of the justice system has occurred that is extensively reported, as in the Guildford Four and Birmingham Six cases, such confidence will be undermined, but the publicity given to such failures helps to create pressure for reform. If the media did not undertake this task, justice could not be seen to be done, abuses of power within the system could go unchecked, and the public would be unable to protest—at election times and outside them—against flaws it perceives within the system. As Bentham put it: 'publicity is the very soul of justice. It is the . . . surest of all guards against improbity'.[8] The European Court of Human Rights captured this idea in *Axen*: 'by rendering the administration of justice visible, publicity contributes to the achievement of the aims of Article 6(1), namely a fair trial'.[9] Similarly, the Commission has found: '[the Convention attaches] importance to the public reporting of trials as one of the means whereby confidence in the courts . . . can be maintained'.[10] These comments impliedly reject the idea that open justice could be secured by allowing public access to court while preventing contemporaneous reporting of the case. Equally, that idea has found no favour in domestic decisions and was expressly rejected when the issue arose by the Supreme Court of Ireland.[11]

In *A-G v Leveller Magazine*[12] Lord Diplock set out the defining constitutional principles at stake:

---

[4] See further T.R.S. Allan, 'Procedural fairness and the duty of respect' [1988] 18 *OJLS* 497, pp 507–10.

[5] For discussion in the US context, see Hon Margaret H. Marshall, 'Dangerous Talk, Dangerous Silence: Free Speech, Judicial Independence and the Rule of Law' [2002] Vol 24(4) *Sydney Law Review* 455.

[6] See the then Lord Chancellor's comments on this point in the 4th RTE/UCD Lecture, 'Reporting the Courts: The Media's Rights and Responsibilities' 1999 at UCD.

[7] (1979) 2 EHRR 245, at para 65.

[8] Quoted by Lord Shaw of Dunfermline in *Scott v Scott* [1913] AC 417, p 477.

[9] *Axen v Germany* (1984) 6 EHRR 195, at para 25.

[10] *Hodgson, Woolf Productions v UK* (1987) 51 DR 136.

[11] *Murphy v Irish Times* (1998) 1 IR 359; (1998) 2 IRLM 161.   [12] [1979] AC 440, pp 449–50.

[t]he English system of administering justice does require that it be done in public . . . If the way that the courts behave cannot be hidden from the public eye and ear this provides a safeguard against judicial arbitrariness or idiosyncrasy and maintains the public confidence in the administration of justice. The application of this principle of open justice has two aspects: it requires that [the proceedings] should be held in open court to which the press and public are admitted and that, in criminal cases, at any rate, all evidence communicated to the court is communicated publicly.[13]

In *R v Felixstowe Justices, ex parte Leigh*,[14] Lord Justice Watkins said: 'no-one nowadays surely can doubt that [the journalist's] presence in court for the purpose of reporting proceedings conducted therein is indispensable. Without him, how is the public to be informed of how justice is being administered in our courts?' Moreover, access to information in this context is almost wholly dependent on the media. In contrast, in other areas of political speech, other sources, such as the leaflets of political groups and pressure groups, are available.

But the value of media discussions and reporting of court proceedings goes beyond informing the public and scrutinizing the workings of the justice system. It is essential in a democracy that there should be free debate as to the workings of the justice system, allowing for the expression of a variety of views regarding conceptions of justice which may be essential to the development of the process of justice. Thus, from the perspective of media freedom, it is clear that reports or discussions concerning the administration of justice amount to speech of the highest significance since it relates to an institution of the first importance in a democracy. As Chapter 1 argues, one of the most influential justifications for free speech arises from the part it plays in furthering democratic principles and values.[15] The argument, which is associated primarily with the American writer Meiklejohn,[16] is simply that citizens cannot participate fully in a democracy unless they have a reasonable understanding of political issues; therefore, open debate on such matters is essential. In the context of court reporting, the furthering of public knowledge as to the operation of the law in practice, and as to the relation between law and policy, is a particularly significant aspect of political speech, broadly defined. Such reporting is thus strongly under-pinned by the argument from democracy. As Cram puts it: 'Of all the arguments for free speech . . . it is the argument from democracy that seems to speak most directly to the matter of court-related speech in liberal democracies and is either implicit or explicit in judicial defences of media reporting across a variety of jurisdictions'.[17]

Reporting related to trials often relates to a range of ongoing public debates,[18] and therefore it can also be viewed as underpinned by the argument from truth, associated

---

[13] See also the comments on the importance of the principles and on the need to limit use of private hearings in *Preston* [1993] 4 All ER 638; 143 *NLJ* 1601.

[14] [1987] QB 582, p 591.   [15] See pp 16–18.

[16] See, e.g., his 'The First Amendment is an absolute' (1961) Sup Ct Rev 245.

[17] I. Cram, *A Virtue Less Cloistered, Courts, Speech and Constitutions*, Oxford: Hart, 2002, pp 10–11.

[18] See Chapter 6 at 280–3.

with J. S. Mill.[19] Its basic thesis is that the truth is most likely to emerge from free and uninhibited discussion and debate. If trial-related examples were withdrawn from a debate, it would be less compelling since it would become a contribution to a purely hypothetical, abstract discussion.[20] It appears that Mill envisaged his argument as applicable mainly to the expression of opinion and debate, but it can equally well be used to support claims for freedom of information, since the possession of pertinent information about a subject will nearly always be a prerequisite to the formation of a well-worked-out opinion on the matter. However, *prima facie*, it may be thought that the theory does not immediately make it clear *when* we need to know the truth about a given subject. Thus, it could be argued that a delay in receiving certain trial-related information during a trial due to fear of creating prejudice to it would not greatly matter, as long as the truth eventually emerged. In response to this, it may be argued that if truth is valued substantively—a position most would assent to[21]—then any period of time during which citizens are kept in ignorance of the truth or form erroneous opinions because of such ignorance, amounts to an evil, thus giving rise to a presumption against secrecy. The presumption could however be displaced in the example given, as discussed further below. If, alternatively or in addition, knowledge of the truth is valued because of its importance for political participation, then clearly it will be most important to know the information at the time that the issue it concerns is most likely to affect the political climate. These arguments could be used to support many forms of speech related to the administration of justice, but they have a particularly pertinent application to the protection for journalistic sources, discussed in Chapter 7.

These arguments are instrumental ones and are therefore vulnerable to defeat by other stronger, competing claims based on the same values. In particular, in so far as a real conflict between free speech and fair trials arises, it might readily be argued that ensuring the fairness of a trial is such a central value in a democracy that free speech claims must be overcome.[22] A similar point may be made in relation to the argument from truth. The Millian argument appears to have less applicability to the dissemination of purely factual information relating to a trial, where it makes no contribution to an ongoing debate, but amounts to mere reportage.[23] If such speech, due to its truthfulness, is damaging in terms of its effect on another competing right, such as the right to a fair trial or to private life, Mill's argument does not provide a strong basis for defending it. This might be said of, for example, disclosure of a defendant's previous convictions in the media, or of disclosure of the identity of a victim-witness who had not revealed his childhood sexual abuse, the subject of a trial, to his family.

---

[19] J. S. Mill, *On Liberty*, in M. Cowling, (ed.), *Selected Writings of John Stuart Mill*, London: Everyman, 1972. See further Chapter 1 at 14–16.

[20] This point echoes Lord Diplock's words in *A-G v English* [1983] 1 AC 116; see Chapter 6 at 280.

[21] Mill, as a utilitarian, would probably not see truth as inherently valuable, but rather as a very important means of ensuring the overall welfare of society.

[22] See Chapter 6 at 261–8.

[23] See Barendt on this point, *Freedom of Speech*, OUP, 2005, Chapter 1. See further Chapter 6 at 283–4.

Thus the justifications from democracy and truth both set out goals for society as a whole and, therefore, would seem reasonably to allow abrogation of speech in the interests of fair trial concerns which may be immediately and directly damaged by the exercise of speech.

It is further argued in Chapter 1 that freedom of speech is necessary in order to enable individual self-fulfilment. It is argued that individuals will not be able to develop morally and intellectually unless they are free to air views and ideas in free debate with each other. However, this rationale does not value speech in itself, but rather, instrumentally, as a means to individual growth. Therefore, in situations where it seems that allowing free expression of the particular material will be likely to retard or hinder the growth of others or of the 'speaker', the justification does not offer a strong defence of speech.[24] Most reporting relating to the administration of justice would not of its nature exhibit this demeaning quality. However, it would be hard to defend the type of trial-related reporting that focuses on the sensational aspects of particular crimes, and assaults human dignity in its presentation of a humiliating caricature of the defendants, by reference to this rationale.[25]

The speech-supporting rationale based on the argument from moral autonomy discussed in Chapter 1 is also engaged by reporting of the justice system. The argument may be viewed as founded on Dworkin's basic postulate of the state's duty to treat its citizens with equal concern and respect.[26] This justification for free expression is centred around the liberal conviction that matters of moral choice must be left to the individual. This justification is less contingent than the others mentioned above, because any restriction on what an individual is allowed to read, see, or hear, clearly amounts to an interference with her right to judge such matters for herself. Thus, the argument consistently defends virtually all kinds of speech and other forms of expression,[27] whereas the arguments from truth and democracy will tend to have a somewhat less comprehensive range of application. This argument extends not only to hearing the expression of opinions, but also to information-based reporting.[28] This account of the value of open debate regarding trials and other proceedings may be considered in terms of both speakers' and audience rights, but this underlying justification for media freedom is in general more applicable to audience rather than speakers' rights.[29]

However, Dworkin's theory is based partly on a desire to protect unpopular forms

---

[24] Barendt (argues in *Freedom of Speech*, 1st edn., Oxford: OUP, 1987, pp 16–17) that justifications for suppressing some forms of speech could be advanced on the basis that human dignity (the value promoted by allowing self-development) would thereby receive protection. He cites the finding of the German Constitutional Court that there was no right to publish a novel defaming a dead person as such publication might violate the 'dignity of man' guaranteed by Art 1 of the German Basic Law (*Mephisto* (1971) BVerfGE 173).

[25] See Chapter 6 at 304–5 on this point.   [26] See Chapter 1, at 13–14.

[27] It also covers material which could only doubtfully be classified as speech, e.g., photographic pornography.

[28] See R. Dworkin, *Freedom's Law: The Moral Reading of the American Constitution*, Harvard University Press, 1996, 199–201.

[29] See Chapter 1 at 20–5.

of speech from the expression of majoritarian preferences, enforced through law. This central concern does not have a strong and direct applicability to trial-related reporting since such reporting is not in general placed in a precarious position for that reason. Moreover, although this is not an instrumental justification, it can be argued that it is not strongly engaged where, rather than allow some forms of trial-related reporting, they should be restricted precisely *in order* to ensure that the state treats all of its citizens with equal concern and respect. This is especially the case in relation to the trial of high-profile and deeply unpopular defendants, such as terrorist suspects belonging to extremist Muslim groups, a matter discussed in Chapter 6.[30] State-based initiation of court proceedings aimed at restraining speech may be necessary in order to ensure equality of access to fair trial rights.

It may be concluded that the freedom of the media to report on the justice system is presumptively valuable in itself, since it may be underpinned by a range of speech-based rationales, but it is also of the highest importance in securing the integrity of the system and public understanding of it. From the perspectives both of media freedom and the fair hearing principle, reports about or linked to court hearings are *prima facie* valuable. However, in reality, such reporting may be far from consonant with the principles discussed. Purely commercial concerns may seek to take advantage of free speech arguments, and therefore the point at which free speech values are largely abrogated in favour of such concerns should be carefully identified in order to downgrade the protection afforded by free speech guarantees. Newspapers and broadcasts do not act as neutral conduits of information; nor would their audiences expect them to do so. But the free speech rights of the media deriving from the 'audience rights' of the readers as an aspect of the Article 10 guarantee (and as a common law principle indicated in statements such as: 'the news media [are] the trustees of the general public whose eyes and ears they are'),[31] mean that the media is expected to engage in accurate and fair reporting of proceedings.

Reportage of criminal proceedings passes through a selective and creative journalistic and editorial process, with the result that the public is informed about particular aspects of it—the most newsworthy ones—and the informing process occurs within a particular interpretation of the pre-trial and trial events. The narrative of the proceedings may be affected, even greatly distorted, by the reporting process. The quality of court reporting is extremely variable. Clearly, some speech bearing upon court hearings is trivial and sensationalist, motivated solely or largely by profit-making concerns. The narrative of the proceedings found in the media may become in fact a media-driven narrative, going well beyond reporting of the facts, and in fact creating a vivid story that eventually bears little relation to the proceedings that are apparently being reported.[32] In general, much press coverage of the criminal justice system creates the impression that the system favours criminals. The tabloid reporting of

---

[30] See pp 254–7.   [31] Brooke J in *A-G v Guardian (No 3)* [1992] 1 WLR 874, p 886.
[32] See B. Naylor, 'Fair trial or free press: Legal Responses to Media Reports of Criminal Trials' [1994] *CLJ* 492.

high-profile arrests or trials, such as the trial of Lee Bowyer in 2001 for affray and causing grievous bodily harm, the arrest of Ian Huntley in 2003 for the murder of two Soham schoolgirls, or the arrests of Premiership footballers in 2003 and 2004 for rape,[33] was often inaccurate, sensationalist, biased, and unremitting. Some of the coverage of the arrests in relation to the London attempted terrorist bombings in July 2005, especially in the tabloids, was potentially prejudicial since it straightforwardly imputed guilt to the suspects.[34] Such reporting, far from enhancing the justice process, detracts from it. The fact that such newspaper coverage constitutes 'speech' should not be allowed to obscure its failure to play any significant part in furthering open justice or informing the public on other matters of public interest. When such reporting creates a likelihood of prejudice to proceedings, no sufficient competing interest is available in order to found the argument that restrictions are unjustified.

It follows that it is legitimate to restrict expression that is likely to create unfairness in the justice process since such speech undermines a central justification for its own existence. In other words, freedom of speech *prima facie* plays a part as an essential aspect of a fair system of justice, but where speech affects the impartiality of a hearing it tends not only to detract from its fairness, but to undermine public confidence in the administration of justice. Therefore it can run counter to its own key role. Moreover, it is a central tenet of a democracy that justice should not be arbitrary, and therefore the state has a duty to ensure that all have equal access to justice. As indicated, under the liberal account of rights which this book is premised upon, rights are underpinned by the notion that the state has a duty to treat all its citizens with equal concern and respect.[35] That notion underlies, it is argued, both free speech and fair trials. If the fair trial of an individual is arbitrarily affected by media coverage, since that individual is accused of a crime which happens to have caught public attention, the state has failed to secure equal access to justice. Therefore restrictions on such coverage may be justified on the basis that the speech which creates such an interference undermines an aspect of its own underlying rationale: it can be viewed as attacking democratic values rather than as upholding them. This argument need not automatically mean, however, that such speech should be wholly suppressed or that it should attract sanctions, since, as discussed below, the primary responsibility for ensuring fairness remains with the trial judge under the current domestic system. But it does place such speech in a precarious position.

Different considerations arise in relation to reporting that is concerned not primarily with a particular court hearing, but with a different aspect of public affairs, while touching upon an issue significant in forthcoming or current proceedings.[36] In this instance, the open justice principle is largely unengaged, but the general justifications

---

[33] See Chapter 6 at 271–2.

[34] For example, *The Sun*'s coverage of the arrests on 27 and 28 July included the headline, referring to the suspects: 'Got the Bastards!'. Thus, guilt was clearly imputed—the assumption was that the right people had been arrested.

[35] See pp 13–14 for discussion of this Dworkinian precept in its application to the media.

[36] See e.g. *A-G v English* [1983] 1 AC 116. See Chapter 6 at 280–1 for discussion of the case.

for media freedom discussed in Chapter 1 are applicable. In such instances a more direct conflict between free speech and fair trials is likely to arise since, except at a very general level, it is hard to view the two as mutually supportive. On the other hand, such speech tends to be less likely to create prejudice since it by its nature it is unlikely to be centrally focused on a particular hearing.

Thus, it may be concluded that legal mechanisms that set out to create a balance between free speech and fair trials should be capable of creating differentiation between speech which furthers openness and fairness in the justice system, speech which informs on another issue of public interest, and speech which fails to achieve either of these aims, either due to its triviality or to its misleading nature and lack of impartiality. Conflicts between media freedom and fair hearings may well arise due to failures in creating such differentiation, but there may also be an area of irreducible conflict, demanding that hard choices are made. The most problematic disputes occur where it appears that a risk to the fairness of the proceedings has arisen, but the speech in question is of value, either specifically in relation to the aim of upholding the integrity of the justice system, or more generally in relation to the role of the media in informing the public on matters of public interest and raising issues for debate.

It is argued then that there is degree of consonance between the values underlying free speech and fair trials, but that in principle where speech runs counter to such consonance, it may justifiably be restricted. In Convention terms, such justification is founded on the difference between Articles 10 and 6 in terms of qualifications: Article 6 is not materially qualified, but restriction of speech should be based firmly upon the principle of proportionality at the heart of Article 10(2). Prejudice-creating speech fails to serve the open justice principle and comes into conflict with the right to a fair trial. The damage to the fairness of a trial may be wholly or partly irretrievable if such speech is published, whereas if it is subject to postponement the damage to the interest of the media in publication may be minor.[37] Where free speech does *not* play a particular role in supporting the fairness of trials, but is of value for other reasons, the impact on each right if the other were to prevail should be carefully scrutinized. Thus legal intervention with a view to protecting, as far as possible, both fair trial and free speech values should, this chapter contends, be capable of taking such factors into account. Such intervention should engage fully, but in a nuanced fashion, with those values: in seeking to protect trials it should not encroach unduly on speech; it should curb speech only where a genuine threat to a trial is apparent, and should be the more willing to do so where the speech itself is also of limited value. Thus the legal tool employed should allow the threat to the trial to come under close scrutiny. But, equally, in seeking to protect speech it should not *assume* the value of the speech claim too readily, thus allowing unfairness to trials to occur. In other words, the legal model for regulation chosen should make it possible to weigh up the value of the speech claim and the damage to the media interest in question that would occur due to the

---

[37] See Chapter 6 at 307–9 for argument against the 'perishable commodity' notion.

intervention. In the light of these findings this chapter moves on to consider the different models underpinning such legal intervention apparent in various jurisdictions, before looking closely at the current models used in England and Wales in the context of a media environment radically different from that in place when those models were under consideration.[38]

MODELS FOR THE REGULATION OF COURT-RELATED SPEECH

As indicated, publications clearly have the ability to create interferences with the course of justice in civil or criminal proceedings. The various ways in which interference can occur are indicated in this chapter and it will be argued that some interferences are far more serious than others. To take an obvious example—if a large number of tabloid newspapers, in pursuit of a newsworthy story, take the view that a defendant in a high-profile trial is guilty, they may slant stories and pictures so that they seem to give that impression, and such coverage may affect the jury since it may create bias against the defendant, undermining—in effect—the presumption of innocence. They may do so on the basis that the margin of interest in the story would be diminished if guilt was not implied or assumed and therefore its newsworthiness would also diminish. Again, the press coverage of the attempted London bombings in July 2005 provides an obvious example. If, as a result of the coverage, some or all members of the jury find it impossible to view the evidence dispassionately before reaching a verdict of guilty, the conviction will have been affected by the partial views of a certain group of people who do not have all the evidence available to them and are influenced by factors other than the concern to ensure fairness in decision-making.

In seeking to avoid such interferences with the course of justice while also affording protection to the freedom of the media, states have chosen to adopt stances that may be termed predominantly 'preventive', 'protective', or 'neutralizing'.[39]

THE PREVENTIVE MODEL

Under the preventive model, the state seeks to prevent the publication of material which might affect the fairness of a particular proceeding, and narrowly focused prior restraints are used to this end. This model is used in a number of European

---

[38] See J. Armstrong Brandwood, 'You Say "Fair Trial" and I Say "Free Press": British and American approaches to protecting defendants' rights in high profile trials' [2000] 75 *New York University Law Review* 1412, pp 1440–2; C. Walker, 'Fundamental Rights, Fair Trials and the New Audio-Visual Sector' [1996] 59 *MLR* 517.

[39] See I. Cram, 'Automatic Reporting Restrictions in Criminal Proceedings and Article 10 of the ECHR' [1998] *EHRLR* 742.

countries.[40] It is also used in England, although, as discussed in Chapters 5 and 6, it is not the dominant model there. This model tends to be used in inquisitorial rather than adversarial systems, since in adversarial ones, lay involvement, especially in the form of juries, is greater, and the need for a broad and general protection for the criminal justice system is therefore perceived as more pressing.

This model may be effective, in a narrow and immediate sense, in protecting the administration of justice, but the danger arises that the media will be inhibited both in the manner and the substance of their reporting of trials. The use of this model may result in over-protection of trials, but also in under-protection of speech. Thus, it may not fully recognize the role of the media in supporting the fairness of trials. This is not inevitable, however. Clearly, it depends on the legal tests used for allowing restraining orders. If they are sufficiently precise, and carefully focused on the harm sought to be prevented, the media will have clear guidance as to the material which temporarily cannot be published. This method may protect expression more effectively than the threat of post-publication sanctions based on broader tests.

THE PROTECTIVE MODEL

Under the protective model, traditionally used in common law jurisdictions,[41] the state seeks, mainly by the use of post-publication sanctions under the law of contempt, to protect the administration of justice from prejudice created by the media. This form of contempt law is intended to act mainly as a deterrent; it is aimed at curbing the publication of potentially prejudicial material while allowing non-prejudicial reporting of proceedings and of discussion relating to them. But the law does not take the full and *direct* responsibility of preventing prejudice from arising and is unconcerned with the question whether prejudice has actually arisen. Therefore prior restraints are the exception; under this model it is assumed that the trial judge has the primary role in ensuring that unfairness does not arise due to the media coverage of the trial. There is in effect an uneasy division of responsibility between contempt law and the trial judge. Although protective laws based on this model are applicable to both civil and criminal actions, centrally underlying them is a fear of the effect of prejudicial material on laypersons, either jurors or magistrates.

This model has the advantage of leaving the media relatively free to publish matter relating to trials, albeit with the risk of attracting sanctions post-publication, but its use may mean that trials are in fact prejudiced, depending on the nature of the test used in determining upon the sanctions, on the likelihood of being able to ascribe responsibility for prejudice to one media organ, and on executive willingness to use the law. If the threshold test for using the sanctions is set at a high level, the threat of

---

[40] See for a comparison with a civil law jurisdiction, Spain, I. Cram, *A Virtue Less Cloistered: Courts, Speech and Constitutions*, Oxford: Hart, 2002, Chapter 6. For examples of the type of prior restraints used, see e.g. *News Verlags* (2001) 31 EHRR 6; *Worm v Austria* (1998) 25 EHRR 454, discussed below at pp 185–9.

[41] See I. Cram, ibid, pp 24–42 and Chapter 3 for discussion of the approaches to prejudicial media comment in these jurisdictions.

using them may not create a sufficient deterrent. Therefore the risk of prejudice may materialize, meaning that the trial judge is placed under pressure to rely heavily on measures intended to neutralize the prejudice, such as staying the trial, which can themselves very readily create a risk of prejudice or impediment to the justice system.[42]

If a trial appears to have been prejudiced by unfair reporting, a successful appeal may be brought on that basis,[43] but this method fails to provide full redress for the defendant or to ensure fairness in the criminal justice system. The result may be that a guilty person may be acquitted or that an innocent one suffers the deeply distressing consequences of being convicted, at least for a period of time.[44] Moreover, a successful appeal plays no necessary part in deterring the media from creating prejudice, thereby leaving open the possibility that trials will be placed at risk in future. This method, therefore, far from preventing prejudice to the administration of justice, merely substitutes one form of unfairness for another.[45]

Thus, one of the aims of affording the media greater freedom than would be available under the preventive model—to recognize its role in enhancing fairness in the administration of justice—may not be realized due to such counter-productive effects. The use of this model may well result in the under-protection of trials, but also at times in the under-protection of speech since it creates a subsequent restraint that can operate in quite an unpredictable fashion. Therefore it can fail to engage fully with the core values underlying both free speech and fair trials.

THE NEUTRALIZING MODEL

Under the neutralizing model, the emphasis is placed on dealing with the potential effects of prejudicial material, by means of procedural devices aimed at ensuring the impartiality of the jury. Such devices include the use of strong directions to the jury, jury challenges to select out of the panel those affected by publicity, changing the trial venue, stays, and sequestration of the jury. If neutralizing measures fail, the remedial measure of acquittal or abandonment of the trial may be the last resort. The use of neutralizing devices themselves may run counter to enhancing the fairness of the trial; for example, delaying the trial may mean not only that witnesses' memories have faded, but also that the ordeal of the victim is prolonged and opportunities for the intimidation of witnesses, including victim-witnesses, are enhanced. The possibility of sequestration may create an additional factor enhancing the unattractiveness of the

---

[42] See D. Corker, and M. Levi, 'Pre-trial Publicity and its Treatment in the English Courts' [1996] *Crim LR* 622.

[43] See the successful appeal on this basis in *Taylor* (1993) 98 Cr App R 361, CA (for discussion, see Chapter 6, at 263).

[44] The Taylor sisters (ibid) were convicted of murder amid widespread, sensationalist, unremitting tabloid publicity. The convictions, which subsisted until the successful appeal, obviously caused them deep stress and humiliation.

[45] See T.M. Honess, 'Empirical and Legal Perspectives on the Impact of Pre-Trial Publicity' [2002] *Crim LR* 719.

prospect of jury service and therefore affecting the profile of those who undertake it. Thus, it is arguable that this cannot be viewed as an effective method of protecting the administration of justice. At first glance, the use of this model appears to reflect a strong recognition of the important role of the media, discussed above, in terms of supporting the fairness of trials, since it maximizes media freedom. However, in itself this method of dealing with the creation of prejudice by the media may create injustice and therefore it may counter the impact of the media in that role. This model is therefore over-protective of speech and under-protective of trials;[46] further, it fails to engage fully with the core values underlying both trial-related speech and the fair trial guarantee.

Since the First Amendment provides an unqualified guarantee of free speech,[47] the emphasis in the USA has inevitably been on using neutralizing measures rather than on sanctions intended to deter the media from publishing potentially prejudicial material.[48] The guarantee of a fair trial under the Sixth Amendment[49] has to be satisfied by a means other than that of curbing free speech. The publicity surrounding the OJ Simpson trial provided the most notorious example of the results of this stance.[50] In *Nebraska Press Association v Stuart*,[51] the Supreme Court held that adverse publicity before a trial would not necessarily have a prejudicial effect on it and that therefore a prior restraint would not be granted. The result of the adoption of this stance is that witness statements may be obtained pre-trial, while assertions of guilt or confessions and hearings to determine the admissibility of evidence[52] may all be made public. The use of procedural devices such as jury selection, delaying the trial, or changing its venue, as an alternative to restraining the media, are not always very effective, leaving open the possibility that defendants may be wrongfully acquitted or

---

[46] See J. Armstrong Brandwood, 'You Say "Fair Trial" and I Say "Free Press": British and American approaches to protecting defendants' rights in high profile trials' [2000] 75 *New York University Law Review* 1412; M. Chesterman, 'OJ and the Dingo: How Media Publicity for Criminal Jury Trials is Dealt With in Australia and America' (1997) 45 *Am Jo Comp Law* 109; H.P. Furman, 'Publicity in High Profile Criminal Cases' (1998) 10 *St Thomas L Rev* 507; see I. Cram, *A Virtue Less Cloistered: Courts, Speech and Constitutions*, Oxford: Hart, 2002, pp 59–66 for discussion of the use of this model in the US.

[47] 'Congress shall make no law . . . abridging the freedom of speech or of the press. . . .'

[48] See *Knapp* (1990) 114 L Ed 2d 763 on the detailed questioning of jury members; see M. Chesterman, 'OJ and the Dingo: How Media Publicity for Criminal Jury Trials is Dealt with in Australia and America' (1997) 45 *Am Jo Comp Law* 109 and I. Cram, 'Automatic Reporting Restrictions in Criminal Proceedings and Article 10 of the ECHR' [1998] *EHRLR* 742 on the US neutralizing approach generally. As the most extreme neutralizing measure, a conviction may be quashed and a retrial ordered. In *Shepherd v Maxwell* (1966) 384 US 333, a retrial was ordered because of the extensive media coverage. For comment on *Shepherd v Maxwell*, see A. Grant, 'Pre-trial Publicity and Fair Trial' (1976) 14 *Osgoode Hall LJ* 275. The neutralizing measure of sequestration of the jury was used in the trial of OJ Simpson in 1995 and attracted widespread criticism in the UK.

[49] 'In all criminal prosecutions, the accused shall enjoy the right to a speedy and public trial, by an impartial jury of the State and district wherein the crime shall have been committed, which district shall have been previously ascertained by law, and to be informed of the nature and cause of the accusation; to be confronted with the witnesses against him; to have compulsory process for obtaining witnesses in his favor, and to have the Assistance of Counsel for his defence.'

[50] See M. Chesterman, ibid.   [51] (1976) 427 US 539.

[52] *United States v Brooklier* (1982) 685 F 2d 1162; *Re Application of Herald Co* (1984) 734 F 2d.

may appeal against conviction and obtain an acquittal owing to the publicity. Certain US commentators therefore favour adoption of aspects of the protective approach used in Britain, although the current law adopted in reliance on that model is seen both as ineffective and as creating unacceptable limitations on media freedom.[53]

CONCLUSIONS

No state relies exclusively on one model. For example, the US relies strongly on neutralizing measures but preventive measures are also used.[54] The intention underlying all the models is that the law should seek to ensure fair hearings, especially fair trials, while protecting freedom of expression, but the first two seek to ensure fairness by curbing media freedom to an extent, the third by seeking to insulate the hearing from potentially prejudicial publications, while leaving media freedom largely intact. In other words, the models use different means to further the same end.

The protective model has traditionally been used in the UK, although aspects of the preventive and neutralizing models are also evident. As discussed in Chapter 5, prior restraints are available to prevent the reporting of specific items of prejudicial information. It cannot be assumed, however, that prior restraints are necessarily 'preventive', while subsequent ones are 'protective': there is a complete ban on the reporting of jury deliberations; it is a protective measure, aimed not at preventing prejudice to particular proceedings, but at preserving the administration of justice by protecting the confidentiality of such deliberations.

Apart from the use of narrowly focused restraints preventing the reporting of specific items of information, English contempt law also provides for the possibility of post-publication sanctions. The underlying aim of such sanctions has traditionally been to protect the administration of justice in a general sense, rather than to ensure the fairness of individual hearings, although specific preventive orders are also used to restrain the reporting of certain material. Since it is not assumed that the use of contempt law alone can or should be able to ensure a fair hearing, certain neutralizing measures, discussed below, are also used to that end,[55] and there has been an underlying tension between the roles of contempt law and of such measures, which, it will be suggested, is currently unresolved. Thus it will be contended that there is a theoretical incoherence in UK law: it reflects a mixture of the models indicated,

[53] See J. Armstrong Brandwood, 'You Say "Fair Trial" and I Say "Free Press": British and American approaches to protecting defendants' rights in high profile trials' [2000] 75 *New York University Law Review* 1412, pp 1442–4; see also Krause (1996) 76 *Boston UL Rev* 357.

[54] See A. Bernabe-Riefkohl, 'Prior Restraints on the Media and the Right to a Fair Trial: A Proposal for a New Standard' 84 *Kentucky LJ* 259, discussing the use of pretrial publication bans in the US. He notes that such bans can be constitutionally valid under very limited circumstances, but argues that the standard by which they are judged is inconsistent and confusing. He considers that an absolute rule protecting the press from prior restraints should be adopted in the US.

[55] See the comments of Simon Brown LJ regarding the differing roles of the judge in contempt proceedings and at trial: *A-G v Birmingham Post and Mail Ltd* [1998] 4 All ER 49; see also the comments of Sedley LJ in *A-G v Guardian Newspapers* [1999] EMLR 904; both are discussed below—see Chapter 6, at 285–6.

resulting in confusion and uncertainty as to the role of important strands of contempt law.

Adherence to this approach is apparent to a variable extent in other common law jurisdictions. When Canada adopted the Charter of Rights and Freedoms in 1982, the Supreme Court considered that the common law stance of affording the fairness of trials priority over free speech had been changed by the Charter and that, therefore, adherence to a neutralizing rather than a preventive model had become appropriate. The Court found that a ban on pre-trial publication should only be ordered when 'alternative measures', such as jury sequestration, could not prevent the risk of prejudice.[56] Pre-Charter, Canada had taken an approach akin to that under the English common law pre-1981 and influenced by English precedents.[57] In particular, no means of undertaking speech/harm balancing had been developed—there was no form of public interest test pre-Charter.[58] The current position in Canada is akin to that taken post-1981 in England where speech/harm balancing does occur, and there is greater reliance on neutralizing measures in both countries. In contrast, Australia has adopted a stance more akin to that of UK common law, although somewhat less restrictive of freedom of expression.[59] The Australian common law does allow for some balancing between free speech and fair trials but the balance appears to lie in favour of the administration of justice,[60] and the factors that will allow a court to find in favour of freedom of expression are not entirely clear, leading to some chilling of speech.[61]

APPROACHES TO THE FAIR TRIAL/FREE SPEECH BALANCE IN ENGLAND AND WALES IN THE HUMAN RIGHTS ACT ERA

INTRODUCTION

This chapter now moves on to concentrate on the stance adopted under the European Convention on Human Rights—the model it predominantly appears to adhere to. The following two chapters compare that stance with that which underpins the

---

[56] See *Dagenais v Canadian Broadcasting Corporation* (1995) 120 DLR (4th) 12, p 37. For comment, see Horwitz, 'Jury selection after *Dagenais*: prejudicial pre-trial publicity' (1996) 42 *CR* 220.

[57] See *Steiner v Toronto Star Ltd* (1955) 114 CCC 117.

[58] See *Re A-G for Manitoba and Radio OB Ltd* (1977) 70 DLR (3d) 311.

[59] For discussion of the Australian approach, which contrasts it with that adopted in the US, see M. Chesterman, 'OJ and the Dingo: How Media Publicity for Criminal Jury Trials is Dealt With in Australia and America' (1997) 45 *Am Jo of Comp Law* 109. In Australia, contempt cannot be committed until proceedings are pending: *James v Robinson* (1963) 109 CLR 593.

[60] See *A-G v Hinch* (1987) 164 CLR 15.

[61] See further I. Cram, *A Virtue Less Cloistered: Courts, Speech and Constitutions*, Oxford: Hart, 2002, pp 107–14.

English domestic provisions. The Human Rights Act brings the two approaches into confrontation with each other.

Strasbourg has had to consider the imposition of restrictions on the media which have been intended to be either protective or preventive, depending on the stance taken in the state in question. It has not yet had to consider the impact on fair trials of the use of neutralizing measures. As indicated above, those measures stemming from signatory countries other than the UK tend to have a preventive role. At Strasbourg, conflicts between free speech and fair trials may be viewed either as a clash between Article 10 and the societal interest in protecting the administration of justice (under the Article 10(2) rubric of 'protecting the authority of the judiciary'), or as a clash between the guarantees of Articles 10 and 6 (the fair trial article). The extent to which a particular proceeding, as opposed to a general interest in the protection of justice, might be affected by a publication will depend on the facts of the case. The question whether the Article 6 guarantee is fully engaged is obviously a very significant one. Article 6(1) provides:

[i]n the determination of his civil rights and obligations or of any criminal charge against him, everyone is entitled to a fair and public hearing within a reasonable time by an independent and impartial tribunal established by law . . .[62]

The presumption of innocence is guaranteed under Article 6(2).[63] Strasbourg has a mechanism for considering the conflict in question which is more nuanced than that available in the US under the First and Sixth Amendments,[64] since under Article 10(2), an interference with the guarantee of freedom of expression can be justified if it is prescribed by law, has a legitimate aim and is necessary in a democratic society. However, as pointed out above, since Article 10 is qualified while the guarantees of impartiality, fairness and the presumption of innocence under Article 6(1) and (2) are

---

[62] In full Article 6 provides: In the determination of his civil rights and obligations or of any criminal charge against him, everyone is entitled to a fair and public hearing within a reasonable time by an independent and impartial tribunal established by law. Judgment shall be pronounced publicly but the press and public may be excluded from all or part of the trial in the interest of morals, public order or national security in a democratic society, where the interests of juveniles or the protection of the private life of the parties so require, or to the extent strictly necessary in the opinion of the court in special circumstances where publicity would prejudice the interests of justice.

2 Everyone charged with a criminal offence shall be presumed innocent until proved guilty according to law.

3 Everyone charged with a criminal offence has the following minimum rights:
   (a) to be informed promptly, in a language which he understands and in detail, of the nature and cause of the accusation against him;
   (b) to have adequate time and facilities for the preparation of his defence;
   (c) to defend himself in person or through legal assistance of his own choosing or if he has not sufficient means to pay for legal assistance, to be given it free when the interests of justice so require;
   (d) to examine or have examined witnesses against him and to obtain the attendance and examination of witnesses on his behalf under the same conditions as witnesses against him;
   (e) to have the free assistance of an interpreter if he cannot understand or speak the language used in court.

[63] See note 62 above.   [64] See notes 47 and 49 above.

not, free speech may receive insufficient protection. Moreover, as Chapter 16 points out, the Strasbourg jurisprudence on clashes of rights remains relatively undeveloped in contrast to that on the conflict between individual rights and societal concerns, although it has been improved as a result of the decision in *Von Hannover*.[65]

INTERFERENCE WITH FREEDOM OF EXPRESSION TO PROTECT THE ADMINISTRATION OF JUSTICE

Action taken against a media body in respect of its coverage of a forthcoming or ongoing action, or of issues impliedly or expressly linked to it, may be justified under Article 10(2) if it has the legitimate aims of protecting the 'rights of others' and/or of 'maintaining the authority and impartiality of the judiciary'. The 'rights of others' exception covers Article 6(1) and (2) rights. The term 'impartiality' refers to the preservation of confidence in the courts by persons engaged in dispute settlement and the public in general.[66] The guarantees of fairness and of impartiality are threatened where a court is influenced by material emanating from outside the court room,[67] such as newspaper articles, and the threat has been found to be especially present where lay jurors are required to determine the key issue of guilt or innocence.[68] The presumption of innocence may be undermined where media coverage assumes guilt,[69] or where government officers make pronouncements that suggest that guilt is established.[70] The 'authority' of the judiciary refers to the acceptance of the courts as the proper forums for the settlement of disputes.[71] This exception was apparently included in the Convention at the instigation of Britain precisely to cover contempt of court.[72] The other European signatories have no clearly comparable law, although laws regulating pre-trial publicity are common.

As discussed below, Strasbourg has taken a different stance depending on the aim in view. If the Court finds that a measure interfering with speech had the aim of preventing a specific threat to a fair trial, it tends to find no breach of Article 10, at times affording a fairly wide margin of appreciation to the state, unless there is a very clear lack of proportionality between the interference and that aim.[73] Where the measure is viewed as having a more general protective role, and is therefore seen as one that need not be characterized as creating a clash of rights, it is much more likely to find such a breach. This approach is revealed by a consideration of the stance taken at Strasbourg

---

[65] [2004] EMLR 21—for a summary and comment, see (2004) 5, EHRLR 593–6. See Chapter 13 at 671–4.

[66] *Fey v Austria* (1994) 16 EHRR 387; *Worm v Austria* (1998) 25 EHRR 454, p 473.

[67] Appls 8603, 8722, 8723, and 8729/79 *Crociani v Italy* D&R 22 (1981) p 147.

[68] See *X v Norway* (1970) Yearbook XIII, 302; *X v Austria* (1963) Coll 11, p 31.

[69] See *Worm v Austria* (1998) 25 EHRR 454.

[70] See *Ribemont v France* (1995) 20 EHRR 557. This argument was put forward but rejected as manifestly ill-founded due to the lapse of time between the pronouncements and the trial in *Wloch v Poland* (2002) 34 EHRR 9, p 191, below.

[71] *Chorherr v Austria* (1994) 17 EHRR 358.

[72] See the Joint Dissenting Opinion in *Sunday Times v UK* (1979) 2 EHRR 245, p 285.

[73] See *News Verlags v Austria* (2001) 31 EHRR 8 discussed below.

to claims that Article 10 has been violated by prosecutions of journalists in respect of publications bearing upon legal proceedings in the line of authority arising from *Sunday Times v UK*,[74] *C v UK*,[75] *BBC Scotland v UK*,[76] *Worm v Austria*,[77] and *News Verlags v Austria*.[78]

The *Sunday Times* case arose from the ruling of the House of Lords in *A-G v Times Newspapers Ltd*.[79] The case concerned litigation arising out of the thalidomide tragedy. The parents of the children affected by thalidomide (which caused severe deformities to the developing foetus) wished to sue Distillers, the company that had manufactured the drug, because they believed that it was responsible for the terrible damage done to their unborn children. Distillers resisted the claims and entered into negotiation with the parents' solicitors. Thus, the litigation was dormant while the negotiations were taking place. Meanwhile, the *Sunday Times* wished to publish an article accusing Distillers of acting ungenerously towards the thalidomide children. The article came close to alleging that Distillers had been negligent, although it was balanced in that it did consider both sides. The Attorney General obtained an injunction in the Divisional Court preventing publication of the article on the ground that it amounted to a contempt of court. The Court of Appeal then discharged the injunction in a ruling which weighed up the public interest in freedom of speech against the need to protect the administration of justice, and found that the former value outweighed the latter: the article concerned a matter of great public interest and, since the litigation in question was dormant, it would probably be unaffected by it.

On appeal, the House of Lords restored the injunction on the ground that the article dealt with the question of negligence and therefore prejudged the case pending before the court. It held that such prejudgment was particularly objectionable as coming close to 'trial by media' and thereby leading to an undermining of the administration of justice; a person might be adjudged negligent by parts of the media with none of the safeguards available in court. The confidence of the public in the courts might be undermined, thus creating a long-term detriment to the course of justice generally. In making such findings, the Law Lords showed, it is suggested, a typical inclination to be over-protective of matters within the judicial sphere, a tendency discussed elsewhere in this book.[80] In response, the editor of the *Sunday Times* applied to the European Commission of Human Rights, seeking a ruling that the imposition of the injunction breached Article 10 of the European Convention,

---

[74] (1979) 2 EHRR 245.   [75] (1989) 61 DR 285.   [76] (1998) 25 EHRR CD 179.

[77] (1997) 25 EHRR 557; (1998) 25 EHRR 454.   [78] (2001) 31 EHRR 8.

[79] [1974] AC 273; [1973] 3 All ER 54; [1973] 3 WLR 298, HL. For case notes, see C.J. Miller, 'The Sunday Times Case' (1974) 37 *MLR* 96; M. O'Boyle, '*A-G v The Times*' (1974) 25 *NILQ* 57; D.G.T. Williams, 'Contempt and the Thalidomide Case' (1973) 32 *CLJ* 177; C.J. Miller, 'Contempt of Court: The Sunday Times Case' [1975] *Crim LR* 132. There is some overlap between the discussion here and the discussion in Chapter 6, but the discussion at this point is necessary since the *Sunday Times* case is so crucial to an understanding of contempt law.

[80] See Chapter 3 (mapping judicial deference) at 144–53.

and five years after the judgment of the House of Lords, the case came before the European Court of Human Rights (*Sunday Times* case).[81]

The Court found that the injunction clearly infringed Article 10(1) and that this was not a trivial infringement—the free speech interest involved was very strong, because the matter was one of great public concern. As it famously said, it was not faced with 'a choice between two conflicting principles but with a principle of freedom of expression that is subject to a number of exceptions which must be narrowly interpreted'.[82] The Court found that the interference with freedom of expression was prescribed by law and served the legitimate aim of preserving the authority and impartiality of the judiciary. It did not consider that the injunction was needed in order to preserve the rights of others. The right in question would have been the right to an impartial hearing of a civil right or obligation. Having characterized the action in this manner, it could proceed on the basis that it was considering a narrow exception to the free expression guarantee, rather than a conflicting right. This was understandable since the litigation in question was dormant.

The key question, therefore, was whether the injunction was 'necessary in a democratic society' in order to achieve the aim in question. In order to make a determination on this point, the Court considered the meaning of the term 'necessary', finding that it implied the existence of a 'pressing social need'.[83] But there could not be such a need if the interference was disproportionate to the aim pursued. In terms of proportionality, the Court balanced the value of the speech in question against the harm caused under quite close scrutiny, an approach that foreshadowed the one it adopted in the later case of *Goodwin*.[84] It weighed up the strength of the free speech interest in considering whether the injunction was disproportionate to the aim of preserving the authority of the judiciary. It found that, although the courts are clearly the forums for settling disputes, this did not mean that there could be no newspaper discussion before a case. The article was couched in moderate terms and explored the issues in a balanced way. Moreover, the litigation in question was dormant and therefore unlikely to be affected by the article. Nevertheless, the injunction created an absolute prohibition on discussion of the issues forming the background to the case.

Thus, on the one hand, there was a strong free speech interest, while on the other, there was quite a weak threat to the authority of the judiciary. If the free speech interest had been weaker, it might have been more easily overcome. The court therefore concluded that the interference did not correspond to a social need sufficiently

---

[81] (1979) 2 EHRR 245. For case notes, see P.J. Duffy, 'The Sunday Times Case: Freedom of Expression, Contempt of Court and the European Convention on Human Rights' 5 *H Rts Rev* 17; F.A. Mann, 'Contempt of Court in the House of Lords and the European Court of Human Rights' (1979) 95 *LQR* 348; W-WM. Wong, 'The Sunday Times Case: Freedom of Expression versus English Contempt of Court law in the European Court of Human Rights' (1984) 17 *NY Univ JIL and Pol* 35.

[82] Ibid, at [65].

[83] The Court ruled that it did not mean indispensable, but connoted something stronger than 'useful', 'reasonable', or 'desirable'.

[84] See Chapter 7 at 334–6.

pressing to outweigh the public interest in freedom of expression. In reaching its conclusion that a breach of Article 10 had therefore taken place,[85] the Court also adverted briefly to the value of the article in furthering the aim of preserving the authority of the judiciary since 'in bringing to light certain facts it might have served as a brake on speculative and unenlightened discussion'.[86] In other words, the speech in question served the ends of justice in a general sense. Although, as an aspect of its application of the requirements of proportionality, the Court took the view that the strong free speech interest outweighed the slight impact on the administration of justice, it might also be said that the speech in question engaged strongly in the debate as to the proper ends of justice, but no countervailing considerations regarding equal access to justice or the creation of unfairness genuinely arose. The margin of appreciation conceded was narrow, since the Court took the view that the notion of the authority and impartiality of the judiciary is an objective one which can, therefore, be closely scrutinized.

Worm v Austria[87] is now the leading authority on balancing expression and fair trial values. Unlike the *Sunday Times* case, it addressed a real clash between the two since in the circumstances the Article 6 guarantees were clearly engaged. The article in question created a high risk of prejudice: it was published during a criminal trial, clearly imputed guilt and made specific allegations against the defendant. In all these respects, therefore, it created a strong contrast with the article at issue in *Sunday Times*. Thus *Worm*, unlike *Sunday Times*, is properly characterized as a clashing rights case. A political periodical had published an article by Worm, a journalist, about the criminal trial for tax evasion of Hannes Androsch, a former Minister of Finance. The article, published while the trial was ongoing, stated that it had been known for a substantial period of time that Androsch was evading taxes and that it had been proved for some time, by the investigating judge, that Androsch was lying on this key point. In general, the article was highly critical of Androsch and clearly evinced a belief in his guilt. Worm was convicted and fined under the Austrian Media Act s 23 which provides for the punishment of those who discuss 'subsequent to the indictment and before the judgment at first instance . . . the probable outcome of those proceedings or the value of evidence in a way capable of influencing the outcome'. There is no need to establish that the proceedings have in fact been influenced. The Vienna Court of Appeal considered that the article had a potential influence on the criminal proceedings since it had the capacity to affect at the least the two lay judges involved. It also found that Worm had intended to influence the proceedings.

The European Court of Human Rights accepted that Worm's conviction constituted an interference with the freedom of expression guarantee. The State argued that the prosecution had the legitimate aims of preserving the authority and impartiality of the judiciary and the 'rights of others'. The Court accepted that the conviction had a link with the Article 6(1) guarantee, although it did not pursue the question whether

---

[85] It may be noted that the Court was divided 11–9 in reaching this determination.
[86] (1979) 2 EHRR 245, at para 66.   [87] (1998) 25 EHRR 454.

the article had created an interference with the rights of others by undermining the presumption of innocence which is guaranteed under Article 6(2). It found:

In this regard, the Court has consistently held that the expression 'authority and impartiality of the judiciary' has to be understood 'within the meaning of the Convention.' For this purpose, account must be taken of the central position occupied in this context by Article 6 which reflects the fundamental principle of the rule of law. The phrase 'authority of the judiciary' includes, in particular, the notion that the courts are, and are accepted by the public at large as being, the proper forum for the settlement of legal disputes and for the determination of a person's guilt or innocence on a criminal charge; further, that the public at large have respect for and confidence in the courts' capacity to fulfil that function. 'Impartiality' normally denotes lack of prejudice or bias. However, the Court has repeatedly held that what is at stake in maintaining the impartiality of the judiciary is the confidence which the courts in a democratic society must inspire in the accused, as far as criminal proceedings are concerned, and also in the public at large . . . It follows that, in seeking to maintain the 'authority and impartiality of the judiciary,' the Contracting States are entitled to take account of considerations going—beyond the concrete case—to the protection of the fundamental role of courts in a democratic society.[88]

As to the question whether the interference was necessary in a democratic society, the Court found that, although the limits of acceptable comment are wider as regards politicians than as regards a private individual, public figures are still entitled to the enjoyment of the guarantee of a fair trial set out in Article 6(1), which in criminal proceedings includes the right to an impartial tribunal. It went on:

this must be borne in mind by journalists when commenting on pending criminal proceedings since the limits of permissible comment may not extend to statements which are likely to prejudice, whether intentionally or not, the chances of a person receiving a fair trial or to undermine the confidence of the public in the role of the courts in the administration of criminal justice.[89]

The Court conceded a certain margin of appreciation to the State in relation to the particular choice made by the domestic authorities in relation to what was needed to protect the administration of justice, since—as it does not adopt the role of a domestic appellate court—it did not second guess the evidence. It accepted that there was no necessity to demonstrate that prejudice to the proceedings had actually arisen. It found that it was:

in principle for the appellate court to evaluate the likelihood that at least the lay judges would read the article to ascertain the applicant's criminal intent in publishing it. It cannot be excluded that the public's becoming accustomed to the regular spectacle of pseudo-trials in the news media might in the long run have nefarious consequences for the acceptance of the courts as the proper forum for the determination of a person's guilt or innocence on a criminal charge.

The sanction was found to be proportionate to the aim pursued since a fairly minor

---

[88] Ibid, at para 40.   [89] Ibid, at para 50.

penalty only—a fine—was imposed and the publishing firm was ordered to be jointly and severally liable for its payment. Thus the proportionality analysis was based on means/ends balancing[90]—the measures taken, it was found, did not go further than necessary to protect the right to a fair trial in the circumstances. No breach of Article 10 was therefore found.

This was an instance in which it could more readily be argued than in the *Sunday Times* case that the speech ran counter to the underlying speech-supporting rationales discussed above, in the sense that it was more likely to cause prejudice to the trial. The Court's approach rested on the possibility that the article had made it very difficult to ensure that the tribunal was impartial. It took the stance that the Article 10 guarantee could be justifiably infringed in order to protect Androsch's right to a fair trial under Article 6(1). But it also spoke of the general principles encapsulated under Article 6. The Court explicitly refused to look at the question whether the proceedings in question had actually been affected by the publication; it refused to consider whether the Austrian Media Law should have concerned itself with that issue. Therefore it explicitly denied that there was a need to show an actual interference with Article 6 rights (or at least a very strong probability that such an interference had occurred) before an interference with the Article 10 guarantee—in the context of political expression—could be justified. Thus, it seemed to adopt both a protective and a preventive approach, though laying more stress on the former. An obvious unfairness was potentially created by the article, but the Court also concentrated on the longer term harm that it might have created to the administration of justice in a broader sense. The state's case was obviously problematic in *Sunday Times* since the litigation in question was dormant. In *Worm*, in contrast, the state had acted to avert a genuine risk to the trial; the Court made it clear that Article 6 will take precedence over Article 10 where it can be said that there is a real likelihood of prejudice.

The stance adopted in *Worm* had been foreshadowed to an extent in the Commission's decisions in *C v UK*[91] and *BBC Scotland v UK*.[92] *C v UK* concerned a broadcast reproducing parts of the appeal in the *Birmingham Six* case. The intention of the broadcasters was that it should be shown before the final judgment in the appeal, but the Court of Appeal hearing the case granted an injunction preventing the broadcast of the programme until after the appeal had been heard. The Commission found no breach of Article 10 on the basis that there was a pressing social need to delay the programme since the portrayal of the hearing by actors would condition the response of the audience since the actors would be bound to communicate suggestions about the reliability of the witnesses they were portraying. Also the Commission accepted the view of the Court of Appeal that while the Courts' judgment would normally be unaffected, the appellants had the right to be assured that the Court had been unaffected by external matters.[93]

The application in *BBC Scotland v UK*[94] arose from the prohibition of a broadcast

---

[90] See Chapter 2 at 91–7.   [91] (1989) 61 DR 285.   [92] (1997) 25 EHRR CD 179.
[93] Ibid, p 294.   [94] (1997) 25 EHRR CD 179.

which featured allegations that prisoners moved to Barlinnie Prison after prison riots had been assaulted there by prison officers. The broadcast 'Beaten by the System' was an up-date on one previously broadcast on the same subject. An indictment had been served on three prison officers alleging that they had assaulted prisoners, about three weeks before the programme was to be broadcast. The Scottish High Court relied on its inherent equitable jurisdiction to issue an order prohibiting the broadcast until the completion of the trial of the officers, on the ground that the programme would create a risk of prejudice to the trial. The risk of prejudice arose, so the High Court found, since at least one of the jurors might have obtained from the programme the impression that the prison doctor interviewed, who was a witness for the prosecution, was a witness of considerable credit. The Court noted that the broadcast was not particularly urgent and that there was a more than minimal risk of prejudice. The applicants complained that the order of the High Court constituted a breach of Article 10.

The Commission accepted that the order constituted an interference with the freedom of expression guarantee. It went on to find that the order had the legitimate aim of protecting the right of the officers to a fair trial; therefore it was for the preservation of the authority and impartiality of the judiciary and for the protection of the 'rights of others'. In considering the question whether the order was necessary in a democratic society it might have been expected that the Commission would have subjected it to that 'most careful scrutiny' which prior restraints demand.[95] Instead, the Commission largely adopted the High Court's assessment of the necessity and proportionality of the order. The Commission appeared to be assessing the reasonableness of the High Court's findings in balancing the free speech and fair trial interests, rather than considering the issues itself. In speaking of the 'balancing act' carried out by the High Court, the Commission clearly did not view itself as applying a principle of freedom of expression subject to exceptions to be narrowly construed. Thus the need for the interference was not subjected to a strict scrutiny. Had it been, it is possible that a breach of Article 10 might have been found, bearing in mind the uncertainty of the risk of prejudice and the probability that the programme would never be broadcast once it had been postponed.

The stance taken in this line of authority was confirmed in *News Verlags v Austria*.[96] At first sight *News Verlags* presents something of a contrast to *Worm v Austria, C v UK* and *BBC Scotland v UK* in terms of the intensity of the review, but ultimately the findings are consistent with the previous ones. The case concerned a somewhat weaker Article 10 claim; the 'rights of others' exception was invoked to justify the restriction on the speech in question, but the application succeeded. The case concerned the prosecution of the News Company for the publication of a photograph of a right wing extremist, B, who was accused of sending letter bombs as part of a political campaign. The text accompanying the photograph accused him of being the

---

[95] *Observer and Guardian v UK* (1991) 14 EHRR 153, at para 60.
[96] (2001) 31 EHRR 8; (2000) 9 BHRC 625.

perpetrator of the attacks. The applicant company complained that court decisions prohibiting it from publishing the photograph in the context of reports on the criminal proceedings against it, violated its right to freedom of expression. The aims pursued were to protect the rights of others and the authority of the judiciary. The Court noted that the 'rights of others' exception was relevant since *inter alia*, the injunctions were intended to protect B against violations of the presumption of innocence, protected by Article 6(2).

The case turned on the proportionality of the interference with the legitimate aims pursued. The Court subjected this question to a detailed review, conceding only a narrow margin of appreciation to the State. It took into account the possible effect on the Article 6(2) rights of B. But it also took account of the facts that he had sought publicity as a Nazi activist and that the offences in question had a political background and were 'directed against the foundations of a democratic society'.[97] Reiterating the significance of the essential function of the press in a democratic society, the Court pointed out that the duty of the press to inform the public extends to reporting and commenting on court proceedings and noted the consonance of its discharge of such a duty with the requirement under Article 6(1) that hearings should be public. The injunctions restricted the choice of the newspaper as to its presentation of reports. The Court in particular took account of the fact that, although objection was taken only to the picture in conjunction with the adverse comments, the injunction created an absolute prohibition on publishing a picture of B with or without such comments. It may be argued that the intensity of the review undertaken in this instance was due partly to the special circumstances of the case, especially the fact that, as a right wing extremist, B had himself sought publicity for his views in the past. But the key point was that the photograph alone was unlikely to cause prejudice to the proceedings and yet the effect of the injunction was to prohibit any publication of it, even if accompanying a fair and accurate factual report of the proceedings. The injunction, therefore, was manifestly over-broad since it caught harmless publications. Thus the proportionality analysis was again based on means / ends balancing[98]— the measures taken, it was found, went further than they needed to do. The Court concluded on that basis that there was no reasonable relationship of proportionality between the interference and the aims pursued.

The injunction also affected the openness of the proceedings, since publication of such reports was found to be consonant with that aspect of Article 6(1). Although it might be argued that the publication of this particular photograph had little impact on open justice, the judgment may be said to protect both the substance and the form of reporting on court proceedings. Thus, the Court made explicit, in a partial sense, the consonance between Articles 10 and 6. That line of argument could have been taken further and the broader harmony between the aims of free speech and the protection for the administration of justice could have been more clearly articulated. *News Verlags* differs somewhat from the previous line of authority in terms of the

---

[97] Ibid, at paras 54 and 55.   [98] See Chapter 2 at 91–7.

intensity of the review that was undertaken, but does not represent a significant departure from it since the potential impact on the trial was thought to be very slight, whereas the effect on media freedom was viewed as quite significant. Moreover, the case concerned an obviously over-broad injunction.

CLAIMS OF SPEECH INTERFERING WITH THE ARTICLE 6 GUARANTEES

The cases considered so far have concerned claims alleging a breach of Article 10 where there has been interference with reporting related to civil or criminal actions. The tendency of the Court is to view its approach to the interests of freedom of expression and the administration of justice as 'the balancing of competing interests'[99] where a claim raising Article 6 issues arises under Article 10, whereas such balancing is far more problematic where a claim alleging a breach of Article 6, but raising Article 10 issues, arises at Strasbourg, since Article 6 is not materially qualified.[100] It is possible that the stance taken in *News Verlags* would have differed had the Austrian Court refused to grant the injunction and *B* had brought a claim to Strasbourg, arguing for a violation of Article 6(2). *Ribemont v France*[101] demonstrated that this would probably have been the case—at least where there was a genuine possibility that the presumption of innocence might have been undermined.

Ribemont concerned a press conference on the subject of the French police budget for the coming years. At the conference the Minister of the Interior, Mr Michel Poniatowski, the Director of the Paris Criminal Investigation Department, Mr Jean Ducret, and the Head of the Crime Squad, Superintendent Pierre Ottavioli, referred to a murder inquiry that was under way. Mr de Ribemont had been arrested in connection with the murder. Two French television channels reported this press conference in their news programmes. In one Mr Ducret was reported as saying, *inter alia*: 'The instigator, Mr De Varga, and his acolyte, Mr de Ribemont, were the instigators of the murder. The organiser was Detective Sergeant Simoné and the murderer was Mr Fréche.' Later the charges against Mr de Ribemont were dropped. He brought the case on the basis that had the trial occurred Article 6(2) would have been breached.

He brought an application to Strasbourg on the basis of a violation of the Article 6(2) guarantee, owing to the effect of the public statements. The Court noted that, 'freedom of expression, guaranteed by Article 10 of the Convention, includes the freedom to receive and impart information. Article 6(2) cannot therefore prevent

---

[99] Ibid, at para 56, relying on the judgment in *Bladet Tromsø and Stensaas v Norway* (2000) 29 EHRR 125; (1999) 6 BHRC 599.

[100] I.e. it has no broad exceptions, unlike Article 10.

[101] (1995) 20 EHRR 557. The Court found that Article 6(2) had been breached by a statement made by the French Minister of the Interior and senior police officers at a press conference in which they named the applicant as involved in a murder. Cf. *X v UK*, No 7452/76, 2 Digest 688, in which the European Commission rejected a similar claim under Article 6 as inadmissible, finding that, despite a great deal of publicity, it had not prejudiced the trial of those involved in the Aldershot bombing since the trial judge had directed the juror to disregard media comment.

the authorities from informing the public about criminal investigations in progress, but it requires that they do so with all the discretion and circumspection necessary if the presumption of innocence is to be respected'.[102] The Court went on to find that the comments made about Ribemont went beyond merely providing information and had created a breach of Article 6(2): 'some of the highest-ranking officers in the French police referred to Mr Allenet de Ribemont, without any qualification or reservation, as one of the instigators of a murder and thus an accomplice in that murder. This was clearly a declaration of the applicant's guilt which, firstly, encouraged the public to believe him guilty and, secondly, prejudged the assessment of the facts by the competent judicial authority.'[103] Once the violation of Article 6(2) was found, the application succeeded since, apart from provisions allowing for the exclusion of persons from a hearing in certain circumstances, Article 6 is not qualified.

In contrast, in *Wloch v Poland*[104] an allegation that numerous newspaper comments shortly after the applicant's arrest had led to a violation of Article 6(2) was rejected on the basis that on the facts it was extremely unlikely that the comments could have affected the judges who were to preside over the trial. Long after the time of publication—a matter of about six years—the judges who would preside over the trial had still not been empanelled. It was clearly highly unlikely that the newspaper comments would be remembered with any clarity by the judges when they were eventually empanelled and even more unlikely that they would have any influence. Thus it was found that there was no evidence that the presumption of innocence had been violated and so this aspect of Wloch's application was dismissed as manifestly ill-founded. This decision is of little value in terms of supporting the argument that the British media have some leeway to comment on the guilt or innocence of a potential defendant, since it could only be utilized where there had been a very significant time lapse between publication and trial. A lapse of around 6 years would not normally occur in the UK.

BALANCE CREATED BETWEEN ARTICLE 6 AND ARTICLE 10

As a preliminary comment on the above jurisprudence, it may be found that where a matter comes before the Court in the form of an Article 10 claim, the Court's reasoning follows the contours of that Article, which require it to afford presumptive primacy to freedom of expression and to regard the administration of justice as an exception to that right. It is perhaps inevitable, then, that the two interests will be viewed, broadly, as competing. Where the same or similar issues arise, exceptionally, in the form of an *Article 6* claim, it appears that there can be no balancing of competing interests,[105] except as regards the requirements of a public hearing in Article 6(1), since Article 6 is otherwise unqualified. The question is merely whether, on the facts, a breach of Article 6 could have arisen due to media comment—no question of

---

[102] Ibid, at para 38.   [103] Ibid, at para 41.

[104] March 2000, Information, note No 16; for the other aspects of the application, see (2002) 34 EHRR 9.

[105] See the discussion of the 'parallel analysis' in *Re S* [2003] 2 FCR 577, CA; [2004] 4 All ER 683; the decision is discussed in Chapter 16.

justification arises. The choices thereby apparent, informing the moral framework of the Convention, indicate that in this context Article 6 takes precedence over Article 10. Therefore, where an infringement of the guarantee under Article 6 might genuinely arise as a result of a publication, the Court is almost bound to find no breach of Article 10, despite the fact that when it is dealing with an Article 10 claim it has to treat an arguable violation of Article 6 as arising, technically, in the form of an exception under Article 10(2).

The Court's statement in *Worm* to the effect that 'the limits of permissible comment may not extend to statements which are likely to prejudice, whether intentionally or not, the chances of a person receiving a fair trial' bears out this finding. This comment suggests that speech (including political speech) which infringes the presumption of innocence, or is likely to infringe it, will readily be overridden by the fair trial guarantee. This is not because it is seen as of low value, but because the competing interest is so weighty.[106] In other words, speech that invades another right protected by the Convention cuts across the established categories of expression as 'political,' 'artistic' and 'commercial'. This is especially the case where the expression affects one of the unqualified, or not materially qualified, rights. Even where the speech is within the category occupying the highest place in the hierarchy of speech, as in *Worm*, that factor does not appear to play a significant role in the stance taken—the value of the speech does not appear to be weighed up against the effect on the other Convention right.

One difficulty with the Court's approach is that it can allow interferences with freedom of expression even where the Article 6 rights of a particular defendant are only doubtfully threatened—as *BBC Scotland* indicates. A further difficulty is that the Court is also prepared to draw the line at allowing comments that 'are likely to . . . undermine the confidence of the public in the role of the courts in the administration of criminal justice'.[107] On the other hand, it avoided such a stance in the *Sunday Times* case. The exception—the 'authority of the judiciary'—is not linked to criminal proceedings alone and many of the comments made by the Court in *Worm* regarding the fear of undermining public confidence in such authority could have equal validity in relation to civil actions. It considered that one aspect of the mischief to be avoided was that of a threat to the administration of justice in a general sense. It justified such a stance by reference to the rule of law principle encapsulated in Article 6 regarding the need to maintain confidence in the courts. In other words, it sought to reconcile the stance taken under Article 10(2) with that taken in relation to Article 6, partly on the basis of infringing Article 10 in order to avoid a concrete harm in Article 6 terms, but also at a broader level of principle. The difference of approach may partly be explicable on the basis that the Court is particularly concerned with the protection of the

---

[106] To a lesser extent this is also the case in relation to privacy-invading speech and speech offensive to religious sensibilities—breaching Article 9. See *Otto Preminger* (1994) 19 EHRR 34 in relation to speech that the Court has viewed as clashing with the Article 9 guarantee of freedom of religion; *Tammer v Estonia* (2003) 37 EHRR 43 and *N v Portugal* (Appl No 20683/92, 20.2.1995) both indicated that quite draconian penalties for invasion of privacy are compatible with Article 10. See further Chapter 13 at 692–3.

[107] (1998) 25 EHRR 454, at para 50.

administration of justice in criminal rather than *civil* proceedings. Clearly, where lay-persons are concerned in the justice process—which is more likely to be the case in criminal proceedings[108]—the risk of unfairness due to the influence of publications may be higher. The fear of 'trial by newspaper' that exercised the House of Lords in *A-G v Times* appears to strike the Court as of especial significance in relation to criminal proceedings.

The Court's differences of approach to Article 10 claims in this context are therefore explicable by reference to the question whether the term 'the authority of the judiciary' can or cannot be viewed as covering interests that are quite closely linked to the concrete demands of Article 6 in that instance. The effect of the margin of appreciation doctrine is variable. Where the rhetoric of 'protection for the administration of justice' in a non-concrete sense is used in relation to a publication that in actuality relates closely to particular proceedings, especially criminal ones, and creates some risk to those proceedings, a margin of appreciation may be conceded in assessing the *degree* of risk. The *Sunday Times* case established that the interference with freedom of expression represented by curbing media freedom to comment on a forthcoming action or on issues linked to it must answer to a pressing social need.[109] Where, as in that instance, the interference is aimed—broadly—at the protection of the administration of justice, but has only a very indirect and uncertain justification in terms of protecting particular litigation, the review of the existence of such a need is likely to be intense. But where the interference appears to be fairly strongly linked to the preservation of Article 6 rights since a particular trial is quite clearly affected, the margin of appreciation doctrine may not have a significant role, and the interference may be found to be justified, as in *Worm* and *BBC Scotland v UK*, since where two rights are viewed as in conflict, the Court will prefer the (almost) unqualified right under Article 6. If, however, the clash is with a qualified Convention right—often Article 8—the Court will assume that the rights are presumptively equal and will seek to balance them against each other. It will not allow one of them to prevail automatically. Chapter 16 considers clashes between Articles 8 and 10 in the context of the general clash between the interest in the administration of justice and media freedom.[110]

It may be concluded, therefore, that where a conflict between free speech and a fair trial arises at Strasbourg as an Article 6 claim, the Convention does not adopt the stance that the two strong individual rights can be balanced against each other on a basis of presumptive equality. Where a direct threat to the fair trial of an individual arises due to a publication, the guarantee under Article 6 will prevail, since it is not materially qualified and the Court has not shown a willingness to find that there is an implied proportionality test within the guarantee where the conflict is with Article 10, as a competing Convention right. This situation is likely to arise infrequently since the national court or appeal court would have a duty to seek to deal with any unfairness

---

[108] In the UK juries are used in certain civil proceedings, notably libel actions and in certain civil actions against the police: see Supreme Court Act 1981 s 69.

[109] (1979) 2 EHRR 245, at para 62.   [110] See pp 823–31.

by the use, if necessary, of neutralizing devices. In the more usual case where the issue arises as part of an Article 10 claim, the Article 6 issue may be considered as an aspect of the 'rights of others' exception under Article 10(2); and the individual right at stake will be afforded recognition by this means, together with the general interest in 'maintaining the authority of the judiciary'. It may be, as in *Worm*, that the Article 6 right at stake will not be considered separately from the general exception. Where both exceptions are at stake, Strasbourg review will tend, as indicated, to be less intense, although where harmony between the primary right and the exceptions can be discerned in terms of their underlying values, this will affect the intensity of the review, as in *News Verlags*.

But where the interference cannot be viewed as directly protecting the interests of specific individuals in fair proceedings, as in the *Sunday Times* case, while its operation clearly directly infringes the individual freedom of expression of certain journalists, the free speech principle will prevail, unless the interference answers to a pressing social need. Thus, under the Strasbourg rhetoric regarding competing interests, some recognition of the consonance between the values underlying them is evident, despite the obscuring effect of the margin of appreciation doctrine. Since the Court must take an overview of the situation that has arisen domestically, on the assumption that all corrective domestic measures have already been exhausted, it may view itself as ill-equipped to consider whether, at trial, the less intrusive neutralizing measures could have been adopted to negate the impact of the media coverage. In other words, the Court appears to have been reluctant to take into account the possible division of responsibilities between preventive and trial measures, although it might have been expected that the possibility of using neutralizing measures would be considered as an aspect of the proportionality doctrine under Article 10(2). Essentially, the jurisprudence reveals a leaning towards the protection of Article 6 rights in specific proceedings where there is a clear risk of prejudice, as in *Worm*. The Court also insists that its concern is with the administration of justice in an abstract sense. It is clear that Strasbourg, unlike the US, does not favour the neutralizing model. But otherwise its stance cannot be characterized as a clearly preventive rather than a protective one. What is clear is that it does not take a strong stance in favour of freedom of expression where a fair trial may be at risk. It accepts the premise that statements in the media may quite readily influence a trial. On the other hand, the speech in question in this context tends to be of significant political value and therefore will tend to overcome the interest in the administration of justice put forward as a general societal concern.

CONCLUSIONS

The following three chapters consider domestic approaches to free speech and the administration of justice. This is a context in which reliance on the Convention under the Human Rights Act provides domestic judges with quite a wide choice as to a number of possible responses. As Chapter 2 indicated, it is a significant feature of Convention case law that in determining the key issue of proportionality,[111] the standard of review varies markedly in accordance with the margin of appreciation doctrine. The strong tendency under Article 10 in this context is to concede a fairly wide margin of appreciation to the state where a clash of rights arises—in this case, a clash between the right to freedom of expression under Article 10 and the right to a fair trial under Article 6(1). In such instances, interferences have not always been rigorously scrutinized (*BBC Scotland*), despite the fact that the speech in question can often be characterized as political expression. Where a real threat to a fair trial arises, Article 6 will prevail (*Worm*). Where the interference with speech has the more general aim of protecting the societal interest in the administration of justice, the margin of appreciation conceded is more circumscribed (*Sunday Times*).

Clearly, the margin of appreciation doctrine, as such, should not be applied by domestic courts,[112] since it is a distinctively international law doctrine. Disregarding the effects of the doctrine might merely mean treating certain judgments as nondeterminative of the points raised at the domestic level. Certainly, domestic courts minded to make an intensive enquiry into questions of proportionality will receive fairly limited guidance from the 'clashing rights' cases described in so doing. Thus, the domestic courts, in applying the Strasbourg jurisprudence have greater leeway than they have in relation to the political expression cases generally. A number of possible approaches are therefore open to the domestic courts. Under the first of these, referred to in Chapter 3 as a 'minimalist' or 'minimal compatibility' approach, the courts, while pronouncing the margin of appreciation doctrine inapplicable, would not take the further step of recognizing and making due allowance for its influence on the cases applied. Thus, judges might merely 'check' the outcome of a domestic case, decided on common law principles, against the relevant Strasbourg jurisprudence. So long as leeway could be found for finding the outcome compatible with the Convention, no more would be attempted.

A further possible approach was referred to in Chapter 3 as 'activist'. Under this approach, judges would regard themselves as required to go beyond the standard of review applied in the relevant Strasbourg jurisprudence,[113] given Strasbourg's view of itself as a system of protection firmly subsidiary to that afforded by national courts. It

---

[111] The focus of concern in nearly all the cases has been on the requirement that interference be 'necessary in a democratic society'. *Hashman v UK* (2000) 30 EHRR 241 is the exception: the issue in that case was the 'prescribed by law' requirement.

[112] *R v DPP, ex parte Kebilene and others* [1999] 3 WLR 972, p 1043, per Lord Hope: '[the doctrine] is not available to the national courts . . .'; see *dicta* to like effect in *R v Stratford Justices, ex parte Imbert, The Times*, 21 February 1999, per Buxton LJ.

[113] In the words of Judge Martens, '[the task of domestic courts] goes further than seeing that the minimum standards laid down in the ECHR are maintained . . . because the ECHR's injunction to further realise human rights and fundamental freedoms contained in the preamble is also addressed to domestic courts.' ('Opinion: Incorporating the Convention: The Role of the Judiciary' [1998] 1 *EHRLR* 3.)

adheres to that stance especially strongly in 'clashing rights' cases.[114] That stance has led it, in almost all instances, to intervene only where the Article 10 guarantee is strongly engaged, while the risk to a fair trial—as guaranteed by Article 6—is only minimal or non-existent. An activist approach would recognize that, as a consequence, the relevant jurisprudence has not in fact required national authorities to demonstrate convincingly in all instances that the test of 'pressing social need' under Article 10(2) has been met. Furthermore, under that approach judges would look, initially, for assistance to the general principles developed by Strasbourg.[115]

One such principle, repeated in a number of cases, is that the right to freedom of expression is one of the foundations of a democratic society[116] and, as Chapter 2 pointed out, it is a marked feature of the Strasbourg jurisprudence that clearly political speech receives a much more robust degree of protection than other types of expression. This is evident in the 'political' speech cases of *Sunday Times*,[117] *Jersild*,[118] *Lingens*,[119] and *Thorgeir Thorgeirson*;[120] in all these instances a very narrow margin of appreciation was conceded, the interference in question was subjected to a very strict scrutiny and Article 10 was found to have been violated.[121] Such an approach would mean that the politically expressive dimension of trial-related speech would obtain greater recognition. But at the same time, the right to a fair trial, guaranteed under Article 6(1), is viewed as one of the most fundamental guarantees offered to an individual under the Convention.[122] Thus, both guarantees represent and encapsulate core Convention values. Once these founding principles are established, the domestic court will not derive extensive guidance from Strasbourg as to the proper resolution of a clash between the two; it has allowed Article 6(1) to prevail, tending to employ the margin of appreciation doctrine to avoid close scrutiny of the questions of necessity and proportionality.

In contrast, the domestic courts, taking the pronouncements at Strasbourg as to the value of these fundamental rights seriously, could make more effort to tease out the free speech and fair trial values genuinely at stake, and go on to employ the tools of

[114] See in particular: *Otto Preminger Institute v Austria* (1994) 19 EHRR 34; *Tammer v Estonia* (2003) 37 EHRR 43; (2001) 10 BHRC 543.

[115] See Chapter 3 at 147–8. As the House of Lords has stressed: 'in the national courts also the Convention should be seen as an expression of fundamental principles rather than as a set of mere rules' (*R v DPP, ex parte Kebilene* [1999] 3 WLR 972).

[116] *Rassemblement Juraiseen v Switzerland* (1980) 17 DR 93, p 119.

[117] *Sunday Times v UK* (1979) A 30.

[118] *Jersild v Denmark* (1994) 19 EHRR 1 concerned an application by a Danish journalist who had been convicted of an offence of racially offensive behaviour after preparing and broadcasting a programme about racism which included overtly racist speech by the subjects of the documentary.

[119] *Lingens v Austria* (1986) 8 EHRR 103 concerned the defamation of a political figure.

[120] *Thorgeirson v Iceland* (1992) 14 EHRR 843 concerned newspaper articles reporting allegations of brutality against the Reykjavik police.

[121] See the discussion of political speech, the margin of appreciation doctrine, and the strictness of review in Chapter 2, at 48–72.

[122] See e.g. Appls 8603, 8722, 8723, and 8729/79 *Crociani v Italy* D&R 22 (1981), p 147. For the full text of Article 6 see note 62 above.

necessity and proportionality to determine the issue, untrammelled by the margin of appreciation doctrine. The clash of such values and the method of their resolution could now be made explicit in the legal discourse surrounding the limits placed on trial-related speech.

Such an activist stance would be particularly appropriate in this context since the courts are not required to abjure a rigorous enquiry into proportionality in deference to the 'area of judgment' or 'discretion' of another body.[123] The preservation of the fairness of proceedings is the courts' own domain. Where such safeguards have been placed on a statutory basis, the courts are, nevertheless, likely to accord some deference to Parliament and the limits of such deference are currently being determined under s 3(1) HRA. But it is now clear that where the courts view themselves as controlling their own domain—protecting the court process—they are prepared to take an especially activist stance under s 3.[124] Where the courts are developing the common law in a context such as this, they may tend to view themselves as having even greater leeway.[125] However, as Chapter 16 points out, judicial activism does not necessarily entail a principled weighing up of the values at stake where individual rights come into conflict with each other. It can mean the re-assertion or re-affirmation of judicial control over a particular area of law with a view to preserving judicial control and resisting interference by outside bodies—in this case, the media. Having considered differences between the Strasbourg and the domestic approach, the next two chapters will evaluate the stance the domestic courts currently appear to be taking, bearing these comments in mind, as they come to an accommodation with the Strasbourg jurisprudence under the Human Rights Act.

The following two chapters situate the domestic interpretation of the current contempt provisions within the Strasbourg jurisprudence. It will be argued that during the 25 years since the Contempt of Court Act 1981 was introduced as a result of the *Sunday Times* case, the domestic fair trial/free speech balance has changed and, perhaps ironically, now fails, for a variety of reasons, to reflect the Strasbourg one. The developments that have occurred and their underlying rationales are examined with a view to considering how far it is desirable or possible to use the Human Rights Act to create a renewed harmony with the Strasbourg balance.

---

[123] See for full discussion Chapter 3 at 146–53. In *ex parte Kebilene* [1999] 3 WLR 972, Lord Hope said: 'In some circumstances it will be appropriate for the courts to recognise that there is an area of judgment within which the judiciary will defer, on democratic grounds, to the considered opinion of [another body or person] whose act or decision is said to be incompatible with the Convention'; see also *Secretary of State for the Home Dept v International Transport Roth GmbH and Others* [2002] 1 CMLR 52; *R v Shayler* [2003] 1 AC 247 (Chapter 19, at 939–45); *R (ProLife Alliance) v BBC* [2004] 1 AC 185 [2003] UKHL 23 (Chapter 11, at 577–92); see also Laws LJ, 'Wednesbury' in C, Forsyth and, I Hare (eds), *The Golden Metwand and the Crooked Cord: Essays in Honour of Sir William Wade QC* (Cambridge, 1998), p 201; D. Pannick, 'Principles of interpretation of Convention rights under the HRA and Discretionary areas of judgment' [1998] PL 545, pp 549–51; Hunt et al. 'Is there a role for the margin of appreciation in national law after the HRA?' [1999] EHRLR 15 at 21–2.

[124] See *R v A* [2002] 1 AC 45; *R v Offen* [2001] 1 WLR 253.

[125] This may eventually occur in relation to common law contempt but it has not yet done so—cf the stance of the Court of Appeal in *A-G v Punch* [2001] 2 All ER 655, discussed in Chapter 6, at 291–4.

5

FREE SPEECH AND FAIR TRIALS: REPORTING RESTRICTIONS

INTRODUCTION

FREEDOM OF EXPRESSION AND OPEN JUSTICE

Chapter 4 considered the values underlying the open justice principle and its relationship with freedom of expression. This chapter considers the range of specific prior restraints on trial-related reporting that has incrementally accumulated in British law. They now form a complex and chaotic web. The large and ever-increasing range of restrictions indicates a well-established UK acceptance of the open justice principle as heavily qualified. As Chapter 4 pointed out, there are two interests at stake underlying the principle.[1] One is that the right to a fair trial is safeguarded by the public nature of trials since a check on its fairness is created.[2] The other is the interest of the public in receiving information via the media regarding trials—in itself a means of safeguarding fairness. It can be argued therefore that any rights of access to hearings and to report upon them should be protected only if they have the consequence of securing a fair trial. If access for reporters and allowing reporting might *interfere* with a fair trial, it could justifiably be curtailed or prevented.[3] It might also be suggested that since these rights are there to aid in securing the right of the parties to a fair trial, the parties themselves could waive them. In fact such a right of waiver has not been accepted in British law in a general sense,[4] although where parties have strong reasons to argue that the hearing should occur in private, or that matters should not be reported, this has on occasion been accepted both in Britain[5] and at Strasbourg.[6]

---

[1] See pp 168–70. [2] See J. Jaconelli, *Open Justice: A Critique of the Public Trial*, Oxford: OUP, 2002.

[3] See further F. Schauer, 'The Speech of Law and the Law of Speech' (1997) 49 *Arkansa LR* 687.

[4] See *Scott v Scott* [1913] AC 417. See further p 199 below. See also the decision of the House of Lords in *Re S* [2005] 1 AC 593, discussed in Chapter 16.

[5] *R v Chandler of Chichester Consistory Court, ex parte News Group Newspapers Ltd*, *The Independent*, 10 September 1991; *R v Richards* (1999) JP 246.

[6] See *Atkinson Crook and the Independent v UK* (1990) 67 DR 244, discussed at p 224 below. See further Chapter 16, at 828.

These exceptional circumstances have tended to be predicated on specific reasons for restrictions in order to serve the ends of justice, which is in accordance with the instrumental nature of reporting rights in relation to trials.

But if a general right of waiver has not been accepted, demonstrating that the right to a fair trial has a public aspect going beyond the immediate preferences of the parties involved, it remains the case that reporting rights, including access rights, can be abrogated where fairness to the trial might be compromised. Barendt argues that the access rights are somewhat precariously supported by free speech values: 'there is no clear explanation why the law should be more willing to uphold free speech access rights to attend legal proceedings, even against the objection of the parties, than they are to uphold rights to attend meeting of government committees . . .'.[7] On the other hand, it is argued that there is a difference between access rights to courts and to meetings of public bodies. The results of such meetings are usually opened to public scrutiny at some point when the deliberations issue forth as policy statements or proposals. At that point the public will be informed of the main purpose of the deliberations, and some indications of the *process* may also become apparent. Access to the meetings by reporters and the public is not therefore essential to the integrity of the decision-making process or as a means of creating accountability.

In contrast, access to trials relates strongly to the integrity of the process and also acts as an assurance to the public that fairness is being maintained. There is no real opportunity after the verdict for the public to impose accountability on the court. There may be an outcry after certain verdicts, but the link between the reaction of the public and the response of the administration of justice system once the trial is over is relatively weak. Upholding the integrity of the criminal or civil process has a significance that transcends its effects in individual trials.[8] It may help to ensure the continued cooperation of the public with the process, by, for example, reporting crimes or coming forward as a witness. More fundamentally, if faith in justice is not maintained, social breakdown may begin to occur as the public perceive that the criminal justice process does not have a greater integrity than criminal activity itself. People may turn to self help methods rather than using the law. Thus there is, it is argued, a strong case for upholding access rights for the press in this context. This is recognized in the US as a right under the First Amendment,[9] and the German Constitutional Court has accepted a right of reporters to attend criminal trials.[10]

In considering the various reporting restrictions in UK law, it will be questioned therefore whether they go beyond what is required to serve the ends of justice. It will also be suggested below that there are so many circumstances in which reporters are not allowed to attend hearings, that it may be a misnomer to speak of general 'rights

[7] E. Barendt, *Freedom of Speech*, 2nd edn., OUP, Oxford: 2005, at 340. See further R. Dworkin, 'Is the Press Losing the First Amendment?' in *A Matter of Principle*, Cambridge, Mass.: Harvard University Press, 1985, 381.

[8] See further on this point at: J. Jaconelli, note 2 above; for general discussion of the effects of maintaining public confidence in the criminal justice system, see A. Sanders, and J. Young, *Criminal Justice* OUP, 2nd edn., Oxford: 2000; R. Clayton and H. Tomlinson, *The Law of Human Rights*, Oxford: OUP, 2000, 1465–6.

[9] *Richmond Newspapers v Virginia* 448 US 555 (1980).   [10] 50 BVerfGE 234 (1979).

of access' to hearings for reporters, despite the provision of Article 6(1). The Strasbourg Court has also accepted a large number of exceptions to the right of access it holds out as guaranteed.[11] Thus despite the common law acceptance of the open justice principle and the constitutional guarantees of free expression and open justice in Articles 6 and 10 HRA, a number of exceptions to the principle have been accepted in UK law. No significant modification of the existing exceptions occurred after the HRA came into force, and they continued to proliferate. The 'constitutionalism' of freedom of expression—its embodiment in the Human Rights Act—has had remarkably little impact on the profileration of these exceptions in a range of statutes. Clearly, it could be argued that the new constitutional guarantees merely reflected the existing common law position. However, the HRA did raise different expectations. Cram argues:

'the enhanced level of constitutional protection accorded to expression [in the HRA and—in Canada—in the Charter of Rights] . . . raises the possibility that previously established boundary lines between speech and administration of justice interests which prioritised the latter may now be constitutionally dubious. . . . [as a result] the workings of the judicial system might emerge more fully from the cloisters . . .'[12]

This chapter will argue that there are few signs of the re-drawing of those boundary lines thus far under the HRA and that therefore scrutiny of the justice system continues to be tramelled.

The reporting restrictions operate as prior restraints and therefore at first sight pose an especial threat to free expression.[13] A number of writers have, however, argued that prior restraints are not inevitably more of a threat to free speech than post-publication sanctions,[14] although this stance was not taken in Chapter 3.[15] A comparison between the preventive measures discussed in this chapter and the post-publication sanctions discussed in the next indicates, unsurprisingly, that where the latter are especially broad and imprecise, they may have more of a 'chilling' effect on the media than prior restraints do. However, the impact of prior restraints is undoubted, even if generalized hostility to them is unwarranted, and the large number of restraints on trial-related reporting that now exist is clearly a matter of concern, even where individual restraints are relatively narrow. It may be concluded that they clearly require careful scrutiny under Article 10 since Strasbourg has taken the view that prior restraints are especially inimical to free expression.[16] This is also the very

---

[11] See B v UK [2001] FCR 221.

[12] I. Cram, A Virtue Less Cloistered: Courts, Speech and Constitutions, Oxford: Hart Publishing, 2002, p 2.

[13] See the seminal work: A. Bickel, The Morality of Consent, Yale University Press, 1975.

[14] See W.T. Mayton, 'Toward a Theory of First Amendment Process: Injunctions of Speech, Subsequent Punishment and the Cost of Prior Restraint Doctrine' (1982) 67 Cornell LR 245; see also the discussions in I. Cram, A Virtue Less Cloistered: Courts, Speech and Constitutions, Oxford: Hart Publishing, 2002, pp 130–4; E. Barendt, 'Prior Restraints on Speech' (1985) PL 253.

[15] At pp 153–7.

[16] See e.g. News Verlags (2001) 31 EHRR 6; Observer and Guardian v UK (1992) 14 EHRR 153; see also Atkinson Crook and the Independent v UK (1990) 67 DR 244, p 224 below. See note 15 above, and see further Chapter 13 at 696–9.

well established stance of the US Supreme Court.[17] In the US this has been very clearly the case in the context of court-reporting;[18] this is less clearly the case at Strasbourg; it has set the limits of 'permissible comment' at the point at which the material creates a *likelihood* of prejudice to the chances of a person receiving a fair trial.[19] This remark was not applied only to the use of post-publication sanctions—it would appear also to cover prior restraints. But there is clearly a strong free speech case for taking a critical look at the many prior restraints discussed in this chapter; they strike at the heart of reporting on matters that are frequently of significant public interest. Taking account of the realities of journalism, restraints imposing anonymity or postponing reports may well mean that the newsworthiness of the story is undermined to such an extent that it is never run. This is justifiable where the ends of justice so demand or another Convention right provides a strong countervailing argument justifying these measures.[20] But a particularly pernicious aspect of a number of the restraints discussed below is their meagre provision of avenues of challenge for the media. This means that the balancing act demanded by Article 10(2) cannot be carried out; it is hard therefore to assess the weightiness of the other countervailing interest. The compatibility of a number of the restraints with Article 10 must remain therefore in doubt.

The open justice principle has long received a degree of legislative recognition in the UK,[21] but until Article 6(1) received further effect in UK law under the Human Rights Act, the principle was not encapsulated in an express constitutional guarantee, as in the USA.[22] However, as discussed in Chapter 4, it could readily be viewed as a fundamental principle recognized by the common law.[23] The principle has a number of aspects: firstly, that court hearings should normally be in public; secondly that judgment should be pronounced publicly, and thirdly that fair and accurate reporting of court proceedings should not be restrained by law. Under the Human Rights Act the first two aspects of this principle are expressly recognized in the Article 6(1) requirement that, in respect of the determination of a 'criminal charge' or of 'civil rights and obligations', everyone is entitled to a 'fair and *public* hearing.' Article 6(1) continues:

Judgment shall be pronounced publicly but the press and public may be excluded from all or part of the trial in the interests of morals, public order or national security in a democratic society, where the interests of juveniles or the protection of the private life of the parties so

---

[17] See in particular *Near v Minnesota* (1931) 283 US 697; *Nebraska Press Assoc v Stuart* (1976) US 427. See further Chapter 3, at 153–7, and Chapter 7, note 166.

[18] See *Press-Enterprise Co v Superior Court of California* (1984) 464 US 501; *Richmond Newspapers v Virginia* 448 US 555 (1980).

[19] *Worm v Austria* (1998) 25 EHRR 454, at para 5.

[20] See further Chapter 14, at 714–15, and Chapter 16, at 843–8.

[21] See Administration of Justice Act 1960 s 12(1); Contempt of Court Act 1981 s 4(1). In both statutes the principle is expressed negatively: see p 210 below.

[22] It is protected under the Sixth Amendment. The relevant part provides: 'the accused shall enjoy the right to a speedy and *public* trial' (emphasis added); for the full text see Chapter 4 p 178 note 49.

[23] The principle that justice should be openly administered is well established in the common law (*Scott v Scott* [1913] AC 417, at 437). See more recently the comments to this effect and on the need to limit the use of private hearings in *Preston* [1993] 4 All ER 638; 143 NLJ 1601. See further Chapter 16 at p 828.

require or to the extent strictly necessary in the opinion of the court in special circumstances where publicity would prejudice the interests of justice.

This guarantee is more widely stated than the principle enunciated by Lord Diplock in *A-G v Leveller Magazine*:[24]

[t]he English system of administering justice does require that it be done in public . . . The application of this principle of open justice has two aspects: It requires that [the proceedings] should be held in open court to which the press and public are admitted and that, in criminal cases, at any rate, all evidence communicated to the court is communicated publicly.

The Article 6 requirement is wider since civil actions are expressly included. However, the guarantee of public hearings is subject to a number of exceptions contained in Article 6(1). The use of the word 'but' in relation to the guarantee that judgment shall be pronounced publicly appears to imply that this is an absolute requirement. However, the Court has held that both requirements are qualified in the same way.[25]

The third aspect of the open justice principle mentioned above—that accurate reporting of court proceedings should not be restrained—is not the subject of an express guarantee under Article 6 but it is clearly covered, in a general sense, by Article 10(1). As Nicol and Rogers argue, although Article 10 does not in general provide a right of access to information from an unwilling provider,[26] there may be a case for suggesting that even where the parties to a hearing wish the information available from attending a hearing to remain private, Article 10 provides a right to such information where an important public interest is at stake.[27] This aspect of the open justice principle is also covered, in a negative and limited sense, by s 4(1) of the Contempt of Court Act 1981 which provides that a fair and accurate factual report of the proceedings, in good faith, will not amount to a contempt.[28]

As the discussion below reveals, the three aspects of the open justice principle are not necessarily linked in British law. The fact that reporters are allowed access to a courts hearing does not preclude the application of reporting restrictions. Conversely, the fact that reporters are not allowed such access does not mean that reporting of the hearing is inevitably penalized. But clearly, allowing reporters access to court hearings is highly significant in allowing them to perform their role in informing the public as to the administration of justice.

---

[24] [1979] AC 440, pp 449–50. Part of this comment is also discussed in Chapter 4 at 169.

[25] *B v UK* [2001] FCR 221.   [26] See *Gaskin v UK* (1990) 12 EHRR 36.

[27] See A. Nicol and H. Rogers, 'Reporting Restrictions', Vol. VI *Yearbook of Copyright and Media Law 2001–02*, p 374. The authority quoted in support of this contention is *Hakansson and Sturesson v Sweden* (1990) 13 EHRR 1, at para 66: It was found that although litigants can waive the right to a public hearing under Article 6(1), waiver is subject to the qualification that it must not run counter to any important public interest. This might be found to apply in other contexts. But see *Atkinson Crook and the Independent v UK* (1990) 67 DR 244; facts given at p 224 below.

[28] Section 4(1), therefore, creates an exception from the strict liability rule under the 1981 Act (see Chapter 6, esp at 257–8) in respect of proceedings held in public, so long as the other elements mentioned are present. It can also be said that in most instances fair and accurate reports of proceedings would not fall within s 2(2) in any event: s 4(1) merely makes this explicit, in statutory form.

It is clear that, domestically, the aspect of the open justice principle reflected in allowing reporting of proceedings goes beyond the principle of openness reflected in Article 6(1) in the guarantee of public hearings. Such reporting is more broadly protected under Article 10 on the basis that, while the exclusion of reporters from the proceedings themselves might be accepted in some circumstances, based on the exceptions specified in Article 6(1), as necessary in a democratic society, restrictions on the *reporting* of the proceedings would be viewed as a more direct and far-reaching interference with freedom of expression. Restrictions relating only to the reporting of proceedings must be scrutinized under Article 10(2). All restrictions preventing journalists attending hearings should now be scrutinized under the HRA in relation to both Article 6(1) and Article 10(2) since they are bound to impair the ability of journalists to report on the hearing. In this respect, Articles 10 and 6 are not in conflict, since Article 10 may be said to require impliedly that restrictions on allowing journalists to attend hearings should be strictly scrutinized. Where such restrictions are intended to protect the privacy of the proceedings, conflict between Article 6(1) (together with Article 10) and Article 8 might arise. Such conflicts are considered in Chapter 16.[29]

The adoption of a different stance under Article 10(2) in relation to these two aspects of media freedom can be justified on the basis that journalists excluded from the hearing would be able to obtain information from witnesses and others, whereas they would be entirely unable to fulfil their role in informing the public if the reporting of private hearings amounted automatically to a contempt.

THE NATURE OF THE PREVENTIVE MEASURES

The range of trial-related prior restraints is the main subject of this chapter, although account is also taken of restrictions preventing reporters from attending hearings. Certain restrictions are aimed mainly at protecting privacy, although they may have links to the administration of justice. Where this is the case they are discussed in Chapters 15 and 16.[30] Certain measures that have a 'mixed' role, in terms of protecting both the privacy of those involved in trials and the administration of justice, are discussed below. As Chapter 6 indicates, the protective approach predominates in Britain under the Contempt of Court Act 1981 as a means of seeking to prevent prejudice to court proceedings. However, the preventive approach also has a role, as this chapter demonstrates. The difference between the two approaches is that specific reporting restrictions are aimed directly at preventing specific forms of interference with proceedings, while protective measures are not aimed directly at *preventing* prejudice to proceedings since that is ultimately the responsibility of the trial judge. They are aimed generally at protecting the administration of justice. They do have, however, a part to play in protecting trials by deterring prejudicial media comment but, as Chapter 6 discusses, the relationship between contempt law and the role of

[29] See pp 813–14.   [30] See pp 715–16, 813–15.

the trial judge remains unclear.[31] The preventive measures take the form of pre- and post- trial publication reporting bans; they are intended to serve as a means of preventing prejudice, but also protect other interests falling within other Convention guarantees. The various measures are considered below, as is their relationship with the protective measures that are discussed fully in Chapter 6. Clearly, the current media environment, which has changed immensely with the rise of the Internet and access to satellite television, raises serious questions about the continued efficacy of such measures.[32]

There has recently been a rapid incremental increase in the range of restrictions. Some of the exceptions apply automatically, while others are qualified. They take the form of court orders or injunctions relating to specific proceedings and of statutory rules delineating the trial-related material that cannot be published (temporarily or permanently). Where such restrictions are intended to protect the fairness of the trial, they indicate that there is an acceptance by the judiciary and Parliament of a partially preventive approach: The media are forewarned that some reports of trial-related material, however fair and accurate, will attract liability, either automatically or subject to certain further qualifications.

The reporting restrictions do *not* relate merely to the question whether the hearing is private, public or semi-public. (The term semi-public is used to indicate those hearings that are technically public but which occur under some restrictions as to entry due to security concerns.)[33] Reports of private hearings are not automatically banned, although they are subject to a range of restrictions which are inapplicable to public hearings. This is made clear by s 12(1) Administration of Justice Act 1960; the provision adheres to the open justice principle in indicating that in general the reporting of private proceedings will not amount to a contempt in itself, before going on to specify the exceptional circumstances in which it will do so. It could therefore be said that in a sense the legal scheme relating to the first aspect of the open justice principle—that court hearings should be public—is more restrictive than that relating to the third—open reporting. Clearly, in practical terms, reporting of private hearings is often likely to be problematic, although those involved or witnesses may disclose matters to journalists, and so doing will not amount to a contempt so long as none of the exceptions under the 1960 Act apply.[34]

It is convenient to delineate three categories of 'preventive' reporting restrictions. In the first are those relating specifically to certain private hearings as detailed in s 12(1) of the 1960 Act. In the second are orders or automatic restrictions temporarily

---

[31] See pp 265–6.

[32] See I. Cram, *A Virtue Less Cloistered: Courts, Speech and Constitutions*, Oxford: Hart Publishing, 2002, Chapter 7; J. Armstrong Brandwood, 'You Say "Fair Trial" and I Say "Free Press": British and American approaches to protecting defendants' rights in high profile trials' [2000] 75 *New York University Law Review* 1412, pp 1446–7. The problems created for both preventive and protective measures by the growth of the new media technology are considered in Chapter 6 at 261–2.

[33] See *Campbell and Fell v UK* (1984) 7 EHRR 165, at paras 86–88.

[34] *Clibbery v Allan* [2001] FLR 819.

postponing the reporting of matters that could prejudice the fairness of forthcoming proceedings, while in the third there are provisions allowing persons involved in court proceedings to remain anonymous. The main restrictions within these groups are discussed below, although an exhaustive list is not attempted. The extent of their compatibility with Article 10 and, in respect of restrictions flowing from lack of access to the hearing, Article 6(1), is also considered. All these exceptions clearly represent interferences with freedom of expression and with the open justice principle. In relation to reporting restrictions, as opposed to restrictions on those who may attend the hearing, a conflict between Articles 10 and 6(1) may arise where the restrictions are aimed at avoiding prejudice to the trial. In relation to restrictions on attending the hearing, Articles 10 and 6(1) may not be fully in harmony since Article 10 can be said to require impliedly that restrictions on allowing journalists to attend hearings should be strictly scrutinized for their necessity in a democratic society, while Article 6 uses the term 'necessary in the opinion of the court.' Reporting restrictions aimed specifically at protecting privacy, rather than the administration of justice, are discussed in Chapter 14[35] and Chapter 16.[36] As indicated below, certain restrictions protect both interests. At a very high level of generality, it can be said that restrictions aimed at protecting privacy also serve the ends of justice since victims in civil and criminal cases with inevitably humiliating elements might refuse to pursue the action otherwise.[37]

This chapter goes on to discuss reporting restrictions falling into these three categories taking account of their implications under the Human Rights Act, Articles 10 and 6(1). The chapter then moves on to consider a particular form of reporting restriction that requires a category of its own—the ban on reporting on jury deliberations under s 8 of the 1981 Act. This ban requires distinct treatment since it is the most far-reaching absolute restriction that this chapter deals with. It is similar to the provisions assuring anonymity since it is not temporary and it is aimed not at preventing prejudice to proceedings, but at protecting the administration of justice in a more general sense. But it is much broader than the anonymity provisions since they do not prevent reporting of the trial in question, but only anonymize the identity of certain parties to them.

PRIVATE HEARINGS

As Chapter 16 points out, all courts have a common law discretion to sit in private, but due to the importance of access rights as an aspect of the open justice principle, the discretion is to be exercised only in exceptional circumstances.[38] The Civil Procedure

---

[35] See pp 714–15.   [36] See pp 813–18 and 825–7.

[37] This is true of instances of allegations of sexual offences in employment or cases of sexual misconduct which are covered by reporting restrictions under s 11(6)(a) and (b) Employment Tribunals Act 1996; anonymity for rape victims is considered below. See. p 226

[38] The rule derives from *Scott v Scott* [1913] AC 417. See further Chapter 16 at 813–14.

Rules 1998 Part 39 provide that a number of categories of hearing may take place in private; the decision whether to hold the hearing in private or in public is for the judge conducting it. Part 39 now places a greater emphasis on the openness of court hearings than previously, and the Practice Direction made under it[39] was amended before the Human Rights Act came fully into force, to provide expressly that judges should have regard to Article 6(1) of the Convention. Clearly, it is hard to see that this adds anything to the duty of a court, as a public authority, to abide by the Convention rights under s 6(1) HRA, but it may have value in terms of drawing the attention of the courts to the Article 6(1) provisions.

Certain statutes expressly provide for hearings to be held in private in relation to matters involving children or official secrets.[40] Courts are highly likely, for obvious reasons, to hold hearings of applications for injunctions to restrain a breach of confidence in private. They will also seek to do so where a private hearing would serve the ends of justice. The courts in exercising their inherent discretion now also have to abide by all the Convention rights under s 6(1) HRA. The most relevant guarantee is clearly the right to a fair trial under Article 6(1) (as Part 39 indicates), but the guarantee of respect for private life under Article 8 and of freedom from inhuman and degrading treatment under Article 3 might also be relevant in the sense that the interests of victims and other witnesses in freedom from humiliation and indignity may be viewed as aspects of the ends of justice in their own right and not merely in relation to ensuring a fair trial. A court might sit in private where, for example, a witness would be so humiliated at having to reveal intimate details that he or she would be unable to give full evidence.[41] However, as Feldman points out, the line between sitting in private to save a witness from embarrassment and in order to serve the ends of justice can be very hard to draw; he argues that some courts have failed to make the effort to distinguish between the two aims and have sat in private on doubtful grounds.[42]

On the other hand, although merely saving a witness from embarrassment may not be a sufficient reason to sit in private, it could be argued that a court's duty to abide by Articles 3 and 8 could possibly be violated where a victim or other witness is asked to reveal very humiliating details in open court. An instance arose in the case of *JM v UK*[43] which concerned a complaint under Article 3 in respect of degrading treatment of a woman in a UK rape trial; it was declared admissible at Strasbourg. The woman was subjected to prolonged cross-examination—over a period of days—by the defendant himself, who was deliberately wearing the clothes in which he had allegedly raped her. The experience was extremely humiliating and distressing for the victim.

---

[39] Practice Direction to CPR Part 39: Miscellaneous Provisions relating to hearings.

[40] Adoption Act 1976 s 64; Magistrates Court Act 1980 s 69(2) as amended by the Children Act 1989 s 97; Official Secrets Act 1920 s 8(4).

[41] *R v Chandler of Chichester Consistory Court, ex parte News Group Newspapers Ltd, The Independent,* 10 September 1991.

[42] D. Feldman, *Civil Liberties and Human Rights in England and Wales,* 2nd ed OUP 2002, p 990.

[43] See case comment at (2001) *EHRLR* 215.

This case partly turned on its particular facts, and the decision was addressed by disallowing defendant cross-examination in such instances.[44] However, it raises the further possibility that Articles 3 or 8 might be found to demand that the revelation of particularly distressing and humiliating details in rape and other cases concerning sexual violence should not occur in open court. In other words, even where the demands of justice now encapsulated in Article 6(1) do not fully or clearly support a decision of a court to sit in private, other Convention guarantees may do so.

The mere fact that a hearing occurs in private does not automatically mean, as indicated above, that reporting of the proceedings is restricted. Under s 12(1) of the 1960 Act it will only be a contempt to report on proceedings held in private where they relate to: wardship, adoption, guardianship, custody, upbringing of or access to an infant; where they are brought under Part VII Mental Health Act 1983 or under any provision of the 1983 Act authorizing an application or reference to be made to a Mental Health Review Tribunal or county court; where the court sits in private for reasons of national security; where the information relates to a secret process or invention at issue in the proceedings; where the court, acting within its powers, expressly prohibits the publication of all information relating to the proceedings or of information of the description which is published.

A report of information relating to all such proceedings is *prima facie* a contempt; it is not *automatically* a contempt since the section preserves all defences a person accused of contempt would normally have. Thus a conviction was not obtained where a newspaper editor published material relating to wardship proceedings without being aware of the connection.[45] It has been found that the press cannot report any aspect of wardship proceedings,[46] but this is not an absolute restriction—it has been found to cover 'statements of evidence, reports, accounts of interviews' and similar information.[47] The restrictions on reporting relating to children are largely intended to protect privacy, although the open justice principle may also be relevant. Therefore, although certain restrictions are considered briefly below, they are looked at more fully in relation to Article 8, in Chapter 16.[48]

POSTPONING REPORTING OF PROCEEDINGS

There a large number of measures allowing for the postponing of reports on proceedings. They are more defensible than complete bans on aspects of such reporting, which are discussed in the next section of this chapter, but they still represent

[44] The experience could no longer recur thanks to the provision of the Youth Justice and Criminal Evidence Act 1999, s 34, introduced as a result of that case.
[45] *Re F (A Minor) (Publication of Information)* [1977] Fam 58.
[46] See *Re X (A Minor) (Wardship: Injunction)* [1984] 1 WLR 1422 (the Mary Bell case).
[47] *Re F (A Minor) (Publication of Information)* [1977] Fam 58, p 105.
[48] At pp 813–14, 823–31, 844–8.

significant encroachments on reporting rights as an aspect of the open justice principle.[49]

RESTRICTIONS ON REPORTING PRE-TRIAL HEARINGS AND PROSECUTION APPEALS

There are a number of measures allowing for the postponing of reporting of proceedings—they fall into two groups—the automatic and the discretionary. The automatic restrictions arising under ss 41 and 37 Criminal Procedure and Investigations Act (CPI) 1996 Part IV prevent the reporting of most matters relating to preparatory hearings and all matters relating to pre-trial rulings. Where the trial is likely to be lengthy or complex, s 37 covers reporting restrictions at the preparatory hearings. Section 37(9) sets out the matters that may be reported in relation to preparatory hearings—they cover only the bare details of the hearing: the identity of the court and judge, brief identifying details relating to the defendants, the offences charged, the date and place of adjournment and whether legal aid was granted.[50] The judge can order otherwise but unless such an order is made, it will be an offence to report anything other than these bare details, until the conclusion of the trial. Section 41 provides similar restrictions, applying generally to pre-trial hearings. Under s 42 it is

---

[49] For a fuller account and further critique of such restrictions see C.J. Miller, *Contempt of Court*, 3rd edn., Oxford: OUP, 2000.

[50] Section 37 provides in full: Restrictions on reporting (as amended by Criminal Justice Act 2003 Pt 13 s 311(6)).

(1) Except as provided by this section—
  (a) no written report of proceedings falling within subsection (2) shall be published in the UK;
  (b) no report of proceedings falling within subsection (2) shall be included in a relevant programme for reception in the United Kingdom.
(2) The following proceedings fall within this subsection—
  (a) a preparatory hearing;
  (b) an application for leave to appeal in relation to such a hearing;
  (c) an appeal in relation to such a hearing.
(3) The judge dealing with a preparatory hearing may order that subsection (1) shall not apply, or shall not apply to a specified extent, to a report of—
  (a) the preparatory hearing, or
  (b) an application to the judge for leave to appeal to the Court of Appeal under s 35(1) in relation to the preparatory hearing.
(4) The Court of Appeal may order that subsection (1) shall not apply, or shall not apply to a specified extent, to a report of—
  (a) an appeal to the Court of Appeal under section 35(1) in relation to a preparatory hearing,
  (b) an application to that Court for leave to appeal to it under section 35(1) in relation to a preparatory hearing, or
  (c) an application to that Court for leave to appeal to the House of Lords under Part II of the Criminal Appeal Act 1968 in relation to a preparatory hearing.
(5) The House of Lords may order that subsection (1) shall not apply, or shall not apply to a specified extent, to a report of—
  (a) an appeal to that House under Part II of the Criminal Appeal Act 1968 in relation to a preparatory hearing, or
  (b) an application to that House for leave to appeal to it under Part II of the Criminal Appeal Act 1968 in relation to a preparatory hearing.

an offence to publish a report of any aspect of the rulings or proceedings in pre-trial hearings.[51] No avenue of challenge to these restrictions is provided for the media. These restrictions will be referred to below as the 'CPI pre-trial reporting restrictions'.

The Criminal Justice Act 2003 s 71(1) (CJA) provides for a similar range of reporting restrictions relating to prosecution appeals,[52] although brief identifying details can be reported.[53] It is an offence to report matters that contravene s 71, under s 72. The Court of Appeal or House of Lords can order that s 71(1) is not to apply, but no

---

[51] Under s 42 the proprietor, editor or publisher of the newspaper or periodical (and the equivalents in respect of a broadcast) can be fined in respect of a contravention of s 41. The consent of the Attorney General is required.

[52]
(1) Except as provided by this section no publication shall include a report of—
  (a) anything done under section 58, 59, 62, 63 or 64,
  (b) an appeal under this Part,
  (c) an appeal under Part 2 of the 1968 Act in relation to an appeal under this Part, or
  (d) an application for leave to appeal in relation to an appeal mentioned in paragraph (b) or (c).
(2) The judge may order that subsection (1) is not to apply, or is not to apply to a specified extent, to a report of—
  (a) anything done under section 58, 59, 62, 63 or 64, or
  (b) an application to the judge for leave to appeal to the Court of Appeal under this Part.
(3) The Court of Appeal may order that subsection (1) is not to apply, or is not to apply to a specified extent, to a report of—
  (a) an appeal to the Court of Appeal under this Part,
  (b) an application to that Court for leave to appeal to it under this Part, or
  (c) an application to that Court for leave to appeal to the House of Lords under Part 2 of the 1968 Act.
(4) The House of Lords may order that subsection (1) is not to apply, or is not to apply to a specified extent, to a report of—
  (a) an appeal to that House under Part 2 of the 1968 Act, or
  (b) an application to that House for leave to appeal to it under Part 2 of that Act.
(5) Where there is only one defendant and he objects to the making of an order under subsection (2), (3) or (4)—
  (a) the judge, the Court of Appeal or the House of Lords are to make the order if (and only if) satisfied, after hearing the representations of the defendant, that it is in the interests of justice to do so, and
  (b) the order (if made) is not to apply to the extent that a report deals with any such objection or representations.
(6) Where there are two or more defendants and one or more of them object to the making of an order under subsection (2), (3) or (4)—
  (a) the judge, the Court of Appeal or the House of Lords are to make the order if (and only if) satisfied, after hearing the representations of each of the defendants, that it is in the interests of justice to do so, and
  (b) the order (if made) is not to apply to the extent that a report deals with any such objection or representations.
(7) Subsection (1) does not apply to the inclusion in a publication of a report of—
  (a) anything done under section 58, 59, 62, 63 or 64,
  (b) an appeal under this Part,
  (c) an appeal under Part 2 of the 1968 Act in relation to an appeal under this Part, or
  (d) an application for leave to appeal in relation to an appeal mentioned in paragraph (b) or (c), at the conclusion of the trial of the defendant or the last of the defendants to be tried.
Section 58 covers the general right of appeal; ss 59 and 64 cover expedited/non-expedited appeals; ss 62 and 63 cover evidentiary rulings significantly weakening the prosecution's case.

[53] Under s 71(8) such details can include the name, age, address of the defendant(s), nature of offence, court in question.

avenue of appeal for the media is provided. Section 71(5)(a) provides that an order should not be made postponing reporting if the defendant objects to the order, and if 'it is in the interests of justice to do so'. It could be argued on behalf of the media that such interests should include the interest in open justice. However, at present no means of putting such an argument is provided in the 2003 Act. Thus there seems to be a potential for incompatibility with Article 10.

POSTPONING REPORTING TO AVOID A RISK OF PREJUDICE

The CPI and CJA provisions may be contrasted with those of s 4(2) of the Contempt of Court Act 1981 which apply much more widely—to all proceedings, including civil ones, but are discretionary. There are also avenues of challenge.

Section 4 provides:

(1) Subject to this section a person is not guilty of contempt of court under the strict liability rule in respect of a fair and accurate report of legal proceedings held in public, published contemporaneously and in good faith.

(2) In any such proceedings the court may, where it appears to be necessary for avoiding a substantial risk of prejudice to the administration of justice in those proceedings, or in any other proceedings pending or imminent, order that the publication of any report of the proceedings, or any part of the proceedings be postponed for such period as the court thinks necessary for that purpose.

(3) For the purposes of subsection (1) of this section . . . a report of proceedings shall be treated as published contemporaneously (a) in the case of a report of which publication is postponed pursuant to an order subsection (2) of this section, if published as soon as practicable after that order expires.

Thus s 4(1) contains an exception to the strict liability rule under s 1 of the Act, discussed in Chapter 6.[54] That rule can be satisfied if, *inter alia*, s 2(2) is fulfilled. Section 2(2) provides: 'the strict liability rule applies only to a publication which creates a substantial risk that the course of justice in the proceedings in question will be seriously impeded or prejudiced'. It may be noted that s 2(2) speaks of the creation of '*serious* prejudice', whereas s 4(2) speaks only of 'prejudice'. So in this respect s 4(2) creates a lower threshold than s 2(2). The effect of s 4(1) is that, even where the contemporaneous publication of a fair and accurate report of court proceedings creates a substantial risk that the course of justice will be seriously impeded or prejudiced (under s 2(2)), the publisher is not to be guilty of contempt of court under the strict liability rule. Clearly, it is highly unlikely in most circumstances that such fair and accurate reporting could cause prejudice. However, this exception is intended to reassure newspaper editors in relation to trial-related reporting.

The freedom of the media to report proceedings is itself then limited, however, by the provision of s 4(2). Section 4(2) provides a discretion to be exercised during any

[54] At pp 251–2.

legal proceeding held in public, allowing a judge to make an order postponing reporting of those proceedings, if such action 'appears necessary for avoiding a substantial risk of prejudice' to the proceedings or any other imminent proceedings, thus creating an exception to s 4(1).[55] In other words, despite the fairness and accuracy of such reporting—and its importance in relation to the open justice principle—there are special circumstances that mean that it should nevertheless be curbed. Section 4(2) is limited in one respect—it only covers reports *of* the proceedings, not reports of extraneous matters *relating to* the proceedings that could create the risk in question. They can be dealt with by way of subsequent sanctions, as discussed in Chapter 6. It is also important to note that reports of the proceedings can be postponed, not because they might affect the proceedings in question, but because *other* proceedings could be affected. Those other proceedings need only be 'imminent', not 'active'. These terms are considered in Chapter 6,[56] and it is clear that the term 'imminent' denotes a longer and more imprecise period of time. Thus the period during which reporting is postponed can be very lengthy.

Lord Taylor CJ found in *R v Central Criminal Court, ex parte Telegraph plc*[57] that s 4(2) contains two requirements for the making of an order. The first is that publication would create 'a substantial risk of prejudice to the administration of justice' and the second is that postponement of publication 'appears to be necessary for avoiding' that risk. He continued: '[i]t has been said that there is a third requirement, derived from the word "may" at the beginning of the subsection, namely, that a court, in the exercise of its discretion, having regard to the competing public interests of ensuring a fair trial and of open justice, considers it appropriate to make an order.' In fact whether the element of discretion is to be regarded as part of the 'necessity' test or as a third requirement, the courts as a matter of practice have tended to merge the requirement of necessity and the exercise of discretion.[58] As regards the second element, it is important to note that the risk in question can concern 'any other proceedings pending or imminent.' This appears to mean that reports that would not satisfy the strict liability rule—since the other proceedings are merely imminent, not *active*[59]—could nevertheless be the subject of a s 4(2) order. The term 'imminent' has been found to cover the possibility that those other proceedings might never in fact arise.[60] Orders under s 4(2) might typically involve the reporting of matters which the defence wished to argue should be ruled inadmissible.

Section 4(3) is not free from ambiguity, but appears to allow an order to be made relating to reports which would have been published—but for the s 4(2) order—some

---

[55] For comment on s 4 of the 1981 Act, see C. Walker, I. Cram and D. Brogarth, 'The Reporting of Crown Court Proceedings and the Contempt of Court Act 1981' (1992) 55 *MLR* 647.

[56] At pp 251, 286–8.   [57] [1993] 1 WLR 980, p 984 D–G.

[58] See *BBC, Petitioners* [2002] SLT 2.   [59] See Chapter 6, at 251.

[60] See *R v Horsham Justices, ex parte Farquharson and West Sussex County Times* [1982] QB 762, p 797 E. In *Galbraith v HM Advocate* [2001] SLT 465, p 468. J-K opinion was reserved on this matter.

time after the proceedings in question had concluded.[61] A right of appeal against such orders in relation to trials on indictment was created by s 159 of the Criminal Justice Act 1988 in order to take account of a challenge under Article 10 at Strasbourg.[62] The position of the media when a s 4(2) order is made in respect of reporting a summary trial is less clear. However, it was established in *R v Clerkenwell Metropolitan Stipendiary Magistrate, ex parte The Telegraph and Others*[63] that in such circumstances, the media have a right to be heard and must be allowed to put forward the case for discharging the order. When the applicants, publishers of national newspapers, became aware of the existence of the order, they were granted a hearing before the magistrate at which they submitted that the court had power to hear representations from them as to why the order should be discharged. The magistrate held that the court had no power to hear from anyone but the parties to the proceedings. The applicants sought a declaration that the court did have the power to hear their representations, and it was determined, relying on *R v Horsham Justices, ex parte Farquharson*,[64] that they had sufficient standing to apply for judicial review. It was found to be implicit in s 4(2) that a court contemplating use of the section should be able to hear representations from those who would be affected if an order was made. In determining whether the order should be maintained, it was found to be necessary to balance the interest in the need for a fair trial before an unprejudiced jury on the one hand and the requirements of open justice on the other. In performing this balancing exercise, the magistrate would need to hear representations from the press as being best qualified to represent the public interest in publicity.

A Practice Direction relating to the use of s 4(2) orders was issued by Lord Lane CJ on 6th December 1982:[65]

... a court may, where it appears necessary for avoiding a substantial risk of prejudice to the administration of justice in the proceedings before it or in any others pending or imminent, order that publication of any report of the proceedings or part thereof be postponed for such period as the court thinks necessary for that purpose. It is necessary to keep a permanent record of such orders for later reference. For this purpose all orders made under section 4(2) must be formulated in precise terms having regard to the decision of *Horsham Justices, ex parte Farquharson* ... and orders under both sections must be committed to writing either by the judge personally or the clerk of the court under the judge's directions. An order must state (a) its precise scope, (b) the time at which it shall cease to have effect, if appropriate, and (c) the specific purpose of making the order. Courts will normally give notice to the press in some form that an order has been made ... and court staff should be prepared to answer an inquiry about a specific case, but it is, and will remain, the responsibility of those reporting cases, and their editors, to ensure that no breach of any order occurs and the onus rests with them to make inquiry in any case of doubt.

The ruling of the Court of Appeal in *Horsham Magistrates, ex parte Farquharson* was

---

[61] See *A-G v Guardian Newspapers* [2001] EWCA Crim 1351 (see below pp 214–15).
[62] *Hodgson, Woolf Productions and NUJ and Channel Four Television* (1987) 10 EHRR 503.
[63] [1993] 2 All ER 183; *The Times*, 22 October 1992.
[64] [1982] 2 All ER 269, [1982] QB 762, (1982) 76 Cr App R 87, CA.   [65] [1982] 76 Cr App R 78.

to the effect that such orders should be made sparingly; judges should be careful not to impose a ban on flimsy grounds where the connection between the matters in question and prejudice to the administration of justice was purely speculative. If other means of protecting the jury from possibly prejudicial reports of the trial were available, they should be used. Moreover, it must be ensured that the ban covers only the matters in question. This ruling was reinforced by the decision in *Central Independent Television plc and Others*.[66] During a criminal trial, the jury had to stay overnight in a hotel and in order that they could watch television or listen to the radio, the judge made an order under s 4(2) postponing reporting of the proceedings for that night. The applicants, broadcasters, appealed against the order under s 159 of the Criminal Justice Act 1988 on the basis that there was no ground on which the judge could have concluded that there was a substantial risk of prejudice to the administration of justice. Further, they argued that the judge had incorrectly exercised his discretion under the sub-section and failed to take proper account of the public interest in freedom of expression and in the open administration of justice. The Court of Appeal found that it had not been necessary to make the order as there was little, if any, evidence of a risk to the administration of justice: the previous reporting of the case had not suggested that reporting on the day in question would be anything other than fair and accurate. Even had there been a substantial risk, it might have been possible to adopt alternative methods of insulating the jury from the media. Where such alternative methods were available, they should be used. Accordingly, the appeal was allowed.

The emphasis in this judgment on the need to restrict reporting only where clearly necessary is in accordance with Article 10 requirements. The convenience of the jury is not a sufficient reason for invoking the sub-section, since it would not fall within one of the legitimate aims of Article 10(2). Similarly, in *ex parte The Telegraph plc*,[67] the Court of Appeal found that even where a substantial risk to proceedings might arise, this need not mean that an order must automatically be made. The court based this finding on the need to consider the two elements of s 4(2) separately; first, a substantial risk of prejudice to the administration of justice should be identified flowing from publication of matters relating to the trial, and, secondly, it should be asked whether it was necessary to make an order in order to avoid the risk. In making a determination as to the second limb, a judge should consider whether, in the light of the competing interest in open justice, the order should be made at all, and if so, with all or any of the restrictions sought. In the case in question, the order should not have been made, since the risk of prejudice was outweighed by the interest in open justice. In *MGN Pension Trustees Ltd v Bank of America National Trust and Saving Association*,[68] the Serious Fraud Office applied for an order postponing reporting of civil actions brought by trustees of the pension fund until after the criminal proceedings were concluded. Six newspapers opposed the application. The judge followed the steps indicated in *ex parte The Telegraph* in determining that no order would be made.

---

[66] [1991] 1 All ER 347.   [67] [1993] 2 All ER 971.   [68] [1995] EMLR 99.

These decisions suggests a concern on the part of the judiciary to prevent a ready use of s 4(2) orders, which would be prejudicial to the principle of open justice.[69] Incidentally, it is of some interest to note that this decision followed closely on that in *A-G v Guardian Newspapers (No 3)*[70] which concerned an article written while a ban on reporting of a major fraud trial was in force, criticizing the alleged propensity of judges in such trials to impose bans. It was held that the article created too remote a risk to constitute a contempt under the strict liability rule (see below), and Brooke J took the opportunity of re-emphasizing the importance of the news media as the 'eyes and ears' of the general public. This approach was developed in *R v Beck ex parte Daily Telegraph*.[71] Beck, who had been a social worker in charge of children's homes, was charged with offences involving sexual abuse, and owing to the number of charges, the trial was split into three. At the first trial, a s 4(2) order was made, owing to the risk of prejudice to the subsequent two trials. On appeal, the Court of Appeal accepted that there was a substantial risk of prejudice, but went on to find that the public interest in the reporting of the trial outweighed the risk. In so finding, the court emphasized the concern which the public must feel because of the particular facts of the case and the right of the public to be informed and to be able to ask questions about the opportunities created for those in public service to commit such offences.

The decisions discussed indicate that pre-HRA the domestic courts were already taking into account the demands of Articles 10 and 6 by reference to the principles underlying those two Articles. The stance taken towards the role of journalists closely parallels that taken at Strasbourg, as indicated in Chapter 4.[72] A further Practice Direction, which also appears to be intended to ensure that the use of s 4(2) is Convention-compliant, was issued in 2002:

From 'Practice Direction (Criminal: consolidated)'[73]
3. *Restrictions on reporting proceedings*
. . .
3.2. When considering whether to make such an order [under s 4(2) or s 11] there is nothing which precludes the court from hearing a representative of the press. Indeed it is likely that the court will wish to do so . . .
[The Order continues in the same terms as the previous order.]

The important point is that this Direction indicates that media representatives should be heard before the order is made, thus allowing them to challenge it in general and also to raise Article 10 points. However, even where the Practice Directions are followed, courts in making s 4(2) orders are under a duty due to s 6 HRA to ensure that the tests of necessity and proportionality under Article 10 are satisfied.

This duty was not explicitly adverted to in the post-HRA decision in *A-G v Guardian Newspapers*[74] in which the reach of s 4(2) was widened and the tension between

---

[69] See also *Saunders* (the Guinness trials) [1990] Crim LR 597; *Barlow Clowes Gilt Managers v Clowes, The Times*, 2 February 1990; *R v Sherwood, ex parte The Telegraph Group plc, The Times*, 12 June 2001.
[70] [1992] 3 All ER 38.   [71] [1993] 2 All ER 177.   [72] See pp 182–90.
[73] [2002] 3 All ER 904, at 906–7.   [74] [2001] EWCA Crim 1351.

s 4(2) and s 2(2) was exacerbated, a point that is returned to in Chapter 6.[75] The order in question in the case had been made in the criminal trial[76] of four Premiership footballers. During the trial the judge had given a direction that there was no evidence of a racial motive in the case. The jury retired to consider their verdicts and were eventually sent home for the weekend, still undecided.[77] That Sunday the *Sunday Mirror* published an interview with the father of the victim which in a double page spread, with photographs, revived the allegations of racism.[78] The judge decided in consequence to discharge the jury. The *Sunday Mirror* article and the halting of the trial attracted a great deal of media publicity in a number of newspapers. The judge ordered that a retrial should take place and provisionally fixed the date for the retrial.

The judge had agreed to make an order under s 4(2) of the 1981 Act imposing stringent reporting restrictions. They covered any reference to material from the offending article and to racist motives in the case.[79] This order under s 4(2) was designed to obviate the possibility of prejudice to the future retrial. This order was the subject of the appeal by a number of newspapers under s 159 Criminal Justice Act 1988 (CJA). The main ground for the appeal was that the terms of the order were not limited to the publication of a report of the proceedings, or part of the proceedings, and therefore the order was made without jurisdiction. Without referring to the HRA, the Court of Appeal found that since the order concerned an article that had led to the halting of the trial: '[a]ny similar reporting or republication of [the *Sunday Mirror*] article or its contents, or discussion of the judge's reasons, after 10th April . . . would albeit indirectly, be a "report of part of the proceedings." ' The order was able to cover reports intended to be published some time after the trial had been halted since it was found that such reporting could be treated as 'contemporaneous' due to the provision of s 4(3). It might have been expected, taking Article 10 into account, that a more media-friendly reading of s 4(3)—affording a more limited meaning to the term 'contemporaneous'—could have been adopted under s 3(1)HRA. However, this judgment

---

[75] See pp 305–6.

[76] The order in question in the case had been made in the trial of four Premiership footballers, Woodgate, Bowyer, Clifford, and Caverney, for offences of affray and causing grievous bodily harm with intent to Sarfraz Najeib. The case had of course attracted a considerable amount of publicity. See for further discussion of the trial and the effect of the *Sunday Mirror* reporting, Chapter 6, p 271.

[77] On 4 April 2001.

[78] It also included comments commending the evidence of a co-accused (who had by that time been acquitted) in suggesting that some of the remaining defendants, in relation to whom the jury were still considering their verdicts, were guilty.

[79] The order was in the following terms:

1. There should be no further publication or broadcast of any matter contained within the headlines or the body of the article which appeared on pages 8 and 9 of the Sunday Mirror on 8 April 2001.

2. There should be no further reference in any publication or broadcast to the said article or headline, save for reference to the fact that this jury was discharged as a result of an article in the Sunday Mirror.

3. No publication or broadcast should make reference to racism or racist motivation in relation to the above proceedings.

4. For the avoidance of doubt, the above Order does not preclude publication or broadcast of any material relating to, or comment upon, the Macpherson Report, or issues of racism generally, provided that no reference in such publications or broadcasts is made to these proceedings.

exhibits the tendency, noted in other chapters of this book, to disregard the HRA even where a Convention article is clearly relevant.

POWERS TO GRANT INJUNCTIONS TO RESTRAIN CONTEMPTS

Section 4(2) orders are limited to restraints on fair and accurate reports of proceedings where 'a substantial risk of prejudice' might arise. This appears to leave a gap in the law since s 4(2) does not cover the gathering of information ancillary to reporting. Powers arising under the Supreme Court Act 1981 allow that gap to be filled, but create at the same time a further, potentially highly significant, curb on media freedom since they are so broad. Injunctions postponing reporting of proceedings and activity ancillary to such reporting can be granted by the High Court under s 37(1) of the Supreme Court Act 1981 (SCA). Section 37(1) grants the High Court the jurisdiction to grant injunctions 'in all cases in which it appears to the court to be just and convenient to do so.' Section 45(4) of the SCA gives the Crown Court only limited jurisdiction in relation to proceedings before it.[80]

Section 37 only expressly gives the power to grant injunctions to the High Court; it does not mention the Crown Court. However, it was found in *ex parte HTV Cymru (Wales) Ltd*[81] that s 45(4) SCA affords the Crown Court the same powers as the High Court as regards the granting of injunctions to avoid contempts.[82] So there is no *general* power in the Crown Court to grant injunctions.

It was made clear in the House of Lords decision in *Pickering v Associated Newspapers Holdings Plc*[83] that where a contempt by way of reporting would consist of impeding or prejudicing the course of justice, an injunction would 'rarely be appropriate.' Two reasons were put forward:

The first is that the injunction would have to be very specific and might indirectly mislead by suggesting that other conduct of a similar, but slightly different, nature would be

---

[80] The relevant parts of s 45(4) provide as follows: '[s]ubject to . . . any provision contained or having effect under this Act the Crown Court shall, in relation to the attendance and examination of witnesses, any contempt of court, the enforcement of its orders and all other matters incidental to its jurisdiction, have the like powers, rights, privileges and authority as the High Court.' The proviso at the beginning of that subsection is important, because it indicates that if there are other provisions in the SCA that deal with particular powers of the High Court, then it is necessary to consider that provision to see whether it also expressly or impliedly grants power or jurisdiction to the Crown Court.

[81] [2002] EMLR 11.

[82] It was found that the wording in s 45(4) indicates that there may be other sections in the SCA that specifically cut down or enlarge the powers of the Crown Court compared with those of the High Court. If other sections do so, then they will govern the powers, rights, privileges and authority of the Crown Court as opposed to the general rule set out in s 45(4). But if they do not expressly deal with the powers of the Crown Court, then the general provisions set out in s 45(4) must prevail. Section 37 was not found to detract from the powers of the Crown Court that are laid out in s 45(4) since it does not state that the Crown Court shall not have the power to grant injunctions for the specific purposes that are referred to in s 45(4) of the SCA. But the Crown Court has the power to grant an injunction to restrain a threatened contempt of court in relation to a matter that is before the Crown Court in question.

[83] [1991] 2 AC 370; [1991] 1 All ER 622.

permissible. The second is that it is the wise and settled practice of the courts not to grant injunctions restraining the commission of a criminal act—and contempt of court is a criminal or quasi-criminal act—unless the penalties available under the criminal law have proved to be inadequate to deter the commission of the offences.

But in *ex parte HTV Cymru (Wales) Ltd* it was found that one of those rare occasions had arisen—there were special circumstances justifying the granting of an injunction. The defendant was being tried for the murder of S. The death of S and the trial of the defendant had been widely reported. HTV was planning to make a documentary on the case which it intended to transmit as soon as the jury had returned a verdict. For this purpose HTV intended to interview at least one witness who had already given evidence on behalf of the Crown. BBC Wales was also considering making a similar programme. The Crown, supported by the defendant, sought an order prohibiting the media from contacting or interviewing any witness who had given or was likely to give evidence in the case on behalf of the prosecution. The judge granted the order and HTV applied for the order to be discharged.

The court found that an injunction could only be granted if it was clear that the alleged acts were going to be carried out, if not restrained. In this case that act—which was clearly going to occur—was the making of the documentary, involving interviewing witnesses. It was also found that the court had to be sure that if the alleged acts were carried out, then they would amount to a contempt of court in that the acts would create a substantial risk that the course of justice in the trial would be seriously impeded or prejudiced. In coming to the conclusion that this test was also satisfied, the court bore in mind the prospect that all the principal prosecution witnesses might have been approached once they had given evidence and that the questioning might have altered the witnesses' view of the evidence that they had already given. It was also possible that some of them might be recalled to give further evidence, after being interviewed by the journalists. The witnesses were viewed as vulnerable and two of them were seen as lacking in intellectual capacity. In the event the grant of the injunction was upheld but it was limited to HTV.[84] It did not cover any other media bodies, although BBC Wales had also indicated that its reporters might want to interview witnesses. In placing limitations on the injunction, the HRA was taken into account; the reasoning on Article 10 is considered below. These powers will be referred to as 'SCA powers to grant injunctions'.

POWERS TO POSTPONE REPORTS: THE EFFECT OF THE HRA

It might appear that the powers discussed would be affected not only by Article 10 under the HRA, but also by s 12. Under s 12(4) HRA, the court 'must have particular

---

[84] The injunction was in the following terms:

'HTV, by themselves, their servants or agents or howsoever are hereby restrained and an injunction is granted prohibiting them from contacting, approaching directly or indirectly, interviewing or collecting evidence from any person who has given evidence or is likely to give evidence in the above case on behalf of the prosecution until the start of closing submissions by Counsel for the Crown or further order (if sooner)'.

regard to the importance of the Convention right of freedom of expression' and 'where the proceedings relate to material which the respondent claims or which appears to the court to be journalistic . . . material to the extent to which . . . it is or would be in the public interest for the material to be published.' It is, however, probable that s 12(4) adds little to the duty already imposed on courts to abide by the demands of Article 10 under s 6.[85] Section 12(3) is also unlikely to be of assistance to reporters. Under s 12(3) HRA orders or injunctions cannot be granted 'so as to restrain publication before trial unless the court is satisfied that the applicant is likely to establish that publication should not be allowed'.[86] Section 12(3) applies in all *civil law* cases.[87] Thus s 12(3) might not apply to injunctions sought by the Attorney-General under, s 4(2) of the Contempt of Court Act, or under the powers of the Crown Court under the SCA s 45(4), discussed below, to prevent a threatened criminal contempt of court.[88] As regards powers to prevent threatened contempts it could be argued that if an order or injunction is not imposed or granted in criminal proceedings themselves, it would not be 'relief in criminal proceedings', but could be relief given 'in relation to' criminal proceedings. The s 37 Supreme Court Act 1981 power to prevent contempts relating to civil proceedings would presumably be covered if an interim injunction was granted. The leading case on the interpretation of section 12(3) is *Cream Holdings Limited and others v Banerjee and others.*[89] It established that interim relief can be granted only where it is more likely than not that the plaintiff would succeed at final trial. However, many of the orders discussed in this chapter are not interim ones and therefore s 12(3) would be inapplicable.

Where reporting restrictions arise under s 42 or s 37 CPI (the CPI pre-trial reporting restrictions),[90] s 4(2) and s 11 of the 1981 Act[91] or—exceptionally—under s 45(4) or s 37 SCA (power to grant injunctions to avoid contempts),[92] intended to ensure the fairness of trials, a conflict between Articles 10 and 6 arises. As Eady J put it in *ex parte Telegraph Group Plc:*[93]

It has become commonplace over the last ten years or so for courts to emphasise the role of the media in court reporting and the need for the wider public to be given fair and accurate information about the administration of justice and the conduct of public servants. These are rights enshrined in Article 10 of the European Convention. Equally, however, the right to a fair and open trial is protected by the principles set out in Article 6. The jurisdiction to

---

[85] On which, see further Chapter 3 at 131–2, and Chapter 16 at 836.

[86] S 12 (1) provides: This section applies if a court is considering whether to grant any relief which, if granted, might affect the exercise of the Convention right to freedom of expression. . . .

(3) No such relief is to be granted so as to restrain publication before trial unless the court is satisfied that the applicant is likely to establish that publication should not be allowed. See further Chapter 3 at 153–7 on s 12(3).

[87] Section 12(5) excludes from the section any 'relief' (which 'includes any remedy or order') that is made 'in criminal proceedings'.

[88] On which, see further Chapter 6 at 306–7.

[89] [2004] 3 WLR 918. For comment see A.T.H. Smith, [2005] 64(1) *CLJ* 4.

[90] See p 208 note 50 above.   [91] See pp 210–16 and 224–5 above.

[92] See pp 216–17 above.   [93] [2001] EMLR 10, at [12].

make a postponement order under s.4(2) of the Contempt of Court Act is therefore inevitably a sensitive one operating, as it must, at the interface between these two vital interests.

A significant concern arising from the use of these reporting restrictions is that in seeking to protect the fairness of trials they may create unacceptable curbs on the freedom of the press and broadcasters. The main safeguard for media freedom is the possibility that the use of the restrictions, in the HRA era, is subject to the tests of necessity and proportionality under Article 10(2). It might be expected that the relevant Article 10 jurisprudence would, increasingly, have an important influence upon the use of orders under s 4(2) and s 11.[94] The cases considered below suggest that the HRA is having some impact on the use of prior restraints, but *A-G v Guardian Newspapers*,[95] discussed below, indicates that judges do not fully accept the need to take the HRA into account in relation to s 4(2) orders. Reporting restrictions under s 42 or s 37 CPI are imposed automatically, as discussed above, and therefore *prima facie* a judge is not asked to comply with s 6 HRA in imposing them. Further, since the provisions are expressed in entirely unambiguous terms, it is unclear that s 3(1) HRA could bite on them. But if a judge decided to allow for some reporting of a pre-trial or preparatory hearing, the duty under s 6(1) would come into play on the basis that in deciding to lift some restrictions but not others, the court is bound by the Convention rights. In particular, in this instance, Articles 10 and (possibly) 6 would be relevant. The restrictions would have to be subjected to the tests of Article 10(2) but, where there was a real link between the restriction and the preservation of a fair trial under Article 6, the fair trial right would be likely to prevail. However, where there was a very tenuous connection, it might be found that the tests of necessity and proportionality were not satisfied by a very minor lifting of the restrictions. The decision in *C v UK*,[96] discussed in Chapter 4, would be relevant, but the case for finding a breach of Article 10 on the basis that the restrictions are disproportionate to the aim in view—the preservation of Article 6 rights would be stronger—since, as Cram argues, dangers posed by televised dramatizations are greater than those posed by unvarnished reporting of the facts.[97] Clearly, if a judge adopted such an argument an anomaly would be created since it would mean that s 6 would bite where a judge partially lifted the restrictions but not where no lifting occurred. The better argument would be that the decision not to lift the restrictions is a decision on which s 6 bites. Therefore it is arguable that a judge is expected, in taking any decision in relation to s 42 or s 37 CPI, to abide by the Convention rights.

Section 4(2) and s 11 of the 1981 Act and the powers to avoid contempts under s 45(4) and s 37 SCA do not contain public interest tests, but any judge considering restraints under these powers is bound by s 6 HRA to comply with the Convention

---

[94] For discussion in the Scottish context, bearing in mind the effect of the ECHR under the Scotland Act 1988, see A. Bonnington, and R. McInnes, 'Scottish Contempt from 1998: Brave New World?,' Vol. VI, *Yearbook of Copyright and Media Law 2001–02*, pp 121–40.

[95] [2001] EWCA Crim 1351.   [96] (1989) 61 DR 285. See Chapter 4, at 187.

[97] See I. Cram, 'Automatic Reporting Restrictions in Criminal Proceedings and Article 10 ECHR' (1998) 6 *EHRLR* 742.

guarantees in so doing. This means that in any instance it is necessary for the judge to ask, using the Article 10(2) tests, whether in the present case the effect on the administration of justice of failing to make the order would be such as to make it both necessary and proportionate in a democratic society that it should be made. In other words, it must be asked whether the threat to the administration of justice from the reporting which would arise, absent the making of the order, is sufficient to make a prior restraint a proportionate response in a society which, as a democracy, values and protects the freedom of the press. If judges show a preparedness to look closely at the question of proportionality, they may be able to tease out the real purpose of making a particular order more effectively. It might be clear that the order is unnecessary or could be more narrowly focused, thus creating less impact on the media. As indicated above, under the current guidelines, these orders should be stated in precise terms. However, the judges are failing in their duty under s 6 HRA if they do not also subject orders to the full rigour of the Article 10(2) tests. It is not enough merely to assume implicitly—as appeared to occur in *A-G v Guardian*, considered below—that the same result would have been reached had those tests been applied.

This approach was, to an extent, adopted in *ex parte HTV Cymru (Wales) Ltd*,[98] discussed above, in which extensive consideration was given to the effect of Article 10 in relation to the grant of an injunction restraining the interviewing of prosecution witnesses for a documentary.[99] It was accepted that the Crown Court, in granting the injunction to restrain the threatened contempt, must comply with s 6 HRA and therefore it must not act in a way that is incompatible with a Convention right, in this instance Article 10(1). It was noted that that right is subject to the limitations set out in Article 10(2) and in particular that it is subject to the restrictions necessary for 'maintaining the authority and impartiality of the judiciary.' Relying on *Sunday Times v United Kingdom*,[100] it was pointed out that that this wording in Article 10(2), broadly interpreted, includes the need to provide protection of the rights of litigants and therefore includes the law of contempt insofar as it serves to protect those rights. The court continued:

However Article 10(2) makes it clear that an injunction should only be granted if it is 'necessary.' . . . In addition there has to be a reasonable relationship of 'proportionality' between the means employed (*i.e.* the injunction) and the aim pursued—*i.e.* the prevention of a threatened contempt: *Handyside v UK*.[101] A fair balance has to be struck between the demands of the general interests of the community and the requirements of the protection of the individual's fundamental Convention rights: *Soering v UK*.[102] In my view the demands of the general interests of the community and the particular interests of the defendant in this case must be to safeguard the integrity of the present trial and to ensure that the threatened contempt does not occur. That must be done with the least possible restrictions on HTV's Convention right to freedom of expression. I have concluded that there is a risk of the course of justice being seriously prejudiced. But I think that this risk exists only so long as there is a possibility of evidence being given by witnesses. Once all the evidence is

---

[98] [2002] EMLR 11.   [99] Ibid, at paras 31–33.   [100] (1979) 2 EHRR 245, p 279.
[101] (1976) 1 EHRR 737, at [49].   [102] (1989) 11 EHRR 439, at [89].

completed, then any risk to the trial by virtue of HTV approaching witnesses for filmed interviews is minimal. So after that point the Convention rights of HTV ought to prevail.

In this instance the court was prepared to apply the Article 10(2) tests as a check on the width on the injunction. But the tests were not applied in determining whether the court had jurisdiction to grant an injunction at all—the matter of uncertainty discussed above. The dangers of according this ability to the Crown Court, as opposed to relying on the strict liability rule under the 1981 Act to deter the media from committing contempts, are apparent. Courts might be tempted, where some evidence was available suggesting that reporters might interview witnesses before the end of the trial, to grant restraining injunctions, thereby in effect demanding that media bodies come before the court to explain their planned reporting. This decision could be viewed as a step on the path toward court censorship of trial reporting. It might also be asked why this power was omitted from the 1981 Act and the more limited power under s 4(2) Contempt of Court Act 1981 (CCA) made available instead. That power only allows for restraints on fair and accurate reporting. The power under s 45(4) SCA would allow for restraints on any type of reporting where a contempt might otherwise be committed—so long as in the particular circumstances the injunction could be framed precisely enough—it therefore seems to stray into the territory covered by s 2(2) CCA. If it appeared probable that a publication might affect the minds of jurors and witnesses during the trial, an injunction could be issued under s 45(4) to restrain it, following the principle from this case. Given the existence of s 2(2) CCA, it could be argued that a power to grant injunctions under s 45(4) SCA is unnecessary and therefore disproportionate to the aim in view—preventing threatened contempts. For all these reasons it is arguable that a restrictive interpretation of s 45(4) and s 37 under s 3(1) HRA should have been adopted to deny Crown courts this jurisdiction.

At the least, however, the decision *ex parte HTV Cymru (Wales) Ltd* shows an acceptance of the need to apply the Article 10(2) tests to the grant of the injunction. Similarly, in *BBC, Petitioners*[103] the importance of reporting proceedings as an aspect of the Article 6(1) guarantee and of freedom of expression under Article 10 was taken into account in relation to a petition to recall a s 4(2) order postponing reporting of proceedings for murder until a decision to charge a further person, Ward, had been taken. The defendant had sought, during his trial, to implicate Ward in the murder. It was found that in the circumstances of the case, an order was not 'necessary' under Article 10(2) in the sense of answering to a 'pressing social need' to deal with the risk of prejudice to the course of justice in any trial of Ward, taking into account the likelihood that jurors would concentrate on the evidence in that trial, rather than on material they had come across in the media some weeks or months before. Therefore the jury would be able to reach a proper verdict in any subsequent trial. Some of the evidence at the accused's trial would have been likely to be replicated at Ward's trial, and the jury would therefore have been likely to base their decision on the version of

---

[103] [2002] SLT 2.

the evidence led at that trial, which would be fresh in their minds, rather than on their recollection of a report of what had been said in the accused's trial. Further, it was found, directions by the judge at any future trial would have been able to deal perfectly adequately with any risk of prejudice from the reporting of the proceedings in the accused's trial.

This was quite a media-friendly ruling, bearing in mind that the order only post-poned reports of the accused's trial for 24 hours after it had ended (with the possibil-ity that the order would be renewed if Ward was charged). No consideration was given to the competing importance of safeguarding Ward's right to a fair trial under Article 6(1). However, bearing in mind the length of time that was likely to elapse before that trial,[104] the court was probably right to conclude that there was no pressing need to continue the order. The decision may be contrasted with that in *ex parte Telegraph Group Plc*[105] in which the opposite result was reached, on fairly similar facts. In that instance the evidence to be given in the second trial had already—in part—been given in the first. A defendant police officer had been charged with the murder of a suspect and at his trial the defendant alleged failures by senior officers in the planning and execution of the operation. The trial of three senior officers for misconduct in public office had been severed to avoid unfairness to them. The judge in the first trial made an order under s 4(2) postponing reporting of first trial until after the verdicts in the second trial. An application was made to the Court of Appeal on behalf of various media groups.

The s 4(2) order, which was upheld, covered not only the reasoning at the first trial in relation to the order itself, but also that of the Court of Appeal. The first trial was clearly of immense public interest due to its subject matter and it was clear that reports of it, however fair and accurate, would be delayed for a very considerable period of time. As Eady J in the Court of Appeal put it:

[i]t is a very striking set of circumstances that a police officer could be tried for murder, by shooting, and yet the wider public be prevented from receiving information about the trial while it is taking place—and, moreover, not even be permitted to know the outcome until the verdicts have been returned in respect of the remaining defendants.[106]

Therefore the free speech arguments in favour of publication during the first trial were very strong. Having decided that the order was necessary in the sense denoted by s 4(2), the Court went on to consider whether it was necessary in 'the second sense; that is to say the sense contemplated by Article 10(2) of the European Convention.' The Court found that even where it had been concluded that there was no other way of eliminating the perceived risk of prejudice, it still did not follow *necessarily* that an order had to be made. The judge would still have to ask whether the degree of risk contemplated should be regarded as tolerable and it would be at this stage that 'value

---

[104] In fact it had become apparent by the time the court considered the order that Ward would not be charged with the murder—the court decided the matter as one of general public interest.

[105] [2001] EMLR 10.   [106] Ibid, at [9].

judgments may have to be made as to the priority between "competing public interests." ' The choice made came down in favour of Article 6. The Court found that in
the unusual circumstances of the case nothing short of an order completely banning
all reporting of the first trial was sufficient in order to ensure that the three defendants
in the second trial had a fair hearing in accordance with the Article 6 guarantee.

The Court was clearly seeking to confine this decision as far as possible to the
particular facts of the case, since otherwise there would be a danger that the reporting
of any trial in which evidence was put forward potentially relating to a future trial
could be the subject of a s 4(2) order. But the Court did not place the same emphasis to
the ability of jurors to disregard previous publicity, especially when properly directed
by the judge, as was afforded in *BBC, Petitioners*. Further, the especially strong free
speech interest in the case did not persuade the Court that a less restrictive order could
have been made—one arguably more in proportion to the aim sought to be achieved.
In fact the test of proportionality was not, in terms, considered. Although the Court
sought to distinguish between what was needed to satisfy the test of 'necessary' under
s 4(2) and that of 'necessary' under Article 10(2), it is suggested that it in fact elided
the two tests since it assumed that once it had been shown that the fair trial of the
defendants was—in its view—genuinely threatened by the reporting of the first trial
and an order banning all reporting was needed in order to avert the threat, no further
factor—such as the very strong interest in allowing the reporting, which could have
been a factor relating to the test of proportionality—was taken into account. The
decision makes it clear that, in making s 4(2) orders, Article 6 takes priority over
Article 10. It will be argued in Chapter 6 that while this stance may be in accordance
with the Convention jurisprudence, it is not reflected in the strict liability rule of the
1981 Act.

ANONYMITY

The anonymity reporting restrictions represent an especially significant infringement
of the open justice principle since the reports are entirely prohibited, rather than
postponed. The provisions allowing for the preservation of the anonymity of those
involved in proceedings have mixed purposes that may relate to strong public interests
or other individual rights. In so far as anonymity is preserved in order to ensure
privacy rather than to serve the end of ensuring the fair administration of justice, the
provisions relating to juveniles are discussed in Chapter 16[107] and in relation to adults
in Chapter 14.[108] Provisions having the mixed purpose of protecting privacy and the
administration of justice since, for example, the fairness of the hearing for a juvenile is
preserved, are considered here.

---

[107] See pp 813–18.   [108] See pp 715–16.

ADULT WITNESSES AND DEFENDANTS

At common law, a judge can order prohibition of a publication in order to prevent, for example, the disclosure of the identity of a witness. Section 11 of the Contempt of Court Act 1981 allows a court which has power to do so to make an order prohibiting publication of names or other matters if this appears necessary 'for the purpose for which it was so withheld'. Thus, s 11 does not *itself* confer such a power and therefore refers to other statutes and common law powers. The leading authority is the House of Lords' decision in *A-G v Leveller Magazine Ltd*[109] in which it was accepted that departure from the principle of openness would be warranted if necessary for the due administration of justice, and that therefore if a court made an order designed to protect the administration of justice, then it would be incumbent on those who knew of it not to do anything which might frustrate its object.

At present, there are signs that a robust interpretation will be given to s 11 similar to that being taken to s 4(2) so that the fundamental importance of open justice will be outweighed only by a very clear detriment which answers to a general public interest flowing from publication of the matters in question—economic damage to the interests of the defendant will not suffice.[110] Nor will a concern to protect the 'comfort and feelings of the defendant.'[111] The courts may be prepared to make anonymity orders to protect the privacy of those involved in proceedings,[112] but only where the failure to afford anonymity would, under strict scrutiny, render the attainment of justice very doubtful.[113] The restrictions on the use of s11 appear to render it compatible with Article 10. In *Atkinson Crook and the Independent v UK*[114] a journalist, Crook, had attempted to challenge a s 11 anonymity order: *Central Criminal Court ex parte Crook*.[115] When the challenge failed, Crook took the case to Strasbourg, arguing for a breach of Article 10. In the circumstances of the trial it had been feared that matters disclosed in open proceedings might put the defendant's family at risk. The Commission found that the interest of the media in reporting arguments about the sentencing of a convicted defendant could be outweighed if on reasonable grounds, the prosecution, the judge, and the defendant himself, wished to hear them in private.[116]

Witnesses are placed in a somewhat different position. There is a clear public interest in encouraging witnesses to come forward and to cooperate in proceedings. Therefore, courts have shown a greater willingness to ensure the anonymity of witnesses.[117] And, clearly, if a court takes measures to protect the anonymity of witnesses,

---

[109] [1979] AC 440; [1979] 2 WLR 247, HL. For comment on s 11 of the 1981 Act see C. Walker, I. Cram and D. Brogarth, 'The Reporting of Crown Court Proceedings and the Contempt of Court Act 1981' (1992) 55 *MLR* 647.

[110] *Dover JJ, ex parte Dover DC and Wells* (1991) 156 JP 433; [1992] Crim LR 371.

[111] *Evesham JJ, ex parte McDonagh* [1988] 1 QB 553, p 562.

[112] See *H v Ministry of Defence* [1991] 2 QB 103; *Criminal Injuries Compensation Board, ex parte A* [1992] COD 379.

[113] *Westminster CC, ex parte Castelli and Tristan-Garcia, The Times*, 14 August 1995.

[114] (1990) 67 DR 244.   [115] (1984) *The Times*, 8 November.   [116] See also Chapter 16 at 813.

[117] See *Watford Magistrates' Court, ex parte Lenman* [1993] Crim LR 388; *Taylor* [1994] TLR 484.

such as sitting in camera or allowing the use of screens, there may be no need to make an express s 11 order. Exceptionally, an injunction granted to protect the anonymity of a child may be extended, on grounds of the doctrine of confidence, once the child reaches 18. This was found in *Venables, Thompson v News Group Newspapers Ltd, Associated Newspapers Ltd, MGM Ltd.*[118] Although such a restraint relates to the administration of justice since it concerns an interference with the reporting of criminal justice matters, the object of the injunction is to protect privacy, not to protect a fair hearing, and therefore it is discussed in Chapter 16.[119]

JUVENILES INVOLVED IN CRIMINAL PROCEEDINGS

A number of reporting restrictions are aimed at the protection of children. These reporting restrictions are also briefly discussed in Chapter 16[120] since they are mainly aimed at protecting privacy. However, it can also be argued that an aspect of the fair trial provision under Article 6(1) is to provide special protections for juveniles in the criminal justice system,[121] whether involved as witnesses or defendants. Under s 39 of the Children and Young Persons Act 1933 (CYPA), a court (apart from a Youth Court) could direct that details relating to a child, 'who was a witness or defendant, including his or her name', should not be reported and that 'no picture of the child should be broadcast or published'. The media could make representations to the judge, arguing that the demands of media freedom outweigh the possibility of harm to the child. Section 49 of the Act, as amended,[122] which relates to Youth Courts, now provides for an automatic ban on publishing certain identifying details relating to a juvenile offender, including his or her name and address, although the court can waive the ban. Under s 45 Crime (Sentences) Act 1997, the court can lift reporting restrictions where it considers that a ban would be against the public interest.[123]

---

[118] [2001] 1 All ER 908, Fam Div.   [119] See pp 814–15.   [120] See pp 813–14.

[121] See *Thompson and Venables v UK* (2000) 7 BHRC 659. It may be noted that Rule 5 of the Beijing Rules recommends that every juvenile justice system emphasize the well being of the juvenile and ensure that all reactions to such offenders are proportionate to the offence. The UN Convention on the Rights of the Child links fairness and privacy in relation to juveniles: Article 40(2)(b) every child has the right to the presumption of innocence, to informed promptly at the charges against him/her, to have the matter determined without delay by a competent and independent body, the right to silence, a right to an appeal, to understand the language used in proceedings and to have their privacy respected at each stage of the trial.

[122] As amended by Schedule 2 to the Youth Justice and Criminal Evidence Act 1999.

[123] S 45 provides: (1) After subsection (4) of section 49 of the 1933 Act (restrictions on reports of proceedings in which children or young persons are concerned) there shall be inserted the following subsections—

(4A) If a court is satisfied that it is in the public interest to do so, it may, in relation to a child or young person who has been convicted of an offence, by order dispense to any specified extent with the requirements of this section in relation to any proceedings before it to which this section applies by virtue of subsection (2)(a) or (b) above, being proceedings relating to—
(a) the prosecution or conviction of the offender for the offence;
(b) the manner in which he, or his parent or guardian, should be dealt with in respect of the offence;
(c) the enforcement, amendment, variation, revocation or discharge of any order made in respect of the offence;

The s 39 restrictions were extended under s 44 of the Youth Justice and Criminal Evidence Act 1999, which now covers children involved in adult proceedings. The 1933 Act did not cover the period before proceedings begin. In contrast, the 1999 Act prohibits the publication once a criminal *investigation* has begun, of any matter relating to a person involved in an offence while he is under 18 which is likely to identify him. Thus, juveniles who are witnesses are also covered. Under s 44(4), the court can dispense with the restrictions if it is satisfied that it is in the public interest to do so. Thus, s 44 brings the restrictions relating to juveniles in adult proceedings into line with those under s 49 relating to youth proceedings, placing the onus on the court to find a good reason for lifting the restriction rather than having to find a good reason for imposing it. The discretion of the court is therefore more narrowly confined.[124] This is clearly an instance in which, as between the demands of press freedom and the interest in the protection of the privacy and reputation of juveniles, the latter interest has prevailed.[125]

VICTIMS OF SEXUAL OFFENCES

A number of special restrictions also apply to the victims of certain sexual offences. Under s 4(1)(a) of the Sexual Offences (Amendment) Act 1976, once an allegation of rape was made it was an offence to publish or broadcast the name, address or photograph of the woman who was the alleged victim. Once a person was accused of rape, nothing could be published by the media which could identify the woman. These restrictions were extended under s 1(1) of the Sexual Offences (Amendment) Act 1992.[126] Section 1(1) covers a number of sexual offences as well as rape, and makes wider provision for anonymity: 'where an allegation has been made that an offence to which the Act applies has been committed against a person,[127] no matter relating to that person shall during that person's lifetime be included in any publication.' This restriction, unlike those considered above, is not subject to any exception. Therefore, in that respect, it affords less recognition to freedom of speech, although it does not prevent the reporting of the case or discussion of it once it is over, so long as details likely to identify the victim are not revealed.

(d) where an attendance centre order is made in respect of the offence, the enforcement of any rules made under section 16(3) of the Criminal Justice Act 1982; or

(e) where a secure training order is so made, the enforcement of any requirements imposed under section 3(7) of the Criminal Justice and Public Order Act 1994.

(4B) A court shall not exercise its power under subsection (4A) above without—

(a) affording the parties to the proceedings an opportunity to make representations; and

(b) taking into account any representations which are duly made.

[124] See the discussion in *Lee* [1993] 1 WLR 103, pp 109–10.

[125] See further I. Cram, *A Virtue Less Cloistered: Courts, Speech and Constitutions*, Oxford: Hart Publishing, 2002, Chapter 4. See also Chapter 16 at 813–14.

[126] As amended by s 48 of the Youth Justice and Criminal Evidence Act 1999 and Schedule 2.

[127] Male victims are also covered, under the Criminal Justice and Public Order Act 1994, s 142.

RESTRAINTS PRESERVING ANONYMITY AND THE HRA

Restrictions on the reporting of proceedings intended to preserve anonymity are likely to create conflict between Article 10, especially in relation to the interest in open justice, and the Article 8 guarantee of a right to respect for private life. The main safeguard for media freedom is the possibility that the restrictions—apart from that of anonymity in relation to certain sexual offences—may be dispensed with in the public interest. In the HRA era, it would be expected that Article 10 jurisprudence would become an increasingly important influence upon the development of the public interest test. The granting of anonymity raises a number of Convention issues. From the perspective of Article 10, the imposition of anonymity clearly limits what can be reported about a case and may inhibit later reporting or discussion of any issues arising out of the case. However, such restrictions may be justifiable within the paragraph 2 exceptions which include 'for the rights of others'. The right to respect for privacy would therefore be covered, as would Article 6 rights. Therefore, the current emphasis on granting anonymity only on the basis that otherwise the administration of justice would suffer, is questionable. Courts are bound by Article 8; therefore witnesses, plaintiffs and defendants are able to argue in certain circumstances that anonymity should be granted even where such administration does not clearly demand it. If an order preserving anonymity is lifted it would appear that a breach of Article 6 would arise if the subject of the order had no means of challenging the lifting of the order, whether on the basis of the potential infringement of Article 8 that might arise or on the basis of his or her welfare within the criminal justice system. This argument was put in *R v Manchester Crown Court, ex parte H and D*[128] in relation to the lifting of a s 39 CYPA order; the lifting of the order was challenged in the Divisional Court which found that it had jurisdiction to restore it under s 29(3) SCA. The Court however considered that clarifying legislation as to the scope of s 29(3) and s 159 CJA was required.

While Articles 6 and 10 may come into conflict in respect of anonymity granted to the defendant, they may have similar demands in respect of anonymity granted to witnesses. Allowing witnesses to give evidence behind screens or by means of a video link clearly raises Article 6 issues, as Strasbourg has accepted.[129] But it also raises Article 10 considerations. Again, argument could be raised under both Articles to the effect that any measures affording anonymity to witnesses should be strictly scrutinized. But while arguments for anonymity might prevail under Article 10 since it is materially qualified, they would be less likely to do so under Article 6. This issue is also considered in Chapter 16.[130]

---

[128] [2000] 2 All ER 166.
[129] See *Doorson v Netherlands* (1996) 22 EHRR 330.
[130] See pp 813–14 and 823–31.

THE BAN ON DISCLOSURE OF JURY DELIBERATIONS

This chapter now moves on to consider a specific preventive measure—the ban on media reporting of jury deliberations. Apart from the various specific restraints on reporting already discussed, there is a complete ban in the 1981 Act on the reporting of jury deliberations; it is aimed not at preventing prejudice to particular proceedings, but at preserving the administration of justice by protecting the confidentiality of such deliberations. Section 8(1) of the Contempt of Court Act 1981 bars the revelation of statements, opinions, arguments or votes of the members of the jury in the course of their deliberations[131] except in very narrow circumstances, to a court, as discussed below. It is accepted that there is a mens rea element of intention—the section refers only to deliberate revelations. A similar rule has prevailed in Commonwealth countries,[132] but it is less absolute than the UK one.[133]

Therefore jurors are prevented from exercising their freedom of expression, except in one narrow circumstance, and the media are barred from discussing such deliberations in two ways. First, the source of information that they would need is withheld from them since it would be an offence for a juror to disclose information about the deliberations, while it would also be an offence under s 8 for a reporter to solicit it. Second, any reporting of the deliberations would itself infringe s 8.[134] Therefore, apart from general and abstract discussions, the media cannot act in their watchdog role[135] in relation to the very significant function of the jury in society. Further, due to s 8 research into the deliberations of jurors in real trials, even if anonymized, is so highly constrained in the UK as to be impossible.[136]

---

[131] S 8 provides in full: 'Confidentiality of jury's deliberations.

(1) Subject to subsection (2) below, it is a contempt of court to obtain, disclose or solicit any particulars of statements made, opinions expressed, arguments advanced or votes cast by members of a jury in the course of their deliberations in any legal proceedings.

(2) This section does not apply to any disclosure of any particulars—
    (a) in the proceedings in question for the purpose of enabling the jury to arrive at their verdict, or in connection with the delivery of that verdict, or
    (b) in evidence in any subsequent proceedings for an offence alleged to have been committed in relation to the jury in the first mentioned proceedings,
    or to the publication of any particulars so disclosed.

(3) Proceedings for a contempt of court under this section (other than Scottish proceedings) shall not be instituted except by or with the consent of the Attorney General or on the motion of a court having jurisdiction to deal with it.

[132] For Australia, see: *R v Andrew Brown* [1907] 7 NSWSR 290; *R v Medici* (Court of Criminal Appeal, Victoria, 5 June 1995); for Canada, see: *R v Pan; R v Sawyer* [2001] 2 SCR 344; for New Zealand, see: *R v Papadopoulos* [1979] 1 NZLR 621.

[133] See Chapter 6 at 273–5 for discussion of research into jury trials in various Commonwealth countries.

[134] See *A-G v. Associated Newspapers* [1994] 2 AC 538, HL.

[135] See the discussion of *Goodwin v UK* (1996) 22 EHRR 123 in Chapter 7, esp at 334–6.

[136] See below at 241–3 and see Chapter 6 at 272–5 for discussion of research into jury trials.

INTERPRETATIONS OF SECTION 8

The pre-HRA stance, from the ruling in *A-G v Associated Newspapers Ltd and Others*,[137] was that s 8 should be interpreted literally. In that instance, jury deliberations were not disclosed directly to the defendant newspaper, but to researchers who made a transcript of them. The paper then used the transcript in order to gather information for the article in question. It was argued on behalf of the defendants that the word 'disclose' used in s 8 is capable of bearing two meanings; it could mean disclosure by anyone, or it could mean disclosure by a member of the jury to the defendant. It was well established in the pre-HRA era that where a statute contains an ambiguous provision, it should be construed so as to conform with the relevant Convention guarantee.[138] On that basis, the narrower meaning should have been adopted, allowing the defendants to escape liability. However, it was found that the word 'disclose' was not ambiguous—in its natural and ordinary meaning, which Parliament clearly intended it to bear, it denoted disclosure to anyone; the defendants therefore clearly fell within its provisions.

The closing up of a potential loophole in s 8 achieved by this ruling means that the important institution of the jury is largely immune from media scrutiny, at least as regards the manner in which it discharges its role.[139] The section does not prevent interviewing of jurors that does not touch upon their deliberations in the jury room, but such inquiries should only be undertaken with the leave of the trial court or after verdict and sentence, by the Court of Appeal.[140] Jury deliberations are clearly a matter of very significant public interest, and it is therefore argued that s 8 should have been framed much less widely. The only current constraint is the requirement of the Attorney General's consent to a prosecution, but even this is not necessary where proceedings are instituted on the motion of a court.

The absolute nature of s 8 means that it may be incompatible with Article 10 since jurors are denied freedom of expression, and media discussion and reporting on a matter of great public interest is so greatly curbed. Section 8 probably answers to the exceptions under Article 10(2), of preserving confidentiality and perhaps 'for maintaining the authority of the judiciary'. But assuming that one of these exceptions applies, the absolute nature of the section means that it creates an interference arguably disproportionate to the end in view. On the face of it it might have been expected therefore that s 8 would be found at some point after 2000 to be *prima facie* incompatible with Article 10 under the Human Rights Act, and s 3 would have had to be invoked to impose a different interpretation on it. Alternatively, it might have been expected that a declaration of the incompatibility would have to be made under s 4 HRA.

---

[137] [1994] 2 WLR 277; [1994] 1 All ER 556; (1994) 142 *NLJ* 1647, HL; [1993] 2 All ER 535; (1993) 144 *NLJ* 195, CA.

[138] See Chapter 3 at 157–63 for discussion of the position under s 3 HRA.

[139] For consideration of the effect of the restriction see the Royal Commission on Criminal Justice Report (1993) Cm 2263, p 2.

[140] *McCluskey* (1993) 94 Cr App R 216, CA. See also *Mickleborough* [1995] 1 Cr App R 297, CA.

The two leading post-HRA cases concerned the compatibility of s 8 with Articles 6 and 10; they indicate that the senior judges are not minded to create exceptions to the section, relying on s 3 HRA, apart from one very narrow one. It seems clear therefore that they would not be prepared to create an exception which would allow for some limited, anonymized disclosure of jury deliberations to the media. In *R v Mirza; R v Connor*[141] the House of Lords largely reaffirmed the accepted understandings as to the interpretation of s 8.[142] However, it was found that s 8(1) does not apply to the trial court or to the Court of Appeal. In other words, there is an exception to s 8 allowing a judge to enquire into a juror's disclosure of impropriety in the jury's deliberations during proceedings. Thus matters can be disclosed without either the juror or court facing liability under s 8. Prior to this decision the general assumption in the English courts was that the terms of section 8(1) were so broad as to apply to any court, whether the trial court or the Court of Appeal (Criminal Division), which might otherwise have wished to inquire into a matter relating to the jurors' deliberations. Section 8(1), it had been thought, in effect ruled out such inquiries by the courts.[143]

Subsequently, in *R v Smith*[144] the House looked further at what form the trial judge's inquiries might take when a matter was drawn to his/her attention during the trial. It was found that it would not be appropriate for a judge to question jurors about the contents of a letter received during proceedings from one of the jurors making allegations about impropriety in the jury deliberations, and a judge was not obliged to do so. In relation to the case it was said: 'If he had gone into the allegations, he would inevitably have had to question them about the subject of their deliberations and whether S was guilty of any of the offences charged'. The common law prohibition against inquiring into events in the jury room extended, it was found, to matters connected with the subject matter of the jury's deliberations. Thus, following *Mirza* and *Smith*, s 8 does not disallow enquiry into the jury's deliberations, but once an enquiry has been made the judge cannot under the common law question the jury as to allegations made. He or she would only have a choice between discharging the jury or redirecting them in terms that took account of the allegations. In *Smith* it was found on appeal that the redirection had not taken sufficient account of the allegations and therefore the appeal was allowed.

Mirza also concerned the admissibility into evidence of jurors' expressed concerns about the jury's deliberations—concerns that suggested that the jury had not acted fairly. The majority determined, by virtue of a long-standing common law rule,[145] that

---

[141] [2004] 1 All ER 925; [2004] 2 WLR 201.

[142] See *R v Qureshi* [2002] 1 WLR 518; *Roylance v GMC (No2)* [2000] 1 AC 311.

[143] See *R v Young* [1995] QB 324, 330.   [144] [2005] 1WLR 704.

[145] There is a long line of decisions holding that it is never permissible to admit evidence of what happened during jury deliberations. See: *Ellis v Deheer* [1922] 2 KB 113, 117–118, *per* Bankes LJ at 121; *R v Thompson* [1962] 1 All ER 65, 66, *per* Lord Parker CJ; *Attorney General v New Statesman and National Publishing Company Ltd* [1981] QB 1,10; *per* Lord Widgery CJ; *R v Miah* [1997] 2 Cr App R 12, 18–19, per Kennedy LJ; *Roylance v General Medical Council (No 2)* [2000] 1 AC 311, 324B, *per* Lord Clyde; *R v Qureshi* [2002] 1 WLR 518, *per* Kennedy LJ. The position is similar in Scotland: *Stewart v Fraser* (1830) 5 Murray 166; *Swankie v H M Advocate* (1999) SCCR 1.

after the jury have returned their verdict, evidence directed to matters intrinsic to the jurors' deliberations is inadmissible.[146] Exceptionally, however, evidence of extraneous influences on the verdict is admissible. So jury concerns could not be admitted into evidence after the conclusion of proceedings unless the jury had been subjected to, for example, bribery. The bar thereby created was found not to be incompatible with the Article 6 guarantee of a fair trial. The residual possibility of a miscarriage of justice was, it was found, the necessary price to be paid for the preservation and protection of the jury system, although Lord Steyn, in the minority, delivered a powerful dissenting judgment. He said:

In my view it would be an astonishing thing for the ECHR to hold, when the point directly arises before it, that a miscarriage of justice may be ignored in the interests of the general efficiency of the jury system. The terms of Article 6(1) of the European Convention, the rights revolution, and fifty years of development of human rights law and practice, would suggest that such a view would be utterly indefensible.[147]

Clearly, the Lords were not concerned with the compatibility of s 8 with Article 10. However, the findings demonstrate that the Lords are not minded to create implied exceptions to s 8 except in relation to the courts themselves; they were prepared to find that a court itself cannot be in contempt of court on the narrow basis that to hold otherwise would be self-evidently absurd and that therefore s 8 must be read as including that exception. Otherwise, the Lords were content to continue the previously established approach.

In the key post-HRA authority, *Attorney General v Scotcher*,[148] the House of Lords reaffirmed the approach in *Mirza* and also found that s 8 is compatible with Article 10. It should be pointed out that *Scotcher* did not concern media free expression—at least, not directly—but the exercise of free speech rights by a juror. The facts of *Scotcher* were as follows. In January 2000 the appellant, Scotcher, was summoned for jury service in the Crown Court. Like all the other potential jurors, Scotcher was informed that disclosing the deliberations of the jury to anyone would be contempt of court under s 8 Contempt of Court Act 1981. The jury convicted the two defendants (brothers) by a majority verdict of ten votes to one.

The appellant then wrote to the defendants' mother, telling her that he had been the one juror who had wanted an acquittal and criticizing the basis on which the other jurors had reached their decision. He said *inter alia* that they had not weighed up the evidence properly and that some of them had convicted merely because they wanted to get home. He also indicated that in his view the police had framed the defendants but that the other jurors had failed to appreciate this. He suggested that she should appeal and also asked her not to disclose the fact that he had sent the letter to the court or to the police. The defendants' mother's solicitor brought the matter to the attention of the Court of Appeal; eventually Scotcher admitted that he had written

---

[146] *R v Hood* [1968] 1 WLR 773; *R v Brandon* (1969) 53 Cr App R 466; *R v Young (Stephen)* [1995] QB 324.
[147] *R v Mizra; R v Connor* [2004] 1 All ER 925; [2004] 2 WLR 201, at [19].
[148] [2005] 1 WLR 1867.

the letter, and he was convicted of the offence under s 8. He appealed, arguing that he had a defence based on the Human Rights Act, and specifically Article 10, on the basis that he had written the letter since he was seeking to prevent a miscarriage of justice. This was of relevance also in relation to Article 6, although that Article was not directly engaged. It was argued that in the particular circumstances of this case, by virtue of s 3 HRA, section 8(1) had to be interpreted as including the defence argued for so as to make it compatible with Article 10 of the European Convention. It was further argued that if this could not be done, then the House should make a declaration of incompatibility under s 4 HRA.

Both sides accepted that, in the terms of s 8, the appellant had revealed 'statements, opinions, arguments or votes' of the members of the jury in the course of their deliberations. It was also accepted that the mens rea for the offence is an intention to disclose those matters and that the appellant had deliberately disclosed these aspects of the jury's deliberations to the defendants' mother. So unless a defence was available to the appellant he was guilty of contempt of court in the terms of section 8(1). Just before the appeal the House of Lords had given judgment in *R v Mirza*.[149] That decision corrected the previous interpretation of section 8(1), which the Divisional Court had applied in Scotcher's case. As a result, the arguments before the House were different from those in the Divisional Court.

The House had held in *Mirza*, however, as indicated above, that if a trial judge was informed about any misconduct during the jury's deliberations, but before they had returned their verdict, then s 8(1) did not prevent him/her from looking into the matter. Since jurors might well not appreciate that they could tell the judge about any misconduct of their fellow jurors, the House suggested that in future they should be given further guidance. This suggestion led Lord Woolf CJ to issue Practice Direction (Crown Court: Guidance to Jurors) in 2004[150] which amended Practice Direction (Criminal Proceedings: Consolidation)[151] so as to provide, *inter alia*: 'Trial judges should ensure that the jury is alerted to the need to bring any concerns about fellow jurors to the attention of the judge at the time, and not wait until the case is concluded.'

However, this amended advice was not available at the time when Scotcher served as a juror—the advice he received was the previous, blanket advice. It was accepted that if he had written his letter to the Crown Court or to the Court of Appeal, he would not have been in contempt of court in the terms of section 8(1). Taking Article 10 and s 3 HRA into account, the defence argued that s 8 should be interpreted as being subject to a defence that it did not apply to a juror who disclosed the jury's deliberations to a third party rather than to the court, if the juror was motivated by a desire to expose a miscarriage of justice and he did not contact the court authorities because he had been told that he could not disclose the deliberations to anyone. Any other argument would, it was suggested, lead to a breach of Article 10 on the ground

---

[149] [2004] 1 AC 118.
[150] [2004] 1 WLR 665.   [151] [2002] 1 WLR 2870.

of the disproportionality of the penalty to the aim pursued. This argument was rejected by the House on the basis that s 3 HRA comes into play only where it is needed in order to make a legislative provision compatible with a Convention right. But when properly interpreted according to ordinary principles of construction (as it was in *Mirza*), it was considered that section 8(1) is compatible with Article 10 of the Convention. Therefore, it was found, section 3 did not apply. So the warnings to the jurors at the time were incorrect, but the statutory provision was not. In any event, the House found, any such potential defence would have been inapplicable to Scotcher since he disregarded warnings not to contact anyone and therefore the warnings could not be viewed as having affected him. Therefore he would not have contacted the court had the warnings been correct. Scotcher's conviction was therefore upheld since the defence argued for in his favour was not found to exist.

BALANCING FREE EXPRESSION AND THE ADMINISTRATION OF JUSTICE IN *SCOTCHER*

A number of comments may be made on this decision in relation to the balance it strikes between free expression and the administration of justice. Although this was not a decision about media reporting of jury deliberations, it is clear that the House had the possibility of disclosures to the media in mind. The Lords appeared to be concerned that the creation of exceptions to s 8, allowing disclosure to anybody apart from a court, might open the floodgates to such disclosures. The discussion will concentrate on the current position in relation to Article 10 and ask whether an absolute bar on disclosure to the media, taking account of the possibility of anonymizing the reporting, is acceptable under Article 10. But it will begin by considering the correctness of this decision in terms of its application of the HRA to the circumstances and facts of this particular case. It will be suggested that a different outcome could have been reached using a somewhat different process of reasoning.

The starting point is to assume that the absolute bar to disclosures to anyone, including the court, apparently applicable at the time of Scotcher's letter, did not answer to the demands of proportionality under Article 10(2). The invasion of speech rights was especially serious due to the importance of the speech in question. The House appeared to proceed on the basis that this might have been the case, but that it was not necessary to reinterpret s 8 in order to create an exception under s 3 HRA since that reinterpretation had already occurred in *Mirza*, albeit without needing to invoke s 3. The next step is to determine the effect of ss 3 and 6 HRA, on the arguable assumption that the penalty imposed on Scotcher was not compatible with the demands of Article 10. The issue concerns the matter of disclosure to others, including relatives of the defendant or the media, under the pre-*Mirza* blanket rule.

The most straightforward argument would have been simply to apply s 3 HRA to import a similar defence into s 8, despite the fact that it would virtually always be unnecessary due to the 2004 Practice Direction. In other words, despite the reinterpretation of s 8 that had occurred in *Mirza* there was still room for argument that s 8

required modification under s 3. The argument would be that if s 8 were not interpreted in this way it would not be compatible with Article 10 since a rare instance
might arise in which a juror seeking to prevent a miscarriage of justice contacted
someone other than the court in the mistaken but honest belief that s/he was barred
from contacting anyone. The imposition of a penalty on such a juror could be viewed
as disproportionate to the aim pursued under Article 10(2). The defence could be
relied upon post-2004 if an administrative error on the part of the court authorities
had occurred in dealing with the jurors, and the fact that a juror could bring the
matter to the attention of the court had not been brought sufficiently to his/her
attention. But in order to cover the circumstances of the instant case the defence could
be framed as applicable if circumstances had led a juror to believe that he could not
disclose the deliberations to anyone. Thus a juror genuinely desiring to expose a
miscarriage of justice, but apparently faced with an absolute bar on disclosure, would
have had a defence whomever he disclosed the material to so long as the person/body
in question was a reasonable one to choose in the circumstances. This defence would
not have opened the floodgates to disclosure to the media since it would only have
had a significant impact in the post-1981 but pre-2004 period. Once s 8 had been
reinterpreted in that way such a defence could have benefited Scotcher.

One other possible, if controversial, argument is that although s 3 HRA was arguably inapplicable on the grounds accepted by the Lords, s 6 was applicable. Thus, the
House (and the lower courts) had a duty under s 6 HRA as public authorities to apply
s 8 CCA—on its understood interpretation at the time when Scotcher sent his letter—
in a manner that ensured compatibility with the Convention, if possible. This point
concerns of course the difficult interface between the functions of ss 6 and 3 HRA
when statutory provisions are in question in relation to a court as a public authority.
The court must *apply* the provisions compatibly with the Convention under s 6, and if
necessary in order to do so must reinterpret them under s 3. Clearly, in many
instances the s 6 duty would then lead to the engagement of s 3. In this instance the
House considered that it did not due to the subsequent reinterpretation of s 8 of
the 1981 Act that had occurred after the Divisional Court decision but before that in
the Lords. But that still left a duty to act compatibly with the rights under s 6 even if
s 3 could not in the particular instance aid the court in its discharge of that duty.[152]

What did the courts' duty under s 6 entail in this instance? It demanded that the
court itself should act compatibly with Article 10. The House in *Mirza* had succeeded
in excluding trial and Appeal courts from the s 8 duty without invoking s 3 HRA and
relying on ordinary principles of statutory interpretation to do so. There is nothing in
s 6 to state that where the public authority is a court and s 3 appears to be inapplicable, s 6 itself cannot be relied upon as an aid to determining the *application* of
statutory words in a particular instance in a manner that might encroach to an extent

---

[152] Possibly s 4 could also have been used whether or not s 3 had previously been invoked, although in
this instance it would arguably have been pointless to invoke s 4 due to the effect of *Mirza*. The point about s 4
is a contentious one, but s 4 itself makes no mention of using s 3.

on the function of s 3.[153] It is contended that therefore the House should have gone further than it did in *Mirza* in this instance, but under s 6 HRA. It could have accepted that this was an exceptional instance since the law had been re-interpreted to become Convention-compatible *after* Scotcher had been affected by the non-Convention compatible law. The *Mirza* reinterpretation obviously did not help Scotcher since he was not told that he could legitimately disclose his concerns to the court. It therefore appeared that, not knowing how he could legitimately disclose them, he disclosed them to the defendants' mother. The House of Lords did not accept this explanation of his conduct, but it is argued that it is plausible. Thus it could be argued that the Lords' duty under s 6HRA meant that in this instance s 8 should have been applied *subject to* the defence argued for on Scotcher's behalf—a defence applicable if a juror was motivated by a desire to expose a miscarriage of justice and he did not contact the court authorities because he had been wrongly told that he could not disclose the deliberations to anyone. Failing to accept this argument meant that Scotcher fell into a lacuna effectively created between ss 3 and 6 HRA. He apparently could not rely on s 3 since the statute had been subject to a different, arguably Convention-compatible, interpretation *after* he had been affected by warnings based on the incorrect interpretation. He could not rely on s 6 since that appeared to involve a reinterpretation of s 8—the job of s 3. Thus in this exceptional circumstance there was an argument for using s 6 HRA in order to apply s 8 as it *should* have been applied to Scotcher via the warnings he was given as a juror.

If either position had been adopted that would not have been the end of the matter since the House considered that the warnings did not affect Scotcher since he disregarded them, and disclosed the material in any event, although not to the court. The House found that since Scotcher had disclosed the deliberations to the defendants' mother despite the application of the blanket rule, the rule had had no effect on him. Therefore although the rule at the time in question was too restrictive, it was not the relevant consideration. However, this conclusion is questionable. The argument could have been put forward that the jurors were faced with a rule banning all communications to anyone. Scotcher wanted to exercise his freedom of expression because he considered that a miscarriage of justice had occurred but he also knew that he was banned absolutely from exercising it. He could not guess that had he contacted the court he would in fact—as it turned out—have incurred no liability. Instead of focusing only on what actually occurred, it is necessary to imagine what *would have* occurred had the amended post-*Mirza* warning been in place. It would appear strange to find that Scotcher would not have contacted the court regarding his concerns had he specifically been told that he could do so without incurring liability (the House did in fact make that finding which, it is contended, was erroneous). In other words,

---

[153] The argument could be put forward that the application of s 3 to s 6 itself could demand this interpretation. However, it is not clear that the Convention rights themselves demand this since the Convention mandates no particular mode of incorporation into domestic law; see further on this point T. Hickman (2005) PL 306, at note 15.

Scotcher did know that he should not disclose matters to anyone and he disregarded that warning. But the converse does not apply—that had he known that he could disclose matters to the court he would have disregarded that possibility and risked liability. This argument could have been used to combat the argument that the incorrect warnings were irrelevant to Scotcher's actions. Any such potential defence would therefore have been applicable to Scotcher.

The lack of such a defence was disproportionate to the aim pursued under Article 10(2) in the circumstances since importing such a defence retrospectively post-2004 would very rarely affect the confidentiality of jury deliberations (due to the effect of *Mirza* on the hypothetical defence in the meantime) and yet the defendant had had a criminal conviction imposed upon him when exercising expression rights. If an absolute bar to the exercise of expression rights appears to be in place due to an erroneous interpretation of the law by the relevant authorities, it is suggested that it is disproportionate to the aim pursued under Article 10(2) to punish a person for exercising those rights in a reaction to the absolute bar in order to serve the public interest in good faith, albeit in retrospect in a misjudged manner. In this instance the invasion was also especially serious due to the importance of the speech in question. In those circumstances, then, it is argued that the application of the rule was incompatible with the demands of Article 10. Therefore the defence should have been accepted and Scotcher's conviction should have been over-turned.

COMPATIBILITY BETWEEN ARTICLE 10 AND SECTION 8

This brings us to the second and more significant issue concerning non-disclosure to others, including the media, under the amended rule. The defence Counsel conceded that, once the 2004 Practice Direction came into force, section 8(1) did not infringe a juror's Article 10 rights, since he would know that he could draw his concerns to the attention of the trial judge before the jury returned their verdict. However, this is questionable. As matters stand at present certain bodies have been exempted from the application of s 8 via interpretation. The exception arose since it appeared strange to hold that a court could itself be in contempt of court.

But, following *Mirza*, a *juror* may avoid liability for contempt if s/he discloses to the court what is said or done during the jury's deliberations with the intention of prompting an investigation. S/he is also exempt from being in contempt of court in terms of section 8(1)—a further exception and one not dependent on the anomaly of finding a court to be in contempt. Jurors can make representations to the court regarding jury deliberations both during and after the trial. Doing so after the trial is however of no efficacy since such evidence is inadmissible, unless the representations concern external influences. Section 8 itself does not appear to import such an exemption for jurors. Once this inroad had been made, it could be argued that in an exceptional instance a further exemption should be created, using the powerful interpretative tool of s 3 HRA. For example, after acquittal, a female juror in a rape trial might come to the conclusion on reasonable grounds that both the court and fellow-jurors were affected by highly sexist views of rape-victims. For example, a juror might have expressed the view that 99 per cent of victims in rape trials are liars. Or a group of jurors might have expressed the view that since the woman was wearing a short skirt and had flirted with the alleged rapist, she must have given consent. If despite her concern about the court's stance, she exposed the sexist views of jurors to the court she would not be acting unlawfully, but her action would have no effect in averting a miscarriage of justice (the wrongful acquittal of a rapist) or in alerting the public to failings in the jury system in rape cases. Her action would be ineffective in relation to miscarriages since the verdict could not be appealed. Even if the law were changed so that it could be, the evidence would be inadmissible as not relating to extrinsic influences. Therefore after an acquittal tainted by sexism the female juror might consider that the only way of exposing this matter, and thus helping to address the very low conviction rate in rape cases, was to contact the media. If a newspaper published her allegations, but anonymized the case itself, it would nevertheless face liability for contempt under s 8, as would the juror.

In a similar instance, if a juror considered that fellow jurors and the court were influenced by racism in reaching a conviction, disclosure to the court would not be unlawful but would not avert a miscarriage of justice since on appeal the evidence would be inadmissible. Lord Steyn gave this example in *Mirza*: 'A juror reveals after verdict that during the jury deliberations it emerged that some members of the jury were associated with a Neo-Nazi group and that they urged the conviction of the accused because he was a black immigrant;' he considered that there could be no serious dispute as to the perversion of justice that would have occurred in that instance.[154] Nevertheless, the disclosure could not be admitted in evidence on appeal. The juror who realized that his/her revelation had had no effect might be tempted to write to a newspaper, revealing what had happened as a matter that the public should be informed about. If he did, he would incur liability under s 8 even if he anonymized his letter.

Under the present state of the law, disclosure by a juror *during* the case of the fact that a juror was evincing sexist or racist views, could be received by the court. But it is clear, following the Lords' decision in *R v Smith*,[155] that it could not lead to an enquiry by the judge into the matter; the judge appears only to have the options of discharging the jury or re-directing them. If a mere redirection was given, which in fact appeared to have little impact, disclosure to the court might be viewed as having been ineffective by the juror. Recourse to the media might appear to be the only way of alerting the public to the miscarriage of justice and also possibly prompting a change in the law.[156] Consideration of such instances indicates that s 8 may be incompatible with Article 10

---

[154] *R v Mirza* [2004] 1 AC 118 [1].   [155] [2005] 1 WLR 704.

[156] A possible change that might be prompted by media outcries would be to allow for enquiries into jury debate to be made by a judge during trial if an allegation of jury prejudice is made by a juror (contrary to the finding in *R v Smith* note 155 above). This would have been valuable in domestic courts in relation to the domestic case (*R v Gregory* Manchester Crown Court between 26 and 28 November 1991; leave to appeal refused) resulting in *Gregory v UK* [1997] 25 EHRR 577, discussed below.

since the free expression of jurors and of the media is severely curbed in relation to jury deliberations.

The position in England prior to the enactment of s 8 is of some interest in this context. *A-G v New Statesman*[157] was the decision that led to the introduction of s 8. Following the acquittal of a prominent politician on a charge of conspiracy to murder, the *New Statesman* magazine published an article, based on an interview with one of the jurors, which gave an account of significant parts of the jury's deliberations. The Attorney General applied for an order for contempt of court against the New Statesman. The Divisional Court held that a juror's disclosure of the jury's deliberations was not a contempt of court unless it 'tended, or would tend, to imperil the finality of jury verdicts, or to affect adversely the attitude of future jurors and the quality of their deliberations'. The court held that the article in question would not have that effect and the Attorney General's application was refused. Lord Widgery CJ found:[158]

The evidence before us shows that for a number of years the publication of jury room secrets has occurred on numerous occasions. To many of those disclosures no exception could be taken because from a study of them it would not be possible to identify the persons concerned in the trials. In these cases, jury secrets were revealed in the main for the laudable purpose of informing would-be jurors what to expect when summoned for jury service. Thus, it is not possible to contend that every case of post-trial activity of the kind with which we are concerned must necessarily amount to a contempt. Looking at this case as a whole, we have come to the conclusion that the article in the 'New Statesman' does not justify the title of contempt of court. That does not mean that we would not wish to see restrictions on the publication of such an article because we would.

These findings suggest that an absolute bar on publication of jury deliberations was not needed and was not being asked for by the court. They also suggest that the courts did not view anonymized publications as problematic, while even nominate ones—as in the *New Statesman* case—were not viewed as imperilling the jury system in a significant manner. These remarks provide a starting point from which to examine the compatibility of s 8 in its current manifestation—post-*Mirza*—with Article 10. It may be noted that in *Scotcher* the House relied on *Gregory v UK*,[159] discussed below, in noting that the European Court of Human Rights had acknowledged that the rule governing the secrecy of jury deliberations is a crucial and legitimate feature of English trial law. The House took the view that this finding was relevant to the compatibility of s 8 with Article 10, Lord Roger of Earlsferry stating:

Therefore, in so far as section 8(1) serves to reinforce that rule by making it an offence for a juror to disclose the information which he receives in confidence from his fellow jurors, the objective is sufficiently important to justify limiting the juror's freedom of expression in this way. The provision is rationally connected to its aim and the means adopted are no more than is reasonably necessary, since the restriction does not apply to bona fide disclosures to the court authorities. The measure is accordingly reasonably justifiable in a democratic society.[160]

---

[157] [1981] QB 1.   [158] At p 11.   [159] (1997) 25 EHRR 577, 594, [44].   [160] At [29].

However, that is not necessarily the end of the matter as far as Article 10 is concerned. *Gregory* concerned the right to a fair trial under Article 6(1) and specifically whether, in the circumstances of the trial in question, impartiality had been achieved so as to satisfy Article 6(1). Article 10 was not in question. On the facts the Court was satisfied that no breach had occurred. The applicant in that case had been tried for robbery and on the final day of the trial the jury had retired to consider their verdict. After some time a note was passed by the jury to the judge. It read: 'Jury showing racial overtones. 1 member to be excused.' The trial judge consulted counsel for the prosecution and defence and decided to redirect the jury as to the need to decide the case on the evidence, although he did not mention racial prejudice specifically. He could not enquire directly into any racial bias on the part of jury members due to s 8. Eventually the jury convicted. The European Court decided that the note was ambiguous and that the judge had taken reasonable measures to ensure that impartiality had been safeguarded. Thus the decision turned on the particular circumstances of the case and did not determine that in all circumstances the application of s 8 on its current interpretation could cause no breach of Article 6 or of Article 10.

If s 8 serves a legitimate aim under Article 10(2) and satisfies the tests for necessity and proportionality in relation to that aim then there is no incompatibility. However, it is suggested that Lord Roger in *Scotcher* did not take full account of all the tests for proportionality or subject s 8 in relation to them to a sufficiently high level of scrutiny, despite citing *de Freitas v Permanent Secretary of Ministry Agriculture*.[161] Clearly, the preservation of jury confidentiality serves a significant societal interest—it can be said that it answers to a pressing social need. It is important that there should be free debate in the jury room; jurors should be able to deliberate without fear of possible future repercussions. Does s 8 go further than is necessary to serve that need? A number of tests for proportionality should be applied (those from *Goodwin v UK*[162] and from *de Freitas v Permanent Secretary of Ministry Agriculture*).[163] It is also suggested that the level of scrutiny to be adopted should be strict, bearing in mind the significance of the speech in question and the importance of the media's role—a juror disclosing material to a newspaper about a miscarriage of justice would be in position analogous to that of a source disclosing malpractice in, for example, the police service. Thus the strict level of scrutiny determined upon in *Goodwin v UK* in relation to source disclosure should apply.[164]

The *de Freitas* tests for proportionality cover first the suitability of the interference in question. In this instance, the penalty under s 8 constitutes the interference. This test is arguably met on the basis that criminal liability for disclosing information is effective while the penalties imposed are not excessive: a custodial sentence is unlikely to be imposed, although a suspended sentence might be. The second test concerns the

---

[161] [1999] 1 AC 69, 80.   [162] (1996) 22 EHRR 123.

[163] [1999] 1 AC 69, 80. The tests are discussed fully in Chapter 2, at 86–106 and Chapter 7, at 335–6 and 359–61.

[164] (1992) 15 EHRR 244. See further Chapter 7 for discussion of the proportionality test used in this instance and for discussion of the standard of scrutiny from *Goodwin*.

need to choose the least intrusive measure. It is arguable that this test is not met since a less intrusive measure—an injunction obtained on grounds of breach of confidence—is available and subject to a public interest test that meets Article 10's demands. More significantly, near-absolute bars to the exercise of expression rights invade the right almost as far as it is possible to do so. A parallel could be drawn with *Open-Door Counselling and Dublin Well-Woman v Ireland* [165] in which the interference with speech rights was also very serious. Pamphlets on the availability of abortions outside Ireland were—in effect—banned by an injunction granted by the Irish courts. The European Court of Human Rights was struck by the absolute nature of the interference—there were no grounds, including that of health, on which it could be waived. On that basis it was found to be a disproportionate interference with expression rights. In the instance of s 8 there is an *absolute* bar to the exercise of *media* expression rights since jurors cannot disclose matters relating to the trial to the media, however significant the public interest involved. Media reports of such matters could adopt anonymity and therefore protect the confidentiality of jury deliberations. Therefore absolute bars to media reporting may be viewed as unnecessarily restrictive. The strictness of the test for scrutiny means that it is not sufficient to find a reasonable relationship between the restrictiveness of s 8 and the aim pursued.

Thirdly, the seriousness of the interference has to be balanced against the importance of the aim sought to be pursued. Clearly, the interference is especially severe, since it amounts to an absolute bar despite the significance of the expression in question. The aim pursued is important—the efficient working of the jury system. But is that efficiency best served by hiding the failings of the system from public scrutiny? Could it be served more effectively by allowing reports of jury deliberations, but anonymized? In coming to a conclusion on this point it would not be enough to be satisfied that the balance struck between the two interests was not manifestly unreasonable. On a stricter level of scrutiny it would appear that the balance struck between the two is not satisfactory since it is does not appear that the serious invasion of expression rights is warranted by the aim pursued. The efficacy of the jury system might ultimately be enhanced by media scrutiny accompanied by the safeguards mentioned: an absolute bar is not therefore needed. Thus it appears that two of the key tests for proportionality are unsatisfied by s 8. If its effects are disproportionate to the aim pursued, they cannot be viewed as necessary in a democratic society under Article 10(2).

REFORM OF SECTION 8

Arguably it would be possible to imply an exception into s 8 via s 3HRA on similar lines to the exception created by the House of Lords in *R v A* [166] to s 41 Youth Justice and Criminal Evidence Act 1999; s 8 could be read subject to the need to ensure compatibility with Article 10 by allowing for a defence where a juror was genuinely

<hr />

[165] (1993) 15 EHRR 244.   [166] [2001] 2 WLR 1546.

motivated by a desire to expose a miscarriage of justice in the public interest and
where the material was anonymized. Such a reinterpretation would not be contrary to
the underlying intention behind s 8 since, as the House accepted in *Scotcher*, the main
intention behind introduction of the section was to prevent the harassment of jurors
by the media. The new exception could be made applicable only where the jury
member had spontaneously contacted the media in the exceptional circumstances
envisaged; thus the exception could be found not to apply where a journalist had
contacted the juror or offered money. There is also a strong Article 10-based argument for creating a further exception covering anonymized research into jury trials on
the basis that the confidentiality of jury deliberations is unlikely to be threatened but
the material discovered is of very high public interest value. The creation of implied
exceptions to s 8 which allow for serious debate as to the fairness of the jury system
would be a desirable result in terms of the values enshrined not only in Article 10 but
also in Article 6 and possibly Articles 8 and 3. If the creation of such exceptions using
s 3 HRA was viewed as too radical, a declaration of incompatibility between Article 10
and s 8 could be made.

Clearly, in order to import these exceptions into s 8 under s 3 HRA, the House of
Lords would probably have to decide in a suitable case to overturn *Scotcher*. The only
alternative in terms of creating compatibility at the domestic level, in the absence of
legislative change, would be for the courts to find that *Scotcher* is confined to its own
special facts. It could be found to be inapplicable to an instance in which a juror *knew*
of the possibility of disclosure to the court and took it but considered that her
concerns were not taken seriously. *Scotcher* could also be viewed as inapplicable to an
instance in which a juror did not express her concerns to the court on defensible
grounds. In both instances recourse to the media could reasonably be seen as the only
effective option. The question of compatibility between Article 6 and the common law
rule on admissibility of allegations of jury impropriety post-verdict is outside the
scope of this book. But the unwillingness of the judiciary in the post-HRA era to
accept that such allegations should be admitted in order to serve the demands of
Article 6 is indicative of their determination to maintain the secrecy of jury deliberations, even in the face of a number of highly significant competing considerations.
The refusal to allow judges to enquire into such allegations during the trial is equally
telling. Thus a judicial determination to narrow down s 8 does not appear to be
present. It is therefore more probable that an adverse ruling may arise eventually at
Strasbourg. It is possible that eventually there will be a finding at Strasbourg that s 8 is
incompatible with Articles 10 or 6, or both. Such a finding would be expected to
prompt review of the section.

A review may eventually occur in any event, as indicated above. The Runciman
Royal Commission on Criminal Justice recommended that s 8 should be amended in
order to allow research to be conducted into the reasoning of jurors in reaching
a verdict.[167] In 2001 Lord Justice Auld recommended that legislation should be

---

[167] (1993) Cm 2263, p 2.

introduced, *inter alia*, to permit enquiry 'into alleged impropriety by a jury, whether in the course of its deliberations or otherwise.'[168] In 2003 the Lord Chancellor indicated in a written answer in the House of Lords that he would publish a consultation paper dealing with Lord Justice Auld's recommendation.[169] *R v Mirza; R v Connor*,[170] as indicated, created a limited exception to s 8 which addressed this issue to an extent. In the wake of *Mirza* the Courts Minister, Chris Leslie, said that the Department for Constitutional Affairs would shortly publish a consultation paper considering whether the Government should allow research to be conducted on jury deliberations and juror impropriety.[171]

It is suggested that a return to the clause originally put forward in the Contempt Bill would go some way towards meeting the Article 10 requirements. That clause would have prevented *inter alia* the disclosure or publication of *details* of a jury's deliberations. It would have protected jurors without preventing legitimate research. It might have allowed for some anonymized reporting of jury deliberations. However, it would be more satisfactory to put media freedom in this context on a surer basis. One possibility would be to introduce a revised section containing an exception arising where a juror was genuinely motivated by a desire to expose a miscarriage of justice, had disclosed the jury impropriety to the court during the trial without adequate effect, or had had reasonable grounds for not disclosing it, and the media body had anonymized the case fully in its reporting of it. Exceptions could also be included (as they were under the clause as originally drafted)[172] which would allow approaches to jurors as part of academic research so long as the proceedings and jurors were not identified.[173]

CONCLUSIONS

The repeal and replacement of s 8 with a revised clause on the lines discussed is warranted, not only on grounds of freedom of speech, but in the interests of justice, since the results of research into the workings of the jury system might lead to reforms which would serve those interests. For example, the use of juries in serious fraud trials

---

[168] Review of the Criminal Courts of England and Wales, Report of October 2001, at para 98.

[169] *Hansard* (HL Debates), Col WA 135, 11 September 2003.

[170] [2004] 1 All ER 925; [2004] 2 WLR 201.

[171] He said: 'The finding is good news . . . it opens the door for the Government to consult more broadly than it otherwise could have, on aspects of jury work. This is desirable in order to ensure that the system is working properly and that jurors feel they have everything they need to do their job properly. The Government regards jury service as one of the most important civic duties that anyone can be asked to perform. Few decisions made by members of the public have such an impact upon society as a jury's verdict. So it is essential that they are given enough information to perform their role as juror and that they have confidence in the judiciary. That is what the Consultation paper will seek to achieve.' See Report at www.spr-consilio. com/artels6.htm.

[172] *Hansard* (HL Debates), Col 416, 20 January 1981.

[173] It is worth noting that the Divisional Court in *A-G v New Statesman* [1981] QB 1 indicated that disclosure of jury room secrets which did not identify the persons concerned could have no adverse effects on the administration of justice.

may be inappropriate and may not serve the interest in convicting the guilty. Such research has been inhibited by s 8.[174] Research into the impact of prejudicial media coverage and into the efficacy of neutralizing measures, such as directions to the jury, is also inhibited in the UK, although as discussed in Chapter 6, it has been conducted abroad in relation to US juries.[175] Such research would serve the ends of justice, since it might aid in ensuring that neutralizing measures were tailored more specifically to the potential for harm in different instances. Thus the values underlying Articles 6 and 10 may be viewed as uniting in the case for reform of s 8.[176]

RELATIONSHIP BETWEEN THE PREVENTIVE AND PROTECTIVE APPROACHES

As indicated in this chapter the preventive approach operates by means of a variety of discretionary or absolute prior restraints, while the protective approach relies on deterrence created by the potential use of subsequent restraints. There is no general provision allowing interested parties, including potential defendants, to seek to avoid prejudicial publicity. The avoidance of such publicity is supposed to occur due to the deterrent effect of such restraints, discussed below. Section 4(2) of the 1981 Act only affords a narrow discretion to make an order restricting fair and accurate reporting relating to proceedings to a judge. Unfair and inaccurate reporting cannot be the subject of prior restraints. On the face of it this is anomalous. Clearly, however, it might be difficult to frame an order or injunction widely enough to cover such reporting without creating an unacceptable curb upon the media. But even where a restraint could be so framed, it is unclear whether s 4(2) covers biased and inaccurate reporting. This gap was revealed in *HM Advocate v Beggs*.[177] In that instance, in the circumstances of the case, the defendant expected that there would be prejudicial publicity and sought a s 4(2) order at the beginning of his trial for murder, in order to ward it off. The accused argued that the exceptional nature of the case might result in responsible court reporting stimulating a 'feeding frenzy' on the part of less responsible elements in the media, including publication of material on web sites, some of which still carried earlier prejudicial material. The order was refused on the basis that s 2(2)[178] is available to deal with such publicity and that s 4(2) is only available to restrict fair and accurate reporting. The court found:

---

[174] The Fraud Trials Committee was unable to conduct research into the experience of juries in fraud trials: *Fraud Trials Committee Report* (1986), HMSO, at para 8.10.

[175] See Simon, 'Does the court's decision in *Nebraska Press Association* fit with the research evidence on the impact on jurors of news coverage?' (1978) *Stanford Law Review* 515. See further Chapter 6 at 275.

[176] See J. Jaconelli, *Open Justice: A Critique of the Public Trial*, Oxford, 2002, Chapter 7 for further discussion and criticism of this provision.

[177] [2002] SLT 135.   [178] See Chapter 6.

Senior counsel for the accused himself said that he had 'no problem' with fair and accurate reporting; his concern lay elsewhere. That acceptance that fair and accurate reporting did not create a problem is plainly fatal to the motion which he made, since, as the Lord Justice General put it in *Galbraith*[179] s.4(2) is intended to deal with fair and accurate reports of proceedings which should nonetheless be postponed, not with material outwith the scope of such reports, to which the strict liability rule could apply under s.2(2) of the Act of 1981.

Exceptionally, as indicated above, s 45(4) or s 37 SCA could be relied upon to allow the Crown Court or High Court to grant injunctions to restrain a threatened contempt. But, as found by the House of Lords in *Pickering v Associated Newspapers Holdings Plc*,[180] an injunction would 'rarely be appropriate.' Thus where it is readily foreseeable that reporting of a particular proceeding is highly likely to amount to a contempt (because, for example, reporting relating to one of the parties involved on a previous and similar occasion—as in *Pickering* itself—had impeded the course of justice in those proceedings) there is little likelihood that an injunction would be granted. Newspapers and others could be reminded by the Attorney General of the relevant provisions of the 1981 Act in the hope that they would be deterred by the threat of criminal or quasi-criminal proceedings, but in most circumstances that would be all. Section 4(2) orders cannot be used to restrain prejudicial publicity *in general* since s 4(2) merely creates an exception to s 4(1) and therefore relates only to the 'fair and accurate' reporting of particular proceedings.[181] This was reaffirmed in *A-G v Guardian Newspapers*,[182] although the reach of s 4(2) was widened, but only in the narrow circumstance where reporting had led to the halting of a trial and therefore could be viewed as indirectly linked to it.

As indicated in this chapter, preventive measures can be used in a manner that encroaches on the role that has been assigned by British law to protective measures. *A-G v Guardian Newspapers* created a small inroad into the role of protective measures. A greater inroad was created by the decision in *ex parte HTV Cymru (Wales) Ltd.* As discussed in the next Chapter, injunctions can be granted, in relation to s 2(2) of the 1981 Act, against publications—although this is very rare—to prevent the risk of prejudice to a forthcoming action arising. But in most instances the only legal means currently available of seeking to prevent prejudice to proceedings is by way of the threat of post-publication sanctions, and these are considered in the next chapter. As that chapter will seek to demonstrate, British law is therefore uneasily poised between the preventive and the protective approach, leaving gaps, uncertainties, and anomalies in the protection for both fair trials and free speech.

This chapter has revealed that a number of reporting restrictions, and especially the ban on reporting jury deliberations, go further than needed to serve the ends of justice or another countervailing Convention right. It is clear that the UK 'preventive'

---

[179] *Galbraith v HM Advocate* [2001 SLT 465.   [180] [1991] 2 AC 370; [1991] 1 All ER 622.
[181] See *Scaresbrook v HM Advocate*, Appeal Court of the High Court of Judiciary, 7 September 2000 (unreported).
[182] [2001] EWCA Crim 1351.

measures have created severe inroads into the principle of open justice. It is hard to discern a clear, unifying principle underlying the range of restrictions discussed in this chapter. It has demonstrated therefore that the attachment to open justice in British law is 'hesitant and qualified'[183] and that the principle readily gives way where a range of other considerations compete with it. But at the same time, the uncertain relationship between protective and preventive measures leads to a failure of the law to focus strongly and consistently on the fair trial values at stake.

[183] E. Barendt, *Freedom of Speech*, 2nd edn., Oxford: OUP, 2005, at 340.

6

FREE SPEECH AND FAIR TRIALS: PREJUDICING PROCEEDINGS

INTRODUCTION

The balance struck between fair trials and free speech has been and remains deeply problematic within the area of law covered by this chapter. The strict liability rule under the Contempt of Court Act 1981 is used to protect the administration of justice from prejudice or impediment by threatening the media with post-publication sanctions if it publishes prejudicial material. The pre-1981 common law developed on the basis that it had the general aim of protecting the administration of justice, rather than the right of the individual to a fair trial. It took, in other words, a protective rather than preventive stance. The 1981 Act, however, reflects a mixture of both approaches, although ostensibly it continues the protective approach. This chapter will argue that an uneasy and confused interweaving of protective and preventive measures is evident within the application of the strict liability rule, and that judicial uncertainty as to its relationship with the use of neutralizing measures continues to bedevil the case law. The result is that the rule fails to focus strongly on either free speech or fair trial values.

This area of contempt law creates interferences with the guarantee of freedom of expression under Article 10. The interference may be justified where it has the legitimate aim of 'maintaining the authority and impartiality of the judiciary' under paragraph 2. This phrase may be taken to cover the preservation of the integrity of the administration of justice, including the rights of litigants.[1] Such rights also fall within the rubric of 'the rights of others' in paragraph 2 and so include, but are not necessarily confined to, Article 6 rights. Since contempt law has a role to play in deterring the media from causing prejudice to proceedings, it could be viewed as a means of protecting Article 6 rights,[2] although, in accordance with domestic tradition, the direct and primary responsibility for providing such protection is seen as falling on

---

[1] The exception referring to the judiciary has been found to cover the rights of litigants: *Sunday Times v United Kingdom* (1979) 2 EHRR 245, at 279.

[2] See Chapter 4 at 181, note 62.

the trial judge.[3] Article 6 is not engaged where the threat is to the administration of justice in a general or long-term sense. As indicated in Chapter 4, at *Strasbourg* restraints on reporting can be justified on the basis of protecting Article 6 rights. But domestically, contempt law is more likely to be viewed as coming into conflict with free expression on the basis of protecting the general societal interest in the administration of justice. The domestic judges tend to look towards neutralizing measures as a *direct* means of protecting Article 6 rights. Thus, a divergence of emphasis can be perceived between the relevant Strasbourg jurisprudence[4] and the traditional domestic stance. There is little sign of this as yet, but the influence of the HRA might eventually encourage domestic judges to acknowledge that contempt law could have a more direct role than they had previously accorded to it in protecting the fairness of trials. In other words, a more overtly preventive approach could be adopted, relying on the Convention, in a departure from the traditional stance of domestic law.

Currently, unless trial-related material is covered by one of the prior restraints considered in the last Chapter—most often an order relating to juveniles, a s 4(2) order under the Contempt of Court Act 1981, or an injunction under s 45(4) or s 37 Supreme Court Act—the media is free to publish it. However, it has to face the possibility of a sanction when the material is likely to create a risk of prejudice to the proceedings. UK contempt law has relied on various tests to indicate to the media where the limits of permissible comment lie. The domestic courts have traditionally been preoccupied with the administration of justice rather than with individual rights to free speech. Therefore the tests under domestic common law contempt prior to the introduction of the 1981 Act strongly favoured the protection of the administration of justice over freedom of expression. The inquiry under the common law always began by considering the law governing the interference with the negative liberty of expression and contained no test allowing account to be taken of the impact on the liberty. Thus, although the approach was technically protective since the law focused on objective rather than actual risks, common law contempt had a significant preventive effect: its breadth and uncertainty operated as a powerful deterrent.

This approach was modified in the pre-HRA era under the Contempt of Court Act 1981. As discussed in Chapter 4, the Act was a response to the finding at Strasbourg in the *Sunday Times* case[5] that common law contempt, as applied by the House of Lords in *A-G v Times Newspapers Ltd*,[6] had failed to afford sufficient weight to freedom of expression. It is generally accepted that the House of Lords' decision gave too much weight to the protection of the administration of justice and too little to the

---

[3] See the comments of Simon Brown LJ regarding the differing roles of the judge in contempt proceedings and at trial: *A-G v Birmingham Post and Mail Ltd* [1998] 4 All ER 49.

[4] See in particular *Worm v Austria* (1997) 25 EHRR 557; (1998) 25 EHRR 454.

[5] (1979) 2 EHRR 245; see below pp 249–50.

[6] [1974] AC 273; [1973] 3 All ER 54; [1973] 3 WLR 298, HL. For case notes, see C.J. Miller, 'The Sunday Times Case' (1974) 37 *MLR* 96; M. O'Boyle, '*A-G v The Times*' (1974) 25 *NILQ* 57; D.G.T. Williams, 'Contempt and the Thalidomide Case' (1973) 32 *CLJ* 177; C.J. Miller, 'Contempt of Court: The Sunday Times Case' [1975] *Crim LR* 132. See the discussion in Chapter 4 at 183–5.

protection of freedom of speech, and that the 1981 Act was intended to bring about a change of emphasis. As Lloyd LJ said in *A-G v Newspaper Publishing*:[7]

... the statutory purpose behind the Contempt of Court Act 1981 was to effect a permanent shift in the balance of public interest away from the protection of the administration of justice and in favour of freedom of speech.[8] Such a shift was forced upon the United Kingdom by the decision of the European Court in *Sunday Times v United Kingdom*.

Common law contempt was preserved under the 1981 Act, but only in a narrow form. The approach adopted under the Act was largely protective rather than preventive. There have been judicial attempts post-1981 to delineate the roles of contempt law and of trial judges more clearly,[9] the latter taking the primary preventive role, by using neutralizing measures. Under the HRA some modification of the current statutory and common law tests may eventually occur, as discussed below, and further clarification of the two roles may occur since domestic judges can consider contempt law in relation to both Articles 10 and 6. The nature and structure of domestic decision-making need not fully follow the Strasbourg model since Article 10, and, at times, Article 6, issues can be considered during a contempt action[10] rather than as aspects of an Article 10 claim—the form in which Strasbourg has normally considered them. Article 6, issues may also be raised during a criminal trial or on appeal as part of an argument that the jury or others would be or had been affected by the publication of prejudicial journalistic material.

In the next sections the shifts in the balance struck between fair trials and free speech pre- and post-1981 and then post-HRA will be considered. The current efficacy of contempt law in protecting both fair trials and free speech will be questioned and possible reforms will be put forward.

DOMESTIC DEVELOPMENTS WITHIN THE PROTECTIVE MODEL—THE PRE-1981 COMMON LAW APPROACH

The orthodox view of criminal contempt at common law was that it was intended to protect the administration of justice; it was not intended to play a direct role in protecting the right to a fair trial. Common law contempt was a crime of strict liability consisting of the following elements: creation of a real risk of prejudice within the *sub judice* period (the *actus reus*) and an intention to publish. The starting point of this

---

[7] [1988] Ch 333, at 382.

[8] This passage was cited and approved of by Collins LJ in *A-G v Guardian Newspapers* [1999] EMLR 904.

[9] See pp 264–6, below.

[10] The implication is not that media bodies are themselves bound to adhere to Article 6—fair trial rights cannot be claimed directly against a media body. In so far as the demands of Article 6 appear to be at stake, the court has a duty to adhere to them under s 6.

period occurred when the proceedings were 'imminent.'[11] This test attracted much criticism because of its vagueness and width; it was obviously capable of applying a long time before the trial and it therefore had an inhibiting effect on the media out of proportion to its value. In particular, it gave rise to the restriction caused by so-called 'gagging writs.' For example, a newspaper might be discussing corruption in a company. If a writ for libel was then issued—although there was no intention of proceeding with the case—the newspaper might find itself in contempt if it continued to discuss the issues. Thus, this method could be used to prevent further comment.

The *actus reus* could be fulfilled if it was shown that the publication in question had created a risk that the proceedings in question might be prejudiced; it was irrelevant whether they actually had been. This distinction was clearly illustrated by *Thompson Newspapers Ltd, ex parte A-G*.[12] While the defendant was awaiting trial, the *Sunday Times* published his photograph and commented on his unsavoury background as a brothel keeper. This was held to amount to contempt. He was convicted and then appealed on the ground that the trial had been prejudiced by the article, but his appeal failed on the basis that jurors had not in actuality been so prejudiced. The effect of common law contempt, however, was clearly indirectly preventive: the creation of liability based merely on establishing such a minimal and imprecise *actus reus* clearly had quite a strong deterrent effect. But in terms of preventive impact the area of liability was clearly over-inclusive since it readily caught material which was unlikely in practice to affect the fairness of the proceedings. Thus common law contempt was flawed. Since it was not targeted precisely at protecting the fairness of proceedings, but at protecting the administration of justice, it entailed the creation of a broad area of liability, inevitably curtailing freedom of expression in a manner which was disproportionate to the benefit created. Its very breadth did create a preventive effect, tending to aid in ensuring such fairness, but the lack of precise targeting encroached too far on media freedom.

REFORM—THE CONTEMPT OF COURT ACT 1981

The need for reform which would, in particular, address the over-breadth of the imminence test thus became apparent, and led to the setting up of the Phillimore Committee in 1974,[13] but it might not have come about without the influence of the European Court of Human Rights. The ruling in *Sunday Times v UK*[14] that UK contempt law had breached Article 10 arose from the decision of the House of Lords in *A-G v Times Newspapers Ltd*,[15] discussed in Chapter 4. The Lords found that the

---

[11] *Savundranayagan and Walker* [1968] 3 All ER 439; [1968] 1 WLR 1761, CA.

[12] [1968] 1 All ER 268; [1968] 1 WLR 1.

[13] See *Report of the Committee on Contempt of Court*, (1974) Cmnd 5794. For comment, see R. Dhavan, 'Contempt of Court and the Phillimore Committee Report' (1976) 5 *Anglo-Am L Rev* 186.

[14] (1979) 2 EHRR 245.   [15] [1974] AC 273; [1973] 3 All ER 54; [1973] 3 WLR 298, HL.

actus reus of common law contempt could be satisfied where a publication was found to have 'prejudged' proceedings. This test was wider than the test of 'real risk of prejudice,' in that where little risk to the proceedings could be shown, it might still be possible to find that they had been prejudged. This test was heavily criticized by the Phillimore Committee; it had a potentially grave effect on freedom of speech because it was very difficult to draw the line between legitimate discussion in the media and prejudgment. Since it was easier to satisfy the prejudgment test than the old test for the *actus reus* of common law contempt, the Phillimore Committee found that the *Sunday Times* ruling strengthened the case for reform.

The prejudgment test can be viewed as based very clearly on the protective rather than the preventive model since any connection between the creation of liability and ensuring the fairness of a trial was even weaker than it was under the 'real risk of prejudice' test. However, since it widened the area of liability even further, it also contributed to the effect of deterrence created by common law contempt. It exacerbated the lack of focus of the common law, and its incoherence. The prejudgement test was not clearly consonant with the imminence test: if the mischief to be avoided was that of the possibility of 'trial by newspaper', why was it significant that a particular proceeding could be viewed as imminent in relation to the publication in question?

However, the problem was that the Strasbourg approach in the *Sunday Times* case also lacked a coherent rationale. The Court merely found, applying the proportionality test under Article 10(2), that the domestic findings in the House of Lords had allowed too great an encroachment on freedom of expression, taking the value of the expression and the dormancy of the litigation into account (speech/harm balancing).[16] But its use of this proportionality test was based implicitly on a preventive approach, although it did not advert expressly to the rationale underlying that approach, appearing to accept that that was not the aim of domestic contempt law. In particular, the dormancy of the litigation was viewed as very significant, although that factor was not significant if the interference with freedom of expression was intended to protect the administration of justice in a general sense, by deterring the media from engaging in 'trial by newspaper'. Thus, the Court used 'protective' language but afforded weight to 'preventive' factors. The Court did not, however, attempt to tease out any inconsistencies in the strands of argument. It made the assumption that contempt law was linked to the protection for a fair trial in particular proceedings, and that assumption was allowed to play a key part in the determinations as to proportionality. No attempt was made in the statute passed in response to the findings, the 1981 Act, to delineate the precise role of contempt law in preventing media encroachment on the fairness of particular trials. The relationship between contempt law and the use of neutralizing measures, such as a stay, was left unclear. Thus, the major failing of the Act lay in its incoherent approach. If it was intended to protect the administration of justice in a general sense, why was it confined to risks created to particular proceedings? If it was intended to prevent such risks, why was it not

---

[16] See Chapter 2 at 101–4 for discussion of this proportionality test.

targeted more precisely at preventing them, by including, in particular, specific provision, going beyond that of s 4(2), for the use of orders and injunctions against the media? The assumption was made, despite the impliedly preventive approach adopted at Strasbourg, that the traditional domestic protective approach would be reflected in the new statute, although preventive aspects would also be present.

Thus, in an incremental fashion, typical in UK legal development, the new statute merely took each common law test for the actus reus of contempt and afforded it a somewhat more precise meaning.[17] The Contempt of Court Act 1981 (CCA) was designed to modify the common law without bringing about radical change. It introduced various liberalizing factors, but it was intended to maintain the stance of the ultimate supremacy of the administration of justice over freedom of speech, while moving the balance further towards freedom of speech.[18] It maintained the 'strict liability rule,' under s 1, but introduced stricter time limits—the 'active' tests[19]—and a somewhat more precise test regarding the necessary risk of prejudice under s 2(2). It did introduce one innovation—a somewhat opaquely worded 'public interest' test designed to allow some material on matters of public interest to escape liability even though it created a risk of prejudice to proceedings. This test, arising under s 5, was a key part of the response to the findings on proportionality at Strasbourg since it gives some weight to the *value* of the speech. Its aptness in that respect will be indicated below.

Under s 1, conduct is contempt if it interferes with the administration of justice in particular proceedings,[20] regardless of intent to do so. Thus, not all publications that

---

[17] See *Report of the Committee on Contempt of Court*, (1974) Cmnd 5794; Green Paper, (1978) Cmnd 7145.

[18] For comment on the 1981 Act see: C.J. Miller, 'The Contempt of Court Act 1981' [1982] *Crim LR* 71; N.V. Lowe, 'Contempt of Court Act 1981' [1982] *PL* 20; J.C. Smith [1982] *Crim LR* 744; G. Zellich, 'Fair Trial and Free Press' [1982] *PL* 343; M. Redmond, 'Of black sheep and too much wool' [1983] 42 *CLJ* 9.

[19] Under s 2(3) proceedings must be 'active.' For criminal proceedings, the active period begins at the point (Schedule 1, paragraph 4 (a–e)) of: the issue of a warrant for arrest, an arrest without warrant or the service of an indictment (or summons or an oral charge); the ending point is acquittal, sentence, any other verdict or discontinuance of the trial. The starting point for civil proceedings occurs when the case is set down for a hearing in the High Court or a date for the hearing is fixed (Schedule 1, paragraphs 12 and 13). In *A-G v Hislop and Pressdram*: [1991] 1 QB 514; [1991] 1 All ER 911; [1991] 2 WLR 219, CA. It was found that s 2(3) was fulfilled because the proceedings in question (an action for defamation) had come into the 'warned' list at the time the articles in question were published. This starting point prevents the use of 'gagging' writs. The end point of the active period for civil proceedings comes when the proceedings are disposed of, discontinued or withdrawn. The precision of these provisions, which allows the media to determine with reasonable certainty the point at which a risk of liability arises, means that they can be viewed as meeting the demands of Article 10. Surprisingly, appellate proceedings are also covered by Schedule 1. The starting point occurs when leave to appeal is applied for, by notice of appeal or application for review or other originating process; the end point occurs when the proceedings are disposed of or abandoned. Section 9 of the Criminal Appeal Act 1995 provides that a reference by the Criminal Cases Review Commission to the Court of Appeal is to be treated as an appeal under the Criminal Appeal Act 1968 for all purposes, and therefore, appellate proceedings become active when such a reference is made.

[20] The proceedings must be 'court' proceedings. This test includes certain tribunals in the contempt jurisdiction. Section 19 provides that 'court' includes 'any tribunal or body exercising the judicial power of the State'. See further, Borrie and Lowe, *The Law of Contempt*, 3rd edn., London: Butterworths, 1996, pp 485–91. The phrase 'the judicial power of the state', employed in s 19 in defining a court, reflected the language of the House of Lords in *A-G v BBC* [1981] AC 303 which held that a local valuation court was not a court in law or of law, as it was fulfilling an administrative function rather than a judicial function. In *General Medical*

deal with issues touching on the administration of justice fall within the 1981 Act. The starting point under s 1 is to ask whether the publication touches upon particular legal proceedings. In other words, if the publication appears to have a long term effect on the course of justice generally, without affecting any particular proceedings, it falls outside the Act. In contrast, under s 6(c) the common law is preserved, if the *mens rea* of intention to prejudice is shown, in relation to interferences in the administration of justice;[21] particular proceedings are not mentioned. Sections 1 and 6(c) read together are indicative of the Act's failures of focus.

Despite the emphasis on particular proceedings, it was clearly not the intention of the 1981 Act to introduce a change of approach towards an overtly preventive one. This is made clear in s 2(2), one of the most problematic sections of the Act. Under s 2(2) the publication must create 'a substantial risk of serious prejudice or impediment to the course of justice in the proceedings in question.'[22] This test, like its predecessor under the common law, is an objective one; it is unconcerned with the question whether prejudice has actually been caused. So under the 1981 Act the uneasy and uncertain relationship between the role of trial judges using neutralizing measures and the role of the law of contempt was continued.

THE ROLE OF THE ATTORNEY GENERAL [23]

The Attorney General has the responsibility under s 7 of the Contempt of Court Act 1981 for initiating statutory or common law prosecutions for contempt against media bodies.[24] Theoretically, superior courts[25] can punish contempts on their own motion. This inherent power is preserved under s 7. In practice, the courts do not exercise this power in respect of publications subject to the strict liability rule. A party to

---

Council v BBC [1988] 1 WLR 1573 it was held that the Professional Conduct Committee of the GMC does not constitute a 'court' since, whilst the committee exercised a function which was clearly judicial in nature, and did so in the public interest with a statutory sanction, it was not exercising the judicial power of the state. It could not therefore be regarded as a court for the purposes of the Act. This concept of 'a court' appears to be narrower than that denoted by the term 'tribunal' and therefore within the field of application of Article 6(1), as delineated by the relevant Strasbourg jurisprudence. In order to qualify as a 'tribunal' a body must have a 'judicial function', not merely an administrative one: see *Belilos v Switzerland* A 132 para 64 (1988). But no qualification relating to the 'judicial power of the state' has been introduced.

[21] See pp 284–96 below.

[22] The test of 'impeding' proceedings is treated in a somewhat more specific fashion. It may be satisfied where the publication can be said to have created a likelihood that the proceedings will be delayed owing to the risk of prejudice: see *A-G v BBC, The Independent*, 3 January 1992.

[23] For discussion, see the National Heritage Committee Second Report (1997) *Press Activity Affecting Court Cases*, pp 36–8.

[24] Section 7 provides: '[p]roceedings for a contempt of court under the strict liability rule shall not be instituted except by or with the consent of the Attorney-General or on the motion of a court having jurisdiction to deal with it.'

[25] In England and Wales, the House of Lords, the Court of Appeal, the High Court of Justice, the Crown Court, the Restrictive Practices Court, the Employment Appeals Tribunal, the Courts-Martial Appeal Court.

proceedings in a superior court could put, through counsel, the argument that a publication is prejudicial. The judge could then refer the matter to the Attorney-General. This would not necessarily mean, however, that proceedings would be brought.[26] Thus, in terms of the division of responsibility, the current approach has the hallmarks of a protective one since a separation between the role of contempt law and the role of judges in protecting the fairness of proceedings is maintained in practice. The Attorney-General is now bound by s 6 of the HRA and therefore has a duty to ensure that both Articles 10 and 6 are satisfied.[27] But the *content* of his duty under Article 6 is inherently limited in this context due to the protective model on which contempt law is partly based, since the responsibility for meeting Article 6 demands lies ultimately with the trial judge. Contempt law does not directly provide a remedy where a publication creates a risk of prejudicing a trial.

However, adherence to the protective model is tempered by elements of a preventive approach. As discussed in the last chapter, the Attorney-General can obtain orders restricting reporting under s 4(2) of the 1981 Act. He can also seek an injunction in reliance on the strict liability rule to restrain a planned publication[28] on the ground that it risks causing prejudice to a forthcoming trial,[29] although such injunctions are very infrequently sought or granted. He may also issue warnings to the media regarding coverage of cases which have attracted public attention.[30] This suggests that Attorney Generals do perceive a role for contempt law in ensuring a fair trial by preventing prejudice, despite its generally protective stance and the fact that neutralizing measures are available.

The duty of the Attorney General under s 6 in relation to Article 6 could be viewed as requiring *further* steps to be taken in developing the preventive role of contempt law, which would probably involve obtaining injunctions against publication pre-trial more often. Greater use of express threats of prosecutions for contempt, where Article 6 rights might otherwise be violated in particular proceedings, might have a deterrent effect. A further step would be to specify the material that cannot be published pre-trial. But if the preventive role of contempt law were to be developed in that way, legislative change would be required.[31] This matter is returned to below.

---

[26] See *R v Taylor and Taylor* (1993) 98 Cr App R 361 (discussed below, p 263).

[27] He may be challengeable under s 7(1)(a) HRA if his actions or inactions breach a Convention right. However, he has been viewed as non-judicially reviewable: see on this issue, note 50 below.

[28] See *A-G v Times Newspapers* [1974] AC 273; *A-G v Steadman*, Feb 1994 (unreported) (preventing a play about Robert Maxwell on the ground that it would prejudice the trial of his sons).

[29] It was made clear by the Court of Appeal in *A-G v News Group Newspapers* [1987] 1 QB 1 that an injunction could be granted to prevent prejudice, although, on other grounds, one was not granted in that instance. An injunction was granted under common law contempt in *A-G v Times Newspapers Ltd* [1974] AC 273.

[30] For example, he issued such warnings in respect of the 'Yorkshire Ripper' case, in the case of Frederick and Rosemary West, in respect of the press coverage of the murders at Soham in summer 2002, again at the time of the trial for the murders of Ian Huntley in December 2003 and in relation to the arrests of alleged terrorists in connection with the discovery of traces of the Ricin toxin in January 2003.

[31] For a number of reasons (including the fact that the HRA cannot create criminal or (probably) quasi-criminal liability—s 7(8) HRA) that are outside the scope of this chapter, the change could not occur solely in reliance on the HRA.

Assigning an enhanced role to contempt law in reliance on the Attorney-General as the initiating agency would, however, be problematic since questions may be raised about the *current* reliance, under s 7 of the 1981 Act, on his role since he is a member of the Cabinet. The 1981 Act potentially brings the Attorney-General, who is closely associated with the government, into direct conflict with newspaper proprietors. Theoretically, he or she should use contempt law to safeguard the administration of justice. In practice, so doing may require him to intervene to protect the fair trial rights of an ordinary citizen who has become involved in a high profile criminal trial, attracting immense press interest. A conflict of interests may well arise when, at the same time, the Prime Minister and his political advisers are seeking to maintain friendly relations with particular newspaper proprietors. A dramatic instance of such a conflict, which was resolved to the detriment of the citizens' fair trial rights—in the sense that the media bodies responsible for prejudicing the trial went unpunished—appeared to occur in *R v Taylor*,[32] which is discussed below.[33]

When government Ministers themselves collude with the press in implying that arrestees or defendants are guilty, the Attorney-General is faced with an even clearer conflict of interests. This may occur in relation to the arrest and trial of suspected terrorists since government policy is at stake. A telling instance of this occurred in *R v McCann*.[34] Three Irish persons were arrested and charged with conspiracy to murder Tom King, the Northern Ireland Secretary. At trial they exercised their right to silence. On the day when counsel for one of the defendants was giving the closing speech, the Home Secretary announced that the government intended to change the right to silence. Tom King gave interviews on the matter, stating that the right allowed terrorist suspects to be acquitted. The defendants were convicted and appealed, partly on the basis that the remarks had prejudiced the trial since Tom King had said in strong terms that a failure of a defendant to answer questions in terrorist cases was tantamount to guilt. The defendants' contention was accepted and the convictions were quashed. No contempt proceedings were brought. In 2003 when seven men were arrested in North London on suspicion of terrorist-related activity linked to the toxin ricin, Tony Blair said that the arrests showed: 'this danger is present and real and with us now and its potential is huge.'[35] The *Express* commented on the arrests: 'Britain's not just embracing terrorists, but housing them at the taxpayer's expense.' The *Sun* declared: 'the poison factory used to make deadly ricin is just 200 yards from the lair of one of Osama bin Laden's henchmen. Police racing against time to smash the terror network fear MORE fanatics may be plotting in the area.'[36] In a manner

---

[32] [1993] 98 Cr App R 361.   [33] See p 263.   [34] (1990) 92 Cr App Rep 239.

[35] See 'There's no chance of a fair trial when Government, press and police get together to damn these "terrorists" ', Nick Cohen, *The Observer*, 12 January 2003.

[36] Ibid. No contempt proceedings were brought in respect of the coverage of the ricin incident, but a s 4(2) order was eventually obtained restricting coverage of the trial. See 'True ricin story could not be told', *Media Lawyer Newsletter* 2005, 57, 14–15. The article reviews the reporting restrictions imposed under the Contempt of Court Act 1981 s 4 up to and during the trial of Kamel Bourgass and others for conspiracy to carry out the chemical attack using ricin. It considers the extent to which the reporting restrictions impeded the media discussion of the Government's anti-terrorist policy.

reminiscent of the instance that arose in *Ribemont v France*,[37] these was a sense that the presumption of innocence was undermined: the implication of Blair's words and of the newspaper coverage was that the arrestees were involved in terrorism and were therefore guilty of the crimes that they were arrested for.

A similar but even more telling example arose in relation to the forthcoming trial of those arrested in respect of the attempted terrorist bombings in London in July 2005. The Home Office Minister, Charles Clarke, was accused of coming very close to prejudicing the trial,[38] while, commenting on the arrests, the *Sun* newspaper's head-line declared: 'Got the Bastards!'.[39] In other words, the persons arrested were guilty of the attempted bombings. Direct assertions of guilt are, in the words of Borrie and Lowe, 'the most serious contempts'.[40] It may be suggested that the *Sun's* words, which were published during the active or *sub judice* period,[41] were tantamount to making such an assertion. As Simon Brown LJ has pointed out:

To publish as fact the guilt of a named person after his arrest and before his trial is not a step to be taken lightly. The risk is, moreover, heightened the more vulnerable the accused, the more high-profile the case, and the less accurate the reporting . . . All those, therefore, in the business of crime reporting should recognise that articles such as these are published at their peril.[42]

The incidents discussed could be viewed as aspects of an unholy alliance subsisting between the government and the press in relation to terrorism. Generally speaking, the government appears to be content for the press to raise the emotional ante—to exacerbate the fear and insecurity caused by the terrorist incidents themselves—thus giving it greater licence to introduce draconian anti-terrorist measures. The press, and the Murdoch press in particular,[43] are influential in setting the political agenda regard-ing the criminal justice system. If that agenda can be said to have changed—even more than the terrorist incidents in themselves might warrant—the government may feel reassured in taking the view that criticism of its policies from others, including

---

[37] (1995) 20 EHRR 557. See Chapter 4 at 190–1.

[38] See e.g. *The Guardian*, 7 October 2005; it reported that the Home Office had published a police 'dossier' detailing their case for detaining suspects without charge for up to three months. The document included details and background of three terrorist cases, including the 21 July attempted London bombings, using them as examples to help to make the case for three month detention without trial. Shami Chakrabarti, the director of *Liberty*, was quoted as stating that she believed that the dossier was 'dangerously close to contempt'.

[39] Part of the *Sun's* coverage of the arrests on 27 and 28 July 2005.

[40] Borrie and Lowe, p 143. It may be noted, however, that since a period of time is likely to elapse before the trial the *Sun's* coverage might not satisfy the test of causing a substantial risk of serious prejudice (s 2(2) 1981 Act, discussed below, pp 257–72).

[41] The proceedings—the trial of the suspects was 'active' since the arrests had occurred (Contempt of Court Act 1981 Sched 1 para 4(a)). See above for active periods under the 1981 Act, Sched 1, p 251, note 19.

[42] *A-G v Unger* (1998) EMLR 280 at 319.

[43] It may be noted that the Murdoch press in the UK (*The Times, Sunday Times, Sun, News of the World*), unlike Sky Broadcasting also owned by Murdoch, is not bound by due impartiality rules in its coverage; see for discussion of the rules, Chapter 20 at 995–1012.

judges, may be muted.[44] In this climate it may be argued that the nature of the Attorney General's position is structurally inadequate to guarantee his independence—since he is a member of the Cabinet he can be dismissed by the Prime Minister. During the period of the Blair government his independence has been called into question.[45] The possibility that the lack of high profile post-HRA contempt cases is attributable to the government's close relationship with parts of the media and the institutional role of the Attorney General cannot be entirely ruled out.

The position of the Attorney General in relation to initiating contempt actions may arguably also be viewed as problematic in Article 6 terms.[46] The Attorney-General does not fulfill the criteria of being an 'independent and impartial tribunal' in Article 6(1) terms; therefore one would not think of him/her as being capable of determining civil rights and responsibilities and/or a criminal charge. However, since he is capable of preventing a prosecution from reaching court in the first place, then in effect his office could be taken to be determinative of certain civil rights and obligations in the sense of actually preventing the court from deciding the issue. So there would probably be an access to justice point that could be raised under Article 6 as well as one relating to bias. This point would be perhaps most pertinent where the dispute did not originate as a matter between private individuals (eg newspaper and plaintiff in a civil action), where the Attorney General could intervene by way of a contempt action to protect the administration of justice, but where it originated in relation to state policy or secrecy and intervention would be to protect that administration, on behalf—in effect—of the state. As in the example of Tom King—if it was possible to

---

[44] See e.g. the comments of Lord Hoffman (dissenting on this point) in *A v Secretary of State* [2005] 2 AC 68; [2005] 2 WLR 87 to the effect that in 2004 no terrorist-created emergency existed and that therefore draconian measures could not be justified. The Prime Minister, Tony Blair, gave a number of broadcast interviews shortly after 7 July 2005, and the later attempted bombings, that implied that in the current political climate Lord Hoffman would not make the same remarks.

[45] This was most notoriously the case in respect of his advice in relation to the Iraq war.

[46] In *McGonnell v United Kingdom* (2000) 30 EHRR 289, it was argued that the position of the Lord Chancellor is unsatisfactory in Article 6 terms; the Court said: 'any direct involvement in the passage of legislation, or of executive rules, is likely to be sufficient to cast doubt on the judicial impartiality of a person subsequently called to determine a dispute over whether reasons exist to permit a variation from the wording of the legislation or rules at issue' (at para 55). These remarks could not be applied directly to the Attorney-General's role in relation to contempt actions. However, it could be argued that an appearance of bias is present since the government is not an entirely disinterested party and the Attorney General is a member of the government. This is most obviously the case when the prejudice is partly or wholly created by the words of an individual Cabinet Minister, as in the Tom King instance. The question of Article 6 compliance might depend on whether a strict approach is taken to the separation of powers doctrine. See further *Kleyn v Netherlands* (2004) 38 EHRR 14; *Pabla KY v Finland*, judgment of 22 June 2004 (available at www.echr.coe.int). See further R. Masterman, 'Determinative in the Abstract?: Article 6(1) and the Separation of Powers', forthcoming *EHRLR* 2005; R. Masterman, 'A Supreme Court for the United Kingdom: Two steps forward, but one step back on judicial independence' [2004] *PL* 48. As indicated in the text the Attorney General has a pivotal role not only in relation to contempt actions, but also in relation to actions for injunctions on grounds of breach of confidence in relation to state secrecy (see Chapter 19 at 948–53); this is also the case in respect of actions on the basis of race and (potentially) religious hatred (see Chapter 9 at 508–27). Thus his role is under pressure—in terms of the need to demonstrate impartiality and independence—in relation to a number of areas of media law.

overcome the 'determinative of civil rights' issue, then the matter of bias should be relatively easy to prove since the Attorney General is a member of the executive.[47]

The question of bias seems to arise most obviously when common law contempt actions are used—in effect—to enforce injunctions against the whole of the media that have been obtained against one media organ on the ground of state secrecy.[48] In such an instance the Attorney General would have obtained the initial injunction on behalf of the state and would also take the decision to institute contempt proceedings against any media body that publishes material covered by the injunction. This has occurred so far in respect of common law contempt, as discussed below,[49] but it could also occur under the strict liability rule if proceedings were active, since the publication by the third party media body could impede the proceedings for the permanent injunction against the first party body. Thus in a range of respects, even if a breach of Article 6 could not be found, the Attorney General's pivotal position in relation to contempt proceedings is in principle problematic.

Therefore any future reforms should take into account the possibility of affording the role of initiating the use of prior or subsequent restraints based on contempt law to a non-governmental body.[50] This would become an even more pressing matter if, under such reforms, contempt law were to take on a more preventive role and the Attorney General obtained an enhanced role in ensuring fairness in the justice system, since any bias might be more starkly revealed. However, clearly, there are obvious reasons to find that the political will to undertake such reforms may be absent.

THE INTERPRETATION AND APPLICATION OF THE 1981 ACT: CREATING A SUBSTANTIAL RISK OF SERIOUS PREJUDICE TO PROCEEDINGS UNDER SECTION 2(2)

Section 2(2) provides: 'the strict liability rule applies only to a publication which creates a substantial risk that the course of justice in the proceedings in question will be seriously impeded or prejudiced'. Section 2(2) on its face answers to the findings on proportionality in *Sunday Times v UK*[51] since in that instance in balancing the value of the speech against the harm it had been found to cause under Article 10(2), it

---

[47] See further *Ringeisen v Austria* No 1 (1971) 1 EHRR 455; No 2 (1972) 1 EHRR 504; No 3 (1972) 1 EHRR 513. Discussion is aided by the work of R. Masterman (2005) ibid, on the separation of powers.

[48] See for discussion pp 289–302 below.   [49] See for discussion pp 284–96 below.

[50] In order to obviate uncertainty any reforms should make it clear that such a body would be judicially-reviewable. The Attorney General's actions or inactions in relation to initiating contempt proceedings were found in a pre-HRA decision to be non-reviewable: see *R v Solicitor-General ex p Taylor and Taylor* [1996] 1 FCR 206. Since the Attorney General is a public authority under the HRA, this would not be the case now under s 7(1)(a) HRA.

[51] (1979) 2 EHRR 245. See for discussion Chapter 4 at 183–5.

was found that the harm caused was quite slight. Section 2(2), in demanding a *substantial* risk of *serious* prejudice presupposes that the harm caused could not be characterized as slight or minimal.

SECTION 2(2) AND APPEALS

The strict liability rule covers civil actions and other proceedings, despite a recommendation of the Phillimore Committee that most appellate proceedings should not be covered.[52] The Committee's recommendation was in accord with the aims of the administration of justice and of media freedom since the ends of justice are unlikely to be served by seeking to stifle media comment that refers specifically to appeals—the openness of the discussion supports confidence in the quality of justice which is unafraid of comment. The misinformed or biased nature of aspects of such discussion would not be expected to affect the judiciary, especially the senior judiciary. Therefore no fear of arbitrariness due to prejudice should arise. As Lord Reid said in *A-G v Times*:[53] '[i]t is scarcely possible to imagine a case when comment could influence judges in the Court of Appeal or noble and learned Lords in this House.'

Nevertheless, Channel 4 was enjoined from broadcasting a re-enactment, in the form of a dramatic 'reconstruction,' of the appeal of the Birmingham Six, until after the decision on the appeal had been taken.[54] This was a doubtful decision, since it was highly unlikely that the judges would have been influenced by the programme. The injunction was therefore obtained on the basis that the public's view of the judgment of the court might have been affected by it. This justification is flawed, since it does not appear to be covered by s 2(2); it could not have been shown that a substantial risk of prejudice to the proceedings—the appeal—would arise. Section 2(2) does not refer to a substantial risk of prejudice to the course of justice in a general sense. Moreover, the public's view of that judgment and of the Appeal Court generally would be more greatly influenced, it is suggested, by the impression given that a ban was necessary in order to prevent the programme from influencing the judges. This is one instance in which the HRA may have an influence. In *Re Lonhro plc and Observer Ltd*,[55] the House of Lords relied on Article 10 in finding that since the possibility that a professional judge would be influenced by media coverage of a case is extremely remote, it would be extremely hard to establish a 'pressing social need', as required by Article 10(2), to suppress the speech in question. This stance is likely to be reinforced by the inception of the HRA since s 2(2) CCA must be interpreted in accordance with Article 10(2), under s 3(1) HRA. Since the Attorney General, as a public authority under s 6HRA is bound by Article 10, it is also suggested that he should be very slow to initiate contempt actions in relation to appeal-related speech.

---

[52] *Report of the Committee on Contempt of Court*, (1974) Cmnd 5794, at para 132.
[53] *A-G v Times Newspapers* [1974] AC 273.
[54] *In re Channel 4 Television Co Ltd, The Times*, 2 February 1988; [1988] Crim LR 237.
[55] [1989] 2 All ER 1100, HL.

FACTORS TAKEN INTO ACCOUNT UNDER SECTION 2(2)

Section 2(2) is by far the most significant aspect of the strict liability rule since, assuming that proceedings are 'active', it determines whether the actus reus of statutory contempt is satisfied. The bulk of the argument will therefore centre on its application in a particular instance. It was made clear in *A-G v MGN*[56] that the 'substantial risk of serious prejudice' test had to be judged by reference to the context at the time of publication. The Court of Appeal found in *A-G v News Group Newspapers*[57] that both limbs of the test under s 2(2) must be satisfied: showing a slight risk of serious prejudice or a substantial risk of slight prejudice would not be sufficient. However, this finding did not give guidance as to the meaning to be accorded to the terms 'substantial' or 'serious.' The discussion below reveals that the key factor in determining the *substantial risk* of serious prejudice is that of proximity in time between publication and proceedings, although audience/circulation figures are also relevant. Perhaps the most problematic matter is the ascription of responsibility for prejudice to a particular publication/broadcast where there has been a great deal of media coverage. But uncertainty is also created due to differing judicial views as to the robustness and integrity of jurors and the effect on them of neutralizing measures, such as, in particular, directions to disregard media coverage. The discussion below reveals that determining whether a 'substantial risk' has arisen is far more problematic than making a finding as to 'serious prejudice'.

(i) Circulation

The circulation of a publication/viewing figures for a broadcast is a relevant factor in relation to the 'substantial risk' limb of the s 2(2) test.[58] This factor potentially has a greater impact on broadcasters than on newspapers, since the viewing figures for popular programmes tend to far exceed the circulation figures of individual newspapers: One broadcast will in general reach far more people than will one article. However, not many prosecutions have been brought against broadcasters, probably because they tend to take a more responsible stance than the press due to the strict regulatory regime to which they are subject, discussed in Chapter 20.[59] An exception arose in *A-G v BBC, A-G v Hat Trick Productions Ltd.*[60] During a programme on BBC2 in the irreverent, satirical series *Have I Got News for You*, remarks were made by

---

[56] [1997] 1 All ER 456.   [57] [1987] 1 QB 1; [1986] 2 All ER 833; [1986] 3 WLR 365, CA.

[58] If a publication has a small circulation, this risk might be seen as too remote. This point was considered in *A-G v Hislop and Pressdram* [1991] 1 QB 514; [1991] 1 All ER 911; [1991] 2 WLR 219, CA, which concerned the effect of an article in *Private Eye* written about Sonia Sutcliffe, wife of the Yorkshire Ripper. She began an action for defamation in respect of the article. Shortly before the hearing of the action, *Private Eye* published two further articles defamatory of Mrs Sutcliffe. The Attorney General brought proceedings for contempt of court in respect of the second articles, and on appeal it was determined that as *Private Eye* had a large readership, many of whom might live in London, where the libel action was held, it could not be said that the risk of prejudice was insubstantial.

[59] At pp 995–1012.

[60] [1997] EMLR 76; *The Times*, 26 July 1996. See also *A-G v LWT* 3 All ER 116; *A-G v Jones and BBC* (1995) (unreported).

celebrities which assumed that the Maxwell brothers were guilty of defrauding the *Daily Mirror* pensioners. The broadcast occurred six months before the trial of the Maxwells, but was viewed by an audience of several millions. An action for contempt was brought and it was found that despite the humorous context, the remarks assuming the guilt of the defendants might have been taken seriously by viewers and that therefore s 2(2) was satisfied.

Clearly, circulation figures cannot be calculated only on the basis of viewing or selling figures. The impact of newspapers depends on their readership, not just their circulation figures. Further, front-page, banner headlines may reach many more people in a range of contexts. The existence of the Internet clearly increases the circulation figures of both newspapers and broadcasts. All newspapers and some broadcasts have their own website on which material is archived. Internet users could access trial-related material on such web-sites, either by putting a key word into Google (or another search engine), or by choosing to search the website of a particular media organ in the expectation that some reporting would cover such material.[61]

(ii) Temporal proximity

The reliance on temporal proximity between publication and proceedings in relation to the 'substantial risk' limb of s 2(2) arguably favours the particular operational methods of the tabloid press. As Chapters 17 and 20 point out, the press are not restrained, as are broadcasters, by quite a strict statutory regime governing privacy and accuracy. The result is that tabloid newspapers are able to rely on sensationalist and frequently misleading reporting as a marketing tool. Such reporting is very unlikely to attract liability under the strict liability rule so long as it occurs some months or even weeks before the proceedings in question. It is very clear from decisions over the last ten years that the time at which coverage is most at risk is getting closer and closer to the time at which the proceedings occur. Prosecutions would probably no longer be brought where a time-lag of the order of ten months between publication and proceedings had occurred. By 2006 it became possible to say that imputations of guilt in the active period probably would not incur liability unless they occurred contemporaneously with the trial.

In 1987 the ruling in *A-G v News Group Newspapers*[62] made it clear that the proximity of the article to the trial is highly relevant to the question of risk. The Court of Appeal held that a gap of ten months between the two could not create the substantial risk in question because the jury would be likely to have forgotten the article by the time the trial came on, and even if it were faintly recollected at the time of the trial, it would be likely to have little impact. Similarly, in *A-G v Independent TV News and Others*[63] one of the factors founding the ruling that s 2(2) was not satisfied was the lapse of time before the trial; the risk that any juror who had seen the offending item

---

[61] See further, C. Walker, 'Fundamental Rights, Fair Trials and the New Audio-Visual Sector' 1996, 59 *MLR* 517.

[62] [1987] QB 1.   [63] [1995] 2 All ER 370.

would remember it was not seen as substantial. ITV News and certain newspapers had published the fact that a defendant in a forthcoming murder trial was a convicted IRA terrorist who had escaped from jail where he was serving a life sentence for murder. However, the trial was not expected to take place for nine months, there had only been one offending news item, and there had been limited circulation of only one edition of the offending newspaper items. In contrast, in *A-G v Hislop and Pressdram*,[64] a gap of three months between publication of the article and the trial of the libel action was not viewed as long enough to negate the risk. A publication during the trial is clearly most likely to create a risk.

In the late 1990s judges began to show a readiness to assume that somewhat smaller time lapses would still diminish the risk in question to the point where it could be viewed as negligible or minimal. In *A-G v MGN*[65] the article in question, discussed further below, was published about three and a half months before the trial in a tabloid with a large circulation. It was found that its impact should be looked at at the time of publication, and at the time of the trial—its residual impact on jurors should be taken into account. Over that period of time its impact would have faded; taking that 'fade factor' into account, it was determined that a substantial risk of prejudice did not arise. A similar stance was taken in *A-G v Unger*.[66] The respondent newspapers, the *Daily Mail* and *Manchester Evening News*, published newspaper articles, relating how the defendant, who was a home help, had been caught red-handed on video stealing money from a pensioner in her care. In other words, they imputed guilt. Simon Brown LJ found that articles of this nature which plainly prejudged guilt could influence jurors. But when he considered the 'crucial' matter of the residual impact of the publication on a notional juror at the time of trial, he attached great significance to the 'fade' factor, the effect of the lapse of time, between publication and trial. Here the time lapse was of the order of nine months. He considered that this would greatly affect the recollections of the article by any juror who had happened to read it. He noted that this factor had been stressed in a number of the cases.[67] He considered that publications are most dangerously prejudicial when they are published contemporaneously with the trial, because then jurors read them with 'particular interest rather than merely as part of an everyday media diet', or when they disclose prejudicial material which is itself inadmissible in evidence, most obviously an accused's previous convictions. Neither of those two factors were present. But in *A-G v Newsgroup Newspapers*,[68] the *Sun* published a serious allegation regarding a defendant in a murder trial at the point at which the jury had retired to consider its verdict. The murder charge was dropped, and the *Sun* was prosecuted, convicted and fined for contempt.

The existence of the Internet is highly relevant to temporal proximity. Trial-related material is often placed on a newspaper's website prior to or early in the active

---

[64] [1991] 1 QB 514; [1991] 1 All ER 911; [1991] 2 WLR 219, CA.   [65] [1997] 1 All ER 456.

[66] *A-G v Unger* (1998) EMLR 280 at 319.

[67] *A-G v NGN* [1987] QB 1; *ex parte Telegraph plc* [1993] 1 WLR 980; *A-G v Independent TV News* [1995] 1 Cr App R 204.

[68] 16 April 1999 (unreported).

period—at the time when the reporting occurs of a high profile investigation or of an arrest. However, that material is likely to remain on the website, whereas the newspaper itself will be discarded by its readers very rapidly, often on the day that it is obtained. Thus the material may still be on the website and accessible as the trial date approaches. Jurors might decide deliberately to search newspapers' websites with a view to discovering more about the trial and, perhaps, the background of defendants. Where publicity is potentially prejudicial, but is subject to a significant fade-factor, newspapers could ensure that such material is removed from the website's archives. However, if they fail to do so they clearly place themselves at risk of a prosecution for contempt, even though there has been a significant time lapse between initial publication and trial. This factor, and the accessibility of the web-based material, should be taken into account when assessing the risk created by press material that has been published some time before the trial. It may be noted that where the Internet Service Provider maintaining a website on which trial-related material is stored is not a domestic newspaper or broadcaster, but is a body outside the jurisdiction, it would not be possible to bring a prosecution even if highly prejudicial material was up-loaded to an easily accessible website and maintained on it before and during the trial. It might be argued that the chance of a juror accessing the website could be viewed as remote, but the rapidly increasing use of the Internet is undermining that argument.[69]

(iii) Totality of the news coverage

Obtaining a conviction under the s 2(2) test as currently interpreted is especially difficult or impossible where a substantial risk of serious prejudice or impediment is created by the totality of the news coverage, rather than by the coverage of a particular article or broadcast. *A-G v MGN*[70] concerned the coverage of a case involving the notorious boyfriend of a soap opera actress, Gillian Taylforth, by five tabloid newspapers, which mentioned his previous criminal record and presented a misleading picture of the incident in question. It was found that none of the articles, considered separately, reached the required threshold under s 2(2). The judge, Schiemann LJ, said that where, in such an instance, the totality of the coverage had prejudiced the trial, it might be proper to stay the proceedings. This decision reveals a weakness in the use of the strict liability rule, since it means that the creation of serious prejudice to a trial by a large number of newspaper articles in combination cannot be addressed by means of contempt law where individual articles just fail to satisfy the strict test of s 2(2) as interpreted in *A-G v Guardian Newspapers*.[71] As discussed below, that decision significantly raised the s 2(2) bar. The use of a stay means that the coverage has had the effect of impeding the course of justice in the proceedings in question, but that the detriment thereby created cannot be laid at the doors of those responsible.

---

[69] See Chapter 12 at 641, note 88.   [70] [1997] 1 All ER 456.
[71] [1999] EMLR 904. See pp 264–5 below.

It is argued that the courts need to distinguish more clearly between 'threshold,' 'generic' and prejudicial publicity.[72] 'Generic' publicity can be taken to indicate coverage that is not in itself prejudicial since it does not relate specifically enough to the trial. But it may have a general and all-pervasive effect in terms of painting 'the defendant with an incriminating brush.'[73] 'Threshold' publicity is merely coverage relating to someone involved in proceedings, making his or her name memorable. The existence of threshold or generic publicity tends to mean that prejudicial publicity has more impact.[74] Therefore such publicity is more, not less, likely to satisfy the s 2(2) test. On the other hand, where a number of newspapers publish material that does relate specifically to a case and which, combined, satisfies s 2(2), it may be difficult to show that any particular publication, alone, satisfies the test.

Some of the prosecutions discussed above, and in particular that in *A-G v BBC, A-G v Hat Trick Productions Ltd*,[75] may be contrasted with the lack of action taken in respect of the facts of *R v Taylor*.[76] A large number of tabloid newspapers published a photograph which was taken of one of the defendants in a murder trial giving the husband of the victim a polite kiss on the cheek; it was distorted in such a way as to give the impression that it was a passionate mouth to mouth kiss and was captioned 'Cheats Kiss.' It was found that this was part of an 'unremitting, extensive, sensational, inaccurate and misleading press coverage' and had led to a real risk of prejudice to the trial. This determination was made on appeal in overturning the convictions of the two defendants. The Attorney-General refused to bring an action against the newspapers for contempt, possibly because he considered that no individual publication would attract liability, and it was found that his decision not to act was non-reviewable.[77] The failure to act did not therefore have to be justified, but the uncertain nature of the s 2(2) test as applied to individual newspapers could be viewed as providing a degree of justification for it. On the other hand, the possibility cannot be ruled out, as argued above, that government reluctance to take on a large number of press proprietors played a part in the decision.

(iv) Reliance on the use of neutralizing directions; ensuring harmony between contempt law and tests for appeals/stays

In a number of the cases discussed below judges have stressed the ability of jurors to

---

[72] See e.g. J.C. Doppelt, 'Generic Prejudice: How Drug War Fervor Threatens the Right to a Fair Trial' (1991) 40 *American University Law Review* 821.

[73] See M. Chesterman, J. Chan, and S. Hampton, *Managing Prejudicial Publicity* (2001), Justice Research Centre, Law and Justice Foundation of New South Wales, p 9.

[74] Ibid, pp 111, 121, 122, 235.   [75] [1997] EMLR 76.   [76] (1993) 98 Cr App R 361, CA.

[77] *R v S-G, ex parte Taylor*, *The Times*, 14 August 1995. For comment on the case, see M. Stephens and P. Hill, 'The Role and Impact of Journalism' in C. Walker and K. Starmer (eds) *Miscarriages of Justice: A Review of Justice in Error*, Blackstone Press, 1997, 263, pp 264–7. For comment and the implications of the case within the European Convention on Human Rights, see Borrie and Lowe, *The Law of Contempt*, 3rd edn., London: Butterworths, 1996, pp 481–2. An action could arguably now be brought against the Attorney General under s 7(1)(a) HRA on the basis that a public authority had failed to seek to protect the Article 6 rights of the appellants (see note 50 above).

disregard media comment, especially when properly directed to do so. In taking the use of such 'neutralizing' directions into account, they have also stressed the need for contempt law to use the same standards as those that would determine the need for a stay or the success of an appeal. The courts have, increasingly, emphasized the unlikelihood that jurors will be unaffected by prejudicial media comment. The probability that the lesser neutralizing measure of warning the jury to disregard media coverage will be employed is increasingly taken into account when a court is considering the risk of prejudice, although two schools of thought can be discerned among the judiciary on this matter—broadly speaking, those of juror susceptibility and juror invulnerability.[78]

It was pointed out in *A-G v Times Newspapers*[79] that jurors are able to ignore possibly prejudicial comment in newspapers. That case concerned a relatively trivial incident which happened to attract publicity because of the fame of one of the persons involved, a factor which jurors might be expected to appreciate, leading them to discount the press coverage. Recently, it has become more common for consideration to be afforded to the likelihood that the jury will be strongly directed to ignore prejudicial coverage of the trial.[80] In *A-G v BBC*,[81] however, Staughton LJ said that he did not have the confidence expressed by certain judges in 'the ability of jurors to disregard matters which they do remember but which they are not entitled to take into account.'

In contrast, in *A-G v Unger*[82] Simon Brown LJ found that the 'fade factor' should be coupled with the presumption that juries would decide cases solely according to the evidence put before them and the directions they were given. He considered that in the case before him, if the accused woman had elected jury trial and had been convicted, she could not have won an appeal on the basis of the published articles. A similar stance was taken in *A-G v Guardian Newspapers*.[83] The case concerned the trial of one Kelly for stealing body parts, apparently for artistic purposes; during the trial The *Observer* published an article suggesting in strong terms that Kelly had had no artistic purpose in stealing the parts, but was motivated merely by a morbid fascination with dead people. The writer linked Kelly's fascination to that experienced by a number of named serial killers. Since Kelly's honesty was a key issue in the trial, the article was very damaging to his case since in the jury's eyes it could have undermined his credibility. Both Collins LJ and Sedley LJ concluded that the article therefore created a risk of serious prejudice.

Sedley LJ wrestled with the question whether the risk should be described as substantial:

In the end, and not without anxiety, I have concluded that it is simply not possible to be sure that the risk created by the publication was a substantial risk that a jury, properly directed to

---

[78] See the National Heritage Committee Second Report (1997) *Press Activity Affecting Court Cases*, pp 33–4.

[79] *The Times*, 12 February 1983.   [80] See e.g. *A-G v MGN* [1997] EMLR 284.

[81] 1 December 1995 (unreported).   [82] (1998) EMLR 280, at 319.   [83] [1999] EMLR 904.

disregard its own sentiments and any media comment, would nevertheless have its own thoughts or value judgments reinforced by the article to a point where they influenced the verdict. As a first cross-check, I doubt whether an appeal would have been allowed had the jury which convicted Mr Kelly read the article. As a second cross-check, it seems to me that the threat from this article, published when it was, to the course of justice in Mr Kelly's trial was not sufficient to make either prior restraint or subsequent punishment a proportionate response in a society which, as a democracy, values and protects the freedom of the press.

In other words, some degree of serious prejudice had been caused, but it was accepted that the degree of risk was likely to be diminished by the use of such directions. Collins LJ also took into account the effect of judicial directions on the jury in terms of neutralizing any prejudice created by the publication, although he differed from Sedley LJ in finding that once it could be assumed that 'serious prejudice' had arisen it would be difficult to be sure that it had been dispelled by the use of neutralizing directions. However, Collins LJ felt that the issue was so finely balanced that he would not dissent from Sedley LJ's conclusion on this point. It was therefore found that the test of 'serious prejudice,' but not that of 'substantial risk,' was satisfied.

Sedley LJ's approach, which appears to be the dominant one, shifts the emphasis impliedly from the protective to the neutralizing stance since it makes the assumption that directions to the jury will be effective and can therefore properly undermine the need for protective measures. That approach also shifts the responsibility for the effect of prejudicial material from the media to judges and jurors. Arguably, that shift of responsibility is not fully in accordance with the Article 10 notion that the 'duties and responsibilities' it mentions in paragraph 1 are placed upon those exercising the right to freedom of expression it protects, that is, the media. As pointed out in Chapter 2, Strasbourg has employed the term, in general, to limit media freedom rather than to enhance it.[84] Any reliance on it in the sense suggested here could also be a development in the *domestic* Article 10 jurisprudence.[85]

There has been uncertainty as to the relationship between s 2(2) and the tests used to make good an appeal against conviction or to found a stay. Simon Brown LJ found in *A-G v Birmingham Post and Mail*:[86] 's 2(2) postulates a lesser degree of prejudice than is required to make good an appeal against conviction. Similarly, it seems to me to postulate a lesser degree of prejudice than would justify an order for a stay'. He went on to conclude that where s 2(2) was satisfied, it would not follow that a conviction was imperilled or that a stay was required, but that the converse was not the case:

I find it difficult to envisage a publication which has concerned the judge sufficiently to discharge the jury and yet is not properly to be regarded as a contempt . . . In short, s.2(2) is

[84] See Chapter 21 at 1074.
[85] A notion of protection only for responsible journalism is already occurring, as discussed in Chapter 21 at 1074–5, 1081, partly in reliance on the wording of Article 10(1).
[86] [1999] 1 WLR 361, at 369H; [1998] 4 All ER 49, at 57, 59. See further *Mcleod, The Times*, 20 December 2000.

designed to avoid (and where necessary punish) publications even if they merely risk prejudicing proceedings, whereas a stay will generally only be granted where it is recognised that any subsequent conviction would otherwise be imperilled, and a conviction will only be set aside . . . if it is actually unsafe.

However, Sedley LJ and Collins LJ in *A-G v Guardian Newspapers*[87] considered that the tests for contempt and for the risk of actual prejudice to a trial should be harmonized. Collins LJ said:

It seems to me that the prejudice required by s.2(2), which must be serious, is not of a lesser degree than that required to make good an appeal against conviction. To establish contempt it needs only be shown that there was a substantial risk that serious prejudice, which must in my view mean such prejudice as would justify a stay or appeal against conviction, would result from the publication. That such prejudice does not in the event result is nothing to the point. Thus uniformity of approach is achieved by requiring that the prejudice within the meaning of s.2(2) must be such as would be likely to justify at least a stay.

These words were echoed in *A-G v Unger*[88] by Simon Brown LJ in something of a departure from his previous stance:

It seems to me important in these cases that the Courts do not speak with two voices, one used to dismiss criminal appeals with the Court roundly rejecting any suggestion that prejudice resulted from media publications, the other holding comparable publications to be in contempt, the Courts on these occasions expressing grave doubts as to the jury's ability to forget or put aside what they have heard or read . . . generally speaking it seems to me that unless a publication materially affects the course of trial in that kind of way, or requires directions from the court well beyond those ordinarily required and routinely given to juries to focus their attention on evidence called before them rather than whatever they may have heard or read outside court, or creates at the very least a seriously arguable ground for an appeal on the basis of prejudice, it is unlikely to be vulnerable to contempt proceedings under the strict liability rule.

Thus a growing perception among the judiciary can be discerned of a need to bring contempt law into line with criminal appeals, so that in Simon Brown LJ's words, the courts do not 'speak with two voices'. This stance, it is argued, encourages newspapers to publish prejudicial material in the hope that the risk it poses to proceedings is not substantial enough. The problem with this approach is that it detracts from the role of contempt law in protecting particular proceedings. It seems to assume that unless the resulting effect might approach one that had to be dealt with by a stay or an appeal, s 2(2) would not be satisfied. This stance undermines the role that s 2(2) seemed to be intended to have—that of setting the threshold before that stage would be likely to be reached, thus protecting the criminal justice system. The fact that the judges are taking this stance is not surprising, given that the division of responsibility between contempt law and trial judge has always been problematic. But arguably it poses an unacceptable level of risk to the system.

---

[87] [1999] EMLR 904.   [88] (1998) EMLR 280, at 319.

(v) Summing-up

On the face of it, the factor of proximity in time cannot be considered in isolation from other relevant ones: the celebrity status of defendants/plaintiffs; the subject matter of the publication; the language used. These three factors may make it more likely that a publication will be remembered even over a fairly substantial period of time. However, temporal proximity, combined with the effect of neutralizing directions, is by far the most important factor. We now seem to have arrived at the point when it is almost possible to say that the active period runs *de facto* only from the start of the trial—from the point at which the jurors are empanelled, since from that point they are likely to take especial interest in articles relating to that particular trial. From that point judges view publications or broadcasts as no longer part of an ephemeral media diet (they have not yet, it seems, taken account of the fact that the use of the Internet means that it is much less ephemeral than it used to be), but as of especial significance. In other words, even where other factors founding a 'substantial risk' are quite clearly present, unless material is disclosed that would be inadmissible in evidence, prejudicial publication/broadcasts, even very close to the trial, but not during it, may not reach the s 2(2) threshold.

This reliance on proximity means that where a high-profile crime, such as the Soham murders in 2002 or the attempted terrorist bombings in London in July 2005,[89] occurs, the tabloids can report on the arrestees in lurid terms, as they did in both instances, in the knowledge that although the proceedings are 'active,' there is likely to be quite a significant time lapse before the trial, and that therefore the risk of prejudice will probably be viewed as diminished to the point where it cannot be regarded as 'substantial'. Therefore newspapers that are—in contrast to broadcasters—already unrestrained in such reporting by a statutory regulatory scheme enjoining accuracy and impartiality on them, are likely to be equally unrestrained by the strict liability rule. In the instance of Soham the Attorney General did issue warnings to the tabloids reminding them of the rule, but no action was taken. Clearly, if the aim of s 2(2) is to protect the fairness of particular trials, it is inevitable that the proximity in time of a publication will be taken into account. But there may be instances, such as that of Soham, or of the terrorist incidents in 2003 and 2005, where the coverage is so extreme and so unremitting at the time of an arrest, that a fair trial, even months later, is likely to be prejudiced. The more recent rulings on temporal proximity suggest that the judges would not accept that s 2(2) was satisfied in such circumstances, especially when the findings from *A-G v MGN* regarding totality of coverage were also taken into account, since it would be difficult to ascribe responsibility for the creation of prejudice to any one newspaper. Once a substantial period of time had elapsed, it would be likely that a potential juror would merely remember an impression, rather than the specifics of the coverage of any one

---

[89] See Chapter 4, at 173 note 34.

newspaper. But that impression—that the arrestees were guilty—might be deep-rooted and insidious.[90]

THE THRESHOLD CREATED BY THE SECTION 2(2) TEST

The decisions on s 2(2) have not fully clarified its meaning, but it may be concluded quite firmly that the threshold to be reached under the test can now be viewed in 2006 as quite a high one *in practice*. Therefore newspapers may risk publishing material concerning high profile trials that they would not have published twenty-five years ago when the 1981 Act was introduced. A steady, if unacknowledged, raising of the bar denoted by the term 'substantial risk' can be discerned from the case law, which can largely be attributed to the influence of Article 10 of the European Convention, even before the HRA had come into force. It will be questioned below whether this raising of the bar is really in accord with Article 10 values, as some of the judges appear to assume.

Two years after the 1981 Act was introduced the bar was placed at a low level. In *A-G v English*[91] Lord Diplock interpreted 'substantial risk' as excluding a 'risk which is only remote,'[92] a finding which still strongly influences the *formal* approach to s 2(2).[93] The finding that only remote risks would be excluded allowed the House of Lords to find that the reference in an article to the mercy-killing of handicapped babies might prejudice the jury in the trial of a consultant charged with the murder of a Down's syndrome baby. The article, published in the *Daily Mail* after the trial had begun, made no direct reference to him, but was written in support of a ProLife candidate, Mrs Carr, who was standing in a by-election. Mrs Carr had no arms; the article referred to this fact and continued: 'today the chances of such a baby surviving are very small—someone would surely recommend letting her die of starvation. Are babies who are not up to scratch to be destroyed before or after birth?'. The Lords considered that jurors would be likely to take the comments to refer to the trial; therefore, the assertion that babies were often allowed to die if handicapped might influence them against the consultant. The timing of the article predisposed the court

---

[90] There would be the possibility of bringing an action for common law contempt in respect of such coverage, but editors would be able to show that due to the lapse of time they did not foresee the creation of a real risk of prejudice as a virtual certainty (oblique intent). So far, it is only in cases in which a newspaper has a personal interest that a desire to prejudice proceedings (simple intent) has been shown: see discussion below pp 284–8.

[91] [1983] 1 AC 116; [1982] 2 All ER 903.

[92] *A-G v English* [1983] 1 AC 116; [1982] 2 All ER 903; for comment, see G. Zellick, 'Fair trial and free press' [1982] *PL* 343 (especially on the question of the degree of risk); A. Ward, 'A Substantial Change in the Law of Contempt?' (1983) 46 *MLR* 85; M. Redmond, 'Of Black Sheep and too much Wool' [1983] 42 *CLJ* 9. It may be noted that aspects of *A-G v English* were the subject of an unsuccessful application to Strasbourg: *Times Newspapers Ltd and others v UK* (1983) 8 EHRR 45, p 54. Bearing in mind the comments in Chapter 2 as to the effect of the Commission on the Convention jurisprudence, especially in its older decisions, it is suggested that this finding of inadmissibility would be unlikely to be repeated today and that the decision is somewhat out of line with the generality of the jurisprudence relating to pre-trial publicity and the reporting of issues relating to litigation.

[93] See G. Zellick, ibid, on this point, p 344.

to find that s 2(2) was satisfied. Nevertheless, on any view the risk was quite low but could be viewed as more than remote. (Incidentally, the consultant was acquitted; therefore, the article presumably did not in fact influence the jurors against him.) The finding that only remote risks are excluded appears to lessen the impact of the term 'substantial', and it is hard to see that there is a difference between this test and the old common law 'real risk' one.

In *MGN Pension Trustees Ltd*[94] it was found that the term meant 'not insubstantial' or 'not minimal' rather than weighty. In *A-G v Independent TV News and Others*,[95] the same view was taken—the risk of prejudice was found to be too small to be termed substantial, although arguably it could have been viewed as more than minimal. The term 'substantial' has been afforded *de facto* a greater weight in the instances discussed below,[96] effectively excluding fairly low but non-remote risks. *A-G v Guardian Newspapers*,[97] *A-G v Unger*[98] and *A-G v MGN*[99] marked the turning point in the approach. These cases were all decided around the time of the inception of the HRA but before it had come into force. The imminent reception of Article 10 into domestic law affected the judicial approach.

In *A-G v MGN*[100] an article creating the inference that a defendant in forthcoming proceedings was guilty was not found in itself to create a sufficiently substantial risk of serious prejudice, despite the fact that that article in combination with others had led the trial judge to stay the proceedings. A straightforward imputation of guilt was made in *A-G v Unger*, but the time lapse led to the conclusion that the risk was not substantial enough. In *A-G v Guardian Newspapers* Sedley LJ in the Court of Appeal considered that he was placing a strong reliance on the Article 10(2) tests as interpreted in *Worm v Austria*[101] in finding that although a risk of serious prejudice arose, it was not certain that it could be viewed as a substantial one.

The previous rulings clearly do not give as much weight to the term 'substantial' as Sedley LJ did. The facts of *Guardian Newspapers*, discussed above, were in some respects far more compelling than those of *English* as far as s 2(2) was concerned. The *Observer* article at issue in *Guardian Newspapers* was centrally about the trial, whereas the comments in the *Daily Mail* article in *English* were only obliquely or inferentially linked to it; they were ambiguous and did not necessarily impute guilt. Both the articles at issue were published contemporaneously with the trial. Yet s 2(2) was found to be satisfied in *English*, whereas in *Guardian Newspapers* the opposing result was reached, indicating the incremental, stealthy raising of the bar that has occurred. The imminent inception of the Human Rights Act, encouraging the judiciary to afford a strong weight to the relevant Article 10 jurisprudence, appears to explain the difference. In *Worm*, which was relied on in *Guardian Newspapers*, the test

---

[94] [1995] EMLR 99. [95] [1995] 2 All ER 370.
[96] See in particular Lord Lane's comments in *A-G v Times Newspapers Ltd, The Times*, 12 February 1983.
[97] [1999] EMLR 904.
[98] *A-G v Unger* (1998) EMLR 280 at 319. The decision is discussed above at 266.
[99] [1997] 1 All ER 456. The decision is discussed above at 261. [100] [1997] 1 All ER 456.
[101] (1998) 25 EHRR 454. See Chapter 4 at 185–7 for full discussion.

used was that of 'likelihood' of risk; as discussed below, this appears to mean that the risk is more likely than not to materialize. This test denotes a higher threshold than does Lord Diplock's test in *English* of excluding only remote risks.

The only case to succeed under the strict liability rule in the late 1990s was *Attorney-General v BBC and Hat Trick Productions Ltd*[102] where the words in question were spoken by celebrities during a popular television programme. Auld L.J. said of them:

The offending words are strikingly prejudicial and go to the heart of the case which the jury are to try, and . . . the offending publicity is great both because of its medium and repetition, and because both the speakers and the victims are already much in the public eye.

Taking account of the case law as a whole, it seems fair to conclude that although the courts continue in most instances to pay lip-service to Lord Diplock's dictum in *A-G v English*, they are not prepared to find that s 2(2) is satisfied on the basis of risks just above the 'minimal' threshold. And, clearly, a strict approach to s 2(2) seemed to be likely to prevail after the Human Rights Act came into force, on the basis that the judiciary in general were likely to accept that the *Guardian Newspapers* approach to the Strasbourg jurisprudence, and especially to *Worm v Austria*, was the correct one.

Following Simon Brown LJ's approach in *Unger* and Sedley LJ's in *Guardian Newspapers*, it seems to be clear that the s 2(2) bar is being raised. Clearly, this is a media-friendly approach. Whether it is protective of free speech values is more open to doubt. Collins LJ said, 'in applying s 2(2) due weight must be given to the protection of freedom of speech.' This assumes a complete convergence between the claims of the media and those of free speech, although it is questionable whether speech that undermines the presumption of innocence has a strong claim to protection, bearing in mind underlying free speech rationales.[103] This approach may also be under-protective of trials since it confuses the role of protective measures with that of neutralizing ones. If the administration of justice is not protected from prejudicial comment on the ground that the courts should not 'speak with two voices' then the criminal justice system is potentially placed under strain. It may be exposed to preju-dicial comment and have to take measures, such as stays, which may themselves cause impairment to trials,[104] in order to protect itself. If the less responsible sections of the media[105] perceive that they can cause prejudice just short of that sufficient to create a demand for a stay, then they will do so, and in pushing at that boundary they may over-step it. In particular they may do so where, amidst a mass of sensationalist, partial reporting, it is very difficult to ascribe responsibility to individual newspapers.

USE OF SECTION 2(2) IN THE POST-HRA ERA

There have only been three post-HRA prosecutions so far and all were in the more clear-cut cases. In two of them liability was not contested. In *A-G v BBC*[106] the BBC

---

[102] [1997] EMLR 76; *The Times*, 26 July 1996.   [103] See Chapter 1 at 12–19.
[104] See Chapter 4 at 177.   [105] Generally, the tabloids in the lower and middle sectors of the market.
[106] [2001] EWHC Admin 1202.

mistakenly released details about a complainant witness during a trial relating to charges of sexual abuse in an approved school, breaching his anonymity. The police had undertaken not to allow such details to be released and his anonymity was protected by s 1(1) of the Sexual Offences (Amendment) Act 1992. The witness was very distressed since his family had not known that he had—as he alleged—suffered sexual abuse. The BBC accepted that the publication of the details had satisfied the tests under s 2(2) and therefore the only question was as to the penalty to be imposed. It was accepted that the publication of the details had resulted from negligence and that the journalist responsible had had an exemplary record in relation to such matters. The penalty—a fine—was not excessive; it was imposed both on the BBC and on the journalist involved. The HRA was not mentioned during the case, although Article 10 would have been relevant to the heaviness of the fine[107] and to the decision to impose a separate penalty on the journalist.

A-G v MGN[108] concerned a somewhat similar instance in that liability was not disputed and the articles in question were apparently published in error. The articles, in the *Sunday Mirror*, concerned the trial of certain Premiership footballers for affray and causing grievous bodily harm with intent. The article revived allegations that the attack was racially motivated. The article was published at the time when the jury was considering its verdicts and, as the publishers recognized, its thrust was at variance with the evidence as presented in the criminal trial. The publishers recognized that the judge had given a clear direction that there was no evidence of a racial motive. The second article concerned a co-accused, Duberry. He had been acquitted, but his credibility and his evidence were still relevant in relation to the guilt or innocence of the four remaining defendants, in respect of whom verdicts had not been returned. Liability was not disputed but the court gave some consideration to the s 2(2) tests, finding that they were satisfied due to the timing of the article and the probability that the jurors might have been influenced for or against the four defendants. The trial had been abandoned as a result of the article and a re-trial ordered. It was found that: ' "substantial" in that context connotes a risk which is more than remote and not merely minimal . . . and it has to be accepted that within the range of strict liability contempts, this case is towards the top end.' This indicates that in terms of wording a test akin to that of Lord Diplock in *A-G v English* is still influencing judges, particularly at first instance. Again the HRA was not mentioned and the fine imposed was high but not excessive.

A somewhat similar instance arose in *A-G v Express.*[109] The *Daily Star* published an article relating to the alleged gang rape of a 17-year old girl at a London hotel by up to eight footballers on September 27, 2003. Between September 30, 2003 and October 22, 2003 the Attorney General and the Metropolitan Police had repeatedly issued advice and guidelines stating that identification was in issue and that suspects should not be identified by name or photograph or other likeness. There was a great deal of

---

[107] See *Tolstoy Miloslavsky v UK* (1995) 20 EHRR 442.   [108] [2002] EWHC 907.
[109] [2005] EMLR 13.

media interest, but the article in the *Daily Star* was unique in that it identified the two potential defendants. The Attorney General contended that it was sufficient to establish a substantial risk that the course of justice would be prejudiced to show that there was a risk that the complainant did not know the identity of the footballers revealed in the *Daily Star*. It was found that at the point when the Daily Star published the article the complainant had not identified to the police either of the two footballers by name or by effective description. The court found that the inference could be drawn therefore that the complainant did not know the identities of the accused at the time of the publication. Accordingly, the publication to millions in the *Daily Star* of items identifying the two individuals created a substantial risk that the course of justice would be seriously impeded or prejudiced. The HRA played no part in the judgment.

Given the nature of these three post-HRA cases, no careful scrutiny of the s 2(2) tests in the light of the HRA was necessary, although it might have been expected that Article 10 would not have been entirely disregarded. The cases were clear-cut: either specific details relating to identity were released, or the prejudicial material was published during the trial. The question of creating bias in the minds of the jury or undermining the presumption of innocence pre-trial has not been addressed post-HRA.

RESEARCH ON THE EFFECT OF COURT-RELATED PUBLICITY

At this point it is worth considering research into the effect of court-related publicity with a view to placing the tests under s 2(2) in that context. Section 2(2) was introduced in 1981, over twenty years ago. It was based, with some modification, on a common law test originating well over 100 years earlier. Since that time the media have changed profoundly. There is now widespread access to the internet, to satellite and cable broadcasting and to 24-hour news channels. The cult of the celebrity also provides a strong motivation for the less responsible sections of the press to publish sensational details of celebrity trials, as has been seen recently—in 2003 and 2004—in relation to charges of assault and of rape brought against a number of Premiership footballers.[110] The fear of Al-Qaida-related terrorist activity post-9/11 and 7/7 has increased the emotional pressure to undermine or depart from fair trial values, and in 2005 tempted a number of UK tabloids to risk prejudice to the fair trial of terrorist suspects.[111] Therefore the question arises—is s 2(2) still a workable tool to use to seek to hold back court-based publicity and to guard against prejudice, when there appear to be a number of forces working in the opposite direction?[112] Answering this question first requires consideration of the most recent research into the effect of pre-trial publicity in the current media climate.

There is currently a substantial body of empirical literature on the effects of

---

[110] See note 109. The rape charges were dropped.   [111] See note 155 below.
[112] See C. Walker, 'Fundamental Rights, Fair Trials and the New Audio-Visual Sector' [1996] 59 *MLR* 517, p 521.

publicity in creating prejudice.[113] UK research into the experiences of actual jurors in the jury room is impossible due to the provision of s 8 of the 1981 Act. Section 8(1), discussed fully in Chapter 5,[114] provides that it is a contempt: 'to obtain, disclose, or solicit any particulars of statements made, opinions expressed, arguments advanced or votes cast by members of a jury in the course of their deliberations in any legal proceedings.' The section does not prevent interviewing of jurors which does not touch upon their deliberations in the jury room, but such inquiries should only be undertaken with the leave of the trial court or after verdict and sentence, by the Court of Appeal.[115]

Thus, s 8 makes it very difficult or impossible to conduct in Britain the kind of research that has been conducted in a number of other jurisdictions.[116] There has, however, been some academic writing that attempts speculatively to apply the lessons from empirical research to actual high profile trials in the UK.[117] Such writing points to the power and impact in general of news reporting since it is presented in simple language, making events intelligible to people of limited education.[118] There is a 'particular salience of pre-trial publicity constituted in a vivid story form,'[119] and when such publicity is presented in emotive terms and creates a compelling narrative, it is argued that jurors have difficulty in disregarding it when weighing up evidence.

A particularly important piece of research was completed five years ago in New Zealand.[120] It relied on the experience of jurors in 48 completed criminal trials, many of them high-profile cases. 19 per cent of the jurors recalled seeing some pre-trial publicity. The main conclusion of the report was that in only one case was there some evidence that pre-trial publicity might have influenced the deliberations of the jury. 34 per cent of jurors recalled encountering publicity *during* the trial but considered that it had had no influence on them. Jurors consciously made an effort to put aside the effects of any publicity, and the researchers said that it was impossible to know

---

[113] See e.g. N.L. Kerr, 'The effects of pretrial publicity on jurors' *Judicature* 78, 120; G.P. Kramer and N.L. Kerr, 'Laboratory simulation and bias in the study of juror behaviour: a methodological note' (1989) *Law and Human Behaviour* 89; G. Moran and B.L. Cutler, 'The prejudicial impact of pretrial publicity' (1991) 21 *Journal of Applied Social Psychology* 345.

[114] See pp 228–43.

[115] *McCluskey* (1993) 94 Cr App R 216, CA. See also *Mickleborough* [1995] 1 Cr App R 297, CA.

[116] See e.g. McConville and Baldwin, 'The Effect of the 1981 Act on Research on Juries' (1981) 145 *JPN* 575; Borrie and Lowe, *The Law of Contempt*, 3rd edn., London: Butterworths, 1996, pp 366–74. Canada has an equivalent of s 8 in s 649 of the Criminal Code. See also note 120 below.

[117] See T.M. Honess, 'Empirical and Legal Perspectives on the Impact of Pre-Trial Publicity' [2002] *Crim LR* 719 (discussing *R v Bowyer (Lee)* (2001) (unreported)); B. Naylor, 'Fair trial or free press: Legal Responses to Media Reports of Criminal Trials' [1994] *CLJ* 492 (discussing the publicity that led to the quashing of the conviction in the *R v Taylor* case (*The Times*, 15 June 1993)). Aspects of both cases are discussed in this chapter (p 263) and the previous one (p 215).

[118] See Naylor, ibid, p 495.

[119] See T.M. Honess, 'Empirical and Legal Perspectives on the Impact of Pre-Trial Publicity' [2002] *Crim LR* 719, p 719.

[120] W. Young, N. Cameron and Y. Tinsley, *Law Juries in Criminal Trials, Part Two: A Summary of the Research Findings*, Law Commission of New Zealand Prelim Paper 37, Vol 2, 1999.

whether this was due to directions from the judge or because they thought that to take such publicity into account would be unfair.

More recent research from New South Wales came to similar conclusions.[121] It may be noted that New South Wales has legislation similar to s 8 of the 1981 Act in place, but it is possible for responsible academic research to be carried out.[122] Until this study was carried out, little empirical research was carried out in Australia, and in some quarters there was clearly a belief that there is no real conflict between fair trials and free speech: the Australian Law Reform Commission has made the bold assertion that there is no such conflict since 'no person involved in a trial . . . is ever actually influenced by publications relating to the trial.'[123] It may be noted that in New South Wales, as in Britain, there are constraints on reporting during the *sub judice* period, and neutralizing measures, such as changing the venue of the trial, are also used; therefore jurors are not likely to be exposed to intense levels of prejudicial publicity. In 8 per cent of the trials (3 out of 40) the researchers thought it likely that the verdict was publicity-driven rather than based on the evidence.[124] In only one of these did the judge and counsel consider the verdict to have been 'unsafe.' A number of matters relevant to the strict liability rule, or to its reform, emerged. A single article, clearly prejudicial, appearing some months before the trial was unlikely to be recalled. Material posted on websites gave rise to special problems since jurors, once empanelled, could decide to seek to obtain access to prejudicial material.[125] The material might have been stored on the site for some time and might well include references to previous convictions. Judicial instructions to jurors to ignore publicity did not appear to be very effective, but judicial directions to concentrate only on the evidence appeared to give jurors the confidence to ignore publicity and form independent judgements based on the evidence.[126]

The researchers explained the general resistance of the jurors to publicity on the basis that they were likely to be able to identify and ignore biased or incomplete coverage; they also found that a significant proportion of jurors conscientiously

---

[121] M. Chesterman, J. Chan and S. Hampton, *Managing Prejudicial Publicity* (2001) Justice Research Centre Law and Justice Foundation of New South Wales.

[122] The relevant Act is the Jury Act 1977. Section 68B deals with disclosure of information by jurors and reads: '(1) A juror shall not, except with the consent or at the request of the judge or coroner, wilfully disclose during the trial or inquest information on the deliberations of the jury to any person. (2) A person (including a juror or former juror) shall not, for a fee, gain or reward, disclose or offer to disclose to any person information on the deliberations of a jury. (3) The deliberations of a jury include statements made, opinions expressed, arguments advanced or votes cast by members of the jury in the course of their deliberations.' The provision which deals with enabling academic research is s 68A (soliciting information from or harassing former jurors). Section 68A(1) makes it an offence to attempt to gain information on deliberations from a juror/former juror. Section 68A(3) reads: 'Subsection (1) does not prohibit a person from soliciting information from a juror or former juror in accordance with an authority granted by the Attorney-General for the conduct of a research project into matters relating to juries or jury service.'

[123] Australian Law Reform Commission, *Contempt*, Report No 35 (1987), at para 246.

[124] Ibid, p 230.

[125] It may be noted in this context that all UK newspapers are now available online.

[126] Ibid, pp 241–2.

scrutinized the evidence and thereby 'managed' the publicity. However, jurors resisted publicity less well where it included an inadmissible and seriously prejudicial item of information such as a prior conviction of the accused for a similar offence.[127]

Research from the US came to a rather different conclusion:[128] it suggested that exposure to negative publicity tended to produce a higher proportion of guilty verdicts. However, '[Consideration of the research must take into account] the virtually unconstrained freedom of the American media to publish overtly prejudicial material right up to the time of the trial. The fact that there are "no holds barred" affects the real-life studies, and an assumption to this effect underlies the experimental studies.'[129] Although neutralizing measures were used, they did not appear to be successful in preventing prejudice probably because, unless the jurors were sequestered, publicity was highly likely to have some impact on them. As indicated, however, publicity in the US is much less constrained than in Britain or other Commonwealth jurisdictions; it tends to be far more highly prejudicial and relentless; specific prejudicial facts may be published. This may explain the difference in the findings.

But the research from the US is of value—it indicates that if s 2(2) was repealed or replaced by much more media-friendly rules—in the sense that far more court-related material could be published—prejudice to trials might occur much more frequently. The body of research in general suggests that far more importance should be attached to the release of specific prejudicial facts than to generalized criticisms of the defendant. The effect of general implications of guilt appears to be more uncertain. The research does not therefore support full abandonment of the partly preventive approach of the strict liability rule, but it does suggest that s 2(2) is needlessly broad and imprecise, creating too much uncertainty in relation to contempt actions. Too much leeway is created for idiosyncratic judicial notions of juror susceptibility—or invulnerability. The current research thus supports the contention of this chapter that the current protective approach is not targeted precisely enough at the real problem. Certain reforms are suggested below intended to take account of the research findings in creating a more precisely targeted scheme.

POTENTIAL IMPACT OF THE HRA

So far the argument has sought to demonstrate that the strict liability rule, based on the protective approach, sets a high threshold, is unworkably imprecise and is therefore ineffective in operation. As a result, in relation to high profile cases, it allows too much strain to be placed on the criminal justice system (and on individual defendants, witnesses and victims) which has to seek to combat the effects of prejudicial

---

[127] Ibid, p 236, at para 510.

[128] See e.g. M. Chesterman, 'OJ and the Dingo: How Media Publicity for Criminal Jury Trials is Dealt With in Australia and America' (1997) 45 *Am Jo Comp Law* 109; C.A. Studebaker and S.D. Penrod, 'Pre-trial publicity: the media, the Law and common sense' (1997) 3 *Psychology, Public Policy and Law* 428.

[129] M. Chesterman, J. Chan and S. Hampton, *Managing Prejudicial Publicity* (2001) Justice Research Centre Law and Justice Foundation of New South Wales, p 22.

publicity by taking neutralizing measures. It has been suggested that the adoption of such measures can create, in itself, unfairness in the system.[130] But at the same time, since the s1 rule is *capable* of going beyond what is necessary to protect fair trials, freedom of expression can be unnecessarily curtailed. (And the very uncertainty of the rule can of course have a chilling effect.) This is especially apparent in relation to those decisions on proceedings, including civil actions, which are heard by a judge or judges, not by a jury or other lay person.

It is arguable that the inefficacy of s 2(2) considered here—in terms of protecting fair trials—might be addressed to an extent by adopting a change of interpretation under s 3(1) HRA. The s 2(2) test, on its face, differs from that accepted at Strasbourg as in harmony with the Convention standards indicated in *Worm v Austria*,[131] *News Verlags*[132] and *BBC Scotland v UK*.[133] As indicated in Chapter 4, Strasbourg sets the limits of permissible comment at the point at which the material creates a *likelihood* of prejudice to the chances of a person receiving a fair trial.[134] This is, on its face, a test that is in one respect close to the old common law one in that it requires only that prejudice, as opposed to serious prejudice, should be caused. In this respect it is less strict than the terms used in s 2(2). However, the requirement of 'likelihood' appears to denote a stricter requirement in terms of risk than the term 'substantial' in s 2(2). 'Likely' appears to mean 'more likely than not',[135] whereas substantial may be taken to mean 'not insubstantial' or not negligible. According to Lord Diplock, the term is cognate with the terms 'more than minimal' or not remote. The domestic courts, following the interpretation adopted by Lord Diplock in *A-G v English*, have, as discussed above, paid lip-service to this interpretation of the term 'substantial'. The test for the degree of risk that could overcome the Article 10 interest from *Worm* therefore could have been viewed, post-HRA, as sounding the death knell for Lord Diplock's interpretation and as imposing a demand for a higher degree of risk under s 2(2). However, the interpretation of s 2(2) adopted in *A-G v Guardian*,[136] influenced by *Worm*, created a much higher threshold for the test, affording full weight to the term 'substantial,' albeit without acknowledgment that a departure from Lord Diplock's interpretation was occurring. It appears that the minimizing interpretation adopted in *A-G v English* does not represent the current test, although the courts have not acknowledged that this is the case. The term 'serious prejudice' has not been afforded a minimizing interpretation. Thus it is clear that there is a difference of emphasis between the domestic and the Strasbourg tests—at least in relation to the need for *serious* prejudice, and probably in relation to the need for a *substantial* risk, on the basis that that term as currently interpreted domestically still denotes on the

---

[130] See D. Corker and M. Levi, 'Pre-trial Publicity and its Treatment in the English Courts' [1996] *Crim LR* 622. See also Chapter 4 at 177.

[131] (1998) 25 EHRR 454.   [132] (2001) 31 EHRR 8.   [133] (1998) 25 EHRR CD179.

[134] *Worm v Austria* (1998) 25 EHRR 454, at para 5.

[135] See *Cream Holdings v Bannerjee* [2005] 1 AC 253; [2004] 3 WLR 918 which in a different context found that the term 'likely to succeed' meant 'more likely than not'. See Chapter 15 at 808.

[136] [1999] EMLR 904.

face of it a lower risk than the term 'likelihood' does. Confusion is created since the courts, as discussed, are not relying *in practice* on establishing only a low level of risk.

A domestic court could ignore the difference between the domestic and the Strasbourg tests on the ground that it is not bound by the Strasbourg jurisprudence under s 2 HRA. Having taken the Strasbourg test from *Worm* into account, it could fail to apply it, reasoning that Strasbourg has to deal with applications as a final port of call, whereas a domestic court can, in this instance, rely on the use of neutralizing measures to deal with the possibility that prejudice has been created. It could find itself entitled therefore to respect the balance Parliament chose to strike between free speech and fair trials in setting the threshold of the test. This would not, however, be a very satisfactory argument since Parliament was seeking to re-balance contempt law in line with the Strasbourg standard.

Alternatively, and more satisfactorily, the domestic courts could rely on the *Worm* test to minimize the term 'serious' and to clarify the meaning of the term 'substantial' with a view to creating greater certainty as to the threshold to be reached under s 2(2). The need to show *serious* prejudice may go too far in protecting speech at the expense of fair trials under Article 6, even taking account of the use of neutralizing measures. At the same time, the high threshold that apparently needs to be reached under the term 'substantial' following *A-G v Guardian* and *A-G v MGN* may also be over-protective of speech, although Lord Diplock's non-remote risks test was under-protective. It is suggested that the test of 'likelihood' from *Worm* should be used under ss 2 and 3 HRA and should be adapted to interpret the term 'substantial' in s 2(2) of the Act. So doing would only involve a minimal departure from Lord Diplock's test since remote risks would still be excluded; it would merely mean that some non-remote risks were also excluded—which has been occurring in practice in any event since the late 1990s.

The result of this change would ultimately be that the strict liability rule could have more impact in curbing prejudicial comment and therefore on the fairness of trials since a greater deterrent effect could be created. The desirability of such a development is considered further below. Clearly, it would exacerbate the likelihood of interfering with freedom of expression unnecessarily since this is inevitable under the protective approach based on a test with a fairly low threshold. It would also be at first glimpse a somewhat ironic development—since the stricter s 2(2) test was adopted as a response to a perception of what was required in order to satisfy Article 10, following the *Sunday Times* case, in which the application of the weaker common law test was criticized. However, it is clear that it would not be an illegitimate development since the test would be based on that from *Worm* which is consistent with *Sunday Times*,[137] and greater protection for speech would be created than was attained under the weaker test created by the Law Lords that was criticized in the *Sunday Times* case.

If the threshold was clarified in this way by interpretation under s 3 HRA, relying on s 2, the courts and the Attorney-General would then have leeway within the broader

---

[137] See Chapter 4 at 185–7.

test to target only those publications which—the research suggests—are genuinely likely to cause prejudice. For example, it would be possible and easier to target individual newspapers even where a number of papers had engaged in prejudicial reporting. Where, amid such reporting, one newspaper had given prominence to a single, highly telling, item of prejudicial information, it would clearly fall within s 2(2), even if it could be assumed that jurors would be told to disregard it. Instead of trying to disentangle the responsibility of individual newspapers from the collective impact of the reporting, the test should be: if one article by itself would have satisfied s 2(2), had there been no other prejudicial publications, liability should be established, taking all the circumstances into account, *including* the effect of generic and threshold reporting in raising the profile of the defendant and in focusing the public mind on the trial. It would be as legitimate to take account of the reporting as a whole in the manner suggested—considering generic reporting but not the cumulative effect of reporting—as it is to take account of the probability that neutralizing measures, in particular, directions from the judges, would minimize the impact of the reporting. All such factors are part of the context within which the potentially prejudicial reporting should be judged. It is arguable that ordinary principles of interpretation could be used to arrive at this result, but the use of s 3(1) and s 2 HRA, bearing the test from *Worm* in mind, would provide a clear under-pinning for this stance, which represents a development from that taken in *A-G v MGN*, discussed above. These arguments have not been considered so far in the meagre post-HRA case-law on s 2(2). So far, under the HRA, no case has arisen in which there has been a full opportunity to consider the tests under s 2(2).

CONCLUSIONS

It has been found that a distinct lack of post-HRA cases is evident, although tabloid coverage of high profile trials still takes the risk of creating prejudice.[138] Some reluctance to bring prosecutions in respect of high profile trials appears to be evident in the post-HRA era, except in very clear-cut cases. This appears to be due to a mixture of factors: the apparently high but uncertain threshold denoted by s 2(2), as interpreted in *A-G v Guardian* by Sedley LJ; the need to show in most instances that the publication was contemporaneous with the trial, coupled with an assumption about the robustness of jurors; the difficulty of ascribing responsibility for prejudice to one particular newspaper, and possibly a general reluctance to antagonize sections of the media by initiating contempt actions. The role of the Attorney General in initiating such actions was considered earlier.[139] Arguably, it is becoming apparent post-HRA that it is institutionally flawed as a means of seeking to ensure the fairness of trials, and that this is especially evident in terrorist cases, where the government's own policies may be viewed as at stake.

The discussion above of the s 2(2) jurisprudence sought to reveal that the

---

[138] See above pp 267–8.   [139] See above pp 252–7.

interpretation of the sub-section is in a state of near-chaos. On the one hand Lord Diplock's interpretation in *English* to the effect that only minimal risks are excluded continues to influence the case law since it is the only House of Lords' decision. On the other, the courts in the late 1990s, taking the inception of the HRA into account, appeared to become uneasy with his test due to its impact on media freedom. So they continued to raise the bar without fully acknowledging that they were doing so, due to adherence to precedent. Therefore adoption of the *Worm* 'likelier than not' test would at least create greater certainty. It would probably *lower* the bar *in practice*, while raising it in formal terms since a clear departure from Lord Diplock's test would occur.

If a test more consistent with that from *Worm* was to be adopted in future under s 2(2), media freedom would be curbed in practice, although it would continue to receive some protection under the 'freedom of expression' provision of s 5 of the 1981 Act, and it is possible that reinterpretation of s 5, as discussed below, under s 3(1) HRA would allow the section to operate more effectively as a means of providing such protection. Thus the *de facto* under-inclusiveness of s 2(2)—in terms of protecting fair trials—could be addressed by recourse to s 3(1)HRA, but its potential for over-inclusiveness—in terms of curbing free speech—could also be corrected.

SECTION 5: PROTECTION FOR GOOD FAITH DISCUSSIONS OF PUBLIC AFFAIRS

Section 5 of the Contempt of Court Act 1981 provides:

A publication made as or as part of a discussion in good faith of public affairs or other matters of general public interest is not to be treated as contempt of court under the strict liability rule if the risk of impediment or prejudice to particular legal proceedings is merely incidental to the discussion.

Section 5 conveys the message to the media that they can create a substantial risk of serious prejudice to a trial without incurring liability so long as they can also satisfy s 5, and they do not have the burden of proof in so doing—s 5 does not provide for a *defence*. The existence of s 5 therefore offers further confirmation that the 1981 Act is partly based on the protective model since it accepts that a substantial risk of serious prejudice to a trial can be created but that no liability may arise. Section 5 may be viewed as based impliedly on the assumption that the prejudice would have to be dealt with by the adoption of neutralizing measures in relation to trials, and it is only by taking that possibility into account that s 5 can be viewed as compatible with Article 6. The findings in *Ribemont* and in *Worm* make it clear—if there could be doubt on the matter—that under the Convention, notwithstanding the demands of Article 10, publications that are likely to create unfairness in a trial can be subject to sanctions, and that a breach of Article 6(1), and possibly of Article 6(2), will arise if the effects of such publications are not addressed in order to obviate the unfairness.

THE SECTION 5 TESTS

If the Attorney-General can show that s 2(2) is fulfilled, he must next seek to establish that s 5 does not apply. Where a piece merely discusses a particular case and makes no attempt to address wider issues, s 5 will clearly be inapplicable (*Daily Express* case).[140] In *A-G v English*,[141] the leading case on s 5, the article in question was about the election of a ProLife candidate, Mrs Carr, and also the general topic of mercy killing. As indicated above, it had been found to prejudice the trial of a Consultant, Dr Arthur, standing trial for the murder of a handicapped baby. The main point of Mrs Carr's candidature was that killing of sub-standard babies did happen and should be stopped; if it had not asserted that such babies were allowed to die, she would have been depicted as tilting at imaginary windmills. Thus the term 'discussion' could include implied accusations. Lord Diplock adopted a two stage approach in determining the sections's applicability. First, could the article be called a 'discussion'? The Divisional Court had held that a discussion must mean the general airing of views and debating of principles. However, Lord Diplock considered that the term 'discussion' could not be confined merely to abstract debate, but could include consideration of examples drawn from real life. Applying this test, he found that a discussion could include accusations without which the article would have been emasculated and would have lost its main point. Without the implied accusations, it would have become a contribution to a purely hypothetical issue. Thus the term 'discussion' was found to include implied accusations.

The Lords went on to find that the risk of prejudice to Dr Arthur's trial was merely an incidental consequence of expounding the main theme of the article, which was the candidate's election policy; Dr Arthur was not mentioned. It was found that the article was therefore the antithesis of the one considered in *A-G v Times Newspapers*,[142] which was concerned entirely with the actions of Distillers—the producers of the drug Thalidomide. It was clearly straightforward to find that the prejudice created could properly be described as incidental to the main theme. Thus, s 5 applied; the article did not, therefore, fall within the strict liability rule. This ruling was generally seen as giving a liberal interpretation to s 5.[143] Had the narrow interpretation of the Divisional Court prevailed, it would have meant that all debate in the media on the topic of mercy killing would have been prevented for almost a year—the time during which the proceedings in Arthur's case were active from charge to acquittal. The findings also made it clear that the discussion can be triggered off by the case itself; it need not have arisen prior to it. However, if this ruling had been taken to mean that s 5 only covered articles that touched obliquely on a trial, in contrast to the

---

[140] *The Times*, 19 December 1981.   [141] [1983] 1 AC 116; [1982] 2 All ER 903.
[142] [1974] AC 273.   [143] See e.g. Robertson, *Media Law*, 3rd edn., London: Penguin, 1999, p 216.

one at issue in the *Sunday Times* case, it would have had quite a narrow application and would not have answered to the findings in that case as to the need to take account of the value of the speech.

However, the ruling in *A-G v Times Newspapers*[144] made it clear that s 5 does cover direct reference to a particular case. The *Sunday Times* and four other newspapers commented on the background of an intruder into the Queen's bedroom at a time when he was about to stand trial. The article in the *Mail on Sunday* about Fagin made various adverse comments which were found to satisfy the s 2(2) test. It was alleged that he had had a homosexual liaison with the royal bodyguard and that he was a 'rootless, penniless, neurotic.' It was thought that the comments would affect the jury's assessment of his honesty. However, they fell within s 5 as they were part of a discussion of the Queen's safety, which was a matter of general public concern. In contrast, the *Sunday Times'* allegation that Fagin had stabbed his stepson could not fall within s 5, as it was irrelevant to the question of the Queen's safety, but had nevertheless been considered in detail.

It can be concluded that the term 'a discussion in good faith of public affairs or other matters of general public interest' has received quite a broad interpretation in the courts. However, this is less clearly the case in relation to the question whether the risk is 'merely incidental' to the discussion. *A-G v TVS Television, A-G v HW Southey and Sons*[145] concerned a TVS programme entitled 'The New Rachman' which made allegations about certain landlords in the South of England, alleging that they were obtaining money by deceiving the DHSS. The programme focused on landlords in Reading and coincided with the charging of a Reading landlord with conspiring to defraud the DHSS. It was found that the focus on Reading landlords meant that the article could not be viewed as creating a merely incidental risk of prejudice. In *A-G v Guardian Newspapers*[146] the article in question dealt with the tendency of judges in fraud trials to impose reporting restrictions, and stated that the judge in a criminal trial in Manchester had banned all reporting of the trial under s 4(2) of the 1981 Act on the ground that it could influence a separate trial involving one of the defendants. When the judge's attention was drawn to the article, he discharged the jury. It was readily found that the effect on the trial, if any, should be viewed as 'merely incidental' to the wider discussion[147] since the inclusion of examples was no more than 'an incidental consequence of expounding the main theme of the article.'[148]

These findings indicate that there is likely to be a difficulty in more borderline cases in drawing lines between the creation of risks in an incidental and a non-incidental fashion. Section 5 impliedly accepts that the discussion, but not the risk of prejudice it creates, need *not* be merely incidental to the trial. Clearly, given that it will already have been shown that the article in question creates a risk of serious prejudice, it is difficult to show that the risk of prejudice is merely incidental if the article relates

---

[144] *The Times*, 12 February 1983.   [145] *The Times*, 7 July 1989.
[146] [1992] 3 All ER 38, CA.   [147] It had already been found that s 2(2) was not satisfied.
[148] [1992] 3 All ER 38, p 49.

largely to the case. But this might not be impossible where the thrust of the discussion could not be said to cause prejudice, while the part which could was capable of being viewed as incidental to the rest. So far the courts appear to have assumed, however, that where the 'discussion of public affairs' is initiated by the case itself and centrally uses the facts of the case as an example, as in *A-G v TVS Television*, s 5 is likely to be inapplicable. Since s 5 was adopted as a response to the *Sunday Times* case, as a measure intended to protect media freedom, it might be expected to be capable of differentiating between two types of prejudicial publications—those consisting of inaccurate, misleading coverage of forthcoming proceedings and those that concern a general issue of public interest where the proceedings are centrally used as an example. It does not fully succeed in creating such differentiation since, although reporting within the latter category would fall within s 5 as 'a discussion of public affairs,' following the ruling in *English*, it would tend to fail the 'incidental' test, as occurred in *A-G v TVS Television, A-G v HW Southey and Sons*.

RE-INTERPRETING SECTION 5 IN THE POST-HRA ERA

Section 5 was intended to afford scope to the speech/harm balancing proportionality test under Article 10(2), as a response to *Sunday Times v UK*. But it fails to do so, since it does not provide a means of weighing up the seriousness of the prejudice against the significance of the speech in question. In contrast to the previous common law position, it clearly does provide a means of affording value to political speech, broadly defined, and to that extent it reflects the value placed upon such speech at Strasbourg. However, it is not the equivalent of a proportionality test since it depends on problematic determinations as to the central focus of a publication, as opposed to its peripheral aspects. The courts are being asked to engage in literary as opposed to legal analysis. The 'incidental' test is not apt to encapsulate the notion of proportionality and it is hard to import that notion through interpretation of the term. It would, however, be possible to go some way in doing so, which could mean stretching the notion of 'incidental' under s 3(1) HRA where a publication would be viewed as of especial value at Strasbourg in terms of the justifications for free expression.[149] If, as discussed above, the threshold under s 2(2) was lowered in reliance on s 3(1), such a development would allow a counter-balancing value to be afforded to media freedom.

The problematic term 'incidental' could only be stretched so far, and if the courts were to seek to adopt a proportionality test within the terms of s 5, they would have to be prepared to depart from the literal meaning of the section and to read words into it.[150] A strong argument for so doing is that the Parliamentary intention behind the introduction of the 1981 Act was to bring English law into compliance with the

---

[149] See Chapter 1 at 14–19.

[150] This might be possible: see *R v A* [2001] 2 Cr App R 21; [[2002] 1 AC 45; for discussion, see Chapter 3 at 157–63. A. Kavanagh's writings on s 3(1) have influenced this analysis. See in particular 'The elusive divide between interpretation and legislation under the HRA' (2004) 24(2) *OJLS* 259. A court could read in the words 'if the proportionality test under Article 10(2) is not satisfied, or' after the word 'if'.

Convention. If the judges were prepared to accept that Parliament had partially failed to achieve its aim, then even reading words into the statute to achieve such compliance could be seen, not as *defeating* Parliament's intention, but as perfecting it. The new interpretation, moreover, does not go against a pervasive feature of the statute.[151] At the same time the reform proposed is largely a matter of interpretation rather than of implying into the statute an entirely new provision that was absent from it.[152] Moreover, the area in question—protecting the judicial process—is one that is clearly within the judicial domain in terms of constitutional competence and role.[153] Parliament is not otherwise addressing this issue—there are no plans at present to reform the 1981 Act.[154] No issues of resource allocation arise; thus there are positive reasons for activism in this context and none for deference.

CONCLUSIONS

Where prejudice has probably been caused and the speech in question consists of reportage with a misleading gloss,[155] s 5 could not be used, under the current interpretation of the section. But the speech might escape liability since it would be probable that no prosecution would be brought for the reasons given above, founded partly on the unsatisfactory nature of s 2(2). The reform proposed under s 5 would not afford greater protection to such speech since its misleading quality would undermine its public interest value. Section 2(2), if interpreted more clearly, as discussed above, could provide an increased protection for fair trials; s 5 could only be viewed as providing a satisfactory countervailing protection for free speech if the courts were prepared to take this course. But the result might be—in something close to a reversal of the current situation—that near worthless and probably prejudicial speech would be caught by an enhanced s 2(2), while speech of the most value in Article 10 terms would be more likely to escape under the reformed s 5. Thus a re-balancing of the statute, based more firmly on both fair trial and free speech principles, could occur. This would accord more strongly with the speech/harm balancing test from *Sunday Times v UK*. Speech of value would be

---

[151] Cf *R (on the application of Anderson) v Secretary of State for the Home Department* [2003] 1 AC 837 in which the Secretary of State's role in sentencing was found to be incompatible with Art 6 since he could not be viewed as an independent and impartial tribunal. However, a declaration of incompatibility was made rather than seeking to use s 3(1) since the Secretary of State's role was such a fundamental feature of the statute as a whole—any other approach would have been against the grain of the statute.

[152] As in the Court of Appeal in *Re S and Re W (Care Orders)*—as discussed in Chapter 3 at 161 the decision was over-turned: it was made clear by the House of Lords [2002] 2 AC 291 that the Court of Appeal had gone too far under s 3.

[153] In terms of both expertise and constitutional role the context is similar to those in *R v A* [[2002] 1 AC 45 and in *R v Offen* [2001] 1 WLR 253; but not that in *Bellinger* [2003] 2 All ER 513—where the court declined to read words into the statute in question under s 3 HRA. For discussion see Chapter 3 at 162–3.

[154] Cf *Bellinger* ibid—where Parliament was about to address the situation at issue regarding the law relating to transsexuals.

[155] E.g. the *Sun* headline 'Got the Bastards!' in relation to the arrests of terrorist suspects in July 2005 referred to earlier, p 272, above.

less likely to be caught but where there was a real possibility of harm to a trial, liability would be more likely to be established. This approach would echo the Strasbourg one as encapsulated in both *Sunday Times* and *Worm* more closely than is the case under the current position, but it would not replicate it. The problem would still remain that Article 10 values can overcome Article 6 ones under s 5 since the section allows speech to cause serious prejudice to a trial but escape liability due to its value. It is only possible to meet this argument by relying on the use of neutralizing measures at trial, but for the reasons already discussed, this is not an entirely satisfactory position.

INTENTIONAL CONTEMPT AT COMMON LAW

So far the discussion has concentrated on the protective approach as reflected in the 1981 Act. The statute, however, left open under s 6(c) the possibility of bringing an action under common law contempt in respect of publications where specific intent to prejudice the administration of justice can be shown. This is an anomalous possibility since, in a departure from domestic tradition, it focuses centrally on the culpability of the media body rather than on the effect on proceedings. Contempts can arise in a myriad of forms, but so far three forms of common law contempt have been identified post-1981: creating bias against defendants; pressurizing litigants; frustrating the purpose of injunction against another media body. All three forms rely on the tests that are discussed below; all three could be dealt with under the strict liability rule so long as the publication in question occurred within the active period. Bearing this in mind, the next sections evaluate the reasons for retaining common law contempt in the post-HRA era.

ELEMENTS OF COMMON LAW CONTEMPT; POTENTIAL INFLUENCE OF THE HRA

Section 6 provides: '[n]othing in the foregoing provisions of this Act—(c) restricts liability for contempt of court in respect of conduct intended to impede or prejudice the administration of justice.' 'Prejudice [to] the administration of justice' clearly includes (and probably solely denotes) prejudice to particular proceedings. Common law contempt—like strict liability contempt—is not based on the preventive approach since it is unconcerned with the question whether prejudice has actually been caused. The link between this form of liability and prevention of prejudice to proceedings is even weaker than it is under the Act since the establishment of *mens rea* is largely unrelated to the prevention of such prejudice, in terms of deterrence. The test is so strict that in most instances, even where it is highly likely that prejudice will be caused, an editor will be able to argue that he or she at most may have acted recklessly, but not intentionally. Indeed, the need to show intent precludes the emergence of the incidental preventive effect that might otherwise have arisen as a result of the ease with which the tests for establishing the *actus reus* can be satisfied.

The test for intention to prejudice the administration of justice was established in *A-G v Times Newspapers:*[156] specific intent is required and therefore it clearly does not include recklessness. Intent can consist either of a desire to prejudice proceedings or of a recognition that causing such prejudice was a virtually certain consequence of publication—oblique intent. All but one of the cases so far have been concerned with the latter form of intent, in which intent has to be inferred from the published material and from any other relevant circumstances.[157] However, in *A-G v News Group Newspapers plc*,[158] discussed further below, it was said that the *Sun* could not have published the articles in question had it not been 'campaigning for a conviction as it clearly was'. The *Sun*'s support for the prosecution in its columns and in funding a private prosecution allowed the inference to be made. A Dr B was questioned about an allegation of rape made against him by an eight year old girl, but eventually the county prosecuting solicitor decided that there was insufficient evidence to prosecute him. *The Sun* obtained the story and decided that it should offer the mother financial help in order to fund a private prosecution. It published various articles attacking Dr B: 'Rape Case Doc: Sun acts'; 'Beast must be named, says MP', etc. The Attorney General brought a prosecution against *The Sun* for contempt. The articles could not come within the strict liability rule because the proceedings in question—the private prosecution—were not active. The contempt alleged, therefore, arose at common law. It was found that intention could be established, either on the basis of a desire to prejudice the proceedings (presumably in order to vindicate the paper's stance) or because the editor must have foreseen that Dr B would almost certainly not receive a fair trial. The judgment would support either view, but probably favours the former. Thus the case appeared to be concerned with desire to cause prejudice, rather than with oblique intent. Clearly, it is hard to infer that such desire is present in a particular instance. Establishing it would probably mean showing personal involvement of the media body. In general the tests for intent are very difficult to satisfy in relation to publications, except in one special instance—the interference by one media body with an injunction against another. This instance is discussed further below. It is in general difficult to infer that a media body desired to prejudice proceedings but it is also very difficult to show that it recognized that such prejudice was a virtually certain consequence of publication—especially where there is a reasonable time-lag between publication and proceedings.

---

[156] [1992] 1 AC 191; [1991] 2 All ER 398; for a report of the Divisional Court proceedings see *A-G v Observer and Guardian Newspapers Ltd, The Times,* 9 May 1989; for comment, see [1989] *PL* 477. For comment on the *mens rea* issue, see Laws LJ, 'Current problems in the law of contempt' (1990) 43 *CLP* 99, pp 105–10. See also *A-G v News Group Newspapers plc* [1989] QB 110. It is clear that 'intention' connotes specific intent and therefore cannot include recklessness (*A-G v Sport* [1991] 1 WLR 1194). This test is based on the meaning of intent arising from rulings on the *mens rea* for murder: see *R v Hancock and Shankland* [1986] AC 455 and *R v Woollin* [1999] 1 AC 82.

[157] See discussion of the *Spycatcher* case *A-G v Times Newspapers* [1992] 1 AC 191 below, pp 290–1.

[158] [1989] QB 110; [1988] 3 WLR 163; [1988] 2 All ER 906.

The development of the tests for common law contempt post-1981 has tended to marginalize the role of the doctrine in terms of seeking to prevent prejudice to proceedings—in the sense of influencing those involved in the proceedings. Its role in that respect is now far more limited than the role of the strict liability rule due to the requirement of intent. But if the requirement of intent *can* be satisfied, it is then easier to establish contempt at common law rather than under the Act since it is only necessary to show 'a real risk of prejudice' and proceedings need only be imminent, not 'active.' There is also no common law equivalent of s 5.

While the test for intent has been strictly interpreted,[159] the test of timing has become more uncertain. At common law, the *sub judice* period began when proceedings could be said to be 'imminent.'[160] This was clearly a less well-defined period than the active period. However, the parameters of the period may be even more uncertain than that. In *A-G v News Group Newspapers plc*[161] it was held *obiter* that where it is established that the defendant intended to prejudice proceedings, it is not necessary to show that proceedings are imminent. In his judgment, Watkins LJ approved of David Pannick's contention:

no authority states that common law contempt cannot be committed where proceedings cannot be said to be imminent but where there is a specific intent to impede a fair trial, the occurrence of which is in contemplation.

It was found that even if the trial was too far off to be said to be pending or imminent, the conduct of the *Sun* in publishing stories at the same time as assisting the mother of the victim in the private prosecution could still amount to contempt. This test— that proceedings need merely be in contemplation or highly likely to occur—is also used in New Zealand.[162]

Bingham LJ concurred with this dilution of the imminence test in *A-G v Sport*,[163] although in the same case Hodgson J considered that proceedings must be 'pending.' He interpreted 'pending' as synonymous with 'active,' an interpretation which would at one and the same time have curtailed the scope of common law contempt, but focused it more closely on the harm caused by deliberately creating prejudice to proceedings. This point, therefore, remains unresolved, leaving the media without a clear guide as to the period during which publication of matter relevant to proceedings will be risky. If proceedings need not even be imminent, it appears that reporting of matters which may give rise to proceedings at some point in the future could be curbed, assuming that the other tests were satisfied. The test of 'imminence' is itself too wide and uncertain, but would be preferable to the uncertainty on this point which was exacerbated by *A-G v Sport*. It is uncertain what the alternative test contemplated by Bingham LJ could be. There cannot be an intention to prejudice something which cannot even be identified as a possibility. Thus the test at its least stringent must be

---

[159] Note 156 above.   [160] *R v Savundranayagan* [1968] 3 All ER 439; [1968] 1 WLR 1761, CA.
[161] [1989] QB 110; [1988] 3 WLR 163; [1988] 2 All ER 906.
[162] *Television New Zealand Ltd v Solicitor-General* [1989] 1 NZLR 1, at 3.   [163] [1991] 1 WLR 1194.

that proceedings can be identified as a possibility before this head of common law contempt can be in question. At the same time it would only be possible to rely on this diluted imminence test in relation to instances of simple rather than oblique intent. Desired consequences can never be viewed as too remote, assuming that they in fact arise, but it would be almost impossible to show that a virtually certain consequence of prejudice had been foreseen in instances of a very lengthy time lag between publication and proceedings. Obviously, even in relation to simple intent, the actus reus of a real risk of prejudice still has to be established, which would also be very difficult in relation to a lengthy time lag, except possibly in exceptional instances such as that in *A-G v News Group Newspapers* itself where the newspaper is personally involved. This development in common law contempt is therefore of little practical significance. It may have some slight curtailing impact on media freedom, but at the same time it is unlikely to protect the fairness of proceedings. The more uncertain the test becomes, the more, it is argued, common law contempt is divorced from a focus on such fairness.

If a suitable post-HRA case ever arises, it is possible that reinterpretation of this common law doctrine as an aspect of the courts' duty under s 6 HRA[164] might reintroduce certainty into the timing test. It is questionable whether the interference with freedom of expression represented by a prosecution for common law contempt could be said to be 'prescribed by law' due to the lack of precision and therefore of forseeability inherent in the current interpretations of the *sub judice* period. As Chapter 2 indicated, an interference must not only have a basis in law, that basis must be of sufficient quality.[165] Probably the most satisfactory method of ensuring that the requirements of quality are met would be to adopt the course suggested by Hodgson J in *A-G v Sport*. The 'active' test is laid down with reasonable precision and would, therefore, probably meet those requirements. It may be noted that, as Hodgson J pointed out, Scottish and Australian cases have held that imminent proceedings are not covered by contempt law.[166] At the least, reinterpretation might demand a return to the original requirement of imminence. Obviously, if the active test was adopted, this would confine common law contempt to instances in which the statute could also be used. It would still have a role since, where intention to prejudice was shown, a much higher fine could be imposed on the media body in question. Such a development would be, it is suggested, appropriate in the post-HRA era since it would prevent the common law, as interpreted in accordance with Article 10 under s 6, from circumventing a statute that had been adopted in order to meet a Strasbourg ruling.[167] If common law contempt could be viewed as prescribed by law, the timing test could nevertheless be narrowed down by reference to the Article 10(2) tests of necessity and proportionality. It could readily be argued that holding open the possibility of liability

---

[164] See *Douglas v Hello!* [2001] QB 967.   [165] See pp 47–8.
[166] See *Hall v Assoc Newspapers Ltd* 1978 SLT 241; *A-G for NSW v TCN Channel Nine Pty Ltd* (1990) 20 NSWLR 368.
[167] In the *Sunday Times* case (1979–80) 2 EHRR 245.

for such an indeterminate length of time was disproportionate to the legitimate aim pursued.

In practice, unless a media body can be shown to have *desired* to prejudice proceedings through a publication, by creating bias in the minds of those involved such as jurors, it is almost impossible to show that such prejudice is a virtually certain consequence of publication if the proceedings are merely imminent but not active. *Virtual certainty* of such prejudice could normally only arise where publication occurred close to the action or during it. Therefore the 'imminence' test is only nominally of significance in most instances—it can be assumed that it may have become virtually otiose and that the strict liability rule will almost always be used rather than the common law in relation to this form of prejudice. The only reason for using the common law during the active period would be to seek a higher penalty where mens rea could be shown. But this could be done in any event if reforms to the 1981 Act abolished this form of common law contempt but allowed for higher penalties to be applied where the media body was shown to have mens rea. There would be an argument for including recklessness. Intentionally or recklessly creating a substantial risk of serious prejudice during the active period could become a new offence, creating an alternative to the strict liability rule, and attracting a higher sentence. The current common law rule might however have a residual relevance in relation to other forms of creating prejudice to proceedings, as discussed below.

The key element of the *actus reus* of common law contempt is that the publication must create 'a real risk of prejudice to the administration of justice.'[168] The test does not refer to 'particular proceedings', but post-1981 it has always been used in relation to such proceedings, not in relation to the administration of justice generally. It has been found to cover a number of highly disparate forms of impediment or prejudice to proceedings. It covers the creation of prejudice in the minds of those involved in the proceedings. In *A-G v News Group Newspapers plc*[169] it was found that there was a risk of prejudice since jurors might have been influenced by the newspaper coverage which came close to imputing guilt to the defendant. This was however a doubtful finding due to the lapse of time between publication and trial. The almost dismissive treatment of the actus reus in that case came close to implying that the *Sun* was being punished for acting reprehensibly in seeking to prejudice the proceedings, rather than in relation to the risk it actually created.

In *Hislop and Pressdram*[170] it was found that the defendants, who were one party in an action for defamation, had interfered with the administration of justice because they had brought improper pressure to bear on the other party, Sonia Sutcliffe, wife of Peter Sutcliffe, the 'Yorkshire Ripper', by publishing material in *Private Eye* intended to deter her from pursuing the action. There was a substantial risk that the articles might have succeeded in their aim; had they done so, the course of justice in Mrs Sutcliffe's action would have been seriously prejudiced, since she would have

---

[168] *Thompson Newspapers* [1968] 1 All ER 268; [1968] 1 WLR 1.   [169] [1989] QB 110.
[170] [1991] 1 QB 514; [1991] 1 All ER 911; [1991] 2 WLR 219, CA.

been deterred from having her claim decided in a court. Counsel for *Private Eye* had argued that defamatory material which the defendant seeks to justify should not be restrained, because until it is clear that the alleged libel is untrue, it is not clear that any right has been infringed.[171] This argument was rejected because the question of pressure did not depend on the truth or falsity of the allegations. The possibility of justification was thus irrelevant.

The particular use of common law contempt at stake in *Hislop* can be viewed as having a preventive role. It represents a clear and quite precisely defined area of liability targeted at a particular mischief. There is no division of responsibility between trial judge and contempt law—if contempt law did not fulfil this role, it could not be fulfilled at all, under the existing law. But it might be considered whether common law contempt is the most suitable tool to be used to protect litigants from pressure. In *Hislop* the relevant tests under the 1981 Act were also satisfied, on the basis that the articles that had been published might have influenced the jury against Mrs Sutcliffe in the forthcoming libel proceedings. But there would be nothing to prevent the Attorney General from beginning a contempt action under the strict liability rule where the creation of prejudice had created a risk, during the active period, of impeding the proceedings by pressurizing a litigant into dropping them. Since this form of liability could be used against the media regardless of the possibility of creating unfairness by affecting the minds of those involved in the proceedings, it is arguable that it should be viewed as a special form of contempt and placed on a new statutory basis.

But the form of common law contempt based on creating bias in the minds of those involved in proceedings seems to be serving no useful purpose, since it overlaps with the use of the strict liability rule, and should be abolished. The imprecision and over-breadth of the tests for the actus reus sit uneasily with the demands of proportionality under Article 10. Since it is now hard to satisfy s 2(2) of the 1981 Act unless a publication occurs close to or during the trial, it is hard to imagine an instance in which it would be useful to invoke the test of imminence—if a publication was merely imminent as opposed to active it would not satisfy the 'real risk of prejudice' test under the more recent s 2(2) rulings on the creation of risk.[172] Possibly, since no cases have been brought in reliance on this form of common law contempt since 1991, it can be assumed that it is becoming a dead letter.

FRUSTRATING THE PURPOSE OF INJUNCTIONS AGAINST OTHER MEDIA BODIES

Common law tests

A further very significant special form of common law contempt can arise if part of the media frustrates a court order (including orders made under s 4(2) of the 1981

---

[171] *Bonnard v Perryman* [1891] 2 Ch 269, at 289.   [172] See pp 268–70 above.

Act)[173] against another part. Usually the order is made to restrain the publication of confidential material.[174] The three tests applicable are the same as those discussed above: proceedings must (probably) be imminent; specific intent to prejudice proceedings must be shown, and a real risk of prejudice must arise. But the last test has had to be interpreted in a very particular fashion in order to allow this particular form of contempt to arise.

This highly significant extension of common law contempt arose from one strand of the *Spycatcher* litigation. In 1985, the Attorney General commenced proceedings in Australia in an attempt to restrain the publication of *Spycatcher* by Peter Wright. The book included allegations of illegal activity engaged in by MI5. In 1986, after the *Guardian* and the *Observer* had published reports of the forthcoming hearing which included some *Spycatcher* material, the Attorney General obtained temporary *ex parte* injunctions preventing them from further disclosure of such material on the ground of breach of confidence.[175] While the temporary injunctions were in force, the *Independent* and two other papers published material covered by them. It was determined in the Court of Appeal,[176] and confirmed in the House of Lords,[177] that such publication constituted the *actus reus* of common law contempt on the basis that publication of confidential material, the subject matter of a pending action, damaging its confidentiality and thereby probably rendering the action pointless, created an interference with the administration of justice. Once the material had been published it was no longer confidential; therefore the subject matter of the action for breach of confidence in which a permanent injunction was being sort had been destroyed. The case therefore affirmed the principle that once an interlocutory injunction has been obtained restraining one organ of the media from publication of allegedly confidential material, the rest of the media may be in contempt if they publish that material, even if their intention in so doing is to bring alleged iniquity to public attention. This case thus allowed the laws of confidence and contempt to operate together as a significant prior restraint on media freedom, and in so doing created an inroad into the general principle that a court order should only affect the party to which it is directed as only that party will have a chance to argue that the making of the order would be wrong.

The decision in *A-G v Newspaper Publishing plc and Others*[178] seemed to represent an attempt to narrow down the area of liability created by the decision in *A-G v Times*

---

[173] S4(1) provides that a fair and accurate report of proceedings held in public published contemporaneously in good faith will not be a contempt. Section 4(2) of the 1981 Act provides that during any legal proceeding held in public, a judge may make an order postponing reporting of the proceedings if such action 'appears necessary for avoiding a substantial risk of prejudice to the administration of justice in those proceedings'. For discussion of s 4, see Chapter 5.

[174] See for discussion of breach of confidence in the context of state secrecy, Chapter 19 at 948–57.

[175] For full discussion of this branch of the litigation see Chapter 19 at 950–4.

[176] *A-G v Newspaper Publishing plc, The Times*, 28 February 1990.

[177] *A-G v Times Newspapers Ltd* [1992] 1 AC 191; [1991] 2 All ER 398; [1991] 2 WLR 994, HL: for comment see *NLJ* (1991) 141 (6516), 1115.

[178] [1997] 3 All ER 159; *The Times*, 2 May 1997, CA.

Newspapers Ltd. The case arose from the reporting of the appeals in the *Ordtech* case,[179] a case which bore strong similarities to the *Matrix Churchill* case.[180] The appellants appealed against their convictions for exporting arms; public interest immunity certificates were issued,[181] but the Court of Appeal ordered that the material covered by them, which was crucial to the appeal, should be disclosed in summarized and edited form to the appellants and their legal advisors. The order restricted the use of the material to the appeal and requested its return on conclusion of the appeal. In court, in directing return of the documents, the Lord Chief Justice indicated that breach of the order would result in the matter being referred to the Attorney General.

In its report of the proceedings, the *Independent* published a small amount of material from the documents which did not also appear in the written copy of the judgment. The Attorney General brought proceedings for contempt against the *Independent*, relying on the ruling in *A-G v Times Newspapers* to the effect that if a third party with the requisite intent acts in a way that frustrates the basis on which a court has determined that justice should be administered, then it will be guilty of contempt. On behalf of the *Independent* it was argued that the *Times* case represented an extension of the law as it had previously been understood, and that the court should be slow to extend the law any further since any such extension represented a further encroachment on freedom of expression and inhibited the media in its function of informing the public. The court did not accept that any conduct by a third party inconsistent with a court order was sufficient to amount to the *actus reus* of contempt—it was found necessary to show that a significant and adverse effect on the administration of justice in the relevant proceedings had occurred. The Court of Appeal used the wording of Article 10 of the Convention in finding that restraints on freedom of expression should be no wider than necessary in a democratic society, and considered that conduct which is inconsistent with a court order in a trivial way should not create the risk of a conviction for contempt. The application of the Attorney-General was therefore dismissed.

The post-HRA position

The principle laid down in the *Times* case was again reconsidered in the HRA era by the House of Lords in *A-G v Punch*.[182] The case arose from the publication by *Punch* magazine of an article by David Shayler. Shayler had served as an officer with MI5 and when he left MI5 he took with him copies of confidential documents containing sensitive information relating to intelligence activities of MI5. According to the Attorney General, Mr Shayler then disclosed some of this material to a newspaper

---

[179] See *Blackledge and Others* (1996) 1 Cr App R 326, CA.

[180] See *The Report of the Inquiry into the Export of Defence Equipment and Dual Use Goods to Iraq and Related Prosecutions*, 1995–96, H.C. 115. See further [1996] *PL* 357–527; PL [1997] 211–214.

[181] Certificates rendering the material covered immune from scrutiny.

[182] [2003] 1 AC 1046; [2003] 2 WLR 49; [2003] 1 All ER 289. For discussion of the case, see A.T.H Smith, 'Third Parties and the Reach of Injunctions' [2003] 62(2) *CLJ* 241.

publisher, Associated Newspapers Ltd. Articles written by Mr Shayler, or based on information provided by him, were published in the *Mail on Sunday* and the *Evening Standard* in August 1997. The Attorney General then intervened and brought civil proceedings against Mr Shayler and Associated Newspapers. Hooper J granted an interlocutory injunction against Mr Shayler based on breach of confidence.[183] A similar order was made against Associated Newspapers. By this order, expressed to continue until the trial of the action, Mr Shayler was restrained from disclosing to any newspaper or anyone else:

any information obtained by him in the course of or by virtue of his employment in and position as a member of the Security Service (whether presented as fact or fiction) which relates to or which may be construed as relating to the Security Service or its membership or activities or to security or intelligence activities generally.

Two provisos were attached to the order. First, the order did not apply to any information in respect of which the Attorney General stated in writing that the information was not information the publication of which the Crown was seeking to restrain. Second, the order did not preclude repetition of the information disclosed in the *Mail on Sunday* on 24 August 1997. Neither Mr Shayler nor Associated Newspapers objected to the making of these orders.

Mr Shayler then began writing for *Punch* magazine; the editor, Mr Steen, was aware of the terms of the interlocutory non-disclosure orders made against Mr Shayler. The article which became the subject of the contempt proceedings dealt with the Bishopsgate bomb in 1993 and the death of WPC Yvonne Fletcher outside the Libyan Embassy in 1984. At first instance, in the contempt proceedings, Silber J concluded[184] that the *actus reus* of common law contempt had been established on the basis that the defendants had published the article in breach of the terms of the injunctions, with the result that the purpose of the court in making those injunctions was subverted and, in consequence, there had been some significant and adverse effect on the administration of justice. The judge held that the purpose of the court in granting the injunctions was not to protect national security, but to ensure that until trial there should be no disclosure of information obtained by Mr Shayler in his employment, so that the confidentiality of the information could be kept intact until the trial of the permanent injunctions.[185] The judge also found that the necessary *mens rea* had been established since Mr Steen knew that publication of the article was a breach of the injunctions, and he intended to act in breach of them. Therefore it was found that he intended by the publication to impede or prejudice the administration of justice by thwarting or undermining the intended effect of the injunctions.[186]

The Court of Appeal, by a three-two majority overturned this decision.[187] Lord Phillips MR characterized the court's purpose in granting the injunctions differently. He found that the correct approach was to proceed on the basis that Hooper J's

---

[183] On 4 September 1997.   [184] *A-G v Punch*, 6 October 2000 (unreported), QB, at para 62.
[185] Ibid, at para 52.   [186] Ibid, at para 78.   [187] [2001] QB 1028; [2001] 2 All ER 655.

purpose in granting the injunctions was 'to prevent the disclosure of any matter that arguably risked harming the national interest.'[188] He noted the Attorney-General's case that the effect of the injunctions was that 'no newspaper could knowingly publish any matter that fell within the wide terms of the Associated Newspapers' injunction without first obtaining clearance from himself or from the court.' Lord Phillips objected to this contention on the basis that it would subject the press to the censorship of the Attorney General. He found that it would result in an imposition of a restriction on freedom of the press that would be disproportionate to any public interest and thus in breach of Article 10 of the European Convention. He further considered that such a proposition could not be reconciled with the duty imposed on the court by s 12(3) HRA.[189] Section 12(3) has established a higher threshold for granting injunctions against the media but it is not applicable in criminal proceedings. Lord Phillips' point appeared to be that if an injunction could be granted which then affected another media body through the threat of criminal proceedings, that would not appear to accord with the spirit of the section. However, he found that the article in question included three items of previously unpublished material which *did* risk harming the national interest and therefore defeated the purpose of the injunction. The *actus reus* of common law contempt was therefore established. Lord Phillips went on, however, to hold that in order to satisfy the test for *mens rea* it had to be shown that Mr Steen knew that publication would interfere with the course of justice by defeating the purpose underlying the injunctions. It was found that the Attorney General had failed to establish this; Mr Steen had contended that he thought that the purpose of the court order was to restrain publication of material dangerous to national security and that he had no intention of publishing any such information.

This decision of the Court of Appeal sought to focus closely on the values and interests at stake and refused to allow an uncertain threat to the administration of justice to overcome freedom of expression. Although the Convention was not relied on extensively and there was virtually no recitation of the relevant jurisprudence, the Court showed itself determined to adopt a stance which relied on close examination of the necessity of the interference in question, eventually concluding that a pressing social need to allow such an interference with freedom of political expression was not present. The Court was not impressed by the claim that it was necessary to preserve this area of liability in order to prevent impediments to the administration of justice. Thus, the Court sought to identify another interest—in this instance national security—which could genuinely support the grave interference with freedom of expression represented by the *Spycatcher* doctrine, and found that the alleged harm was not serious enough to justify such a grave interference with media freedom. In some rare instances it might be possible to show that the journalist or other person in question, due to his or her background and/or specialist knowledge, did recognize that publication of the material in question would be likely to damage national

---

[188] Ibid, at para 100.

[189] For the provision of s12(3) and discussion see Chapter 3 at 153–7 and Chapter 15 at 807–8.

security. It may be noted that the Official Secrets Act 1989 s 5 presupposes that it will sometimes be possible to show that a person in the position of a journalist recognized that possibility.[190]

Nevertheless, this decision would have narrowed down and virtually destroyed the *Spycatcher* area of liability, since if the purpose of interim orders was accepted to be to prevent disclosure of any matter that arguably risked harming the national interest, then proof of *mens rea* for contempt would involve proving to the criminal standard that third parties, including editors and journalists, knew that materials published arguably risked harming that interest. This would probably have proved to be a difficult, if not impossible, task for the Crown in most instances. Editors would have been able to insist that they had no reason to believe that even arguable damage to national security might result from such publication. Since the *mens rea* required is specific intent, it would not be possible merely to show that a reasonable person in the defendant's position would have known that such a risk arose—a possible means of satisfying the test required under the Official Secrets Act 1989 s 5. Thus, the result would have been that the grant of such injunctions in most circumstances could not have lead to the imposition of criminal liability against third parties such as Mr Steen.

However, the House of Lords overturned the decision of the Court of Appeal. Lord Nicholls, in a speech with which the other Law Lords agreed, found that the underlying purpose of the Attorney General, as the plaintiff in the proceedings against Mr Shayler, in seeking the order against Mr Steen was irrelevant. He said:

The reason why the court grants interim protection is to protect the plaintiff's asserted right. But the manner in which this protection is afforded depends upon the terms of the inter-locutory injunction. The purpose the court seeks to achieve by granting the interlocutory injunction is that, pending a decision by the court on the claims in the proceedings, the restrained acts shall not be done. Third parties are in contempt of court if they wilfully interfere with the administration of justice by thwarting the achievement of this purpose in those proceedings. This is so, even if in the particular case, the injunction is drawn in seemingly over-wide terms.[191]

In that instance, he found, the remedy of the third party whose conduct is affected by the order is to apply to the court for the order to be varied. He also pointed out that the act in question would only be contemptuous if the act done has some 'significant and adverse effect on the administration of justice in the proceedings.' Lord Hope characterized the purpose of the interim injunction in similar terms:

'[i]ts purpose is to ensure that the other party to the dispute does not assume the res-ponsibility of deciding for himself whether the material is of such a nature that the Attorney-General is entitled in law to protection against its publication.'[192]

In the instant case the Lords found that the purpose of the judge in making the order was to preserve the confidentiality of the information specified in the order pending

---

[190] See Chapter 19 at 934–5 for discussion of s 5.
[191] [2003] 1 AC 1046; [2003] 2 WLR 49; [2003] 1 All ER 289, at paras 43 and 44.   [192] Ibid, at [114].

the trial so as to enable the court at trial to adjudicate effectively on the disputed issues of confidentiality arising in the action. It was to ensure that the court's decision on the claims in the proceedings should not be pre-empted by disclosure of any of the information specified in the order before the trial. The *actus reus* of contempt was satisfied by the thwarting of this purpose by destruction of the confidentiality of the material, through its publication in *Punch*, which it was the purpose of the injunction to preserve. Mr Steen had accepted that the publication of the offending magazine article had constituted the *actus reus* of contempt. Bearing in mind the purpose of the injunctions as already established, Lord Nicholls went on to find that the *mens rea* of common law contempt was also satisfied and so concluded that contempt of court was established. He said:

The facts speak for themselves. Mr Steen . . . knew that the action against Mr Shayler raised confidentiality issues relating wholly or primarily to national security. He must, inevitably, have appreciated that by publishing the article he was doing precisely what the order was intended to prevent, namely, pre-empting the court's decision on these confidentiality issues. That is knowing interference with the administration of justice.[193]

Clearly, the finding of contempt represented an interference with freedom of expression as guaranteed by Article 10. However, Lord Nicholl's consideration of the impact of the HRA was brief and superficial. He noted, before coming to the argument as to the purpose of the injunction, that national security, one of the list of exceptions in Article 10(2), can justify a restraint on freedom of expression. He then went on to find, '[t]he rule of law requires that the decision on where this balance lies in any case should be made by the court as an independent and impartial tribunal established by law' and in the meantime the court must be able to prevent the information being disclosed. He went on to find that therefore:

the law must be able to prescribe appropriate penalties where a person deliberately sets the injunction at nought. Without sanctions an injunction would be a paper tiger. Sanctions are necessary to maintain the rule of law; in the language of the Convention, to maintain the authority of the judiciary.

This analysis did not address the questions of necessity and proportionality; it implied that once a court had decided that material should be kept confidential before the trial of a permanent injunction and had imposed an interim injunction with that object in mind, it would *always* be justifiable to restrict freedom of expression by way of common law contempt in order to provide a sanction against publication of the material by third parties where publication would have a significant and adverse effect on the administration of justice in that trial. But the need to show such an effect does not necessarily satisfy the requirements of proportionality since the adverse effect would always be caused by publication of material covered by the injunction which was not already, or not to a significant extent, in the public domain. Further, in such

---

[193] Ibid, at paras 51 and 52.

circumstances the *mens rea* requirement would virtually always be satisfied since journalists would normally be aware that the material was covered by an injunction against another body or person.

Lord Hope gave brief consideration to the question of proportionality, but without citing any Strasbourg jurisprudence, although he came to the same conclusion as Lord Nicholl. He found that there can be no objection to an interim injunction against the publication of information on the ground of proportionality if three requirements are satisfied. He considered that the general principles from which the requirements are to be derived are well established and are indicated in three leading cases: *R (Daly) v Secretary of State for the Home Department*,[194] *R (Pretty) v Director of Public Prosecutions*,[195] *R v Shayler*.[196] He found that in the context in question the requirements are: first, that there is a genuine dispute as to whether the information is confidential because its publication might be a threat to national security; second that there are reasonable grounds for thinking that publication of the information before trial would impede or interfere with the administration of justice and third, that the interference with the right of free speech is no greater than is necessary. Lord Hope concentrated on the third requirement and found that the requirements of proportionality were satisfied since the opening words of the interim injunction were qualified by the proviso allowing newspapers to apply to the Attorney General to publish innocuous material; the extent of the injunction remained subject to the further order of the court and that court itself would have to observe the principle of proportionality when it dealt with any application before the trial for the relaxation of the scope of the injunction.[197] He insisted that in each instance the analysis of proportionality should be fact-sensitive.

However, objection can be made to his findings on the basis that all interim injunctions would satisfy the second and third of these requirements and the first is open to the objection that it places a power of censorship in the hands, not only of a member of the executive, but also in those of one party to the original and forthcoming actions, creating an appearance of bias. The Attorney General is the very person (or office) whose rights are being upheld by the threat of the invocation of the contempt of court jurisdiction. To determine whether liability under that jurisdiction can be justified as an interference with freedom of expression, partly by reference to his powers to allow publication, does not appear to provide an adequate safeguard for the media. This was far from the hard look at the proportionality that one would expect of a court which took its duty under s 6(1) HRA seriously.

CRITIQUE OF *PUNCH* AND THE COMMON LAW DOCTRINE

The requirements of both the *actus reus* and *mens rea* of common law contempt, as interpreted by the House of Lords in *Punch*, do little to temper the rigour of this

---

[194] [2001] 2 AC 532, at 547A–B, *per* Lord Steyn.   [195] [2001] 3 WLR 1598, at 1637A–B.
[196] [2002] 2 WLR 754, at 783F–H, 786A–B.   [197] *A-G v Punch* [2003] 1 AC 1046, at paras 114–120.

doctrine. In particular, the demands of proportionality do not appear to be satisfied when it is borne in mind that if the party to whom the interim injunction was originally addressed published material covered by it, it would only be subject to civil sanctions, whereas third parties such as *Punch* who published such material would be criminally liable. It is clearly anomalous that this should be the case. In the instant case the Attorney-General had fair warning that *Punch* was likely to publish Shayler material and could have sought a separate injunction, backed up by civil sanctions, against it.[198]

The requirements of proportionality could have been satisfied by accepting the test put forward by the Court of Appeal. That test clearly did depart from the test for common law contempt established in the *Spycatcher* case since it focused on the underlying as opposed to the expressed purpose of the injunctions. But it is the duty of the courts under s 6 HRA to develop the common law by reference to the Convention rights,[199] taking account of the jurisprudence (s 2 HRA). In this instance the scrutiny afforded to the proportionality review would be expected to be particularly intense since the expression to be suppressed was political expression.

Possibly—although this is a much more problematic argument—the demands of proportionality could also have been answered to by taking account of the question whether the initial injunction was over-broad, and by affording greater weight to the requirement of s 12(3) that a temporary injunction should not be issued in the original proceedings for breach of confidence unless the plaintiff is *likely* to succeed at final trial.[200] Where it is arguable that the initial injunction is either over-broad or unlikely to be sustained at final trial, it could be contended that criminal liability should not be imposed since the initial injunction either should not have been granted or should have been granted in narrower terms. The likelihood that the injunction would eventually be sustained was hardly touched on by Lord Nicholls; had it been, the 'public interest' test under the breach of confidence doctrine[201] and the effects of Article 10 at the final trial could have been taken into account. In other words, since the material had public interest value, it was arguable that the injunction would not be likely to be sustained since the material would have been published in the public interest. The taking of this stance in relation to the initial granting of the injunction takes into account the effect of Article 10 as applied under s 12(4) and s 6(1) HRA. But it asks courts to dispute the judgment of another court outside the context of an appeal, something they are clearly very reluctant to do. But the

[198] It is in fact arguable that if the first party violated an injunction as indicated, it could be punished under the law of criminal contempt in the sense that it had interfered with the administration of justice in the proceedings against itself, but since the civil sanction is available, this sanction is not used in such circumstances *A-G v Punch* [2003] 1 AC 1046, at paras 114–120.

[199] The position is more complex where both parties are private; for discussion see Chapter 3 at 124–44.

[200] See *Cream Holdings v Bannerjee* [2005] 1 AC 253—the test 'likely to succeed' was taken to mean normally 'more likely than not', departing from the *American Cyanamid* doctrine. For further discussion, see Chapter 15 at 807–8.

[201] See, in a different context, discussion of the test in Chapter 15 at 780–800.

alternative is to expect the media to apply to the Attorney General to have injunctions varied, something that—it appears—they will only be able to do if the original order makes provision for such applications,[202] and an avenue that the Court of Appeal saw in any event as amounting almost to executive vetting and censorship. Where the original order made no such provision there would appear to be a strong case for asking the court in contempt proceedings to take account of the over-breadth of the original order.

In so far as some protection for the rights of litigants in this context is needed, it would often be available under liability for contempt for aiding and abetting a breach of an order by the person against whom the order was made. That form of liability would be preferable in terms of media freedom since the area of liability would be narrower. Proceedings could be brought only where there was a direct connection between the party subject to the interim order and the third party. Such proceedings could have been brought in respect of the facts of the *Punch* case itself, although not in respect of those in the *Spycatcher* case. In so far as the *Spycatcher* doctrine is of value in preserving national security, whether that is viewed as an indirect or direct effect of its application, such liability would also provide protection against disclosures that might harm national security, and of course liability could also arise under s 5 of the Official Secrets Act 1989.[203] The Attorney General could merely seek injunctions against each media body separately on grounds of breach of confidence if it seemed likely that it would publish the material in question. Thus the continuance of this form of liability overlaps in most instances with other possible remedies or sanctions.

The net result of the House of Lords' ruling is that the *Spycatcher* contempt principle has been re-affirmed, unchanged, in the HRA era. The cursory treatment of the HRA is perhaps the most interesting aspect of the ruling. It had little impact on the reasoning and none on the outcome. The immense implications of the *Spycatcher* contempt principle for media freedom went largely unrecognized in the Lords' findings. Those findings mean that the whole of the media can continue to be threatened with a criminal sanction for an indefinite period of time—a period that could well exceed one year—as a result of civil proceedings for an interim injunction within which media third parties are not represented. The contrast with other leading cases on journalistic speech, such as *Reynolds*,[204] discussed in Chapter 21,[205] is particularly striking in this regard; in that case the central point was to mark out discussion of important public affairs in the media, as deserving of special protection under the common law and the European Convention because of its vital role in maintaining a democratic society.

---

[202] Arguably a third party could invoke s 7(1)(a) HRA as a route to seek variation of the original order. A third party could also seek permission to publish some of the material covered by the injunction (see *A-G v Observer Ltd, Re An Application by Derbyshire CC* [1988] 1 All ER 385), but of course this would be likely to be denied since such publication would amount to the actus reus of common law contempt unless a minimal amount of confidential material was included.

[203] For discussion of s 5 see Chapter 19 at 934–5.   [204] [1999] 4 All ER 609.

[205] See pp 1076–86.

The value of the speech in question was hardly touched upon in the rulings. The rich Strasbourg jurisprudence on political speech was not referred to. The Lords managed to decide the case without mentioning one Strasbourg precedent. A clear preference for referring to UK precedents decided post-HRA, such as *R v Shayler*,[206] was evinced. Free speech jurisprudence on the matter from other jurisdictions played no part in the decision. The approach of their Lordships in general was so narrow and blind to the free speech values at stake, that the judgment as a whole cannot but leave an advocate of such values with a sense of strong unease. Despite the inception of the HRA, their reasoning proceeded largely on the basis of an orthodox approach to an analysis of the common law with a brief nod in the direction of Article 10.

This is essentially not only a minimalist but a defensive approach to the HRA. Under this approach a case is decided by reference to established common law principle. The outcome is then checked briefly against HRA standards in order to ensure that incompatibility with the relevant Convention right is not clearly manifest. If a reasonable person could come to the conclusion that compatibility has been achieved, that appears to be sufficient. This approach compares strikingly with that taken in *Simms*[207] and *Reynolds*,[208] decided prior to the inception of the HRA. In those decisions, freedom of expression, both as a common law 'constitutional right' and as embodied in Article 10 of the Convention, was 'the starting point' of legal reasoning.[209] *Reynolds* included extensive citation and consideration of relevant Convention jurisprudence.[210] The values underpinning freedom of expression in general, and those particularly engaged by the instant case were identified; in *Simms* the demands of freedom of expression were treated as the touchstone by which the legality of subordinate legislation was to be assessed, and were found to demand a reading of it which ran clearly counter to its literal meaning. The explicit treatment of the free speech dimension in *Punch* was one which sought its marginalization. Lord Hope made token references to it, although there was no consideration of Strasbourg jurisprudence, despite the fact that a number of relevant cases were cited to their Lordships in argument—again a sharp contrast with the approach of the House of Lords in the leading pre-HRA free speech cases.

Lord Nicholls appeared to be uninterested in the Convention and the HRA—the latter was mentioned only once in a lengthy speech of 63 paragraphs. He claimed that his view of the law was not inconsistent with Article 10 since paragraph 2 provides exceptions to the right, but he made little attempt to apply the Article 10(2) tests; he stated that third parties 'must' respect the rule of law—i.e. the effect of an interim injunction against another party—but, as pointed out above, he did not subject this contention to a Convention-based analysis, by establishing a pressing social need

---

[206] [2003] 1 AC 247; see further Chapter 19 at 939–45.   [207] [1999] 3 All ER 400.

[208] [1999] 4 All ER 609.

[209] See *Ex Parte Simms* [1999] 3 All ER 400, at 407, *per* Lord Steyn and at 412, *per* Lord Hoffman (referring to 'fundamental rights' generally); *Reynolds* [1999] 4 All ER 609, at 629, *per* Lord Steyn.

[210] (1999) 4 All ER 609, at 621–622, *per* Lord Nicholls, at 628 and esp 635, *per* Lord Steyn, at 643, *per* Lord Cooke.

to enforce such respect and by considering the demands of proportionality. Lord Hoffman similarly showed a marked unwillingness to engage with the HRA and the Article 10(2) tests, merely remarking that 'national security is a well-established exception to the freedom conferred by Article 10.' However, the pertinent exception in question was that relating to 'maintaining the authority of the judiciary' if, as their Lordships were contending, the purpose of the injunction was to preserve the right of the Attorney-General to have an effective hearing of the final injunction rather than to safeguard national security. So the wrong exception was identified and in any event, the well-established status of the exception is beside the point; since it is expressly mentioned in Article 10(2) it is clearly 'well established'; the question was whether in the circumstances it was necessary to achieve the end of maintaining the authority of the judiciary by continuing the *Spycatcher* doctrine and, in the instant case, by imposing liability for contempt on Mr Steen.

This superficial approach to Article 10 was applied also to the HRA itself. Lord Hoffman's approach echoed that of all the other Law Lords, in ignoring the question of the *content* of the courts' duty under s 6 HRA when developing the common law. Section 12 was also ignored by Lords Nicholls and Hoffman and this was all the more remarkable since Lord Hoffman did embark on some consideration of the effect of *American Cyanamid*, a decision which has been superseded by s 12(3) HRA.[211] Although this was a case with the gravest of implications for media freedom, consideration of the meaning and effect of s 12(4)[212] played no part in the majority of the speeches. Lord Hope merely repeated the words of the statute in noting that s 12(4) demands that particular regard should be had to freedom of expression. He did not consider whether this adds anything to the duty the court is already under due to s 6 to apply Article 10. He was content to find that s 12(4) and Article 10 had been satisfied since 'the restriction on the publication of the information before trial can be justified as being in the public interest in a democratic society.' He gave some consideration to proportionality, as discussed above, but none to necessity or to the particular 'public interest' involved. It is now reasonably clear that s 12(4) is being treated judicially either as a means of drawing other Convention rights into consideration in private law cases or—as far as the demand to have particular regard to Article 10 in its opening words are concerned—as an unnecessary and superfluous reminder of the effect of Article 10.[213] Since s 6 covers both effects in any event, the latter stance is probably the correct one. In other words, in essence s 12(4) is being found—in effect—to add nothing to the demands of Article 10 and s 6 combined. However, at the time of deciding *Punch* one would have expected their Lordships to

---

[211] See *Douglas v Hello!* [2001] QB 967. It is now clear after the House of Lords' decision in *Cream Holdings v Bannerjee* [2005] 1 AC 253; [2004] 3 WLR 918 that s12(3) raised the bar for awarding an injunction—the test is that the injunction is more likely than not to be awarded at final trial; for further discussion, see Chapter 15 at 807–8.

[212] S12(4) provides that the court must have 'particular regard' to the importance of Article 10. For full citation of the sub-section and further discussion, see Chapter 3 at 131–2.

[213] See Chapter 16 at 836–8.

consider the question whether s 12(4) could have had any significant impact in the instant case. Having marginalized s 12(4), they proceeded in effect to do the same with Article 10. Whatever s 12(4) means, this stance appears to represent the converse of the intention behind it.

Their Lordships were content with the idea that while the right of freedom of expression and the public's right to know are of great importance, their exercise can on one view be subject in effect to the dictat of the Attorney General. Freedom of expression under Article 10 is subject to exceptions to be narrowly construed. It must be questioned whether the scope of the exception re-affirmed in this case can be viewed as narrow. In terms of the acceptance or non-recognition of the anomalies created and the likelihood that in many instances, once an interim injunction is obtained, the material in question will lose its newsworthiness, their Lordships showed no awareness of the practical realities of media freedom. Not only does this approach display a characteristically exaggerated attachment to the value of the right to bring litigation, it also exemplifies the tendency of English judicial reasoning to assume a narrow and technical basis, abstracted from any meaningful context.

CONCLUSIONS

The effect on third parties of the *Spycatcher* doctrine flows from findings in hearings for interim relief in which the burden on the Attorney-General is not weighty, as discussed in Chapter 19.[214] Bearing in mind the relative ease with which such relief may be granted—despite the effect of s 12(3)HRA[215]—it must be questioned whether this is a satisfactory basis for the consequential far-reaching impact on the media. One unsatisfactory consequence of the continuance of this doctrine has already been pointed out—that third parties who publish information covered by an interim injunction can be subject to a harsher penalty than would be available if the first party published the same information. A further anomaly arises: the litigant who has obtained the interim injunction is thereby placed, in effect, in a more advantageous position than he or she will be in if the final injunction is obtained, since the *Spycatcher* doctrine has been found to cease to have effect once that injunction is granted.[216] In a sense, the litigant who has obtained the interim injunction obtains a very significant benefit, not enjoyed by the litigant who wins the final action, since the whole of the media will be deterred from publication of the confidential material during the period between the interim and the final injunction. In other words, the litigant is worse off after establishing his substantive right to confidentiality at trial. Clearly, in instances in which no final injunction is obtained since the other party—usually a newspaper—does not continue to contest the interim injunction because the information in

---

[214] See pp 950–3.

[215] As mentioned above, note 135, s 12(3) as interpreted in *Cream Holdings and Bannerjee* [2005] 1 AC 253 has raised the bar for the grant of injunctions.

[216] *Jockey Club v Buffham* [2003] 2 WLR 178; [2003] EMLR 5.

question loses its newsworthy quality, a greater anomaly is created because the period of time during which the *Spycatcher* doctrine is applicable is likely to be longer. The applicability of that doctrine in relation to interim but not final injunctions follows logically from the emphasis on preserving the litigant's right to the final hearing of the action. However, if the emphasis was instead on the underlying purpose of the injunction, as the Court of Appeal in *Punch* advocated, it would still be possible in a narrow range of circumstances that a third party could attract liability for criminal contempt by undermining the final order in the sense of negating its purpose in protecting national security by publishing material covered by it. This would be less anomalous than the current position.

This form of common law contempt remains of very doubtful compatibility with Article 10, bearing in mind the emphasis placed upon the role of the media in *Goodwin v UK*[217] by the European Court of Human Rights. Although trivial or technical breaches of court orders made against other parties will not attract liability, the area of liability which remains creates a curb on media freedom which is out of accord with the crucial role of the press in a free society.[218] It is unlikely after *A-G v Punch* that reform can be expected in the domestic courts and therefore it can now only come from Strasbourg or Parliament. If a Strasbourg ruling eventually leads to abolition of this form of common law contempt, certain instances of the *Spycatcher* type could still fall within the statutory strict liability rule, if—which would rarely occur—the hearing of the permanent injunction had been set down at the time of publication. In such instances, however, s 5 would apply; therefore liability might be avoided, depending on a difficult application of the 'incidental' test where the information had public interest value.

For obvious reasons the political will to introduce reform to abolish this head of common law contempt is likely to be absent. From the government perspective the doctrine remains valuable as a means of creating secrecy that is in executive hands in terms of instigation—since in the *Punch* and *Spycatcher* category of case the initial temporary injunction will be sought by the Attorney-General. Having obtained it on the basis of a test satisfied with relative ease, he need do nothing more to ensure that all the rest of the media are silenced on the matter at hand since criminal contempt at common law, after *Punch*, will do the job for him. If reform of this area of contempt eventually occurs as a result of a Strasbourg ruling, it will represent an indictment of the stance of a number of the senior judiciary in relation to a fundamental freedom in a democratic society. *A-G v Punch* is one of the most disappointing rulings there has been so far under the HRA: it represents a judicial acquiescence to the executive's predilection for secrecy, coupled with a determination to cling to anti-speech values reflected in common law doctrine even where they fly in the face of Convention principles.

---

[217] *Goodwin v UK* (1996) 22 EHRR 123.
[218] These issues are discussed further in Chapter 19 at 950–3, in relation to the breach of confidence issue, the other strand of the *Spycatcher* litigation.

EFFICACY OF STATUTORY AND COMMON LAW CONTEMPT IN PROTECTING FREE SPEECH AND FAIR TRIALS

It has been argued in this chapter that contempt law is failing as a means of protecting fair trials, but also that it is not sufficiently effective in protecting freedom of expression. A rarely enforced rule of a high but uncertain threshold such as that under s 2(2) inevitably tends to leave the ultimate responsibility for avoiding unfairness with trial judges. The current division of responsibility, almost inevitable under a partly protective model, between contempt law and trial judges, is deeply problematic. The current position may mean that freedom of expression is not fully protected since the media are uncertain at times whether or not a publication might infringe the imprecisely expressed rule under s 2(2). But at the same time the existence of the rule fails to provide protection for trials. Certain newspapers, especially the less responsible sections of the press, at times engage in reporting at the outer limits of what can be tolerated under s 2(2). They may do so in the knowledge that if a number of newspapers are involved, it may be hard to identify the responsibility of any particular one. Or they may merely take a risk, motivated by determination to maintain commercial advantage, on the basis that the uncertainty of the s 2(2) test (and of the common law test of real risk of prejudice), and the high threshold it appears to represent, make it difficult for a prosecution to succeed and quite probable, therefore, that it will not be undertaken.

The imprecision of the s 2(2) test is exacerbated precisely because the roles of contempt law and of the trial judge overlap. Judges in contempt cases must take account of the likelihood that neutralizing measures will be or have been used. The use of such measures, including directions to the jury, make it hard to determine whether the risk in question at the time of publication still subsisted at the time of trial. Different judges take varying views as to the efficacy of such measures and the ability of the jury to disregard media comment. Thus contempt law is failing to delineate the boundary between the use of protective and of neutralizing measures and it is therefore allowing too much pressure to be placed on the criminal justice system in high profile cases. Possibly that boundary cannot be delineated effectively unless, as discussed below, a far more precise 'protective' test is adopted and preventive measures are used more extensively, accompanied by robust safeguards for media freedom. Most worryingly, parts of the media may rely, not merely on the uncertainty of s 2(2), but on some kind of complicity with the government in relation to their coverage, especially in terrorist cases. The uncertainty of s 2(2), and the high bar it appears to create in practice, clearly aid the Attorney General in justifying refusals to prosecute. As indicated above, such refusals probably do not in any event have to be justified in court.[219]

---

[219] See above note 50 and pp 255–7.

This overview of this form of contempt also gives rise, it is argued, to the conclusion that at present, it is out of accord with Convention values and requirements in terms of both law and practice. Although, as discussed above, its jurisprudence in this context is open to criticism, certain thematic strands can be discerned. As *Worm*, *Ribemont*,[220] *News Verlags*[221] and *Sunday Times* indicate, Strasbourg seeks to protect fair trials where they appear to be genuinely threatened by media coverage. Where the threat is nebulous and the value of the speech in question is high, restraints on the media are not found to be justified. A comparison between the *Taylor*[222] and the *Spycatcher* or *Punch* cases[223] suggests that both statute and common law are insufficiently focused on the core Convention values at stake. In *Taylor*, the individual's right to a fair trial under Article 6 was genuinely threatened; at the same time, the speech in question was of virtually no value in Article 10 terms, since it was misleading. Yet no prosecution was forthcoming. In contrast, *Spycatcher* and *Punch* concerned political speech to which Strasbourg accords the highest value, while in both instances the Article 6 guarantee was only doubtfully engaged. A successful prosecution for contempt in *Taylor* on the basis that the trial in question had been severely affected by relentless and misleading publicity could almost certainly have been justified under Article 10(2) as proportionate, in terms of speech/harm balancing, to the aim pursued—that of protecting the Article 6 rights of the defendants. The reverse is true, it is contended, of both *Spycatcher* and *Punch*.

A possible explanation for current practice in these and other similar instances is that where speech is directly critical of a part of the executive and therefore, impliedly, of government itself, the interests of the government in stifling it are most obviously engaged. Such an instance arose in both *Spycatcher* and *Punch*, arguably providing an example of the failure of Attorney-Generals to ensure that an appearance of distance from the government was maintained. In contrast, as in *Taylor*, when the trial of an obscure personage, accused of a highly publicized crime, is in question, there is little or no political advantage to be gained in seeking to prevent or punish interferences with it. But there may be quite severe political disadvantage in appearing to attack the massed ranks of the tabloids. As indicated above, it is not entirely possible to dismiss misgivings as to the ability of Attorney-Generals to distance themselves fully from their political colleagues, who are likely to have such considerations in mind.

The problems created by the willingness of newspaper proprietors to damage the fairness of trials in pursuit of competitive advantage are likely to continue so long as they view contempt actions as improbable. Certain trials, such as those of the Taylor sisters, of Harold Shipman in 2000, the trial in 2001 of the suspect charged with the murder of the television presenter Jill Dando, the arrest of the terrorist suspects in connection with the Ricin incident in 2003, the trial of Ian Huntley for the Soham murders in 2003 and the arrest of terrorist suspects in July 2005, tend to attract a misleading and sensationalist media coverage, which has, in the case of a number of

---

[220] (1995) 20 EHRR 557. See Chapter 4 at 190–1.   [221] (2001) 31 EHRR 8.
[222] [1993] 98 Cr App R 361. See p 263 above.   [223] See above pp 290–6.

newspapers, little connection with free speech values, but is motivated merely by profit-making concerns. Obviously, horrifying incidents, especially terrorist ones, will be reported in extensive detail using untempered language, but the aim of some of the coverage appears to be to come closest to expressing the baser instincts of readers, however prejudicial to a fair trial such expression might be. Assuming that in the very competitive media market, one newspaper is unlikely to forego the chance of attracting readers by its coverage of such cases, further intervention by Parliament appears to be essential if the criminal justice system and certain deeply unpopular defendants are not to bear the burden created by the demands of the media market.

RELATIONSHIP BETWEEN PREVENTIVE AND PROTECTIVE APPROACHES

This chapter and the previous one have considered the relationship between the preventive and protective approaches under contempt law as currently interpreted. That relationship is exemplified by the demarcation between s 4(2) and s 2(2) of the 1981 Act (although, as indicated in Chapter 5, s 4(2) is not the only relevant provision). Section 4(2) allows for orders restraining fair and accurate reports of proceedings on the basis that a substantial risk of serious prejudice would otherwise be created. But it does not provide a mechanism for restraining biased and unfair reporting that might create that risk. Restraints on such reporting are supposed to be created by the deterrent effect of s 2(2). This is an anomalous and unsatisfactory position since it means that fair and accurate reports of proceedings can be subject to prior restraint, despite attracting the highest level of protection under Article 10, since all the free speech rationales are engaged, and such reporting is supported also by the open justice principle. In contrast, as argued in the introduction to Chapter 4, partial, unfair and distorted reporting is, axiomatically, unsupported by that principle and only lightly by those rationales. Yet it is subject to post-publication sanctions only which are arguably close to unworkable and are not consistently applied. At the same time the research considered suggests that certain pieces of information reported in the media at certain points in the trial process are likely to cause prejudice. The Strasbourg case-law discussed—in particular *Ribemont* and *Worm v Austria*—suggests that the introduction of further neutralizing measures, as opposed to further preventive measures, might not satisfy the demands of Article 6, and that Strasbourg is content with a preventive approach so long as the demands of Article 10 are also met. Where the two guarantees genuinely clash, Article 6 will prevail.

In domestic law at present, anomalously, the Article 10 guarantee receives greater recognition in relation to post-publication sanctions than it does in relation to prior restraints. This point is exemplified by comparing *ex parte Telegraph Group Plc*[224]—on a s 4(2) order—with *A-G v English* or *A-G v Times*[225] in relation to s 2(2) and s 5. In *ex parte Telegraph Group*, once it was found that a fair trial was genuinely threatened, it

---

[224] [2001] EMLR 10.   [225] *The Times*, 12 February 1983.

was decided that the order had to be sought. This stance does not comport well with the findings in *A-G v Times* since even where it was found that the fairness of the trial was threatened by the reporting, it was also found that a sanction did not need to be applied due to the free speech argument under s 5. The two decisions taken together make it clear that in making s 4(2) orders Article 6 takes priority over Article 10, but that in applying the strict liability rule, *Article 10* can prevail. The stance under s 4(2), but not that under the strict liability rule, appears to be in accordance with the Convention jurisprudence.

PROPOSED REFORMS

It is argued therefore that the relationship between the preventive and protective approaches should be re-visited with a view to reform. At present there are no governmental plans for a radical reform. Some of the political reasons why the government might be unreceptive to reform have already been explored. Therefore consideration must be given as to what can be done with the tools to hand—the strict liability rule as interpreted under s 3(1) HRA. The sole tool to be employed in most instances is the rule since liability under the common law is almost always ruled out by the requirement to prove intention. As discussed above, it would be possible to argue that the threshold of the test under s 2(2) should be modified and clarified in accordance with the findings in *Worm*. At the same time s 5, given a broad interpretation, could take on the role of a proportionality test in order to seek to ensure that some valuable speech could escape liability. The statute could therefore be re-balanced in a manner that would focus it more closely on the true issues at stake. Arguably, if combined with reform of the initiation of contempt actions—taking them out of the hands of the Attorney General—prejudice created by unbridled accusations of guilt aimed at defendants in high profile terrorist or criminal trials could be curbed. Near-worthless, trial-impairing speech would be caught,[226] while speech genuinely in the public interest could escape under s 5. Although at first sight the creation of a risk of prejudice to trials by speech that is in the public interest does not appear to be accord with the demands of Article 6, the potential effect of neutralizing measures should also be taken into account in relation to the demands of proportionality under a reconfigured s 5, in terms of speech/harm balancing. Moreover, as the discussion reveals, it is not normally reporting that has public interest value that poses the greatest threat to fair trials.

The use or threat of criminal sanctions need not be the only means of preventing prejudice to trials. As discussed above, it would be possible to increase the use of injunctions against the media, pre-trial, under the strict liability rule, as contemplated in *A-G v MGN*[227] and under the Supreme Court Act s 37(1) by the House of Lords in

---

[226] See the example of the *Sun*'s coverage of the arrests for the attempted terrorist bombing in July 2005, note 155 above.

[227] [1997] 1 All ER 456. See above pp 261–3.

Pickering v Associated Newspapers Holdings Plc[228] (and under s 45(4) SCA in *HTV Cymru (Wales) Ltd).*[229] The problem is that at present reliance would have to be placed on the Attorney General to initiate actions for injunctions. The media would be able to challenge the orders made under s 5 interpreted consistently with Article 10.

The modifications of the strict liability rule proposed would allow it to take on a more preventive role and would therefore ease the strain on the criminal justice system, since the need to adopt neutralizing measures would become less pressing. Such a change would mean not only that fair trials received more effective protection, but that political expression, as opposed to misleading coverage of trials, also received greater protection.

The judicial willingness to undertake such a modification of the strict liability rule under s 3(1) HRA may be present on the basis that ensuring the fairness of trials is clearly within the judicial domain. They view that area as peculiarly within their purview; it includes the fields of sentencing and the admissibility of evidence, where they have been most proactive under s 3(1).[230] Clearly, the media would view such a change as problematic and it is fair to say that it is flawed in that newspapers might find themselves hampered in their coverage of a forthcoming trial due to the presence of orders disallowing the reporting of certain matters relating to it. For this reason it would be preferable to undertake the full reform discussed below. But since the injunctions as prior restraints would have to be strictly scrutinized for compliance with Article 10, it could be expected—perhaps optimistically—that only those matters, such as publication of previous convictions, that have been shown by the relevant research to pose a genuine risk to the fairness of the trial, would be restrained.

However, although there are signs that the judges (on occasion) consider that the strict liability rule can be used directly to *prevent* prejudice, it is clear that it is not really suitable for the job due to its imprecision—even after reinterpretation. There is a strong argument therefore for repealing the provisions governing the strict liability rule and introducing a new statute. It is contended that under it an overtly *preventive* but narrowly defined approach should be adopted. The underlying rationale would be that media freedom should be preserved as far as possible, but that the main responsibility for preventing the most specific and pernicious forms of prejudice to trials should rest with the new provisions, not the trial judge, although neutralizing measures could also be used. The new provisions should be based fully on recent research into the impact of media activity on jurors and others.

Three possible forms of restraint are suggested: automatic bans on publication; discretionary orders restraining the publication of certain material; trial participants could also be banned from releasing potentially damaging information in the first place.[231] The possibility of prescribing specific items of information that have been

---

[228] [1991] 2 AC 370; [1991] 1 All ER 622. See Chapter 5 at 216–17. [229] [2002] EMLR 11.

[230] See *R v A* [2002] 1 AC 45 and *R v Offen* [2001] 1 WLR 253.

[231] See J. Armstrong Brandwood, 'You Say "Fair Trial" and I Say "Free Press": British and American approaches to protecting defendants' rights in high profile trials' [2000] 75 *New York University Law Review* 1412, pp 1446–7.

shown to be most damaging by the research was suggested by the Australian Law Reform Commission in 1987.[232] Clearly, the introduction of further prior restraints is not something that should be undertaken lightly—the media already consider that their reporting of trials is unduly tramelled by the incrementally increasing introduction of such restraints, especially in relation to juveniles, as discussed in Chapter 16.[233] At present prior restraint is available under the doctrine of common law contempt to protect the rights of litigants in breach of confidence cases, but it is not—in a broad sense—available to restrain prejudicial reporting. There are practical difficulties. It might be hard to frame an injunction precisely enough and its use might suggest that other closely similar reporting would not attract sanctions. But, as discussed above, bans on the reporting of certain specific items of information, including inadmissible material, and—where prejudice might otherwise occur—names of witnesses or defendants, would be feasible. The post-HRA instances in *A-G v Express*[234] in which disclosure of the potential defendants' identity occurred despite pleas from the Attorney-General to the media to preserve their anonymity, would provide an example of the kind of material that could be covered. It is unclear that broad prior restraints should be available in relation to confidentiality but not in order to prevent prejudice to trials. The one value is surely as important as the other.

Automatic bans would require that certain, listed, matters, such as the defendant's previous convictions and other inadmissible material, could not be published for a short period pre-trial or during the trial. Further, at pre-trial hearings trial judges should be able to impose bans on coverage likely to mislead the jury as to a key issue in the trial (such as that in *Taylor*), meaning that such material could not be published for a certain period of time before and during the trial. The new 'active' periods should take into account the unlikelihood that media coverage would affect jurors over a period of months. The media would be provided with an avenue of challenge to both forms of restraint in particular instances where disclosure of the matter in question would be in the public interest, despite the risk to the trial. Special rules would have to be introduced for websites since trial-related material might have been posted on a site at a much earlier point. The limitations of a *domestic* statute in the context of web-based material would, however, have to be recognized.[235] So long as the banning provisions were tightly defined they would be compatible with Article 10, following the decisions in *News Verlags* and *Worm v Austria*.

If such legislative reforms were undertaken, the possibility of creating prejudice to proceedings by reporting would of course still remain. There are an infinite variety of ways of creating such prejudice—especially in the modern media environment—and clearly many of them are too unpredictable to be caught by prior restraints. In order to avoid the introduction of ever-broader automatic bans, the neutralizing measure of

---

[232] Australian Law Reform Commission (1987) *Contempt* no 35.   [233] See pp 813–15.

[234] [2005] EMLR 13. See above pp 271–2.

[235] Walker argues that websites and new technology cannot entirely be controlled via current laws—what is needed is governance—trans-frontier regulation such as European-based multi-lateral treaties: C. Walker, 'Fundamental Rights, Fair Trials and the New Audio-Visual Sector' [1996] 59 *MLR* 517.

jury selection and screening on the US model could also be adopted. The idea would be to insulate the jury, not the public, from the trial-related information and reporting. This idea is in particular driven by the inception of the Internet and satellite television. In fact jury screening is used in Britain—but infrequently[236]—and the Court of Appeal has recently said that juries should not be questioned about the incident which is the subject matter of the trial.[237] This appears to be a matter for Parliament, but, clearly, selection and screening could be used, not only in relation to empanelling the jurors,[238] but also in relation to ordering retrials. For example, in the *Sunday Mirror* case[239] the jurors could merely have been asked if they had read the offending *Sunday Mirror* article. If none of them had read it the trial need not have been aborted. This is not an argument for the introduction of neutralizing measures *as opposed* to preventive ones. It is an argument for a more effective use of such measures in specific instances where preventive measures have failed—or were in any event inapt—to prevent prejudice. The use of neutralizing measures on the US model does not appear to prevent prejudice, as discussed above, and the nature of the UK media, especially the tabloid section of it, with its market-driven predilection for partial, intense, unremitting and sensationalist coverage of high profile trials, makes it highly unlikely that neutralizing measures would be any more effective here.

The form of common law contempt reaffirmed in *A-G v Punch* remains a serious anomaly; it should be abolished by a new statute on the basis that it does not, as argued above, satisfy the test of proportionality under Article 10(2). As discussed, it creates in effect a wide-ranging form of prior restraint. If the media is to be restrained in this broad fashion, it is suggested that Parliament should consider the strength of the principle that is being given such effective protection. Consideration should be given instead to introducing a statutory test which would reflect that put forward by the Court of Appeal in *Punch*. The common law test of intentionally prejudicing proceedings should be abolished as unworkably imprecise as a test for criminal liability and as serving no useful purpose, except in relation to the placing of undue pressure on litigants as in *A-G v Hislop*.[240] The requirement of intention should be retained but the test should focus specifically on the degree of pressure that is unacceptable. A statutory public interest test should apply both to the new 'pressurising' test and to the narrower residual *Spycatcher* doctrine of liability.

If no reforms are undertaken, either by the judiciary using the HRA or by Parliament, the result is likely to be a continuance of the shift from protective to neutralizing measures. Section 2(2) is likely to be viewed, increasingly, as unworkable and ineffective, thereby throwing further and further responsibility onto trial judges and creating greater strain on the criminal justice system. The argument would tend then to veer

[236] In the Maxwell case (*R v Maxwell*, 25 May 1995 (unreported)) the jurors were questioned extensively about their attitudes and selection was based on the questioning.

[237] *R v Andrews (Tracey)* [1999] Crim LR 156.

[238] See D. Corker and M. Levi, 'Pre-trial Publicity and its Treatment in the English Courts' [1996] *Crim LR* 622, pp 628–9.

[239] Note 108 above.   [240] [1991] 1 QB 514; [1991] 1 All ER 911.

towards the possibility that Britain should move over more overtly to a neutralizing stance as in the US. These two chapters have sought to suggest that while that would be an entirely unwelcome development, the current situation is unsatisfactory. The reforms suggested here are intended to refocus contempt law on the values at stake in a movement away from the currently unfocused protective stance. The intention is not to advocate a slavish adherence to the Strasbourg jurisprudence—its imprecision fails in any event to lend itself to such adherence—but to achieve a protection for fair trial values under Article 6 which creates a minimal impairment of expression, taking into account its role in underpinning the open justice principle. The approach advocated is a nuanced one, which refuses to assume that all trial-related speech is worthy of full protection, or that prejudice to trials is readily created.

7

PROTECTION OF
JOURNALISTIC SOURCES

INTRODUCTION — VALUE OF PROTECTING SOURCES

FREE SPEECH VALUES AND SOURCE PROTECTION — NATIONAL AND INTERNATIONAL RECOGNITION

As the Strasbourg Court put it in the seminal case of *Goodwin v UK*: 'Protection of journalistic sources is one of the basic conditions for press freedom'.[1] It is readily apparent that informed journalism depends crucially on the use of sources. An 'insider' — someone working in or associated with the concern to be reported upon — usually provides the best and most effective source of information. As Lord Denning has put it: '[the journalist] can expose wrong-doing and neglect of duty which would otherwise go unremedied . . . the mouths of his informants will be closed to him if it is known that their identity will be disclosed. .'.[2] These remarks were, ironically, made in considering the entitlement journalists would wish to put forward to avoid source disclosure, before denying that they possessed any such privilege at common law. In various jurisdictions this dependency of journalists on sources is recognized in laws sometimes known as journalistic 'shield laws' or source protection laws. They are laws that shield the identity of sources by giving journalists qualified immunities in criminal and other proceedings allowing them to refuse to answer questions that would lead to revealing the identity of a source. This chapter sets out to subject all the stages in a source disclosure case to an intense Human Rights Act analysis in order to seek to determine the extent to which source protection now exists in the UK.

There are a number of instances documented in this book in which it is argued that the promotion of media freedom is opposed to free speech values.[3] This chapter argues that the protection of journalistic sources is not one of them, if the protection of sources is viewed against the backdrop of the public interest in receiving truthful information.[4] As this chapter indicates, it is generally accepted in democracies by commentators and by courts that the protection of sources is vital to the watchdog

---

[1] (1996) 22 EHRR 123, at [39].   [2] *A-G v Mulholland and Foster* [1963] 2 QB 477 at 489.
[3] See Chapter 4 at 170–5 and Chapter 16 at 844–53.
[4] See *Society of Professional Journalists: Ethical Code* (1996), note 10 below.

role of journalists. Where the media exposes institutional or executive malpractice it performs a significant constitutional role, and when it reveals corporate wrong-doing it can play a very important part in creating corporate accountability. In general, therefore, the speech generated is of great value in a democracy and is viewed as of the first importance within Article 10 ECHR. But such speech is highly dependant on receiving information from sources. Thus in this instance the link between speech of the highest value in public interest terms and an aspect of media freedom is very strong. As discussed in Chapter 19 there is now a Freedom of Information Act in the UK. But private companies are not covered by it unless, exceptionally, they are performing services contracted out by public authorities. Although public authorities are covered, the type of information that has been disclosed in the past would often tend to be covered by one of the many exceptions in the new FoI Act.[5]

Having suggested that source protection is largely in harmony with free speech values, it is necessary to look somewhat more closely at that argument. Information deriving from sources is not *intrinsically* of any greater value than information obtained by other means. Sources, especially those linked to government, may have their own agenda; this may also be true of corporate sources. Source-based information may consist of a slanted mixture of substance and disinformation. The government may well wish to leak information into the public domain for a range of purposes, such as that of 'smearing' political opponents or those whose published opinions run counter to an important aspect of government policy. It is suggested below that the well-known US *Judith Miller* case in 2005,[6] linked to the 'evidence' of WMD justifying the war in Iraq, may provide an example of the latter tendency of governments. In that instance it appeared that Miller's source had leaked information to her deliberately designed to discredit an insider who had challenged evidence of Saddam Hussein's possession of WMD. Clearly, the Bush administration wanted to rely on that evidence in order to justify the war in Iraq. Therefore the administration had a strong motivation to leak information to journalists that in some way aided in its attempts to justify its stance on the war. Miller was eventually found to be in contempt of court when she refused to reveal her sources. This was not an instance— it appeared—in which a journalist was acting to protect her source in order to serve the public interest, but one in which such protection led to the promulgation of misinformation and so was opposed to that interest. On the other hand, Miller went to prison rather than reveal her source, sending a general message to sources about journalists' commitment to their ethical code.

Chapter 1 argues that one of the most influential justifications for free speech

---

[5] See further Chapter 19 at 969–85. For example, in *Ashworth* (note 48 below) the data could not have been obtained by a third party because so doing would have contravened the Data Protection Principles under the Data Protection Act 1998 (see s 40 Freedom of Information Act 2000).

[6] *Judith Miller, Petitioner v US and M Cooper and Time inc, Petitioners v US*, Supreme Court (2005) No 04–1508; opinion of the court of appeals (Miller Pet. App. 1a–77a; Cooper Pet. App. 1a–85a) is reported at 397 F.3d 964. The case is discussed further below.

arises from the part it plays in furthering democratic principles and values[7]—citizens can only participate fully in a democracy if they have a reasonable understanding of political issues. This argument supports source protection in so far as it leads to the furthering of public knowledge as to government policy and political issues generally. But, clearly, where source protection leads to the promulgation of misinformation it runs counter to that argument. The same could be said of the underpinning provided by the argument from truth, associated with J S Mill.[8] Mill's argument can be used to support claims for freedom of information, since the possession of pertinent information about a subject will nearly always be a prerequisite to engagement in ongoing debates. Mill considered that in the market-place of ideas truth would win out.[9] But if the background information informing the formation of ideas is incorrect, this process may be hampered. Thus the participation of source protection in free speech protection must be viewed with a degree of caution since it may not inevitably harmonize with key free speech rationales. Ultimately, the questions involved are a matter of balancing journalistic ethics that are unlikely to see the inside of a court room. Journalists have a duty to their sources but their ultimate duty is to the public. If the sources provide flawed, 'spun' information, or straightforward disinformation, it would appear to accord with journalistic ethics to challenge it and probe it. Such ethics demand that, if necessary, they should be prepared to reveal an untrustworthy or manipulative source, or at the least disassociate themselves from such a source and repudiate the information.[10] This chapter is, however, about the application of the law and the Human Rights Act in particular. It may well be the case that the most difficult struggles with ethical issues for journalists will not be played out in the arena of a court. But when these matters do come to light in the form of litigation, the extent to which free speech values are truly at stake must be probed, and it is argued below that the proportionality test under Article 10(2) provides a reasonably effective tool as the means of doing so.

So it may be concluded that while there is a harmony of interests between free speech and source protection, it must not be viewed uncritically. Source protection has received a fairly high degree of national and international recognition in terms of statutory protection and judicial decisions. But in certain jurisdictions such

---

[7] See Chapter 1 at 16–18.

[8] J.S. Mill, *On Liberty*, in M. Cowling (ed.), *Selected Writings of John Stuart Mill*, London: Everyman, 1972. See further Chapter 1 at 14–16.

[9] See Chapter 1 at 14.

[10] Extracts from *Society of Professional Journalists: Ethical Code* (1996), from website spj.org/ethics_code. asp: journalists should:

Test the accuracy of information from all sources and exercise care to avoid inadvertent error. Deliberate distortion is never permissible.

Identify sources whenever feasible. The public is entitled to as much information as possible on sources' reliability.

Always question sources' motives before promising anonymity. Clarify conditions attached to any promise made in exchange for information. Keep promises.

Journalists should be free of obligation to any interest other than the public's right to know.

Be wary of sources offering information for favors or money; avoid bidding for news.

protection may be viewed more as a journalistic privilege than an aspect of a free speech claim. An acceptance of a harmony of interest between the two can be found at the international level. Article 10 includes the right to receive and impart information, as does Article 19(2) ICCPR. Article 19 expressly includes the right to *seek* information; that right is not clearly implicit in Article 10,[11] but it is clear that Article 10 covers source protection—it was viewed as of the first importance in securing the role of a free media in the Strasbourg case of *Goodwin v UK*.[12]

The statement of principle from *Goodwin* was recently re-stated in the current leading UK domestic decision of *Ashworth*.[13] In the US the value of source protection is also recognized, but not as a free speech claim. The Supreme Court found in *Branzburg*[14] that the First Amendment does not confer protection for sources. *Cohen v Cowles Media Co.*[15] cited *Branzburg* for the proposition:

the First Amendment [does not] relieve a newspaper reporter of the obligation shared by all citizens to respond to a grand jury subpoena and answer questions relevant to a criminal investigation, even though the reporter might be required to reveal a confidential source.

The *Branzburg* rule was recently confirmed in the *Judith Miller* case.[16] However, statutory protective or 'shield' laws for journalists had been enacted by some states prior to the *Branzburg* decision and more were enacted by a number of states and by Congress after it. Thus the US takes the stance that source protection is not synonymous with speech; instead it can be viewed as a 'background' right. The situation in Australia is fairly similar; there is still no national Bill of Rights, so the issue of formal constitutional protection for sources does not arise, but some Australian state legislatures have enacted so-called 'shield laws', recognizing more or less limited rights to confidentiality.[17] In contrast, there are currently, no 'shield' laws in Canada that protect journalists. If a journalist does not comply with a court order to divulge the identity of a confidential source, the journalist can be faced with legal charges, including the threat of jail.[18] It appears then that in the US and Australia, in contrast to the ECHR stance, there is a significant doubt as to the harmony of interests between free speech and source protection. Source protection in these states appears to be seen as a journalistic privilege, not viewed as worthy of the high levels of protection accorded to speech, despite the linkage between the two.

---

[11] See the discussion of this point in Chapter 2 at 44–5.

[12] (1996) 22 EHRR 123. See also Recommendation No. R (2000) 7 of the Committee of Ministers to Member States on the right of journalists not to disclose their sources of information, adopted on 8 March 2000, Principle 4.

[13] [2002] 4 All ER 193.

[14] See *Branzburg v Hayes* 408 US 665 (1972) in which the Supreme Court made this finding.

[15] 501 U.S. 663, 669 (1991).   [16] Note 6 above. The case is discussed further below.

[17] See further W. Bacon and C. Nash, 'Confidential Sources and the Public Right to Know', 1999: *Australian Journalism Review*, Vol 21(2), August, pp 1–26.

[18] See the Report *Investigative Journalism and the State* by G. Cho, available online at journalism. ryerson.ca/online/scribe/smack/schofeature.htm.

SOURCE PROTECTION AND THE ROLE OF THE MEDIA

If a journalist's ability to promise a source that anonymity will be protected is infringed, with the result that the source declines to pass on information, the journalist's right to receive information has been impaired, and as a consequence so has the right of the readers of the newspaper, since reporting of a particular story is likely to be curbed or prevented. Recognizing that the protection of sources serves a vital function in relation to the role of the media, journalists view themselves as morally obliged to protect the identity of their sources, a principle that is recognized worldwide in various press codes.[19] It is stated in paragraph 15 of the UK Press Commission Code;[20] while the Code of Conduct of the UK National Union of Journalists states: 'A journalist shall protect confidential sources of information'. The US *Society of Professional Journalists: Ethical Code* states that journalists should keep promises to sources but adds: 'Always question sources' motives before promising anonymity. Clarify conditions attached to any promise made in exchange for information'.[21]

The sources of the information are often insiders—employees of the concern in question—since they are best placed to be aware of malpractice. They may be motivated by conscience in the sense that they feel that they can no longer stand by and allow the practice in question to continue unchecked. They may view publicity and resulting public awareness as the first step on the road to creating such a check. Or they may have much more doubtful motives, but may nevertheless provide valuable information to journalists that has a public interest dimension. If sources do not believe that their identity will be protected they will not normally cooperate with journalists, or contact them, and therefore the most potent source of information, that of a person who is, in some sense, an 'insider', will be denied to the media and therefore to the public. As Lord Woolf put it in *John and Others v Express Newspapers Limited and Others*:[22]

The reason for the rule [that the identity of sources should not be disclosed] is that it is vitally important, if the press is to perform its public function in our democracy, that a person possessed of information on matters of public interest should not be deterred from coming forward by fear of exposure. To encourage such disclosures, it is necessary to offer a thorough protection to confidential sources generally.

A Canadian journalist, Stevie Cameron, put this very tellingly after she had been fined for refusing to disclose a source:

---

[19] See *Databank for European Codes of Journalism Ethics*. Press Codes in European Countries differ quite significantly as to the extent to which source protection is mentioned explicitly. The German Press Code explicitly enjoins the protection of sources, in Article 5. The French and Swedish Codes are more general and do not cover source protection specifically, although the French Code speaks of maintaining professional secrecy.

[20] 'Journalists have a moral obligation to protect confidential sources of information.' For further comment on the Code, see Chapter 14 at 708–9. Clearly, the promise of confidentiality is not always kept: see K.M. Kase, Note, 'When a Promise is Not a Promise: The Legal Consequences for Journalists Who Break Promises of Confidentiality to Sources', 12 *Hastings Comm. & Ent. L.J.* 565, 576–577 (1990).

[21] See note 10 above.   [22] [2000] 1 WLR 1931; [2000] 3 All ER 257.

We don't live in a free and open society when it comes to investigative reporting, especially with regard to government corruption or white collar crime involving powerful people, organizations or companies. . . . They are not inclined to be open because they are threatened by the disclosure of information.

She concluded that many Canadian journalists end up killing stories because the protection they receive is very slight, 'while the consequences of facing expensive lawsuits and offending powerful people are all too severe'.[23] If the courts are readily able to force journalists to reveal their sources, a promise to keep his or her identity secret to a source from a journalist would be an empty one. Journalists would be likely to want to adhere to their ethical code, but would often be unable to do so while running investigative stories based on source disclosure. Dropping the story would tend to be the only viable option, as is clearly sometimes the case in Canada. In the UK the courts can, in certain circumstances, seek to force journalists to reveal sources. This ability places journalists in an extremely difficult position since they are then faced with a choice between the imposition of a sanction or a breach of the promise to the source. Clearly, the difficulty of the position depends in part on the nature of the sanction. Journalists have been prepared to go to prison rather than reveal a source, but clearly the prospect of a custodial sentence increases the likelihood that stories reliant on confidential sources may be 'killed'.

It is clear from everything that has been said so far that there are two issues at stake here. First, and most importantly, there is the argument that if sources do not believe that their identity will be secure, they will be reluctant to come forward. If a source is aware that the courts may seek to force a journalist to disclose her identity, she may also be aware that the journalist is unlikely to comply—as the outcomes in the cases below indicate, but she may not be prepared to rely on the willingness of a journalist to take the risk of a custodial sentence. In fact, the courts have given some rather reluctant and grudging recognition to the values underlying the protection of sources by declining to impose custodial sentences.[24] However, this is a matter that remains at their discretion. Further, the levying of large fines obviously also has a coercive effect on journalists, especially when they work on a freelance basis[25] or for minor, specialist publications. Second, the courts' attitude is likely to have an impact on journalists themselves—they are likely to wish to avoid the invidious situation they may be placed in whereby they are faced with a choice between breaking a promise to a source and disobeying a court order, with the possibility of imprisonment or a heavy fine. Journalists may refuse to follow up some stories even where a source has come forward and so information becomes less likely to be placed before the public.

---

[23] See note 18 above.

[24] In *A-G v Mulholland and Foster* [1963] 2 QB 477 two journalists were sent to prison for refusing to reveal their sources in relation to the Vassall spy ring inquiry. The modern practice is merely to fine. Cf the result in the recent controversial US case of *Judith Miller, Petitioner v US and M Cooper and Time inc, Petitioners v US*, Supreme Court (2005) No 04–1508; Miller was jailed for four months for refusing to reveal her source (CNN 6 July 2005). The information related to the Bush administration's attempts to justify the war in Iraq.

[25] This was the case in *Goodwin*; see pp 332–3 below.

Information from sources frequently relates to matters of grave public interest such as improper practices in large commercial organizations, in which case the source is likely to be an employee who is prepared to 'blow the whistle'. Such an employee would now have some protection from dismissal under the Public Interest Disclosure Act 1998, but nevertheless is, for obvious reasons, likely to want to protect her identity. The business pages of newspapers frequently depend on information from insiders in companies, and the subsequent articles represent a means of counter-balancing the rosy pictures of companies' market fortunes put forward on their behalf by a range of corporate image consultants. The possibility of revelations of malpractice followed by adverse media publicity, and potential damage to a company's brand image, may be a highly valuable method of creating corporate accountability.[26]

The question of protection for sources arises in a range of other contexts, including that of state secrecy, although cases do not arise as frequently. The matters in question may relate to governmental matters or national security. In the only case touching on matters of national security, *Secretary of State for Defence v Guardian Newspapers*,[27] the source was a civil servant who was activated by conscience in seeking to disclose an apparent government cover-up relating to Cruise missiles. At first glimpse, it might seem surprising that there is a dearth of cases regarding sources and political cover-ups since 'leaking' in order to damage an opponent or to gain advantage in some other respect is a common feature of UK political life.[28] Such leaks from government sources tend to consist of a mixture of 'spin' and revelation. The source remains hidden and cannot therefore be called to account in respect of the 'facts' revealed in the story. The lack of case law may well be explained on the basis that it is not in the interests of any of the parties concerned to bring legal actions, even where the leak is disadvantageous to one of them in the short term. Therefore, it might appear that in this context legal source protection does not necessarily serve to enhance accountability. However, the picture is more complex than that. Leaks would be likely to occur in any event, relying on the protection of powerful political players, even without legal forms of source protection, while stories that might counter-balance government claims might not see the light of day. Thus, the relationship between source protection and political accountability remains a nuanced and complex one.

An incident, referred to above, that in some respects exemplifies the nature of the issues at stake arose in the controversial US case of *Judith Miller, Petitioner v US and M Cooper and Time inc, Petitioners v US*.[29] Miller had written a number of articles for the *New York Times* that relied on sources to provide information supporting the war

---

[26] See the Interbrew saga, pp 342–4 below. Interbrew backed down and desisted in its action only when its brand image was threatened, not at this point by the revelations themselves, but by its attempt to force disclosure of the source. It may be noted that the Financial Services Authority (FSA), which governs the securities market in the UK, began a criminal investigation into the leak in question. Under the Financial Services and Markets Act 2000, a maximum sentence of seven years may be imposed for issuing false and misleading documents.

[27] [1984] 3 All ER 601; [1985] AC 339, 347, HL.

[28] See Peter Hennessy, *Whitehall*, 1989, pp 363–4.   [29] Supreme Court (2005) No 04–1508.

in Iraq. In the course of so doing she had attacked the opinions of a former US diplomat, Wilson, who had challenged the evidence for the possession of WMD by Saddam Hussein. Wilson was married to CIA agent Valerie Plame Wilson, and Plame was utilized, it appeared, in an attempt to discredit Wilson or to attack him indirectly. In 2003 columnist Robert Novak first published Valerie Plame Wilson's name; he cited as his sources two anonymous senior administration officials. Plame was a covert agent working in the area of anti-proliferation of weapons of mass destruction. Miller also relied on sources within the Bush administration in publishing articles supportive of the need to go to war in Iraq, although she did not name Plame. The sources were in fact, it appeared, seeking to smear Wilson (who had service in Africa), who had challenged the Bush claim that the Saddam Hussein regime in Iraq had involvement in Africa in seeking to purchase uranium yellowcake, needed for nuclear weapons. This claim formed a very significant part of the weapons-of-mass-destruction rationale that Bush had employed to lead the country into war against Iraq in 2003.

It appeared that the purpose of leaking Plame's name and occupation was to characterize her, with her husband, as an anti-Bush co-conspirator. The intention in so doing appeared to be to discredit his information on the Bush uranium claim. A special prosecutor attempted to compel Miller to tell a grand jury how the name of Plame was made public in July 2003, since the outing of Plame appeared to constitute a criminal offence. She was subpoened to reveal the identity of her sources. She refused to do so and after losing her appeals[30] was eventually jailed for four months. After spending a substantial period of time in a federal jail, Miller testified about the identity of one of her sources, who turned out to be I. Lewis Libby, chief of staff to Vice President Richard Cheney.[31] Miller consistently characterized her stance in refusing to disclose the identity of her source as one that was strongly linked to the public's right to know.[32] It may be noted that after this revelation Libby was forced to resign—an interesting instance in which disclosure of the identity of a source led to greater governmental accountability, not less.

The lesson to be learnt from the *Miller* case is not, it is argued, that shield laws for journalists should be repealed. Journalists the world over appear to agree that source protection is vital to their role. The case indicates that some free speech arguments in favour of source protection must be treated with caution, since otherwise the claims of already powerful players will be enhanced, to the detriment of furthering true speech values.

---

[30] See US Court of Appeals No 04–3138, 15 February 2005 and note 6 above. Another reporter, M. Cooper, who identified Plame after Novak, eventually avoided the jail term that was given to Miller. He had been held in civil contempt earlier for refusing to testify before the grand jury, but after appeal to the Supreme Court he did testify on the basis that his source had contacted him to give him specific, unambiguous permission to reveal details of their conversations to the grand jury.

[31] See e.g. *Guardian Unlimited* 18 October 2005.   [32] See e.g. her website: Judithmiller.org.

KEY ISSUES

This chapter turns to focusing on the UK stance on protection for sources, placing it in the context of the above comments. It will be contended that the recognition afforded to the protection of sources under UK law has traditionally been inadequate. There has been a rise in the levels of protection available—some further protection was provided under s 10 of the Contempt of Court Act 1981,[33] and the Human Rights Act facilitated enhancement of that protection. The reception of Article 10 into domestic law persuaded the judges to focus more strongly on the Article 10 requirements, and in particular on the higher level of protection provided for sources at Strasbourg.[34]

Nevertheless, in the post-HRA era it will be argued that the judiciary have still not shown a determination to take a hard look at the question of proportionality with a view to applying the Strasbourg standard in giving weight to the free speech values at stake. They remain more readily preoccupied with the harm done to businesses and other institutions if confidential information is leaked. Their attitude is, it will be argued, informed by a set of values that are peculiarly associated with the British judiciary, and which have remained largely undisturbed by the inception of the Human Rights Act—a theme which runs throughout this book. It will be argued that the stance taken towards the protection of sources at common law still lingers on. The strong and continuing attachment of the judiciary to the values and ideas underpinning their previous common law stance, even in the face of countervailing Convention values, forms a central theme of this chapter, and indeed of this book.

Thus this chapter begins by considering the traditional common law stance and moves on to consider the jurisdictional basis of orders for disclosure, which has not changed significantly in the HRA era. It then examines the effect of s 10 of the Contempt of Court Act, which introduced in effect a statutory 'shield' for journalists. It looks at the interpretation of s 10 pre- and post-HRA, concluding by critiquing the position that has currently been reached post-HRA. This lengthy section sets out to subject the pre and post-HRA authorities to an intense Convention-based analysis. A model of judicial reasoning under the HRA is then put forward that is, it is contended, more closely based on the Strasbourg stance. The Chapter then moves on to a brief examination of specific methods of obtaining journalistic material as part of a criminal or a terrorist investigation, arguing that the availability of these methods undermines the protection provided for sources under s 10. Finally it puts forward some conclusions as to the point that source protection has reached in the UK.

---

[33] For comment on s 10, see Allan [1991] *CLJ* 131; C.J. Miller [1982] *Crim LR* 71, p 82; S. Palmer [1992] *PL* 61.

[34] As demonstrated by the fact that the findings in *X v Morgan Grampian* [1991] 1 AC 1 were found to breach Article 10 in *Goodwin v UK* (1996) 22 EHRR 123; this point has, however, been disputed domestically—see pp 341–2 below. But it seems to have been accepted in the post-HRA decisions, see Sedley LJ in *Interbrew SA v Financial Times Ltd* [2002] EMLR 24 at [97].

THE COMMON LAW STANCE

Prior to the inception of the 1981 Act, the values and ideas underpinning the prevailing common law stance were clearly revealed in *British Steel Corp v Granada Television*.[35] British Steel was involved in a steel strike, and Granada made a documentary about the strike which put forward allegations of mismanagement by British Steel and of government intervention. British Steel sought an order that Granada disclose the identity of an informant who had provided them with copies of a confidential document that they had used in the television programme. The majority of the House of Lords found that it would be opposed to the public interest to recognize any journalistic privilege.[36] Lord Dilhorne considered that journalists should be treated as being in the same position as other citizens. Lord Wilberforce considered that: 'this case does not touch upon the freedom of the press even at its periphery'.[37] He recognized that a public interest in the free flow of information exists but considered that it did not take the form of a journalistic privilege; he viewed it merely as a matter that could be taken into account in exercising the judicial discretion to order disclosure. The House of Lords went on to find that disclosure of the identity of the source was required of Granada in the interests of justice, since in their view British Steel had suffered a very serious wrong in which Granada had actively participated.

This was the first time for almost twenty years that a court had sought to force a media organization to reveal its confidential sources.[38] In coming to this judgment the House of Lords showed a clear concern to protect the interests of a large commercial concern. The judges could obviously envisage quite clearly—in concrete terms—the damage that could be done to British Steel if the informant, left in place as a protected source, revealed further secrets. They seemed less able to envisage the consequences for journalism if the order of disclosure was made. In other words, they were being asked to weigh up two differing interests, one of which appeared to strike them as specific and as immediately pressing, while the other of its nature was much more nebulous and rooted in a particular free expression value—informing the public as to corporate wrong-doing—that has not traditionally had much hold upon their imagination. As Palmer puts it, 'the benefit to the community [of the free flow of information] is attenuated and diffuse . . . The harm to the public interest caused by a loss [of this information] cannot by definition be quantified . . . The loss is hypothetical . . .'.[39] It therefore became apparent that statutory intervention was required in order to create a more equitable balance between the two interests. In a manner reminiscent of the stance of the House of Lords in the *Sunday Times* case,[40] a number

---

[35] [1981] AC 1096. See also p 317 above.   [36] At 1181.   [37] At 1168–9.

[38] In *A-G v Mulholland, A-G v Forster* [1963] 2 QB 477, the Court of Appeal ordered the imprisonment of journalists who refused to reveal information leading to the naming of sources, in relation to the Vassall spy ring. The journalists were lauded for their refusal to breach the moral obligation they owed to the sources, even in the face of imprisonment.

[39] S. Palmer, 'Protecting Journalists' Sources' [1992] PL 61–72, at 71.   [40] See Chapter 4 at 183–5.

of the senior British judiciary had once again demonstrated their failure to understand the significance of the media watchdog rule. Thus there was a clear failure to recognize a journalistic privilege at common law.

THE JURISDICTIONAL BASIS OF ORDERS FOR DISCLOSURE

Under the common law there are—imprecisely defined—circumstances in which a journalist can be ordered to disclose the identity of a source. Questions may be asked in existing legal proceedings that might lead to disclosure,[41] and orders for disclosure outside such proceedings are based on the jurisdiction established by the House of Lords in *Norwich Pharmacal Co. v Customs and Excise Commissioners*.[42] It is generally accepted that the *Norwich Pharmacal* jurisdiction is discretionary, and in its exercise the court, pre-1981, was both entitled and bound to perform a balancing exercise weighing the public interest in advancing the course of justice against any countervailing feature of the public interest.[43] That balancing exercise is now conducted in accordance with s 10 Contempt of Court Act 1981, discussed below.

Under the pre-HRA cases, on one view the jurisdiction was exercisable where the defendant (normally this will be the journalist) had become 'mixed up' in the tortious acts of the source so as to facilitate his/her wrongdoing, and as a result had to cooperate in righting the wrongs he had unwittingly facilitated (*Norwich Pharmacal Co*;[44] *British Steel Corp v Granada Television*).[45] The wrong-doing would normally consist of breaching confidence although, as the cases discussed below indicate, there are other possibilities. Typically, a source would divulge confidential information to a journalist, thus potentially incurring liability under the equitable doctrine of breach of confidence.[46] The journalist would become 'mixed' up in the wrong-doing if he or she published the information. But it was unclear precisely what was meant by 'facilitating' the wrong-doing, although it did appear to be clear that the person under the liability to make disclosure did not have to be a joint wrong-doer. However, in some instances the defendant journalist would not have *facilitated* any wrongdoing since

---

[41] However, under the common law a court order to disclose sources would not be made in the context of the preliminary proceedings in a defamation action: see *Adam v Fisher* (1914) 110 LT 537; *Hennessy v Wright* (1888) 21 QBD 509. See further P. Wilmo and W. Rogers (eds) *Gatley on Libel and Slander*, 9th edn., London: Sweet and Maxwell, 1998, para 30.112.

[42] [1974] AC 133. See Matthews and Malek, *Discovery*, London: Sweet and Maxwell, 1992 on the law and practice relating to this jurisdiction.

[43] See [1974] AC 133; 175, *per* Lord Reid; pp 181 and 182, *per* Lord Morris of Borth-y-Guest; pp 188 and 190, *per* Lord Dilhorne; pp 198–199, *per* Lord Cross of Chelsea; and p 205, *per* Lord Kilbrandon.

[44] [1974] AC 133 at 175, *per* Lord Reid.   [45] [1981] AC 1096.

[46] See Chapter 14 at 721–50 for discussion of the doctrine. As the chapter argues, it appears to have undergone a transformation in order to become the tort of misuse of private information. But in terms of commercial and state secrets, it appears to have retained its original form and ingredients (see Chapter 19 at 948–54).

she might merely have received the confidential information. It could be said that in such instances there would be no involvement in the source's activities and so no jurisdiction to make the order. But on the later view of the *Norwich Pharmacal* jurisdiction, allowing for discovery to find the identity of any wrongdoer, it is available against anyone who is mixed up in the justiciable wrongful acts of others, either innocently or as a joint-wrong-doer.[47]

This latter position was reiterated and clarified in the post-HRA decision in *Ashworth Hospital v Mirror Group Newspapers*.[48] The case, which is discussed further below, concerned the revelation of information relating to the Moors' murderer, Ian Brady. The information was leaked from within the hospital by, it appeared, an employee; therefore there was a clear breach of medical confidentiality. Thus potential liability for breach of confidence arose. The reason for seeking the order for disclosure was to discipline the person responsible for the leak, which in practice would have meant that that person would be dismissed. MGN had argued that Ashworth had failed to establish that the unpublished material in Ian Brady's records was truly confidential in the sense that it was secret or not in the public domain. Further, MGN had argued that as all the published information had been placed in the public domain by Ian Brady himself, MGN was not a tortfeasor in publishing the extracts from the records.

These contentions were not accepted by the Lords. It was found that the jurisdiction recognized in *Norwich Pharmacal Co. v Customs and Excise Commissioners* to order disclosure of the identity of a source of information or documents does not depend on whether the person against whom the order is sought—almost always in practice the journalist—has committed a tort, a breach of contract or other civil or criminal wrong. The House of Lords found that while the Court of Appeal had almost certainly been correct in concluding that the defendant was liable for breach of confidence, such a finding in favour of the claimant was not necessary. It was sufficient that the source was a wrong-doer and that the defendant had been involved in the wrong-doing. As Lord Woolf found:

The *Norwich Pharmacal* case clearly establishes that where a person, albeit innocently, and without incurring any personal liability, becomes involved in a wrongful act of another, that person thereby comes under a duty to assist the person injured by those acts by giving him any information which he is able to give by way of discovery that discloses the identity of the wrongdoer.[49]

Thus it was reaffirmed that it is sufficient to show that the defendant—the journalist—had 'participated' or been 'involved', albeit innocently, in the wrongdoing which is the basis of the application for discovery. In *Ashworth*, MGN had published the information which had been wrongfully obtained, and therefore they had clearly been involved in the wrongdoing. If MGN had merely *received* the information but had not

---

[47] *X Ltd v Morgan-Grampian Ltd* [1991] 1 AC 1 at 40B–D.   [48] [2002] 1 WLR 2033.
[49] Ibid, at [26].

yet published it, it still could have been argued successfully that disclosure could be ordered. The argument would have been that receipt of the information could be viewed as innocent involvement. That was the situation in *Morgan Grampian*,[50] which can probably therefore be viewed as having been confirmed on that issue. The wrong-doing of the source need not be tortious as had previously been thought to be the case—it extends, following *Ashworth*, to a range of justiciable wrongs, including breach of copyright,[51] breach of confidence or of contract by an employee.[52] Further, it was found in *Ashworth* that the *Norwich Pharmacal* jurisdiction is not limited to cases where the injured person intends to sue the wrongdoer, but extends to cases in which he intends to obtain some other form of lawful redress.

Thus the current nature of the jurisdiction in the post-HRA era remains relatively unchanged since it has undergone no significant narrowing in that era, and indeed has arguably broadened. The courts have reserved to themselves a very broad jurisdiction allowing for the potential to order disclosure, although, as discussed below, they have also accepted that greater weight should be given, post-HRA, to the countervailing media interest. A rule that allows plaintiffs to demand that journalists reveal the identity of a source on such broad grounds hardly facilitates the media's watchdog role. The House of Lords in *Ashworth*[53] made it clear that all the possible limitations of the *Norwich Pharmacal* rule that had been put forward and argued for on behalf of the newspaper must be rejected. This stance is criticized below on the basis that as a common law doctrine the *Norwich Pharmacal* jurisdiction could have been narrowed down in reliance on the courts' duty under s 6 HRA, taking account of s 2. It is also argued that on grounds of common law principle alone, a doctrine that places a defendant under an onerous duty, with criminal sanctions attached, and yet arises independently of harm caused by him or her, is inherently flawed. However, this very broad jurisdiction is subject to certain important curbs, as discussed below.

SECTION 10 CONTEMPT OF COURT ACT 1981

INTRODUCTION

The protection of sources received, as indicated above, a very limited and precarious recognition at common law pre-1981. But in 1981 s 10 of the Contempt of Court Act 1981 gave some formal recognition to the media's watchdog role, in relation to the protection of journalistic sources. Section 10 thus afforded some express statutory recognition to the important constitutional role of the media.[54] The provision that

---

50 [1991] 1 AC 1.   51 *Ashdown v Telegraph Group plc* [2001] EWCA Civ 1142.
52 *British Steel v Granada TV* ibid; *X Ltd v Morgan-Grampian Ltd* [1991] 1 AC 1.
53 [2002] 4 All ER 193.   54 See further Chapter 1 at 4–12.

became s 10 was introduced into Parliament in the wake of the outcry that followed the result in *British Steel v Granada*[55] and therefore it represented a significant depart-ure from the stance adopted in that case. Section 10 provides:

No court may require a person to disclose, nor is any person guilty of contempt of court for refusing to disclose, the source of information contained in a publication for which he is responsible, unless it be established to the satisfaction of the court that disclosure is neces-sary in the interests of justice or national security or for the prevention of disorder or crime.

Section 10 covers any speech, writing, broadcast or other communication in whatever form, which is addressed to the public at large or any section of the public.[56] Thus, it is clearly not confined to journalists, but obviously it is of most benefit to them, and in fact, unsurprisingly, all the s 10 cases so far have concerned attempts by professional journalists to protect the identity of their sources. It was determined in *Secretary of State for Defence v Guardian Newspapers*[57] that s 10 applies to the disclosure of docu-ments which might reveal the identity of the source, not merely to direct disclosures. It was also made clear that it applies even where there is a mere likelihood that the identity of the source will be revealed. The protection it offers therefore extends to an order for the disclosure of any material, or information directly or indirectly disclosing, or likely to facilitate the disclosure of a source's identity.

Clearly, s 10 did not provide any new power to require a journalist to disclose the identity of a source. It does not enlarge the *Norwich Pharmacal* jurisdiction discussed above. As Lord Diplock put it in *Secretary of State for Defence v Guardian Newspapers*, the leading pre-HRA case:

Section 10 confers no powers upon a court additional to those powers, whether discretion-ary or not, which already existed at common law or under rules of court, to order disclosure of sources of information, its effect is restrictive only. . . . Further, s10 clearly does not provide that the court has merely to decide whether the information is necessary to serve any one of the enumerated purposes and, if so, grant the order, nor does it alter or qualify the fact that the remedy is discretionary, to be approached on a case by case basis.

Lord Scarman, in *Secretary of State for Defence v Guardian Newspapers*,[58] referred to the profound importance of s 10, which prompted him to ask whether English law should move in the direction of a Bill of Rights. He suggested that s 10 did not precisely introduce a constitutional right, but gave statutory recognition to a funda-mental right. Section 10 gave statutory form and greater force to the existing

---

[55] The provision that is now section 10 was introduced into the Contempt of Court Bill in Committee by Lord Scarman, following the *British Steel* decision. Lord Scarman based his proposal on Lord Salmon's dissenting speech in that case in favour of much stronger protection. He put forward two proposed exemp-tions from a general privilege for journalists' sources: national security and the prevention of disorder or crime; he explained that they were derived from Article 10(2) of the European Convention on Human Rights. He withdrew his amendment when Lord Hailsham L.C. promised to consider the issue, and Lord Morris thereafter introduced the clause that became section 10, including 'the interests of justice' as a further exception.

[56] Ss 2(1) and 19, 1981 Act.   [57] [1984] 3 All ER 601; [1985] AC 339, 347, HL.

[58] Ibid, at p 361.

recognition of a public interest in the confidentiality of sources as a part of the balance to be weighed in the exercise of a judicial discretion. That public interest was recognized, albeit without great enthusiasm, in the *British Steel* case. Its underlying purpose, as expressed post-1981 by Lord Diplock in *Secretary of State for Defence v Guardian Newspapers*, was to ensure that 'informers could be confident that their identity would not be revealed [since otherwise] sources of information would dry up.'[59]

In performing the weighing up exercise to determine what is necessary in the interests of justice or in relation to one of the other exceptions, s 10 implies that the courts are expected to start from the premise that there is an established and clear public interest in the confidentiality of the source, subject to exceptions to be narrowly applied. In other words, s 10 indicates that the courts should attribute great weight to the interest in protecting sources in comparison with the public interest in advancing the interest encapsulated in the relevant exception in a particular case. Section 10 thus creates presumptive priority for the speech interest in sources as compared to the other enumerated interests in s 10. In this sense s 10 is in keeping with the values encapsulated in Article 10.[60] The reasoning process under it is structured in the same way as that undertaken under Article 10, since freedom of expression is subject to exceptions to be narrowly construed, except where another competing Convention right is engaged.[61] Section 10 thus creates a qualified privilege allowing journalists and others to refuse to answer questions or disclose documents in court which would lead to revealing the identity of a source of information. In practice this means that journalists have a special privilege which can override the general presumption that rules of evidence are designed to elicit and determine truth in court proceedings. The courts take the view, however, that the privilege is based on the public interest in receiving information and not on a special protection for journalists.[62]

Nevertheless, s 10 represented a significant breakthrough for journalists. But its protection for sources is subject to four overlapping and potentially very broad exceptions which may, however, be invoked only where it is established to the satisfaction of the court that disclosure is necessary. Having taken a step in the direction of protecting sources, s 10 nevertheless leaves the courts quite a broad discretion which is structured by its presumption of inequality. The exceptions, which create limitations on the privilege, act as gateways to disclosure. Under s 10, courts have to take two steps when considering whether to order disclosure, bearing in mind that they will already have considered the legal basis of the order of disclosure—the *Norwich Pharmacal* jurisdiction—and its width and applicability in the instant case. Firstly the courts have

---

[59] [1985] AC 339 at 349, per Lord Diplock.   [60] See Chapter 2 at 40–1.

[61] See Chapter 16 at 832–6 and see further below, pp 369–70.

[62] This was found in the pre-s 10 case of *British Steel* [1981] AC 1096 at 1168–9, and in *Interbrew* [2002] EMLR 24, Sedley LJ provided a similar exploration of the principles involved. His view can be summed up as a finding that the media enjoy, by virtue of s 10 of the Contempt of Court Act 1981, a high level of presumptive protection, not in their own right, but in the public interest.

to consider whether the case falls within the scope of the exception in question. Secondly they have to consider the necessity of ordering disclosure in order to serve the aim indicated in the exception.

INTERPRETATION OF THE SECTION 10 EXCEPTIONS IN THE PRE-HRA ERA

Under s 10 disclosure of the identity of the source may be necessary in four exceptional circumstances—'in the interests of justice or national security or for the prevention of disorder or crime'. The crucial findings as to the exceptions—in terms of resisting attempts to afford them a narrow and precise meaning—have been made in relation to the terms 'the interests of justice' and 'national security', especially the former. The terms 'disorder or crime' have not generated any significant case law. The term 'the interests of justice' is clearly potentially extremely broad, by far the widest of the four exceptions. The inclusion of the term suggested that Parliament had existing case law in mind, particularly the *British Steel* case.[63]

The term 'interests of justice' could be interpreted either broadly, relating to the general needs of justice, or narrowly, by asking what justice requires in the context of an existing legal action. In other words, it could refer either to the administration of justice in particular, existing legal proceedings[64] or, in a case based on the *Norwich Pharmacal* jurisdiction, to a civil action which could potentially be brought against a wrongdoer who has not yet been identified. Lord Hailsham has said of this exception: 'What are the interests of justice? I suggest that they are as long as the judge's foot'.[65] But the possibility of taking quite a narrow and precise approach to the meaning of the term did emerge in the pre-HRA era. Two schools of thought became apparent in the case law as to its meaning. It was found by Lord Diplock in *Guardian Newspapers*[66] that the term refers to 'the technical sense of the administration of justice in the course of legal proceedings'. Thus on this view there would have to be *existing* legal proceedings. This would have narrowed down the meaning of the term very significantly and would have prevented this exception in most instances from operating in conjunction with the *Norwich Pharmacal* jurisdiction. Adopting the narrower meaning of the term would have meant that the jurisdiction could have continued to operate in relation to the other exceptions, but the 'interests of justice' exception could only have been invoked where proceedings were already in existence and source disclosure became warranted in those interests.

But in *X v Morgan Grampian*[67] this narrow interpretation was rejected. A confidential plan had been stolen from the plaintiffs, a company named Tetra. In 1989 the plaintiffs wished to raise additional capital and a number of their senior officers, with

---

[63] [1981] AC 1096, at 1171 and 1173–1175, *per* Lord Wilberforce. See also Lord Haldane in *Scott v Scott* [1913] AC 417.

[64] Cf. *Handmade Films (Productions) Ltd v Express Newspapers plc* [1986] FSR 463.

[65] HL Deb, Vol 416, col 162 (10 February 1981).   [66] [1985] AC 339.   [67] [1991] 1 AC 1.

the assistance of their accountants, were engaged in preparing a corporate plan for submission to prospective lenders. Much of the information in the plan was highly confidential and its publication pending the finalization of the negotiations for the purpose of which it was being prepared was likely to cause severe damage to the plaintiffs. Information apparently from the plan was leaked by an unidentified source by phone to Goodwin, a journalist. The plaintiffs obtained an injunction preventing further publication on grounds of breach of confidence; they also applied for an order requiring Goodwin to disclose the source, and sought discovery of his notes of the phone conversation in order to discover his or her identity.

It was argued on behalf of the defendants that the phrase 'the interests of justice' does not include merely assisting the plaintiff to pursue a claim against a third party, but is of more restricted scope.[68] It was argued that the plaintiff's claim was not serious enough to require the disclosure of the source since the exceptions based on the interests of justice must be of the same order of seriousness in terms of the well-being of the whole community as the other potentially overriding exceptions—national security or the prevention of disorder or crime. Therefore it was contended that the 'interests of justice' must refer to an interest of greater public import than advancing private litigation: the term should refer to the efficacy and integrity of the trial process. The House of Lords rejected this argument; it was found that the application of the exception should allow persons to 'exercise important legal rights and protect themselves from serious legal wrongs, whether or not resort to legal proceedings in a court of law will be necessary to attain these objectives'.[69] This was obviously a broader interpretation that that argued for on behalf of the defendants, and that accepted in *Guardian Newspapers*, although the use of the words 'serious' and 'important' had some potential narrowing effect. The other aspects of the case are discussed below.

The definition proffered in *Morgan Grampian* clearly gave the term one of the widest of the possible interpretations open to it, leading to complaints that this exception will apply wherever a court is moved by the complaint of the aggrieved party.[70] A further attempt put forward by the defendants in the post-HRA decision in *Ashworth*, which is discussed below, to narrow down the 'interests of justice' exception in accordance with Lord Diplock's test, was again rejected.[71] One factor underlying this prevailing judicial stance appears to be the notion that it would be artificial and burdensome to expect a claimant to institute legal proceedings merely in order to bring itself within the meaning of the term for the purposes of disclosure.[72] However, the damage done instead to the interest in protecting sources and journalistic freedom more generally has not been taken into account since that issue has been relegated to a later stage in the argument. By combining the term 'interests of justice' with the *Norwich Pharmacal* jurisdiction, the courts have in a sense destroyed any narrowing effect that the term might have had: since that jurisdiction will virtually always apply

---

[68] See *Secretary of State for Defence v Guardian Newspapers* [1985] AC 339, 347, *per* Lord Diplock.
[69] [1991] 1 AC 1 at 43.   [70] See *Goodwin v UK* (1996) 22 EHRR 123, discussed below.
[71] P 347 below.   [72] See *Morgan Grampian* note 91 at pp 332–4.

where a source has disclosed material, it can always be said to be presumptively in those interests to allow the plaintiff to seek to obtain disclosure of his identity.

An attempt by Lord Justice Sedley in the Court of Appeal in *Interbrew*[73] to confine the 'interests of justice' exception to the disclosure of information relating to potential civil actions only, as opposed to including identifying information relating to criminal proceedings, was rejected in the House of Lords, by Lord Woolf, in *Ashworth*.[74] In *Interbrew*, both Lightman J and Sedley LJ concluded that the principle was limited to the disclosure of information which identified someone against whom the applicant meant to bring a civil action or otherwise assert its rights. Sedley LJ rejected the idea that it extended to the detection of crime, on the basis that such detection is the business of specialized agencies who have been granted special statutory rights of search and seizure, representing a carefully crafted balance between societal needs and individual rights. Lord Woolf took a different view in *Ashworth*, finding that if persons can be identified for the purpose of serving the aim of bringing civil actions, there could be no justification for not requiring the wrongdoer to be identified where he or she has committed a criminal act.

A source disclosure order can be viewed at first glance as having two purposes— first, to seek to prevent further disclosures and second to allow for legal (or other) action to be taken against the source. If the identity of the source is disclosed he/she may be unlikely to be able to leak any more information, while the body about whom information has been revealed can take action against him or her. However, the first purpose cannot always be satisfied by a source disclosure order. The journalist may refuse to reveal the source and, in any event, the source may already have leaked further information to a media body (or bodies) which it is holding, unpublished. An injunction usually provides a more effective means of preventing further disclosures. Thus, one aim of the 'interests of justice' exception partially overlaps with the purpose behind the action for breach of confidence—to obtain an injunction in order to prevent disclosure of information.

A disclosure will almost inevitably involve a breach of confidence—especially as that doctrine now encompasses a much broader range of disclosures.[75] It is now established that a newspaper that publishes material obtained by a source in breach of confidence *also* itself commits a further breach of confidence by publishing the material, since the newspaper is viewed by the law as coming under the same duty to maintain confidence as the source.[76] Thus a claimant who acts swiftly enough to obtain an injunction against the newspaper may be able to prevent a disclosure of the material obtained by the source, or at least any further disclosure. In most of the cases discussed in this chapter the remedy of an interim injunction had already been obtained with the aim of preventing further disclosures of the same information or any other information that had been leaked to the newspaper by the source. Any such injunction would subsist until the trial of the final injunction. Due to the effect of s 12(3)

---

[73] [2002] EMLR 24.   [74] P 347 below.   [75] See Chapter 14 at 740–8.
[76] *A-G v Guardian Newspapers* [1990] 1 AC 109 (*Spycatcher* litigation).

HRA it is now somewhat harder to obtain an interim injunction on grounds of breach of confidence than it was pre-HRA, but the plaintiff only has to surmount the hurdle of showing that it is more likely than not that the injunction will be granted at final trial.[77] Once an injunction has been obtained against one organ of the media in this way, any other organ that repeats the material which is the subject matter of the injunction will be in contempt.[78] So the main purpose served by invocation of the 'interests of justice' exception is to force a journalist into helping the plaintiff to identify its own disloyal employee or other. The question might be raised whether the court system should be used in this way at all. Court time is extremely expensive—it might be asked whether it is appropriate for it to be used where, for example, a company has failed to institute an enquiry into a leak or where its security has been lax?

This exception overlaps with all the other three and arguably renders them redundant. It is hard to envisage a situation in which a disclosure could be viewed as necessary to prevent crime or disorder, or to protect national security, in which it could not also be said that disclosure was necessary in order to prevent legal wrongs or enable the exercise of legal rights. It is now clear after the interpretation that this exception has received that its operation in combination with the *Norwich Pharmacal* jurisdiction leaves only the demands of the test of necessity in s 10 to provide any protection for sources. That jurisdiction will almost inevitably arise in a source disclosure case since at the least a breach of confidence will have occurred, and therefore a potential cause of action will almost always be in place to be served by disclosure.

The 'prevention of crime' exception has also received a wide interpretation and would cover the interpretation placed on the 'interests of justice' exception by Lord Woolf. It was relied on in *Morgan Grampian* at first instance, but it was found unnecessary to deal with it. 'Crime' has been found to bear a wide interpretation: it refers to the public interest in deterring crime generally, as opposed to the interest in preventing the commission of a specific and identifiable crime.[79]

The term 'the interests of national security' has always been afforded a broad meaning by the UK judiciary, in the sense that they have been prepared to accept executive claims that such interests are engaged in a wide range of situations,[80] but in this instance the stance they have taken is particularly all-encompassing. The only case involving this exception so far is *Secretary of State for Defence v Guardian Newspapers*.[81] A document classified 'secret' was prepared in the Ministry of Defence. Seven copies of the document were sent from the Ministry to the Prime Minister, for senior Ministers, the Chief Whip and the Secretary of the Cabinet. A junior civil

---

[77] *Cream Holdings v Bannerjee* [2005] 1 AC 253; [2004] 3 WLR 918 in which it was found that the term 'likely to succeed' in s 12(3) meant 'more likely than not'. See further Chapter 3 at 153–7.

[78] As recently reaffirmed by the House of Lords in *Attorney General v Punch Limited and Another* (also referred to as *A-G v Steen*) [2003] 1 AC 1046; [2003] 2 WLR 49; [2003] 1 All ER 289. See further Chapter 6 at 291–6.

[79] See *X v Y* [1988] 2 All ER 648; In *re An Inquiry under the Company Securities (Insider Dealing) Act 1985* [1987] BCLC 506, *per* J. Hoffmann and [1988] AC 660, 673, *per* Slade L.J., and at pp 681–2, *per* Lloyd L.J.

[80] *Rehman v Secretary of State for the Home Dept* [2001] 3 WLR 877.   [81] [1985] AC 339.

servant, who considered that Parliament was being misled by the Conservative government as regards the timing of the arrival of cruise missiles in Britain, sent a photocopy of the document regarding the timing to *The Guardian*, who published some of the details. The Secretary of State, the plaintiff, wished to discover the identity of the civil servant and sought the return of the photocopy, since it was expected that it would probably reveal his or her identity. Clearly, the arrival of Cruise Missiles is on its face quite a serious matter in national security terms. However, the Lords proceeded on the basis that the information disclosed by the source was in itself innocuous since, presumably, relevant foreign powers would already be in possession of the information.

The Secretary of State claimed that the national security exception under s 10 applied since the very fact that a secret document with restricted circulation relating to defence had come into the hands of a national newspaper was of great significance in terms of the maintenance of national security. A majority in the House of Lords accepted this interpretation. Lord Bridge found:

An unidentified member of [a small group of civil servants] was prepared, for motives which could not be known before identification, to make unauthorised disclosure to the public of a document which those responsible had thought fit to classify as 'Secret.' That the presence of such a disloyal servant in such a position represents a potential threat to national security seems to me self-evident.[82]

However, it appeared that the disclosure of the material in question had no possible bearing on national security in a more specific sense since the document in itself was innocuous. Lord Scarman said on this point:

Serious though a breach of trust by a Crown servant is, it does not, however, necessarily follow that national security has been endangered . . . the evidence of danger to the security system is meagre and full of omissions . . . Indeed, I cannot find in the evidence any grounds which could reasonably satisfy a court that national security was endangered by the unauthorised disclosure of this document, the contents of which, if leaked, constituted no danger, to national security. We do not know . . . whether the memorandum was filed or processed in the same system as sensitive defence documents . . . The Court of Appeal thought the link [with national security] 'blindingly obvious.' I do not; nor did Scott J. It is no part of the judge's function to use his common sense in an attempt to fill a gap, which can be filled only by evidence. Common sense as a substitute for factual information is a dangerous weapon at any time.[83]

The majority in the Lords took the view taken by Lord Bridge—that the mere fact of the leak could in itself create a sufficient basis for invoking the exception, since it suggested that further leaks could occur from the same untrustworthy person. There was in fact no evidence that this was likely—it was purely a matter of speculation. As Lord Scarman pointed out, there was no evidence that the public servant in question had access to sensitive documents. So the Lords took the view that national security

---

[82] At 373.   [83] At 366.

was threatened, not by disclosure of the contents of the document, but due to the potential for further disclosures that might pose such a threat. The identity of the source was duly discovered when the photocopy was returned and she was prosecuted.[84] She turned out to be a junior clerk. She was, it appeared, activated by conscience.

In this context, the twin notions that the discloser of information is in a senior or key position in the concern in question, and is also highly likely to disclose further information, is in effect an article of judicial faith—as is evident from the discussion in this chapter of a number of these cases. These notions are a matter of judicial 'common sense'—they are not beliefs that have been found to have a sound objective basis. No attempt has been made to consider the different circumstances in question in the various instances which might appear to make it more or less likely that the unknown source was a senior figure or would be likely to engage in further disclosures. In the *Guardian* case it might have been expected that the person in question would only have risked disclosure due to the especial significance of the event in question, which was not likely to recur.

Ironically enough, in *Guardian Newspapers*, the House of Lords knew of the identity of the source before they decided the case and, with some disquiet, had to engage in the solipsistic exercise of deciding it on the basis of the factors apparently before the Court of Appeal, even though those 'factors' were mere judicial beliefs, whereas the Lords were in possession of the true facts. But the findings from the case could well have an application going beyond matters that have a significant link with national security. Its net result appears to be that the 'interests of national security' exception will generally apply when the information appears to emanate from a governmental body or Department that has a link with matters that could have a national security dimension, regardless of the significance of the actual link, so long as a colourable argument can be made that national security might potentially be at risk. The key point in terms of invoking this exception is that since the source remains unidentified, as will of course always be the case, the assumption tends to be made that he/she may leak much more sensitive material in future. That is the only link with national security required. Lord Bridge has said that where a case concerns national security or the prevention of crime the court will virtually always decide that disclosure is necessary.[85] There are very narrow exceptions to this rule in respect of the prevention of crime (and these possibilities could probably be extended to the preservation of national security); courts would not order disclosure in relation to a trivial offence or where the life of the journalist would be placed in danger.[86]

THE TEST OF NECESSITY PRE-HRA

In the pre-HRA era, having broadened the s 10 exceptions through interpretation, the judges then went on to devise a test for necessity (it must be established that

---

[84] See Chapter 19 at 925.   [85] *X Ltd v Morgan Grampian Publishers* [1991], AC 1, at 43.
[86] *Re an Inquiry under the Companies Security (Insider Dealing) Act 1985* [1988] AC 660, at 670.

disclosure is 'necessary' to serve the aim of one of the exceptions) that would almost always be met in respect of the national security exception and would often be met in relation to furthering the interests of justice. It was found in *Secretary of State for Defence v Guardian Newspapers*[87] that disclosure of the identity of the source would only be ordered where other means of identification were not reasonably readily available; if they were they should be used. On the other hand, this did not mean that all other means of inquiry that might reveal the identity of the source had to be exhausted before disclosure would be ordered. The term 'necessary' was found in *Re an Inquiry under the Companies Security (Insider Dealing) Act 1985*[88] to mean something less than indispensable, but something more than useful. Lord Griffiths said: '. . . whether a particular measure is necessary, although described as a question of fact for the purpose of section 10, involves the exercise of a judgment upon the established facts of the particular case . . . The nearest paraphrase I can suggest is "really needed" '.[89] This phrase is, of course, very similar to the term 'pressing social need' used by Strasbourg in relation to Article 10(2).[90]

In *Guardian Newspapers* the evidence of a threat to national security did not convince the minority in the House of Lords, but the majority accepted it, Lord Bridge stating that any threat to national security ought to be eliminated by the speediest and most effective means possible. The majority, therefore, took the traditional stance of failing to afford a rigorous scrutiny to imprecise and flimsy claims of a threat to national security made by the executive. However, the House of Lords did suggest that more convincing evidence would be needed in future. It is hard to see that disclosure was 'really needed' in this instance, or that any genuine balancing act between media freedom and national security occurred. The Lords clearly elided the tests for applying the national security exception and for finding that disclosure was 'necessary'.

The House of Lords clarified the nature of the balancing exercise to be carried out under s 10 in *X v Morgan Grampian Publishers and Others*.[91] The House of Lords had to consider the application of s 10 to the leak of a highly confidential plan, as indicated above. It found that when a journalist relies on s 10 in order to protect a source, it must be determined whether the applicant's right to take legal action against the source is outweighed by the journalist's interest in maintaining the promise of confidentiality made to him or her. The House of Lords took into account various factors in balancing these two considerations. Lord Bridge found first, that the protection of sources is itself a matter of high public importance. As to the criterion of necessity, he found that in relation to the interests of national security and the prevention of crime the test would be readily satisfied once the exception had been found to apply. He said:

For if non-disclosure of a source of information will imperil national security or enable a crime to be committed which might otherwise be prevented, it is difficult to imagine that any judge would hesitate to order disclosure. These two public interests are of such overriding importance that once it is shown that disclosure will serve one of those interests, the

[87] [1985] AC 339.   [88] [1988] 1 All ER 203.   [89] 704A–E.   [90] See Chapter 2 at 54–9.
[91] [1991] AC 1; [1991] 2 All ER 1, HL.

necessity of disclosure follows almost automatically . . . But the question whether disclosure is necessary in the interests of justice gives rise to a more difficult problem of weighing one public interest against another. It will not be sufficient, per se, for a party seeking disclosure of a source protected by section 10 to show merely that he will be unable without disclosure to exercise the legal right or avert the threatened legal wrong.[92]

In conducting the balancing exercise demanded by the term 'necessary', Lord Bridge took account of a number of factors relevant on both sides of the scale. He found that an important factor would be the degree of public interest value in the information obtained from the source. However, he found that another 'and perhaps more significant factor' would be the manner in which the information was itself obtained by the source. He considered that if the information was obtained illegally, that would diminish the importance of protecting the source, unless that factor was counterbalanced by a very strong public interest in publication of the information—classically, in exposing iniquity. In the instant case he found that the importance to the plaintiffs of obtaining disclosure lay in the threat of severe damage to their business, and consequentially to the livelihood of their employees, which would arise from disclosure of the information contained in their corporate plan while their refinancing negotiations were still continuing. That threat, he found, could only be defused if they could identify the source whom he viewed as the 'time bomb ticking away under the plaintiff's business'.[93] Thus the threat to the plaintiffs' business and the complicity of the source in 'a gross breach of confidentiality' were the key factors that were taken into account and weighed in the balance in favour of disclosure. Thus Lord Bridge, with whom the other Law Lords unanimously agreed, found that the interest of the plaintiffs in identifying the source outweighed the interests of the journalist in protecting it. Goodwin refused to reveal the identity of the source and was fined £5,000 for contempt in refusing to obey the court's order.

The findings in the Lords were significant since they made it clear that a newspaper publishing information deriving from an employee of the plaintiff body in question would very frequently be ordered to disclose his or her identity, since the factors identified by Lord Bridge would almost always apply. In such instances there would almost always have been a breach of confidence (the judiciary are remarkably unwilling, in this context, to find that the public interest defence could have been made out)[94] and there would almost always be a threat, based on speculation, to the company. It would almost always be virtually impossible to rule that threat out, and the

[92] At p 44.
[93] At [45]: The importance to the plaintiffs of obtaining disclosure lies in the threat of severe damage to their business, and consequentially to the livelihood of their employees, which would arise from disclosure of the information contained in their corporate plan while their refinancing negotiations are still continuing. This threat, accurately described by Lord Donaldson of Lymington MR ante p 23E, as 'ticking away beneath them like a time bomb' can only be defused if they can identify the source either as himself the thief of the stolen copy of the plan, or as a means to lead to the identification of the thief and thus put themselves in a position to institute proceedings for the recovery of the missing document.
[94] See pp 362–5 below.

judiciary, as noted earlier, have not required any evidence to accept that the threat actually exists in any given instance—the mere fact that one disclosure has occurred is apparently sufficient. Clearly, an employee who has leaked information on one occasion might leak it again, but the likelihood of that occurring requires scrutiny, depending on the facts.

Thus, following the *Morgan Grampian* findings, the 'balancing' exercise appeared to be virtually a misnomer since once the factors identified were in the equation, it was unclear that they would ever be likely to be outweighed by the value of the information.[95] The term 'necessary' was being afforded very little weight: the key question was in reality whether the 'interests of justice' could be viewed as being at stake at all, and, as contended above, they inevitably would be. The Lords did find that very clear cases of exposing iniquity might mean that disclosure would not be ordered on the basis that the factors identified could be outweighed, but they made it clear that in most instances—outside such clear-cut cases—disclosure would be ordered. Lord Bridge mentioned the interest in protecting sources. However, when it came to conducting the balancing exercise, he considered that the public interest value of material would be a relevant factor, but he did *not* avert to the *general* and constant public interest in protecting sources in order to serve the interests of investigative journalism. That was the key error in the analysis. He did not set *that* factor against the need of the company to identify the untrustworthy employee. Since both interests would almost always be present in a source disclosure case they would always tend to need to be balanced against each other.

When Goodwin took his case to Strasbourg, it was made clear, it is argued, that the House of Lords had indeed failed to give proper weight to the term 'necessary' in s 10. Goodwin applied to the European Commission on Human Rights[96] which gave its opinion that the order against Goodwin violated his right to freedom of expression under Article 10 of the Convention on Human Rights. When the case came before the Court it found that there was a vital public interest in protecting journalistic sources, since so doing was essential to the maintenance of a free press.[97] Thus, the margin of appreciation was circumscribed by that interest. It considered that limitations placed on the confidentiality of such sources would require the most careful scrutiny. Was the vital public interest in protecting sources outweighed by Tetra's interest in eliminating the threat of damage due to the dissemination of confidential material? The injunction was already effective in preventing the dissemination of such material and therefore the additional restriction on freedom of expression entailed by the disclosure order was not supported by sufficient reasons to satisfy the requirements of

---

[95] However, in *Chief Constable of Leicestershire v Gravelli* [1997] EMLR 543, DC, a case concerning revelations of malpractice in the police, it was found that in the circumstances of the case in question—disciplinary proceedings—it appeared that the interests of justice would not in fact be served by requiring the journalist to name her source. In other words, there could be no necessity to make such a demand when it was viewed as of no, or virtually no, utility in the particular context that arose.

[96] *Goodwin v UK* (1994) No 17488/90 Com Rep.

[97] *Goodwin v UK* (1996) 22 EHRR 123. See also *Fressoz and Roire v France* (1999) 5 BHRC 654.

Article 10(2). Tetra's interest in disclosure, including its interest in unmasking a disloyal employee, was not outweighed by the public interest in the protection of journalistic sources. Taking these matters into account, it was found that the order was disproportionate to the purpose in question and therefore could not be said to be necessary. A breach of Article 10 was therefore established. The Court found:

> The court recalls that freedom of expression constitutes one of the essential foundations of a democratic society and that the safeguards to be afforded to the press are of particular importance. Protection of journalistic sources is one of the basic conditions for press freedom, as is reflected in the laws and the professional codes of conduct in a number of contracting states and is affirmed in several international instruments on journalistic freedoms. Without such protection, sources may be deterred from assisting the press in informing the public on matters of public interest. As a result the vital public watchdog role of the press may be undermined and the ability of the press to provide accurate and reliable information may be adversely affected. Having regard to the importance of the protection of journalistic sources for press freedom in a democratic society and the potentially chilling effect an order of source disclosure has on the exercise of that freedom, such a measure cannot be compatible with article 10 of the Convention unless it is justified by an overriding requirement in the public interest.[98]

Thus *Goodwin* made it clear that in *this* context the strictest form of scrutiny should be afforded to the application of the tests for proportionality. As Chapter 2 indicates, less strict forms can be applicable.[99] *Goodwin* relied largely on speech/harm balancing as the proportionality test.[100] In other words, the seriousness of the harm caused by the disclosure of Tetra's confidential information was weighed up against the weightiness of the expression interest. The Court insisted on looking closely at the state's case regarding the degree of harm that Tetra had suffered, and took a view of it that differed significantly from that of the state. The interference was very severe, bearing in mind the significance for free expression of protection for journalistic sources. In coming to this conclusion the Court applied a strict test for scrutinizing the balance between the two interests—had it conceded a wider margin of appreciation to the national authorities, it might have been satisfied that the balance struck between the two was not manifestly unreasonable. Thus the Court found that the proportionality test had not been met

The Court did not fully refer to the tests for necessity and proportionality that answer to the *de Freitas*[101][102] three stage test discussed in Chapter 2, but it is worth placing the facts of *Goodwin* within that reasoning framework in order to demonstrate that the application of the key *Goodwin* proportionality test, as opposed to the key *de Freitas* tests, may well lead to a different outcome. Following *de Freitas*, it is first necessary to ask whether a significant and pressing interest, falling within one or more of the Article 10(2) exceptions, has been identified since so doing is part of the test for

---

[98] At [39].   [99] See Chapter 2 at 50–61.   [100] See Chapter 2 at 101–4.
[101] From the decision of the Privy Council in *de Freitas v Permanent Secretary of Ministry of Agriculture, Fisheries, Lands and Housing* [1999] 1 AC 69, 80.
[102] See Chapter 2 at 91–3.

'necessary' under para 2. That is the first test, and impliedly it was not met in *Goodwin* since the Court did not find that the harm caused to Tetra outweighed the value of protecting the source. The second and third *de Freitas* tests cover the issue of proportionality. Under the second it is necessary to consider the suitability of the interference in question—the extent to which it is rationally connected to the aim pursued. In this instance, the source disclosure order constituted the interference; the Court did not address this question directly, but in many source disclosure cases this is a relevant issue. It is relevant, for example, where an injunction would probably be effective in preventing further disclosures, or where, due to the circumstances, little likelihood of a further disclosure by the same source arose. In *Goodwin* an injunction had already been obtained and the Court could have adverted specifically to the question of its efficacy in the circumstances.

The third *de Freitas* test concerns the need to choose the least intrusive measure— the measure that creates a minimal degree of harm to the primary right consistent with affording protection to the aim pursued. The seriousness of the interference has to be balanced against the importance of the aim sought to be pursued. This is means/ end balancing—if there is another way of achieving the aim pursued that is less restrictive, it should be used. This can also be termed 'the least intrusive' means test. The Court's judgment might be viewed as implying that this test had not been met since a less intrusive measure—the injunction—was available and had been used. The problem is that this test does not lend itself readily to the principled analysis of the harm caused in relation to the value of the speech that can occur under the *Goodwin* speech/harm balancing test.[103] It remained to be seen whether the domestic courts would apply this test under a strict level of scrutiny.

In order to comply with this ruling, it might have been thought to be necessary to amend the 'interests of justice' head of s 10. The then Conservative Government stated, however, in response to the ruling, that it had no plans to amend the 1981 Act.[104] Thus, before the HRA came fully into force it appeared that under s 3(1) HRA, when a suitable case arose, s 10 would be found to require re-interpretation; clearly, the established interpretation of the term 'necessary' did not accord with the test for necessity under Article 10(2). But in any event it was probable that the judges would react to the ruling in *Goodwin*, regardless of the HRA, although there was subsequently disagreement among them as to the effect of *Goodwin*. The argument that the UK stance on source disclosure differed from that taken at Strasbourg was far from fully accepted.[105]

Therefore it appeared to be quite possible that before the HRA was in force, the judges would already have brought about harmony between the established domestic interpretation of s 10 and the demands of Article 10 as indicated by

---

[103] This point is discussed in Chapter 2 at 98–106. It depends on the interpretation of the means/end balancing test. If the *nature* and extent of the interference is examined, it overlaps with the speech/harm balancing test.

[104] *Hansard* (Lords) 13 April 1996 Vol 571, Col 6147, Written Answer.   [105] See pp 341–2, below.

Goodwin. However, in *Camelot Group Ltd v Centaur Communications*[106] the Court of Appeal allowed the 'necessary in the interests of justice' exception under s 10 a scope which was arguably as wide as that afforded to it in *X v Morgan Grampian*. The company, Camelot, runs the UK national lottery. An anonymous source sent Camelot's draft accounts to the newspaper, which published them. It appeared that Camelot was misleading the public regarding the dedication of the funds generated to charitable concerns. Camelot sought return of the documents in order to identify the source, and the newspaper relied on s 10.

Camelot had already obtained an injunction preventing any further dissemination of its accounts. Once the injunction had been obtained against Centaur, any other newspaper that published information covered by it would have risked liability for contempt of court as a result of the contempt ruling in the *Spycatcher* case, discussed in Chapter 6.[107] Therefore the disclosure order might have been viewed as disproportionate to the end in view. This was found to be the case in *Goodwin* in similar circumstances. The significance of the information itself might also have been taken into account in reaching this finding, since it concerned the accountability of a large and very profitable company, engaged, at least to an extent, in funding public and community services. On the *Goodwin* model the Court of Appeal could have balanced the weightiness of the expression interest against the degree of harm caused. In relation to the expression interest it could have taken account, not only of the significance of protecting sources, but also of the issues of public interest that are raised by the question of the proportion of lottery money that is diverted to community projects, and the like, and the proportion which is straightforward profit. There is clearly an important political dimension to Camelot's activities that might not arise to the same extent in respect of the activities of many private companies. In relation to the question of harm, it could have taken account of the effect of the injunction that was already in place.

Schiemann L.J, with whom the other judges concurred, concentrated, not on the public interest value of the information, but on the speculative harm to Camelot that might arise in future if the employee who had leaked the information perpetrated further leaks:

There is no threat now posed to the plaintiffs by further disclosure of the draft accounts. Such threat as there was has been dealt with by injunction or undertaking in relation to that material and the passage of time. There is however a continuing threat of damage of a type which did not feature significantly in the *Goodwin* case or in the *X v Morgan Grampian* case ... Clearly there is unease and suspicion amongst the employees of the company which inhibits good working relationships. Clearly there is a risk that an employee who has proved untrustworthy in one regard may be untrustworthy in a different respect and reveal the name of, say, a public figure who has won a huge lottery prize.[108]

This speculative threat of damage was found to be sufficient to outweigh the interest in protecting sources. On the question of necessity the court found that the interests

---

[106] [1998] EMLR 1; [1999] QB 124.   [107] See pp 290–1.   [108] At 138.

of Camelot in ensuring the loyalty of its employees and ex-employees should out-weigh the public importance attached to the protection of sources. In the present instance, the Court considered that in any event, there was no public interest in protecting the source.[109] The Court of Appeal took the view that in reaching this finding it was applying the same test of necessity as was applied by the European Court of Human Rights in *Goodwin*.

Clearly, the term 'necessary in the interests of justice' used in s 10 leaves room for varying interpretations. Nevertheless, the determinations as to necessity in *Camelot* and in *Goodwin* do not, it is contended, afford equal weight to the role of the media in informing the public. In asking whether the interference in question was proportion-ate to the legitimate aim pursued, the Strasbourg Court in *Goodwin* unpacked the 'harm' apparently caused, and applied a very high weight to the speech interest. In *Camelot* the court did not consider the question of proportionality as a distinct aspect of necessity and did not accord a high weight to source protection or look closely at the harm caused by the leak. Further, since the European Court of Human Rights allowed the domestic authorities a margin of appreciation (albeit highly circum-scribed) in determining the issue of proportionality in *Goodwin*, one might have expected an even stricter view of the issue to be taken at the domestic level. It is argued that this threat did not provide a weighty enough basis for finding that the key *Goodwin* test for proportionality was satisfied, taking account of the strict scrutiny required. Bearing the use of the injunction in mind, it could also have been argued that the *de Freitas* means/end balancing test was not satisfied. In fact in *Goodwin* there was the same speculative harm.

Greater weight was, however, accorded to the term 'necessary' in two further pre-HRA decisions, and the balance struck was more in accord with that endorsed in *Goodwin*. Both concerned apparent leaks from lawyers' offices. In *Saunders v Punch Ltd*,[110] in which an injunction had been granted to restrain use of the information in question, it was found that the interests of justice were not so pressing as to require the statutory privilege against disclosure to be overridden. Saunders had been the subject of interviews by the DTI in relation to a criminal prosecution that had eventu-ally been challenged under Article 6 at Strasbourg.[111] No report made by the inspec-tors to the DTI had been published, but the inspectors' deliberations had got to that stage at which extracts of their provisional findings had been sent to those persons potentially affected by them, including Mr. Saunders. He took legal advice and had a number of meetings with solicitors and leading counsel. An article appeared in *Punch* magazine that led Mr. Saunders to think that confidential material as to communica-tions between him and his solicitors had been leaked and he began proceedings against *Punch*. An injunction restraining further publication was immediately granted and its continuation until judgment was not resisted by *Punch*. However, Mr. Saunders wanted *Punch* to be compelled to disclose its source for the information in the article.

---

[109] See e.g. p 139 of the judgment.   [110] [1998] 1 WLR 986.
[111] *Saunders v UK* (1996) 23 EHRR 313.

The article stated that Mr. Saunders was expected 'to fight tooth and nail to prevent publication of the report by DTI inspectors', and it then raised the question why that should be the case, concluding that Saunders was trying to protect his earning power at the last stages of his career.[112]

The judge, Lindsay J, found that an issue of legal professional confidence arose, but that there was some public interest in knowing why, so many years after the relevant events, no report had been published regarding the DTI prosecutions, a matter that presumptively should be reported upon by a free press. He also took into account the more general public interest against disclosure, as summed up in *Goodwin v UK*. He found that there was a relatively insubstantial risk of foreseeable future damage and a relative unlikelihood of repetition. The 'residual threat of damage through dissemination'[113] was much less weighty, he found, than it had been in *X Ltd*.[114] He found that the great importance of the protection of sources constituted 'a very substantial counterweight' and, conducting the balancing act under s 10, he found that relief going beyond that provided by the injunction already granted, in the interests of justice, was not of such preponderating importance as to override the statutory privilege against disclosure. This was a pre-HRA case, but Lindsay J conducted, without using that terminology, the speech/harm balancing act required by the proportionality test from *Goodwin*.

In *John v Express Newspapers*,[115] a similar approach was taken by the Court of Appeal. The first four claimants, who included the well known singer, Elton John, were involved in litigation in which their solicitors, the fifth claimants, had instructed counsel to advise them. A copy of counsel's draft advice was leaked to a journalist; the Chambers did not institute an internal enquiry into the leak. A source disclosure order was made, but on appeal Lord Woolf, in giving the leading judgment, found that disclosure of a journalist's source might be necessary to protect the interests of justice pursuant to s 10 of the 1981 Act, but that, before the courts would require journalists to break what they regarded as a most important professional obligation to protect a source, the minimum requirement was that other means of identifying that source should be explored; it could not merely be assumed that it would not be possible to identify the culprit. He indicated that the failure of the plaintiffs to take other steps to find out the identity of the source (such as instituting an internal enquiry) was very significant since it affected the assessment of what was 'necessary' in the circumstances. He found that the first instance judge had attached insufficient importance to the failure of counsel's chambers to conduct an inquiry into the leak, and too much significance to the threat that that single incident posed to legal confidentiality.

Therefore the claimants had not established that disclosure of the journalist's

---

[112] The article went on: 'The answer lies in previous unpublished records of meetings between Saunders and his then lawyers in 1996. The documents show that Saunders was worried that the DTI would choose to publish immediately after the verdict from the European Court last October and that his real fear was that this would affect his earning power in the last few years of his business career.'

[113] He took the phrase from *Goodwin v UK* (1996) 22 EHRR 123, 145.

[114] [1991] AC 1, discussed above.   [115] [2000] 1 WLR 1931; [2000] 3 All ER 257.

source was necessary in the interests of justice and, in any event, the judge should have exercised his discretion to refuse disclosure. Lord Woolf laid emphasis on the role of the press in exposing corruption and stressed the importance of protecting sources in order that that role should be fulfilled. These findings clearly refer to aspects of the *Goodwin* tests for proportionality discussed above. Thus it may be concluded that these two decisions took some account of such tests, rather than focusing on identifying and stressing the countervailing need to order source disclosure to further the aim in question. However, the different context in these two cases, as compared to that in *Camelot* appeared to be of relevance. *John* and *Saunders* did not concern an employee of a company—someone who might potentially leak confidential information in future. In both instances it appeared probable that the leak would not recur. Thus in both instances the judges seemed to view themselves as free to impose a strict standard of scrutiny—they were not trammeled by the concern to protect a business from an untrustworthy employee—the 'ticking bomb' notion—that exercised the courts so much in *X v Morgan-Grampian* and in *Camelot*.

The discussion indicates that although there were signs that a different balance was being struck between the value of protecting of sources and the interests of justice in the immediate pre-HRA period, the domestic approach was still flawed. In deciding whether or not to order disclosure of sources the test of necessity demanded that the court then had to balance the public interest in confidentiality of sources against that of advancing the cause in question. But the interpretation of the test of 'necessary in the interests of. . . .' did not appear to depend sufficiently on differentiation between the concepts of necessity and proportionality, especially in *Camelot*. The pre-HRA test was not therefore fully in harmony with that under Article 10(2) since the factor of proportionality was not being given full weight. It was also apparent that the test for necessity appeared to differ depending on the exception being invoked, a weaker test operating under the 'national security' exception than under that concerning the 'interests of justice'. This stance has some basis in the Strasbourg jurisprudence under Article 10(2),[116] but it is nevertheless unclear that the readiness with which this weaker test has been satisfied in this context would be acceptable at Strasbourg.

THE IMPACT OF THE HUMAN RIGHTS ACT, ARTICLE 10 ECHR

INTRODUCTION

This chapter has argued that a number of the leading pre-HRA cases—*Secretary of State for Defence v Guardian Newspapers*, *British Steel* and *Camelot*—reveal that a media-friendly stance was not adopted by the judiciary in respect of the step-by-step analytical

---

[116] See Chapter 2 at 55.

exercise to be taken in a source disclosure case. Those steps are: first, that jurisdiction must be established; second, the applicability of a s 10 exception must be determined; third the necessity of ordering disclosure to serve the aim of the exception must be considered. As cases arose under the HRA, bearing in mind the importance accorded at Strasbourg to the protection of sources under Article 10 as a vital part of the media's role, it was reasonable to expect at the least that the reasoning on the question of necessity—the third step—would be affected by a determination to afford a stronger weight to the various media interests at stake[117] by applying the *Goodwin* test for proportionality under a strict form of scrutiny. It appeared possible that an order to disclose the identity of a source would only be obtained in the most exceptional of circumstances and that Article 10 under the Human Rights Act would satisfy the role that had been assigned by some to s 10 of the 1981 Act, but which it had not fulfilled.

It never appeared to be very likely that the judges would use Article 10 to affect the first two steps in a source disclosure case. The exceptions under s 10 regarding national security and the prevention of crime answer to the similarly worded exceptions to Article 10. The term 'the interests of justice' does not appear in para 2 of Article 10, although it is probably covered by the exception for the preservation of confidentiality or, more rarely, for the prevention of crime. The term 'the preservation of the authority and impartiality of the judiciary' and—as it has been interpreted domestically—the 'rights of others' exception might also apply. As discussed above, the 'interests of justice' exception was not narrowed down by interpretation pre-HRA, but instead remained an extremely broad and imprecise concept.[118] Under the HRA the term had to be interpreted compatibly with para 2 of Article 10. The precedents set by the House of Lords could have been overridden relying on s 3(1) HRA. However, the term 'protecting the rights of others' in Article 10(2) is on its face even broader than the phrase 'the interests of justice',[119] thus giving leeway to the domestic courts to continue to adopt a broad approach. So it was always probable that the judiciary would continue to interpret the phrase broadly.

Therefore under the HRA attention was always likely to turn exclusively to the s 10 term 'necessary', which now clearly covered the Article 10 tests of necessity and proportionality. It was in this respect, after *Goodwin*, that Article 10 of the Convention most clearly demanded a greater protection for sources than had been provided under domestic law. This was partly due to the Strasbourg Court's insistence on the constant interest in protecting sources, and partly to the strictness of the standard of scrutiny applicable to the use of the tests for proportionality. The argument that *Goodwin* established a stricter standard than *Morgan Grampian* was put forward in *Camelot Group plc v Centaur Communications Ltd*[120] and rejected by Schiemann LJ; he held

---

117 See, for example, David Feldman in *Civil Liberties and Human Rights*, 2nd edn., Oxford: OUP, 2002, p 856.

118 *X Ltd v Morgan-Grampian Ltd* [1991] 1 AC 1 at 43.

119 But see the interpretation of the phrase the 'rights of others' in *Chassagnou v France* (2000) 29 EHRR 615, p 359, below.

120 [1999] QB 124 (pp 337–8 above) at 135.

that the different result merely reflected the fact that different courts can reach different conclusions while applying the same legal principles to the same facts. However, Sedley LJ commented on this point in the post-HRA decision in *Interbrew SA v Financial Times Ltd*[121]: 'the decisions of the European Court of Human Rights demonstrate that the freedom of the press has in the past carried greater weight in Strasbourg that it has in the courts of this country'.

But it was already apparent that the strong established domestic traditions governing the approach of the courts ran counter to the Strasbourg jurisprudence. Therefore the possibility of departure from the jurisprudence, while appearing to adhere to it in a superficial or tokenistic fashion, became apparent. The key issue, therefore, in the post-HRA era was whether the interpretation of the term 'necessary' in s 10 would become fully consonant with the Strasbourg view of what is 'necessary in a democratic society' in order to further the aims in question.

THE POST-HRA DECISIONS

Interbrew SA v Financial Times Ltd[122] is the post-HRA case that can be most readily pointed to as indicating that the HRA has not produced significantly more protection for journalists. The claimant, the company Interbrew, maker of Stella Artois lager, was contemplating a possible takeover bid for another company, S. Interbrew's advisers prepared a presentation which they submitted to the company. Subsequently an unidentified person obtained a copy of the presentation. The document referred to the intention of Interbrew to launch the bid. Most of the document was genuine, but whoever leaked it also doctored it to include a fabricated offer price and timetable. He or she then sent copies of the doctored version to various news media, including the defendants. The defendants then published articles about the takeover bid. The claimants applied for a *Norwich Pharmacal* order requiring the defendants to deliver up the copies of the presentation which they had received in order to attempt to identify the source. The defendants invoked section 10 of the Contempt of Court Act 1981, but the judge made the order sought. He took the view that the doctored leak had been perpetrated in order to affect S's share price. Since this would, on the face of it, be a criminal act he considered that it would be in the public interest for Interbrew to be given the documents to try to trace the source. The defendants appealed.

The appeal therefore concerned the scope of the right of a newspaper to refuse to reveal its sources within the bounds of Article 10, applied under ss 3 and 6 HRA. The source had passed on information which he must have known was confidential, and therefore a breach of confidence was made out. Each defendant, by disseminating the leaked information, had innocently lent itself to the source's wrongful purpose. It was found that the jurisdiction recognized in *Norwich Pharmacal Co v Customs and Excise Commissioners*[123] allowed the court to make an order requiring the yielding up of the

---

[121] [2002] EMLR 24 at [97].   [122] [2002] EMLR 24; [2002] EWCA Civ 274, CA.
[123] [1974] AC 133.

documents. The appellants argued that even if there was jurisdiction to grant the order it should not have been granted, taking into account s 10 of the Contempt of Court Act 1981 and Article 10 ECHR, under the HRA.

The Court began by considering the effect of reading and applying s 10, so far as possible, compatibly with the Convention rights under s 3(1) HRA. Lord Justice Sedley said, on the question of the meaning of the term 'interests of justice' in s 10 of the 1981 Act, that the Court of Appeal in *Ashworth*[124] (discussed below) had followed the line of authority now accepted as dominant which attributes a broader meaning to the phrase 'the interests of justice' in section 10 of the Contempt of Court Act 1981 than was initially given to it in *Secretary of State for Defence v Guardian Newspapers*,[125] where Lord Diplock had limited it to the technical interests of the administration of justice in court proceedings. He said: 'By common consent our approach is that of Lord Bridge in *X v Morgan-Grampian*:[126] the phrase is large enough to include the exercise of legal rights and self-protection from legal wrongs, whether or not by court action.' He further found that the term 'interests of justice' in section 10 means 'interests that are justiciable' and said that he could not envisage any such interest that would not fall within one or more of the catalogue of legitimate aims in Article 10(2). This approach to the first and second steps to be taken in a source disclosure case was the expected and readily predictable one.

The Court went on to consider whether the use of the disclosure order was necessary and proportionate to the aim in view—to protect the interests of justice, and one or more of the Article 10(2) aims. Lord Justice Sedley went on to find that the term 'necessary' within section 10 must mean what is 'necessary in a democratic society' within Article 10(2). He found that this meant, 'to be necessary within what is now the meaning of section 10, disclosure must meet a pressing social need, must be the only practical way of doing so, must be accompanied by safeguards against abuse and must not be such as to destroy the essence of the primary right.' This last proportionality test is closer to the means/end balancing test from *de Freitas* test than it is to the speech/harm balancing test from *Goodwin*. Clearly, an interference that goes further than it needs to do to serve the end in question may destroy the essence of the right—speech. He also asked whether the importance of disclosure outweighed the public interest in protecting journalist's sources. He went on to find that it was clear that a democratic society accepts the need to protect press sources. Therefore it must be possible to identify a strong countervailing 'pressing social need' to set on the other side of the scale. The need was, he found, in terms of section 10, to enable Interbrew to restrain by court action any further breach of confidence by the source and possibly to recover damages for losses already sustained. In terms of Article 10(2) it was to protect the rights of Interbrew. No less invasive alternative had to be available—which appeared to be the case. So there were two significant interests on both sides of the scale. On the one hand, then, it was found that there was 'the legitimacy of Interbrew's

---

[124] [2001] 1 WLR 515; 1 All ER 991, CA.   [125] [1985] AC 339 at 350.   [126] [1999] 1 AC 1 at 43.

intended resort to law.' On the other there was a constant public interest in the confidentiality of media sources.

The critical factor identified by the court in determining where the balance lay between the two interests was the source's evident purpose. Lord Justice Sedley found that it was clearly a malevolent one. The public interest in protecting the source of such a leak was not, he considered, sufficient to withstand the countervailing public interest in letting Interbrew seek justice in the courts against the source. Therefore the order of disclosure was upheld, and the House of Lords refused leave to appeal[127] on the ground that the issues had been dealt with in the *Ashworth* case, below.

As will be contended in more detail below, this judgment did not fully apply the *Goodwin* speech/harm balancing test. It did not examine the two interests at stake in a sufficiently rigorous fashion. In particular it appeared to give less weight to the unvarying and strong interest in protecting sources than *Goodwin* did—in a fairly similar situation—although in *Goodwin* the source did not seem to be activated by malice. As part of the subsequent saga, lawyers for Interbrew immediately wrote to the organizations demanding that the document be handed over. Interbrew went on to ask the High Court to seize the *Guardian*'s assets for refusing to hand over a copy of the leaked document. However, after an outcry against the company in the media and in government, which might have affected its brand image, Interbrew withdrew its threat to seize the assets. It announced that it had abandoned its legal action against the *Guardian* and three other media organizations, the *Financial Times, The Times*, the *Independent* and Reuters, in the attempt to recover the leaked documents.[128] The newspapers stated that they intend to take the case to the European Court of Human Rights.[129]

The decision attracted adverse comment from a range of sources in the press, from civil libertarians, the House of Commons and abroad.[130] An interesting analogy might be drawn between Interbrew's actions in seeking to seize *the Guardian*'s assets and those of the Turkish government in the Strasbourg case of *Ozgur Gundem v Turkey*.[131] The Court found in that instance that a search operation at the newspaper's premises, which resulted in newspaper production being disrupted for two days, constituted a serious interference with the applicants' freedom of expression under

---

[127] On 11 July 2002. [128] On 26 July 2002. [129] See *The Guardian*, 12 July 2002.

[130] Aidan White, General Secretary of the Brussels-based International Federation of Journalists, said that the decision created further intolerable pressure on journalistic ethics from corporate interests. John Wadham, the (then) Director of *Liberty*, said that the principle of press freedom, 'a fundamental protection for democracy', would be substantially eroded if journalists had to disclose their sources. Chris Mullin, Chairman of the all-party Commons Home Affairs Committee, commented: 'The right to protect sources is a fundamental part of a free press. I am very disappointed that the courts have not recognised this.' Tom Watson, a member of the all-party Commons Home Affairs Select Committee, said: 'This legal action is corporate bullying.' Jeremy Dear, General Secretary of the National Union of Journalists, attacked the decision: 'The idea that a brewer is prepared to send a team of accountants to sequestrate and run a newspaper is one of the biggest threats to press freedom for decades.'

See *The Guardian* website—guardian.co.uk.

[131] (2001) 31 EHRR 49. See further p 378 below.

Article 10. No justification had been provided for the seizure of the newspaper's archives, documentation and library. The Turkish case was concerned with state actions, Interbrew with those of a large corporate body. But arguably media freedom was severely threatened in both instances. Judges in a mature democracy such as that in the UK recognize the threat posed by the *state* to that freedom; they appear to be less ready at present to recognize the threat posed by multi-nationals.

In the ruling in *Ashworth Hospital Authority v MGN Ltd*[132] a somewhat stricter approach was taken, under the HRA, to the interests of the media in protecting sources, although the process of reasoning and the outcome were similar to those in *Interbrew*. The appeal concerned the right of a newspaper to refuse to reveal its sources. It arose from the publication of an article in the *Daily Mirror* which included extracts from the medical records of Ian Brady (one of the Moors murderers), a patient at Ashworth Security Hospital ('Ashworth'). He was, at the time of the publication, engaged on a hunger strike which had received a great deal of publicity.[133] In April 2000, Rougier J ordered the defendant, MGN Ltd, the publisher of the *Daily Mirror*, to make and serve upon the authority a witness statement aimed at identifying the source who had passed on the medical records.[134]

In the course of their appeal against that order, MGN contended that Rougier J had no jurisdiction to grant the order, but that if he did have such jurisdiction, he was not entitled to do so in the circumstances of this case. The *Daily Mirror* reporter stated that he did not know the identity of the initial source of the information, but that he assumed it to be an employee of Ashworth. However, he accepted that he did know the identity of the intermediary who supplied the material to him. It was also accepted that knowledge of the intermediary would in all probability lead to the identity of the original source. The reporter had previously dealt with the intermediary on the understanding that he would be paid for stories supplied.

It was found by the Court of Appeal (and was not later disputed in the House of Lords), that it was overwhelmingly likely that the source provided the intermediary with a print-out from Ashworth's computer database which was used to record data about patients ('PACIS'). This meant that the source was probably an employee of the authority. The importance of the confidentiality of medical records was emphasized when a new member of staff was engaged at Ashworth and the contract of employment

---

[132] [2002] 1 WLR 2033; [2002] 4 All ER 193 HL; [2001] 1 WLR 515; 1 All ER 991, CA.

[133] On 2 February 2000, Ian Brady obtained permission to apply for judicial review, in order to challenge the continuing decision to force-feed him (see *R (Brady) v Ashworth Hospital Authority* [2000] Lloyd's Med R 355; (2001) 58 BMLR 173). Maurice Kay J ruled that force-feeding was lawful since it was reasonably administered as part of the medical treatment given for the mental disorder from which Ian Brady was suffering.

[134] The statement, to be served within two working days, demanded of the publisher that it: (i) explain how it came to be in the possession or control of any medical records kept by the claimant in respect of Ian Brady whether that possession or control be of originals, copies or extracts;

(ii) identify any employee of the claimant and the name of the person or persons (and any address, telephone and fax numbers known for such a person or persons) who were involved in the defendant acquiring possession or control of the said records.

included a confidentiality clause. It was accepted that leaks to the press have a detrimental effect on security, treatment of patients and staff morale for a number of reasons: they may inhibit proper recording of information about patients; may deter patients from providing sensitive information about themselves; may damage the patient-doctor relationship, which rests on trust; may lead to assaults by patients on a patient about whom information is disclosed; may create an atmosphere of distrust amongst staff, which is detrimental to efficient and cooperative work; and they may give rise to fear of future leaks.

The Court of Appeal found that the jurisdiction to order the disclosure of the identity of a wrongdoer did not have to be confined to cases involving tort but should be of general application. The Court considered the approach that should be taken to s 10, taking into account the requirements of the HRA. It considered that there is no difference in principle between English law and Article 10,[135] and that in interpreting s 10 the court should, where possible, (a) equate the specific purposes for which disclosure of the source was permitted under s 10 with 'legitimate aims' under Article 10 of the Convention, and (b) apply the same test of necessity as that applied by the European Court. Applying that test to the instant case, it was found that in general the disclosure of confidential medical records to the press was misconduct which was contrary to the public interest. The exceptional circumstances making this argument more compelling were stressed: it was said that there is a very clear need to protect patient confidentiality, especially the confidentiality of medical records, which should be safeguarded in any democratic society and, further, in this case it was considered that there was a risk of further leaks. So the Court of Appeal dismissed the appeal and disclosure was ordered.

When MGN appealed, it argued in the House of Lords that the order should not have been granted, taking account of s 10 of the 1981 Act and Article 10. The House of Lords found that both section 10 and Article 10 have a common purpose in seeking to enhance the freedom of the press by protecting journalistic sources. They relied on the approach of the European Court of Human Rights as to the role of Article 10 as set out by the Court in *Goodwin v United Kingdom*,[136] and in particular on these phrases from the judgment:

Protection of journalistic sources is one of the basic conditions for press freedom . . . source disclosure cannot be compatible with article 10 of the Convention unless it is justified by an overriding requirement in the public interest.[137]

It was accepted that the same approach should be applied equally to section 10 since

---

[135] It found that two views had been expressed in the House of Lords as to the meaning of the expression 'interests of justice'. As discussed above, in *Defence Secretary v Guardian Newspapers* [1985] AC 339 at 350, Lord Diplock had sought to confine the exception to the administration of justice in the course of existing court proceedings. But in *X Ltd v Morgan Grampian* [1991] 1 AC 1 at 43, Lord Bridge had found that this interpretation was too narrow and that the exception included facilitating the exercise of legal rights even where resort to legal proceedings was not occurring, and whether or not it would need to do so. The Court of Appeal favoured Lord Bridge's much broader approach.

[136] (1966) 22 EHRR 123.   [137] At [39].

Article 10 is part of domestic law under the Human Rights Act. It had to be determined whether it was a necessary precondition of the exercise of the jurisdiction to make an order of disclosure that the applicant (Ashworth) should have begun, or had an intention to begin, legal proceedings in respect of the allegedly wrongful act against the source. The Lords relied on the speeches in *British Steel Corp v Granada Television Ltd*[138] and in particular on the judgments of Lord Denning MR,[139] and of Templeman LJ,[140] in the Court of Appeal in finding that this was unnecessary. Lord Woolf confirmed that the approach of Lord Bridge in *Morgan Grampian* was the correct one.[141] In other words, it was confirmed that s 10 allows for the making of orders in the interests of justice, and such interests are widely defined—they are not confined to the administration of justice within legal proceedings, and it is not necessary that such proceedings should be brought. This was, clearly, a crucial finding, demonstrating that, despite the effect of the HRA and Article 10, the Lords were determined to keep open the possibility of seeking source disclosure orders in a very wide range of circumstances.

The Lords considered whether the use of the disclosure order was necessary and proportionate to the aim in view—to protect the interests of justice, under s 10 and Article 10. On the interpretation of the term 'necessary in the interests of justice', Lord Woolf said:

Construing the phrase 'in the interests of justice' in [the sense determined upon] immediately emphasises the importance of the balancing exercise. It will not be sufficient, *per se*, for a party seeking disclosure of a source protected by section 10 to show merely that he will be unable without disclosure to exercise the legal right or avert the threatened legal wrong on which he bases his claim in order to establish the necessity of disclosure. The judge's task will always be to weigh in the scales the importance of enabling the ends of justice to be attained in the circumstances of the particular case on the one hand against the importance of protecting the source on the other hand. In this balancing exercise it is only if the judge is satisfied that disclosure in the interests of justice is of such preponderating importance as to override the statutory privilege against disclosure that the threshold of necessity will be reached.[142]

The hospital had to establish 'an overriding public interest, amounting to a pressing social need, to which the need to keep press sources confidential should give way' since, as Laws L.J. had pointed out in the Court of Appeal,

the public interest in the non-disclosure of press sources is constant, whatever the merits of the particular publication and the particular source. It is in no way lessened and certainly not abrogated, simply because the case is one in which the information actually disclosed is of no legitimate, objective public interest.[143]

Lord Woolf found that any restriction on the otherwise unqualified right to freedom of expression must meet the requirements under Article 10(2) of answering to a

---

[138] [1981] AC 1096. [139] At p 1127. [140] At p 1132. [141] At [39]
[142] At [39]. [143] At [101].

'pressing social need' and also the restriction should be proportionate to a legitimate aim which is being pursued.[144] In this instance, it was found, an overriding public interest could be identified, as Lord Woolf determined:

The situation here is exceptional, as it was in *Financial Times Ltd v Interbrew SA* and as it has to be, if disclosure of sources is to be justified. The care of patients at Ashworth is fraught with difficulty and danger. The disclosure of the patients' records increases that difficulty and danger and to deter the same or similar wrongdoing in the future it was essential that the source should be identified and punished. This was what made the orders to disclose necessary and proportionate and justified. The fact that Ian Brady had himself disclosed his medical history did not detract from the need to prevent staff from revealing medical records of patients.

Lord Woolf also referred to the approach of the European Court to medical records in relation to Article 8 in *Z v Finland*.[145] The Court had found that:

the protection of personal data, not least medical data, is of fundamental importance to a person's enjoyment of his or her right to respect for private and family life as guaranteed by Article 8 of the Convention. Respecting the confidentiality of health data is a vital principle in the legal systems of all the contracting parties to the Convention. The domestic law must therefore afford appropriate safeguards to prevent any such communication or disclosure of personal health data as may be inconsistent with the guarantees in Article 8 of the Convention.

Taking account of the significance of preserving the confidentiality of health data, Lord Woolf went on to dismiss the appeal. He did not examine the question of proportionality in detail, but appeared to assume impliedly that since there was such a pressing need to protect medical records in the instant case, the measure in question was proportionate to the aim pursued. Thus he did not engage in a full application of the *Goodwin* proportionality tests under a strict level of scrutiny.

The other Law Lords agreed with his findings. Therefore the order of disclosure was upheld. The test of necessity from *Ashworth* may be taken to have superseded the test from *Interbrew* in so far as the two decisions differ on this point. The Lords, however, appeared to take the view that they do not differ significantly since they refused leave to appeal in the *Interbrew* case. The nature of the current domestic tests for pro-portionality and its consonance with the Strasbourg tests is considered further below.

Ackroyd v Mersey Care NHS Trust[146] arose as a result of the findings in the *Ashworth* case. MGN proceeded to disclose the identity of the intermediary through whom it had obtained the notes—Ackroyd. He was an investigative journalist who had been involved in previous investigations into mismanagement at the hospital; he therefore had an established and lengthy interest in it. Some of Mr Ackroyd's revelations about failings at the hospital had previously led to the Fallon Inquiry which produced the Fallon Report.[147] The conclusion of the Report had been that Ashworth should close

---

[144] At [62].   [145] (1998) 25 EHRR 371 at [94] and [95].   [146] [2003] EMLR 820.

[147] *The Report of Committee of Inquiry in the Personality Disorder Unit at Ashworth Special Hospital* (1999).

due to poor management. In evidence, Ackroyd said that over the years he had developed contacts with a number of sources at the hospital and that in the instance in question in *Ashworth* he had not paid the source for the notes. The claimant, Ashworth, brought proceedings against the defendant, Ackroyd, seeking an order for disclosure of his source. He resisted, relying firstly on an argument that the *Norwich Pharmacal* jurisdiction was not applicable. He argued that the source would have had a public interest defence to a claim by the hospital for breach of confidence or contract and that therefore he was not 'mixed up' in wrong-doing by the source since there was no wrong-doer.

He also relied on s 10. Ashworth argued that Mr Ackroyd's position was indistinguishable from that of *The Mirror* in the *MGN* case and that the decision of the House of Lords had concluded the issue. Ackroyd argued that the facts relevant to an application for an order for disclosure against him were materially different from those advanced by *The Mirror* in the *MGN* case. The judge took the view that the issues had been settled by the *MGN* case, and made the order of disclosure sought. The view was taken that the expressed purpose of the order made in the *MGN* case would be subverted if Mr Ackroyd were to succeed in keeping his source anonymous on the basis that the judgments in that case, to which Mr Ackroyd was not a party, were determinative of his defence also.

Ackroyd appealed, contending as his ground of appeal that the judge had been wrong to find that he had no real prospect of successfully resisting the claim that he should be ordered to disclose the source of the clinical notes. He put forward an argument based on the public interest in the disclosures, which went both to establishing that there was no jurisdiction to make the disclosure order and to the s 10 contentions. In support of this argument he said in evidence that he had been approached by sources at Ashworth and provided with information, including the PACIS notes covering Brady's first month on hunger strike. He had promised not to reveal the identity of the sources.

The sources were not, Ackroyd said, motivated by monetary gain; he had made no payment to them; their purpose in providing him with information was: 'to enable the public disclosure of the way in which Mr Brady had been treated, which, consistent with the findings of the Fallon Report in other matters, had not been disclosed by Ashworth'.[148] Thus, according to Ackroyd, the sources were acting in the public interest since they were exposing various serious flaws in the running of the hospital. In particular, they had revealed that the treatment of Brady was improper. Ackroyd had relied on a number of confidential journalistic sources in order to help him expose incompetence at the hospital and to subject the institution to public scrutiny. The Fallon Report had revealed that there was a history of secrecy and non-disclosure of reports at the hospital. Therefore, exposure of improper practices at the hospital might not have occurred had sources not made revelations to Mr Ackroyd. He further argued that in any event the hospital had failed to establish an overriding public

---

[148] At [36].

interest in disclosure of the identity of the source, making it necessary for that identity to be revealed in the interests of justice under s 10, and Article 10, HRA.

The Court of Appeal found that that it was not necessary to reach any conclusion as to whether Ackroyd might be able to establish, on the facts presented, that the source who provided the clinical notes to him might have had a public interest defence to a claim by the hospital for breach of confidence or contract. The Court accepted that, if this were established, a *Norwich Pharmacal* claim would not have been available for want of a 'wrong-doer', but also accepted that if the defence was not established the source had clearly acted in breach of confidence and in breach of contract.[149] The Court went on to find that if its inquiry was confined to disclosure of the clinical notes alone, a public interest defence might be difficult to sustain. However, it did not decide that question since it found that the 'separate public interest defence', depending on s 10 and Article 10 encompassed the same facts and considerations and provided 'a more promising defence'. It was clearly found that a failure to establish that the source had a public interest defence would *not* have meant, automatically, that the hospital would be able to establish that their public interest in disclosure was sufficient to override Mr Ackroyd's public interest in maintaining the confidentiality of his source. The difference between the two arguments was indicated in the findings of the Court in relation to the effect of Article 10 on the protection of sources.

The Court relied on the statement of principle in the judgment of the European Court of Human Rights in *Goodwin*[150]—re-stated in the *Ashworth v MGN* case—that protection of journalistic sources is one of the basic conditions of press freedom, and since an order of source disclosure undermines the exercise of that freedom, such a measure cannot be compatible with Article 10 unless it is justified by an overriding requirement in the public interest.[151] The Court found that it might be hard to identify a particular public interest in the disclosure of Brady's clinical notes in the context in which they were disclosed and looked at alone since Brady had himself already published the details that they contained. Further, it was found that the notes did not contain matter giving rise to legitimate criticism of the hospital. The argument had been advanced, relying on the decision of the European Court of Human Rights in *Fressoz and Roire v France*,[152] that the notes provided 'much needed corroboration of what would otherwise be Brady's own bald and unconvincing narrative'. This argument was rejected, partly on the basis that the *Mirror* article did not use the notes for that purpose. However, this argument was found in any event to be redundant since, relying on *Goodwin*, it was clear that Ackroyd did not have to establish an overriding public interest in his source's disclosure of the clinical notes. On the contrary, the hospital had to establish 'an overriding public interest, amounting to a pressing social need, to which the need to keep press sources confidential

---

[149] The Court noted that Lord Woolf had said in [32–34] of his Opinion in the *MGN* case, that Lord Phillips was almost certainly correct in coming to this conclusion.

[150] At p 143, [39].   [151] At [66] of the *Ackroyd* judgment.

[152] *Fressoz and Roire v France* (2001) 31 EHRR 2, para [55].

should give way', since it was clear, relying on Laws LJ's comments in the *MGN* case, that the public interest in the non-disclosure of press sources was established and unvarying.[153]

This was found to be the basis for accepting that Ackroyd could argue plausibly that his case differed from the MGN one. The Court went on to consider the differences between the two cases and the factors that might be capable of swinging the balance from the preservation of confidentiality in patient records, to preserving the anonymity of sources in order to further the ends of journalism. In so doing the Court did in fact identify a public interest *other than* that in protecting sources, despite its earlier remarks on the point. The factors identified included: the unhappy history at the hospital which did not feature prominently in the *MGN* case, but was very significant in Ackroyd's; Ackroyd's arguable entitlement to enlarge the ambit of his defence to encompass other sources on the basis of the chilling effect of a requirement to disclose one source that might extend to other sources whom the hospital was not seeking to have identified; the fact that Mr Ackroyd's sources received no payment. The Court also noted that Ackroyd might be entitled to argue that, in the different circumstances of his case, the finding of the need for disclosure of his source in order to deter other breaches of confidence ought to be reconsidered.

The Court concluded that Mr Ackroyd had established a sufficient case to entitle him to a trial since the focus of his defence was significantly different factually from that of MGN. Therefore the decision in that case should not have been regarded as summarily determinative of his case under the Civil Procedure Rules.[154] An order for source disclosure would only be compatible with Article 10 of the European Convention if justified by an overriding requirement in the public interest. There was a clear public interest in preserving the confidentiality of medical records, but that alone could not be regarded as an *automatically* overriding requirement without examining the facts of a particular case. It would only be in exceptional circumstances that a journalist could be ordered to disclose the identity of his source without the facts of *his* case being fully examined. The nature of the subject matter was therefore found to indicate that there should be a trial in most cases.

---

[153] At [67] of the judgment.

[154] For the purposes of Pt. 24 of the Civil Procedure Rules (CPR). It was also found that he was entitled to point to Pt.24.2(b) CPR to the effect that there was another compelling reason why the case should be disposed of at a trial. Part 24 CPR provides: The court may give summary judgment against a claimant or defendant on the whole of a claim or on a particular issue if—(a) it considers that: (i) the claimant has no real prospect of succeeding on the claim or issue; or (ii) that the defendant has no real prospect of successfully defending the claim or issue; and (b) there is no other compelling reason why the case or issue should be disposed of at a trial. This conclusion of the Court was reached without according the CPR itself a Convention-friendly interpretation under s 3(1) HRA, but that would have been a possibility.

FLAWS IN THE POST-HRA JUDICIAL REASONING

The discussion above reveals that post-HRA a stance unsympathetic to the media's watchdog role was still found in relation to the first two steps in a source disclosure case—those of finding jurisdiction and applying one or more of the s 10 exceptions. The discussion of the findings in the leading post-HRA decision in *Ashworth* makes this clear. The key post-HRA change occurred in the last step—the determination as to the test of necessity—due to the influence of Article 10 under the HRA, a change that was prefigured in *John v Express Newspapers* and in *Saunders v Punch*. In relation to the first two steps the judges have always taken and continue to take, the approach that at one and the same time enhances the chances of ordering disclosure and tends to keep the argument open, thereby preserving maximum judicial discretion—a tendency that is constantly evidenced in domestic legal reasoning. The strong preference evinced is to avoid allowing the argument to be closed down at the jurisdictional stage or at the stage of considering the ambit of the exceptions in relation to an instant case. At both stages such closure would have disallowed engagement by the courts in a balancing exercise between the interest in question and the interest in protecting sources.

The tendency to take a very broad approach at these first two stages of the argument was unaffected, then, by the inception of the HRA. This is at first glance legitimate in relation to the question of the applicability of the aim—since the legitimate aims under Article 10(2) are even broader.[155] But it can be more strongly contended that it is not legitimate in relation to the jurisdictional argument which should itself be considered in relation to Article 10 under s 6 HRA since it concerns a common law doctrine. The third stage, the question of necessity, inevitably represents the crucial stage of the argument in almost all instances due to the tendency identified. It is at this stage that the stance of the judges has undergone, to an extent, a change that appears to be directly linked to the inception of the HRA.

The decisions discussed concerned two very different interests which were opposed to the public interest in media freedom and the protection of sources. In *Ashworth* (and in *Ackroyd*) there was a risk of further leaks and the source had revealed confidential medical records. A number of reasons for preserving the confidentiality of such records, especially in a hospital treating dangerous patients, were taken into account. In *Interbrew*, on the other hand, the decision protected a company's interest in bringing a legal action against a person who had leaked confidential information (although the institution of the action was not essential to the obtaining of the order—a very important point, discussed further below). The decisions in *Interbrew* and in *Ashworth* took account of the effect of the Human Rights Act and the courts

---

[155] However, it is argued below at pp 365–6 that a different approach could be taken to the aims under the HRA.

considered that the outcomes were consistent with the demands of Article 10 of the Convention, as interpreted in *Goodwin*.[156]

Nevertheless, the decisions clearly do not offer reassurance to sources who are uncertain whether to come forward. It could be argued that the source in the *Interbrew* case came forward for his or her own (arguably improper) motives and was hardly in the position of the source who wishes to reveal wrong-doing but is afraid of the repercussions. But potential sources are unlikely to understand the nuances of the decisions, but may merely receive the message that the protection for their anonymity is in jeopardy. It might appear in general that the courts are over-zealously protecting the right of institutions or companies to bring actions against employees and others. Their tendency to envisage the potential harm that could be done to companies in clear and concrete terms remains very apparent, although they now also afford at least an appearance of recognition to the interest in source protection. Although it is understandable that the courts would want to protect the right to bring an action where there is a legitimate grievance, the net result may be that companies are aided in seeking to maintain effective cover-ups.

Although the outcome in *Ashworth* is arguably less significant than the test it laid down, and the outcome should not become the main focus of writings on the matter, it is fair to suggest that the senior judiciary have developed an understanding of the tests under Article 10, but not yet a full grasp of its spirit. In particular, they tend to adopt a narrow approach to the doctrine of proportionality, failing both to subject the justification for source disclosure to a strict enough scrutiny or to apply all the *Goodwin* and *de Freitas* tests. The doctrines of necessity and proportionality tend to be elided. In *Ashworth*, wrong-doing was not perceived as being revealed. It appears that unless it is revealed, freedom of expression may be at risk of being outweighed by varying public interests in disclosure of the identity of the source, *despite* the unvarying nature of the interest in protecting sources. This point is of significance in the discussion below in which particular criticisms are offered of judicial reasoning in the post-HRA period in this context.

FAILINGS IN THE NECESSITY AND PROPORTIONALITY ANALYSES

The findings in *Ashworth* and in *Interbrew* stand in contrast to each other, to an extent. In *Ashworth*, now the leading decision, the importance of protecting sources was recognized in the test laid down for determining the 'necessity' of ordering

---

[156] The demands of Article 10 in relation to source protection are a matter of interpretation and do not arise from the wording of para 2 itself, so they could have been departed from, since under s 2 HRA the jurisprudence itself is not binding; it is the rights themselves which must be adhered to if at all possible under s 3(1), not the jurisprudence. Thus the leeway that existed to allow departure from the Strasbourg standard in the pre-HRA era, still existed post-HRA. Nevertheless, the judges post-HRA stated, possibly disingenuously, that they were following *Goodwin* rather than refusing to treat the case as binding, despite the established tendency within the pre-HRA domestic jurisprudence to afford less weight to source protection than that afforded at Strasbourg.

disclosure. If the protection of sources is regarded as an inherent and constant public interest, the other party is forced into the position of seeking to establish very weighty reasons for displacing that interest. Thus the judgment of the court has to focus on the particulars of that other party's claim. This was a significant departure from *Interbrew* since in that instance the focus of the decision was on the source's culpability rather than on identifying a clear public interest in disclosure of his or her identity. In *Ackroyd* the test from *Ashworth* was applied, resulting in the finding that the need to preserve patient confidentiality could not represent an automatic justification for ordering disclosure—it would be necessary to consider the facts in any particular instance.

This is also a criticism of *Ashworth* itself: if the decision purported to lay down clear tests for necessity and proportionality to be used in future instances, it failed to do in a number of respects. In particular, it did not subject the facts to the intense form of scrutiny demanded by *Goodwin*, and the judgment failed to distinguish fully between the tests of necessity and proportionality. The findings in *Ashworth* went to the issue of necessity—the pressing social need to preserve the confidentiality of medical records in the circumstances. In itself, establishing that need did not mean that the measure taken was proportionate to the aim pursued, although those findings could be viewed as of relevance in relation to the third aspect of the *de Freitas* test. It is possible that the demands of proportionality were satisfied, but that matter should have been subjected to greater and separate scrutiny, applying all three aspects and focusing intensely on speech/harm balancing as in *Goodwin*.

The House of Lords in *Ashworth* purported to do what the European Court did in *Goodwin*, but, it is argued, mis-weighed both the harm done to the privacy interest and the value of the speech. The Lords took the view that the protection of sources is in *itself* a highly significant public interest, regardless of the specifics of the case in question and the objective value of the information disclosed. That finding, relying on *Goodwin*, was clearly correct. But the point was not made clearly enough that the *converse* finding does not apply. In other words, where the information *is* of value in public interest terms it should weigh in the calculus as *another* weighty factor in favour of non-disclosure of the source, meaning that the other party would have to provide reasons of an exceptionally weighty nature pointing in the direction of disclosure. This point is of relevance to the key *Goodwin* proportionality test—weighing up the seriousness of the interference with speech against the importance of the aim that the plaintiff is seeking to pursue, and the harm done to that interest. The seriousness can be judged in terms of its *extent* or its nature or both. In this instance both aspects were at stake. In terms of *nature* the interference was serious for the reasons indicated: two weighty speech-based arguments went in favour of non-disclosure of the source's identity—the general interest in protecting sources, affirmed in *Goodwin*, and the public interest value of the information. In terms of extent, the interference was also serious (the third *de Freitas* test) since, unlike an injunction which can be tailored to a particular situation, a source disclosure order is an all-or-nothing measure. The consequences for the source would have been very serious and other sources at the hospital would have been deterred from coming forward. Thus it is arguable that, on strict scrutiny, this test would not have been found to be satisfied in *Ashworth*, meaning that the infringement of Article 10 would not have been viewed as justified.

This analysis is now, however, complicated where another Convention Article— usually Article 8—can be invoked as part of the justification for source disclosure. This was the case in *Ashworth*, as the House of Lords impliedly indicated in its references to *Z v Finland*. The term 'parallel analysis' was not used, but after the House of Lords' decisions in *Campbell*[157] and in *Re S*,[158] it is now clear that this is the proper means of weighing up two Convention Articles against each other,[159] except possibly in certain narrowly defined (and anomalous) exceptional circumstances.[160] In fact, prior to *Ashworth*, it had already been found in *Douglas v Hello!*[161] that this was the proper method of proceeding where an apparent clash of rights arose. It might be thought at first sight that where another Convention right is engaged the standard of scrutiny from *Goodwin* is not applicable since *Goodwin* was not a clash of rights case, but a case in which an exception based on a societal concern had to be narrowly construed. At Strasbourg a wide margin of appreciation tends to be afforded in the case of clashing rights and therefore the standard of scrutiny is less strict.[162] However, as argued in Chapter 16, this is not and should not be the approach taken at the domestic level.[163] There are a number of reasons why the approaches at the domestic and the international levels inevitably differ. The most valuable precedent is that of the House of Lords in *Campbell* in which in a case of a clash of rights a strict standard of scrutiny was adopted.[164] The precedent of *Von Hannover*[165] could also be taken into account, in which, unusually, Strasbourg did not concede a wide margin of appreciation in a case of a collision between Articles 8 and 10.

Had the parallel analysis been fully conducted in *Ashworth*, as arguably it should have been, it would have reached the stage of balancing the underlying values of both Articles 8 and 10 against each other. It would have been necessary to examine the restriction each Article proposed to lay on the other and to ask which right would suffer the greater harm if the other prevailed. The question whether the invasion of Article 10 (the source disclosure order) went further than necessary to protect the Article 8 right at stake should have been asked. In terms of extent, the interference with the Article 8 rights of Brady as a patient was quite serious, since his medical records had been disclosed without consent. However, it could arguably be assumed

---

[157] [2004] 2 WLR 1232; see Chapter 15 at 784–6 for further discussion of the decision.

[158] [2005] 1 AC 593; [2004] UKHL 47. See Chapter 16 at 828–32 for further discussion of the decision.

[159] See Chapter 15 at 784–5 and Chapter 16 at 842–4 for a full discussion of the use of the 'parallel analysis'.

[160] See Chapter 16 at 829–30 for further discussion. It now appears that the courts may decide that there are no exceptional circumstances—there are merely instances in which the speech in question is especially valuable since it related to the open justice principle (see pp 830–1).

[161] [2001] QB 967. See Chapter 16 at 828 for further discussion of the decision.

[162] See Chapter 16 at 832–6 for discussion.   [163] See Chapter 16 at 832–8 for discussion.

[164] See Chapter 15 at 785–6 for discussion.

[165] (2004) App no. 59320/00, judgment of 24 June 2004; see in particular paras 63, 64, 65, 66.

that consent could be implied, given Brady's own actions in disclosing his notes. In terms of nature, the interference was in general terms very serious since the preservation of the confidentiality of medical records is itself recognized at Strasbourg as an unvarying and consistent public interest.[166]

But in terms of *this particular context* the interference was of a less serious nature. The history of mal-management at the hospital was not viewed as relevant in *Ashworth* for various reasons. In fact it was highly relevant in relation to the weightiness of the patient confidentiality claim *and* the claim for non-disclosure of the source. It was relevant to the former claim due to the particular context in question in which the key argument for preserving patient confidentiality was put forward. It could readily be argued that where patients themselves have deliberately breached their own confidentiality in order to serve a more pressing cause—to reveal the abuses suffered by patients at the hospital—that creates a particular focus from which to view the interest in preserving confidentiality. In the instance in question two patients, including Brady himself, had breached confidentiality with that end in view. In general, in terms of the experience of being in a secure hospital and in terms of treatment, patients are likely to view the interest in confidentiality as outweighed by the interest in preventing the suffering and humiliation of patients due to maltreatment. In the hierarchy of interests relating to the hospital experience, the prevention of maltreatment—by exposing it—looms higher than the preservation of confidentiality.

It must be re-emphasized that this argument is being applied to the value of preserving patient confidentiality in a highly context-sensitive fashion, and on the basis, endorsed by *Goodwin*, of an intense scrutiny. It is undoubted that there is *general* value in enabling persons to be reassured that their medical records will remain confidential, and the Lords were clearly right to refer to that value. It has since been endorsed by the European Court of Human Rights in *Plon (Société) v France*[167] as an interest that can win out even when opposed by the countervailing interest in political speech. But while the Lords were right to place weight on the *general* value of preserving patient confidentiality, they failed to examine the very particular context in question which, it is argued, undermined that value as an individual right, or countered it. Thus, the general societal interest in preserving medical confidentiality remained of significance, but the interference with Brady's Article 8 right was of less significance than it would have been in a different context. The value of the parallel analysis and of concentration on the speech/harm balancing test from *Goodwin* is precisely that this method teases out the values genuinely at stake.

In the context of maltreatment, then, the preservation of patient confidentiality, generally of very high importance, may be viewed as a near-meaningless abstraction divorced from the idea of serving any worthwhile purpose. Indeed, it came close to being used in *Ashworth* in a perversion of its original purpose. Preservation of patient confidentiality is rooted in ideas about the intimacy of details of medical treatment—

---

[166] See *Plon (Société) v France* No. 58148/00.
[167] No. 58148/00, 18 May 2004. The decision is discussed and criticized in Chapter 13 at 696–9.

in itself linked to notions of humiliation and embarrassment. If that treatment itself directly causes humiliation—as was alleged in abundance in relation to Ashworth Hospital—then the underlying basis for maintaining confidentiality is undermined. Although it was true that the *Mirror* article in question did not directly concern mal-management at Ashworth, disclosure of the identity of the source was clearly likely to aid in the continuing attempt of the Ashworth management to cover up the failings there, documented in the Fallon Report. Thus the ruling preserved patient confidentiality in a technical or formal sense without succeeding in examining the *real* value of that confidentiality in the circumstances. Lord Woolf relied on *Z v Finland* in relation to the value of confidentiality of medical records encapsulated in Article 8. But he failed to take account of other competing values underlying Article 8, including the preservation of dignity and privacy of patients in hospitals such as Ashworth, or the general interest in the prevention of harm to patients, which would have pointed in the direction of protecting the source in order to aid in uncovering abuses of power in the hospital. However, there are precedents in a different context for weighing up such competing values.

In a series of cases the courts have recognized that the public interest in protecting patients, or potential patients, from harm outweighs the interest in maintaining the confidentiality of medical records.[168] In *Re A (Disclosure of Medical Records to the GMC)*,[169] it was found that production of medical records could be justified on the ground of protecting persons from possible medical misconduct, even where the risk of such conduct is not established. Similarly, in *A Health Authority* v *X*,[170] at first instance, it was found that there was a public interest in the disclosure of health care records in order to aid in an investigation into a certain GP. Serious allegations had been made of misconduct and unsatisfactory standards of care, although these had not been substantiated. Further, in *Woolgar* v *Chief Constable of Sussex*[171] a patient in a nurse's care had died in suspicious circumstances. Disclosure of the medical records was authorized for disciplinary purposes to the United Kingdom Central Council for Nursing, Midwifery and Health Visiting on the basis of the general public interest of the proper regulation of the nursing profession in the interests of those receiving nursing care.

It was essential in *Ashworth* to identify the relevant Article 8 values at stake, under a strict level of scrutiny, in order to determine the seriousness of the interference, weighing it against the importance of the speech, without affording either value presumptive priority. In this instance, although interference with patient confidentiality had occurred, the more significant value at stake was that of the humiliation and indignity suffered by patients at the hospital, especially Brady. Publicity *aided* in addressing that matter and thus affected both aspects of the speech/privacy balancing analysis. The more significant privacy interest—the humiliation suffered by patients,

---

[168] This has also been recognized legislatively: the Data Protection (Processing of Sensitive Personal Data) Order 2000 (SI 2000/417), Schedule, para 2, allows disclosure for regulatory purposes if in the public interest.
[169] [1998] 2 FLR 641, 644.   [170] *X* [2001] 2 FLR 673, 677.   [171] [1999] 3 All ER 604 at 615.

which sought publicity—overcame, it is argued, the interest in confidentiality. There-fore the interference with the right to respect for private life—the disclosure of the notes to the newspaper—was proportionate to the legitimate aim pursued, that of preserving the Article 10 rights of the newspaper (under the Article 8(2) 'rights of others' exception). No breach of Article 8 occurred on this analysis.

In terms of the second half of the parallel analysis, conducted under Article 10(2), it is clear that under a strict scrutiny a very serious interference with speech rights occurred which was not justified by the aim pursued—the Article 8 rights of others. The discussion reveals that the unhappy history of the hospital was relevant to the claim for non-disclosure of the identity of the source in *Ashworth* on a basis other than that of the general interest in protecting sources—thus there was a *heightened* interest in non-disclosure. That interest arose in the context of a matter of grave public interest—a context that the House of Lords was aware of but chose not to place weight on. The fact that in the instance in question the revelations arguably did not add much of significance to discussions of the situation at Ashworth was not the end of the matter. Any order of disclosure was bound to have some broad stifling effect in a number of respects in relation to a matter of grave public interest. In other words, their Lordships should have looked beyond the specifics of the revelations in question, to that general effect in such a significant context. Had these factors been taken into account, and then weighed up in the calculus of proportionality, under the speech/harm balancing test, it is argued that the decision would have gone the other way since the doubly strong public interest on the side of non-disclosure would have out-weighed the relatively weak public interest—in the particular context—of preserving patient confidentiality. The values enshrined in Article 3 could also have been taken into account in the balancing act since the disclosures were relevant to the use of degrading treatment.[172] Revelations leading to the uncovering of Article 3 treatment should surely be placed in a protected position.

Despite purporting to take account of Article 10, and in particular of the test of necessity, the House of Lords' decision fell into the trap, typical of British judicial reasoning, of assuming a narrow and technical basis, divorced from the realities of the context in question. Further, in terms of the third limb of the *de Frietas* test, it may be argued that the source disclosure order went further than was needed to serve the end of preserving the value of confidentiality since an action for breach of confidence was available against the newspaper (although it might have failed on public interest grounds), and therefore the interference was disproportionate to the end pursued. Therefore it should have been found that a breach of Article 10, but not of Article 8, would occur if the source disclosure order was upheld.

In following *Ashworth*, *Ackroyd* dealt more fully with the proportionality aspects of the instance before it, although the parallel analysis was not conducted. The decision

---

[172] For example, Brady was quite seriously injured in the course of subjecting him to force-feeding, and a child was allowed unsupervised visits in the hospital and was subjected to sexual abuse on a number of occasions. Article 3 provides 'No-one shall be subjected to torture or inhuman or degrading treatment'.

focused on the lack of payment to the source and the chilling effect on other sources at the hospital if disclosure was ordered. If the interest in protecting sources is viewed as constant, those are significant factors in terms of *heightening* that interest. The unhappy history of mismanagement and abuse of power at the hospital was considered in relation to the nature of the interference, but it should have been taken into account both in relation to the preservation of confidentiality *and* in respect of the claim for non-disclosure of the source, as argued above. In other words, it potentially affected both sides of the speech/harm equation, diminishing the importance of the aim pursued (medical confidentiality) and enhancing the significance of the interference with freedom of expression. Following this argument, *Ackroyd* reached the right result.

If the more complete version of the doctrine of proportionality argued for here—speech/harm balancing—had been applied to the facts of *Interbrew*, there is a strong argument that a breach of Article 10 would have been found. In *Interbrew* any weighing up of Articles 10 and 8 against each other would have had to concern the 'privacy' of a company. Although companies may have certain rights to private life and to protection for correspondence,[173] that argument has been accepted at Strasbourg only in relation to search and seizure of material from a company's premises.[174] It is unlikely that disclosure of information relating to a company could be viewed as 'private' information. Revelations as to share prices and the like are *prima facie* of a public character: Article 8 would be found to be unengaged or only peripherally engaged in such an instance. In *Interbrew* then it may be argued that the Article 10 claim did not have to be balanced by a strong—or any—Article 8 claim. So the case was arguably correctly viewed as one in which Article 10 had presumptive priority, subject to exceptions to be narrowly construed.

Since another Convention right was not at stake, or barely at stake, the parallel analysis was not applicable, and the interests of Interbrew were rightly viewed by Sedley LJ as protected only by Article 10(2) exceptions to be narrowly construed. The exception in question appeared to be that of 'the rights of others'. In this context, the case of *Chassagnou v France*[175] is of relevance. The Court said in that case that when dealing with 'rights of others' that are not themselves competing Convention rights, 'only indisputable imperatives can justify interference with enjoyment of a Convention right.' *Chassagnou* was not referred to in *Interbrew*, but it might be asked whether Interbrew's interest in bringing a legal action was an indisputable imperative. In any

---

[173] See *R v Broadcasting Standards Commission ex p BBC* [2000] 3 WLR 1327 (concerning the privacy of the company Dixons). The decision is discussed further in Chapter 17 at 865.

[174] In *Societe Colas Est v France* (2002) Application no. 37971/97 at [41] the Court found: 'the time has come to hold that in certain circumstances the rights guaranteed by Article 8 of the Convention may be construed as including the right to respect for a company's registered office, branches or other business premises . . .'. However, as Chapter 17 points out at pp 876–7, the protection at present extends only to physical searches of the company's premises; it would not appear to cover information relating to it or held by it (although obviously the company personnel would have individual Article 8 rights to their own private information held in the company's files).

[175] (2000) 29 EHRR 615.

event, the public interest involved in requiring source disclosure was clearly less significant than that in *Ashworth* since an individual Convention right was not involved, and therefore the case for allowing it to outweigh the interest in protecting the confidentiality of media sources was less strong. Following *Goodwin* that is a strong and unvarying interest; it would have had to be outweighed by a very compelling countervailing interest if it was to be overcome; on the facts that did not appear to be the case.

It must be noted that *aside* from the interest in source protection, the speech in *Interbrew* was *not* of high value since it appeared to be intended to be misleading; therefore it ran counter to the truth-based rationale. (In making this point it must be borne in mind that although it is possible or even probable that the source had behaved reprehensibly and from reprehensible motives, his or her motives could not be known since (obviously) he or she could not come to court to answer accusations.) In this respect the speech differed from that at issue in *Ashworth* which was of a higher value in terms of all the speech-based rationales. But that factor did not detract from the general significance of protecting sources.

Lord Justice Sedley relied partly on a test akin to means/end balancing in conducting the proportionality analysis. But such a test does not provide a sufficiently effective or nuanced mechanism for weighing up the value of the speech in relation to the harm caused. Moreover, in applying this test he did not take account of the possibility that an injunction on grounds of breach of confidence could have been obtained against the newspapers banning publication of similar material from the same source. If other newspapers had then published such material they would have faced liability under the doctrine of common law contempt.[176] Clearly, an injunction would not have covered the doctored part of the document published by the newspapers, but it is argued that no source disclosure order should have been made in relation to that part in any event since the *Norwich Pharmacal* jurisdiction was not available in relation to it (this point is discussed further below).

Lord Justice Sedley purported to use the *Goodwin* speech/harm balancing test, but when it came to weighing up the two interests against each other he allowed the apparently malevolent attitude of the source to undermine the interest in protecting sources, despite accepting at an earlier point in the judgment that that interest should be viewed as constant. If that interest had been viewed as constant it is argued that it would have outweighed the interest of Interbrew in resorting to law since source disclosure cases inevitably involve a desire to seek legal redress: thus there was no especially pressing need in this instance to aid Interbrew in seeking such redress. He said on this point: 'the relatively modest leak of which they are entitled to complain does not diminish the prospective seriousness for them of its repetition'.[177] This point could also have been made in *Goodwin*; it was highly speculative, and relied only on a possibility of future harm. It is suggested that this nebulous possibility of harm should

---

[176] See Chapter 6 at 289–96. If it had been published during the 'active' period under the Contempt of Court Act 1981 they could also have faced liability under the strict liability rule.

[177] At [54].

not have been allowed to outweigh the constant interest in protecting sources. Had the *Goodwin* test been properly applied at this crucial point in the analysis, it is argued that a different outcome would have been reached.

The *Interbrew* decision is likely to deter those who have, *prima facie*, purer motives for leaking information—to expose malpractice in a powerful corporate player. Arguably, if the *Goodwin* speech/harm balancing test is applied, it is clear that the impact of such deterrence was not given sufficient weight when balanced against the interest of the company in the right to pursue an action for breach of confidence. Moreover, the other possible sanctions which could be brought to bear in relation to this (arguably successful) attempt to 'rig' the market, by the Financial Services Authority (FSA) could have been taken into account and afforded greater weight in the reasoning on proportionality in relation to the 'least intrusive means' enquiry. In other words, in so far as wrong-doing had occurred, another means of redress was potentially available which was likely to deter many persons from seeking to promulgate financial misinformation. The interests of Interbrew were not therefore without protection due to the existence and powers of the FSA. Therefore, not only was the speech interest more weighty than the countervailing interest of Interbrew, but the interference represented by the source disclosure order went further than necessary to pursue the aim of protecting those interests.

The argument here is not only that an intense focus on the true values at stake in any particular instance is necessary in the proportionality analysis. It is also that judges should be wary of making unfounded assumptions about sources. Although, following *Ashworth*, the protection of sources has been accepted as a strong and unvarying interest, it appears that particular factors in a situation can strengthen the free speech claim under the *Goodwin* proportionality test. In *Ackroyd*, for example, they did so. But in *Interbrew* they were viewed as weakening it, and this appears now to be an illegitimate stance to take since it takes no account of the general deterrent effect on potential sources of source disclosure in a particular instance. This point may be made about a number of the cases discussed in this chapter; it is further enhanced since the matters that have sometimes tipped the balance in relation to the test of necessity often turned out to rest on judicial 'commonsense' and assumptions. Many of the pre and post-HRA cases discussed rested on uncertain assumptions, which then turned out to be erroneous.[178] In *Ashworth*, the assumption was made that the source was a dishonest employee motivated by greed. *Ackroyd v Mersey Care NHS Trust* showed that the sources were in fact motivated by the desire to expose malpractice at the hospital. The assumption is also often made that the source, if undetected, will continue to leak confidential information. But, as argued above, *Guardian Newspapers* indicated that this is not necessarily the case.

---

[178] For example, as mentioned earlier, the assumption was made in *Guardian Newspapers* that the source was a senior civil servant, which turned out not to be the case.

FAILURE TO APPLY ARTICLE 10 (AND OTHER CONVENTION ARTICLES) AT THE JURISDICTIONAL STAGE

The judicial reasoning in the post-HRA cases is, it is argued, also flawed in a further respect. The cases considered rested on the *Norwich Pharmacal* jurisdiction—in order to consider whether a journalist was mixed up in wrong-doing it was necessary to examine the claim for breach of confidence (or of contract) in relation to the source. If no justiciable claim had been found to exist there could be no wrong-doing for the journalist to be mixed up in and therefore no jurisdiction to make the disclosure order. But the courts failed to recognize that they have a duty under s 6 HRA to develop common law and equitable doctrines in order to render them compatible with Article 10.[179] Indeed, theoretically, s 6 makes *greater* demands on the 'public' common law in terms of modification, than s 3 does on statutes since there is no provision in s 6 equivalent to s 3(2)HRA[180] in relation to the common law. This duty should have affected their approach to that jurisdiction; rather than merely following the pre-HRA authorities as to its nature, they should have considered whether it itself should be modified post-HRA. In this instance this means firstly taking account of post-HRA developments in the doctrine of confidence, and secondly applying s 6 to the jurisdiction itself.

The Court of Appeal in *Ackroyd* considered whether the source would have a defence to an action for breach of confidence based on public interest, but did not need to come to a conclusion on the subject. The Lords in *Ashworth* did not consider this point. It is argued that they should have done so, taking account of the post-HRA breach of confidence jurisprudence. So doing means, where Article 8 is engaged in relation to the confidentiality claim (which would not inevitably be the case in this context), conducting a parallel analysis based on Article 8(2) and Article 10(2).[181] Since *Ashworth* concerned an important privacy interest the Court should have considered whether the balancing of Articles 10 and 8—as in *A v B*[182] (and now, *Campbell*)[183] would have resulted in a finding that no wrong-doing had occurred. If a case such as that of *Ashworth* arises in future post-*Campbell* this is the course that should be taken. The public interest defence has been subsumed within the consideration of the Article 10 claim. The argument at this stage is not the same as at the latter, s 10, stage since the unvarying interest in protection of sources is not yet at stake—the speech case at *this* point depends on the public interest dimension of the information disclosed by him or her. Therefore, as the Court correctly pointed out in *Ackroyd*, the failure to put forward a convincing public interest argument at this point would affect but not preclude the success of the s 10 argument later on.

The argument then is that a court in an action for source disclosure appears to be in

---

[179] See Chapter 3 at 124–44.

[180] See Chapter 3 at 123–44 on this point. It may be noted that as Chapter 3 at 131 points out, s 12 HRA in any event puts paid to any doubts as to the duty of the court in relation to Article 10 and the common law.

[181] See Chapter 16 at 828–31, 842–3.   [182] [2002] 3 WLR 542.

[183] [2004] 2 WLR 1232; (2004) UKHL 22. For comment see J. Morgan, 'Privacy in the House of Lords— Again' (2004) 120 *LQR* 563–66. See further Chapter 15 at 785–6.

the unfortunate position of having to take the steps that would be taken in the hypothetical breach of confidence action—where that cause of action would constitute the wrong-doing in question. Where any other claim—such as a claim for breach of contract—has a link to the preservation of privacy, those steps would also be applicable, by analogy with the confidence jurisprudence, since contract doctrine is clearly also subject to modification via s 6 HRA where a Convention right is engaged. Although *Campbell* concerned a breach of confidence claim, the balancing act would surely bring about the same outcome in relation to breach of contract. On the face of it, had this step been taken in *Ashworth* the chance of identifying a 'wrong-doer' would have been *enhanced*, since the parallel analysis enhances the privacy claim; as Chapter 16 argues, the analysis is based on the view that Articles 8 and 10 are presumptively equal. On the face of it this would obviously be an unwelcome argument for the defendant to pursue.

However, subjecting the privacy claim to the intense scrutiny of the parallel analysis allows its true value to be revealed. As argued above in relation to Article 10, there were compelling Article 8 and 10-based reasons in favour of disclosure of the conditions at Ashworth, had the arguments relating to disclosures of malpractice at the hospital figured more fully in the case. On the face of it a strong Article 8 claim could have been identified, based on the significant privacy interest in preserving the confidentiality of medical records—as in fact it was, based on *Z v Finland*, but *Z* was not considered at the jurisdictional stage of the argument. However, bearing in mind the arguments above as to the *true* value in the circumstances of such preservation of confidentiality, it is argued that the balancing act—using the parallel analysis—would have come down on the side of Article 10 since other Article 8 values—in preventing humiliation and preserving dignity—would have spoken in favour of publicity, even without assistance from the strong argument in favour of protecting sources. Thus, having conducted the parallel analysis, it could be found in a case such as *Ashworth*, that no jurisdiction for making the source disclosure order could be found as the source could not be viewed as a wrong-doer.

As indicated above, not all confidentiality cases in this context engage Article 8. In *Interbrew* it was unnecessary to weigh up Articles 10 and 8 against each other at the jurisdictional stage on the basis that the 'private life' of a company was not engaged[184]—for the reasons already discussed. Article 10 had presumptive priority, subject to exceptions to be narrowly construed; therefore the speech argument could have prevailed at the jurisdictional stage—in relation to the potential confidentiality claim. However, that argument was not considered at that stage. It is possible that the case could have been decided merely on the basis that there was a lack of jurisdiction to make the order. The fact that there was no competing Article 8 right in question would clearly have *enhanced* the possibility that any potential breach of confidence action would have failed.[185]

[184] See p 359 above regarding the extent to which companies can claim Article 8 rights.
[185] As Chapter 16 discusses (pp 836–8), whenever a common law doctrine coincides with the area covered

Thus the hypothetical breach of confidence action offering the restraint of an injunction represented an interference with the Article 10 rights of the newspaper that had to be necessary and proportionate to the aim pursued—that of the preservation of confidentiality, narrowly construed. It is argued that the true grievance of Interbrew was that the disinformation was promulgated and the share price went down. But, as Sedley LJ noted, the disinformation presumably emanated largely from the *source itself* and therefore would not qualify in itself as confidential information. Possibly Interbrew might have argued on this point that some of the information was confidential and that in order to deter persons from producing doctored information it was necessary to pursue the breach of confidence action, even though the confidential information leaked was in itself innocuous. But could it not be argued that the pursuit of such an action would have been disproportionate to the aim pursued, under a strict level of scrutiny,[186] on the basis that the remedy was not suitable for the purpose (the second limb of the *de Freitas* test) since the appropriate remedy answering to the true grievance of Interbrew lay with the FSA? It could also be argued that the speech/harm balancing test from *Goodwin* was not satisfied—since part of the information—the more significant part—was not confidential the importance of the aim pursued was thereby undermined. If the general value in protecting sources (the speech interest) had been balanced against the harm done to the confidentiality of the information, it might have been found that the latter outweighed the former.

On this basis it could be argued that in *Interbrew* the source would have had an answer based on the application of Article 10 to the potential breach of confidence action and therefore should not have been viewed as a wrong-doer. With no wrong-doer the journalist could not have been viewed as mixed up in wrong-doing and so no jurisdiction to make the order would have arisen. Clearly, the reason for this arguable flaw in the reasoning is that although Article 10 was taken properly into account at the later stage in the reasoning, it was not taken fully into account at the earlier stage—when the *Norwich Pharmacal* rule was being considered. Had Article 10 been allowed to affect both the statutory and the common law rule, the outcome might have been different.

There is a further possible argument that a new Convention-based interpretation could be applied to a different aspect of the *Norwich Pharmacal* jurisdiction, in order to narrow it down, based on the duty of the court under ss 6 and 2 HRA. This argument must be put forward very tentatively since the European Court in *Goodwin* at no point took issue with the *Norwich Pharmacal* jurisdiction. Even assuming that

by a Convention right(s), it may need to be modified by reference to the demands of that right(s). But the modification that must occur differs depending on whether the doctrine protects (a) a legitimate interest that has to be viewed as an exception to a competing interest arising in the form of a right (in *Interbrew* the interest was that of a company in preserving confidentiality under that exception in Article 10(2)) or (b) where a common law doctrine covers a right, not a societal interest.

[186] On the strict level of scrutiny deriving, not from *Goodwin* since no source disclosure action is at this point in contemplation, but from the Strasbourg cases defending the media's watchdog role. See Chapter 2 at 54–5, 67–8, 70–1 for discussion of such cases.

the source *has* been involved in wrong-doing, having taken account of a potential public interest test, one could readily question the breadth of the jurisdiction in its applicability to the *journalist*. It could be argued, relying on s 6 HRA, that there is a case for finding that the journalist should not be viewed as 'mixed up' in the wrongful act of the source where he or she is not a joint-wrong-doer—that it should be an essential part of the doctrine that some form of wrong should be attributable to the journalist. If the jurisdiction is the equivalent of tortious doctrine, it is anomalous that there is no such requirement, and yet the journalist can be subjected ultimately to a fine or even imprisonment once the jurisdiction is found to arise. Allowing the *Norwich Pharmacal* jurisdiction to extend to instances of a journalist's innocent involvement in another's arguably tortious acts creates a *prima facie* breach of the Article 10 guarantee of the right to receive information. It is hard to see that there is a sufficiently pressing social need under Article 10(2) to justify the extensiveness of the jurisdiction. Even if there is such a need, it is suggested that the interference represented by the existence of the jurisdiction is disproportionate to the aim pursued on the basis that the third limb of the *de Freitas* test is not satisfied.

Once it was established in UK law that a further breach of confidence is committed by a journalist who passes on confidential information received by him or her[187] it is unclear that the further remedy of source disclosure orders is needed at all and certainly not in instances of innocent involvement by the journalist. Clearly, if the jurisdiction was reined back it would mean that in an instance of non-publication, the body in question would not be able to identify the source (probably one of its own employees), but it could prevent publication of the information via an injunction. Arguably such a response is proportionate to the aim pursued—of preventing further dissemination—bearing in mind the general significance of protecting sources.

ARTICLE 10, SECTION 3 HRA AND THE SECTION 10 EXCEPTIONS

There is also a possible argument that the reasoning process in the post-HRA decisions fails to apply Article 10 fully to the s 10 exceptions. The Lords in *Ashworth* and Sedley LJ in *Interbrew* took the view that the exception in favour of the 'interests of justice' would be covered, readily, by one or more of the Article 10(2) exceptions. But the judges failed to appreciate that on one interpretation of the demands of Article 10 it can be argued that *all* the steps of Article 10(2), including the tests of necessity and proportionality, should have been applied, not merely the wording of the para 2 exceptions, due to the requirements of s 3(1) HRA. The compatibility with Article 10 of words in a statute—s 10—depends on a full application of all the Article 10 tests. Had the test of proportionality been applied using the strictest form of scrutiny, the narrower interpretation of the test 'interests of justice'—Lord Diplock's version—could have been adopted on the basis that thereby only a minimal

---

187 In *A-G v Guardian Newspapers* [1987] 3 All ER 316. See Chapter 19 at 951–3 for discussion.

impairment of the primary right would occur. Clearly, this is quite a technical and also speculative argument that asks courts to look at the words 'the interests of justice' in isolation. But given their extreme importance in aiding in the creation of a wide exception to the s 10 'shield', it is suggested that it is worth raising this argument. The Strasbourg Court did not find the broad interpretation given to s 10 domestically problematic,[188] but it was more straightforward, in the circumstances of the case, to decide it on the issue of proportionality.

Adopting a narrower interpretation of the term 'the interests of justice' would also address the unreality of a situation in which the interests of justice are apparently served by giving the company or body in question the technical ability to take action against the source. That may be a possibility in certain instances, but the courts tend to close their eyes to the unlikelihood that the source will eventually be revealed. The only punishment is usually reserved for the journalist and it is unclear that the interests of justice are thereby served. In fact, in virtually all the instances discussed in this chapter the body in question was not able in the end to take action against the source since the journalist refused to reveal his or her identity. The courts could take that factor into account under Lord Diplock's test in considering the real likelihood that the action might succeed. The doctrine of proportionality requires under Article 10(2) inter alia that measures are not taken that have an impact on a primary right, but at the same time are unlikely to be capable of serving the end in question since they are not rationally connected to it. As discussed above, this is the second limb of the *de Freitas* test. Clearly, this argument carries the danger that it could be used to press for harsher punishments for journalists, including imprisonment, rendering source disclosure more effective. However, imprisonment would be more likely to be seen to be disproportionate to the aim pursued on other grounds—the possibility of imprisonment would do so much damage to the s 10 'shield' law as to impair its efficacy very considerably. It could be condemned both under the means/ends balancing test from *de Freitas* and the speech/harm balancing test from *Goodwin*.

If the approach suggested was followed, changing the interpretation of s 10 under s 3 HRA, it would mean that the exception for the 'interests of justice' could only be used in instances outside the application of the *Norwich Pharmacal* doctrine—where court proceedings were already in existence and source disclosure was necessary for their fair and effective administration. The other s 10 exceptions could be used in such instances, and in instances covered by that reconfigured doctrine, subject to the test for proportionality applied under s 3 HRA on the lines discussed.

---

[188] At [140] the Court noted that Lord Diplock's interpretation had been replaced by that of Lord Bridge without any adverse comment.

A NEW FRAMEWORK FOR REASONING
UNDER THE CONVENTION

Below, the steps that should be taken under the HRA in a source disclosure case are outlined. In contrast to the current position, the Convention is taken into account at each stage under either ss 3 or 6 HRA. It is acknowledged that the courts are likely to remain very reluctant, in cases concerning disclosures by a source that engage Article 8, as in *Ashworth*, to conduct the parallel analysis at the jurisdictional stage. They are likely to confine it to the question of necessity under s 10—if indeed they are prepared to conduct it at all. Conducting it at two stages of the argument is highly likely to strike them as an over-technical approach. Since the privacy interest is more likely to counter-balance the speech interest, the jurisdiction is in any event more likely to arise, on the basis—using the terminology of breach of confidence rather than that of the tort of misuse of private information[189]—that no sufficiently strong public interest defence defeats the hypothetical breach of confidence claim. Thus, since taking this approach means that the argument is less likely to be closed down at this stage, the reasons for conducting the parallel analysis at this point become less compelling. However, where Article 8 is *not* engaged, as in *Interbrew* or *Camelot*, there is a stronger argument for considering the public interest at the jurisdictional stage since there is clearly a greater likelihood that it will be found, having done so, that no jurisdiction to make the source disclosure order arises. One of the main contentions of this chapter is that apart from the question of necessity, the tests, as interpreted so far, are in effect empty ones. The following section attempts to reinvigorate them—to give them real bite—by reference to the Human Rights Act.

THE APPLICATION OF THE *NORWICH PHARMACAL* JURISDICTION

The application of the jurisdiction at present depends on showing first, that the source has been involved in justiciable wrong-doing and second, following *Ashworth*, that the journalist is 'mixed up' in that wrong-doing, whether innocently or not. In relation to the first step, the source will not have been involved in wrong-doing if, in a hypothetical action against him or her for breach of confidence or contract, the information disclosed was of significant public interest value, since then the Article 10 claim would outweigh the societal interest in question (one of the enumerated exceptions under Article 10(2)), and might well outweigh the Article 8 claim (assuming that Article 8 was applicable). Clearly, the claim for jurisdiction could *prima facie* be more readily resisted in the former instance. The courts would have to consider

---

[189] See *Campbell* [2004] 2 WLR 1232; (2004) UKHL 22. See Chapter 14 at 732–40 for discussion of the decision. In *Campbell* of course the Article 10 claim did *not* prevail. But see Chapter 15 at 780–4 for instances in which the public interest defence defeated the breach of confidence claim (either put forward as a societal interest or as a private information claim).

previous Convention-based rulings in breach of confidence cases, the leading decision being that of the House of Lords in *Campbell*.[190] In a breach of contract case the court should itself conduct the balancing act in accordance with its duty under ss 6 and 2 HRA, bearing in mind the applicability of Article 10. It is important to point out that the engagement of Article 10 is *not* confined to the revelation of wrong-doing. Having considered the effect of the Convention in the hypothetical case, it might be found that there was no jurisdiction to make the order since the source had not perpetrated a civil wrong. That would be the end of the source disclosure case.

In practice a court would probably only be prepared to consider public interest arguments at two stages of the analysis if such arguments were very strong, making it unlikely that even a *prima facie* breach of confidence case could arise. But, as pointed out above, the speech-based arguments are *not* the same at both stages since at the second the unvarying interest in source disclosure *as well as* the public interest value of the information is relevant. A court might consider that the defendant should wait for the stage when she can put her strongest Article 10-based argument forward. But such a stance does not take full account of the duty of the court under s 6 HRA where the case could be closed down at the jurisdictional stage.

If a court considered that a *prima facie* breach of confidence case *did* arise, it could then move to a possible further stage of the *Norwich Pharmacal* argument and apply Article 10 and *Goodwin* (via ss 6 and 2 HRA) to the nature and extent of the jurisdiction itself. As argued above, that jurisdiction could be narrowed as a result, where in terms of necessity and proportionality it was unjustifiable to allow the jurisdiction to extend to the particular factual situation before it. This might be found where it was not established that the journalist was a joint tort-feasor with the source, and so could be said to have become innocently involved in wrong-doing. At the least, a court could re-consider whether it sits well with the demands of Article 10 to extend the jurisdiction to instances of entirely innocent involvement—as where a journalist has merely received the information without soliciting it. If the jurisdiction was narrowed in this way, it could then fail at this stage.

SECTION 10 EXCEPTIONS—BREADTH

Assuming that the *Norwich Pharmacal* doctrine was found to be applicable, the next stage could be to consider the applicability of the relevant s 10 exception, taking account of s 3(1) HRA and Article 10. If the test of proportionality is applied to the 'interests of justice' exception (by far the most commonly invoked exception), a narrower interpretation of the test—the version put forward by Lord Diplock, demanding existing legal proceedings—could be adopted. As indicated above, the case of *Chassagnou v France*[191] is of relevance at this point. It was established that 'only indisputable imperatives' as non-Convention 'rights of others' can overcome the

---

[190] See Chapter 15 at 779–92 for discussion, taking account of this change of terminology.
[191] (2000) 29 EHRR 615.

primary right. In source disclosure cases, the exception most often invoked under Article 10(2) is the preservation of confidentiality. But it is arguable that if an injunction has already been issued—which is usually the case in respect of the information that has already been leaked—that aim is already being served. The source disclosure order is much more tenuously linked to preserving confidence. On this argument it can be suggested that the most pertinent aim to be served by an order is 'the rights of others'. But where those rights do not answer to another Convention right—most often Article 8—it would be necessary to show that the right claimed was an indisputable and imperative one. Given the speculative nature of a number of the source disclosure cases, it might be difficult to argue in a number of circumstances that the right to bring court or other action was indisputable.

NECESSITY AND PROPORTIONALITY TESTS UNDER ARTICLE 10 AND SECTION 10

Since it is now established under the post-HRA cases that s 10 and Article 10 must be used together, it must be asked whether the interference with freedom of expression is necessary to serve the aim in question (the s 10 aim equated to one of the Article 10 aims) and whether it is proportionate to that aim. A clear distinction should be drawn between the 'pressing social need' and the proportionality aspects of the exercise. Where Article 8 is engaged the balancing exercise should be conducted by means of the parallel analysis from *Campbell.* That would mean in effect interpreting s 10 by reference to Article 8 under s 3 HRA in order to place the two rights on a basis of presumptive equality. Since, as argued above, the *de Freitas* tests provide a useful template for conducting the proportionality exercise, combined with the speech/harm balancing test from *Goodwin,* there should be a full application of all those tests under both Article 10(2) *and* under Article 8(2), using a strict standard of scrutiny.[192] In practice that would mean weighing up Articles 8 and 10 against each other on a basis of presumptive equality, taking account of the weightiness of the interest on both sides and the extent to which each right would be damaged were the other allowed to prevail. It would mean subjecting the measure of source disclosure to a strict scrutiny in order to determine its appropriateness Although on its face this would mean that where a privacy interest was involved, as in *Ashworth,* s 10 would be weakened as a protection for sources, the proper application of the parallel analysis should mean that an effective teasing out of the true values at stake would be achieved.[193] As discussed above, it might be found, in a typical whistle-blowing case with a range of privacy interests at stake, that both Articles 8 and 10 spoke in favour of publicity for the information and non-disclosure of the source.

The *Goodwin* and *de Freitas* tests, applied on a strict standard of scrutiny, would also be applicable where Article 8 was *not* engaged, but the balancing act would be carried out only under Article 10(2), and the para 2 exception should be narrowly

---

[192] See above note 102 and pp 335–6 for discussion.   [193] See Chapter 16 at 842–8.

construed. In conducting the balancing exercise the courts should take account of all the circumstances, taking a broad view of the context, and should avoid—as in *Ashworth*—ruling out relevant circumstances at the outset. In particular, the court should be careful to bear in mind, not only the general and unvarying interest in protecting sources, but also, where relevant, the *particular* public interest served by such protection in the instance before it (in *Ashworth* and *Ackroyd* the need to facilitate the uncovering of serious misconduct at the hospital). The plaintiff would have the burden of seeking to show that the aims relating to the exception in question were particularly pressing on the facts, but the especially valuable nature of the speech would not need to be viewed as weighing only on that side of the equation: it could be taken into account in a more positive sense as well and would weigh in favour of non-disclosure in order to avoid inhibiting the production of such speech.

For clarity, the tests to be applied are set out here in a step by step fashion. Following *de Freitas*,[194] it is first necessary to ask whether a significant and pressing interest, falling within one or more of the Article 10(2) exceptions, has been identified. The question here would be—are the aims pursued by the source disclosure order sufficiently weighty and serious to justify the interference with the expression interest, in principle? Turning to the question of proportionality, it is necessary to consider whether the particular measure chosen is proportionate to the aims put forward. Under the second *de Freitas* test it is necessary to consider the suitability of the interference in question—the extent to which it is rationally connected to the aim pursued. The third *de Freitas* test concerns the need to choose the least intrusive measure that will serve the aim pursued. This is means/end balancing—if there was another way of achieving the aim pursued that would have been less restrictive, it should have been used.

Finally it may often be valuable to apply the key *Goodwin* speech/harm balancing proportionality test—balancing the value of the speech interest against the harm caused to the other interest. The higher the value of the speech interest, the harder it will be to outweigh it by reference to the harm caused. The full application of this final test is crucial—the application of the *de Freitas* tests do not fully tease out the values at stake since they rely on considering the nature of the interference in question, rather than the real extent of the harm it was protecting against or remedying. Further, they do not provide an effective means of considering the value of the speech—the extent to which the free speech rationales are engaged. In applying these tests the level of scrutiny is crucial. Following *Goodwin* it must be strict. Therefore, for example, it would not be sufficient to find, in applying the third test, that among the measures available that could have been used, it was not unreasonable in the circumstances to choose the one in question, even though a less restrictive one was available.

---

[194] From the decision of the Privy Council in *de Freitas v Permanent Secretary of Ministry of Agriculture, Fisheries, Lands and Housing* [1999] 1 AC 69, 80.

SEIZURE OF JOURNALISTIC MATERIAL

So far this chapter has considered the general jurisdiction to seek source disclosure. It moves on to look at the seizure of journalistic material in order to aid in criminal or terrorist investigations. Clearly, journalists will quite frequently possess material in the form of documents or film obtained as a result of pursuing a particular investigative story. The next section considers a selection of the key powers allowing for the seizure of journalistic material. In each case the information obtained might include material identifying sources. Even where that is not the case, seizure of such material affects press freedom, not only because it hampers the collection of information, but also because if journalists are viewed as likely to be forced to aid police investigative efforts, contacts and others may refuse to cooperate with them. Journalists might also be put at risk when, for example, trying to film or report on demonstrations, since those involved would be likely to be concerned about the use to which the material gathered could be put.

A partial 'shield' against seizure of journalistic material is provided in the key seizure power under the Police and Criminal Evidence Act 1984. But despite the significance of the other powers, they contain no express protection for media freedom. No common law privilege against seizure of press material exists[195] and it appears, as discussed below, that where sources might be revealed by such seizure s 10 of the 1981 Act nevertheless does not apply to any of the powers. However, some protection for press material could be imposed upon them since all these powers should of course be rendered compatible with Article 10, taking account of *Goodwin*, under s 3(1) HRA if at all possible. Following *Goodwin* some mechanism should be available within these powers to allow for the weighing up of the interest in protecting sources against the countervailing public interest in preventing crime or protecting national security that the power in question seeks to serve. Article 8 may also be applicable. As indicated above, Strasbourg has found that companies may have certain rights to private life and to protection for correspondence in the context of search and seizure of material from their premises.[196] A search and seizure of journalistic material could therefore engage both Articles. Further, since all those involved in using the powers are public authorities (the police, the courts, civil servants), they should, under s 6 HRA, comply with Article 10 and 8 in exercising them. The real possibilities of protecting the identity of sources where the varying powers are exercised are discussed below.

---

[195] See *Senior Holdsworth ex p Independent TV News* [1976] 1 QB 23.

[196] In *Societe Colas Est v France* (2002) Application no. 37971/97 at [41], the Court found: 'the time has come to hold that in certain circumstances the rights guaranteed by Article 8 of the Convention may be construed as including the right to respect for a company's registered office, branches or other business premises . . .'.

SEARCH AND SEIZURE OF JOURNALISTIC MATERIAL UNDER THE POLICE AND CRIMINAL EVIDENCE ACT 1984

The main search and seizure powers are provided in the Police and Criminal Evidence Act (PACE) 1984, Part II.[197] The orders allowed for are intended to force journalists to disclose material where so doing is likely to assist in a criminal investigation, but certain restrictive conditions have to be met. Under s 9 PACE a search warrant cannot be issued in respect of journalistic material; a production order has to be sought under Sched 1, which can be challenged in an *inter partes* hearing before a circuit judge on the basis that the access conditions have not been met. This position is similar to that applying in the US, where such a hearing can be held, if necessary, and investigators cannot obtain the specified material by applying only for a search warrant.[198]

The protection is afforded to journalists against seizure of journalistic material by designating it as either excluded or special procedure material and then placing special conditions on obtaining access to it. Section 11 governs excluded material. Such material consists *inter alia* of documentary journalistic material[199] held in confidence[200] and can only be seized if the special restrictions under Sched 1 of the Police and Criminal Evidence Act are satisfied. The provisions allow for production orders to be made by a judge only if there is reasonable suspicion that the material is on the premises specified and that but for s 9(2)PACE it would have been possible and appropriate for a search warrant to have been issued.[201] Under s 14 non-confidential journalistic material is termed special procedure material and can only be seized if a serious arrestable offence has been committed, the material is on the premises and is likely to be of substantial value to the investigation. It must also be in the public interest to make the order, taking account of the benefit to the investigation and the circumstances under which it is held.[202] It is clearly of significance that the public interest requirement only applies to non-confidential journalistic material. It was intended as a safeguard but it has been subverted by judicial interpretation; pre-HRA it appeared that it would always be assumed to be served where the material would be of substantial benefit to the investigation or relevant in evidence.[203] However, this

---

[197] For comment on these provisions see: R. Stone, *The Law of Entry: Search and Seizure*, London: Sweet and Maxwell, 4th edn., Oxford: OUP, 2005; M. Zander, *The Police and Criminal Evidence Act 1984*, 4th edn., 2003; D. Feldman, *The Law Relating to Entry, Search and Seizure*, 1986; Stone [1988] *Crim LR* 498.

[198] 94 Stat 1879 (1980).

[199] Defined in s 13 as material created or acquired for the purposes of journalism—a circular definition that obviously is unhelpful in determining the limits of the privilege. It clearly covers material gathered for such purposes even if the material itself is not eventually published. See further D. Feldman ibid on this point at 104–6.

[200] S 11(1)(c). Journalistic material is not afforded as much protection as legally privileged material, covered by s 10; no access to such material is allowed at all.

[201] Sched 1, para 3.   [202] Sched 1, para 2.

[203] See: *R v Bristol Crown Court ex p Bristol Press and Picture Agency Ltd* (1986) 85 Cr App R 190; *Chief Constable of Avon and Somerset Police v Bristol United Press, Independent*, 4 November 1986.

interpretation renders the inclusion of the public interest requirement otiose. This point is discussed further below.

Section 8(1) PACE covers general powers of search and seizure for material other than excluded material (s 8(1)(d)). The ruling in *Guildhall Magistrates' Court ex p Primlacks Holdings Co (Panama) Limited*[204] made it clear that a magistrate must satisfy him or herself that there are reasonable grounds for believing that the items covered by the warrant does not include material subject to the special protection. The Criminal Justice and Police Act 2001 (CJP) s 50 extends the power of seizure very significantly. The further new power of seizure under s 50(2) allows the person in question to seize material which he has no power to seize but which is attached to an object he does have the power to seize, if it is not reasonably practicable to separate the two, and this includes the specially protected material.[205] Section 50 may serve to undermine the protection for certain journalistic material since where such material is part of other material and cannot practically be separated, it can be seized.

Sections 50, 54 and 55 CJP taken together provide avenues to the seizure and use of journalistic material.[206] The provisions thus circumvent the limitations placed on the seizure of excluded material and, most importantly, mean that information contained in the material, identifying sources, will have been passed to the police even though the material is subsequently returned. It can be said that for the first time journalistic material has lost part of the protection it was accorded under PACE. These wide CJP powers are 'balanced' by the provisions of ss 52–61 which provide a number of safeguards.[207] Under s 60 a duty to secure the property arises which includes the obligation under s 61 to prevent *inter alia*, copying of it. But despite these safeguards, it is unclear that the new powers, especially to seize and use journalistic material, are

---

[204] [1989] 2 WLR 841. The magistrates had issued search warrants authorizing the search of two solicitors' firms. Judicial review of the magistrates' decision to issue a warrant was successfully sought; it was found that the magistrate had merely accepted the police officer's view that s 8(1)(d) was satisfied rather than independently considering the matter.

[205] The further powers of seizure it provides in s 50 apply to police powers of search under PACE and also to powers of seizure arising under a range of other statutes and applicable to bodies other than police officers, as set out in Schedule 1 of the CJP. This provision is significant since *inter alia* it allows police officers to remove items from premises even where they are not certain that—apart from s 50—they have the power to do so. Thus a number of items can now be seized from media premises although no power of seizure—apart from that now arising under s 50—in fact arises. It can also be seized where a police officer takes the view on reasonable grounds that it is something that he has the power to seize, although it turns out later that it falls within one of the special categories.

[206] Special provisions are made under the 2001 Act for *inter alia* the return of excluded material. Under s 54 such material must be returned unless it falls within s 54(2). Section 57(3) provides that ss 53–56 do not authorize the retention of property where its retention would not be authorized apart from the provisions of Part 2 of the CJP. Under s 62 inextricably linked property cannot be examined or copied, but under subsection 4 can be used to the extent that its use facilitates the use of property in which the inextricably linked property is comprised.

[207] Notice must be given to persons whose property has been seized under s 52, and under s 59 he or she can apply to the 'appropriate judicial authority' for the return of the whole or part of the seized property, on the ground that there was no power to seize, or that excluded material is not comprised in other property as provided for in ss 54 and 55.

compatible with the requirements of the Convention under the HRA, as discussed below.

PRODUCTION ORDERS UNDER THE TERRORISM ACT 2000; REQUIREMENTS TO PROVIDE INFORMATION UNDER THE TERRORISM LEGISLATION

Schedule 7 para 3(5) of the Prevention of Terrorism (Temporary Provisions) Act (PTA) 1989 provided for the production of material relating to terrorism if such production would be in the public interest. When inquiries relating to terrorist offences were made, Sched 7, para 3(5) allowed access to special procedure and excluded material. This provision was replaced by an equivalent provision under the Terrorism Act 2000 (TA), Sched 5. The judge only needs to be satisfied that there is a terrorist investigation in being, that the material would substantially assist it and that it is in the public interest that it should be produced. This procedure creates an exception to the PACE Sched 1 special access conditions[208] and so can be viewed as undermining the PACE shield provisions. A police officer of the rank of superintendent or above can authorize a search if satisfied that immediate action is necessary since the case is one of great urgency.[209] It appears that once the first two requirements are satisfied, it will be rare to find that the third is not.[210]

It was assumed in *Director of Public Prosecutions v Channel Four Television Co Ltd and Another*[211] that the existence of the Sched 7 provision meant that the making of an order precluded a defence under s 10 Contempt of Court Act. The potential danger of Sched 7—now 5—in terms of media freedom was shown in that case. Channel 4 screened a programme in its Dispatches series called 'The Committee', which was based on the allegations of an anonymous source (Source A) that the RUC and Loyalist paramilitaries had colluded in the assassination of Republicans. The police successfully applied under Sched 7 para 3(5) for orders disclosing information which would probably uncover the identity of Source A. Channel 4 refused to comply with the orders on the ground that to do so would expose Source A to almost certain death and it was then committed for contempt of court. It attempted to rely on the public interest provision of Sched 7 in arguing that it was in the public interest for the identity of Source A to be protected, but this was rejected on the following grounds. Channel 4 should not have given an unqualified assurance of protection to the source even though had it not done so, the programme could probably not have been made, because so doing was likely to lead to flouting of the provisions of the Prevention of Terrorism (Temporary Provisions) Act. Thus, giving such assurances could inevitably undermine the rule of law and therefore, it was held, help to achieve the very result that the terrorists in Northern Ireland were seeking to bring about. Channel 4 was therefore fined for non-compliance with the orders. In determining the amount of the

---

[208] This is also the case in respect of drug trafficking: see Drug Trafficking Act 1994 ss 55, 56.
[209] Para 31.   [210] See above note 203.   [211] [1993] 2 All ER 517.

fine, it was borne in mind that the defendants might not have appreciated the dangers of giving an unqualified assurance, but a warning was given that this consideration would be unlikely to influence courts in future cases of this nature.

This ruling fails to accord sufficient weight to the public interest in the protection of journalistic sources in order to allow the media to fulfill its role of informing the public. The comment that the assurances given to Source A as a necessary precondition to publication of this material would undermine the rule of law, ignores the possibility that undermining of the rule of law might be most likely to flow from the behaviour alleged in the programme—it might appear that nothing would be more likely to undermine the rule of law than collusion between State security forces and terrorists. The decision not to impose a rolling fine on Channel 4 or make a sequestration order may be welcomed in the interests of press freedom, but it is clear that such indulgence may be refused in future, thereby creating a significant curb on investigative journalism. Schedule 7 para 3(5) as interpreted in that instance arguably breached Article 10. The power under the Terrorism Act 2000 affords primacy to national security without explicitly providing a defence for journalists. It now must be interpreted compatibly with Article 10, in a manner which may impliedly provide such a defence. Some means of conducting the balancing act demanded by Article 10(2) should be imported if possible, as discussed below.

The current terrorism legislation provides a number of provisions criminalizing failures to disclose information. They contain no journalistic shields at all, although they could clearly have an application to journalists. On their face the obtaining of journalistic material is treated in precisely the same way as seizure of other material. Under Section 19 TA it is an offence to fail to report information to the police that comes to one's attention in the course of a trade, profession, business or employment and which might be of material assistance in preventing an act of terrorism or in arresting someone carrying out such an act.[212] Section 38B Anti-Terrorism Crime and Security Act 2001 broadens this provision immensely—it makes it an offence, subject to an un-explicated defence of reasonable excuse, for a person to fail to disclose to a police officer any information which he knows or believes *might* be of material assistance in preventing an act of terrorism or securing the apprehension or conviction of a person involved in such an act. A further wide range of people are potentially subject to criminal penalties under s 58(1) TA, the provision relating to the collection of information, which is based on section 16B PTA. Section 58(1) provides: 'A person commits an offence if (a) he collects or makes a record of information of a kind likely to be useful to a person committing or preparing an act of terrorism, or (b) he possesses a document or record containing information of that kind'. The offence lacks any requirement of *knowledge* regarding the nature of the information or any requirement that the person *intended* to use it in order to further the aims of terrorism, although a defence of 'reasonable excuse' is provided.

---

[212] Subsection (5) preserves an exemption in respect of legal advisers' privileged material.

POWERS UNDER THE OFFICIAL SECRETS ACT 1989 SECTION 8(4)

The Official Secrets Act 1989 s 8(4) makes it an offence for a person (this would normally be a journalist) to fail to comply with an official direction for the return or disposal of information which is the subject of s 5, and which is in their possession or control. Section 5, discussed in Chapter 19,[213] is headed 'information resulting from unauthorized disclosures or entrusted in confidence'. This is not a new category of information. Information will fall within s 5 if it falls within one or more of the previous categories (under ss 1,2,3,4, discussed in Chapter 19) and it has been disclosed to the defendant by a Crown servant or falls within s 1 of the Official Secrets Act 1911. Section 5 is primarily aimed at journalists who receive information leaked to them by Crown servants, although it could of course cover anybody in that position.[214]

Since s 5 is aimed at journalists and potentially represents an interference with their role in informing the public, it requires a very strict interpretation under s 3(1)HRA, in accordance with Article 10, bearing in mind the emphasis placed by Strasbourg on the importance of that role.[215] The fact that journalists were included at all in the net of criminal liability under s 5 has been greatly criticized on the basis that some recognition should be given to the important role of the press in informing the public about government policy and actions.[216] In arguing for a restrictive interpretation of ss 8(4) and 5 under s 3 of the HRA, a comparison could be drawn with the constitutional role of the press recognized in America by the *Pentagon Papers* case.[217]

HUMAN RIGHTS ACT IMPLICATIONS

Where journalistic material is seized, potentially revealing the identity of sources, Article 10 is engaged, as *Goodwin* made clear. The powers discussed, apart from the PACE power, make no express provision themselves for balancing the needs of criminal investigations against the requirements of Article 10. The powers must, however, be read and applied under the HRA compatibly with Article 10. If a source might be revealed by the exercise of the power, it would appear *prima facie* that s 10 of the Contempt of Court Act would apply. In *Secretary of State for Defence v Guardian Newspapers*,[218] it was found that on its true construction, section 10 applied to all judicial proceedings irrespective of their nature, or the claim or cause of action in

---

[213] See pp 934–5.

[214] It is also aimed at the person to whom a document is entrusted by a Crown servant 'on terms requiring it to be held in confidence or in circumstances in which the Crown servant or government contractor could reasonably expect that it would be so held' (s 5(1)(ii)). The difference between entrusting and disclosing is significant in that, in the former instance, the document—but not the information it contains—will have been entrusted to the care of the person in question.

[215] See, e.g. *Goodwin v UK* (1996) 22 EHRR 123.

[216] See, e.g. Ewing and Gearty, *Freedom under Thatcher*, Oxford: Clarendon, 1990 Chapter 6, pp 196–201.

[217] *New York Times Co v US* (1971) 403 US 713. The Supreme Court determined that no restraining order on the press could be made in order to protect the role of journalism in relation to government scrutiny.

[218] [1984] 3 All ER 601; [1985] AC 339, 347, HL.

respect of which they had been brought.[219] However, the later decision in *Director of Public Prosecutions v Channel Four Television Co Ltd and Another* found otherwise, in relation to the Terrorism Act production power. Thus, by analogy it might be argued, if the question of source disclosure arose, that s 10 does not apply to the other provisions, in PACE and the Official Secrets Act. One way out of this problem would be to argue that since there is ambiguity as to the question of the applicability of s 10 to all the powers discussed, it should be taken to apply, over-ruling the *Channel Four* case on that point. It is a pre-HRA case and therefore subject to over-ruling via s 3 HRA. The argument would be that s 10 should be read, in reliance on s 3(1), as applying to all provisions requiring the production of material, where that would lead to the disclosure of the identity of a source.

If this argument is not accepted in a suitable case, it could in any event be argued that Article 10 could be applied to the provisions via ss 6 and 3 HRA, and since s 10 has been rendered virtually synonymous with Article 10, as discussed in the main part of this chapter, source protection could be made available by that route. Clearly, the problem would be that these provisions do not make specific provision for source protection, so the courts would have to seek to read into them defences that do not exist. It could be argued at the least that it would be anomalous, given the protection offered to sources by both Article 10 and s 10, to consider ordering the seizure of journalistic material, revealing sources, without taking account of the free expression implications as a specific and distinct exercise. So where the provisions offer any discretion to the court as to application or sentence, the factor of source protection should be influential via s 3 and 6 HRA. That factor affected the sentence, as discussed, in the *Channel Four* case.

The special procedure under s 9 and Sched 1 of PACE allow for production orders to be made only if the material is likely to be of *substantial* value to the investigation. That term could be used to limit the authorizing of such orders where the identity of sources might be likely to be disclosed. A similar argument could be used in relation to the production power under the Terrorism Act 2000, Sched 5 since it can be invoked only if the material would substantially assist the investigation. Further, and more significantly, it must be in the public interest under PACE sched 1 para 2 and under the TA for the order to be made. That term would allow leeway to a court to impose an Article 10-based interpretation on the provisions, relying on s 3 HRA, Article 10 and *Goodwin*. The public interest could be read as requiring that the court should balance the needs of the investigation against the public interest in source protection. Indeed, Sched 1 para 2 lends itself to this interpretation since it requires the court to consider the benefit to the investigation *and* the circumstances under which the material was held. In other words, a strong countervailing public interest would have to be shown in order to overcome the strong and constant interest in protecting sources. Indeed, Sched 1 para 2 lends itself to this interpretation since it requires the court to consider the benefit to the investigation *and* the circumstances

---

[219] At pp 349B–D, 356E–F, 362D–G, 368G–369A, 372A–C.

under which the material was held.[220] In other words, a strong countervailing public interest would have to be shown in order to overcome the strong and constant interest in protecting sources.

Where journalistic material was seized *without* revealing the identity of a source, Article 10 would still be applicable via ss 3 and 6 HRA, but the strong interest in protecting sources would not be engaged. It must be noted that it is not a prerequisite of the engagement of Article 10 that the seizure of the material would inevitably reveal the source; it is sufficient that it would be likely to do so.[221] The provisions under the terrorism legislation requiring provision of information are subject to defences of a reasonable excuse for failing to comply. That term would allow leeway to a court to impose an Article 10-based interpretation on the provisions, relying on s 3 HRA and Article 10. Once a journalist had put forward the excuse that the material had been collected for the purposes of journalism, this would enable a court to balance the value of the information in revealing terrorist activity against the public interest in protecting journalistic material in determining its reasonableness.

As mentioned above, companies can claim Article 8 rights to private life and to protection for correspondence where search and seizure of material from their premises has occurred.[222] Where a search and seizure of journalistic material takes place on the premises of a media organization, Article 10 as well as Article 8 is relevant. Even where a production order had been properly obtained, argument could be raised regarding the *effects* of the search, as *Ozgur Gundem v Turkey*[223] demonstrates. The Court found that the search operation at the newspaper's premises, which resulted in newspaper production being disrupted for two days, constituted a serious interference with the applicants' freedom of expression. It accepted that the operation was conducted according to a procedure 'prescribed by law' for the purpose of preventing crime and disorder within the meaning of the second paragraph of Article 10. It did not, however, find that a measure of such dimension was proportionate to this aim. No justification had been provided for the seizure of the newspaper's archives, documentation and library.

It has been argued that the judiciary have not provided sufficient protection for journalistic material.[224] Both Articles 8 and 10 could be relied upon in arguing that a production order under s 9 and Schedule 1 PACE should not be issued on grounds of disproportionality. This occurred in *R v Central Criminal Court ex parte Bright*.[225] Judicial review was sought of production orders under s 9 Police and Criminal

---

[220] Sched 1, para 2.

[221] In *Guardian Newspapers* ibid, Lord Bridge said (at 372): 'secondly, is it sufficient to attract the protection of the section that the order of the court in dispute *may*, although it will not necessarily, have the effect of disclosing a 'source of information' to which the section applies? In agreement with Griffiths L.J. and with all your Lordships I would answer both these questions in the affirmative for the reasons given in the judgment of Griffiths L.J. [1984] Ch 156, and in the speeches of my noble and learned friends, Lord Diplock and Lord Roskill, with which I fully agree.'

[222] See *Societe Colas Est v France* (2002) Application no. 37971/97 at [41], note 174 above.

[223] (2001) 31 EHRR 49.   [224] R. Costigan [1996] *Crim LR* 231.   [225] [2001] 2 All ER 244.

Evidence Act 1984. The orders concerned material relating to David Shayler, a former employee of MI5 who had made allegations about the involvement of MI6 in a plot to assassinate Colonel Gadafy. The *Guardian* had published an emailed letter from Shayler; the *Observer* had published an article about his allegations; production orders were sought to obtain material from both newspapers regarding Shayler.

The court had to consider the principles to be applied. Lord Justice Judge found that the judge personally must be satisfied that the statutory requirements have been established. The question to be asked was not whether the decision of the constable making the application was reasonable, nor whether it would be susceptible to judicial review on *Wednesbury* grounds. He found that this followed from the express wording of the statute: 'if ... a Circuit Judge is satisfied that one ... of the sets of access conditions is fulfilled', and considered that, 'The purpose of this provision is to interpose between the opinion of the police officer seeking the order and the consequences to the individual or organisation to whom the order is addressed, the safeguard of a judgment and decision of a circuit judge.'[226] Further, the material to be produced or disclosed could not be merely general information which might be helpful to police inquiries, but relevant and admissible evidence. Once it was found that the relevant set of access conditions was fulfilled, it was made clear that the judge is empowered, but not bound, to make the order. The basis for refusing the order was found in the conditions stated to be relevant to the 'public interest' in paragraph 2(c). It was found that this provision allows the judge to take account of matters not expressly referred to in the set of relevant access conditions, including fundamental principles.

In adopting this approach the judge relied on *R v Bristol Crown Court, ex p Bristol Press and Picture Agency Ltd*[227] in which Glidewell L.J. noted with approval that the judge at the Crown court had rightly taken into account both 'the importance of the impartiality and independence of the press', and 'the importance of ensuring that members of the press can photograph and report what is going on without fear of their personal safety'. In the case of journalistic material the judge considered that the potential stifling of public debate could be taken into account. He did not consider that it was necessary to take account of Article 10 of the European Convention on the basis that the principles it encapsulates are: 'bred in the bone of the common law'.[228] Taking the public interest in freedom of expression into account, the judge decided that the orders must be quashed. The findings in that case were made just before the HRA came fully into force. The comments of Mr Justice Judge as to the relationship between the ECHR jurisprudence and common law principle provide encouragement to argument that under the HRA such orders should not be made where the journalistic material is sought and there is a strong public interest in the material in question. The judge making the order would be bound by s 6 HRA and therefore he or she would have to take account of Strasbourg jurisprudence, unless it was clear that a result consistent with that required by Article 10 would be arrived at by following

---

[226] At [73] of the judgment.   [227] (1987) 85 CAR 190.   [228] At [82] of the judgment.

common law principles. Where the material revealed the identity of sources that jurisprudence should be relied on since it provides the strongest statement of principle, as discussed above, regarding the significance of protecting sources.

CONCLUSIONS

Where s 10 of the 1981 Act applies, source protection has been enhanced in the UK post-HRA. But it is clear that where it does *not*, journalistic material that may reveal the identity of a source may be obtained under coercion in a range of circumstances, and that little leeway for Article 10 arguments has so far been made available. The duties of the courts under ss 6 and 3 HRA makes this position no longer sustainable; where scope is available under the relevant provisions for speech/harm balancing, it must be explored, and in particular the 'public interest' provision under Sched 1 para 2 PACE requires reinterpretation.

In relation to s 10, the inception of the Human Rights Act has made a difference to source protection in the sense that efforts are being made to ensure that the tests for necessity and proportionality under Article 10 are being fully applied when examining the need for ordering disclosure of the identity of a source. But no narrowing of the *Norwich Pharmacal* jurisdiction or re-interpretation of the s 10 exceptions has occurred, and this is due, it is argued, to the strong and well established attachment of the judiciary to values opposed in this instance to journalistic ones. The tests devised for the determination of jurisdiction and for the applicability of the s 10 exception 'in the interests of justice' show a hollow judicial attachment to the values at stake since they are almost invariably fulfilled due to the very nature of the case. The new framework for judicial reasoning under the HRA outlined here would allow for a very different approach—one that would demand a lot more of the plaintiff.

The pre-HRA domestic decisions discussed above reveal that despite the introduction of s 10 the domestic courts were not affording the same weight to media freedom in examining the need for source disclosure as that afforded at Strasbourg, as revealed in the strong judgment in the *Goodwin* case. In particular, the 'interests of justice' exception was being applied in a manner that afforded greater weight to the right of institutions to take legal action than to the principle of freedom of expression. This approach has now been modified by the decision in *Ashworth*, which did evince a determination to apply Article 10 under the HRA correctly since it fully recognized the constant and unvarying interest in protecting sources. The findings in *Ashworth* demonstrate, however, that there is still a failure to engage fully with the Strasbourg reasoning process in respect of the doctrine of proportionality. The courts' approach to this journalistic privilege still appears to depend very much on the *nature* of the other interest at stake. The real *extent* to which it might be damaged still appears to be a largely subordinate consideration. If an employee of a company appears to be the source, that fact continues to have a very significant influence on the judicial response, while the stance taken under the national security exception presumably would not differ significantly from that taken in *Guardian Newspapers*.

The judges consider that the stance they are now taking is in accordance with the Strasbourg one. This chapter has argued that this is not the case—the judges have misapplied *Goodwin*. *Interbrew* suggests that they appear to prefer the means/end balancing proportionality test from *de Freitas* rather than the speech/harm balancing act. Where speech/harm balancing has occurred, as in *Ashworth*, the level of scrutiny adopted has not been strict enough. If that level of scrutiny was used, and use was made of the parallel analysis from *Campbell* where Article 8 is engaged, the analytical tools made available to the judiciary would allow for a more effective teasing out of the values at stake in any particular instance. The true value of confidentiality in the circumstances could be gauged. But on the other side of the coin, where sources appeared to be motivated by a desire to 'spin', or doctor, the information in question, the general interest in source protection would remain unvarying, but other speech arguments, based on the public interest value of the information, would be undermined since the speech rationale from truth would be lightly engaged at best.

The judicial reasoning in source disclosure cases is typical of that found in other common law areas covered by this book, such as common law contempt and breach of confidence. There is a strong tendency to erect apparent legal barriers that in reality can inevitably be crossed, thus giving the appearance of protection to an interest that the judges are not in sympathy with. The first barrier is normally created by the *Norwich Pharmacal* jurisdiction, but its demands will inevitably be satisfied since it is hard to imagine a source disclosure case in which a breach of confidence will not have occurred. The court then considers the next apparent barrier—the need to show that one of the s 10 exceptions applies. But the 'interests of justice' exception will always apply since a possible action for breach of confidence will always be available. The need to show that a *serious* legal wrong has occurred appears to have no inhibiting effect at this stage; it appears to be assumed that a breach of confidence is always a serious matter. Pre-*Goodwin* the courts would always then find that disclosure was necessary. Even in *Interbrew* Sedley LJ was preoccupied by the 'legitimacy' of Interbrew's intended resort to law—which of course would always be a factor for the reasons given. In the vast majority of cases considered in this chapter, including the post-HRA ones, disclosure has been ordered. So has any further protection for sources really been created due to *Goodwin* and the inception of the HRA?

In relation to the question of necessity a change has occurred. The difference, post-*Goodwin*, is that the Strasbourg Court has found that there is an unvarying interest in source protection. So there has to be a clear and strong interest to set on the other side *other than* the plaintiff's apparent desire to bring an action. The unvarying interest in protecting sources cannot be outweighed by the legitimacy of a resort to law alone since that would always be a factor. In *Interbrew* the other special feature was the malevolent purpose of the source; in *Ashworth* it was the interest in medical confidentiality. In both instances it is arguable that the courts did not examine the nature of that other factor closely since they were inclined towards the outcome achieved.

There has been no post-HRA case yet where it would be difficult to identify a special factor *but* the source might perpetrate further leaks (unlike the situation in *Saunders* and in *John*). *Camelot* arguably provided an example pre-HRA. How would the courts react in such an instance? In reality two interests would be opposed. First there would be the interest of the company or institution in protecting its confidential information—something that the judges take very seriously. On the other side there would be an imported notion, from *Goodwin*, of the need to protect sources—a matter that has not traditionally struck the judiciary as appealing. If a *Camelot* type of case arose post-*Ashworth* it would pose an interesting dilemma for the judges.

It may be asked *why* the British judiciary are traditionally disinclined to protect sources. Firstly, it seems to be for the reason given earlier—that they can readily envisage the concrete harm done to a company by a leak—the 'ticking bomb' argument—but the opposing interest strikes them as much more nebulous. Secondly there appears to be a suspicion of s 10. It was introduced by a Labour government as a deliberate means of overturning a House of Lords' decision in the wake of a case with a controversial political dimension. The judges appear to view s 10 with some suspicion, partly because they may have expected the *government* to have been the main beneficiary of the protection s 10 offers—since leaking information is often associated with government activity.[229] No exception contained in s 10 would have covered leaked governmental information, unless there was a national security dimension, without the broad interpretation given to the interests of justice exception which would now cover it. Thus the courts have removed some of the protection government may have arrogated to itself for its own purposes.

These closing remarks suggest that the protection for sources is still fairly precarious and is not embedded fully in the judicial consciousness as a common law principle to which they are strongly wedded. It may be concluded that in the UK investigative journalism relying on sources has received some encouragement from legal developments—in comparison with the situation in Canada the judges have eventually created an appearance of adhering to a principle of source protection. This chapter has set out to subject *all* the stages in a source disclosure case to an intense HRA analysis. Its use has helped to reveal flaws in the pre- and post-HRA judicial reasoning; an appearance of source protection has been created that is not fully borne out by the reality.

---

[229] In *Interbrew* note 122 above, at [7] Sedley LJ said: 'It should not be forgotten that in this country, then as now, the principal source of unattributable leaks to the media—in the form of off-the-record briefings—and therefore the principal beneficiary of a rule protecting the secrecy of sources, was government itself.'

PART III

MEDIA FREEDOM, OFFENCE, MORALITY, AND HATE SPEECH

This Part begins with Chapter 8 by considering theoretical issues raised by sexually explicit and/or otherwise offensive speech. It sketches the approaches of Strasbourg, the US, and Canada to this notoriously difficult and controversial issue. It then goes on to consider the criminal offence that delineates the boundaries of acceptable expression—the offence of obscenity. Chapter 8 also considers offences of indecency—where the concern is with the public *display* of explicit material rather than singling out the material that must be subject to criminal sanctions. Chapter 9 examines the offences of blasphemy and race hatred, before moving on to consider the new and controversial offence of religious hatred. Having evaluated the basic criminal offences that set the boundaries of explicit and offensive expression, the Part moves on to consider their reflection in the regulation of the visual media. Chapter 10 considers the theoretical issues raised by the regulation of the visual media and the position of regulation, as opposed to law, in relation to Article 10 of the European Convention on Human Rights. Chapters 11 and 12 consider the forms of regulation applied to broadcasting, films, and the Internet.

8

PORNOGRAPHY:
'HATE SPEECH'?

*The particulars given are that . . . the accused conspired together . . . by means of . . .
advertisements, 'to induce readers thereof to meet those persons inserting such
advertisements for the purpose of sexual practices taking place between male persons and
to encourage readers thereof to indulge in such practices, with intent thereby to debauch
and corrupt the morals as well of youth as of divers other liege subjects of Our Lady
the Queen.'*
Charges against persons publishing a gay 'contacts' magazine,
in *Knuller v DPP* (1973).

'persons of deviant sexuality and homosexuals and other perverts'
from the headnote in *DPP v Jordan* (1976).

*To impose [through obscenity laws] a certain standard of public and sexual morality,
solely because it reflects the conventions of a given community, is inimical to the exercise
and enjoyment of individual freedoms.*
from *R v Butler* [1992] 1 SCR 452, 492.

INTRODUCTION

This chapter is concerned with the age-old and ever more normatively complex
argument surrounding the widely felt need by states to suppress or at least strongly
regulate sexually explicit expression. To traditional concerns that such expression
may undermine moral values and the institution of marriage have been added
feminist arguments that it amounts to a damaging attack upon core human rights
values such as dignity, equality, and the right of all to have their voices heard.
Such feminist concerns some time ago stepped out of the pages of academic
journals and books into the legislature[1] of one US state and the Supreme Court of

---

[1] The Indianapolis Anti-Pornography Ordinance; it was successfully challenged as incompatible with the
First Amendment. For the first instance decision, see *American Booksellers Assoc. etc v Hudnitt III, Mayor, City
of Indianapolis et al* 598 F Supp 1316; for the (unsuccessful) appeal, see 771 F 2d 323.

Canada.[2] On the other hand, as we will see, the very argument as to the political character of pornography—that it portrays a particular ideological message, which is harmful, has itself raised fresh counter-arguments from anti-censorship groups and scholars: if pornography, rather than just being mindless 'smut', carries a 'political message', surely it is not for the state to suppress it, on the ground that the message is seen as undesirable or wrong. Many of the arguments in this chapter revolve around the particular dual nature of pornography—its strongly commercial nature and the fact that it is intended predominantly to arouse (often, to be used as an aid to masturbation); as such, the arguments are unique to sexually explicit literature. Similarly, issues of public display of such material and the offence that this may cause, as opposed to the *damage* it may do, are confined to pornography. At this point, a brief point as to terminology is necessary: this chapter is concerned principally with sexually explicit material, which could be considered either obscene[3] or indecent or both; however, the English law notions of both concepts include immoral or shocking non-sexual matter, as will appear below.

In this area, as we shall see, English law, based primarily upon authorities handed down in the 1970s, themselves based upon an Act of 1959 that has its roots in a judgment from the Victorian era,[4] has not begun even to engage with these complexities. Indeed, as we will argue, it is based upon a notion of endangering the morals of individuals that is completely unworkable in a pluralistic society in which agreement as to sexual morality as a substantive value[5] has wholly fragmented—a society in which gay rights activists rub shoulders with conservative Muslims; 'swingers' with Evangelical Christians. The judiciary continues to avoid the problem of defining the legal restrictions represented by the immensely vague statutory and common law 'principles' by hiding behind the role of the jury, leaving the criminal liability of the artist as well as the pornographer in the hands, in Dicey's striking phase, of the moral judgment of 'twelve shopkeepers'.[6] The law, we will argue, is enormously over-broad in its potential application, as well as plainly internally inconsistent in the view that it takes of the role of artistic or other merit as a defence to *prima facie* obscenity or indecency. It is only kept within manageable limits by *de facto* decisions by prosecutors to use it only against the most extreme forms of material, although it appears even there that little principled attempt is made to distinguish between material

---

[2] See the leading decision in *R v Butler* [1992] 1 SCR 452 on the constitutionality of the anti-pornography provisions of the Criminal Code, which is based at least in part upon feminist arguments as to the adverse effects of pornography upon the image and therefore the role and treatment of women in contemporary society.

[3] The word 'obscene', in English law, connotes that which will morally corrupt an individual; 'indecent' connotes that which is merely shocking and repulsive.

[4] *R v Hicklin* (1868) 3 QB 360.

[5] That is, a sexual morality which argues for an approach to sexuality which goes beyond the limits placed by the criminal law upon sexual *acts*, i.e. the proscription of incest, sex with children, and non-consensual sex.

[6] 'Freedom of discussion is in England little else than the right to write or say anything which a jury, consisting of twelve shopkeepers, think it expedient should be said or written.' A. V. Dicey, *Introduction to the Study of the Law of the Constitution*, 10th edn. London: Macmillan, 1959, Chapter VI.

concerned with violence, coercion, and criminality on the one hand, and the merely 'hard-core', in the sense of graphic depiction of sexual activity not in itself illegal, on the other. In this area, as we will demonstrate, Strasbourg, through deployment of the margin of appreciation doctrine in its most extreme form, has sought to avoid entanglement—even engagement—with these difficulties, while at the same time, by legitimizing state action through 'no breach' findings, has effectively endorsed a traditional, moralistic view of the role of obscenity and indecency law. If judicial reform of the law is to come about in this area, it appears that it can come not through application of the Strasbourg case law, but by recourse to the very general Convention free speech principles, and the drawing of inspiration from other jurisdictions, such as Canada.

The inception of the HRA means that the UK courts are now faced squarely with the difficult theoretical problems associated with a positive right to freedom of expression as opposed to a negative liberty.[7] This is a matter that is especially pertinent in relation to the forms of expression considered in this chapter. Instead of merely determining whether a particular statute or a doctrine of the common law applies to a factual situation, the courts must consider the *weight* to be given to a particular manifestation of expression, when considering the claim that an interference with it is justified. As Chapter 3 indicated, they were already going down this path in creating a common law right to freedom of expression.[8] But they will now have to consider such a right in a much wider range of situations, and will have to grapple with the doctrinal constraints of the Article 10(2) exceptions. The use of a range of laws, such as those aimed at suppressing obscene works, at the protection of public decency, and at protecting religious sensibilities, will all have to be considered in relation to the Article 10 freedom of expression guarantee. In other words, in instances in which, previously, the free speech argument would hardly be heard, defendants will argue that it should take a central place. The theorizing of judgments in all sorts of areas of law that have had a largely unrecognized effect on expression *may* begin to take place. However, it should be stressed again that, because of the very wide discretion that the relevant case law allows to the executive authorities, this is now a *possibility* generated by the HRA, rather than something it directly imposes.

As the above will have indicated, this chapter, while expounding the law, is intended primarily to engage in an energetic critique of it: it is difficult to think of another area of British law affecting media freedom that is in such a neglected, inconsistent, and downright indefensible state. The chapter will rely on Canadian law in particular, but will also consider US law as a means of illustrating alternative, more sophisticated, alternatives to the UK approach. But it will also critique those other approaches, with a view to revealing their flaws and the unresolved issues inherent in them. The critique of the Strasbourg 'approach', already indicated in Chapter 2, will be as robust as that of domestic law. In particular, it will be found that the so-called 'hierarchy' of speech, in

---

[7] See Chapter 1 at 4–12 for discussion of this point.   [8] See p 109.

which 'artistic' expression is relegated to a relatively low level of protection, together with the slippery geometry of the margin of appreciation,[9] has given rise to profoundly unsatisfactory tendencies in judgments that offer little or nothing by way of inspiration for domestic judicial law reform in this area. It is for these reasons that this chapter has such a strongly comparative flavour: the Strasbourg case law, quite simply, adds very little, save in terms of a different formal doctrinal approach, to the existing flawed domestic approach. Inspiration must therefore be sought elsewhere.

This chapter will approach the topic as follows. It will firstly consider briefly the evidence linking pornography with sexual offences and other types of harmful behaviour, then go on to survey the intense theoretical debate surrounding the permissibility of, and rationales for, restrictions upon freedom of expression in this area. It will then go on to consider critically the Strasbourg jurisprudence in this area, building upon the approach outlined in Chapter 2. The discussion will then turn to UK obscenity law, considering the main statutory and common law offences, in the light of the preceding discussion of the Convention explicit expression jurisprudence. The approach of the Canadian Supreme Court to this issue will be introduced, to indicate a contrasting way forward, inspired by the feminist perspective, and evaluated against the current British and other possible approaches. The law governing indecency will finally be considered, before the conclusion offers a number of alternative proposals for reform.

PORNOGRAPHY — THE EVIDENCE OF HARM

It is unreal to discuss objections to the availability of extreme and violent pornography, and arguments about consequent legal restrictions, without some idea in mind of the nature of the problem. A recent government paper gives this disturbing sketch:

There are hundreds of internet sites offering a wide range of material featuring the torture of (mostly female) victims who are tied to some kind of apparatus or restrained in other ways and stabbed with knives, hooks and other implements ... Some material contains sexualised images of women hanging by their necks from meat hooks, some with plastic bags over their heads. There is also extensive availability of sites featuring violent rape scenes. Within this category there is a growing trend for scenes purporting to be filmed in real time which heightens their impact. Depictions of necrophilia and bestiality are also widely available.[10]

---

[9] The phrase owes something to Lord Lester, who has commented that 'The concept of the margin of appreciation has become as slippery and elusive as an eel.' A. Lester, 'Universality versus Subsidiarity: A Reply' [1998] EHRLR 73.

[10] Home Office, *Consultation: on the possession of extreme violent pornography* (2005), at [5]; available http://news.bbc.co.uk/1/shared/bsp/hi/pdfs/30_08_05_porn_doc.pdf

In terms of the possible access of children to such sites, according to a major UK research study published in April 2005,[11] 75 per cent of 9–19 year olds surveyed had accessed the internet from a computer at home and 57 per cent of all 9–19 year olds surveyed who use the internet at least once a week had come into contact with pornography online. Plainly, coming into contact with pornography may have traumatic and other psychologically damaging effects on children, although the evidence on this matter remains inconclusive.[12] There is a widespread consensus as to the need to protect children from sexually explicit materials.[13] But what is the effect of pornography, particularly violent pornography, on adults? Proving a link between the availability and consumption of pornography and sexual offences has not yet been possible. The evidence remains equivocal. Some evidence has been produced of a link, although this evidence is disputed by other studies.[14] The recent conclusions of the Fraser Report[15] could not postulate any causal relationship between pornography and the commission of violent crimes, the sexual abuse of children, or the disintegration of communities and society. On the other hand, the Attorney General's Commission on Pornography in the US, reporting in 1986, found that:

the clinical and experimental research 'virtually unanimously' shows that exposure to sexually violent material increases the likelihood of aggression toward women; and that the available evidence strongly supports the hypothesis that substantial exposure to sexually violent materials . . . bears a causal relationship to antisocial acts of sexual violence and, for some subgroups, possibly to unlawful acts of sexual violence.[16]

This is in contrast to the findings of the MacGuigan Report.[17] As the Canadian Supreme Court put it in *R v Butler*.[18]

While a direct link between obscenity and harm to society may be difficult, if not impossible, to establish, it is reasonable to presume that exposure to images bears a causal relationship to changes in attitudes and beliefs. The Meese Commission Report,[19] concluded in respect of sexually violent material (vol. 1, at p 326):

. . . the available evidence strongly supports the hypothesis that substantial exposure to

[11] *UK Children Go Online*, Sonia Livingstone and Magdalena Bober: www.children-go-online.net
[12] See Chapter 12 at 633–4 for a brief consideration of this matter.   [13] See Chapter 10 at 541–5.
[14] Evidence for a causal link is quoted in C. MacKinnon, *Feminism Unmodified*, Cambridge, Mass: Harvard University Press, 1998, pp 184–91, while a recent UK study which finds against such a link: G. Cumberbatch and D. Howitt, *A Measure of Uncertainty—the Effects of the Mass Media*, J. Libbey, 1989. The findings of this latter study were published in the *Daily Telegraph*, 23 December 1990. Eckersley discusses the issue ('Whither the feminist campaign? An evaluation of feminist critiques of pornography', 15 *Int J Soc of Law* 149 at 161–3). See also C. Itzen, (ed), *Pornography: Women, Violence and Civil Liberties*, Oxford: OUP, 1993, which puts forward a body of evidence supporting a causal link.
[15] *Pornography and Prostitution in Canada*, 1985.
[16] Extracts appear in T. Mappes and J. Zembaty, *Social Ethics: Morality and Social Policy*, 5th edn., New York: McGraw-Hill, 1997, at 212–17.
[17] Report on Pornography by the Standing Committee on Justice and Legal Affairs 1978.
[18] [1992] 1 SCR 452.
[19] The Attorney General's Commission on Pornography (the 'Meese Commission'), *Final Report* (US, 1986), vol. 1.

sexually violent materials as described here bears a causal relationship to antisocial acts of sexual violence and, for some subgroups, possibly to unlawful acts of sexual violence.

Although we rely for this conclusion on significant scientific empirical evidence, we feel it worthwhile to note the underlying logic of the conclusion. The evidence says simply that the images that people are exposed to bears a causal relationship to their behaviour. This is hardly surprising. What would be surprising would be to find otherwise, and we have not so found. We have not, of course, found that the images people are exposed to are a greater cause of sexual violence than all or even many other possible causes, the investigation of which has been beyond our mandate. Nevertheless, it would be strange indeed if graphic representations of a form of behaviour, especially in a form that almost exclusively portrays such behaviour as desirable, did not have at least some effect on patterns of behaviour.[20]

This sounds like common sense; however, if taken literally, it would also have serious implications for the screening of films that portray serious violence in a glamorous light. Obvious recent examples include the *Kill Bill* films, *Sin City, Natural Born Killers*, and *Pulp Fiction*, to name only a few. But such a view is *not* taken in relation to the depiction of violence, which is relatively freely allowed, in comparison to the graphic depiction of rape, which is rarely seen in films and certainly not depicted in a light-hearted way, as the violence often is in the above films.[21] It is apparent immediately therefore that on the face of it there is some inconsistency in the singling out of *sexual* violence as particularly problematic.

The UK Government, in a paper advocating an extension of the law to catch simple possession of certain kinds of extreme pornography, has recently conceded:

We are unable, at present, to draw any definite conclusions based on research as to the likely long term impact of this kind of material on individuals generally, or on those who may already be predisposed to violent or aberrant sexual behaviour.[22]

In short, it appears that the evidence linking consumption of certain types of pornography with sexual offences and/or with changes in attitudes to women is uncertain, but that such a link cannot be ruled out. Barendt's common-sense conclusion on this is:

What perhaps can be stated with confidence is that the relationship (if any) between pornography and conduct is better determined by a legislature than by a court, even by a court accustomed to considering sociological evidence.[23]

This is probably the case: but courts are bound to be, and already have been, drawn to an extent into the 'evidence' question, as the discussion below reveals. The 'evidence' issue will be referred to at various points in the discussion below.

---

[20] Cited in *Butler*, op cit, at 502.

[21] A recent film which did feature a prolonged and graphic rape scene, *Irreversible*, was found by the BBFC to treat rape with great seriousness, and not in a way that would be likely to titillate; had it been found to have treated it otherwise, cuts might have been imposed. See Chapter 12 at 629.

[22] Consultation paper, op cit, at [31].

[23] Barendt, *Freedom of Speech*, 2nd edn., Oxford: OUP, 2005, at 374.

A further, distinct argument concerns the harm that may be done to the participants in the making of 'hard core' pornographic films. This will depend on the nature of the pornographic industry in the particular jurisdiction. If such films portray a variety of actual sexual acts, including sado-masochistic ones, the participants may suffer psychological or even physical harm. This point is of especial pertinence to women since, typically, the female participants are subjected to sexual acts in which they are more victim than perpetrator.[24] For example, a typical scenario might include one woman having sex with a large number of men, sometimes simultaneously. In such circumstances, it is arguable that the woman's consent may be undermined owing to uncertainty as to what will occur, intimidation into accepting certain acts, such as anal sex, and, more generally, owing to the power disparity between the (typically) young woman and the (generally) male directors of such films. If, for example, a woman is alone with a group of men in a house at which filming is taking place and has already been bullied and intimidated, the question whether she is continuing to give informed consent to a variety of sexual acts, which have been occurring for a period of time, begins to lose any reality.[25] If it was fairly clear that she was no longer giving such consent, it is hard to imagine that it would be possible, in practice, for her to seek the protection of the law, a fact of which she, and the film makers, will be aware. The film makers are under commercial pressures to push participants into accepting more extreme acts. If it appears from the nature of a film that participants may have been intimidated and subjected to actions verging on sexual abuse (owing to the circumstances, including the duration of one session), feminists, liberals, and conservatives would all, on the arguments indicated below, accept regulation. On this argument, films depicting potentially harmful sado-masochist and other sexual acts would not necessarily be banned completely, but the conditions under which such filming could take place would be subject to rigorous controls, with the welfare of the participants in mind, and designed to be certain that full, informed consent had always been given. But where it was apparent that such controls had not been in place, and that harm, such as psychological trauma, had occurred, censorship would arguably be warranted, except in exceptional cases owing to the strong artistic merits of the film. Where it could only be said that a risk of such harm was possible, it could be viewed as a further factor to be weighed in the balance, along with those identified above. While it is not

[24] The most disturbing account is given by the star of the film *Deep Throat*: L. Lovelace, (with M. McGrady), *Ordeal*, Secaucus, N.J.: Citadel Press, 1980.

[25] During the compilation of a documentary into the making of hard-core pornographic films in Los Angeles, *Hard Core* (broadcast on Channel 4 on 7 April 2001), the Director of the Channel 4 documentary intervened when it appeared that due to bullying and intimidation by the director of the pornographic film, the woman participant was no longer capable of giving informed consent. She had already been subjected to painful and humiliating acts to which it appeared probable that she had not given consent. In other words, consented-to acts had verged into actions going beyond the apparent boundaries of what she had consented to beforehand. Despite her distress occasioned by painful, forceful oral sex, the director wished to continue filming and she was told that she must next participate in a group orgy scene in which she would be the only woman. She appeared to acquiesce, but after the intervention, she, and the film crew, had to leave immediately. See further *The Times*, 9 April 2001, p 27.

the general job of the law on freedom of expression to protect the working conditions of those in the pornography industry, the law could certainly take into account the fact that certain films appeared to show actual acts of abuse or criminal violence taking place.

LAW AND PORNOGRAPHY: THEORETICAL CONSIDERATIONS

The question as to how far sexually explicit speech deserves the same protection as other forms of expression, and if it does not, how far and for what reasons it should be suppressed, has, as Barendt notes, '. . . almost certainly elicited more academic commentary than any other [free speech] topic'.[26] As striking as the amount of writing on the subject is the failure by academics of different persuasions to reach a consensus view. Thus, for example, conservatives,[27] liberals,[28] and feminists[29] have all attacked the findings of the famous William Committee, appointed in 1977 to review obscenity law findings, and all for different reasons. In addition, even to speak of 'feminist' and 'liberal' positions necessitates a conscious simplification, because these two opposing positions, at first sight monolithic, are in fact riven by internal debate; in particular, the feminist camp displays a conspicuous lack of unanimity.[30] Nevertheless, an attempt will be made, in what follows, to outline briefly the 'core' of each stance and evaluate the strength of their arguments, both against each other and directly on the subject of the permissibility of censorship in this area.

THE CONSERVATIVE POSITION

The conservative position, which in the popular consciousness is probably most associated with the former campaigner for 'family values', Mary Whitehouse, finds its

---

[26] Op cit, at, 352.

[27] See, e.g., the comments of Mary Whitehouse in *The Sunday Times* that, as a result of the Committee's report, '. . . we are going from a quicksand into . . . a very, very mucky quagmire . . .', quoted in A. W. B. Simpson, *Pornography and Politics: The Williams Committee in Retrospect*, Waterlow Publishers, 1983, p 44; he also quotes (p 45) a *Daily Telegraph* leader which criticized the 'some would say excessively liberal principle' it endorsed.

[28] See, e.g., the detailed analysis in R. Dworkin, 'Do we have a right to pornography?', in *A Matter of Principle*, Cambridge, Mass: Harvard University Press, 1985, in which he broadly endorses the Committee's conclusions, but argues that these cannot be supported by the arguments they deployed.

[29] The whole approach of the feminists is hostile to the broadly liberal stance adopted by the Committee; see, e.g., S. Brownmiller, *Against Our Will*, Ballantine Books, 1975, where it is asserted that all previous value systems, including the liberal tradition, have worked against the interests of women. For explicit criticism of the Committee by a more moderate feminist, see R. Eckersley, 'Whither the feminist campaign? An evaluation of feminist critiques of pornography', 15 *Int J Soc of Law* 149. Eckersley dismisses Williams as having 'simply fail[ed] to register the feminist objection' (p 174).

[30] For comments on the divisions in the feminist critique of pornography, see Eckersley, ibid. See also N. Lacey, 93 *JLS* 93.

academic and somewhat more abstract exposition in Lord Devlin's work, *The Enforcement of Morals*.[31] In essence, Devlin's view is that since a shared set of basic moral values is essential to society, it is as justified in protecting itself against attacks on these values (such as that mounted by pornography) as it is in protecting itself against any other phenomena which threaten its basic existence, such as violent public disorder. On this thesis, moral corruption of the individual is to be prevented in order to ensure the ultimate survival of society. Devlin's position is clearly not compatible with most existing UK law.[32] It could neither support nor even account for the existence of the public good defence in section 4 of the Obscene Publications Act 1959,[33] or indeed any similar defence: it would appear somewhat absurd to argue that material which threatened the very survival of society should be allowed to circulate freely on the grounds that it was somehow also in the public good.[34]

Devlin's position also appears to have been placed in doubt on the theoretical level by Hart's incisive critique.[35] Briefly, Hart's objections are as follows: on the more favourable reading of Devlin's position, he is not assuming, but trying to establish, the truth of the proposition that a shared set of moral standards (going on Devlin's account far beyond simple prohibitions on violence, theft, etc.) is an essential attribute of society. If this is the case, argues Hart, Devlin fails to establish the proposition for the simple reason that he offers no empirical evidence to support it. This leads one, Hart continues, to the suspicion that Devlin actually *assumes* the truth of the proposition and thus builds his theory on a tautology: having defined society as a system of shared beliefs, he then concludes, with perfect logic but some futility, that if those shared beliefs change radically or unanimity is lost, the society has disintegrated. Devlin's position therefore does not seem a compelling one. Moreover, it is plausible to say that any consensus—any 'moral glue'—relating to sexual attitudes has *already* disappeared, as contended above. There is a 'thin' consensus that sex should not be coercive and should not involve minors, but those attitudes are, of course, *already* protected by the criminal law on rape, the age of consent, and sexual offences. But there is no moral consensus that an obscenity law could or should protect from 'corruption' on issues such as adultery, promiscuity, gay sex, minority or alternative sexual lifestyles[36]—what used to be known as 'sexual perversion'. Given the widely different views held on these matters by people, depending upon their age, religious

[31] London, New York, and Toronto: Oxford University Press, 1965.

[32] It may find reflection in some of the more obscure common law offences such as conspiracy to corrupt public morals and outraging public decency. The Lords, in *Knuller v DPP* [1973] AC 435; [1972] 3 WLR 143; (1972) 56 Cr App R 633, a much criticized decision, arguably gave some support to the Devlin thesis. For discussion of the decision, see below, at 445–7.

[33] For discussion of the defence, see below, pp 438–41.

[34] Under the 1959 Act, the defence of public good only comes into play once it has been decided that the material is likely to deprave and corrupt: *Penguin Books* [1961] *Crim LR* 176 (the *Lady Chatterley's Lover* trial).

[35] For a summary of Hart's critique, see 'social solidarity and the enforcement of morality', in *Essays in Jurisprudence and Philosophy*, Clarendon, 1983.

[36] For example, transvestism, and what may be referred to as BDSM: bondage, domination, sadism, and masochism.

belief, ideology, and sexual preferences, there simply is no unified set of contemporary moral standards. Devlin's position has therefore either been proved wrong (society has survived), or societal collapse, on one level, has already come about. Whichever is the case, it now seems implausible to argue that the availability or otherwise of pornography will have any effect on the matter.

There is, however, a less absolute conservative view on pornography as a source of cultural pollution or corruption. As Barendt points out:

[Such a] view is taken not only by unthinking moral conservatives. It has been entertained by such a distinguished constitutional lawyer as Professor Alexander Bickel. In 1971 he wrote in a passage quoted by Burger CJ in the *Paris Adult Theatre* case: '[The problem] concerns the tone of society, the mode, or to use terms that have perhaps greater currency the style and quality of life, now and in the future. Moreover, just as great books reflect the values of a civilized community and may ennoble and inspire generations, so the very existence of pornography lowers (it may be claimed) our sensitivities and debases society's moral outlook. The state has every right to eradicate it.[37]

However, Barendt himself disputes the force of this argument:

More strongly, it may be said that broad anti-pornography rules cannot be justified by recourse to moral tone arguments, because the commitment to free expression on sexual matters itself represents an integral aspect of a liberal community's morality.[38]

Another difficulty with Bickel's view is that it leaves the door wide open to anyone who believes—even a majority who believe—that the acceptance of certain ideas will lower the moral tone of society generally, or make its common life less valuable. The problem is in singling out sexually explicit material from, say, violent films, intolerant political discourse in the tabloid newspapers, or celebrity magazines, all of which, it can be argued, 'lower our sensitivities and debase our moral outlook'.

Practically speaking, it may also be said that it is simply wholly unrealistic to talk of 'eradicating' pornography, or displays of nudity and erotica, for the general good. As the vast amount of material available on the internet,[39] the widespread popularity of what might be termed sub-pornographic magazines in the UK such as *FHM, Loaded, GQ*, various tabloid newspapers, and the ubiquity of pop videos featuring scantily dressed female and male dancers indicates, our society is quite thoroughly saturated with sexuality in a commodified form. Plainly, in practical terms, it would be almost impossible for the law to *eradicate* pornography, as Bickel advocated, or the effect of the constant display of (generally female) flesh in various media. The question is, are any kinds of pornography so harmful that the law is in principle justified in being deployed against them, and are there are any arguments in favour of pornography's free availability that outweigh whatever harms it is claimed to cause?

---

[37] Op cit, at 364.   [38] Ibid.

[39] See Chapter 12 regarding the difficulties of dealing with the availability of pornography on the internet.

THE LIBERAL POSITION

The liberal position on pornography is broadly united around general opposition to censorship in the absence of clear evidence of a concrete harm caused by its free availability.[40] However, unanimity does not exist as to the rationales for free speech most applicable to defending a liberty to read or view pornographic material. There certainly *was* for some time general agreement that Meiklejohn's argument from participation in democracy[41] is of little relevance; as Dworkin caustically remarks, 'No one is denied an equal voice in the political process ... when he is forbidden to circulate photographs of genitals to the public at large'.[42] The contention that pornography makes no contribution to directly political speech may readily be conceded; however, we will consider below a plausible argument to the effect that pornography *does* amount to more than mere 'smut'—that it does, in short, convey ideas. As we shall see, paradoxically, this argument has gained most ground as a result of the position of some of the most bitter opponents of pornography—the radical feminists.

A variant of Mill's argument from truth[43] was avowedly the free speech justification adopted by the Williams Committee convened in 1979 to report on obscenity; although they expressed some scepticism at Mill's perhaps rather naïve conviction that in a *laissez faire* market of ideas, truth would always win out,[44] they endorsed the main thrust of his theory. Interference with the free flow of ideas and artistic endeavour was unacceptable since it amounted to ruling out in advance possible modes of human development, before it was known whether or not they would be desirable or necessary. Since they also reached the conclusion that '... no one has invented or in our opinion could invent, an instrument that would suppress only [worthless pornography] and could not be turned against something ... of [possibly] a more creative kind',[45] they concluded that this risk of suppressing worthwhile creative art ruled out censorship of the written word. (They regarded standard photographic pornography as not expressing anything that could be regarded as an 'idea' and so as unprotected by the argument from truth.)

Ronald Dworkin has mounted a sustained attack on this rationale;[46] it rests, he contends, on the instrumental justification that allowing the free circulation of ideas is necessary to enable individuals to make intelligent and informed choices about how they want to lead their lives and then flourish in them. He finds that such an argument is unable to support its own conclusion against censorship; for, he urges, it must be accepted that allowing the free availability of pornography will 'sharply limit' the ability of some (perhaps the majority) to shape their cultural understanding of sexuality in a way they think best—a way in which sexuality has dignity and beauty. His

---

[40] See J. Feinberg, *The Moral Limits of the Criminal Law: Offence to Others*, Oxford: OUP, 1985. See above for a brief discussion of the possible link between pornography and the commission of sexual offences.

[41] See Chapter 1 at 16–18.   [42] R. Dworkin, op cit, at 336.   [43] See Chapter 1 at 14–16.

[44] Report of the Committee on Obscenity and Film Censorship (Williams Committee), Cmnd 7772, 1979, at [5.20].

[45] Ibid, at [5.24].   [46] R. Dworkin, op cit.

argument appears to conclude that the justification from self-development does not argue conclusively against censorship, because of the plausible case that forbidding some pornography will for many people greatly *assist* in their self-development. Dworkin is surely correct when he concludes that not self-development but the straightforward argument from moral autonomy amounts to the strongest case against censorship in this area. This argument points out that judging for an individual what will and will not be beneficial for him or her to read represents a clear invasion of the individual right of an adult to decide moral issues concerned with one's own life for oneself,[47] what Dworkin refers to as one's 'moral independence'. Such an invasion could therefore only be justified if a serious risk of substantial damage to the concrete well-being of society was shown.[48] Since the law does not posit such a risk, censorship is unacceptable. Whether this argument also provides a convincing answer to the radical feminist objections to free access to pornography will be considered below; this position must first be sketched out.

Before turning to the feminist position, however, it is worth revisiting the question dismissed by Dworkin and the Williams Committee: does pornography, in some sense, convey ideas? Barendt points out that Schauer sees this as *the* crucial issue, in terms of the protection of pornography under free speech guarantees, such as the First Amendment.

Schauer has . . . argued convincingly that the question whether the material is offensive to the majority of society is really irrelevant [citing Schauer, F. 'Response: Pornography and the First Amendment' (1979) 40 *Univ of Pittsburgh Law Rev* 605, 610.] If it is wrong for the Court to take into account the degree of offensiveness or hurt occasioned to people when determining whether intemperate political discourse enjoys the coverage of the First Amendment, so it should be in the case of sexually explicit material. The constitutional question is whether such material is 'speech' at all, and the degree of offensiveness is irrelevant to its answer; what matters is whether there is a genuine communication of ideas or information.[49]

In relation to Schauer's point, there is an argument, as Barendt puts it:

that all, or at least virtually all, pornography should be treated as speech, because sexually explicit material does convey ideas—that sex is fun, that it need have nothing to do with permanent relationships, that it is good to be erotically aroused whenever one wants, and so on. The message of such material can only be put across effectively by the distribution of hard-core pornography. Another way of putting the case is to suggest that one of the purposes of pornography, whether gay or straight, is to explode the distinction between the private and the public in the discussion and portrayal of sexual activity; on this view, the proscription of hard-core material artificially excludes one perspective from public discourse.[50]

---

[47] See Chapter 1 at 12–14.

[48] It is submitted that Dworkin's other possible justifications for abrogating speech are not in most instances applicable here.

[49] Barendt, op cit, at 369.   [50] Ibid, at 358.

This applies, for example, to subversive (as they once were) novels like *Lady Chatterly's Lover*. Barendt instances a case in which a New York statute, 'improperly restricted the circulation of ideas' [since it required] 'the state to refuse a licence for the exhibition of a film which portrayed acts of sexual immorality as desirable or acceptable'. Plainly the statute sought to render the expression of certain moral views about sexuality impermissible. Barendt refers to such speech as 'ideological obscenity', noting that it should be protected as speech, 'because it does appeal to the intellect or artistic sensitivity'.[51]

On the other hand, Barendt argues that it is also somewhat unreal or fanciful to regard most standard pornography as in some way conveying 'ideas'. First of all, there is the issue of motive:

Almost all of it is written and published simply to make money. Its publishers have no intention of communicating information or opinions. While even the shabbiest politician wants his audience to believe what he has to say or to vote for him, a porn merchant simply wants consumers to purchase his wares.[52]

This leads on to the argument that:

. . . it would be ludicrous to claim of all hard-core pornography, particularly pictorial literature, that it is implicitly saying something about politics or social relationships. Most pornography is essentially non-cognitive; it does not make claims which might be true . . . Rather, the intention of its publishers, and its effect, is to create sexual excitement, to provide material for the indulgence of fantasy . . . an aid to masturbation. Indeed, there is little significant distinction between the impact of a picture magazine, depicting sexual intercourse in close detail, and that of a plastic sex aid or a visit from a prostitute. Now it may be that the public availability of all three means of taking pleasure should be immune from regulation. But that is not a free speech argument. A pornographic picture magazine no more involves communication than these other two means of achieving sexual satisfaction.[53]

Barendt suggests that, insofar as there is a speech argument, it could be that enjoyed by the recipient. But there are two objections to this. One is put by Barendt himself:

But it may be difficult to characterize pornography as speech solely because of the recipient's interest in its purchase, when the speaker's claim to exercise freedom of expression is so transparently bogus.[54]

This does not seem to be a particularly compelling point: the recipient may have a genuine autonomy or self-developmental interest in choosing for him- or herself what pornography or explicit literature he or she wishes to use, whatever the motives of the 'speaker'. If the potential recipient of, say, gay pornography is unable to receive it, due to societal disapproval and the fact that the producer of it acts only from the profit motive, his moral independence has been invaded, and possibly his sexual self-development

---

[51] Ibid, at 361.   [52] Ibid, at 360.   [53] Ibid, at 357.   [54] Ibid, at 360.

hampered.[55] The second argument is that, certainly in the case of standard pictorial pornography, the user's interest, as Barendt points out, is perhaps primarily a privacy right, to enjoy (generally solitary) sexual activity in the privacy of his or her own home, with whatever aids (i.e. pornography) he or she chooses to use. There is no doubt that there is a privacy interest here: but equally, on Barendt's own earlier argument, there is a case to be made that even 'hard core' pornography does convey ideas, even if this is not the producer's motive or primary purpose.

The two questions that matter therefore are: (a) whether the material can be said to be communicative in any way, and (b) whether it may reasonably be thought to cause harm in some way, which can include attitudinal changes that threaten the dignity and equal respect of persons. In relation to (a), there is what may be termed a 'specific' and a 'general' communicative argument. The former would look at the item in question and ask whether it could reasonably be thought to convey ideas—clearly this would be far more likely to happen in a work of any literary or sociological merit. Thus, scenes, particularly in novels or short stories, of extreme sexual conduct, perhaps even involving illegal acts, such as sexual torture, bestiality, etc., could be viewed, within the context of the work as a whole, as conveying ideas about human sexuality. The second is the more difficult, philosophical argument: that *all* pornography, in a sense, conveys ideas. It may force the viewer to re-assess attitudes to the body and to nudity and as to the types of sexual acts that are acceptable (e.g. by arousing him or her by depicting acts that the viewer had previously thought repellent, such as sado-masochistic practices, or perhaps group sex). It may, as Barendt argues, be seen as conveying the simple message that sex is 'fun' and should not be confined by any form of social or religious morality. Confrontation with pornography might also have the effect of radicalizing women (and, perhaps, men) in terms of gender politics. It may provoke strong convictions about the objectification of the female body and thus contribute to a person's intellectual and moral development. This may seem a perverse argument: pornography's very objectionable nature may count as one of its 'advantages'. This is not so, if it is recalled that we are discussing not whether society would be better off without certain forms of pornography, but whether the objections to it are strong enough to justify criminalization. One can perfectly consistently object strongly to the sexist message of some pornography whilst being opposed to the use of the criminal law to combat it, as Dworkin is; similarly, in a different area of law—holocaust denial—Noam Chomsky has furiously defended the right of a holocaust revisionist in France[56] to be free to propagate his views, whilst being wholly opposed to their substance.[57] At times, opponents of pornography appear to think that they

[55] One of the arguments put forward by lesbian and gay groups to the Canadian Supreme Court in the *Little Sisters* case was that pornography is particularly important for homosexuals, since it affirms and celebrates their sexuality, and may assist them in developing it, in a hostile or unsympathetic, certainly heterosexual-dominated environment: see *Little Sisters and Art Book Emporium v Canada* [2000] 2 SCR 1120 at [247].

[56] See *Robert Faurisson v France* (1997) IHRR 4(2) 444.

[57] See: www.mit.edu/activities/safe/writings/chomsky-on-free-expression

have proved their point regarding criminalization when they show that certain kinds of pornography convey undesirable ideological messages. This would, to many on the left, also justifying criminalizing *The Daily Mail.*

Whilst the arguments that pornography conveys ideas, and that its offensiveness is irrelevant, are not without force, one must be realistic and accept that they are highly unlikely to be accepted by courts, since they would allow for the virtually unrestricted production of pornography, save in cases in which persons were harmed making it, or where there was clear evidence of harm in terms of a causal link with sex crimes (which there is not, as discussed above). Such arguments would, however, allow for restrictions in terms of display and availability to ensure that it was only exposed to the willing and consenting. It is hard to deny that pornography *may* have communicative value; however, it is likely that in the vast majority of cases it is used, non-cognitively, simply as a masturbation aid. While a general speech value *may* attach to it, it must be accounted a fairly low one, at least in the case of standard pictorial pornography. Such value is relatively easily outweighed by the possibility of harm occurring through extreme forms of pornography and, in terms of public display, by the shock and offence caused to those unwillingly confronted with it.

It should finally be noted that liberals are willing to support restrictions on the outlets and public display of pornography[58] on the grounds that such restrictions do not necessarily spring from contempt for those who read pornography, but may simply reflect the genuine and personal aesthetic preferences of those who would rather not have to suffer the continual and ugly spectacle of publicly displayed pornography.[59] Unwanted public displays can be regulated just as neighbours who play loud music can be: as a public nuisance. The solution is to ensure that those who want pornography can access it, whilst those who do not want to be confronted with it are free from that offence: thus, access to pornography is justifiably limited to licensed sex shops and cinemas and through film classifications and warnings about explicit content.

THE PRO-CENSORSHIP FEMINIST POSITION

The views of feminist writers on the harms pornography does, on the justifications offered for allowing its free availability, and on what, if anything, the law should do about it are many and varied.[60] However, the pro-censorship feminist position on the

---

[58] Such as, e.g., the recommendations of the Williams Committee; see their 'Summary of our proposals', op cit.

[59] See R. Dworkin, op cit, at 355–8, where he broadly endorses the Williams Committee's proposals.

[60] For feminist writers who take a different stance on pornography from that broadly examined here, see any of the following: the chapters on pornography in C. Smart, *Feminism and the Power of Law,* Taylor & Francis Ltd, 1989, in which the author expresses distrust of using the law to control pornography; D. L. Rhode, *Justice and Gender,* 1989, in which the extent to which feminism has framed a puritanical ideology of sexuality and pornography is deplored: it is argued that women who find explicit depictions of, e.g., bondage or anonymous sex highly arousing do not 'need more sexual shame, guilt and hypocrisy, this time served up as feminism'. See also Jackson, 'Catherine MacKinnon and feminist jurisprudence: a critical appraisal' (1992) *JLS,* pp 195–213, for a moderate critique, particularly of MacKinnon's views on the impossibility of

possibility of legal control of pornography is generally equated with the views of
Catherine MacKinnon and Andrea Dworkin, who framed an Indianapolis Ordinance
giving rise to civil liability for trafficking in pornography or forcing it upon unwilling
recipients; its constitutionality was successfully challenged on the grounds of incompatibility with the First Amendment.[61] We devote some time to considering this
view precisely because of the influence it has had—unsuccessfully in the US, but
successfully in Canada, as will appear below. It has also been particularly influential
academically. As one dictionary of philosophy puts it:

[the MacKinnon] approach has provoked particular interest and discussion among both
liberals and feminists, and has come to constitute a dominant framework for much of the
contemporary debate between liberals and feminists over pornography.[62]

The essence of this variant of feminist thought is that while some argue that pornography causes harm to some individual women, by causing some individual men to
perpetrate rape, battery, and sexual abuse,[63] pornography causes a far more subtle and
all-pervasive harm to all women. It is on the latter argument that the remainder of the
discussion will concentrate.

In some of their more terse, dramatic statements, such as 'Pornography is violence
against women',[64] and 'We define pornography as a practice of sex discrimination',[65]
it sounds as if MacKinnon and Andrea Dworkin regard the very existence of pornography as a concrete harm to women which goes far beyond mere offence and yet is
not a physical harm. However, in the more precise explanations they offer, it seems
clear that the harm is caused through the effect it has on men's view of women: 'Men
treat women as who they see women as being. Pornography constructs who that is.' In
other words, the argument does remain, as Ronald Dworkin claims, 'a causal one'.[66]
At this point, having posited a link between pornography and the way men treat
women, the explanation draws in the more general radical feminist thesis that men
have near total power over women and that consequently, 'the way men see women
defines who women can be'.[67] Elsewhere, MacKinnon explains that this power is
generated by the fact that men have managed to establish the total 'privileging' of
their interests and perceptions and the concomitant complete subordination of
women, and then passed this off as reality or 'just the way things are'. MacKinnon

---

non-coercive heterosexual activity in contemporary society; V. Burstyn, (ed.), *Women Against Censorship*,
Vancouver: Douglas and MacIntyre, 1985.

[61] For the first instance decision, see *American Booksellers Assoc, etc v Hudnitt III, Mayor, City of Indianapolis et al* 598 F Supp 1316. For the (unsuccessful) appeal, see 771 F 2d 323.

[62] 'Pornography and Censorship' in the *Stanford Encyclopedia of Philosophy* at [4.1].

[63] See, e.g., C. MacKinnon, *Feminism Unmodified*, pp 184–91.

[64] The basic thesis of A. Dworkin, *Pornography: Men Possessing Women*, Cambridge, Mass: Harvard
University Press, 1979, quoted in Simpson, op cit, p 71.

[65] MacKinnon, op cit, at 175. The quotation given refers specifically to the Indianapolis Ordinance, but
equally summarizes MacKinnon's analysis of pornography.

[66] R. Dworkin, 'Liberty and pornography', *The New York Review of Books*, 15 August 1991, p 12.

[67] MacKinnon, op cit, at 172.

calls the resulting illusion 'metaphysically nearly perfect'.[68] Several more moderate feminists have pointed out[69] that this view places feminism in the bizarre position of having to deny the possibility of its own existence, because it entails assuming that all available modes of thought and perception are male, although masquerading as neutral. If this were true, it is hard to see how women could even come to realize that they were oppressed, let alone frame proposals for affirmative action to free themselves from male dominance. MacKinnon has indeed asserted that 'Feminism affirms women's point of view by . . . explaining its impossibility',[70] but since MacKinnon herself has in fact somehow managed to construct a substantive and highly influential feminist point of view—including the analysis of pornography under consideration— this reply seems rather unconvincing. It might be thought at this point that since acceptance of the radical feminist thesis on pornography is apparently only possible if one also accepts a metaphysical theory which seems both to deny its own existence and to involve acceptance of the most comprehensive conspiracy theory ever devised, the thesis can be summarily dismissed.

This, it is submitted, would be premature. The most significant feminist point with respect to pornography is the effect it is said to have on men's view of women and therefore on the way they treat them. One does not have to accept the general radical feminist thesis in order to give *some* consideration to the proposition that pornography, through the effect it has on men, oppresses women. Consequently, the discussion will now turn to considering whether the feminist thesis can still provide a justification for restrictions on the freedom to consume pornography even if the notion of total female subordination is rejected.

The oppression of women caused by pornography is claimed to manifest itself in the following three distinct ways. First, women are discriminated against, sexually harassed, and physically assaulted in all walks of life; this constitutes a denial of their civil right to equality. Secondly, women are denied their positive liberty, their right to equal participation in the political process because of the image in men's minds constructed by pornography, which 'strips and devastates women of credibility',[71] and consequently prevents women's contributions from being taken seriously. Finally, pornography 'silences' women—even their negative freedom from restrictions on their speech is denied because they are not seen as fully human agents, but rather as dehumanized creatures who 'desperately want to be bound, battered, tortured, humiliated and killed'.[72] The argument that the State should, therefore, seek to

---

[68] See 'Feminism, Marxism, method and the State', in Bartlett and Kennedy (eds), *Feminist Legal Theory*, Boulder, Co: Westview Press, 1991, p 182.

[69] See, e.g., Sandra Harding's introduction to MacKinnon's 'Feminism, Marxism, method and the State', in S. Harding, *Feminism and Methodology*, Oxford: OUP, 1987.

[70] C. MacKinnon, in *Feminist Legal Theory*, p 181.   [71] MacKinnon, op cit, at 193.

[72] MacKinnon, op cit, at 172. Cf Andrea Dworkin's description of the view that rape law evinces of women as one in which rape is not really against a woman's will, 'because what she wants underneath is to have anything done to her that violates or humiliates or hurts her': *Pornography: Men Possessing Women*, E. P. Dutton, 1979.

ban pornography on the basis of furtherance of equality, just as it seeks to outlaw discrimination in employment, is developed in *Only Words.*[73]

Two points may be made in response to the above. First, this thesis attributes to men a uniformly passive and receptive attitude to all pornographic images.[74] Nowhere in a long essay on pornography[75] does MacKinnon appear to advert to the possibility that many men may completely reject the 'message' of violent misogynistic pornography, even though some may be aroused by it. Her theory thus, in effect, amounts to a profound refusal to recognize the immense difference that men's backgrounds, education, and life experiences will have on their responses,[76] and more generally, the enormous variety of human responses to any given phenomenon which will be found even amongst those of similar backgrounds; ultimately, her theory denies (male) free will and with it men's individual voices.[77] Sadurski has made a similar point here, arguing that such a stance:

... denies the autonomy and individual responsibility of the hearers, and ... imagine[s] that once the hateful speech is uttered, it somewhat mechanically induces negative changes in the hearers' opinions ... they are seen as thoughtless receivers of ideas imposed upon them by speakers.[78]

The second point is that if one leaves aside the extreme idea of the total control of men over women described above, it then becomes impossible to accept the immense influence that is attributed to the consumption of pornography. The idea, for example, that pornography silences women in all walks of life remains quite simply, 'strikingly implausible'[79] perhaps precisely because it is so eloquently expressed, and it is hard to take seriously the notion that pornography denies women the right to participate in political life. One could only accept such arguments if one regarded women as defined completely by the images of pornography; as has been seen, that argument in turn could only have force if one first accepted that men's view of women is almost wholly constructed by pornography and then could agree to the assertion that men's view of women is all that women are. The impossibility of accepting such counter-intuitive propositions means, it is submitted, that the radical feminist argument does not convincingly establish that the availability of pornography represents or causes actual infringements of the rights of women.

---

[73] C. MacKinnon, *Only Words*, Harvard University Press, 1993.

[74] Andrea Dworkin attributes a similarly monolithic character to men; consider, e.g., the following description of the male sex: 'Terror issues forth from the male; illuminates his essential nature and his basic purpose' (*Pornography: Men Possessing Women*, 1979, at 74).

[75] MacKinnon, *Feminism Unmodified*, Chapter 14.

[76] For criticism of this characteristic failing in MacKinnon's work generally, see Jackson, op cit.

[77] An ironic point, since MacKinnon often talks of men 'silencing' women.

[78] W. Sadurski, 'On "Seeing speech through an equality lens": a critique of egalitarian arguments for suppression of hate speech and pornography' (1996) 16(4) *OJLS* 713, 717.

[79] R. Dworkin, op cit, at 14; Rhode also asks how, if women are silenced by pornography, a small group of feminists managed to mount a challenge to some of the most cherished principles of American constitutionalism and one of its most successful entertainment industries: D. L. Rhode, *Justice and Gender*, Harvard University Press, 1989.

Similarly, the attempt to define pornography not as *persuasive* speech, which it is difficult to justify restricting simply because of its undesirable message, but as a form of 'speech-act' also seems lacking in plausibility.[80] The latter class of 'speech' is referred to as 'illocutionary' speech—that is, speech that does not create effects, as is generally the case, by persuading others to a different point of view, or by giving them information, but by performing actions. Such actions can include subordinating others. Examples, given by Sadurski, include statements such as: ' "blacks are not permitted to vote"; "Hispanics need not apply"; "Women are not allowed in the [bar area]." '[81] Such speech-acts '*constitute* unequal treatment'. Generally, only governments can perform discriminatory speech-acts, as the South African government did under apartheid.[82] But as Sadurski concedes, some private bodies have effective powers to do so. Umpires in sporting games who shout 'foul' or 'no-ball' are one example; so clearly are private clubs that bar female members. However, it would be very difficult to see a form of general expression (pornography) in magazines, books, and films as constituting such speech-acts. Langton's argument that it does is as follows:

Just as the speech of the umpire is authoritative within a certain domain—the game of tennis—so pornographic speech is authoritative within a certain domain—the game of sex. The authors of pornographic speech are not mere bystanders to the game, they are speakers whose verdict counts ... Pornographers tells its hearers which moves are appropriate and permissible; it tells them that certain moves are appropriate because women want to be raped, it legitimates violence.[83]

This, as Sadurski makes clear, cannot mean merely that pornography *persuades* readers that certain 'moves', for example sexual violence, are 'appropriate'; this would amount to describing speech as performing its normal, persuasive function. As a recent Liberal Democrat policy paper observed, it is not a 'function of the law to impose restrictions on freedom of expression because sexually explicit material may misinform men about women's sexual desires. These are matters appropriately addressed by enhanced debate and discussion (including about the roles of men and women in society) and by ensuring that young people have positive and accurate sex education.'[84] Rather, it means that Langton, to make out her argument that pornography is a 'speech-act', would have to show that pornographers are recognized (as an umpire is) as having the authority to define rightful conduct. The very recognition of speech-acts presupposes that the person speaking has already been given the official status to make what they say authoritative and binding: if someone from the crowd watching a tennis game shouts 'Out!', as the ball lands, their 'call' is not a speech-act, simply because they are not recognized as having the authority to bind the participants by their determination of the matter. Similarly, if a friend were to read out the wedding service to a couple and then 'pronounce' them 'husband and wife',

---

[80] This thesis is put forward by R. Langton, 'Speech Acts and Unspeakable Acts' (1993) 22 *Philos. and Pub. Aff* 293 and critiqued by Sadurski, op cit.

[81] Op cit, at 718.   [82] Op cit, at 103.

[83] Op cit, at 109.

[84] *Censorship and Freedom of Expression*, Policy Paper 65, at [3.7(4)].

her speech would lack the performative quality it would have if she were to be pre-recognized as having the authority to perform marriage ceremonies. Thus, for Langton's theory to be correct, readers of pornography would have to attribute to pornographers the authority to decide for them the rules of sexual conduct—rather like a judge pronouncing sentence. As Sadurski puts it, even to ask whether the readers of pornography view its creators in this way has 'an air of absurdity' about it. The proposition is so implausible as scarcely to need further refutation. However, if further argument is needed, it may be pointed out that if we are using the analogy of sex as a game with referees, there can be only one referee; her metaphorical equivalent is a *genuine* speech-act relating to sexual conduct, which is *correctly* seen as authoritatively determining the permissible and impermissible in sexual conduct. Collectively, such a speech-act is represented by the criminal law, which, of course, proscribes rape and all other forms of sexual assault. The attempt then to present pornography, using the 'speech-act' argument, as a '*practice* of sex discrimination' fails resoundingly.

However, another, perhaps more moderate, variant of the feminist 'silencing' argument may be considered. As Harel puts it, it may be argued that: 'A society that does not restrict pornographic speech is less inclined, in turn, to understand, accept, and be shaped by women's speech and women's values.'[85] She goes on:

If the aim of the First Amendment is to encourage the *exercise* of the right to free speech, we must calculate the impact that some speakers' uninhibited exercise of the right to speak will have on the exercise of that same right by others. If a restriction on certain forms of speech is likely to produce more speech than it will deter, the restriction is justified. Moreover, the protection of speech is meaningless unless the speech is guaranteed some opportunity to shape the life of the community. The second component of the silencing argument requires courts to take into account not only the degree to which the right of free expression is exercised by individuals but also the degree to which it has a fair opportunity to influence the community.[86]

There are a number of points to make in response to this. First of all, what is being suggested here is a right to 'effective speech'; this might be of relevance to broadcasting policy, where 'must carry' and 'due impartiality' requirements do aim at ensuring a fair representation of a range of views, but can scarcely be of relevance to the general law.[87] As Barendt puts it:

... to concede a right to *effective* communication risks blurring the line between speech and action. In some circumstances, violence may be used to protest against a political policy or to communicate the strength of feelings on particularly controversial issues, for example, the abortion laws or participation in a war. But an argument that violence in those circumstances amounts to speech cannot be upheld; its acceptance would make nonsense of any distinction between speech and conduct.[88]

Second, in relation to the 'silencing' argument, the converse could of course be the

---

[85] Harel, 'Bigotry, Pornography and the First Amendment: a theory of unprotected speech' (1992) 65 *South Cal L.R.* 1887, at 1908.

[86] Op cit, at 1909.   [87] See, generally Chapter 10.   [88] Op cit, at 359.

case: encountering some particularly revolting pornography might actually radicalize a woman, who, hitherto, while of course engaging in normal social and personal communication, had been unengaged politically. In the same way, a gay man, who has not been politically active in promoting gay rights, might be radicalized into doing so by being the subject of homophobic abuse, or reading an anti-gay diatribe in a morally conservative publication. Moreover, as Harel herself puts it:

The advocates of restriction fail to explore the exact quantitative impact that different forms of speech have upon different groups, compare them, and base their position on this comparison. It is doubtful whether such comparisons are possible, even in theory.[89]

It may further be argued in relation to the 'silencing' argument that it does not pertain solely to pornography, in other words, that it does not identify a harm distinctive to pornography. For example, the widespread dissemination of 'ProLife' expression, claiming that abortion is murder, would be bound to have some silencing effect upon *some* pro-choice members of a community that was strongly ProLife. Moreover, there are other kinds of 'silencing' which are precisely designed to strip credibility from opponents: for example, speech that ridicules creationists as deluded, backward religious fanatics with a sinister fundamentalist agenda is deliberately intended to strip their position, and thus their own speech, of credibility. As Ronald Dworkin puts it: 'Creationists, flat-earthers, and bigots, for example, are ridiculed in many parts of America now; that ridicule undoubtedly dampens the enthusiasm that many of them have for speaking out and limits the attention others pay to what they have to say.'[90] Conversely, speech by US right-wingers, which portrays 'liberal' opponents of the war in Iraq as unpatriotic, defeatist, and filled with self-loathing, is intended to strip the arguments of such people of their credibility and persuasiveness. In fact, such speech has this 'silencing' outcome as its primary aim and is therefore, arguably more pernicious: this outcome is (if it occurs at all) but a side-effect of pornography, which generally has as its primary aim simply the making of money.

There is a further point. Just as the 'silencing argument', upon examination, is not unique to pornographic speech, so the more general feminist thesis about the possible pernicious effects of pornography upon women's interests fails to distinguish pornography from other forms of expression concerning women, which are arguably more damaging. As Ronald Dworkin puts it:

Sadistic pornography is revolting, but it is not in general circulation, except for its milder, soft-porn manifestations. It seems unlikely that it has remotely the influence over how women's sexuality or character or talents are conceived by men, and indeed by women, that commercial advertising and soap operas have. Television and other parts of popular culture use sexual display and sexual innuendo to sell virtually everything, and they often show women as experts in domestic detail and unreasoned intuition, and nothing else. The images they create are subtle and ubiquitous, and it would not be surprising to learn, through whatever research might establish this, that they indeed do great damage to the way women

---

[89] Op cit, at 1910. [90] 'Women and Pornography', *New York Review of Books* (1993) XL/17.

are understood and allowed to be influential in politics. Sadistic pornography, though much more offensive and disturbing, is greatly overshadowed by these dismal cultural influences as a causal force.[91]

Despite the fact that the internet now makes access to sadistic pornography much easier, his basic argument still seems persuasive. Moreover, to the cultural influences he cites, one should add women's fashion and lifestyle magazines, of which it is regularly complained that they induce an atmosphere of obsession with female appearance, particularly their weight, plausibly linked to the growing incidence of eating disorders, obsession with dieting, and low self-esteem even amongst women of normal weight. One study found that 7 out of 10 women recorded feeling 'angry and depressed' after seeing images of fashion models; girls as young as 8 are now dieting; adolescent girls report being more afraid of gaining weight than of cancer, nuclear war, or losing a parent.[92] A US health foundation specializing for 10 years in the treatment of eating disorders states flatly on its website: 'The influence of the media on the proliferation of eating disorders cannot be refuted.'[93] Evidence of such a link appears in a number of published studies, one of which concludes: 'magazine reading and television viewing, especially exposure to thinness-depicting and thinness-promoting media, significantly predict symptoms of women's eating disorders'.[94] A well-known and striking piece of evidence relates to the effect of the introduction of US television into Fiji, featuring (amongst other things), the usual plethora of thin, beautiful actresses, singers, and models. Three years after its introduction, in 1998, nearly 12 per cent of teenage girls were found to be suffering from bulimia, a condition that was hitherto unknown there.[95] Clearly, no-one suggests making it a criminal offence to publish such magazines, or show such television programmes, even though it may be plausibly asserted that such publications do more harm to women than the consumption of pornography by men and that the evidence is in fact much clearer.[96] Of course, there are pragmatic reasons for criminalizing pornography and not these other damaging forms of expression: deciding the exact basis on which (say) the regulation of women's magazines could occur would be enormously problematic, if not impossible. Moreover, societies have been accustomed since time immemorial to having constraints placed upon sexually explicit literature. In a sense, therefore, it is understandable why pornography is seen as a legitimate target for legal regulation when these other materials are not. But the question nevertheless remains as to why

---

[91] Dworkin, 'Liberty and Pornography', op cit.

[92] Source: Rader Programs (a foundation for treating eating disorders): http://www.raderprograms.com/media.htm.

[93] Ibid.

[94] K. Harrisson, 'The Relationship Between Media Consumption and Eating Disorders,' published in the *Journal of Communication*; and 'Does Interpersonal Attraction to Thin Media Personalities Promote Eating Disorders?' published in the Autumn 1997 issue of the *Journal of Broadcasting & Electronic Media*.

[95] S. Orbach, 'Body hatred is becoming a major export of the western world', *The Guardian*, 20 December 2005.

[96] See J. Cocks, *The Oppositional Imagination*, London: Routledge, 1989, for a survey of a number of cultural sources which damage women.

pornography is so remorselessly singled out for particular opprobrium and legal attack by feminists. One suspects this is at least partly because of its generally low status in society: the fact that it is seen as a shameful, seedy product, which many people with traditional moral values—often flatly opposed to other aspects of feminism—would equally like to see suppressed.[97] It is, in other words, a convenient and easy target. State legislatures and courts find time to deal with complaints from feminists about pornography when equally worthy, but less tempting, targets of concern to feminism, such as the provision of child-care, are neglected. As one pro-pornographer feminist puts it: 'People were looking for a scapegoat for every perceived moral and ethical failing in our culture, and pornography fit the bill.'[98]

THEORETICAL CONSIDERATIONS: SOME TENTATIVE CONCLUSIONS

What conclusions can be drawn from the above? Every position seems problematic, although the old-fashioned conservative one appears to have the least intellectual justification. The feminist pro-censorship argument based upon damage to the dignity and equality of persons is more attractive than the old-fashioned arguments about protecting moral tone or social cohesion, but runs into a host of difficulties upon closer examination: its more radical claims seem simply implausible.[99] Its more moderate arguments seem not to be confined to the case of pornography—as in the claim that pornography 'silences' women, and may cause them damage in terms of social attitudes, both of which, we have found, can be seen to apply to a wide range of materials and points of view. What remains, however, is the notion that pornography *may* cause serious harm, through a link with sex-crimes and harassment, and that it may also, although not uniquely, damage women more generally.

To set against the feminist argument for restrictions, there *is* a clear liberal-based autonomy argument for moral independence—for leaving it to the individual to decide as to the material he or she finds offensive or degrading, rather than having such a choice imposed upon him or her by the state. While the autonomy argument is conceded, it may plausibly be argued, however, that some invasions of autonomy—those which interfere with choices that go to the core of the individual's identity—*must* be more grave than invasions with respect to more peripheral areas. Interference with the individual's choice to view violent pornographic films with no pretension to artistic expression is arguably considerably less of an infringement of his or her autonomy than, say, interfering with the right of the individual to have homosexual relations. It follows that the autonomy interest here is not particularly strong. We noted above a further anti-censorship argument to the effect that pornography may be seen as

[97] The 'unholy' alliance formed between feminists and the moral right over anti-pornography laws is well known: see Antoniou, below.

[98] L. Antoniou, 'Defending Pornography', *The Harvard Gay and Lesbian Review*, Summer 1995, Vol. II, No. 3, pp 21–2.

[99] That is, the arguments that pornography is a 'speech-act' and that it directly constructs women through the automatic effects it has in men's minds, and in doing so strips them of credibility and humanity.

conveying ideas, and that therefore it should not be characterized purely as low-grade commercial speech, but as speech with an ideological message about sexuality. However, as previously discussed, it would be unrealistic to pretend that this is anything but a peripheral—almost accidental—effect in relation to standard types of visual pornography. This speech interest must also therefore be seen as a fairly weak one, in the absence of any particular feature of the material under consideration which may plausibly be viewed as conveying a *particular* message. In contrast, explicit material that appeared to be concerned genuinely with confronting taboos, and challenging conventional sexual norms, rather than merely the mundane and mechanical production of arousal through standard images, might well qualify for some kind of public good or artistic merits defence.

These two points, taken together, would suggest that the liberal anti-censorship case in respect of violent non-artistic pornography is not a particularly strong one. This case must then be balanced against the possibility of a link between pornography and the commission of sexual offences and/or general discriminatory and damaging attitudes. The argument as to this link is still ongoing, and it is submitted that a proper evaluation of the evidence in this area falls within the ambit of the social sciences rather than a study of media freedom. It is suggested as a provisional conclusion that until a consensus on the evidential question emerges, the law is entitled, given the relative weakness of the argument for protecting violent pornography, to take a pragmatic stance and allow narrow and selective censorship of at least the portrayal of sexual violence for pornographic purposes, subject to an artistic merits defence; it would also support criminal controls over such material, as suggested below. It would seem unattractively doctrinaire to insist that pornography should be unrestricted until the hypothesized link with sex offences has been established beyond reasonable doubt. We thus adopt a pragmatic stance, which falls well short of accepting the general pro-censorship feminist position, but allows for some regulation in a way that Ronald Dworkin's liberal position would not. Whether this stance should be converted into law by means of a broadly based definition of pornography based on degradation of women or offence to values of dignity and equality, as adopted in Canada, or by means of a more tightly framed prohibition is a point we consider below. Once the various legal options for the control of pornography have been considered, we will be in a position to come to more detailed conclusions as to the best way forward for law reform in this area.

LEGAL RESPONSES TO EXPLICIT EXPRESSION: GENERAL CONSIDERATIONS

That the above conclusions on pornography are not in general accepted by states is revealed by the fact that almost all Bills or Charters of Rights, apart from the US Bill of Rights, contain an exception to the free speech clause which *inter alia* allows restraint on freedom of speech on the broad ground of protection of morality. The 'absolute' nature of the First Amendment, in contrast, has led the US courts to interpret the First Amendment so as to exclude obscene speech from the category of protected speech.[100] Both Canada[101] and New Zealand[102] allow for restrictions on expression in relation to the regulation of obscenity and pornography. The justification borne in mind in interpreting such exceptions is the harm to be guarded against, which seems to include four possibilities: the corruption of persons, particularly children, as the more vulnerable; the shock or outrage caused by public displays of certain material; damage to constitutionally protected values such as equality and dignity through the proliferation of violent and/or degrading pornography; the commission of sex crimes.[103] The development of UK law has been based on the avoidance of the first two possibilities, whilst, as we shall see, Canadian law now focuses primarily upon the third. On the ground of causing shock, the public display of certain publications can be regulated, while others viewed as having the potential to corrupt can be prohibited entirely, either by punishment of those responsible after publication or by being suppressed or censored before publication.

The type of restraint used tends to depend on the type of publication in question because it seems to be accepted that the harm that may be caused will vary from medium to medium. The print media are subject to a far more lax regime than the visual media. Printed matter, including magazines, newspapers, and books, is not subject to a system of restraint on the model of the one operating for films and broadcasting before screening or transmission;[104] there is, however, the possibility of forfeiture under the Obscene Publications Act, which operates as prior restraint, as discussed below, Criminal sanctions are also available afterwards if indecent or corrupting material is published. Books containing only text are now in practice free from the criminal law, on the basis that something with no visual impact is less likely to cause harm. Films and broadcasts *are* censored because of their visual nature[105]—as discussed in detail in Chapters 10–12 of this Part—and they are also subject to the general criminal law.[106] The theatre, however, is in an odd position; it has not been censored since 1968 despite its visual impact, though of course criminal sanctions

---

[100] See *Roth v US* (1957) 354 US 476; *Memoirs v Massachusetts* (1966) 383 US 413. The US position is considered briefly below.

[101] *R v Butler* (op cit).

[102] *Society for Promotion of Community Standards Inc v Waverley International (1988) Ltd* [1993] 2 NZLR 709.

[103] These were the key notions of harm considered by the Williams Committee appointed in 1977 to review obscenity and indecency law (Williams Report, Cmnd 7772, 1979). Broadly, the Committee endorsed regulation of pornography with a view to preventing the second of the harms mentioned.

[104] See Chapter 10 in relation to broadcasting and Chapter 12 in relation to films and videos.

[105] It may be noted that broadcasters exercise prior restraint mainly on the basis of self-censorship, since the regulator, OFCOM, can only act after the fact: it cannot prevent a programme being broadcast: see Chapter 11 for discussion. The BBFC (the film regulator) *does* censor films, but rarely these days imposes cuts on them; this, however, is partly due to the fact that film makers seeking an 18 rating will self-censor, to achieve this: see Chapter 12.

[106] Subject to various exceptions, as discussed.

may arise after the event.[107] As indicated in Chapter 12, the internet is also in an anomalous position: although it is a visual medium, it is not subject to the same regime as broadcasting or cinemas, despite the fact that technology now allows for the viewing of films via the internet, and that it is now one of the most significant media for accessing graphic content, including child pornography and violent material.[108]

THE STRASBOURG STANCE

The Government has recently confidently asserted that, 'the present test [for obscenity] is consistent with our obligations under Article 10 of the European Convention on Human Rights'.[109] As discussed in Chapter 2, even 'hard-core' pornography has been found by the Commission to fall within the scope of Article 10(1).[110] Under Article 10(2), an interference with the guarantee of freedom of expression under Article 10 can be justified if it is prescribed by law, has a legitimate aim, and is necessary in a democratic society. Given the breadth of paragraph 2, it is unnecessary to seek to draw lines in Article 10(1) between artistic erotica and forms of pornography aimed at entertainment alone, even assuming that such line-drawing has any validity.[111] Instead, the jurisprudence under Article 10 in this context, as in others, concentrates on the para 2 tests. Interferences with explicit expression may be justified if they have the legitimate aim of providing for the protection of morals.[112] The use of laws on obscenity and indecency against explicit expression or regulation of the media with a view to upholding 'standards of taste and decency' are matters that will now have to be considered in the light of Article 10, under the HRA. Specific possibilities are considered in this and succeeding chapters, at relevant points. Here, the general Strasbourg stance on the application of Article 10 to explicit expression is considered.

As Chapter 2 of this book indicated, Strasbourg takes a sharply differentiated stance towards different types of expression: political or public interest speech in the media is afforded strong protection; artistic speech, particularly where it raises issues regarding the protection of morality, is treated very differently.[113] Not only does speech without obvious public/political content rank considerably lower in the hierarchy than political speech; Strasbourg regards the aim of protecting morals both as one that is difficult to define with any objectivity (in contrast, for example, to the protection of the authority of the judiciary)[114] and one in which considerable cultural

---

[107] See Chapter 12.   [108] Under the Theatres Act 1968.
[109] Consultation paper, op cit, at [13].
[110] *Hoare v UK* [1997] EHRLR 678; *Scherer v Switzerland* A 287 (1993) Com Rep.
[111] See further the discussion in Chapter 10 of this Part, relating particularly to the visual media and the Convention case law.
[112] See P. Kearns, 'Obscene and blasphemous libel: misunderstanding art' [2000] *Crim LR* 652.
[113] See esp. pp 56–60.
[114] See the judgment of the E Ct HR in the *Sunday Times* case (1979) 2 EHRR 245, discussed at 53–5.

diversity across Europe is apparent. The absence therefore of clear criteria for assessing the necessity of restrictions based on morality, of a common European consensus upon the types of restrictions thought acceptable, and the presence of sharply differing cultural attitudes to matters such as the portrayal of nudity, sexuality, homosexuality, and religious subjects, are all factors that have led the Court to apply a highly attenuated form of review in this area. It is one in which proportionality as a test is all but abandoned, and the 'pressing social need' test replaced with one that asks whether the state reasonably thought—or was not unreasonable in thinking—that there was such a need.[115]

The decisions of the *Court*—as opposed to those of the Commission—in this area indicate an eagerness to defer to the decisions of national authorities which results in a clear disregard for the principle of moral autonomy, as well as a reluctance to attach appropriate weight to what in some cases was fairly significant artistic or other ideological expression. It is convenient to start with the well-known *Handyside* case,[116] in which the Court had to consider the validity of English obscenity law as a restriction upon freedom of expression. We have already considered this decision in some detail in Chapter 2, and readers are referred to that discussion.[117] A book called *The Little Red Schoolbook*, which contained chapters on masturbation, sexual intercourse, and abortion, was prosecuted under the Obscene Publications Act 1959 on the basis that it appeared to encourage early sexual intercourse. The publishers applied for a ruling under Article 10 to the European Commission and the case was referred to the Court, which determined that the book fell within Article 10(1). In a famous passage, which strongly favours freedom of artistic or creative expression (the expression of information or ideas), it found:

Freedom of expression constitutes one of the essential foundations of a democratic society, one of the basic conditions for its progress and for the development of every man. Subject to paragraph 2 of Article 10, it is applicable not only to information or ideas that are favourably received, or regarded as inoffensive but also to those that offend, shock or disturb the state or any sector of the population. Such are the demands of that pluralism, tolerance and broadmindedness without which there is no democratic society.[118]

However, as this passage indicates, the interference could be justified under para 2. The Court then considered the protection of morals provision under Article 10(2), in order to determine whether the interference with the expression was necessary in a democratic society. It suggested that the 'protection of morals' exception refers to the corruption of individuals rather than to an effect on the moral fabric of society.[119] The Court found that the requirements of morals vary from time to time and from place to place and that the domestic authorities were therefore best placed to judge what was needed. They must 'make the initial assessment of the reality of the pressing social need implied by the notion of necessity in this context'.[120] The judgment thus

---

[115] See in particular pp 56–60.   [116] (1976) 1 EHRR 737.
[117] See pp 61–3 and 74. The points made in that discussion are briefly reprised here.
[118] Ibid, at [49].   [119] Ibid, at [52].   [120] Ibid, at [48].

accepted that domestic authorities would be allowed a wide margin of appreciation in attempting to secure the freedoms guaranteed under the Convention in this area, although this was not to be taken as implying that an unlimited discretion was granted: the power of appreciation 'goes hand in hand with a European supervision' which concerned the legislation in question—the Obscene Publications Act—and the decision applying it. The Court placed particular weight on the fact that the book was aimed at children between the ages of 12 and 18 and that it might encourage them 'to indulge in precocious activities harmful for them or even to commit certain criminal offences'.[121] Thus, the English judges were entitled to find that the book would have a 'pernicious effect on the morals' of the children who would read it. In finding that the tests under para 2 were satisfied, it was said that the fact that the book was circulating freely in the rest of Europe was not determinative of the issues, owing to the application of the margin of appreciation doctrine. The thinking behind the *Handyside* decision can find some parallels from the US[122] and Canada.[123] In the US, however, there has been a greater concentration on the question whether restrictions aimed at children might impinge also on the freedom of expression of adults and on the extent to which this should be tolerated,[124] a matter which was in issue in *Handyside*, although not afforded any weight by the Court.

In Chapter 2, we pointed out that the decision was noteworthy for its refusal to recognize the type of expression in question as being in fact political in nature: the book took a liberal stance on issues such as drug-taking, pre-marital sex, and homosexuality, and it was partly because of these attitudes that it was censored by the British authorities.[125] As we pointed out: 'the perception of the English authorities that the book had a tendency to "deprave and corrupt", that is, create a moral change for the worse in its readers, proceeded purely from the fact that the book's message was, not one devoid of intellectual content and designed purely to arouse, but simply one that the authorities ideologically disagreed with';[126] it was a message reflected ultimately in 'the sexual revolution' in the 1960s. We suggested that this marked *mis*-characterization of the speech in question arose from two causes: first, the general desire of the Court to avoid interfering with the decisions of the national authorities where the culturally sensitive and (it found) subjective notion of 'protecting morals' was in question; second, the fact that there was at least a colourable argument that the state had acted to prevent damage to the well-being of children, rather than that of consenting adults. Thus *Handyside*, apart from the famous statement of principle that it contains, is not of great assistance in resolving issues about the rights of autonomous *adults* in respect of sexually explicit or immoral expression. What it does do, however, is signal clearly that Strasbourg review in this area will be highly deferential to the judgments of state authorities and be characterized by a refusal to apply a

---

[121] Ibid, at [52].   [122] *Ginsberg v New York* 390 US 629 (1968).

[123] *Irwin Toy Ltd v AG (Quebec)* [1989] 1 SCR 927 (broad limitation on broadcast advertising aimed at children).

[124] *Reno v American Civil Liberties Union* (1997) 521 US 844.   [125] See in particular pp 61–3.

[126] See p 63.

rigorous proportionality test: in Convention terminology, a wide margin of appreciation will be conceded to the national authorities, with all the attendant consequences discussed in Chapter 2.[127]

The case law arising subsequent to *Handyside* on the protection of morals and religious feelings in relation to *adults* exhibits a curious tendency: the Commission has tended to take a more liberal line than the Court.[128] In each of the three modern leading cases in the area—*Otto Preminger*,[129] *Müller*,[130] and *Wingrove*[131]—the Commission found a breach of Article 10,[132] only to be overruled by the Court.[133] In fact, the only liberalizing judgment to stand is that given by the Commission in *Scherer v Switzerland*[134]—a case that never reached the Court, due to the death of the applicant. It is therefore difficult to know how much weight can safely be attached to *Scherer*, given that it runs against the dominant trend of the jurisprudence, and might itself have been overruled by the Court had the case got that far. *Scherer* can in any event be distinguished from the other cases on its facts, as indicated below.

Scherer concerned a sex shop, which sold magazines, books, and video films. There was no question of indecent display: as the Commission commented:

The nature of the establishment was not apparent to passers-by, but customers knew about it through advertisements to be found in specialist magazines or at homosexuals' meeting-places.

Explicit films consisting almost entirely of depictions of homosexual sex activity were shown in a room to which access was obtainable by men on payment of an entrance fee. There was no advertising of these films—customers apparently heard about them 'by word of mouth'. The applicant was convicted of publishing obscene items and fined; the films were confiscated. The test for obscenity in Swiss law was that works are obscene 'which offend, in a manner that is difficult to accept, the sense of sexual decency; the effect may be to arouse a normal person sexually or to disgust or repel him'. The Court of Cassation found:

On the basis of the facts which led to the conviction complained of, there was no risk of anyone being confronted with the film in question unintentionally, or even against their will ... It is beyond doubt that the sex shop in question and, a fortiori, the separate projection room adjoining it were visited only by individuals who were aware of what awaited them and intended to see a film of this kind ... If the sole objective is in fact indirectly—by means

---

[127] See esp. pp 79–81.

[128] The Commission did not of course take a liberal line in the admissibility decision in *Gibson v UK*, Appl No 17634, a case which therefore never reached the Court.

[129] (1994) 19 EHRR 34.   [130] (1991) 13 EHRR 212.

[131] No. 17419/90 (1995). See also discussion in Chapter 12.

[132] In relation to *Müller*, the Commission found a breach in relation to the confiscation of the paintings, but not the conviction of the artist.

[133] In *Handyside* itself, this pattern was not so apparent: the Commission declared the application admissible, but by a relatively narrow margin of 8 votes to 5, found no violation of Article 10. The Court's near unanimous no-breach finding, by 13 votes to 1, was somewhat more emphatic.

[134] A 287 (1993) Com Rep. See also discussion in Chapter 10.

of criminal proceedings instituted against the applicant—to prevent adults from seeing the film in question although they wish to do so and are aware of its subject-matter, no 'pressing social need' for such a measure can be perceived. If it were thought that there was a pressing need to protect individuals from their own desire to see obscene publications, it would logically be necessary to punish private showings of such films too. That is not the case, however.

This was classic proportionality reasoning: the Swiss Court found that the law as applied in this context would not be rationally linked to the objective (of preventing individuals from 'harming themselves') since it allowed individuals to see the same films in private.

But the Federal Court overruled this, stating:

It is impossible to see why the morals of adults (who include weak, easily influenced individuals) and consequently the morals of society as a whole should not also be protected. At all events, this view lies within the margin of appreciation which the European Court of Human Rights recognises that member States have and takes due account of the different opinions that may prevail in a democratic society as to the requirements of the protection of morals.

The Federal Court also held that for the applicant to invoke the right to freedom of expression when his obvious intention was merely to derive substantial financial profit from trading in pornography was an abuse of process.

The Commission declared the application admissible, finding a violation of Article 10. It was founded on the principle that: 'Where no adult is confronted unintentionally or against his will with filmed matter, there must be particularly compelling reasons to justify an interference.'[135] A critical factor in the case was that there was no possibility that either minors or adults who were unaware of the nature of the films could view them. In the circumstances, there were no 'compelling reasons' justifying the interference. The Commission referred to this principle in its decision in the *Wingrove* case,[136] which concerned the refusal of a certificate to a video mixing erotic and religious elements, and which was deemed by the English authorities to be probably blasphemous.[137] In that case, the Commission said:

An important element of the Commission's examination of this type of case is whether the offending material is on open display to the general public. [A violation was found in *Scherer*] because there was no danger of adults being confronted unwillingly with the film. Nor was there any question of minors having access to it.[138]

Such reasoning *does* uphold a clear autonomy rationale and strikes directly against pure moral paternalism—that is, against protecting consenting adults from the deleterious effects upon their own morals that state authorities might consider would result from their viewing certain kinds of material. As just seen, the Swiss Federal Court founded precisely upon such paternalism, arguing that it was legitimate to

---

[135] Comm. Report 14.1.93, Eur Court HR, Series A no. 287, p 20.   [136] No. 17419/90.
[137] The case is considered fully in the next chapter.   [138] Op cit, at [62].

protect the morals of what might be 'weak, easily influenced individuals', in order to protect 'the morals of society as a whole'. The Commission was, then, prepared to challenge the views of the national courts on the protection of morals directly. If such a principle could confidently be said to flow clearly from the Strasbourg case law taken as a whole, it would be one in strong tension with UK obscenity law, which founds directly upon the need to protect adults against moral harm, and does not take willing consent to view certain items as a defence. As will appear once we have discussed the *totality* of the case law, however, this is unfortunately not the case.

Hoare v UK,[139] another Commission decision, *does* provide endorsement of the principle established in *Scherer*, although the decision went against the applicant. The Commission pronounced as a general rule: 'Where no adult is confronted unintentionally or against his will with filmed matter, there must be particularly compelling reasons to justify an interference [citing *Scherer*]'. The case concerned a producer of pornographic videos, many of them highly unpleasant, containing scenes of violent sado-masochistic conduct, coprophilia, and bestiality, who was convicted on various counts of obscenity.[140]

The applicant's *modus operandi* as to distribution is described below:

The Commission notes that the applicant went to considerable lengths to prevent cassettes from falling into the 'wrong hands': in the first place, he arranged for advertisements to be placed in a newspaper, thereafter a leaflet was sent to interested parties and only then would a cassette be distributed. It was thus very unlikely that the cassettes would be purchased accidentally.[141]

Nevertheless, the Commission found:

On the other hand, it is in the nature of video works that once they have been distributed, they can, in practice, be copied, lent, rented, sold and viewed in different homes, thereby escaping any form of control by the authorities [citing *Wingrove*, at [63]).[142] The Commission considers that it cannot therefore be said with any degree of certainty that only the intended purchasers of the film would have access to it and not minors.[143]

The Commission noted that 'no claim is made for any artistic merit in the applicant's video cassettes', and concluded that in the circumstances, 'the applicant's conviction for publishing obscene works was proportionate to the legitimate aim pursued'. This finding appeared to depend upon a straightforward balancing act between the value of the speech (low, because no artistic merit was claimed for the films) and the importance of the aim—fairly high, because there was the possibility of minors seeing the films: there was virtually no means/ends proportionality reasoning. What is noteworthy is that the Commission spent no time considering the harms the films might do, either to consenting adults, to those taken by surprise, or to minors. Certainly, as to the middle category, many might be expected to react to seeing such a

---

[139] [1997] EHRLR 678. See also Chapter 10.
[140] Descriptions of some of the contents of the films appear below at note 145 and p 435.
[141] Op cit.   [142] For discussion of *Wingrove*, see Chapter 9.   [143] Ibid.

film inadvertently with simple shock, followed by immediate cessation of viewing. Strasbourg's stance, in examining the issue with the benefit of no expert evidence—or even argument—on the possible harmful effects of the items under consideration, echoes the stance of British law on the matter, in which, somewhat strangely and anomalously, expert evidence is actually proscribed.[144]

However, it is also notable that the rationale for the decision in *Hoare* is consistent with the autonomy principle espoused in *Scherer*. The Commission did *not* decide *Hoare* on the basis that the pornography in question fell outside Article 10, either because it was simply not 'expression', or on the grounds that what it portrayed was fundamentally offensive to basic Convention values, such as the equality of women; and the nature of the films certainly raised serious issues in relation to this issue.[145] Nor was it decided on the basis of the protection of the morals of those who might *voluntarily* encounter it. In other words, the Commission rejected both what we shall term the 'constitutional morality'[146] route, and the 'moral paternalism' approach. It founded solely upon the principle of autonomy—that whilst adults may be permitted to view such material, the conditions under which they do so must ensure that only those genuinely wishing to see it are exposed to it.

However, the decision of the *Court* in *Müller v Switzerland*[147] cannot, it is suggested, be reconciled with the above principles. The case concerned the criminal conviction of an artist and others arising from the exhibition of shocking and explicit paintings in an art gallery. The decision was considered in detail in Chapter 2 in relation to the standard of scrutiny applied by the Court.[148] However, it is necessary briefly to reiterate the approach of the Court in that case, and make some additional points. Müller, an artist with an international reputation, produced three large paintings for an exhibition. The catalogue contained a photographic reproduction of the paintings, which amounted to explicit portrayals of a variety of sexual acts between men, women, and animals. He was prosecuted for obscenity. It seemed that the prosecutor had acted following a complaint 'by a man whose daughter, a minor, had reacted violently to the paintings on show; some days earlier another visitor to the exhibition had apparently thrown down one of the paintings, trampled on it and crumpled it'.[149] The artist and others were convicted of obscenity under the Swiss Criminal Code and the paintings were seized by the authorities. A number of points specifically relevant to obscenity are of note. First of all, it must be recognized that the pictures were of a particularly shocking nature. The following, critical description by the Swiss Courts gives an idea of the content of the paintings:

---

[144] See below at 427–8.

[145] For example, one of the films, which the British jury requested to be stopped after 10 minutes, was described as follows: 'This bondage film started off with a scene of a girl tied to a table, two masked men, and I need only say that you saw that girl being whipped vigorously, both on her back and on her front, in every area and you saw the use of clothes pegs both on the breasts and on the [genitals]. . . . you had an image for some time of a male urinating over the face and into the mouth of this girl who was tied up.' (*Hoare*: op cit,).

[146] For discussion, see below at 418–19.   [147] (1991) 13 EHRR 212.

[148] See Chapter 2 at 56–60.   [149] Op cit, at [12].

All the persons depicted are entirely naked and one of them is engaging simultaneously in various sexual practices with two other males and an animal. He is kneeling down and not only sodomising the animal but holding its erect penis in another animal's mouth. At the same time he is having the lower part of his back—his buttocks, even—fondled by another male, whose erect penis a third male is holding towards the first male's mouth. The animal being sodomised has its tongue extended towards the buttocks of a fourth male, whose penis is likewise erect.[150]

Of critical importance to the case, given the above point about the protection of adult autonomy, is that the paintings were displayed in a gallery to which the public had access, that there were no warnings as to the content of the pictures, and that minors could—and did—gain access: as noted above, one of the complaints was from a man whose 15-year-old daughter had been upset by the paintings. In other words, the finding by the Court that it was permissible within Article 10 to impose some criminal sanctions upon the artist *could* narrowly be seen as turning upon the fact that the applicant could *not* argue that this was a case of paternalist interference with the freedom of adults to choose what they wished to view. The applicant was legitimately punished, on this view, *not* for producing morally shocking works of art, but for failing to ensure that unwitting adults and minors were protected from them. If this reading exhausted the judgment, this decision could comfortably be read consistently with the *Scherer* principle. Nevertheless, even under this reading, the decision cannot be seen as a strong defence of artistic freedom of expression. No evidence of widespread outrage is reported in the case, whereas the artist was a reputable one. The Court thus allowed freedom of artistic expression to give way to the right not to be offended or shocked in public.

Unfortunately, there are further difficulties with the case. As noted in Chapter 2, the action taken by the Swiss authorities also included the confiscation of the paintings, which remained out of circulation for a total of 8 years.[151] This action by the Swiss authorities plainly amounted to an interference both with the right of the artist to show them to consenting adult audiences (using an appropriate warning and measures to bar minors from access), *and* with the rights of consenting adults to view them. Thus an obvious point of principle at which to draw the line would have been between the conviction—which was arguably justifiable given the failure of the organizers of the exhibition to safeguarded unwilling adults and children from confrontation with very shocking material—and the confiscation, which amounted to censorship, for a very long period, in relation to the entire adult population of Switzerland. This indeed was precisely the distinction that the Commission drew, finding the conviction, but not the confiscation, to be justifiable under paragraph 2 of Article 10.[152] The *failure* of the Court to draw such a principled distinction *prevents* the drawing of any clear principle as to the protection of autonomy from the case. Further than this, however, the difficulty lies in the fact that the Court simply ignored the point that confiscation required particular justification: it produced no reasoning to justify its finding that

---

[150] Ibid, at [16].   [151] For the details, see 56–60.   [152] No. 10737/84 (1986).

both the conviction *and* the confiscation were justifiable under Article 10(2). Instead, it simply said, disingenuously: 'The same reasons which justified [the conviction] also apply in the view of the Court to the confiscation order made at the same time'. Plainly, this was not the case. The fact that the Court simply refused to acknowledge the need to examine the two penalties separately means that whatever justification the judges had in mind for the outright censorship exercised in this case remained shrouded in obscurity. In *Otto Preminger v Austria*,[153] discussed in Chapter 2 and Chapter 9,[154] a similar stance was taken towards confiscation, in that instance of an allegedly blasphemous film: the proportionality review conducted by the Court was equally attenuated. In that instance also the Commission found a breach of Article 10.

Thus the *confiscation* of works upheld by the Court in *Müller*,[155] and in *Otto Preminger*,[156] had the effect of depriving consenting adults all across Switzerland and Austria from seeing works which, moreover, could be viewed as having serious artistic merit—unlike the 'hard-core' pornography at issue in *Scherer*. Nevertheless, the Court found no violation in either case: a consistent application of the autonomy principle to both would surely have found a violation in both cases in respect of the confiscation, as the Commission did in both instances. Therein lies the weakness of the Strasbourg explicit or offensive expression jurisprudence taken as a whole: it is very difficult to extract from it a *strong, consistent* principle in favour of adult autonomy, against moral paternalism. Counsel seeking to derive this principle from the case law would have to pitch certain Commission admissibility decisions against full findings on the merits from the Court—scarcely an attractive position to have to take.

Thus far, then, we have argued that review in this area, constrained by the margin of appreciation doctrine, is heavily deferential to state authorities, and that the case law does not yield a clear defence of adult autonomy. An important analysis of the jurisprudence in this area suggests that there is a further lack of clarity. Nowlin[157] argues that the ECtHR may be seen as embracing two wholly different conceptions of 'morality' in Article 10(2). One is the traditional notion of a conservative morality based upon Christianity; the other is what Nowlin and the Canadian justices in *Butler*[158] refer to as a 'constitutional morality'—the maintenance of the rights and freedoms of all, which in itself requires a pluralistic approach. Nowlin suggests that this ambivalence may be seen in the *Handyside* judgment itself. The Court, he notes, ringingly espoused a constitutional morality in its famous dicta cited above: 'Freedom of expression constitutes one of the essential foundations of a democratic society . . . .'. Similarly, *part* of its reason for finding that the suppression of *The Little Red Schoolbook* was justified was the apparent danger that the book would encourage children to engage in behaviour

---

[153] (1994) 19 EHRR 34.   [154] See p 80.   [155] (1991) 13 EHRR 212.
[156] (1994) 19 EHRR 34.
[157] C. Nowlin, 'The Protection of Morals under the European Convention for the Protection of Human Rights and Fundamental Freedoms' (2002) 24(1) *HRQ* 264.
[158] [1992] 1 SCR 452.

harmful to themselves and others, some of which could be criminal (e.g. under-age sex). As Nowlin puts it:

This thinking reflects a concern for the health and welfare of children that could feasibly be construed as a concern for the human rights of children . . .

On the other hand, Nowlin points out that the Court also seemed to take into account the apparent danger of good 'morals' being threatened by the book, 'and implied that "traditional moral values" were worth considering in the overall analysis'.[159] As Nowlin puts it, by doing so: 'In effect the ECtHR made one conception of the good life, one based on "traditional moral values", partly determinative of the scope of a citizen's constitutional rights.'[160] This simply allows proponents of one set of moral convictions (for example, against 'free love', and gay sex) to use the criminal law to enforce their views against those holding more liberal (or permissive) ones. The unacceptability of this approach if writ large becomes clear if one imagines a prosecution of a reading of the Bible or the Koran on the ground of corrupting public morals by facilitating the development of intolerant, misogynistic, or homophobic views. It could very readily be argued that encouraging such views amounts to a 'moral change for the worse'. More prosaically, some would regard the kinds of views commonly espoused in *The Daily Mail* about, for example, asylum seekers, as likely to engender a moral change for the worse in its readers.[161] But it is highly unlikely that readings from the Bible, Koran, or *Mail* could lead to prosecution under future conceivable manifestations of the criminal law.[162] Outside the realm of obscenity law, it is not generally seen as being the role of the state to criminalize certain forms of expression in the UK, on the ground that they may lead others astray morally.

The question again, therefore, is why sexually explicit speech is being singled out from other kinds of morally damaging speech. The finding in *Müller*, it should be remembered, related to the Swiss Code's prohibition of materials that were liable 'grossly to offend the sense of sexual propriety of persons of ordinary sensitivity'. As Nowlin points out, in finding such a prohibition unobjectionable in Convention terms, 'the Court implied that the scope of artistic freedom under [Art 10] is circumscribed by majoritarian proclivities and tastes'.[163] The Court, points out Nowlin, 'did recognise that there is a natural link between protection of morals and protection of the rights of others', but didn't specify what those rights might be. But, as he finds, those rights, 'by the logic of *Handyside*, do not include a right simply not to be offended, shocked or disturbed'.[164] Confirmation that the autonomy of some citizens

---

[159] Nowlin, op cit, at 480.   [160] Op cit, at 480.

[161] See discussion in Chapter 1 at 28–9.

[162] The possible role of religious hatred law in relation to religious documents is discussed in Chapter 9, but it is almost inconceivable that a prosecution would be brought against either the Bible or the Koran on this ground, despite the fact that some Muslim or Christian extremists no doubt do view either document as deeply offensive to their religious sensibilities, and possibly as inciting religious hatred. In any event, legal change allowing for their prosecution on the ground of corrupting morals is, it is argued, inconceivable in a democracy.

[163] Op cit, at 281.   [164] Ibid.

should not be interfered with simply on the basis that others find what they do offensive is found in a key passage in *Dudgeon*, which concerned the proscription of homosexuality in Northern Ireland:

Although members of the public who regard homosexuality as immoral may be shocked, offended or disturbed by the commission by others of private homosexual acts, this cannot on its own warrant the application of penal sanctions when it is consenting adults alone who are involved.[165]

This is a clear statement in favour of the moral independence of the minority from laws giving effect to majoritarian disapproval. However, as discussed above, the effect of the penalty imposed in *Müller* was precisely to deny consenting adults across the whole of Switzerland the ability to view the artist's paintings, purely because a few people had been shocked and offended by them; nevertheless, no breach of Article 10 was found. Nowlin's point, in other words, is that Strasbourg's approach lacks consistency: on occasions it seems to interpret the 'morals' exception in Article 10(2) as connoting a 'constitutional morality', such as the protection of children; but on the other hand, it allowed a *substantive* conception of morals to trump adult autonomy and artistic freedom in *Müller*. To this we would add our finding that its protection of adult autonomy is plainly inconsistent: *Müller* cannot be squared with the finding in *Scherer* and the statements supporting *Scherer* in *Hoare*.

A further comment may be made on the Court's approach to offensive speech. As noted in Chapter 2,[166] one of the principal reasons that the Court concedes a wide margin of appreciation to states in this area, is its finding that no European consensus on morality exists. This absence of a consensus, in other words, is used to justify a 'hands off' approach by the Court, when states prosecute individuals for offensive speech in the name of protecting morality. We would[167] suggest that an alternative approach could be taken: the absence of a consensus as to the necessity for protecting particular 'morals' could be seen as an argument *against* the alleged necessity for doing so, not the other way around. The absence of a European consensus on a substantive sexual morality, in other words, could be taken to weaken the position of the morality-enforcing state, *not* the dissentient individual. Thus an alternative approach for the Court to have taken would have been to limit the 'morals' which a state could use to restrict freedom of expression justifiably to those on which there *is* a relatively clear consensus—at least in Western Europe. Broadly speaking, this consensus could be identified as being one of *tolerance*, providing that all the parties involved are consenting adults. In other words, the European consensus on morality could be said to be one that holds non-consensual activity, or that involving animals or children, to be both morally repugnant and unlawful, whilst it is also considered intolerant and therefore morally wrong to punish consensual sexual activity (e.g. gay sexual relationships) even though quite large numbers of people continue to find them morally abhorrent or distasteful. This Europe-wide moral consensus on the

---

[165] 4 E Ct HR 149 (1981).   [166] See pp 73–4.
[167] As discussed in Chapter 2 in relation to *Handyside*: 73–4.

desirability of tolerance in relation to consensual sexual activity could be applied in relation to depictions of it and to explicit expression more generally. Instead, the Court has chosen to focus *not* upon this in fact quite strong consensus of tolerance, but instead upon the *variations* within European states on the question of sexually explicit representation.

To summarize—the Court's approach in this area lacks a clear principled basis. The Commission has identified a principle upholding the moral autonomy of consenting adults; its stance has, however, been blurred, if not overridden, by the Court in the judgments discussed above. Moreover, aspects of the Court's reasoning quite clearly endorse—if only through the restrained review flowing from the margin of appreciation—the notion that states may enforce substantive moral views through the criminal law. The Court has *not* taken the opportunity in the area of explicit speech to sketch out a constitutional European morality, as it did in *Dudgeon* in the area of the decriminalization of homosexuality. The bold statement of principle in *Handyside* that Article 10 protects speech that 'shocks, offends or disturbs' has been radically undercut by decisions that allow the banning of works precisely on those grounds, and no others. It cannot be pretended that this is a satisfactory platform of human rights jurisprudence from which a domestic court can build a principled judicial reform of the obscenity and indecency laws. There *is* a strand of principle from *Scherer* which can be relied upon; but a much weightier principle, in terms of pedigree, emerges from the major *Court* decisions, which permit censorship on the grounds of shock and offence, and which, moreover, repeatedly state that it is for the national authorities to set their own standards in this area. Whilst there is, theoretically, European 'supervision' of this standard setting, it was argued above that the extraordinary laxness of the proportionality reading in *Müller*, replicated in *Otto Preminger*, amounts in practice to the virtual abnegation of this responsibility.[168]

The new rules of the Court in relation to admissibility,[169] and the enormous growth in cases coming before it,[170] mean that it may be doubted whether it is likely in future to hear fresh cases concerning non-political offensive speech. Since in its view such cases do not engage the core values of Article 10, and it has established a fairly clear approach in the decisions mentioned above, it is perhaps unlikely to see them as raising sufficiently important issues of principle to deserve consideration. Moreover, its illiberal and deferential stance to date is likely to discourage applicants from bringing cases to Strasbourg. It is quite likely, therefore, that no fresh and significant jurisprudence will emerge in this area, at least for some time. Innovation, if there is to be any, will probably therefore have to come from the domestic courts, building upon

---

[168] This is also Lester's conclusion; see his 'Universality versus Subsidiarity: A Reply' [1998] *EHRLR* 73 at 80. See Chapter 1 pp 6–7 for a discussion of the possible, unexplicated reasoning underlying the Court's flawed stance in this context.

[169] See Protocol 14, Articles 7–9.

[170] Over 40,000 applications were lodged with the Court in 2005, with a backlog of over 80,000. See figures on the Council of Europe's website: http://www.echr.coe.int/NR/rdonlyres/A1B76D3F-67C5-41F2-A254-1EC49C946F21/0/stats2005.pdf

the slender thread of liberal principle apparent in *Scherer* and affirmed in *Hoare v UK*.[171] But it is much more probable that the Strasbourg jurisprudence will be seen as merely affirming the general Article 10 compliance of existing UK law.[172] It is to that law that we now turn.

OBSCENITY LAW

STATUTORY OBSCENITY

The Obscene Publications Act 1959 law operates primarily as a subsequent restraint and is largely used in relation to books, magazines, and other printed material, material posted on web-pages, or videos.[173] The powers of forfeiture (seizure) contained under the Act, however, allow for the suppression of material, rather than punishment of those distributing it, and therefore amount to prior restraint. Theoretically, obscenity law could also be used against broadcasts and films,[174] although, as discussed in Chapters 11 and 12, the standards applied by broadcasters and film makers in complying with regulation are so much more stringent than those represented by the criminal law that the possibility of a prosecution in respect of a broadcast or a film is remote.

The harm sought to be prevented under the 1959 Act is that of a corrupting effect on an individual. In other words, it is thought that an individual will undergo a change for the worse after encountering the material in question. The rationale of the law is thus overtly paternalistic. The idea of preventing depravity and corruption had informed the common law long before the 1959 Act; it sprang from the ruling in *Hicklin*.[175] Determining whether material would 'deprave and corrupt' was problematic, especially as it was unclear to whom the test should be applied. Two cases in 1954 showed the uncertainty of the law. In *Martin Secker and Warburg*[176] it was determined that the test applied to persons who might encounter the material in question. But at the same time, in *Hutchinson*,[177] the court held that the test should be applied to the most vulnerable person who might conceivably encounter the material and that the

---

[171] [1997] EHRLR 678.

[172] This is not to say that there may be no room for narrowly drawn Convention-based arguments, for example relating to non-discrimination as between the criminalization of gay and straight pornography, an argument considered further below: see 466.

[173] In *AG's Reference (No 5 of 1980)* [1980] 3 All ER 816, CA, it was found that a video constituted 'an article' for the purposes of the 1959 Act. 168 of the Criminal Justice and Public Order Act 1994 added the transmission of electronically stored data to the Obscene Publication Act's definition of 'publication'. See Chapter 12 for discussion of the application of obscenity law to videos and to the internet.

[174] See Chapters 11 and 12 for discussion of the application of obscenity law to broadcasting and to films, respectively.

[175] (1868) 3 QB 360.   [176] [1954] 2 All ER 683; [1954] 1 WLR 1138.

[177] (1954), unreported. For an account of the proceedings, see St John Stevas, *Obscenity and the Law*, London: Secker and Warburg, 1956, p 116.

jury could therefore look at the effect it might have on a teenage girl. Moreover, the jury could find that something that could merely be termed shocking could deprave and corrupt.

The 1959 Act was passed in an attempt to clear up some of this uncertainty, although it made no attempt to specify the meaning of the term 'deprave and corrupt', which is used in the statute, without explication. The *actus reus* of the offence involves the publication for gain (s 2(1)) or possessing with a view to such publication (s 1(2) of the Obscene Publications Act 1964) an article which tends, taken as a whole,[178] to 'deprave and corrupt a significant proportion of those likely to see or hear it' (s 1(1)). This is a crime of strict liability: there is no need to show an intention to deprave and corrupt, merely an intention to publish. The Act does not cover live performances on stage, which fall within the similarly worded Theatres Act 1968. It does, however, cover broadcasting, cinemas, and publishing on the internet.[179] Section 1(1)(3) of the 1959 Act provides that 'publishes' means:

(b) in the case of an article containing or embodying matter to be looked at or a record, shows, plays or projects it, or, where the matter is data stored electronically, transmits that data.

In *R v Waddon*,[180] it was held that an article is published in the UK when it is accessed here, regardless of whether the web server is out of the jurisdiction—in that case, in the US.[181] (The use of obscenity law in relation to the internet is discussed in detail in Chapter 12.) The need for publication means that the 1959 Act does not cover simple possession of pornography, however extreme, although possession of child pornography is an offence under separate legislation.[182]

The Government is currently consulting on proposals to fill this gap by introducing a new offence of possession of certain classes of extreme hard-core pornography.[183] Possession of the following would be an offence:

explicit pornography containing actual scenes or realistic depictions of:

   i)   intercourse or oral sex with an animal;

   ii)   sexual interference with a human corpse;

   iii) serious violence in a sexual context; and

   iv)   serious sexual violence.[184]

---

[178] 'Or where it comprises two or more distinct items, the effect of one of the items.' This is a very significant provision in respect of magazines (see *Anderson* [1972] 1 QB 304, discussed below on this point at 427) since it means that a magazine can be condemned as obscene in respect of a single item, although a novel could not be. A book containing short stories, a film, or a web site consisting of a number of distinct and discrete episodes/items would also appear to fall within this rule.

[179] See s 1(4); see also notes 105 and 108 above.   [180] (2000) WL 491456.

[181] The Court reserved judgment on 'what the position might be in relation to jurisdiction if a person storing material on a website outside England intended that no transmission of that material should take place back to this country' (op cit at [11]).

[182] The Protection of Children Act 1978, as amended: see below, at 467–70. See further Chapter 12 at 650–2.

[183] Home Office, *Consultation: on the possession of extreme violent pornography* (2005). See also Chapter 12.

[184] Ibid, at [39].

There would be no 'public good', or artistic merits, defence under these proposals. It may be noted that the material intended to be covered is limited to 'actual scenes or realistic depictions of' the above; therefore drawings, including cartoons, would not be caught. Plainly, written descriptions would also fall outside the new offence. It is thus relatively narrowly drawn. It would not affect the media directly, since it would criminalize possession only: the material that it is intended to cover would incur liability under existing law if it was published for gain or possessed with intent to so publish.

'Deprave and corrupt'

This is the central test under the 1959 Act. It is clear from the ruling in *Calder (John) Publishing v Powell*[185] that it is not confined to descriptions or representations of sexual matters; it was applied to a disturbing book on the drug-taking life of an addict. This ruling was followed in *Skirving*,[186] which concerned a pamphlet on the means of taking cocaine in order to obtain maximum effect. In all instances, the test for obscenity should not be applied to the type of behaviour advocated or described in the article in question, but to the article itself. Thus, in *Skirving*, the question to be asked was not whether taking cocaine would deprave and corrupt, but whether the pamphlet itself would. Clearly, however, the two are strongly linked: the pamphlet could only deprave and corrupt in encouraging people to take cocaine: there must then be found to be something harmful or immoral about cocaine-taking for an article encouraging it to be found to be itself corrupting.

   This test is hard to explain to a jury and uncertain of meaning, with the result that directions such as the following have been given: '. . . obscenity, members of the jury, is like an elephant; you can't define it, but you know it when you see it.'[187], However, it is clear from the ruling of the Court of Appeal in *Anderson*[188] that the effect in question must be more than mere shock or revulsion. The trial judge had directed the jury that the test connoted that which was repulsive, loathsome, or filthy. This explanation was clearly defective, since it would have merged the concepts of indecency and obscenity, and it was rejected by the Court of Appeal on the basis that it would dilute the test for obscenity which, it was said, must connote the prospect of *moral harm*, not merely shock. The conviction under the Act was therefore overturned because of the misdirection. The House of Lords in *Knuller v DPP*[189] considered the word 'corrupt' and found that it denoted a publication which produced a 'real social evil'—going beyond immoral suggestions or persuasion. However, this suggestion was watered down by *DPP v Whyte*.[190] The owners of a bookshop which sold pornographic material were prosecuted. Most of the customers were old men who had encountered the material on previous occasions, and this gave rise to two difficulties. First, the old men were unlikely to engage in anti-social sexual behaviour and therefore the

---

[185] [1965] 1 QB 159.   [186] [1985] QB 819.   [187] Robertson, note 198, at 45.
[188] [1972] 1 QB 304.   [189] [1973] AC 435; [1972] 3 WLR 143; (1972) 56 Cr App R 633, HL.
[190] [1972] AC 849; [1972] 3 All ER 12, HL. Successive references are to the AC report.

meaning of 'corrupt' had to be modified if it was to extend to cover the effect on them of the material. It was found that it meant creating a depraved effect on the mind that need not actually issue forth in any particular sexual behaviour. Secondly, it was suggested that the old men were already corrupt and therefore would not be affected by the material. The Justices who heard the case saw the regular customers to the shop, as to which there was some evidence, as:

inadequate, pathetic, dirty minded men, seeking cheap thrills, addicts to this type of material, whose morals were already in a state of depravity and corruption. They consequently entertained grave doubts as to whether such minds could be open to any immoral influences which the articles were capable of exerting.[191]

On this basis, the shopkeepers were acquitted. The Prosecutor appealed, and the case eventually came before the House of Lords. It is important to note here, therefore, that the Lords were correcting a view taken that had led to an acquittal. Their Lordships found first of all that the material was 'pornography of the hardest quality, or, in the ordinary sense of the word, obscene'.[192] They went on to hold that corruption did not connote a once-only process: persons could be 're-corrupted'.

The Act is not merely concerned with the once-for-all-corruption of the wholly innocent; it equally protects the less innocent from further corruption, the addict from feeding or increasing his addiction.[193]

More cogently, perhaps, it was found that the Justices' finding:

assumes the possibility of corruption by the articles in question, indeed the fact of it is found, and argues from that to an absence of corrupting tendency. The passage contains its own refutation. These very men, it states, are depraved and corrupted by these very articles. In itself it proves the case: it should have led to conviction.[194]

As Lord Cross put it, he could not believe:

that the staunchest supporters of the 'permissive' view meant it to be a defence for a bookseller to say: 'I have been selling books of this sort to this group of readers for a long time. I admit that as a result of their reading they have become depraved. Fortunately for me, however, they have now reached such a state of depravity that further reading of my books— though they still excite them—cannot be said to make them any worse than they are already.' I would not be prepared to read the words 'tends to deprave and corrupt' so as to lead to such a ludicrous result unless I was convinced that they admitted of no other construction. To my mind, they are well able to include 'maintaining' in a state of depravity and corruption.[195]

As to the argument that because the men were old, any effect that the articles had would not lead to undesirable sexual conduct, his Lordship said trenchantly:

. . . there is no basis for the argument that even if the effect was only on the mind and not,

---

[191] Ibid, at 853. [192] Ibid, at 860. [193] Ibid, at 863. [194] Ibid.
[195] Ibid, at 871.

directly, upon action, that is outside the Act. At least since *Reg v Hicklin* . . . and, as older indictments clearly show, from earlier times, influence on the mind is not merely within the law *but is its primary target* . . .[196]

Thus it is confirmed that the evil to which the Act is directed is a moral change for the worse in the minds of the readers or consumers of the material in question. Lord Pearson was equally clear:

The words 'deprave and corrupt' in the statutory definition refer, in my opinion, to the effect of an article on the minds (including the emotions) of the persons who read or see it. Of course, bad conduct may follow from the corruption of the mind, but it is not part of the statutory definition of an obscene article that it must induce bad conduct.[197]

Given then that the test relates purely to mental effects, it is important for the defendants to be able to argue quite specifically as to the probable effect that the material will have on its audience. One principle established by the case law is that the 'deprave and corrupt' test will not be satisfied if the material in question causes feelings of revulsion from the immorality portrayed. This theory, known as the 'aversion theory', derives from *Calder and Boyars*,[198] which concerned the novel *Last Exit from Brooklyn*; it was found that the horrific pictures it painted of homosexuality and drug-taking in New York would be more likely to discourage than encourage such behaviour. The Court noted that:

This description was compassionate and condemnatory. The only effect that it would produce in any but a minute lunatic fringe of readers would be horror, revulsion and pity; it was admittedly and intentionally disgusting, shocking and outrageous; it made the reader share in the horror it described and thereby so disgusted, shocked and outraged him that, being aware of the truth, he would do what he could to eradicate those evils and the conditions of modern society which so callously allowed them to exist. In short, according to the defence, instead of tending to encourage anyone to homosexuality, drug-taking or senseless, brutal violence, it would have precisely the reverse effect.[199]

The failure to put this possible way of looking at the material—the view urged upon the Court by the defendants, in fact—amounted to a serious misdirection to the jury, with the result that the conviction was quashed. In *Anderson*[200] also, the judge failed to put to the jury the argument that in particular some of the illustrations of sexual activity were:

. . . so grossly lewd and unpleasant that they would shock in the first instance and then would tend to repel. In other words, it was said that they had an aversive effect and that far from tempting those who had not experienced the acts to take part in them they would put off those who might be tempted so to conduct themselves.[201]

---

[196] Ibid, at 873.   [197] Ibid, at 864.
[198] [1969] 1 QB 151; [1968] 3 WLR 974; [1968] 3 All ER 644; (1968) 52 Cr App R 706. For comment, see Robertson, *Obscenity*, Weidenfeld and Nicholson, 1979, pp 50–3.
[199] [1969] QB 151, 169.   [200] [1972] 1 QB 304.   [201] Ibid, at 315.

However, in later Court of Appeal decisions, *O'Sullivan*[202] and *Elliot*,[203] the aversion theory was somewhat marginalized. The Court said it agreed with the trial judge in the latter case that it might have relevance to books (as in *Calder*), but not to videos:

It is not a question of whether [the material] is disgusting or offensive or shocking . . . The question you have to decide is whether it would have a defiling effect on those likely to see it. Will it debase the watchers or hearers; will it make them worse morally, will make them more rotten, will it taint them and defile them?

The application of the 'aversion theory' to visual material therefore remains in doubt.

The effect of the article as a whole on persons likely to encounter it should be considered, not merely the effect of specific passages of a particularly explicit nature. However, in *Anderson*[204] it was made clear that where the article consists of a number of items, each item must be considered in isolation from the others. Thus, a magazine containing a variety of different articles or photographs which is, on the whole, innocuous, but contains one obscene item, can be suppressed, although a novel containing one obscene scene could not be.

A novelist who writes a complete novel and who cannot cut out particular passages without destroying the theme of the novel, is entitled to have his work judged as a whole, but a magazine publisher who has a far wider discretion as to what he will, and will not, insert by way of items is to be judged under the 1959 Act on what we call the 'item by item' basis. This was not done in this case. Our main concern in mentioning the point now is to ensure that it will be done in future. To consider the article as a whole did no harm to the defence in the present case, but the proper course to be taken in future is the item by item approach for magazines and other articles comprising a number of distinct items.[205]

How is the corrupting effect of an article to be proved? *DPP v Jordan*[206] considered the issue of *evidence* of corruption. On this, it found:

When the class of likely reader has been ascertained, it is for the jury to say whether the tendency of the material is such as to deprave or corrupt them, and for this purpose, in general, no evidence, psychological, sociological or medical may be admitted . . . The jury consider the material for themselves and reach their conclusion as to its effect. They cannot be told by psychologists or anyone else what the effect of the material on normal minds may be.[207]

The ruling in *Anderson* was to like effect: that in sexual obscenity cases and normally in other obscenity cases, the defence cannot call expert evidence as to the effect that an article may have on its likely audience: 'In the ordinary run of the mill cases in the future, the issue "obscene or no" must be tried by the jury without the assistance of expert evidence on that issue.'[208] In that case, at trial a psychologist had given evidence of the use of sexual images to create aversion against the acts portrayed (seemingly, homosexual acts)—in other words, to show that such images might not cause a

---

[202] [1995] 1 Cr App R 455 at 464.   [203] [1996] 1 Cr App R 432.   [204] [1972] 1 QB 304.
[205] Ibid, at 312.   [206] [1977] AC 699.   [207] Ibid, at 717.   [208] Op cit, at 309.

change for the worse, but create revulsion in the minds of those seeing them It was found that such evidence is inadmissible. Thus, the view taken in *DPP v A and BC Chewing Gum Ltd*[209] that such evidence would be admissible may be regarded as arising only due to the very specific circumstances of that case. As the Court put it, in *Anderson*:

That case, in our judgment, should be regarded as highly exceptional and confined to its own circumstances, namely a case where the alleged obscene matter was directed at very young children, and was itself of a somewhat unusual kind.[210]

In other words, in that case, the jury could not be expected to decide as to the possible effect of the material without assistance.

However, it was decided in *Skirving*[211] that in cases concerned with alleged depravity and corruption arising from factors *other than* the sexual nature of the material, expert evidence will, exceptionally, be admissible, although the evidence can only be as to the effects of the behaviour described in the material, not as to the likely effects of the material itself. Thus, generally, where the material deals with matters within their own experience, the jury will receive little help in applying the test.

What are the standards that are to be applied in deciding whether a moral change for the worse has come about? Given the divergence of sexual standards in contemporary society, this is an important question. The answer to it is clear in doctrinal terms, although, it will be argued below, the test is effectively unworkable. A jury is meant to apply what they consider to be 'contemporary standards' of morality (from *Calder and Boyars*). Thus, they are able to take into account changing standards of morality in considering what will deprave and corrupt. The concept of obscenity is, therefore, theoretically, able to keep up to date. The application of these tests was seen in the trial for obscenity of the book *Inside Linda Lovelace*,[212] which suggested that a prosecution brought against a book of any conceivable literary merit would be unlikely to succeed. Thus, in December 1991, the DPP refused to prosecute the Marquis de Sade's *Juliette*, even though it was concerned (fictionally) with the sexualized torture, rape, and murder of women and children. No prosecution was brought in relation to the book *American Psycho*, which contains the most appallingly graphic scenes of sexual assault, torture, and murder, though arguably in a work of considerable literary merit. It appears that, *de facto*, the written word is free from the constraints of obscenity law, unlike the situation in, for example, Canada. More generally, it may be said on the contemporary standards test that because the jury are simply told to apply what they consider to be contemporary standards, without further guidance, and without the benefit of expert evidence, there is the danger of a huge variation in standards, depending upon the make-up of the jury. Such variation can make the application of the law in practice arbitrary and unpredictable. It is arguable that under the HRA, to avoid claims of discriminatory prosecutions, more guidance

---

[209] [1968] 1 QB 159.   [210] Op cit, at 313.   [211] [1985] QB 819.
[212] For comment see (1976) *NLJ* 126. The prosecution failed.

will have to be given to juries as to how to make this determination. These points are considered in more detail below.

The notion of 'relative' obscenity

An important point to be made about the test for obscenity is that it is a relative one, depending upon the particular likely audience of the material in question. The test in section 1(1), it will be recalled, was that the material is likely to deprave and corrupt 'a significant proportion of those *likely to see or hear it*'. The jury must therefore consider the likely reader in order to determine whether the material would deprave and corrupt him or her, rather than considering the most vulnerable conceivable reader. As the House of Lords put it in *Whyte*: 'the Act has adopted a relative conception of obscenity. An article cannot be considered as obscene in itself: it can only be so in relation to its likely readers.' Their Lordships went on:

One reason for this was no doubt to exempt from prosecution scientific, medical or sociological treatises not likely to fall into the hands of laymen, but the section is drafted in terms wider than was necessary to give this exemption, and this gives the courts a difficult task. For, in every case, the magistrates, or the jury, are called upon to ascertain who are likely readers and then to consider whether the article is likely to deprave and corrupt them.[213]

The Court of Appeal took a like stance in *R v Clayton and Halsey*,[214] in which it was said:

This Court cannot accept the contention that a photograph may be inherently so obscene that even an experienced or scientific viewer must be susceptible to some corruption from its influence. The degree of inherent obscenity is, of course, very relevant, but it must be related to the susceptibility of the viewer.[215]

In that case, where the only proven publication was to police officers, who admitted that they had no reaction to the pictures whatever, the conviction was quashed. Similarly, in *Knuller*, both Lord Wilberforce and Lord Pearson gave the example of a medical treatise, dealing perhaps with sexual deviance, kept in the library of a university and intended only for the perusal of scholars of medicine and psychology. In such a case, the item would not be considered obscene, although if it was made available more widely it could be. (It should be noted that a 'public good' defence—see below—would probably also be available in such an instance.)

It was held in *Whyte* that in order to make a determination as to the type of consumer in question, the Court could receive information as to the nature of the relevant area, the type of shop, and the class of people frequenting it. Thus, in that case, their Lordships found it important that the bookshop was a general one in an 'ordinary shopping area'. In *Penguin Books*,[216] which concerned the prosecution of *Lady Chatterley's Lover*, the selling price of the book was taken into account and the fact that being in paperback, it would reach a mass audience. It was determined in *Calder*

---

213 Op cit, per Lord Wilberforce at 860.   214 [1963] 1 QB 163.   215 Ibid, at 167.
216 [1961] Crim LR 176; see C.H. Rolph, *The Trial of Lady Chatterley*, London: Penguin, 1961.

and Boyars[217] that the jury must determine what is meant by a 'significant proportion', and this was approved in *DPP v Whyte*, Lord Cross explaining that 'a significant proportion of a class means a part which is not numerically negligible, but which may be much less than half'. This formulation was adopted in order to prevent sellers of pornographic material claiming that most of their customers would be unlikely to be corrupted by it. As Lord Pearson put it:

There is the danger, for instance, of leading a bookseller to believe that, so long as he sells a comparatively large number of copies of a pornographic book to persons not likely to be corrupted by it, he can with impunity sell a comparatively small number of copies to persons who are likely to be corrupted by it. In such a case, if the comparatively small number of copies is not so small as to be negligible, the statutory definition should be applied according to its terms.[218]

A study of the contemporary application of the Act found a direction in which the jury were told that 'a significant number' meant simply 'more than a negligible handful of people'.[219] As Barendt comments:

Theoretically, therefore, it is possible for a publication to be successfully prosecuted in England merely because a large number of the sexual deviants at whom it is aimed are liable to be further corrupted by looking at it; it is immaterial that ordinary people would find it inoffensive or just ridiculous.[220]

Obscenity law in Canada takes a markedly contrasting stance to the issue of determining who is the 'audience' or 'consumers' of the material in question. Thus, in *Towne Cinema Theatres Ltd. v The Queen*,[221] a decision of the Supreme Court of Canada, Dickson CJ said:

The cases all emphasize that it is a standard of *tolerance*, not taste, that is relevant. What matters is not what Canadians think is right for themselves to see. What matters is what Canadians would not abide other Canadians seeing because it would be beyond the contemporary Canadian standard of tolerance to allow them to see it. Since the standard is tolerance, I think the audience to which the allegedly obscene material is targeted must be relevant. The operative standards are those of the Canadian community as a whole, but since what matters is what other people may see, it is quite conceivable that the Canadian community would tolerate varying degrees of explicitness depending upon the audience and the circumstances. [Emphasis in original.].[222]

Wilson J said:

It is not, in my opinion, open to the courts under s 159(8) of the *Criminal Code* to characterize a movie as obscene if shown to one constituency but not if shown to another . . . In my view, a movie is either obscene under the *Code* based on a national community standard of tolerance or it is not. If it is not, it may still be the subject of provincial regulatory control.[223]

Canadian law thus embraces a national standard of obscenity, not the unpredictably

[217] [1969] 1 QB 151.   [218] Op cit, at 865.   [219] Edwards, note 239, at 850.
[220] Op cit, at 366.   [221] [1985] 1 S.C.R. 494.   [222] Ibid, at 508–9.   [223] Ibid, at 521.

variable one created by the OPA. The OPA clearly does not depend upon notions of *taste* or upon the individual's *own* idea of what he or she should see. It creates a varying standard since it depends upon the jury's estimate of the effect of the material on a small proportion of the *likely* audience.

As suggested above, the internet is now one of the most important media enabling access to pornography, including extreme and violent pornography. Probably it has become the most important medium in this respect. The question raised is: which persons constitute the 'likely audience' of material that is available on the web? Presumably, where 'Age-Check' technology is used, and/or a credit card is required to gain access, publishers will be able to claim that the likely audience does not include children. However, the recent decision in *R v Perrin*,[224] discussed further in Chapter 12,[225] deals with the issue of material displayed on the internet without the use of such restrictions. It suggests that, given the now widespread availability of access to the internet, and the fact that most children have access,[226] often unsupervised, it will be assumed readily that material on the internet could be seen by the 'vulnerable', including children. In that case, a prosecution was brought in relation to an obscene web page openly accessible as a preview page for an adult subscription site. It was viewed by a police officer in order to gather evidence of its nature and content, but no evidence was led by the prosecution as to other persons who might have visited it. The case turned on whether vulnerable people might have seen the material—that is, those vulnerable to corruption by it. The applicant argued that the prosecution needed to show specific evidence that the persons likely to view the particular site were vulnerable. The court disagreed, reiterating first that the prosecution only needed to show that a more than negligible number of persons visiting the site would be corrupted. Given this, it was plausible to think that enough vulnerable people to make up more than a negligible number might have seen the material. It was not necessary to show that anyone deemed vulnerable had in fact seen it.

... we emphasise that section 1(1) of the 1959 Act only requires the jury to be satisfied that there is a likelihood of vulnerable persons seeing the material. The prosecution does not have to show that any such person actually saw it or would have seen it in the future.[227]

Perrin therefore seems to indicate that in principle, courts will *presume* that children have access to pornographic material on the internet, so that the question to be asked will be whether children are likely to be depraved and corrupted by the material there displayed. Since a vast amount of pornographic pictures, including 'hard-core' images, are in fact obtainable on the internet without any Age-Check technology or requirement to use a credit card, it would seem that prosecutions for internet pornography will, since *Perrin*, be more readily successful, even in respect of material that is not particularly extreme.[228]

---

[224] (2002) WL 347127.   [225] See pp 649–50.

[226] Government statistics show that as of July 2005, 55% of households in the UK have internet access: see www.statistics.gov.uk/cci/nugget.asp?id=8. See p 389 above.

[227] Ibid, at [22].   [228] See further Chapter 12.

The problematic nature of the 'deprave and corrupt' test in contemporary society

A. W. B. Simpson, a former member of the Williams Committee appointed in 1977 to review obscenity law, recalls that: 'Before, during and after the Committee sat, the chorus of abuse against the law continued; virtually everyone claimed that it was unworkable.'[229] The authors would strong agree. The central legal test in this area is ultimately derived from the decision in *Hicklin*—a decision made in Victorian times, when any item likely to produce arousal and thoughts of sexual pleasure was considered immoral. As Lord Pearson said in the leading decision of *Whyte*:

The definition in section 1(1) [of the 1959 Act] of an obscene article is evidently based on the traditional test of obscenity which was formulated by Cockburn C.J. in *Hicklin*.[230] In that case, for example, Cockburn CJ referred to as obscene an article that, 'would suggest to the minds of the young of either sex, or even to persons of more advanced years, thoughts of a most impure and libidinous character.'

In other words, the current law is based upon a legal definition advanced at a time in which any arousal of sexual desire by published material was regarded as corrupting. This puritanical definition was applied by Lord Pearson in the 1970s in *Whyte*, a decision taken over a hundred years later, after the advent of the contraceptive pill, the sexual revolution, and the decriminalization of homosexuality, in a society in which pre-marital sex was becoming the norm. Nevertheless, his Lordship actually repeated the very words used in the Victorian judgment:

In the words, of Cockburn C.J. in *Reg v Hicklin*, at p 371, the pornographic books in the respondents' shop suggested to the minds of the regular customers 'thoughts of a most impure and libidinous character.'

It was as if the sexual revolution had never occurred, as far as the courts were concerned. Similarly, the *Anderson* case in 1972 dealt with a magazine that contained some anodyne stories and cartoons, as well as certain items found to be obscene. One, an advertisement for a magazine called *Suck*, the judge described thus:

It is a salaciously written account of the joys from the female aspect of an act of oral sexual intercourse. It deals with the matter in great detail. It emphasises the pleasures which the writer says are to be found in this activity, and there is in it no suggestion anywhere which would imply that this was a wrong thing to do or in any way induce people not to do it.[231]

Clearly, therefore, in the judge's view, oral sex is simply 'wrong'—or at least deriving pleasure from it is. In *Whyte*, reference was made to descriptions in the materials in question of 'such deviant sexual behaviour as intercourse per oram [oral sex], intercourse per anum [anal sex] as well as homosexual acts between both men and women'. Clearly, all these acts were regarded as morally wrong. Lord Pearson said of the same books:

---

[229] A. W. B. Simpson, *Pornography and Politics: The Williams Committee in Retrospect*, Waterlow Publishers, 1983, p 80.
[230] Op cit, at 864.   [231] Op cit, at 231.

If the contents of the pornographic books had been confined to normal sexual behaviour the case would have been of a different kind and I express no opinion as to what the decision should be in a case of that kind. In the present case the contents of the pornographic books were as stated. There could hardly be anything more obviously obscene than that collection of pornographic books exposed for sale and sold in that shop.[232]

As Spinola J commented in the Canadian decision of *Butler*:

The *Hicklin* philosophy posits that explicit sexual depictions, particularly outside the sanctioned contexts of marriage and procreation, threatened the morals or the fabric of society. In this sense, its dominant, if not exclusive, purpose was to advance a particular conception of morality. Any deviation from such morality was considered to be inherently undesirable, independently of any harm to society.[233]

Lord Wilberforce, in contrast, did show some awareness of the difficulties of applying the test in contemporary society and was highly critical of it:

No definition of 'deprave and corrupt' is offered—no guideline as to what kind of influence is meant. Is it criminal conduct, general or sexual, that is feared . . . or departure from some code of morality, sexual or otherwise, and if so whose code, or from accepted or other beliefs, or the arousing of erotic desires 'normal' or 'abnormal,' or, as the justices have said, 'private fantasies.' Some, perhaps most, of these alternatives involve deep questions of psychology and ethics: how are the courts to deal with them? Well might they have said that such words provide a formula which cannot in practice be applied . . . I have serious doubts whether the Act will continue to be workable in this way, or whether it will produce tolerable results.[234]

The 'deprave and corrupt' test made sense in a society in which there was a strong consensus as to substantive sexual morality, one based upon a puritanical interpretation of Christian teaching: sex and sexual desire was morally permissible only in marriage, and homosexual sex was absolutely wrong; to produce a publication likely to arouse *hetero*sexual desire was generally therefore to corrupt *per se*; any attempt to arouse homosexual desire was doubly so. In contemporary society, however, agreement as to appropriate sexual morality has fractured spectacularly, aside from a basic remaining consensus that sexual activity should be confined to consenting adults. There are some Christians who retain an allegiance to a basically Victorian morality,[235] whilst many Muslims would take, a similar view. Beyond a relatively small group of very strict, or extreme, religious adherents, there is a vast range of views based on personal preference, taste, and conviction. For example, there has been a rapid revolution in terms of attitudes towards, and the legal treatment of, homosexuality; a significant minority continue to take the view that consenting homosexual intercourse between adults is morally wrong, or at least repugnant, albeit perhaps something that should be tolerated. Given the plethora of varying views as to what might be meant by

---

[232] Op cit, at 865.   [233] Op cit, at 492.   [234] Op cit, at 862.

[235] The Christian Institute, for example, campaigns against recognition of gay rights in the sphere of sexuality. See Chapter 12, note 166 for its stance in relation to the broadcast in 2005 of *Jerry Springer: the Opera*.

moral corruption, to ask a jury to apply 'contemporary standards' to sexually explicit material is to ask of them the impossible. In making this point it must be borne in mind that such standards are not necessarily linked to those enforced by the criminal law governing sexual relations—photographs of persons engaging in non-simulated illegal sexual acts might be likely to be deemed obscene, but this cannot be said with certainty of digitally created photographs or simulations of such acts.[236]

As an example of how standards have changed, it was noted above that in *Calder and Boyars*, evidence was led in an attempt to show that exposure to images of homosexuality would not in fact corrupt, because it could avert men from homosexuality, rather than encourage any tendencies that they had. Today, somewhat ironically, such an argument could be turned on its head: using images to create revulsion against homosexuality could be seen by many *now* as depraving and corrupting—as making people morally worse in the sense of inducing prejudice, intolerance, and revulsion against a natural disposition. Thus is the unworkable and paradoxical nature of the Act, in a society in which there is no moral consensus on the limits of consensual sexuality, revealed.

Our conclusion is that the test of 'deprave and corrupt', in relying upon what a jury or magistrates consider would produce a 'moral change for the worse', with no substantive degree of consensus on what such a change might mean, is intolerably uncertain, potentially broad, and arbitrary. Its effects are kept within tolerable limits since prosecutions are brought only in relation to the most extreme forms of material, as indicated in the next section. But since 'obscenity' provides the basic standard from which the offence-based regulation of films and broadcasting stems, the uncertainty and unworkability of the test remains a matter of grave concern.[237] As discussed in Chapter 12, the BBFC, the film regulator, has to take a stance on the question whether films might be obscene in determining the point at which it would not award an R18 certificate without cuts, or at all.[238] We consider how the test could be judicially reinterpreted later in this chapter.

The application of the Act in practice: prosecutions

The problematic nature of the Act is further reflected in the fact that it is, seemingly, markedly underused. In a debate in 1996, the Lord Bishop of Bristol said:

[The Act] is not used by the CPS. . . . It is believed to be too subjective and there are therefore declining numbers of prosecutions and an unwillingness to prosecute.[239]

---

[236] If such depictions included children they would be likely to be caught by the Protection of Children Act 1978, as amended (see below at 467–70); they might also be viewed as obscene.

[237] See discussion in Chapter, 10–12. As discussed in those chapters, such regulation is intended to set the boundaries of acceptable viewing at a level 'higher' than that denoted by the OPA 1959. Therefore a reasonable degree of certainty as to the statutory standard is needed.

[238] See Chapter 12 at 621–2.

[239] HL Deb Vol. 576, col. 1599 (18 Dec 1996) per Lord Bishop of Bristol. This quote is cited in S. Edwards, op cit, 'On the Contemporary Application of the Obscene Publications Act 1959' [1998] *Crim LR* 843 at note 1, to whom the authors are indebted for the material that follows.

It is something of an exaggeration to say that the Act is 'not used', but correct to say that there has been a sharp fall in the number of prosecutions under the Act. The Government recently noted[240] that the number of prosecutions under the Act has fallen from 309 in 1994 to 39 in 2003. This in itself indicates a lack of confidence in the legal test used by the Act, as does the evidence given to the Lord Bishop.

In terms of the threshold of obscenity, as judged by the prosecutions brought, the picture that emerges from a recent study of the practical operation of the law[241] is that only fairly extreme types of material are prosecuted. However, it appears that no clear distinction is drawn between highly explicit and extreme but legal and apparently consensual practices on the one hand, and violent, illegal, and seemingly non-consensual practices on the other. For example, *Hoare v UK*[242] concerned a number of counts of alleged obscenity, as follows:

On a number of occasions during the course of fairly vigorous activity, you saw men and women inserting not only fingers into the vagina of various women, but also the whole hand and, indeed, on one or two occasions, the whole fist up to the wrist.[243]

A second count involved explicit scenes of buggery and ejaculation on the women's faces or hair. Now, whilst many people might find (some of) these practices personally distasteful, they are not illegal, are practised with enjoyment by many couples, and therefore are arguably not to be compared with the violent pornography prosecuted. Some of this is described as including:

Sex with animals and acts of violence including wooden chisel handles being pushed into the vagina and anus and lighted cigarettes being applied to the vagina, electrical shock and torture, and scenes involving a tyre lever being inserted into the anus, objects and animals inserted into the vagina and anus, beating and ball-gags to the mouth . . .[244]

Other counts deemed obscene included a film of a woman consuming faeces, of a woman inserting eels into the vagina and anus of another woman, and of a woman being whipped vigorously all over her body—a film that the jury found so distressing to watch that they asked that it be stopped within the first ten or twelve minutes.[245]

The author of the survey concludes that in the only jury acquittal following a full trial, the nature of the material could be clearly distinguished from depictions of illegal and violent acts, in that it only involved 'explicit sex, fisting, urination and mild bondage'. If such distinctions are being drawn by juries generally, this is to be welcomed, but the analysis above suggests that in some cases prosecutors, at least, are not drawing distinctions between mere shockingly explicit depictions of lawful acts (e.g. 'fisting'), and depictions of rape, violence, and torture. To prosecute the former kind of material suggests a reliance upon the distinctions encapsulated in the notions of 'soft' and 'hard' core material. In other words, the former material appears to be viewed as 'hard core' material and therefore possibly obscene, since it is especially

---

240 Consultation paper, op cit, at [15].   241 Ibid.   242 [1997] EHRLR 678.
243 Ibid.   244 Edwards, op cit, at 848.   245 Ibid, at 849. See note 145 above for further details.

explicit. Distinctions between material termed 'soft' and 'hard' core pornography traditionally turned primarily upon whether shots of genitals, particularly the erect penis, and actual penetration, were shown. Such distinctions *are* still important in the classification of films: it is only very recently, for example, that an actor's penis could be shown erect in films for mainstream release,[246] and such scenes are still very rare. Although prosecutions for obscenity would not now be brought in relation to such material, the idea that the more explicit the material, the more likely it is to be obscene still appears to be prevalent. It appears that such material is not necessarily treated as distinct from material that depicts sexual violence and illegal forms of sexual activity, in terms of the application of the law on obscenity.

We would suggest that the extent to which material is *explicit* is irrelevant in terms of its moral impact. Distinctions between items of material based on such a test would appear to us to be irrelevant to the corruption of morals. Most people are not celibate, and could—in effect—view the material depicted, such as close-ups of genitals, simply by looking at their own and partner's bodies during sexual intercourse. Why a visual representation of that which is done and observed nightly by millions of adults should be deemed to be corrupting to morals is not, in the authors' view, explicable. There is something incongruous in a statement by the law that adults may lawfully engage in certain activities, such as anal intercourse or group sex, but may *not* watch films *depicting* such activities. Yet one of the films mentioned above was found impliedly to be quite close to the boundary delineated by the test for obscenity, although it depicted nothing more than one of the more common of these lawful activities. Recently, the BBFC, the film regulator, required a cut in a French film, *The Pornographer*, to remove a shot in which semen was visible on a woman's face, following oral sex.[247] The implication was that without the cut it would not have been classified for viewing in mainstream cinemas, although it might have obtained an R18 classification.[248] By way of contrast, in the case of films depicting extreme violence, it is commonplace for much of the action to concern the very graphic depiction of the most serious criminal offences of violence. The same can be said of filmic depictions of drug-taking. Such films are readily classified for mainstream viewing and the possibility of criminal proceedings is remote. It is hard to escape the idea that in law, as well as in feminist writing, sexually explicit material is being unfairly singled out; this would not be surprising, given that, as we have seen, the law is normatively of Victorian pedigree.

Forfeiture proceedings

The vast majority of actions against allegedly obscene material take the form of forfeiture proceedings. Forfeiture, in leading to the destruction of items, and therefore

---

[246] On the standards applied by the BBFC in relation to sex, see further Chapter 12 at 623–7.

[247] See Chapter 12 at 629.

[248] See Chapter 12 at 621–4 for an explanation of this classification. Without the cut it could only have obtained an 'R18' classification if the BBFC had not viewed the film as obscene; it is unclear from the ruling whether that was the case. The cut was required in order to obtain an '18' classification.

preventing them from reaching their audience, is a form of prior restraint. Nevertheless, under s 3 of the 1959 Act, safeguards are extremely limited. Magazines and other material, such as videos, can be seized by the police if it is suspected on reasonable grounds that they are obscene and have been kept for gain.[249] A magistrate signs a seizure warrant if satisfied that such grounds exist and then can order the articles to be forfeited if satisfied that they are obscene.

No conviction is obtained; if found to be obscene, the material is merely destroyed; no other punishment is imposed and therefore s 3 may operate at a low level of visibility. During the process of *seizure*, the safeguards provided by the Act are bypassed: no consideration is given to the possible literary merits of such material because the public good defence is not taken into account in issuing the seizure warrant. The merits of an article should be taken into account in the forfeiture hearing in determining whether it out-balances its obscenity, but there is not much evidence that magistrates take a very rigorous approach to making such a determination. They do not need to read every item, but need only look at samples selected by the police[250] and seem, in any event, more ready than a jury to defer to police

---

[249] Section 3—Powers of search and seizure:

(1) If a justice of the peace is satisfied by information on oath that there is reasonable ground for suspecting that, in any premises or on any stall or vehicle, being premises or a stall or vehicle specified in the information, obscene articles are, or are from time to time, kept for publication for gain, the justice may issue a warrant under his hand empowering any constable to enter (if need be by force) and search the premises, or to search the stall or vehicle and to seize and remove any articles found therein or thereon which the constable has reason to believe to be obscene articles and to be kept for publication for gain.

(2) A warrant under the foregoing subsection shall, if any obscene articles are seized under the warrant, also empower the seizure and removal of any documents found in the premises or, as the case may be, on the stall or vehicle which relate to a trade or business carried on at the premises or from the stall or vehicle.

(3) Subject to subsection (3A) of this section any articles seized under subsection (1) of this section shall be brought before a justice of the peace acting [in the local justice area in which the articles were seized, who may thereupon issue a summons to the occupier of the premises or, as the case may be, the user of the stall or vehicle to appear on a day specified in the summons before a magistrates' court acting in that local justice area to show cause why the articles or any of them should not be forfeited; and if the court is satisfied, as respects any of the articles, that at the time when they were seized they were obscene articles kept for publication for gain, the court shall order those articles to be forfeited: Provided that if the person summoned does not appear, the court shall not make an order unless service of the summons is proved. Provided also that this subsection does not apply in relation to any article seized under subsection (1) of this section which is returned to the occupier of the premises or, as the case may be, to the user of the stall or vehicle in or on which it was found.

(3A) Without prejudice to the duty of a court to make an order for the forfeiture of an article where section 1(4) of the Obscene Publications Act 1964 applies (orders made on conviction), in a case where by virtue of subsection (3A) of section 2 of this Act proceedings under the said section 2 for having an article for publication for gain could not be instituted except by or with the consent of the Director of Public Prosecutions, no order for the forfeiture of the article shall be made under this section unless the warrant under which the article was seized was issued on an information laid by or on behalf of the Director of Public Prosecutions.

(4) In addition to the person summoned, any other person being the owner, author or maker of any of the articles brought before the court, or any other person through whose hands they had passed before being seized, shall be entitled to appear before the court on the day specified in the summons to show cause why they should not be forfeited.

[250] *Crown Court at Snaresbrook ex p Metropolitan Police Comr* (1984) 148 JP 449.

judgment and find that an item is obscene.[251] It seems, therefore, that the protection afforded by the 1959 Act to freedom of speech may depend more on the exercise of discretion by the police as to the enforcement of s 3, or on the tolerance of magistrates, rather than on the law itself. However, s 3 can be used only in respect of material which may be obscene rather than in relation to any form of pornography; it was held in *Darbo v DPP*[252] that a warrant issued under s 3 allowing officers to search for 'sexually explicit material' was bad on its face, as such articles would fall within a much wider category of articles than those which could be called obscene. Nevertheless, the forfeiture procedure exemplifies an unhappy paradox: the most drastic interference certainly with audience rights—prior restraint—is accompanied by a lower level of safeguards than are in place in relation to criminal proceedings. Moreover, given that magistrates are not representative of the population as a whole, and are probably more conservative, it is not clearly apparent that contemporary standards are observed in making the determination as to obscenity.

The defence of public good

This defence, which arises under s 4 of the 1959 Act[253] and s 3 of the Theatres Act 1968, was intended to afford recognition to artistic and other merit. Thus, it may be seen as a highly significant step in the direction of freedom of speech, acknowledging the force of a variant of the argument for free speech from truth which was also used by the William Committee.[254] Under the 1959 Act, s 4, it is a defence to a finding that a publication is obscene if it can be shown that 'the publication of the article in question is justified as for the public good in that it is in the interests of science, literature, art, learning or of other objects of general concern'. Under the 1968 Act, the similarly worded defence which covers 'the interests of drama, opera, ballet or any other art or of literature or learning' is somewhat narrower as omitting the concluding general words. Under s 53(6) of the Criminal Law Act 1977, which amended s 4 of the 1959 Act, this narrower defence is applied to films. Expert evidence will be admissible to prove that one of these possibilities can be established and it may include considering other works. It may be noted that this turns the Convention approach on its head: under Article 10, any interference must be justified; under obscenity law, the publication of any obscene material must be justified by the public good defence, a point returned to below.

It was determined in *Penguin Books*[255] in respect of *Lady Chatterley's Lover* that the jury should adopt a two-stage approach, asking first whether the article in question is

[251] Bailey, Harris, and Jones note (op cit, at 328) that comment arose when forfeiture proceedings of an edition of the magazine *Men Only* coincided with the jury acquittal of the editors of *Nasty Tales* of the offence under s 2 ((1973) 127 JPN 82). Robertson argues (*Obscenity*, 1979, p 96) that as the hearing is before a tribunal which has already decided that the material is—at least *prima facie*—obscene, it is likely to have an appearance of unfairness. The Bench may be unlikely to be convinced that, in effect, it was wrong in the first place in issuing the summons.
[252] (1992) *The Times*, 4 July; [1992] Crim LR 56.
[253] As amended by s 53 of the Criminal Law Act 1977.   [254] See above, at 395.
[255] [1961] Crim LR 176.

obscene and, if so, going on to consider whether the defendant has established the probability that its merits are so high as to outbalance its obscenity so that its publication is for the public good. The failure of the prosecution was seen as a turning point for literary freedom, and the jury allowed it to be known that the second stage of the test afforded the basis on which the novel escaped suppression. In *DPP v Jordan*,[256] the House of Lords approved this two-stage approach and the balancing of obscenity against literary or other merit. However, the House also rejected an attempt to widen the test. The main question was whether the articles in question—hard-core pornography—could be justified under s 4 as being of psychotherapeutic value for persons of deviant sexuality in that the material might help to relieve their sexual tensions by way of sexual fantasies. It was argued that such material might provide a safety valve for such persons, which would divert them from anti-social activities and that such benefit could fall within the words 'other objects of general concern' in s 4. The House of Lords, however, held that these words must be construed *ejusdem generis* with the preceding words 'art, literature learning, science'. As these specific words were unrelated to sexual benefit, the general words which followed them could not be construed in the manner suggested. It was ruled that the jury must be satisfied that the matter in question made a contribution to a recognized field of culture or learning which could be assessed irrespective of the persons to whom it was distributed. As Lord Wilberforce put it:

the structure of the section makes it clear that the other objects, or, which is the same argument, the nature of the general concern, fall within the same area, and cannot fall in the totally different area of effect on sexual behaviour and attitudes, which is covered in s 1. The judgment to be reached under s 4(1), and the evidence to be given under s 4(2), must be in order to show that publication should be permitted in spite of obscenity—not to negative obscenity. Section 4 has been diverted from its proper purpose, and indeed abused, when it has been used to enable evidence to be given that pornographic material may be for the public good as being therapeutic to some of the public.[257]

Although the test of public good has clearly afforded protection to freedom of expression in relation to publications of artistic merit, it has been criticized. Section 4 requires a jury to embark on the very problematic task of in some way weighing a predicted change for the worse in the minds of the group of persons likely to encounter the article, against literary or other merit. Thus, an effect or process must be imagined, entirely without the benefit of expert evidence, which, once established, must be measured against an intrinsic quality. As the Court of Appeal put it in *Calders*:

In the view of this court, the proper direction on a defence under s 4 in a case such as the present is that the jury must consider on the one hand the number of readers they believe would tend to be depraved and corrupted by the book, the strength of the tendency to deprave and corrupt, and the nature of the depravity or corruption; on the other hand, they

---

[256] [1977] AC 699.   [257] *DPP v Jordan*, op cit.

should assess the strength of the literary, sociological or ethical merit which they consider the book to possess. They should then weigh up all these factors and decide whether on balance the publication is proved to be justified as being for the public good.[258]

The Court went on:

A book may be worthless; a book may have slight but real merit; it may be a work of genius. Between those extremes the gradations are almost infinite. A book may tend to deprave and corrupt a significant but comparatively small number of its readers or a large number or indeed the majority of its readers. The tendency to deprave and corrupt may be strong or slight. The depravity and corruption may also take various forms. It may be to induce erotic desires of a heterosexual kind or to promote homosexuality or other sexual perversions or drug-taking or brutal violence. All these are matters for the jury to consider and weigh up; it is for them to decide in the light of the importance they attach to these factors whether or not the publication is for the public good. The jury must set the standards of what is acceptable, of what is for the public good in the age in which we live.[259]

It is clear, given this extraordinarily open-ended guidance on how the jury are to perform their task, that Dicey's quip that the 'right to free speech' in Britain is merely the right to publish what 12 shopkeepers think ought to be published, remains startlingly apt in this area. The jury is presented with a disparate bundle of ephemeral considerations, and simply told to come to a conclusion, attaching whatever weight they see fit to the matters that they must consider, and using whatever reasoning process they care to adopt. Geoffrey Robertson has said on this point, 'the balancing act is a logical nonsense [because it is not] logically possible to weigh up such disparate concepts as "corruption" and "literary merit"'.[260] Moreover, the test at first sight appears to imply a paradox: it assumes that an individual can be corrupted, which suggests a stultifying effect on the mind, and yet can also experience an elevating effect due to the merit of an article. However, such an interpretation of the test is open to two objections. First, a person could experience corruption in the sense that her moral standards might be lowered, but she might retain a sense of literary or artistic appreciation. Secondly—and this might seem the more satisfactory interpretation— the 'message' of the publication and its general artistic impact (through, for example, its influence on other works which followed it) might be for the public good although some individuals who encountered it were corrupted. Thus the term 'publication' in s 4 must mean publication to the public at large, not only to those who encounter the article if the test is to be workable.[261]

The Court of Appeal in *Calder* adverted to precisely this point:

The legislature can hardly have contemplated that a book which tended to corrupt and deprave the average reader or the majority of those likely to read it could be justified as being for the public good on any ground.[262]

---

[258] [1969] 1 QB 151, 172.   [259] Ibid.   [260] Robertson, op cit, at 164.
[261] The House of Lords in *Jordan* [1977] AC 699 appeared to take this view. See also Robertson, op cit, on the point (pp 168–9).
[262] Op cit, at 711.

In response to this comment, it is noted that under s 1(1) it is necessary that an article have a tendency to corrupt 'a significant proportion' of those who read it. This does not in fact avoid the paradox that where a court found that an item *would* be likely to corrupt the average reader, or a majority of those who read it, it might still avoid giving rise to liability through the application of the s 4 defence. It should finally be noticed that, as discussed below, the defence can be avoided by bringing a charge of indecency at common law; as *Gibson*[263] demonstrated, the merits of an obscene object may, paradoxically, prevent its suppression while the merits of less offensive objects may not, because there is no 'public good' defence to indecency offences.

There are further difficulties with s 4. As just seen, it does not allow for consideration of any claimed benefits of pornography; moreover, it may be inapt to take into account 'new art at the cutting edge of art development':[264] judges are perhaps not best placed to recognize the value of innovative forms of art, which might to them simply appear bizarre and sensationalist. On the other hand, the words, 'or other object of general concern', must be taken to mean *something* since otherwise they are otiose. We discuss below the potential effect of Article 10 ECHR on obscenity law, but it may be noted here that those very general words, even construed as they were in *Jordan*, provide the most obvious 'entry point' for Article 10 to act upon the statute, via s 3(1) HRA. This possibility has the potential to remedy the basic defect of the Act indicated in the direction from *Calder* (above): it contains no reference to considering the value of freedom of expression *per se*.

It is useful at this point to consider how other jurisdictions deal with this point. In Canadian law, the basic test for obscenity is as follows:

For the purposes of this Act, any publication a dominant characteristic of which is the undue exploitation of sex, or of sex and any one or more of the following subjects, namely, crime, horror, cruelty and violence, shall be deemed to be obscene.[265]

The defence is expressed as follows:

No person shall be convicted of an offence under this section if he establishes that the public good was served by the acts that are alleged to constitute the offence and that the acts alleged did not extend beyond what served the public good.[266]

Sopinka J sums up the 'internal necessity' or 'artistic defence' as:

Assess[ing] whether the exploitation of sex has a justifiable role in advancing the plot or the theme, and in considering the work as a whole, does not merely represent 'dirt for dirt's sake' but has a legitimate role when measured by the internal necessities of the work itself.[267]

Two comments may be made about the Canadian defence as it compares to s 4 OPA. First, it is a genuine 'public good' defence, in that it uses that broad, expansive term,

---

[263] [1990] 2 QB 619; [1991] 1 All ER 439; [1990] 3 WLR 595, CA.
[264] P. Kearns, 'Obscene and blasphemous libel: misunderstanding art' [2000] *Crim LR* 652, p 654.
[265] s 163, Canadian Criminal Code.   [266] s 163(3).   [267] *Butler*, at 482–3.

rather than the relatively narrow wording of s 4, as interpreted. Second, as Sopinka's dicta make clear, the defence allows for an assessment of whether the sexual content has a meaningful relationship with the work as a whole: it serves as a starting point, therefore, for distinguishing material intended purely to arouse, from that which links the portrayal of human sexuality to broader themes. However, it is interesting to note one problem that this approach raises: a book which had as its theme the intense and liberating experience which some women and men, homosexual or heterosexual, might find in submissive, masochistic sexual practice[268] and used explicit material to further that theme should not, from one particular feminist perspective,[269] be permitted any more than one which used such a scene for purposes of mere titillation. The former would be likely, if anything, to do more harm to attitudes to women (if attributing submissive sexual desires to some women is harmful to all women) than the latter. From that perspective, then, more significant or serious works would be *less* likely to be viewed as being 'for the public good'.

The other point to be made about the Canadian approach is that it appears to leave little room for books, short stories, or films that consist primarily of explicit sexual content to benefit from the defence. As the Supreme Court has explained;

The need to apply [the defence] only arises if a work contains sexually explicit material that by itself would constitute the undue exploitation of sex. The portrayal of sex must then be viewed in context to determine whether that is the dominant theme of the work as a whole. Put another way, is undue exploitation of sex the main object of the work or is this portrayal of sex essential to a wider artistic, literary, or other similar purpose? Since the threshold determination must be made on the basis of . . . whether the sexually explicit aspect is undue, its impact when considered in context must be determined on the same basis. The court must determine whether the sexually explicit material when viewed in the context of the whole work would be tolerated by the community as a whole. Artistic expression rests at the heart of freedom of expression values and any doubt in this regard must be resolved in favour of freedom of expression.[270]

This suggests that the judges are called upon to apply a rather crude form of sexual-literary proportionality: the amount of explicit content in a work must not be out of proportion to the work as a whole. It might be asked in response—on what basis is it the role of judges to determine how much sexual content a literary or other work should contain? Is a work that chooses to focus almost exclusively upon sexuality to be pre-judged as obscene? Such judgments are very fine ones, and many will be unhappy at the thought of them being made mainly by elderly, male judges, however much they claim to be applying 'community standards'. But, as Barendt points out, the inclusion of any kind of 'public good' defence makes some such exercise inescapable:

it would go too far in the other direction automatically to exclude from the reach of pornography laws any material for which the status of literature or art can be claimed. Some

---

[268] Examples would be the French classic *Story of O*, described by Graham Greene as 'A rare thing, a pornographic book without a trace of obscenity' and the controversial Lesbian S/M erotica of Pat Califa.
[269] See note 315 below.   [270] Ibid, at 486.

assessment of that claim is inescapable. Otherwise the law must abandon the attempt to control the dissemination of sexually explicit material. As the Supreme Court of Canada has said, the courts should be generous in their application of the defence of artistic merit. Any work which can *reasonably* be treated as art or literature should be entitled to the defence.[271]

This chapter now moves on to consider the anomalous common law offence of conspiracy to corrupt public morals, an offence that seems to cover the same territory as the OPA, but the notion of a 'public good' or artistic necessities defence will be returned to in the consideration given below to reform of this area of law.

THE COMMON LAW OFFENCE OF CONSPIRACY TO CORRUPT PUBLIC MORALS

The offence of conspiracy to corrupt public morals is aimed at essentially the same mischief as is the Obscene Publications Act, but was 'developed' under the common law by the judges some time *after* the Act was passed. The existence of this offence is perhaps the most unsatisfactory aspect of this unsatisfactory area of law. It lacks the key safeguards contained in the statutory offence, is 'defined' in extremely broad and imprecise terms, and creates serious anomalies in this area of law taken as a whole. As discussed below, all these strictures can also be levelled at the somewhat similar offence of outraging public decency. In *Shaw v DPP*,[272] the House of Lords determined that the offence of conspiring to corrupt public morals existed, partly on the basis of some disputed and ancient authorities, and partly on the basis of some statements (since largely disavowed) that the law confers a general discretion to punish immoral (not merely criminal) conduct which could injure the public. The defendants had published the 'Lady's Directory', a pamphlet giving descriptions of call-girls and details of the services that they could provide. The offence that the judges discovered to exist, which they could then use to punish the defendants, is enormously broad: all that is needed by way of the *actus reus* is an agreement to carry out an action that is likely to lead people morally astray—in *Shaw*, the agreement to publish the Directory. The harm is in the agreement (the conspiracy); it may be unnecessary for any objectively verifiable act to occur, such as publication of material, so that even if the agreed-upon act is never performed, there will still be liability. However, although *Shaw* is not entirely clear on this point, it appears that the act must be one, which, if carried out, would be likely to lead people morally astray. The *mens rea*, however, is quite specific: there must be intention to corrupt public morals, that is, a desire or aim to cause such corruption, or realization that it was virtually certain that such corruption would occur.[273] Both states of mind are difficult to prove in this

---

[271] Barendt, op cit, at 384.

[272] [1962] AC 220; [1961] 2 WLR 897, HL; for comment, see (1961) 24 *MLR* 626; (1964) 42, *Canadian Bar Review* 561.

[273] This is based on the normal definition of simple and oblique intention in criminal law: *R v Woolin* (1999) 1 AC 82.

context. Clearly, the prosecution would have to proceed by way of inference. In the case of simple intent, defendants who, for example, agreed to publish explicit material, would be likely to say that their aim or desire had been simply to provide arousing material to aid masturbation, and that they had not envisaged, or believed in, the possibility of any corrupting effect.[274] If it was accepted that it was impossible to disprove this contention by relying on inferential material, the prosecution would have to show oblique intent: to do so they would have to show that the conspiracy was to commit acts that were virtually certain to cause corruption and that the defendants (subjectively) realized this. In most instances, it is hard to see that either of these elements could be proved to the criminal standard in this context and in this respect the offence is more restrictive than the offence under the OPA, which only requires an intention to publish.

The over-breadth of the offence lies in the fact that it simply requires an agreement to lead others astray morally: the fact that the defendants are seeking to encourage or entice people into what is in fact lawful conduct provides no defence. Indeed, this point was expressly adverted to in *Shaw* itself. Viscount Simmonds, speaking at a time before homosexual intercourse was decriminalized, said:[275]

Let it be supposed that at some future, perhaps early, date homosexual practices between adult consenting males are no longer a crime. Would it not be an offence if, even without obscenity, such practices were publicly advocated and encouraged by pamphlet and advertisement? Or must we wait until Parliament finds time to deal with such conduct? I say, my Lords, that if the common law is powerless in such event, then we should no longer do her reverence.

Thus the offence has been especially criticized on the basis that it left it unclear whether an agreement to commit adultery could amount to a criminal conspiracy.[276] Counsel gave a striking example in a later case of the difficulties stemming from the fact that the offence allows for the punishing of conspiracy to do that which is it itself lawful:

Until the Sexual Offences Act 1967, all forms of abortion were illegal. By the Act of 1967, certain forms of abortion were made legal. But the astonishing consequence of the present case is that if advertisements are placed in newspapers putting persons in contact with abortion clinics which only deal with the types of abortion that come within the province of the Act of 1967, all those concerned with publishing the advertisements might be found guilty on indictment of the offence of conspiracy to corrupt public morals, for the judge trying such a case would have no option but to leave the case to the jury. That is the great difficulty in this branch of the law, that all such cases would have to be left to the jury and therefore one has a vague and undefined branch of the criminal law in which juries in different parts of the country might take different views of the same conduct. For to take the abortion example, there might well be certain parts of the country where juries consider that abortion is an immoral act.[277]

---

[274] However, since intention is in any event always inferred from the evidence, juries might well merely disbelieve a defendant who claimed that he had not intended to bring about a corrupting effect.

[275] [1962] AC 220, at 268.   [276] See Robertson, op cit, at 215.

[277] *Knuller v DPP* [1973] AC 435; [1972] 3 WLR 143; (1972) 56 Cr App R 633, HL.

In *Knuller v DPP*,[278] from which the above passage is taken, the offence arose out of the placement in a magazine of gay 'contact' advertisements. It was pointed out for the defence that it was a strange anomaly to make it an offence to place advertisements allowing men to meet each other and then, if they chose, engage in homosexual acts where, if two people met without such advertisements, and then agreed to engage in such acts, the acts would not be unlawful. Nor, logically, could the agreement between two such people in those circumstances to engage in homosexual acts be unlawful: for if one makes it lawful to engage in homosexual acts, one must also make it lawful to agree to engage in them, otherwise the startling result would be that this offence would have the effect of rendering otiose the statute decriminalizing homosexual sex. (Clearly it could not render only male homosexual intercourse undertaken *without agreement* lawful: that would mean, ludicrously, that only male rape, not consensual homosexual sex, would be lawful.)

As Counsel put it:

The real vice here is that this offence gives rise to complete uncertainty in the law because it is impossible to ascertain whether a given act is contrary to public morals until a jury has given its verdict upon it. An example of this could be a society issuing a pamphlet advocating the practice of euthanasia. It is one of the cardinal rules of the criminal law that the law should be certain . . . In this branch of the law, any co-operative conduct is criminal if a jury consider it *ex post facto* to have been immoral. If all that has to be proved is that more than one person has led another morally astray then this offence has no bounds.[279]

This indeed was the basis of Lord Reid's dissenting judgment in *Shaw*, in which he argued that the decision offended against the principle that the criminal law should be certain; his Lordship said that it would be very difficult to determine beforehand what a jury would consider to fall within the area of liability created.

Having dissented in *Shaw*, Lord Reid said in *Knuller* that he thought *Shaw* had been wrongly decided, but that he would not now support changing the law again, to abolish the offence that the Lords had discovered to exist. But he did suggest certain clarifications to the offence:

In the first place conspiracy to corrupt public morals is something of a misnomer. It really means to corrupt the morals of such members of the public as may be influenced by the matter published by the accused.[280]

This clarification of course actually broadens the potential scope of the offence, since, rather than the morals of 'the public' at large, only the small readership of a particular publication would have to be placed at risk. The other clarification suggested by Lord Reid was to import the 'contemporaneous standards test':

I think that the jury should be told in one way or another that although in the end the question whether matter is corrupting is for them, they should keep in mind the current standards of ordinary decent people.[281]

---

[278] Ibid.   [279] Ibid, at 443.   [280] Op cit, at 456.   [281] Ibid, at 457.

The other major objection to the offence is that, contrary to the spirit of the Obscene Publications Act, their Lordships held that no public good defence applied. This clearly created the possibility that the common law offence would be used so as to circumvent the safeguards of the Act: the public good defence and the requirement to take the work as a whole. It also of course opened up the possibility that the offence might be used against serious works of art or literature. However, it should be recognized that the finding on this point was, in both cases, strictly *obiter*, since no colourable argument was raised that either publication could come under some common law equivalent of the public good defence. In an often-overlooked dicta dealing with this point, Lord Morris in *Knuller* said:

It was not suggested that the advertisements in the present case (nor was it suggested that the directory in *Shaw's case*) could be regarded as publications which were justifiable as being for the public good. *It may be that if a publication could be so justified, a conspiracy designed to effect, or which contemplated, such a publication would not be a criminal conspiracy* (emphasis added).[282]

Nevertheless, the dominant wisdom is that no such defence applies.[283] The result was that the DPP could use this form of liability in instances where the material in question appeared to fall outside the Obscene Publications Act, or add a charge of conspiracy to corrupt public morals to a charge of obscenity as an alternative in case the obscenity charge failed. In response to fears that the offence would be charged in substitution for the statutory offence, with its greater safeguards, an undertaking was given by the Solicitor-General in the House of Commons on 3 June, 1964, that a conspiracy to corrupt public morals would not be charged so as to circumvent the statutory defence in subsection (4) of section 2 of the Obscene Publications Act 1959.[284] Lord Reid commented in *Knuller*, however:

But I am bound to say that I was surprised to learn that nothing effective had been done to bring this undertaking to the notice of the legal profession. Very experienced senior counsel in this case had never heard of it. It was not said that the course of the present case would have been different if counsel had known of the undertaking. But I cannot avoid an uneasy suspicion that ignorance of it may have affected the conduct of some other prosecution for this crime.[285]

Arguably this offence was simply used in *Knuller* by the prosecuting authorities and the judiciary as an alternative means of criminalizing homosexuality, thereby undermining the liberal reform carried out by Parliament in 1967. It appears plain that this offence, being not only overtly paternalistic, but of very doubtful legitimacy in terms of its antecedents, and without a clear public good defence, should be judicially abolished, or at least substantially modified, if an opportunity presents itself. The duty

---

[282] Ibid, at 465. (emphasis added)

[283] See, e.g. Robertson and Nicol, *Media Law*, 3rd edn, London: Penguin,1992, at 156. In discussing the offence no mention is made of a possible 'public good' defence.

[284] See Hansard, Vol. 695, col. 1212.   [285] Op cit, at 456.

of the courts to act compatibly with Convention rights under s 6 HRA allows for this possibility, an issue discussed further below. It is probable, however, that its anomalous nature means that it is becoming a dead letter, in which case prosecutions are unlikely.

At this point, having completed our survey of what may be termed UK 'obscenity'—as opposed to indecency—law, it may be useful to compare the English position with that in the US and in Canada. We will lay particular emphasis upon the latter, since it amounts to a conceptually different approach, one which has sought directly to answer to the feminist analysis of pornography in developing the rationale for the law's intervention in this area. Having considered this contrasting approach, the possible routes forward for judicial reform of the law will be considered.

COMPARISONS: US AND CANADIAN OBSCENITY LAW

US LAW ON OBSCENITY

The US test for obscenity[286] is as follows. It must be asked, applying contemporary standards:

(a) whether the material appeals to prurient interest;

(b) whether it depicts or describes in a patently offensive way sexual conduct specifically defined by the relevant state law;

(c) whether, taken as a whole, the material lacks serious literary, artistic, political, or scientific value.

The Supreme Court in *Miller*[287] gave a number of examples of material that could properly be regulated by the states under the test of obscenity:

patently offensive representations or descriptions of ultimate sexual acts, normal or perverted, actual or simulated, [and] patently offensive representations or descriptions of masturbation, excretory functions, and lewd exhibition of the genitals.

The Court has consistently emphasized that the *average person* must find the material offensive under *contemporary community standards* for this limb of the obscenity definition to be satisfied. It is readily defensible to assess a publication by reference to its impact on an average person rather than on a particularly vulnerable or sensitive person (a paedophile or a nun, for example), since otherwise the availability of reading matter would be determined by the standards of a small minority.[288] However, as Barendt puts it,

---

[286] From *Miller v California* 413 US 15 (1973).   [287] (1973) 413 US 15.
[288] Op cit, at 366.

Any definition of 'obscenity' in terms of 'offensiveness to contemporary community values' necessarily raises questions about the size and character of the *community* whose judgement is to be considered, as well as about the more obviously contentious concept of 'offensiveness'. The larger the community, the less likely that its members will share common values, except the fashionable faith in the virtues of pluralism.[289]

Given the enormous diversity in US society, in particular between the Christian mid-West and the liberal East and West Coast cities, the notion of there being an 'average' US citizen, in terms of attitudes towards the depiction of sexuality, must be considered a fairly naked legal fiction. It is immediately apparent that there are a number of strong parallels between US and English law here, as well as a couple of interesting contrasts. Both share what may broadly be termed a 'public good defence', although under the US test the state has the burden of disproving the presence of literary or other merits; both apply contemporary standards in making the crucial assessment of obscenity. However, the two diverge upon both the nature of the essential test and upon the audience who must judge it. Firstly, the US test is limited to material that appeals to the 'prurient interest', that is, material intended to produce sexual arousal. As we have seen, English law is not specifically confined in this way. Second, under US law, the test is whether the material is 'patently offensive', not, as under English law, whether it would tend to deprave and corrupt. This is evidently an easier test to satisfy. However, under the US test, as seen, the offensiveness of the work must be tested by the standards of the average citizen. Convictions cannot therefore be obtained, as in the UK, by showing that particularly vulnerable viewers were likely to encounter the work, as in *Perrin*.[290] The US test is narrower in that it only applies to sexually explicit literature, and, as the discussion below indicates, one of the main decisions in this context,[291] finding the output of *Playboy TV* not to be 'obscene', suggests that the average citizen is deemed to be a relatively sophisticated and tolerant viewer. However, using 'offensiveness' as the test, is, in some respects, as problematic as using the test of 'deprave and corrupt'. Granted, the area of unprotected speech is limited to speech likely to arouse, in contrast to the position under British law,[292] but, even so, a legal test determining the protection of expression based purely on its patently offensive nature is both potentially very broad and runs directly counter to the basic principle that offence is not a valid reason for denying free speech. On its face, US obscenity law is much closer to English indecency law, which *is* based upon offence, but which is only concerned with the public display of offensive material.[293]

Notably, obscene speech falls outside the First Amendment altogether. Where sexually explicit speech is considered not obscene it may be regulated 'only where the restriction advances a substantial government interest in a proportionate manner and does not inadvertently chill political speech'.[294] This notion, as Cram explains, is

---

[289] Barendt, op cit, at 368.   [290] See above at 431.

[291] *United States v Playboy Entertainment Group Ltd*, 529 US 803 (2000).   [292] See above at 424.

[293] See below at 467 *et seq.*

[294] I. Cram, 'Beyond Madison? The US Supreme Court and the Regulation of Sexually Explicit Expression' [2002] *Public Law* 743, at 747.

based on the perception that sexually explicit speech may convey 'messages' about sex or sexual conduct that are at odds with the 'official' view, or which 'challenge prevailing norms'. It was on this basis, as he explains, that the Supreme Court struck down the MacKinnon/Dworkin-inspired Indianapolis anti-pornography ordinance, since it 'attempted to establish and enforce an approved view of women and relations between the sexes, which violated the First Amendment'.[295]

As an example of a Supreme Court ruling on non-obscene but explicit speech, Cram discusses the decision in *United States v Playboy Entertainment Group Ltd.*[296] The case concerned a challenge by the Playboy Group to an Act requiring cable operators to limit transmission of sexually explicit programmes to the time between 10pm and 6am, in order to protect children. The Court found the statute to be overbroad in its restriction upon expression, and therefore unconstitutional and void. First, there was research showing that, prior to the Act, 30–50 per cent of such programming was viewed before 10pm, so that there would, the Court found, be a substantial interference with adult autonomy once such viewing became impossible under the Act. Second, the majority reasoned that a less restrictive interference with the expression in question was available that could achieve the desired aim of protecting children, namely the ability of parents to opt out of the programming by means of a request to their cable operator.

The dissent, as Cram points out, took a very different view. It firstly found the material to be lacking an obviously informational character, and therefore to have a relatively low speech value. Second, it stressed that the content was, in any event, not banned, but merely restricted to the hours between 10pm and 6am, when it could be presumed that only adults would be viewing. Third, the minority, focusing closely upon the practical realities, found that the parental opt-out was not, as claimed by the majority, an effective way of protecting children. They cited research showing that 5 million children were left without parental supervision at home every week and pointed out, moreover, that the exercise of the opt-out relied upon a number of factors, including parental awareness of the right to exercise it, knowledge or suspicion that their children were watching the explicit programmes and 'a prompt response from cable operators to a blocking request', something which could not, apparently, be relied upon. This reasoning, in its combination of a rigorous, evidence-based proportionality, together with a realistic appraisal of the relatively low value of the speech in question, seems attractive. The approach of the majority, in contrast, is startling in comparison to the approach in this area of English judges: it reveals a clear preparedness to risk children coming into contact with sexually explicit material, in order to avoid interfering with adult autonomy. It also reveals that the judges afforded a relatively high level of protection to what was plainly speech inspired primarily by profit, with no pretensions to artistic or other merit. Perhaps of most interest, in terms of the themes of this book, is that the case concerns the use of free speech arguments

---

[295] Ibid, at 747.
[296] 529 US 803 (2000). We are indebted to Cram, op cit, for the discussion of the decision that follows.

by a major, powerful corporate player, purely, it is contended, in order to further its commercial position.[297] In treating the Playboy Group as equivalent to an individual speaker seeking to protect her freedom of expression, the Supreme Court lapsed into formalism of a particularly unhelpful sort. Whether the case had very much to do with free expression, in human rights terms, must be doubted.

THE CANADIAN POSITION

Introduction

The Canadian approach has firmly disclaimed the protection of 'morality', in the old-fashioned and still British sense of the word, as its focus. Rather, the focus is upon material that may cause harm to society, in various ways, one of which is to expose certain classes of its members, particularly women, to dehumanization, with a concomitant damage to their actual equality in society, as well as encouraging the development of truly deviant forms of sexuality that could cause real harm to others (for example, encouragement of non-consensual sexual fantasies). It was to an extent inspired by the analysis of pornography by MacKinnon and Dworkin, and their definition of pornography is therefore worth noting:

[Pornography is] the graphic sexually explicit subordination of women through pictures and/or words that also includes one or more of the following: (i) women are presented dehumanized as sexual objects, things, or commodities; or (ii) women are presented as sexual objects who enjoy pain or humiliation; or (iii) women are presented as sexual objects who experience sexual pleasure in being raped; or (iv) women are presented as sexual objects tied up or cut up or mutilated or bruised or physically hurt; or (v) women are presented in postures of sexual submission, servility or display; or (vi) women's body parts—including but not limited to vaginas, breasts, and buttocks—are exhibited, such that women are reduced to those parts; or (vii) women are presented as whores by nature; or (viii) women are presented being penetrated by objects or animals; or (ix) women are presented in scenarios of degradation, injury, torture, shown as filthy or inferior, bleeding, bruised or hurt in a context that makes these conditions sexual.[298]

This analysis informed the Indianapolis Ordinance put forward by MacKinnon and Dworkin.[299] Note in particular '(v) women are presented in postures of sexual submission, servility or *display*'. Virtually all erotic photography, including that shown in relatively 'respectable' magazines, such as *GQ*, *FHM* etc, show women in postures of 'sexual . . . display'. The ordinance was not, therefore, narrowly tailored. Note also that the definition is, on its face, directly discriminatory: it does not catch any depictions of men, however degrading, offensive, or violent. These points may be noted in

---

[297] See further Chapter 1 at 23.

[298] C.A. MacKinnon, 'Pornography, Civil Rights, and Speech, 20 *Harvard Civil Rights-Civil Liberties L.R.* 1.

[299] As noted above, its constitutionality was successfully challenged on the grounds of incompatibility with the First Amendment. For the first instance decision, see *American Booksellers Assoc, etc v Hudnitt III, Mayor, City of Indianapolis* et al, 598 F Supp 1316. For the (unsuccessful) appeal, see 771 F 2d 323.

relation to the discussion below of the conception of pornography developed by Canadian judges, when proceeding from a not dissimilar underlying philosophical approach. It should be noted that the ordinance did *not* impose criminal sanctions, unlike Canadian law, but would have given rise to claims in civil liability by women against pornographers for provable harm.

Canadian law, under the influence of the MacKinnon and Dworkin strand of feminist thinking, rejected the traditional 'moral' approach to obscenity law. Sopinka J for the majority said in *R v Butler*:[300]

I agree with Twaddle J.A. of the Court of Appeal that [the objective of preventing moral harm] is no longer defensible in view of the *Charter*. To impose a certain standard of public and sexual morality, solely because it reflects the conventions of a given community, is inimical to the exercise and enjoyment of individual freedoms, which form the basis of our social contract.[301]

The statutory test which the Supreme Court was considering was as follows:

For the purposes of this Act, any publication a dominant characteristic of which is the undue exploitation of sex, or of sex and any one or more of the following subjects, namely, crime, horror, cruelty and violence, shall be deemed to be obscene.[302]

The Canadian Courts were seeking to go beyond the UK approach, which was implicitly criticized in *Brodie v the Queen*,[303] where the court referred to 'tests which have some certainty of meaning and are capable of objective application and which do not so much depend as before upon the idiosyncrasies and sensitivities of the tribunal of fact, whether judge or jury'.[304] Wright J in *Butler* was of the view that legislation which seeks to proscribe a fundamental freedom must have as its objective a more precise purpose than simply to control the morals of society or to encourage decency. He said:

The aim must be directed more specifically to objectives such as equality concerns, or other Charter rights, or particular human rights; otherwise, the basic freedoms in the Charter will be subject to restrictions that arise from very personal and subjective opinions of right and wrong that will be impossible to identify. . . . Examples of more precise aims or bases for restrictions will be . . . the prevention of the circulation of pornographic material that effectively reduces the human or equality or other Charter rights of individuals. This may arise, and often will arise, in material that mixes sex with violence or cruelty, or otherwise dehumanizes women or men.[305]

The question, as ever, was where to draw the line between merely sexually explicit material, which is not likely to reach children, or be thrust upon unwilling or unwarned recipients, and material which promotes harm. At first instance in *Butler*, Wright J drew what was an explicable and relatively easy to apply distinction:

---

[300] [1992] 1 SCR 452, 492.   [301] Ibid.   [302] Section 163, Canadian Criminal Code.
[303] [1962] S.C.R. 681.   [304] Ibid, at 702.
[305] (1989), 50 C.C.C. (3d) 97, at 121. Wright J also gave as permissible aims: '(1) The protection of people from involuntary exposure to pornographic material; [i.e. public indecency concerns] and (2) The protection of the vulnerable, for example children, from either exposure or participation.'

Applying these standards . . . only those materials which contained scenes involving violence or cruelty intermingled with sexual activity or depicted lack of consent to sexual contact or otherwise could be said to dehumanize men or women in a sexual context were legitimately proscribed under s 1.[306]

On the non-obscene side of the equation, he boldly placed virtually all other forms of pornography:

I am unable to conclude that the depiction of the human body or any of its parts, no matter how explicitly presented, or the visual presentation of masturbation, group sex or other heterosexual or homosexual activity, including incestuous relations, *prima facie* relate to sufficiently specific concerns which are pressing and substantial in a free and democratic society to justify restricting or limiting the basic freedom permitting them to be expressed. The same reasoning applies in respect of the material before the court described as sexual toys or devices.[307]

The advantage of this approach is its relative simplicity or predictability; rather than relying simply upon the view taken by 12 random persons, or magistrates (the English law approach) or of some more abstract notion of degrading or dehumanizing portrayals of (generally) women, these categories of proscribed material are *relatively* easy to apply. When the case came to the Supreme Court, however, Sopinka J upheld a more expansive definition of pornography:

Pornography can be usefully divided into three categories: (1) explicit sex with violence, (2) explicit sex without violence but which subjects people to treatment that is degrading or dehumanizing, and (3) explicit sex without violence that is neither degrading nor dehumanizing.[308]

Justice Sopinka went on:

The courts must determine as best they can what the community would tolerate others being exposed to on the basis of the degree of harm that may flow from such exposure. Harm in this context means that it predisposes persons to act in an anti-social manner as, for example, the physical or mental mistreatment of women by men, or, what is perhaps debatable, the reverse. Anti-social conduct for this purpose is conduct which society formally recognizes as incompatible with its proper functioning. The stronger the inference of a risk of harm the lesser the likelihood of tolerance. The inference may be drawn from the material itself or from the material and other evidence. Similarly evidence as to the community standards is desirable but not essential.[309]

Sopinka J then cited the Report on Pornography by the Standing Committee on Justice and Legal Affairs;[310] the influence of feminist thought on the Committee's findings are plain:

The clear and unquestionable danger of this type of material is that it reinforces some unhealthy tendencies in Canadian society. The effect of this type of material is to reinforce

---

[306] Ibid.   [307] Ibid, at 124–5.   [308] Op cit, at 484.   [309] Op cit, at 454.
[310] (MacGuigan Report) (1978), at p 18:4.

male-female stereotypes to the detriment of both sexes. It attempts to make degradation, humiliation, victimization, and violence in human relationships appear normal and accept-able. A society which holds that egalitarianism, non-violence, consensualism, and mutuality are basic to any human interaction, whether sexual or other, is clearly justified in controlling and prohibiting any medium of depiction, description or advocacy which violates these principles.[311]

Problematizing the Canadian position

Such aims on their face sound far more appealing to human rights lawyers than the old-fashioned moralism of UK law. However, when they are examined more closely, a number of thorny questions immediately arise. If society is justified in 'controlling and prohibiting *any* . . . . advocacy' which violates the principle of 'egalitarianism, non-violence and consensualism' then is it not justified in outlawing any expression of strongly sexist, or homophobic, views? Do conservative Muslim clerics who con-demn homosexuality as 'an abomination' and call for the death penalty for sodomy not fall within the above definition?[312] Or utterances by the Christian Right, which call for women to obey their husbands and stay in the home? Canadian law does not at present makes the propagation of misogynistic, or homophobic, views, whether by religious leaders or otherwise, an offence. Why then is the direct propagation of misogynistic or homophobic views permitted, whereas the implication of such atti-tudes in sexually explicit material is not? Is misogyny acceptable provided there is no sex involved? It is no answer to say that such speech is permitted because it is 'political speech', which has a higher level of protection. Such speech appears to amount to a fundamental attack upon basic constitutional values, which under both Canadian[313] and Strasbourg expression law, may be proscribed.[314] Harel describes the MacKinnon/ Dworkin feminist argument as follows:

The subordination of women in pornographic literature is an example of speech that may be characterized as non-political but which clearly conveys political-ideological messages and values. The sexist values pornography reinforces do not remain within the viewer's mind: they extend to his bedroom, to the ways he treats his wife and his employees; they infect his pattern of voting and may determine which policies he supports. Sexism conveyed in pornography penetrates all dimensions of life, including the paradigmatically political dimension.[315]

This, of course, is an empirical claim. It also begs the question as to why a citizen may spend all day writing newspaper articles or distributing pamphlets which claim that

---

[311] Cited at *Butler*, op cit, at 492–3.

[312] For example, Dr Yusuf al-Qaradawi, controversially invited to speak in London by Mayor Livingstone, has denounced homosexuality as 'perverted' and 'abominable'. He has called it an 'aberration' and an 'unnatural, foul and illicit practice', rightly punishable by death in Islamic states. Source: http://www.petertatchell.net/religion/qaradawi.htm. It may be noted that a number of Islamic states currently invoke the death penalty for homosexual acts.

[313] *R v Keegstra* [1995] 2 SCR 381.   [314] See e.g. *Norwood v UK* (2005) 40 EHRR SE11.

[315] A. Harel, 'Bigotry, Pornography and the First Amendment: A Theory of Unprotected Speech', 65 (1992) 65 *S. Cal L.Rev* 1887, 1897.

women are inferior to men and should be confined to the home, and yet may not distribute materials that only tenuously and indirectly convey a sexist message, but which are sexually explicit.

It may further be asked: who is to judge the 'message' of explicit sadomasochistic pornography, which depicts the women it describes as aroused by taking on a sexually submissive role, a not uncommon phenomenon? Should it be those women who have this orientation, who might describe it as enormously liberating and fulfilling? Or should it be those who find this form of pornography incomprehensible and repulsive, and therefore label it 'degrading and dehumanizing'? As Pat Califa says: 'The things that seem beautiful, inspiring and life-affirming to me seem ugly, hateful, and ludicrous to most other people.'[316] This might be viewed, and many in the radical lesbian S/M community would view it, as another example of the imposition of moral majoritarian views on a small, unpopular, and misunderstood minority, analogous to the view taken of homosexuality, which was only relatively recently decriminalized.

As seen above, the test used in Canada asks whether a publication is likely to encourage anti-social behaviour.[317] But is, for example, consensual sado-masochistic, or dominant/submissive play, 'anti-social conduct'? Some level of sado-masochistic sexual activity is permitted by law in Canada. In the UK, the line is drawn (roughly speaking) at behaviour that causes actual bodily harm, although the decision that set this limit[318] has been subject to much criticism. If the conduct itself is not illegal, then it is not necessarily clear that an explicit film that depicts and may be seen to encourage it should be illegal. If presenting sexual violence in an attractive way is opposed to fundamental constitutional values, what should be said of films that are simply violent, which associate extreme graphic violence with glamour, with characters presented as sympathetic, and which place extreme violence in no moral context?[319] It appears somewhat strange that such films tend to be lawful, whereas a graphic film of, for example, *The Story of O*, would not be, even though the acts it depicted would be far less anti-social than the acts portrayed in the violent films instanced. The association between sex and violence in the visual media, *and* the tendency to allow extreme forms of the latter but not the former is one that is readily open to question. It may be noted that *The Story of O* is in fact one of the books that has been seized by Canadian customs authorities as obscene, along with works by internationally acclaimed authors such as Marguerite Duras, *The Man Sitting in the Corridor*, Jean Genet, *Querelle*; Jane Rule, *Contract With the World* and *The Young in One Another's Arms*; Sarah Schulman, *Girls, Visions, and Everything*; Dorothy Allison, *Trash*; Joe Orton, *Prick Up Your Ears*; Kathy Acker, *Empire of the Senseless*.[320]

---

[316] *Macho Sluts*, Los Angeles: Angelo Books, 1988, 'Introduction' at 9. Pat Califa is a lesbian sado-masochistic writer.

[317] Op cit, at 454.   [318] *R v Brown* [1993] 2 All ER 75.

[319] We have already mentioned as examples such fashionable films as the *Kill Bill* series, *Sin City*, *Natural Born Killers*, and *Pulp Fiction*.

[320] See *The New York Times*: 'Canada's Morals Police: Serious Books at Risk?' There is a relatively 'soft porn' film of *Story of O* which has recently shown for the first time on television by Film Four.

Gonthier and L'Heureux-Dube JJ in *Butler* added that some material in their category 3 (above)—non-dehumanizing (or violent) sexually explicit representation—may be obscene, depending upon its mode or manner of representation to the public.[321] Gonthier J instanced an explicit scene of a couple making love on a billboard, pointing out that it would be unexceptionable in a book, more problematic in a magazine, but downright unacceptable in that context. Many would accept this conclusion, but his reasoning—that it takes sex out of its context and thus distorts it[322]—is surely highly questionable. A book could do this. Rather, it is surely the fact that the viewer—the passer-by, that is, is deprived of any choice as to whether to view the material: it is thrust in front of his or her gaze. Moreover, the enforced viewing of a pornographic image, particularly for a woman, perhaps surrounded by men, is liable directly to engender feelings of humiliation, embarrassment, degradation, in the way that it could not if she either viewed the material privately or, *a fortiori*, if it was simply viewed by some men in private, without her knowledge, as is likely to be the case, people generally being desirous of keeping their predilection for pornography private.

A key question, clearly, is—whose standards are to be used to judge as to those categories of pornography to be proscribed? In relation to the three categories outlined above,[323] Justice Sopinka held:

Some segments of society would consider that all three categories of pornography cause harm to society because they tend to undermine its moral fibre. Others would contend that none of the categories cause harm. Furthermore, there is a range of opinion as to what is degrading or dehumanizing . . . Because this is not a matter that is susceptible of proof in the traditional way and because we do not wish to leave it to the individual tastes of judges, we must have a norm that will serve as an arbiter in determining what amounts to an undue exploitation of sex. That arbiter is the community as a whole.[324]

The obvious problem, of course, is that 'the community as a whole' consists in fact of a fractured range of diverse voices and views. Any notion that 'the community' can be expressed through the views of the judges is very doubtful. Inevitably it will be the judicial view of what 'the community' can tolerate that will in fact be used as the standard. It also seems odd that the actual, current standards of tolerance are used as the legal test; this means that rather than the law setting a standard of tolerance, it simply follows its perception of that of the average Canadian. This seems a strangely majoritarian view of human rights protection: courts are there not to protect inoffensive speech, which is not under threat in any event, but precisely that speech that does 'offend, shock or disturb' the average citizen. The noble idea of re-orienting the law on obscenity around the protection of fundamental constitutional values seems at this point to be in danger of collapsing into the reinforcement of majoritarian proclivities.

---

[321] Op cit, at 518–19.   [322] Op cit, at 518–19.

[323] '(1) explicit sex with violence, (2) explicit sex without violence but which subjects people to treatment that is degrading or dehumanizing, and (3) explicit sex without violence that is neither degrading nor dehumanizing' (*Butler*, op cit, at 484).

[324] Ibid.

The overall question that arises, then, is whether the Canadian position escapes being simply that of moral censorship in new dress. Ferg J, for example, addressed the notion that one type of obscenity lies in the dehumanization or degradation of women in *R v Ramsingh*.[325] The judge described in graphic terms the type of material that qualified for this label.

Among other things, degrading or dehumanizing materials place women (and sometimes men) in positions of subordination, servile submission or humiliation. They run against the principles of equality and dignity of all human beings. In the appreciation of whether material is degrading or dehumanizing, the appearance of consent is not necessarily determinative. Consent cannot save materials that otherwise contain degrading or dehumanizing scenes. Sometimes the very appearance of consent makes the depicted acts even more degrading or dehumanizing. This type of material would, apparently, fail the community standards test not because it offends against morals but because it is perceived by public opinion to be harmful to society, particularly to women. While the accuracy of this perception is not susceptible of exact proof, there is a substantial body of opinion that holds that the portrayal of persons being subjected to degrading or dehumanizing sexual treatment results in harm, particularly to women and therefore to society as a whole . . .'[326] It would be reasonable to conclude that there is an appreciable risk of harm to society in the portrayal of such material.[327]

Such material is objected to because it portrays women as '. . . exploited, portrayed as desiring pleasure from pain, by being humiliated and treated only as an object of male domination sexually, or in cruel or violent bondage'.[328] The difficulty here is that there is a large body of literature, some literary, such as *The Story of O*, or de Sade's *Juliette*, that precisely portrays women in this way. There is also a huge 'sub-culture' literature, which portrays the undoubted proclivities of at least a proportion of the population towards dominance or submission in sexuality, combined with lesser or greater degrees of sado-masochism.[329] The internet teems with chat-rooms in which individuals explore such desires. Much of this literature may awaken latent desires in the readers to be treated, or to treat others, in sado-masochism fashion. It is not clear that the legality of the material should turn on the fact that it is presented in print rather than in video format. If the ideas themselves are thought to be illegitimate, and to run against core Charter (liberal democratic) principles, much in the way that the avowal of openly racist or pro-Nazi views would do, then what is the basis for permitting literary works or, say, 'blogs' describing personal experience of such activities as intensely enjoyable or arguing for the legitimacy of such activities? As Harel puts it:

---

[325] (1984), 14 C.C.C. (3d) 230 (Man. Q.B.).

[326] See also: Attorney General's Commission on Pornography (the 'Meese Commission'), *Final Report* (U.S., 1986), vol. 1, at pp 938–1035; Metro Toronto Task Force on Public Violence Against Women and Children, *Final Report* (1984), at p 66; *Report of the Joint Select Committee on Video Material* (Australia, 1988), at pp 185–230; *Pornography: Report of the Ministerial Committee of Inquiry into Pornography* (New Zealand, 1988), at pp 38–45.

[327] Op cit, at 479.   [328] *R v Ramsingh* (1984), 14 C.C.C. (3d) 230 (Man. Q.B.)

[329] For example, the *Nexus* series of novels, generally concerned with sexually submissive women, at sale in virtually all bookshops in the UK.

But when the arguments [against sexually explicit 'hate speech'] are scrutinized, they often justify even broader restrictions than those advanced by their advocates. The plausibility and force of the arguments often rely upon the initial, arbitrarily limited scope of the proposed restriction, but the logical implications extend well beyond that scope.[330]

This may be seen particularly clearly if we return to the conclusions of The Standing Committee Report on pornography, which said:

A society which holds that egalitarianism, non-violence, consensualism, and mutuality are basic to any human interaction, whether sexual or other, is clearly justified in controlling and prohibiting *any medium of depiction, description or advocacy* which violates these principles.[331]

This comes very close to saying that there are basic principles which simply may not be gainsaid, even in terms of rational argument: something that could be termed a form of totalitarian defence of liberalism. As suggested above, these dicta appear to draw no distinction between visual and written material, nor between sexually explicit and non-explicit expression. In this respect, Ronald Dworkin[332] cites a key passage in *R v Butler*:

The proliferation of materials which seriously offend the values fundamental to our society is a substantial concern which justifies restricting the otherwise full exercise of the freedom of expression.

He comments:

That is an amazing statement. It is the central, defining, premise of freedom of speech that the offensiveness of ideas, or the challenge they offer to traditional ideas, cannot be a valid reason for censorship; once that premise is abandoned it is difficult to see what free speech means.

Barendt, similarly, argues that the censorship approved in the *Butler* case is straight-forward content-based censorship, flowing from judicial disapproval of the message of the 'speech':

The portrayal of women in, say, sexually submissive poses is treated as a harm society is entitled to avert, precisely because it is wrong to regard women in this light. That is a moral view or perspective, reflecting contemporary standards of gender equality. In comparison, speech disparaging, say, vegetarians or meat-eaters would not be treated as occasioning harm, because there is no conventional moral view that such attacks infringe any widely shared moral perspective concerning the position of vegetarians or their opponents. It is hard in fact to see how this version of the harm rationale adds anything to the inadmissible argument that society is entitled to preserves its moral values against challenge.[333]

Professor Moon has argued that in *Butler*, '[judicial] subjectivity (value judgment) is

---

[330] Op cit, at 1903.   [331] Cited op cit, at 473.
[332] 'The Coming Battles over Free Speech' (1992) 39(11), *New York Review of Books*.
[333] Op cit, at 380.

simply dressed up in the objective garb of community standards'.[334] Another (female) Canadian commentator remarks: 'Feminists who rejected outdated "morality-based" censorship had, perhaps inadvertently, given the authorities a new justification to repress sexual material that went outside normative bounds.'[335]

The Canadian route to reform: evaluation. Are these commentators right? Is the Canadian position, while more attractive than the British one, just a form of moral censorship in new dress? A number of points may be made, bearing in mind our discussion of the feminist position above, which has much in common with the Canadian position. First, it is established that it is acceptable under Article 10 ECHR and in English law to proscribe direct attempts to stir up racial hatred.[336] As discussed in the succeeding chapter, the UK Parliament has recently passed legislation prohibiting stirring up religious hatred.[337] Given that one's gender is not a matter of choice,[338] whereas one's religious beliefs are (at least to an extent), it might seem in principle acceptable also to have a law that in some way sought to proscribe attempts to stir up hatred against women. Certain kinds of pornography could be viewed as effectively inciting sexual violence (generally against women). Ronald Dworkin would not accept this, since it would be a content-based restriction on speech, but as Europeans we would not find the idea wholly alien. The difficulty that remains is one we have raised earlier: if we believe that such a message should simply be unacceptable, why is it only proscribed when it is, as it were, transmitted through sexually explicit material? Whilst it is true that one of the major forms of discrimination that women suffer is sexual violence and harassment, there are other major areas of disadvantage: domestic violence,[339] discrimination in the work place unrelated to sexuality,[340] pay inequality, pensions inequality, and so on. Why single out sexually explicit literature that implicitly advocates hatred or unequal treatment of women to be proscribed? As discussed earlier, a wide range of types of expression, including women's magazines, advertising, mainstream films, and television contribute to the notion that women should be valued in large part for being attractive and slim, with probable damaging effects upon millions of girls and women, but no-one even considers restricting or banning them.[341] As a society, we are a long way from banning sexist speech and/or images, whether it be promulgated by religious leaders, magazines such as *Glamour*, conservative politicians, or men's lifestyle magazines, such as *FHM*. While publications such as *FHM* are the subject of feminist criticism, no-one suggests banning them: yet the

---

[334] *R v Butler*: The Limits of the Supreme Court's Feminist Re-Interpretation of Section 163' (1993), 25 *Ottawa L. Rev.* 361, at 370.

[335] Z. Margulis, 'Canada's Thought Police', *Wired Magazine*, 1995.

[336] For discussion of the relevant law, see Chapter 9 at 513–16.

[337] For discussion, see Chapter 9 at 516–27.

[338] Save, to an extent, in the exceptional cases of transsexuals who have undergone gender reassignment.

[339] We are not of course discounting the fact of male rape and also domestic violence directed by women against men; our point is simply that both rape and domestic violence are disproportionately suffered by women, to a very significant degree.

[340] As well as sexualized discrimination, e.g. sexual harassment.

[341] Some practical reasons why this is the case are conceded and discussed above at 406.

'message' of female 'sexual display'—to quote MacKinnon and Dworkin's ordin-ance[342]—is the same whether or not the model is naked or wearing underwear. It is at this point that we believe a confusion or cross-over has occurred between old-fashioned notions of decency or morality and the new values of equality and dignity. The result is that pornography is (to some) arbitrarily selected out of the great mass of sexist and harmful speech going on around us, to be criminalized.

A further objection relates to the enormous discretion that such laws inevitably vest in police, prosecuting authorities, and magistrates. As one Canadian commentator puts it: '*Butler*'s more dramatic flaw is that police are left to determine the boundaries between freedom and constraint, between expression and degradation.'[343] This reminds us that, however noble the aim of a law may be, its actual enforcement will rest in the hands of those who may well turn it to regressive and/or discriminatory ends, as was found to have occurred in Canada in the *Little Sisters Bookshop* case.[344] The owners of a lesbian and gay bookshop, which carried a range of sexually explicit material aimed at the gay community generally, complained that erotica destined for their shop, which was imported from the US, was routinely and wrongfully inter-cepted by Customs officials. It was found that:

Customs officials had wrongly delayed, confiscated, destroyed, damaged, prohibited or misclassified materials imported by the appellant bookstore on numerous occasions, but that these errors were caused by the 'systemic targeting' of the store's importations.[345]

As Binnie J for the majority found:

The administration of the [customs legislation] . . . was characterized by conduct of Customs officials that was oppressive and dismissive of the appellants' freedom of expression. Its effect—whether intended or not—was to isolate and disparage the appellants on the basis of their sexual orientation.[346]

In short, as the trial judge found in that case, 'untrained Customs officials were too quick to equate homosexuality with obscenity'. Plainly, the more broad and open-ended the definitions used by the law are, the more discretion is vested in the enforcement authorities: a definition that uses words such as 'degrade or dehumanize' is wide open to abuse, just because such judgments will inevitably be coloured by the personal standards and tastes of the individuals making the judgments.

We believe that the discussion above reveals the Canadian approach—and the feminist thinking on which it is based—to be highly problematic, both in theory and in terms of practical implementation. Given, however, that this is an area in which *all* positions seem to be open to objection, we nevertheless consider that there may be room for a narrow and selective approach to the regulation of certain kinds of porn-ography, based broadly upon 'equality' principles rather than on 'moral' concerns.

---

[342] The definition of pornography includes images in which: '. . . (v) women are presented in postures of sexual submission, servility or display': for the full definition, see above note 298.

[343] Z. Margulis, 'Canada's Thought Police', op cit.

[344] *Little Sisters Book and Art Emporium and ors v Canada (Minister of Justice)* [2000] 2 SCR 1120, at [37].

[345] Ibid (headnote).   [346] Ibid, at [40].

Five possible justifications for such an approach come to mind. The first is that pornography may often be equated with commercial speech, where it is apparent that its *primary* aim is profit-making.[347] As Sopinka J noted in *Butler*:

In my view, the kind of expression which is sought to be advanced does not stand on an equal footing with other kinds of expression which directly engage the 'core' of the freedom of expression values. This conclusion is further buttressed by the fact that the targeted material is expression which is motivated, in the overwhelming majority of cases, by economic profit.[348]

Such expression, like advertising, is generally given less protection under free speech guarantees.[349] While it may carry an implicit message, it is peripheral, in the same way that advertising may carry various messages about lifestyles and values underneath the specific brand promotion.[350] Where the pornography in question was the product of a small enterprise, aimed at a minority, and intended partly at least to provide materials sustaining and affirming the sexual identity of that minority, it could be classified differently, as speech with a genuine communicative content. Equality principles would not be violated by permitting publications which had that role. It may be recalled that Raz[351] argues that one important function of free expression in the area of lifestyles, rather than politics, is to 'validate' the styles of life portrayed. Conversely, censorship is not only an 'insult' to the persons leading the lifestyle censored—a point which sounds very like Dworkin's argument for freedom of expression based on equal respect for citizens[352]—but it also, in a more instrumental vein, denies those living the lifestyle the opportunity for reassurance, the sense that they are not alone in their lifestyle and its problems, and also the chance for the public to learn about the widest possible range of lifestyles, thus maximizing their freedom of choice.[353] This argument seems particularly apt in relation to sexual minorities. One of the arguments put forward by Lesbian and Gay groups to the Canadian Supreme Court in the *Little Sisters* case was that pornography is particularly important for homosexuals, since it affirms and celebrates their sexuality, and may assist them in developing it, in a hostile or unsympathetic, certainly heterosexual-dominated, environment.[354] Lucy Williams has argued that 'pornography depicting "perversions" (e.g., butch/femme lesbian sex, BD and SM, and bisexuality) should not be censored since viewing it may help to raise important and useful questions about the characterization of sexual normality and the standard categories of sexual practice that are used to discuss these

---

[347] Of course magazines such as *Vogue*, *Glamour*, and *FHM* are also run to make a profit, as are newspapers, but it could plausibly be claimed that they have a wide variety of other purposes.

[348] Op cit, at 500–1.   [349] See Chapter 2 at 60–1.

[350] See the discussion in Chapter 20 at 1033–5.

[351] J. Raz, 'Free Expression and Personal Identification' (1991), 11(3) *OJLS* 303, 310. This rationale is discussed more generally in Chapter 1 at 18–20.

[352] R. Dworkin, 'Do we have a right to pornography?', in *A Matter of Principle*, Cambridge (Mass): Harvard University Press, 1985, at 272–4.

[353] Raz, op cit, at 312.

[354] *Little Sisters and Art Book Emporium v Canada* [2000] 2 SCR 1120, at [247].

questions.'[355] In other words, both the *status* of the producer of pornography—whether it is a mainstream, commercial company, like Playboy Group Second,[356] or, in contrast, a small, minority interest book store or film company, *and* the nature of the material in question may be taken into account. But in many cases, it may be relatively easy to conclude that the speech can be classified as commercial. If this is the case, it may be assigned a relatively low weight.

The second point we would wish to make is that perhaps the reason why the sexually explicit expression of, for example, misogynistic views of women is criminalized, but not its non-sexualized expression, is that the message is carried, as it were, subliminally—through the fusion of arousal and ideology: as MacKinnon puts it, 'the eroticisation of dominance and submission'.[357] While there is undoubted communicative content in some pornography, it is not put as an appeal to reason: possibly for this reason, it should attract less protection as a contribution to an ideological debate, albeit an offensive one. If pornography conveys its 'message' in an insidious way that arguments against it cannot combat, it becomes less susceptible to the principle that speech conveying an oppressive message is best combated not by censorship or the criminal law but by more speech. The *Stanford Encylopedia of Philosophy* claims:

Studies suggest, among other things, that exposure to violent pornography can significantly enhance a subject's arousal in response to the portrayal of rape, that exposure to films that depict sexual violence against women can act as a stimulus for aggressive acts against women, and that prolonged exposure to degrading pornography (of a violent or non-violent sort) leads to increased callousness towards victims of sexual violence, a greater acceptance of 'rape-myths' (for example, that women enjoy rape and do not mean no when they say 'no'), a greater likelihood of having rape-fantasies, and a greater likelihood of reporting that one would rape women or force women into unwanted sex acts if there was no chance of being caught.[358]

Clearly, the evidence from these studies is disputed by others, as discussed above;[359] what would probably be undisputed is that the effects that the studies claim are produced by viewing violent pornography would *not* be brought about by listening to reasoned argument or even skilful non-sexual propaganda seeking to inculcate the same attitudes. The point is that pornography acts in such a way so as to build an association between sexual arousal and violent or degrading treatment of women; that arousal may then overcome both moral and social inhibitions leading eventually to sexual violence or harassment. This may provide a rational ground for singling out sexually explicit material as requiring special controls.

The third point is that, as argued above,[360] the invasion of the moral autonomy of

[355] L. Williams, 'Pornographies on/scene, or diff'rent strokes for diff'rent folks', in Lynn Segal and Mary McIntosh (eds), *Sex Exposed: Sexuality and the Pornography Debate*, London: Virago Press, 1992, 233–65; see also her 'Second Thoughts on Hard Core: American Obscenity Law and the Scapegoating of Deviance', in Pamela Church Gibson and Roma Gibson (eds), *Dirty Looks: Women, Pornography and Power*, London: BFI Publishing, 1993, 46–61.
[356] See p 449 above.   [357] MacKinnon, 'Feminism unmodified', op cit.
[358] 'Pornography and Censorship', at [5.1].   [359] See 388–90.   [360] See 407.

the consumer whose freedom to view certain types of violent pornographic films is interfered with is of a relatively low order, compared with the interference with other, more weighty choices. Fourth, there is the clear *possibility* of a link between such pornography and the commission of sex crimes, of sexual harassment, abuse, and discrimination against women; these are weighty interests to be ranged against the permissive view, albeit only as possibly or probably present.[361] It does not appear that what may be termed non-violent pornography is linked with the nurturing and legitimization, in offenders' minds, of the desire for rape and violent sexual conduct, which could give a reason for singling out violent pornography.[362]

Fifth, while the justification for it may not be wholly convincing,[363] it is now widely accepted in many jurisdictions that different rules apply to the written word compared to the visual media.[364] If this is accepted in relation to sexually explicit material, as it is at present, then only the visual media will be affected by obscenity laws. Therefore, for those who want to experiment with, read, discuss, and explore the darker aspects of human sexuality, there is a medium open to them—fiction and written erotica, as well as the new forum of internet discussion sites. The drawing of such a distinction may not be wholly satisfactory in logic, but pragmatic solutions appear to be the only ones available. It does also equate to a rough proportionality argument: in responding to the possible danger posed by violent, sexually explicit expression, the state would be taking a measured and fairly minimal response, outlawing only what were seen as the most dangerous forms of that expression—films and photographs. Not only is there some evidence that these media have a greater impact upon those who view them,[365] films do, after all, require human actors to make, harm to whom is an issue to be considered, as discussed above.[366] Moreover, allowing the written word to be free in this respect would mean that the 'message' of those who participate in minority sexual communities could still be disseminated. Only the medium would be controlled. On the above arguments, a modified version of the Canadian position may be seen as perhaps the least unsatisfactory of those available. Whether some form of it could be adopted by UK judges, under the guise of the HRA by relying on Strasbourg jurisprudence, is the question to which we now turn.

OBSCENITY LAW: THE EFFECT OF THE HRA

Having surveyed UK law, the Strasbourg jurisprudence, and the alternative sources of inspiration available from Canada and the US, we may now consider the possible

---

[361] Depending upon the view taken on the available evidence.

[362] Of course, harms may flow from anti-egalitarian speech, e.g. stating publicly that homosexuality should be punished by death.

[363] See Chapter 10 at 563–5.

[364] For discussion, see Chapter 10 at 542–5. The exception, in relation to the obscenity laws, is Canada.

[365] See Chapter 12 at 633–5.

[366] See the discussion above as to the harm sometimes done to women participating in the making of pornographic films pp 391–2.

effect of the HRA on this area of domestic law. Clearly, any prosecutions under the 1959 Act or forfeiture actions constitute interferences with the Article 10 guarantee of freedom of expression under the HRA,[367] although subject to justification. In relation to any particular decision, the public authorities involved are bound by s 6 of the HRA to ensure that the tests under Article 10 are satisfied, while the provisions of the 1959 Act must be interpreted consistently with Article 10 under s 3 of the HRA. As Chapter 3 indicated, s 12 of the HRA does not apply to criminal proceedings. Forfeiture proceedings have the hallmarks of criminal proceedings in certain respects, although a conviction is not obtained, and therefore they are almost certainly outside the ambit of s 12.

It will already be apparent that the Strasbourg jurisprudence provides little clear impetus for change in the existing law. The decisions considered above at Strasbourg on the 1959 Act and the Swiss Law challenged in *Scherer*[368] and *Müller*[369] indicate that the statutory regime relating to publication of an obscene article under s 2 OPA is broadly in harmony with Article 10 of the European Convention. This was the approach recently taken in *Perrin*,[370] the only obscenity case so far to consider Article 10 in any detail. The defendant claimed that his conviction breached that guarantee; thus the Court was confronted directly with the necessity of evaluating domestic law against the guarantee of freedom of expression—it was given an opportunity, in other words, to break with the past. As discussed above, the major cases on the Act date from some time ago, and display attitudes that would in contemporary society appear both prudish and, in some cases, bigoted.[371] However, there are no dicta in *Perrin*, decided in 2002, to the effect that decisions of the appellate courts in the 1960s and 1970s must now be treated with caution, given the more plural, tolerant society we now live in and the revolution since that time in discrimination law and policy as applied to homosexuality. In making this point, it should be borne in mind that the material at issue in *Perrin*[372] was of quite an extreme pornographic nature and that material on the website made available only to adults was not found to be obscene. There is some consideration of the ECHR case law (and, perhaps surprisingly, of US jurisprudence), but it is very rapidly dismissed. Notably, Kennedy LJ, giving the judgment of the Court, directly relies upon pronouncements in *Müller* and *Otto Preminger* as to the wide margin of appreciation to be granted to national authorities in cases of offensive speech, without once adverting to the different position of itself, as a domestic court. Instead, his Lordship relies on *Kebeline*[373] and *HM Advocate v McIntosh*[374] as to the deference to be afforded to Parliament in difficult cases of balancing

---

[367] Except possibly in the case of certain very extreme forms of material—see below.

[368] See above at 413–15.   [369] See above at 416–18.

[370] (2002) WL 347127. See above at 431 for the facts; and Chapter 12 at 449–50 for further discussion.

[371] As in the frequent references to homosexuality as a 'perversion': see e.g. the examples in the quotes at the beginning of this chapter.

[372] See note 370 above.   [373] *R v DPP, ex parte Kebilene* [2000] 2 AC 326.

[374] [2001] UKPC D1.

individual rights and interests with societal concerns, effectively adopting the non-interventionist stance of the Strasbourg court. His Lordship's conclusion, in terms very similar to that used by the European Court, was that: 'Parliament was entitled to conclude that the prescription was necessary in a democratic society.'[375] The attenuated standard of review adopted by Strasbourg on the grounds of deference to European cultural diversity was thus applied *within* a particular jurisdiction by English judges to the British Parliament, in a textbook example of the misapplication of the margin of appreciation.[376] The lack of precise proportionality reasoning, as required by *Daly*,[377] is evident in the following, very general 'balancing' exercise:

No-one has argued that the protection of minors and other vulnerable people is not an important issue to be addressed. On the other side of the balance sheet, apart from the general right to freedom of expression, there is no public interest to be served by permitting a business for profit to supply material which most people would regard as pornographic or obscene.[378]

This decision, then, gives very little ground for optimism that the HRA may lead to a liberalization or rationalization of the law in this area.

Theoretically, however, the 1959 Act is open to a revised interpretation. It is plainly not one that flows directly from the HRA, because it does not proceed from the Strasbourg jurisprudence, but could be undertaken in accordance with the notion that the advent of Article 10 in UK law requires a new approach. The moral 'change for the worse' to be protected against could be taken by the judges to mean *not* the raising of libidinous thoughts or 'perverted' desires but rather, *inter alia*, the encouragement of harmful attitudes towards women, along the lines of the Canadian jurisprudence. There is in fact a hint of this in the domestic judgment in the *Hoare* decision. The Judge commented on the nature of the film in question:

You very rarely, if at all, saw the faces of the people, and one of the matters relied upon quite properly by the Crown here in saying to you that you should find these to . . . have a tendency to deprave and corrupt, is what is, perhaps you think, the utter dehumanisation of the people concerned, *particularly the women* . . .[379]

In other words, the test of whether the material could cause a moral change for the worse, which is itself left entirely at large by the wording of the Act, could be reinterpreted so that it asked whether the material in question is such as to undermine certain core constitutional values, such as respect for women, egalitarianism, and human dignity. The inspiration for such a change could clearly be drawn directly from the Canadian jurisprudence examined above. It could also be based on more general Strasbourg principles: there are indications that advocacy of positions directly opposed

---

[375] Op cit, at [52].   [376] See Chapter 3 at 145–51.

[377] *R v Secretary of State for the Home Department ex parte Daly* [2001] 2 WLR 1622. The UK Court's approach to proportionality is examined in detail in the subsequent chapter.

[378] Op cit, at [50].

[379] [1997] EHRLR 678, under 'A.—The Particular Circumstances of the Case' (emphasis added).

to foundational Convention values may fall outside the ambit of Article 10(1). In one recent decision[380] concerning a poster linking all Muslims with the 9/11 attacks, the Strasbourg Court remarked:

Such a general, vehement attack against a religious group, linking the group as a whole with a grave act of terrorism, is incompatible with the values proclaimed and guaranteed by the Convention, notably tolerance, social peace *and non-discrimination.*

Given that direct, abusive advocacy of racialist views was found to fall outside the scope of Article 10(1) in *Jersild v Denmark,*[381] it would not be a major step for a domestic judge to find that certain extreme forms of misogynistic pornography, such as those depicting the sexual torture and murder of women as described in the Government's consultation paper above,[382] were unprotected by Article 10 completely. More positively, such a notion of a 'constitutional' morality could be used as the touchstone for obscenity, substituting the current ad-hocery of jury determinations with a more consistent and principled test. Inspiration could be sought for *liberalizing* the law's stance towards very explicit but non-misogynistic or violent pornography from the famous dicta in *Handyside* to the effect that Article 10 covers offensive and shocking speech, and from the clear stance taken in favour of adult autonomy in *Scherer,* which should be applied to cases in which such material was effectively confined to access by consenting adults. This in fact appeared to be the approach taken in *Perrin* to the material on the website that was only accessible with a credit card, and therefore presumptively safely shielded from access by children.[383]

Acceptance of such a stance, however, would require a sophisticated judicial approach towards the Strasbourg jurisprudence, entailing awareness of the way in which the decisions in *Müller*[384] and *Otto Preminger*[385] wholly failed to apply any form of meaningful proportionality test. In contrast to these cases, a fairly rigorous investigation of proportionality was carried out by the Supreme Court of Canada in *Butler*—its conclusion was as follows: 'The final question to be answered in the proportionality test' is 'whether the effects of the law so severely trench on a protected right that the legislative objective is outweighed by the infringement.' As to this, the Court concluded:

The infringement on freedom of expression is confined to a measure designed to prohibit the distribution of sexually explicit materials accompanied by violence, and those without violence that are degrading or dehumanizing. As I have already concluded, this kind of expression lies far from the core of the guarantee of freedom of expression. It appeals only to the most base aspect of individual fulfilment, and it is primarily economically motivated. The objective of the legislation, on the other hand, is of fundamental importance in a free and democratic society. It is aimed at avoiding harm, which Parliament has reasonably concluded will be caused directly or indirectly, to individuals, groups such as women and children, and consequently to society as a whole, by the distribution of these materials. It

---

[380] *Norwood v UK* (2005) 40 EHRR SE11.   [381] (1994) 19 EHRR 1.   [382] See p 388.
[83] Op cit, at 109.   [384] Op cit.   [385] Op cit. See also Chapter 2, at 56–60.

thus seeks to enhance respect for all members of society, and non-violence and equality in their relations with each other. I therefore conclude that the restriction on freedom of expression does not outweigh the importance of the legislative objective.[386]

It would be refreshing to see reasoning such as the above imported into English law. As suggested above, the combination of the open-ended 'deprave and corrupt' test, the public good defence, and the ability to reinterpret the law using the HRA allows for the opportunity for this to take place, although it would be naïve to be optimistic about the prospects.

There is the possibility of a more specific effect of the HRA: it is plain from cases such as *Knuller* and *Jordan* that British judges and prosecutors have traditionally been much more likely to see gay pornography as obscene. However, under the HRA, restrictions upon freedom of expression must not only be necessary and proportionate under Article 10(2), they must also comply with Article 14, which provides for the enjoyment of Convention rights without discrimination.[387] In order for Article 14 to bite, the situation of the person claiming its protection must be 'within the ambit' of another Convention right,[388] in this case, Article 10. It appears plain that where the allegation was that gay pornography was being prosecuted or subject to forfeiture in an instance in which it appeared that heterosexual material of the same nature would not have been, Article 10 would be engaged, therefore activating the protection of Article 14. Assuming that no substantial justification could be found for it, less favourable treatment of gay pornography in comparison to its heterosexual equivalent would surely amount to a violation of the Article 14 rights of both the producers of the pornography, and, arguably, the gay consumers of it. The HRA could therefore at the very least have the effect of putting a stop to the openly homophobic approach taken by the judiciary in cases such as *Knuller*.

The UK forfeiture regime has not itself been tested at Strasbourg. The HRA requirements may be especially pertinent in relation to forfeiture: the magistrates conducting the proceedings are, of course, bound by Article 10 and therefore would be expected to approach the task with greater rigour. In particular, it is arguably necessary to examine each item, even where a large-scale seizure has occurred, rather than considering a sample of items only.[389] But since, in practice, a vast amount of material is condemned as obscene in legal actions for forfeiture, the practical difficulties facing magistrates make it possible, especially initially, that the impact of the HRA will be more theoretical than real. It seems probable that, in practice, magistrates will not examine each item and will give only cursory attention, if any, to considering the

---

[386] Op cit, at 509.

[387] Article 14 provides: 'The enjoyment of the rights and freedoms set forth in this Convention shall be secured without discrimination on any ground such as sex, race, colour, language, religion, political or other opinion, national or social origin, association with a national minority, property, birth or other status.'

[388] For a recent discussion of the application of this test, see R. Wintemute, ' "Within the Ambit": How Big *Is* the "Gap" in Article 14 European Convention on Human Rights?' [2004] *EHRLR* 366

[389] It was found that such sampling was acceptable in *Snaresbrook Crown Court ex p Comr of the Metropolis* (1984) 79 Cr App R 184. For discussion, see R. Stone [1986] *Crim LR* 139.

application of the somewhat elusive Strasbourg case law. However, if on occasion publishers seek to contest s 3 orders before a jury, the proportionality of the measures adopted may receive more attention.

INDECENCY OFFENCES[390]

The concept of indecency, as opposed to obscenity, is contained in certain statutes and also exists at common law. The idea of prohibiting indecency is, essentially, to prevent public displays of offensive material or the possibility that such material will impinge in some way on the general public, or a part of it. Such prohibition is aimed at protecting persons from the shock or offence occasioned by encountering certain material without consent, rather than at preventing moral deterioration. Therefore, except perhaps in a very broad sense, it may be said not to be aimed at the protection of morals and so might not fall within that exception to Article 10. The general lowering of moral standards or attacks on the moral fabric of society must occur—if it is assumed that it is likely to occur at all—through the medium of individual persons who are affected by encountering obscene material;[391] it would seem, therefore, that the 'moral fabric of society' would be unaffected by material which only serves to shock. However, it might be very broadly argued on a conservative view that indecent material might have a corrupting effect if it was repeatedly encountered because it might lead at each encounter to less outrage as sensibilities became blunted. In any event, the European Court of Human Rights has found that material which was, arguably, merely shocking, fell within the protection of morals exception. As appears above, Swiss Law plainly rests upon a notion of indecency, rather than obscenity, but was found to fall squarely within the protection of morals exception in *Müller v Switzerland.*[392]

Indecency is easier to prove than obscenity because there is no defence of public good, there is no need to consider the whole article, and there is no need to satisfy the difficult test of 'deprave and corrupt'. Prosecuting authorities have taken note of these distinctions and have therefore tended at times to rely on the law against indecency where, arguably, the article in question could be said to be obscene.[393] It will be seen that the existence of these two strands of law has led to some anomalies.

[390] See Robertson, op cit, Chapter 7; G. Robertson and A.G.L. Nichol, *Media Law*, London: Penguin, 1992, pp 115–24.

[391] For criticism of the view that preventing the lowering of the moral tone of society justifies censorship, see above at 394.

[392] (1988) 13 EHRR 212. See Chapter 2 at 56–60.

[393] This trend is reflected in Lord Denning's comments in *GLC ex parte Blackburn* [1976] 1 WLR 550, p 556.

THE TEST FOR 'INDECENCY'

The test for indecency was discussed in *Knuller v DPP*,[394] it was determined by Lord Reid that it was satisfied by material which creates outrage or utter disgust in 'ordinary decent-minded people'. This statement, coupled with the general tenor of Lord Reid's comments, suggests that the level of shock would have to be fairly high. In *GLC ex p Blackburn*,[395] Lord Denning approved the simple test, 'is this indecent?', since he considered that if jurors were asked the more complex question 'will it deprave and corrupt?' they would allow very offensive articles into circulation. It seems that the test is not confined to sexual material; Lord Reid in *Knuller* considered that 'indecency is not confined to sexual indecency'.[396] This is supported by the finding in *Gibson*,[397] considered below, that the use of freeze-dried foetuses as earrings on a model of a head was indecent.

Sir Robert Megarry has said that 'indecency' is too subjective and emotional a concept[398] to be workable as a legal test. In particular, uncertainty arises as to whether the term 'indecency' denotes a relative concept: a concept which, like that of relative obscenity, depends on its context or on the nature of the audience or recipient. According to the ruling of the Court of Appeal in *Straker*,[399] such considerations are irrelevant: indecency is an objective quality discoverable by examination in the same way that, for example, a substance might be discovered to be a certain chemical. However, *Wiggins v Field*[400] suggests otherwise; the ruling specifically demanded that the circumstances in which the alleged indecency occurred should be taken into account. A prosecution was brought in respect of a poem on the basis of a charge of using indecent language in contravention of a local bylaw. The judgment indicates the nature of the circumstances.

During the reading of the poem the word 'fuck' was read once by the defendant in a phrase 'Go fuck yourself with your atom bomb'. The poem was entitled 'America' and was written by the American poet Alan Ginsberg. The poem was a genuine work and had been published in both America and England. In England it was published in a Penguin and had been available to the public since 1964. The phrase in question appeared in the fifth line of a long poem and was the only time the word 'fuck' appeared in the poem.[401]

The Divisional Court held that if the context was considered—this was the work of a recognized poet, read without any intention of causing offence—the charge of indecency could not be supported. Lord Parker said:

whether a word or words is or are capable of being treated as indecent language must, as it seems to me, depend on all the circumstances of the case, what the occasion was when it was spoken, how it was spoken, in the course of what was it spoken, and maybe up to a

---

[394] [1973] AC 435, p 457; [1972] 3 WLR 143; (1972) 56 Cr App R 633.   [395] [1976] 3 All ER 184.
[396] [1973] AC 435, p 458.   [397] [1990] 2 QB 619; [1991] 1 All ER 439, CA.
[398] *A Second Miscellany at Law*, p 316.
[399] [1965] Crim LR 239; this approach was affirmed by the Court of Appeal in *Stamford* [1972] 2 WLR 1055; [1972] 2 All ER 427.
[400] [1968] Crim LR 50.   [401] Ibid.

certain extent what the intention was though that is certainly not conclusive. But in these circumstances there was a serious reading of a poem, and the justices went so far as to get the defendant to recite the relevant part to them to see if he, by gesture or emphasis or anything was exaggerating or drawing attention to the words; they came to the conclusion that there was nothing in the case and they dismissed it. I agree.[402]

A similar stance was taken by the Court of Appeal in *AG ex rel McWhirter v IBA*;[403] it was agreed that the film in question, 'taken as a whole', was not offensive, although a small percentage of it depicted indecent incidents. Thus it may be that the *Straker* ruling, to the effect that indecency may be treated as an objective concept, is confined to cases arising under what is now the Postal Services Act 2000,[404] but the point cannot yet be regarded as settled. However, it is clear that the notion of indecency will vary from generation to generation and that the jury will be expected to apply current standards.[405]

SPECIFIC STATUTORY OFFENCES

The word 'indecent' is contained in a number of statutes and bylaws. Therefore, only specific areas are covered, but if no statute affects a particular area, the gap may be filled by the common law. Taking an indecent photograph or film of a person under the age of 18 is prohibited under s 1 of the Protection of Children Act 1978 (as amended by the Sexual Offences Act 2003), as is possessing it with a view to sale, showing it, or distributing it. The only intention needed is the intention to take a photograph; whether the photograph is indecent depends on the view of the jury regarding recognized standards of propriety.[406] No artistic merits defence is available, although the distributor of the photographs, not the taker of them, can seek to show that he had a 'legitimate reason' for distributing or showing the photographs or for having them in his possession. Section 84 of the Criminal Justice and Public Order Act 1994 amended the 1978 Act to add 'pseudo-photographs' of children in order to cover digitally created photographs.[407] It also amended the Act so that the storage of data on computer disk or by other electronic means capable of conversion to a photograph is covered. Section 160 of the Criminal Justice Act 1988 created an additional offence of merely possessing the indecent picture of a child without a view to sale, display, or distribution. The offence under either the 1978 or the 1988 Act can be committed merely by downloading an image onto a computer;[408] automatic storage of an image on a hard disk would not amount to making a photograph or pseudo-photograph.[409] Further, it has been found that possession requires knowledge.[410]

---

[402] Ibid.   [403] [1973] QB 629.   [404] S 85; formerly under the Post Office Act 1953.

[405] *Shaw v DPP* [1962] AC 220, p 292. This approach was accepted in *Stamford* [1972] 2 WLR 1055; [1972] 2 All ER 427.

[406] *See R v Graham-Kerr* (1988) 88 Cr App R 302: this offence is discussed in Chapter 12 at 625–7 in relation to films.

[407] See further C. Manchester, 'Criminal Justice and Public Order Act 1994: obscenity, pornography and videos' [1995] *Crim LR* 123, pp 123–8.

[408] *R v Bowden* [2000] 2 All ER 418.   [409] *Atkins v DPP* [2000] 2 All ER 425.   [410] Ibid.

The breadth of these offences was illustrated when the Saatchi Gallery in London was threatened with prosecution in March 2001 for showing pictures of children playing naked on the beach, taken by their mother, a professional photographer, as what one commentator called 'a celebration of the wonderment and joie de vivre of her children'.[411] The prosecution did not materialize, apparently on the basis that no element of lewdness was present. Similarly, when the Mapplethorpe Exhibition was shown at the Hayward Gallery in London in Autumn 1996, the Gallery took legal advice owing to the sexually explicit nature of some of the exhibits. Prosecution under the 1959 and/or under the 1978 Act appeared to be a possibility. It decided not to show three photographs, one of which was of a child.[412]

Offensive displays fall under the Indecent Displays (Control) Act 1981.[413] The Act provides, under s1(1): 'If any indecent matter is publicly displayed the person making the display and any person causing or permitting the display to be made shall be guilty of an offence.' The Act provides in s 1(2) that 'Any matter which is displayed in or so as to be visible from any public place shall, for the purposes of this section, be deemed to be publicly displayed.' 'Public place' is then defined as 'any place to which the public have or are permitted to have access (whether on payment or otherwise) while that matter is displayed'.[414] There are various exceptions to the definition of 'public places': the Act does not apply to the theatre, cinema, broadcasting, museums, art galleries, local authority or Crown buildings (s 1(4)). Shops which display an adequate warning notice are exempted[415] as far as adults are concerned; thus, as will be seen below, art galleries are, anomalously, more constrained in their displays than sex shops, in that they will fall within the common law on indecency and will not be able to take advantage of this exception.

Mailing of obscene or indecent items is covered by section 85 of the Postal Services Act 2000;[416] sexual literature in luggage is covered by s 49 of the Customs and Excise Management Act 1979. In the 1970s, customs officials interpreted the term 'indecency' widely; in 1976, for example, they seized and destroyed 114,000 books and magazines and 4,000 films. It also appeared that the test was being used in an arbitrary and indiscriminate manner. For example, in 1985 books ordered by the bookshop 'Gay's the Word' were impounded, including books by Oscar Wilde and Gore Vidal. The trial was about to commence, but the proceedings were withdrawn because of the ruling of the European Court of Justice in *Conegate Ltd v Customs and Excise Comrs*.[417] It was held that under Article 36 of the Treaty of European Union[418] Britain could not apply a more stringent test—indecency—to imported goods when the equivalent in terms of domestically produced ones could circulate freely because they

---

[411] See *The Guardian*, Report, 10 March 2001, p 9.

[412] See further Warbrick, 'Federalism and free speech', in Loveland (ed.), *Importing the First Amendment*, Oxford: Hart Publishing, 1997, pp 177–9 and 190–2.

[413] For discussion of the effect of the Act, see (1982) *Stat LR* 31; (1981) 45 *MLR* 62; (1981) 132 *NLJ* 629.

[414] S 1(3).   [415] S 1(3)(b).   [416] Formerly, the Post Office Act 1953, s 11.

[417] [1987] QB 254; [1986] 2 All ER 688. Figures quoted by Robertson, *Obscenity*, 1979, p 193.

[418] Formerly Art 30 of the Treaty of Rome.

were not obscene. Thus, where obscenity or indecency existed as alternatives, the easier test should not be used to favour domestic goods since that would amount to arbitrary discrimination on trade between Member States contrary to Article 36. Customs officers now apply this ruling but not just to EU imports, because it would be too impracticable to apply different tests to imports from different countries. This ruling has therefore resulted in a major relaxation of censorship. 'Hard-core' pornography is, however, still seized; this is justifiable under Article 36 because it would also be prohibited if disseminated internally under the Obscene Publications Act.

EFFECT OF THE HRA

Prosecutions under these provisions will normally constitute interferences with freedom of expression under the HRA. The public authorities involved are bound by s 6 of the HRA to ensure that the tests under Article 10 are satisfied, while the provisions of the various statutes must be interpreted consistently with Article 10 under s 3. As Chapter 2 indicated, State interference with the Article 10 guarantee must be in accordance with the law, under para 2, if it is to be justified. This requirement covers not only the existence of national law, but its quality. In *Kopp v Switzerland*[419] the Court clearly stated that the essential requirements of a national legal basis are those of accessibility and foreseeability. These requirements demand precision so that, in this context, the citizen is sufficiently aware of the meaning of the term 'indecency'. It is suggested that, as currently interpreted, the term is so uncertain that there is at least room for argument that these statutory provisions do not meet the 'prescribed by law' requirement. Arguably, the concept of indecency considered in *Knuller v DPP*,[420] which depends on considering whether material would disgust 'ordinary decent-minded people' is extremely imprecise; as pointed out above, doubts have been expressed as to the suitability of such a concept as a basis for criminality. It would, of course, be a bold domestic court that was prepared to find such a significant flaw in a large number of statutory provisions (and in respect of common law indecency, discussed below). The Commission has had the opportunity of making such a finding but has not done so,[421] and neither did the Court in *Müller*.

In terms of substantive compatibility with Article 10, there might appear to be an argument that preventing shock resulting from 'indecency', rather than harm to morals, is not an interest falling within Article 10, which mentions the latter but not the former. However, it must be said that at present, the European Court has not always drawn a clear distinction between the two mischiefs: in *Müller v Switzerland*,[422] it will be recalled, paintings were prosecuted under Swiss Law, under which material was obscene if it was liable to 'grossly offend the sense of sexual propriety of persons of ordinary sensitivity'. This sounds like indecency rather than corruption, but the Court blurred the distinction between the two, in implying that the former would

---

[419] (1999) 27 EHRR 91, at [70–71].   [420] [1973] AC 435, p 457; [1972] 3 WLR 143.
[421] *Gibson v UK*, Application No 17634.   [422] (1991) 13 EHRR 212.

merge with the latter once a certain level of offensiveness was reached. That level may be reached, it is suggested, by speech which may best be termed 'very shocking', as in the paintings in *Müller*. Certainly, the Court had little difficulty in finding that the Swiss authorities had acted for the legitimate aim of protecting morals and/or the rights of others.

A more workable possible argument is that certain aspects of this statutory regime will be found to be disproportionate to the legitimate aim pursued, either in terms of the provisions themselves or in respect of decisions made under them. It is suggested that the interference with expression represented by the provisions of s 160 of the Criminal Justice Act 1988, affecting the downloading of indecent pseudo-photographs of persons under 18 onto a computer, presumably from a website, might be viewed as disproportionate to the aim in view, although no court has yet taken that view.[423] The provisions criminalize a person merely for possessing a photograph, or its equivalent, which has been created without the involvement of a minor. The breadth of the offences under the Protection of Children Act was indicated by the possibility of prosecution in respect of the Saatchi Exhibition. Arguments regarding proportionality could be raised in a similar instance, especially regarding the lack of an artistic merits defence or a defence of legitimate reason applicable to the creator of the photographs, so that the taking and distributing of photographs of children by paedophiles is not distinguished from taking them for artistic or scientific purposes. Plainly, the concept of 'indecency' is broad enough to allow Article 10 concerns into adjudication on these cases, in the way that free speech concerns were, essentially, allowed to determine the outcome in *Wiggins v Field*,[424] as discussed above. The Indecent Displays Act appears to be broadly in harmony with the adult autonomy principle flowing from *Scherer*. More problematic in this respect is the common law indecency offence.

THE COMMON LAW OFFENCE OF OUTRAGING PUBLIC DECENCY

In *Knuller v DPP*,[425] which, as seen, concerned publication of homosexual contact advertisements, the House of Lords, as well as confirming the existence of the offence of conspiracy to corrupt public morals, also held that there was a separate offence of outraging public decency and conspiring to commit it. This offence overlaps with the statutory indecency offences, just as the 'conspiracy to corrupt public morals' offence does with statutory obscenity. The harm in this case is only that of causing 'outrage' to public decency; the *mens rea* is merely awareness of the content of the publication or item, and knowledge that it is being made available to the public: no intention to outrage public decency need be shown. The House of Lords ruled in *Knuller* that the necessary 'public' element would be present even if the indecency was not

---

[423] See A. Gillespie, 'Sentences for Child Pornography' (2003) *Crim LR*, 81 for a survey of recent case law.
[424] [1968] Crim LR 50.   [425] [1973] AC 435; [1972] 3 WLR 143; (1972) 56 Cr App R 633, HL.

immediately visible, since it appeared on an inside page, so long as there was an express or implied invitation to go beyond the cover and partake of the lewd contents; therefore there must be a reference on the cover to the contents. Furthermore, the contents must be so offensive that the sense of decency of the public would be outraged by seeing them. Whether or not a member of the public would be so outraged would be determined by reference to that section of the public likely to frequent the place where the publication in question was sold. In *Knuller*, Lord Simon gave the rationale of the offence as follows:

I would add, lastly, that, subject to the riders to which I refer later, it does not seem to me to be exorbitant to demand of the law that reasonable people should be able to venture into public without their sense of decency being outraged.[426]

But this basic rationale—that one should be free to go about one's business without being shocked or repulsed by objects involuntarily encountered—is incompatible with the holding that a magazine which invites you to look inside it to see the shocking object should attract liability: in such a case, the essential element of *unwilling* exposure to the shocking material is lost. It is one thing for someone to complain, say, of a sexually explicit billboard or an image on the front of a newspaper, seen on the stands of newsagents; it is quite another to say, that having been given notice by a magazine that homosexual images were to be found within, the person who then looks through the magazine to find them and is then putatively outraged, has been *involuntarily* exposed to shocking material. The person investigating the magazine further, having been given notice of the contents, surely has only him- or herself to blame for exposure to the material; a 'decent' citizen would surely have shunned the invitation to 'open the cover and partake of the lewd contents'.

Lord Reid in *Knuller* thought that there was no offence of outraging public decency. He said:

If there were in any book, new or old, a few pages or even a few sentences which any jury could find to be outrageously indecent, those who took part in its publication and sale would risk conviction. I can see no way of denying to juries the free hand which *Shaw's* case gives them in cases of conspiracy to corrupt public morals. There would be no defence based on literary, artistic or scientific merit. The undertaking given in Parliament with regard to obscene publications would not apply to this quite different crime. Notoriously, many old works, commonly regarded as classics of the highest merit, contain passages which many a juryman might regard as outrageously indecent. It has been generally supposed that the days for Bowdlerising the classics[427] were long past, but the introduction of this new crime might make publishers of such works think twice.[428]

Lord Diplock agreed that there was no such offence.

. . . Previously it was possible for a citizen to regulate his conduct in the knowledge that if

---

[426] [1973] AC 435, 493.
[427] That is, the practice of removing words or passages considered indecent.   [428] Op cit, at 458.

what he was minded to do was not specifically prohibited by a criminal statute and did not fall within any of those equally specific categories of conduct which had already been held to constitute offences at common law, he could do it without risk of incurring punishment even though most of his fellow citizens might be shocked at it as immoral or indecent. As a result of *Shaw's case* it would seem that any conduct of any kind which conflicts with widely held prejudices as to what is immoral or indecent, at any rate if at least two persons are in any way concerned with it, may *ex post facto* be held to have been a crime.[429]

Despite these powerful dissents, a majority of the House of Lords upheld the existence of the offences. As to their content, Lord Simon said:

It should be emphasised that 'outrage,' like 'corrupt,' is a very strong word. 'Outraging public decency' goes considerably beyond offending the susceptibilities of, or even shocking, reasonable people. Moreover the offence is, in my view, concerned with recognised minimum standards of decency, which are likely to vary from time to time . . . I think the jury should be invited, where appropriate, to remember that they live in a plural society, with a tradition of tolerance towards minorities, and that this atmosphere of toleration is itself part of public decency.[430]

The above passage does at least import a 'contemporaneous standards' test, but the offence, it is suggested, remains deeply problematic. Firstly, and unlike conspiracy to corrupt public morals, which might now be seen as a dead letter,[431] the offence has been successfully prosecuted comparatively recently, as will appear below. Second, it operates substantially to undermine the various safeguards built into the Indecent Displays Act, including the saving for establishments in which appropriate warning signs are displayed and minors excluded. It also undermines the exclusion of art galleries from the statutory offence; they may, of course, display works by artists who make use of the power to shock and offend in order to convey their artistic vision.

This anomaly was highlighted in the case of *Gibson*.[432] The defendants were convicted of outraging public decency after displaying in an art gallery a model of a human head with earrings made out of freeze-dried human foetuses of three to four months' gestation. The artist explained that he intended the use of the foetus earrings to symbolize the commodification of human life. As Kearns put it:

although *prima facie* Gibson's creations might appear distasteful, they bear the message that life is now so cheap that aborted foetuses can even be used as mere ornamentation in the superficial world of postmodernism.[433]

The Court of Appeal reaffirmed the ruling of the House of Lords in *Knuller* as to the ingredients of the offence. It may be noted that, at first instance, the jury was directed that they were entirely free to use their own standards in deciding whether the model was indecent. Argument on appeal centred on s 2(4) of the 1959 Act which provides

---

[429] Ibid, at 480.   [430] Ibid, at 495.
[431] It does not appear to have been prosecuted since *Knuller*.
[432] [1990] 2 QB 619; [1991] 1 All ER 439; [1990] 3 WLR 595; for comment, see Childs [1991] *PL* 20–29.
[433] Op cit, at 657.

that where a prosecution is brought in respect of an obscene article, it must be considered within the Act, *not* at common law, 'where it is of the essence of the offence that the matter is obscene'. 'It was therefore crucial to determine the meaning of "obscene" in this context.' There were two possible meanings, the Court found. First, 'obscene' could be used in a broad, everyday sense, to denote something which disgusted the public; second, it could be used to mean something which had a tendency to corrupt; if it carried the first meaning, the 'foetus earrings' could be said to be obscene (since the sculpture might disgust many who saw it). If this was the case, then prosecution at common law would be unlawful, given the terms of s 2(4); it would have to be brought under the 1959 Act—meaning that the defence of 'public good' would be available. Clearly, it would have been pleaded in *Gibson* itself. However, the second, more restricted meaning of the word 'obscene' was that used in the Act itself, in section 1(1), namely an item that had a tendency to 'deprave and corrupt'. If this was the case, then section 2(4) only prohibited the prosecution at common law of articles that tended to deprave and corrupt. There was no suggestion that the exhibition of the earrings had a tendency to corrupt; therefore, if this meaning of 'obscene' was adopted, then the prosecution could go forward at common law. It would be being brought not because the earrings were obscene but because they were indecent: it would not therefore fall within the prohibition against common law obscenity prosecutions contained in section 2(4). Lord Lane, perhaps not surprisingly, held that the meaning of 'obscene' in section 2(4) was the same as its meaning in section 1(1): that the item in question must have a tendency to deprave and corrupt.

'the plain wording of this part of the Act is incontrovertible ... If we were to hold the contrary, it would mean that in section 2 where the word "obscene" is used three times, two of those occasions would have the restricted meaning, and one of those occasions, namely, section 2(4) alone, would have a meaning quite different.'[434]

Therefore, the prosecution at common law did not fall within the prohibition in section 2(4) and was permissible. The conviction was upheld. Clearly, if the defence argument on the meaning of obscene had been accepted, the prohibition on using common law offences in section 2(4) would have been greatly expanded; with that route blocked, a greater number of publications would have fallen only under the Obscene Publications Act and could have benefited from the section 4 defence. Since this would have meant the effective abolition of the common law offences of indecency, it is perhaps not surprising that this interpretation was not adopted. However, the outcome of *Gibson* means the continuation of the paradoxical and anomalous situation in which those who produce publications or items which more seriously breach normal moral standards—items that may corrupt—can plead the 'public good' defence, including their artistic merit, whilst those who produce less offensive objects (merely indecent items) cannot.

What is striking about the *Gibson* judgment, upon reading it, is the seemingly

---

[434] [1990] 2 QB 619, 625.

complete lack of judicial awareness that the law is at this point punishing people for artistic expression; in other words, that it is, on one view, striking at the heart of the individual's right to communicate his or her vision of the world to others. The judgment consists entirely of narrowly based statutory construction, on the one hand, and the orthodox analysis of precedent (to decide whether there was any requirement of intention to outrage public decency). The comparison, for example with the judgment in *Derbyshire*,[435] is striking. In that case, it will be recalled, the Court of Appeal found, by reference to Article 10 ECHR, that because of the importance of political expression, the common law should be developed, under the influence of the Convention, so as to prohibit a right of action in defamation for local authorities. The House of Lords reached the same decision, relying solely on the common law, *regardless* of the requirements of the Convention. In *Gibson*, in a decision handed down at about the same time, there is no reference either to Article 10, or the value that the common law attaches to freedom of expression. It is as if the case simply did not register with the judges as one which amounted to an attack on free speech.

The decision of the Commission,[436] to whom those convicted applied, alleging a breach of Article 10, is scarcely more encouraging. The inherent uncertainty of the offence was dismissed simply on the basis of the decision in *Knuller*. 'The Commission finds, therefore, that the applicants did have an indication, sufficient in the circumstances, of the existence of the offence of outraging public decency.' There was, however, no analysis of the *quality* of law here, as, for example, in *Hashman v Harrup*,[437] in which the content of the law and its inherent uncertainty was given proper consideration.

On the substance of the argument, the Commission in *Gibson* was even more disappointing. The applicants argued:

that the restriction on their freedom of expression was disproportionate, given the limitations on their defence to the charge of outraging public decency. They submit, *inter alia*, that their conviction will have a chilling effect on the artistic community as a whole, with art galleries being extremely cautious in the future to exhibit controversial work for fear of such prosecutions. The balanced protection of the Obscene Publications Act 1959 can now be circumvented by framing a prosecution on the basis that the article is offensive and disgusting rather than obscene, a distinction which, in their view, is impossible in reality to make.[438]

The Commission started simply by noting 'the wide margin of appreciation afforded to States in the protection of morals, given the absence of any uniform European conception'. It was found that:

As regards the facts of the present case, the Commission notes that the second applicant's sculpture used two freeze-dried foetuses of three to four months' gestation as earrings. The sculpture was displayed in an exhibition which was open to, and sought to attract the public. In the circumstances, the Commission does not find unreasonable the view taken by the

---

[435] [1993] AC 534.   [436] *Gibson v UK*, Appl No 17634.
[437] (2000) EHRR 24. See Chapter 2, at 47–8.   [438] Ibid.

English courts that this work was an outrage to public decency. Having regard to the margin of appreciation left to them under Article 10 para. 2 of the Convention, the domestic courts were entitled to consider it 'necessary' for the protection of morals to impose a fine on the applicants for exhibiting the piece.[439]

And that is that. It may be seen that, exactly in line with the tendencies identified in Chapter 2, the Commission used one of the lowest possible standards of review.[440] First, there was no examination of the evidence for thinking that there was a 'pressing social need' to punish the applicants, in the form, for example, of details of complaints by members of the public or other evidence of widespread shock or outrage. Second, there was no examination of proportionality: the Commission instead employed a *Wednesbury* type test, finding merely that the authorities were 'entitled to consider it necessary' to impose a fine. Also striking, although of course fairly typical of Commission decisions on admissibility, was the almost complete absence of justificatory reasoning on the matter. Finally, the *decision* of the Commission was to declare the application inadmissible as manifestly ill-founded, in other words as not raising seriously arguable issues as to a breach of Article 10—an extraordinary finding. In short, this decision, far from requiring the authorities to adduce strong and cogent reasons, backed by clear evidence, to justify the decision to interfere with freedom of expression, placed the burden on the applicant to show that the State had acted unreasonably. It therefore dismissed the argument—that the offence was bad in Convention terms because there was no real means of bringing Article 10 into adjudication upon it—with no evidence or real analysis. Indeed, in one of the only points the Commission made, it appeared to be satisfied with the finding that Article 10 'was not wholly irrelevant' to the offence.

A domestic court, confronted with a common law indecency case, would be bound by its own duty under s 6 HRA[441] to ensure that the law it was applying and the outcome of the case was compatible with Article 10. It would be easy for such a court simply to note cases such as *Müller* and *Gibson* at Strasbourg and conclude that the law as it stood was not incompatible and therefore required no change. But an activist court could take the opportunity to take a hard look at this area of common law, question the rationale for its existence, given the statutory offences, and at the very least, import into it something akin to a defence of public good: giving consideration to the question whether prosecuting the offence in a particular instance was necessary in a democratic society would require giving some consideration to the content of the expression in question. Where it could be said to have clear artistic merit, that factor should make it much harder for the state to justify a conviction: in proportionality terms, the more valuable the speech, the greater is the justification required for interference with it.

---

[439] Ibid.   [440] See pp 79–81.

[441] This would not a horizontal effects situation, since the case would be a criminal one.

CONCLUSIONS

The law on indecency is not as troubling as that governing obscenity, simply because its purpose is not the suppression of speech, but merely its restriction to venues in which it will be seen only by a willing audience. There are major concerns over the width of the law relating to indecent photographs of children, as discussed above, which could be dealt with judicially, simply by adopting a narrower interpretation of 'indecency' in that context. The statutory offences[442] do not include a public good defence, but it is submitted that the notion of 'indecency' is sufficiently flexible to allow for consideration of the nature and value of the expression in question, as occurred to a limited degree in *Wiggins v Field*.[443] One change very clearly required is the abolition or substantial judicial reform of the common law offence of indecency, as just discussed.

In terms of obscenity, we see five major policy options for reform. These stem from the basic options of retention, transformation, or abolition of the law of obscenity; in relation to two of these cases, however, there is a choice between judicial and legislative action. The options, as we see it, are as follows. First, retain the status quo: the law captures anything that a jury thinks could cause a moral change for the worse. This is enormously broad, and, as a reason for censorship, quite unjustifiable in a democracy. In practice, the breadth of the law is mitigated by applying it to a narrow band of highly explicit visual material, which broadly encompasses violent pornography, bestiality, and what may be termed 'disgusting' or 'degrading' acts. If nothing else is done, at the very least the common law offence of conspiracy to corrupt public morals should be abolished, as discussed above.

A second option would be a limited reform, which would ameliorate at the least the breadth and uncertainty of the current law: this would involve taking the Government's consultation paper on extreme pornography and using it as the basis for a fresh Obscenity Act, which would replace the current general definition of obscenity with the narrow category of materials outlined therein.[444] It is noteworthy that Liberty has very recently given broad support to the Government's proposals in this area.[445]

The third option would be for the judges to use section 3(1) HRA and, relying on broad Strasbourg principles, rather than the specific 'protection of morals' jurisprudence of the Court,[446] replace the notion of 'depraving and corrupting' with that of using the law to protect what Nowlin refers to as a 'constitutional morality'.[447] In other words, UK law could adopt a position akin to the Canadian one, through

---

[442] Under the Protection of Children Act 1978, as amended.
[443] [1968] Crim LR 50. See above at 468.   [444] The categories are set out above at 423.
[445] See Liberty's response to the Consultation Paper (2005), available: http://www.liberty-human-rights. org.uk/resources/policy-papers/2005/extreme-pornographic-material-ho-consultation.PDF. It should be noted that the organization has some concerns as to the width of some of the proposed categories.
[446] The Commission decisions in *Müller* and *Otto Preminger* and in *Scherer* could also be relied upon.
[447] See above at 418–19.

judicial re-interpretation of the existing statutes; under such a course, the harm to be remedied would become not any kind of moral change for the worse, as assessed by a jury or magistrates, but attacks upon fundamental values of equality and dignity. There are clear difficulties with this position, as discussed above; primarily there is a doubt as to the legitimacy of singling out pornography for proscription, and there is the danger that the law will be used to stifle the sexual expression of minorities. However, in founding upon a basic set of internationally agreed values, underlying all liberal democracies, rather than a particular, substantive, and conservative view of morality, this approach would be preferable to the present one from a human rights perspective, if applied and interpreted in a selective and discerning manner. In practice, much of the same material might be caught, although material which was simply explicit and shocking (e.g. 'fisting'), rather than that which was violent and/or degrading would not be.

A fourth alternative would be to enact fresh legislation specifically re-orientating the law around the defence of equality and human dignity; the MacKinnon/Dworkin[448] definition would be unacceptable as it is overtly discriminatory, but something like it could be used. Such a reform, if preceded by a public debate and thorough consideration in Parliament, would give the change greater legitimacy and there would be a chance of enacting a much more precise definition than would be likely to be arrived at by judicial re-interpretation of the 1959 Act. Such a law should make it as clear as possible that a contextual and holistic view was to be taken in assessing sexually explicit material. It should be framed in such a way as not to catch material, which, although shocking and presenting sexuality in ways that did not on their face conform to notions of equality and dignity, was a genuine exploration of sexual identity or fantasy and not in fact likely to inculcate damaging sexual attitudes. The offence should of course contain a robust and general public good defence, and, as suggested above, should overtly *exclude* the written word. This would not only continue the literary freedom that Britain has enjoyed since the *Lady Chatterley* trial, it would also represent a relatively narrow and proportionate response to the problem of violent pornography.

The final, and perhaps most radical, option would be the fifth, in which general obscenity laws would be abolished[449] and replaced with laws which:

(a) strictly regulated the public display and public access to explicit materials, in particular to ensure that minors were prevented from coming into contact with such material;

(b) made it an offence to show or possess any material in which any of the participants were actually harmed or coerced;

(c) made it an offence to display or possess any material made with the participation of children;

---

[448] See above at text to note 298. The authors did make clear that it could apply to men also, but it would appear strange if a definition intended to protect women from harmful social constructions of their identity was used to suppress e.g. soft gay porn.

[449] As in Denmark, which abolished its obscenity laws in the late 1960s.

(d) (probably) prohibited child pornography absolutely, even if made without the participation of actual children (i.e., using only pseudo-images of children).[450]

This chapter has in the end concluded that the fourth option would be the best solution to the problem; however, if in future further research substantially undermines the claim that violent pornography *is* associated with dangerous attitudinal changes, we would submit that the fifth option should be adopted. Simple moral disapproval of the depiction of certain activities cannot be a justifiable reason for interfering with freedom of expression and the moral autonomy of the audience.

What, finally, are the prospects for reform? As seen above, the government's latest proposals contain no suggestion to overhaul the law in this area in any systematic way but, in a manner typical of legislative changes in the UK, simply to add another offence to those that already exist. The proposed new offence is relatively unobjectionable compared to the existing ones—it is narrowly tailored and captures only fairly extreme material[451]—but it is profoundly disappointing that the Government proposes to leave all the current anomalies and injustices of the current law fully in place. To conclude, the Parliamentary route to reform appears to be thoroughly unpromising; Strasbourg is most unlikely, for reasons we have already explored, to take decisions leading to liberalization of the law in this area; the only route to reform that is possibly still open is from the appellate domestic courts relying on the HRA. However, the disappointing conclusion must be that one of the areas of law most urgently in need of reform is least likely to receive it.

---

[450] The alternative would be to decriminalize pseudo child pornography and instead use other methods to discourage paedophile activity, such as the use of 'grooming' offences. Such a move would, however, be virtually politically impossible.

[451] Though see Liberty's concerns as to possible over-breadth in the definition: op cit.

9

BLASPHEMY, RACIAL HATRED, AND RELIGIOUS HATRED

'In an increasingly plural society, such as that of modern Britain, it is necessary not only to respect the differing religious beliefs, feelings and practices of all, but also to protect them from scurrility, vilification, ridicule and contempt.'[1]

[Article 9 ECHR] is 'a precious asset for atheists, agnostics, sceptics and the unconcerned'.[2]

'Experience shows that criminal laws prohibiting hate speech and expression will encourage intolerance, divisiveness and unreasonable interference with freedom of expression.'[3]

The area of blasphemy law and the linked area of incitement to religious hatred present some similar, and some very different, issues from those raised in the preceding chapter. Blasphemy law is of ancient origin, discriminatory (in this case overtly so), potentially of enormous reach, and arguably anachronistic in contemporary, pluralistic society. In all these respects it bears a striking resemblance to the English law on obscenity and indecency. It further resembles obscenity law, in that it has, nevertheless, been for all intents and purposes legitimized and buttressed in its attempt to survive in the modern world by judgments at Strasbourg. Such judgments have not only found the law itself to be a justifiable limitation upon free expression rights, but have given it new legal strength and normative force by holding that laws protecting against religious offence actually protect another Convention right—freedom of religion.[4] The difference in this area of law is that its reform has just been undertaken by Parliament at the time of writing, in the form of an Act which introduces a new offence of incitement to religious hatred. This proposal *ought* to be accompanied by the abolition of the law of blasphemy, but it appears at present that this is unlikely. But this reform may, alternatively, afford impetus to *judicial* abolition, or, at least, radical reform of this archaic criminal offence.

---

[1] Lord Scarman, *Whitehouse v Lemon* [1979] AC 617 at 658.

[2] *Kokkinakis v Greece* (1993) A 260-A, at [8].

[3] Soli Sorabjee, former Attorney General of India; quoted in Select Committee on Religious Offences in England and Wales (2003), (HL 95), Ch4, at [52], hereafter 'Select Committee'.

[4] See below, at pp 488–94.

BLASPHEMOUS AND SEDITIOUS LIBEL[5]

Blasphemy is an offence unique in English law in that it prescribes that treatment of certain subjects—objects and figures sacred in Anglicanism—in an unduly disrespectful manner will be a serious criminal offence. The existence of the offence stems from the 17th century, when it was tried in the Ecclesiastical courts. It was then thought to be a form of sedition due to the close relationship between the Church and the State. Therefore it only protected the Anglican Church; other sects of the Christian Church such as Catholicism, or other religions, received no protection. As Lord Diplock put it in the leading case:

In the post-Restoration politics of 17th and 18th century England, Church and State were thought to stand or fall together. To cast doubt on the doctrines of the established church or to deny the truth of the Christian faith upon which it was founded was to attack the fabric of society itself; so blasphemous and seditious libel were criminal offences that went hand in hand.[6]

The basis of the offence, which derives from *Taylor's* case,[7] was that the defendant had aspersed the Christian religion. By the middle of the 19th century, and in particular after the case of *Ramsay and Foote*,[8] it became clear that the basis of blasphemy had changed: it required a scurrilous attack on Christianity rather than merely reasoned and sober arguments against it. It was thought by 1950 that the offence was a dead letter:[9] there had been no recorded prosecution since 1926. However, it was resurrected in *Lemon*.[10] *Gay News* published a poem—'The Love that dares to speak its name'—by a professor of English literature, James Kirkup. It expressed religious sentiment in describing a homosexual's conversion to Christianity and in developing its theme it ascribed homosexual practices with the Apostles to Jesus. As Lord Diplock described the poem:

[It] purports to describe in explicit detail acts of sodomy and fellatio with the body of

---

[5] General reading: see G. Robertson and A. Nichol, *Media Law*, London: Penguin, 1999, Ch, pp 124–7; S. Bailey, D. Harris, and B. Jones, *Civil Liberties: Cases and Materials*, London: Butterworths (4th edn., 1995) pp 591–8; J.A. Robillard, *Religion and the Law*, Manchester: Manchester University Press, 1984, Ch 2; E. Barendt, *Freedom of Speech*, Oxford: OUP (2nd edn., 2005), pp 186–92; for historical discussion of the development of blasphemy law, see C.S. Kenny, 'The evolution of the law of blasphemy' [1992] CLJ 127–42 and N. Walter, *Blasphemy Ancient and Modern*, London: Rationalist Press Association, 1990. For a discussion of the theoretical issues lying behind blasphemy law, see J. Feinberg, *Offense to Others*, New York: OUP, 1985 and, in the context of possible reform, see Law Commission Report No 145, *Offences against Religion and Public Worship* (1985).

[6] *R v Lemon* [1979] AC 617, 633–34.   [7] (1676) 1 Vent 293.   [8] (1883) 15 Cox CC 231.

[9] This was Lord Denning's description of it in *Freedom under the Law*, London (1949), at 46, also *The Hamlyn Lectures*, Series 2, 1950.

[10] [1979] AC 617; [1979] 2 WLR 281; [1979] 1 All ER 898, HL.

Christ immediately after His death and to ascribe to Him during His lifetime promiscuous homosexual practices with the Apostles and with other men.[11]

Mary Whitehouse, a campaigner for standards of decency and Christian morality, well known at the time, obtained leave to bring a private prosecution against *Gay News*, and the editor and publishing company were convicted of the offence of blasphemous libel.

The Court of Appeal held that the intention or motive of the defendants was irrelevant since blasphemy was a crime of strict liability. There was no defence of publication in the public interest; serious literature could therefore be caught. The work in question need not be considered as a whole. All that needed to be shown, it was found, was that the material in question, which was published with the defendant's knowledge, had crossed the borderline between moderate criticism on the one hand and immoderate or offensive treatment of matter sacred to Christians on the other. It was only necessary to show that resentment would be likely to be aroused, not that it actually was aroused. The past requirement to show that a breach of the peace might be occasioned by publication of the material was no longer necessary. The case was considered by the House of Lords on the question of the mental element required. The judgment confirmed the Court of Appeal ruling that it was only necessary to show intent to publish the material. This was in spite of the fact that it was open to the House on the existing authorities to take the view that specific intention was required,[12] and that such an approach had been adopted in one of the most prominent 19th-century cases, by Lord Coleridge C.J. in *R v Ramsay and Foote*.[13] As Lord Russell, one of the judges in the majority, conceded:

The authorities embrace an abundance of apparently contradictory or ambivalent comments. There is no [House of Lords] authority on the point. The question is open for decision.

Lord Scarman, also in the majority, agreed that the matter could be decided as one of principle:

The history of the law is obscure and confused. The point is, therefore, open for your Lordships' decision as a matter of principle and in deciding the point your Lordships are not saying what the law was in the past or ought to be in the future but what is required of it in the conditions of today's society.[14]

There were, in fact, strong arguments, based upon the overall direction and therefore coherence of the criminal law, in favour of requiring specific intent. As Lord Diplock, one of the dissenting judges, powerfully put it:

My Lords, if your Lordships were to hold that Lord Coleridge C.J. and those judges who

---

[11] [1979] AC 617, 632. The poem can be read in full at http://www.petertatchell.net/religion/blasphemy. htm. Christian and Muslim readers are warned that they may find it offensive.

[12] Op cit, at 635, per Lord Diplock.   [13] (1883) 15 Cox CC 231, 236, per Coleridge CJ.

[14] Op cit, at 662.

preceded and followed him in directing juries that the accused's intention to shock and arouse resentment among believing Christians was a necessary element in the offence of blasphemous libel were wrong in doing so, this would effectively exclude that particular offence from the benefit of Parliament's general substitution of the subjective for the objective test in applying the presumption that a man intends the natural consequences of his acts; and blasphemous libel would revert to the exceptional category of crimes of strict liability from which, upon what is, to say the least, a plausible analysis of the contemporaneous authorities, it appeared to have escaped nearly a century ago.[15]

As his Lordship went on to point out:

The usual justification for creating by statute a criminal offence of strict liability, in which the prosecution need not prove mens rea as to one of the elements of the actus reus, is the threat that the actus reus of the offence poses to public health, public safety, public morals or public order. The very fact that there have been no prosecutions for blasphemous libel for more than 50 years is sufficient to dispose of any suggestion that in modern times a judicial decision to include this common law offence in this exceptional class of offences of strict liability could be justified upon grounds of public morals or public order.[16]

Similarly, Lord Edmund-Davies in his dissent, despite what he called his 'revulsion over this deplorable publication', was forced to the 'reluctant' view that, 'to treat as irrelevant the state of mind of a person charged with blasphemy would be to take a backward step in the evolution of a humane code.'[17]

The majority, however, took the opposite view. Most notably, the speeches of Viscount Dilhorne and Lord Russell contain no acknowledgment whatever that this is an unusual offence, both in its recent disuse and in the fact that it criminalizes pure expression of satirical or offensive ideas, without more. There is no mention of freedom of expression generally, still less of Article 10 ECHR. Their speeches consist entirely of consideration of the historical precedents, without ever any consideration of the wider issues at stake in terms of the general tendency of the criminal law to move away from crimes of strict liability towards a requirement of subjective intention. Lord Scarman was the only one of the majority to consider the broader issues, stating that he did not agree that the law of blasphemy 'had no useful purpose in the modern law:'

On the contrary, I think that there is a case for legislation extending it to protect the religious beliefs and feelings of non-Christians. The offence belongs to a group of criminal offences designed to safeguard the internal tranquillity of the kingdom. In an increasingly plural society such as that of modern Britain it is necessary not only to respect the differing religious beliefs, feelings and practices of all but also to protect them from scurrility, vilification, ridicule and contempt.[18]

In a remarkably prescient passage, considering the later decision of the European Court of Human Rights in *Otto Preminger*,[19] Lord Scarman also went on to say:

---

[15] Op cit, at 637–8.   [16] Ibid, at 638.   [17] Ibid, at 656.   [18] Ibid, at 657.
[19] (1994) 19 EHRR 34; see below at 488–94.

By necessary implication [Article 9] imposes a duty on all of us to refrain from insulting or outraging the religious feelings of others ... The exercise of [Article 10] 'carries with it duties and responsibilities' ... It would be intolerable if by allowing an author or publisher to plead ... the right of free speech he could evade the penalties of the law even though his words were blasphemous in the sense of constituting an outrage upon the religious feelings of his fellow citizens. This is no way forward for a successful plural society.[20]

This line of reasoning is considered and critiqued below: what may be said initially is that at least Lord Scarman directed his mind to the broader issues and founded his judgment upon values that all would accept—the maintenance of a tolerant, pluralist society—although many would disagree with the conclusions he drew from those values.

The decision in *Lemon* has been much criticized:[21] it leaves the law in a state of considerable uncertainty as to how far the satirical treatment of Christianity may go,[22] especially as regards the treatment of sexuality in relation to aspects of the Anglican religion by writers and broadcasters. The 1st Report of the Select Committee on Religious Offences in England and Wales makes the point in para 1 that the *actus reus* of blasphemy is so uncertain as to be virtually unworkable.[23]

In common with other parts of the common law, the offence allows the Obscene Publications Act to be circumvented because it admits of no public good defence. *Lemon* also, of course, maintained the anomaly that the law of blasphemy only protects Christianity, a situation plainly out of line with the best defence of the law of blasphemy, as put forward by Lord Scarman: singling out one religion for protection denied to others is, to use his words, 'no way forward for a successful plural society'.

Gay News applied to the European Commission on Human Rights on a number of grounds, including that of a breach of Article 10.[24] This application was ruled inadmissible in a cautious judgment. It was found that the Article 10 guarantee of freedom of expression had been interfered with, but that the interference fell within the 'rights of others' exception of Article 10(2). Was the interference necessary in a democratic society? It was found that once it was accepted that the religious feelings of citizens may deserve protection if attacks reach a certain level of savagery, it seemed to follow that the domestic authorities were best placed to determine when that level was reached. In other words, just as in the line of cases on sexually explicit speech,[25] a very wide margin of appreciation was allowed, with the result that no rigorous scrutiny was given to the questions of the necessity or proportionality of the offence.

---

[20] Ibid, at 665.

[21] See G. Robertson, *Obscenity*, London: Weidenfeld and Nicolson, 1979, at 242; Law Commission Report, 1985.

[22] It is said that legal advice was taken in relation to the Monty Python Film, *The Life of Brian*; one QC reportedly considered that it was blasphemous, one that it was not, and one that it was not possible to predict the matter with any certainty.

[23] Op cit, at [1].   [24] *X and Y Ltd v the United Kingdom* (1979) 5 EHRR 123.

[25] In particular *Müller v Switzerland* (1991) 13 EHRR 212; *Handyside v UK* (1976) A24; see Chapter 2 at 56–60, 80–2, 95–6, and Chapter 8 at 410–22.

It seemed fairly clear in the pre-HRA era that this offence was unlikely to be extended beyond Anglicanism. The Law Commission in their 1985 Report[26] concluded, rather, that it should be abolished, in finding that an offence of wounding the feelings of adherents of any religious group would be impossible to construct because the term 'religion' could not be defined with sufficient precision. The argument in favour of extension of the offence was put and rejected in *R v Chief Metropolitan Magistrate ex parte Choudhury*,[27] a case which arose out of the publication of Salman Rushdie's *The Satanic Verses*.[28] The applicant Muslims applied for judicial review of the refusal of a magistrates' court to grant summonses against Salman Rushdie and his publishers for, *inter alia*, the common law offence of blasphemous libel. The Court of Appeal found that the expression of views in an artistic context would not prevent them from amounting to a blasphemous libel, a finding that has been criticized as revealing a 'lack of judicial awareness of the right to artistic expression and its theoretical basis ... [and an ignorance of] the autonomy of art as a specific cultural category with its own symbolic methods'.[29] But it was determined after reviewing the relevant decisions that the offence of blasphemy was clearly confined only to publications offensive to Christians. Extending the offence would not only amount to retrospective criminalization of previously lawful conduct, but would also, it was found, create great difficulties since it would be virtually impossible to define the term 'religion' sufficiently clearly. Freedom of expression would be curtailed as authors would have to try to avoid offending members of many different sects.

The applicants did not, however, rely only on domestic law; during argument that the offence should be extended, it was said that UK law must contain a provision to give effect to the Convention guarantee of freedom of religion under Article 9.[30] In response, it was argued and accepted by the Court of Appeal that the Convention need not be considered because the common law on the point was not uncertain. However, the respondents nevertheless accepted that in this particular instance, the Convention should be considered—they wanted the Convention arguments to receive an airing so that various points could be settled. It was found that the UK was not in breach of the Convention because extending the offence of blasphemy would breach Articles 7[31] and 10; the exceptions of Article 10(2) could not be invoked, as nothing in the book, it was found, would support a pressing social need for its suppression. Furthermore, Article 9(1) could not be treated as absolute;

---

[26] Report No 145, Offences Against Religion and Public Worship. This was preceded by the Law Commission Working Paper No 79 of the same title (1981). See Robertson [1981] *PL* 295; Spencer, J.R. [1981] *Crim LR* 810; Robillard (1981) 44 *MLR* 556 for comment on the 1981 Working Paper. The direction reform might take is considered further below.

[27] [1991] 1 QB 429; [1991] 1 All ER 306, DC; for comment, see M. Tregilgas-Davey (1991) 54 *MLR* 294–99.

[28] For discussion of Muslim and Western reactions to publication of *The Satanic Verses*, see R. Abel, *Speech and Respect*, London: Stevens and Sons/Sweet and Maxwell, 1994, Chapter 1 (iii).

[29] See P. Kearns, 'Obscene and blasphemous libel: misunderstanding art' [2000] *Crim LR* 652, at 656.

[30] For discussion of the particular question whether blasphemy law can be defended by reference to the rights of others to freedom of religion, see below, pp 488–94 and 505–8.

[31] The prohibition on retrospective law-making—see below, note 101.

implied exceptions to it must include the lack of a right to bring criminal proceedings for blasphemy where no domestic law had been infringed. Article 9 might be infringed, it was found, where Muslims were prevented from exercising their religion, but such restrictions were not in question. It should be noted that that last finding and probably the finding regarding Article 10(2) may arguably be said to be wrong, as a matter of Convention law, in the light of the subsequent findings in *Otto Preminger*[32] in the Strasbourg Court (below), although this point is by no means free from doubt.

On behalf of the applicants, it was further argued that even if Article 9 provided no protection for Muslims, they had suffered discrimination in the exercise of their freedom of religion and therefore a violation of Article 14 had occurred. This interpretation of Article 9, read alongside Article 14, had been rejected by the European Commission in the *Gay News* case.[33] In this case, it also failed on the ground that the envisaged extension of UK law to protect Islam would involve a violation of Article 10, which guarantees freedom of expression. Such an extension was not, therefore, warranted. It seems clear from this ruling and from statements made by Lord Scarman in the House of Lords in *Lemon*,[34] which were relied upon in the *Choudhury* case, that the judiciary are not minded to extend this offence, considering that only Parliament should do so.

The applicants also argued that the crime of seditious libel would extend to the image of Islam presented by *The Satanic Verses*. This offence at one time seemed to cover any attack on the institutions of the State, but in modern times it has been interpreted to require an intention to incite violence against the State and that the words used must have a tendency to incite such violence.[35] It was not, therefore, apt to cover the offence caused to Muslims by the book, which could be said to be intended to arouse general hostility and ill will between sections of the community, but not against the public authorities. This finding, which was contrary to the ruling in *Caunt*,[36] means that incitement to religious hatred is not covered by any part of the common law, although attacks on Anglicanism would in most instances fall within the ambit of blasphemy, while attacks on religious groups that are also racial groups would fall within the offence of incitement to racial hatred.[37]

An application was made to the European Commission on Human Rights by the applicants in *Choudhury*,[38] but it was declared inadmissible on the ground that Article 9 does not include a positive obligation on the part of the State to protect religious sensibilities. This, however, is a finding that can now only doubtfully stand with the reasoning in *Otto Preminger*,[39] discussed below. The discriminatory application of blasphemy law therefore remains a source of discontent among Muslims. Parliament had the opportunity of abolishing the offence of blasphemy in 1994 when a Bill was

---

[32] (1994) 19 EHRR 34.   [33] (1982) 5 EHRR 123.

[34] [1979] AC 617, p 620. Lord Scarman considered that there was a case for extension, however.

[35] *Burns* [1886] 16 Cox CC 333; *Aldred* (1909) 22 Cox CC 1.   [36] (1947) 64 *LQR* 203.

[37] See further below at 512.   [38] *Choudhury v UK* (1991) No 17349/1990; (1991) 12 HRLJ 172.

[39] (1994) 19 EHRR 34.

put forward by Lord Lester which would have achieved this. However, it was withdrawn after the government opposed it,[40] partly on the ground that no clear consensus as to the value of abolishing this offence could be discerned.

THE FUTURE OF BLASPHEMY LAW: IMPACT OF THE HUMAN RIGHTS ACT

THE STRASBOURG JURISPRUDENCE

Consideration of the Strasbourg jurisprudence suggests that the inception of the HRA will not bring about reform of UK blasphemy law since such reform is not seemingly required in order to ensure harmony with Article 10 of the Convention, as interpreted at Strasbourg. This suggestion is borne out by the findings of the European Commission in the *Gay News* case. But the most significant ruling is that of the European Court of Human Rights in *Otto-Preminger Institut v Austria*.[41] An order was made by the Austrian authorities for the seizure and forfeiture of a film, *Das Lieberkinzil* (Council in Heaven), which caricatured aspects of Christianity, on the basis that it disparaged religious doctrines and was 'likely to arouse justified indignation'. The film was based on a satirical play by Oskar Panizza, published in 1894. The play bases itself on the assumption that syphilis was God's punishment for man's fornication and sinfulness at the time of the Renaissance. The film begins and ends with a depiction of Panizza's trial for blasphemy in 1895 in respect of the play. It shows the performance of the play, by the Teatro Belli in Rome, which portrays God as a senile old man, prostrating himself before the Devil. Jesus is portrayed as a mental defective and is shown attempting to kiss and fondle his mother's breasts. God, Jesus and the Virgin Mary agree with the Devil to punish the world; the Devil suggests infecting the world with a sexually transmitted disease; as his reward, he demands freedom of thought. Apart from satirizing aspects of religious belief, the film explores the idea of the limitations of artistic freedom in relation to the trial of the author of the play. Importantly, it should be noted that the film was not in fact shown—it was seized before the intended projection date.

In an Opinion that strongly emphasized the need to protect artistic freedom, the Commission found a breach of Article 10.[42] In considering whether the interference was necessary in a democratic society for protecting the right to freedom of religion under Article 9, the Commission took into account the role of works of art in a democratic society and relied on the observation in *Müller*[43] to the effect that:

---

[40] HL Deb Cols 1891–1909, 16 June 1994.   [41] (1994) 19 EHRR 34.   [42] No. 13470/87 (1993).
[43] (1991) 13 EHRR 212.

those who create, perform, distribute or exhibit works of art contribute to the exchange of ideas and opinions which is essential for a democratic society. Hence, the obligation of the State not to encroach unduly on their freedom of expression.

It was noted that a warning had been given to the public as to the nature of the film, and, although access was not specifically restricted, the film was to be shown in a 'cinema of art' at a late hour. Therefore, it was unlikely that young children would be present. These factors strongly affected the Commission's view. The Commission considered that recourse to certain artistic methods (satirization and caricature) would not 'justify the imposition of a restriction on a work of art even if it deals with religion'.[44] As a general statement of principle, it said:

satirical texts or films can normally not be completely prohibited even if some restrictions concerning minors or people unaware of the contents may be possible.[45]

In other words, the possibility of religious offence at a satirical treatment of sacred subjects *cannot* 'normally' justify complete censorship—although the state may reasonably require that precautions be taken to avoid giving offence to the unprepared. The Commission concluded:

A complete prohibition, which excludes any chance to discuss the message of the film, must be seen as a disproportionate measure, except where there are very stringent reasons for such an act. In the Commission's view such reasons have not been established.[46]

The Court took a strikingly different stance. It took into account the lack of a uniform conception in Europe of the significance of religion in society in finding that it was not possible to arrive at a comprehensive definition of what constitutes a permissible interference with freedom of expression to protect religious feelings. It therefore left a wide margin of appreciation to the Austrian Government in respect of assessing the extent of the interference necessary. It did recite its usual mantra to the effect that the necessity for the restriction 'must be convincingly established'; however, it must be doubted whether its approach in fact required this. The Court did not give a specific reason for finding that the case for adopting the measures against the film had been convincingly established, merely asserting that the Austrian authorities had not overstepped their margin of appreciation. In finding that the seizure and forfeiture were necessary, the Court accepted the view of the Austrian authorities that the offensive nature of the film was not outweighed by its artistic merits, and left them a wide margin of appreciation in determining the measures needed in the light of the local situation, bearing in mind the fact that the Roman Catholic religion was the dominant religion in the local region, the Tyrol. No breach of Article 10 was therefore found.

Most significantly in terms of the justification for the censorship of the play, the Austrian Government maintained, and the Court accepted, that the seizure and forfeiture were aimed at protecting the 'rights of others' within Article 10(2). The Court found that 'the manner in which religious doctrines are opposed or denied is a matter

---

[44] (1994) 19 EHRR 34, at [12].   [45] Op cit, at [75].   [46] Ibid, at [77].

which may engage the responsibility of the State, *notably its responsibility to ensure the peaceful enjoyment of the right under Article 9*' (emphasis added).[47] The most problematic passage in the whole judgment is the following: that the Court found that the responsibilities of those exercising the right under Article 10 include:

an obligation to avoid as far as possible expressions that are gratuitously offensive to others *and thus an infringement of their rights* and which *therefore* do not contribute to any form of debate capable of furthering progress in human affairs (emphasis added).[48]

There are three separate, highly controversial propositions here. First, there is the question whether the 'offence' caused here was 'gratuitous'. The use of this term is presumably meant to convey the notion that the offence was inflicted for its own sake, with no good reason or purpose. In a film of artistic merit, it is surely contentious for a court to find that the offensive elements served no purpose. The artist, and others, would no doubt assert that the satirical treatment found to be offensive was not 'gratuitous' at all, but an important aspect of the film's *raison d'être*.

Second, the Court asserted, without argument, that gratuitously offending others is 'an infringement of their rights'. This statement runs clearly counter to the famous and foundational statement of principle in *Handyside* that freedom of expression extends to ideas that 'offend, shock or disturb':[49] if there is a right not to be offended there is no right to offensive speech. This must surely be right in general terms; what the Court sought to do was to justify, in effect, special treatment of religious feelings, so that offence to them was treated differently from offence to other beliefs or views. Its reasoning on this point was as follows:

. . . the manner in which religious beliefs and doctrines are opposed or denied is a matter which may engage the responsibility of the State, notably its responsibility to ensure the peaceful enjoyment of the right guaranteed under Article 9 to the holders of those beliefs and doctrines. *Indeed, in extreme cases, the effect of particular methods of opposing or denying religious beliefs can be such as to inhibit those who hold such beliefs from exercising their freedom to hold and express them.* . . In the *Kokkinakis* judgment the Court held, in the context of Article 9, that a State may legitimately consider it necessary to take measures aimed at repressing certain forms of conduct, including the imparting of information and ideas, judged incompatible with the respect for the freedom of thought, conscience and religion of others. The respect for the religious feelings of believers as guaranteed in Article 9 can legitimately be thought to have been violated by provocative portrayals of objects of religious veneration; and such portrayals can be regarded as a malicious violation of the spirit of tolerance, which must also be a feature of democratic society.

The measures complained of were based on section 188 of the Austrian Penal Code, which is intended to suppress behaviour directed against objects of religious veneration that is likely to cause 'justified indignation'. It follows that their purpose was to protect the right of citizens not to be insulted in their religious feelings by the public expression of views of other persons. Considering also the terms in which the decisions of the Austrian courts were

---

[47] Ibid, at [47].   [48] Ibid, at [49].   [49] *Handyside v UK* (1976) A24, at [49].

phrased, the Court accepts that the impugned measures pursued a legitimate aim under Article 10 para. 2, namely 'the protection of the rights of others.'[50]

The above passage contains a number of strands. One is the notion that Article 9 requires citizens to show respect for the religious feelings of others, and that this respect can be violated by 'provocative portrayals' of sacred subjects. No argument is offered here as to why religious feelings deserve a level of protection that, say, deeply held secular convictions do not. The only substantive argument made is in the first paragraph and relates to Article 9 protection. It asserts that 'the effect of particular methods of opposing or denying religious beliefs can be such as to inhibit those who hold such beliefs from exercising their freedom to hold and express them'. This statement is presumably to be classified as one of human psychology: it suggests that satirical attacks upon religious beliefs can hamper a person's ability to hold them. Presumably this statement is not intended to mean simply that a person may be persuaded out of their religious faith by doubt induced by religious satire or argument: to uphold this as a reason for restricting speech would be to strike at the very heart of the values underlying Article 10. If what is meant is that a person who experiences shock or outrage about satirical treatment of his religious views may be inhibited in holding such views in some other way, we would observe that, intuitively, one would think the contrary: that such experiences can actually lead to greater religious fervour. For example, the Christians who complained about the broadcast of the satirical *Jerry Springer: The Opera* on television[51] did not complain that their faith had been shaken or made more difficult to hold by the opera, but rather, simply, that it was outrageous or offensive to show it.[52] It *is* perhaps plausible to think that a religious person in an environment in which expression of religious views would be greeted with ridicule (for example at school) might become more unwilling to express them, but, as discussed in the preceding chapter, this applies to a great deal of speech about secular matters, and yet that has not been accepted as a good reason for suppressing such speech.[53] For example, at certain points, Conservative Party viewpoints were widely portrayed in parts of the media as deeply unfashionable, old-fashioned, 'nasty'[54] and regressive; no-one would suggest that the possible 'silencing' effect this might have on persons holding Conservative views could count as a legitimate reason for punishing or silencing such speech. Moreover, whilst sustained ridicule and hostility for (say) expressing Islamic beliefs in a school environment might inhibit expression of such beliefs by pupils frightened of bullying, it seems highly unlikely that the performance of one satirical play in a very Catholic area, Tyrol, could possibly have affected the willingness of Catholics living there to express their beliefs. Further, it is very important to recall that, given that a clear warning

---

[50] Op cit, at [57] (emphasis added).

[51] For details of this episode, see Chapter 11 at 605–6 and below at 509–10.

[52] See e.g. http://www.christianvoice.org.uk/springer.html.   [53] See p 405.

[54] As notoriously said by then Chair of the Party, Teresa May, at the Conservative Party conference in October 2002.

as to the satirical nature of the film was given, and that it was never in fact shown, the offence being protected against appears to have been either self-inflicted (Catholics going to see a film they *knew* would offend them) or to arise not from being confronted with the material itself, but simply from knowing that it was being expressed. Overall, the rationale that religious satire can inhibit the exercise of Article 9 rights seems simply implausible in the context of the *Otto-Preminger* case and generally unpersuasive and unsound, particularly in relation to the right to *hold* religious views.

Finally, we may return to the additional argument made by the Court that offensive religious expression, *because* it amounts to an 'infringement of rights' 'do[es] not contribute to any form of debate capable of furthering progress in human affairs'.[55] This is a remarkable statement: in ruling out in advance the possibility that offensive religious speech *can* contribute to worthwhile debate, it is astonishingly sweeping and arbitrary. Numerous possible examples of the provoking of worthwhile debate by such speech come to mind: believers may debate the offensive matter in question, some persuading others that, while deeply offensive to them, it should be tolerated, given (say) the importance of separating Church from State. For example, as Barendt points out:

One noted theologian argues that it is wrong for Christians to take offence when their faith is abused, and that the law should play no part in compelling respect for what should be a matter of personal commitment.[56]

Agnostics may be swayed one way or the other by such speech; others still may debate the merits or otherwise of using religious satire as a means of expression. For a court to decide that a particular class of speech *cannot* in principle lead to worthwhile debate amounts to authoritarianism of a particularly objectionable kind. It, in effect, prescribes for all an official attitude towards the treatment of religious matters. Such a view also reveals a failure to understand the principle of moral autonomy, which demands that citizens should be free, not only to choose to view works of art, but to decide for themselves whether they have value.[57]

Bearing in mind the gravity of the interference with religious expression in the *Otto Preminger* case—it made it permanently impossible to show the film anywhere in Austria—and its theoretical basis, this judgment is, it is argued, entirely unsatisfactory in the light of the free speech justifications discussed in the Introduction to this book.[58] The Court appeared to afford little weight to the value of the speech in question in terms of providing worthwhile dissent from established thought. In attacking the *manner* of the dissent from established religious ideas, the Court, in contrast to the Commission, failed to understand the nature of artistic endeavour,

---

[55] Ibid, at [49].

[56] Op cit, at 189; he cites K. Ward in *Law, Blasphemy and the Multi-Faith Society* (report of seminar held by CRE and Inter Faith Network of the UK (1989), 34–6).

[57] See the statement to this effect in the well-known free expression decision in the US: (1966) *Ginzburg v US*, 463, 498.

[58] See Chapter 1 at 12–20.

which often uses techniques such as satire in order to make an impact on an audience.[59] In this respect, it disregarded its own earlier statement to the effect that 'Article 10 protects not only the substance of the ideas and information but also the form in which they are conveyed'.[60] It further failed to differentiate between conceding the possibility that the expression in question had value, based on an understanding of the free speech justifications, and assessing that value itself.[61] Clearly, the Court possesses no special expertise allowing it to arbitrate as to the artistic worth of films.

The judgment was also unsatisfactory in a more technical sense, relating to the proportionality of the *sanctions* imposed. The Court ought to have considered the relationship between the end sought (preventing serious religious offence to Catholics living in the local area) and the means used to achieve that end—seizure and confiscation of the film. As to this, the Court said that it:

cannot disregard the fact that the Roman Catholic religion is the religion of the overwhelming majority of Tyroleans. In seizing the film, the Austrian authorities acted to ensure religious peace in that region and to prevent that some people should feel the object of attacks on their religious beliefs in an unwarranted and offensive manner. It is in the first place for the national authorities, who are better placed than the international judge, to assess the need for such a measure in the light of the situation obtaining locally at a given time. In all the circumstances of the present case, the Court does not consider that the Austrian authorities can be regarded as having overstepped their margin of appreciation in this respect.

The foregoing reasoning also applies to the forfeiture, which determined the ultimate legality of the seizure and under Austrian law was the normal sequel thereto. Although the forfeiture made it permanently impossible to show the film anywhere in Austria, the Court considers that the means employed were not disproportionate to the legitimate aim pursued and that therefore the national authorities did not exceed their margin of appreciation in this respect.[62]

In fact, of course, 'the foregoing reasoning', resting as it does upon a local factor—the unusually high proportion of Roman Catholics in the area in which the film was to have been shown—was *logically incapable* of justifying a measure, forfeiture, that had the effect of permanently banning the film across all of Austria,[63] especially as the ban covered areas where there might be few believing Catholics. Plainly, additional arguments, which could justify permanently preventing anyone in Austria seeing the film, were needed, over and above those adduced to justify its initial seizure based on the particular religious characteristics of Tyroleans. In pretending in effect that this local factor, which could perhaps justify the banning of the film in one particular area, could justify the film's *forfeiture*, which prevented it from being seen anywhere at all, the Court not only failed wholly to apply any meaningful form of proportionality reasoning to the forfeiture, it lapsed into downright intellectual dishonesty. Such an

---

[59] It may be noted that, in contrast, Ofcom, the broadcast regulator, made precisely this point in relation to *Jerry Springer: The Opera*; see Chapter 11 at 605–6.

[60] *Oberschlick v Austria* (1991) 19 EHRR 389.

[61] See further D. Pannick, 'Religious Feelings and the European Court' (1995) PL, 7–10.   [62] Op cit.

[63] The Court explicitly conceded that the forfeiture argument would have this effect: op cit, at [57].

approach cannot be characterized as due deference, or an 'application of the margin of appreciation': it amounts to a straightforward failure to require the State to justify a direct act of censorship by reference to the standard of proportionality laid down by the Convention. In short, this was an unconvincing, under-theorized judgment of the Court which is unworthy of its freedom of expression jurisprudence in general. The Opinion of the Commission was, it is suggested, far more in tune with that jurisprudence.

The judgment of the Court in *Wingrove v UK*[64] shows very similar tendencies. Again, the decision can be contrasted with the finding of the Commission in that case that there had been a violation of Article 10.[65] Strasbourg had to consider whether a refusal of the BBFC to issue a certificate licensing a video, *Visions of Ecstasy*, constituted a breach of Article 10. The film depicts erotic visions experienced by St Theresa of Avila, a 16th-century Carmelite nun. In the short, silent film she is depicted first stabbing her hand with a nail, then smearing the blood over her naked breasts, spilling a chalice of communion wine during her writhing and licking it up from the ground, before losing consciousness. The second part shows her in a white habit, her wrists bound by a cord, being erotically embraced by her own psyche, represented by a near-naked woman. That scene is intercut by scenes showing St Theresa, as part of her fantasies, kissing and embracing Christ who is fastened to the cross. She kisses his wounds and sits astride him in a manner reflecting intense arousal. 'For a few seconds, it appears that Christ responds to her kisses;'[66] his fingers also appear to twine themselves around hers in the final seconds of the film.

The BBFC, the film regulator, took the view that if the video had been granted a classification certificate and shown in the UK, a private prosecution for blasphemy might have been brought successfully, principally because 'the wounded body of the crucified Christ is presented solely as the focus of, and at certain moments a participant in, the erotic desire of St Teresa'.[67] The applicant's argument was that:

the video is not concerned with anything which God or Jesus Christ did, or thought or might have approved of. It is about the erotic visions and imaginings of a sixteenth-century Carmelite nun—namely St Teresa of Avila. It is quite plain that the Christ figure exists in her fantasy as the Board expressly accepts.[68]

The refusal to issue the certificate meant that the video could not be distributed. The Court found that the restriction was prescribed by law—the BBFC was acting within its powers under s 4(1) of the Video Recordings Act 1984[69]—and that no general uncertainty was apparent as to the definition of blasphemy formulated in the *Lemon* case.

---

[64] Opinion of the Commission: (1994) 19 EHRR CD 54. Judgment of 25 November 1996, Case 19/1995/525/611; (1996) 24 EHRR 1. For further discussion, see S. Ghandi and J. James, 'The English law of blasphemy and the European Convention on Human Rights' [1998] *EHRLR* 430.

[65] *Wingrove v UK* (1994) 76-A DR 26.   [66] Ibid, at [9].

[67] From the transcript of the BBFC's decision letter, quoted ibid, at [13].

[68] Ibid, at [16]—quoted from the applicant's letter to the Video Appeals Council.

[69] See Chapter 12 at 630–5.

The refusal of the certificate had the aim, it was found, of protecting the rights of others within Article 10(2) and was consonant with the aim of the protection afforded by Article 9 to religious freedom. In considering the necessity and proportionality of the restriction, the Court went on to find that while the margin of appreciation allowed to States would be narrow in relation to political speech, it would be wide in relation to offending 'intimate personal convictions within the field of morals or, especially, religion'.[70] It also placed strong emphasis on the fact that views hostile to Christianity could lawfully be expressed within English law, given the narrow scope of the offence of blasphemy:

it is the manner in which the views are advocated rather than the views themselves which the law seeks to control . . . The high degree of profanation that must be attained [is] . . . itself a safeguard against arbitrariness.[71]

The Court recognized that 'the case involves prior restraint [and thus] calls for special scrutiny by the Court' (citing *Observer and Guardian v UK*).[72] Nevertheless, it found, having viewed the video, that the decision of the BBFC that it would outrage and insult the feelings of believing Christians could not be said to be arbitrary or excessive. The national authorities had not overstepped their margin of appreciation: no breach of Article 10 had occurred.

Looking at the decision in a little more detail, and bearing in mind the analysis of proportionality in Chapter 2,[73] it is worth asking how the Court arrived at the view that there was a 'pressing social need' to interfere with expression in this area, as required by its jurisprudence. Its conclusion was that:

. . . the fact remains that there is as yet not sufficient ground in the legal and social orders of the Member States of the Council of Europe to conclude that a system whereby a State can impose restrictions on the propagation of material on the basis that it is blasphemous is, in itself, unnecessary in a democratic society and thus incompatible with the Convention.[74]

This is a remarkable passage: it completely overturns the burden lying on the state to justify its actions. As Ghandhi and James point out:

With the greatest respect to the Court, to argue that certain restrictions have not been shown to be unnecessary, is not at all the same thing as showing there is a 'pressing social need' to curtail freedom of expression. First, the former is purely a negative argument and secondly, it seems to reverse the burden of proof and impose on the applicant to show it was unnecessary, whereas logically surely it must be for the Government to show that there is a positive 'pressing social need' . . . The apparent reversal in the burden of proof is completely unjustified.[75]

This judgment strongly resembles that in *Otto-Preminger* in revealing a strange failure in a court of human rights to understand or afford weight to the familiar free speech

---

[70] Op cit, at [58].   [71] Ibid, at [60].   [72] (1991), A216, at [60]. See Chapter 3 at 156–7.
[73] See esp. 94–6 et seq.   [74] Op cit, at [57].
[75] S. Ghandhi and J. James, 'The English Law of Blasphemy and the European Convention on Human Rights' (1998) 4 *EHRLR* 430, 443.

justifications. The judgment also reveals an inability to appreciate that a complete ban on a film is especially difficult to defend if the principle of moral autonomy is to be given any weight at all. It failed to understand the value of allowing dissent, not only from established views of religious figures, but also from conventional views as to the way in which they may be portrayed. In placing so much emphasis on the question of the manner of the portrayal, it shows a readiness to stifle artistic initiative, thereby preventing the free debate of the ideas the film portrays and also curbing the outgrowths in terms of further artistic exploration of similar ideas that it might have fostered.

Moreover, although the Court accepted that it was most unlikely that any believing Christians would ever purchase the film—especially if it had been licensed as fit for sale only in registered sex shops, as would have been possible—it found that:

it is in the nature of video works that once they become available on the market they can, in practice, be copied, lent, rented, sold and viewed in different homes, thereby easily escaping any form of control by the authorities.[76]

The Court acknowledged the drastic nature of the penalty imposed:

It is true that the measures taken by the authorities amounted to a complete ban on the film's distribution. However, this was an understandable consequence of the opinion of the competent authorities that the distribution of the video would infringe the criminal law.[77]

This, however, is a non-sequiter: it was of course understandable that the BBFC would not allow the distribution of a film it viewed as probably infringing the criminal law; but that is not a relevant matter in Strasbourg terms. The question should be, not whether the actions of the authorities were understandable, but whether the law, under which they so acted, is *justifiable*. The fact is that a range of sanctions are available in respect of offensive expression: the least restrictive ones entail imposing requirements as to the distribution, availability and packaging of the work in such a way as to render it highly unlikely to reach an audience that would be offended by it: in this case that would have amounted to licensing it for distribution in registered sex shops only. The next most restrictive measure would have been a criminal prosecution; the most restrictive was a total ban. The UK authorities chose the most restrictive: this should have been considered in relation to the harm threatened by the work in question, not whether, given the state of the much-criticized English law of blasphemy, it was understandable that a certificate was refused. As Judge Pettiti put it in his concurring judgment:

The fact that the legislation on blasphemy, profanation or defamation may give rise to a prosecution does not in itself justify, under Article 10 (art. 10) of the European Convention, a total ban on the distribution of a book or video.[78]

It was this point, in fact, that the Commission had founded upon: the severity of the sanction—a total ban—measured against the relative lack of likelihood that anyone

---

[76] Ibid, at [63].   [77] Ibid, at [64].   [78] Op cit.

likely to be offended by the film would ever actually see it. It was not likely that anyone would stumble across the film inadvertently, as had happened in relation to works of art in *Muller v Switzerland*[79] and nor would the film be on display to the general public, as in *Otto-Preminger*.[80] As to the notion that offence would be caused by the mere knowledge that the film existed, the Commission was clear:

The fact that certain Christians, who had heard of the existence of the video, might be outraged by the thought that such a film was on public sale and available to those who wished to see it, cannot, in the view of the Commission, amount to a sufficiently compelling reason to prohibit its lawful supply.[81]

The interference with Article 10 was therefore disproportionate to the aim pursued: the drastic restriction upon freedom of expression represented by prior restraint could not be justified by the very minor risk that anyone would be confronted with the film who would be seriously offended in their religious feelings by it. As Ghandi and James put it, whilst it was conceivable that someone might copy the video and it could thus fall into the hands of Christians, who would be offended by it:

. . . In practice it is inconceivable that anyone would have gone to such lengths to reproduce an 18-minute experimental 'soft-core' pornography video, when far more explicit erotica and 'hard-core' pornography is so readily available on the British market. No doubt such an occurrence [it being viewed by someone who would be offended by it] would be possible, but it is suggested that it would have been a very remote likelihood that a significant number of persons would have been so affected as to warrant control by prior restraint [which] . . . is such a serious derogation from freedom of expression that it should not be tolerated except in the clearest possible case.[82]

What should, however, be noted is that the Court did *not* follow the reasoning in *Otto-Preminger* as to the applicability of Article 9 to the present case. Admittedly the Court said that the aim pursued by the UK in this case was 'fully consonant with the aim of the protections afforded by Article 9 to religious freedom', but it based the legitimate aim not upon protecting Article 9 rights, but generally as relating to 'the rights of others exception in Article 10(2)'. This was noted in the concurring judgment of Judge Pettiti, who said emphatically:

Article 9 is not in issue in the instant case and cannot be invoked. Certainly the Court rightly based its analysis under Article 10 on the rights of others and did not, as it had done in the *Otto-Preminger-Institut* judgment, combine Articles 9 and 10, morals and the rights of others, for which it had been criticised by legal writers.[83]

This suggests the possibility of a retreat from the controversial stance taken in *Otto-Preminger*—something of great significance for the future course of the English law of blasphemy, as considered below.

---

[79] (1991) 13 EHRR 212.   [80] Op cit, at [67].   [81] Ibid, at [68].   [82] Op cit, at 446.
[83] Op cit.

DOMESTIC APPROACHES TO BLASPHEMY LAW UNDER THE HRA

The state of the law in this area was recently reviewed by the Select Committee on Religious Offences in England and Wales (herein 'the Select Committee'); perhaps surprisingly it concluded that it could be said that the current law reflects the 'underlying sense of identity of the British people, their innate respect for the values of a fair and just society resting on ... Christian teachings'.[84] The Committee identifies some traditionalists as likely to feel a 'real sense of loss which might easily be turned to anger, if the delicate balance ... of our nation were to be destroyed too roughly by legislation for which there has ... been no public surge of demand'.[85] Where the European Court of Human Rights leaves a wide margin of appreciation to Member States in determining the extent of the exceptions to a Convention right, this could be taken to imply that, at least until a common European conception of the width of the exception emerges, States have the main responsibility for ensuring that rigorous human rights standards are maintained. It is suggested that the ease with which publications can infringe blasphemy law in the UK does not represent a maintenance of such standards and that therefore, reform of blasphemy law should be attempted, now that the HRA is in force, by domestic judges who are not trammelled by the margin of appreciation doctrine. Moreover, given the widespread criticism of the decisions in *Otto-Preminger* and *Wingrove*, and the failure to apply basic principles of protection for freedom of expression that they reveal, there are strong grounds for arguing that the domestic courts should not follow them, but should look for guidance to the Commission in both instances, and to courts in other jurisdictions in order to achieve a more developed understanding of those principles.

For example, in the well-known judgment in *Cohen v California*,[86] the US Supreme Court found that a political view expressed in profane terms was protected by the First Amendment. The Court said:

much linguistic expression serves a dual communicative function: it conveys not only ideas capable of relatively precise, detached explication, but otherwise inexpressible emotions as well ... words are often chosen as much for their emotive as their cognitive force. We cannot sanction the view that the Constitution, while solicitous of the cognitive content of individual speech, has little regard for that emotive function which, practically speaking, may often be the most important element of the overall message sought to be communicated.

These words would clearly be equally applicable to a film such as *Council in Heaven*, which had both an emotive and a cognitive function, or to *Visions of Ecstasy*, which had a largely emotive function.

There are at least two clear reasons why some change is needed in the current law.

---

[84] Op cit, Ch 4, at [34].   [85] Ibid, at [35].

[86] (1971) 403 US 15, 25–6. The decision, regarding the words 'Fuck the draft' could be viewed as affected by being taken in the context of political speech. Nevertheless, lower courts have applied the words regarding emotive communication to visual expression that cannot be regarded as political expression: *Cinevision Corp v City of Burbank* 7456 F 2d 560, p 569 (concerning music) and *Birkenshaw v Haley* (1974) 409 F Supp 13 ED Mich (concerning mime).

First, from a pragmatic point of view, the present situation, since it is perceived by Muslims as unfair, is a considerable source of racial tension: it both engenders feelings of anger and alienation in the Muslim community and, when these feelings are expressed through such activities as book burning and attacks on booksellers stocking *The Satanic Verses*, increased feelings of hostility towards Muslims in certain sections of the non-Muslim population. In particular, many Muslims, for whom faith and religious belief is of paramount importance (often much more so than for many who would define themselves as Christians), highlight the fact that 'prejudice and hostility against Islamic communities are prevalent in all European Member States, and have often led to discrimination against Muslims and their exclusion from mainstream socio-economic activities'.[87] Secondly, from the standpoint of a liberal democracy, it is indefensible that the State should single out one group of citizens and protect their religious feelings while others are without such protection. The peculiarity of the law in singling out Anglicans becomes ever more glaring: '[They] are not a community at particular risk in this country, so there is no possible justification for privileging them at law. Unlike Muslims, [they] have [their] own special schools, a monarch to defend [their] faith and . . . automatic seats in Parliament.'[88] The Select Committee also pointed out, however, that 'most Muslim groups . . . are opposed to the repeal of the law of blasphemy'; the Muslim Council of Britain views abolition alone as 'negative equalization'. In other words, Muslims favour extension of the law to cover Islam. The Board of Deputies of British Jews believes, it may be noted, that extension would 'raise inherent contradictions' and that the law should be retained as it stands.[89] It may be borne in mind that Jews are to an extent protected indirectly from attacks on their faith by the race hatred laws.[90] Nevertheless, the argument of principle as to abolition remains: the Law Commission in 1985 pointed out that 'it should not be the policy of the law to seek to assert the truth of any particular religion by means of the criminal law'.[91]

In what follows, therefore, the question whether blasphemy law should be extended, abolished or replaced by an offence of incitement to religious hatred, will be considered from the point of view of the philosophical justifications which would support each alternative. The probable effect of each course of action on racial tension will also be briefly considered. This discussion is premised upon the importance of freedom of expression and the principle that it should be infringed only if a similar individual right is threatened by speech, or if the values which lead us to support free speech are not at issue in the instant case, or if the speech carries a real risk of damage to the wellbeing of society.

When blasphemy law is considered in suitable instances under the HRA, the arguments for its abolition or extension are likely to be canvassed. Since blasphemy is a

---

[87] Lord Ahmed, quoting the European Monitoring Centre on Racism and Xenophobia, HL Deb Col 319 (30 January 2002).

[88] Sara Maitland, *The Independent*, 27 November 1997.   [89] Op cit.   [90] See below at 512.

[91] Report No. 145, 'Offences Against Religion and Public Worship' (1985), at [2.24].

common law doctrine, the judges are in principle at liberty to abolish, extend or curtail it, under s 6 of the HRA. The argument to extend the blasphemy law to cover other faiths would clearly find support in principle if the present law is viewed as having a firm basis in Convention values.[92] It receives strong support, it is suggested, from the decision in *Otto Preminger*, which would have to be taken into account by the domestic judiciary, under s 2 HRA, in a suitable case. It could be argued that since the Strasbourg Court has found that Article 9 covers a right to be free from the knowledge that expression offensive to one's religious beliefs is occurring in one's locality, and that that right further covers a ban on such speech that covers the whole country, the reach of Article 9 has been greatly extended. As noted above, the Court held in that case that, 'in extreme cases, the effect of particular methods of opposing or denying religious beliefs can be such as to inhibit those who hold such beliefs from exercising their freedom to hold and express them'.[93] Muslims could readily argue that the sale of a book or showing of a film with a theme similar to that of *The Satanic Verses* amounts on this argument to a violation of their Article 9 rights and that a complete ban, as opposed to a very restricted sale, confined to certain localities, would therefore be warranted. Article 14 could also be invoked in conjunction with Article 9. The argument of the European Commission on Human Rights in *Choudhury*,[94] to the effect that Article 9 does not include a positive obligation on the part of the State to protect religious sensibilities, may be doubted on the basis that positive obligations have been accepted under Article 8.[95] On the other hand, as noted above, the Court did not base its decision in *Wingrove* on the notion that Article 9 was engaged, and one of the concurring judges explicitly denied that it was.[96] UK courts confronted with such a case could therefore plausibly assert that, when considering the issue, and their duty to take account of the Convention jurisprudence under section 2(1), they are not obliged to follow *Otto-Preminger* in this respect. Of course, section 2(1) does not make the Convention jurisprudence binding, in any event, but it will be recalled[97] that in *Alconbury*, Lord Steyn stated that UK courts 'should follow any clear and constant jurisprudence of the European Court of Human Rights'.[98] It may well be

---

[92] For general discussion of this issue, see 'Speech, religious discrimination and blasphemy' (1989: Proceedings of the American Society of International Law, p 427 *et seq*) and, in particular, Reisman's article, pp 435–9: he makes out an elegant thesis that attempts such as Ayatollah Khomeni's, to punish and deter unorthodox references to the Koran amount to a 'claim of the right to exclusive control of major symbols of global culture and the prerogative of deciding how they are to be used artistically' (p 437). He expresses concern over 'the support lent by religious leaders in the West' to this claim and the criticism of Rushdie expressed by some of them. He warns that imposing censorship on artists or forcing them to internalize such censorship through insisting that free expression amounts to a form of religious intolerance will lead to the deterioration of the arts: creative endeavour will become a kind of 'communal Rubik cube in which a limited number of approved elements are moved feverishly round in an ever decreasing number of "new" combinations' (p 439).

[93] Op cit, at [57].   [94] *Choudhury v UK* (1991) No 17349/1990; (1991) 12 HRLJ 172.

[95] See Chapter 13 at 668–74.   [96] Op cit, at [497].

[97] The point is discussed further in Chapter 3 at 145, esp note 230.

[98] *R (on the application of Alconbury Developments Ltd) v Secretary of State for the Environment, Transport and the Regions* [2003] 2 AC 295, at [26].

argued that the principle in question—that Article 9 gives rise to a positive right to be free from having one's religious feelings outraged—cannot be seen to amount to a 'clear and constant' aspect of the Strasbourg jurisprudence. It was expressed only in a single case, denied by the Commission in another (*Choudhury*),[99] and not followed by the Court in a subsequent decision (*Wingrove*) where one judge explicitly interpreted that absence of affirmation of the approach to Article 9 in *Otto Preminger* as implicit disapproval of it. If this argument is accepted, it would be open to a UK court to decide the question on its merits.

Given the Court of Appeal decision in *Choudhury*, the fact that Parliament has recently considered the matter, but neither abolished blasphemy law nor extended it,[100] and the retrospectivity issue (considered below), it would, perhaps depressingly, be likely that a domestic court would make only minor changes to the status quo. Amongst these could be the introduction of the requirement of some form of *mens rea*, and of a 'public interest defence' under Article 10. Given, however, that the UK law of blasphemy *without* these features was found to be compatible with Article 10 in *Wingrove*, a conservative judge would be unlikely to make any changes at all, citing *Wingrove* as respectable grounds for so doing.

Judicial *extension* of the law of blasphemy to cover other religions would plainly raise an issue under Article 7 of the Convention, which prohibits the retrospective application of the criminal law. The decision in *S.W. and C.R. v United Kingdom*[101] suggests that Strasbourg is prepared to give some leeway to domestic courts in common law countries to develop the criminal law, particularly in a Convention-friendly direction, as in that case. However, the finding in that case that there had been no breach of Article 7 by the judicial abolition of the 'marital rape exemption' was based primarily upon the finding by the Court that the change in the law was reasonably foreseeable, if necessary with appropriate advice, as a series of decisions had undermined the scope and credibility of the marital rape exemption. No such argument could be made in the instant case, since the decision of the domestic court

---

[99]   *Choudhury v UK* (1991) No 17349/1990; (1991) 12 HRLJ 172. But see also some comments by the Court in *Murphy v Ireland* [2003] ECHR 352 at [65] to the effect that among a speaker's duties under Article 10 is 'a duty to avoid as far as possible an expression that is, in regard to objects of veneration, gratuitously offensive to others and profane' (citing *Otto Preminger* at [46, 47 & 49]). There is a reference in the same paragraph to such duties also including a 'requirement to ensure the peaceful enjoyment of the rights guaranteed under Article 9', which could sound like a return to *Otto Preminger* reasoning (i.e. implying an Article 9 right not to be offended). However, the Court does not specifically state that offensive expression about sacred matters violates Article 9 rights, merely implying that speech *can* interfere with peaceful enjoyment of those rights. We may, for example, imagine a person bursting into a religious service and disrupting it with heckling and obscenities: that would arguably violate rights under Article 9, but not in the *Otto Preminger* manner. *Murphy* was not a blasphemy case, and plainly not decided as a 'clashing rights' case; overall, it does not appear to be a case that can be argued in support of the *Otto Preminger* approach to blasphemy offences.

[100]   In considering the Religious Offences Bill 2005: specific votes were taken on the abolition of blasphemy law, but not carried. See HC Deb at 8 November 2005, col 520 *et seq*.

[101]   (1996) 21 EHRR. This decision arose out of an application by two men convicted of raping their wives following the decision in *R v R* [1992] 1 AC 599, [1991] 4 All ER 481, which confirmed the removal of the ancient 'marital rape exemption' by the courts.

in *Choudhry*, the only case to address the point, firmly ruled out extending the blasphemy law to Islam.[102]

There would also be practical difficulties, based on the nature of the HRA, in seeking to rely on Article 9 in relation to a bookseller or a film producer or a broadcaster. A Muslim group would not be able to bring an action under s 7(1)(a) based on a free-standing application of Article 9 since the other party would not be 'a public authority'.[103] There would be the possibility of bringing an action based solely on Article 9 where a public authority, such as a media regulator, or possibly the BBC,[104] was involved. If a remedy was available, it would presumably take the form of an injunction, or an award of damages for violation of Article 9, since the Convention cannot be used to create criminal liability.[105] But the most obvious, and, as indicated, probably the only, vehicle existing in domestic law on which to base an Article 9 argument is blasphemy law. The result of an attempt to use the blasphemy law might end in an application for judicial review, as in *Choudhury*. A Muslim group would base their application on the ordinary standing rules, as in *Choudhury*, and then rely on s 7(1)(b) HRA in order to argue that their Article 9 and 14 rights should be afforded recognition.

Clearly, from a legislative point of view, these issues would not arise. At present it appears that the Government is not minded to bring forward proposals to abolish the law of blasphemy. As recently as March 2005, in a written answer a government spokesperson said:

If material or conduct is gratuitously offensive to Christians, and is prosecuted as such, a finding of blasphemy may be the appropriate response by a court to ensure that the rights of others under Article 9 [of the Convention] are protected.[106]

In debate on the religious hatred Bill, however, the Government did recognize that there was a serious issue to be considered in relation to the abolition of the law of blasphemy, but took the view that that Bill was not the right vehicle to achieve it,

---

[102] It would appear virtually impossible that the exception under Article 7(2) could be invoked successfully. The exception provides: 'This Article shall not prejudice the trial and punishment of any person for any act or omission which, at the time when it was committed, was criminal according to the general principles of law recognised by civilised nations.' The fact that, as the Court noted in *Wingrove*, op cit, at [57], 'the application of [blasphemy laws in Europe] is becoming increasingly rare and several States . . . have recently repealed them altogether . . .' would make it almost impossible to argue that making blasphemous statements against Islam was criminal according to such general principles of law. In the US, the First Amendment provides expressly that 'Congress shall make no law respecting an establishment of religion, nor prohibiting the free exercise thereof' and in *Joseph Burstyn Inc v Wilson* (1952) 343 US 495, an attempt to stop the screening of a film on the ground that it was blasphemous failed. The decision made it clear that the offence of blasphemy could not be sustained since it was entirely opposed to First Amendment principles. See also the famous 'Nazis at Skokie' decisions: *Collin v Smith* (1978) 578 F 2d 1197, 7th Cir, (1978) 436 US 953, (1978) 439 US 916; *Skokie v Nat Socialist Party* (1978) 373 NE 2d 21; they raised issues which have parallels with those in *Otto Preminger*.

[103] See Chapter 3 at 112–22.

[104] For the possibility that the BBC would be treated for some purposes as a public authority under the HRA, see Chapter 3 at 114–15 and 119–22.

[105] Per s 7(8) HRA.   [106] *Official Report*, 3 March 2005; col WA 40.

further consultation and consideration being necessary.[107] However, as Lord Avebury, who chaired the Select Committee on Religious Offences, which examined the whole issue of reform of this area of law, said bluntly:

The Minister repeated what the Home Secretary has said elsewhere: that he does not want to move to legislate on the matter until there has been proper consultation. I do not know what we were doing for a year in the Select Committee: We took evidence from everyone: the Church of England, the Catholics, the Methodists, the Muslims, the Sikhs, the Hindus—you name it, they all came. We spent a whole year examining just this question. Now the Minister wants us to start on another round of consultation. That is an excuse for procrastination.[108]

In terms of extension, there remain other, formidable difficulties, many of which have been pointed out by the Law Commission.[109] As two commentators have put it:

In a multi-cultural British society presumably protection would have to extend beyond the obvious cases of Islam, Buddhism, Judaism and Hinduism to include also Zoroastrianism and the Bahai faith and many other minority religions. It is interesting to note that, on the particular facts of the cases before it, the European Commission on Human Rights has found no need to decide whether Scientology, the Divine Light Zentrum and Druidism were religions.[110]

Inevitably, decisions excluding certain 'religions' from the protection of blasphemy laws would attract immediate complaint that the practitioners thereof were being discriminated against in the exercise of their Article 9 rights. There are further problems:

Although an English jury might be expected to understand the doctrines of Christianity, this may not be so with other religions, particularly some of the more obscure ones. Expert evidence would no doubt have to be called for both prosecution and defence. Furthermore, if different sects of the same religion had differing views, e.g. Sunni and Shia Muslims, and the published materials scandalised one sect but not the other, would that be blasphemous? Since the only mental requirement in the offence is, according to the Gay News case, an intention to publish the words complained of, the width of the offence would be impossibly wide and there would be a grave danger that a publication might scandalise some obscure sect or religion unknown to the author of the works.[111]

But, practical issues aside, the key issue of principle concerns the validity of the arguments that freedom of expression should give way to a right to freedom of religion that includes the right not to be offended by the promulgation of expression that offends against religious sensibilities. To evaluate the force of this argument, it is necessary first to identify which, if any, of the rationales for blasphemy law would provide support for both its continued existence and extension, and which would not. Three rationales will be considered in turn: the argument from the

---

[107] See HL Deb, col 540 (8 November 2005).   [108] Ibid, at col. 542.
[109] Report No. 145 (1985) 'Criminal Law: Offences against Religion and Public Worship'.
[110] Ghandhi and James, op cit, at 448–9 (references omitted).   [111] Ibid, at 449.

protection of society, the argument from preventing individual distress, and the argument from the right to religious freedom. The point of view which sees blasphemy law as protecting those shared beliefs of a society which are essential to its survival[112] would not, it is submitted, support the extension of the law to cover other faiths; the law would then be protecting a whole set of conflicting beliefs and thus supporting religious pluralism, not the survival of religious conformity. It may be argued that the law should uphold religious pluralism as a shared belief, but abolition of the offence of blasphemy would do this far more simply and effectively than extension.

The argument that blasphemy laws are justified because they protect individual believers from mental anguish immediately runs into a host of problems over extension of the law. For if one is concerned to protect individuals from the mental distress which can flow from attacks on deeply held beliefs,[113] it is not readily apparent that society should not also outlaw attacks upon deeply held non-religious beliefs, such as a deep belief in the equality of the sexes.[114] But one would then arrive at a position in which the criminal law would be being used to prevent people from attacking or insulting the deep beliefs of others. Arguably, such a law would be unworkable, since it would require judgments to be made about indeterminable matters such as the depth at which a belief was held. More importantly, not only would such a law represent a major infringement of the individual's freedom of speech, offering only the prevention of distress as a justification, it would be philosophically indefensible besides. If we are really committed to the notion that free discussion is the best way to arrive at the truth,[115] it seems nonsensical to abandon that position when our most important beliefs are at stake; if anything, we should be most concerned precisely to encourage free discussion of our deep beliefs since, almost axiomatically, it is our deepest beliefs which we most wish to be true. In this respect it is rather alarming that one of the judges in *Wingrove*, Judge Pettiti, in his concurring judgment expressed the clear view that:

Profanation and serious attacks on the deeply held feelings of others or on religious or secular ideals can be relied on under Article 10 para. 2 (art. 10–2) in addition to blasphemy.

---

[112] Lord Devlin is usually associated with the thesis that society may justifiably protect its shared moral beliefs through the criminal law: see his *The Enforcement of Morals*, Oxford University Press, 1965, considered briefly in Chapter 8 at 392–4. It is arguable that the protection of society was, historically at least, one of the purposes of blasphemy law: see, e.g., *Taylor's case* [1676] 1 Vent 293 in which it was said: 'For to say, Religion is a cheat is to dissolve all those obligations whereby civil societies are preserved.'

[113] Note, e.g., the *dicta* of Lord Scarman in *Lemon* [1979] AC 617, p 620 that 'there is a case for legislation extending [blasphemy law] to protect the religious beliefs and feelings of non-Christians'. Arguably, however, he saw protection of feelings as ultimately aimed at 'the internal tranquillity of the Kingdom'. See above, at 484–5.

[114] Recognizing this, a number of commentators have attempted to frame definitions of 'religious belief' in which the term includes both actual religious convictions and those beliefs which hold a place in people's minds analogous to that held by religious belief. See, e.g., Clements, 'Defining "religion" in the First Amendment: a functional approach' (1989) 74 *Cornell LR* 532.

[115] For an exposition of this theory, see Chapter 1, pp 14–16.

He went on to give an example:

the use of a figure of symbolic value as a great thinker in the history of mankind (such as Moses, Dante or Tolstoy) in a portrayal which seriously offends the deeply held feelings of those who respect their works or thought may, in some cases, justify judicial supervision so that the public can be alerted through the reporting of court decisions.[116]

One would only have to add Marx or Lenin to this list to arrive at a perfect recipe for totalitarian censorship of anti-communist speech, on the grounds of the offence caused to deeply committed Marxist-Leninists. This is not an instance in which a 'levelling-up' of the protection given to religious believers in order to extend it to secularists is desirable.

It is submitted that the only justification for continuance of the blasphemy law which could offer it even *prima facie* support is the argument from the right to religious freedom, which is protected under Article 9 of the Convention. The need to provide such protection is also viewed as falling within the 'rights of others' exception to Article 10 and, therefore, arguably justifies the banning of publications that might offend religious sensibilities, as the Court of Human Rights found in *Otto-Preminger* and *Wingrove*. It is contended that the *particular* argument accepted by the Court that such publications infringe Article 9 is deeply flawed, as discussed above. At a more general level, the defence of such a view has been put forward by Poulter, who contends that:

Freedom of religion is . . . a valuable human right and it may be doubted whether it can be fully enjoyed in practice if the State allows religious beliefs to be vilified and insulted in a gratuitous manner.[117]

The first assertion made here, about the value of religious freedom, is of course readily conceded. However, the argument, as expressed by the Court of Human Rights, then goes on to assume that the State is under a positive duty to facilitate the full enjoyment in practice of its citizens' right to freedom of religion, taking that term to encompass a duty to prevent attacks on religion which take a certain objected-to form. This is surely a mistaken view; rather, it is submitted, the right to religious freedom is violated if one is not free to choose, express and manifest one's religious beliefs:[118] the right is not so violated simply because one is not protected from mental suffering caused by verbal attacks upon one's religion or offensive portrayals of it. As Van Dijk and Van Hoof put it in one of the leading texts:

this decision [in Otto-Preminger] is mistaken. The screening of the film in no way

---

[116] Op cit.

[117] S. Poulter, 'Towards legislative reform of the blasphemy and racial hatred laws' [1991] *PL* 371, p 376.

[118] Thus, Article 18 of the Universal Declaration of Human Rights provides that: 'Everyone has the right to freedom of thought, conscience and religion; this right includes freedom to change his religion or belief and freedom . . . in public or private to manifest his religion or belief in teaching, practice, worship and observance.' Both the International Covenant on Civil and Political Rights (Article 18) and the European Convention (Article 9) contain very similar provisions.

would have limited or inhibited Roman Catholics in manifesting their religion ... a right [not to be insulted in one's religious views] is not included in Article 9 but is on the contrary inconsistent with the 'pluralism indissociable from a democratic society'[119] embedded in Article 9.[120]

Even if it were to be accepted for the purposes of argument that the religious freedom of those from Christian faiths should be protected by the blasphemy law, it is denied that this finding would be a conclusive argument for continuing or, *a fortiori*, extending the protection. If Poulter's contention, and that of the Court of Human Rights, are correct, then we are confronted by a situation in which two important individual rights—freedom of religion and freedom of speech—come into conflict with each other. In such a situation, it is surely reasonable, not simply to assume that freedom of religion should override freedom of speech, but rather to attempt to weigh up the extent to which right would be infringed if the other was given precedence. In other words, which would suffer most? If this is done, the argument runs as follows: if there was no offence of blasphemy, this might mean that on occasion some distress, perhaps acute, would be associated with the practice of one's religion, although those aware that they might suffer distress could normally take steps to ensure that they did not encounter the offending publication. If there *was* such an offence, it might mean that use of the coercive sanctions of the law would damage the liberty to write creatively or speak one's mind freely on religious matters.[121] Clearly, the damage done to freedom of religion if there is no blasphemy law is less than the damage done to freedom of speech if there is one.

In any event, the argument that regards a blasphemy law as essential because the right to religious freedom demands it, immediately runs into difficulties since it is clearly necessary to define religion. One could not follow the path described above and define religion to include secular but deeply held beliefs, as one would then be placed in the absurd position of defending secular ideas from attack by reference to a right to religious freedom. Nor could one overcome this difficulty by adopting a pragmatic stance and framing a statute protecting only the five major world religions. If the individual's right to religious freedom demands protection against vilificatory attacks upon her religion,[122] and since presumably members of less well known religions are as entitled to religious freedom as members of the major religions, it follows that they must also be entitled to protection against such attacks. Clearly, therefore, a satisfactory definition of religion would have to be arrived at. The difficulties of framing such a definition have already been noted. The most pressing difficulty is that there does not exist a common definition of 'religion'. A host of definitions of the

[119] *Kokkinakis v Greece* A 260-A, p 18.
[120] P. Van Dijk and F. Van Hoof, *Theory and Practice of the European Convention on Human Rights*, London: Kluwer, 1998, p 551.
[121] Poulter concedes that his proposed extension of the blasphemy law (see op cit, at 378 *et seq*) might well have caught *The Satanic Verses* (at 384–5).
[122] This proposition is not conceded as indicated. It is put forward by Poulter, op cit.

word 'religion' exist from the Oxford English Dictionary,[123] decided cases[124] and academic writings,[125] but some of these fail to deal with certain faiths many would accept as religions, such as those which embrace polytheism.[126] The Government, when addressing the reform of the law of charities[127] wished to ensure that 'faiths that are multi-deity (such as Hinduism) or non-deity (such as some types of Buddhism)'[128] should be considered religions (and thus able to achieve charitable status). In its reply to the Select Committee report on Religious Offences, which emphasized the difficulties of a lack of a precise definition of religion,[129] the Government recognized that 'any legal drafting would need to take into account the Human Rights Act 1998, for example, the probable need to protect non-belief and doctrines whose status as religions is debatable'.[130] In this connection, it is also worth recalling that the UN General Assembly Declaration on the Elimination of All Forms of Intolerance and Discrimination Based on Religion and Belief, as one commentator notes, 'does not seek to define religion or belief'. He explains: 'This is because no definition could be agreed upon, as none could be agreed when the texts of Article 18 of the Universal Declaration and Article 18 of the ICCPR were drafted.'[131] Since, therefore, the impossibility of framing such a definition seems to be well attested to, it may reasonably be concluded that the project to extend blasphemy law to cover other faiths is fraught with difficulty.

On all these grounds, it is concluded that the argument that freedom of religion demands a blasphemy law fails. It follows, if this view is accepted, that the abolition of the current law can readily be defended on Article 10 grounds without fear of offending against Article 9. Christian beliefs and doctrines could, therefore, be placed in the same position as Islamic or deeply held secular beliefs in that their adherents could choose to avert their eyes from distasteful portrayals of their beliefs, and to combat what they regard as untrue or unfair representations of Christianity with—in their view—more truthful or more inspirational speech.

Abolition of the blasphemy law would also tend to ease racial tension since at least it

---

[123] 'The belief in a superhuman controlling power, esp in a personal God or gods entitled to obedience and worship', Concise Oxford Dictionary, 8th edn. OUP (1990).

[124] *Church of the New Faith v Commissioner for Pay-roll Tax* (1983) where the Australian Supreme Court considered any 'belief in a supernatural Being, Thing or Principle' to be sufficient, holding that scientology was charitable under the head of 'religion'.

[125] The Association of Muslim Lawyers in their submission to the Select Committee defined the beliefs to be protected by reference to a deity. Select Committee on Religious Offences in England and Wales (2003), Ch 4, para 45.

[126] See the definition of religion from Statutory Instrument 2003 No.1660, the Employment Equality (Religion or Belief) Regulations 2003 s 2(1) where 'religion or belief' is defined as meaning 'any religion, religious belief or similar philosophical belief'.

[127] Cabinet Office Strategy Unit, 'Private Action, Public Benefit' (Cabinet Office, 2002).

[128] Ibid, para 4.34.   [129] Select Committee at [46].

[130] The Government Reply to the Report from the Religious Offences Committee (2003), HL Paper 95, para.21(iii).

[131] K. Boyle, 'Religious intolerance and the incitement of hatred', in Coliver (ed.), *Striking a Balance: Hate Speech, Freedom of Expression and Non-Discrimination*, Human Rights Centre, University of Essex, 1992.

would be clear that all religions were being accorded an equal lack of protection. This would be the better solution, since it is by no means clear that extending blasphemy law would ease the problem. Indeed, it is possible that if, for example, Muslims had been able to use an extended blasphemy law to suppress *The Satanic Verses*,[132] considerable resentment might well have been engendered in the non-Muslim community. The justified grievance felt by Muslims about the unfairness of the present law would, to a certain extent, be remedied if blasphemy was abolished altogether as an offence.

It may finally be noted that secularists decided to mark the 25th anniversary of the conviction in *Lemon* of the publishers of *Gay News* and Professor Kirkup for blasphemy in relation to the poem 'The Love that Dares to Speak its Name' by reading the poem publicly in Trafalgar Square.[133] On 22 July 2002, 11 speakers,[134] including writers, academics and MPs, each took a turn to read a verse of the poem. The event was intended as an act of civil disobedience, both to protest against the infringement of free speech represented by the original prosecution, and in effect to defy the prosecuting authorities either to bring a prosecution, or declare the offence 'dead'. The police took no action against those reading the poem, but filmed the event and sent the film to the DPP, who decided not to bring a prosecution. Whilst the episode does not indicate that the offence no longer exists, it may indicate that only in the most extreme possible circumstances would it nowadays be prosecuted, if ever. The fact that no blasphemy prosecution was brought in respect of the screening by the BBC of the *Jerry Springer Opera*, despite the evident widespread outrage that it caused to Christians,[135] is further evidence of this.

INCITEMENT TO RELIGIOUS HATRED: EXTENDING THE OFFENCE OF INCITEMENT TO RACIAL HATRED?

INTRODUCTION

The current atmosphere of concern about the success of multi-culturalism and tolerance of and between different religious groups renders the question whether such an extension to the law should be made a particularly sharp one. Four recent examples of religious tension may be highlighted. The first was the shocking murder by an Islamic extremist of the film-maker Van Gogh in Holland, following release of his film *Submission*, which was about Islam and violence against women,[136] and used images of

---

[132] See Poulter, op cit.

[133] See the account given at http://www.petertatchell.net/religion/blasphemy.htm.

[134] Namely, Barry Duke, Shirely Dent, Jim Herrick, Jonathan Meades, George Melly, Professor Richard Norman, Sam Rimmer, Brian Sedgemore MP, Hanne Stinson, Peter Tatchell, and Keith Wood.

[135] See below at 509–10 and Chapter 11 at 605–6.

[136] It told the story of four Muslim women who were beaten, raped, and forced into marriage, and were calling upon Allah for help.

words from the Koran being projected onto a woman's body. It provoked a strong reaction in Europe, with headlines such as 'Dutch find the strength to take on their "new Nazis" ',[137] raising the fear of an all-out confrontation between the Western tradition of free speech and artistic expression and Islamic fundamentalism—a re-run of the Rushdie affair. But a remarkable feature of the affair was an article appearing on Index on Censorship's website written by one Rohan Jayaskera as follows:

Van Gogh . . . with Somalia-born Dutch MP Ayann Hirsi Ali . . . made a furiously provocative film that featured actresses portraying battered Muslim women, naked under transparent Islamic-style shawls, their bodies marked with texts from the Koran that supposedly justify their repression. Van Gogh then roared his Muslim critics into silence with obscenities. An abuse of his right to free speech, it added injury to insult by effectively censoring their moderate views as well.

So without fear of further disturbing already ravaged public sensitivities, applaud Theo van Gogh's death as the marvellous piece of theatre it was. A sensational climax to a lifetime's public performance, stabbed and shot by a bearded fundamentalist, a message from the killer pinned by a dagger to his chest, Theo van Gogh became a martyr to free expression. His passing was marked by a magnificent barrage of noise as Amsterdam hit the streets to celebrate him in the way the man himself would have truly appreciated. And what timing! Just as his long-awaited biographical film of Pim Fortuyn's life is ready to screen. Bravo, Theo! Bravo![138]

Another *Guardian* columnist appeared to hold the makers of the film at least partly responsible for the reaction to it:

In the midst of this tinderbox, insisting on their right to speak freely and with the support of many Dutch people, Hirsi Ali and Van Gogh scattered their sparks—a blistering critique of Islam—with magnificent disregard for the feelings they might be offending.[139]

Such reactions to the horrific murder of an artist, purely for the ideas expressed in his art and the imagery used, perhaps indicate the level of unease and confusion into which 'liberals' have fallen in relation to speech offensive to Muslims. Plainly, some such liberals come at least close to regarding such expression as racist, a viewpoint which to others betrays the essence of the right to free speech—the freedom to attack an ideology, such as Islam—and the conflation of such criticism with attacks upon a human characteristic—race—which cannot be changed so that attacks on it can only be the expression of prejudice and a desire to dominate.

Another issue is equality: some see a willingness to bow to intolerant religious fundamentalism when expressed by ethnic minorities such as Muslims, on the grounds of racial sensitivity, while when it is expressed by Christians it is condemned simply as old-fashioned intolerance. The event which, to some, exemplified this dichotomy was the second of our examples, the decision by the BBC, upheld by Ofcom, to show on terrestrial television the satirical opera *Jerry Springer*, something

---

[137] *Telegraph*, 10 November 2004.
[138] Published in November 2004: the piece is no longer available on Index's website.
[139] 'I feel terribly guilty', John Henley, *Guardian*, 4 November 2004.

which attracted the greatest ever number of complaints about a broadcast: some 55,000 people complained to the BBC before the broadcast and a further 8,860 complained afterwards. Despite the seemingly scurrilous treatment of sacred subjects in this film,[140] Ofcom found no breach of the relevant standards Code.[141] Many were moved to question whether the BBC would have dared to broadcast a show similarly satirizing Mohammed.[142]

A third significant episode was the closure by the organizers of a run of the play *Behzti,* a play about sex abuse and murder in a Sikh temple, after hundreds of protesting Sikhs gathered outside the theatre and sought to storm the building. According to news reports, 'more than 800 people had to be evacuated, security guards were attacked and thousands of pounds' worth of damage was caused'.[143] The organizers, explaining the decision to close the play, said that they could not guarantee public safety if its run continued.

The fourth, and perhaps most significant, event was the so-called 'cartoon' row, which exploded across Europe and then the wider Muslim world in February 2006. One commentator described the ongoing episode thus, speaking of the notorious cartoon showing Mohammed with a bomb-shaped turban with the fuse fizzing:

There has almost certainly never been a more incendiary cartoon in the history of comic illustration. It's this image, among the now infamous Danish cartoons, that is deemed the greatest insult to Islam and, by extension, the world's Muslim population. Such is its apparent potency that thousands have rioted across the globe. Embassies have been burned and protesters shot.[144]

The day before, on 18th February, 16 people were killed in Nigeria, as protesting Muslims burned down churches.[145] Anthony in the *Observer* wrote:

As the cultural critic Kenan Malik, author of *The Meaning of Race*, observes: 'We already live in a climate in which institutions are afraid of giving offence. For instance, John Latham's work God is Great was removed from the Tate gallery.[146] They hadn't received any complaints but they thought it might offend Muslims and so it had to be removed. Self-censorship has become part of the fabric of our lives.'

Surely all those who counsel that the right to freedom of speech is sometimes better not exercised have a strong case? Malik disagrees: 'One of the underlying assumptions of the debate about the cartoons is that in a plural society free speech must necessarily be less free. I believe the opposite. In a plural society it is both inevitable and important that we do give offence. Important because any kind of major political, intellectual, artistic change has always offended deeply held beliefs and that's all for the good.'

---

[140] Including the portrayal of Jesus in a nappy.   [141] See note 135 above.

[142] See, for example, the remarks of Salvation Army spokespersons, reported at 'British Church leaders in Jerry Springer row' http://www.religionnewsblog.com/14000/British-Church-leaders-in-Jerry-Springer-row.

[143] See 'Theatre Attacks Sikh Play Protest' http://news.bbc.co.uk/1/hi/england/west_midlands/4109315.stm

[144] A. Anthony, 'The End of Freedom?' Review, *Observer*, 19 February 2006.

[145] See 'Nigeria Cartoon Riots Kill 16', *Observer*, 19 February 2006.

[146] See http://news.bbc.co.uk/2/hi/entertainment/4281958.stm.

It's likely that fewer people will now want to risk offending Islam . . .[147]

No British newspaper published the cartoons. There is at the moment at least a perception of growing militancy and intolerance by a number of religious denominations, which is heightened by the current preoccupation with, and continuing violent attacks by, Al-Qadi, and its sympathizers, most relevantly and recently, of course, in London on 7 July 2005. This atmosphere pulls both ways: on the one hand, many defenders of freedom of expression perceive it as particularly important to stand firm in defence of traditional Western liberal values and liberties, at a time when radical Muslims, at least, appear to be most hostile to them, and to avoid the kind of self-censorship deprecated above. On the other hand, the very tragedy of alienation and hatred against Western values by its own Muslim citizens revealed by the actions of the British London Tube-bombers and the Madrid bombings in March 2004 leads others to call for urgent action to demonstrate to the Muslim community that society and the government takes its concerns seriously. David Blunkett, then Home Secretary, indeed responded to the events of September 11th by announcing proposals to bring forward a law on incitement to religious hatred:

Regrettably, there are those who are prepared to exploit the tensions created by the global threat [of international terrorism]. Racists, bigots, and hotheads, as well as those associating with terrorists, are prepared to use the opportunity to stir up hate. It is therefore my intention to introduce new laws to ensure that incitement to religious, as well as racial, hatred will become a criminal offence.[148]

There does indeed appear to be a well-founded fear that incidents such as 9/11 and 7/7 result in a significant back-lash in terms of revenge attacks upon the Muslim community. As a House of Commons research paper notes:[149]

The European Monitoring Centre on Racism and Xenophobia commented on the situation in the United Kingdom in a report covering the immediate aftermath of the attacks on the World Trade Centre (to the end of 2001):

'A significant rise in attacks on Muslims was reported across a range of media in the immediate aftermath of September 11. Numbers of incidents of violent assault, verbal abuse and attacks on property were noted, some of which were very serious.'[150]

The International Covenant on Civil and Political Rights, to which the UK is a signatory, requires Contracting States to prohibit the advocacy of 'national, racial or religious hatred that constitutes incitement to discrimination, hostility or violence' (Article 20, emphasis added). Moreover, the Committee of Ministers of Council of Europe (COM-COE) has called upon member states to combat:

statements which may reasonably be understood as hate speech, or as speech likely to

---

[147] A. Anthony, 'Amsterdamned', *Observer*, Part Two, 5 November 2004.
[148] HC Deb, Col 923 (15 October 2001).   [149] *The Racial and Religious Hatred Bill* (no. 95/48) 2005.
[150] The full report is available at http://eumc.eu.int/eumc/material/pub/anti-islam/Synthesis-report_en.pdf.

produce the effect of legitimising or promoting racial hatred, xenophobia, anti-Semitism or other forms of discrimination based on intolerance.[151]

The justification sometimes put forward for abrogating free speech in this area is that prohibiting the advocacy of racial and religious hatred does not strike at the core value of free speech because neither individual self-fulfilment, nor the opportunity to arrive at the truth through free discussion, nor the chance to participate meaningfully in democracy[152] seem to be strongly threatened by such a prohibition. Such an extension, of course, still represents an interference with the individual's moral autonomy, since it amounts to judging for her what is and is not fit for her to hear. However, on one influential viewpoint, the State is supposed to leave such judgments to the individual because to do otherwise would be to violate the individual's basic right to equal concern and respect,[153] and it may be argued that the present situation, in which the advocacy of hatred against Muslims is allowed, while Sikhs and Jews (as racial groups) are protected from such speech,[154] itself amounts to a denial of equal respect for Muslims.[155] Moreover, as stressed further below, there is arguably a pressing *social* need to take measures to protect against further deterioration in relations between certain sections of the Muslim and non-Muslim population. Accordingly, there appears to be an arguable case for the extension of the Public Order Act provisions dealing with racial hatred to cover religious hatred: the interference with moral autonomy involved is necessary to avoid discrimination and there is an argument that the free speech interest involved is relatively weak; in addition, there are strong utilitarian arguments that such a measure would considerably ease racial tension. As one Bishop has put it, 'what is at issue is not the right of free speech, no religion ought to have anything to fear from fair scrutiny and honest debate . . . what is at issue is the abuse of free speech to incite fear, prejudice, contempt and violence.'[156] FAIR (the Forum Against Islamophobia and Racism), in its submission to the Select Committee, pointed to evidence that BNP 'campaigns against Islam and Muslims are deliberate and pre-meditated . . . devised to sit within existing laws'.[157] Often such campaigns

---

[151] Recommendation No. R   [152] See Chapter 1 at 12–19.

[153] See, e.g., R. Dworkin, op cit, and Chapter 1 at 13–14.

[154] To quote from the Select Committee at ch. 2, note 12: 'The law was defined in 1983, when the House of Lords (in *Mandla v Dowell Lee* [1983] 2 AC 548) held that the Sikh community could be described as having an "ethnic origin" under s. 3(1) of the Race Relations Act 197 . . . The Jewish community have since been treated as having the same protection because the House of Lords, in seeking a meaning for "ethnic origin", relied on a New Zealand decision on the same point under similar legislation, concerning a pamphlet published with the intent to incite ill-will against the Jews (*King-Ansell v Police* [1979] 2 NZLR 531). Since then gypsies/travellers/Romanies (the Court of Appeal used these words inter-changeably) have obtained a similar status (*Commission for Racial Equality v Dutton* [1989] 1 All ER 306).'

[155] It might be argued from this that all measures prohibiting incitement to racial hatred should be repealed, but this is not a practicable possibility and would involve the UK in an even clearer breach of Article 20 of the ICCPR than is currently being committed by the lack of protection for Muslims.

[156] Lord Bishop of Birmingham, HL Deb, col 322 (30 January 2002).

[157] Select Committee on Religious Offences in England and Wales (2003), Memorandum from the Forum Against Islamophobia and Racism (FAIR).

are, in reality, aimed simply at Asians, but hide behind criticism of Islam to avoid generating any liability under the current law.

The argument above is, however, predicated on the assumption that the prohibition of incitement to racial hatred under the Public Order Act does not already create an unacceptable infringement of freedom of speech. But, as pointed out below, it may be argued that the offences as currently conceived go beyond the mischief that they are intended to prevent. There is an argument that some provision should be available to prevent some forms of racist speech owing to its special propensity to lead to serious social tensions, racism and violence, and that such protection should be extended to religious groups, but it is argued that one could comfortably support the addition of incitement to religious hatred to Public Order Act offences only once they had been reformed to encompass a much more narrowly targeted area of liability.

HATE SPEECH: STIRRING UP RACIAL HATRED [158]

Domestic provisions [159]

The offence of stirring up racial hatred was introduced under s 6 of the Race Relations Act 1965, in order to meet public order concerns and protect persons from the effects on others of provocative and inflammatory racist expression. The Public Order Act 1936 was amended in order to include this offence, but Part III (ss 17–23) of the Public Order Act 1986 extends its ambit. Section 18 provides that liability will arise if threatening, abusive or insulting words or behaviour are used or written material of that nature is displayed, intended by the defendant to stir up racial hatred or which make it likely that racial hatred will be stirred up against a racial group (not a religious group) in Great Britain.[160] Where intent is not shown, it is necessary to show that the accused realized that the words used might be threatening, abusive or insulting.[161] Section 18(2) catches private or public meetings (unless held in a 'dwelling'). Section 19 makes it an offence to publish threatening, abusive or insulting material, either intended by the defendant to stir up racial hatred or which make it likely that racial hatred will be stirred up against a racial group. Section 21 extends the offence to the distributing, showing or playing of visual images or sounds. Section 20 makes it an

---

[158] For general discussion of this offence and its background, see G. Bindman (1982) 132 NLJ 299; Cotterell, op cit; Williams, DGT [1966] Crim LR 320; Leopold, P. [1977] PL 389; W. Wolffe [1987] PL 85.

[159] For discussion of racial hatred in the context of freedom of speech, see Robertson and Nichol, op cit, Chapter 3, pp 129–32; Barendt, op cit, 177–87, and generally R. Cotterell [1982] PL 378; Dickey [1968] Crim LR 489. For the argument that the State should seek to ban racially motivated hate speech on the basis of furtherance of equality just as it seeks to outlaw discrimination in employment, see MacKinnon, *Only Words* (Cambridge (Mass): Harvard University Press, 1993). For criticism of the argument, see W. Sadurski, 'On "Seeing speech through an equality lens": a critique of egalitarian arguments for suppression of hate speech and pornography' (1996) 16(4) OJLS 713, considered in Chapter 8 at 400–5.

[160] See note 154 above.

[161] Section 18(5). Awareness as used in the 1986 Act seems to mean subjective recklessness.

offence to stir up racial hatred in the public performance of a play, but the likelihood that hatred will be stirred up must be judged by reference to 'all the circumstances' and 'in particular taking the performance as a whole'. Therefore, the context in which, for example, a character is racially abused must be considered: where the message of the play as a whole could not be viewed as one aimed at stirring up racial hatred, the offence will not be committed. Thus, plays that explore the theme of racism in society should escape liability.

Section 22 makes it an offence to use threatening, abusive, or insulting visual images or sounds in a programme, intended by the defendant to stir up racial hatred, or which make it likely that racial hatred will be stirred up against a racial group. Section 164(2) of the Broadcasting Act 1990 amended s 22 so that it covers 'programme services', including cable programme services. The offence under s 22 can be committed by the programme producer, director, the television company and any person 'by whom the offending words or behaviour are used'. This is a broadly worded offence which encourages caution in producing programmes about the problem of racism, since it can be committed without any intent on the part of the producer or the company, and does not contain any express defence whereby no offence is committed provided that the programme as a whole distances the broadcaster from any racist content. Whether racial hatred is likely to be stirred up must be assessed by reference to all the circumstances, however, so that, where any racist material (e.g. interviews) is placed in a context in which its message is balanced and undercut by other material, it could be concluded that there was no such likelihood. Section 23 of the 1986 Act places further obstacles in the way of those producing programmes about racism, particularly historical programmes. Section 23 creates an offence of possessing racially inflammatory (threatening, abusive or insulting) material with a view, in the case of written material, to publication or distribution and, in the case of a recording, to its being distributed, shown, played or included in a programme service, intended by the person possessing it to stir up racial hatred or which makes it likely, having regard to all the circumstances, that racial hatred will be stirred up.

These offences have a number of elements in common. None of them requires a need to show that disorder was caused, or that there was an intent to cause disorder, and there is no need to show that racial hatred is actually stirred up. It is not an essential ingredient to show that there was an intent to stir up racial hatred. It is sufficient to show that hatred might actually be stirred up. In that circumstance, s 18 imports an element of *mens rea*—awareness that the words were threatening, insulting, or abusive—but the other sections do not, a very significant difference.[162] The offence might be committed by broadcasting or using or promulgating words or material by the methods indicated above, threatening, abusive, or insulting matter

---

[162] See above, at note 161. The other sections provide a defence—in effect, a reversed *mens rea*: the defendant has a defence if he can prove that he was not aware of the content of the recording/material/broadcast and had no reason to suspect that it was threatening, etc.

which, objectively speaking, is incapable of stirring up racial hatred so long as the accused intended that it should do so. It may be noted that the section 18 offence is the only public order offence which may be committed by words alone unaccompanied by the need—as an essential ingredient—to show any likelihood that they would cause distress, since the offence could be committed by uttering words which were greeted with delight by those who heard them. But of most significance is the possibility that criminal liability can arise owing to the promulgation of material likely to stir up racial hatred unintentionally.

These offences represent a restriction based on manner rather than content due to their specific requirements. Reasoned argument of a racist nature would probably not incur liability, since the racist words or material must be threatening, abusive or insulting. Further, the term 'hatred' is a strong one: merely causing offence or bringing a racial group into ridicule is not enough and nor is racial harassment. Thus, the offences are narrowly conceived; although they cover political expression, they concentrate on the manner of the expression. Further, it is hard to conceive that the type of speech caught—threats, abuse, insults—could itself be defended by reference to the free speech justifications discussed in Chapter 1 of this book. Where the threat, etc., is thematically appropriate since it is placed within a context, such as a play or film touching on the theme or subject of racism, it will probably fall outside the area of liability, since all the circumstances must be taken into account. However, the breadth of the offences relating to broadcasting could, as suggested above, have the effect of deterring the production of documentaries dealing with the subject of racism.

Impact of the HRA on race-hatred offences

Is expression likely to stir up racial hatred covered by Article 10(1)? In other words, would it be viewed as protected expression at all? In *Lehideux and Isornia v France*[163] it was found that if material is directed towards attacking the Convention's underlying values, it will be outside the protection of Article 10.[164] In that instance, the material supported a pro-Nazi policy. However, in *Kuhnen v FRG*,[165] Article 10 was found to cover the conviction of the applicant for advocating the reinstitution of the Nazi Party, although the interference was justified under Article 10(2). Similarly, Article 10 applied in *Glimmerveen and Hagenbeeck v Netherlands*.[166] The applicants had been convicted of possessing leaflets which incited racial discrimination. The interference was found to be justified under Article 10(2). In that instance, Article 17 was relied upon. Where racist expression is concerned, reliance on Article 17, either in addition to Article 10(2) or alone, tends to produce the same result: the interference is found to be justified and the review is not intensive.[167] The Canadian Supreme Court has made a similar finding in the case of *R v Keegstra*.[168]

---

[163] (1998) 5 BHRC 540. See further Chapter 2 at 46. [164] Ibid, at 558.
[165] (1988) 56 DR 205. [166] (1979) 18 DR 187.
[167] See *X v Germany* (1982) 29 DR 194; *T v Belgium* (1983) 34 DR 158; *H, W, P and K v Austria* (1989) 62 DR 216. For the text of Art 17, see below at note 194.
[168] [1990] 3 SCR 697.

Jersild[169] is the most directly applicable Article 10 case. It concerned an application by a Danish journalist who had been convicted of an offence of racially offensive speech after preparing and broadcasting a programme about racism which included overtly racist speech by members of the racist group, 'the Greenjackets', the subjects of the documentary. A breach of Article 10 was found. The interference with expression was found to be disproportionate to the aim pursued—protecting the rights of others. The Court stressed that its finding was directed to the value of enabling the media to act as a public watchdog. The news value of the programme was a matter that could be best assessed by professional journalists. The Court also considered that the mode of presenting the broadcast should be determined by journalists. Had the racists who spoke on the programme applied to Strasbourg, their own convictions would have been found to give rise to no breach of Article 10.

It seems to be clear that persons directly using threatening or abusive or insulting speech likely to stir up racial hatred would not obtain any benefit by invoking Article 10. But the position of those who aid in the dissemination of such speech, who do not have the purpose of stirring up racial hatred, is different. It is arguable that UK law does not draw a sufficiently clear distinction between the two groups. *Jersild* suggests that the restrictions on broadcasting in relation to racial hatred are open to challenge under the HRA since it would seem possible that if an equivalent situation arose in the UK, the presenter and producer of the programme could be convicted of the offence under s 22 of the 1986 Act. Possibly television researchers involved could also be convicted of the broader offence under s 23. No prosecutions have been brought against broadcasters, and are highly unlikely ever to be brought, but the relevant point is the *breadth* of the racial hatred provisions: at their widest, they allow for conviction of a BBC researcher who has in their possession racist videos made by the BNP, excerpts from which it is intended to include in future broadcast, where it was likely that that broadcast might stir up racial hatred (e.g. amongst those with racist tendencies who watched the programme). In this respect, the relative *narrowness* of the new religious offence now enshrined in law is a strong and welcome contrast, given the much greater potential scope of the notion of religious, as opposed to racial, hatred. Had the new offence been modelled on the racial hatred provisions, as originally intended, the scope of the new offences would have been broad indeed.

THE RACIAL AND RELIGIOUS HATRED ACT 2006

Ghandhi and James point out in an article published in 1998 that parliamentary attempts to reform or abolish the law of blasphemy and/or replace it with some other offence have 'had a remarkable lack of success'.[170] The pattern has continued since

---

[169] *Jersild v Denmark* (1994) 19 EHRR 1. The decision is discussed further in Chapter 2 at 46.

[170] They point out that: 'In 1885 Professor Kenny introduced a Bill abolishing the common law offence of blasphemy and replacing it with a statutory offence penalising intentional insults to religious feelings based on the Indian penal code. In 1889 it was dropped in favour of Bradlaugh's Bill, drafted by Sir James Fitzjames Stephen, abolishing all laws relating to blasphemy and not replacing them. This Bill was not passed. Similar

then, with the 2006 Act representing only a partial bucking of the trend in introducing a new offence, but failing to reform or abolish the blasphemy laws. The 2005 Bill represented the fourth attempt in recent years to introduce an offence of inciting religious hatred. The first was in Lord Avebury's Bill in 2000, which was remitted to the Select Committee on Religious Offences for consideration; the second attempt was made via clause 38 of the 2001 Anti-Terrorism Bill, which was defeated by the Lords; the third attempt appeared in the Serious and Organised Crime Bill 2004; the provision was dropped in order to allow the remainder of the Bill to go through Parliament before the end of the Parliamentary session for the 2005 General Election. The controversy surrounding the reform remains as keen as ever: there was a sustained media campaign against it, with fears expressed that everything from stand-up comedy to proselytizing preaching could be affected by the Bill.

On the whole, the print media, as might be expected, have opposed the introduction of the new offence strongly. Whilst the determination to protect freedom of expression in the increasingly contested and important area of religious belief is heartening, it must be said that much of the criticism has been ill-informed, and essentially equates the proposed new offence with a blasphemy law. In fact, as will appear below, the two are very different, for a number of reasons. First of all, there is a fundamental difference of purpose or essence: a blasphemy law identifies certain beliefs as having a special status, due to their sacred nature, such that they cannot be attacked, or not attacked in a certain way. The essence of a blasphemy law, in other words, is to protect believers from the offence of having their sacred beliefs attacked. In contrast, a religious hatred law aims not to prevent offence—offence to the believer not being the gravamen of the offence—but to prevent hatred being stirred up against those who subscribe to the belief. As the Select Committee put it: 'the offences have different targets: blasphemy concerns sacred entities or beliefs while incitement relates to people or groups who belong to a particular faith'.[171]

Thus, for example, poking fun at certain religious doctrines might be found deeply offensive by strong, traditionalist believers, but would be hardly likely to stir up *hatred* against those believers. The satirical Monty Python film, *The Life of Brian*, for example, did cause offence to certain Christians at the time of its release, and some contemporaneous legal advice was apparently to the effect that it might contravene the blasphemy laws. But it would be very hard to make out any kind of plausible argument that it incited *hatred* against Christians, or Jews, however much it may have

---

Bills were introduced in 1923 and 1925. When the Government of the day introduced an amendment to one of them to include the statutory offence of outraging religious convictions, the Bill was dropped. Other Bills introduced by Lord Willis and latterly Tony Benn in 1989 failed also. In 1994, a House of Lords amendment to a Bill that would have abolished the offence of blasphemy was withdrawn in the face of Government Opposition. Ten years after the majority view of the Law Commission recommending abolition in 1985 Lord Avebury introduced yet another Bill to abolish the law of blasphemy. The draft Bill attached to the Law Commission's Report was adopted by Lord Avebury as his model. This Bill failed also.' ('The English law of blasphemy and the European Convention on Human Rights' [1998] EHRLR 430, at 449–50.)

[171] Op cit, at [3].

offended them. There are strong *Pepper v Hart* statements stressing this distinction by the Lord Chancellor. In the second reading debate in the House of Lords, Lord Falconer said that the Bill 'is not about protecting . . . beliefs. It is not, despite what some might say, a new blasphemy law.'[172] Lord Falconer pointed out that Sikhs are in fact protected under the existing race hatred laws, but that:

the existing offence did not last year inhibit the staging of the play 'Behzti', which is set in a Sikh gurdwara, and . . . the play was not prosecuted for inciting hatred against Sikhs, even though it caused intense offence to some Sikhs.[173]

Thus, the underlying rationales of the two offences are quite different. A religious hatred offence is essentially intended to preserve harmony in a multi-ethic, multi-faith society; the other is to privilege the beliefs of a certain religion from the normal rough and tumble of political and artistic discourse, including satire and ridicule.

The second key distinction between the two types of offences is that the relevant target audience is different as between blasphemy laws and incitement to religious hatred. Speech likely to stir up religious hatred is speech aimed not at the believers themselves, but at *others*. The fact that the believer finds the speech offensive will not be relevant: it is the likely or intended response of the *non*-believer that is relevant. This is certainly intended to be the distinction between the two offences: as appears below, the position may not be as clear-cut as this, depending on how the new offences are interpreted by the courts.

Assuming (as will be argued below) that this distinction *should* be accepted, there are certain positive, Convention-based arguments for the change, if accompanied (even eventually) by abolition of the blasphemy laws, which may be outlined before the detail of the Bill and the criticisms of it are considered. First, its aim—to protect people from bigotry and fear—is one which is in harmony with the Convention, whereas a blasphemy law is arguably in direct conflict with it, whatever the views of the Court in *Otto-Preminger*. The Government has said that in its view, whilst incitement to religious hatred is not commonplace:

It exists it has a disproportionate and corrosive effect on communities, creating barriers between different groups and encouraging mistrust and suspicion. At an individual level this can lead to fear and intimidation. It can also lead indirectly to discrimination, abuse, harassment and ultimately crimes of violence against members of our communities. It is legitimate for the criminal law to protect citizens from such behaviour.[174]

Second, the proposed offence would satisfy the Convention principle of equality, in that all religious groups—and non-religious ones—are covered, whereas the present offence is overtly discriminatory in being confined to the Christian faith. Third, by being more narrowly focused, the proposed offence should offer much less of a threat to freedom of expression than a blasphemy law.

---

[172] HL Deb col 163 (11 October 2005).   [173] Ibid, at col. 166.

[174] Quoted in the 8th Report of the Joint Committee on Human Rights, HL 60/HC 388 (2004–05), at [2.57].

Moreover, the impact of the proposed new provisions on freedom of expression can be minimized. Prosecutions for the offences of stirring up racial or religious hatred can only be brought with the consent of the Attorney-General, which has so far been sparingly given in respect of race hatred, whereas a blasphemy conviction can be, and has been, procured by private prosecution.[175] The offence of incitement to racial hatred has resulted in only 44 convictions in the 18 years between 1986 and 2004. Since the Attorney-General is a public authority under the HRA, he or she will be required to give careful consideration to Article 10 before giving consent to a prosecution. While this is a *de facto* safeguard against abuse of the new offences, it may lead to pressure being brought on the Attorney-General, and itself to lead to alienation of certain groups whose expectations of prosecutions being brought on their behalf are frustrated. As Lord Lester has pointed out:

It should cause concern to the Government, for example, that Sir Iqbal Sacranie OBE, the leader of the Muslim Council of Britain, still believes, according to his public utterances, that the new offences will enable Salman Rushdie to be prosecuted for publishing his novel *The Satanic Verses*.[176]

He went on to predict:

The Attorney-General's highly political decision would be a source of mischief and resentment among extremists and mischief makers ... [His] decision to refuse consent will be used by extremists as evidence of the discriminatory operation of the law and will leave embittered those whose expectations were not fulfilled.[177]

If this reaction is to be avoided or at least minimized, it is important that prosecutions are brought only in the most extreme cases, for clearly articulated and defendable reasons, and that prosecutorial decisions are made on a consistent basis of principle.

The offences: an outline

In practical terms it has long been noted that it would be fairly straightforward to amend ss 17–23 of Part III of the Public Order Act 1986, discussed above, to include religious groups.[178] At the time of writing, the Racial and Religious Hatred Act 2006 has just received Royal Assent. The new provisions, as enacted, do not take the route, as first drafted, of simply amending Part III of the 1986 Act to add 'religious hatred' to the offences set out therein, though they are broadly modelled on them. Instead, as a result of a series of important amendments, carried in the House of Lords and accepted by the Commons in a rare rebellion against the Government,[179] the 2006 provisions are much narrower than their equivalents in the POA, and include a

---

175 As in the leading case of *R v Lemon*, op cit.   176 HL Deb col 173 (11 October 2005).

177 Ibid, at 174.

178 This was the route taken by the previous two Government attempts to introduce the new offence in 2001 and 2004: see text following note 170.

179 In dramatic votes on 31 January 2006, the Commons accepted, by one vote, various amendments intended to liberalize the offence, introduced by the Lords, discussed further below.

specific defence for freedom of expression. The Bill sidesteps the problem of definition of religion, and the accompanying possible problems of discrimination between
different religious groups and between such groups and non-believers by defining
religious belief extraordinarily widely: 'religious hatred means hatred against a group
of persons defined by reference to religious belief or lack of religious belief.'[180] Clearly,
such a provision hands an enormous discretion—and responsibility—to the courts,
while avoiding the problem of legislative definition. The issues surrounding the difficulties of defining what religions or beliefs are to be protected are canvassed
above;[181] it may be noted here that the Bill will plainly apply to wide range of religious
and non-religious groups. The Explanatory Notes to the Bill state:

> It includes, though this list is not definitive, those religions widely recognised in this coun-
> try such as Christianity, Islam, Hinduism, Judaism, Buddhism, Sikhism, Rastafarianism,
> Baha'ism, Zoroastrianism and Jainism. Equally, branches or sects within a religion can be
> considered as religions or religious beliefs in their own right. The offences also cover hatred
> directed against a group of persons defined by reference to a lack of religious belief, such as
> Atheism and Humanism.[182]

However, as Lord Falconer pointed out in Parliament, 'Religion is not defined also in
relation to discrimination on the grounds of religion and belief in the Employment
Equality (Religion or Belief) Regulations 2003'.[183] The problem is not, in other words,
unique to this area of law.

As originally introduced by the Government, the Bill simply added 'religious hatred' onto the five main ways in which the racial hatred offence could be committed. In
all, the offence was committed by the display or use of threatening, abusive or insulting words or behaviour with intent to stir up religious hatred or whereby it was likely
to be stirred up. The five basic offences, mirroring those concerning racial hatred, are:

- the use of such words or behaviour or display of written material (Schedule 1,
  section 29B);

- publishing or distributing such written material (section 29C);

- the public performance of a play (section 29D);

- distributing, showing or playing a recording (section 29E);

- broadcasting or including a programme in a programme service (section 29F);
  and

- possession of relevantly inflammatory material with a view to its broadcast
  (section 29G).

However, the original Bill made it significantly easier to obtain a conviction in relation

---

[180] Sched 1, s 29A.   [181] See 506–7.
[182] Explanatory Notes to the Bill, at [13], available http://www.publications.parliament.uk/pa/ld200506/
ldbills/015/en/06015x—.htm
[183] HL Deb col 167 (11 October 2005).

to all of these situations than under the Public Order Act. Under that Act, as discussed above, the offence can be committed either by means of specific intent—if the 'speaker' 'intends thereby to stir up racial hatred'—*or* if, 'having regard to all the circumstances, racial hatred is likely to be stirred up thereby'.[184] This part of the Act, allowing for a conviction without intention to incite racial hatred, and indeed, in situations in which no racial hatred was in fact stirred up[185] has been subject to criticism. But the 2005 Bill proposed making the offence even easier to commit, at the same time, of course, as widening its scope to include incitement to religious hatred. The Bill proposed to make both offences (racial and religious hatred) committable either through intent, as before, *or* where the words, play, recording or broadcast were '*likely* to be heard or seen by any person in whom it is *likely* to stir up racial or religious hatred' (emphasis added).[186] This would have made it easier to obtain convictions. It would have been possible, for example, to convict where the words were heard by no-one, or where they were only in fact heard by a person or persons very unlikely to be incited thereby to hatred, although it had been likely that a person likely to have been so incited would have heard the words. This would have been a worrying development. Fortunately, as noted above, the provisions were radically amended in the House of Lords.

The crucial amendments introduced by the House of Lords are as follows. First, the new offence was made a free-standing one, not achieved by amending the Public Order Act. Given the broad scope of those offences, as discussed above, this is a major change of substantive, not technical, significance. Second the words 'abusive' and 'insulting' were removed from the offence, leaving only 'threatening words or behaviour' capable of prosecution. Since what is 'insulting' or 'abusive' is open to much broader, subjective interpretations than what is threatening, this represents a crucial narrowing of the scope of the offence. For example, a devout Muslim might take any publication critical of Mohammed or Islamic doctrine as *per se* 'insulting': it would be harder to argue that such publications were 'threatening'.[187] Third, the offence, as enacted, can only be committed with *specific intent*: the offence is only committed if the person 'intends thereby to stir up religious hatred.'[188] This makes the offence much narrower than the race hatred offences considered above, and sharply lowers the possibility of comedians, satirists, artists, and preachers merely teaching the truth of their own religion being caught by the Bill. It applies across the board, to all the offences.

The fourth important amendment is what may be termed a 'saving' clause for freedom of speech in section 29J of Schedule 1:

---

[184] Section 18 POA 1096; similar wording is used in all the other offences in ss 19–22.

[185] Possible because the Act only requires that it be likely that hatred be stirred up, not that it actually was.

[186] This was the wording in the Schedule to the Bill as originally introduced: it would have amended sections 18–22 in slightly different ways, to make them all subject to this basic test.

[187] The Government has indicated that it is unhappy with this change, as reducing the coverage of the offence too greatly: HL Deb col 511 (8 November 2005).

[188] Schedule 1: the requirement of intention appears in each of the various ways in which the offence can be committed.

Nothing in this Part shall be read or given effect in a way which prohibits or restricts discussion, criticism or expressions of antipathy, dislike, ridicule, insult or abuse of particular religions or the beliefs or practices of their adherents, or of any other belief system or the beliefs or practices of its adherents, or proselytising or urging adherents of a different religion or belief system to cease practising their religion or belief system.

The intention behind this amendment—to protect robust debate about religious matters, using the full range of discursive method, including satire, ridicule and vigorous criticism—is to be welcomed, as is the specific saving for proselytizing.[189] The problem, in our view, is that by allowing expressions of 'antipathy' towards the beliefs and practices of adherents, it is arguably inconsistent with the main thrust of the offence itself. Whilst in theory it allows for a distinction between saying, 'I hate Muslims' and saying 'I hate the fact that Muslims think/do/believe . . .', in practice, any statement of hatred for Muslims would be founded upon hatred of their beliefs or practices. Moreover, 'antipathy' is very close in meaning to 'hatred', if not synonymous with it. In other words, the defence threatens to swallow up the mischief captured by the offence. In a sense, therefore, it is evidence of the difficulty of seeking to draft such provisions in such a way as to draw a line between robust criticism and satire, on the one hand, and stirring up hatred, on the other.

Compatibility with Article 10

It may be noted that the 2005 Bill was accompanied by a statement of compatibility under section 19 of the HRA. However, such a statement leaves the judges free to consider compatibility afresh, if necessary, by using section 3(1) HRA to narrow the scope of offences that threaten to trench too far upon freedom of expression. The view of the Joint Committee on Human Rights on the compatibility of the Bill as originally drafted with Article 10 was as follows:

We accept the existence of a serious, albeit limited, problem of incitement to hatred on religious grounds. We consider that the measures proposed in the Bill are unlikely to give rise to any violation of the right to freedom of expression under Article 10 of the ECHR.[190]

The recent decision in *Norwood v UK*,[191] is further evidence of the above view. The applicant belonged to the BNP. The facts were as follows:

Between November 2001 and 9 January 2002 he displayed in the window of his first-floor flat a large poster . . . supplied by the BNP, with a photograph of the Twin Towers in flame, the words 'Islam out of Britain—Protect the British People' and a symbol of a crescent and star in a prohibition sign.[192]

He was convicted in a magistrates court of the offence under section 5 of the Public Order Act of displaying 'any writing, sign or other visible representation which is threatening, abusive or insulting, within the hearing or sight of a person likely to be

---

[189] As explained below.   [190] 8th Report, op cit, at [2.59].   [191] (2005) 40 EHRR SE11.
[192] Ibid, at [A.]

caused harassment, alarm or distress thereby'. He was moreover convicted of having committed the offence in religiously aggravated way. He unsuccessfully appealed his conviction to the High Court,[193] which found that the restriction upon his freedom of expression right represented by the offence was proportionate to the legitimate aim of protecting the rights of others, given also the fact that the speech arguably fell within Article 17 ECHR.[194] One of the applicant's arguments was that there was in fact no evidence that any Muslim had actually seen the poster.

The Strasbourg Court, in a brief judgment, found the application inadmissible; in doing so it referred to Article 17:

Such a general, vehement attack against a religious group, linking the group as a whole with a grave act of terrorism, is incompatible with the values proclaimed and guaranteed by the Convention, notably tolerance, social peace and non-discrimination. The applicant's display of the poster in his window constituted an act within the meaning of Article 17, which did not, therefore, enjoy the protection of Articles 10 or 14.[195]

Given this judgment, which admittedly concerned a fairly clear attempt to stir up hatred against Muslims, it seems likely that prosecutions under the proposed new law, provided they were used only in sensible cases, would be found to be compatible with Article 10. Nevertheless, given that the current blasphemy laws have been found to be compatible with Article 10, this should not be taken to indicate positive approval of the proposal.

Evaluation

The authors' view is that the proposals amount to a potentially serious threat to freedom of expression, depending upon how they are interpreted—and upon the prosecutorial policy of successive future Attorney-Generals. The term 'hatred' should be given full weight, as should the term 'threatening', which should, it is argued, be interpreted as meaning threatening to the reasonable, tolerant religious adherent rather than in relation to adherents of a particular sect (or group within a religion) which may be of an extreme nature. In other words, convictions should only be found where the material lacks any credible intention of provoking debate or criticism of religious doctrines and has the intent merely of threatening members of a religious community and stirring up hatred against them.

There is, however, a more basic interpretative issue to be resolved. While it was argued above that speech which a given community itself found to be offensive could not be taken to incite hatred against that community, and thus would not fall within the scope of the new offence, it would be possible to interpret the legislation differently, given its actual wording. Let us imagine that, in response to the Danish

---

[193] *Norwood v DPP* (2003) WL 21491815.

[194] This provides: 'Nothing in [the] Convention may be interpreted as implying for any State, group or person any right to engage in any activity or perform any act aimed at the destruction of any of the rights and freedoms set forth herein or at their limitation to a greater extent than is provided for in the Convention'.

[195] Op cit.

cartoons, and with the motive of provoking a debate as to the limits of satirical treatment of Islamic subjects, a UK magazine or newspaper commissioned a fresh series of cartoons, intended to be as provocative as the Danish ones, although perhaps less crude. It could be argued that the offence had been committed as follows: first, such words *can* be interpreted as 'threatening'. On one view, something that attacks something fundamental to one's identity is threatening. As regards intention, whilst the publisher could truthfully say their aim or desire was not to stir up hatred, and would not therefore have what is known as 'core' or 'simple' intent to do so, they might well be found to have what is known as indirect or oblique intent. This is satisfied, where (a) the forbidden consequence (in this case the stirring up of hatred) is a virtually certain consequence of their actions; and (b) the publisher is aware that this is the case.[196] In such an instance, a jury may 'infer' that the defendant intended the consequence.[197] Would such cartoons be virtually certain to stir up hatred? They would not seem apt to stir up hatred of Muslims by non-Muslims. But it seems, after the events of the past few weeks, impossible to deny that they would be very likely indeed to stir up hatred by Muslims against non-Muslims. Indeed, it would not be implausible to say that, after seeing the world-wide Muslim reaction to the publication of the Danish cartoons in various newspapers across Europe, anyone publishing further such cartoons must know that stirring up hatred is a virtually certain consequence of so doing. Of course, there would still be the possibility of the publisher being saved by the 'freedom of expression' clause. But the protective coverage of the clause, whilst it allows for 'expressions of antipathy, dislike, ridicule, insult or abuse of particular religions or the beliefs of practices of their adherents' must at some point run out. It cannot be interpreted so far that it swallows up the whole substantive offence. There must therefore be a point at which expressions of antipathy become expressions of hatred. The line between them is not a bright or clear one.

What, however, would be wrong with such a situation? Simply this: the mischief of the Act is, presumably, to protect religious minorities having hatred stirred up against *them*. What the framers of the legislation had in mind, surely, were publications that, under the guise of attacking Islamic practices or beliefs, in reality attack Muslims in a way intended to make people hate them. As Lord Falconer put it, in his Second Reading speech for the Government: the mischief to be addressed is a situation in which a person is:

addressing people *other than* the people whom [he is] insulting or abusing with a view to stirring up hatred among them against a particular religious group. That is not currently covered by the criminal law, and that is why there is a gap that needs to be covered (emphasis added: HL Deb, 11 Oct 2005, col. 162).

---

[196] This is taken from the standard test for intention in criminal law: *R v Woollin* [1999] 1 Cr App R 8, HL.

[197] A classic instance is the man who fires from his sitting room, through his own closed window, at his enemy in the garden outside. He does not *want* to break his own window but, in deliberately acting to bring about an inevitable consequence of his wish to do something else (shoot his enemy) he may be said to intend to break the window.

It would seem perverse, surely, if such a law were used to protect Muslims from being stirred into hatred against others. The secular cartoonist—the person intending to stir up hatred—would then be prevented from publishing cartoons for fear that others would hate him for it. This would seem absurd. The law—or at least its interpretation by the courts—ought in some way to provide that grossly unreasonable responses to material—such as being stirred to violent hatred by merely satirical treatment of doctrine—should not result in criminal liability.

But to conclude that the offence could *never* be interpreted in such a way would be too hasty. A judge might well reason as follows: the aim of this legislation is the preservation of racial, religious and cultural harmony, the inner tranquillity of the Kingdom, as Lord Scarman put it in *Lemon*.[198] As the Religious Offences Committee put it:

It is ... important to recognise that continued tranquillity depends not only upon con-tinued mutual tolerance but, equally, on equality of protection from intolerance on the basis of religion or belief or no belief.[199]

Where provocative portrayals of religious objects, such as the Prophet or the Koran, are published or displayed, the effect is to whip up hatred against the perpetrators—and Western society and 'values' generally—by Muslims, particularly extremists. *This in turn* leads to a negative image of Muslims being implanted in the minds of other groups—as when radicals march calling for the beheading of those who insult Islam and calling down another 7 July on London.[200] The effect therefore is sharply to *increase* tension between racial and religious groups. This is the mischief the legisla-tion is designed to prevent. Therefore, it may be argued, the publication of the original cartoons—the spark for the whole controversy—*is* within the mischief of the Act. It is important that such an interpretation is energetically rejected by the judiciary: the clear argument of principle against it is that it amounts to punishing the publisher of the original, provocative images for the extreme reactions of those offended by it, which in turn stir up hatred. The law should instead be used against those extreme reactions: it is those who call for people who insult Mohammed to be beheaded who are stirring up religious hatred (as well as inciting violence), and it is they who should be prosecuted.

Assuming then that the above interpretation *is* rejected, the requirement of specific intent *and* the extended defence for various forms of free discussion of religion should in practice be enough to ensure that no such liability would result, and that robust debate on religious matters, satire, proselytizing and irreverent comedy would all be clearly and unequivocally protected.

This is therefore a radically narrower offence than that of blasphemy, with its absence of *mens rea* and any public interest defence. What further differentiates it

---

[198] Above at 484.   [199] Op cit, at [13].

[200] As in the now notorious march of 3 February 2006 during the 'cartoon' crisis: see 'British Muslims protest over cartoons', *Guardian*, www.guardian.co.uk/religion/Story/0,,1701518,00.html.

from offences of obscenity and blasphemy is that there is, in the authors' view, at least, a plausible argument as to pressing social need that can be put forward. No-one can doubt that the issue in particular of the effective reconciliation of the UK's Muslim community with the non-Muslim majority and their cultural practices is an urgent and very serious problem: the events of 7 July, and the evidence of support from some actions amongst a minority of the British Muslim population plainly demonstrate this to be the case. A Populus poll for *The Times*, published on 2 February 2006[201] found that 7 per cent of British Muslims thought that further such attacks in the UK would be justified. With a Muslim population of 7 per cent, this indicates a possible support base for such attacks of over 100,000.[202] It is also plausible to assume that the presence of material published by organizations such as the BNP, which seeks to incite hatred against Asians, but avoids the current law by framing its attacks on Muslims or Islam, has the potential directly to inflame racial tensions, and increase the risk of radical alienation of sections of the Muslim community, leading to further terrorist or racial violence—which of course, in turn, creates greater hatred against Muslims in some quarters, so risking a vicious circle. This is a serious and credible possibility, with potentially grave, even catastrophic consequences. In these particular circumstances, the standard liberal distrust of curbs on freedom of expression might, at least temporarily, have to give way to urgent, pressing, and genuine societal needs, bolstered of course by claims of individual rights not to suffer racial or religiously motivated violence, harassment and ultimately loss of life.

Finally, it is the case that much of the extreme material, such as that of the BNP, intended to be caught by the new offence would, in Convention terms, at the lowest be seen as speech the interference with which could very readily be justified; alternatively at least some of it could be regarded as speech that falls outside the protection of Article 10 altogether, on the authority of *Jersild*,[203] on the basis, as the Government has suggested,[204] of Article 17 ECHR, which prohibits the claimed exercise of a Convention right in such a way as to destroy or undermine the other Convention rights. As the European Court held in *Norwood v UK*,[205] this saving in Article 17 can be seen to apply to expression which is 'incompatible with the values proclaimed and guaranteed by the Convention, notably tolerance, social peace and non-discrimination'. Bearing in mind all the above points, this books takes the view that the proposals as amended by the House of Lords are justifiable as a narrow restriction upon freedom of expression rights, and in harmony with key Convention values. However, there are, in our view, *no* persuasive arguments for the retention of the discriminatory and flawed law

---

[201] www.populuslimited.com/poll_summaries/2006_02_07_times.htm

[202] 7 per cent of 1.6 million is 112,000. The figure is close to that found in a *Guardian* poll carried out shortly after the 7 July attacks, which found that 5 per cent expressed such support, indicating a figure of around 80,000.

[203] Op cit.   [204] See 8th Report of the Joint Committee, op cit, at [2.58].

[205] No. 23131/03 (2004).

of blasphemy, which should be repealed, as a corollary of the enactment of the new proposals. If it is not, judicial reform of it, as canvassed above, would become an urgent necessity, when a suitable case arises.

POSTSCRIPT: 'GLORIFYING TERRORISM'

The Terrorism Act 2006[206] includes a new offence, which directly curbs freedom of expression, and has been highly controversial from the start. According to the Home Secretary, it aims to fill a gap in the law. As the Joint Committee put it:

In his view, the law already outlaws incitement to commit a particular terrorist act, such as the statement 'Please will you go and blow up a tube train on 7 July in London?', but not a generalised incitement to terrorist acts such as 'We encourage everybody to go and blow up tube trains'.[207]

The basic offence is set out in section 1(1) of the Act and provides:

This section applies to a statement that is likely to be understood by some or all of the members of the public to whom it is published as a direct or indirect encouragement or other inducement to them to the commission, preparation or instigation of acts of terrorism or Convention offences.[208]

An offence in similar terms is also committed under section 2 by the dissemination of a terrorist publication, which is defined as one that is likely to encourage or induce as above. 'The public', as defined by the Act, 'can include the public of any part of the United Kingdom or of a country or territory outside the United Kingdom':[209] thus there need be no intention (or likelihood) that any terrorist activity within the UK or even by persons living in the UK would be encouraged by the statement. The offence thus could catch any praise of any group using political violence anywhere in the world, a point we will return to below.

This very broad principle is then qualified in a number of ways. First of all, the person publishing the statement[210] or disseminating the publication[211] has to:

intend members of the public to be directly or indirectly encouraged or otherwise induced

---

[206] This version of the Act was finally accepted by the House of Lords on 22 March 2006; it has therefore been possible to include only a brief treatment of it.

[207] Third Report, 'Counter-Terrorism Policy and Human Rights: Terrorism Bill and related matters' HL 75-I/HC 561 (2005–06) at [21].

[208] 'Convention offences' are defined in section 20 as those listed in Schedule 1: they include offences relating to the causing of explosives, of developing, using etc. nuclear, biological or chemical weapons, offences against internationally protected persons (i.e. diplomatic and other agents), hostage taking, hijacking, offences involving nuclear material, offences under the Aviation and Maritime Security Act 1991 relating to the endangering of ships, aerodromes, etc., directing terrorist organizations under section 56 Terrorism Act 2000 or offences concerned with fund-raising under sections 16–18 of that Act.

[209] S 20(3)(a).   [210] S 1(2).   [211] S 2(2).

by the statement to commit, prepare or instigate acts of terrorism or Convention offences . . . (s 1(2)(b)(i)).

or be 'reckless' as to that consequence. The House of Lords rejected the originally contained[212] definition of recklessness as including 'any case in which he could not reasonably have failed to be aware of that likelihood'—that is, a definition which made it clear that *objective* recklessness, or gross negligence, would suffice. Therefore, it is clear that the offence can only be committed intentionally or by someone who sees an obvious risk that the forbidden harm will be brought about, but who goes ahead anyway.

Second, and of particular concern to the media, what was previously only a narrow defence of innocent publication for those who host websites has been extended by Lords' amendments to cover all such innocent publications. The original defence applied only where the statement was published electronically, and was intended to benefit those who run websites, on which such statements might be published without the webmasters' knowledge or consent. This would have left broadcasting bodies, or magazines or newspapers which carried interviews with extremists, open to the possibility of committing the offence, since they would have 'published a statement' under section 1(1) and might at least be found to be reckless as to the effect that the interview might have on listeners. This might have had the possibility of 'chilling' the willingness of media bodies to carry such interviews, and also would have fallen foul of the *Jersild* principle, discussed above,[213] that where media outlets carry interviews with those inciting hatred, but themselves merely report the *fact of* such views being held, they should themselves not be convicted of offences. Under the Bill as amended, therefore, it is now, per s 1(6),[214] a defence—where no intention can be shown—for the accused to show:

(a) that the statement neither expressed his views nor had his endorsement (whether by virtue of section 3 or otherwise); and

(b) that it was clear, in all the circumstances of the statement's publication, that it did not express his views and (apart from the possibility of his having been given and failed to comply with a notice under subsection (3) of that section) did not have his endorsement.

A like defence applies to the section 2 dissemination offence.[215] In other words, mere reportage of another's words or views, where the media distance themselves from the reportage, does not constitute an offence. The reference to section 3 is to an exception to the defence, in other words, to a situation in which someone can be held liable for publishing a statement, even though he does not himself endorse it. Section 3 is a complex provision, but essentially applies to a case in which a statement or article falling within section 1 or 2 has been published electronically, i.e. on

---

[212] That is, in the Bill as printed on 10 November 2005.   [213] At p 516.
[214] In section 2, under ss (9).   [215] Per s 2(9).

a website and, per section 3, a constable has given notice that in his view (a) the statement is one that falls within section 1 or 2;[216] (b) required the person to make sure that it is no longer available to the public (that is, removed from the website) or modified so that it is no longer unlawful; (c) warned the person that failure to comply with the notice within two days will result in the person now being deemed to endorse the statement; and (d) explained how he will then commit an offence.[217] Thus failure to comply with such a notice (i.e., not removing or modifying the statement or article) within two working days of receiving the notice implies endorsement of the views expressed therein and thus removes the possibility of relying on the defence under section 1(6) or 2(7). There is a defence of 'reasonable excuse' under section 3(2) for failing to comply with such a notice, which seems to be made out when the person has taken 'every step he reasonably could'[218] to prevent the statement being re-made.[219]

The key question, then, is what 'encouraging' or otherwise 'inducing' terrorism means. It will be recalled that the Act refers to 'direct or indirect encouragement or other inducement'. 'Direct encouragement' is perhaps relatively straightforward: in the House of Lords debates a consensus emerged that, as Lord Lloyd said, 'it is already covered by the existing law of incitement'.[220] The controversy surrounded what 'indirect encouragement' meant, and it is here that the key dispute as to the inclusion or otherwise of 'glorification' of terrorism within the definition of indirect encouragement occurred. The House of Lords had insisted upon confining the definition of such conduct to 'the making of a statement describing terrorism in such a way that the listener would infer that he should emulate it'. However, the House of Commons four times voted in favour of the glorification definition, with increasing majorities,[221]

---

[216] That is, direct or indirect encouragement or other inducement of terrorism etc., which, per ss 8A, includes 'glorification', as defined in ss 1 and 2.

[217] The above uses the correct sub-paragraph numbers in ss (3), but is a paraphrase: the full text is as follows:

'(3) A notice under this subsection is a notice which—
  (a) declares that, in the opinion of the constable giving it, the statement or the article or record is unlawfully terrorism-related;
  (b) requires the relevant person to secure that the statement or the article or record, so far as it is so related, is not available to the public or is modified so as no longer to be so related;
  (c) warns the relevant person that a failure to comply with the notice within 2 working days will result in the statement, or the article or record, being regarded as having his endorsement; and
  (d) explains how, under subsection (4), he may become liable by virtue of the notice if the statement, or the article or record, becomes available to the public after he has complied with the notice.'

[218] S 3(5).

[219] It may be noted that the House of Lords had inserted an important amendment to this provision, under which no notice could be served unless leave had been given by a judge, who was satisfied that the material in question fell under ss 1 or 2. This was disagreed to by the Commons and dropped by the Lords in their debate on 28 February: HL Deb cols 165 ff (28 Feb 2006).

[220] HL Deb col 144 (28 February 2006).

[221] In Committee, on 2 November 2005 (majority—16), on Report, on 9 November 2005 (majority, 25), at Commons consideration of Lords Amendments on 15 February (majority, 38), at second Commons consideration of Lords Amendments on 16 March (majority 59): see the speech of Lord Scotland, HL Deb, 22 March, col 246.

and after twice insisting otherwise, the Lords finally conceded the point. Thus, per s 1(3):[222]

... statements that are likely to be understood by members of the public as indirectly encouraging the commission or preparation of acts of terrorism or Convention offences include every statement which—

(a) glorifies the commission or preparation (whether in the past, in the future or generally) of such acts or offences; and

(b) is a statement from which those members of the public could reasonably be expected to infer that what is being glorified is being glorified as conduct that should be emulated by them in existing circumstances.

Glorification, section 20 tells us, '*includes* any form of praise or celebration'.[223] As was pointed out in the Lords, this definition 'does not say "comprises", but "includes", which suggests that glorification is wider than any form of praise or celebration. That in itself indicates how vague the concept is.'[224] Such a statement is to be taken as a whole and looked at in all the circumstances in which it was made.[225] It is not necessary to show—indeed it is irrelevant—whether anyone was actually 'encouraged or induced' to commit any relevant offence by the statement.[226] Conviction on indictment carries a hefty maximum sentence of 7 years.

Thus, the House of Lords' amendments have partially curtailed the scope of the offence—in allowing for convictions only where the person concerned had intention or subjective recklessness as to the encouragement of terrorism, and in providing for a defence of innocent publication or dissemination. However, serious concerns remain. The Joint Committee on Human Rights had grave reservations about both the breadth and vagueness of the original provisions.[227] In terms of compatibility with Article 10, the Joint Committee considered that under the existing Strasbourg case-law:

restrictions on *indirect* incitement to commit violent terrorist offences are also capable in principle of being compatible with Article 10, provided they are

- necessary
- defined with sufficient precision to satisfy the requirements of legal certainty, and
- proportionate

to the legitimate aims of national security, public safety, the prevention of crime and the protection of the rights of others.[228]

In terms of necessity, whilst the Committee thought that general statements encouraging terrorism might well fall within the existing law on soliciting murder,[229] it accepted that 'there is some uncertainty about the scope of the existing offences' and therefore that:

---

[222] The like definition appears in other relevant parts of the Act.   [223] S 20(2).
[224] HL Deb col 159 (28 February 2006).   [225] S 1(4).   [226] S 1(5)
[227] Third Report, op cit.   [228] Op cit, at [20].
[229] Under the Offences Against the Person Act 1861, s 4.

A clarification of the law is therefore in principle justifiable, even if it overlaps to some extent with other existing offences. We therefore accept, on balance, that the case has been made out by the Government that there is a need for a new, narrowly defined criminal offence of indirect incitement to terrorist acts.[230]

However, as enacted, the new offences fail to address many of the Committee's recommendations designed precisely to ensure such a 'narrow' offence. Four objections to the new offences may still be made: first, the use of 'glorification' to define the offence remains; second, the definition of terrorism remains the enormously broad one in the Terrorism Act 2000; third, there is no requirement that any encouragement to commit terrorist acts is actually caused; fourth, there is no general defence of public interest. The third and fourth of these points are perhaps self-explanatory: the first two require a little more explanation. The use of 'glorification' in the definition of the offence was perhaps the main concern of the Committee: 'The legal certainty concern is that terms such as glorification, praise and celebration are too vague to form part of a criminal offence which can be committed by speaking.' The Committee pointed out that the Home Secretary rested upon a distinction between:

encouraging and glorifying on the one hand and explaining or understanding on the other. The last two, he says would not be caught by the new offence, because they do not amount to encouraging, glorifying, praising or celebrating.[231]

The Committee was unconvinced by this reasoning:

In our view, the difficulty with the Home Secretary's response is that his distinction is not self-executing: the content of comments and remarks will have to be carefully analysed in each case, including the context in which they were spoken, and there will be enormous scope for disagreement between reasonable people as to whether a particular comment is merely an explanation or an expression of understanding or goes further and amounts to encouragement, praise or glorification. The point is made by the vast range of reaction to the comments of both Cherie Booth Q.C. and Jenny Tonge M.P. about suicide bombers. Some reasonable people thought they fell on one side of the Home Secretary's line, other reasonable people thought they fell on the other.[232]

As Lord Goodhart explained in the House of Lords,[233] the difficulty is that it is uncertain whether the reference to glorification is intended to extend the meaning of 'indirect encouragement' of terrorism. If it is not, then the reference to 'glorification' is harmless. But if it *is* intended to extend the notion of 'encouragement', in other words, to make people guilty of the offence who would not otherwise be thought to have encouraged terrorism in what they said, then 'enormous uncertainty' is opened up, given the vagueness of the term 'glorification'. Moreover:

How can it be possible to justify treating as a criminal offence glorification that does not in the ordinary meaning of the word amount to indirect encouragement of terrorism?[234]

---

[230] Op cit, at [25].   [231] Ibid, at [27].   [232] Ibid.
[233] HL Deb, 22 March, col 248.   [234] Ibid.

Lord Goodhart also pointed out the somewhat absurd genesis of the 'glorification' provision:

Why is it that the Government are so obsessed with outlawing glorification? The answer can only be described as being to save face—their own and that of the Prime Minister. He said that glorification must be made a crime and it was put into the manifesto . . . [But] it . . . became obvious that glorification, as a freestanding offence, would be in itself an absurdity. The definition of terrorism is so wide that it extends to the actions of Robin Hood and his merry men or the War of American Independence . . . The Government therefore backed down half-way and made glorification a sub-species of encouragement instead of an independent species of its own. At that point, the Government should have recognised that all that was needed here was a simple offence of direct or indirect encouragement of terrorism, an offence which we [Liberal Democrats] accept as necessary and which we support. But the Government had become so committed to glorification that they had to stick it in.[235]

While the Government constantly paraded UN Security Council Resolution 1634,[236] which spoke of 'Condemning also in the strongest terms the incitement of terrorist acts and repudiating attempts at the justification or glorification . . . of terrorist acts that may incite further terrorist acts', it was pointed out by Lord Lester that none of the signatories of that Resolution had sought to make such 'glorification' a criminal offence, save for Spain, the Supreme Court of which had found the offence unconstitutional.[237]

The second main problem identified by the Committee was that of overbreadth. The offence uses the definition of 'terrorism' in the 2000 Terrorism Act, which is notoriously wide. Section 1(1) of that Act provides that 'terrorism' means the use or threat, 'for the purpose of advancing a political, religious or ideological cause', of action 'designed to influence a government or to intimidate the public or a section of the public', which involves 'serious violence against any person or serious damage to property, endangers the life of any person, or creates a serious risk to the health or safety of the public or a section of the public, or is designed seriously to interfere with or seriously to disrupt an electronic system'. This extraordinarily wide definition covers such action occurring anywhere in the world (under s 1(4)). The Government thus accepts that 'the effect of the clause as drafted is to criminalise expressions of support for the use of violence [including violence against property] as a means of political change anywhere in the world'. However, rather extraordinarily, it argued that 'there was nowhere in the world where such where resort to violence, including violence against property, could be justified as a means of bringing about change'.[238] What is bizarre about this argument is that it seeks to argue not just that nowhere in the world should violence or serious damage to property be used to bring about such change, but suggests that anyone who disagrees with this view—as the Joint Committee itself does—and express support for such violence, say against a murderous dictatorship, as in Burma, should be guilty of a criminal offence. It thus elevates one view

---

[235] HL Deb, col 143 (28 February 2006).   [236] September 2005.
[237] See HL Deb, col 155 (28 February 2006).   [238] JCHR, 3rd Report, at [29].

of contemporary global politics—essentially a pacifist one—into dogma, the challenge to which is made a criminal offence. The Government's only defence of this position, when the Joint Committee renewed its concerns about it, was to say, rather facilely: 'The Government opposes terrorism wherever it may occur . . . [it] does not believe it is appropriate to distinguish between "good terrorists" and "bad terrorists".'[239] The issue, of course, is not the enormously complex one of when and whether political violence, including war, may be justified, but whether it can possibly be justifiable to criminalize any expression of support for such violence anywhere in the world. Such an offence, even reformed as it is, represents an extraordinary attack upon freedom of expression which we consider most unlikely to be compatible with Article 10 of the Convention.

[239] JCHR, 10th Report, HL 114/HC 888, Appendix 1.

10

CENSORSHIP AND REGULATION OF THE VISUAL MEDIA ON THE GROUND OF AVOIDING OFFENCE: GENERAL ISSUES OF LAW AND POLICY

UNDERPINNING THEORETICAL CONSIDERATIONS

As Chapter 8 discussed, the question as to how far explicit, erotic, and sexually violent expression deserves the same protection as other forms of expression, and if it does not, how far and for what reasons it should be restrained or suppressed, has proved highly contentious.[1] This chapter, introducing the regulation of the visual media, must be read in the light of the discussion of the theoretical considerations relating to offensive speech and the domestic and Strasbourg jurisprudence outlined in Chapter 8. The position of the visual media is particularly difficult in relation to such forms of expression. From a liberal standpoint, cuts in film or broadcast material on the basis of avoiding offence may be condemned as an infringement of autonomy, especially where they go beyond what is demanded by the criminal law.[2] There is general opposition to such censorship in other mediums in the absence of clear evidence of the concrete harm caused by the material.[3] However, explicit images conveyed in the print as opposed to the visual media may not only have less impact on people, but the encounter with them may represent more of a genuine choice. Liberals are willing to

---

[1] See Chapter 8, esp at 392–408.

[2] See F. Schauer, *Free Speech: A Philosophical Enquiry*, Oxford: OUP, 1982, Chapters 5 and 6; D. Feldman, *Civil Liberties and Human Rights*, 2nd edn., Oxford: OUP, 2002, 13.2; D.F.B. Tucker, *Law, Liberalism and Free Speech*, Totowa, NJ: Rowman & Allan, held 1985, 11–56; E. Barendt, *Freedom of Speech*, Oxford: OUP, 2005, 2nd edn., Chapter 1; see also Chapter 8 at 395–9.

[3] See J. Feinberg, *The Moral Limits of the Criminal Law: Offense to Others*, Oxford: OUP, 1985. For a brief discussion of the possible link between pornography and the commission of sexual offences, see Chapter 8 at 388–90.

support restrictions on the outlets and public display of explicit material[4] on the ground that such restrictions do not necessarily spring from contempt for those who wish to view such material, but may simply reflect the genuine and personal aesthetic preferences of those who would rather not be confronted unexpectedly with offensive images.[5] The position of the broadcast media, film, the Internet is more problematic since adults can normally protect themselves from offence.

Following the liberal argument from autonomy,[6] the provision of information and advice in order to warn persons of the content of particular films or broadcasts is clearly acceptable. Provision of such information, far from infringing personal auto-nomy, upholds it. But the mere *restraint* through cuts or outright bans of visual material aimed at adult audiences beyond the requirements of the criminal law represents a failure to respect the right of adults to choose their own diverse forms of entertain-ment, within the law. (Clearly, the relevant criminal law also creates infringements of autonomy, as discussed in Chapter 8.)[7] It fails to hold the balance between upholding the autonomy of those who do not wish to be confronted unexpectedly by offensive images and those who wish to be able to make a choice to view them. The use of the watershed continuum in broadcasting—the scheduling of explicit, adult material to later periods in the evening (normally after 9.00pm) is defensible since it does not involve the banning of such material from the screen. Age restrictions for films are more controversial, although again they are defensible since the material is not entirely withheld from adult audiences. But mandatory restrictions on films and videos may be viewed as infringing the autonomy of children and in Chapter 12 it is questioned whether, as in most of Europe, they should be advisory only.[8]

The current age classification regime for videos is based largely on the idea of parental responsibility, thereby offering the probability that children will view films that they could not view in the cinema. At the same time, as discussed below, the warning contained in the classification of videos is not assumed to be enough to ensure that children under the age of eight, for example, will not watch explicit material. There is also an infringement of adult autonomy since films and videos must not contain material that prevents them from achieving a classification, but the infringement goes furthest in relation to videos. Clearly, since broadcasts come into the home and the viewer may be confronted inadvertently with offensive images, there is a fairly strong case under the argument from autonomy for instituting a special regime relating to explicit broadcast material. Such a regime would typically include showing explicit material after the 'water-shed', accompanying it with detailed warn-ings or encoding it. The warnings regime could probably be taken further under the developing technology so that people were extremely unlikely to be confronted with

---

[4] Such as, e.g., the recommendations of the Williams Committee (*Report of the Committee on Obscenity and Film Censorship*, Cmnd 7772, 1979) briefly discussed in Chapter 8 at 395; see their 'Summary of our proposals'.

[5] See R. Dworkin, 'Do we have a right to pornography?' in *A Matter of Principle*, 1985, pp 355–8, where he broadly endorses the Williams Committee's proposals.

[6] See Chapter 1 at 13–14.   [7] See Chapter 8 at 422–9. See also Chapter 9.

[8] See Chapter 12 at 622–3.

material that they find offensive. However, at present the regulation of broadcasting goes further, and in the interests of protecting those few people who might inadvertently be confronted by images they find offensive, infringes the autonomy of those who wish to exercise a choice to view explicit material within what the criminal law allows.

Thus, the regulation of broadcasting goes further in the direction of paternalism than does the regime for films and videos, since autonomy is to a greater extent removed from parents and handed to a regulator—now Ofcom. The regime affecting broadcasting in the interests of preventing offence to viewers clearly curbs the freedom of broadcasters to impart information and expression; it also curbs the freedom of viewers to receive broadcast expression. It is a compromise between protecting children and protecting adult autonomy. It will be contended that the regime for both films and broadcasts fails to differing degrees to adhere to the Dworkinian precept, discussed in Chapter 8, that the argument from moral autonomy amounts to the strongest case against restraint and censorship in this area.[9] Under it restraint can only be justified if a serious risk of substantial damage to the concrete well being of society was shown.[10] At present the test for cutting broadcast material, based on the readily satisfied notion of causing offence, is very far from satisfying the Dworkinian test.

Plurality and diversity in broadcasting is in general served by regulation, but not in the case of offence avoidance. In that instance conservative values are, essentially, upheld since regulations designed to avoid offence protect the majority from having their views on sexual propriety challenged in ways that they might find shocking and offensive. Thus the regulatory schemes, especially the one for broadcasting, discussed in the following two chapters, do not support diversity. But the broadcast regulatory scheme creates diversity in accordance with all the free speech justifications in relation to requirements to broadcast minority programmes, due impartiality rules and 'must carry' requirements. This is the paradox of 'command and control' regulatory regimes.[11] Thus this Part tends to attack regulation, whereas Part 6, Chapter 20 tends to support it.[12] This paradox appears at present to be an inevitable concomitant of broadcast regulation in the UK, in contrast to the effect of free market policies in the US.[13]

---

[9] See Chapter 8 at 395–7.

[10] The justifications for abrogating speech in this context do not approach the level of stringency of this test: see generally Chapters 8 and 9. See Chapter 8 at 388–90 for consideration of the possible link between pornography and sexual offences.

[11] The term is considered in Chapter 12 at 618.

[12] See Chapter 20 at 993–5.

[13] See Chapter 20 at 993–4; the US Supreme Court strikes down 'must carry' requirements.

CRIMINAL LAW AND REGULATION [14]

The criminal law affecting forms of explicit expression described in Chapters 8 and 9 applies equally to the visual mediums of film and broadcasting. But they are also subject to a further layer of restraint via forms of regulation, monitored by media regulatory bodies. The regulatory regimes in place mean that the visual media are restrained beyond the demands of the criminal law. Such regulation has the effect of ensuring that these media tend not to test the boundaries of the criminal law fully in relation to forms of expression since one aim of regulation is to avoid approaching too close to those boundaries. In other words, the use of regulation creates an unexplored territory between the limits of criminal liability and the regulated area. If in this context expression falls within that territory, it would not attract criminal liability, but might be censored or attract the post-publication sanctions that the relevant media regulator has at its command. Theoretically, prosecution of broadcasters or film-makers under the Obscene Publications Act 1959[15] or the Protection of Children Act 1978, as amended, is possible, but the regulatory regime applied to them has so far obviated this possibility, except where the regime itself is evaded, as in the case of unclassified 'hard-core' pornographic DVDs and videos. This Part covers the Internet since it is not only very much a visual medium, it also has many links with the other media discussed here. But since the Internet is not subject to a regulatory body, it follows that web-based material is far more likely to come directly into conflict with the criminal law than the other forms of visual material discussed here.

As discussed in Chapter 8, three justifications for the use of the UK criminal law to control and curb explicit expression in order to protect persons from encountering offensive material are usually relied upon: the corruption of persons, particularly children as the more vulnerable; the shock or outrage caused by public displays of certain material; the perceived link with the commission of sex crimes.[16] As discussed in Chapter 8, Canadian law now focuses primarily upon a fourth justification: damage to constitutionally protected values such as equality and dignity.[17] The development of UK criminal law in general has been based on the avoidance of the first two possibilities mentioned, as Chapter 8 points out, although in relation to the visual media, the third has had some influence. On the ground of causing shock, the display of certain publications attracts sanctions, while others viewed as having the potential

---

[14] For a comprehensive treatment see: D. Goldberg, T. Prosser, and S. Verhulst, *Regulating the Changing Media: A Comparative Study*, Oxford: OUP, 1998; T. Gibbons, *Regulating the Media*, 2nd edn., London: Sweet & Maxwell, 1998; T. Gibbons, *Regulating the Media*, 2nd edn., London: Sweet & Maxwell, 1998.

[15] The Obscene Publications Act, s 1 covers these media under s 1(2) since the Broadcasting Act 1990, s 162, has brought radio and television within its ambit.

[16] See the Williams Committee appointed in 1977 to review obscenity and indecency law (Williams Report, Cmnd 7772, 1979).

[17] Pp 450–62.

to corrupt can be prohibited entirely, either by punishment of those responsible after publication or by being seized and suppressed before publication.

Apart from the third justification, which appears to play a part in the censorship of films, regulation, in contrast, has been underpinned by a different aim. It has been aimed at offence avoidance in situations in which the public can in general exercise choice, whereas it is difficult to avoid displays on billboards or posters. The stricter system of controls for the visual media seems to have been adopted in answer to the view that owing to their particular impact on audiences, it is appropriate to subject films, videos and broadcasting to regulatory restraint.[18] The visual media have been seen quite readily as possible sources of harm. It will be argued in the following chapters, however, that the aims of regulation are changing—the paternalistic aim of general offence-avoidance is giving way to that of protecting children in all sectors of the visual media.[19] At the same time, a growing recognition of the need to protect the choices of the adult audience is evident. The emphasis on offence-avoidance has meant that regulation has created a greater curb on the visual media than the criminal law would do if it was the sole regulatory mechanism. Now that the emphasis on offence avoidance *per se* is diminishing, regulation is likely to come closer to following the borders of the criminal law and therefore the regulated area that goes beyond the boundaries of that law is receding.

But the use of media regulators means that the criminal law remains in general far less significant in this context than it is in relation to the print media, although it can be viewed as setting very basic minimal standards. Regulation continues to place broadcasting and films in a very different position from that of the print media, although their positions have converged in one respect since newspapers and magazines are being forced at present to accept legal restraint imposed outside their preferred self-regulatory regime in the context of privacy.[20] In the context under discussion convergence has not occurred. Printed matter, including magazines, newspapers and books, is not subject to licensing and regulation, although explicit material can be subject to forfeiture and to subsequent criminal sanctions, as discussed in Chapter 8. Books are much less likely to be punished than magazines because it is thought that print material that has a visual impact is more likely to cause harm. The still greater visual impact of films and broadcasts is thought to justify a relatively strict censorship and regulation regime. While this chapter therefore concentrates on regulation, it does consider certain specific aspects of the criminal law, including those aspects that create particularly difficult issues for regulators. As will be discussed, film and video makers, manufacturers and distributors now face an enhanced possibility

---

[18] See Chapters 11 and 12, esp 563–4. The theatre is in an anomalous position; it has not been censored since 1968 despite its visual impact (see Chapter 8 at 423). Possibly this is partly due to the idea that theatre audiences are more sophisticated and less likely to be affected by what they have seen than cinema audiences. Further, films can use special effects and create realistic explicit images that go far beyond what can be achieved in a theatre.

[19] See below pp 543–5 and see Chapter 11 at 600–2 below.

[20] See Chapter 14.

of criminal liability in relation to particular films due to changes introduced under the new Sexual Offences Act 2003, which recently came into effect.[21]

REGULATORY CONVERGENCE; THE INFLUENCE OF THE EUROPEAN UNION

The notion that visual material might be available on a computer screen or on a video that cannot be broadcast is anomalous to an extent. The Internet and videos both come into the home, as broadcasting does, and create the possibility that children might encounter harmful material. It is probably still true that people are more likely to view offensive images inadvertently on television, although that possibility is diminishing as discussed in Chapter 11. Therefore there is still a case for imposing a somewhat more restrictive regime on broadcasting. As discussed in the following chapters, the developing regulatory law and policy reflects an acceptance that this anomaly should be addressed by relaxing controls on broadcasting in respect of adults, while seeking to ensure the protection of children across the audio-visual sectors. Thus, especially at the EU level, there is receptivity among policy-makers to the idea that greater convergence should be achieved, not only in the standards applied by the EU member states, but between the standards applied to explicit and disturbing material in the various audio-visual sectors. This chapter explores the emerging convergence between the regulatory schemes affecting the different sectors, but points out that the schemes still differ from each other quite significantly in a range of respects. In particular, while further controls over the Internet are envisaged, in order to seek to protect children, there is no proposal to seek to bring it within a regulatory scheme such as that which applies in the UK to broadcasting.

As the following chapters reveal, UK content-based media regulation has, typically, a statutory underpinning, setting up a regulatory body which then promulgates a Code or Guidelines to which the regulated body or bodies must adhere. The regulator may subject the output of the regulated body to prior or subsequent restraint. In the latter instance, non-adherence may attract penalties—usually fines or requirements to publish adjudications—imposed by the regulatory body. Court intervention tends to be very limited—the regulator itself polices adherence to its Code or guidelines. The regulated bodies can challenge regulatory decisions in court by way of judicial review as can special interest groups and members of the public, although in practice such challenges are relatively rare. But the different audio-visual sectors currently adhere to this model to very varying extents.

Broadcasting and videoworks are subject to regulatory schemes which are largely statute-based in the case of broadcasting, and partly statute-based in respect of videos.

---

[21] It came into force in May 2004. The change is to the definition of a 'child' under the Protection of Children Act 1978; see Chapter 12 at 625–7.

Films are subject to a largely self-regulatory regime, as is the Internet and advertising, although self-regulation of the Internet is far less well established and no one body has responsibility. All sectors are affected by Codes or Guidelines, although again these are far less well established or effective in relation to the Internet. Broadcasting, videoworks, films and advertising are subject to formal or informal sanctions for non-adherence to such quasi-legal rules, but in the case of films and advertising such adherence is self-imposed, although the rules governing films have greater *de facto* force due to their connection with Local Authority licensing powers and broadcasting decisions.[22] There is quite a complex relationship between the regulation of films and various statutory powers even though such regulation has no full statutory basis. Its position may be compared with that of the Advertising Standards Authority which has far less statutory interaction. The Press Complaints Commission (PCC) is an even weaker (*de facto*) regulator—its decisions have no force; its only interaction is with the HRA which mentions the PCC's code in s 12(4).[23] The Internet Watch Foundation is in a weaker position still, as discussed in Chapter 12.[24] The film industry is not subject to *positive* obligations regarding content, as the broadcast media is in certain respects. Films and videos are subject—in effect—to prior restraints. A new and more detailed regulatory regime was introduced for broadcasting in 2003, as explained in Chapter 11. Like the previous regime it is based almost entirely on subsequent restraints, leading to self-censorship and/or the application of sanctions post-transmission. The standards applied to broadcasting nevertheless mean that it is the most heavily regulated and restrained sector.

Broadcasting has for some time been the most significant medium in terms of audience reliance. Over the last fifty years it has risen to its present position of 'cultural supremacy'.[25] It has been termed 'the defining medium of the age'.[26] In general, people rely on broadcasting for entertainment far more than they do on films, since broadcasting comes into the home. But the fact that broadcasting is an 'intruder' into the home is also highly significant in terms of regulation. Broadcasting is at one and the same time of immense significance in terms of audience reliance and is also more highly regulated than any other medium. This is especially the case in relation to restraints on broadcasting on the ground of offensiveness. That special level of restraint may have been justifiable in the past, when choice was circumscribed and persons were more likely to be confronted inadvertently with offensive images. It is less defensible now that the development of broadcast technology has meant that a very wide range of channels are available, some with encoding, and a vast amount of information regarding broadcasts can be obtained via interactive remote control. Films (including videos and DVDs) are regulated to a much greater extent than print material but do not attract the level of regulation to which broadcasting is subject.

---

[22] See Chapter 12 at 619, Chapter 11 at 602.
[23] See Chapter 14 at 756–7, Chapter 15 at 796, Chapter 3, note 1.   [24] See Chapter 12 at 654–7.
[25] See M. Feintuck, *Media Regulation, Public Interest and the Law*, Edinburgh University Press 1999 p 3.
[26] See E. Herman and R. McChesney, *The Global Media*, London: Cassell, 1997, p 2.

Thus when films are broadcast, a further level of regulation is applicable. As indicated, the Internet is in an anomalous position: Although it may be viewed as broadly analogous to the other visual media, it is not subject to one single regulatory scheme, or indeed to any one *effective* regime, due to the difficulty of imposing national regulation on a medium that relies on the provision of websites on an international basis. None of the current regulatory models available in the UK for the other visual media have so far been viewed as feasible or appropriate for the Internet. It is largely governed in this context by the criminal law only.

In 2000 an opportunity arose to achieve greater convergence between the various visual sectors. The government published a White Paper, *A New Future for Communications*,[27] which set out its vision and objectives for the 21st century. The statute that emerged, the Communications Act 2003, did not create a radical departure from the previous regulatory model in terms of content regulation. The key concern of the 2003 reforms is to create a dynamic and competitive communications and media market. The Act adopts, in essentials, the current regulatory model for broadcasting, recognizing the convergence environment by applying it to telecommunications as well as broadcasting, but not to the Internet or to films. The Communications Act 2003 created one super-regulator, Ofcom, which now has the responsibility for maintaining standards for offence-avoidance in relation to broadcasting alone.

It will be argued that the reforms do not fully challenge previously established notions as to the unacceptability of certain forms of explicit material for broadcasting. In particular, pre-2003, videos or websites could contain explicit material that was not viewed as suitable for broadcasting, and the reforms do not address this partial anomaly with any clarity. Following the decision of the High Court in *R v VAC of the BBFC ex parte BBFC*[28] 'hardcore' pornography on videos became legally available in 'sex establishments' under the R18 video classification. This placed the government in a difficult position regarding the proscription of foreign satellite channels broadcasting such material, as explained below. But it also raised questions as to the lack of availability of such material on licensed subscription services in the UK, bearing in mind the more liberal stance of European broadcast regulators. The 2003 Act failed to offer clear answers to these questions. The traditionally paternalistic stance taken in the UK towards providing protection from 'offensive' material is coming increasingly under pressure in relation to a generation that has grown up with the Internet and which has, partly for that reason, a greater awareness of global standards of visual freedom of expression. The notion of creating greater restraints on such expression in the UK than in a number of other European countries is becoming increasingly problematic. Moreover, the use of an archaic and virtually unworkable test—of 'obscenity'[29]—as the basis for the regulation of explicit material on the internet and as the ultimate, albeit unchallenged, standard by which to judge the censorship of films and of programmes for broadcasting, looks increasingly bizarre from a global perspective.

---

[27] Published 12 December 2000; www.communicationswhitepaper.gov.uk.
[28] [2000] COD 239.   [29] See Chapter 8 at 424–34.

The EU is currently creating pressure for harmonization, both between the various audio-visual sectors and across the member states of the EU, and such pressure is likely to intensify. *The Council Recommendation concerning the protection of minors and human dignity*[30] was the first legal instrument at EU-level that concerned the content of audiovisual and information services covering all forms of delivery, from broadcasting to the Internet. The Recommendation was intended to allow for the development of competitiveness in such services by promoting national frameworks aimed at achieving a comparable and effective level of protection. Clearly, if parity was not achieved between the levels of protection, competition would be undermined. At the same time the pressure for parity between national frameworks was intended to lead to convergence and harmony between the different audiovisual media in terms of content. The Recommendation takes a cross-media approach to the protection of minors and emphasizes the cross-border exchange of best practice. It also favours the development of co-regulatory and self-regulatory mechanisms. A co-regulatory approach is one that involves public authorities, the industry and the other interested parties, including consumers. This approach is favoured, since the Commission views it as more 'flexible, adaptable and effective than straightforward regulation and legislation. With regard to the protection of minors, where many sensibilities have to be taken into account, co-regulation can often better achieve the given aims'.

As an aspect of the *Recommendation* the Commission had to present an evaluation report[31] on the application of the Recommendation in the Member States, to the European Parliament and the Council, and in order to do so it commissioned a study[32] which examined the issue of comparative content rating systems in the various media—television, film, interactive games, the Internet. It found that ratings differed, not only between EU and EEA Member States, but also within Member states. So the same film was sometimes rated in a different way within a particular Member State, depending on the distribution medium. This is, of course, the case in the UK, as the following chapters show, although at the same time some recent movement towards harmonization of the various media in terms of ratings can be found, especially in film and broadcasting. The main conclusion of the study was that, while there was no strong pressure from the audio-visual industry or from consumers for homogeneity, the structural pressures of globalization and convergence were tending towards greater consistency.

The Commission found that the development of digital media—the Internet, digital broadcasting and video games—continued to create a significant challenge to

---

[30] 24 September 1998, 98/560/EC, OJ L 270, 7 October 1998, p 48.

[31] In accordance with section III of the Recommendation, paragraph 4. The implementation of the Recommendation was evaluated for the first time in 2000, and the first report was published in 2001: Evaluation Report to the Council and the European Parliament on the application of Council Recommendation of 24 September 1998 on protection of minors and human dignity COM(2001) 106 final, 27 February 2001. Parliament adopted a resolution on the report on 11 April 2002: C5–0191/2001–2001/2087(COS), in which it called on the Commission to draw up a further report preferably before 31 December 2002.

[32] *Study on the rating practice used for audiovisual works in the European Union:* http://www.europa.eu.int/comm/avpolicy/stat/studi_en.htm#rating.

the European Union's audiovisual policy, especially in relation to the protection of children. This policy was reflected in the 'Television Without Frontiers' (TVWF) directive,[33] the main legislative instrument at EU level concerning audiovisual services, which deals with the protection of minors from harmful content disseminated via broadcasting. The TVWF was revised in 1997 to take account of technological and market developments. As discussed in Chapter 12 the European Parliament and the Council had already taken measures in 1999 with a view to protecting minors from harmful material on the Internet.[34] The replies received by the Commission from the member states showed that self-regulation and co-regulation continues to be less strong in broadcasting than in relation to the Internet. Although the Commission found that the regulatory schemes in place were reasonably effective, it also found that insufficient effort was being made to involve consumer associations and other interested parties in the establishment of codes of conduct and other self-regulatory initiatives. A number of the findings of the Commission are considered in relation to the UK regulatory schemes for broadcasting, film and the Internet in the following two chapters.

The Commission proceeded to propose an additional Recommendation: *Proposal for a recommendation of the European Parliament and Council on the protection of minors and human dignity and the right to reply in relation to the competitiveness of the European audiovisual and information services industry.*[35] It is notable that due to the subject matter the Commission considered that the Recommendation should come from the European Parliament and the Council,[36] rather than from the Commission itself,[37] thereby affording it greater prominence. The additional Recommendation builds upon the original 1998 Recommendation and was proposed in order to keep up with the challenges posed by technological developments. The proposal covers a number of matters, including media literacy and the right of reply across the various media, and, interestingly, action against discrimination based on sex, racial or ethnic origin, religion or belief, disability, age or sexual orientation in all audio-visual media. In passing, it is worth noting that although the stance in relation to human dignity is welcome in this context, it appears that it will not affect the press—the media sector

[33] Council Directive 89/552/EEC, as amended by Directive 97/36/EC of the European Parliament and of the Council, adopted in 1989. See Chapter 11 at 567–8, 572.

[34] See pp 652–4. See also note 39, below.

[35] COM(2004) 341 final 2004/0117 (COD) 30 April 2004, press release 04/598. The legal basis proposed for the Recommendation is Article 157 of the EC Treaty.

[36] It was reported on 26 January 2005 on the website *EU Audio-visual policy: the regulatory framework*: 'On 16 November 2004, concerning the Commission proposal for a recommendation on protection of minors and the right of reply, the Council took note of the general approach which was adopted as a result of prior discussions in the Council's Audiovisual Working Party under the Dutch Presidency. The Presidency concluded by noting that the Council unanimously reached a general approach on this proposal.'

[37] Para 4 of the Recommendation: 'the European Parliament has fully backed the need to protect minors and human dignity in its resolution of 11 April 2002 (C5–0191/2001–2001/2087(COS)), on the first evaluation report on the recommendation. Therefore, it seems appropriate to fully involve the European Parliament in the discussion and adoption of the recommendation. The involvement of the European Parliament will result in more public debate and a bigger impact of the Recommendation.'

that, it is contended, presents far more of a threat in this respect. This may be said, not only in relation to its propensity to invade privacy, but also in respect of the insidious effects of the biased and partial portrayal of women, of a number of minority groups, and even of aspects of government policy,[38] found in much of the UK press.

The Recommendation 'calls on the Member States, industry and interested parties, as well as the Commission, to take steps to enhance the protection of minors and human dignity in the broadcasting and internet sectors'.[39] For the purposes of the following two chapters, the recommendations as to cooperation and the sharing of experience and good practices between co- and self-regulatory bodies dealing with the rating or classification of audiovisual content are of most significance.[40] The proposed Recommendation focuses on such content in all forms of delivery, from broadcasting to the Internet; its implications will be assessed in relation to the various regulatory bodies in the different media sectors. But clearly it implies, most importantly, that the recent re-visiting and re-envisioning of the audio-visual sector in the Communications Act 2003 does not go far enough. Far from creating an inclusive scheme with one super-regulator, the new regime created under the Act leaves the Internet, films and videoworks unaffected. Thus it leaves the question of harmonization—in terms of content—between the sectors open to interpretation by Ofcom.

This chapter is not advocating the creation of one super-regulator with government appointees; the Recommendation does not in any event support the creation of such bodies in the member states. But this chapter and the following two will argue that harmonization of rating systems for content, regardless of the mode of delivery, is overdue in the UK. Therefore the chapters argue for the creation of mechanisms for cooperation between the regulatory bodies, the sharing of best practice and, above all, for the sweeping away of anomalies whereby the mode of delivery determines restraint on content. The proposed Recommendation succeeds, it is argued, in reconciling the protection for minors and human dignity with freedom of expression in a number of respects. It places the emphasis on co- or self- regulation, as opposed to regulation via legislation with a government appointed regulatory body. Further, the emphasis of the original and of the proposed Recommendation is on the protection of minors, as opposed to the imposition of 'standards of taste and decency' more gener-

---

[38] Distorted reporting related to groups such as asylum seekers can directly assault human dignity, but it also tends to misrepresent aspects of such policy.

[39] Para 2 of the proposal for a recommendation; it continues: 'Illegal, harmful and undesirable content and conduct on the Internet continues to be a concern for law-makers, industry and parents. There will be new challenges both in quantitative (more "illegal" content) and qualitative terms (new platforms, new products). Taking into account the ever-increasing processing power and storage capacity of computers, and the fact that broadband technologies allow distribution of content such as video on 3G mobile telephones, the need for a safe environment is greater than ever.'

[40] The Recommendation calls on the industries and parties concerned: (1) to develop positive measures for the benefit of minors, including initiatives to facilitate their wider access to audiovisual and information services, while avoiding potentially harmful content, including a 'bottom-up' harmonization through cooperation between self-regulatory and co-regulatory bodies in the Member States, and through the exchange of best practices concerning such issues as a system of common, descriptive symbols which would help viewers to assess the content of programmes . . .

ally. (The phrase is taken from the previous regime affecting the content of broadcasting.)[41] This emphasis is reflected in the Communications Act, s 319, but only in relation to one audio-visual sector. There are no express mechanisms for co-operation with the sectors not covered by the Act; the matter is left to the discretion of Ofcom. As Chapter 11 indicates, Ofcom is taking steps in the direction of harmonization; in particular its stance in relation to the broadcasting of films differs sharply from that adopted by the previous regulatory bodies. But the legal basis for so doing remains weak.

CONVERGENCE ACROSS VARIOUS MEDIA—THE ADVERTISING STANDARDS AUTHORITY

The regulators of the visual media discussed in the following two chapters are medium-specific. They have developed very differently and provide differing models of regulation depending on the medium to be regulated. The historical reasons for the differences are explored in the relevant chapters. But the regulation of advertising undertaken by the Advertising Standards Authority (ASA) is now consistent across all media, including the print media. Until November 2004 it did not regulate broadcast advertising, but now, as discussed in the next chapter, Ofcom has contracted out its broadcast advertising remit to the ASA.[42] The ASA now provides one model for regulation across various media sectors and in this sense it is unique among UK media regulators. It does not vary greatly across the media in terms of its Codes[43] and its sanctions.

The ASA is an independent, self-regulatory body set up by the advertising industry itself in 1961. It resembles the film regulator—the BBFC—in that it was set up by the industry in order to evade external regulation.[44] The Advertising Association established what became the Committee of Advertising Practice (CAP), the industry body that sets the rules for advertisers, agencies and media. The foreword to the first edition of the British Code of Advertising Practice stated: 'The function of advertising is the advocacy of the merits of particular products or services . . . and this Code seeks to define practices considered undesirable by the organisations which have subscribed to

---

[41] See Chapter 11 at 574–5.

[42] See Chapter 11 at 593–4; see also A. Willis, 'The Future Regulation of Broadcast Advertising' *Ent L Rev* (2004), 15(8), 255–6.

[43] The British Code of Advertising, Sales Promotion and Direct Marketing (the CAP Code) applies to all non-broadcast advertising, including online 'paid for' space, such as banner and pop-up advertisements; cinema adverts; bill-boards. It has separate Codes for broadcasting. For discussion of the offence avoidance aspects of its different Codes, see Chapter 12 at 646–7 and Chapter 11 at 594.

[44] In the 1960s the Molony and Reith Committees (see note 46 below) proposed a tax on advertising in order to finance an independent advertising watchdog. The advertising industry evaded this threat by readily setting up a voluntary Code and the Advertising Standards Authority to administer the Code. See Chapter 12 at 619–20 for discussion of the inception of the BBFC.

it.' The following year, the industry established the Advertising Standards Authority under an independent Chairman, to adjudicate on complaints about advertising that appeared to breach the Code.

In terms of the regulatory models described in the following chapters, the ASA probably most resembles the BBFC in its role in relation to films as opposed to videos. The ASA, like the BBFC, does not possess statutory powers to regulate films and both were set up by the relevant industries with a remit as self-regulatory bodies.[45] As explained in Chapter 12, the BBFC has *de facto* power in relation to the statutory power to licence films of local authorities. The ASA stands in a somewhat similar relationship to Ofcom, in relation to broadcast advertising

The advertising industry, through the Committee of Advertising Practice (CAP), supports the ASA. Self-regulation appears to have the support of the government, and of Official Reports. An official report on Consumer Protection by the Molony Committee rejected the case for an American-style Federal Trade Commission to regulate advertising by statute. 'We are satisfied that the wider problem of advertising ought to be, and can be, tackled by effectively applied voluntary controls,' reported the Committee.[46] However, the Molony Committee did consider that there was a need for tighter advertising regulations for the sake of consumer protection, and advocated the setting up of an independent watchdog body. The rapid setting up of the ASA averted that possibility. This model also operates at the EU level.[47] The UK judiciary have been broadly supportive of the ASA in challenges to the ASA's adjucations. For example, the High Court recently dismissed an application for an injunction to prevent publication of its adjudication on television advertising by Jamba! GmbH. In his ruling, the judge, Mr Justice Lloyd-Jones, accepted the ASA's arguments that the public interest was best served by publishing the adjudication immediately, notwithstanding Jamba's request for an Independent Review.[48]

The ASA's remit has developed over the last fifty years; in particular after regulating non-broadcast marketing communications over a number of years, the ASA also became the regulator for broadcast advertising when Ofcom contracted that aspect of regulation out to the ASA. As described in Chapter 11, commercial television, including broadcast advertisements, are subject to statutory standards codes, and have been

[45] See further C.R. Munro, 'Self-Regulation in the Media' [1997] *PL* 6. See also E. Barendt, *Freedom of Speech*, 2nd edn., 2005, Chapter 11.

[46] The Molony Committee on Consumer Protection (1959–61); see also the Reith Commission on Advertising (1966). Both bodies pressed on post-war British public opinion the need for tighter advertising regulations for the sake of consumer protection.

[47] The European Advertising Standards Alliance is a body that brings together national advertising self-regulatory organizations and organizations representing the advertising industry in Europe. The EASA co-ordinates cross-borders advertising complaints and promotes self-regulation in Europe.

[48] Judgment of 22 September 2005. In 1998 Advertiser SmithKline Beecham took the ASA to the High Court over the Authority's upheld adjudications against Ribena Toothkind advertising. See *SmithKline Beecham plc v Advertising Standards Authority* [2001] EWJ No. 49 Queen's Bench Division, Administrative Court, 17 January 2001. The judge upheld the adjudications and supported the self-regulatory system in finding that there was no real risk or danger of bias on the part of the ASA.

since 1955. Thus the ASA now has a regulatory role in broadcast advertising and it will be working in a co-regulatory partnership with Ofcom.

The standards laid down in the ASA codes are intended to protect consumers and also to create a level playing field for advertisers, aiding competitiveness. All advertisements, regardless of the medium they appear in—broadcasting, the Internet, Cinema, press—are required to meet the standards set by the ASA codes of conduct. The Codes are administered by the ASA; they are intended to prevent advertising that is either misleading[49] or offensive. Since 1988, self-regulation has been backed up by statutory powers given to the Office of Fair Trading under the powers of the Control of Misleading Advertisements Regulations.

Advertisements are not allowed to cause serious or widespread offence. Special care is taken in relation to the grounds of sex, race, religion, sexuality and disability. This requirement is included in the ASA Broadcast Codes and in the British Code of Advertising, Sales Promotion and Direct Marketing (the CAP Code) which applies to all non-broadcast advertising, including on-line 'paid for' space, such as banner and pop-up advertisements, cinema adverts, bill-boards.[50] It must be noted that the rules only apply to 'advertisements'—the question whether material is part of an advertisement or part of an editorial may sometimes be in issue. It appears that the ASA's opinion on this matter will be decisive so long as it is based on reasonable grounds.[51] The context of the advertisement is significant; the factors taken into account include: the medium that the advertisement appears in, the audience, the product and generally

---

[49] Advertisements may be found to mislead consumers if the advertiser does not hold evidence to prove the claims made about the relevant products or services before an advertisement appears. The CAP (non-Broadcast) Code states: *Substantiation*

3.1 Before distributing or submitting a marketing communication for publication, marketers must hold documentary evidence to prove all claims, whether direct or implied, that are capable of objective substantiation.

[50] For the offence-avoidance requirements, see para 5.1 of the CAP (non-Broadcast) Code and para 6.1 of the Television Broadcast Code. The Codes are considered in Chapter 11 at 594 and Chapter 12 at 646–7, respectively.

[51] This question arose in *In R v Advertising Standards Authority Limited, ex parte Charles Robertson (Developments) Limited* [2000] EMLR 463. The applicant operated a number of retail stores and had often bought space in various regional newspapers. In those spaces the applicant advertised its products. The space included an 'editorial' column written by the applicant's chairman which contained a mixture of political, cultural, and social comments. Complaints were made to the Advertising Standards Authority that a column published in two newspapers was racist, offensive, and could incite violence. The complaints were upheld by the ASA. The applicant applied for judicial review of the ASA's decision, contending that the ASA had no jurisdiction to consider the matter because the column was not an advertisement. In support of this contention, the applicant argued that the ASA's jurisdiction was confined to that which was properly to be regarded as commercial expression, and did not include material that expressed political views. It was found that the ASA's view that the editorial column was part of the advertisement would be upheld unless it was found not to be based on reasonable grounds, and that in the alternative, if the court itself had to form a view on the matter, it would find that the editorial gave the impression, due to its appearance, of being part of the advertisement. It was concluded that it was for the ASA to determine whether the columns were part of an advertisement and their conclusion could not be impugned. Thus the ASA had jurisdiction. The HRA was not in force at the time, but the court noted that the ASA's jurisdiction to consider political as opposed to commercial expression might be called into question once it came into force: 'it may well be that the right of the ASA to interfere with advertisements which express political opinions, even though those opinions are expressed within an advertisement, will have to be revisited' under the HRA.

accepted standards of conduct at the time. The ASA states on its website: 'Over time, the boundaries of offensiveness change. The challenge is to patrol the boundaries of expectation, not to try to enforce absolute standards of taste'.[52] This approach is similar to that used by Ofcom in relation to offence-avoidance in broadcasting. An advert that has the 'principal function of influencing voters in local, regional, national or international elections or referendums' is exempt from the CAP Code.[53]

If a complaint is made that appears to indicate that a serious breach of the relevant Code has occurred, a formal investigation may be needed. This is undertaken by the ASA Council which will then rule on the matter. The ASA Council is the body that adjudicates on formally investigated complaints. It has an independent Chairman and the majority of its members come from outside the advertising industry; they are members of the public, recruited by public advertisement. The Council decides whether the Codes have been broken and their adjudication is then published on the ASA website. There is also an Independent Review Procedure in place which can ask the Council to reconsider its original decision if a substantial flaw of process or adjudication is apparent, or where additional relevant evidence becomes available subsequent to the Council's findings.

Once the Council has made a decision, the advertisers must ensure that the ruling has been adhered to. That may mean that an advertisement must be altered or withdrawn. This is an infringement of freedom of expression and so must be 'prescribed by law' under Article 10(2). The ASA's Code was found to satisfy that demand in *R v Advertising Standards Authority Ltd, ex parte Matthias Rath BV.*[54] The ASA has various sanctions at its command that ensure that its rulings are complied with. The publication of the ruling on the ASA website may create adverse publicity for the advertiser. The advertiser can be referred to the Office of Fair Trading in relation to misleading advertisements, and broadcasters can be referred to Ofcom for persistently breaching the rules. Media owners and broadcasters will refuse to run advertisements that breach the Codes.

Thus the ASA does not possess formal sanctions as Ofcom itself does, but relies on informal ones or on reference to other bodies. The strength of its self-regulatory system lies in the perception from consumers and the industry that the ASA is independent, and also it appears to have the support and commitment of the advertising industry, through the Committee of Advertising Practice (CAP), to the standards of the codes. Regulation by the ASA covers certain matters outside the scope of this book—the efficacy of advertising in relation to effective consumerism is not a concern of this book. However, as discussed in Chapter 20, some advertising engages to an extent with free speech rationales and therefore its regulation is a matter of concern.[55]

---

[52] See asa.org.uk.

[53] See para 12.1 of the CAP Code. Political advertising, apart from Party Election Broadcasts and political broadcasts, is banned from broadcasting (see Chapter 20 at 1012–20) but can appear in print, film, or online.

[54] [2001] EMLR 22.

[55] See Chapter 20 at 1022, 1033–4, and Chapter 2 at 60. See also *R(British American Tobacco UK) v Secretary of State for Health* (2004) WEHC 2493 on the ban on tobacco advertising.

As Barendt argues, the desire of consumers for information does not 'remotely establish that there is a *free speech right* to receive, or impart, this information'.[56] However, as he accepts, commercial advertising that goes beyond the mere promulgation of information has been found to fall within the free speech rights of consumers.[57] The impact of the ASA is considered at various points in this book alongside the work of the media-specific regulators[58] and in relation to the question of banning political advertising in broadcasting.[59]

REGULATION AND ARTICLE 10 EUROPEAN CONVENTION ON HUMAN RIGHTS

Regulation of the visual media in order to avoid offence clearly creates a significant restraint on expression—a restraint that, as indicated, goes beyond the demands of the criminal law. Chapters 8 and 9 discussed the place of restraints created by the criminal law on explicit expression in relation to the free speech guarantee of Article 10. This chapter focuses mainly on the place of media content-based *regulation* within Article 10 and the possibilities it offers of affecting the different regulatory regimes under the Human Rights Act. As Chapters 8 and 9 pointed out, almost all Bills or Charters of Rights, apart from the US Bill of Rights,[60] contain an exception to the free speech clause which *inter alia* allows restraint on freedom of speech on the broad ground of the protection of morality or the rights of others. For example, section 14 of the New Zealand Bill of Rights protects freedom of expression, but the protection is subject to such 'reasonable limits prescribed by law as may be justified in a free and democratic society'. Such limits include the regulation of explicit expression in the visual media.[61]

The inception of the Human Rights Act means that the UK courts and regulatory bodies as functional public authorities[62] are faced with the difficult theoretical

---

[56] See Barendt 2005 p 401; cf the controversial dicta of Lord Woolf in *A v B* [2002] 3 WLR 542, see chap 15, pp 795–8.

[57] See Chapter 2, pp 60–1. See further, in favour of including advertisements as aspects of free speech: C. R. Munro, 'The Value of Commercial Speech' (2003) 62 *CLJ* 134; A. Kozinski and S. Banner, 'Who's Afraid of Commercial Speech?' (1990) 76 *Virginia Law Rev* 627 148–55.

[58] See Chapter 11 pp 593–5, Chapter 12 pp 646–7.   [59] See Chapter 20 pp 1014–15.

[60] The 'absolute' nature of the First Amendment, in contrast, has led the US courts to interpret the First Amendment so as to exclude obscene speech from the category of protected speech: see *Roth v US* (1957) 354 US 476; *Memoirs v Massachusetts* (1966) 383 US 413. See further Chapter 8 pp 447–50.

[61] *Society for Promotion of Community Standards Inc v Waverley International (1988) Ltd* [1993] 2 NZLR 709.

[62] See Chapter 3 pp 112–22 and Chapter 11 pp 607–8. It is highly probable—although there is no post-HRA authority—that the British Board of Film Classification is a public authority in relation to its classification of films. It is almost certain that this is the case in relation to its classification of videos. See further Chapter 12 pp 635–6. As discussed in Chapter 3 p 117, regulators tended to be judicially reviewable pre-HRA. Equally, the ASA is probably a functional public authority on the same basis—that if it did not exist the government would set up a watchdog body with statutory powers in its place. In *R v Advertising Standards Authority Ltd, ex parte Matthias Rath BV* (note 54 above) it was found: 'The court would require much persuasion that the ASA was not a public authority'.

problems associated with a positive right to freedom of expression as opposed to a negative liberty. This is a matter that is especially pertinent in relation to the forms of expression considered in this chapter since in this instance the restrictions are largely in the hands of media regulators rather than in those of the courts. Instead of merely determining whether and how far a statutory or Code provision applies to a factual situation, the various media regulators must consider the value of the expression, in determining whether a particular interference with it is justified. Free speech claims are tending to take a more central place in the Codes promulgated by regulators and in their rulings.[63]

The impact of the HRA in these areas is likely to be very variable and its effects are complicated by the fact that a number of the media bodies involved are private bodies, while the regulatory bodies are public authorities. The likelihood that sweeping change in the current UK regulatory regime governing films and broadcasts will not occur in this context under the HRA is partly due to the Strasbourg stance in relation to explicit expression in general, indicated below. In principle, the uncertainty and weakness of the Convention explicit expression jurisprudence need not deter domestic policy makers from adopting a more rigorous approach, based on the general principles underlying Article 10 and also on human rights jurisprudence in other jurisdictions. Those principles provide indications as to the policy that could be adopted in relation to erotic and explicit material of artistic merit aimed at a consenting adult audience.[64] But since the regulatory regimes are in most respects almost certainly within the margin of appreciation conceded to the member state, it is less likely that the judiciary would be inclined to bring about significant changes in them, through interpretation. Moreover, the very significant post-HRA House of Lords' decision in *ProLife Alliance v BBC*,[65] discussed in Chapter 11, is unlikely to encourage the judiciary to take a strongly liberalizing stance. If radical change is to come about, it is probable that it will have to be brought about by Parliament.

JUSTIFYING THE REGULATION OF EXPLICIT EXPRESSION UNDER ARTICLE 10(2)

Under Article 10(2), as Chapter 2 discussed, interferences with explicit expression may be justified if they have the legitimate aim of providing for the protection of morals or—in certain circumstances—the 'rights of others'. Regulation of the visual media with a view to avoiding offence, and underpinned by the laws on obscenity, indecency or blasphemy, is a matter that must meet Article 10 standards under the HRA. The compatibility of those laws with Article 10 is considered in Chapters 8 and 9. Specific

---

[63] See e.g. Ofcom's ruling in 2005 in relation to *Jerry Springer: The Opera*—Chapter 11 at 605, note 166.
[64] See pp 418–22.
[65] [2004] 1 AC 185; [2003] 2 All ER 977. See Chapter 11 at 577–92.

possible areas of incompatibility created by the regulatory regimes are considered below, at relevant points. Here, the Strasbourg stance on the application of Article 10 to the regulatory regimes governing explicit expression is considered.

(I) AMBIT OF ARTICLE 10(1)

Article 10(1) of the Convention specifically provides that the free expression guarantee 'shall not prevent States from requiring the licensing of broadcasting, television or cinema enterprises'. It is significant that this provision arises in the *first* paragraph of Article 10, thereby providing a limitation of the primary right that on its face is not subject to the test of para 2. However, a very restrictive approach to this sentence has been adopted at Strrasbourg. It has been found to mean that a *licensing system* is allowed for on grounds not restricted to those enumerated in para 2; the State may determine who is to have a licence to broadcast.[66] But in general, other decisions of the regulatory bodies who normally grant licences and oversee broadcasting, etc, are not covered by the last sentence of para 1 and must be considered within para 2.[67] Thus, content requirements must be considered under para 2. The preservation of a State monopoly on broadcasting also has to be considered within para 2.[68]

The European Court of Human Rights has found that commercial speech is covered by Article 10 (1),[69] but also refuses to view expression as commercial, when it covers matters of significant public interest. This was made clear in *Barthold v Germany*[70] in relation to an interview by a vet which sought to highlight the absence of a proper veterinary night service in the city in question, while indicating that he did offer such a service. The Court held that the application of the German advertising restrictions on professionals advertising their own services could deter such persons from contributing to public debate where it could appear that they were engaging in such advertising. In *Open Door Counselling and Dublin Woman v Ireland*[71] the Court did not view advertisements for abortion services as merely commercial speech, in finding that restrictions on it were incompatible with Article 10. In *VGT v Switzerland*[72] a Commercial Television Company refused to broadcast an advert with an animal rights message on the basis that the advert was clearly political in nature. The Court found that the advert could not be viewed as commercial speech—as the Swiss authorities had somewhat disingenuously sought to argue, since it was part of a debate about animal rights. As it represented political speech, a narrow margin of appreciation only was afforded; a wider margin would have been conceded had it been characterized as purely commercial speech.[73]

---

[66] *Groppera Radio AG v Switzerland* (1990) 12 EHRR 321.
[67] *Groppera Radio AG v Switzerland*, ibid; *Autronic AG* (1990) A 178.
[68] *Informationsverein Lentia v Austria* (1993) 17 EHRR 93.
[69] *Jacubowski v Germany* A 291A (1994).   [70] (1985) 7 EHRR 383.
[71] (1992) 15 EHRR 244.   [72] (2002) 34 EHRR 159.   [73] See Chapter 20 at 1021–3 on this point.

(II) EFFECT OF ARTICLE 10(2)

It was indicated in Chapter 2 that[74] Strasbourg has contemplated the possibility that material gratuitously offensive to religious sensibilities,[75] or certain depictions of sexual activity in broadcasts or videos intended merely for entertainment,[76] may fall outside the scope of Article 10(1). But on the other hand, 'hard-core' pornography has been found by the Commission to fall within Article 10(1).[77] This is the more defensible stance; given the breadth of para 2, it is unnecessary to seek to draw lines between artistic erotica and forms of pornography aimed at entertainment alone, even assuming that such line-drawing has any validity.[78] As Chapter 8 indicated, the jurisprudence under Article 10 in this context, as in others, concentrates on the para 2 tests and, clearly, in principle, Article 10(1) should retain as broad an ambit as possible in relation to the content of expression; its *quality* should not take it outside Article 10(1) since the para 2 necessity and proportionality tests are clearly capable of recognizing the low value of certain forms of expression.[79] So it appears to be reasonably clear that explicit broadcasts and films of little or no artistic value fall within Article 10(1).[80]

Under the familiar formula discussed in Chapter 2, an interference with the guarantee of freedom of expression under Article 10(1) can be justified, under Article 10(2), if it is prescribed by law, has a legitimate aim and is necessary in a democratic society. The legitimate aim under Article 10(2) would be either the protection of morals or of the rights of others. The regulation of the visual media in relation to offensive material is largely aimed at protecting persons from the shock or offence occasioned by encountering certain material, rather than at preventing moral deterioration.[81] The European Court of Human Rights has found that material which was, arguably, merely shocking, falls within the protection of morals exception.[82] The Court's stance therefore differs from that taken under the Obscene Publications Act 1959.[83] The Court is also content in this context to invoke the 'rights of others' exception—a 'right' not to be offended.[84] Possibly this is merely an instance in which Strasbourg has failed to distinguish carefully between the exceptions to be applied.[85]

In establishing the necessity and proportionality of a particular interference, the

---

[74] At pp 411–22. It did not ultimately adopt this stance.

[75] *Otto Preminger Institut v Austria* (1994) 19 EHRR 34.

[76] In *Groppera Radio AG v Switzerland* (1990) 12 EHRR 321, it was thought that mere entertainment might not fall within Article 10(1). But this presumably cannot be taken to mean that a television broadcast should not be viewed as a form of expression.

[77] *Hoare v UK* [1997] EHRLR 678; *Scherer v Switzerland* A287 (1993) Com Rep.

[78] See P. Kearns, 'Obscene and blasphemous libel: misunderstanding art' [2000] *Crim LR* 652.

[79] See further Chapter 2.   [80] See *Wingrove v UK* (1997) 24 EHRR 1.

[81] See Chapter 8 at 416–18 on the relation between Article 10(2) aims and criminal offences based on the concept of indecency rather than obscenity.

[82] *Müller v Switzerland* (1988) 13 EHRR 212.   [83] See Chapter 8 at 424.

[84] *Otto Preminger Institut v Austria* (1994) 19 EHRR 34, para 56. Strasbourg tends not to delineate the specific 'rights' of others with any precision. See e.g. *Steel v UK* (1998) 28 EHRR 603.

[85] This can be found in relation to a number of its decisions under the other qualified Articles. See e.g. *Zana v Turkey* (1999) 27 EHRR 667; *Buckley* (1997) 23 EHRR 101.

type of expression is highly significant. As indicated in Chapter 2, Strasbourg views the scope for interference with *political* expression in the media as very limited.[86] Artistic expression appears to have a lower place in the hierarchy of expression.[87] Expression aimed merely at entertainment, of no artistic value, occupies a lowly place in the hierarchy, but may be of higher value than some forms of purely commercial expression, such as advertisements.[88] Nevertheless, in relation to artistic and entertainment-based expression it is arguable that there is some reluctance at Strasbourg to defend restrictions on the freedom of artistic expression of *adults*, as the discussion below indicates, except in respect of sexually explicit expression where a risk to children is *also* present, or in the context of offending religious sensibilities. This reluctance is, however, more apparent in the decisions of the Commission than of the Court. The exception is *Gibson v UK*.[89] Neither of these factors were present and yet the restraint on artistic expression was upheld. At present, the explicit expression jurisprudence is meagre and impoverished and therefore the conclusions drawn from it below are tentative.

In its explicit expression jurisprudence Strasbourg has not drawn a distinction between the print and the visual media, and has made it clear that the visual expression of a message renders it more vulnerable to restriction.[90] As discussed in Chapter 8,[91] its stance can also be characterized as a pro-censorship one in respect of all forms of media in terms of the *outcomes* of decisions. The line of authority stemming from the *Handyside* case[92] suggests that although disturbing, explicit and erotic expression, including some or most pornographic expression, is protected within Art 10(1), interference with it can be justified quite readily. This seems to be the case *even where* such expression could be termed political. It is clear that the margin of appreciation conceded to the state in such instances is particularly broad.

The *Handyside* case is considered in full in Chapters 2 and 8. The judgment accepted that domestic authorities would be allowed a wide margin of appreciation in attempting to secure the freedoms guaranteed under the Convention in this area, although this was not to be taken as implying that an unlimited discretion was granted: the power of appreciation 'goes hand in hand with a European supervision' which concerned the legislation in question—the Obscene Publications Act—and the decision applying it. The Court placed particular weight on the fact that the book in question was aimed at children between the ages of 12 and 18 and that it might encourage them 'to indulge in precocious activities harmful for them or even to commit certain criminal offences'.[93] Thus, the English judges were entitled to find that

---

[86] See pp 50–5.   [87] See pp 56–60.

[88] See Harris, O'Boyle, and Warbrick, 397–406. Some forms of commercial expression fall outside Article 10(1). It was found in *Jacubowski v Germany* (1994) 19 EHRR 64 that commercial expression is only covered by Article 10 if it is aimed at furthering the interests of persons or commercial bodies through the promulgation of advertisements or other information.

[89] See pp 476–7.   [90] *Murphy v Ireland* (2004) 38 EHRR 13, paras 69 and 74.

[91] See pp 410–22.   [92] Eur Ct HR, A 24; (1976) 1 EHRR 737.   [93] Ibid, para 52.

the book in question would have a 'pernicious effect on the morals' of the children who would read it. In finding that the tests under para 2 were satisfied, it was said that the fact that the book was circulating freely in the rest of Europe was not determinative of the issues, owing to the application of the margin of appreciation doctrine.

Subsequent decisions in this line of authority concerned expression that could be categorized far more readily as artistic or entertainment-based. Thus, although *Handyside* is often seen as creating the foundational basis for those decisions, it could perhaps be viewed more aptly as an aberrational and unfortunate decision within its political expression jurisprudence. The stance taken in the subsequent decision in *Müller v Switzerland*,[94] discussed fully in Chapter 8, was similar to that of *Handyside* in terms of the width of the margin of appreciation conceded and the concern regarding children.[95] These two decisions give a strong indication as to the stance taken by the Court in respect of Art 10, para 2 in this context, but may be viewed as turning on their special facts, particularly the fact that children might have been affected. The thinking behind the *Handyside* decision can find some parallels from the US[96] and Canada.[97] In the US, however, there has been a greater concentration on the question whether restrictions aimed at children might impinge also on the freedom of expression of adults, and on the extent to which this should be tolerated,[98] a matter which was in issue in *Handyside*, although not afforded weight by the Court.

These decisions at Strasbourg do not determine the question of the consumption of explicit visual material solely or mainly by a willing adult audience—a matter that is especially pertinent in relation to films and videos, bearing their age classifications in mind. That question was considered in *Hoare v UK*,[99] looked at in detail in Chapter 8,[100] which concerned the possession of 'hard core' pornographic videos. The applicant had been convicted of possessing obscene material under s 2 of the Obscene Publications Act 1959. The Commission found quite easily that the restriction on his freedom of expression had the legitimate aim of protecting morals and was not disproportionate to that aim. But the decision was largely based on the risk that children might view the videos since once they had left the applicant's possession he would not have been able to control their eventual audience. The Commission may have been influenced by the nature of the material—it had no artistic or political value and therefore the justifications underlying freedom of expression, referred to in Chapter 1, were not present, apart from the justification based on moral autonomy. That decision was broadly in harmony with that of the Commission in *Scherer v*

[94] (1991) 13 EHRR 212. See Chapter 8 at 416–21.   [95] See pp 416–18.

[96] *Ginsberg v New York* 390 US 629 (1968).

[97] *Irwin Toy Ltd v AG (Quebec)* [1989] 1 SCR 927 (broad limitation on broadcast advertising aimed at children).

[98] *Reno v American Civil Liberties Union* (1997) 521 US 844.

[99] [1997] EHRLR 678.   [100] Pp 415–16.

[101] A 287 (1993) Com Rep (the case was discontinued in the Court owing to the death of the applicant).

Switzerland;[101] it was found that the conviction of the proprietor of a sex shop for showing obscene and explicit videos had breached Article 10, since access was restricted to adults and no one was likely to confront them unwittingly. *Scherer* demonstrates that Strasbourg (or at least, the Commission) is prepared to defend adult autonomy in relation to the consumption of explicit material, so long as control is retained over the ultimate consumer of the material. The difference between *Hoare* and *Scherer* related to the question of the restrictions on access to the material; in *Hoare* the penalty imposed was proportionate to the aim pursued since it was viewed as capable of protecting the 'rights of others'—the rights appeared to be those of minors to be protected from harmful material; in *Scherer* such rights could not be protected by the imposition of the penalty since they were not threatened by the showing of the videos.[102] Thus, in contrast to the stance taken in the US,[103] Strasbourg is clearly content to restrict the expression rights of adults in order to protect children.

In *Otto Preminger Institut v Austria*,[104] discussed fully in Chapter 9,[105] the Court considered the question of restrictions on freedom of expression in respect of a film where the expression was aimed at a willing adult audience. A warning had been given and therefore viewers knew what to expect. Nevertheless, owing to the shock caused to particular religious sensibilities in the local region, it was found, in a much criticized decision,[106] that the interference could be justified despite the fact that the measure had the effect of preventing the showing of the film across the whole country. That decision can be contrasted with the findings of the Commission in the case that Article 10 had been violated.[107]

As Chapter 8 argues, the defence of autonomy in *Scherer* is undercut by the clear failure of the *Court*, especially in *Otto Preminger* and *Handyside*, to defend the principle by finding no breach of Article 10 in the line of cases in which prosecutions or forfeiture of the contested items had the effect of denying consenting adults across the entire state from accessing them.[108] Those cases, it may be pointed out, concerned

---

[102] In *Hoare* the Commission, having found that the material fell within Article 10(1), went on to find under Article 10(2): 'In the present case, the sole question which arises in the context of the relationship of proportionality between the interference with the applicant's right to freedom of expression and the aim pursued is the question of whether, given that the applicant only distributed his video cassettes to people who expressed a clear interest, it can be said that the penalty imposed was capable of protecting the "rights of others" (see, in this context, *Scherer v Switzerland*, Comm. Report 14.1.93, ECHR, Series A no. 287, p 20, para 65). Where no adult is confronted unintentionally or against his will with filmed matter, there must be particularly compelling reasons to justify an interference (above-mentioned Scherer Report, p 20, para 65). The Commission considers that it cannot therefore be said with any degree of certainty that only the intended purchasers of the film would have access to it and not minors. To that extent the present case is different from the case of *Scherer*, where the only adults who saw the applicant's videos were those who had access to his shop (above-mentioned *Scherer* Report, p 19, para 62).'

[103] See Chapter 12 at 647–8.   [104] (1994) 19 EHRR 34.   [105] See pp 488–94.

[106] For an incisive critique see D. Pannick, 'Religious feelings and the European Court' [1995] *PL* 7.

[107] See also *Wingrove v UK* (1996) 24 EHRR 1; *Gay News v UK* (1982) 5 EHRR 123.

[108] See pp 421–2.

works of artistic merit, unlike the material at issue in *Scherer* and *Hoare*, rendering the denial of autonomy even more problematic.

(III) APPLYING THE STRASBOURG JURISPRUDENCE UNDER THE HUMAN RIGHTS ACT

The decisions in this line of authority confirm that where there is a chance that children might be affected or religious sensibilities offended, Strasbourg is particularly cautious. Even accepting the effect of the margin of appreciation doctrine, its stance is very significantly out of line with that taken under a number of national Bills of Rights at the end of the 20th century and the beginning of the 21st. It is one of the weakest and most out-dated areas of its jurisprudence, which entirely fails to follow up the principles established in *Handyside* in relation to Article 10(1). However, as discussed further in Chapter 8, *Scherer* provides a basis of sorts from which to attack the current censorship of films for cinematic release in the UK since age restrictions are in place and are enforced. That decision, and the jurisprudence in general, provides on its face no basis for attacking the regulation and censorship of videos and broadcasting since there is a risk that children will encounter the material. In general the Strasbourg jurisprudence in this area does not set precise standards that could be followed effectively by regulators or by the courts; the standards may readily be referred to as 'soft-edged'. But clearly it can be argued that the Convention was never intended to set such standards since it provides a 'floor', not a 'ceiling', of rights.

The expectation deriving from the margin of appreciation doctrine is that the state, via legislation, decisions of the courts and the practice of regulators, will devise its own standards which will be higher than those maintained at Strasbourg. Only where the margin of appreciation is over-stepped—as in especially restrictive decisions—is Strasbourg expected to intervene. Thus, used at the *domestic* level under the HRA, the Strasbourg jurisprudence can be misleading and could be used to underpin a very restrictive stance since it could be applied without regard to the influence of the margin of appreciation doctrine on it; the *outcome* of decisions such as *Handyside*, rather than the free speech pronouncements, could be influential. (However, so far, in judicial reasoning under the HRA there has been no recognition of the need to 'strip away' the margin of appreciation aspects of Strasbourg decisions before applying them domestically.) Therefore, in the next two chapters, although the jurisprudence is referred to, it is not fully relied upon as though it provided, or was intended to provide, a definitive set of standards.

Restrictions based on the idea of avoiding offence or maintaining certain standards of taste and decency tend to have a greater impact on 'artistic' rather than political expression—using the term 'artistic' very broadly. As indicated, the margin of appreciation doctrine has an especially significant impact on such expression due to the lack of consensus in Europe as to the proper extent of restrictions on it intended to prevent offence. So if the established Strasbourg hierarchy of expression is rigidly applied in relation to such restrictions they can be justified quite readily. However, if the justifications for freedom of expression considered in Chapter 1 are taken into account, particularly those from truth and self-fulfilment, it is suggested that there is no convincing basis for relegating 'artistic' expression to a lowly place in such a hierarchy. Possibly its place should be below that of political speech, but too sharp a distinction should not be drawn. Moreover, it is readily apparent that some forms of political speech are clearly less valuable than some forms of artistic speech. For example, a number of classic films that fall outside the category of political speech engage a number of the justificatory free speech arguments more strongly than do the more minor manifestations of political speech. An autonomous free speech jurisprudence in the UK under the HRA could begin to grapple with this matter more effectively than Strasbourg is able to do due to the effects of the margin of appreciation doctrine. There is little sign as yet, however, that such a development is likely to occur in relation to post-HRA regulatory decisions. But at the Strasbourg level there may be developments in the explicit expression jurisprudence. The effects of EU-driven harmonization may begin to influence the margin of appreciation doctrine; if greater consistency of standards in this context can be discerned in the EU member states, the case for conceding such a broad margin of appreciation to state authorities may come to be viewed by the Strasbourg Court as less compelling.

CONCLUSIONS

The following two chapters reveal that regulation is subject to rapid change which to an extent reflects the rapidly changing technological environment in the visual as opposed to the print sector. But it will be suggested that regulation has not kept pace with such technological change and in particular with the impact of the Internet and with developments in Western broadcasting. Both developments have lead to a globalization of outlook in the current younger generation—an expectation that standards relating to explicit expression in the more progressive Western countries will be broadly in harmony with each other, while strongly differing standards will not be apparent across the different audio-visual sectors. The following chapters reveal that such expectations are not being met, while justifications for maintaining anomalous differences between the sectors, or for taking a specifically UK-based stance on offence-avoidance, have not been forthcoming. At present, it will be suggested, the government is tending to avoid the difficult questions that harmonization in both respects would create, in particular the question of the effects of non-regulation of the Internet. The judiciary continues to prefer to defer to the decisions of regulators rather than accepting that it has a duty under the HRA to call them to account in terms of maintaining free expression standards. However, the weakness of the Strasbourg explicit expression jurisprudence, documented especially in Chapters 8 and 9, combined with the acceptance by the Strasbourg Court that restriction of the audio-visual media is more acceptable than restriction of the print media,[109] do not offer domestic judiciary a high free speech standard to adhere to in this context.

The following chapters will concentrate on the decisions of a number of regulators of the visual media, rather than on court findings. Courts merely decide in relation to obscenity and indecency whether the law has been breached, whereas regulators have a broader role in ruling not only as to breaches of the relevant rules, but also in enhancing speech since they can take account of a wider range of considerations, including those of diversity and plurality.[110]

---

[109] In *Murphy v Ireland* (note 90 above) the Court stated (at para 74): 'The prohibition concerned only the audio-visual media. The State was, in the court's view, entitled to be particularly wary of the potential for offence in the broadcasting context, such media being accepted by this Court (see paragraph 69) and acknowledged by the applicant, as having a more immediate, invasive and powerful impact including, as the Government and the High Court noted, on the passive recipient. In making this finding the Court relied on *Jersild v Denmark* (1994) A298 at 31.' For the facts of *Murphy* and further discussion see Chapter 20 at 1024.

[110] See Chapter 11 at 565 and Chapter 20 at 993–4.

11

REGULATING BROADCASTING ON GROUNDS OF AVOIDING OFFENCE

INTRODUCTION

This chapter evaluates one sphere of content-based regulation of broadcasting in the UK—that founded, essentially, on the notion of offence-avoidance. In the UK that notion covers protections intended to prevent children viewing 'adult' material and the general maintenance of standards of decency. These twin ideas have been traditionally, and still are, a significant feature of broadcast regulation, although the latter is declining in significance in favour of the former. Acceptance of the regulation of broadcasting on this basis presupposes that it should not enjoy free speech rights as extensive as those enjoyed by the print media. This stance is adopted in the UK and in Europe generally,[1] and the UK judiciary appear to find it non-controversial, as indicated by the commitment to the idea of regulation that they demonstrated in *ProLife Alliance v BBC*.[2] It is more controversial in the US, due to the existence of the First Amendment,[3] but even there content-based regulation of broadcasting, on the ground of preventing the use of indecent language, has been accepted as constitutional by the Supreme Court in *Federal Communications Commission v Pacifica Foundation*,[4] although such a curb would not have been upheld had it been imposed on the press. Indeed, recent developments—after the bizarre and notorious 2004 'Nipplegate' incident—suggest that US broadcasting is subject to a *stricter* regulatory regime than that applicable in the UK.[5]

---

[1] See below pp 567–8 for the EU stance. See also *Murphy v Ireland*, Chapter 10 at 553, 557.

[2] [2004] 1 AC 185; [2003] 2 All ER 977.

[3] See E. Barendt, Chapter 3 'The First Amendment and the Media' in I. Loveland (ed.) *Importing the First Amendment*, Oxford: Hart Publishing, 1998. For the text of the First Amendment see text at note 16, Chapter 2.

[4] (1978) 438 US 726. See also *Red Lion Broadcasting Co v FCC* (1969) 395 US 367.

[5] On 1 February 2004, on MTV on prime-time television, a female celebrity, Janet Jackson, exposed a nipple when her dress was displaced. The exposure of the nipple was apparently unintentional. The camera cut away from the exposed nipple almost immediately. There was a national outcry and thousands of complaints were received. The television station was fined $550,000 by the Federal Communications Commission—the

There appears to be, then, a degree of consensus in the West as to the non-controversy in free speech terms of this form of content-based regulation of commercial broadcasting. This idea seems to be predicated partly on an assumption that the free speech rights in question are enjoyed by the broadcasters rather than by the audience.[6] However, the more compelling argument, based on the speech-supporting rationales, is that the audience has a right to receive broadcasts from a willing broadcaster free from interference by a regulator. This chapter seeks then to challenge the idea that broadcast regulation based on offence-avoidance is non-problematic in free speech terms, and to suggest some of the reasons why it might have arisen. In terms of three of the free speech rationales—the arguments from truth, democracy and self-fulfillment[7]—the regulation of broadcasting per se *is* non-controversial. Indeed, it is beneficial. In theory, such regulation interferes in the broadcast market in such a way as to create a real market place of ideas—a true market place, rather than a false one that is dominated by the agenda of a few powerful corporate players. Regulation, preventing the dominance of the market by such players, fosters a diversity of viewpoints, exposing the audience to a range of ideas in public interest debates.[8] At first sight, the only free speech rationale not necessarily furthered by regulation of the broadcast market is that of autonomy: those persons in the broadcast audience who desire to be confronted by homogenized, bland, mainstream speech and images, reflecting uncontroversial, majoritarian viewpoints might have plurality imposed upon them. But this argument could of course be countered by pointing out that autonomy may most clearly be served by maximising consumer choice in broadcasting, and that those consumers even in quite heavily regulated broadcast markets are still likely to encounter a satisfactory diet of homogenous images.

Market-based broadcast regulation is, however, accompanied or even premised upon, regulation on grounds of taste and decency. This could be justified on the basis that if media bodies obtain access to a scarce resource, the airwaves, they should accept obligations to adhere to societal obligations, including the obligation to abide by generally accepted standards of taste and decency. Even leaving aside the fact that the resource has become less scarce,[9] the problem is that while the three speech-based rationales, the arguments from truth, democracy and self-fulfillment, are applicable to

---

broadcast regulator. The comments made by the FCC regarding the ruling had, according to commentators, a 'chilling effect' on broadcasters; the FCC indicated that stringent fines would be imposed on broadcasts on strict taste and decency grounds if they did not take self-censoring action (see Julie Hilden ' "Nipplegate" risks chilling free speech', 20 February 2004 CNN.com). For further comment on the findings and their impact on US broadcasting, see M. Dorf, 'Does the First Amendment Protect Janet Jackson and Justin Timberlake? A Brief Primer on the Constitutional Law of TV Decency Regulation' (4 February 2004 CNN.com).

[6] See *Red Lion Broadcasting Co v FCC* (1969) 395 US 367.   [7] See for discussion Chapter 1 at 13–19.

[8] See further M. Feintuck, *Media Regulation, Public Interest and the Law*, Edinburgh: Edinburgh University Press, 1998, esp Chap 3.

[9] Digital technology has expanded enormously the number of channels that each household can receive. In 1996, 18 per cent of households received satellite, cable, or digital channels. By 2002, the figure had risen to 44 per cent (figures from National Statistics online).

broadcast schemes in their market-regulatory function, they are inapplicable to such regulation in its function of promoting general standards of decency. In terms of those rationales *this* function of regulation answers to a societal, not an individual, concern and runs counter to the creation of a true market-place of ideas since it curbs the broadcasting of controversial, explicit and disturbing speech. The speech-based rationale founded on autonomy counters regulation intended to impose standards of decency on broadcasting since it imposes moral choices on consumers. The argument from autonomy is classically applicable when the law curbs moral choice by, for example, criminalizing the consumption of forms of pornography.[10] Its application, however, to inadvertent, brief encounters with offensive images is highly doubtful (or at most paper-thin)—it is unclear that there is any right not to be offended. Thus this function of broadcast regulation—to impose curbs on broadcasting in the name of avoiding offence—is founded solely on a societal concern to protect consumers from inadvertent confrontation with offensive images. But, as this chapter argues, the broadcast environment has changed so significantly that such inadvertent encounters are far less likely now than they were even ten years ago.[11] Nevertheless, as discussed below, that rationale is still viewed as placing broadcasters in a different position from that of the press in terms of imposing constraints on them via regulation, since in theory persons have a greater choice as to the images that they encounter in the press.

From a UK perspective the application of regulation to broadcasting, but not to the press, sets up an interesting anomaly. In the UK press, it is suggested, there is no true market-place of ideas: the market is heavily dominated by a number of corporate players who determine the political agenda and effectively exclude other players. As Feintuck argues, 'The regulatory system is essentially reactive and in respect of owner-ship patterns largely fails to establish an alternative agenda to that which results from the exercise of market forces, and therefore offers flimsy protection to citizen-ship values.'[12] At the same time, although very explicit images are unlikely to be encountered inadvertently in the print sector, consumers are frequently likely to encounter pictures of semi-naked women on the front pages of tabloids, displayed on news-stands. The pervasive cultural pollution created by this objectivization of wom-en's bodies in the tabloid press is uncontrolled by the law,[13] or by any form of regulation. Conversely, as far as broadcasting is concerned, the weak attempts at market-regulation of commercial broadcasting only partially succeed in creating a true market-place of ideas, while curbs based on notions of imposing standards of taste and decency *are* effective, despite running counter to all the speech-supporting rationales. So in the UK situation the *lack* of regulation of the press fails to further free

---

[10] See Chapter 8 at 395–6.   [11] See pp 601–2 below.

[12] M. Feintuck, *Media Regulation, Public Interest and the Law*, Edinburgh: Edinburgh University Press, 1998, p 118.

[13] Prosecutions under the Indecent Displays Act 1981 or under the common law doctrine of outraging public decency have not been brought so far against these displays, and therefore they appear to be viewed as lawful by the prosecuting authorities; if the tabloids went further and began displaying entirely naked breasts on front pages, prosecutions might be brought. See further on the indecency offences, Chapter 8 at 467–77.

speech objectives, while the current forms of broadcast regulation also fail to do so. This is to over-state the argument slightly, but not grossly.

This chapter is not concerned with the success or otherwise of broadcast regulation in creating a true market place of ideas by regulating the market itself. There is already quite a significant body of literature covering that issue.[14] It is concerned with the extent to which current UK broadcast regulation runs counter to all the free speech rationales. In the UK there is no significant body of legal literature covering that issue,[15] so this chapter is the first to examine this function of content-based regulation in such depth. Media regulation in a range of jurisdictions is covered in the comparative free speech literature,[16] while the domestic provisions are covered briefly in civil liberties texts.[17] But the domestic *media* literature concentrates on market regulation.[18] Possibly the lack of domestic or Strasbourg case law[19] and the uninspiring minutiae of the broadcast offence-avoidance regulation has deterred writers. This is a subject that is very much Regulator- rather than jurisprudence-driven.

In pursuit of an attempt to situate regulatory curbs within the free speech rationales, this chapter traces developments in content-based broadcast regulation in the UK. It begins by considering the rationales put forward for broadcast regulation based on offence-avoidance and moves on to consider market de-regulation under the Broadcasting Act 1990 and then the Communications Act 2003, placing the legislation in the context of the Television Without Frontiers Directive.[20] It moves on to introduce the current content-based regulatory regime under the 2003 Act, beginning by placing it in the context of the previous regime and examining the effect of the only significant decision on the free speech implications of that regime, *ProLife Alliance v BBC*.[21]

[14] See M. Feintuck, *Media Regulation, Public Interest and the Law*, Edinburgh: Edinburgh University Press, 1998; D. Goldberg, T. Prosser, and S. Verhulst, *Regulating the Changing Media: A Comparative Study*, 1998; T. Gibbons, *Regulating the Media*, 2nd edn, London: Sweet & Maxwell, 1998.

[15] It was considered in 1999 from a sociological perspective in C. Shaw, *Deciding What We Watch: Taste, Decency and Media Ethics in the UK and US*, Oxford: OUP, 1999.

[16] See the leading work—E. Barendt, *Broadcasting Law: A Comparative Study*, Oxford: OUP, 1995; see also: E. Barendt, *Freedom of Speech*, 2nd edn., Oxford: OUP, 2005; see also D. Goldberg, T. Prosser, and S. Verhulst, *Regulating the Changing Media: A Comparative Study*, Oxford: OUP, 1998; I. Loveland (ed.) *Importing the First Amendment*, op cit; L. Hitchens, 'Approaches to broadcasting regulation: Australia and the UK compared' (1997) 17(1) *LS* 40.

[17] See: Bailey, Harris, and Ormerod, *Bailey, Harris and Jones, Civil Liberties Cases and Materials*, Oxford: OUP, 2001, Chapter 5, Part 3; D. Feldman, *Civil Liberties and Human Rights*, 2nd edn., Oxford: OUP, 2002, Chap 14; H. Fenwick, *Civil Liberties and Human Rights*, 3rd edn., Oxford: Cavendish, 2002, Chap 4.

[18] This is true of both the legal and the media studies literature; see note 14 above and see, for example, D. McQuail, *Media Accountability and Freedom of Publication*, Oxford: OUP, 2003.

[19] There is little Strasbourg case law on regulation of broadcasting. See Chapter 8 at 410–22 for discussion of the line of case law on restraints based on protecting morals or the rights of others. Strasbourg has found that there is no right to broadcast and that therefore an argument that an absolute bar to the broadcasting of a particular group breached Article 10 was manifestly ill-founded: *United Christian Broadcasting* Appl 44802/98 (2000) Admissibility only. An outright ban on advocacy advertising was found to breach Article 10 in *VGT v Switzerland* (2002) 34 EHRR 159; the decision is discussed in Chapter 20 at 1021–3.

[20] Council Directive 89/552/EEC, as amended by Directive 97/36/EC of the European Parliament and of the Council, adopted in 1989.

[21] [2004] 1 AC 185; [2003] 2 All ER 977.

The chapter then moves on to compare the new Ofcom regime with the previous one, examining the special position of the BBC, and placing the new regime in the context of free speech principles under the Human Rights Act.

RATIONALES FOR BROADCASTING REGULATION[22]

Historically, in the UK the scarcity of frequencies was thought to provide part of the rationale for broadcast regulation.[23] But it is not apparent that this rationale can support content-based curbs, although it might support rights of access to a scarce resource[24] of such significance in terms of the efficacy of expression. However, cable and satellite television have enormously increased the number of actual and potential channels. Digital technology is continuing to increase the number of channels available. There are far more channels available at present in the UK than there are individual newspaper titles. The high level of regulation to which broadcasting continues to be subject must now therefore be attributed mainly to the fact that it is an *audio-visual* medium and to its status as the most influential means of communication.[25] Since it comes into the home and since so much time is spent watching television, it has been viewed as having a unique impact on people and particularly on children, who form a large part of the broadcast audience, especially at certain times of the day. Further, the potential for flouting viewer expectations by inadvertently causing offence when people tune in and out of programmes is thought to provide a cogent rationale for content regulation.[26] In other words, a viewer might be unexpectedly confronted by offensive broadcast material. That is the main reason usually advanced for providing a different and stricter regime for broadcasting as opposed to

---

[22] See, generally, E. Barendt, *Freedom of Speech*, 2nd edn., OUP, 2005, Chapter 12; D. Goldberg, T. Prosser, and S. Verhulst, *Regulating the Changing Media: A Comparative Study*, Oxford: OUP, 1998; E. Barendt and L. Hitchens, *Media Law: Cases and Materials*, Longman, 2000, Chapter 8; T. Gibbons, *Regulating the Media*, 2nd edn, London: Sweet & Maxwell, 1998; Robertson and Nichol, *Media Law*, 1999, Chapter 15; T. Ballard, 'Main Developments in Broadcasting Law', *Yearbook of Copyright and Media Law* 329, OUP, 2001/02; T. Ballard, 'Survey of the Main Developments in the Field of Broadcasting Law in 1999', *Yearbook of Copyright and Media Law* 367, OUP, 2000; C. Munro, *Television, Censorship and the Law*, Saxon House, 1979; N. Reville, *Broadcasting*, London: Butterworths, 1991; C. Horrie and S. Clarke, *Fuzzy Monsters: Fear and Loathing at the BBC*, London: Heinemann, 1994; Bailey, Harris, and Ormerod, *Bailey, Harris and Jones, Civil Liberties, Cases and Materials*, Oxford: OUP, 2001, Chapter 5, Part 3; D. Feldman, *Civil Liberties and Human Rights*, 2nd edn. 2002, Chap 14; Reville, *Broadcasting: The New Law*, 1991; I. Loveland (ed.) *Importing the First Amendment*, op cit, E. Barendt, chapter 3; E. Barendt, *Broadcasting Law: A Comparative Study*, Oxford: OUP, 1995; A. Briggs, *The History of Broadcasting, Vols 1 and 2*, Oxford: OUP, 1961 and Oxford: OUP, 1965; L. Hitchens, 'Approaches to broadcasting regulation: Australia and the UK compared', Oxford: OUP, 1997, 17(1) *LS* 40. For discussion and criticism of the Broadcasting Act 1996, see M. Feintuck (1997) Regulating the Media Revolution: In Search of Public Interest 3(2) *European Public Law*, 201.

[23] See A. Briggs, *The History of Broadcasting*, op cit, Vols 1 and 2, 1961 and 1965; Barendt and Hitchens, op cit, note 22.

[24] See the discussion of the US Supreme Court on this point in *Red Lion Broadcasting Co v FCC* (1969) 395 US 367.

[25] See Barendt and Hitchens, op cit, note 22, pp 5–9.   [26] See text to note 29 below.

videos. But, as this chapter will reveal, the UK regulatory regime has incrementally moved away from the *general* imposition of certain standards of 'taste and decency' on broadcasting, in favour of curbs premised mainly, although not solely, on protection for children. Thus it has focused more on the use of protective devices—such as the use of the watershed[27] or of encryption—as opposed to outright bans on the showing of explicit and offensive material. Nevertheless, broadcasting is still restrained to a greater extent than other media.

Adherence to a regulatory regime aimed at the avoidance of offence has been viewed as part of a 'contract' for the privilege of coming directly into the home which should be adhered to by responsible broadcasters. The Broadcasting Standards Commission made this point by referring in its Code on Standards to an implied contract between viewer and broadcaster about the terms of admission to the home.[28] Lord Hoffman pointed out in *ProLife Alliance v BBC*[29] that a similar point was made by Stevens J giving the opinion of the United States Supreme Court in *Federal Communications Commission v Pacifica Foundation*[30] in a case about the use of obscene language on sound radio:

> the broadcast media have established a uniquely pervasive presence in the lives of all Americans. Patently offensive, indecent material presented over the airwaves confronts the citizen, not only in public, but also in the privacy of the home, where the individual's right to be left alone plainly outweighs the First Amendment rights of an intruder . . . Because the broadcast audience is constantly tuning in and out, prior warnings cannot completely protect the listener or viewer from unexpected program content. To say that one may avoid further offence by turning off the radio when he hears indecent language is like saying that the remedy for an assault is to run away after the first blow.

However, although these points may have been valid in 1978, they are losing their cogency today, at least in relation to television, as it becomes more and more interactive. Viewers usually tune in and out of programmes using a menu, which also provides them with consumer advice on programmes. 'Adult material' can be Pin-protected or made available on pay-per-view channels only, decreasing the chance that children could access it and obviating the risk of coming across it inadvertently. Thus the chances of inadvertent encounters with offensive material have diminished; the argument that children should be protected from material that they deliberately choose to view, continues to retain some cogency.[31] As the interactivity of television broadcasting and the provision of consumer information increases, while improvements occur in the use of security devices such as encoding, its position comes closer to that of the internet which also comes into the home. Therefore, as discussed in Chapter 12, there is a degree of tension in free speech terms between the lack of

---

[27] The broadcasting of adult material and '18'-rated films later in the evening. The provision of warnings and of consumer advice has also become much more prevalent. See pp 601–3 below.

[28] Para 2 of the Code. The Code is discussed at p 576 below.

[29] [2004] 1 AC 185; [2003] 2 All ER 977.   [30] (1978) 438 US 726, 748–749.

[31] See the 2005 research conducted by Ofcom on the efficacy of PIN protection systems, note 161, below.

regulation for the internet and the high level of content-based regulation to which broadcasting is currently subject.[32]

As indicated in the introduction, a very different rationale can be advanced to argue that regulation is necessary in order to preserve pluralism—in order to seek to ensure that a range of views, including a variety of political ones, are heard.[33] This can be achieved by imposing requirements to broadcast minority interest programmes, 'must carry' requirements,[34] or by imposing more general responsibilities that tend to support diversity, including impartiality requirements. The unregulated press are openly partisan in the UK, and right wing and anti-liberal views predominate.[35] Therefore a significant threat to free expression—in terms of diversity—comes not from government, but from private corporate bodies. As Barendt puts it, referring to the free speech rationale from truth:[36]

'it is . . . reasonable to doubt whether any truth will emerge from an unregulated market-place in which a handful of media corporations draw up the agenda of political and social discourse and carefully limit the access of individuals and groups which dissent from their programme'.[37]

Therefore this argument provides a rationale for broadcast regulation, even in the context of a rapidly changing technological landscape, in so far as plurality and impartiality can be ensured by this means. It does not, however, provide a necessary justification for restraints based on offence-avoidance. Indeed, such restraints tend to run *counter* to the enhancement of plurality and diversity since they may curb the more controversial forms of broadcast speech, including that reflective of the practice of sexual minorities. The regulatory regimes for broadcast regulation in the UK have tended at one and the same time to impose curbs based on generally accepted standards of taste and decency, while making some efforts in the direction of diversity. The contradiction between the two goals appears to have gone unrecognized both by the legislation and by the regulators.

[32] See p 642.

[33] See M. Feintuck, *Media Regulation, Public Interest and the Law*, Edinburgh: Edinburgh University Press, 1999.

[34] See Communications Act 2003 ss296 and 309. Under s296 C4C has obligations in relation to school programming. Under s 309, 10 per cent of the air time must be allocated to a range and diversity of independent productions in digital services.

[35] Feintuck ibid, at 54–6; T. Gibbons, 'Freedom of the Press: ownership and editorial values' (1992) Summer *PL* 279. The *Telegraph*, the *Mail*, and the *Sun* are the highest-selling newspapers in their different sections of the market. Editorially, they tend towards the right and to anti-liberal views.

[36] See Chapter 1 at 14–16.

[37] See *Importing the First Amendment*, Oxford: Hart Publishing, 1998; I. Loveland (ed.) E. Barendt, op cit, chapter 3, at p 46.

MARKET-BASED 'DEREGULATION' IN THE UK

The Broadcasting Act 1990 brought about the so-called 'deregulation' of independent television, a trend culminating at present in the Communications Act 2003. The trend represents a movement towards enhancing the influence of media regulators but exerted post-transmission in terms of content, as explained below. An underlying policy objective of de-regulation was that of enhancing the ability of corporate bodies to maximize commercial success by furthering and developing concentrations of media power, especially in the sectors of the press and satellite broadcasting. The 1990 Act raised questions about the influence of the owners of broadcasting stations who might wish to use broadcasting as a means of exerting political influence. The Broadcasting Act 1996 further eased some of the restrictions on media ownership created by the 1990 Act, with a view to balancing 'proper commercial demands and the wider public interest which includes plurality, diversity of opinion'.[38] The dominant theme governing the regulatory regime is the continuance of light-touch regulation, in terms of commercial freedom, which was introduced under the Conservative government's 1990 Act. The changes introduced by the Labour government's Communications Act 2003 continue to represent a business-oriented scheme that recognizes the convergence of the separate technological sectors. It favours corporate interests, not necessarily those of plurality and diversity. It does not address substantive media freedom issues. For example, while corporate advertising remains central to the commercial viability of independent television, political advertising is still disallowed. Thus, in so far as groups such as Greenpeace or Amnesty may wish, *inter alia*, to criticize and challenge corporate interests by means of such advertising, they are unable to do so.[39]

The Communications Act 2003 is influenced by the 'Television Without Frontiers' (TVWF) directive,[40] as discussed below, and is based to a significant extent on the model of deregulation put in place by the 1990 Act.[41] This continued movement away from market regulation may have the effect of *detracting* from the exercise of creative freedom since small independent broadcasters may be unable to gain a foot-hold in the market, while investigative journalism (especially investigations into corporate matters) and alternative film-making may be marginalized and discouraged in the pursuit of commercially safe, but bland, homogenous broadcasting, in the form of game shows, soap operas, gardening and home decorating programmes. On this view, further movement towards privatization of the means of communication,

---

[38] V. Bottomley, Dept of National Heritage Press Release DNH 219/96. For discussion of regulation of cross-media ownership and concentrated media ownership, see Feintuck note 33 above; H. Fleming (1997) 60(3) *MLR* 378; Hitchens (1994) 57 *MLR* 585.

[39] See Chapter 20 at 1012–20.

[40] Council Directive 89/552/EEC, as amended by Directive 97/36/EC of the European Parliament and of the Council, adopted in 1989. See pp 1015–20.

[41] See also the proposals in the White Paper *A New Future for Communications*, Cm 5010, published 12 December 2000.

deregulation and the freer expression of commercial values is unwelcome. Moreover, it provides a strong argument for retaining the licence fee for the BBC, and its independence, on the basis that certain programmes would not be made if BBC programming was subject to a largely or wholly market-driven regime. Further, programmes made under such a regime—and the choices underlying the selection of programmes—are likely in themselves to have an impact in influencing the public's choices. Therefore leaving BBC programming largely to market forces by removing the licence fee would tend to have a pro-corporate, anti-plural impact. The contemporary political agenda would be more likely to go unchallenged, while the anti-liberal agenda apparent in much of the press would have a greater chance of gaining ascendancy since programmes challenging it might not be made.

The thesis can be put forward that in general regulation is an essential precondition for securing the objectives inherent in the familiar free speech justifications,[42] although this argument is not applicable to the current offence-avoidance rules. As Feintuck argues, media regulators are concerned to limit 'the ability of corporate media giants to further their own commercial ends while acting in ways that run counter to maximizing the provision of information upon which the claim is premised'.[43] However, the ethos underlying the regulatory regime considered below is unclear, although it could be broadly expressed as intended to be in the public interest. It is suggested that intervention cannot be assisted by the failure to identify a meaningful guiding principle for media regulation.

European broadcasting law and policy has a significant impact on the form taken by the broadcasting regulatory regime in the UK. However, as discussed in Chapter 10, at the EU level broadcasting policy is only one aspect of the European Union's increasingly integrated audiovisual policy,[44] whereas at the UK level, despite the inception of the Communications Act, the medium of delivery remains extremely significant. Thus this chapter and the next will consider the effect of EU instruments on broadcasting in isolation from their effect on the mediums of film and the Internet, while recognizing that so doing is out of accord with the trend of EU policy.

The EU's role in UK broadcasting regulation reflects the various values that are being balanced. It may be argued that since economic integration is a central constitutional value for the EU, its regulatory agenda might be expected to bear more resemblance to that of the US, in terms of economic values, than to the public interest values evident in the regimes of its Member States.[45] At the same time EU audiovisual policy reflects the values embodied in Articles 8 and 10 ECHR; in particular it focuses on the protection of minors and of human dignity. These varying—and arguably conflicting—values are reflected in the 'Television Without Frontiers' (TVWF) directive,[46] which deals with the protection of minors from harmful content

---

[42] See Part III, Chapter 10, and see further Barendt, op cit, note 22, above.
[43] See Feintuck, op cit, note 33.   [44] See pp 539–45.   [45] Feintuck, ibid, p 170.
[46] Council Directive 89/552/EEC, as amended by Directive 97/36/EC of the European Parliament and of the Council, adopted in 1989. See Chapter 10 at 543–4.

disseminated via broadcasting. Technological and market developments necessitated the revision of the TVWF in 1997, as discussed below. The need to ensure the effective protection of minors was also reflected in the Recommendation adopted in 1998,[47] and in the Commission's proposal for an additional Recommendation in 2004.[48]

The TVWF, the original and the proposed Recommendation, seek to reconcile the protection for minors and human dignity with both freedom of expression and market freedom. One aspect of such reconciliation is reflected in the focus on the protection of minors, as opposed to the imposition of 'standards of taste and decency' on programmes aimed at adults. It will be made clear below that this emphasis is reflected in the Communications Act 2003, s 319, and in the current policy of Ofcom, the broadcast regulator. This is quite a significant departure from the stance adopted under the previous regime. However, as discussed in Chapter 10,[49] the Act provides no clear mechanisms for co-operation with the sectors not covered by the Act, in particular that of film. The Act leaves Ofcom to determine how far content regulation in broadcasting should be harmonized with that relating to film. No express guidance on that matter is provided, save for that which can be viewed as flowing implicitly from the provisions of s 319.[50] This is acceptable under the TVWF, but it does not appear to accord with the aims of the proposed 2004 Recommendation.

Thus the reforms that have occurred under the Communications Act 2003 may already have been shown to be inadequate since the question of harmonization of content regulation across the various media sectors has not been addressed. The new regulatory regime created under the Act leaves the Internet, films and videoworks unaffected since the decision was taken to leave such sectors outside Ofcom's remit. While this decision is readily defensible, since it means that regulation in those sectors can remain flexible and sensitive to the particular needs of consumers and the industry involved, it means that both freedom of expression and the protection of minors may not receive effective protection. On the one hand Ofcom may continue the previous practice of indicating to broadcasters (via its Code) that the broadcast of a film may not be appropriate without cuts, or at all, even though it has been released on video with an 18 classification. On the other, the availability of (arguably) harmful material on the Internet may pose a danger to children[51] and may also call into question disharmony between restraints on Internet and broadcast content.

The EU creates pressure for harmonization, not only across the member states of the EU, but also between the various audio-visual sectors. The promotion of national frameworks aimed at achieving an effective level of protection for minors can, clearly, come into conflict with the promotion of competitiveness within and between those

---

[47] *The Council Recommendation concerning the protection of minors and human dignity*, 24 September 1998, 98/560/EC, OJ L 270, 7.10.1998, p 48.

[48] *Proposal for a recommendation of the European Parliament and Council on the protection of minors and human dignity and the right to reply in relation to the competitiveness of the European audiovisual and information services industry*, COM(2004) 341 final 2004/0117 (COD) 30.4.04, press release 04/598. The legal basis proposed for the Recommendation is Article 157 of the EC Treaty.

[49] See pp 541–5.   [50] See note 145, p 597 below.   [51] See Chapter 12 at 643–57.

sectors. Further, the extent to which public interest values can be furthered in broadcasting while promoting competition is debatable. 'Must carry' requirements[52] can be viewed as anti-competitive, as can regulation via a legislative scheme as opposed to self or co-regulation.[53] The Human Rights Act may have a role to play in relation to broadcast regulation in terms of providing a counter to the expression of commercial values, although that role should not be over-stated. If the public interest has so far been defined within the regulatory regime considered below in too nebulous a manner, the Strasbourg jurisprudence might provide a means of creating greater certainty, in terms of the part to be played by media regulation in a democratic society. The jurisprudence of the European Convention on Human Rights, especially that relating to Art 10, is centrally premised on the notion that the purpose of the Convention is to 'maintain and promote the ideals and values of a democratic society'.[54] Article 10 arguments, taking such jurisprudence into account, could be raised in relation to the adjudication of Ofcom, the super-regulator set up under the Communications Act 2003, since it is bound by s 6 HRA.[55] It is at least arguable that the infusion of clear substantive values into media regulation, organized around the concept of the public interest, could occur under the HRA. At the least, the HRA could play a part in allowing such an infusion to occur since it provides media regulators with a benchmarking document with its jurisprudential accretions—domestic and international[56]—which is highly relevant to the argument that a version of media freedom informed by Strasbourg principles is not necessarily coterminous with market freedom.

CONTENT REGULATION ON GROUNDS OF OFFENCE AVOIDANCE

As discussed above, arguments based on pluralism and autonomy do not underpin the ethos of the current broadcasting *content* regulatory regime, particularly the continued offensive material restrictions, now contained in the Communications Act 2003. Further, since the restrictions apply to all forms of broadcasting, including political broadcasting, a matter discussed further below, they militate against plurality

---

[52] Requirements to carry certain forms of material in broadcasting, usually imposed in the interests of ensuring impartiality (see Chapter 20 at 995–1009) or in order to serve minority interests; see Chapter 20, note 32.

[53] See Chapter 10 at 542–3.

[54] *Kjeldsen v Denmark* (1976) 1 EHRR 711, p 731; see also the comments of the Court in *Socialist Party v Turkey* (1999) 27 EHRR 51 as to the need for pluralism in a democracy.

[55] As a regulator of private sector broadcasting set up under statute, it can be classified as a core public authority (or at the least, a functional one) on the basis that it is acting in a governmental capacity: see below 607 and Chapter 3 at 113–17.

[56] See *Sunday Times v UK* A 30 (1979); *Jersild v Denmark* (1994) 19 EHRR 1; *Lingens v Austria* (1986) 8 EHRR 103; *Thorgeirson v Iceland* (1992) 14 EHRR 843. But note *Murphy v Ireland*: see Chapter 10 at 553, 557.

since they may mean that minority forms of expression are curbed. This chapter seeks to challenge the notion that the extent to which a medium is influential should necessarily be linked to the degree to which it should be regulated in terms of content.

In terms of restrictions on grounds of offence avoidance, the UK has traditionally operated one of the strictest regulatory regimes for broadcasting within Western Europe. The constraints created by the imposition of content-based responsibilities on broadcasters have inevitably meant that their creative freedom is curtailed. The Government had the opportunity to overhaul the regime in 2000 when it was considering the changes to the regulatory regime that eventually came about under the Communications Act 2003,[57] but it drew back from seeking to bring about radical change. The traditional particularly strict regime in relation to matters of taste and decency was continued with some modification and presented in more detail under Part 3 of the 2003 Act. It is a regime that would clearly appear intolerable if applied to the print media. Broadcasting has also been subject to greater restraints than have videos, and such greater restraint may tend to continue under the new post-2003 regime, depending on the stance of Ofcom—the new broadcast regulator—under its new Code. This special regime can only be justified by reference to the notion of intrusion into the home, discussed above. Previously, s 6(1)(a) of the Broadcasting Act 1990 imposed on independent broadcasters an obligation to ensure that programmes contained nothing that offended against good taste and decency or was likely to be offensive to public feeling, and the BBC Charter and Agreement 1996 contains equivalent provisions. The Broadcasting Act 1996 gave statutory recognition to the Broadcasting Standards Commission which was set up to monitor standards of taste and decency in public sector and independent broadcasting, and its role was then taken over by Ofcom, which under the 2003 Act now has to set standards whereby the public is protected from offensive material.

The emphasis placed on protection from offence rather than on adult autonomy was not seriously questioned in the White Paper preceding the 2003 Act, *A New Future for Communications*,[58] and the current statutory regime does not differ from the previous one in essentials. There are, however, certain significant differences which may, depending on their interpretation by Ofcom, tend in the direction of liberalization. Proportionality issues must now be considered when creating standards under the new Act under s 3(3)(a); the notion of maintaining standards of 'taste and decency' has been replaced by a duty to avoid offence and harm,[59] judged by context and by generally accepted standards; Ofcom has an express duty to abide by free expression principles in relation to that duty.[60] However, this of course adds nothing to the duty it is already under, as a public authority, under s6HRA.

In making decisions as to offence-avoidance Ofcom is faced with choices on a spectrum of extreme liberality or extreme restraint. It can either deny all viewers the

---

[57] See the White Paper, *A New Future for Communications*, published 12 December 2000; www.communicationswhitepaper.gov.uk.

[58] Ibid.   [59] Sections 3(2)(e) and 319.   [60] s 3(3)(g).

chance of watching explicit or disturbing material, or it can operate a highly liberal regime, allowing broadcast audiences the freedom to view such material but expecting them to protect themselves from offence. It is clearly arguable that people have a responsibility to protect themselves from offensive material merely by accessing information via a remote control before tuning into a programme where such material might be present. As warnings, encoding, Pin protection and consumer advice become more effective, this argument becomes more compelling. The small burden placed on viewers in expecting them to take responsibility for their own viewing could readily be viewed as proportionate to the aim of allowing others auton-omy in terms of choosing for themselves what they wish to see or hear. In other words, the small chance that someone might inadvertently view something they find offen-sive provides a doubtful justification for the infringement of autonomy involved in denying all viewers the chance to watch unexpurgated disturbing or sexually explicit material, within the limits created by the criminal law. This argument would apply in particular to the showing of films on television since they would already have been subject to the possibility of cuts to achieve a particular rating.

The warning contained in the classification of videos which also come into the home is viewed as going a long way towards providing a basis for ensuring that young children will not watch explicit material: the regime for videos is founded largely on the idea of parental responsibility, although there is of course some infringement of adult autonomy since videos must not contain material that prevents them from achieving a classification.[61] Broadcasting is based on the same foundation—since 'adult' material is shown after the watershed—but the offence-avoidance regime dis-cussed below is potentially more restrictive than that in place for videos, and therefore goes further in the direction of paternalism. This regime affecting broadcasting in the interests of preventing offence to viewers clearly curbs the freedom of broadcasters.

The pervasive notion that broadcasts, as opposed to video-based material, are aspects of an 'intrusive' medium is largely based, it is suggested, on an out-of-date model for television. The large number of channels currently available and the increased possibilities of interactivity (in particular, checking on information about a programme via a remote control) undermine the idea of intrusiveness. In the past the small number of channels made it more probable that in tuning in and out of pro-grammes a viewer might inadvertently encounter offensive material. The possibility of encoding also offers protection to those who do not wish to view such material. At present two issues in particular arise. Under the previous regulatory regime for broad-casting '18' rated films were shown but normally long after the cinematic or video release, when the '18' rating had in general become less significant, as standards changed.[62] Since such films are viewed in the home on videos, is there any basis for refusing to show them on general television channels without cuts and not long after

---

[61] See Chapter 12 at 621–3.

[62] See Chapter 12 at 620–30 for discussion of the standards applied to films by the BBFC and the ratings system.

the video release, so long as adequate consumer advice is provided? Secondly, if videos classified 'R18' (which now do contain 'hard core' material, as discussed in Chapter 12)[63] can be bought from restricted outlets, are there cogent reasons for barring the showing of such material on domestic or EU-based television subscription channels, using encoding as a protection for children? There are indications that a different stance is being taken towards such issues under the new Ofcom regime. An approach based not on general restrictions intended to avoid offence, but on the protection of minors only will become more firmly established if the Recommendation under the *Television without Frontiers* Directive is adopted.

In the next sections this chapter will focus on the question how far the current model of broadcast regulation, as compared with the previous one, comports with free speech principles. It will consider what part, if any, is played by the European Convention on Human Rights under the HRA in guaranteeing media freedom and media responsibility in the context of the maintenance of broadcasting standards relating to offence-avoidance. This is a context, however, in which it will be suggested that the HRA as mediated by the judiciary has not had and will not have a radical impact as far as modifying the general statutory regime governing explicit or violent expression in broadcasting is concerned. It may, however, have an impact as regards specific decisions taken under that statutory regime by courts and regulators. Although the regime is governed by a post-HRA statute—the Communications Act 2003—the Act itself was not, it is argued, heavily influenced by the European Convention on Human Rights. As discussed in Chapter 20, the 2003 Act was *not* declared compatible with the Convention under s 19 HRA. However, the presumed incompatibility is due to the continuance of the ban on political advertising under ss 321 and 319(g),[64] and it can be assumed that the rest of the provisions are intended to be compatible. Case law on the Act's provisions governing broadcast content is, however, likely to be sparse, providing few opportunities for examining its compatibility with the Convention rights.

THE BASIC REGULATORY REGIME

In the 1950s, with the advent of commercial television, it was considered necessary to impose direct statutory regulation on broadcasting. Special duties were imposed on independent broadcasting to maintain standards of taste and decency and of impartiality; the responsibility for maintaining standards was given to the Independent

---

[63] At pp 632–4.

[64] The s 3(1)HRA obligation applies to s 321 of the 2003 Act as it would to any statutory provision. Therefore in a challenge to the ban, a judge would be free to re-examine the presumptive incompatibility. This would be of particular significance if relevant developments had occurred since 2003 in the Strasbourg jurisprudence. But in any event, it would be open to a judge to seek to reinterpret the relevant provisions in order to determine whether exceptions to the ban could be created. See Chapter 20 at 1026–7 for discussion of this possibility.

Broadcasting Authority (IBA), established in 1954. Prior to the introduction of the Broadcasting Act 1990, the IBA was charged with the regulation of independent television. As part of the policy of deregulation of television, the 1990 Act set up the Independent Television Commission (ITC) to replace the IBA as a public body charged with licensing and regulating non-BBC television services.[65] The function of the ITC in this respect was similar to that of the Radio Authority (RA), which had the statutory function, under Part III of the 1990 Act, of licensing and monitoring the independent radio stations.

The regime established under the 1990 Act, and then taken further under the 1996 Act, represented an attempt to deregulate broadcasting, in the sense of enhancing market freedom, especially by affording further leeway to cross-media ownership, that is, ownership in more than one media sector. In contrast, in terms of creative freedom, it would be misleading to speak of 'deregulation' when the system not only led to the establishment of an overlapping and strict set of controls over broadcasting, but also had a tendency to suppress diversity. As Gibbons puts it: '[the 1990 Act created the danger that cross-media ownership would] create pressure for more homogenized editorial positions or, as has occurred, cross-media promotion.'[66]

Section 106 of the Broadcasting Act 1996 established the Broadcasting Standards Commission; as discussed below, the Commission until recently monitored BBC and independent programming. Its role was taken over in 2003 by the new regulator, Ofcom, which created legally enforceable controls over public broadcasting for the first time. Thus, until the Communications Act 2003 came into force, *independent* broadcasting was governed by the Broadcasting Acts 1990 and 1996.

Public broadcasting was, and—to an extent—still is, governed by the Royal Charter of the BBC which partly comprises a Licence Agreement.[67] The 1996 Act drew the BBC partly into the regulatory regime, as discussed below, and the 2003 Act takes that process somewhat further, but still leaves many regulatory matters to the BBC Charter and Agreement, which are to be renewed at the end of 2006. Thus the BBC still operates under this Agreement and also under the terms of its Charter.[68] This included the undertaking to comply generally with the statutory duties placed on the IBA and then the ITC.[69] The current position under the 2003 Act in relation to Ofcom is discussed below. Under the Charter and Agreement, the Board of Governors of the BBC has the responsibility for maintaining standards of taste and decency and of impartiality. The current (1996) Charter and Agreement, amended in 2003, set out in more detail the obligations of the BBC as a public broadcaster operating by means of

---

[65] For discussion of the change in regime introduced under the 1990 Act, see T. Jones, 'The deregulation of broadcasting' (1989) 52 *MLR* 380–88.

[66] 'Aspiring to pluralism: the constraints of public broadcasting values on the deregulation of British media ownership' (1998) 16 *Cardozo Arts and Entertainment Journal*, 475, p 485.

[67] Cmnd 8233.   [68] Cmnd 8313.

[69] This undertaking is annexed to the Corporation's licence agreement. This includes the requirement to observe due impartiality. See T. Gibbons, 'Impartiality in the media' (1985) *Archiv für Rechts- und. Sozialphilosophie*, Beiheft, Nr 28 pp 71–81.

the licence fee, in particular its obligation to maintain independence. Although it is commercially funded, Channel 4 also has a public service remit governed by statute—previously s 25 of the 1990 Act—and now contained in s 265 of the 2003 Act.

Thus, under the pre-2003 regime, commercial broadcasting was subject to dual, overlapping regulation from the ITC and BSC. The key difference under the pre-2003 regime, between the regulators, was in terms of sanctions: the BSC could only require a broadcaster found to be in breach of its code to broadcast its findings and an apology if appropriate; the ITC could, in addition to these sanctions, fine a broadcaster, and, in extreme cases, withdraw its licence. The BBC was still largely self-regulatory, although it was regulated by the BSC in relation to taste and decency and privacy.[70] Thus the BBC was under a much 'lighter touch' scheme of regulation than the commercial broadcasters. As indicated below, the Ofcom regime has harmonized these regimes to an extent, but the BBC remains self-regulatory in terms of its public service remit.[71]

REGULATION ON GROUNDS OF TASTE AND DECENCY UNDER THE BROADCASTING ACTS 1990 AND 1996; THE BBC'S EQUIVALENT OBLIGATIONS

Under the previous regulatory regime—pre-2003—the BBC and independent broadcasting were placed, formally, in very different positions in relation to regulation on grounds of taste and decency. That distinction is preserved, to an extent, under the current regime. In response to its duty arising under paragraph 5(1)(d) of its Agreement with the Secretary of State for National Heritage (1996),[72] the BBC has produced a code, entitled 'The BBC Producers' Guidelines', Chapter 6 of which deals with issues of taste and decency and imposes standards similar to those imposed on independent broadcasting. As discussed below, the obligation to respect such standards was imposed on independent broadcasting by the ITC under the 1990 Act. Thus the BBC was and is subject to a comparable, but non-statutory, obligation by virtue of its 1996 Agreement, to be superseded in 2006. However, the Broadcasting Act 1996 placed the BBC and independent television in the same position in relation to taste and decency requirements as far as the Broadcasting Standards Commission was concerned.

(I) THE PRE-2003 STATUTORY REGIME

Under s 6(1)(a) of the Broadcasting Act 1990 (now superseded by similar but more extensive provisions under s 319, Part 3 Communications Act 2003, below) the

---

[70] See Chapter 17 for discussion of broadcast regulation and privacy.
[71] See First Report of Select Committee on Culture, Media and Sport (2004) A Public BBC HC 82–I.
[72] Cmnd 3152, esp para 157.

Independent Television Commission (ITC) had to attempt to ensure that every licensed television service included nothing in its programmes 'which offends against good taste and decency or is likely. . . . to be offensive to public feeling'. Clearly, these were terms which were intended to leave a good deal of leeway to broadcasters as regards their interpretation. However, the ITC Programme Code, discussed below, fleshed out these requirements, sometimes in very specific and prescriptive terms, and therefore editorial decisions were not fully left to individual broadcasters. Section 6(1)(a) invited consideration of explicit material in the context in which it was shown, so that what might be offensive in one setting and with one particular audience in mind, was not so in another. Under s 7 of the 1990 Act the ITC had to draw up a Code giving guidance as to standards; it drew up its Programme Code in 1991 (the last version dated from 2001) giving guidance as to complying with standards of good taste and decency. The ITC had a number of sanctions to use against a company which failed to abide by the Programming Code, ranging from a requirement to broadcast an apology, to the power to revoke its licence. The financial penalties available were very severe but they were very rarely used.

These 1990 legislative arrangements for independent broadcasting could be said to represent a slackening of restraint on what could be broadcast in the sense that the television companies no longer had to submit their controversial programmes to an outside body for preview and censorship. As the Annan Committee pointed out in 1977,[73] the previous system (pre-1990) meant that programmes might be subject to dual censorship in being considered first by the IBA and then by the company concerned. After 1990 such censorship was placed solely in the hands of the companies themselves, the regulators wielding only post-transmission sanctions. The provisions under the 2003 Act have to be placed in the context of the regime created under the 1990 Act.

The role of the ITC in this respect was to an extent duplicated by the Broadcasting Standards Council, set up in 1988 to monitor the standards of taste and decency being maintained in programmes.[74] Section 106 of the Broadcasting Act 1996 established the Broadcasting Standards Commission (BSC), which was made up of a merger of the Broadcasting Standards Council and the Broadcasting Complaints Commission. The Broadcasting Standards Commission was set up with a view to imposing further controls on broadcasting. It was charged with the duty of drawing up a Code in respect of programme standards in relation to taste and decency under s 108 of the Broadcasting Act 1996—the 'Standards Code'.[75] The Commission was under a duty to monitor programmes (s 109), including BBC programmes, in relation to taste and decency, especially the portrayal of sex and violence, and to consider complaints regarding these matters (s 110). If a complaint was upheld, the BBC and independent

[73] Report of the Committee on the Future of Broadcasting, chaired by Lord Annan, Cmnd 6753.
[74] Under s 152 of the 1990 Act, the BSC had a duty to draw up a code relating to broadcasting standards covering the BBC, independent television, and radio broadcasting.
[75] Section 108 re-enacted the former s 152 of the 1990 Act.

broadcasters were under a legal obligation to publish it (s 119). The main sanction was contained in the adverse publicity.

(II) THE ITC PROGRAMME CODE AND THE BSC STANDARDS CODE

The taste and decency provisions in the ITC Programme Code were headed 'Family Viewing Policy, Offence to Good Taste and Decency, Portrayal of Violence and Respect for Human Dignity' (s 1.2). The provisions are discussed in detail below[76] and compared with those under the current Ofcom Code. The provisions placed restrictions on the material that could be broadcast, which went quite a long way beyond those applicable to video works.

The BSC Standards Code substantively reflected the ITC Code restrictions in a number of respects, although the detail of the provisions differed somewhat. The BSC Code laid down a number of key free expression principles. In particular, it made it clear that editorial responsibility remained with the broadcasters themselves, and that the Code was therefore to be treated as a guide, rather than as a rigid set of rules. Nevertheless, it acknowledged that in particular instances the Code drew attention to specific issues and offered clear advice.[77] In those instances, then, broadcasters clearly laid themselves open to the possibility of an adverse adjudication for breach of the code if they did not follow the guidance; it therefore appeared that those parts of the Code that give such specific direction had to be treated as having a quasi-legal status. The Code took brief account of the HRA, providing: 'the Human Rights Act 1998 ensures that broadcasters have a right to impart creative material, information and ideas, and that viewers have a corresponding right to receive these.'

The BSC Code was clearly based on the principles of allowing for creative freedom but protecting persons from the non-consensual viewing of offensive material, and in that respect it was in part in keeping with the liberal free speech account of restrictions on broadcasting discussed above. It stated: 'The most frequent reason for viewers or listeners finding a particular item offensive is that it flouts their expectations—expectations about what sort of material should be broadcast at a certain time of day, on a particular channel and within a certain type of programme, or indeed whether it should be broadcast at all; and whether the intentions of the programme are signalled in advance.' Therefore certain forms of broadcasting were more restricted than others; as the Code noted: 'Trailers and advertisements come upon audiences without warning, so that people cannot make informed choices about whether or not to be exposed to them.'

In seeking to strike a balance between the principles involved, it is suggested that both the ITC and BSC Codes placed too little emphasis on the need to avoid imposing paternalistic decisions on adults, as far as possible, within the criminal law. The right of television audiences to receive broadcast expression was not afforded as much emphasis as was the editorial freedom of broadcasters. The ability of people to take

---

[76] At pp 600–4.   [77] Para 3 BSC Code.

responsibility for protecting themselves from offence was emphasized, but there was nevertheless an acceptance of the idea that people need protection from the inadvertent viewing of offensive images. Such protection was more strongly emphasized than was the principle of seeking not to interfere with the ability of adults to choose to watch (potentially) disturbing, shocking or explicit material. While there are cogent reasons for restricting the content of advertisements, and arguably of trailers, the restrictions placed on films or docu-dramas, even shown well after the watershed and accompanied by extensive warnings and advice, were less defensible. Such films suffered from greater restriction than do videos, under the regime for videos discussed in Chapter 12.

Thus, as far as independent broadcasting was concerned, a dual and overlapping system was in place, imposing a confusing and onerous burden on the companies. In 2005 the ITC Code was superseded by the new Code under the Ofcom regime. In 2004 the BSC Code only applied to the BBC and Channel 4; it was also superceded by Ofcom's own code. This chapter goes on to discuss *ProLife Alliance v BBC*,[78] in which the taste and decency provisions of the pre-2003 regime were considered against Article 10 standards. The decision is considered at length since it is one of the most significant (and disappointing) post-HRA House of Lords' free speech decisions,[79] and has very important implications for the current Ofcom regime. The divergent approaches towards political expression, the effect of the HRA and the stance as to the impact of the taste and decency rules in the House of Lords, as compared to that taken by the Court of Appeal, make this decision remarkable.

(III) POLITICAL BROADCASTING AND TASTE AND DECENCY RESTRAINTS: *R (ON THE APPLICATION OF PROLIFE ALLIANCE) V BBC*

Background

Restraints created by regulation based on maintaining standards of 'taste and decency' are especially problematic in relation to political broadcasting. Many types of political expression in the form of documentaries, discussions, interviews with politicians are broadcast, but the opportunities for political groups to speak directly to television audiences by producing their *own* programmes for broadcasting are very constrained. As discussed in Chapter 20, political advertising is prohibited in independent broadcasting and the BBC is prohibited from accepting payment in return for broadcasting.[80] Party Broadcasts (PPBs) and Party Election Broadcasts (PEBs), transmitted free,

---

[78] [2003] 2 WLR 1403; [2003] 2 All ER 977.

[79] There are five other such decisions; they are are: *A-G v Punch*, see Chapter 6 at 291–301; *Campbell*, see Chapter 14 at 732–40; *R v Shayler*, see Chapter 19 at 939–45; *Re S*, see Chapter 16 at 825–7, 836–7. Interestingly, in all but the last one, speech 'lost'. All, except *Campbell* and, to an extent, *Ashworth* (see Chapter 7 at 345–8), are heavily criticized in the relevant chapters as very disappointing examples of post-HRA judicial reasoning.

[80] See p 1016.

are an exception to this rule. These PPBs and PEBs provide the only opportunity for political parties to have access to television to obtain broadcast time for programmes they produce in order to promote their party and their political agenda. But this narrow opportunity for this particular form of political communication is on its face restricted by the taste and decency requirements, which in this instance operate as a *prior* restraint since the broadcasters have the opportunity to reject material or insist on cuts to the proposed broadcast beforehand.

The taste and decency provisions of the BSC Standards Code, the ITC Code and the BBC Agreement applied to all forms of broadcasting expression, including political expression. Therefore PPBs and PEBs were covered (and are still covered under the new regime, as discussed below). This position was endorsed by a document produced jointly by the BBC and the independent broadcasters entitled 'Guidelines for the Production of Party Election Broadcasts' which indicated that PEBs had to comply with the ITC Programme Code and the BBC Producers' Guidelines, 'having regard to the political context of the broadcast'. Paragraph 4 of the BBC *Producers' Guidelines* 'Impartiality and Accuracy', states: 'The content of party political broadcasts, party election broadcasts, and ministerial broadcasts (together with Opposition replies) is primarily a matter for the originating party or the Government and therefore it is not required to achieve impartiality. The BBC remains responsible for the broadcasts as publisher, however, and requires the parties to observe proper standards of legality, taste and decency.' Paragraph 4.2 of the ITC Programme Code stated:

Editorial control of the contents of [PPBs and PEBs] normally rests with the originating political party. However, licensees are responsible to the ITC for ensuring that nothing transmitted breaches the Programme Code, notably the requirements on matters of offence to good taste and decency set out in section 1 . . . Licensees should issue parties with general guidelines on the acceptability of content . . . These guidelines, which are agreed between all relevant broadcasters, are designed to reconcile the editorial standards of the broadcaster, and audience expectations, with the freedom of political parties to convey their political messages.

The Guidelines for the Production of Party Election Broadcasts issued by the broadcasters for the 2001 election stated that PEBs had to comply with the ITC Programme Code and the BBC *Producers' Guidelines* relating to taste and decency and the codes concerning fairness and privacy, 'having regard to the political context of the broadcast'.

The application of these constraints to political broadcasting was challenged in *R (on the application of ProLife Alliance) v BBC*.[81] The case arose from a refusal of a PEB by the BBC and independent broadcasters; eventually the House of Lords had to consider the application of the taste and decency provisions to a PEB—the first time that such restraints had been looked at by the senior judiciary.

The ProLife Alliance is a registered political party which opposes abortion. At the 1997 general election the applicant put up enough Parliamentary candidates to qualify for a party election broadcast. The applicant submitted a video showing *inter alia*

---

[81] [2003] 2 WLR 1403; [2003] 2 All ER 977.

an abortion being carried out. The broadcasters refused to broadcast the video on the grounds that it offended against good taste and decency and would cause widespread offence. The applicant's application for permission to seek judicial review was refused by Dyson J. and by the Court of Appeal, and its application to the European Court of Human Rights was declared inadmissible by the Commission.[82]

At the 2001 general election the applicant put up enough parliamentary candidates to qualify for a PEB in Wales. The rules governing PEBs, and the fact that abortion is not at present available in Northern Ireland, obviously dictated the tactical choice of Wales for the ProLife Alliance since the cost would be far less when the candidates lost their deposits than it would have been had candidates been put up in England.[83] The loss of deposits was almost certainly inevitable in the case of an extremist single issue party, and in the event all the deposits were duly lost.[84] The applicant submitted a modified form of the video which it had submitted in 1997; it had been edited to remove the most graphic images but still showed aborted foetuses in a mutilated state. The video described the processes involved in different forms of abortion, and included, as Simon Brown LJ put it: 'prolonged and graphic images of the product of suction abortion: aborted foetuses in a mangled and mutilated state, tiny limbs, a separated head, and the like'. Again, representatives of the broadcasters refused to screen the images as part of the proposed broadcast. They did not raise any objection, however, to the soundtrack proposed. Therefore the ProLife Alliance was able to make various anti-abortion points verbally. Eventually a version of the video was submitted by the Alliance and unanimously approved by the broadcasters. It replaced the offending images with a blank screen on which the word 'censored' appeared, and which was accompanied by a sound track describing the images shown in the banned pictures. This version was then broadcast in Wales before the General Election.[85]

[82] See: *R v British Broadcasting Corpn, ex parte ProLife Alliance Party* (unreported) 24 March 1997; *R v BBC ex parte Quintavalle* (1997) 10 Admin LR 425; *ProLife Alliance v United Kingdom* (Application No 41869/98) 24 October 2000.

[83] S 36 of the 1990 Act provides that licences for certain descriptions of broadcasters must include 'conditions requiring the licence holder to include party political broadcasts in the licensed service' (subsection (1)(a)) and to observe 'such rules with respect to party political broadcasts as the [ITC] may determine' (subsection (1)(b)). The BBC is not under a formal obligation to offer party political broadcasts or party election broadcasts but has agreed to the same rules of allocation. Section 4 of the ITC Programme Code contains the rules for PPBs and PEBs. PPBs are offered to the major parties in Great Britain (the Labour, Conservative, and Liberal Democrat parties and, in Scotland and Wales respectively, the Scottish National Party and Plaid Cymru) at the time of significant events in the political calendar. PEBs are offered at election times. In the 2001 general election, the major parties were each offered a separate series of PEBs in each of the four nations of the United Kingdom. A smaller party could qualify for a PEB for transmission in the territory of any nation if it fielded candidates in at least one-sixth of its seats. Thus a party could qualify if it put up 88 candidates in England, 12 in Scotland, 6 in Wales, 3 in Northern Ireland. These rules and the fact that abortion is not at present available in Northern Ireland obviously dictated the tactical choice of Wales for the ProLife Alliance.

[84] The six Alliance candidates in Wales received a total of 1,609 votes, or 0.117 per cent of the total votes cast.

[85] It may be noted that had the Alliance succeeded in the application discussed below, and put the offending version of the same video forward for broadcasting in the 2005 election campaign, the broadcasters would have had to broadcast it if the Alliance had put up enough candidates to qualify for a PEB.

The ProLife Alliance then applied for permission to seek judicial review of the broadcasters' refusal to broadcast the original version of the video, showing the offending images. The application was dismissed by Scott-Baker J. Like Dyson J., Scott-Baker J. held that the broadcasters' decision was not irrational, and the applicant appealed. The challenge was not to s 6(1)(a) of the Broadcasting Act 1990, imposing the requirement to adhere to the taste and decency standards, itself, or the equivalent standards of the BBC's Licencing Agreement, as inconsistent with Art 10 under the HRA; so a declaration of the incompatibility of s 6(1)(a) with Art 10 was not sought under s 4 HRA. (Given that the case was brought against the BBC which was not subject to s 6(1)(a) it is hard to see that a declaration could have been made, in any event. This point was avoided by the judges in the proceedings.) The applicant argued rather that the broadcasters had not properly *applied* those standards, on the basis that they had failed to attach sufficient significance to the electoral context—a context in which freedom of expression was especially crucial.

The Court of Appeal ruling

The Court of Appeal found that under the HRA it itself had to decide whether the censorship (as it put it) in question was justifiable under Art 10(2) of the European Convention. The prohibition of the claimant's PEB was found to be 'prescribed by law' since the broadcasters' obligations arose under the Agreement between the BBC and the Secretary of State and under s 6(1) Broadcasting Act 1990. It was further found that they did not offend against the required standard of legal certainty. The factors of taste, decency and offence were found to be capable of justifying a prohibition upon free expression under Article 10(2) since they could be viewed as aspects of the 'rights of others'—a term that required, it was found, a broad interpretation: the 'rights' were not limited to the Convention rights.[86] In considering the necessity and proportionality of the interference with the freedom of expression of the Alliance and the potential audience, Laws LJ for the majority examined the question of deference, considering that 'the degree of deference which the court would pay to the view of the legislature in imposing requirements of taste and decency, and to the expertise of the broadcasters, depended on the context'. In the context of broadcast entertainment, he found, a very high degree of respect to the broadcasters' judgment would be accorded, while the broadcasters' margin of discretion would be only slightly diminished in the context of day-to-day news reporting. However, in the context of a general election the broadcasters' margin, it was found, would be *very* constrained since the court's duty to protect political speech would be viewed as 'over-arching'.[87]

Citing the *Bowman* case,[88] Laws LJ went on to find that under the Strasbourg jurisprudence the state in principle possesses very little discretion to interfere with free political speech, especially at election time. But he acknowledged that a wide

---

[86] *Müller v Switzerland* (1988) 13 EHRR 212; *VGT v Switzerland* (2002) 34 EHRR 159 and *Chapman v United Kingdom* (2001) 33 EHRR 399 applied.
[87] Para H7 4.   [88] *Bowman v UK* (1998) 26 EHRR 1.

margin of appreciation is conceded to states in the context of speech liable to offend against personal moral or religious convictions, on the basis that the signatory States are in such instances at greater liberty to choose between more restrictive or more liberal regimes. Therefore, he concluded, the national authorities in question can make choices as to the approach to be taken to restrictions on political speech, where such convictions may also be at stake. In other words, impliedly, the courts themselves could make choices on this matter and an aspect of so doing was found to involve the development of a domestic human rights jurisprudence:

[as] a coherent and principled domestic law of human rights[89] . . . The need to make good an autonomous human rights jurisprudence is prompted by a further consideration. Treating the ECHR text as a template for our own law runs the risk of an over-rigid approach. Travelling through the words of provisions like Article 10(2), with stops along the way to pronounce that this or that condition is met or not met, smacks to my mind of what Lord Wilberforce once condemned as the 'austerity of tabulated legalism' . . .[90]

Laws LJ went on to find that the domestic courts had already developed a strong jurisprudence protecting freedom of expression, especially in the political field.[91] He considered that in extreme cases concerns regarding taste and decency might prevail even over political speech, but found that this was not the case in the instance before him. Such an instance might, he found, involve factors of gratuitous sensationalism and dishonesty, rather than the mere promulgation of graphic and disturbing images. Having decided that gratuitous sensationalism was not present, Laws LJ found that considerations of taste and decency could not prevail over the freedom of speech of a political party at election time, except wholly exceptionally—and this instance did not, he found, require an exception to be made. Very little deference to the broadcasters' expertise and experience was accorded by the court.[92] A declaration was made that the BBC's refusal to broadcast the ProLife Alliance's party election broadcast was unlawful.

Laws LJ clearly did not consider that the Alliance had shown dishonesty in creating the video or that the images had been chosen for their sensational qualities. It may be suggested that both points are in fact arguable since most of the images appeared to be from later (post-first trimester) abortions, although the vast majority of abortions in the UK occur in the first ten-twelve weeks of pregnancy, when tiny limbs would not be discernable. Thus the Alliance video may have presented the material in a misleading fashion in order to seek to drive home its message as sensationally as possible, taking into account widespread ignorance of the reality of the majority of abortions.

But this was a seminal free speech ruling. It was entirely consistent with the

---

[89] *R (on the Application of the ProLife Alliance) v British Broadcasting Corporation* [2002] 2 All ER 756, paras [33] and [34].

[90] See *Ministry of Home Affairs v Fisher* [1980] AC 319 at 328.

[91] That stance is discussed in Chapter 15, esp at 782–90.

[92] For discussion and criticism of this decision see: A. Geddis, 'What Future For Political Advertising on The United Kingdom's Television Screens?' [2002] *PL* 615. See also J. Rowbottom, 'Freedom of Expression in Election Campaigns' (2002) 152 *New Law Journal* 679.

argument expressed at the beginning of this chapter, that content-based regulatory schemes trend to run counter to free speech rationales. It was a principled ruling that looked closely at the importance of the type of speech in question and found that flexibility had to be imposed on the regulatory scheme in order to accommodate it. Taking account of the high value of the speech, it found that it could not be treated in a monolithic fashion, despite the fact that the regulatory scheme implied that it could. It rejected the idea of deference to a regulator where speech of this nature was in question.

The House of Lords ruling

The BBC then appealed to the House of Lords.[93] The majority in the Lords considered that the Court of Appeal decision amounted to a finding that the taste and decency standards should not be applied to Party Election Broadcasts. However, they found that Parliament had decided that such broadcasts should not be exempt from those standards—despite the importance of free speech at such times—and that decision of Parliament as encapsulated in the Broadcasting Acts 1990 and 1996 (in respect of both the ITC and BSC) had not itself been challenged—although it could have been, under ss 3(1) and 4 HRA. Thus, according to the majority in the Lords, once it was accepted that those standards should be applied to PEBs, the question was whether the broadcasters had applied them wrongly. That did not appear to be the case on the facts, bearing in mind the clear findings of expert broadcasters; and in giving weight to their views the Lords made it clear that a degree of deference should be accorded to the broadcasters on the basis that, due to their audience research, they were likely to be thoroughly in touch with audience expectations.

Several significant points for political expression generally, and for the application of the taste and decency standards in particular, were made in the speeches of the Lords in the majority. Lord Nicholls of Birkenhead and Lord Hoffman, who gave the leading speeches, considered the scope of the application of Article 10 in the context in question. Whereas the Court of Appeal had treated the BBC's findings as censorship, both agreed that Article 10 does not provide an entitlement to make television broadcasts: it provides, they found, a right to expression, but not a right to have access to a particular medium—broadcasting—in order to exercise that right.[94] However, a right to broadcast a PEB had already been provided by the relevant legislation to those who qualified. Therefore, Lord Nicholls found:

the principle underlying article 10 requires that access to an important public medium of communication should not be refused on discriminatory, arbitrary or unreasonable grounds . . . or . . . granted subject to discriminatory, arbitrary or unreasonable conditions.[95]

---

[93] [2004] 1 AC 185; [2003] 2 All ER 977.

[94] See para 8 of the judgment. See also the decisions of the European Commission of Human Rights in *X and the Association of Z v United Kingdom* (1971) 38 CD 86; *Haider v Austria* 83–A DR 66; *Huggett v United Kingdom* 82–A DR 98.

[95] Para 8 of the judgment.

Both accepted that a restriction on the content of a PEB had to be justified under Art 10(2). They also accepted that this was a particularly pressing matter in relation to political communication at election time, especially where, as in the instant case, the restriction operated as a prior restraint.[96]

In relation to the question of justification Lord Nicholls considered that two questions appeared—at first glance—to arise. Firstly, he asked whether the content of party broadcasts should be subject to the same restriction on offensive material as other programmes. He said that, clearly, this was the case since the statutory and non-statutory regimes in question demanded that they should be. (In fact, it is suggested that questions could be raised about the legal status of the non-statutory BBC regime in relation to the HRA—a matter that all the judges decided not to consider, making the assumption that nothing turned on the distinction between the two regimes. This matter is returned to below.) He found that in considering this question at all, the Court of Appeal had fallen into error:

> The flaw in this broad approach is that it amounts to rewriting, in the context of party broadcasts, the content of the offensive material restriction imposed by Parliament on broadcasters. It means that an avowed challenge to the broadcasters' decisions became a challenge to the appropriateness of imposing the offensive material restriction on party broadcasts . . . this was not an issue in these proceedings.[97]

He said that the Court of Appeal had 'carried out its own balancing exercise between the requirements of freedom of political speech and the protection of the public from being unduly distressed in their own homes', but that the court had done so illegitimately since Parliament had already decided where the balance should be struck. The second question was whether, on the basis that the restrictions applied, the broadcasters had applied the right standards in the instant case.

So the only pertinent question to consider, in Lord Nicholls' view, was the second one. In viewing the matter in this way, however, he ignored the effect of s 3(1) HRA. The judges themselves are under an obligation to render legislative provisions compatible with the Convention; whether the applicant had challenged the provision itself or not should therefore have been viewed as irrelevant. It is argued that there were in fact *three* questions to be answered; the second one should have concerned the proper interpretation, in the light of Art 10, of the taste and decency provisions when applied to political communication. It could have been argued that they should have been given a narrow interpretation in that context, under s 3(1) HRA in relation to the demands of Art 10, and then the third question would have been whether the broadcasters had correctly applied those standards once they had been subjected to that more narrow interpretation.

Lord Nicholls assumed impliedly that there was no need to consider the effect of

---

[96] The BSC and ITC operated, as explained above, by way of *subsequent* restraint only in relation to matters of taste and decency, arising in contexts outside the PEB one, and this continues to be the case under the new 2003 regime.

[97] Para 15.

s 3(1) since the ProLife Alliance had accepted that the taste and decency regimes were not incompatible with its Article 10 right. Therefore he considered that the Court of Appeal had been wrong to find that the regimes could only rarely and exceptionally be relied upon in censoring a PEB. Lord Hoffmann, however, did examine the question of the interpretation of the statutory (and, by implication, the non-statutory) rules. He considered that the thrust of the applicant's submissions, which the Court of Appeal had been receptive to, was that the statute should be 'disregarded' or taken lightly. However, it must be pointed out that the application of s 3(1) HRA to a statute, narrowing, if necessary, the meaning of a provision in order to achieve compliance with the Convention, does not amount to *disregarding* it. Lord Hoffman was the only judge who considered the compatibility of Art 10 with the taste and decency rules; he considered that despite its apparent stance on compatibility in relation to s4 HRA, this was really the gravemen of the ProLife Alliance argument. He agreed with Lord Nicholls in finding that Article 10 does not provide a right of access to the broadcast media, relying on *Haider v Austria*.[98] In that instance the Commission found:

The Commission recalls that article 10 of the Convention cannot be taken to include a general and unfettered right for any private citizen or organisation to have access to broadcasting time on radio or television in order to forward his opinion, save under exceptional circumstances, for instance if one political party is excluded from broadcasting facilities at election time while other parties are given broadcasting time.

Lord Hoffman found that under Art 10, 'The emphasis, therefore, is on the right not to be denied access on discriminatory grounds,'[99] not on a right to broadcast. He considered whether the Strasbourg jurisprudence would require the taste and decency requirement to be regarded as unreasonable or discriminatory. ProLife Alliance was claiming that the requirements did not operate as 'neutral' or non-discriminatory restrictions. They applied on their face to all PEBs of any party, but the ProLife Alliance wished to express a particular message which, it claimed, had to be presented visually in order to depict the reality of abortion and therefore to arouse people against it. It inevitably breached the rules which therefore, it claimed, bore unfairly upon it alone since it was unable to present its political message in its chosen manner. On this basis it may be noted that the taste and decency rules could be viewed as discriminatory in relation not only to the Alliance PEB, but potentially in relation to any PEB dependent on visual material likely to cause offence.

   Lord Hoffman accepted that the rules had a *prima facie* discriminatory effect. So the next question was whether they could be objectively justified. In considering this matter, Lord Hoffman analysed the proportionality of the restrictions in relation to the political value of the Alliance PEB. He noted that the broadcast time allocation for PEBs had been introduced in order to further informed choice in general elections. However, he found that the ProLife Alliance message was not related to making such a choice since abortion is not a party political issue in the UK. In his view the message

---

[98] (1995) 83–A DR 66.   [99] At para 61.

was significant only in relation to the six Welsh constituencies in which the party's candidates were standing since, having seen the broadcast, the electorate in those constituencies could have chosen to vote for those candidates. Therefore the value and significance of the PEB was limited if considered in the context of the purpose behind providing for PEBs in general. That limited value then had to be weighed up, he said, against the right of viewers of broadcasts not to be shocked and offended in the privacy of their homes. It was, he considered, legitimate for Parliament to lay down certain conditions governing PEBs to protect those viewers' rights.

He noted that in *VGT Verein gegen Tierfabriken v Switzerland*,[100] in which a ban on political advertising was found to be discriminatory, the European Court of Human Rights had made it clear that it was not considering a case in which the objection to an advertisement was that its content was offensive. He also considered the response of the Court to the complaint of the Alliance about the previous rejection of its PEB in the 1997 election. The Registrar of the court had written to the Alliance, stating: 'in accordance with the general instructions received from the court' he drew their attention to 'certain shortcomings' in the application. The indication given by the Registrar was that the court might consider that the taste and decency requirements were not an 'arbitrary or unreasonable' interference with the access of the Alliance to television. The Court then rejected the application as inadmissible as not disclosing 'any appearance of a violation of the rights and freedoms set out in the Convention. . . .' Lord Hoffman concluded therefore that there 'is no public interest in exempting PEBs from the taste and decency requirements on the ground that their message requires them to broadcast offensive material.'[101]

Thus Lords Nicholl and Hoffman came to the same conclusion—that the only significant question was whether the broadcasters had applied the taste and decency rules correctly. Having arrived at that finding, with which Lords Millett and Walker agreed, the outcome of the case became virtually inevitable. Once Lord Nicholls had configured the issue as indicated he found that it resolved itself into one question only: 'should the court, in the exercise of its supervisory role, interfere with the broadcasters' decisions that the offensive material restriction precluded them from transmitting the programme proposed by ProLife Alliance?' He answered this question by considering the broadcasters' decision and went on to find that the broadcasters' application of the statutory criteria was not at fault. He noted that the broadcasters would have accepted that some images of abortion could be included to convey the message, but that the images put forward were too graphic and prolonged. The BBC representative had stated: 'What is unacceptable in your client's broadcast is the cumulative effect of several minutes primarily devoted to such images.' The broadcasters had, Lord Nicholls found, applied an appropriate standard in assessing the question whether transmission of the images in question would be likely to cause offence to viewers. In other words, if the only matter at issue was the application by

---

[100] 34 EHRR 159, at para 76, p 177. The decision is discussed in Chapter 20 at 1021–3.
[101] At para 73.

the broadcasters of the statutory criteria, not the *interpretation* of those criteria, then it appeared that the broadcasters had taken the correct stance.

Lord Hoffman arrived at the same conclusion. Having found that Parliament was entitled to impose standards of taste and decency which were 'meant to be taken seriously', he went on to consider the application of those standards by the broadcasters. In considering the standards applied he rejected the idea that they could be 'a matter of intuition on the part of elderly male judges' and took into account the expertise of the broadcasters and the audience research they had conducted.[102] He also took account of the feelings of women who had had abortions who might have viewed the PEB inadvertently. He found that the broadcasters were well placed to determine whether members of the public would be likely to find the images offensive, and that they had found that the images did not fall at the margin of acceptability, but well below it. He therefore accepted that the broadcasters' decision should not be interfered with.

Lord Millett adopted Lord Nicholls' reasoning. Lord Walker of Gestingthorpe also concluded that there were no grounds for finding that the broadcasters' decision was unjustified, even after subjecting it to close scrutiny. Lord Scott of Foscote dissented, although he accepted that the question on appeal was the narrow one identified by Lord Nicholls, not the broader one identified by the Court of Appeal. But he then found that the broadcasters had not applied the taste and decency standards reasonably, taking account of the ProLife Alliance's Article 10 right to put forward their anti-abortion message, as a form of political expression. So the appeal of the BBC was allowed.

Critique

Before moving on to criticism of the House of Lords' stance it is worth pointing out here that, technically, a route was available which would have allowed the decision to reach a different outcome. The case concerned the BBC and therefore did not directly concern the statutory regime under the 1990 Act applied to independent broadcasters, although all the judges treated it as though it did.[103] They thereby succeeded in treating the decision as a test case for all the broadcasters and avoided difficult questions about the mechanics of the HRA and their application to the non-statutory BBC regime. The question whether the BBC is in fact a public authority under s 6 HRA and, if so, the much more difficult question as to which of its functions are caught by the Act,[104] was not addressed directly, although the decision can be viewed as proceeding on the assumption that it is a public authority when it acts as a regulator. The House of Lords' argument about the need to respect statutory provisions was not therefore directly applicable. Clearly, all the judges concerned decided to elide

---

[102] Paras 78–80.

[103] S108 of the 1996 Act relating to the standards Code of the Broadcasting Standards Commission was relevant (see above p 575) but the discussion as to the effect of s 3(1) HRA focused on s 6(1)(a) of the 1990 Act.

[104] Under s 6 (3) HRA. See further discussion in Chapter 3 at 114–22.

the position of the BBC with that of the independent broadcasters, and it is difficult to avoid the conclusion that they did so partly in order to avoid the difficult and technical HRA questions that otherwise probably would have arisen. The Alliance was not, as indicated above, seeking a declaration of incompatibility under s 4 HRA since they perceived a declaration as valueless. But ss 3 and 4 are not applicable to quasi-legal agreements such as that of the BBC. The House of Lords could readily have implied terms into the Agreement creating compatibility—as far as the application of the taste and decency rules to PEBs was concerned—relying on its own duty under s 6(1) HRA to act to enforce Art 10 of the Convention, untrammelled by the provision of s 6(2), which was also inapplicable, since on the facts legislative provisions were not involved.

This decision placed the taste and decency rules in an anomalous position in relation to s 3(1) HRA. As indicated above, the majority and minority judges in the House of Lords failed to apply the HRA since the effect of s 3(1) was misunderstood. The striking thing about their ruling was the extraordinarily contorted reasoning: it verged on dishonesty to suggest that ProLife was challenging the statute itself—seeking to set it aside. Section 3(1)'s very function is to create compatibility with the Convention rights and, as discussed, this would not have involved damaging the statute, let alone setting it aside.

It may be argued that the Court of Appeal also did not deal with s 3(1) effectively since Laws LJ appeared to assume that the statutory rules on taste and decency could be disapplied—in almost all instances—as far as PEBs were concerned. Section 3(1) has not been interpreted as affording a means of disapplying statutory provisions, although the House of Lords has come close to that position, in all but name, where the statute in question appeared to provide them with a gateway for such disapplication.[105] The statutory taste and decency rules do not provide such a gateway since they contain no exceptions, although the statutory terms are very clearly open to interpretation; they cannot, it is argued, be completely disregarded. (Of course, in the case of the BBC's Agreement, such a gateway would not in any event have been needed since it does not have statutory force—a point which was not relied upon by the Alliance and which all the judges chose to disregard.) But this was not an instance in which it was necessary to seek to straddle the difficult line between interpreting and legislating since terms such as 'good taste and decency' and 'offensive' are themselves so open-ended. So the Court of Appeal could have used s 3(1) HRA[106] to narrow down the application of the rules to PEBs on the basis of the great importance accorded to political expression under Article 10. Laws LJ argued that in the context of PEBs the public is prepared to accept that images could properly be more explicit than in other contexts, without finding that standards of taste and decency had been violated. Thus it would not have been necessary to utilize s 3(1) to read words into s 6(1)(a)

---

[105] See the discussion of s 3 in Chapter 3 at 157–63 and in particular the consideration of *R v A* [2001] 3 All ER 1 in the House of Lords.

[106] On the assumption that it was applicable—as discussed, s 3(1) was not *directly* applicable, although the BBC had accepted the s 6(1)(a) obligations and was subject to BSC taste and decency monitoring.

Broadcasting Act 1990; the requirement that standards of taste and decency should be context-dependent seems to be self-evident. But Laws LJ appeared to go further in implying that the taste and decency rules could be virtually disregarded or rendered otiose, thus seeming to overstep the line between legislating and interpreting. Moreover, he did not appear to think that he was relying on s 3(1) HRA in making this argument but on common law principle. Had s 3(1) been employed to interpret the taste and decency rules as suggested—in a highly context-dependent manner—far less damage would have been done to the statute than has been done under the HRA in other House of Lords' rulings.[107]

So the decisions of the two courts stand at opposite ends of the spectrum, not only as far as the use of s 3(1) is concerned, but also in relation to the value accorded to political expression. But had the House of Lords found that the taste and decency rules could be narrowed down in their application to PEBs (and perhaps to other forms of political broadcasting, to a lesser extent), the *outcome* of the decision might still have been the same on the basis that the broadcasters had found that the showing of the video would have created a grave rather than a marginal breach of the rules. In other words, it might have been argued that even a narrow application of the rules would still have led the broadcasters to the same decision: any other outcome might have been viewed as tantamount to a disapplication of the statute.

The outcome would also have been the same had the House of Lords accepted that s 3(1) *could* be used to narrow down the rules, but come to the conclusion that the Strasbourg jurisprudence did not require that the broadcasters' decision should be declared unlawful. It could have been argued that the effect of s 3(1) HRA would depend on the application of the tests of proportionality and necessity under Article 10(2) in relation to the conditions applied to the Alliance's PEB. (The argument that there is no right to broadcast air-time under Article 10(1) is irrelevant since the Alliance had already qualified for a PEB.) Lord Hoffman appeared to be of the view that the jurisprudence gave little support to the Alliance's claim, although he did not make it clear that his argument was linked to the potential effect of s 3(1). He made two points in relation to his proportionality argument. The first was that the value of political expression in this instance was limited. This argument has been roundly condemned by two of the academics who have commented on the House of Lords' decision,[108] and, although it was argued that the Court of Appeal decision makes more 'appeal to rhetoric than to reason',[109] its findings on the matter were preferred.

---

[107] See Lord Steyn's ruling in *R v A* [2001] 3 All ER 1.

[108] See E. Barendt, 'Free Speech and Abortion' (2003) *PL* 580–591 and I. Hare, 'Debating Abortion—the Right to Offend Gratuitously' (2003) 62(3) *CLJ* 525–528. J. Rowbottom, 'Article 10 and Election Broadcasts' (2003) 119 *LQR* 553–557 favours the House of Lords' approach. A. MacDonald's analysis appears to favour the stance of the House of Lords, but concentrates on the general issue of 'the role, if any, of judicial "deference" in a democratic constitution': *R (on the application of ProLife Alliance v BBC* 6 EHRLR 651–657. A. Geddis, 'If Thy Right Eye Offend Thee, Pluck it Out' (2003) 66 *MLR* 885–893 strongly favours the House of Lords' approach and attacked that of the Court of Appeal in 'What future for political advertising on the UK's television screens?' (2002) *PL* 615.

[109] I. Hare, ibid, at 527.

However, Lord Hoffman's argument cannot be dismissed without making some effort to tease out the different values underlying forms of political expression.

A central argument of this book is that in relation to its underlying value freedom of expression cannot be viewed in monolithic terms. That argument is of course very well established in the jurisprudence at the domestic and international levels.[110] However, as this book has argued, *within* the different categories of expression, a further hierarchy can be discerned. Political expression is, it is argued, divisible in normative terms. Laws LJ in the Court of Appeal was surely right in finding that free speech at election times is of very high value. But Lord Hoffman's finding that the Alliance's speech was almost coincidental with the election, rather than an inherent aspect of it, had some merit. Lord Hoffman considered that the applicant was not seriously attempting to participate in the election campaign, but to use the PEB loop-hole in the political advertising ban in order to obtain broadcast time to promote its anti-abortion message. The Alliance presumably recognized that the estimated commercial value of the free airtime would greatly exceed the cost of the lost candidate deposits in one sixth of the seats.[111] Thus, the extent to which the video could be viewed as a part of the general election campaign was debatable. It must be acknowledged that if creating informed choice is the *central* value in election-related expression, that value was not—except in the most tenuous and uncertain sense—at stake in relation to the Alliance's video. Other, more peripheral but still significant, election-related values were however at stake, such as the possibility that minority, single issue parties can only obtain greater influence in future via election-related publicity.

But leaving aside the issue of its linkage to the General Election, the applicant's video was a form of political communication and therefore still of particular significance in Art 10 terms. Moreover, as discussed in Chapter 20, the advertising ban itself almost certainly breaches Art 10,[112] and therefore the fact that the Alliance appeared to be exploiting a loop-hole in it would not in itself weaken their Art 10 claim. Where Lord Hoffman fell into error, was in his dismissal of the speech in question as of limited value. It remained a form of highly significant political expression, partly due to its very nature and partly due to the less central election-related values underlying it. Therefore there was a strong case for narrowing down the taste and decency rules where they led to a restriction on such expression. This was the case that the majority in the House of Lords failed to acknowledge,[113] while at the same time Laws LJ in the Court of Appeal arguably over-stated it.

[110] See Chapter 1 at 12–20, 27–32.

[111] This concern was raised in a report published in 2003, *Party Political Broadcasting: Report and Recommendations*, the Electoral Commission. It considered that there was a case for deterring organizations from fielding candidates so as to qualify for a PEB for their own publicity purposes rather than for genuine electoral purposes. Lord Hoffman also noted this concern in *ProLife Alliance v BBC* [2004] 1 AC 185, at para 35.

[112] See pp 1020–9.

[113] Lord Hoffman touched on this point but did not, it is argued, give enough weight to political speech. He appeared to take the stance that even political speech of the highest value could be restricted or banned in response to the application of taste and decency rules: 'Even assuming that the Alliance broadcast had been

Lord Hoffman's second point was linked to his first. He found that Strasbourg endorsed his view that the form of political expression in question was of low value, meaning that interferences with it could readily be justified. In coming to this conclusion he relied most strongly on the adverse Strasbourg admissibility decision against the Alliance in respect of their 1997 video.[114] (In strong contrast, the Court of Appeal made little attempt to engage with the relevant jurisprudence, deciding the case largely on the basis of common law free speech principles.) Lord Hoffman did not take account of the less offensive nature of the 2001 video and, more importantly, ignored the impact of the margin of appreciation doctrine on the jurisprudence, and the fact that under s2HRA it is non-binding. The failure to deal with the impact of the margin of appreciation doctrine was most significant. As argued elsewhere in this book, the stance of the UK judiciary in relation to the implications of the effects of this doctrine amounts to one of their most significant failures in confronting the application of the HRA.[115] The line of cases stemming from *Handyside*[116] is deeply affected by this doctrine, which is not applicable at the national level. Therefore the admissibility decision relied upon by Lord Hoffman should have been applied—as far as that is possible—after stripping away the effects of the doctrine upon it. Since it was a decision upon admissibility alone, the decision would have been rendered almost an empty one once that process had been undertaken. It may be noted that the Court of Appeal accepted—correctly—that this admissibility decision was non-determinative of the issue before it. Had the Lords taken that stance that would have left the judges with little guidance as to the Strasbourg stance on the matter, except from the *Handyside* line of authority and from general Strasbourg free speech principles.

Lord Hoffman noted that *VGT Verein gegen Tierfabriken v Switzerland*,[117] in which a breach of Art 10 was found in relation to discrimination in allocation of broadcast time, did not deal with an instance in which the objection to an advertisement was that its content was offensive. However, that left the point at issue open. Therefore the general principle from *Handyside* should have been applied, bearing in mind that *Handyside* was itself to an extent in point in relation to the instant case. It dealt with speech that could be termed political, if that term is broadly interpreted, including information about abortion, taking impliedly a pro-abortion stance. The book in question in *Handyside* informed children and teenagers about matters related to sexuality, and its implicit message could be viewed as a liberal one. As discussed in Chapter 8, the Court took a strong stance in favour of offensive speech under Art 10(1) but then applied the tests of necessity and proportionality under Art 10(2) in a manner that was heavily influenced by the margin of appreciation doctrine. If the influence of that doctrine on the decision was to be disapplied at the domestic level, the decision could be taken to endorse a very restrictive role for rules aimed at

---

an ordinary PEB, relevant to the general election, I do not think it would have been unreasonable to require it to comply with standards of taste and decency' (para 70).

[114] *ProLife Alliance v United Kingdom* (Application No 41869/98) 24 October 2000.
[115] See Chapter 3 at 145–9.   [116] Eur Ct HR, A 24; (1976) 1 EHRR 737. See Chapter 8 at 410–22.
[117] 34 EHRR 159, at para 76, p 177.

avoidance of offence in relation to semi-political speech. *A fortiori* the decision would endorse such a role in relation to political speech of *higher* value—as in the *ProLife Alliance* case.

Therefore, if the effects on the findings of the margin of appreciation doctrine could have been disapplied, *Handyside* would arguably favour a stance closer to that of the Court of Appeal than that of the House of Lords, although whether, bearing in mind the view taken by the BBC of the gravity of the offence that would be caused by the video, it could have supported the findings of the Court of Appeal as to the *outcome*, is debatable. (The *outcome* in *Handyside* itself would, arguably, lend some support to the House of Lords' decision since Strasbourg accepted that the direct censorship of political/ideological speech was justifiable under Article 10(2)—admittedly in the context of protecting children.) It must be acknowledged that the *Handyside* case does not lend itself readily to the idea of "stripping" away its margin of appreciation aspects. The effect of the doctrine on the reasoning was so pervasive that this would have been difficult. Most of the reasoning was directed to refuting arguments that the interference was disproportionate to the aim pursued. No evidence of pressing social need or of proportionality was demanded by the Court.[118] However, the House of Lords could merely have taken the view that it had to take a much harder look at the application of those tests, since as a domestic court it was unaffected by the margin of appreciation doctrine. It is concluded that the treatment of the Strasbourg jurisprudence in both the House of Lords and Court of Appeal was flawed: Lord Hoffman did not take account of the effects of the margin of appreciation doctrine and severely understated the value placed by Strasbourg on speech in general and political speech in particular, while the Court of Appeal failed to analyse the implications of the jurisprudence relating to such speech, choosing instead to rely on more familiar common law principles.

The House of Lords' judgment does nothing to mitigate the dangers of content-based regulatory schemes in free speech terms, discussed at the beginning of this chapter. In this instance all the free rationales were engaged in relation to ProLife itself as a speaker and in relation to the audience. Lord Hoffman's key point was that deference should be paid to the expertise of the regulator, as well as to Parliament. Presumably therefore even if he had explicitly rejected the effects of the margin of appreciation doctrine on Strasbourg jurisprudence, he would still have been wedded to a domestic doctrine of deference. But it is argued that the notion of deferring to a regulator needs to be unpacked. Regulators have expertise as to matters of fact and can also give expert opinions. In this instance the regulator—the BBC—had expertise as to accepted standards of taste and decency in broadcasting and therefore as to audience expectations. Therefore it was entitled to take the stance that the ProLife video infringed those standards, and it was reasonable for the court to defer to those findings. But the regulator did not have expertise in *balancing* the concerns relating to taste and decency against free speech. That was a normative exercise for the court,

---

[118] See further on these points Chapter 8 at 411–13.

basing itself on Strasbourg principles. It is precisely the role of the courts to conduct that balancing exercise under Article 10(2) between the right to freedom of expression and societal concerns. Lord Hoffman fudged the issue—he elided the issue of deference on the basis of expert findings with the question of balancing those findings against free speech demands. Lord Hoffman made much also of deference to Parliament. But Parliament had enacted not only s 6(1)(a) of the 1990 Act, but also the HRA and had placed a responsibility on the judges to abide by the Convention rights, under s6. Lord Hoffman appeared almost to abrogate his responsibility as a judge to conduct the necessary balancing exercise. His motivation appeared to be a determination to avoid subjecting a regulator's decision to a real, systematic Convention scrutiny.[119]

The general impact of this decision in terms of the HRA and the media is discussed further in Chapter 3,[120] while its significance in relation to political expression in broadcasting is considered in Chapter 20.[121] Its implications in terms of the *current* taste and decency rules are considered below.[122]

REGULATION ON GROUNDS OF AVOIDING OFFENCE UNDER THE COMMUNICATIONS ACT 2003

(1) THE STATUTORY REGIME

The BSC's and ITC's roles in relation to the maintenance of standards of taste and decency were taken over in 2003 by Ofcom, the inclusive regulator set up under powers provided for in the Office of Communications Act 2002 and with the powers and duties designated under the 2003 Act.[123] They include the licensing[124] and regulation of broadcasting and of telecommunications. Thus the regime was

---

[119] For further criticism of Lord Hoffman's findings on deference in this instance, see Lord Steyn 'Deference is a tangled web' (2005) *PL* 346–359.

[120] At pp 151–3, and Chapter 17, at 867–9.   [121] See pp 1024–7.   [122] See pp 607–12.

[123] Section 2 (1). As from such date as the Secretary of State may appoint for the coming into force of this section, the functions that are set out in Schedule 1 (functions of the Secretary of State and of the pre-commencement regulators) shall become functions of Ofcom in accordance with that Schedule.

(2) References in any enactment to a person who is a person from whom functions are transferred by virtue of this section are to have effect, so far as necessary for the purposes of the transfers, as references to Ofcom.

[124] Television Licensable Content Services and the licensing regime which applies to them are described in ss 232–240 of the Communications Act 2003. They replace the separate categories of satellite television services and licensable programme services which were established under the Broadcasting Act 1990 (as amended by the Broadcasting Act 1996). A television licensable content service is a service provided in digital or analogue form broadcast from a satellite or distributed using an electronic communications network that is to be made available for reception by members of the public and consists of television programmes (which for this purpose also comprises text services) or electronic programme guides, or both. It does not constitute a service which is a television multiplex service, a restricted television service, a digital television programme service, a service provided under a Channel 3 licence, a service provided under the Channel 4 licence, a service provided under the Channel 5 licence, a service provided under the public teletext licence or an additional television service.

rationalized under the 2003 Act, and the dual system of control—by the ITC and BSC—was modified: during 2004-early 2005 independent television only had to refer to one Code—the ITC Programme Code monitored by Ofcom. In 2005 the ITC Code was superceded by Ofcom's own Code once it came into force.

Section 325 Communications Act 2003 covers observance of the Code in licensed TV services. Under s 325 the conditions included in Broadcasting Act licences must ensure that the s 319 standards for offence avoidance (see below) are observed in the service provision, and a duty is imposed on Ofcom to establish procedures for handling and resolving complaints regarding adherence to the standards. Section 237 allows for the imposition of penalties, including financial penalties, for the contravention of licence conditions or of directions given by Ofcom. If Ofcom is satisfied that a licensee has contravened a provision of a licence, or failed to comply with a direction from Ofcom, a penalty can be imposed.[125]

Under its own penalty guidelines[126] Ofcom states that the amount of any penalty must be appropriate and proportionate to the contravention in respect of which it is imposed. It states that it must have regard to any representations made by the regulated body in breach, and accepts therefore that in setting the level of penalty, it will consider all relevant circumstances. In particular it states that it will take account of the seriousness of the contravention, precedents set by previous cases, and the need to ensure that the threat of penalties will act as a sufficient incentive to comply. The penalty will be higher where there are repeated contraventions by the same regulated body, where the contravention continues after the body becomes aware of it, or after it has been notified of it by Ofcom.[127]

(II) THE ROLE OF THE ADVERTISING STANDARDS AUTHORITY

In November 2004 Ofcom contracted out its broadcast advertising remit to the ASA.[128] Thus the ASA is now the sole regulator for advertising and it will be working in a co-regulatory partnership with Ofcom in relation to broadcast advertisements. The commercial TV channels and radio stations must continue to observe Ofcom's Code, but if broadcast advertisements cause offence or distress, the matter will be dealt with first by the ASA, not by Ofcom.[129] The Broadcast Committee of

---

[125] This cannot exceed a fine of £250,000. Section 392 requires Ofcom to prepare and publish a statement containing the guidelines they propose to follow in determining the amount of penalties imposed by them under the Act or any other enactment, apart from the Competition Act 1998. By virtue of s 392(6) of the Act, Ofcom must have regard to the statement for the time being in force when setting the amount of any penalty under this Act or any other enactment (apart from the Competition Act 1998).

[126] From its website: www.Ofcom.org.uk/codes_guidelines/penalty.

[127] In considering raising the penalty Ofcom will also take account of the extent to which senior management knew, or ought to have known, that a contravention was occurring or would occur, and of the absence, ineffectiveness or repeated failure of internal mechanisms or procedures intended to prevent contravention by the body concerned.

[128] See Chapter 10 at 545; see also A. Willis, 'The Future Regulation of Broadcast Advertising', Ent L Rev (2004), 15(8), 255–6.

[129] See Chapter 12 at 646 for discussion of the ASA Code.

Advertising Practice Television Advertising Standards Code covers offence avoidance under s6.[130]

The status of the Codes covering broadcast advertising content differs from that of the Code covering advertising in the non-broadcast media. Other media are also bound by the law in relation to misleading claims, but compliance with the offence-avoidance standards laid down by Ofcom, based on those of the 2003 Act, is a condition of broadcasters' licences, so Ofcom has retained its legal powers over the broadcasters in that respect. No such condition applies to other media, and therefore the parts of the ASA regime dealing with advertising in the non-broadcast media have no relationship with Ofcom on matters of advertising content. The public deals with the ASA in relation to handling complaints, but ASA's self-regulatory system has recognised the

---

[130] The Broadcast Committee of Advertising Practice

Television Advertising Standards Code

6.1 Offence

Advertisements must not cause serious or widespread offence against generally accepted moral, social or cultural standards, or offend against public feeling

Notes:

(1) Although no list can be exhaustive, and values evolve over time, society has shared standards in areas such as:
- *(a) the portrayal of death, injury, violence (particularly sexual violence), cruelty or misfortune*
- *(b) respect for the interests and dignity of minorities*
- *(c) respect for spiritual beliefs, rites, sacred images etc*
- *(d) sex and nudity, and the use of offensive language. (For further information see the ITC research reports* Nudity in Television Advertising *and the ASA/ITC report* Delete Expletives. *The latter reports on attitudes to swearing and offensive language.)*

(2) The ASA and BCAP do not judge cases simply, or even primarily, on the number of complaints received. It makes judgements about the likelihood of widespread offence as well as taking into account the possibility of deep, usually unintentional, offence to sections of the audience which have particular vulnerabilities.

(3) Particular circumstances can result in otherwise unobjectionable material causing offence. For example, a joke may cease to be acceptable if it seems to refer to a recent tragedy or if it appears close to a programme about a serious, related issue. On the other hand, if material might be on the edge of acceptability for a general audience but would be perfectly acceptable to, for example, young adults, careful scheduling in 'youth' programmes may be sufficient to avoid causing offence.

(4) Whilst commercials for media products such as CDs and videos must not mislead about their content, any extracts from the products should not cause offence.

6.2 Violence and cruelty
- (a) Advertisements must not encourage or condone violence or cruelty
- (b) Gratuitous and realistic portrayals of cruel or irresponsible treatment of people or animals are not acceptable

Notes to 6.2:

(1) Careful judgements are needed in this area. 'Theatrical' violence (for example, the mayhem common in action/adventure films) is generally acceptable, as is violence which has a stylised 'cartoon' or slapstick quality. Problems are more likely to arise where the violence seems to take place in everyday life and to involve ordinary people. However, care should be taken to avoid giving young viewers the impression that copying wrestling, martial arts etc would be safe, harmless fun.

(2) Advertisements must not appear to condone people using violence or aggression to get their own way in everyday life.

(3) Jokes about or involving violence require care and will usually need to be distanced from everyday life by being, for example, in cartoon form.

(4) Scenes which would otherwise be inappropriate may be acceptable to the audience in, for example, charity advertising or newsreel footage in advertisements for news media.

(5) Timing restrictions are necessary for advertising featuring violence.

differences between licensed broadcasters and non-broadcast media non-licensed services by setting up separate decision-making structures to deal with broadcast and non-broadcast advertising.

(III) THE OFCOM REGIME AND THE POSITION OF THE BBC

Ofcom also affects public sector broadcasting.[131] Such broadcasting was also regulated under the BSC regime, but the BSC did not have the power to impose financial penalties on the BBC. This power, introduced under the current regime, represents a highly significant change from the previous regime. It undermines the BBC's independence and brings the BBC far more into conformity with independent television. But at the same time the new statutory regime represents a compromise between BBC editorial freedom and greater regulation by a government regulator[132] since the regime for the BBC has to operate within the parameters of its Charter and Agreement. Section 198 provides that Ofcom may impose financial penalties on the BBC within the powers conferred by the Charter and Agreement if it contravenes the provisions of Part 3 2003 Act or of its Charter and Agreement.[133] The Agreement was amended in 2003 in anticipation of the changes to be introduced under the 2006 Agreement, the new amendment coming into force in 2004. Clause 13 of the amended BBC Agreement allows Ofcom to impose penalties, including financial ones, on the BBC[134] if it contravenes a 'relevant enforceable requirement'. A 'relevant enforceable requirement' includes the new Ofcom Code. Thus complaints about harm and offence may be addressed by the BBC, by Ofcom, or by both.

When the BBC's Charter is renewed at the end of 2006 this system will change, but not radically. The Green Paper reviewing the BBC's Royal Charter[135] stated that the government intends to create a new body called the BBC Trust to take on the oversight

---

[131] Section 198 (1) It shall be a function of OFCOM, to the extent that provision for them to do so is contained in—

    (a) the BBC Charter and Agreement, and
    (b) the provisions of this Act and of Part 5 of the 1996 Act,
    to regulate the provision of the BBC's services and the carrying on by the BBC of other activities for purposes connected with the provision of those services.

[132] See further First Report of Select Committee on Culture, Media and Sport (2004) *A Public BBC* HC 82–I.

[133] Section 198 (2) For the purposes of the carrying out of that function OFCOM—

    (a) are to have such powers and duties as may be conferred on them by or under the BBC Charter and Agreement; and
    (b) are entitled, to the extent that they are authorised to do so by the Secretary of State or under the terms of that Charter and Agreement, to act on his behalf in relation to that Charter and Agreement.

The maximum penalty that can be imposed is £250,000 (s 198(5)), although the 2003 Act also confers power on the Secretary of State to substitute a different sum (s 198 (6)).

[134] See Chapter 20 at 1002–3, 1006–7 for further discussion of the position of the BBC in relation to Ofcom.

[135] Review of BBC's Royal Charter *A strong BBC, independent of government*, published May 2005. The White Paper was published in 2006 (see Chapter 20 at 1006, note 65). It may be noted that parts of the Green Paper are to be treated as 'White', including the part on governance and accountability. See HL Paper 50–I, 15.3.05 at [47].

role currently discharged by the Governors.[136] The responsibility currently shared between Ofcom and the Governors for ensuring offence-avoidance will from January 2007 be shared between the BBC Executive and Ofcom, the Trust having an oversight role. This is also true of complaints about fairness and privacy, as discussed in Chapter 17. But, as discussed in Chapter 20, if a complaint relates to the accuracy and impartiality of a programme, the BBC will remain finally responsible.[137] The BBC Trust will deal with such complaints from January 2007 onwards—for the ten years of the new Charter's life. The background to the renewal of the Charter, including the Hutton Report,[138] is discussed fully in Chapter 20. The BBC is now subject to a dual and overlapping system for complaints regarding offence, and this will continue to be the case from 2007. This system hardly makes for clarity in terms of content-based control and could lead to a confused and even conflicting application of standards. In its response to the Green Paper Ofcom proposed that the Government should move towards greater clarity and consistency in content; it argued that the current arrangement, dividing regulation between Ofcom and the BBC, 'risks implying to the public that there are no common standards of acceptability and quality . . .'.[139] The effect of this change on the BBC's traditional independence depends to quite a significant extent on the stance that Ofcom takes under its Code. The possibilities open to Ofcom are discussed below.

(IV) PROTECTION FROM OFFENSIVE MATERIAL UNDER S319 COMMUNICATIONS ACT

The key provision under the 2003 Act in terms of curbing the broadcasting of offensive material is s 319.[140] Section 319(1) of the 2003 Act requires OFCOM to set standards whereby the public is protected from offensive material.[141] The standards objectives for the Code are set out in s 319(2)[142] and include protection for children

---

[136] Ibid at p 10, para 3.1.   [137] See pp 1006–9.

[138] Lord Hutton, Report of the Inquiry into the Circumstances Surrounding the Death of Dr David Kelly C.M.G. (hereafter 'the Hutton Report'). For comment on the Report see G. Smith and D. Sandelson, 'The Future Shape of the BBC—the Hutton Inquiry, Charter Review and the Challenges Facing the BBC and the Government' [2004] Ent LR 15(5) 137–146. See further Chapter 20 at 1004–6.

[139] House of Lords Select Committee on BBC Charter Renewal, HL Paper 50–I, 15.3.05 at [104].

[140] See also s 3(2)(e), concerning the general duty of Ofcom to secure the application of standards to television and radio services, 'that provide adequate protection for members of the public from the inclusion of offensive and harmful material in such services'. That duty is then encapsulated in more detail in s 319.

[141]

(1) It shall be the duty of OFCOM to set, and from time to time to review and revise, such standards for the content of programmes to be included in television and radio services as appear to them best calculated to secure the standards objectives.

[142]

(2) The standards objectives are—
   (a) that persons under the age of eighteen are protected;
   (b) that material likely to encourage or to incite the commission of crime or to lead to disorder is not included in television and radio services . . .

and a warning that responsibility must be exercised in relation to the content of religious programmes.[143] The specific obligation set out in s 319(2)(a), to protect persons under the age of eighteen, is new; the 1990 Act contained no such obligation.

The most general restriction is contained in s 319(2)(f) which provides that 'generally accepted standards are applied to the contents of television and radio services so as to provide adequate protection for members of the public from the inclusion in such services of offensive and harmful material'. The term 'generally accepted standards' can be assumed to refer to changing contemporary ideas of what is offensive material. In contrast, the BSC arguably appeared to work on the assumption that absolute standards could be discerned and maintained as opposed to steadily changing ones.[144]

Section 319(4) gives further guidance as to the matters to be taken into account by Ofcom in securing the standards objectives;[145] they are particularly pertinent in relation to the objective of s 319(2)(f). Section 319(4) does not contain an exhaustive list of the matters that Ofcom must take into account in setting or revising the standards referred to, and, while minimum standards must be apparent under s 319(5)(a) which impliedly reflect the matters listed, Ofcom can take the listed matters into account to the extent that it deems them to be relevant to the securing of the standards objectives. Ofcom is warned not to be too interventionist since it must bear in mind the desirability of maintaining the independence of editorial control over programme content. At the same time it has to consider the extent to which harm or offence may be caused by the inclusion of certain forms of material in programmes.

A distinction is drawn in s 319(4) between material which could give offence in programmes generally, or where it is included in programmes of a particular description. Clearly, this is a crucial distinction: some forms of material may be viewed by

(e) that the proper degree of responsibility is exercised with respect to the content of programmes which are religious programmes

(f) that generally accepted standards are applied to the contents of television and radio services so as to provide adequate protection for members of the public from the inclusion in such services of offensive and harmful material;

[143] In relation to the statutory obligation regarding religious sensibilities, see Ofcom's ruling on the BBC's broadcast of *Jerry Springer: The Opera* in 2005, note 166 below.

[144] BSC Annual Report 1988–89 and Code of Practice 1989, p 41. For comment on the work of the BSC, see F. Coleman, 'All in the best possible taste—the Broadcasting Standards Council 1989–1992' [1992] *PL* 488.

[145] Section 319(4) provides: 'In setting or revising any standards under this section, OFCOM must have regard, in particular and to such extent as appears to them to be relevant to the securing of the standards objectives, to each of the following matters—the degree of harm or offence likely to be caused by the inclusion of any particular sort of material in programmes generally, or in programmes of a particular description; the likely size and composition of the potential audience for programmes included in television and radio services generally, or in television and radio services of a particular description; the likely expectation of the audience as to the nature of a programme's content and the extent to which the nature of a programme's content can be brought to the attention of potential members of the audience; the likelihood of persons who are unaware of the nature of a programme's content being unintentionally exposed, by their own actions, to that content; the desirability of securing that the content of services identifies when there is a change affecting the nature of a service that is being watched or listened to and, in particular, a change that is relevant to the application of the standards set under this section; and the desirability of maintaining the independence of editorial control over programme content.'

Ofcom as too offensive or harmful to be broadcast at all, whereas in most instances the context is the determining factor. The issues most often encountered are likely to concern the suitability of showing particular forms of material before the watershed, or at what point after it, or in the context of a particular type of programme. Context clearly strongly influences audience expectations, and Ofcom is enjoined to take those expectations into account. In coming to such decisions as to contextual suitability, Ofcom must take into account the probable size and composition of the potential audience for particular radio and television programmes. But Ofcom also has to consider the nature of the audience for television and radio services generally. This appears to mean that Ofcom must look beyond the audience that might be attracted to, for example, a sexually explicit film shown late at night and take account of the expectations and wishes of the more general audience who might happen to tune in to it. Clearly, this provision might encourage Ofcom to take a more restrictive approach. The possibility that persons might be unintentionally exposed to the content of a prog-ramme, and the extent to which the nature of a programme's content can be brought to the attention of potential members of the audience, are specifically identified as relevant factors, but it is clearly implicit in this approach that even where a person could take steps to ascertain the content of a programme beforehand (ie outside the context of trailers or adverts which come upon the audience without warning), the programme makers must take their susceptibility to offence into account.

Section 319 has nothing to say about the responsibility of audience members to seek to avoid shock or offence by looking up the guidance given as to the nature of the programme beforehand or using interactive features to do so. The nod in the direc-tion of editorial freedom in s 319(4)(f) does not amount to the far more comprehen-sive guidance which could have been given as to the showing of material at the boundaries of acceptability, such as material from films with an '18' rating which are towards the further end of the '18' classification band.[146] For example, specific guid-ance could have been given as to the conditions under which such material could be broadcast. The use of the term 'offensive' clearly implies that the material covered falls well outside the boundaries of criminal liability created by the common law, statutory indecency provisions, or the Obscene Publications Act 1959,[147] taking account of the 'public good' defence under s 4.[148] As discussed in Chapter 8, those provisions set variable but higher bars in terms of establishing the impact of the material in order to attract liability than is inherent in the term 'offensive'. Section 319 therefore indicates that there is a body of material that cannot be broadcast although it lies well outside the boundaries created by the criminal law relating to explicit expression. At present, the statutory emphasis on the possibility that persons might view such material unawares appears to outweigh the emphasis on seeking to ensure that willing adult

[146] The nature of the '18' rating is discussed in Chapter 12 in relation to the current stance of the British Board of Film Classification (BBFC). See pp 621–30, 632–5.

[147] Under s 162 Broadcasting Act 1990 the 1959 Act is applied to broadcasting; s 162 was not repealed by the Communications Act 2003.

[148] See Chapter 8 at 438–43.

audiences can view such material. It is arguable that a full plurality of standards is not being maintained.

As indicated, it is extremely unlikely that a broadcast could fall foul of the Obscene Publications Act 1959. However, given the 'likely audience' test used in obscenity law, as discussed in Chapter 8,[149] an argument could conceivably be made that the transmission of a film on television changes the analysis of that audience, since individuals, including children or teenagers, switching between channels at random, could be confronted by explicit images without warning. Since obscenity is a relative concept, judged by its effect on a significant proportion of the likely audience, a televised film could be adjudged obscene where that would not be the case if it was made available only by hiring a DVD, since the publicity material on the DVD case, together with the age rating for the film, would give the individual some warning of its likely content. It would be even less likely that the same film could be viewed as obscene when shown in the cinema, since entrance to the cinema would be age-restricted;[150] further, the advertisements for the film would provide a warning. Given therefore, that when a film is broadcast on television, there is the possibility of a number of younger people stumbling upon it unawares, it is possible to conceive of a particular broadcast being deemed obscene, though the film itself obviously had not been—by the film regulator, the BBFC.[151] Since 'hard core' pornography—film material rated R18—is not broadcast on television under the current regulatory regime,[152] this is highly improbable, but the possibility cannot be completely ruled out. However, it could be dealt with using the various protective devices discussed below.

(V) OFCOM'S BROADCAST CODE[153]

Until 2005 Ofcom relied on the ITC Code and on the BSC Standards Code, although it was in the process of developing its own new Code. The new Code now applies[154] to programmes, advertisements[155] and text broadcast on all forms of television services and radio, including satellite and cable channels. Ofcom made a deliberate decision to discard the ITC and BSC Codes on offence-avoidance and to make a fresh start with its own Code. Clearly, one option would have been merely to adopt the ITC Programme Code as it stood, with some modifications due to Ofcom's broader remit.

---

[149] See pp 429–31.   [150] See Chapter 12 at 621–3.

[151] For the standards the BBFC currently uses in classifying films see Chapter 12 at 621–35. Clearly, it would not classify a film that might be obscene within the meaning of the OPA 1959.

[152] See p 602 below.

[153] Under s 324(1), before setting standards under s 319, Ofcom was under a duty to publish a draft of the Code which sets the standards. It was also under a duty to consult with the bodies affected by the Code before finalising it. They included the licensees, the BBC, persons appearing to Ofcom to represent the interests of those who watch television programmes, and persons appearing to Ofcom to represent the interests of those who will have to take account of the contents of the proposed standards for advertising or sponsorship. During 2004 and early 2005 Ofcom promulgated a draft Code and engaged in the process of consultation.

[154] It came into force on 25 July 2005.

[155] As noted above, pp 593–5, broadcast advertisements are under the remit of the Advertising Standards Authority, working in partnership with Ofcom.

The ITC Code would have had the advantage of familiarity as far as the independent broadcasters were concerned, and also it had evolved over a number of years, taking into account the ITC's experience in monitoring it. It had also undergone an incremental process of liberalization. However, Ofcom decided instead to make a clean break and to introduce a new Code which, while it retains certain basic features of the ITC Code, differs from it significantly in a number of respects.

Ofcom's new Code places the emphasis more strongly than the ITC Code did on the avoidance of harm, rather than on the imprecise and subjective idea of avoidance of offence and the maintenance of standards of 'good taste'. It also places greater emphasis on the use of warnings rather than on restricting the broadcast of certain forms of material. Thus it assumes up to a point that the audience can exercise choice and protect itself from shock. It further assumes that people are entitled to view a wide and diverse range of programmes. It is less comprehensive and detailed than the last (2003) version of the ITC Code and, clearly, it is possible that Ofcom will have to make it more detailed in future when it issues revised versions of the 2005 Code.

The Code places quite a strong emphasis on free expression principles and on editorial responsibility since it is less extensive and prescriptive than the ITC and BSC Codes. Nevertheless, in a number of specific instances it is very precise and provides clear and unequivocal rules.[156] The prescriptive terms used indicate that a number of the rules are mandatory rather than advisory or discretionary. In those instances, then, broadcasters clearly lay themselves open to the possibility of an adverse adjudication for breach of the Code if they do not follow the rules. However, the use of clear and precise rules, so long as their restraining effect is kept to a minimum, does obviate the potentially chilling effect of imprecision.

The Code is more firmly based on the principle of allowing for creative freedom than the two previous Codes were. To this end, Ofcom's Code creates a clear dividing line between provisions applicable to children and to adults, whereas the ITC Code provisions applied on their face to both children and adults, and various rather clumsy qualifications were introduced in order to clarify the application of the provisions. The ITC Programme Code, s 1.2 was headed 'Family Viewing Policy, Offence to Good Taste and Decency, Portrayal of Violence and Respect for Human Dignity'. It attempted to strike a balance between preserving good taste and decency on the one hand and avoiding too great a restraint on freedom of speech on the other. It therefore allowed sexual scenes under s 1.6 so long as they were defensible in context. (Under the previous version of s 1.6 sexual scenes had to be presented with 'tact and discretion'.) Under the family viewing policy set out in s 1.2 (and reflected in s 1.6), the ITC accepted that a compromise was necessary between protecting children and ensuring that a wide range of programmes suitable for adults were broadcast. It did not seek to ensure that unsuitable material would never be viewed by a few children. The rules assumed a 'progressive decline throughout the evening in the proportion of children present in the audience'.

---

[156] See e.g. ss 1.1, 1.2, and 1.5 of the Code.

Section 1 of Ofcom's Code is headed 'Protecting the under-Eighteens', while s 2 relates to protection from harmful or offensive material generally. It can be assumed therefore that s 2 relates mainly, although not exclusively, to adults. Ofcom's stance is welcome since it allows for a greater focus on the need for restrictions applicable largely to adult programming, and on their basis. Since the ITC Code did not create a clear dividing line between such programming and that aimed at children it appeared more restrictive—there appeared to be a greater possibility that adult viewing would be restricted in order to protect children. Ofcom's Code also lays greater emphasis—depending on Ofcom's interpretation of it in practice—on protecting persons from the inadvertent viewing of offensive material, not by barring it from broadcasts, but by requiring that it is accompanied by extensive warnings.

Ofcom's Code places a strong emphasis on protecting children, not by restricting or banning the showing of explicit material completely, but by showing it at certain times, either after the watershed, or by avoiding times when 'children are particularly likely to be listening'. Ofcom's Code is also more specific than the ITC one in relation to what should not be shown when children are likely to be viewers. Only 'material that might *seriously* impair the moral, mental or physical development of children (emphasis added)' must not be broadcast.[157] (The wording is taken from the Television Without Frontiers Directive, 1997, Art 22.1.)[158] In other words, the Code is focused on the avoidance of serious and specific harms to children (defined as those under 15). But under s 1.2 material that might merely *impair* their development in the ways specified *can* be shown so long as 'appropriate scheduling or technical devices' are used. The reference to scheduling means, following ss 1.3 and 1.4, that the material must be shown after the watershed and the probable number and age of the children present in the audience must be taken into account. If encoding is not used, 'a clear verbal warning' must be given prior to the programme. Encoding clearly provides an effective means of protecting children while allowing adults to view a range of material, including explicit or potentially disturbing material. The possibility of using encoding was not given as much prominence in the ITC code.

The use of the term 'seriously impair' creates on its face a more liberal standard than that used in the Obscene Publications Act 1959 with its use of the terms 'deprave and corrupt'. In other words, material that might *merely* impair, but not to a serious extent, can be broadcast, whereas material that creates any level of depravity or corruption is, at first sight, caught by the OPA. In fact, the test under the OPA is not currently interpreted in this fashion,[159] but the apparent closeness of the boundaries between the two tests is of interest since, taking the previous regime into account, one would expect a broadcast regulatory body to impose standards lying well within the borders of the basic OPA test.

However, Ofcom's Code also speaks of appropriate scheduling for 'material

---

[157] Section 1.1.   [158] Dir 89/552 as amended by Directive 97/36.

[159] See Chapter 8 at 431–6; see also S. Edwards, 'On the Contemporary Application of the Obscene Publications Act' (1998) *Crim LR* 843.

unsuitable for children'—a much more imprecise term than the terms used in the Directive. Like the ITC Code, the new Code makes it reasonably clear in s 1.4 that such material can be shown later in the evening, but its stance is equally imprecise, leaving broadcasters uncertain as to what can be shown and in what context. The ITC Code s 1.3 also set out the wording from the Television without Frontiers Directive, but indicated that the requirement regarding 'suitable' material to show children was *additional* to it. Ofcom's Code begins with the Directive's wording, indicating that it is focusing on the avoidance of serious harms, whereas the ITC Code began with the wording from s 6(1)(a) of the 1990 Act concerning the avoidance of material offensive to good taste and decency.

In general, the emphasis of Ofcom's Code as regards children is on the use of various devices to protect them (the use of the watershed, detailed warnings, Pin protection and encoding of material), rather than on bans or on making cuts in the material. '18'-rated films can be shown at any time while 'adult–sex' material can be shown between 2200 and 0530 so long as protections are in place to ensure that children cannot view the material.[160] A very clear distinction is drawn between pay-per-view and ordinary broadcasting, although 'R18' material still cannot be broadcast since Ofcom finds, on the basis of research it recently conducted, that the current Pin security environment does not provide an effective safeguard against children accessing such material or its equivalent.[161] The convergence that appears to be occurring between video and 'pay per view' broadcasting suggests that the current distinction between what can be shown on the two media is likely eventually to disappear. In fact, ironically, it may now be less likely that children would view R18 material in Pin-protected broadcasts than on video, once videos are brought into the home by adults.

Section 2 of the Code, focussing more on adult viewing, is aimed at ensuring that broadcasters provide 'adequate protection for viewers and listeners from the inclusion of harmful or offensive material', judged against 'generally accepted standards'. It is noticeable that the 'protection' to be provided in s 2 centres more on the provision of

---

[160] **1.23** Pay per view services may broadcast up to BBFC 18-rated films or their equivalent, at any time of day provided: there is a protection system pre 2100 and post 0530 (a mandatory PIN or other equivalent protection), that seeks satisfactorily to restrict access solely to those authorised to view when material other than BBFC U-rated or PG-rated or their equivalents is shown; information is provided about programme content that will assist adults to assess its suitability for children; there is a detailed billing system for subscribers which clearly itemises all viewing including viewing times and dates; and those security systems which are in place to protect children are clearly explained to all subscribers. **1.24** Premium subscription services and pay per view/night services may broadcast 'adult–sex' material between 2200 and 0530 provided that in addition to other protections mentioned above: there is a mandatory PIN protected encryption system, or other equivalent protection, that seeks satisfactorily to restrict access solely to those authorised to view; and there are measures in place that ensure that the subscriber is an adult. **1.25** BBFC R18-rated films or their equivalent must not be broadcast.

[161] In May 2005 Ofcom conducted a research study, *Research into the Effectiveness of PIN protection systems in the UK.* It found that a high percentage of children (about 50 per cent of those in the relevant houses surveyed) knew that a PIN number was needed to access blocked channels, and of those children about 50 per cent knew of their parents' PIN number; of those just under half had used the number to access pay per view programmes without their parents' permission. Ofcom concluded that security methods in the current PIN environment are not likely to prevent children from accessing 'R18' material.

information, rather than on making cuts in the material. This is made clear in s 2.3. At the same time s 2.3 makes it clear that if the use of potentially offensive language and material—in particular, the inclusion of scenes of violence or sex, sexual violence, or scenes of humiliation, distress or the use of discriminatory treatment or language must be justified by the context, implying that otherwise they should not be broadcast or should be cut. The term 'context' refers *inter alia* to a number of the factors outlined in s 319 (4)(a),(b),(c), and (d) of the Communications Act.[162] But s 2.3 also accepts that if information is included—presumably in the form of consumer advice and detailed warnings as to content—it can assist in preventing offence.

The ITC Code left less discretion to the broadcasters. Under s 1.6 of the ITC Code sexual scenes were not to be shown until after 9 pm except in the case of nature programmes, educational programmes or where the representation was non-graphic. Graphic portrayal of sexual violence was only exceptionally justifiable. Violence in general was covered by s 1.7, which set out a number of factors to be kept in mind, including the content of the programme schedules as a whole and the policy of family viewing time. The s 1.7 rules were not in general very specific, but they did provide that violence should not be shown for its own sake and that ingenious, easily imitated methods of inflicting pain or injury should not be included. The previous version of s1.6 concluded: 'In so sensitive an area risks require special justification. When in doubt, cut.'

Section 2, in contrast to the provisions of the ITC Code, is far more specific. After the general provisions regarding the broadcasting of explicit material in ss 2.1 and 2.3, it focuses, in the following sections, on a range of specific harms to be avoided.[163]

---

162 See above note 145, p 597.

163

2.4 Programmes must avoid anything that individually, and/or taken as a whole and in context, is likely to encourage violent, dangerous or seriously antisocial behaviour.

2.5 The means or methods of suicide and self harm must not be included in programmes except where the context, scheduling and likely audience can justify them.

2.6 Demonstrations of exorcism, the occult, the paranormal, divination and related practices must be treated with due objectivity. Entertainment programmes that contain such demonstrations must be clearly labelled as such for the audience. No potentially life changing advice may be given. (Religious programmes are exempted from the rule about life-changing advice but must, in any event, comply with the provisions in the section regarding religious programmes in this Code.) (Please also note the scheduling restrictions contained in section 1 of this Code.) Films, dramas and fiction generally are not bound by this rule.

Meaning of 'life-changing':
Life-changing advice includes advice about health, finances, employment, relationships etc.

2.7 Broadcasters must prevent hypnosis being induced in susceptible viewers and listeners.

2.9 Programmes must not use techniques which exploit the possibility of conveying a message to viewers or listeners, or of otherwise influencing their minds, without their being aware, or fully aware, of what has occurred.

2.10 Television broadcasters must minimise the risk to viewers who have photosensitive epilepsy. . . .

3.1 Material likely to encourage or incite crime, or likely to lead to disorder must not be included in television or radio services.

3.2 Material that enables viewers or listeners to commit crime must not be included in television or radio services. . . .

Beginning with the opening words about taste and decency in s 1.1, the ITC Code was more general and much more extensive.[164] The difference between the provision in the two Codes regarding feature films is especially striking. The ITC Code laid down a series of very specific provisions in relation to the scheduling of films which depended on the age classification. Section 1.4 of that Code provided that the BBFC video classification—not the classification for the cinematic release—should always be used as a guide, if one existed. As discussed below, the video classification tends to be stricter, since different considerations apply to videos under the Video Recordings Act 1984. Under s 1.4, which covered feature films, it set out rules which followed the guidelines laid down by the British Board of Film Classification BBFC for films and videos (see Chapter 12): '18' rated films could be shown, but only after 10 pm;[165] '15' rated films were not normally to start before 9 pm, while '12' rated films were not to start before 8 pm. In contrast, Ofcom's Code provides, in s 1.20: 'No version of a film or programme refused certification by the British Board of Film Classification (BBFC) may be broadcast.' Material rated 'R18' cannot be shown; '18' rated films can be shown after 9.00 but even after that point they may be viewed as 'unsuitable' (s. 1.21). As to suitability, Ofcom presumably takes the view that the provisions relating to the portrayal of sex and violence, and the showing of disturbing material in general in s 1 regarding children and in s 2, cover the scheduling of films. But it is clear that Ofcom's

---

3.6 Material must not be broadcast that could endanger lives or prejudice the success of attempts to deal with a hijack or kidnapping.

164

1.6 Sex and Nudity
Similar considerations apply. Much great fiction and drama have been concerned with love and passion which can shock and disturb. Popular entertainment and comedy have always relied to some extent on sexual innuendo and suggestive behaviour but gratuitous offence should be avoided.

Careful consideration should be given to nudity before the watershed but some nudity may be justifiable in a non-sexual and relevant context.

Representations of sexual intercourse should not occur before the watershed unless there is a serious educational purpose. Any portrayal of sexual behaviour must be defensible in context. If included before the watershed it must be appropriately limited and inexplicit.

Sex scenes of a more adult nature, which are more graphic and prolonged, should be limited to much later in the schedule. (See also s 1.3(i))

1.7 Violence
The real world contains violence in many forms. It is reasonable for television to reflect this but it is clear that the portrayal of violence, whether physical, verbal or psychological, can upset, disturb and offend and can be accused of desensitising viewers, of making them unduly fearful or of encouraging imitation. These are legitimate public concerns requiring careful consideration whenever violence, real or simulated, is to be shown. The treatment of violence must always be appropriate to the context, scheduling, channel and audience expectations.

a) Offensive violence
At the simplest level, some portrayed acts of violence may go beyond the bounds of what is tolerable in that they could be classified as material which, in the words of the Broadcasting Act, is 'likely to be offensive to public feeling'.

165 e.g. s 1.4 (c) 'No "18" rated version should start before 10pm on any service. This rule may be relaxed if the classification was made more than 10 years ago and the film is now clearly suitable for earlier transmission.'

Code is somewhat less prescriptive in this respect and leaves greater discretion to the broadcasters. But the BBFC standards are regarded as minimum ones; the mere fact that a film has an '18' certificate is not to be taken as implying that it is clearly proper to broadcast it.

It can be said that Ofcom's Code accords with the liberal free speech account of restrictions on broadcasting discussed above in so far as it concentrates on the avoidance of specific harms, and largely avoids the use of broad statements about ensuring the promotion of 'good taste and decency'. It strikes a balance between offence avoidance and the right of adult television audiences to receive a diverse range of broadcast expression, which differs somewhat from the balance struck under the superceded Codes. The ability of people to take responsibility for protecting themselves from offence is more strongly emphasized. The restrictions placed on films shown on television appear to be more in line with those placed on videos, as discussed in Chapter 12, although it remains the case that 'hard core' pornography cannot be broadcast. Since videos and the internet also come into the home this relaxation of the rules is readily defensible.

An indication of the stance Ofcom is currently taking was given when, in 2005, Ofcom cleared the BBC of flouting the BSC Code in relation to *Jerry Springer—the Opera*. 16,801 complaints had been received in relation to the programme which satirized features of Christianity.[166] Ofcom considered in particular the question of

---

[166] The BBC's Governors Programme Complaints Committee had also considered the complaints; it found: 'in all the circumstances, the outstanding artistic significance of the programme outweighed the offence which it caused to some viewers and so the broadcasting of the programme was justified'.

Extracts from Ofcom's adjudication: **Sections 26 and 27—Respect and Dignity.** The Code states that 'challenging and deliberately flouting the boundaries of taste in drama and comedy is a time-honoured tradition. Although these programmes have a special freedom, this does not give them unlimited licence to be cruel or to humiliate individuals or groups gratuitously'. Ofcom recognises that a great number of complainants felt that the Opera denigrated the Christian religion. The show was created as a caricature of modern television. Importantly, in Ofcom's view the Opera did not gratuitously humiliate individuals or any groups and in particular the Christian community. Its target was television and fame. *Conclusion: The programme did not contravene these sections of the Code.* **Sections 43–45—Offences against Religious Sensibilities.** The Code states that 'Although religions should not be exempt from (the) critical scrutiny . . . particular care should be taken when referring to religion in entertainment'. Many complainants accused the BBC of committing the crime of blasphemy. However, criminal law is not a matter for Ofcom but for the courts. Ofcom is not required to determine whether the BBC committed blasphemy, but whether, in this case, the provisions of the Code had been contravened. . . . Ofcom has sought to achieve the appropriate balance between, on the one hand the standards set in the Code (ex-BSC Code on Standards) and the need to apply those standards to give adequate protection from harmful and offensive material, and on the other hand the need, as appropriate, to guarantee freedom of expression. Freedom of expression is particularly important in the context of artistic works, beliefs, philosophy and argument. . . . Their main concern arose from the depictions of figures at the heart of the complainants' religious beliefs. In considering offence against religious sensibilities, Ofcom took into account the clear context of the Opera. The fictional Jerry Springer lay dying in a delusional state. As he hallucinated, this character was asked to pitch Jesus against the Devil in his own confessional talk show. This '*dream*' sequence was emphasised by the fact that the same actors, who played guests on his show in the first act played the characters in the second act. What resulted was a cartoon, full of grotesque images, which challenged the audience's views about morality and the human condition. The production made clear that all the characters in the second act were the product of the fictional Springer's imagination: *his* concepts of Satan, God, Jesus and the others and modelled on the guests in his show. . . . In light of this, Ofcom did not

offence against religious sensibilities and balanced the possibility of offence against the need to protect freedom of expression. In coming to this finding, Ofcom took into account the significance of the work. This was a very important and telling decision, bearing in mind the subject matter of the programme and the extremely large number of complaints; it may be taken to indicate that Ofcom is taking a robust stance in relation to creative freedom. However, this was not borne out recently by Ofcom's stance in relation to the timing of the broadcast of *Pulp Fiction* by the BBC.[167]

It may be concluded that in so far as the ITC Code in its various manifestations was gradually becoming more liberal, Ofcom's Code takes this process further. But although the Code is on its face a liberalizing measure when compared with the ITC and BSC's Codes, a number of open-ended terms are used and the level of detail of those Codes is missing. Thus Ofcom has a great deal of leeway to take a range of approaches in terms of liberality and the preservation of creative freedom when it

---

believe that the characters represented were, in the context of this piece, conveyed as faithful or accurate representations of religious figures, but were characterisations of the show's participants. . . . It is not within Ofcom's remit to record a contravention of the Code on the basis that Christianity, as opposed to another faith, was the subject of *Jerry Springer: The Opera*. In considering freedom of expression, Ofcom recognises the UK's long-standing tradition of satirising political and religious figures and celebrities. Ofcom must consider each programme on its merits. No contravention was found. Ofcom broadcast bulletin 34, 9 May 2005. See Ofcom's website 10.5.05. An application to seek judicial review of the BBC's decision to screen the film, by the Christian Institute and other groups, was refused by the Honourable Mr Justice Crane, judgment dated 27 May 2005.

[167] **Report:** *Pulp Fiction BBC 2, 7 August 2004, 21:10*
Nine viewers complained about the transmission of this film. The majority were concerned that its transmission shortly after the 21:00 watershed, when young people watch television, could encourage anti-social behaviour. Overall, viewers felt that the strong content, including graphic violence, seriously offensive swearing and scenes of drug abuse, made the film unsuitable at a time in the evening when young people and children were still part of the audience.

    Response: The BBC believed that, as this film was arguably one of the most influential and best-known films of the last ten years, it was unlikely to surprise or offend BBC2 viewers. The BBC had shown this film on five previous occasions and complaints had steadily declined, with this transmission attracting only one complaint to the BBC. The BBC said that the film was a serious cultural achievement and deserved to be made available to a wide audience. Even for this fifth BBC screening, the BBC stated that it did not neglect its obligation to alert viewers who were unfamiliar with the film. It had provided written and broadcast warnings about aspects of the content that some viewers might not have found to their taste.

    Decision: Ofcom has no issue with the points the BBC wish to make about the editorial and cultural merits of the film. The film has been shown before on BBC2. However, all other transmissions on BBC2 were at 21:45 or later. We acknowledge the steps taken to warn viewers about the content of this film and we know that audience research suggests that viewers are more tolerant of adult content in films, preferring them to be unedited. However, this has to be balanced against the expectations of the general audience, who are available to view terrestrial television at this time and the context of the material, on that evening, within the schedule. On this occasion, the film was shown at 21:10 on a Saturday night. Audience figures show that 8% (124,000) of the audience for this film were aged 15 years and under. A combination of seriously offensive language, graphic violence and drug-abuse occurred early in the film, before 21:30. Under the relevant Code, 18 films are not prohibited but the content should be suitable for the time of transmission. Such intense material is not normally expected so soon after the watershed. We believe the scheduling of this film at 21:10 was too early, given the strong, adult content from the start. **The scheduling of this film was in contravention of the Code**

    Note: This case has been appealed three times by the BBC. This decision was made by the Content Board following the BBC's third and final appeal.

adjudicates on alleged breaches of the Code. It also has a lot of room for manouevre in drafting future manifestations of the Code. Since it is unlikely that there will be much or any court intervention in Ofcom's regulatory scheme, after the *ProLife* decision, the provisions of the Code and Ofcom's stance towards them provide the key mechanisms for protecting free speech in broadcasting. Nevertheless, it is to the possibilities of court intervention under the HRA that this chapter now turns.

THE POTENTIAL EFFECTS OF THE HUMAN RIGHTS ACT AND THE IMPLICATIONS OF THE *PROLIFE ALLIANCE* DECISION FOR THE CURRENT REGIME

THE PUBLIC AUTHORITY/PRIVATE BODY DISTINCTION

Ofcom and the public sector broadcasters are susceptible to challenge under the Human Rights Act. Ofcom is probably a core public authority under s 6(1)HRA; it has clear governmental functions since is a regulator set up by government. In any event, it is clearly a functional public authority.[168] In discussing the meaning of 'public function' under s 6(3)(b) HRA, Chapter 3 pointed out that the BBC is almost certainly a functional public authority under s 6(3) HRA.[169] It can be viewed as a governmental body in being set up under a Royal Charter. Acceptance of its status as a functional public authority appeared to be implicit in *ProLife Alliance*, although, as discussed, the judges were reluctant to engage in argument as to the mechanisms of the HRA.

Assuming that the BBC is a functional public authority, there is then immense room for argument as to those functions it has that are 'public'. There is nothing inherently public about broadcasting, and if the BBC were to be viewed as acting publicly in relation to all aspects of programme-making, this would set up a clear anomaly in relation to the private broadcasters since they would be performing the same function but would not bound by the HRA. Clearly, a distinction could be drawn between the BBC's function as a broadcaster and as a regulator, finding that it is providing a public function in the latter role but not the former. This would be a sensible line to draw, although it is not without its difficulties. This stance can be viewed as implicit in *ProLife*. This would mean that when the BBC regulates its *own* programmes it is performing a public function. Thus, decisions as to filming techniques and the making of programmes might not be viewed as 'public', while decisions to allow a programme to be broadcast taken at senior level would be.[170] Decisions taken in relation to offence-avoidance could be viewed as public as so closely associated with the BBC's core role in providing programming for public consumption. Clearly, s 6 HRA inevitably creates difficult decisions and anomalies in

---

[168] See Chapter 3 at 112–22.   [169] See pp 114–22.   [170] See Chapter 3 at 120–2.

relation to the public/private divide. The BBC provides an especially difficult example. But it must be noted for the purposes of this chapter that, assuming it is a public authority in relation to decisions to broadcast, it is hard to imagine a situation in which a Convention right could be invoked against it in response to a positive decision to broadcast a programme that then caused offence. There is no Convention right not to be offended—the only possible candidate would be Article 9 in relation to offending against religious sensibilities.[171] The public/private function divide is far more significant in relation to invasion of privacy, discussed in Chapter 17.

Channel 4 may possibly have the status of a functional public authority since it has public service functions, but the independent broadcasting companies are almost certainly private bodies for HRA purposes. Thus the independent broadcasters cannot be challenged directly under the HRA. However, in any court action against Ofcom or the BBC concerning relevant sections of the 2003 Act, an interpretation of the provisions should of course be adopted, under s 3(1) HRA, which accords with the demands of Article 10. Any resultant modification of the Act by interpretation, or as a result of a declaration of incompatibility under s 4 HRA, would then affect the independent broadcasters. If s 319 itself were affected in this way the effect would be indirect—as a result of a change in Ofcom's stance. Also, as public authorities, Ofcom and the BBC must take the demands of Article 10 into account in coming to any decisions relating to content restrictions.

The *ProLife Alliance* decision, with its strong emphasis on deference to the regulatory scheme and the regulator, gave little encouragement to the use of the HRA as a means of challenging restrictive decisions relating to broadcast material or the restrictions themselves. However, using a different approach, or on other, more compelling, facts a successful challenge remains a possibility. Overly restrictive decisions of public sector broadcasters and of Ofcom under the 'offensive material' provisions of s 319 of the 2003 Act and the current Code could theoretically be challenged by a programme-maker under s 7(1)(a) HRA, relying on Article 10. A challenge to Ofcom's use of its powers would normally have to occur after the event since Ofcom does not have censorship powers.

ARTICLE 10 JURISPRUDENCE

There are some grounds for thinking that the inception of the Human Rights Act might have called the previous regime into question and might still do so as regards the current one. In this context the restraints on broadcast expression relate to offence-avoidance. Such restraints can be justified only where they meet the Art 10(2) tests.[172] In particular they would have to be proportionate to the aims of protecting morality or the rights of others. On the face of it, one might not expect the restrictions on the basis of avoiding offence—essentially of a similar nature under the previous

---

[171] See *Otto Preminger* (1994) 19 EHRR 34, discussed in Chapter 9 at 488–94.
[172] Discussed in Chapter 2.

and the current regimes—to meet those tests since the term 'offence' is so broad and imprecise. However, as discussed in Chapter 8, the Convention jurisprudence interpreting Article 10(2) notoriously does not uphold freedom of expression very strongly where restrictions protecting children from offence in respect of non-political speech are concerned. Thus the possibility of mounting challenges to the decisions of regulators or broadcasters in court was always likely to be problematic since the regulatory regime tends to have its greatest impact on artistic rather than political speech. The message of political expression can frequently, although not invariably, be conveyed without the use of potentially offensive words or images. As discussed, a strong pronouncement was made in *Handyside*[173] to the effect that Art 10(1) covers speech which some might find offensive, but the Court went on to find that in the instance before it such speech (albeit of ideological significance) could justifiably be suppressed, and it reached this decision on the basis of conceding a wide margin of appreciation to the state since there is no uniform European conception of moral standards.[174] It can therefore readily be said in this context that the Article 10 standard is 'soft-edged': applied domestically, it very clearly leaves room for the adoption of either an activist or a minimalist approach, and *ProLife* adopted the latter approach. It might well support quite far-reaching restrictions on broadcasting owing to the possibility that children might be affected.

But, as discussed in Chapter 8, in the line of authority stemming from *Handyside*,[175] a broad margin of appreciation was conceded to the state in finding against the applicant, especially where offensive 'artistic' speech was concerned—using that term loosely.[176] The pronouncement in *Handyside* to the effect that Art 10(1) covers offensive speech runs presumptively directly counter to the previous provision against such speech in broadcasting in s 6(1)(a) 1990 Act, aspects of the BBC's Agreement, s 108 1996 Act, and now s 319 of the 2003 Act. Since the domestic courts are not required to concede a margin of appreciation to the state, there is a case for expecting them to take a stricter stance in relation to restraints on broadcast speech. But, as discussed earlier, the *ProLife* decision has in effect replaced the margin of appreciation doctrine in this context with a domestic deference doctrine.

But the use of the Convention jurisprudence on both political and—if afforded a creative interpretation—artistic expression,[177] has in principle the potential, applied domestically, to challenge accepted conceptions of offence-avoidance in broadcasting. This argument is reasonably strong in relation to restrictions on all forms of broadcasting on the ground of offence-avoidance, including soap operas, 'reality' TV programmes, and films. It is even stronger in relation to forms of political broadcasting, such as Party Political Broadcasts, Election Broadcasts, news programmes and documentaries since, as Chapter 3 discussed, the Strasbourg jurisprudence defends political

---

[173] See p 411.   [174] See pp 411–12.   [175] See pp 413–22.

[176] As discussed, the effect of the doctrine should be irrelevant in the domestic courts since the margin of appreciation doctrine is an international one with no application domestically. See Chapter 3 at 145–7.

[177] See Chapter 2 at 37–44, 50–71.

expression in the media very strongly—as decisions such as that in *Jersild*[178] demonstrate. *Handyside*, as discussed above, concerned expression that could be viewed only as a very marginal form of political speech. Mainstream, 'core', political expression, even accompanied by explicit images, could in principle be treated as far more analogous with the expression in *Jersild*, which concerned the broadcast of a programme containing grossly racist language. If this argument were to be accepted, restraints based on offence-avoidance, particularly if applied to such speech, would be found to breach Article 10 as impermissibly over-broad.

CURRENT EFFECTS OF *PROLIFE* AND ITS UNREALIZED POTENTIAL

Before the *ProLife Alliance* decision it would have appeared to follow from the Strasbourg free speech principles that the Ofcom regulatory regime upholding offence-avoidance standards might have been found to conflict with the standards maintained by Article 10 in the realm of political speech. The balance to be struck in this instance between freedom of expression and the responsibilities of Ofcom and the broadcasters in relation to allowing for the intrusion of offensive material into the home might have been re-determined by the courts. Changes to the relevant Code might have had to be made as a consequence, differentiating between forms of political broadcasting and pure entertainment. The result of such a challenge could have led to an extension of editorial freedom in one sense since there was a possibility that explicit and disturbing material which would previously have been rejected could be broadcast. On the other hand, the broadcasters' understanding of the balance in question and their semi-autonomous policing of it could have been viewed as undermined. However, the *ProLife Alliance* decision now appears to render improbable a successful challenge to the regime governing offence-avoidance.

The appeal of the BBC in the *ProLife Alliance* case was allowed on the basis that there was no ground for interfering with the decision reached by the BBC as regulator and the broadcasters, taking account of their special expertise. The outcome means that the broadcasters' freedom within that particular statutory framework—which in essence is now encapsulated in s 319 of the 2003 Act—was re-affirmed. The HRA did not operate as a mechanism enabling the courts to wield (or claim) significantly greater powers of interference in broadcasters' decisions as to their responsibilities in respect of maintaining standards of taste and decency—even in respect of political speech. The same stance is now likely to be taken in respect of the new statutory framework if a similar case arises.

Thus Ofcom, and to an extent the broadcasters, are still largely free to decide on the balance between freedom of expression and fulfilling their responsibilities to avoid violating viewers' expectations based, under s 319(2)(f), on current standards of offensiveness and taste and decency as to what can be shown. But a further freedom—to escape in certain contexts from the constraints of such standards—has not been

---

[178] (1994) 19 EHRR 1. See further Chapter 2 at 46, and Chapter 9 at 516.

achieved. Of course, in relation to Party Election Broadcasts—where the broadcasters' own editorial freedom is not at stake—they might not immediately see the value of such a freedom, valuing instead their own control over broadcasting. However, in other contexts concerning political speech, broadcasting creativity and editorial independence might be viewed as more obviously at stake. If, for example, an independent broadcaster wished to broadcast a documentary which relied on very disturbing, explicit images from a war or disaster zone, but it was clear from Ofcom's Code that so doing would be likely to attract a financial penalty, the broadcaster could, as a last resort, mount a challenge under Art 10 against Ofcom, relying on s 7(1)(a) HRA. The *ProLife Alliance* decision, however, suggests that such a challenge would be unlikely to succeed due to the high level of deference conceded to the expert regulator, and therefore indirectly to Parliament.

SUCCESSFUL CHALLENGES TO THE CURRENT REGULATORY REGIME?

Nevertheless, successful HRA challenges to the current regime under the 2003 Act are conceivable, despite the *ProLife* decision. A claim could occur in relation to any form of broadcasting affected by the offence-avoidance Code rules, but clearly it would be most likely to succeed in the context of political broadcasting. It is nevertheless important to point out that the following remarks could also apply to, for example, films of strong artistic merit if the relevant Art 10 jurisprudence was applied, but the effects of the margin of appreciation doctrine were disapplied[179] at the domestic level. Thus while the strongest impetus for change could come in the realm of political expression, it is not ruled out in relation to other forms.

A departure from the *ProLife Alliance* decision could come about if a case on a similar factual basis arose but the challenge was to the new statutory framework itself—specifically s 319—as requiring re-interpretation under s 3 (1) HRA in order to achieve compatibility with the demands of Art 10. The decision in *ProLife Alliance* does not stand in the way of such a reinterpretation since the House of Lords deliberately considered only the application of the statutory provisions and not the provisions themselves.[180] The 2003 Act does not exempt PEBs from the s 319 requirements or the Ofcom Code, which applies to all forms of broadcasting. Thus, post-HRA Parliament did make the deliberate decision to continue to subject PEBs to the offence-avoidance requirements. Courts will inevitably consider that they should pay some deference to that decision, following *ProLife*. Nevertheless, the majority in the House of Lords left open the possibility that a challenge to the equivalent provisions under the previous regime might have succeeded. It may be noted that, as discussed

---

[179] As discussed in Chapter 8, a case can be made for arguing that comments at Strasbourg sometimes support forms of artistic expression fairly strongly, but inconsistently. See pp 415–16.

[180] If a challenge was mounted to the application of the rules themselves the outcome would probably be the same as in *ProLife* unless the decision to ban an election video was a far more marginal one.

above, the 2003 Act was *not* declared compatible with the Convention rights under s 19 HRA.[181] However, it can be assumed that the rest of the Act was viewed by Parliament as compatible with Article 10 and therefore it should be treated in the same way as any other Act of Parliament.[182]

Section 3(1) HRA could be used to impose a different interpretation on s 319, reducing its impact quite dramatically in relation to PEBs or other forms of political broadcasting. As a result, where such forms were concerned, quite a radical modification of ss1 and 2 of Ofcom's Code could be brought about by interpretation. The demands of offence-avoidance as a standards objective could be minimized in the context of political broadcasting. Such a modification may be possible since, although s 319 does cover PEBs, it is more nuanced and goes into more detail regarding context and audience expectations than s 6(1)(a) of the 1990 Act or s108 of the 1996 Act did. Such matters were only taken into account previously by the ITC Programme Code and the BSC Standards Code. Section 319(4)(a)–(d) could be viewed as a gateway to allowing the radical re-interpretation suggested. For example, the term 'generally accepted standards' used in s 319(f) in relation to the protection of the public from 'offensive material' could be interpreted to mean that greater leeway should be accorded to PEBs since such standards can be assumed to accord particular weight to the non-tramelling of political expression. The comments of the Court of Appeal in *ProLife* as to the greater public tolerance of controversial and explicit images in the context of serious political speech should be borne in mind.[183] There is a case for limited deference to Parliament here since the re-interpretation argued for would not go against the grain of the statute or necessitate reading words into it, and the question of balancing the societal interest in maintaining standards of decency in broadcasting against the demands of free speech, is very much one within the Courts' constitutional sphere under the HRA.[184]

Such a re-intepretation of s 319(f), and the resultant effect on ss1 and 2 of the Code, could also affect other forms of political broadcasting. Such a result would in one sense enhance the freedom of broadcasters since it would widen choice as to what could be shown in documentaries, discussion programmes etc. In relation to PEBs it would tend to remove some control from their hands in relation to their interpretation of their responsibilities and place it in the hands of the courts. Challenging and explicit images could be shown, if justified by context. A more effective representation of a plurality of views, including the views of minority groups, in broadcasting might occur.[185]

---

[181] As noted earlier, the lack of a declaration was due to the view taken that s 321(2) (the ban on political advertising) was incompatible with Article 10. This decision was based on the decision of the ECHR in *VGT v Switzerland* [2001] ECHR 408. See Chapter 20 at 1021–3.

[182] Indeed, it is argued that the lack of a statement of compatibility under s 19(1)(b)HRA has no effect on the ability of judges to seek to achieve compatibility under s 3(1) in relation to s 321(2)).

[183] See above pp 580–2.

[184] See for further discussion of the use of s 3 Chapter 3 at 152–3 and 160–3.

[185] As a further resort, there would also be the possibility of issuing a declaration of the incompatibility under s 4 HRA between Article 10 and s 319. Amendment in relation to PEBs might then come about in reliance on the s 10 procedure.

EU-BASED SATELLITE BROADCASTING

In the 1990s, the regulatory regime controlling broadcasting was confronted with the dissemination of material by methods which seemed to fall outside its compass since the material originated from outside the UK, but could be accessed from within it. The concern was that obscene or indecent material would be disseminated by non-terrestrial broadcasters outside the jurisdiction of the UK. The difficulties of attempting to regulate material when it is transmitted by these means, since it is outside the regulatory regime for broadcasting, are discussed below. EU-based satellite broadcasting created particular difficulties, in the view of the government, difficulties that, it will be argued, are currently being evaded rather than resolved.

The ITC Code did not apply to broadcasters who were not licence holders of the ITC. Under s 43 of the 1990 Act, a satellite service was required to hold an ITC licence if it was a 'domestic satellite service' or a 'non-domestic satellite service'. A domestic service was defined as one that used direct broadcasting by satellite on one of the five frequencies allocated to the UK at the World Administrative Radio Conference in 1977. A non-domestic satellite service was one which either used a lower powered satellite to transmit programmes from the UK, or transmitted from outside the territory of prescribed countries, but a UK supplier dictated the service. 'Non-domestic' satellite services were not subject to the same regime as domestic services in the sense that they had to transmit on allocated frequencies and had public service responsibilities.

If a service is licensed from within an EU Member State, it must receive freedom of reception within other Member States under the EU Directive on Transfrontier Television, *Television without Frontiers* (89/552/EEC). In *Commission of EC v UK*[186] it was found that s 43 of the Broadcasting Act 1990 applied different regimes to domestic and non-domestic satellite services, and that in exercising control over certain broadcasters falling under the jurisdiction of other Member States, the UK had failed to fulfil its obligations under Arts 2(1),(2), and 3(2) of the Directive. Thus, in 1997, the distinction between domestic and non-domestic services was abolished: only one category was created—satellite television services.[187] Section 89 of the Broadcasting Act 1996 amended s 45 of the 1990 Act to allow for the immediate revocation of the licence of a satellite television service which breached s 6(1)(a) of the 1990 Act. These sections in both statutes were repealed by the Communications Act 2003. Under ss 232–240 of the 2003 Act satellite services are 'television licensable content services'. That term replaces the separate categories of satellite television services and licensable programme services which were established under the Broadcasting Act 1990, as amended.

---

[186] Case 222/94 [1996] ECR–I 4025.
[187] Satellite Television Service Regulations 1997 SI 1997/1682. Further amendment was made under the Television Broadcasting Regulations 1998 SI 1998/3196.

But satellite services licensed from within another EU Member State are not licensable services and are not therefore covered by Ofcom's broadcast Code. Therefore material that might infringe the Code, particularly 'hard core' pornography, could be received in the UK via EU satellite broadcasting. The solution adopted in the Broadcasting Act 1990 was to allow for the proscription of such material. The government took the view in the 1990s that although such material was available in other EU countries, it should not be available in the UK. It appeared at the time that the use of proscription would not infringe EU law. Dir 89/552 was amended by Directive 97/36 to provide that member states must not restrict retransmissions on their territory of broadcasts from other member states for reasons within the fields co-ordinated by the Directive, but it allowed them to derogate provisionally from the obligation to allow the free movement of broadcasts where a broadcast 'manifestly, seriously and gravely' infringes Art 22 and/or Art 22a. Art 22 allows for restrictions where programmes might 'seriously impair the physical, mental or moral development of minors'. This is not confined to their violent or sexual content, and individual nations have a wide margin of discretion in relation to such matters.

Proscription orders are made under ss 177 and 178 of the 1990 Act.[188] Proscribing a channel is not, formally speaking, a means of banning it. When a channel is proscribed it becomes an offence for it to advertise in the UK or to supply (or offer to supply) any decoding equipment primarily for the purpose of enabling the reception of the proscribed service within the UK. Proscription therefore does not prevent the channel from broadcasting, but in practical terms it means that UK citizens are unable to access it. Once the television service in question has been drawn to the attention of the Secretary of State he or she can only make an order if satisfied that it is in the public interest and compatible with any international obligations of the UK (s 177(3)). S177 was not repealed by the 2003 Act and the ITC's role in this respect has now been taken over by Ofcom. Under s 177 of the 1990 Act, the ITC could draw 'unacceptable' foreign satellite services to the attention of the Secretary of State if satisfied that 'there is repeatedly contained on programmes included in the service matter which offends against good taste and decency or is likely to . . . be offensive to public feeling'. This procedure was thought to be allowed for by Art 2a of the *Television without Frontiers* Directive. Under s177 the National Heritage Secretary has issued a number of proscription orders against satellite channels from EU Member States which beam 'hard core' pornography into Britain. Channels proscribed have included *Eurotic Rendezvous* in 1999 and *Eros TV* in 1998.[189] But proscription orders have not been issued since 2000, and this is probably due to their doubtful compatibility with EU law.

---

[188] Note that ss 329–332 of the 2003 Act allows for the use of proscription orders by the Secretary of State at the instigation of Ofcom, but not against satellite broadcasts.

[189] See *R v Secretary of State for Culture Media and Sport ex parte Danish Satellite TV* 9.7.99 (CD) in which the Court of Appeal held that the Secretary of State was entitled to proscribe the service *Eurotic Rendez-vous*; it was found that the order was based on the protection of minors and not on wider grounds. Some of the images shown on the service were so explicit that if shown in the cinematic or video release of a film, an R18 certificate would not have been granted (see Chapter 12 at 622, 629). *Eros TV* was proscribed under SI 1998 No 1865.

So far, the question whether proscription orders breach EU law has not been addressed by the European Court of Justice. Art 22 presupposes that there is a reasonable likelihood that minors would be affected, and it is arguable that the likelihood is minimal. Thus it seems possible that a breach would be found, taking account of the wording of Art 2a, since children would be highly unlikely to be exposed to the broadcast of hardcore pornography due to recent advances in technology. Channels can be digitally encrypted and scrambled so that non-subscribers are unable to view any signal. It is possible to PIN protect channels to prevent unauthorized access.[190] Adult supervision of the equipment provides a further level of protection. Where the service is transmitted very late at night and accessible only by using a smart card—as was the case in respect of *Eurotic Rendez-vous*—it seems to be improbable that children would be affected. The provisions relating to the protection for children under the Directive are likely in themselves to be amended in 2005 in the light of such technological developments.[191]

At present the evidence that children would be harmed to any significant extent if they were exposed to hardcore material is inconclusive.[192] This was highlighted by the High Court ruling in 2000 in *R v Video Appeals Committee of the BBFC ex parte BBFC*,[193] discussed in Chapter 12; the BBFC lost their judicial review in relation to the promulgation of hard core material on videos largely because they had not provided cogent evidence of any harm to children caused by such material. That decision led to the relaxation of BBFC Guidelines in relation to videos. Since hard-core material is now legally on sale under the R18 classification on DVDs and videos from more than 120 licensed sex shops in the UK, the claim by the Government that such material would seriously impair the development of children would probably fail in the European Court of Justice. Its availability from UK shops means that the risk that children might view 'hard-core' videos cannot be entirely ruled out. It is also hard to sustain the argument that greater protection should be available for children in the UK than in other parts of the EU. The Italian hardcore channel *Satisfaction TV* was recommended for proscription by the ITC in December 2000. However, no proscription order has yet been raised. In itself this is telling since if harm to children was genuinely likely it would not appear to be acceptable to delay the order. It is also notable that the old notion of maintaining 'taste and decency' is applied as the basis for raising proscription orders, while domestic services are subject to the current apparently less stringent offence-avoidance standard, under the 2003 Act, as discussed above. Since the legalisation of 'hard-core' material on the BBFC R18 video classification in 2000 the government appears to have abandoned proscription of foreign satellite channels.

---

[190] The most recent Sky systems have PIN protection by default on adult channels, as does Telewest; the PIN can be automatically disabled after three failed attempts at access.

[191] Commission: *Second Evaluation Report on the application of Council Recommendation of 24 Sept 1998 concerning the protection of minors and human dignity.* COM (2003) 776 final (12.12.2003).

[192] See BBFC News Release, 26 October 2000, *Abused children most at risk from pornography*, Chapter 12 at 632–4, note 51.

[193] (2000) EMLR 850. See p 633 below.

The government presumably has concerns that using an order would breach EU law, in the light of the factors identified.

The possibility that some proscription orders may be incompatible with Article 10 under the HRA should be considered. The protection of children is a significant theme running through the Convention explicit expression cases discussed in Chapter 8,[194] and restrictions on such expression tend to be readily justified under Art 10(2) at the Strasbourg level. It is theoretically possible for the domestic courts to apply a strict proportionality analysis in this context, which Strasbourg has never done due to the effects of the margin of appreciation doctrine. This is possible since the domestic courts are not bound by that doctrine. However, as discussed above, this need not be the case at the domestic level if the requirements of proportionality are applied absent the effects on them of the margin of appreciation doctrine. It could be argued that the restriction created by a proscription order was disproportionate to the harm to be avoided since the risk to children appeared to be minimal. It would arguably be acceptable under Article 10 to distinguish between modern satellite subscription services under which viewing is very restricted, and open to air broadcasts where any viewer can access any programme. The rights of others to be protected from offence under Article 10(2) would be only minimally at stake due to the impact of such restrictions. However, as discussed in Chapter 3,[195] the domestic judiciary have not so for shown a tendency to disapply the effects of the margin of appreciation doctrine in this fashion.

CONCLUSIONS

The discussion above suggests that a number of matters should have been addressed with greater clarity under the 2003 reforms. Over the last fifteen years broadcasting content regulation has moved from a system based on censorship under the IBA, to one based on post-transmission sanctions reflecting standards of taste and decency under the ITC and BSC, to the use of such sanctions to ensure offence avoidance and to protect minors, under Ofcom. The vexed question as to the basic standard to be used in relation to material aimed at adults was left open by the 2003 Act and, as discussed, it is still largely unanswered, despite the promulgation of the new Code. The current controls over broadcasting appear to be aimed more at preserving market rather than creative freedom. Their tendency is to make for cautious rather than explorative and challenging broadcasting.

When the power of the owners of the television companies to influence the nature of broadcasting is compared with that of the media regulators or of the public service broadcasters, a human rights scheme in which the exercise of the powers of the latter,

---

[194] See e.g. *Müller v Switzerland* (1991) 13 EHRR 212; *Scherer* A 287 (1993) Com Rep; for discussion see Chapter 8 at 416–20.

[195] At pp 145–7.

but not the former, can be challenged on free expression grounds looks fundamentally flawed. There is clearly a mismatch between the areas in which the HRA can intervene and the location of the main influences over the medium of most significance in terms of its cultural and opinion-forming impact. But the impact of the HRA on broadcasting is unlikely to be radical. This is in part because the regulatory regime already adheres to free expression principles in a reasonably comprehensive and advanced fashion. Nevertheless, this chapter has described quite significant restraints to avoid causing offence contained in Ofcom's Code and the 2003 Act. Currently broadcast material is subject both to special regulation in terms of a regime based on warnings, and use of the 'watershed', and *also* to restraint which in effect amounts to a form of censorship since the broadcasters must exercise self-censorship in order to adhere to the offence-avoidance aspects of Ofcom's Code. Despite quite significant liberalization relative to the old ITC and BSC Codes, the new Code is potentially quite restrictive in certain respects, depending on Ofcom's interpretation of it. Ofcom retains significant leeway in adopting a range of free expression standards. At present, it appears to be taking a liberal stance, as evidenced in its decision on *Jerry Springer: The Opera*. This regime is not applied to any other medium and since, as discussed in Chapter 12, the BBFC appears to be operating a regime in respect of films and videos that has recently become much more liberal, the differences between the regimes for films and for broadcasting are becoming more marked. As technology advances, the range of channels widens and a wider range of information about programmes becomes more readily available to viewing audiences, these differences are arguably becoming less defensible. Although it might appear that Art 10 under the HRA could play a part in bringing about a greater liberalization of the current offence-avoidance regime, it is probable, for the reasons discussed above, that its effect will continue to be marginal, especially after the *ProLife* decision. Regulation of UK broadcasting is in effect insulated from free speech principles applied by means of the HRA due to the excessive deference to the regulators enjoined upon the courts by *ProLife*. In any event, Strasbourg has readily accepted restraints on non-political and offensive expression, especially in the context of broadcasting, and Chapters 8 and 10 point out.[196]

Clearly, Parliament has had a strong input—the area is littered with legislation—but the very fact that there is a paucity of case law at both the domestic and Strasbourg levels, coupled with a lack of academic interest appears to have led to an impoverishment of Parliamentary debate. It appears that it is still correct to find that the freedom of broadcast speech is significantly curtailed in comparison with that of other media. The remedy does not appear to lie with Strasbourg or the domestic courts under the HRA.

[196] See pp 410–21 and 553, 557–8.

12

REGULATION OF FILMS, VIDEOS, AND THE INTERNET

INTRODUCTION [1]

Regulation of films, videos and the Internet differs sharply from the 'command and control' model of regulation provided by the Ofcom system. Regulation of films for cinematic release has some features in common with the self-regulation of the Internet since it was originally entered into voluntarily by the film-makers themselves. However, the regulation of films is far less fragmentary and has achieved far greater recognition than the system for the Internet. In relation to videoworks, the film regulatory scheme does bear quite a strong resemblance to the Ofcom one. Generally, film regulation does not have a *full* statutory under-pinning, but is strongly associated with a number of statutes. As discussed below, a range of bodies set up by Internet Service Providers, such as the Internet Watch Foundation, provide a self-censoring service for the Internet. None of these bodies has a statutory underpinning or have so far received any statutory recognition. Nor can they be viewed as affecting the Internet in a comprehensive fashion since, unlike the system for films, they do not apply controls at source but are consumer-driven. In other words, they rely on a voluntary engagement with their services by the public or by institutions, whereas films and videos are affected by regulation prior to release. The remit of the Advertising Standards Authority[2] now not only covers broadcasting, but runs across all these different media; it is most significant in relation to the Internet. It will be discussed in the different contexts, below.

---

[1] See generally: E. Barendt, *Freedom of Speech*, 2nd edn., Oxford: OUP, 2005, Chaps 10, 12, and 13; G. Robertson and D. Nichol, *Media Law*, London: Penguin, 1999, Chapter 14; Bailey, Harris, and Jones, *Civil Liberties and Human Rights Cases and Materials*, Oxford: OUP, 2002, Chap 6, at 650–67; P. Carey and J. Sanders, *Media Law*, 3rd edn., London: Sweet & Maxwell, 2004, Chaps 5 and 9 (basic guide); T. Gibbons, *Regulating the Media*, London: Sweet & Maxwell, 1998; Y. Akdeniz, C. Walker, and D. Wall (eds.), *The Internet, Law and Society*, Longman, 2000; for background see N. Hunnings, *Film Censors and the Law*, London: Allen and Unwin, 1967.

[2] Its role is discussed in Chapter 10 at 545–9.

THE BRITISH BOARD OF FILM CLASSIFICATION

Classification and censorship of films and videoworks is undertaken by the British Board of Film Classification (BBFC), a self-censoring body set up by the film industry itself in 1912. It is an independent, non-governmental body which is funded by the fees it charges to those who submit films, videos, DVDs for classification. The video release of films has a firmer statutory under-pinning deriving from the Video Recordings Act 1984, and so the regulation of videos has a greater resemblance in that respect to the system for broadcasting.

The BBFC provides an interesting example of a body that does not possess statutory powers—in relation to the cinematic release of films—and yet its decisions as to film classification are adhered to as though they had statutory force. It was originally set up in response to the Cinematograph Act 1909 (now Cinemas Act 1985), which allowed local authorities to grant licences in respect of the films to be shown in their particular area; the idea was that the film industry would achieve a uniformity of decision-making by local councils by providing authoritative guidance to them. So when the BBFC classifies films it does so, formally speaking, on behalf of the local authorities who license cinemas under the Cinemas Act 1985. The idea behind this system, from the point of view of the film-makers and distributors, was that they would have a guide as to whether a film would be shown and as to where to make cuts in order to achieve a wider audience.

Statutory powers to control what is shown at cinemas still remain with local councils who may over-rule any of the Board's decisions. Thus, films—not videos—can be classified on two levels: first, the BBFC may insist on cuts before issuing a certificate allowing the film to be screened or may refuse to issue a certificate at all. Second, the local authority may on occasion decide to depart from the BBFC classification or may refuse to allow a film to be shown despite the fact that it has received an '18' classification. Clearly, this is an anomalous system since it means that films are the only medium subject to censorship on a local level. But although the BBFC originates from an arbitrary and now out-dated system, it performs a function that would otherwise be performed by a regulator such as Ofcom with statutory powers. The BBFC is not a creation of statute although, as discussed below, it does have statutory powers in relation to videos. Arguably, a regulator that has worked closely with the industry for a substantial period of time and which is not a governmental creation, or subject to government appointments, may be able to take a more effective, sensitive and nuanced stance in relation to classification and censorship than a government body— a point that is returned to below. The matter of self-censorship by film companies prior to submission to the BBFC must not be disregarded, but over the last ten years the BBFC appears to have adopted an increasingly liberal attitude to censorship: in 1995, 27 films were censored; in 2005, the figure was four.[3] However, at present, as the

---

[3] Source—*The Guardian*, 13 September 2005. The figure of four in 2005 is based on decisions from January to September 2005. However, the figure is unlikely to rise significantly: only five films were censored in 2004.

BBFC itself accepts, films and videos are particularly heavily censored in the UK. The reasons for this and the current pressure for change form a central focus of the discussion below.

Below, the general classification and censorship system operated by the BBFC is considered, before turning to the differences between the way films are treated for cinematic release and for release on videoworks.

THE CLASSIFICATION AND CENSORSHIP SYSTEM

The BBFC classifies and censors films and videos against the background of the relevant criminal law,[4] including the Obscene Publications Act 1959.[5] S4(1)(a) Video Recordings Act 1984, as amended,[6] requires the BBFC to apply an additional test with regard to the classification of videos—that of suitability for viewing in the home. This requirement reflects the fact that, in the BBFC's words: 'unlike cinema films where age restrictions may be "policed" by box office staff, videos in the home are more likely to be viewed by younger age groups and could be replayed many times with individual scenes taken out of context and repeated in slow motion or even frame by frame'.[7] In relation to videos there is a right of appeal from the decisions of the BBFC to the Video Appeals Committee (VAC). No such right exists in relation to films.

The BBFC makes its decisions on the basis of published Guidelines.[8] As it acknowledges, the application of the Guidelines goes further in terms of creating restraints than the relevant law itself does. It states in the Guidelines that it is complying with the requirements of the European Convention on Human Rights to make the classification criteria clear. It considers that it has fulfilled this duty by the publication of the Guidelines and their availability on the BBFC website or directly from the Board. However, the mere fact that the Guidelines can be readily accessed clearly does not mean that the criteria are sufficiently clear, and it is arguable that in a number of respects sufficient clarity has not been achieved. This is an especially significant matter since the BBFC is the only UK media regulator which operates by means of prior restraint: it can order cuts in films before they can be seen by the public.

---

[4] The relevant criminal law is discussed in Chapters 8 and 9. Note also that the Cinematograph Films (Animals) Act 1937 makes it illegal to show any scene if animals were treated cruelly in the making of that scene.

[5] The Obscene Publications Act 1959 does not apply in Scotland; the Civic Government (Scotland) Act 1982 makes it an offence to publish obscene material, and prosecution is the responsibility of the Procurator Fiscal Service. Under the Scotland Act 1998, Scottish criminal law generally has been devolved and this includes the law on obscenity; however, the Video Recordings Act has been reserved to the UK Parliament. The Obscene Publications Act does not extend to Northern Ireland; nor do the relevant provisions of the Local Government (Miscellaneous Provisions) Act 1982. Obscene material, including videoworks, is generally dealt with under the common law offence of publishing an obscene libel.

[6] Discussed below at pp 631, 634.

[7] See the 2000 BBFC Response to the Home Office Consultation Paper on *the Regulation of R18 Videos* at para 2.1.

[8] Available from the BBFC website—http://www.bbfc.co.uk.

Adherence to the Guidelines is intended to mean—and so far has meant—that the producers or distributors of a film are very unlikely to be prosecuted under the Obscene Publications Act 1959 (OPA) or other provisions imposing criminal liability in respect of explicit expression. Thus, as is the case in relation to broadcasting, it is probable that films do not fully explore the boundaries of the criminal law, but stop instead somewhere short of them.

(I) AGE RESTRICTIONS

Films and videos are classified by age, creating a number of categories that restrict viewing. The age restrictions are more significant, for obvious reasons, in relation to films as opposed to videos. Clearly, children and teenagers under 15 or 18 may well be able to view videos privately that have the higher age rating; they are able to do so much more readily than in the cinema. This is a matter that the BBFC takes into account in its classification. There are seven classification categories. 'U' and Uc films are open to anybody as, in effect, are 'PG' (parental guidance) classified films. These categories are advisory only. After that are '12'/'12A', '15' and '18' certificate films. 12A is a new, recently introduced, category which allows children under 12 to see '12' rated films at their parents' discretion; it requires such children to be accompanied into the cinema by an adult. Children over 12 will be able to see the film unaccompanied, as previously. Thus the 12A rating recognizes that parents have a better understanding of the particular sensitivities of their individual children than a regulator can have. The introduction of the 12A rating is a step in the direction of recognizing the applicability of the free speech autonomy rationale to children as well as to adults.

The advice at the '18' rating is obviously crucial since it represents the outer limits of acceptability for mainstream films and sets the boundaries for most adult viewing. The '18' rating does not fully perform that function in relation to videos since the BBFC takes into account the possibility that people under 18 may see the film, although that is far from meaning that only material suitable for, say, 15 year-olds is promulgated. 'R (restricted viewing) 18' films are intended for viewing only on segre gated premises. The R18 classification certificate was introduced by the BBFC following the introduction of the 1982 Local Government (Miscellaneous Provisions) Act which required the licensing of all cinema exhibitions operated for private gain, including those clubs which showed films containing more explicit sexual depictions than would be acceptable in the public adult—18—category. This classification is also used in the context of classifying sexually explicit videoworks since the implementation of the Video Recordings Act 1984.There are strict controls on the sale of videoworks which are given an R18 classification. Under s 12 of the 1984 Act, such videos can only be sold in a licensed sex shop to adults aged 18 and over. They cannot be legally sold by mail order, supplied through ordinary video outlets, or shown on television. Their supply other than in a licensed sex shop is a criminal offence.[9]

---

[9] The offence is subject to a fine of up to £5,000, six months' imprisonment, or both.

The issue of an 'R18' certificate means that the BBFC considers that the film or video would survive an Obscene Publications Act (OPA) prosecution; it will refuse a certificate if a film is thought to be obscene within the meaning of the Act.[10] Thus BBFC decisions as to the borderline between what can be shown in an R18 film and what would fall foul of the OPA are probably the best guide to the meaning and application of the problematic term 'obscenity' available in the UK. The BBFC may of course err on the side of caution: it may not wish to patrol very closely to that borderline, and the very uncertainty of the term 'obscenity'[11] is likely to engender caution.

R v Video Appeals Committee of the BBFC ex p BBFC,[12] discussed further below, marked a very significant change in the use of the R18 certificate for videos. The decision resulted in the promulgation of new, more relaxed Guidelines for 'R18' videos by the BBFC. The BBFC nevertheless takes the view that despite this relaxation the UK 'still probably has the strictest Guidelines of any European or Western nation'.[13] Since film-makers outside the pornography industry obviously do not want to receive a 'R18' rating for their work, the vast majority of films aimed at adults must respect the BBFC Guidelines as far as the UK cinema release of films is concerned in order to secure the UK adult mainstream market. The BBFC states that it 'respects the right of adults to chose their own entertainment, within the law. It will therefore expect to intervene *only rarely* in relation to "18" rated cinema films' (emphasis added).[14]

In coming to its decision, the BBFC will take the 'public good' defence under s 4(1A) of the 1959 Act, as amended, into account.[15] This defence is the more restricted defence under s 3 of the Theatres Act 1968; s 4(1A) provides that a film or soundtrack can be justified as being for the public good 'on the ground that it is in the interests of drama, opera, ballet or any other art or of literature or learning'. Therefore, the BBFC may grant a certificate on the grounds of artistic merit to a film which contains some obscene matter.

The 12A–R18 classifications are mandatory, not recommendatory. In most of Europe and in the US the age classifications are intended to provide guidance to parents and to children, but (in the US, depending on the theatre owner and the area) children under the age in question can enter the cinema and view films in the 'older' category. For example, in the US the 'PG13' rating is roughly the equivalent of the '12A' rating in the UK, but younger children can view 'PG13' rated films in the US. In the UK they can only do so if accompanied by an adult. Thus in this respect the autonomy of children and teenagers is more fully acknowledged than it is in the UK.

---

[10] See Chapter 8 at 424–34.   [11] See Chapter 8 at 424–8.

[12] (2000) EMLR 850. The appeal to the VAC was brought by Sheptonhurst Ltd and Prime Time Promotions (Shifnal) Ltd and involved seven titles: *Horny Catbabe, Nympho Nurse Nancy, T.V. Sex, Office Tart, Carnival International Version (Trailer), Wet Nurses 2 Continental Version* and *Miss Nude International Continental Version*.

[13] See the 2000 BBFC Response to the Home Office Consultation Paper on *the Regulation of R18 Videos* 28.7.00.

[14] BBFC Guidelines, '18' ratings.   [15] See further Chapter 8 at 438–43.

This restriction relating to cinemas is not—in effect—applicable to videos and, as discussed further below, influences the BBFC in relation to determining the classification of videos and in deciding on cuts.

Most film distributors have no interest in achieving only a restricted publication for a film and are therefore prepared to make cuts to achieve a wider circulation. This is especially the case in relation to the R18 certificate. But profitability is also highly significant and determinative of pre-censorship: the system of control may be driven largely by commercial motives; studios may make relatively stringent cuts in order to ensure that, for example, a film receives a '15' certificate and so reaches a wider audience. The BBFC normally avoids having to impose cuts because film directors effectively pre-censor films in order to fall within a particular classification.

(II) PROBLEMATIC AND DISTURBING CONTENT; EXPLICIT DEPICTIONS OF SEX AND VIOLENCE

The BBFC states in its Guidelines that the acceptability of a particular theme at levels of classification is determined by 'the context and sensitivity of its presentation'. The Guidelines state that the very problematic themes such as drug abuse or paedophilia are almost bound to be unacceptable below the '15' level of classification. Therefore it is accepted that in principle *any* theme could be viewed as acceptable if properly handled at '18' or even at '15'. But this must now be read subject to new restrictions, discussed below, on the depiction of teenage sexuality created by the inception of the Sexual Offences Act 2003. The Guidelines state that the portrayal of human sexual activity is not permitted at 'U', 'Uc' or 'PG'; it may be implied in '12' rated video works and in '12A' cinema works. Thereafter, 'progressively more graphic portrayal' may be included at the '15' and '18' classifications,[16] but the extent of the portrayal is context-dependent, and the emphasis given to 'responsible, loving and developing' relationships will be relevant. In taking this stance the BBFC lays itself open to the charge that it is engaging in ideological censorship—in other words, only an authorized view of sexuality is acceptable. Again, the effect of the 2003 Act is to create a further age-based constraint even within the depiction of such relationships. Certain

---

[16] At '12A'/'12': 'sexual activity may be implied. Sexual references may reflect the familiarity of most adolescents today with sex education through school'. At '15' 'sexual activity and nudity may be portrayed but without strong detail. The depiction of casual sex should be handled responsibly.' At '18' the Board may cut or reject the 'more explicit images' of sexual conduct unless, exceptionally, they are justified by context. The following are not acceptable, even at R18: 'any material which is in breach of the criminal law; material (including dialogue) likely to encourage an interest in abusive sexual activity (e.g., paedophilia, incest) which may include depictions involving adults role-playing as non-adults; the portrayal of any sexual activity, whether real or simulated, which involves lack of consent; the infliction of pain or physical harm, real or (in a sexual context) simulated. Some allowance may be made for mild consensual activity. Any sexual threats or humiliation which do not form part of a clearly consenting role-playing game are disallowed, as are the use of any form of physical restraint which prevents participants from withdrawing consent, for example, ball gags, penetration by any object likely to cause actual harm or associated with violence, activity which is degrading or dehumanising (examples include the portrayal of bestiality, necrophilia, defecation, urolagnia)'.

forms of simulated consenting heterosexual or homosexual sexual behaviour can no longer be shown involving 16 or 17 year old actors, or (possibly) older actors portraying younger people if digital change has occurred. The 'R18' category is primarily reserved for explicit videos of consenting sex between adults. In contrast, nudity, providing there is 'no sexual context or sub-text', is stated to be acceptable at all classification levels.

Significantly, the Guidelines state that the standards set for *legal* heterosexual and homosexual behaviour are equal (emphasis added). The use of the term 'legal' is important: in the past there has been differentiation between legal and illegal homosexual behaviour which was not replicated to the same extent in relation to heterosexual behaviour. For example, the age of consent for heterosexual intercourse is 16, whereas until 1994 it was 21 for homosexual intercourse. Until quite recently it was 18.[17] However, under very recent legislative changes the two forms of behaviour are now equal under the law. Under the Sexual Offences (Amendment) Act 2000 s 1 the age of consent was equalized at 16. When the Sexual Offences Act 2003 came into force,[18] a range of forms of heterosexual and homosexual sexual behaviour were placed on an equal footing. These changes could potentially have an important impact on depictions of homosexual behaviour on film, and a significant liberalization in terms of what can be shown may occur, due indirectly to changes in the criminal law. Films rarely depict actual as opposed to simulated sexual acts, including intercourse. The film *9 Songs*, however, achieved an '18' rating in 2004 for the cinematic release despite frequent and graphic portrayals of non-simulated sexual intercourse. Previously, *Ai No Corrida* was classified '18' in 1991, as were *Romance* (1999) and *Intimacy* (2001)—all three films contain images of non-simulated intercourse. No '18' rated film has yet depicted actual homosexual intercourse (the term is used here to include oral sex as well as anal intercourse). This difference is only indirectly linked to the legal age of consent: the previous legal inequality probably had more of an educative effect in terms of cultural expectations; the mere fact that the age of consent is now equal is unlikely imminently to have a significant influence on the decisions of either the BBFC or film-makers.

The equalization of the age of consent is, of course, relevant only to the age of the actors engaged in the film and it is very unlikely at present that a seventeen year old actor would be viewed on screen engaging in actual heterosexual intercourse. It is impossible to determine how far the inequality in the age of consent has influenced cultural expectations which themselves influence the decisions of film-makers. But lack of equality in this respect may have underpinned a cultural norm within which depictions of homosexual, as opposed to heterosexual, intercourse

[17] Under the Sexual Offences Act 1967 s 1, the age of consent was 21; this was amended by the Criminal Justice and Public Order Act 1994 s 143 to 18. Until recently, when the Sexual Offences Act 2003 came into force, there were a number of legal differentiations between illegal heterosexual and homosexual acts/ behaviour, apart from that stemming from the age of consent; the more restrictive laws applied to homosexual behaviour. See further H. Fenwick, *Civil Liberties and Human Rights*, 3rd edn., London: Cavendish, 2002, pp 738–741.

[18] On 1 May 2004.

are viewed as more disturbing. If this is the case, such cultural expectations may change, and may be, in turn, reflected in BBFC decisions; change is, however, likely to be slow.

Any liberalizing effects of the change in the age of consent under the 2003 Act were curbed at the same time as far as films are concerned. The Act makes a very important change in this context, which also has implications for the distribution of films and videos made prior to 2003. The change concerns the definition of a 'child' under the terms of the Protection of Children Act 1978 (PCA), discussed in Chapter 8.[19] Previously the 1978 Act s 7(6) defined a 'child' as a person under 16 years of age and made illegal the manufacture, possession and distribution of indecent photographs of children under 16. Section 45(2) of the new Sexual Offences Act amended the PCA by raising the age of a 'child' for the purposes of this Act to 18. The effect of this is retrospective, applying to all such images, regardless of when they first came into circulation. The Act in effect bans from the screen all depictions of sexual activity involving someone under 18 that could fall within the term 'indecent'. It is uncertain whether older actors whose features have been digitally manipulated to make them appear to be under 18 could be used since this might amount to the use of a 'psuedo-image' of a child.[20] Section 51 of the 2003 Act introduced a new offence of 'facilitating' child pornography. The new restraints are mainly aimed at Internet pornography, but place film-makers exploring depictions of teenage sexuality in a very difficult position, and mean that 16 and 17 year olds are constrained in relation to viewing people of the same age involved in sexual activity.

Sexual intercourse between over-16s is legal, and other forms of sexual activity short of intercourse were legal even before the age of consent was raised to 16, but although the acts themselves are legal, depictions of them may not be. It is anomalous, to say the least, that heterosexual or homosexual intercourse between 16 year olds or with adults, is lawful, whereas depictions of forms of sexual activity involving 16 or 17 year old actors, falling far short of intercourse, might not be. Clearly, depictions of some forms of sexual activity involving 16 and 17 year-old actors would not attract criminal liability, but the 2003 Act has created a number of grey areas in relation to such depictions which did not previously exist. The BBFC may find itself seeking to classify films that could fall foul of the PCA 1978.

Clearly, the key question is whether the depiction of the 'child' could be viewed as 'indecent'. Whether a photograph is indecent depends on the view of the jury regarding recognized standards of propriety.[21] In *Oliver, Hartrey and Baldwin*[22] the Court of

---

[19] See pp 469–70.

[20] Section 84 of the Criminal Justice and Public Order Act 1994 amended the 1978 Act to add 'pseudo-photographs' of children in order to cover digitally created photographs. This would of course depend on whether in the context the image would be seen as 'indecent'. See further Chapter 8 at 469.

[21] *R v Graham-Kerr* (1988) 88 Cr App R 302. See further: C. Manchester, 'Criminal Justice and Public Order Act 1994: obscenity, pornography and videos' [1995] *Crim LR* 123, pp 123–8; I. Cram, 'Criminalising Child Pornography—a Canadian Study' [2002] 66 *J Crim L* 359.

[22] [2003] Cr App R 28.

Appeal found that pornographic images were to be categorized by the following levels of seriousness: (1) images depicting erotic posing with no sexual activity; (2) sexual activity between children, or solo masturbation by a child; (3) non-penetrative sexual activity between adults and children; (4) penetrative sexual activity between children and adults; and (5) sadism or bestiality. Thus level (1), covering a very wide range of images,[23] represents the 'lowest' level at which an image of a child could be termed 'indecent'. A number of films have depicted teenage actors, most frequently those aged between 16–18, in the situations described in (1)–(3).[24] The definition of indecency is obviously context-dependent. Where *Gillick*-competent child or teenage actors above the age of 13 engage in depictions of fairly restrained, non-nude, consensual heterosexual activity with each other, it may perhaps be assumed that this would not violate recognized standards of propriety. Clearly, the older the teenager, the more clearly this would be the case. The fact that a teenage actor of 18 had been made up or (perhaps) digitally altered to look, say, 13 could also be taken into account in relation to a determination as to indecency. But the uncertainty of the definition of indecency hardly favours erotic creativity and places film-makers and the BBFC in a difficult position. The Court of Appeal will no doubt have to revisit its definition of indecency under the PCA due to the effect of the 2003 Act. The retrospective effect of the new definition of a 'child' is also highly problematic since certain cinematic depictions of sexuality, using sixteen or seventeen year old actors, would not have fallen foul of the constraints of the 1978 Act at the time.[25]

After the equalization of the age of consent it would have been possible to depict

---

[23] See Warbrick, 'Federalism and free speech', in Loveland (ed.), *Importing the First Amendment*, Oxford: Hart Publishing, 1997, pp 177–9 and 190–2.

[24] A number of examples could be given; in *The Ice Storm* a sequence depicted actors Elijah Wood and Christina Ricci 'dry-humping'; another scene depicted Christina Ricci and Adam Hann-Byrd half-naked and kissing in bed together. All three actors were very young teenagers at the time. Both scenes appear to fall within level (2) from *Oliver, Hartrey and Baldwin*. In *The Name of the Rose*, Christian Slater, who was 17 at the time and depicting a teenager, had simulated sex with an adult woman. The film *Kids* depicted a number of teenagers engaging in sexual activity. In *Trainspotting*, Kelly McDonald, 17 at the time, engaged in simulated intercourse with an adult male actor, Ewan McGregor. The key question of course would be whether such scenes in the context of acting, and taking account of the fact that the actors were teenagers and *Gillick*-competent, would violate accepted standards of propriety and so be viewed as 'indecent'.

[25] The change might not be compatible with the demands of Article 7(1) ECHR in Sched 1 HRA. Article 7 provides: '(1) No one shall be held guilty of any criminal offence on account of any act or omission which did not constitute a criminal offence under national or international law at the time when it was committed. Nor shall a heavier penalty be imposed than the one that was applicable at the time the criminal offence was committed. (2) This Article shall not prejudice the trial and punishment of any person for any act or omission which, at the time when it was committed, was criminal according to the general principles of law recognised by civilised nations. Article 7 was found to have been breached in *Welch v UK* (1995) 20 EHRR 247. Before the trial of the applicant for drug offences, a new provision came into force under the Drug Trafficking Offences Act 1986, making provision for confiscation orders. This was imposed on the applicant, although the legislation was not in force at the time when he committed the offences in question. It clearly had retrospective effect and was found to constitute a 'penalty' within Art 7(1). The 2003 Act was declared compatible with the Convention under s 19(1)(a)HRA, so the government legal advice must have been to the effect that Art 7 had been complied, probably on the basis that the exception under Art 7(2) applied. The declaration is not, however, conclusive; compatibility is a matter for the judiciary to determine.

consenting homosexual acts (including simulated or actual intercourse) between sixteen or seventeen-year old actors or between such actors and an adult. But if viewed as indecent such acts cannot be seen on screen despite the equalization of the age of consent. This is now also true of heterosexual acts, and in this sense the effect of the 2003 Act was to 'level down' in terms of equalizing cinematic depictions of sexuality involving teenagers or apparent teenagers. But it is probable that homosexual acts might be more likely to be seen as indecent, and in this sense BBFC decisions might—in effect—indirectly discriminate against depictions of homosexuality. This point is pursued below in relation to the HRA.

This might also be true even outside the purview of the 1978 Act, where other criminal law provisions are or might be applicable, including the anomalous common law doctrine of outraging public decency.[26] Such other provisions create differentiation in the legal position, thereby creating difficulties affecting depictions of homosexual behaviour short of intercourse, and simulated sexual acts, even between actors on screen, since such acts might be more likely to be viewed as indecent. Therefore depictions of homosexual behaviour on films have been, and still appear to be, subject to greater restriction.

The classification system also addresses the degree and nature of violence depicted in films,[27] while accepting that violence is an inevitable aspect of entertainment at all ages, 'an element in many serious representations of the human condition'. But the Guidelines advise against the portrayal of violence as 'a normal solution to problems' and against callousness to victims or the encouragement of aggression. The guidelines state that works which 'glorify or glamorise violence' will receive a more restrictive classification and may be cut. Sexual violence is of particular concern. The BBFC states that it has a strict policy on rape and sexual violence. Cuts may be made in material that associates sex with non-consensual restraint, pain, or humiliation. If a portrayal eroticizes or endorses sexual assault, the Board is likely to require cuts at any classification level. Cuts are more likely in video rather than film portrayals due to the possibility of repeat viewing of video scenes. The guidelines indicate that portrayals of the use of weapons easily accessible to young people will be restricted, and imitable combat techniques may be cut, as may imitable detail of criminal techniques. Works that promote or encourage or glamorize the use of illegal drugs will not in general receive even an '18' classification. Clear instructive detail as to drug use is only acceptable at the '18' classification 'if there are exceptional considerations of context'.

The Guidelines highlight the use of expletives in films, a matter that is more problematic in relation to UK film audiences than it is in the rest of Europe. The

---

[26] See Chapter 8 at 472–7.
[27] At '12A'/'12': 'Violence must not dwell on detail. There should be no emphasis on injuries or blood. Sexual violence may only be implied or briefly indicated and without physical detail.' At '15': 'Violence may be strong but may not dwell on the infliction of pain, and of injuries. Scenes of sexual violence must be discreet and brief.' There should be no 'detailed portrayal of violent or dangerous acts which is likely to promote the activity.'

BBFC finds that the degree of offence caused by the use of expletives varies according to age, background and beliefs; ethnicity may also be relevant. The context will also be significant. In the light of these variables it offers only general guidance rather than providing a comprehensive listing of unacceptable words. Specific terms are advised against at different classification levels only where there is a reasonable consensus of opinion.[28]

THE THEATRICAL RELEASE OF FILMS

The BBFC Guidelines discussed are applied somewhat differently to films in relation to the cinematic and the video release. Since cinema films are viewed by an adult, willing audience who has access to information about the nature of the film, it might have been expected that '18' rated films would fall just outside the boundaries of criminal liability as determined by the Obscene Publications Act as amended, and common law offences. There is a greater risk, in relation to videos, that children might view adult films. The difficulty with the availability of the R18 classification in relation to the cinematic release is that it may mean that the BBFC are not exploring the boundaries of the legal definition of obscenity in adult films in general, those that receive the 18 classification. The R18 classification may, in effect, drive a wedge between such films and the outer limits of acceptability under the criminal law.

Consideration of recent decisions by the BBFC suggests that there is some basis for these concerns. However, at the PG–15 levels the BBFC has shown a willingness in some instances to place films within a non-restrictive category, even where they fall at the outer limits of that category. For example, the BBFC took a creative approach in 2001 to the classification of *The Lord of the Rings—the Fellowship of the Ring*. The Board found that the battle violence and fantasy horror in the film were a matter for concern since children under the age of 8 might be frightened or disturbed. However, it decided to give the film a 'PG' rating on the basis that the film's distributor had agreed that all advertising and publicity for the film would carry the consumer advice that the film contains scenes which may not be suitable for children under eight years of age. Most films do not carry such advice, over and beyond the classification rating; the only other films to carry consumer advice on all publicity and advertising were *Jurassic Park* and *The Lost World—Jurassic Park*, both of which were rated 'PG'.[29] The BBFC was presented with greater difficulties in relation to the film *Spiderman*. It was aimed at a young audience by the film-makers, and Hollywood had marketed it with

---

[28] The Guidelines state, at '12'/'12A': 'The use of strong language (e.g. "fuck") should be rare'. At '15' 'there may be frequent use of strong language; the strongest terms (e.g. "cunt") are only rarely acceptable. Continued *aggressive* use of strong language and sexual abuse is unacceptable.' At '18' there are no constraints on language.

[29] See BBFC press release 22.11.01.

that audience in mind. But the BBFC considered it 'possibly the most violent film . . . aimed at a young audience that the BBFC has classified.' Therefore the Board considered that it was clearly unsuitable for a 'PG' rating since very young children would then be able to view the film. Classifying it as '12', the BBFC found that the film '[carries] . . . a clear message that the use of violence is the normal and appropriate response when challenged.'[30] The '12A' rating was not available at the time.

At the '18' level the BBFC has to deal with the even more problematic issue of censorship of material aimed at adults, as opposed to the issues raised by restrictive age classifications. In 2002 the BBFC decided to classify the French film *Irreversible* as '18' uncut for the cinema release. The film centres around a graphically depicted rape and its consequences. The Board found, in line with its current classification guidelines, and having taken advice from a clinical forensic psychiatrist, that the depiction of the rape did not eroticize or appear to endorse sexual violence. The Board considered that the rape scene was a harrowing and vivid portrayal of the brutality of rape which was not designed to titillate.[31] In contrast, in the same year the BBFC passed the French language cinema film, *The Pornographer*, as '18' but required a cut to a graphic unsimulated sex scene in which a woman was seen with semen on her face following oral sex.[32] This cut was in line with the BBFC's Guidelines at '18' which state that the Board may cut or reject 'the more explicit images of sexual activity—unless they can be exceptionally justified by context'. The Board did not find that the context justified the scene. As mentioned above, the film *9 Songs* obtained an '18' rating in 2004 for the cinematic release although it depicted actual as opposed to simulated sexual intercourse. The Board decided that the film's sensitive exploration of the relationship between the two people provided sufficient contextual justification. The consumer advice provided a warning of the content.

The emphasis on context as providing a justification for portrayals of sexual activity or violence is questionable since it depends on value judgments made by the Board members as to 'acceptable' contexts. Films are a very significant medium for the exploration of controversial themes and such themes may depend on the use of images from outside the boundaries of those contexts. There is a case for arguing that the R18 classification should be abolished for the theatrical release of films and that mainstream films should therefore be able to explore the boundaries created by the criminal law more vigorously and closely. If a film viewed only by adults is to be cut, the starting point should be the demands of the criminal law. Clear justification based on the avoidance of specific harms—as opposed merely to offence avoidance—should be available for cuts made reaching beyond those demands. The possibility of more extensive use of detailed consumer guidance should be pursued in order to avoid the causing of offence.

The second level of classification is operated, as discussed above, by local authorities under the Cinemas Act 1985 which continues the old power arising under the

---

[30] See BBFC press release 13.6.02.   [31] See BBFC press release 21.10.02.
[32] See BBFC press release 2.4.02.

Cinematograph Act 1909. The local authority will usually follow the Board's advice; authorities are reluctant to devote resources to viewing films and will tend to rely on the BBFC's judgment.[33] But authorities may, on occasion, choose not to grant a licence to a film regardless of its decision. Films which have been licensed but which nevertheless have been banned in some areas include *A Clockwork Orange, The Life of Brian, The Last Temptation of Christ* and *Crash*. Conversely, local authorities may come under pressure to change the classification of a film in order to make it less restrictive. Two local authorities down-graded *Spiderman* to a PG rating for that reason, since some parents had been disappointed by the '12' rating.[34] There is no requirement of consistency between authorities and thus discrepancies have arisen between different local authority areas. It is notable that the cinema is the only art form subject to moral judgment on a local level and clearly it may be asked why it should be so singled out. This dual system of censorship was criticized unavailingly over twenty-five years ago by the Williams Committee in 1979,[35] partly on the ground of the anomalies caused by having two overlapping levels of restraint and partly due to the inconsistency between local authorities. It considered that a unified system should be adopted. In particular, it criticized a system which allowed adult films to be censored beyond the requirements of the Obscene Publications Act.

STATUTORY REGULATION OF VIDEOWORKS

The Video Recordings Act 1984 was introduced after a campaign about the dangers posed by 'video nasties' to children. The campaign, by the *Daily Mail* and a group called the Festival of Light, managed to convince Parliament that legislation was necessary in order to address the problem.[36] Under the Video Recordings Act 1984, the BBFC was established as the authority charged with classifying videos for viewing in the home.[37] It currently classifies videos, DVDs and some digital works under the 1984 Act. Videoworks[38] are classified and therefore censored in almost the same way as films, and under s 9 of the 1984 Act, it is an offence to supply a video without a classification certificate, unless it is exempt on grounds of its concern with education, sport, music or religion. Under s 2(2) the exemption will not apply if the video portrays human sexual activity or gross violence or is designed to stimulate or encourage this. Section 4 of the 1984 Act requires that the BBFC should have 'special regard to the likelihood of video works being viewed in the home'. Thus, makers of

---

[33] See Holbrook (1973) 123 *NLJ* 701.   [34] See BBFC press release 13.6.02.

[35] See Williams Committee on Obscenity and Film Censorship, which conducted a review of the area, Cmnd 7772, 1979.

[36] See J. Petley, *Screen*, Vol 25 No 2, p 68.

[37] After the introduction of the Video Recordings Act 1984, the President and Vice-Presidents of the Board were designated by the Home Secretary under section 4(1) as the authority responsible for applying the statutory classification system for videoworks set out in the Act.

[38] When the term 'videowork' or video is used it will be used to cover video material presented on DVDs and digital games.

videos may find that videos are censored well beyond the requirements of the Obscene Publications Act.

The regime in respect of videos was made potentially more restrictive in 1994. Fears that children might be more likely to commit violence after watching violent videos[39] led the government to include a number of provisions in the Criminal Justice and Public Order Bill 1994, which was then before the Commons. Under s 90 of the Criminal Justice and Public Order Act 1994, inserting s 4A into the 1984 Act, the BBFC must have 'special regard' to harm which may be caused to 'potential viewers or through their behaviour to society' by the manner in which the film deals with criminal behaviour, illegal drugs, violent behaviour or incidents, horrific incidents or behaviour or human sexual activity. These criteria are non-exhaustive. The BBFC can consider any other relevant factor. 'Potential viewers' include children, but it is not necessary to show that children had in fact viewed the video. The kind of harm envisaged, to a child or to society, is not specified and nor is the degree of seriousness envisaged, although the use of the word 'may' implies that there must be some likelihood of harm. Once the Board has taken the above factors 'into account', s 4A does not prescribe the Board's response.[40] Section 89 of the 1994 Act also amended s 2(2) in respect of the scope of the exemptions mentioned above. These exemptions will not apply if a video 'depicts techniques likely to be useful in the commission of offences' or 'criminal activity likely to any significant extent to stimulate or encourage the commission of offences'. It is not necessary to show that the video is *designed* to stimulate or encourage the activity mentioned above, but only that it is likely to do so. If the BBFC considers that a particular work is unacceptable for viewing, it can, and does, refuse to issue a classification certificate altogether. This has the effect of banning the videowork concerned since under the 1984 Act ss 9–11 it is a criminal offence to supply, offer, or possess for supply an unclassified video. It is also an offence to supply a video in breach of the classification certificate issued by the BBFC.[41]

A right of appeal from the decisions of the BBFC to the Video Appeals Committee (VAC), which operates as a Tribunal, was created under the provisions of s 4(3) of the 1984 Act.[42] No other party has the right of appeal under the Act. The Home Secretary

[39] See further, Home Affairs Committee, *Video Violence and Young Offenders*, Fourth Report (1994) HC 514.

[40] See, on this issue, C. Manchester, 'Criminal Justice and Public Order Act 1994: obscenity, pornography and videos' (1995) *Crim LR* 123, pp 129–30.

[41] It may be noted that it is a defence under the Video Recordings Act 1993 to a charge of any offence under the 1984 Act to prove that the offence was due to the act or default of another person or that the accused took all reasonable precautions to avoid the commission of the offence 'by any person under his control'.

[42] Under section 4(3) of the 1984 Act the Home Secretary must be satisfied that the designated authority (in practice this meant the principal officers at the BBFC) have adequate arrangements for appeals against classification determinations which producers or distributors feel are too restrictive. This may be because the video works in question have been given too high a classification or because they have been refused a classification altogether. The 1984 Act itself is silent as to the nature of the appeals body but the BBFC itself set up the VAC. The BBFC was responsible for the mechanics of recruitment and appointment of its members.

has sought to intervene in this classification and appeals scheme, with the result that in the 1990's the BBFC and the VAC came into conflict in respect of a number of explicit videos which depicted actual, rather than simulated, sexual scenes. The Board relaxed their guidelines in 1997 and classified a number of videos containing more explicit material than had been classified before, including scenes of actual penetration and oral sex. The Home Secretary was apparently concerned that this action would create a potential conflict with the enforcement policies of both Customs and Excise and the police, who may seize material of similar explicitness for forfeiture proceedings via Magistrates' Courts under the Customs Consolidation Act 1876 and the Obscene Publications Act 1959 respectively. He instructed the Board to rescind their policy change. The Board set up an Enforcement Sub Group which was established to consider the issue of consistency of standards between the Board and the prosecuting authorities.[43]

In 1998 the Board refused to classify an explicit sex video, *Makin' Whoopee*, to which they had given, but subsequently withdrawn, an interim classification certificate under their revised guidelines. The publishers appealed to the VAC who found in their favour, rejecting arguments that the video might be obscene within the meaning of the 1959 Obscene Publications Act. The Board classified the video in the R18 category but did not accept that the judgement, which was limited to the issue of obscenity, set a precedent for consideration of similar videos.[44] A further seven videos were subsequently refused classification certificates and the Board then faced appeals against their decisions in respect of the videos. The VAC found in favour of the appellants and the Board subsequently sought leave to apply for judicial review of the VAC's judgement: *R v Video Appeals Committee of the BBFC ex parte BBFC*.[45] The Board was unsuccessful on the basis that the VAC had taken all the relevant factors into account, including any risk to children. It was thought that since the videos were to be sold in adult sex shops, the risk that they would come into the hands of children and the risk that they would cause harm to them was very slight. In the proceedings, Mr Justice Hooper concluded: 'I have no doubt that the conclusion "that the risk of [the videos in question] being viewed by and causing harm to children or young persons is, on present evidence, insignificant" is one that a reasonable decision maker could reach . . .'. He found that the VAC had acted reasonably in reaching the decision which they did on the basis of the arguments put before them, and dismissed the Board's application. In other words, it could not be said that this was a decision that no reasonable regulator could have come to—the familiar low threshold. Thus the judgment was based on the *Wednesbury* unreasonableness standard only, not on Art 10 demands, and indicated quite a high degree of deference, common in this context, to the expert decision-maker—the VAC.[46] It was *consistent* with the view that

---

[43] See BBFC Response to the Home Office Consultation Paper on the *Regulation of R18 Videos*, paras 2.3 and 1.4.

[44] Ibid.   [45] (2000) EMLR 850.

[46] See further Chapter 3 at 149–53 on deference in this context.

the access of adults to explicit material should not be prevented on the basis that there was an unquantifiable risk of harm to children if it happened to come into their hands. However, it would be over-stating the matter to find that the judgment laid down a statement of principle of this nature.

The then Home Secretary, Jack Straw, was angered by the decision of the VAC, and the Home Office published a Consultation Paper indicating that new legislation on the VAC, and the use of the R18 classification, might be necessary.[47] The possibility that the VAC could be set up under statute, with government appointed officers, was raised.[48] In response the BBFC did not accept the government's criticisms of the VAC, but recommended that its jurisdiction should be confined to deciding whether the Board, as the Designated Authority under the Video Recordings Act, had been 'fair, consistent and legally correct in the application of its published policy and Guidelines'.[49] It may be noted that the VAC has not always been so bold: it did not reverse the decision of the BBFC in relation to the video *Visions of Ecstasy*, on the basis that it was possibly blasphemous (this decision turned, however, on the problematic nature of the law of blasphemy; it is discussed further in Chapter 9).[50]

The decision in *R v Video Appeals Committee of the BBFC ex parte BBFC* highlighted one of the problems inherent in the 1984 Act, a flaw that became especially apparent in relation to R18 rated videos, under the more relaxed Guidelines. S4A of the Act operates on the assumption that children may be harmed if they view sexually explicit or very violent videos. However, there is no firm evidence that this is the case in relation to explicit depictions of sexuality,[51] as the government itself

---

[47] Home Office Consultation Paper on the *Regulation of R18 Videos*, 28.7.00; see also *The Guardian*, 17 May 2000.

[48] Home Office Consultation Paper on the *Regulation of R18 Videos*, paras 3.16–3.21.

[49] BBFC Response to the Home Office Consultation Paper on the *Regulation of R18 Videos*.

[50] See pp 494–7.

[51] BBFC News Release, 26 October 2000, *Abused children most at risk from pornography*: 'The BBFC commissioned the research in response to the Video Appeals Committee's ruling that the Board had failed to provide sufficient evidence of harm to children from viewing pornography in an appeal to the VAC by two porn distributors in 1999. The research was focused on finding out whether pornography by itself harmed children ... The majority of those interviewed [child psychologists] believed that viewing pornography would be harmful to any child, and that they should be protected from it. They were, however, able to quote very little in the way of evidence to support this belief, either from their own case loads or those of their colleagues. Some felt that viewing pornography depicting consensual sex would *not* be harmful to children who were well cared for and not being harmed in other ways. Determining the harm pornography does is not easy because it is difficult to disentangle it from other features of a child's situation, especially as the majority of children who are exposed to pornography are usually being harmed in other ways. Several of the experts argued that pornography was less regulated and more readily available in Europe and the USA. Yet they were not aware of any evidence that a higher proportion of children in those countries needed professional help because seeing pornography had upset them. Nor were related outcomes like teenage pregnancies or marital breakdowns higher in countries where pornography circulated more freely. . . . Robin Duval, Director of the BBFC, said: '. . . this research shows that there is in fact little clear evidence to support the natural view that "accidental" viewing will have seriously harmful effects. It is reasonable to assume that a sample of 38 leading professionals would have been able to cite more anecdotal evidence from their caseloads if harm to children, outside abusive or negligent situations, were significant or common . . .'

accepts,[52] and therefore it is very difficult to establish that harm is likely. Also, the connection between violence on film and violent behaviour in children has not been firmly established. It appears to be possible that there is a greater likelihood, not that children may perpetrate violence as an immediate reaction to exposure to violent films, but that they may be de-sensitized to violence in a long term sense if they watch a great deal of it.[53] However, psychologists disagree as to the creation of this effect and there is no clear consensus among them as to the general proposition that watching violent films harms children.[54]

Likelihood of harm should arguably be established on the balance of probabilities,[55] and on the basis of the current research it is unclear that it can be. If a greater risk of harm could be established it would at the least support the continuance of the restrictions on the sale of R18 videos. There are clearly two separate issues— that of the likelihood of harm and of the likelihood that children might view the video. The small chance that they might do so in respect of videos with the R18 classification due to the restrictions on sale makes it difficult to give effect to s 4A in relation to such videos, as the High Court accepted in *R v Video Appeals Committee of the BBFC ex parte BBFC*. It could also be argued that it is difficult to give legal effect to s 4A, even in relation to videos classified 15 or 18, since although there is a higher probability that children may view them, it is even harder to establish that they might be harmed if they do. Possibly s 4A has become legally ineffectual. Therefore it is unclear that there is a sound legal basis for creating distinctions between videos and films in terms of cuts at those classification levels

The 1984 Act places the BBFC in the position of official censors and in that role their work has in the past been criticized as over-strict and arbitrary.[56] Taking account of s 4 of the 1984 Act, the BBFC uses cuts and restrictive classification more stringently with videos than with films, partly because of the greater possibility that younger children will view them despite the age classification, and also because—as it states—certain techniques, such as the use of weapons or of drugs, can be watched repeatedly 'until the lesson is learned'. The possibility of repeat viewings may also, in the Board's view, be a matter of concern in relation to sexually explicit and violent scenes. So the age classifications may be used more restrictively in relation to videos and cuts are more likely to be made to videos before being rated '18'. For example, after taking specialist advice, the BBFC required a cut of one minute 28 seconds to the video version of *A Ma Soeur!*, a film about the rape of a young girl, to achieve an '18' rating. The Board had previously passed the film version '18' uncut. The Board took

---

[52] Home Office Consultation Paper on *The Regulation of R18 Videos*, para 1: 'There is little conclusive evidence of harmful effects'.

[53] See further, Home Affairs Committee, *Video Violence and Young Offenders*, Fourth Report (1994) HC 514.

[54] See M. Barker and J. Petley, *Ill Effects: The Media Violence Debate*, London: Routledge, 1997.

[55] See further Chapter 8 at 408 on this point in a different context.

[56] See N. Hunnings, 'Video censorship' [1985] *PL* 214; G. Robertson, *Freedom, the Individual and the Law*, London: Penguin, 1993, pp 263–72.

the advice of a leading consultant clinical psychologist who considered that the rape scene was similar to material which paedophiles use to groom their victims.[57] This was perceived as more of a problem in relation to the video, as opposed to the cinematic, release due to the possibility that the scene in question could be played repeatedly and in a private context.

THE IMPACT AND INFLUENCE OF THE HUMAN RIGHTS ACT

The stance of the BBFC is obviously influenced by the composition of the Board. Its effect on film makers has been criticized as militating against creativity. It has been suggested that a cosy relationship has developed with film-makers that is insufficiently challenging—that acceptable boundaries are not fully explored or delineated in the name of artistic integrity and creative freedom.[58] Although there has been liberalization, it is still arguable that commercial judgments rather than artistic considerations tend to dominate. The most pressing consideration for distributors is to find the widest possible audience, which may mean instituting cuts in order to obtain a 15 or 12A certificate. The fact that the classifications are mandatory is also relevant, since distribution in the UK is therefore more restricted by age restraints than in countries in which it is recommendatory. Children under the age in question are still part of the targeted market in such countries. The relationship between 'artistic' and commercial considerations is, clearly, a complex one. There is clear commercial mileage in obtaining the widest possible release of a film by way of the PG certificate. But there may also be commercial advantage in producing sexually explicit and controversial films. In both instances, in a very competitive market where backers and distributors are unwilling to take commercial risks, directors and producers may be forced to institute cuts for the UK release of a film where clearly they would prefer to release it uncut. The BBFC accepts that its application of its Guidelines leads to a more restrictive censorship and classification of films in the UK than in almost all of Europe or the US.

It seems possible that the inception of the HRA could have some impact on this situation, although ultimately by far the most significant matter is the stance of the BBFC. For example, a film maker whose film was refused a classification without certain cuts, could refuse to institute the cuts and seek to challenge the decision of the BBFC or, in the case of a video, that of the VAC, if it upheld the BBFC's decision. The VAC is a body set up under statute with a public function in the sense of hearing appeals regarding the classification of material to be promulgated to the public; it is

---

[57] See BBFC press release 25.6.02.   [58] See Robertson and Nichol, op cit, note 1, p 593.

also subject to judicial review. It is therefore almost certainly a functional public authority under s 6 HRA. The BBFC has a public function which is also statutory in respect of providing classification certificates for videos. Its function in relation to films is not statutory, but can clearly be termed public. Had it not undertaken the classification of films, the government would have been likely to set up a statutory body.[59] It is suggested therefore that it is also almost certainly a functional public authority under s 6.[60] If this is correct, private bodies or persons could bring an action against either body under s 7(1)(a) of the HRA, or by way of judicial review, relying on Art 10. In such an action, a court would have to give effect to s 12(4) HRA.[61]

Assuming that the VAC and BBFC are public authorities and so bound by the Convention rights under s 6, they should also ensure that their decisions do not breach Art 10, or any other relevant Article. For example, a film-maker whose film portraying actual homosexual intercourse or other explicit homosexual activity did not receive a certificate, could put forward the argument that Art 10 read with Art 14 (the freedom from discrimination Article)[62] should affect the interpretation, under s 3 HRA of the term 'indecency' in the PCA (if one of the actors was 17) or 'obscene' in the OPA. The argument would be that the same standards should be applied as would be applied to films showing explicit heterosexual activity. Importantly, as a public authority, the VAC cannot be confined to considering only whether the BBFC's decisions are 'fair, consistent and legally correct'; it also has to consider whether its own decisions on appeals might breach Article 10. It can of course be argued that 'legally correct' includes consideration of the BBFC's own duty under s 6 (1) HRA not to breach Article 10 in its decisions, and therefore the VAC must decide whether the BBFC has acted compatibly with the demands of Article 10. Nevertheless, the VAC has a duty in relation to Article 10 under the HRA distinct from that of the BBFC itself. The 1984 Act, as amended, must be interpreted compatibly with the Convention

---

[59] See further Chapter 3 at 112–22, on functional public authorities.

[60] The BBFC takes the view that because of its public functions in respect of the statutory classification of videoworks, it is a 'public authority' under the HRA. In taking this view it has not distinguished between its function in relation to videos and that in relation to films. Clearly, it would be anomalous if such a distinction was drawn given the similarity of the two functions. (See the 2000 BBFC Response to the Home Office Consultation Paper on *The Regulation of R18 Videos* at para 1.16.) See further Chapter 3 at 113–14, 120–1, on regulators as functional or core public authorities.

[61] See further Chapter 3 at 126, 131–2, on the provisions of s 12(4), and see Chapter 16 at 836 on the stance that the courts have taken towards it.

[62] Article 14 provides: 'The enjoyment of the rights and freedoms set forth in this Convention shall be secured without discrimination on any ground such as sex, race, colour, language, religion, political or other opinion, national or social origin, association with a national minority, property, birth, or other status.' Thus, Article 14 does not provide a general right to freedom from discrimination, only that the rights and freedoms of the Convention must be secured without discrimination. In the context under discussion Article 14 could be employed in order to argue that the right under Article 10 should be secured without discrimination on grounds of sexual orientation. This ground of discrimination is clearly covered by Art 14 (*Salgueiro da Silva Mouta v Portugal* Judgement of 21 December 1999); the question that would arise in this context would be whether differentiation between film-makers' output on the grounds of the *nature* of the output would be covered.

rights under s 3(1) HRA. Given that a number of its terms are very open-ended, there is room for a range of interpretations.

However, in the case of a sexually explicit or violent film, the problem would be, as indicated above, that the Strasbourg jurisprudence appears to support quite far-reaching restrictions. It might be argued that where the risk of children viewing the cinema release of a film is very slight due to the use of age restrictions, *and* the question of offending religious sensibilities does not arise, the jurisprudence could be viewed as supporting the availability of even very explicit films.[63] This contention would be based on the unavailability of the margin of appreciation doctrine at the domestic level, and also derives from the principles underlying the jurisprudence, which, as indicated in Chapter 8, relate, as far as Article 10(1) is concerned, to the familiar free speech justifications, including that of self-fulfilment.[64]

But it must be acknowledged that this argument is not situated firmly in the Strasbourg jurisprudence at present. It rests mainly on one decision of the Commission—that of *Scherer*.[65] The decisions of the Court, in particular those of *Handyside*[66] and *Otto Preminger*,[67] lend it only highly speculative support. The Court may have found it easier, in those decisions, to rest its argument on risks to children or to religious sensibilities, rather than enter the extremely difficult debate as to the proper limits of adult autonomy in relation to controversial, offensive and explicit speech. The argument that decisions at Strasbourg heavily influenced by the margin of appreciation doctrine should be applied domestically 'stripped' of its effects, is an appealing and compelling one that has been canvassed elsewhere in this book.[68] But the judges have shown little receptivity to it under the HRA so far.[69]

If a suitable case in this context arose domestically—which in itself is unlikely—a judge who wanted to impose a liberalizing interpretation on the domestic law would have to have a *pre-existing* determination to take a liberal stance in relation to the PCA 1978 or the OPA 1959. If so, he or she would be able to find some, admittedly meagre, support in the jurisprudence for that stance. But equally the opposing, conservative stance could be taken and could find greater support in the jurisprudence, particularly from *Gibson v UK*.[70] The OPA itself clearly takes an overtly paternalistic stance since it assumes that judgments can be made and imposed on others as to what might deprave and corrupt them. The HRA could be viewed as legitimizing this existing

---

[63] See Chapter 8 at 411–16.   [64] See Chapter 1 at 18–19 and Chapter 8 at 411.

[65] A 287 (1993). See for discussion Chapter 8 at 413–15.

[66] (1976) 1 EHRR 737. See for discussion Chapter 8 at 411–13.

[67] (1994) 19 EHRR 34. See further Chapter 9 at 488–94.   [68] See Chapter 3 at 145–9.

[69] For example, in *R v Perrin* [2002] EWCA Crim 747, a recent case on the OPA 1959 (discussed at pp 649–50 below) in relation to the Internet, *Handyside* and other relevant Strasbourg decisions were fully considered. The court noted that the margin of appreciation doctrine was relevant in them, especially *Handyside*. But it did not appear to appreciate that by applying *Handyside* without seeking to disregard as far as possible the parts of the decision affected by the doctrine, it was in effect allowing the doctrine to have an impact on domestic law. See further Chapter 3 at 145–7.

[70] See Chapter 8 at 476–7. For discussion of the domestic case see M. Childs 'Outraging Public Decency' (1991) *PL* 20.

position since the Strasbourg jurisprudence, especially the decisions of the Court on explicit expression, is itself paternalistic. Recent caselaw on the OPA and PCA in the context of Internet pornography indicates that the courts are taking the latter stance. On the other hand, in this context, courts are likely to defer to the expertise of the regulators,[71] rather than rely on the Strasbourg jurisprudence, however it could be interpreted. So if the BBFC adopts a liberal stance—and it appears, increasingly, to be doing so[72]—the courts are unlikely to interfere with its decisions.

On the assumption that the relevant Strasbourg freedom of expression juris- prudence lends a degree of support to adult autonomy in this context, it can be argued that there is fairly limited scope under Art 10(2) for interferences with the freedom of expression of film-makers in respect of the theatrical release of films targeted at adults. It would be expected that they would be afforded an 18 certificate and appropriate warnings should be posted at cinemas and on the Internet so that an unwitting viewer would not be offended. Art 10 might be viewed as underpinning the policy of awarding R18 certificates to films not viewed as obscene since there is virtually no chance of children viewing them due to the restrictions.

Taking account of *Scherer*[73] and *Hoare*,[74] different considerations might appear to apply to *videos*, owing to the possibility that, despite the restrictions on sale, they might be viewed by children in the home, but this argument should be considered carefully, in terms of its impact on adults. The effect of the margin of appreciation doctrine on those decisions should be taken into account, following the argument discussed above and in Chapter 3.[75] The question of the harm that might be caused should also be considered, bearing in mind the lack of evidence mentioned above regarding a connection between behaviour seen on film and actual behaviour. The mere invoca- tion of the possibility that children might view a video might not appear to be enough to satisfy the demands of proportionality, although it was found to be enough in *Hoare*. Theoretically, a domestic court could take a harder look at those demands than the Commission did in *Hoare*, since the margin of appreciation doctrine would be inapplicable. In practice, as discussed, the court would probably defer to the BBFC or VAC decision as in *R v Video Appeals Committee of the BBFC ex parte BBFC*; possibly the HRA would add little in this context to the reasonableness standard applied in that instance, although a nod in the direction of proportionality would be expected. In respect of videos, the small chance that children might view a video with an R18 certificate (bearing in mind the controls on buying such videos), and the unquantifi- ability of the risk that a child might be harmed by it, could be taken to mean that refusing to classify a video at R18, even where it is not obscene, would be dis- proportionate, under Art 10(2), to the aim pursued. Guidance on this matter might

---

[71] This is strongly indicated by the House of Lords' decision in *ProLife Alliance v BBC* [2004] 1 AC 185; [2003] 2 All ER 977 (for discussion see Chapter 11 at 577–92) and by the *R v Video Appeals Committee of the BBFC ex parte BBFC* decision [2000] EMLR 850.

[72] See note 3 above.   [73] A 287 (1993) Com Rep.   [74] [1997] EHRLR 678.

[75] At pp 145–9.

also usefully be sought from other jurisdictions,[76] since it is not a matter that Strasbourg has inquired into in any depth.

The stance taken by Strasbourg in relation to films likely to offend religious sensibilities was indicated in the leading decision: *Otto-Preminger*.[77] The decision is considered in detail in Chapter 9.[78] The film in question was not likely to be viewed by children, but was found to be offensive to religious sensibilities. The seizure and forfeiture of the film was not found to breach Art 10. Further guidance derives from the decision of the Court of Human Rights in *Wingrove v UK*.[79] It concerned a decision of the BBFC, upheld by the VAC, to refuse a certificate to the short, explicit film, *Visions of Ecstasy*. The Court found that the decision to refuse a certificate was within the national authorities' margin of appreciation. But the film, which was to be promulgated as a short video, was viewed as offensive to religious sensibilities and as quite likely to come to the attention of children, since it could be viewed in the home.[80] No breach of Art 10 was found.

CONCLUSIONS

The view of the Williams Committee on Obscenity and Film Censorship, which conducted a review of the area in 1979,[81] was that the censorship of films should continue. The Committee considered that in the light of some psychiatric evidence to the effect that violent films might induce violent behaviour, a policy based on caution was justified.[82] The point has often been made, however, that the evidence that films have a very different impact from books or magazines is not strong; the difference in treatment may be due to historical reasons: new forms of expression take time to gain the acceptance accorded to traditional mediums and are viewed with some suspicion.[83] Many of the BBFC guidelines are aimed at preventing specific forms of harm which might come about as a result of the viewing of films. Clearly, the causal relationship between the viewing and the harm in many instances may be debatable, but the BBFC does have the prevention of particular harms—over and above the causing of offence—in mind. For example, rejecting or cutting the depiction of imitable combat techniques in films aimed at children is defensible on that basis. Glamorization of images of sexual violence, including rape, may have some effect on the incidence of male aggression towards women, or other men. However, the avoidance of

---

[76] See Chapter 8 at 447–62.   [77] (1994) 19 EHRR 34.   [78] See pp 488–94.

[79] (1996) 24 EHRR 1. The question of the validity of taking the stance adopted in *Wingrove* and *Otto Preminger* is considered in Chapter 9 at 489–97.

[80] See paras 61 and 63 of the judgment.

[81] Cmnd 7772, 1979. See Simpson, note 82, pp 35–38.

[82] See A.W.B. Simpson, *Pornography and Politics: The Williams Committee in Retrospect*, Waterlow Publishers, 1983, p 37.

[83] See e.g. E. Barendt, *Freedom of Speech*, note 1, p 125.

specific harms cannot be said to be the sole aim of cutting explicit sexual images in films aimed at adults, where they are not linked to non-consensual acts or violence. If such images are not obscene—although, admittedly, as Chapter 8 points out, that concept creates its own grave difficulties of interpretation—the basis for cutting them is unclear.

Although the BBFC clearly has in mind the invasion of adult autonomy created by imposing constraints on films beyond those demanded by the criminal law, it continues to accept that such constraints are necessary even though they create a stricter censorship regime in the UK than in the rest of Europe. Such constraints are partly based on necessarily subjective interpretations of the contextual validation of explicit images. In taking its particular stance towards the censorship and classification of films the BBFC appears to an extent to be bowing to government pressure, as the story behind *R v Video Appeals Committee of the BBFC ex p BBFC* reveals. The possibility of mounting successful challenges to restrictive BBFC decisions in reliance on Art 10, as discussed above, remains open and would provide a counter to the paternalistic stance sometimes taken by the government.

But it is not suggested that the only consideration that should inform BBFC decisions is that of moral autonomy. In dealing with the portrayal of sexuality the BBFC is in a position to shift the focus from traditional concerns as to offence and the undermining of traditional moral values, to the protection of what Chapter 8 termed 'constitutional morality'.[84] Indeed, there are some signs in the stance it takes to the classification of films portraying sexual violence that it is already beginning to do so. In other words, on the model provided by the Supreme Court of Canada, which reconceptualized the concern of obscenity law as focused on the protection of foundational values such as equality and dignity,[85] the BBFC could increasingly bring such factors into its deliberations as to the portrayal of sexual activity in film.

THE INTERNET: VOLUNTARY REGULATION

INTRODUCTION [86]

The Internet is already a highly significant medium in terms of the provision of both information and entertainment. Its current and future significance as a medium cannot be over-stated—it will probably eventually overtake broadcasting as the culturally supreme medium. Its role in providing information has been recognized for some time; its role in relation to entertainment has perhaps been less emphasized. Many websites seek to provide both information and entertainment by the provision

---

[84] See Chapter 8 at 478–9.   [85] See Chapter 8 at 451–3.

[86] See generally: E. Barendt, *Freedom of Speech*, 2nd edn., Oxford: OUP, 2005, Chap 13; Y. Akdeniz, C. Walker, and D. Wall (eds), *The Internet, Law and Society*, London: Longman, 2000; G. Graham, *The Internet: A Philosophical Inquiry*, London: Routledge, 1999.

of video clips, photographs, narrative. The association between the use of the Internet and the other media considered here is very strong; for example, a number of websites, official and unofficial, are dedicated to a range of films and broadcasts and show trailers, advertisements, and clips.

But the internet is also a strongly *participatory* medium;[87] it not only enables ideas to be expressed by individuals in their live journals or on websites and discussion forums, it also affords—more significantly—efficacy to such expression in terms of audience access.[88] The internet is taking on a new and important role as a platform for the mass expression and exchange of ideas, globally. Individuals in general are largely excluded from mainstream discourse in the media. Journalists may claim to speak for them, and also their views find a very limited opportunity for expression in 'Letters' pages or audience-participation broadcasts, but such expression hardly overcomes the dominance of the media by professionals, meaning that it is unrepresentative, especially of the views of women and minority groups, since journalism in general, and the higher positions in the media hierarchy, still tends to be a white male domain. In this sense the Internet can be compared to public protest since protest also provides a means of affording efficacy to the speech of individuals, and particularly of minority or excluded groups.[89] The German Supreme Court, in the *Brokdorf* case,[90] viewed participation in protest as a form of 'active engagement in the life of the community'.[91] But the Internet provides opportunities for the mass exchange of ideas that far transcend the role of protest since it allows for such engagement with the global community, providing a means of exchanging views across national boundaries that has never existed before with such efficacy. Further, such ideas include, but are not confined to, the political arena. As Barendt notes, 'The Net certainly affords much more equal opportunities for communication than the traditional press and broadcasting media, where the entry costs are high and which are in practice for the most part available only to professional journalists and to the political and social elite'.[92] It may be said therefore that it engages with the broadly based speech justifications, engaging values of autonomy[93] and self-development.[94]

---

[87] See Barendt 2005, note 1, at p 451.

[88] According to a major research study published in April 2005 (*UK Children Go Online*, Sonia Livingstone and Magdalena Bober, April 2005: www.children-go-online.net), 75 per cent of 9–19 year olds surveyed had accessed the Internet from a computer at home. The Guardian reported in October 2005 that one third of UK teenagers had their own website or live journal.

[89] See H. Fenwick, *Civil Liberties and Human Rights*, 3rd edn., Cavindish, 2002, at 493–4; D.G. Barnum, 'The Constitutional Status of Public Protest Activity in Britain and the US' [1977] *PL* 310; E. Barendt, op cit, at 9, 14–15; D. Williams, *Keeping the Peace: The Police and Public Order*, London: Hutchinson, 1967, at 10 and 130–1; see also Sherr, *Freedom of Protest, Public Order and the Law*, Oxford, 1989, at 10–12.

[90] 69 Bverfge 315, 343–347 (1985).   [91] E. Barendt, op cit, at 15.

[92] See E. Barendt, *Freedom of Speech*, 2nd edn, OUP 2005, Chap 13, p 452.

[93] See generally, R. Dworkin, 'Do We Have a Right to Pornography?' in *A Matter of Principle*, London: Harvard University Press, 1985; T. Scanlon, 'A Theory of Freedom of Expression' (1972) 1 *Phil. & Pub. Aff.* 216.

[94] See generally, C. Emerson, 'Towards a General Theory of the First Amendment' (1963) 72 *Yale L.J.* 877, at 879–80; M. Redish, *Freedom of Expression*, Indianapolis: Michie Co, 1984, at 20–30; and K. Greenwalt, (1989) 89 *Columbia Law Review* 119, at 143–5.

There might appear then to be a strong case for viewing regulation of the internet with suspicion in free speech terms. The US Supreme Court has found that it should not be equated with broadcasting in relation to regulation, but, impliedly, with the print media.[95] The argument that the choice that can be exercised over encountering on-line expression differentiates it from broadcasting is reasonably persuasive, although as argued in Chapter 11, it is becoming increasingly possible to exercise greater choice over broadcast expression as it becomes more interactive.[96] In other words, it is becoming less of an intruder into the home and more of a deliberately invited visitor. Thus there is an argument for relaxing the regulation of broadcasting—which Ofcom appears to accept—but not for extending that model of regulation to the internet.

But the strength of the internet—its ready accessibility and susceptibility to choice— can also be viewed as its weakness. Its use by groups excluded from the mainstream media is not necessarily benign. For example, a range of racial hatred offences can be committed by broadcasters, film-makers or playwrights under the Public Order Act 1986 ss20, 21, 22 and 23. These offences have now been amended to include religious hatred under the Racial and Religious Hatred Act 2005.[97] The Public Order Act offences have not been specifically amended to apply to the internet, although s 21 probably covers it, but in any event the general difficulty of prosecuting Internet Service Providers (ISPs), discussed below, would apply. Hate speech can be available from websites which would not appear in UK newspapers and could not appear in broadcasting due to Ofcom's regulation, and it can also be much more rapidly disseminated throughout the world. The ready dissemination of hate speech (and possibly of extreme depictions of sexual violence) arguably cannot be supported by the free speech argument from self-fulfilment.[98] Thus, as Barendt puts it: 'it is surely wise at least to retain those controls on Internet speech which are justifiable in the case of speech disseminated by other means. The mere facts that the Internet is easy and cheap for most people to use, and that they enjoy equal access as speakers and receivers on it, does not constitute an argument for a bonfire of controls'.[99] The discussion below of law and regulation of the internet is not therefore premised on the desirability of a complete relaxation of control over the internet.

This concern as to the 'weakness' of the internet particularly exercises the authorities in relation to the availability of pornography and the protection of children. This is the case at EU level and in relation to the UK government, as discussed below. As a UK government Consultation Paper put it in 2005:

[The Internet is a] spectacular communications development . . . transforming our lives, offering unparalleled opportunities to communicate, to discover and to learn. Alongside these benefits, the Internet also brings challenges for, amongst other things, the regulation of

---

[95] *Reno v ACLU* 521 US 844. For further discussion of this point, see above, note 1, Barendt 2005, Chap 13, p 455.

[96] For discussion see Chapter 11 at 564–5.   [97] For discussion see Chapter 9 at 508–13, 516–27.

[98] For discussion see Chapter 1 at 18–19.

[99] See Barendt, *Freedom of Speech*, 2nd edn, OUP, 2005, Chap 13, p 454.

potentially illegal pornographic material which is readily accessible . . . In pre-Internet days, individuals who wished to view this kind of material would need to seek it out, bring it into their home or have it delivered in physical form as magazines, videos, photographs etc, risking discovery and embarrassment at every stage. Now they are able to access it from their computers at home . . .[100]

Concern about the use of the internet is not confined to the availability of extreme or child pornography. It expresses itself in the UK partly through prompting developments in the criminal law, but also in supporting other initiatives aimed at regulation. Below, issues relating to UK law and regulation of the internet are considered, followed by consideration of the current efforts at regulation and the application of the current and proposed criminal law, taking account of free speech arguments.

APPLYING LAW AND REGULATION TO THE INTERNET

Internet advertising is regulated in the UK by the Advertising Standards Authority (ASA),[101] but otherwise the Internet is not at present regulated in accordance with any of the models considered above. In the White Paper, *A New Future for Communications*,[102] the government did not propose a means of drawing the Internet within the Ofcom regime in relation to the regulation of programme services on the Internet, or otherwise. Visual images available on a service provided by the Internet *prima facie* fall within the definition, in the 2003 Act, of a 'licensable programme service', but such services also appear to fall within the exception provided for 'two-way' services, depending on the interpretation given to that exception. It is clearly intended to cover Internet services. However, even on the very doubtful assumption that it could do, Ofcom, like the ITC,[103] has not sought so far to apply its powers to the Internet; there would be severe practical difficulties in doing so, although it could do so in relation to broadcast material placed on websites by licensed broadcast services already under its purview. The result is that material is shown on various websites that clearly could not be shown in a broadcast.[104]

The Internet provides a complex global communications network which cannot be fully subject to regulation applied within the boundaries of one State. The Government has recognized the problems of seeking to apply regulation on the Ofcom model

---

[100] *Consultation Paper on The Possession of Extreme Pornographic Material*: Home Office 30.8.05–URL: news.bbc.co.uk/1 shared/bsp/hi/pdfs/30 08 05 porn doc.pdf.

[101] See Chapter 10 at 545–9 for discussion of the ASA as a regulator.

[102] Published 12 December 2000; www.communicationswhitepaper.gov.uk.

[103] See the ITC website http://www.itc.co.uk.

[104] For example, Channel 4 has shown material on its website that has been excluded from films broadcast on television. See e.g. *Guardian Unlimited Special Report* 27.4.04.

to the Internet.[105] It has been contended that: 'By creating a seamless global-economic zone, borderless and unregulatable, the internet calls into question the very idea of a nation-state.'[106] But in considering controls over the Internet, as over the other media considered here, it is necessary to distinguish between the application of the ordinary law and the use of a general regulatory regime monitored and policed by a regulatory body. In relation to the use of the law, a range of views have been expressed. It has been argued that the Internet is not inherently unregulatable, even at the national level, on the ground that 'the Internet creates new contexts for old problems rather than new problems *per se*'.[107] Robin Duval, President of the BBFC from 1999–2004, has also argued that the Internet can be regulated, pointing out that corporations have successfully brought actions against ISPs on commercial grounds.[108] This is also the stance of the EU Commission, which is discussed further below. But as the UK government pointed out in a recent Consultation Paper,[109] the general application of the criminal law in one jurisdiction to ISPs based abroad faces almost insuperable problems, as discussed below. The solutions being canvassed at present include reaching international agreements, particularly on the availability of pornography, and adapting or developing offences aimed at consumers and only indirectly at ISPs.

The availability of explicit and pornographic material on the Internet has prompted significant changes in EU audio-visual policy. *The Council Recommendation concerning the protection of minors and human dignity*[110] was the first legal instrument at EU level that concerned the content of material on the Internet. The European Parliament and the Council had already taken measures in 1999 with a view to protecting minors from harmful material on the Internet.[111] But in 2002 the Commission found that the development of the Internet was continuing to create difficulties in relation to the policy of protecting children.[112] It noted that the volume of material

---

[105] See *Regulating Communications: The Way Ahead*, June 1999, www.dti.gov.uk/convergence-statement.htm at para 3.20.

[106] J.P. Barlow, 'Thinking locally, acting globally' (1996) *Cyber-Rights Electronic List*, 15 January.

[107] Y. Akdeniz, C. Walker, and D. Wall, (eds), *The Internet, Law and Society*, Longman, 2000, Chap 1; Y. Akdeniz, C. Walker, and D. Wall, 'The Internet, Law and Society', p 17.

[108] See RSA lecture 21.2.01, available from the BBFC website, www.bbfc.co.uk.

[109] *Consultation Paper on The Possession of Extreme Pornographic Material*, Home Office 30.8.05–URL: news.bbc.co.uk/1 shared/bsp/hi/pdfs/30 08 05 porn doc.pdf.

[110] 24 September 1998, 98/560/EC, OJ L 270, 7.10.1998, p.48.

[111] In order to promote a safer Internet, the European Parliament and the Council adopted on 25 January 1999 a multi-annual Community Action Plan on promoting safer use of the Internet by combating illegal and harmful content on global networks, Decision No 276/1999/EC, OJ L33, 6/2/1999, p 1 (the 'Safer Internet Action Plan'). On 16 June 2003, the European Parliament and the Council adopted a two-year extension to the Safer Internet Action Plan, Decision No. 1151/2003/EC amending Decision No 276/1999/EC, OJ L 162, 1.7.2003, p 1.

[112] In accordance with section III of the Recommendation, para 4. The implementation of the Recommendation was evaluated for the first time in 2000, and the first report was published in 2001: Evaluation Report to the Council and the European Parliament on the application of Council Recommendation of 24 September 1998 on protection of minors and human dignity COM(2001) 106 final, 27.2.2001. Parliament adopted a resolution on the report on 11 April 2002: C5–0191/2001–2001/2087(COS), in which it

on the Internet is immense in comparison to broadcasting and also that in traditional broadcasting (analogue or digital) it is not difficult to identify the individual broadcaster, while it may be impossible to identify the source of content on the Internet. At the same time access to harmful and illegal content is very easy and may even be unintentional. As a result the Commission proceeded in 2004 to propose an additional *Recommendation*[113] which calls on the Member States, the industry and other interested parties to:

take steps to enhance the protection of minors and human dignity in the .. internet sector ... Illegal, harmful and undesirable content and conduct on the Internet continues to be a concern for law-makers, industry and parents. There will be new challenges both in quantitative (more 'illegal' content) and qualitative terms (new platforms, new products) ... [states should take] into account the ever-increasing processing power and storage capacity of computers ...'.[114]

The original and the proposed *Recommendations* favour the development of co-regulatory and self-regulatory mechanisms for the Internet rather than regulation based on the imposition of an external regulatory regime via legislation. Such approaches, especially the co-regulatory one, are viewed by the Commission as more likely to be 'flexible, adaptable and effective ... with regard to the protection of minors'.[115] At present the approach in the UK is largely self- rather than co-regulatory. At the same time it may be said that self-regulation is giving way to an extent to co-regulation at present since a loose co-operative framework covering public authorities, the industry and the other interested parties, including consumers, is becoming apparent, as indicated below.

So in accordance with the EU stance, which is reflected in current government policy as indicated below, Ofcom is likely to continue to take the approach that the ITC took—that it will support and contribute to the voluntary regulation of the Internet in relation to television programme material and advertisements on websites.[116] It will be argued below, however, that current policy may not result in the creation of the level of protection for minors envisaged in the proposed 2004 *Recommendation*. A more overt and formal movement towards co-regulation may be necessary.

---

called on the Commission to draw up a further report preferably before 31 December 2002. This was produced in 2003: Second Evaluation Report From the Commission to the Council and the European Parliament on the application of Council Recommendation of 24 September 1998 concerning the protection of minors and human dignity, Brussels, 12.12.2003, COM(2003) 776 final.

[113] *Proposal for a recommendation of the European Parliament and Council on the protection of minors and human dignity and the right to reply in relation to the competitiveness of the European audiovisual and information services industry,* COM(2004) 341 final 2004/0117 (COD) 30.4.04, press release 04/598.

[114] Para 2 of the proposal for a recommendation.

[115] Note 113 above, Introduction.

[116] See further: T. Ballard, 'Main Developments in Broadcasting Law', *Yearbook of Copyright and Media Law* 329, at 334–335, OUP 2001/02; T. Ballard, 'Survey of the Main Developments in the Field of Broadcasting Law in 1999', *Yearbook of Copyright and Media Law,* 367, at 373–374, OUP, 2000.

The remit of the Advertising Standards Authority covers standards of taste and decency in internet advertising. But the ASA does not seek to apply the British Code of Advertising, Sales Promotion and Direct Marketing (the CAP Code) to all Internet advertising. It only applies it to online advertisements in 'paid for' space, such as banner and pop-up advertisements[117] and advertisements in commercial e-mails and sales promotions wherever they appear online (including in organisation's websites or in e-mails). It does not apply the CAP Code, which includes requirements of offence-avoidance and 'decency' in advertising,[118] to organizations' claims on their own web-sites. This is mainly because it would be almost impossible to apply sanctions effectively for breach of the Code in such advertising. When the ASA and CAP apply sanctions against companies that do not co-operate with their requests, they usually rely on third parties, such as the owners of newspapers, magazines and poster sites, to enforce decisions by refusing to accept advertising by the company in question. As the ASA acknowledges on its website: 'the direct relationship between the internet user and the organization bypasses any middleman and makes the medium almost impossible to regulate effectively'.[119] The ASA also views the relationships between consumers who visit an organization's own website as direct rather than involuntary: 'the information is therefore "pulled to" rather than "pushed at" them unlike traditional forms of advertising'. In relation to the forms of on-line advertising that it does seek to regulate, it appears to have a very high compliance rate.[120] It reacts to consumer complaints, if upheld, by contacting the organizations in question and requesting changes to internet adverts.[121] The advertisers appear to perceive commercial advantage in complying with the CAP Code—on the tit-for-tat principle. If one advertiser defaults by refusing to

[117] In relation to these forms of internet advertising, the ASA states: 'There are a number of different online advertising formats (or Interactive Marketing Units (IMUs) as they are sometimes called) that are available to marketers. Banner advertisements are probably the best known, but other forms of IMUs include interstitials, superstitials, buttons, pop-ups, skyscrapers, floating ads, advertorials and text links. A banner is an advertisement found on a website page. Banners appear on a rotating basis in windows, usually at the top, bottom or side of web pages, and are used by marketers to make consumers aware of their products and services and to drive consumers directly to a particular website'.

[118] The Code states: *Decency (ie avoiding serious or widespread offence).*

5.1 Marketing communications should contain nothing that is likely to cause serious or widespread offence. Particular care should be taken to avoid causing offence on the grounds of race, religion, sex, sexual orientation or disability. Compliance with the Code will be judged on the context, medium, audience, product and prevailing standards of decency.

5.2 Marketing communications may be distasteful without necessarily conflicting with 5.1 above. Marketers are urged to consider public sensitivities before using potentially offensive material.

5.3 The fact that a particular product is offensive to some people is not sufficient grounds for objecting to a marketing communication for it.

[119] See asa.org.uk.

[120] See *Compliance Report: Internet banner and pop-up adverts Survey* (2002), available from the ASA website: asa.org.uk.

[121] The ASA upheld its first complaint against a banner advertisement in May 2000. The advertisement, by an internet service provider, appeared on a financial webpage and a complaint was upheld on the grounds that the advertiser did not make it sufficiently clear that the banner was an advertisement, not editorial content. Since that time, complaints against a further six banner advertisements have been upheld by the ASA.

comply, others are also likely to do so, thus damaging the level-playing field for marketers within each sector. Also the ASA could seek to apply sanctions against that company's advertising in other media sectors where middle-men can be utilized.

Thus the ASA has informal, commercial sanctions that can be brought to bear in relation to on-line advertising. They are aimed more at misleading adverts rather than at offensive ones. A general UK internet regulator would not have such sanctions at its command. Nor could it have the licensing power that Ofcom possesses or the classification power of the BBFC since ISPs may well be based outside the jurisdiction. The Internet is clearly not as susceptible to control on the basis of offence-avoidance as the other visual media are. In relation to explicit and pornographic speech in films and photographs on websites, the Internet has the potential in a sense to undermine the regulatory regimes applied to the other media, precisely because no regulatory body stands between it and the criminal law, creating a regulated 'no-go' area beyond the requirements of the law. In other words, there is no one regulator monitoring explicit internet material via a code with sanctions attached—a code that would, on the Ofcom model, impose standards for offence-avoidance going beyond those demanded by the relevant criminal law. This is not an argument for seeking to impose regulation on that model on the internet—even assuming that that could be done. The argument is that the availability of legal, explicit material on the internet that at present could not be broadcast, places Ofcom's regulation under pressure.

Since there is no regulatory regime on the broadcasting model, material posted on the Internet is more likely to come directly into conflict with the criminal law in relation to explicit expression. The Internet is subject to the criminal law just as the other media considered here are, although the law has required adaptation in order to bring websites within its ambit. Procedurally and substantively speaking, there are problems in securing convictions in respect of web-based material which do not arise in relation to broadcasts or films. The use of the criminal law to strike directly at the consumer of pornography, rather than at the supplier, immediately engages speech-based autonomy arguments balanced against weaker countervailing justifications, as discussed below.

APPLYING CRIMINAL LAW TO WEB-BASED MATERIAL

The US has sought to suppress and restrict sexually explicit expression on the Internet. The US sought to regulate the Internet by means of the Communications Decency Act 1996, but its main provisions were struck down as unconstitutional on the basis of over-breadth.[122] In so doing, the Supreme Court found, following a

---

[122] *Reno v ACLU* 521 US 844. For further information on the struggle between the American Civil Liberties Union (ACLU) and official attempts to curb expression on the Internet, see the ACLU site: www.aclu.org/

number of precedents relating to other media, that if restraints aimed at protecting children also affect adults disproportionately, they may not be used as the means of denying children access to sexually explicit material. In other words, traditional free speech principles were applied to the Internet. So a more narrowly targeted provision in terms of cybercensorship was needed, if it was to survive challenges. The 1996 Act was followed by the more narrowly drafted Child Online Protection Act 1998.

In contrast, no statute with special application has so far been introduced in the UK. Instead, amendments have been made to existing statutes creating criminal liability in relation to explicit expression in order to apply them to web-based material. The situation is similar in Australia where the Broadcasting Services Amendment (Online Services) Act 1999 (Cth) drew the Internet within the generally applicable prior restrictions on sexually explicit expression.[123] As discussed in Chapter 8, explicit web-based material can be considered within the Obscene Publications Act 1959, as amended (OPA). Section 168 of the Criminal Justice and Public Order Act 1994 added the transmission of electronically stored data to the Obscene Publication Act's definition of 'publication'. Creating a link from a UK-based web-page to another in another jurisdiction on which obscene material is posted arguably amounts to 'publication'.[124] In *Graham Waddon*,[125] the defendant was convicted of the offence under s 2(1) of the 1959 Act on the basis that he had maintained a website in the USA onto which he had uploaded obscene material from the UK. Thus the fact that the material was placed on a US-based website did not prevent the defendant from being charged and convicted of the s 2(1) offence in England.

But in general there are, in practice, particular problems in applying the Obscene Publications Act (and its equivalent in Scotland—the Civil Government (Scotland) Act 1982) to web-based material. For example, the definition of obscenity is a relative one, dependent on the susceptibilities of those who are likely to encounter the material.[126] Web-based erotic and pornographic material, including material from '18' or 'R18' rated films, is available on a range of websites to any user who possesses a computer of the correct specification, although a credit card would often have to be used to gain access to it. Children can therefore gain access to such material and images, and the question of the obscenity of the material might therefore have to be determined by reference to that likely audience, depending on the circumstances, including the nature of the website and the likelihood that children would be able to

issues/cyber/hmcl.html, 2000. The CDA made it a crime, punishable by up to two years in jail and/or a $250,000 fine, for anyone to engage in speech that is 'indecent' or 'patently offensive' on computer networks if the speech can be viewed by a minor. The ACLU argued that the censorship provisions are unconstitutional because they would criminalize expression that is protected by the First Amendment and because the terms 'indecency' and 'patently offensive' are unconstitutionally overbroad and imprecise. See Vick, D. [1998] 61 *MLR* 414 on the Supreme Court decision.

[123] For discussion and criticism of the Act see Chen, P. 6(1) *UNSWLJ*.

[124] See Y. Akdeniz, 'To link or not to link?' (1997) 11(2) *International Review of Law, Computers and Technology* 281.

[125] (1999) Southwark Crown Court, 30 June; appeal dismissed 6 April 2000.

[126] See Chapter 8 at 429–34.

access it. It would be harder to establish the extent of the likelihood that children might access the information than it is to make the same calculation in relation to print material, although probably it would be as hard as it is in relation to videos. But videos are of course regulated by the BBFC, and it is an offence in itself to publish an unclassified video, without reference to its obscenity or indecency. Further, the BBFC has already taken the decision to continue to censor video films beyond the demands of the criminal law, thereby obviating the possibility of a prosecution under the 1959 Act, a decision which is, in effect, as discussed above, a compromise between defending adult autonomy and risking the promulgation of pornography to children. Since the Internet is not subject to the policing of an equivalent regulator, this problem is more significant in that context.

Although the thrust of UK policy in relation to web-based pornography is against individual consumers under the OPA, where the manager of the ISP happens to be in this jurisdiction, successful prosecution can occur. At least one successful prosecution has been brought against a web-page provider—*R v Perrin*.[127] In that judgment a number of findings were made that were intended to adapt obscenity law so as to catch web-based pornography, addressing some of the issues discussed above. The defence argued that the only relevant publication of the web page was to the police officer who had down-loaded it, and therefore it was wrong to test obscenity by reference to others who might have gained access to the preview page, and it was very unlikely that it would be visited by accident. However, the Court of Appeal accepted that there was publication whenever anyone accessed the preview page. No evidence that children would be likely to access it or had accessed it was put forward, but the Court appeared to assume that this was a possibility and that therefore the obscenity of the material could be judged against that likely audience. The lack of interest in the evidence in relation to children could be viewed as creating an appearance of departure from the basic principle of relative obscenity. The Court also rejected the suggestion that a prosecution should only be brought against a publisher where the prosecutor could show that the major steps in relation to publication were taken within the jurisdiction of the court. The possibility that the main steps towards publication might have occurred in another jurisdiction with less restrictive laws (the US) was not accepted as relevant. In relation to Article 10 the Court found: 'In the result we are satisfied that the statutory provision relied upon does fall within the scope of Article 10(2). For a legitimate purpose the offence was prescribed by law. Parliament

---

[127] [2002] EWCA Crim 747, CA. This case involved a French national based in the UK who was publishing from abroad (in the USA). The appellant was convicted of publishing an obscene article and appealed. The obscene article in question was a web page on the Internet. It depicted people covered in faeces, coprophilia or coprophagia, and men involved in fellatio. That web page was in the form of a trailer, a preview, available free of charge to any one with access to the Internet. Anyone wanting more of the type of material which it displayed could click on to a link marked 'subscription to our best filthy sites' and could gain access to a further web page by providing credit card details. The preview web page was accessed by an officer with the Obscene Publications Unit. To reach it a viewer would have to type in the name of the site, or conduct a search for material of the kind displayed.

was entitled to conclude that the prescription was necessary in a democratic society.' In other words, the Court refused to look beyond the balance that Parliament had struck in amending the OPA in 1994 order to include the internet. This was a highly restrictive interpretation of Art 10 since the Court refused to accept that it itself had a responsibility, under s 6 HRA, to examine the application of the law, taking the requirements of proportionality into account, in the instant case.

In general, the gravest problem facing the UK authorities is the practical one of seeking to bring prosecutions against ISPs operating abroad. Clearly, jurisdictions differ greatly as to the speech that they criminalize. This potentially places both the national authorities and the Internet Service Providers in a difficult, almost impossible, position. If national laws *could* be enforced against ISPs regardless of jurisdiction, they would be forced to limit the provision of material on websites very severely since they would have to obey the most draconian and restrictive of the speech laws available.[128] As Barendt points out: 'Website operators and other senders may have no idea who picks up their messages and which jurisdiction they live in, so the law imposes a great burden on them if they can be prosecuted whenever, say, a sexually explicit communication is accessed by a child, or extremist speech is accessed by anyone living in a country with strict hate speech laws'.[129] On the other hand, the national authorities are placed in an impossible position since they may well be unable to enforce sanctions against ISPs who are in another jurisdiction that is unlikely to aid in the enforcement of stricter national laws than it itself recognizes. Such countries would be likely to have little interest in prosecuting. Publishers might take the main steps towards Internet publication in countries with the most relaxed laws. According to the UK government, very little potentially illegal pornographic material found on the Internet originates from within the UK.[130] It appears probable that the lack of UK-hosted material is the result of the deterrent effect of the OPA and the Civil Government (Scotland) Act 1982.

Thus the UK is a more restrictive jurisdiction which the government views as in an especially difficult position in terms of holding the line against internet material hosted on websites outside the jurisdiction. The UK is addressing these problems, as discussed below, partly by enforcing laws against explicit expression against the ultimate consumer rather than against the ISP, and partly through voluntary regulation of the internet. In relation to extreme adult pornography the government stated recently

---

[128] This was pointed out on behalf of the defence in *R v Perrin* [2002] EWCA Crim 747, CA, referring to 'the world wide accessibility of the internet' and the opinion of the United States Court of Appeal was relied on to the effect that (Third Circuit) in *ACLU v Reno (No 3)* [2000] 217 F.3d 162 at 168–169 any court or jury asked to consider whether there has been publication by a defendant of a web page which is obscene should be instructed to consider first where the major steps in relation to publication took place, and only to convict if satisfied that those steps took place within the jurisdiction of the court. As discussed above (pp 649–50), this argument was not accepted by the Court of Appeal.

[129] See E. Barendt, *Freedom of Speech*, 2nd edn, OUP, 2005, Chap 13, p 452.

[130] It notes in its 2005 Consultation Paper (note 135 below) that the Internet Watch Foundation (IWF) received no reports of UK-hosted material in 2003 or 2004.

in its *Consultation Paper on The Possession of Extreme Pornographic Material:*[131] 'the global nature of the Internet means that it is very difficult to prosecute those responsible for publication who are mostly operating from abroad'. The paper is consulting on the introduction of a new offence of mere possession of 'extreme pornographic' material—an offence that has not existed previously in UK law. In its *Consultation Paper* the government noted that it is already illegal to publish such material under the Obscene Publications Act 1959 and, in Scotland, under the Civic Government (Scotland) Act 1982. However, it pointed out that the global nature of the Internet means that it is very difficult to prosecute those responsible for publication who tend to operate from abroad.

So the proposal is to make illegal the possession of a limited range of extreme pornographic material featuring adults. The intention is that the new legislation would introduce provisions to operate alongside the OPA that would mirror the provisions already in place in respect of indecent photographs of children.[132] A new offence would be created of 'simple possession of extreme pornographic material which is graphic and sexually explicit and which contains actual scenes or realistic depictions of serious violence, bestiality or necrophilia'. The intention is not to add an offence of possession to the OPA but to create a new free-standing offence to operate alongside the OPA 1959 and the Civic Government Act, and to increase the sentence for publishing under those other two statutes in order to emphasize the difference between possession and publication. The Consultation paper states: 'We believe the material which is under consideration would be abhorrent to most people and has no place in our society. Our intention in proposing a possession offence is to try to break the demand/supply cycle'. The offence would be limited to explicit actual scenes or realistic depictions of the specified types of material. The term 'explicit' indicates that the offence would cover activity which can be clearly seen and is not hidden, disguised or implied. The intention is also only to cover actual images or realistic depictions of the activities listed. It is not intended therefore to cover text or cartoons. This follows the precedent of the Protection of Children Act (PCA) 1978, s 1 of which covers pseudo-photographs.

The similar child pornography offence under the PCA s 1 requires possession for gain. However, as far as the Internet is concerned, possession has been criminalized since down-loading child pornography from the internet is covered by the Protection of Children Act 1978 (PCA); it has been found to constitute the 'making' of a photograph or pseudo-photograph.[133] It is not intended that the new offence will depend on bringing the material within the definition of 'obscenity'. The aim is to close a gap in the Obscene Publications Act 1959 (OPA): at present it only covers possession for gain. Thus, down-loading adult pornography is not covered by the OPA since making

---

[131] Home Office, 30 August 2005—URL: news.bbc.co.uk/1 shared/bsp/hi/pdfs/30 08 05 porn doc.pdf.

[132] The offence of possession of child pornography under the Protection of Children Act 1978 s 1, discussed in Chapter 8 at 469–70.

[133] *R v Bowden* [2000] 2 All ER 418. See further Chapter 8 at 469.

a photograph not for gain is not covered. The new offence would close that gap and bring the OPA into line with the PCA. It would also possibly criminalize the possession of some material that might not be deemed obscene. The obscenity of material is judged by reference to its likely audience;[134] the current proposal appears to proceed on the basis that some material should not be possessed, regardless of the likelihood that it would be encountered by anyone other than members of a willing audience. The new offence is aimed at the internet, but would not be confined to it. It would represent an extremely significant extension of the law relating to explicit speech. The justifications for its introduction are weak: it is unlikely that it would break the demand/supply link since the ISPs involved would still have an audience in a range of countries with less restrictive laws. The evidence that the availability of such material causes harm is inconclusive, as the government admits in the Paper.

VOLUNTARY REGULATION

The UK, in accordance with EU policy, has followed the path of self-regulation of the Internet, against the backdrop of the relevant criminal law. Thus, in the UK there has been so far no general attempt to draw the Internet within the system of restraints used for broadcasting, or the system used for films. Instead the Internet is restrained, as discussed above, by the general criminal law relating to expression, and also by self-regulation. The White Paper, *A New Future for Communications*,[135] and the Communications Act itself endorse this self-regulatory approach.

Section I(1) of the EU Council *Recommendation*[136] provides that the Member States should encourage the establishment of national frameworks for self-regulation by operators of on-line services. A number of UK Internet Service Provider Associations (ISPAs) are established in the UK, and in a number of member and accession States.[137] The ISPAs from eight member states, including those from the UK, are members of the European Internet Service Providers Association organization (EuroISPA).

---

[134] See further Chapter 8 at 429–31.

[135] White Paper, para 6.10: 'OFCOM should ensure continuing and effective mechanisms for tackling illegal material on the Internet, such as those being pursued under the auspices of the Internet Watch Foundation. It will also promote rating and filtering systems that help Internet users control the content they and their children will see. 6.10.1: The Government sees enormous benefits in promoting new media, especially the Internet. But it is important that there are effective ways of tackling illegal material on the Internet and that users are aware of the tools available, such as rating and filtering systems, that help them control what they and their children will see on the Internet. Research suggests that this is what people want in relation to the Internet, rather than third party regulation.'

[136] Note 113 above.

[137] The member states are: Belgium, Germany, Spain, France, Ireland, Luxembourg, Netherlands, Austria, Sweden, Hungary, Estonia, Slovenia, Turkey, Iceland, and Norway have also established ISPAs. In Denmark, Greece, Portugal, and Finland, the ISPs are represented through other trade organizations (Commission Report, see note 113 above).

Section II (2) of the Recommendation proposes that the industries and the parties concerned should draw up codes of conduct for *inter alia* the protection of minors and human dignity, in order to create an environment favourable to the development of new services.[138] The United Kingdom has stated that codes of conduct have been established and has also proposed to the Commission[139] that such codes should be drawn up by the industry representatives, rather than within a cooperative venture, involving public authorities. In a number of the member states, in contrast, including Germany and France, public authorities have been involved in drawing up the codes.

A number of the member states also have in place additional specific legal requirements dealing with the operators' obligations in relation to any illegal content on the Internet. This includes, for example, the imposition of positive obligations to prevent the further distribution of information clearly covered by the provisions of the country's Penal Code or obligations to preserve data in order to assist in investigations and prosecutions. This is not the case at present in the UK. The Commission has also encouraged the development of 'notice and take down' procedures in relation to illegal content on the Internet.[140]

The development of rating systems is encouraged by the Commission. They allow the carers of children to decide for themselves whether particular websites are suitable for children to access. The systems can be voluntary or mandatory. The United Kingdom relies on a voluntary system established by the Internet Content Rating Association (ICRA); under it website managers can apply for a rating on a voluntary

---

[138] The Commission has given guidance as to the content of such Codes. In particular, the Codes should cover the complaints mechanisms, with a view to facilitating the making and handling of complaints. They should also facilitate a co-regulatory approach by covering the procedures for ensuring cooperation between the operators and the public authorities. These should address the issues of basic rules (i) on the nature of the information to be made available to users, its timing and the form in which it is communicated, (ii) for the businesses providing the on-line services concerned and for users and suppliers of content, (iii) on the conditions under which, wherever possible, additional tools or services are supplied to users to facilitate parental control, (iv) on the handling of complaints, encouraging operators to provide the management tools and structures needed so that complaints can be sent and received without difficulty and introducing procedures for dealing with complaints, and (v) on cooperation procedures between operators and the competent public authorities (op cit, note 113 above, para 3.1.1).

[139] These should address the issues of basic rules (i) on the nature of the information to be made available to users, its timing and the form in which it is communicated, (ii) for the businesses providing the on-line services concerned and for users and suppliers of content, (iii) on the conditions under which, wherever possible, additional tools or services are supplied to users to facilitate parental control, (iv) on the handling of complaints, encouraging operators to provide the management tools and structures needed so that complaints can be sent and received without difficulty and introducing procedures for dealing with complaints, and (v) on cooperation procedures between operators and the competent public authorities (op cit, note 113 above, para 3.1.1).

[140] See note 113 above. These are methods of receiving complaints from members of the public via hotlines, which can then be screened and passed on to the police or to an Internet service-provider. One of the key aims of the Safer Internet Action Plan 1999–2004 (ibid, para 3.1.2, 9) was the creation of a European network of hotlines to span the EU. The Commission found that although hotlines had been established in a number of states, no respondents appeared to have made provision for assessing the efficiency of the hotlines in practice.

basis. Once this rating is available, parents and others, such as teachers, can use it to restrict access to websites with the most suitable rating. ICRA receives funding under the Safer Internet Action Plan and has produced a content rating system that is viewed as suitable for the EU. Rating systems can also be accompanied by filtering systems—systems that block access to certain websites, in the interests of protecting minors.[141] Once a quality charter of websites has been drawn up filter programmes can ensure that users in a particular forum, such as a library or school, are restricted to the websites on the list and such programmes are used in a number of the member states.

The Internet Watch Foundation (IWF) has produced a Consultation Paper on developing the use of rating systems in the UK to block undesirable Internet content.[142] Thus its activities appear to be extending beyond the enforcement of the criminal law; they may have a hidden ideological basis and may in particular invade the expression of sexual minorities. It is argued that government backing should be withdrawn from the IWF unless its activities, and any apparent ideological predilections, are subject to some form of accountability.

The above discussion indicates that the UK favours a regime that is towards the 'lighter touch' end of the spectrum, in comparison with the regimes established in a number of the other member states. The regime relies on a number of voluntary bodies and the involvement of public authorities in the UK has so far been very low-key. While this regime creates flexibility and avoids an overly restrictive approach to website access where controlled by public authorities, it also opens the way to misuse of power by the voluntary bodies in question. In the UK, a self-regulatory system for the Internet is being established by a number of voluntary bodies, including in particular the Internet Watch Foundation, with a remit to reduce the availability of illegal material on the Internet.[143] The IWF was founded by the UK Internet Industry in 1996. It is funded by the EU and the UK Internet industry;[144] it also has the support of the DTI and the Home Office.[145] In its own words the IWF:

is the only authorised organisation in the UK which provides an internet 'hotline' for the public to report their exposure to illegal content online. We aim to minimise the availability of internet content that contains: child abuse images originating anywhere in

---

[141] A particular filtering system utilizes 'walled gardens', consisting of special portals allowing access only to sites of guaranteed quality.

[142] 'Rating and Filtering Internet Content—A UK Perspective', March 1998, at www.internetwatch.org.uk/rating.html.

[143] For further information see: www.iwf.org.uk.

[144] This includes Internet Service Providers (ISPs), Mobile Operators and manufacturers, Content Service Providers (CSPs), and telecommunications and software companies.

[145] See the DTI statement Secure Electronic Commerce Statement (London 1998, at www.dti.gov.uk/CII/ana27p.html) para iv; Memorandum by John Battle MP, Minister for Science, Energy and Industry, House of Commons Adjournment Debate 'HMG Strategy for the Internet' 18 March 1998, www.dti.gov.uk/Minspeech/btkspch3.htm.

the world; criminally obscene content hosted in the UK; criminally racist content hosted in the UK.[146]

Rating, or vetting,[147] and filtering systems[148] can be used as an aspect of the self regulation of the Internet. Filtering systems are commonly used in the US by state bodies such as schools or Universities and also by parents. Such systems are supported by the government in the UK[149] and also by the EU.[150] Rating or filtering systems are problematic in free speech terms since they limit consumer choice and are frequently over-inclusive. They may also be under-inclusive in the sense that they do not affect a number of aspects of Internet-related communication, such as the use of chat-rooms. Thus, the objective of protecting children by the use of rating or filtering systems may not in fact be met, while at the same time adults may be prevented from accessing material posted on the Internet. The free speech implications of the use of filtering software by state bodies was considered in the US in *Mainstream Loudoun v Board of Trustees*.[151] The Loudoun County public libraries provided Internet access to their patrons subject to a number of restrictions; in particular, library computers were equipped with site-blocking software to block all sites displaying child pornography and obscene material and material deemed harmful to juveniles. The plaintiffs and the intervenors alleged that this policy violated their First Amendment rights since it 'impermissibly discriminates against protected speech on the basis of content and constitutes an unconstitutional prior restraint'. It was found that the policy should be subject to strict scrutiny; having examined it it was found that the policy was not necessary to prevent sexual harassment or access to obscenity or child pornography since other, less intrusive measures could have been adopted. Further, it was found that it was not narrowly tailored to meet the objectives asserted since less restrictive means were available to further the defendant's interests.[152]

The decision in *Loudoun* indicates that the pursuit of self-regulation by the use of rating or filtering systems by public authorities, such as schools, libraries or Universities could be viewed as incompatible with rights of expression under Article 10. Clearly, as discussed above, the standards demanded under Article 10 at Strasbourg

---

[146] It claims on its website that the use of its hotline reporting system has reduced the amount of illegal content hosted in the UK from 18 per cent in 1997 to less than 1 per cent in 2003. Under this system, ISPs can combat abuse of their services by operating a 'notice and take down' service which alerts them to any illegal content found on their system; they can report material to the IWF, which then passes on any relevant details to the law enforcement agencies.

[147] The Platform for Internet Content Selections is a vetting system that prevents the display on the computer of certain material. It can cover a range of specified material and is added by an independent vetting body, the publisher of the material, or an ISP.

[148] Filtering software, such as Cyberpatrol, can also be used to block or limit access to certain websites.

[149] See notes 113 and 135 above.

[150] See European Commission Communication, *Illegal and Harmful Content on the Internet* (COM(96) 487, Brussels, 1996); but cf. the Opinion of the Economic and Social Committee of the European Commission—OJEC, 98/C 214/08, 1998 at 29–32. See also Y. Akdeniz, 'The EU and illegal and harmful content on the Internet' (1998) 3(1) *Journal of Civil Liberties* 31.

[151] 2 F.Supp.2d 783 (E.D.Va 1998) 24 F.Supp.2d 552 (1998).

[152] *Sable Communications of California, Inc. v FCC*, 492 US 115 (1989) was relied upon.

where children might be affected by explicit speech, are not as high as those main-tained under the First Amendment. However, if, rather than use a filtering system, less restrictive measures were available in order to protect children, while leaving adults unaffected, state bodies might be expected to adopt them, although it must be noted that the European Court of Human Rights has not yet used the 'less restrictive meas-ures' test in the context of explicit material.[153] This is an instance in which, if a successful challenge to the policy of a particular public authority, such as a library, was mounted under Article 10, using s 7(1)(a) HRA, the body would merely have to change its policy; it would not be able to rely on s 6(2)HRA since no legislation mandates the use of filtering systems or provides public authorities with a discretion as to their use. However, as discussed in relation to films, it is unlikely that a challenge would be successful since the relevant Art 10 jurisprudence is so weak in its defence of explicit speech.

A less restrictive approach might involve relying on the Internet Content Rating Association (ICRA). The ICRA is an international, non-profit-making organization of internet leaders. It states that its objective is to make the internet safer for children, by warning parents and others of the content of websites. It believes in an approach it terms:

user empowerment—giving families the tools to control their online experience. When used voluntarily, tools like ICRA's empower families to match their online experience with their values, without compromising free expression or undermining other users' access to information and while respecting the rights of content providers.

The ICRA claims to make no ideological judgement about various sites. This labelling system would be less restrictive than a general filtering system such as the one used in *Loudoun* since the questionnaire used is specific.[154] However, it would still create the problem of blocking adult access to sites in pursuit of the objective of protecting children.[155]

It is perhaps understandable that the UK government has not sought so far to follow the example of the US government in terms of seeking to impose cybercensor-ship. But concerns may be raised as to the regulation by the IWF. It is a private, not a public, body although it could be viewed as having a public role of sorts, since it has government backing. But its role as an essentially private self-regulatory body means that it is not formally accountable to the public. In particular, any infringement of free speech principles by its activities would probably be outside the Human Rights Act

---

[153] See Chapter 3 at 98–9 and Chapter 8 at 410–22.

[154] It employs 'the ICRA questionnaire'. This asks content providers to check which of the 45 elements in the questionnaire are present or absent from their websites. This then generates a short piece of computer code known as an ICRA label that the webmaster then adds to his/her site. Users can then use filtering software to allow or disallow access to websites, based on the information declared in the label. The ICRA does not itself rate Internet content; the content providers do that, using the ICRA labelling system.

[155] See further L. Lessig and P. Resnick, 'Zoning Speech on the Internet: A Legal and Technical Model' (1999) 98 *Michigan Law Rev* 395, discussing methods of seeking to ensure that ISPs can recognize that the recipient of a communication is a child.

since it may not be a functional public authority[156] and no statute governs its activities.

CONCLUSIONS

The experience in the US indicates that forms of self-regulation provide a more sensitive, nuanced and, arguably, more effective form of restraint than creating broad criminal sanctions relating to explicit material on websites. However, the restraints on the Internet described above indicate that the situation in the UK is a confused and anomalous one. The criminal law has been applied in an arguably over-inclusive fashion. An imprecise and archaic law—the Obscene Publications Act—has been afforded a very broad interpretation in *R v Perrin*[157] that applies it to a relatively new medium. The same could be said of the interpretation of the PCA in *R v Bowden.*[158] The OPA creates restrictions in the UK that are not duplicated in a number of other jurisdictions; if the new possession offence is introduced, that position will be exacerbated. At the same time public authorities, such as libraries and schools, are drifting into a situation similar to that appertaining in the US, whereby rating and filtering systems are used to block access to a number of websites, without full enquiry into the over-inclusiveness of such systems or the value judgments underlying them. The decision so far of the UK government not to follow the dubious US example in seeking to introduce general legislation to protect children in this context is a readily defensible one, but the lack of government intervention or—it appears—of recognition of the potential problems could lead to an overly-restrictive stance. The analogy of book-burning has been used quite frequently[159] to describe the scenario that might arise in the UK, whereby cyber-censorship creates the same effect, but in a hidden fashion, in relation to controversial and explicit expression in cyberspace.

---

[156] In particular, it is not strongly linked to a core public authority, although, as indicated, it does have the support of government departments. It is the weakest regulator discussed in this book, but it is similar in some respects to the Press Complaints Commission, which probably is a public authority. For example, they both have no statutory underpinning or association with statutes, apart from the recognition of the PCC in the HRA, s 12. See further Chapter 3 at 112–22 on the emerging legal explanations of the functional public authority concept.

[157] [2002] EWCA Crim 747, CA.   [158] [2000] 2 All ER 418.

[159] See the ACLU Report www.aclu.org/issues/cyber/burning.html, 1997.

PART IV

MEDIA FREEDOM AND THE PROTECTION OF PRIVACY

This Part begins with Chapter 13, by analysing the approach of the Strasbourg case law to both the protection of privacy against the media and the means by which the conflict with media freedom this raises should be resolved. Having set out this basic framework, which is of relevance to all the chapters in this Part, it then goes on in Chapter 14 to consider the development in English law of rights to informational privacy against the press, focusing primarily upon recent dramatic developments in breach of confidence. Chapter 15 deals with the issues of defences to privacy actions, particularly dealing with the issues raised by the claims of media freedom in this area. Chapter 16 considers the particular issue of the protection of children's privacy against the media, whilst Chapter 17 examines the new regulatory framework for the protection of privacy in relation to the broadcast media.

13

PRIVACY AND FREEDOM OF EXPRESSION: STRASBOURG JURISPRUDENCE IN UK COURTS

INTRODUCTION

Article 8(1) ECHR provides a 'right to respect for . . . private and family life, [the] home and . . . correspondence'; paragraph (2) states, 'There shall be no interference by a public authority' with the exercise of this right', a guarantee subject to a number of general exceptions.[1] The purposes of this chapter, which introduces this Part on the protection of privacy against media intrusion, is to draw out some general themes in Strasbourg jurisprudence on this Article that are of relevance to all the chapters in this Part. There has for some time been quite a developed Strasbourg jurisprudence on Article 10, its scope, the values underpinning it, and on the different weighting to be afforded to the various kinds of speech protected under it. This case law is explored in detail in Chapter 2. However, until recently, there was very little *clear* guidance on two critical issues, which are the concern of this chapter. The first is the question whether Article 8, directed as it is primarily against *state* interference with the right to respect for private life,[2] could or should be interpreted as imposing a positive obligation on the state to intervene between private parties and provide a remedy where one (the media) invades the privacy of the other. The second was how, if Article 8 were to be so interpreted, the issue of the acute apparent clash with media freedom it raises was to be resolved. This latter issue is of particular difficulty and controversy. As is well known, different jurisdictions in the West have come to radically different conclusions on it; for example, US law, under the influence of the absolutist First Amendment,[3]

---

[1] Interferences must be 'necessary in a democratic society' for a number of specified purposes including protection of the rights of others—which clearly includes their Article 10 right to freedom of expression, for the prevention of crime and protection of public health.

[2] Note that paragraph 2 of Article 8 states that 'There shall be no interference *by a public authority* with the exercise of this right' save for the various exceptions enumerated above.

[3] US law also lacks any countervailing *constitutional* right to informational privacy. The US Constitution has of course been judicially interpreted as implicitly providing for a broadly based right to *substantive*

tends to give sweeping protection for truthful, privacy-invading disclosures in the press where there is any colourable public interest ('news-worthiness') justification.[4] French law is firmly in the opposite camp, giving, to Anglo-Saxon eyes at least, almost startlingly high levels of protection for the privacy of even major political figures.[5] For some time, it was impossible to discern a clear stance from Strasbourg on this key issue; now, however, the cases of *Peck v UK*[6] and *Von Hannover v Germany*[7] give some fairly clear, albeit not yet comprehensive, guidance as to how the conflict between these two fundamental rights may be resolved. Before turning to examine the Strasbourg case law, however, it is necessary first to say something about the notion of 'privacy' itself.

A RIGHT TO 'PRIVACY' DEFINED

Any discussion of enhancing legal protection for 'privacy' must indicate the sense in which that vexed term is being used.[8] Our aim is simply to locate our usage of the term within the still unresolved academic debate over its meaning and scope, and in particular to identify what should count as a legally actionable invasion of privacy. Here we follow Wacks, who suggests that the most useful course for the academic in this field is to 'identify what *specific interests* of the individual we think the law ought to protect'.[9] A necessary first step is to draw a distinction between what may be termed 'substantive' and 'informational' autonomy. The former denotes the individual's interest in being able to make certain substantive choices about personal life—for example, over abortion and sexual activity—without state coercion and therefore falls outside the direct concerns of this chapter. 'Informational autonomy', on the other hand, refers to the individual's interest in controlling the flow of personal information about herself, the interest referred to by the German Supreme Court as 'informational self-determination.'[10] Thus Westin describes privacy as the 'claim of

privacy, that is, the right of the individual to make morally controversial decisions about private life free from state interference, most famously in *Roe v Wade*, 410 US, 113 (1973).

[4] For a critical review, see D. Anderson, 'The Failure of American Privacy Law', in B. Markesenis (ed.) *Protecting Privacy*, Oxford: Clarendon, 1999.

[5] See, e.g. Picard, 'The Right to Privacy in French Law', in Markesenis, ibid; C. Dupre, 'The Protection of Private Life Against Freedom of Expression in French Law' (2000) 6 *EHRLR*, 627–49. For a recent decision on French law, which had imposed a permanent ban on the distribution of a book published after the death of former President Mitterrand, and containing details about his health, see *Plon (Société) v France*, no. 58148/00, 18 May 2004, discussed below.

[6] (2003) 36 EHRR 41.

[7] (2004), [2004] EMLR 21—for a summary and comment see (2004) 5, EHRLR 593–6.

[8] It is not our intention to attempt any 'new' definition of privacy and, indeed, we concur with Raymond Wacks in finding that 'the voluminous [theoretical] literature on the subject has failed to produce a lucid or consistent meaning of [the] concept': 'Introduction' in Wacks (ed.) *Privacy*, Volume 1, Hong Kong: Dartmouth, 1993, xi.

[9] Ibid, xii.   [10] BGH, 19 December 1995, BGHZ 131, 322–46.

individuals, groups or institutions to determine for themselves when, how, and to what extent information about them is communicated to others'.[11] Arthur Miller's definition is similar: 'the individual's ability to control the circulation of information relating to him'.[12] Beardsley has dubbed this the right to 'selective disclosure'—to decide when and how much information about ourselves we will make known to others,[13] a value also identified as foundational by Rachels.[14] As Lord Hoffman has put it, speaking extra-judicially, 'Meddling with such matters [personal information] is metaphorically an invasion of my territory, a violation of the castle of my personality'.[15] While some of these commentators talk simply of 'information relating to an individual', we would suggest a narrower definition, namely 'personal information', by which we mean, following W.A. Parent's definition, 'facts about a person which most individuals in a given time do not want widely known about themselves' and 'facts which though not generally considered personal, a particular person feels acutely sensitive about.'[16] In accordance with these views, and those of other scholars,[17] we propose this interest as the primary concern of the law in this area.

This definition has however been attacked: it is said to necessitate making the counter-intuitive assessment that if one voluntarily disclosed the whole of one's personal life to another, this would entail no loss of privacy, because control had been exercised, not infringed.[18] We suggest in response that since we are seeking a definition intended to identify a legal *harm*—what is to count as an 'invasion of privacy'—we need not be concerned if that definition does not appear to capture voluntary actions, which intuitively, one might describe as 'losses' of privacy but which could never be of concern to the law.[19] Moreover, the individual evaluation of such voluntary actions will vary widely: one person's loss of privacy is another's gain in intimacy. The only harm which can be *objectively* identified is the removal of, or interference with, a person's ability to apply his or her own standards of openness which occurs when personal information about someone is disclosed against their will.

---

[11] *Privacy and Freedom*, New York: Athenaeum, 1967, at p 7.

[12] *Assault on Privacy*, Michigan: University of Michigan Press: Ann Arbor, 1971, p 40.

[13] 'Privacy: Autonomy and Selective Disclosure' in *Nomos XIII* 54.

[14] J. Rachels, 'Why Privacy is Important' (1975) *Philosophy and Public Affairs* 323.

[15] 1996 Goodman Lecture, 'Mind Your Own Business', 22 May (unpublished).

[16] W. A. Parent, 'A New Definition of Privacy for the Law', *Law and Philosophy* 2 (1983) 305, 306–7, collected in Wacks (ed.) *Privacy*, Aldershot, Hong Kong: Dartmouth, 1993.

[17] Wacks, *The Protection of Privacy*, London: Blackstones, 1980, 10–21; Ruth Gavison's definition of privacy—'a limitation of others' access to an individual' has three aspects: information; attention; physical access ('Privacy and the Limits of Law' (1980) 89(3) *Yale LJ* 421); see H. Gross's similar definition: 'The Concept of Privacy' (1967) 42 *NYULR* 34, 36. We consider the issue of physical access to be adequately dealt with by the law of trespass and deal in this book only with the issues of information and attention.

[18] Wacks, 'The Poverty of Privacy' (1980) 96 *LQR* 73, 76 (acknowledging the point as from unpublished work by Ruth Gavison (see his note 30)). W.A. Parent agrees (op cit, 326). It should be noted, however, that he simply asserts that such a person *has* lost privacy by so doing without a word of explanation. Intuitively, it is perhaps doubtful whether the position is as clear-cut as this. While most people would probably agree that someone who, for example, disclosed the whole of their private life in a newspaper article had lost privacy, it is by no means clear that someone who discloses intimate secrets to their spouse has 'lost privacy'.

[19] See Gavison, op cit, at 427 and note 23.

W. A. Parent has complained that a conception in which attention can invade privacy is far too broad, because it means that we lose privacy every time we step outside the house and hence become the subject of at least some attention from strangers;[20] this, however, misses the point that privacy need not be an absolute state of affairs[21] to be valuable and that in fact our everyday lives are a constant trade-off between sociability, human interaction, the formation of relationships on the one hand, and the maintenance of a reasonable degree—not an absolute state of—privacy on the other. A legal *right* to privacy seeks to give the individual the ability to apply his or her own standards in terms of information and attention, within ordinary societal constraints, though, as we shall, see, the particularly vexed issue of privacy in public places has resulted in radically different findings from different jurisdictions, with, in particular, an acute divergence between American and European judicial thinking on this matter.

Some judicial recognition of informational autonomy as the founding principle in this area may be seen in a number of *dicta*. In *R v BSC ex parte BBC*,[22] in a case concerning the secret filming of a transaction in a shop, Lord Woolf observed: The fact that it is secret prevents those who are being filmed from taking any action to prevent what they are doing being filmed.[23] As Hale LJ put it:

Notions of what an individual might or might want to be kept 'private', 'secret' or 'secluded' are subjective to that individual. Someone who had declared publicly that he would 'never be seen dead' in Dixons, or who did not wish it to be known that he was buying a present for his wife there, might have excellent reasons for wanting to keep secret a visit to Dixons but be quite relaxed about a visit to an Ann Summers shop. For others, the position would be the reverse. The infringement consists in depriving the person filmed of the possibility of refusing consent.[24]

In other words, the wrong lies in the plain violation of autonomy. As Stanley Benn comments: 'Covert observation—spying—is objectionable because it deliberately deceives a person about his world, thwarting, for reasons that *cannot* be his reasons, his attempt to make a rational choice'.[25] Recently *dicta* of Lord Hoffman in the House of Lords' decision in *Campbell v MGN*[26] has authoritatively confirmed the values underlying privacy in this area: As his Lordship put it:

What human rights law has done is to identify private information as something worth protecting as an aspect of human autonomy and dignity ... the right to control the dissemination of information about one's private life ...[27]

---

[20] 'A New Definition of Privacy for the Law', *Law and Philosophy* 2 (1983), 305–338; collected in Wacks (ed.) *Privacy*, Aldershot, Hong Kong: Dartmouth, 1993.

[21] Gavison suggests that an individual 'enjoys perfect privacy when he is completely inaccessible to others' (op cit, p 428) without suggesting that this is anything other than an unrealistic and extreme scenario. Not absolute but a reasonable degree of privacy is the aim.

[22] [2001] QB 885.   [23] Ibid, at 898.   [24] Ibid, at 899.

[25] 'Privacy, Freedom and Respect for Persons (1971) in J. R. Pennock and J. W. Chapman (eds), NOMOS XIII *Privacy*, New York: Atherton Press, 1971, at 10.

[26] [2004] 2 WLR 1232.   [27] Op cit, at [50]–[51].

The ability to exercise informational control also affords some indirect protection to other privacy-related values: one is personal dignity, which must be diminished when information relating to intimate aspects of a person's life is widely published, giving rise to feelings of violation, shame, and embarrassment. Substantive autonomy may also be indirectly protected: as Feldman[28] has pointed out, 'If people are able to release [private] information with impunity, it might have the effect of illegitimately constraining a person's choices as to his or her private behaviour, interfering in a major way with his or her autonomy',[29] a link that has also been recognized by some American commentators.[30] It is worth noting that a significant reason for the finding of the majority of their Lordships in *Campbell*, as we shall see, was that the revelation of the details of Campbell's treatment at Narcotics Anonymous was likely to deter her from further treatment.[31] Clearly thinking in this vein, Lord Woolf has observed:

> To my mind the privacy of a human being denotes at the same time the personal 'space' in which the individual is free to be itself, and also the carapace, or shell, or umbrella, or whatever other metaphor is preferred, which protects that space from intrusion.[32]

Informational control also protects what Feldman identifies as the value in forming those spheres of social interaction and intimacy—work, friends, family, lovers—which are essential to human flourishing;[33] as Fried, notes, privacy is essential for 'respect, love friendship and trust'—'without it they are simply inconceivable'.[34] Those spheres, through their role in maintaining civil society, also, of course, serve a broader, social purpose.[35] The intimacy that such relationships entail is clearly predicated upon the individual's ability to ensure that information which may be circulated within one sphere is not, without consent, given to another sphere or the outside world. The Strasbourg court has recently stated that Article 8 'is primarily intended to ensure the development, *without outside interference*, of the personality of each individual in his relations with other human beings.'[36] It is clear that control over personal information, especially information relating to personal relationships, is essential, not only as an aspect of human dignity and autonomy, but also as a means of ensuring

---

[28] D. Feldman, 'Secrecy, Dignity or Autonomy? Views of Privacy as a Civil Liberty' 47(2) *CLP* 42, 54.

[29] Ibid, at 51. Feldman argues that privacy protects persons operating in a given sphere of existence from unjustified interference by those outside it. Within each different sphere, privacy is said to operate in four dimensions—'space ... time; action; and information' (ibid, 52). We deal here only with 'information': control over 'space' is dealt with by the law of trespass and property; the 'action' and 'time' categories clearly raise issues of substantive autonomy, and, at least for legal purposes, we regard the attempt to bring both informational and substantive autonomy under one definition as unhelpful: see Parent, op cit, 309 and 316 and Wacks, op cit, esp 79.

[30] Fried, 'Privacy' (1968) 77 *Yale LJ* 477, 483; see also J. Rachels, 'Why Privacy is Important' (1975) 4 *Philosophy and Public Affairs* 4, 323–33; E. F. Paul, F. D. Miller, and J. Paul, *The Right to Privacy*, Cambridge: Cambridge University Press, 2000, esp at 34–42.

[31] Op cit, at [157 and 169]. See Chapter 14 at 744–8.   [32] *ex parte BBC* (op cit, at 900).

[33] Ibid, at 51–69.   [34] 'Privacy' (1968) 77 *Yale LJ* 477, 483.

[35] Feldman has emphasized the strong *social* utility of privacy interests: D. Feldman, 'Privacy Related Rights and their Social Value' in R. Birks (ed.) *Privacy and Loyalty*, Oxford: Clarendon, 1997, 16–28.

[36] *Botta v Italy* (1998) 26 EHRR 241, at [32].

such unimpeded development. Particularly where the formation of such relations, and certain modes of development, may be controversial in the 'judgment of the mob,'[37] privacy allows for the exercise of individual liberty, for what DeCew has termed 'experiments in living'.[38] Whilst control over private property allows for the physical space in which such 'experiments' can occur, if there was no ability to withhold information about them from the disapproving majority, not only would such exercises of individual choice be penalized by the reaction of others, many would be likely to be deterred by the anticipation of it—Feldman's autonomy point again. In terms of effects upon substantive autonomy, the example of a person who wishes to explore their sexual identity being deterred from visiting a gay bar for fear of being 'outed' is plain to see. As Gavison puts it, without privacy, 'We also shall have [fewer] chances to experiment . . . through trial and error, and fewer opportunities to experiment with behaving differently.[39]

Barendt has nicely summed up the various values that we have suggested are in play here:

[Privacy] provides space for individuals to think for themselves and to engage in creative activity, free from observation and supervision. Further, personal relationships could not develop if participants felt that every move was watched and reported . . . Like the right to reputation protected by defamation laws, privacy is an aspect of human dignity and autonomy. It enables individuals to exercise some degree of independence or control over their lives.

A privacy *law* gives the individual a legal remedy to insist upon respect for, or compensation for breach of, the above state of privacy.

THE SCOPE OF ARTICLE 8

INTRODUCTION

It is perhaps not surprising that the question whether Article 8 requires a remedy for invasion of privacy between private individuals was resolved only very recently, given the controversial nature—at least in some countries[40]—of laws that impose

---

[37] Barber, 'A Right to Privacy' [2003] *PL* 602, 605.

[38] J. W. De Cew, 'The Scope of Privacy in Law and Ethics' (1986) 5 *Law and Philosophy* 145, at 166–70.

[39] R. Gavison, 'Too Early for a Requiem: Warren and Brandeis were right on privacy *vs* free speech' (1992) 43(3) *South Carolina Law Review* 437, 461.

[40] Whilst the existence of legal protection for privacy against the media has been long and firmly established in, for example, Germany and France, it remains highly controversial, as a restriction on First Amendment Rights, in the US; New Zealand has only very recently seen the judicial creation of a tort (*Hosking v Runting and others* (2004) CA 101/03), whilst in Australia the issue of how far breach of confidence can protect privacy, and whether there should be a common law privacy tort, is still unresolved, following the decision in *ABC v Lenah Game Meats* [2001] HCA 63: see D. Lindsay, 'Playing Possum? Privacy, Freedom of Speech and the Media Following *ABC v Lenah Game Meats*: Parts 1 and 2' (2002) 7(1) *Media & Arts Law Review*, pp 1–15, and op cit 7(3) pp 161–9; M. Richardson, 'Whither Breach of Confidence: A Right of

liability upon truthful publications on the grounds of invasion of privacy. There are, moreover three factors, amongst others, that generally cause Strasbourg to be reticent in developing the scope of a Convention right: first, where a complainant seeks to lay a positive obligation on the state; second, where the harm complained of flows from the action of a private party, rather than the state itself, so that the so-called 'horizontal effect' of the Convention is in issue; third, where there is a potential conflict with another Convention right. Where these factors arise contiguously—all three are necessarily present in privacy cases against the press—it is not surprising that Strasbourg was for a long time slow to find that Article 8 *required* development to provide a remedy for invasion of privacy by a private individual. A typical early case was *Winer v UK*,[41] which for many years was taken by many English scholars as indicating that Article 8 did *not* require any private law privacy remedy.[42] In a well-known decision, the Commission declared inadmissible the complaint of an applicant who, having sued in defamation in respect of disclosures[43] concerning his private life in a book, argued that his lack of a remedy in respect of the truthful ones violated Article 8. The judgment stated briefly that no positive obligation to provide further remedies in respect of the truthful statements should be imposed, bearing in mind the limitation of the Convention right to freedom of expression which such remedies would entail. In this case, so wide a margin of appreciation[44] was applied, due to the three factors mentioned above, that the Commission, in effect, found that the whole issue of whether a privacy law was required at all by Article 8 lay within it.

As we shall see in a moment, even when this issue was eventually resolved decisively, in *Von Hannover*, the Court in that decision provided virtually no reasoning to explain why this enormously important step was being taken. This being the case, we approach our exegesis of the issue in the following manner:

Privacy for Australia?' 26 *Melb. U. L. Rev.* 381 (2002). For an excellent recent comparative survey, see B. Markesinis, C. O'Cinncide, J. Fedtke, and M. Hunter-Henin, 'Concerns and Ideas about the Developing English Law of Privacy (and How Knowledge of Foreign Law Might Be of Help)' (2004) LII(1) *American Journal of Comparative Law* 133.

[41] 48 IR 154 (1986).

[42] See e.g. P. Carey, *Media Law*, 2nd edn., London: Sweet and Maxwell, 1999, 79–81; I. Leigh, 'Horizontal Rights, the Human Rights Act and Privacy: Lessons from the Commonwealth?' (1999) 48 *ICLQ* 57 at 86. Van Dijk and Van Hoof, *Theory and Practice of the European Convention on Human Rights*, 3rd edn., London: Kluwer, 1998 has no discussion at all of the application of Article 8 to the press (ibid, 489–504).

[43] He had settled a defamation case in respect of some of the statements made.

[44] As explained in Chapter 2, the essence of the doctrine of the margin of appreciation is that in assessing compliance with the Convention, the Court will afford states a certain latitude, principally in deciding what kinds of interferences with Convention rights are necessary in a democratic society. A wider or narrower margin may be afforded, depending upon the Court's assessment of how intensive a review of a state's actions is appropriate in the particular context. This tends to be associated with the delivery of rather unsatisfactory and potentially misleading judgments, as in *Winer* and a number of the other decisions discussed below. For analysis of the doctrine, generally, see Harris, O'Boyle, and Warbrick, *The European Convention on Human Rights*, London: Butterworths, 1995, at 12–15, and Van Dijk and Van Hoof, op cit, at 87–95.

we first of all track the emergence of the 'horizontal'[45] application of Article 8 in this area through the Strasbourg case law prior to *Von Hannover*. Given the lack of reasoning in *Von Hannover* this exercise, we suggest, remains important, in order to illustrate that there was some foundation in earlier decisions for its eventual horizontality finding. Secondly, the decision in *Von Hannover* itself is subject to critical analysis. Finally, we seek to provide a rationalization, or justification, for the Court's finding in that decision, something not provided by the Court itself.

THE STRASBOURG JURISPRUDENCE

Strasbourg's stance on this matter was obscure for some time, probably as a result of the margin of appreciation doctrine, which led to seemingly contradictory decisions. Thus, the decision in *Winer*, as just discussed, appeared to suggest that no specific remedy for invasion of privacy by private persons was required by Article 8. However, as the authors argued some time ago,[46] it left open the possibility of imposing an obligation on the state to provide a remedy for invasion of private life in an instance in which exclusively truthful publicity was given to private matters and no national remedy was available at all, an action in defamation being impossible. Such an inference was supported, nine years later, by the decision in *N v Portugal*.[47] A magazine publisher's application complained of a breach of Article 10 after being convicted of defamation and invasion of privacy in respect of the publication of photographs of a well-known businessman engaged in sexual activities. The sentence imposed was draconian, amounting to imprisonment. Nevertheless, the Commission rejected the application as manifestly ill-founded; it found that the sanction was proportionate and necessary for the protection of the rights of others, one of which was clearly the right to protection from invasion of privacy through publication of true facts by other private individuals. This possibility was affirmed in *Barclay v United Kingdom*,[48] in which the Court accepted that a lack of a remedy in respect of the filming of a private home by reporters *could* constitute a breach of Article 8, although on the facts no invasion of private life had occurred.[49] It thus appeared that there was no bar, in principle, upon the application of the Court's

---

[45] Strictly speaking, it is inapt to talk of horizontal effect at the Strasbourg level: the State is the only possible respondent to an application, and therefore, of course, the only party that may be imposed with liability for breach of the Convention. It is more correct to speak of the State being imposed with a positive obligation to provide a remedy between private parties: however, the effect of such a finding is, of course, that a remedy must be introduced, which will impose liability on private parties, and therefore a horizontal application of the Convention in *domestic* law. Nevertheless, the term 'horizontal effect' or 'horizontality' is used in the text as a convenient shorthand.

[46] G. Phillipson and H. Fenwick, 'Breach of Confidence as a Privacy Remedy in the Human Rights Act Era' [2000] 63(5) *MLR* 660–693.

[47] no. 20683/92 (1995)   [48] (1999) no. 35712/97 (admissibility only).

[49] Reporters filmed the island of Brecqhou, owned by the Barclay brothers. They had no home there, and were not present when the filming occurred.

general approach to interferences with personal information[50] to the actions of private bodies.[51]

Prior to the recent decision in *Von Hannover*, the clearest indication of the 'horizontal' scope of Article 8 was *Earl Spencer v United Kingdom*.[52] A number of (truthful) stories had appeared in the English press relating to the bulimia and mental health problems of Countess Spencer, including photographs taken of her walking in the grounds of a private health clinic. The Commission dismissed as inadmissible the Spencers' claim that the UK had failed to protect them from invasions of privacy by the press on the basis that they had failed to exhaust domestic remedies, namely breach of confidence. This judgment accepted that an interference with the right to respect for privacy had arguably occurred, and required a remedy, but that the doctrine of confidence would have provided one and should have been used. Had the Commission considered that the pleaded facts disclosed no arguable breach of Article 8, it would simply have so held and would not have instead decided the case on non-exhaustion of domestic remedies.[53] Thus *Spencer*, far from suggesting that Article 8 did *not* require the UK to develop a privacy law, seems to have been decided on the assumption that it already had one (albeit at a relatively early stage of development). The Commission would not 'exclude' the possibility that 'the absence of an actionable remedy in relation to the publications of which the applicants complain could show a lack of respect for their private lives.' In other words, the Commission at this point appeared to leave the question open, though, as seen above, its decision to dismiss the application on grounds of non-exhaustion of domestic remedies indicated a positive answer. In the same paragraph of the judgment, however, the Commission went on to say that it 'has regard to:'

... the Contracting State's obligation to provide a measure of protection to the right of privacy of an individual affected by another's exercise of their freedom of expression.[54]

This clear reference to an obligation on the state to provide protection *against other individuals* appears to answer the question decisively: but the sting lies in what counts as a 'measure of protection.' In *Winer*, as we saw, defamation was found to provide the

---

[50] See below at pp 674–7.

[51] The very brief admissibility decision in *Stewart-Brady v UK*, no. 36908/97 (1998), did not indicate the contrary. The notorious murderer was photographed non-consensually by a journalist outside the mental hospital at which he was detained. His complaints to the PCC and to national courts on judicial review were dismissed on the basis that publication of the photograph was justified in the public interest and was, in any event, unobjectionable. The Commission noted that Article 8 could apply in such situations but then simply adverted to the above facts and dismissed the application.

[52] 25 EHRR CD 105 (1998).

[53] The former Article 26 (which provided the rule as to exhaustion of domestic remedies before Protocol 11 came into force) makes it clear that the remedy must be effective. Harris, O'Boyle, and Warbick point out that 'An applicant is only required to have recourse to remedies which are capable of providing an effective and sufficient means of redressing the alleged wrong. If pursuit of a particular remedy would be futile it need not be exhausted', *Law of the European Convention on Human Rights*, London: Butterworths, 1995, at 611 and 619.

[54] Op cit, at 112.

requisite protection, although this was quite evidently an unsatisfactory finding, given the clear analytical distinction between privacy and reputation interests. It should be noted that the use of the margin of appreciation at Strasbourg, so influential in these cases, is precisely premised upon an acceptance of the notion that sufficient remedies do and should exist in domestic law. As Harris et al put it in relation to the efficacy of domestic remedies for exhaustion purposes: 'in common law systems it [is] incumbent on an aggrieved individual to allow the domestic courts the opportunity to develop existing rights by way of interpretation'.[55]

It is worth noting that the Court itself, in a judgment in 2002, confirmed that *Spencer* indicated the possible horizontal application of Article 8:

The Court recalls that Article 8 taken in conjunction with the obligation to secure the effective exercise of Convention rights imposed by Article 1 of the Convention, may involve a positive obligation on the State to provide a measure of protection for an individual's private life in relation to the exercise by third parties of the right to freedom of expression bearing in mind the duties and responsibilities referred to in Article 10. The absence of a remedy in relation to the publication of information relating to private affairs may constitute a lack of respect for private life (cf. *Earl and Countess Spencer v the United Kingdom* . . .)[56]

An important recent decision is that of *Peck v United Kingdom*,[57] of great significance for this area of law, but not one that provides a direct answer to the specific question we are considering here. *Peck* does, however, make it clear that media intrusion into privacy can at least *lead* to a breach of Article 8. The applicant had been captured on Council CCTV cameras, wandering through the street carrying a knife, immediately after he had attempted to commit suicide by cutting his wrists. This footage was passed by the local authority on to a news broadcast and a popular television programme, *Crime Beat*, both of which showed extracts from the CCTV footage, from which the man was recognizable, to an audience of hundreds of thousands. The Court found a breach of Article 8. Thus *Peck* establishes that for a public authority to release footage portraying private acts without consent to the broadcast media is *prima facie* a breach of Article 8 (subject of course to a freedom of expression defence). It can surely be extrapolated from this that if a broadcaster *which was itself* a public authority— such as (perhaps) the BBC[58]—had produced the film itself, using its own reporters and cameramen, and then broadcast it, there would have been a breach of Article 8 in that instance too. *Peck* does *not* make it clear whether Article 8 would have been breached had a private, commercial broadcaster, such as ITV or Channel 5, made and broadcast such a film, and the Court expressly declined to consider whether such bodies could be considered organs of the state. However, the breach of Article 8 in such a case arises from the failure of the state to afford victims a proper remedy against such bodies, regardless of their status.

---

[55] Harris, O'Boyle, and Warbrick, op cit, at 611.   [56] *Shussel v Austria* no. 42409/98 (2002).
[57] (2003) 36 EHRR 41. For comment, see J. Welch, [2003] *EHRLR* (Privacy Special) 141
[58] See discussion in Chapter 3 as to whether the BBC is a hybrid (functional) public authority and as to those functions that may be considered public functions, pp 114–22.

A further recent decision supporting such an inference is *Campany Y Diez de Revenga v Spain*.[59] A Spanish magazine and radio programme had carried a story about what it described as 'a new sex scandal between an attractive aristocrat and a banker from this country'. The story described the parties, including the aristocrat's husband, and was accompanied by pictures of both parties and details of their tryst in a hotel in Madrid 'where they were caught by the photographer in two compromising situations', the first at the hotel entrance and the second during a romantic encounter in the hotel corridors. The Duchess brought a successful civil action against the applicant, for unlawful interference with her right to honour and to respect for her private life under Spanish law. Both damages and an order to print the full text of the judgment in print as large as that of the original story were given as remedies. The applicant applied to Strasbourg alleging a breach of Article 10. The application was declared inadmissible, as manifestly ill-founded, on the basis that the penalty imposed by the Spanish courts was a necessary and proportionate measure taken to protect the private life of the Duchess. This, although only a decision on admissibility, and not dealing directly with Article 8, logically implied that Article 8 was engaged in such situation.

Now, however, following the 2004 decision of the European Court of Human Rights in *Von Hannover v Germany*,[60] it is clear beyond doubt that Article 8 is not only *engaged* but requires a remedy in national law—a finding significantly different from a decision that such remedies merely do not violate Article 10. The case represented the culmination of a long legal fight by Princess Caroline of Monaco to stop pictures of herself and her children, obtained by paparazzi, without consent, appearing in various newspapers and magazines across Europe. The pictures themselves, as discussed further below, were relatively anodyne shots of the Princess engaged in various everyday acts: shopping, horse-riding, at a beach club, a restaurant, and so on. The Court found, unanimously, that the failure of the German courts to provide her with a remedy in relation to these pictures amounted to a breach of Article 8: the positive obligation of the state to intervene between private parties in this area of private life was thus uncontrovertibly established:

In the present case there is no doubt that the publication by various German magazines of photos of the applicant in her daily life either on her own or with other people falls within the scope of her private life.[61]

What is rather startling about the finding here is the almost entire absence of justificatory reasoning. This is in spite of the fact that, as the Court noted, in previous cases it had 'had regard to whether the photographs related to private or public matters' and that there is 'a zone of interaction of a person with others, even in a public context, which may fall within the scope of 'private life'.[62] These dicta suggested that

---

[59] 54224/00.   [60] No. 59320/00 [2004] EMLR 21.

[61] Op cit, at [53]. As discussed below, the German courts *had* afforded a privacy remedy to the Princess in relation to the more intrusive photographs complained of—see pp 677–8.

[62] Ibid, at [50]. The decisions referred to are *PG and JH v United Kingdom*, App. No.44787/98, (2001), at [56], and *Peck v United Kingdom* (2003) 36 EHRR 41, at [57].

an applicant would need to show that the photographs dealt with an aspect of private life recognized under Article 8[63] and that photographs taken in a public context will only exceptionally engage that Article,[64] as where they are disseminated to a much wider audience than would have been anticipated. As one commentary puts it:

In *Von Hannover* the Court accepted almost without question that Art.8 was engaged by the publication of the photographs. This might be thought to sit rather ill with its own judgment in *Peck*, where it seemed to be the fact that CCTV footage of the applicant was disseminated to a much wider audience than he could 'possibly have foreseen' together with the nature of the act he was engaged in (an unsuccessful suicide attempt) that led the Court to find that Art.8 was engaged.[65]

In light of these considerations, it is rather surprising that the Court did not identify *why* the photographs in question related to private life; they did not, in many cases fall into a 'zone of interaction . . . with others' as many (those picturing her alone) did not concern her relations with anyone.

Not only does the judgment, as we will discuss further below, thus radically extend the scope of 'private life' in Article 8; it also confirms, with very little argument or analysis, the engagement of Article 8 in litigation between purely private bodies, a matter that, as discussed above, had been regarded as in doubt and consequently hotly debated for years. As noted above, as recently as 2002, the Court was only prepared to say that, 'The absence of a remedy in relation to the publication of information relating to private affairs *may* constitute a lack of respect for private life.'[66] The Court now confirms that such an absence *does* constitute a breach of Article 8. In fact it goes much further than this: in *Von Hannover* it actually found that a jurisdiction— Germany—that *did* provide such a remedy, but had merely excluded from it certain rather anodyne pictures, partly because of the need to protect press freedom, had violated Article 8.[67] In spite of this, there is remarkably little reasoning to explain *why* it is taking this highly significant step: indeed, on closer inspection, such 'reasoning' as there is consists merely of a cut and pasting exercise, whereby well-worn (and very general, almost vague) phrases from previous judgments are put together to give a semblance of justification.

Thus we have the following:

The Court reiterates that although the object of Article 8 is essentially that of protecting the individual against arbitrary interference by the public authorities, it does not merely compel the State to abstain from such interference: in addition to this primarily negative undertaking, there may be positive obligations inherent in an effective respect for private or family life. These obligations may involve the adoption of measures designed to

---

[63] For example, intimate relations, health and medial treatment; sexuality.
[64] By the use of the words '*even* in a public context' (emphasis added).
[65] (2004) 5 EHRLR, 593–596 (case comment).   [66] See note 56 above (emphasis added).
[67] See e.g. [57].

secure respect for private life even in the sphere of the relations of individuals between themselves.[68]

These principles are all well known and have appeared in numerous judgments. The Court goes on to say:

The boundary between the State's positive and negative obligations under this provision does not lend itself to precise definition. The applicable principles are, nonetheless, similar. In both contexts regard must be had to the fair balance that has to be struck between the competing interests of the individual and of the community as a whole; and in both contexts the State enjoys a certain margin of appreciation.[69]

We have here only the invocation of two well known principles: 'fair balance' and the margin of appreciation doctrine. Nevertheless, the court immediately proceeds to the issue of balancing Article 8 against the right to freedom of expression.[70] We therefore in fact have no reasoning at all to justify the horizontality finding, only the stitching together of various well-known Convention principles (positive obligations, the requirement, sometimes, of intervention between private relations, 'fair balance' and margin of appreciation) without more. There is nothing to explain here *why* this enormously important step has been taken—nothing in the way either of normative or analytic reasoning. From a positivist point of view, the Court does nothing to explain how this development is in fact rooted in previous, well-established principles. From a Dworkinian point of view,[71] again it does nothing to satisfy the criterion of 'fit' with existing principles; but neither does it produce an argument explaining how this interpretation of Article 8 is an attractive one, normatively, in the light of broad principles animating the Convention as a whole. Such arguments can readily be made—but the Court does not attempt them.

Another point worth noting is that whilst the Court refers briefly to the margin of appreciation,[72] it is not clear that the doctrine—found to preclude an obligation to provide a remedy at all in *Winer*[73]—plays any role in the judgment at all. The Court appears simply to substitute its view for that of the German courts—on when there may be a legitimate expectation of privacy, on the meaning of 'private life' itself, and on whether the photographs had any part to play in contributing to any debate of general interest, that is on the proper resolution of the conflict with freedom of expression. This is all the more remarkable, given that the three factors noted above that tend to lead to a wide margin of appreciation being granted were all present in *Von Hannover*: namely a situation in which (a) a complainant seeks to lay a positive obligation on the state, (b) where the harm complained of flows from the action of a

---

[68] Ibid, at [57]. The phrases are taken from: *X and Y v the Netherlands*, judgment of 26 March 1985, Series A no. 91, p 11, § 23; *Stjerna v Finland*, judgment of 25 November 1994, Series A no. 299–B, p 61, § 38; and *Verliere v Switzerland* (dec.), no. 41953/98, ECHR 2001–VII).

[69] Ibid. The court cites, among 'many other authorities', *Keegan v Ireland*, judgment of 26 May 1994, Series A no. 290, p 19, § 49, and *Botta v Italy* 1998–I, p 422, § 32.

[70] In the succeeding paragraphs 58–60.

[71] See, e.g., *Taking Rights Seriously*, London: Duckworths, 1977, chapters 2–4.   [72] At [79].

[73] See above p 667.

private party, rather than the state itself and (c) where there is a conflict with another Convention right. In this case, a positive obligation was being imposed to intervene in private relations to prevent a harm imposed by a private party and there was an admitted conflict with freedom of expression; nevertheless the margin of appreciation appears to have been cut to vanishing point. Moreover, it is well known that, as Markesinis *et al* have recently pointed out, the German courts have developed a sophisticated and nuanced analysis of the levels of protection properly due to differing classes of public figure and how that protection should be balanced against the demands of freedom of expression.[74] One might therefore have expected rather more deference to have been paid to this expertise in the striking of such relatively fine balances: it should be recalled once again that case concerned only the particular line drawn by the German courts as to when the interest in press freedom outweighed that in privacy, not whether such publications engaged the right to private life at all.

Nevertheless, the finding in *Von Hannover* is unequivocal—the horizontality question is finally answered. We consider the very wide *scope* given to Article 8 by this decision further below. In the next section, however, we seek to do what the Court did not, and indicate some of the arguments, normative and analytical, that might be used to support its finding in *Von Hannover*.

GIVING 'HORIZONTAL EFFECT' TO ARTICLE 8: JUSTIFICATION

Going back to first principles, the question at issue is as follows: do the state's positive obligations under Article 8 to afford 'respect' to private life require the court to offer a remedy against intrusion into private life by a non-state actor? Now it has been clear for some time that the state's Convention duties under *Article 10* are engaged where court orders, particularly injunctions amounting to prior restraint, infringe free speech regardless of whether such orders are made in the context of litigation between two private parties: the numerous cases on defamation, including *Tolstoy*[75] and *Bladet Tromso*[76] establish that this is the case. However, justifying a positive obligation flowing from Article 8 to afford a remedy against the press, when it invades a person's privacy, in order to satisfy the duty on the state to show 'respect' for private life, is a much more difficult issue.

It is clear law that the actions of public authorities in gathering, storing and using personal information, including photographs, engage Article 8.[77] The collection and publication of personal information by the press is but one manifestation of—largely uncontrolled[78]—data collection and processing.[79] One cannot of course

---

[74] Markesinis, O'Cinneide, *et al.*, op cit, at 146–7 and 185–91.

[75] *Tolstoy Mioslavsky v UK* (1995) 20 EHRR 442.   [76] *Bladet Tromso v Norway* (1999) 29 EHRR 125.

[77] See, e.g., *Leander v Sweden* (1987) 9 EHRR 433; *McVeigh, O'Neill and Evans v United Kingdom* (1981) 45 EHRR 71; *Murray and Others v United Kingdom* (1995) EHRR 193.

[78] Uncontrolled, at least, before the introduction of the Data Protection Directive.

[79] The press will be regarded as data controllers under the Data Protection Act 1998 (s1(1) though conditionally exempted from its key protective provisions: see Chapter 14, at 717–21.

infer the simple transposition of Convention obligations of public authorities onto private agents; however, in *X and Y v Netherlands* the Court observed that Article 8 obligations 'may require the adoption of measures even in the sphere of relations between individuals'.[80] In other words, the state may be under a positive obligation to provide legal protection for the individual against the actions of other private bodies[81] although given that the state merely has to show 'respect' for private life, its discretion in determining the means of so doing may be increased.[82] In short, the strength of the jurisprudence on interferences with personal information by public authorities indicates that the interest in being free from such intrusion is one which, in general terms, does fall within the ambit of Article 8. As a leading text in the area puts it: 'the obligation of the state to respect private life by controlling the activities of its agents [in collecting personal information] ought to extend also to similar operations by private persons such as . . . newspapers'.[83] It may be noted that, Resolution 428 (1970) of the Council of Europe states that the right to privacy under Article 8 should extend to 'interference by private persons including the mass media,' a finding reaffirmed in Resolution 1165 of 1998. As Clapham has noted, such resolutions may be taken into account by the ECtHR as a source of 'soft law'.[84]

There are further arguments of principle. As the House of Lords has stressed: 'the Convention should be seen as an expression of fundamental principles rather than as a set of mere rules.'[85] Strasbourg has found that the purpose of the Convention is to 'promote the ideals and values of a democratic society,'[86] and to provide 'rights that are practical and effective' rather than 'rights that are theoretical or illusory'.[87] The Convention must be given an 'evolutive interpretation'[88] which takes account of current standards in European countries,[89] in which legal protection for privacy is the norm.[90] It has been remarked that: 'The Court has not perceived the rights in Article 8 in wholly negative terms—the right to be left alone. Instead it has acknowledged that states must ensure . . . the effective enjoyment of liberty'.[91] As a number of scholars

---

[80] (1985) 8 EHRR 235.   [81] As the Court in *Von Hannover* noted.

[82] See *JS v UK* Appl No 191173/91, 3 January 1993. The Commission rejected an application in which it was alleged that an insurance company had carried out a clandestine surveillance in investigating a claim.

[83] Harris, O'Boyle, and Warbrick, *Law of the European Convention on Human Rights*, Butterworths: London, 1995, 310.

[84] A. Clapham, *Human Rights in the Private Sphere*, Oxford: Clarendon, 1993, 102–3.

[85] *R v DPP ex parte Kebilene* [1999] 3 WLR 972.

[86] *Kjeldsen v Denmark* (1976) 1 EHRR 711, 731; *Socialist Party v Turkey* (1998) no. 20/1997/804/1007.

[87] *Airey v Ireland* (1979) 2 EHRR 305, 314.   [88] *Johnstone v Ireland* A 112 (1986), at [53].

[89] *Tyrer v UK* A 26 (1978), at [31].

[90] Developed privacy laws exist in leading European countries such as Germany, France, Italy, Denmark, and the Netherlands: see (on German law), B. Markesenis and N. Nolte, 'Some Comparative Reflections on the Right of Privacy of Public Figures in Public Places', in P. Birks (ed.) *Privacy and Loyalty*, Oxford: Clarendon, 1997; in relation to Germany, France, and Italy, see chapters 2–4 of Markesenis, *Protecting Privacy* op cit; *The Calcutt Committee on Privacy and Related Matters* (1990 Cmnd 1102), at [5.22]–[5.28] discusses privacy protection in Denmark and the Netherlands.

[91] Harris, O'Boyle, and Warbrick, op cit, at 303.

have pointed out,[92] effective enjoyment of liberty cannot occur when persons are constantly afraid of betraying information to the media, and forced to order their choices in life as a consequence, and it would appear to be a hallmark of a democratic society that it seeks to protect a person from such curtailment of liberty.[93] Moreover it is hard to see how a complete absence of legal protection for privacy against the media could constitute that 'fair balance' of individual and societal interests which Article 8 requires.[94]

Nevertheless, it remains the case that the gathering and subsequent publication of personal information by the press does not *necessarily* have to be regarded as engaging Article 8, as it would if carried out by a public authority and, as we have seen, Strasbourg pursued the notion of a duty to intervene between private parties cautiously, until its decision in *Von Hannover*. Aside from the reasons for such caution given above, and the influence of the margin of appreciation doctrine,[95] there may be a good reason for this: there is a respectable argument for what could be termed 'horizontal asymmetry' here; by this is meant the unequal application of Articles 8 and 10 in the private sphere. The argument is this: a court order restraining publication by a newspaper is quite evidently a *direct state interference* with freedom of expression: the court order directly causes the interference, by preventing publication. As noted above, defamation cases, including *Tolstoy*[96] and *Bladet Tromso*,[97] establish that this is the case. In contrast, a *refusal* by a court in a case involving privacy interests to grant an injunction restraining publication does *not* directly cause the harm to private life: the *court* does not invade the person's privacy: the *newspaper* does so, by publishing the offensive words, while the court merely declines to intervene. Thus the fact that Article 10 applies horizontally does not automatically mean that Article 8 does so also. The applicability of the latter to this situation must fall to be determined by asking whether the court would, in principle, show a lack of 'respect' for private life by failing to act in such a situation? Again, this is a not a straightforward question. As the European Court of Human Rights has repeatedly said:

The concept of 'respect' [in Article 8] is not precisely defined. In order to determine whether such [positive] obligations exist, regard must be had to the fair balance that has to be struck between the general interest and the interests of the individual.[98]

However, the Strasbourg court has also recently spoken of Article 8 as 'primarily intended to ensure the development, *without outside interference*, of the personality of each individual in his relations with other human beings.'[99] If this is indeed the principle underlying Article 8, this is a good reason for it encompassing media intrusion, since the prying into and reporting of private life may well have an adverse effect

---

[92] See, e.g. D. Feldman, 'Secrecy, Dignity or Autonomy? Views of Privacy as a Civil Liberty' 47(2) *CLP* 42, 54 and 'Privacy Related Rights and their Social Value' in Birks (ed.) op cit.

[93] The right to privacy appears in Article 12 of the Universal Declaration of Human Rights, and Article 17 of the International Covenant on Civil and Political Rights.

[94] See, e.g. *Botta v Italy* (1998) 26 EHRR 241, at [33].   [95] See pp 667–8.

[96] *Tolstoy Mioslavsky v UK* (1995) 20 EHRR 442.   [97] *Bladet Tromso v Norway* (1999) 29 EHRR 125.

[98] *Botta v Italy* (1998) 26 EHRR 241, at [33].   [99] Ibid (emphasis added).

on the individual's ability to develop intimate relationships with others.[100] Moreover, the Court in the same decision sketched out a test for deciding whether a positive obligation in the sphere of private relations should be inferred. It observed that: 'a State has [positive] obligations of this type [under Article 8] where [the Court] has found a direct and immediate link between the measures sought by an applicant and the latter's private and/or family life.'[101] Under this test, therefore, one would ask whether remedies sought by private individuals in respect of intrusive publications have a 'direct and immediate link' with their private life? Since the purpose of such remedies is to prevent, or discourage the publication of information, often about highly intimate aspects of private life,[102] such as sexual behaviour—consistently treated by Strasbourg as engaging a particularly important aspect of private life[103]—it is clearly apparent that the answer to the question is 'yes'. It is to be regretted that the Court did not pose the question of horizontality in *Von Hannover* in this, as it had earlier suggested, nor advert to many of the arguments outlined above in reaching its conclusion on the issue in that case. To have done so would not only have legitimized its decision, but also strengthened and clarified the finding, in making it clearer what was to be the mischief averted by engaging the State's responsibility in this area.

THE SCOPE OF PRIVATE LIFE AFTER *VON HANNOVER*

The findings and reasoning

We noted briefly above that this decision represents, to say the least, a radical extension of the Court's jurisprudence. As discussed, the decision was remarkable in finding a breach of Article 8 on the basis, not of the *absence* of a remedy in domestic law for invasion of privacy by the press—an issue it had hesitated over only two years earlier,[104] but of a particular finding by German courts that the publication of certain photographs could be justified, given the countervailing interest in press freedom.

To bring this point out, it is necessary, at this point, to recall the facts of the case in a little more detail. The photographs about which Princess Caroline of Monaco complained in this case showed her engaged in various, mainly everyday activities, including: having dinner in a garden restaurant with a boyfriend; riding on horseback; being out with her children; canoeing; shopping with her boyfriend and son, on a skiing holiday; kissing a boyfriend; leaving her home in Paris; playing tennis, and dressed in a swimsuit at a beach club. The German courts had allowed her to recover only in relation to pictures which captured her in moments in which, whilst technically in a public space, she had clearly 'sought seclusion' (e.g. by withdrawing to a quiet corner

---

[100] See Feldman, op cit ('Secrecy').   [101] Op cit, at [31].

[102] *N v Portugal* and *Campany Y* (above) concerned sexual life, as did a number of the English decisions on privacy, including *Theakston v MGN* [2002] EMLR 22 and *A v B* [2002] 3 WLR 542, while *Campbell v MGN* [2004] 2 WLR 1232 concerned publication of details of therapeutic treatment for drug addiction, which relate to health and medical treatment.

[103] See e.g., *Dudgeon v UK* (1981) 4 EHRR 149, 165, para 52, and *Lustig Prean v UK* (1999) 9 EHRR 548.

[104] *Shussel v Austria* no. 42409/98 (2002).

of the garden restaurant with her boyfriend).[105] On final appeal, the Federal Constitutional Court found that the pictures with her children should additionally be entitled to protection, because the right to family protection was also engaged. However, they dismissed her complaint in relation to the remainder of the photographs. This was primarily on the basis that:

as a figure of contemporary society '*par excellence*', the applicant had to tolerate the publication of photos in which she appeared in a public place even if they were photos of scenes from her daily life and not photos showing her exercising her official functions. The public had a legitimate interest in knowing where the applicant was staying and how she behaved in public.[106]

Thus it is important to note that the European Court was concerned *not* with the pictures of the Princess with her children or those of her dining with her boyfriend in the garden restaurant, but with the less sensitive remainder of the pictures: those showing her shopping, playing tennis, leaving her apartment, and so on. These were *not* then photographs that portrayed her engaged in some 'private act' in the sense in which we have been discussing it so far. The position is clearly markedly different from the situation in *Peck*, in which the applicant was photographed in a public place at a moment of great sensitivity and emotional distress. Moreover, the wording of the judgment in *Peck* had appeared to indicate that private life will only exceptionally be engaged in a public space: 'There is, therefore, a zone of interaction of a person with others, *even in a public context*, which may fall within the scope of "private life" ' (emphasis added).[107] This suggests that there may need to be exceptional factors present to give rise to a finding that Article 8 applies. In *Peck*, these were clearly the intensely personal and emotional moment captured by the CCTV cameras. In *Von Hannover*, not only was the applicant in a public place, but the activities she was engaged in did not, at first blush, appear to concern private facts at all. Nevertheless, the court expressed no hesitation at all in making its key finding:

In the present case, there is no doubt that the publication by various German magazines of photos of the applicant in her daily life either on her own or with other people falls within the scope of her private life.[108]

In light of the above considerations, it is rather surprising that the Court does not identify *why* the photographs in question relate to private life; they did not, in many cases fall into a 'zone of interaction . . . with others' as many (those picturing her alone) did not concern her relations with anyone. No distinction is drawn by the Court between the different photographs in this respect.

---

[105] The Federal Court defined a secluded place as 'away from the public eye—where it was objectively clear to everyone that [the couple] wanted to be alone and where, confident of being away from prying eyes, they behaved in a given situation in a manner in which they would not behave in a public place. Unlawful interference with the protection of that privacy could therefore be made out if photos were published that had been taken secretly and/or by catching unawares a person who had retired to such a place', quoted in *Von Hannover*, at [23].

[106] Ibid.   [107] *Peck v UK* (2003) 36 EHRR 41 at [57].   [108] Ibid, at [53].

The problem perhaps is that the words 'public' and 'private' are being used by the Court (without explication or argument) to mean something very much more expansive than their normal meaning in legal discourse. The word 'private' appears to be being used to describe all those aspects of a person's life that do not relate to their official duties. So, for example, a civil servant is engaged in her private life all the time, except when carrying out her duties as a civil servant. Buying groceries, is, in this sense, a part of her private life. There is certainly one sense in which we understand this to be the case: a basic distinction between public (in the sense of 'official') and personal or private life. That this is the sense in which the words have been used is indicated by a passage in which the court 'points out' that:

the photos of the applicant in the various German magazines show her in scenes from her daily life, thus engaged in activities of a purely private nature such as practising sport, out walking, leaving a restaurant or on holiday.[109]

The word 'private' here is clearly being used to mean 'non-official'; the word 'public' to mean, 'part of one's official life or duties'.

The difficulty is that there is another way in which the words are commonly used— perhaps the way that we would expect in this context and in which the other judicial decisions examined so far have used them. In this sense of the word, 'private life' means those aspects of a person's non-official life for which they would generally seek seclusion, intimacy or confidentiality: sexual life, nudity and bodily functions; health, private finance, family life and any activity carried on within the home. Moreover, the word 'public' in discourses about privacy, is usually used not only to mean 'official' (although we do sometimes use it in that way, when talking of 'public life'); it also often means a public *location*: that is, publicly accessible spaces in which the individual can exert no control over who sees her. We would not expect the right to private life to extend to such spaces unless, as the German courts said,[110] a person had sought seclusion for the enjoyment in public of an aspect of private life, for example, sun-bathing topless on a secluded beach. Alternatively, there could be a privacy complaint where, although the location was highly public, the activity in question was particularly sensitive—leaving an abortion clinic, perhaps, or, in Campbell's case,[111] a branch of Narcotics Anonymous, or experiencing the aftermath of a suicide attempt, as in *Peck*. But absent some such particularly personal or intimate aspect, normal activities carried on in public—walking, shopping, eating, riding a cycle or horse, are not, in this sense, generally seen as part of 'private life' in the Article 8 sense. Scholars tend to define 'private facts' much more restrictively. W.A. Parent's proposed definition of personal information, for example, is 'information about a person which most individuals in a given time do not want widely known [or which] though not generally considered personal, a particular person feels acutely sensitive about.'[112] The fact that one has been shopping, or riding a horse would not appear to fall into either

---

[109] Ibid, at [61].　[110] Above, note 105.　[111] *Campbell v MGN* [2004] 2 WLR 1232.
[112] W. A. Parent, 'A New Definition of Privacy for the Law' (1983) 2 *Law and Philosophy* 305, 306–7; see p 663 above.

category, although in relation to Princess Caroline, there is an argument that it falls into the second category—a restrictive reading of the Strasbourg Court's judgment that will be considered in a moment. This was indeed precisely the reason why the applicants in the recent decision in *Hosking v Runting*,[113] although they succeeded in persuading the New Zealand Court of Appeal that there was a tort of invasion of privacy, lost their case on the facts. The complaint was of the publication of pictures taken without consent of a celebrity couple's young children in a busy street. The action failed both because of the very public location in which the pictures were taken, and because they revealed nothing sensitive or intimate about the couple or the children themselves. While aspects of the decision are open to criticism, its whole approach is that only particular aspects of a person's life will be considered to fall within the sphere of 'private life' in human rights terms. As Gleeson CJ put it in the dicta discussed above from *Lenah Game Meats*: '*Certain kinds* of information about a person, such as information relating to health, personal relationships, or finances, may be easy to identify as private, as may *certain kinds* of activity'.[114]

To give an example, it could be argued along these lines that a photograph simply showing a person coming out of a supermarket with a trolley of shopping does not engage private life: it merely reveals the anodyne fact that the person in question has shopped for groceries—scarcely an intimate or sensitive matter. However, if, for example, a reporter surreptitiously followed a woman shopping in a chemist and managed to record that she had purchased a particular prescription drug, or contraceptives, or a pregnancy testing kit, then publication of such information *would* engage private life—because the items purchased all relate to highly personal and intimate matters: health, sexual life and reproduction. Moreover, the customer buying them would not expect the details of her purchases to be seen except by a very few others in the shop. Such distinctions, it may be suggested, are fine but vital ones, if the meaning of 'private life' in public is to be kept within manageable limits. Remarkably, the Strasbourg court here draws no such distinctions.

Interpreting *Von Hannover*

What principle then does the decision in *Von Hannover* stand for? On the reasoning discussed so far, bearing in mind the anodyne nature of the photographs at issue in the case, and the very broad scope to 'private life' discussed therein, this decision appears to take the view that any publication of an unauthorized photograph specifically taken of a particular person[115] engaged in an everyday activity outside their official duties will involve a *prima facie* violation of Article 8. We shall refer to this reading of the case as 'the absolutist view'. However, there is another possible reading. Whilst the judgments of the Strasbourg court cannot strictly be broken down into

---

[113] [2005] 1 NZLR 1.

[114] *Australian Broadcasting Corporation v Lenah Game Meats* (2001) 208 CLR 199, at [42].

[115] The words 'specifically taken of a particular person' are used because this judgment would presumably not apply to photographs of normal street scenes in which individuals happen to be caught.

'ratio' and 'obiter dicta', it may be observed that the inferences to be drawn from the finding of a breach in *Von Hannover* and the reasoning the Court gives to support that finding, are very different. The holding of the case, *given the facts*, is that the systematic and persistent pursuit and photographing of a person going about their everyday life and the publication of those photographs in mass circulation newspapers can give rise to a breach of Article 8. This is not, perhaps, a particularly radical proposition, given the degree of harassment present in the particular case, and the feeling it induced in the applicant of being under constant, albeit unofficial surveillance. As the Court put it, under the view taken of Princess Caroline's case by the German courts, the Princess simply 'has to accept that she might be photographed at almost any time, systematically, and that the photos are then very widely disseminated'. The Court indeed makes clear that it had this factor very much in mind in coming to the decision it did:

[The Princess] alleged that as soon as she left her house she was constantly hounded by paparazzi who followed her every daily movement, be it crossing the road, fetching her children from school, doing her shopping, out walking, practising sport or going on holiday.[116]

Indeed the court makes the influence of this factor on its judgment explicit:

The context in which these photos were taken—without the applicant's knowledge or consent—and the harassment endured by many public figures in their daily lives cannot be fully disregarded.[117]

And again:

Furthermore, photos appearing in the tabloid press are often taken in a climate of continual harassment *which induces in the person concerned a very strong sense of intrusion into their private life* or even of persecution (emphasis added).[118]

The italicized words are of particular significance: they suggest that it is not any one particular photograph, or what it reveals, that induces the sense of intrusion into private life, but, as the court puts it, 'a climate of continual harassment'. This suggests that what we actually have here is a judgment that combines two elements in coming to a finding that Article 8 is engaged: (a) the fact that the pictures relate to the Princess's everyday life, not her official functions, *and* (b) the constant intrusion that the persistent photographing represents. This more restrictive reading would dovetail nicely with the second part of the definition of private facts proposed by Parent: 'information about a person which . . . though not generally considered personal, a particular person feels acutely sensitive about.'[119] The photographs, in other words, fall within Article 8 because, while not revealing anything generally considered personal, they induce an acute feeling of intrusion because of the persistent campaign of low-level intrusion of which they are a part. Looked at this way, the judgment in *Von*

---

[116] *Von Hannover v Germany* (2005) 40 EHRR 1, at [44].   [117] Ibid, at [68].   [118] Ibid, at [59].
[119] Parent, 'A New Definition of Privacy', above notes 112, 307.

Hannover does not, necessarily, imply that *any* photograph taken without consent of a person in their private capacity will engage Article 8; rather the question will be either whether the photograph taken of the person reveals or exposes some intimate aspect of their life (as in *Campbell* or *Peck*) *or* whether the cumulative impact of the persistent taking and publishing of such photographs is such as to give rise to a level of intrusion sufficient to breach Article 8.

It is conceded immediately that this is only one reading of the judgment: it is quite evident that the Court nowhere states that it is the cumulative effect of the photography that in this case was the *decisive* factor. Nevertheless, it would be a perfectly defensible course of action for the English courts to interpret *Von Hannover* simply as a finding that the systematic pursuit and photographing of a person as they go about their daily life can, in sufficiently serious circumstances, amount to a breach of Article 8.

What view *ought* to be taken? There are attractions to the absolutist view of *Von Hannover*. No-one denies that the press is enormously intrusive, that much of the diet it churns out of photographs of celebrities with comments on their fashion sense, or bodies, or health, is of extremely low value, in speech terms and arguably quite culturally corrosive.[120] It might be asked why the press should be able to engage in such low-level but systematic harassment and pursuit of people, simply in order to fulfil consumer demand, and thereby serve their own commercial interests. There is certainly something deeply distasteful about the press using Article 10 in defence of such activity.

However, our sense is that such a development in English law would be too radical to be brought about by the judiciary. Were the popular press to find that the courts had developed the common law to the extent that publication of any photograph of a particular person engaged in every day life exposed them to liability, there would be the most vicious media back-lash imaginable, against both the judiciary and the Convention, which might well weaken popular support for the maintenance of privacy rights and the HRA generally. It should be recalled that whilst it was envisaged at the time that the passage of the HRA might lead to the developments of privacy rights against the media,[121] there was no clear authority at Strasbourg that this was required by Article 8 and the 'horizontal effect' point was shrouded in obscurity. For the Act to lead to such a massive extension in media liability, without a clear mandate from Parliament, would be an outcome of doubtful legitimacy. On another level, in the case of publication of a particularly anodyne photograph of someone simply walking down a street, it is hard to escape the feeling that characterizing it as a violation of human rights is to risk devaluing human rights discourse by associating it with trivial complaints. UK public and popular culture is profoundly different from that pervading in France, in which such a level of protection exists. Moreover, given the inherent difficulty and contestability of the normative exercise entailed in balancing speech and privacy rights, it would seem desirable not to extend the notion of privacy

---

[120] See further J. Seaton, 'Public, Private and the Media' (2003) *Political Quarterly* 174.
[121] See Chapter 3 at 123.

so widely that virtually all cases brought would *prima facie* disclose a cause of action, leaving all the work in judicial adjudication to be done in weighing up the two rights together. There needs to be some form of preliminary, definitional filter. Overall therefore, we believe that adoption of the 'absolutist' view of *Von Hannover* would not be one that should be taken by the domestic courts. The developments to date should be given time to mature and gain greater public acceptance. Certainly, however, where publication of a photograph has been obtained in a context of harassment and intrusion, this is a matter that can—and should—be taken into account by courts adjudicating the resulting claims.[122]

FREEDOM OF EXPRESSION AND THE PROTECTION OF PRIVACY: PRINCIPLE AND CASE LAW

In this section, we consider the Strasbourg jurisprudence on the complex and difficult issue of the balance to be struck between expression and privacy issues, and the way in which it has been at times mis-applied by English courts under the Human Rights Act; its application in the specific areas of breach of confidence cases and children's privacy is considered in detail in the succeeding chapters. We consider first how far the theoretical justifications for expression in general support speech that reveals private facts; the subsequent section examines the reflection of these conclusions in English and Strasbourg expression jurisprudence generally. We then turn to consider the Strasbourg case law on approaching the speech/privacy balance, in terms both of structuring the reasoning process and the means of assessing the value of the speech. Finally we make some preliminary observations on how the domestic courts have tackled this matter. In order to give this discussion some theoretical context, and in order to understand *why* Strasbourg has been quite ready to allow expression rights to be abridged in particular cases by the claims of privacy, in strong contrast to the approach of the US courts, noted above,[123] we start, then, by looking at how the claims of the two rights may be approached at the theoretical level.

FREE SPEECH THEORIES AND PRIVACY [124]

The Introduction to this work introduced the main justifications for freedom of speech: in the words of Lord Steyn: 'First it promotes the self-fulfilment of individuals in society. Secondly, in the famous words of Holmes J (echoing John Stuart Mill),

---

122 See the following chapter for how this could be done.

123 See note 40 above.

124 On the influence upon Strasbourg Article 10 jurisprudence of these theories, see the discussion in Chapter 2. Some of the points made in that chapter are briefly reprised here, in the specific context of the clash with privacy interests under Article 8.

"the best test of truth is the power of the thought to get itself accepted in the competition of the market . . . Thirdly, freedom of speech is the lifeblood of democracy'.[125] These, and another important justification will be examined in turn. It will be argued that, upon examination, privacy-invading speech is often unsupported by the key rationales underlying free speech theory, an insight which unfortunately often goes unrealized, so that as Gavison puts it, 'we often find a tendency to assume that all speech performs all the many functions of free speech so that any limitation on any speech endangers all these functions.'[126]

The theory that freedom of speech is necessary for the discovery of truth[127] has been a strong influence in US jurisprudence[128] but not historically at Strasbourg[129] or in the UK courts.[130] It has been persuasively argued that this rationale has little application to the paradigmatic privacy case, in which intimate facts about an individual are revealed; as Barendt has argued, 'Mill's argument . . . applies more strongly to assertions of opinion . . . than to . . . propositions of fact'.[131] Thus, since privacy actions attempt to stop the publication of private facts only, and not general expressions of opinion, they will pose very little threat to that free and unhindered public debate about matters of importance which Mill's argument seeks to protect. Schauer[132] makes a related point in this area, arguing that one way in which one may fail to possess knowledge—'justified true belief'—is simply through having 'no belief at all'[133] and he asks, 'Is it necessarily the case or generally the case that knowledge is better than ignorance?' On finding out a new fact, it may not replace a previously false belief but merely to what was previously 'epistemological empty space'.[134] Schauer's

---

[125] R v Secretary of State for the Home Department ex parte Simms [1999] 3 All ER 400, 408.

[126] R. Gavison, 'Too Early for a Requiem: Warren and Brandeis were right on privacy vs free speech' (1992) 43(3) South Carolina Law Review 437, at 463.

[127] J. S. Mill, On Liberty in M. Cowling (ed.) Selected Writings of John Stuart Mill, Cambridge: CUP, 1968, 121; for discussion see K. Greenwalt, 'Free Speech Justifications' (1989) 89 Columbia Law Review 119, 130–41.

[128] See, for example, the famous dicta of Judge Learned Hand in United States v Associated Press 52 F. Supp. 362, 372 (1943) that the First Amendment '. . . presupposes that right conclusions are more likely to be gathered out of a multitude of tongues, than through any kind of authoritative selection' and the comments of Holmes J., dissenting but with the concurrence of Brandeis J., in Abrams v United States 250 U.S. 616, 630 (1919), arguing that '. . . the best test of truth is the power of the thought to get itself accepted in the competition of the market.'

[129] Though note the repeated reference by the ECtHR to freedom of expression being one of the 'basic conditions for [society's] progress' (see e.g. Otto Preminger Institute v Austria (1994) 19 EHRR 34, para 49).

[130] ex parte Simms, op cit, at 408.   [131] Freedom of Speech, Oxford: Clarendon, 1985, 191.

[132] F. Schauer, 'Reflections on the Value of Truth' (1991) 41 Case Western Reserve Law Review, 699, 708.

[133] Ibid, 708. His other categories are: 'one's belief may be unjustified [though possibly true]; [and] one's belief can be false'.

[134] He gives the example of glancing at a diet magazine and learning that someone has lost 200 pounds while on a diet of bat guano (p 709). It could of course be argued that even such a trivial fact as this could replace or modify a previous false belief, although Schauer specifically states that in such a case 'I have not modified a previous belief (except possibly the belief that no-one ever lost 200 pounds on a diet of bat guano)' (p 709); the argument will hang on how narrowly or broadly one defines the category of previously held beliefs which may be modified by the new piece of information. If one defined the category as 'those beliefs previously held which related to the relationship between bat guano and diet', then it would

point that certain increases in knowledge have no—or at least virtually no—value at all has some relevance to privacy, in that much intrusive journalism merely gives a set of often trivial facts about a given celebrity.[135] It can fairly confidently be said that at best, such communications, as opposed to, say, the reporting of scientific discoveries or political controversies, are but very weakly supported by any argument from 'truth', simply because it is very hard to maintain plausibly that the simple acquisition of factual information about a given person has any inherent truth value. Schauer's distinction between filling up empty epistemological space and replacing mistaken beliefs could be given some practical force: where a figure in the public eye has deliberately held themselves out as standing for a certain set of values (e.g. the traditional family) the revelation that they in fact have an illegitimate child or are homosexual may be said to dispel a false and possibly influential perception about that person and thus have a higher speech value than a similar revelation about someone in relation to whom no pre-existing opinions had been formed. In cases involving political figures, however, the essence of the argument for the correction of false impressions is one that collapses into the argument from self-governance (below).

The justification for speech which may be referred to as the argument from autonomy[136] arguably also has minimal application in this area, and indeed the values it espouses actually point to a reasonable degree of privacy protection. The basic thesis is that matters of substantive moral choice must be left to the individual as an autonomous, rational agent (subject of course to his duty to respect the basic rights of others); therefore the state offends against human dignity, or treats certain citizens with contempt, if the coercive powers of the law are used to enforce the moral convictions of some upon others by, say, banning certain kinds of pornography or extreme political discourse.[137] It is immediately apparent that much privacy-invading speech, by both directly assaulting informational autonomy and indirectly threatening the individual's freedom of choice over substantive issues,[138] far from being *bolstered* by the autonomy rationale, is in direct conflict with it. The state, in restricting what one citizen may be told about the private life of another, is not acting out of a

---

probably be an empty category, and thus the new information would indeed merely add to one's stock of knowledge. If, however, the category was taken to be 'opinions about diets', then one could see the information as replacing a previous belief: one could have held the view that no-one ever lost weight on diets, or that all diets involved artificial substances etc. Indeed, it is probably hard to think of any belief which will literally just fill up previously empty space and not be at least capable of modifying or qualifying some previous belief.

135 Magazines such as *Hello, OK!, Heat,* and *Closer* in particular seem to be obsessed with the sole aim of passing on a mass of detail about the daily lives of such people to their readers.

136 The argument has been most recently and influentially put by writers in the revived tradition of deontological liberalism. Whether relying on John Rawls' hypothetical social contract *A Theory of Justice,* Oxford: Clarendon, 1972, or Ronald Dworkin's basic postulate of the state's duty to treat its citizens with equal concern and respect, *Taking Rights Seriously,* London: Duckworth, 1978, the thrust of the resultant principle, as described in the text, is similar.

137 The particular concern of Thomas Scanlon's influential approach set out in 'A Theory of Freedom of Expression' (1972) 1 *Phil. & Pub. Aff.* 216.

138 See above, at pp 665–6.

paternalistic desire to impose a set of moral values thereby, but rather to assure an equal freedom to all to live by their own values: in other words, it is protecting, not attacking autonomy. It is perhaps in relation to this justification that we may most clearly see the truth of Emerson's remark that, far from being invariably in conflict, the twin rights to freedom of speech and to privacy 'are mutually supportive, in that both are vital features of the basic system of individual rights'.[139]

The argument from self development—that the freedom to engage in the free expression and reception of ideas and opinions in various media is essential to human development[140]—has received some recognition at Strasbourg[141] and recently in the House of Lords.[142] As with the argument from autonomy, it is immediately apparent that this justification, since it seeks to facilitate human flourishing, far from inevitably opposing the right to privacy, must support it to some extent since, as argued above [143] a reasonable degree of privacy is a *requirement* for individual self development, particularly the ability to form intimate relationships, without which the capacity for individual growth would be severely curtailed.

Moreover, as Barendt has argued,[144] it is implausible to view most newspapers reporters as serving their own human need for self development. Moreover, even if there is some plausible argument that an individual journalist would personally gain from being able to discuss issues arising from facts she has discovered about someone else's private life, it is not possible to argue that her needs in this respect require her to be able to publish the material complained of in a mass-circulation newspaper. The focus must therefore be on the *readers* of such material. Raz has proposed a theory of freedom of expression which he argues provides a reader-based justification for expression and is concerned not with 'serious' public debate but with the type of speech which is 'often overlooked' or seen as 'trivial'.[145] He points out that much public expression in the media portrays and expresses aspects of forms of different lifestyles: 'Views and opinions, activities, emotions etc, expressed or portrayed are an aspect of a wider net of opinions, sensibilities, habits of action or dressing, attitudes etc which taken together form a distinctive style of form of life';[146] such portrayal, he argues, 'validate the styles of life portrayed.' Conversely, censorship is not only an 'insult' to the persons leading the lifestyle censored—a point which sounds very like

---

[139] C. Emerson, 'The Right of Privacy and the Freedom of the Press' (1979) 14(2) *Harvard Civil Rights— Civil Liberties Law Review* 329, 331. As will be seen below, autonomy issues may arise in relation to the self-government justification.

[140] For example, Emerson argues that the right to free expression is justified as the right of the individual to realize his character and potentialities through forming his own beliefs and opinions; see C. Emerson, 'Towards a General Theory of the First Amendment' 1963 72 *Yale LJ* 877, 879–80; M. Redish, *Freedom of Expression*, Indianapolis: Michie Co, 1984, 20–30, and Greenwalt, op cit, at 143–5.

[141] The ECtHR has repeatedly asserted that freedom of expression is one of the 'essential foundations for the development of everyone' (e.g. *Otto Preminger*, note 194 above, para 49).

[142] *ex parte Simms*, op cit, at 498.   [143] See pp 666–7.

[144] Barendt, op cit, at 68; he concedes that such arguments may have some applicability to the writers of 'fringe or underground journals'.

[145] J. Raz, 'Free Expression and Personal Identification' (1991) 11(3) *OJLS* 303, 310.   [146] Ibid.

Dworkin's argument for freedom of expression based on equal respect for citizens[147]—but it also, in a more instrumental vein, denies those living the lifestyle the opportunity for reassurance, the sense that they are not alone in their lifestyles and its problems, and also the chance for the public to learn about the widest possible range of lifestyles, thus maximizing their freedom of choice.[148]

Clearly, insofar as the *raison d'etre* behind supporting such expression is reassurance and validation to those portrayed in it, then expression that has the reverse effect of distressing and humiliating those portrayed, through the use of detail about their private life, falls wholly outside the aim in question. Insofar as it aims to reassure those living a similar type of lifestyle to the person reported on, that is, promote a feeling of solidarity, such a feeling surely cannot be promoted through perusing the fruits of a violation of a privacy; indeed the spectacle of one member of the particular group being subjected to intrusion and mass publicity about the details of their personal life would surely promote feelings, not of solidarity but alarm and unease. Raz himself considers that his argument does not in general justify revelations about particular individuals, but may do so in relation to 'individuals who have become symbols of certain cultures, or ideologies, or . . . styles of life.'[149] It is clear, however, that if speech which invades the privacy of such individuals is restricted, the 'message' sent by the state thereby, far from suggesting condemnation or contempt for the lifestyle revealed, in fact displays respect for the ability of the individual to decide for himself whether he wishes to share his life-decisions with the public at large. Moreover, the reassuring knowledge that control of such information rests with the individual will surely further the core aim of the self-fulfilment justification—the ability of persons to make free choices to experience and experiment with the widest possible range of lifestyles and activities. Conversely, the *inability* of the individual to exercise such control would, as argued above, amount to a significant 'chilling effect' upon the willingness of individuals to make controversial choices about their personal lives. On both deontological and consequentialist arguments, then, this justification tends to support a reasonable degree of protection for informational autonomy.[150]

The 'self governance' or argument from democracy has been described by Barendt as 'the most influential theory in the development of twentieth century free speech law',[151] an assertion supported by examination of the approach of UK and Strasbourg judges. The basic argument[152] is that since citizens cannot participate fully in a democracy unless they have a reasonable understanding of political issues, open debate on such matters is essential to ensure the proper working of a democracy; as Lord Steyn

---

[147] Dworkin, op cit, esp 272–4.   [148] Raz, op cit, at 312.   [149] Ibid, at 316.

[150] Schauer suggests that only under the most crudely utilitarian accounts would the pleasure of those who (say) read about the sex lives of celebrities outweigh the distress caused to the celebrity: 'Increases in knowledge that admittedly increase the pleasure of the knower are necessarily valuable only under a theory that treats pleasurable punchings of others as valuable . . .' (op cit, at 711).

[151] Op cit, at 68.

[152] See A. Meiklejohn, 'The First Amendment is an Absolute' (1961) *Sup. Ct. Rev.* 245 and (1960) *Political Freedom*, esp 115–24.

has recently put it, 'freedom of speech is the lifeblood of democracy.'[153] Since democracy rests upon ideas both of popular participation *and* accountability to the people, the argument from democracy may be seen to encompass also the function which a free press performs in exposing abuses of power,[154] thereby allowing for their remedy and also providing a deterrent effect for those contemplating such wrong-doing.[155] This latter aspect, since it concerns abuses of *state* power, such as corruption,[156] misuse of governmental agencies,[157] the exercise of foreign policy in contravention to declared policies[158] and the like, will be unlikely in the vast majority of cases ever to come into conflict with privacy rights, engaging rather the right to reputation.[159] The instances in which it may be likely to create such a conflict involves complex issues, considered below.

GENERAL APPROACHES TO SPEECH IN STRASBOURG AND THE UK

The high regard in which freedom of speech and particularly press freedom is held at Strasbourg is well known and considered in detail in Chapter 2. The Court has repeatedly asserted that freedom of expression 'constitutes one of the essential foundations of a democratic society,'[160] and that it 'is applicable not only to 'information' or 'ideas' that are favourably received or regarded as inoffensive . . . but also to those that 'offend, shock or disturb'.[161] Particular stress has been laid upon 'the pre-eminent role of the press in a State governed by the rule of law' which, in 'its vital role of 'public watchdog' has a duty 'to impart information and ideas on matters of public interest' which the public 'has a right to receive'.[162]

However, as discussed in that chapter, while the rhetorical attachment to free speech is always strong, it is a marked feature of the Strasbourg jurisprudence that clearly political speech, which more directly engages the self-government rationale, receives a much more robust degree of protection than other types of expression, such as artistic speech. Thus the leading 'political' speech cases of *Sunday Times v UK*[163]

---

[153] *ex parte Simms*, op cit, at 408.

[154] The argument has most powerfully been put by V. Blasi, 'The Checking Value in First Amendment Theory' (1977) *Am. B. Found. Res. J* 521.

[155] As Greenwalt puts it, 'what people do is partly dependent on what they think will become known. Most particularly, persons are less likely to perform acts that are widely regarded as wrong and that commonly trigger some sanction unless they are confident that they can keep the acts secret.' 'Free Speech Justifications' (1989) 89 *Columbia Law Review* 119, 143.

[156] As in the 'Cash for Questions' scandal in 1994, which led to the setting up of the *Committee on Standards in Public Life* under Lord Nolan.

[157] As in the notorious Watergate scandal.

[158] For example, the undeclared change in the Conservative administrations policies towards arms-related exports to Iran and Iraq investigated in the subsequent Scott Inquiry (HC 1995–96) 115.

[159] As in *Reynolds v Times Newspapers* [1999] 4 All ER 609, in which the former Irish Taoiseach sued newspapers which published reports accusing him of lying to the Irish Dail.

[160] *Observer and Guardian v the United Kingdom* A 216 (1991), para 59.

[161] *Thorgeirson v Iceland* (1992) 14 EHRR 843, para 63.   [162] *Castells v Spain* A 236 (1992), para 43.

[163] A 30 (1979). The case concerned a contempt of court action brought against the newspaper in respect of revelations it published concerning the dangers of the drug thalidomide.

Jersild v Denmark,[164] *Lingens v Austria*[165] and *Thorgeirson v Iceland*[166] all resulted in findings that Article 10 had been violated and all were marked by an intensive review of the restriction in question, in which the margin of appreciation was narrowed almost to vanishing point. By contrast, in cases involving artistic speech, supported by the values of autonomy and self-development rather than self-government, an exactly converse pattern emerges: applicants have tended to be unsuccessful and a very deferential approach to the judgments of the national authorities as to its obscene or blasphemous nature has been adopted.[167] As one of the leading works on the Convention concludes: 'It is clear that the Court ascribes a heirachy of value' to different classes of speech, attaching 'the highest importance to the protection of political expression . . . widely understood'; artistic expression is firmly in the second rank.[168]

A similar pattern may be discerned in the domestic jurisprudence: the most lofty rhetorical assertions of the importance of free speech and the strongest determination to protect it have been evident in cases where journalistic material raises political issues, broadly defined.[169] In such cases, the courts have either overtly adopted the Strasbourg principles described above[170] or have strongly emphasized the high status freedom of speech holds in the common law, as 'a constitutional right', or 'higher legal order foundation'.[171] Earlier pronouncements to the effect that: 'The media . . . are an essential foundation of any democracy'[172] have recently been emphatically reinforced by explicit recognition of their duty to inform the people on matters of legitimate public interest.[173] As Lord Nicholls recently put it: 'freedom to disseminate and receive information on political matters is essential to the proper functioning of the system of parliamentary democracy cherished in this country.'[174] The contrast with cases of artistic speech, in which the approach of the courts to the issues of free

---

[164] (1994) 19 EHRR 1. The case concerned an application by a Danish journalist who had been convicted of a racially offensive offence after preparing and broadcasting a programme about racism which included overtly racist speech by the subjects of the documentary.

[165] (1986) 8 EHRR 407. The case concerned the defamation of a political figure.

[166] (1992) 14 EHRR 843. The case concerned newspaper articles reporting allegations of brutality against the Reykjavik police.

[167] The following cases all concerned artistic speech which was restricted by the national authorities on the basis either of protection of public morals or religious feelings, or both: *Müller v Switzerland* (1991) 13 EHRR 212; *Gibson v UK* no. 17634 (declared inadmissible by Commission); *Otto Preminger*, op cit; *Gay News v UK* (1989) 12 EHRR 123; *Wingrove v UK* (1997) 24 EHRR 1, esp [58].

[168] Harris, O'Boyle, and Warbrick, *Law of the European Convention on Human Rights*, London: Butterworths, 1995, pp 397 and 414. The third rank is commercial speech, e.g. advertising.

[169] *Reynolds*, op cit; *Derbyshire County Council v Times Newspapers* [1993] AC 534; *Simms* (op cit). However, deference to widely drafted primary legislation (*Secretary of State for Home Affairs ex parte Brind* [1991] 1 AC 696 and *R (on the application of ProLife Alliance) v BBC* [2003] 2 WLR 1403) or arguments of national security *Attorney General v Guardian Newspapers* [1987] 1 WLR 1248 and *Brind* have resulted in the ready upholding of restrictions on directly political speech.

[170] See the Court of Appeal in *Derbyshire* (ibid) and *ex parte Leech* ([1994] QB 198), the House of Lords in *Reynolds* (op cit), 621–2, 628, 635, 643 and *Simms* (op cit), 407 and 419–20.

[171] *Reynolds*, ibid, 628–9, per Lord Steyn; *Simms*, ibid, 411, per Lord Steyn and 412, per Lord Hoffman.

[172] *Francome v Mirror Group Newspapers* [1984] 1 WLR 892898, per Sir John Donaldson.

[173] *Reynolds*, op cit, 633–634, per Lord Steyn.   [174] Ibid, at 621.

expression concerned has been either cautious[175] or downright draconian could not be clearer.[176] Press freedom in relation to political expression has clearly been recognized as having a particularly high value in UK law and Convention jurisprudence.

Two key points emerge from the above discussion. First, political speech, which, as just noted, receives the highest level of protection, is by its nature unlikely to conflict with the right to privacy. In many cases it will not raise privacy issues at all, as where it consists of the discussion of political ideas, institutions and policies and the discharge by politicians of their public office. Where political speech *does* concern individuals, as where it reveals abuse of state power, the conflict is more likely to be with reputation than privacy.[177] Thus the main libel cases which Strasbourg has considered, in which the Court has insisted on a high degree of protection for speech, all concerned revelations of matters of the highest public importance, including the alleged Nazi sympathies of the Austrian Prime Minister,[178] police brutality[179] and involvement with war crimes.[180] Other, non-libel cases have involved serious journalism exposing matters such as the resurgence of extreme racism in Danish society,[181] and the serious risk posed to public health in the UK by a new drug.[182] The speech in these seminal cases thus lay at the very core of that class of expression which the court regards as most essential for the survival and progress of a democratic society.

Second, speech which *does* invade privacy paradigmatically involves the personal, not the public-political affairs of its subjects, usually involves celebrities rather than public servants, and is often driven by purely commercial considerations. Such publications generally raise no serious speech issues, and simply do not engage core Article 10 values such as the furtherance of a democratic society or the press's right to impart 'information on matters of serious public concern'.[183] As discussed above, such speech is additionally unlikely to gain support from the arguments from autonomy, truth and self-development, so there will often be little or no justification at the level of principle for allowing it to override privacy.

APPROACHES TO THE SPEECH-PRIVACY BALANCE: THE STRASBOURG CASE LAW

Some imbalance between speech and privacy claims may *prima facie* be suggested by the strength of the 'speech' jurisprudence at both the Strasbourg and domestic levels, discussed above. In *ex p Simms*,[184] Lord Steyn referred to free speech as 'the primary right . . . in a democracy', in *Central Independent Television plc*,[185] Hoffmann LJ in an oft-quoted statement said: freedom of speech is 'a trump card which always wins'; and

---

[175] See e.g. *Gibson* [1990] 2 QB 619.
[176] *Knuller v DPP* [1973] AC 435 and *Lemon* [1979] AC 6170, HL.
[177] As in *Reynolds*; see also e.g. *Lingens v Austria* (1986) 8 EHRR 407 and *Thorgeirson* (op cit).
[178] *Lingens v Austria*, op cit.   [179] *Thorgeirson v Iceland*, op cit.
[180] *Tolstoy Miloslavsky v UK*, op cit.   [181] *Jersild v Denmark* (1994) 19 EHRR 1.
[182] *Sunday Times v UK* (op cit).   [183] *Bladet Tromso*, op cit, at [59].
[184] Op cit, at 407.   [185] [1994] Fam 192 at 203 and 204.

some commentators take the view that Article 10 attracts an especially high level of protection at Strasbourg.[186] Moreover, section 12(4) HRA, which enjoins the court to have 'particular regard' to Article 10 when making any order which might infringe it, appears on its face to suggest a higher weighting for speech interests. At least before, *Von Hannover, Peck* and the House of Lord's decision in *Campbell v MGN*,[187] therefore, it appeared possible that English law under the HRA might come to replicate the position in the US where, as Wacks puts it, 'It is widely acknowledged that the . . . "newsworthiness" defence has effectively demolished the private-facts tort'.[188]

This however, would have amounted to a mis-reading of Strasbourg jurisprudence, even before *Von Hannover*. Save for admitting the distinction between those rights stated in absolute or near-absolute terms, such as Arts 2,3,4,6 and 7, and those subject to generalized qualifications (in particular Arts 8–11), Strasbourg has never sought to establish a hierarchy of Convention rights. In this respect it is in accord with the stance in other jurisdictions, such as Germany, France and Canada which have rejected any notion of establishing an *a priori* ranking of rights.[189]

It is fair to say that in some extreme instances clashes can be resolved by refinements of the definition of the ambit of the right. For example, as has recently been argued, speech which 'amounts to a *gross* invasion of privacy . . . [is] considered [by the Commission] to have little or no informational value worth protecting (emphasis added).'[190] But in general, as indicated below, where rights collide, Strasbourg speaks of taking account of both and striking a fair balance under paragraph 2 of the Article pleaded before the Court. While the reasoning process inevitably follows the structure demanded by the Article(s) invoked by the applicant at Strasbourg, the other Convention right is given greater weight at the stage of determining the necessity of the interference (to support that right) in a democratic society, since it is axiomatic that all the Convention rights must be afforded a high value in such a society. This contrasts with the general Strasbourg approach to Arts 8–11 which is that where *societal* interests potentially threaten the primary guarantee, the issue is not 'a choice between two conflicting principles but . . . a principle . . . that is subject to a number of exceptions which must be narrowly interpreted'.[191] Although Strasbourg has not made this difference of approach explicit, it is clearly consistent with the Convention's foundational values to assume that a Convention right, albeit considered under the

---

[186] I. Leigh and L. Lustgarten, 'Making Rights Real: The Courts, Remedies, and the Human Rights Act' [1999] 55(3) *CLJ* 509, 524 and note 79.

[187] [2004] 2 WLR 1232.

[188] Wacks, op cit, 113; see also D. Anderson, 'The Failure of American Privacy Law' op cit, at 167.

[189] The German Supreme Court has remarked of the right to protection of personality (including privacy) and of free expression that 'neither can claim precedence in principle over the other' (BVerfGE 35, 200). For the Canadian approach, see *Hill v Church of Scientology* [1995] 2 SCR 1130, 1179 and the recent decision in *Les Editions Vice Versa Inc v Aubry* [1999] 5 BHRC 437; for the French approach, see E. Picard, 'The Right to Privacy in French Law' in Markesinis (ed.) *Protecting Privacy*, Oxford, Clarendon, 1999, at 93–6.

[190] M. Tugendhat, QC and I. Christie, *The Law of Privacy and the Media*, Oxford: OUP, 2002, 420–1.

[191] *Sunday Times v UK* (1979) 2 EHRR 245, para 65.

paragraph 2 exceptions, must be viewed as a conflicting principle rather than as a narrow exception to the primary guarantee.

Otto-Preminger Institut v Austria[192] provides a striking example of this approach. The Court found that the seizure and forfeiture of a film mocking Christianity was aimed at protecting the 'rights of others' within Art 10(2). The Court found that 'the manner in which religious doctrines are opposed or denied is a matter which may engage the responsibility of the State, notably its responsibility to ensure *the peaceful enjoyment of the right under Article 9*' (emphasis added).[193] The Court found that the responsibilities of those exercising the right under Art 10 include 'an obligation to avoid as far as possible expressions that are gratuitously offensive to others and thus an infringement of their rights and which therefore *do not contribute to any form of debate capable of furthering progress in human affairs*' (emphasis added).[194] The Court considered that the necessity for the restriction 'must be convincingly established' but did not give a specific reason for finding that this was the case, merely asserting that the Austrian authorities had not overstepped their margin of appreciation. Although the reasoning as to the *applicability* of Article 9 in this judgment is viewed by a number of commentators as deeply flawed,[195] the decision demonstrates, it is argued, that the Court follows a different approach within para 2 of Arts 8–11 where the 'rights of others' exception that is engaged concerns another Convention right.

Similar reasoning has informed the protection of Article 8 rights where there is a conflict with Article 10. Initially it seemed possible in *Winer v UK*[196] that the presence of such a clash might lead to a narrowing down of the ambit of 'private life' under Art 8(1) in order to avoid interfering with the guarantee of freedom of expression.[197] However, a different stance was taken in *Spencer (Earl) v United Kingdom*:[198] it was indicated impliedly not only that the conflict of rights should not be resolved by re-defining the ambit of the primary right to respect for private life, but also that a clash with Article 10 still leaves the privacy right with significant protection. The decisions in *Tammer v Estonia*,[199] *N v Portugal*[200] and *Barclay v United Kingdom*[201] also support this stance.

Tammer v Estonia is an especially significant decision in this context since the process of reasoning and the outcome is highly reminiscent of those in *Otto-Preminger*. The journalist applicant had been subject to a criminal penalty in respect of the publication of a hard-hitting interview relating to a former political aide, alleging that she had broken up the Prime Minister's marriage by having an affair with him and had deserted her own children. His application under Article 10 failed before the Court, which found that the remarks in question related to the former aide's private life; the restriction upon the journalist's Article 10 rights, taking into account

---

[192] (1994) 19 EHRR 34.   [193] Ibid, para 47.   [194] Ibid, para 49.
[195] See e.g. Harris, O'Boyle, and Warbrick, op cit, at 402.   [196] (1986) 48 DR 154.
[197] The facts are given above, at 667.
[198] (1998) 25 EHRR CD 105. The facts are given above, at 669–70.
[199] (2003) 37 EHRR 43; (2001) 10 BHRC 543.
[200] *N v Portugal*, Appl No. 20683/92, 20 February 1995. The facts are given above, at 668.
[201] (1999) Appl No. 35712/97 (admissibility only).

the lightness of the penalty imposed, was therefore a necessary and proportionate response to the need to uphold the privacy of the aide. In coming to this conclusion the Court afforded a very wide margin of appreciation to the national authorities since the case concerned a clash of rights:

'In considering the way the domestic authorities dealt with the case, the Court observes that the Estonian courts fully recognised that the present case involved a conflict between the right to impart ideas and the reputation and rights of others. It cannot find that they failed properly to balance the various interests involved in the case'.[202]

Peck v United Kingdom[203] provides further confirmation that the Court is prepared to find a breach of Article 8 rights even where significant restrictions on Article 10 rights are thereby created. The case concerned CCTV footage of an attempted suicide in the street which was then shown on national television. The decision is of significance, not only because it allowed for the suppression of freedom of expression on a matter of some significant public interest, but also because it demonstrates that freedom of expression can be curbed even where the speech suppressed is already partly in the public domain. It might have been found, taking account of *Observer and Guardian Newspapers v UK*,[204] that the suppression of speech in such circumstances was disproportionate to the legitimate aim pursued. But *Guardian Newspapers* was not a case that concerned a clash between two opposing individual rights. Rather, it concerned a clash between societal interests—in national security and the authority of the judiciary—and freedom of expression. The comparison between *Peck* and *Guardian Newspapers* provides a further indication that the Court is prepared to adopt a different approach—one that more readily accepts interferences with freedom of expression—where another individual Convention right is at stake.

The decision in *Von Hannover*, it is suggested, is one that emphatically establishes the presumptive equality of the two rights; going further, it also, as will appear below, comes close to identifying a category of speech that will *generally* be overridden by privacy interests. In *Von Hannover*, the court was confronted with a clear clash between the desire of Princess Caroline to be free from intrusive publications about her private life and the press interest in being free to report on her. As noted above, it was on the basis of the public interest in free reportage on the matter that the German Constitutional court had refused to grant relief in respect of the complained-of photographs, finding that, 'The public had a legitimate interest in knowing where the applicant was staying and how she behaved in public.'[205] The Constitutional Court here founded upon an explanation of the role that even the popular press could play in a democratic society:

Nor can mere entertainment be denied any role in the formation of opinions. That would amount to unilaterally presuming that entertainment merely satisfies a desire for amusement,

---

[202] Op cit, at [69]. It may be noted that a civil penalty could have been imposed rather than a criminal conviction for insulting the aide.

[203] (2003) 36 EHRR 41.   [204] (1991) 14 EHRR 153.   [205] Quoted ibid, at [25].

relaxation, escapism or diversion. Entertainment can also convey images of reality and propose subjects for debate that spark a process of discussion and assimilation relating to philosophies of life, values and behaviour models. In that respect it fulfils important social functions. . . .

The same is true of information about people. Personalization is an important journalistic means of attracting attention. Very often it is this which first arouses interest in a problem and stimulates a desire for factual information. Similarly, interest in a particular event or situation is usually stimulated by personalised accounts. Additionally, celebrities embody certain moral values and lifestyles. Many people base their choice of lifestyle on their example. They become points of crystallisation for adoption or rejection and act as examples or counter-examples. This is what explains the public interest in the various ups and downs occurring in their lives.[206]

This is a relatively subtle and sophisticated view of the legitimate role of the media in a democracy, which goes well beyond the overt discussion of political matters or of politicians. As one American commentator has put it, '[The] media uses people's names, statements, experiences, and emotions to personalise otherwise impersonal accounts of trends or developments.'[207] To quote Lord Cooke, 'Matters other than those pertaining to government and politics may be just as important in the community'.[208] Such speech, which can 'inform the social, political, moral and philosophical positions of individual citizens',[209] could include revelations relating to matters as diverse as eating disorders, abortion, attitudes to sexuality, education and the like; it will often concern not politicians, but celebrities, their relatives and those who for a short time and for a particular reason only are thrust into the public gaze. Some of the key free speech cases at Strasbourg did not in fact involve directly political speech, but speech of broader public interest.[210] However, instead of acceding to the above argument to the effect that details as to private lives *could* form part of a discourse with important public significance (what the German courts referred to as 'infotainment'), the Strasbourg Court in *Von Hannover* draws a sharp (and perhaps somewhat simplistic) distinction:

The Court considers that a fundamental distinction needs to be made between reporting facts—even controversial ones—capable of contributing to a debate in a democratic society, relating to politicians in the exercise of their functions, for example, and reporting details of the private life of an individual who, moreover, as in this case, does not exercise official functions. While in the former case the press exercises its vital role of 'watchdog' in a democracy by contributing to 'impart[ing] information and ideas on matters of public interest . . . it *does not do so* in the latter case.[211]

---

[206] Ibid.

[207] D. Anderson, 'The Failure of American Privacy Law' in B. Markesenis (ed.), *Protecting Privacy*, Oxford: Clarendon, 1999, at 142.

[208] *Reynolds v Times Newspapers* [1999] 4 All ER 609, at 640.

[209] D. Zimmerman, 'Requiem for a Heavyweight: A Farewell to Warren and Brandeis's Privacy Tort' (1983) 68 *Cornell Law Review* 291, 346.

[210] See Chapter 2 at 51–3 and Chapter 21 at 1060–7.

[211] *Von Hannover v Germany* (2005) 40 EHRR 1 at [63] (emphasis added).

Note that the Court states flatly, 'it does not do so': this is a blanket denial of the place of reportage of private facts within the press's legitimate, watchdog function. Applying this test in the instant case, the court found:

The situation here does not come within the sphere of any political or public debate because the published photos and accompanying commentaries relate exclusively to details of the applicant's private life.[212]

The Court's finding, on its face, is quite striking: publications concerning private life will *for that reason* lack any public interest and thus attract only a low weight under Article 10. What we have here is a form of definitional balancing. The Court does not deny that Article 10 is *engaged*: the phrase, 'In these conditions freedom of expression calls for a narrower interpretation', would seem to suggest that perhaps this type of celebrity reportage falls outside the scope of Article 10 altogether, but this would be a radical departure from the court's previous approach to speech, in which even hard-core pornography has been seen as falling within paragraph 1 of Art 10.[213] Rather, the court seems to concede that Article 10 is *engaged*: if it were not, there would be no need for any balancing exercise at all, but as just noted, it refers to 'the decisive factor in balancing the protection of private life against freedom of expression'.[214] However it appears clear that the type of speech in question will, as a matter of principle, be afforded a very low weight. This is a species of definitional balancing, because it lays down a general rule to be applied to a particular type of speech, and states that in such circumstances, Article 10 is *as a general rule* to be 'narrowly interpreted', a happier construction of which would be, 'afforded a low weight'.

The Court goes on to find:

. . . the publication of the photos and articles in question, of which the sole purpose was to satisfy the curiosity of a particular readership regarding the details of the applicant's private life, cannot be deemed to contribute to any debate of general interest to society despite the applicant being known to the public.[215]

Since the photographs and publications 'made no contribution' to a debate of general interest, the interest in press freedom under Article 10 had to give way to the Princess's privacy interests. In Strasbourg's view, it appears, if the complainant in a privacy case performs no official functions and the photographs merely convey details of their private life, the result is a foregone conclusion: the interest in press freedom gives way to the protection of private life. To put it another way, there is generally no (legitimate) public interest in the publication of such photographs.

Such a view, in ruling out almost in advance the possibility of any speech value in the discussion of private facts, amounts to a strikingly restrictive view of the role of the press. And this is not a position which is properly argued for in the judgment. As Sanderson notes, the Court throughout its reasoning in fact relies upon an assertion

---

[212] Ibid, at [64].   [213] *Hoare v UK* (1997) no. 31211/96.
[214] *Von Hannover v Germany* (2005) 40 EHRR 1, at [76].   [215] Ibid, at [65].

made early on in the judgment that 'public figures' are those that perform official functions. Once it then finds that the Princess performs no such function, she is automatically excluded from the definition of a public figure, and thus reportage on her private life falls outside the scope of contributing to a debate of general interest, which, Sanderson notes, the Court simply treats as being synonymous with debate on purely political matters including the performing of official functions.[216] In other words, the court makes one substantive assertion—that public figures should be considered to be only those that perform official functions, and then simply reverts to circularity, in finding that the Princess is not such a figure, and that *therefore* information about her cannot contribute to a debate of general interest.[217]

We return below to criticism of both the *Von Hannover* decision and that of the German courts in the same case. First of all, however, a further point of clarification should be noted. It is clear that the court does not pre-ordain that *any* reportage of private life will result in Article 8 rights prevailing over Article 10: it states that 'in certain special circumstances, [the public's right to be informed] can even extend to aspects of the private lives of public figures, particularly where politicians are concerned'.[218] The example that the Court had in mind[219] was its earlier decision in *Plon* (*Société*) v *France*.[220] The facts of this case are remarkable, and the decision notable. The case concerned what in France was known as 'the great secret'—the fact that throughout nearly all of his Presidency, Mitterand had known that he was suffering from prostrate cancer, a fact that was concealed from the French public for around 10 years. The application to the Court was brought by the publishers of a book giving details of the President's medical condition and treatment over many years, using information provided by a former physician to the President, M. Gubler. The book was published only after the President's death, but proceedings were brought against both M. Gubler and the publishers. The former was convicted in the criminal courts of breach of medical confidentiality, something he appears to have been clearly guilty of, according to the strict French law. A claim in privacy by M Mitterand's family was eventually dismissed on appeal, on the grounds that privacy was a right that could be claimed only by the living. However, an award of damages against M. Gubler and the publishing company was upheld, as was a permanent ban on the distribution of the book in France. This permanent ban continued an interim injunction granted to restrain any further distribution of the book.

It should first of all be noted that the book clearly contained information that would normally be regarded as highly confidential. As described by the Strasbourg court it 'contained the following':

very detailed information of a strictly medical nature concerning the symptoms of François

---

[216] Sanderson, 'Is *Von Hannover v Germany* a Step Backward' [2004] 6 EHRLR 631. Sanderson points out that the court tends to use 'general interest', 'political', and 'official duties' as interchangeable synonyms for 'public'.

[217] Ibid, at 640–1.   [218] *Von Hannover v Germany* (2005) 40 EHRR 1, at [64].

[219] Ibid, at [60].   [220] No. 58148/00, 18 May 2004.

Mitterrand's illness; an account of the medical examinations which he had undergone and their outcome and frequency; a description of a treatment protocol and the manner in which the treatment had been administered; an indication of the medicines used; a description of physical disorders and the side-effects of the treatment; an account of an operation; an account of conversations between Dr Gubler and his patient; a description of operations, consultations and treatment carried out by other practitioners; a description of the circumstances in which certain health bulletins concerning François Mitterrand were drawn up; and information about the private life of François Mitterrand's wife and children.[221]

However, the book was, as noted, published only after the President's death (albeit only ten days after it) and also, of course concerned not only an extremely important story about the former head of state, but also details of a vast deception that had been practised upon the French people. As the Court found:

... the book was published in the context of a wide-ranging debate in France on a matter of public interest, in particular the public's right to be informed about any serious illnesses suffered by the head of State, and the question whether a person who knew that he was seriously ill was fit to hold the highest national office. Furthermore, the secrecy which President Mitterrand imposed, according to the book, with regard to his condition and its development, from the moment he became ill and at least until the point at which when the public was informed (more than ten years afterwards), raised the public-interest issue of the transparency of political life.[222]

Clearly, in Article 10 terms, the speech was of the 'highest value', since it went to the heart of the political process in France. Moreover, the clash was not, as such with privacy (since the President was dead), but with a duty of confidentiality: in other words, this was not a clash of Convention rights, but of speech of the highest importance under Article 10 with a competing societal interest. Moreover, the applicants' main complaint related to the injunctions granted to prevent distribution of the book—to prior restraint, in other words, which the Court has found, because of 'the dangers which [they] pose for a democratic society' to 'call for the most careful scrutiny on the part of the Court'.[223] All of these factors might have led one to expect an emphatic finding of a breach of Article 10, at least in respect of the injunctions. But this was by no means the case. The Court considered the interim and permanent injunctions separately, as in the *Observer and Guardian* case;[224] it found a breach only in relation to the latter.

The *interim* injunction, to restrain publication of the book before a full hearing on the merits could be arranged—banning it for 9 months as it turned out—was held to be justified under Article 10(2). The reasoning of the Court justifies this finding primarily on the basis that the distribution of the book only 10 days after the President's death 'could only have intensified the grief of the President's heirs following his very recent and painful death.'[225] Banning the whole of the French people from reading a book of such vital political importance on the basis of the intensification of

---

[221] Ibid, at [35].   [222] Ibid, at [44].   [223] Reiterated, op cit, at [42].
[224] (1991) 14 EHRR 153. See Chapter 3 at 156–7.   [225] Ibid, at [48].

grief of the President's family seems questionable enough; however, the judgment also seems to miss the point that such grief was presumably being felt in any event: 40,000 copies of the book had been sold before the injunction was granted, and extracts from it appeared in the magazine *Paris-Match*, of which one million copies had sold. Since the injunction was ineffective in preventing such grief, it was arguably therefore impossible for it to be proportionate.[226]

The other reason given by the Court for finding the interim injunction to have been justified is that the 'damage caused by the book to the deceased's reputation was particularly serious in the circumstances' of the emotion generated by his death. This reasoning is, frankly, opaque. The long-term damage to Mitterand's reputation was not related to the emotion of his death, and, in any event, the judgment gives the impression that any such damage was justified—in other words, that the book was truthful. The Court also notes that the issuing of the interim injunction 'did not prejudge the outcome of the subsequent dispute between the parties on the merits'. But this is surely always the case with interim injunctions.

In short, the judgment upholds prior restraint of a book that revealed that the French public had for ten years been seriously deceived as to the health of their president. If ever a case concerned private life but raised serious speech concerns, this was such a one. The decision seems extraordinary, and given the ineffectiveness of the injunction in protecting the family from grief, particularly hard to justify. The injunction had the effect of restraining publication of the book for 9 months (from January to October 1997).

The Court does however find that the issuing of the permanent injunction in October—nine months after the President's death, was disproportionate.

In the Court's opinion, as the President's death became more distant in time, this factor [the effect of the book on the grief of the family] became less important. Likewise, the more time that elapsed, the more the public interest in discussion of the history of President Mitterrand's two terms of office prevailed over the requirements of protecting the President's rights with regard to medical confidentiality.[227]

In other words, the Court was prepared to find that, although at the time immediately after the President's death, his right to medical confidentiality prevailed over the right to freedom of expression, this was not so 9 months later, particularly as the extensive publication of the book that had already happened (40,000 copies sold and 1 million copies of *Paris-Match*, carrying extracts as well as publication on the internet) rendered the information in it 'to a large extent ... no longer confidential'. This is scarcely a ringing endorsement of press freedom: it would have been bizarre to uphold a permanent injunction on *confidentiality* grounds after such widespread publication elsewhere, as well as clearly inconsistent with the ruling in *Observer and Guardian v UK*.[228] The authors of this work are enthusiastic proponents of a right to privacy, but this judgment, with its very weak defence of speech that lies at the very core of Article 10,

---

[226] See the discussion in Chapter 2 at 97–100.   [227] Ibid, at [53].   [228] Op cit.

is liable only to fuel the fears of those who see in the development of a privacy law a threat to investigative journalism.

The Court's comment on this case in *Von Hannover* is that 'in certain special circumstances, [the public's right to be informed] can even extend to aspects of the private lives of public figures, *particularly* where politicians are concerned'[229] raises an interesting point. This statement is arguably in tension with an important statement of principle from the court's decision in *Thorgeirson v Iceland*[230] to the effect that there is no warrant in its case law for 'distinguishing between political discussion and discussion of other matters of public concern'. The whole tenor of the judgment in *Von Hannover* is against there being a legitimate public concern in issues arising from the private lives of others, with politicians (and presumably others holding important public office) being adduced as the key exception. However, if there is no warrant for distinguishing between political speech and speech on other matters of legitimate public concern, and given that the private lives of non-political actors such as celebrities *can* furnish examples to stimulate debate on matters of serious (although not political) concern, it is evident that a consistent application of the Court's jurisprudence should afford a rather broader defence of privacy-invading speech than the Court appears to admit here.

Perhaps one reason why the Court seemed so unreceptive to the notion that privacy-invading speech may sometimes have a legitimate role in contributing to public debate was that in this case, the argument was very weak on the facts. In other words, whilst the German Courts rightly pointed out the important role of 'infotainment' in stimulating debate on matters of public concern in general, it was very hard to see just *what* topics might thus be stimulated through such anodyne photographs of Princess Caroline, still less why a ceaseless parade of such pictures was needed. Whilst there may be *some* legitimate role for the revelation of private facts in fuelling debate on matters of serious concern, it is difficult if not impossible to see how the publication of gossipy, bland pictures of a celebrity's everyday activities could begin to fulfill that role. Thus the Strasbourg court was arguably not confronted with any plausible argument as to the utility of the particular pictures and articles concerned in stimulating public debate and thus did not need to engage with it. Paradoxically indeed, the very fact that the photographs were *not* particularly intrusive could also be said to be the reason why they contributed to no debate of general interest. In contrast, pictures of a celebrity emerging from a brothel, or a drug treatment centre, or an abortion clinic could, whilst more intrusive, *also* could be argued to make a contribution to a serious public debate—on prostitution, drug addiction, or abortion, as the case may be.[231] It

---

[229] Op cit, at [64] (emphasis added).

[230] (1992) 14 EHRR 843. See the discussion on this point in Chapter 2 at 51–3 and Chapter 21 at 1060–7.

[231] Sanderson makes a similar point, speculating whether the perverse outcome of *Von Hannover* may be to encourage journalists to uncover more disreputable facts relating to celebrities, in the hope of thereby being able to benefit from a more plausible 'public interest argument': Sanderson, 'Is *Von Hannover v Germany* a Step Backward', op cit. The decisions in *Tammer v Estonia* (2001) 37 EHRR 857, and *Campmany Y* ((2000) no. 54224/00), however, would give little encouragement to such a course of action.

would therefore be interesting to see how Strasbourg would respond to a case such as *Campbell*, in which the picture and articles in question, whilst clearly strongly engaging private life, also *did* relate to such a matter of serious public concern, as well as engaging the notion of the importance of the public's not being misled by previous untruthful statements by the applicant. However, its very partial and cautious upholding of press freedom in *Plon Société*, a case which, by any standards raised issues of public interest of immeasurably greater importance than the details of Campbell's treatment for drug addiction, would strongly suggest that had the Court of Appeal decision against her been the final one in domestic law, and Campbell had gone to Strasbourg, there would have been a resounding finding of breach of Article 8, an outcome that the authors would of course, fully endorse.

RESOLVING THE CONFLICT IN DOMESTIC COURTS BY IMPORTING STRASBOURG PRINCIPLES

While the approach of the English courts in particular cases to resolving the conflict with privacy that such public interest concerns raise is examined in detail in the succeeding chapters, it is appropriate to set out in the final part of this chapter the general principles that have now been established on this matter.

The satisfactory resolution of the potential conflict between Articles 8 and 10 in domestic privacy cases must, it is suggested, be found at two levels. First there is the issue of the *structure* of the reasoning process by which the balancing act between the two rights is undertaken. Second, there is the issue of substance: what principles should the court use to weigh the two rights against each other when carrying out this process? We have seen that Strasbourg has given a certain amount of guidance in relation to both of these issues, particularly the latter; nevertheless, the different position of the domestic courts requires this issue to be considered from their perspective.

Approaches to the speech-privacy balance: structure

How, then, should the courts structure the competing claims of speech and privacy? *Reynolds*[232] was a defamation case in which, as in confidence actions, speech considerations function as a defence. However, the House of Lords did not treat free speech as an exception to the primary right to reputation. 'The starting point,' Lord Steyn stated,[233] 'is now the right of freedom of expression, a right based on a . . . higher legal order foundation. Exceptions . . . must be justified as being necessary in a democracy. In other words, freedom of expression is the rule, and regulation of speech is the exception requiring justification'.[234] These findings are in line with the general Strasbourg approach discussed in Chapter 2, that where other interests potentially threaten free speech, the issue is not 'a choice between two conflicting principles

---

[232] *Reynolds v Times Newspapers* [1999] 4 All ER 609. The decision is discussed in detail in Chapter 21.
[233] See also Lord Nicholls: 'My starting point is freedom of expression' (*Reynolds*, ibid, at 621).
[234] Ibid, at 629.

but . . . a principle of freedom of expression that is subject to a number of exceptions which must be narrowly interpreted'.[235] However, if this approach were to be applied in domestic privacy cases, the result would be that privacy would lose its Convention status as a fully-fledged right, becoming instead merely a narrowly interpreted exception to the right of freedom of expression. Such an approach, we have consistently argued,[236] could not be right. It would introduce a striking asymmetry whereby the protection of the right to privacy would have to be justified as necessary in a democratic society, while the claims of free speech would be simply assumed. Where a restriction on a Convention right is justified not as serving one of the societal interests the Convention enumerates, such as economic well-being or protection of morals, but in order to protect another primary Convention right, a different approach should be followed. In cases where Convention rights have clashed, Strasbourg, as discussed above, has still formally followed the standard approach, treating one right as primary, so that restrictions upon it by a competing right have to be justified as necessary in a democratic society. However, this is because when Strasbourg hears cases brought by individuals alleging a violation of a Convention right, competing rights figure only as possible means of justification for the respondent State and thus as an exception to the primary right whose infringement is alleged. At the same time, Strasbourg does not view the other right as an exception to be interpreted narrowly but in practice conducts something more akin to a balancing act between the two, if both are found to be engaged. The position of a domestic court is fundamentally different: both sides before it are individuals (or private bodies); both will claim that their rights as individuals are equally in issue. It would therefore be perverse for such a court, by a prior ordering, to assign one right (speech) a position as the primary norm, and the other (privacy) that of a mere exception to it. To put it another way, to treat privacy rights under Article 8 in the same way as the societal interests enumerated in Article 10(2) simply collapses the basic scheme of the Convention, which, as a human rights treaty is, axiomatically, to afford human rights a special status over other interests.

It was this precisely this mistaken approach, however, that was followed in the bulk of the case law prior to the House of Lords decision in *Campbell*. It is perhaps most strikingly illustrated by the judgment in *Venables v News Group Newspapers*.[237] In that decision, the court cited with approval[238] dicta of Sedley LJ in *Douglas v Hello*[239] against the affording of any presumptive priority to Article 10 over 8. But the way in which those dicta were applied amounts to the most comprehensive endorsement of the presumptive priority of Article 10, not only over Article 8, but of other Convention rights, that could be imagined. Butler Sloss P stated:

The onus of proving the case that freedom of expression must be restricted is firmly upon the applicant seeking the relief. The restrictions sought must . . . be shown to be . . .

[235] *Sunday Times v UK*, op cit, at [65].   [236] Phillipson and Fenwick, op cit (*MLR*), at 686.
[237] *Venables and another v News Group Newspapers* [2001] 1 All ER 908.   [238] Ibid, at 920.
[239] [2001] QB 967, CA, at 1004.

justifiable as necessary to satisfy a strong and pressing social need, convincingly demonstrated, to restrain the Press . . . and proportionate to the legitimate aim pursued.[240]

The judge went on:

I am satisfied that I can only restrict the freedom of the media to publish if the need for those restrictions can be shown to fall within the exceptions set out in Article 10(2). In considering the limits to the law of confidence, and whether a remedy is available to the claimants within those limits, *I must interpret narrowly those exceptions.*[241]

In this case, however, the relevant exceptions were *other Convention rights*—the rights to life, to be free from inhuman treatment and to privacy. In other words, the judge regarded herself as being bound to make sure that Convention rights other then Article 10 were 'narrowly interpreted' and, crucially, that claimants wishing to enjoy these other Convention rights may only lawfully be allowed to do so if they can show that this is 'necessary.' The judgment took us to the bizarre situation in which a claim of Article 10 automatically relegates all other Convention rights—including the rights to life and to freedom from torture—to the status of narrowly construed exceptions. Such an approach, giving freedom of expression presumptive priority over all other Convention rights, amounts to a radical distortion of the basic Convention scheme.

This approach was followed in a number of other decisions. In *Mills v MGN*,[242] the court simply recited the new orthodoxy: 'To be justified, any curtailment of freedom of expression must be convincingly established by a compelling countervailing consideration, and the means employed must be proportionate to the end sought to be achieved . . . Freedom of expression is the rule and regulation of speech is the exception requiring justification.[243] (Logically therefore, protection of privacy is the exception, requiring justification). In *Theakston*,[244] the court approved the straightforward application of the above dicta from the *Sunday Times* case, accepting, in effect, that the right to privacy figured solely as a "narrowly construed" exception to Article 10.'[245]

A v B plc[246] contains contradictory dicta on point: on the one hand the Court cites as 'useful guidance' Council of Europe Resolution 116 5 of 1998 which includes the following important statement of principle:

The Assembly reaffirms the importance of every person's right to privacy, and of the right to freedom of expression, as fundamental to a democratic society. *These rights are neither absolute nor in any hierarchical order, since they are of equal value* (emphasis added).[247]

The significance of the final paragraph is obvious: it would suggest that any prior configuration of the two rights such that Article 8 figures only as an exception to Article 10 would be mistaken. However, the court also goes on to say:

Any interference with the press has to be justified because it inevitably has some effect on the

---

[240] Ibid, at 921.   [241] Ibid, at 931 (emphasis added).   [242] [2001] EMLR 41.
[243] [2001] EMLR 41, at [15].   [244] [2002] EMLR 22.   [245] [2002] 3 WLR 542, at [11(xiii)].
[246] [2002] 3 WLR 542.   [247] Ibid, at 553A.

ability of the press to perform its role in society. This is the position irrespective of whether a particular publication is desirable in the public interest. The existence of a free press is in itself desirable and so any interference with it has to be justified.[248]

On its face, this sounds unobjectionable. The problem, it is suggested, is the lack of mention of the commensurate status of Article 8, as affirmed in the Council of Europe resolution above. Implicitly, the right to privacy figures only as an exception, which must be argued for to justify the interference with press freedom. There is no statement balancing the *dicta* above, to the effect that any interference with private life *likewise* stands to be justified, and as will appear below, it is this part of the judgment, rather than the Council Resolution also cited by the court, that appears actually to determine the approach taken in determining how to weigh the two rights against each other.

The approach of the Court of Appeal in the recent decision in *D v L*[249] was even more unbalanced: there was, quite simply, no mention of Article 8 anywhere in the judgment. Thus the court made no attempt therefore even to assess whether its proposed course of action would be compatible with Article 8, let alone considering whether therefore to deviate from that course. The radically unbalanced nature of the judgment appears in the fact that the Court referred extensively to Article 10 during its judgment, and one of its reasons for refusing relief in the case was the defendant's rights under Article 10 to publish the information received. Instead of engaging in any kind of balancing act, even between *confidentiality* and expression, it appeared to be assumed that the defendant's right to publish details as to the applicant's sexual proclivities automatically trumped any confidentiality in the material. In other words, the approach to balancing Articles 8 and 10 was not even one of presumptive priority for the latter: it was simply to deny implicitly the very existence of the privacy side of the scales.

However, the need for a different approach has now found recognition following the House of Lords decision in *Campbell*, and, very recently in *Re S*,[250] building on the approach of earlier decisions. In *Douglas*, the argument as to the structural priority to be given to freedom of expression was evidently put to the court and—in perhaps the most important aspect of the judgments—it was rejected. This is in spite of the fact that s 12(4) HRA instructs the courts, among other things to have 'particular regard' to freedom of expression. But Sedley LJ's reasoning on this point was emphatic:

The European Court has always recognised the high importance of free media of communication in a democracy, but its jurisprudence does not—and could not consistently with the Convention itself—give Article 10(1) the presumptive priority which is given, for example, to the First Amendment in the . . . United States. Everything will ultimately depend on the proper balance between privacy and publicity in the situation facing the court.[251]

---

[248] Ibid, at 549E.

[249] [2004] EMLR 1. The case concerned an application by D against his former partner, to prevent misuse of a tape-recording made by her in which he spoke of his sexual proclivities.

[250] [2005] 1 AC 593. The decision is discussed in detail in Chapter 16.   [251] Op cit, at 1004.

Support was leant to this view by dicta of Simon Brown LJ in *Cream Holdings Ltd v Bannerjee*[252] and of Lindsay J in *Douglas II*, to the effect that 'there is no "presumptive priority" given to freedom of expression when it is in conflict with another Convention right.'[253]

This approach has now been decisively endorsed by the House of Lords, both in *Campbell* and in their recent decision on the appeal from *Re S*. All of their Lordships—including Lord Nicholls and Lord Hoffman, who found against Campbell—rejected the notion of Article 10 having any presumptive priority, such that Article 8 was treated merely as an exception to it. As Lord Nicholls put it:

The case involves the familiar competition between freedom of expression and respect for an individual's privacy. Both are vitally important rights. Neither has precedence over the other . . .[254]

Lord Hoffman was more emphatic:

There is in my view no question of automatic priority. Nor is there a presumption in favour of one rather than the other. The question is rather the extent to which it is necessary to qualify the one right in order to protect the underlying value which is protected by the other. And the extent of the qualification must be proportionate to the need: see Sedley LJ in *Douglas v Hello! Ltd* . . .[255]

Lord Hope took the same view:

Any restriction of the right to freedom of expression must be subjected to very close scrutiny. But so too must any restriction of the right to respect for private life. Neither article 8 nor article 10 has any pre-eminence over the other in the conduct of this exercise.[256]

Lady Hale agreed,[257] endorsing her own approach in the Court of Appeal decision in *Re S*.

In the House of Lords decision in *Re S*, Lord Steyn, giving the unanimous opinion of the House, helpfully distilled the approach we have been discussing into four key principles which he said, 'clearly emerge[d] from the speeches given in *Campbell*:

First, neither article has as such precedence over the other. Secondly, where the values under the two articles are in conflict, an intense focus on the comparative importance of the specific rights being claimed in the individual case is necessary. Thirdly, the justifications for interfering with or restricting each right must be taken into account. Finally, the proportionality test must be applied to each.[258]

As Lady Hale explained in *Campbell*:

[The correct balancing approach] involves looking first at the comparative importance of

---

[252] [2003] Ch 650 at [54]. The case concerned an application for an interim injunction to restrain commercially confidential material, and in particular the construction of s 12(3) HRA.
[253] [2003] 3 All ER 996 at [185 cv]   [254] Op cit, at [12].   [255] Ibid, at [55].
[256] Ibid, at [113]. He also cited Sedley's dicta contrasting the ECHR position with that under the First Amendment—above, note 251.
[257] Ibid, at [111] and [138].   [258] Note 250 above, at [17].

the actual rights being claimed in the individual case; then at the justifications for interfering with or restricting each of those rights; and applying the proportionality test to each.[259]

Under this approach, the court considers the issue of any conflict with press freedom from two perspectives. The court asks first whether Article 10 would be engaged by injuncting the complained of publication and, if so, the standard Convention tests are followed, asking whether the interference with it proposed by the applicant would be necessary in a democratic society and proportionate to the legitimate aim of protecting private life. But the court then considers the issue from the *opposing* perspective, with the rights *reversed* in position so that the speech interest is treated as an exception to the primary right to respect for privacy under Article 8; the same enquiries as to necessity and proportionality are then made from this opposing perspective. The court can then compare the results of the two previous stages. If one right had been preferred whichever analysis was used, the outcome would be clear. If a different conclusion was reached depending upon which right was afforded initial priority as the primary right, the strength and clarity of the two conclusions may be compared. In this way, useful insights can be gleaned by asking, for example, *both* whether the publication in question was more intrusive than was necessary to its legitimate aim of provoking discussion on matters of public interest, *and*, conversely, whether the remedy sought by the applicant went further than was necessary in order to protect the legitimate privacy interest. In a manner reminiscent of the approach of the German[260] and Canadian courts,[261] the claims of both parties are thus subject to a searching, but balanced examination. Such an approach has been endorsed by Tomlinson and Rogers, who argue that the approach of the courts to date neglects the need to conduct such a 'parallel analysis' into the necessity of infringing the claimant's Article 8 right.[262] It had also received some early judicial endorsement: Sedley LJ remarked in *Douglas* that both Articles (8 and 10) were qualified by each other and that when balancing the two against each other, 'the outcome . . . is to be determined principally by considerations of proportionality.'[263]

This was precisely the approach taken by the Strasbourg Court in the recent Article 8 case of *Peck*. The Court undertook a careful assessment of whether the public

[259] Ibid, at [141]. Note that had section 12(4) been interpreted as affording primacy to Article 10 instead, it would probably have necessitated a declaration of the incompatibility of s 12(4) with Article 8. The subsection can now be viewed therefore either merely as a (superfluous) reminder of the demands of Article 10, or as a means of drawing in the conflicting right under Article 8 since s 12(4) clearly covers Article 10(2) as well as Article 10(1). Arguably, the former view accords more comfortably with the notion of presumptive equality. See on this point, Sedley LJ in *Douglas v Hello!* [2001] QB 967, 1003 at para 137. S12(4) is not needed to perform the task of drawing Article 8 into the frame since it is performed by s 6; however, Sedley LJ's interpretation accords with the impact of s 3 (which applies to s 12(4)) and refutes the notion that s 12(4) affords presumptive priority to Article 10. Lord Hope in *Campbell* approved of this approach to s 12(4): op cit, at [111].

[260] See Markesenis and Nolte, op cit, at 122–4.   [261] See note 189 above.

[262] Op cit.

[263] Op cit, at 1005 (emphasis added). This approach was also adopted by Hale LJ in her decision in *Re S*, discussed at length in Chapter 16.

interest claimed by the Council—that of publicising the effectiveness of CCTV and thus deterring crime—justified the intrusion into the applicant's private life. It found that it did not, principally because showing images that revealed the applicant's iden- tity could not be seen to be a *necessary* part of furthering that admittedly 'strong' public interest.[264] The Council, it found, had other means—means that would not have involved such disclosure—of furthering the interest in deterring crime: the intrusion into private life therefore went further than was necessary.[265]

Following such an approach has, it is suggested, two main effects. First, because any proportionality enquiry ultimately requires a court to balance one interest against another by reference to the particular factual context, the court has to make some attempt to assess how far the particular exercise of speech it was considering engaged the values underlying Article 10, in order to assess its relative strength against that of the privacy claim. In short, the Article 10 claim must be *evaluated*, rather than simply taken as a given, as occurred in many of the decisions. Second, this approach forces the court to enquire into the level of intimate detail disclosed by the publication in question and ask whether the *level of intrusion* that detail entailed could in fact be justified. The difference that these two exercises make in practice is drawn out by analysis of the particular decisions considered in the next three chapters.

[264] Op cit, at [79].   [265] Ibid, at [80]–[85].

14

PROTECTION FOR PRIVACY AGAINST THE PRESS IN THE HUMAN RIGHTS ACT ERA[1]

'Photos appearing in the tabloid press are often taken in a climate of continual harassment which induces in the person concerned a very strong sense of intrusion into their private life or even of persecution'[2]

INTRODUCTION

THE CONTEXT

The lack of a clear legal privacy remedy in respect of the non-consensual disclosure of personal information has long been both criticized[3] and, simultaneously, held up as a triumph for press freedom; self regulation has been held out by both the press itself and successive governments as the solution to any privacy issues raised by the activities of the press.[4] The need for such a remedy has been clear since Warren and Brandeis' famous comment in the nineteenth century upon the press's ability and willingness to inflict through invasions of privacy 'mental pain and distress far greater than could be inflicted by mere bodily injury.'[5] That analysis is alarmingly applicable today, over one hundred years later, save that the parabolic microphone and the

---

[1] This chapter and the succeeding one draws in places upon the following articles by the authors: G. Phillipson and H. Fenwick, 'Breach of Confidence as a Privacy Remedy in the Human Rights Act Era' [2000] 63(5) *MLR* 660–693 and 'Confidence and Privacy: A Re-examination' [1996] 55 *CLJ*, 447; G. Phillipson, 'Transforming breach of confidence? Towards a common law right of privacy under the Human Rights Act', (2003) 66(5) *MLR* 726 and 'Judicial Reasoning in Breach of Confidence Cases under the Human Rights Act: not taking privacy seriously?' [2003] *EHRLR (Privacy Special)* 53.

[2] *Von Hannover v Germany* (2004), App no. 59320/00, 24 June 2004 [2004] EMLR 21.

[3] It was condemned by the Court of Appeal in *Kaye v Robertson* [1991] FSR 62, CA, said to give rise to 'serious, widespread concern' by Lord Nicholls in *R v Khan* [1997] AC 558, 582; and referred to as a 'glaring inadequacy' by the Law Commission: *Breach of Confidence* (Law Com. No. 110), para 5.5: 'the confidentiality of information improperly obtained . . . may be unprotected'.

[4] See below at 709–10.   [5] 'The Right to Privacy' (1890) IV(5) *Harvard Law Review* 193, 196.

telephoto lens now give the press far more easy access to our more intimate moments. As commentators have noted, 'A vast array of surveillance devices are available, including detectors that can scan underneath clothing and through walls and micro-phones and transmitters that can hear through walls and at great distances.'[6] While a ubiquitous complaint about the British media is its oft-noted penchant for publishing what one journalist has described as 'toe-curlingly intimate details' about the sexual lives not only of celebrities but of 'quite obscure people,'[7] such intrusive prurience is not the only complaint. Victim Support has detailed a large number of case histories in which ordinary victims of crime and their families had their suffering markedly exacerbated by intrusive publications in local and national newspapers, describing their plight in quite needless detail, causing in some cases diagnosable psychiatric harm and making others feel forced to move from the area where the crime had been committed; causing all intense emotional distress.[8] In contrast to the position in virtually every other Western democracy, such injuries, up until recently attracted no legal remedy in this country. However, the thesis of this chapter is that the decision of their Lordships in *Campbell v MGN Ltd*[9] has now given rise to such a remedy, when taken together with the protection available under various statutes. The purpose of this chapter and the succeeding one is to examine both the adequacy of this remedy and whether protection for privacy has been achieved in a way that avoids compromising the legitimate role of the press in a democracy.

LEGAL PROTECTION FOR PRIVACY: THE POLICY OPTIONS

In principle, there are four main routes by which the historic absence of privacy remedy in UK law might be remedied. First, the matter could be left in the hands of the Press Complaints Commission (PCC), which polices a code protecting privacy, but has no compensatory or restraining powers.[10] Second, Parliament could introduce a general, statutory right to privacy. Third, the courts could introduce such a right, through development of a new, free-standing common law tort, as the New Zealand judges have very recently done.[11] Fourth and finally, the courts could continue to develop existing remedies to provide greater protection, under the influence of the

---

[6] E. Paton-Simpson, 'Privacy and the Reasonable Paranoid: The Protection of Privacy in Public Places' (2000) 50 *University of Toronto Law Journal* 305, at 330; she cites B. Phillips, 'Privacy in a Surveillance Society' (1997) 46 *UNBLJ* 127, 129 and A. J. McClurg, 'Bringing Privacy Law Out of the Closet: A Tort Theory of Liability for Intrusions in Public Places' (1995) 73 *NCL Rev.* 989.

[7] Andrew Marr, *The Independent*, 25 April 1996.

[8] *Fourth Report of the National Heritage Select Committee on Privacy and Media Intrusion*, Appendix 24, HC 294–II (1993).

[9] [2004] 2 AC 457. For comment see: David Lindsay, 'Naomi Campbell in the House of Lords: Implica-tions for Australia' (2004) 11(1) *Privacy Law & Policy Reporter*, 4, 4–11; Jonathan Morgan, 'Privacy in the House of Lords—Again' (2004) 120 *Law Quarterly Review*, 563, 563–6.

[10] That is, it cannot restrain publication and nor can it award damages in respect of publications found to have breached the PCC Code.

[11] *Hosking v Runting and others* (2004) CA 101/03.

introduction[12] into UK law by the Human Rights Act 1998 ('HRA') of Article 8, providing for a right to respect for private life.

Taking these possibilities in turn, we should first consider the arguments of those who consider that regulation of the press through the PCC is a better system for privacy protection than any that may be achieved through development of a *legal* remedy. This has been most recently made by Lord Wakeham, former Chair of the PCC,[13] ever a stubborn defender of the system of which he was until recently in charge. Confidence in his views on a matter concerning the law are not inspired by his rather eccentric account of the genesis of the HRA. These include the mysterious assertion that Britain did not incorporate the ECHR earlier because it 'was not yet a member of the EU',[14] and the proposition that the inclusion of courts within the definition of 'public authorities' in the Act, thus making them bound to uphold Convention rights 'caused wholesale erosion of Parliamentary sovereignty.' How this could be so, given that the significance of this inclusion lay in its impact on the common law,[15] is not explained. Nor does Wakeham seek to tell us how a change in UK law brought about by an Act of Parliament that may itself be repealed by Parliament in the normal way, may be said to 'erode' Parliamentary sovereignty.

His arguments on the specific issue of self-regulation versus legal remedy are threefold: first, that a legal privacy remedy would be inaccessible to all but the rich, able to afford the requisite legal fees; second, that if a privacy law was substituted for self-regulation, newspapers might actually be less restrained than they are now, calculating that a person whose privacy they had invaded might not be prepared for the trouble and expense of legal action;[16] third, that a privacy law would mean that, 'injunctions would be effortlessly deployed against newspapers undertaking legitimate investigative journalism.'[17]

In short order, Wakeham's first argument is irrelevant; his second is founded on an obvious factual misconception; his third simply misstates the legal position. The first argument is irrelevant because it is a general argument against all legal remedies. Wakeham might equally argue well that the law of defamation should be abolished, because only the rich can invoke it, and replaced by the PCC, with power to order apologies; for that matter, perhaps we should abolish the right of consumers to sue for damage caused by faulty implements and replace that with a Code of practice drawn up by manufacturers policed by a Commission able to publish reprimands, but demand no compensation. His argument also ignores the symbolic role of a privacy

---

[12] The term 'introduction' is used since it is arguably inaccurate to speak of the 'incorporation' of the ECHR; see A. Marshall, 'Patriating Rights: with Reservations', in Hare and Forsyth (eds) *Constitutional Reform in the United Kingdom: Practice and Principles*, Oxford: Hart, 1998, 75, and G. Phillipson, 'The Human Rights Act, "Horizontal Effect" and the Common Law: A Bang or a Whimper?' (1999) 62(6) *MLR* 824, 834–5.

[13] 'Press, Privacy, Public Interest and the Human Rights Act' in Tambini and Hayward, *Ruled by Recluses? Privacy, Journalism and the Media after the Human Rights Act*, London: IPPR, 2002.

[14] Ibid, at 27.   [15] The courts' duties in relation to statutes is governed by section 3 HRA.

[16] Op cit, at 25–6.   [17] Op cit, at 26.

law; in the same way as the law prohibiting racialist speech, such a law authoritatively conveys society's disapproval of wanton invasions of privacy.

As to his second argument, it relies on the mysterious premise that the development of any legal remedy would *replace* the PCC. Why this should be, he does not bother to suggest. In fact, of course, it would run alongside it, just as with defamation. Arguments in favour of developing the common law to protect privacy are not arguments for replacing the PCC system, but for complementing it. All the advantages of the PCC—speed, lack of cost, informality and so on, would thus continue. Wakeham himself in a later section refutes the view that the inception of a de-facto legal remedy under the HRA has lead to the PCC becoming bypassed.[18] This argument, then, amounts to tilting at imaginary windmills.

Wakeham's third argument would be a legitimate one if soundly based; however it relies on a view of the law that, quite simply, does not correspond to reality. There are no cases in which injunctions have been 'effortlessly' secured on privacy grounds to stifle 'legitimate investigative journalism.' This would be impossible, given the duty lying on courts to protect the press's legitimate rights under Article 10 to inform the public on matters of serious public concern, as the discussion below will clearly indicate. Wakeham is either straightforwardly ignorant of the legal position or he is scare-mongering.

Finally, it is, in any event clear from the decision in *Peck v UK*[19] that self-regulation is not and cannot be considered an adequate way of protecting Article 8. In *Peck*, a violation of Article 8 was found in relation to the release by a local authority of CCTV pictures of Peck in the street carrying a knife in distressed state having just attempted suicide. Footage was shown, *inter alia*, on a popular television programme, *Crime Beat*. The broadcast media are of course subject to a tough regulatory regime on privacy matters—and one that, unlike, the PCC, has actual sanctions—fines, ultimately the threat of removal of licence. In other words, there *was* protection against invasion of privacy by broadcasters, through real sanctions, unlike under the PCC. Nevertheless, the finding of the Court as to whether these sanctions amounted to adequate protection for Article 8 purposes was clear:

The Court finds that the lack of legal power of the Commissions to award damages to the applicant means that those bodies could not provide an effective remedy to him. It notes that the ITC's power to impose a fine on the relevant television company does not amount to an award of damages to the applicant[20].

This finding has quite evidently been accepted by the English courts, who would not have taken such drastic steps in developing the law of confidence to protect privacy had they believed that the PCC satisfied the requirements of Article 8. So Wakeham's argument for self-regulation as a system precluding the need for further protection is

---

[18] '. . . There is absolutely no evidence that people have "by-passed" the PCC in any way. Indeed, last year the PCC received 3,030 complaints, a record number' (ibid, 33).
[19] (2003) 36 EHRR 41.   [20] Op cit, at [109].

an argument that has already been lost legally speaking: the UK is *obliged* by the ECHR to provide a remedy in damages to those whose privacy is invaded by the press. That does not of course mean that self-regulation cannot provide a valuable service to those who merely want to obtain an apology and are not interested in going to court: it can of course run along side a system of legal redress; but it does mean that any argument that self-regulation should *be a substitute* for legal redress is academic: it is now absolutely clear that such a system would violate the UK's obligations under the ECHR.

As to the second and third possibilities (of judicial or legislative creation of a fully fledged tort of invasion of privacy), while the notion of respect for individual privacy had seemingly developed into a clear underlying common law value[21] by the last decade of the twentieth century, it was equally clear that the courts had declined to give it expression through a new tort. The excitement generated by Sedley LJ's groundbreaking pronouncement in *Douglas and Zeta Jones v Hello!*: 'We have reached a point at which it can be said with confidence that the law recognises and will appropriately protect a right of personal privacy'[22]—has faded entirely away, given the lack of judicial use since then of his Lordship's bold dicta and the preponderance of strong judicial disapproval of such a course. Most importantly and recently, in *Wainwright v Home Office*,[23] the House of Lords unanimously declined to hold that there was any tort of invasion of privacy, as such, in English law. As Lord Hoffman put it:

There seems to me a great difference between identifying privacy as a value which underlies the existence of a rule of law (and may point the direction in which the law should develop) and privacy as a principle of law in itself.[24]

The Court of Appeal in the same case saw formidable 'definitional difficulties and conceptual problems in the judicial development of a "blockbuster" privacy tort vaguely embracing such a potentially wide range of situations'.[25] Buxton LJ was firmly of the view that, 'on grounds not merely of rationality but also of democracy, the difficult social balance that the tort [of invasion of privacy] involves should be struck by Parliament and not by the judges,' because:

---

[21] See *Attorney General v Guardian Newspapers (No 2)* [1990] 1 AC 109, 255 (hereafter *A-G v Guardian*), *per* Lord Keith: 'The right to personal privacy is clearly one which the law [of confidence] should seek to protect'; *R v Department of Health, ex parte Source Informatics Ltd, The Times* 21 January 2000, CA, *per* Simon Brown LJ: '[In cases of personal information], the concern of the law [of confidence] is to protect the confider's personal privacy'; *R v Khan* (op cit), in which three of their Lordships left open the question whether English law already recognized a right to privacy; dicta of Laws J in *Hellewell v Chief Constable of Derbyshire* [1995] 1 WLR 804, 807; *Francome v Mirror Group Newspapers* [1984] 1 WLR 892; *Stephens v Avery* [1988] Ch 449 (discussed below).

[22] [2001] QB 967, 997. In the recent judgment on the trial of the case, Lindsay J declined to make any finding that English law now recognized a right to privacy: [2003] 3 All ER 996, at [229].

[23] [2003] 3 WLR 1137. Note that the decision of their Lordships was an appeal from a decision arising from a set of facts that pre-dated the coming into force of the HRA. Their Lordships were not therefore deciding whether the HRA required the introduction of a general tort.

[24] Ibid, at [31].   [25] [2002] QB 1334, 1351, Mummery LJ.

in areas involving extremely contested and strongly conflicting social interests, the judges are extremely ill-equipped to undertake the detailed investigations necessary before the proper shape of the law can be decided.[26]

Woolf CJ, speaking *obiter* in *A v B plc*, strongly steered the lower courts away from considering the development of a free-standing tort of privacy,[27] whilst Lindsay, J, invited in *Douglas II*[28] to declare a general right to privacy, was of the same view:

So broad is the subject of privacy and such are the ramifications of any free-standing law in the area that the subject is better left to Parliament which can, of course, consult interests far more widely than can be taken into account in the course of ordinary *inter partes* litigation. A judge should therefore be chary of doing that which is better done by Parliament.[29]

On closer examination, however there is something a little odd going on here. The judges, as the above *dicta* disclose, firmly abnegate any judicial role in developing a fully-fledged right to privacy, announcing that it should be left to Parliament. Parliament, of course, cannot act on such a matter without full government backing for any Bill, and, although intermittent governmental interest over recent years in statutory protection for privacy has perhaps distracted the courts with the chimera of possible legislative action,[30] no government in the past has actually grasped this nettle, doubtless due to the fear of press hostility.[31] That such hostility exists is not in doubt. Press coverage of the introduction of the Human Rights Bill was sensationalist, and overwhelmingly dominated by fears that the Act would introduce a right to privacy against the press 'through the back door'. As Lord Ackner remarked during the Bill's debate in the House of Lords:

[the inclusion of Article 8] . . . resulted suddenly in an outburst in the media and, if one looks at the report of our Second Reading debate and at the speech of . . . the Lord Chancellor, one finds that a very large part of his speech was devoted to trying to pour oil on ruffled waters. The press were so indignant that a right to privacy might appear, that they suggested that Article 8 be omitted.[32]

Governmental deference to such hostility may most recently be seen in the Govern-

---

[26] Ibid, 1365.   [27] [2002] 3 WLR 542, 550B.

[28] [2003] 3 All ER 996; this is the decision of the High Court in the final trial of the action for damages, the Court of Appeal having found that no injunction should be granted: *Douglas and Zeta Jones and ors v Hello!* [2001] QB 967, CA. The appeal from this High Court decision will be referred to as *Douglas III* [2005] EWCA Civ 595.

[29] Op cit, at [229(iii)].

[30] The Younger Committee (*Report of the Committee on Privacy* (1972 Cmnd 5012), *Calcutt Committee on Privacy and Related Matters*, hereafter 'Calcutt' (1990 Cmnd 1102), *Review of Press Self Regulation* (Cm 2135), *National Heritage Select Committee Report* HC 294 II (1993) and a Lord Chancellor's Green Paper (CHAN J060915NJ.7/93) all proposed the introduction of statutory measures to protect privacy.

[31] See e.g. S. Rasaiah, 'Current legislation, privacy and the media in the UK' (1998) 3(5) *Communications Law* 183.

[32] HL Deb. Col. 473 (18 November 1997).

ment's response[33] to a Report of Select Committee on Media Culture and Sport on this issue.[34] The Committee's conclusion was:

we firmly recommend that the Government reconsider its position and bring forward legislative proposals to clarify the protection that individuals can expect from unwarranted intrusion by anyone—not the press alone—into their private lives.[35]

The Government immediately rejected this proposal, stating that, 'legislation is not only unnecessary but undesirable'. It went on, in a wonderfully ironic counterpoint to the views on this matter of the Court of Appeal in *Wainwright*:[36]

The weighing of competing rights in individual cases is the quintessential task of the courts, not of Government, or Parliament. Parliament should only intervene if there are signs that the courts are systematically striking the wrong balance; we believe there are no such signs.[37]

What the courts see as something that they are 'extremely ill-equipped to undertake'[38] is, to the Government, 'quintessentially' their task. What to the courts is the legitimate province of Parliament is something that, to the Government, ought to be left to the judiciary. Between two bodies determined to bow to each other's greater expertise and legitimacy in this area, it seems reasonably clear that no general tort of invasion of privacy is to be expected, either as a result of judicial activism or legislative innovation. Jonathan Morgan's appeal for the current re-moulding of *existing* actions such as breach of confidence into privacy remedies to be abandoned, in favour of the direct horizontal application of Article 8 ECHR,[39] is likewise quite evidently one that is doomed to fall on deaf judicial ears: as chapter 3 indicated, the judges have shown no enthusiasm whatever for adopting Wade's controversial interpretation of their duties under sections 6(1) and (3) HRA and there are strong dicta against it, most recently in *Campbell*,[40] in which the speeches of their Lordships all but rule out this approach,[41] and in *Douglas III*.[42]

  This leaves us with the fourth possibility. As Mummery LJ in *Wainwright* put it, in a typically English judicial spirit:

A more promising and well trod path is that of incremental evolution, both at common law and by statute (e.g. section 3 of the Protection from Harassment Act 1997), of traditional nominate torts pragmatically crafted as to conditions of liability, specific defences and appropriate remedies, and tailored to suit significantly different privacy interests and infringement situations.[43]

Or, as Lindsay J rather less enthusiastically put it:

---

[33] *The Government's Response to the Fifth Report of the Culture, Media and Sport Select Committee on 'Privacy and Media Intrusion'*, HC 458–1 (2002–2003), Cm 5985.

[34] Fifth Report, *Privacy and media intrusion*, HC 458 (2002–03).

[35] Ibid, at [111].   [36] See note 25 and 26 above.   [37] Ibid, at [2.3].

[38] *Wainwright* (CA) op cit, at 1365.

[39] J. Morgan, 'Privacy, confidence, and horizontal effect: "Hello" trouble' (2003) 62(2) *CLJ* 444.

[40] [2004] 2 WLR 1232.   [41] See Chapter 3 at 134–40.

[42] [2005] 3 WCR 881 at [50]; quoted Chapter 3, p 142, note 212.   [43] Op cit, at 1365.

if Parliament does not act soon, the less satisfactory course, of the Courts creating the law bit by bit at the expense of litigants and with inevitable delays and uncertainty, will be thrust upon the judiciary.[44]

Breach of confidence and trespass are the common law actions most likely to assist a litigant complaining of disclosure of personal information, obtained either surreptitiously or through conversations with friends or others.[45] The former will be dealt with in detail below; it is clear that the latter is of very limited utility as a privacy remedy[46] since it can bite only where there is physical intrusion, and journalists often gather information without perpetrating any such intrusion.[47] This limitation of the action of trespass clearly currently leaves a gap in the protection of Article 8 rights that cannot be directly remedied without the introduction of a general tort.[48] Nevertheless, as the authors predicted as far back as 1996,[49] the most suitable action for judicial development aimed at providing greater protection for privacy has proven to be breach of confidence and it is to that action that we turn in a moment. Before turning to the common law, however, it is necessary to examine briefly the forms of statutory protection for privacy that are available and which may serve to supplement the protection available at common law.

PRIVACY STATUTES

There are a number of statutes that either potentially or actually provide a measure of protection for privacy. First of all, a number of statutory provisions provide specific protection for those caught up in the criminal justice system, in the course of which they may have to reveal extremely intimate details about themselves, as, for example, in cases involving sexual offences. It is common-place to hear broadcasters referring to alleged victims of crime 'who cannot be named for legal reasons'. Often these are minors; the position of children and young persons is dealt with in detail in Chapter 16 and readers are referred there for an in-depth analysis of the courts' current approach to balancing the needs of open reporting of the criminal justice system with the privacy rights of victims and witnesses. But a number of these restrictions also concern

---

[44] Op cit, at [229(iii)].

[45] Nuisance is not adverted to since its effect is likely to be even more marginal—(see *Bernstein of Leigh v Skyviews & General Ltd* [1978] QB 479). Moreover, any possible relevant effect has probably been subsumed in the Protection from Harassment Act 1997.

[46] See Prescott, 'Kaye v Robertson: a Reply' (1991) 54 *MLR* 451 for an argument as to how it could be used more extensively and imaginatively than generally realized, but still only in cases where there is physical intrusion.

[47] Recent advances in technology can render such intrusion unnecessary; also private information may be obtained by interviewing friends and acquaintances of the applicant. For discussion of such technology and its implications for the legal control of police surveillance, see the JUSTICE report by Madeline Colvin, *Under Surveillance*, London, 1998.

[48] But see above at 711–12.   [49] See note 1 above.

adults, the most well known of which concerns victims (and alleged victims) of sexual offences.[50] It is a specific offence to publish a picture of the alleged victim, or her name and address, once an allegation of a rape offence[51] has been made.[52] Once a person has been charged with a rape offence, no matter or article likely to lead members of the public to identify an individual as the complainant in relation to the offence may be published.[53] However, the courts do have powers to direct the restrictions to be removed; this may be done on the narrow ground of encouraging witnesses to come forward,[54] or on the broader ground that a refusal to lift the restrictions 'would impose a substantial and unreasonable restriction upon the reporting of proceedings at the trial and it is in the public interest to remove the restriction'. This clearly allows a judge to undertake a broad balancing act between the privacy rights of the woman—and the policy of encouraging women to bring cases to trial, given that rapes are notoriously under-prosecuted—and the media interest in reporting on trials, including, specifically the open justice principle. The manner in which the courts approach this balancing act is discussed fully in Chapter 16[55] in relation to children and young persons.

There are a number of other statutory reporting restrictions, including stringent limitations upon the reporting of pre-trial hearings,[56] details of vulnerable witnesses,[57] and the reporting of assertions made about others during a plea in mitigation. An order may be made prohibiting the reporting of such assertions where:

an assertion forming part of the speech or submission is derogatory to a person's character (for instance, because it suggests that his conduct is or has been criminal, immoral or improper), and . . . that the assertion is false or that the facts asserted are irrelevant to the sentence.[58]

This provision, in catching derogatory and false allegations, is clearly intended primarily to safeguard the *reputations* of those caught up in the commission of criminal offences; it could cover, for example, an assertion that an individual had been unfaithful to her partner, put forward in a plea of mitigation about violent conduct towards that individual. But, where the allegation is true, but irrelevant, the interest protected may be privacy, if, of course, the allegation relates to the person's private life, as in the example given. Again, the court has a discretion (it '*may* make an order') rather than a binding duty to order the restriction: presumably under these

---

[50] The restrictions arise under the Sexual Offences (Amendment Act) 1976, s 4.

[51] This includes male rape (created by the Criminal Justice and Public Order Act 1994) and offences of incitement, attempt, conspiracy, and so on.

[52] S 4(1)(a).   [53] S 4(1)(b).

[54] Upon the application of the person accused or rape; the defendant must additionally show that his defence is likely to be substantially prejudiced without such a direction.

[55] Principally in *Re S* [2005] 1 AC 593.

[56] Ss 37 and 38, Criminal Procedure and Investigations Act 1996.

[57] Under section 25 of the Youth Justice and Criminal Evidence Act 1999.

[58] S 58(4), Criminal Procedure and Investigations Act 1996.

provisions also, the open justice principle may be balanced against any relevant privacy or reputational interests.[59]

A further statute that affords potential protection to privacy is the Protection from Harassment Act 1997. It was of course intended primarily for use against stalkers, but it has the potential to be used against journalists engaged in persistent 'door-stepping' or the intrusive pursuit and questioning or photographing of a person. It may therefore be of relevance to those who feel 'hounded' by reporters, and is therefore of interest, given the decision of the European Court of Human Rights in *Von Hannover*,[60] discussed in the previous chapter. Under the Act, it is both a criminal offence and a statutory tort to engage in harassment of another. 'Harassment' is undefined. The Act simply states:

> S 1(1) A person must not pursue a course of conduct—
>
> (a) which amounts to harassment of another, and
>
> (b) which he knows or ought to know amounts to harassment of the other.
>
> (2) For the purposes of this section, the [harasser] . . . ought to know that [his conduct] amounts to harassment of another, if a reasonable person in possession of the same information would think the course of conduct amounted to harassment of the other.

A 'course of conduct' must be conduct that has occurred on two or more occasions.[61] Damages as well as injunctions are available. In terms of media freedom, its potential applicability against journalists is obvious. The Act includes no explicit defence for journalists, but there is a defence of 'reasonableness' in all the circumstances,[62] which could be used to draw in Article 10 protection in cases involving journalistic pursuit which were alleged to amount to harassment under the Act.[63]

The Act remains untested at present in relation to its application in such a context, but in one case it was found, remarkably to be applicable to actual publication in a newspaper. In *Thomas v News Group Newspapers Ltd*,[64] the *Sun* newspaper published a critical story about allegations of racism made by the applicant against certain police officers, who were then subjected to disciplinary proceedings and had their salaries and rank cut as a result. The article gave details about Ms Thomas's place of work and described her as 'black'. The *Sun* then published a series of letters from readers attacking Ms Thomas alongside a brief article reporting readers' 'fury' over the incident and then published a follow-up third article. Ms Thomas gave evidence that she had also received hate mail, as a result of the *Sun*'s coverage of her, and was afraid to go to work. She subsequently changed her place of work as a result of her fears. She commenced proceedings against the publishers of the *Sun*, and the defendants applied

---

[59] It should also be noted that the so-called 'inherent jurisdiction' of the High Court to protect juveniles caught up in the criminal justice system, discussed in Chapter 16, has recently been extended to cover vulnerable adults with mental health problems: *In Re A Local Authority (Inquiry: Restraint on Publication)* [2003] EWHC 2746 (Fam); [2004] 2 WLR 926 at [66] and [86–97].

[60] [2004] EMLR 21.   [61] S 7(3).   [62] S 2(3)(c).

[63] It was found by the Court of Appeal in *Thomas* [2002] EMLR 4 that this defence should be interpreted compatibly with press freedom under Article 10 ECHR.

[64] [2002] EMLR 4.

to have the action struck out as disclosing no real prospect of success. The Court of Appeal found that it would only exceptionally be the case that press criticism of an individual could amount to harassment: 'In general, press criticism, even if robust, does not constitute unreasonable conduct and does not fall within the natural meaning of harassment.'[65] But in this case it had been unnecessary to refer to Ms Thomas's colour and the newspaper had not disassociated itself from the vitriolic letters it had published. In the circumstances, the case should be allowed to go forward to trial. The Court found:

The respondent has pleaded an arguable case that the appellants harassed her by publishing racist criticism of her which was foreseeably likely to stimulate a racist reaction on the part of their readers and cause her distress.[66]

In making this finding, it explicitly adverted to its duty as a court under the Human Rights Act to act compatibly with Article 10 ECHR and to interpret the 1997 Act compatibly with the Convention.[67] Clearly, the offence will only apply exceptionally to newspaper coverage, and the decision gives us no guidance as to its possible application to the activities of journalists in gathering news through door-stepping, unwanted photography and the like. But the Act's potential for use against unreasonable and intrusive journalistic behaviour, at least in extreme cases, might turn out to be significant in providing protection where the informational actions[68] cannot bite, because the complaint is of journalistic conduct in newsgathering, rather than in any publication.

The most important of the privacy statutes is undoubtedly the Data Protection Act 1998, which was enacted to give effect to an EU Directive, one of the stated purposes of which was to protect rights of personal privacy.[69] We compare the DPA with the common law of confidence further below, but it will be useful to give a brief outline of the Act, as it applies to the media, at this point. The Act protects against the wrongful processing of 'personal data'. 'Data' is caught by the Act either if it is held on any electronic storage system, typically a computer, or if it forms part of a filing system.[70] 'Personal data' simply means 'data which relate to a living individual who can be identified (a) either from those data', or (b) 'from those data and other information which is in the possession of, or is likely to come into the possession of, the data

---

[65] Ibid.   [66] Ibid.   [67] Under ss 6 and 3 HRA respectively.

[68] That is, the statutory reporting restrictions, breach of confidence, and the Data Protection Act 1998 (below).

[69] Directive 95/46 EC of the European Parliament and the Council. Recital 10 reads: 'Whereas the object of the national laws on the processing of personal data is to protect fundamental rights and freedoms, notably the right to privacy, which is recognised both in Article 8 of the European Convention for the Protection of Human Rights and Fundamental Freedoms and in the general principles of Community law . . .'

[70] s 1(1) DPA: ' "*data*" *means information which*—

(a) is being processed by means of equipment operating automatically in response to instructions given for that purpose,

(b) is recorded with the intention that it should be processed by means of such equipment,

(c) is recorded as part of a relevant filing system or with the intention that it should form part of a relevant filing system, or

controller.' Photographs of an individual would therefore clearly fall within the Act. However, the Court of Appeal's decision in *Durant v Financial Services Authority*[71] has narrowed somewhat the *prima facie* meaning of these terms. It was held that the interpretation of personal data should be guided by the principle of respect for privacy. Thus it was held that, to be personal, data about an individual must go beyond 'the recording of the putative data subject's involvement in a matter or an event that has no personal connotations'.[72] Thus a picture recording a person as one amongst many attending, for example, an official occasion, would not fall under the Act. Moreover:

> The information should have the putative data subject as its focus rather than some other person with whom he may have been involved or some transaction or event in which he may have figured or have had an interest.[73]

Thus, for example, a picture of a general street scene, in which a number of individuals caught, would not enable all the individuals in the picture to claim, without more, that the picture represented personal data for each of them. This would still of course mean that the vast majority of pictures taken of specific people (nearly always celebrities) with comments about them, relating e.g. to their weight, appearance, clothing, partners etc, would fall within the definition in the Act. As Auld J put it, 'In short, [personal data means] information that affects [the subject's] privacy, whether in his personal or family life, business or professional capacity.'[74] The Court, then, gave the definition of personal data a purposive approach, such that it covers data that has some bearing on private life, highlighting the Act's raison d'etre as the protection of privacy.

The Act covers the 'processing' of data, which is defined extremely widely; of particular significance for the media is the fact that the definition covers both the obtaining and the publishing of data.[75] The 'data' controller—the person who has responsibilities under the Act—is the person who[76] controls the manner in which and the purposes for which the data is processed. In relation to newspapers, this will generally be the editor or editorial board.

Under the Act, personal data must be processed in accordance with the Data Protection Principle; that which is defined as 'sensitive personal data' must be processed in accordance with some particularly stringent conditions. The definition of 'sensitive personal data'[77] includes, as one would expect, information relating to sexual life,

---

[71] [2003] EWCA Civ 1746; [2004] FSR 28.
[72] Ibid, at [28].   [73] Ibid.   [74] Ibid.
[75] 'processing', in relation to information or data, means obtaining, recording or holding the information or data or carrying out any operation or set of operations on the information or data, including—

   (a) organisation, adaptation or alteration of the information or data,
   (b) retrieval, consultation or use of the information or data,
   (c) disclosure of the information or data by transmission, dissemination or otherwise making available, or
   (d) alignment, combination, blocking, erasure or destruction of the information or data; 'using' or 'disclosing', in relation to personal data, includes using or disclosing the information contained in the data.

[76] Either alone or in company with others.
[77] Contained in section 2 of the Act.

health, religious beliefs and so on. It also includes some other, more wide-ranging categories of information, including information relating the racial or ethnic origin of the data subject, his or her political opinions, membership of a trade union and information relating to the commission by the individual of any offence and any proceedings relating to that offence.[78]

Given the stringency of the conditions for lawful and fair processing of data, particularly sensitive personal data as defined, the Act might be thought to lay serious restrictions upon the media's watchdog role. However, as we shall see in a moment, the media will often, although not invariably, be able to claim one or more exemptions from the obligations imposed under the Act. Nevertheless, it remains plainly applicable to a number of the privacy cases we consider in this chapter. It was pleaded by Naomi Campbell alongside breach of confidence in her case against Mirror Group Newspapers[79] after the *Mirror* had published details of her treatment for drug addiction with Narcotics Anonymous, including surreptitiously taken photographs. Her victory at first instance was overturned by the Court of Appeal,[80] but recently reinstated by the House of Lords.[81] The case confirmed the application of the Act to the media. At first instance it was found:

Under s 1(1), the claimant was a 'data subject', the information, including the details and photographs, that the claimant was receiving therapy at Narcotics Anonymous was 'personal data', the defendant was the 'data controller', the obtaining, preparation and publication of the claimant's personal data was 'processing'.[82]

These findings were not questioned on appeal; the Court of Appeal in fact specifically confirmed that the publication of hard copies of newspaper does fall within the definition of processing of data.[83]

Subject to the exemptions, *all* personal data must be processed in accordance with the Data Protection Principles.[84] The most important of these is the First Principle, which states that 'personal data shall be processed fairly and lawfully' and only provided that certain conditions are met. In the case of all data, one of the conditions in Schedule 2 must be met. In the case of sensitive personal data, one of the conditions in Schedule 3 must also be met. Part II of Schedule 1 deals with interpretation of the principles and makes the following provision in relation to the First Principle:

1. (1) In determining for the purposes of the first principle whether personal data are processed fairly, regard is to be had to the method by which they are obtained, including in particular whether any person from whom they are obtained is deceived or misled as to the purpose or purposes for which they are to be processed.

In relation to the media, it was found in *Campbell* at first instance, that the obtaining

---

[78] Per s 2, the definition includes: (g) the commission or alleged commission by him of any offence, or (h) any proceedings for any offence committed or alleged to have been committed by him, the disposal of such proceedings or the sentence of any court in such proceedings.

[79] The first instance decision is reported as *Campbell v MGN* [2002] EMLR 30 (QB).

[80] [2003] QB 633, CA.   [81] [2004] 2 AC 457.   [82] [2002] EMLR 30, at [85].

[83] [2003] QB 633, at [107].   [84] These are set out in Schedule 1 of the Act.

of information by surreptitious photography was unfair, and that if information is obtained in breach of confidence, it will not be obtained 'lawfully.'[85] As to the conditions in Schedule 2, at least one of which must be satisfied in relation to the processing of all personal data, one is consent by the data subject, which would rarely be present in a privacy case, while the only other condition that could be fulfilled by a media body is that:

6(1). The processing is necessary for the purposes of legitimate interests pursued by the data controller or by the third party or parties to whom the data are disclosed, except where the processing is unwarranted in any particular case by reason of prejudice to the rights and freedoms or legitimate interests of the data subject.

While this provision is rather vague and open-ended, it would appear, in the context of press publication, to require the Court to examine, in the light of Articles 8 and 10, whether it was 'necessary' to publish the complained of data for the purposes of exercising the Article 10 right to freedom of expression. Thus it might be relied upon by the press generally, to argue that the data had been gathered and published in order to carry out the press's legitimate role as watchdog.[86] However it will not assist a newspaper which had obtained information surreptitiously, as will often be the case in privacy cases, and which therefore cannot claim to have obtained it 'fairly'.

In relation to 'sensitive personal data', the position of the media is even more difficult. Under Schedule 3, unless the media body in question can show that the data subject has given 'explicit consent' to the processing or that the data in question have been deliberately 'made public' by the subject, it will have to seek to bring itself within the tough conditions set out in the Data Protection (Processing of Sensitive Personal Data) Order 2000, which essentially requires a very weighty 'public interest defence' involving the revelation of criminality, dishonesty, malpractice or mismanagement.[87] It would clearly be very difficult to make out such a defence in a normal case concerning the revelation of private facts; it was not, for example, made out in *Campbell*.[88]

The issue of remedies is dealt with in the next chapter, but it should briefly be mentioned that the remedies under the Act for breach of the Data Protection

---

[85] [2002] EMLR 30, at [108]–[110].   [86] It was not, however, accepted in *Campbell*: ibid.
[87] The only circumstances which could normally apply to journalism under Schedule 3 are:
'3.—(1) the disclosure of personal data—
   (a) is in the substantial public interest;
   (b) is in connection with—
      (i) the commission by any person of any unlawful act (whether alleged or established),
      (ii) dishonesty, malpractice, or other seriously improper conduct by, or the unfitness or incompetence of, any person (whether alleged or established), or
      (iii) mismanagement in the administration of, or failures in services provided by, any body or association (whether alleged or established);
   (c) is for the special purposes [of, *inter alia*, journalism] as defined in section 3 of the Act; and
   (d) is made with a view to the publication of those data by any person and the data controller reasonably believes that such publication would be in the public interest.'
[88] As the Court of Appeal confirmed: op cit, at [88]–[89].

principles include a right to compensation[89] and a right to prevent processing likely to cause damage or distress.[90] However, there is a specific exemption designed to benefit the media in section 32 of the Act. In essence, it both prevents the media from being subject to interim injunctions preventing the publication of personal data[91] and allows them to be exempted from the Data Protection Principles[92] if the media body in question was acting for journalistic purposes and the data controller reasonably believed publication to be in the public interest and that he could not comply with the provisions of the Act, given the journalistic purposes he was carrying out. This provision has been held, controversially, to apply both before and after publication,[93] so that it provides a comprehensive media defence. In the result, the DPA gives the public broad rights against the publication of sensitive personal data without consent by the press and against the publication of any unfairly obtained personal data, subject however to a broad defence of public interest. As we shall see below, it may provide one of the few ways that English law can provide a remedy for the publication of anodyne photographs that might not attract the protection of the law of confidence.[94] However, it has not proved popular with litigants. It *was* pleaded, as just seen in *Campbell*, but virtually ignored by the House of Lords in its decision on the appeal. It is probable that its lack of popularity is due at least in part to the fact that interim injunctions cannot be obtained under it against the media. In contrast, breach of confidence has burgeoned in use as a privacy remedy in recent times.

DEVELOPMENT OF BREACH OF CONFIDENCE AS A PRIVACY REMEDY: INTRODUCTION

This chapter will argue that legal protection for privacy against intrusion by the press through a radically re-modelled breach of confidence action is now an established fact, finally remedying the 'signal shortcoming' in English law' bemoaned by the judges in *Kaye v Robertson*,[95] and providing some protection against what Sedley LJ has termed 'an increasingly invasive social environment.'[96] As this chapter will illustrate, the action for breach of confidence is now being used as the basis for regular orders by the courts

---

[89] Section 13: it applies either where the individual suffers damage as a result of unlawful processing under the Act or suffers distress and the processing is done for the purposes of (*inter alia*) journalism.

[90] Under s 10.

[91] See s 32(4)–(5), under which the Court *must* stay any proceedings under the DPA relating to the publication of hitherto unpublished material, including proceedings under section 10(4) (obtaining an order preventing processing—i.e., an injunction) *if* the data is being processed for journalistic purposes with a view to publishing it.

[92] Except for Principle 7, which, however, merely provides that the data controller shall take appropriate measures against accidental loss of or damage to data or unauthorized processing of it.

[93] *Per* the finding of the Court of Appeal in *Campbell*: op cit, at [129–131].

[94] See below at 767–8.   [95] [1991] FSR 62, CA.

[96] *Douglas and Zeta Jones and ors v Hello!* [2001] QB 967, 997, CA, Sedley LJ.

with the clear aim and effect of affording a remedy against unauthorized publication of personal information by the media. In engineering this quiet revolution, the courts have fused common law development with inspiration from Article 8 of the European Convention on Human Rights, which gives a right to respect for private and family life, despite the fact that newspapers are not 'public authorities' and therefore not bound, under the Human Rights Act ('HRA'), to act compatibly with the Convention rights.[97] The recent House of Lords decision in *Campbell v MGN*[98] has finally put a seal of the highest authority upon these developments and the greater protection for privacy they entail. The case law is now considerable, and some of it, consisting of unreported decisions, requires some introduction to illustrate the range of circumstances in which the courts are now giving legal relief against intrusive journalism.

In March 2001, a famous pop singer successfully sought injunctions preventing publication of pornographic photographs of herself taken at a younger age.[99] In *Beckham v MGN*,[100] the Beckhams obtained an injunction to prevent the publication of photographs of their home, and in *Blair v Associated Newspapers*[101] Cherie Blair was granted a series of injunctions against various parties to prevent the publication of details of her domestic arrangements, provided by a former nanny. In *Holden v Express Newspapers Ltd*[102] an actress and her husband obtained an interim injunction to prevent publication of photographs of themselves relaxing by the swimming pool of a hotel, taken from outside the hotel grounds using a long-range lens. The action was eventually settled, with the newspaper paying damages of £40,000 plus costs. In *Jaqueline A v The London Borough of Newham*,[103] a judge awarded damages for mental distress against Newham Council, in a case based on breach of confidence and the Data Protection Act, for using the photograph of a child, without permission, in a brochure warning of the dangers of AIDS. More recently, Angus Deayton obtained an injunction against the *Mail on Sunday* in respect of threatened revelations relating to his private life,[104] while Sara Cox obtained substantial damages in a settlement

---

[97] Per section 6(1). See Chapter 3 and, generally, B. Markesenis, 'Privacy, Freedom of Expression, and the Horizontal Effect of the Human Rights Bill: Lessons from Germany' (1999) 115 *LQR* 47; I. Leigh, 'Horizontal Rights, the Human Rights Act and Privacy: Lessons from the Commonwealth?' (1999) 48 *ICLQ* 57; R. Singh, 'Privacy and the Media after the Human Rights Act' (1998) *EHRLR* 712; S. Grosz and N. Braithwaite, 'Privacy and the Human Rights Act' in M. Hunt and R. Singh (eds) *A Practitioner's Guide to the Impact of the Human Rights Act*, Oxford: Hart, 1999 (only partially concerned with media intrusion); Sir Brian Neill, 'Privacy: A Challenge for the Next Century' in Markesenis (ed.) *Protecting Privacy*, Oxford: Clarendon, 1999; J. Wright, 'How Private is My Private Life?' in L. Betten (ed.), *The Human Rights Act 1998: What it Means*. London: Martinus Nijhoff, 1999.

[98] [2004] 2 WLR 1232. For comment see D. Lindsay, 'Naomi Campbell in the House of Lords: Implications for Australia' (2004) 11 *Privacy Law & Policy Reporter* 4–11; J. Morgan, 'Privacy in the House of Lords—Again' (2004) 120 *LQR* 563–66.

[99] Judgment of MacKay. The case is entirely unreported.

[100] *Beckham v MGN*, 28 June 2001, Eady J (unreported).

[101] Case no HQ0001236—a no of unreported decisions were delivered in 2001.

[102] (QBD), 7 June 2001, Eady J, unrep. I am indebted to Tugendhat and Christie, *The Law of Privacy and the Media*, Oxford: OUP, 2002, at 218 for the description of this case.

[103] (2001) WL 1612596.

[104] See 'Newspaper to challenge Deayton gagging order', *The Guardian*, 10 June 2002.

with the publishers of the *Sunday People* after it had published surreptitiously taken pictures of her and her husband sunbathing nude on her honeymoon.[105] *Archer v Williams*[106] was perhaps more of an orthodox breach of confidence case: a former employee of Lady Archer published a story based on information faxed by the employee to another newspaper, revealing, amongst other things Lady Archer had had a face-lift. An injunction was granted to prevent further revelations, together with damages for injury to feelings. The judge held that the information concerned fell 'very low on the scale of public interest' while the 'matters which the defendant seeks to disclose represent a substantial intrusion into [the claimant's] and her family's private life'.[107] The recent decision in *Jagger v News Group Newspapers*[108] was much more of a 'pure' privacy action: Jade Jagger gained an injunction preventing the *News of the World* from publishing any further pictures of herself in an intimate embrace inside the front door of a West End night club taken by a CCTV camera. In contrast, in a recent, unreported decision, the Beckhams were denied an injunction in relation to a story detailing problems within their marriage, including very intimate material, provided by their former nanny in clear breach of contract, apparently at least partly on the grounds of the 'public interest' of the story.[109] Likewise, a recent attempt to restrain publication of a story revealing that the Chair of Britain's Olympic bid team, Sebastian Coe MP, had had an affair also failed: the matter was determined to be one of legitimate public concern.[110]

More well known are the following decisions: in *Venables v News Group Newspapers*[111] Butler Sloss P granted unprecedented injunctions *contra omnes*, based on breach of confidence, preventing publication of any material which might reveal the identity and whereabouts of Venables and Thompson, the juvenile killers of Jamie Bulger.[112] She more recently granted identical injunctions giving lifelong protection to the identity of Mary Bell and her daughter. In *Mills v News Group Newspapers*,[113] the court found that the threatened publication of the applicant's address in the *Sun* raised a serious issue of invasion of privacy and breach of confidence, although on the facts relief was withheld. Jamie Theakston's fortunes, in seeking to restrain both photographs and a story giving details of his encounter with prostitutes were mixed: the judge granted an injunction restraining the use of photographs, but refused to restrain publication of the story.[114] In *Douglas and Zeta Jones and ors v Hello!*,[115] the Court of Appeal found that that the proposed publication of surreptitiously-obtained photographs of the couple's wedding arguably amounted to a breach of confidence, and Sedley LJ, found, of the couple's right to privacy;[116] an injunction was withheld, but *Hello!* was recently found liable in damages for breach of confidence by

---

[105] See *The Guardian*, 7 June 2003.   [106] [2003] EMLR 38.   [107] Ibid, at [61].
[108] (2005) unrep—see 'Jagger's Girl Wins Ban on CCTV Pictures' *The Telegraph*, 10 March.
[109] See *The Guardian*, 25 April 2005, http://media.guardian.co.uk/site/story/0,14173,1471125,00.html
[110] *Coe v Mirror Group Newspapers* (unrep), 29 May 2004.
[111] *Venables and another v News Group Newspapers* [2001] 1 All ER 908.
[112] *X (A woman formerly known as Mary Bell) v SO* [2003] EWHC 1101.   [113] [2001] EMLR 41.
[114] *Theakston v MGN* [2002] EMLR 22.   [115] Op cit.   [116] Ibid, at 997.

Lindsay J.[117] In *A v B plc*,[118] the Court of Appeal overturned injunctions granted by Jack J[119] preventing women with whom a premiership footballer had had an affair from publishing details of it in a tabloid newspaper. Naomi Campbell's case is well known and will be discussed extensively below.

The aim of this chapter is to make a thorough analysis of the 'new' style breach of confidence action and its efficacy as a privacy remedy,[120] drawing on insights from other jurisdictions, including the jurisprudence generated by the American 'private facts' tort[121] and commentary thereon. The chapter following this one will consider defences to the new action, in particular the critical issue of balancing effective privacy protection with the legitimate demands of media freedom. The general thesis of this chapter will be that judicial development of the action, culminating in the House of Lords' decision in *Campbell v MGN*, has resulted in a substantial level of protection for privacy and that while, as we suggested in 2000, any legal action that seeks to balance a right to privacy against press freedom is bound to become 'a legal porcupine, which bristles with difficulties',[122] that workable and principled solutions to such problems have been incrementally developed, as in other jurisdictions,[123] despite numerous wrong turnings.

Nevertheless, our stance will not be wholly adulatory of the judicial role in this area. We will argue that, whilst developments in these areas have led to a potentially radical transformation of the ability of the confidence action to protect privacy, one may also detect in many of the judgments a marked degree of equivocation between the values—and terminology—of privacy and confidentiality, an equivocation which it will be suggested is partly attributable to a judicial failure to appreciate the significance of the differing principles underlying these two concepts and partly to what it will be suggested is the absence of a proper resolution of the role the Convention rights should play in private law. The House of Lords decision in *Campbell* should have the effect, if faithfully applied, of resolving many of these problems, but only

---

[117] [2003] 3 All ER 996 (*Douglas II*).

[118] [2002] 3 WLR 542. All references to '*A v B plc*' are to this judgment, unless otherwise stated.

[119] The judgment of 30 April 2001 in which the initial injunction was granted is unreported. The subsequent decision on an application by the newspaper concerned to discharge the injunction is now reported as *A v B plc* [2002] EMLR 7.

[120] It concentrates on the print media but has application to all the media, although the BBC and possibly Channel 4 will be 'public authorities' per s 6(1) of the HRA and so bound directly by the Convention: see Chapter 3.

[121] See below, note 237 and associated text for a definition of the tort. Emphasis is placed on the American tort since, in comparison with other common law jurisdictions, the case law is particularly rich, having been generated over a considerable period of time; further, the American tort had its genesis in the Warren and Brandeis reading of a number of English decision, including some breach of confidence cases (in particular, *Prince Albert v Strange* 1 McN & G 25 (1849), *Duke of Argyll v Duchess of Argyll* [1967] 1 Ch 302; *Pollard v Photographic Company* (1888) Ch 345), and therefore is particularly relevant to the development of a cause of action growing from the same roots.

[122] The term is borrowed from some famous dicta in an administrative law case: *R v Inner London Education authority ex parte Westminster City Council* [1986] 1 WLR 28.

[123] Markesenis (in Markesinis, note 97 above, vi) notes that privacy laws in other jurisdictions have been developed, 'incrementally and cautiously' by judges.

time will tell whether that is its ultimate effect. Before plunging into the details of the confidence action itself, however, it is necessary to pause to turn to recall the issue of the role of Articles 8 and 10 in this private context.

THE ROLE OF THE CONVENTION RIGHTS UNDER THE HUMAN RIGHTS ACT

INTRODUCTION

The issue of the impact of the Convention on private law, such as breach of confidence, is discussed in detail in Chapter 3 and readers are referred to that discussion. Only a couple of points need be made here. The first is that whilst the judgments as a whole, particularly *Campbell*, leave no clear doctrinal answer to the questions raised by the horizontal effect debate, it is clear that *all* of their Lordships—including the dissenters, Nicholls and Hoffman—seemed determined to remould breach of confidence so as to provide the necessary protection under Article 8. In practice, we have in this judgment something closer to strong indirect horizontality, in the way that Convention principles were applied through the common law.

Moreover, unresolved though it is, the difference between the 'strong' and 'weak' models of horizontal effect[124] now seems unlikely to be of significance. The difference between the two models would clearly be of most practical importance if a clear imperative from the Convention clashes with a well defined pre-existing common law rule or principle. In such circumstances, a judge accepting an absolute duty to render the common law compatible with the Convention rights[125] would be *bound* to override the common law, whereas under the weaker model, the Convention would provide only a *reason* for so doing. It now appears tolerably clear, however, that such a direct clash is most unlikely in the area with which we are concerned: the action for 'breach of confidence' has been reformulated into such a simple and broad test that the possibility of a clear conflict with Convention requirements seems now to be very small. As the 'cause of action' is re-moulded into a more and more Convention-friendly form, it ceases to have any sharp edges to conflict with the Convention rights. Indeed, what would conceptually have seemed to be the likely points of conflict have already been overcome without detailed consideration of the necessity—in terms of the courts' duties under the HRA—of doing so.

While it would have been preferable to have had such consideration, there are in any event strong arguments of principle to justify a judge treating the Convention rights only as relevant principles nevertheless to afford them an especially high weight when dealing with invasions of privacy by the media,[126] thus minimizing the differ-

---

[124] See Chapter 3 at 130. [125] That is, the 'strong model'.
[126] For the full argument, see Phillipson, op cit ('Horizontal Effect') at 846–7.

ence between the stronger and weaker models of horizontal effect discussed. The power of the media to invade informational privacy is at least equal to that of the state, rendering the drawing of a sharp, formalistic distinction, whereby rights are upheld against the state but not the private actor, unjustified at the level of principle. Lord Hoffman recognized precisely this point in *Campbell* when he remarked:

I can see no logical ground for saying that a person should have less protection against a private individual than he would have against the state for the publication of personal information for which there is no justification.[127]

Moreover, whereas in certain instances in the private sphere a applicant might have freely agreed to a diminution of his rights by another, weakening or negating his claim subsequently to rely upon them,[128] the invasion of individual rights by the media is generally as involuntary as if perpetrated by the state, giving a strong reason for allowing him or her to assert his rights in such a context through the common law.

HORIZONTAL EFFECT UNRESOLVED: THE IMPACT ON JUDICIAL REASONING

Nevertheless, the failure of the Courts to resolve this issue clearly has not been without its effects. It is suggested at various points in the discussion that follows that this failure may be at least partly responsible for what, it is argued, is a lack of a thorough engagement in many of these cases with principles deriving from Article 8. But while this is probably part of the explanation, it is almost certainly not the whole story. Reading many of these judgments, the impression is given that even where the courts *do* appear to accept that they must act compatibly with Article 8—or at least take account of it—this in practice often has very little impact on the reasoning and findings. There are perhaps three reasons for this; the first was the absence, prior to *Von Hannover*,[129] of clear findings in the Strasbourg jurisprudence that a remedy against press intrusion into privacy is required under Article 8, as discussed in Chapter 13. The second reason, perhaps related to the first, is that principles deriving from Article 8 and its jurisprudence that *could* have provided useful guidance on issues such as the relative weight of different privacy interests simply did not figure in many of the judgments, despite the fact that section 2 HRA requires courts to have regard to such decisions. No such jurisprudence is discussed or even mentioned in the Court of Appeal judgments in *A v B plc*,[130] *Campbell*[131] or *D v L*,[132] or in the High Court judgments in *Theakston*[133] and *Douglas II*.[134] In fact, as will appear below, prior

---

[127] Op cit, at [50].

[128] E.g. where a schoolteacher accepted a job at a private Catholic school on the basis that s/he would not publicly deny any of the fundamental doctrines of the Catholic Church. Strasbourg has accepted such agreements as a legitimate ground for curtailing Convention rights: see *Rommelganger v Germany* (1980) 62 D&R 151 (no violation of Article 10 when employee of Catholic hospital dismissed for expressing pro-abortion views); *Ahmed v UK* (1982) 4 EHRR 125; *Stedman v UK* (1997) 23 EHRR CD 128.

[129] [2004] EMLR 21—for a summary and comment see (2004) 5, *EHRLR* 593–596.

[130] Op cit.   [131] Op cit.   [132] [2004] EMLR 1.   [133] Op cit.   [134] Op cit.

to the House of Lords decision in *Campbell*, a single decision of the Australian High Court—*Lenah Game Meats*[135]—was exerting far more influence on the development of confidence as a privacy remedy than any principles derived from Article 8. In other words, even where there was a *formal* acceptance of the duty to apply Article 8 under the HRA, it had little noticeable place in the reasoning. Thus, in a sense, the above-noted failure to decide which of the 'strong' or 'weak' versions of indirect horizontal effect should be followed remained moot, since in most cases, the courts did not even go as far as enquiring explicitly whether the common law was in harmony with the Convention, let alone determining what should be done if it was not. Once again, the House of Lords' decision in *Campbell* is a welcome exception, and it is to be hoped that subsequent cases will follow its lead in this respect.

A third reason for the lack of influence of Article 8 in these cases, it will be argued, is that there remains in the judgments a noticeable tendency to gravitate back towards confidentiality principles, even as the new role of Article 8 is apparently accepted: this results in a certain equivocation in the judgments as between the values of confidentiality on the one hand, and privacy on the other. Now this, it is suggested, takes us to the heart of the meaning of horizontal effect. A thorough-going application of Article 8 in confidence cases[136] would, it is contended, have the effect of meaning that breach of confidence was treated simply as an empty shell into which Article 8 principles could, as it were, be poured. In other words, when considering issues that raise Convention points, the court's engagement with breach of confidence would stop at the point at which it had satisfied itself that the bare doctrinal requirements of the action could be seen to be satisfied—and it will be suggested below that those requirements as reconfigured in *Campbell* mean that those requirements can in principle be very readily satisfied in the vast majority of case involving personal information. The court would then turn for guiding principles to Article 8, its jurisprudence, and values flowing from an acceptance that the protection of *private life* was the overall aim. This, it will be argued below, was more or less the methodology adopted in *Campbell*.

Cases prior to this decision, however, reveal a marked contrast: the approach in many of them was to treat breach of confidence not only as providing the formal cause of action necessary for the applicant to get his case into court: its principles then continued, through-out the judgments, to exercise a strong gravitational pull upon both the reasoning and outcome, such that in some cases, what might be termed 'confidentiality values' in fact trumped privacy values and those flowing from specifically from Article 8 if, indeed, the latter are mentioned at all. That such normative and analytic tensions should arise when an incorporating instrument brings together two very different sources of principle—common law and an international convention—is not surprising. The question after *Campbell* is whether the approach their Lordships

---

[135] *Australian Broadcasting Corporation v Lenah Game Meats* [2001] HCA 63.

[136] Such an approach would seem to follow under Hunt's strong version of indirect effect (op cit); however, it could also be used under the author's weaker version (op cit, "Horizontal Effect") if Article 8 principles were afforded 'an especially high weight' in common law adjudication, as we have suggested should be the case: see pp 725–6.

adopted in terms of judicial reasoning will be consistently adopted by lower courts, or whether the pre-*Campbell* tendencies noted above will reappear in subsequent judgments.

'THE ACTION FORMERLY DESCRIBED AS BREACH OF CONFIDENCE':[137] A *DE FACTO* PRIVACY TORT?

The House of Lords in *A-G v Guardian Newspapers (No. 2)*[138] found that the decision in *Coco v A N Clark (Engineers) Limited*[139] conveniently summarized the three key elements of the law of confidence: 'First, the information itself . . . must have the necessary quality of confidence about it.[140] Secondly, that information must have been imparted in circumstances importing an obligation of confidence.' The third requirement identified was 'unauthorised use of [the] information to the detriment of the [confider]'; however, subsequent case law suggests either that unwanted revelation of private facts *per se* may constitute detriment for the purposes of the law of confidence,[141] or, alternatively that detriment might not always be necessary.[142] Where the above elements are made out, publication will still be lawful if justified as in the 'public interest' or under Article 10—an issue considered in the following chapter.

Given that showing 'unauthorised use' of the information will generally be a formality, the two requirements traditionally accepted as essential, then, were that the information must have the quality of confidence about it, and that there must be circumstances imposing an obligation of confidentiality. Both of these elements, particularly the latter, had been subject to radical development prior to *Campbell*; but Campbell itself consolidates and, in some respects, takes these developments even further in the direction of 'pure' privacy protection. We will consider the second of them first.

CIRCUMSTANCES IMPOSING AN OBLIGATION OF CONFIDENCE: NOW A REDUNDANT LIMB OF THE ACTION?

Developments prior to *Campbell*

Under the traditional model of confidence, one of two ingredients had to be satisfied for an obligation of confidentiality to arise. The first was that, at least in cases

---

[137] This remarkable phrase was used by the Court of Appeal in *Douglas III*, at [53].

[138] [1990] 1 AC 109.   [139] [1969] RPC 41, 47.

[140] This element is considered below; see also Fenwick and Phillipson, 'Confidence and Privacy: A Re-examination' [1996] 55(3) *CLJ* 447, 449–50.

[141] *A-G v Guardian*, op cit, at 265, *per* Lord Keith.

[142] Ibid. Lord Goff explicitly left the point open (ibid, 281–2); Lord Griffiths (ibid, 270) thought detriment was required. The remainder of the House did not address the point. In *X v Y* ([1988] 2 All ER 650, 651 and 657) it was held *per curiam* that actual or possible detriment was not a requirement. The recent *Source Informatics* case (op cit), left the point open.

involving personal, as opposed to commercial information, there had to be some identifiable, pre-existing, intimate or necessarily confidential relationship between confider and confidant, such as a professional relationship of trust,[143] or a marriage,[144] from which the obligation of confidence could be inferred. As Lord Hoffman recently put it:

Breach of confidence was an equitable remedy and equity traditionally fastens on the conscience of one party to enforce equitable duties which arise out of his relationship with the other. So the action did not depend upon the personal nature of the information or extent of publication but upon whether a confidential relationship existed between the person who imparted the information and the person who received it.[145]

As such its limitations were obvious: 'a doctrine centred around a relationship of confidence could not hope to offer effective privacy protection where, as was increasingly occurring, the wrong complained of was a deliberate and even surreptitious taking [of information] with a view to publication'.[146] However, since *Stephens v Avery*,[147] the existence of such a relationship was no longer 'the determining factor.'[148] Instead, confidentiality was enforced simply on the ground that the information was received 'on the basis that it is confidential', since to allow such a recipient to reveal the information would be 'unconscionable', an approach confirmed in a number of successful actions where there had been no prior relationship between the parties.[149]

The alternative ingredient traditionally required for a duty of confidence to arise was an agreement of confidentiality; either express,[150] or implied—that is, unspoken, but mutually assumed between the parties. This requirement also sharply limited the applicability of the action to only those specific instances in which information was voluntarily *communicated* in confidence. It seemingly could not cover the paradigm case of invasion of privacy, where reporters *surreptitiously* acquired information with a view to publication, because in such cases there is no possibility of agreement between the parties (express or implied), or promise of confidentiality: it would be

---

[143] *W v Edgell* [1990] Ch 59 (doctor-patient); *X v Y* (op cit); *Attorney General v Guardian Newspapers* [1987] 1 WLR 1248 (both employer-employee).

[144] *Duchess of Argyll v Duke of Argyll*, op cit.   [145] Op cit (*Campbell*), at [44].

[146] M. Richardson, 'The Private Life After *Douglas v Hello*' [2003] *Singapore Journal of Legal Studies*, 311, 326.

[147] Op cit: the applicant brought an action against a friend to whom she had confided that she had had a lesbian affair, who had then sold the story to a newspaper; thus the relationship between the parties was one of friendship only.

[148] Ibid, 482, *per* Browne-Wilkinson, VC.

[149] *Francome v Mirror Group Newspapers*, op cit (information obtained by means of a telephone tap); *Shelley Films v Rex Features Limited* [1994] EMLR 134 (injunction granted to prevent the use of a photograph taken surreptitiously on the film set of *Frankenstein*) and *Creation Records Ltd v News Groups Newspapers Ltd* [1997] EMLR 444 (injunction granted to prevent publication of a photograph of a new *Oasis* album cover design taken surreptitiously on the set); *Hellewell v Chief Constable of Derbyshire*, op cit ('mugshot' of the applicant taken by police and later passed to shopkeepers: duty of confidence imposed but overridden in public interest).

[150] See Law Commission, op cit, at [6.11]: for an obligation to be imposed, 'any confidant must agree to treat the information as confidential'.

absurd to say that the defendant journalist had 'agree[d] to treat the information as confidential'[151] when his purpose is to publish it to the world, while the applicant 'confider' is unaware that any communication is taking place at all.[152]

However, decisions well before the HRA had also made it clear that there need be nothing recognizable as any *communication* between the parties—as in a situation where the defendant surreptitiously acquires the information without the plaintiff being aware that this has occurred.[153] This was possible because the notion of an 'implied agreement' of confidentiality had been radically reinterpreted: it was now implied into the dealings between the parties, *not* on the basis of a mutual, though unspoken agreement on the matter, but on the basis that the *reasonable man* in the position of the defendant would have assumed such an obligation,[154] a bold re-casting of the common law. Nevertheless, the crucial point was that there still had to be something *over and above the quality of the information itself* in order to put the hypothetical reasonable person on notice that he or she was assuming an obligation of confidentiality, something such as the warning signs forbidding photography in *Shelley Films*.

However, for the doctrine to attain full utility as a remedy against intrusive journalism, it was clear that it would need to dispense not only with the requirement of a promise or agreement of confidentiality, but also with the need for any express indications by the claimant that the information in question was confidential.[155] For the obvious fact is that not only will people generally refrain from developing relationships of trust and confidence with intrusive journalists, they will also not carry warning signs upon their person, expressly putting journalists on notice that they consider what they are doing as confidential. If such requirements were to be dispensed with, so that the obligation could be imposed simply on the basis of the private nature of the material itself, then it could fairly be said that at the conceptual level, breach of confidence would be substantially transformed into a privacy tort. The point may be illustrated by the distinction Sedley LJ drew in

[151] The requirement the Law Commission thought necessary (ibid).

[152] It may be noted that even in its traditional guise, the action *could* offer protection for privacy in the many cases in which the press obtain information about individuals not through surreptitious means, but from interviewing friends and acquaintances of the applicant in whom he or she has confided. In these cases an obligation of confidence may be imposed upon the newspaper on the orthodox basis that they knew or ought to have known that they had received the fruits of a broken confidence: *Michael Barrymore v News Group Newspapers Ltd* [1997] FSR 600 (a friend with whom Barrymore allegedly had a homosexual affair passed the details to a newspaper); *Stephens v Avery*. See also *Attorney General v Guardian Newspapers* (op cit), esp. 1265; dicta of Nourse LJ in *A-G v Observer Ltd, The Times*, 26 July 1986; Law Commission report op cit, at [4.11].

[153] See e.g. *Francome*, [1984] 1 WLR 892, (information obtained through the use of an unlawful telephone tap); *Shelley Films v Rex Features Limited* [1994] EMLR 134 (injunction granted to prevent the use of a photograph taken surreptitiously on the film set of Frankenstein); *Creation Records Ltd v News Groups Newspapers Ltd* [1997] EMLR 444 (injunction granted to prevent publication of a photograph of an album cover design taken surreptitiously on the set).

[154] This test was explicitly used in both *Shelley Films* and *Creation Records* (above).

[155] As in *Shelley Films* and *Creation Records*, ibid.

Douglas between the traditional conceptions of confidence on the one hand and privacy on the other:

What a concept of privacy does, however, is accord recognition to the fact that the law has to protect not only those people whose trust has been abused [as in confidence cases] but those who simply find themselves subjected to an unwanted intrusion into their personal lives.[156]

If an obligation of confidentiality could be imposed simply on the basis of the obviously private nature of the information, then the law of 'confidence' *would* now protect those who simply find themselves subjected to intrusion into personal life: any idea that, in some sense, trust must be abused, would simply disappear. Given, however, that such a 'development' would in effect dispense with what is the key requirement of the confidence action—the very requirement indeed that distinguishes it from a straightforward privacy tort[157]—it is perhaps not surprising that the case law prior to *Campbell* had disclosed a certain amount of ambiguity on this issue.

Douglas, despite the excitement it generated, in fact made little contribution here. Given the elaborate security arrangements put in place by the couple to prevent unauthorized photographs being taken,[158] the case could have been decided straight-forwardly under the principle applied in the pre-HRA decisions in *Shelley Films*[159] and *Creation Records*:[160] that the intruder was explicitly put on notice that the occasion was confidential. It was on this basis indeed, that Lindsay J eventually imposed liability for damages in *Douglas II*.[161] While clearly recognizing the force of this argument however,[162] Brooke and Sedley LJJ also appeared to take the strangely old-fashioned view that 'if the photographer was an intruder with whom no relationship of trust or confidence had been established,'[163] this could be fatal to the couple's claim.[164] The decision thus added nothing substantial to the development of the law here.

In contrast, *Venables and Thompson*[165] was the most transparently radical of the decisions prior to *Campbell*. As is now well known, the court granted an injunction against the world, forbidding any media outlet from publishing information which could identify the two boys and/or reveal their current location. Butler-Sloss P was

---

[156] *Douglas and Zeta Jones and ors v Hello!* [2001] QB 967, CA, 1011.

[157] Note that the definition of the US privacy tort (see text to note 237 below) stipulates only as to the quality of the information itself.

[158] These included searches of all guests for cameras, and confiscation of any cameras found, as well as very tight security procedures for identifying legitimate guests.

[159] Op cit.   [160] Op cit.

[161] The images of the wedding 'were, so to speak, radiated by the event were imparted to those present, including [the photographer] and his camera, in circumstances importing an obligation of confidence': op cit, at [197].

[162] Op cit, 984: Brooke LJ: 'People were being trusted to participate in this private occasion . . . on the strict understanding that they might not take photographic images of what they saw,'; thus 'unauthorised photographs [of the occasion would be obtained] in breach of his or her duty of confidence'; see also dicta at 988.

[163] Ibid, 984; see Sedley LJ's like dicta at 998.

[164] See the numerous cases in which surreptitious takers with no relationship to the person from whom they acquire the information have been fixed with an obligation of confidentiality: note 159 and 160 above.

[165] Op cit.

quite explicit that any newspaper receiving such information from whatever source, however obtained, would be bound by an obligation of confidence.[166] What then were, to quote the test in *Coco Engineering*, the 'circumstances imposing an obligation of confidence'? As the court in *Venables* recognized, *there were no such circumstances*: this was neither a case of someone giving the information to the newspaper in breach of a relationship of trust and confidence, nor the newspaper surreptitiously obtaining the information in circumstances where it was obvious that it should be treated as confidential. Rather, the whole point of the blanket injunction was that it applied *regardless of how the information was obtained*. Now it could be argued that that the 'circumstances' imposing the obligation were the boy's notoriety, the death threats made against them, and the consequent danger to their lives should the information be published. But this information was relevant because it went to the issue of whether publication of the information would be likely to lead to a violation of the boys' right to life under Article 2 ECHR. Thus in cases where the publication would *itself* cause an intrusion into private life, engaging Article 8, then that 'circumstance'—possible violation of a Convention right—would be present *simply by virtue of the nature of the information itself. Venables* thus specifically affirms that a court may grant an injunction against the publication of information, regardless of the circumstances in which it is obtained, based solely upon the damage that disclosure of the information in question may do to the Convention rights of the person to whom the information relates.[167] As the Court of Appeal noted in 2005,

A remarkable feature of this decision was that the nature of the information alone gave rise to the duty of confidence regardless of the circumstances in which the information might come to the knowledge of a person who might wish to publish it.[168]

The Court of Appeal decision in *Campbell* also yields little guidance on point. The facts of *Campbell* are quite well known, given that the House of Lords' decision is the third reported judgment in the case, but in brief, Naomi Campbell complained in an action both in breach of confidence and under the Data Protection Act 1998 after the *Mirror* newspaper had published details of her treatment for drug addiction with Narcotics Anonymous, including surreptitiously-taken photographs of her leaving the clinic and hugging other clients. Importantly, this photo made the location of the NA centre that Campbell had been attending clearly identifiable to anyone familiar with the area.[169] In the trial the information in question was divided into five classes as follows:

---

[166] Ibid, at 939.

[167] While it was thought that this might be a case that turned upon its very particular facts—the peculiar notoriety of Venables and Thompson and the extent of the evidence of a threat to their safety (op cit, at 933 and 937)—the recent granting of an injunction to preserve the life-long anonymity of Mary Bell (*X (A woman formerly known as Mary Bell) v SO* [2003] EWHC 1101) and her daughter, based solely upon their Article 8 rights (see [16]–1[9]), suggests otherwise. The judge found that Mary Bell was at 'considerable risk of press intrusion and harassment, public stigma and ostracism' and particularly required protection against this, because she was a 'vulnerable personality with mental health problems' (at [9]).

[168] *Douglas III*, at [69].   [169] As Lord Nicholls found: op cit, at [5].

(1)   the fact of Miss Campbell's drug addiction;

(2)   the fact that she was receiving treatment;

(3)   the fact that she was receiving treatment at Narcotics Anonymous;

(4)   the details of the treatment—how long she had been attending meetings, how often she went, how she was treated within the sessions themselves, the extent of her commitment, and the nature of her entrance on the specific occasion; and

(5)   the visual portrayal [through photographs] of her leaving a specific meeting with other addicts and being hugged before such a meeting by other members of the group receiving treatment.[170]

The applicant had conceded that the *Mirror* was entitled to publish the information in categories (1) and (2)—the vital fact that Campbell was a drug addict and was receiving treatment for her addiction;[171] the dispute therefore centered around whether publishing the further details and the photographs (categories (3)–(5)) could attract liability. The Court of Appeal found that the extra details in these categories were too insignificant to warrant the intervention of the courts, a finding discussed further below. But as to the issue of imposing an obligation of confidentiality, it was plain that most of the 'information' in the case—the fact of, and details of the treatment —were evidently provided to the *Mirror* by another patient at Narcotics Anonymous or one of Campbell's staff, actors who would clearly be caught even under the traditional style doctrine of confidence.[172] But what about the photographs—evidently covertly taken? Morland J found that the taking of such photographs imposed an obligation of confidentiality.[173] The Court of Appeal reversed this finding *only* on the basis that the photographs disclosed no fresh confidential information; Phillips MR left undisturbed the judge's finding that the covert taking of the photographs fulfilled the second limb of the doctrine of confidence—the imposition of an obligation of confidentiality.[174] It could therefore be argued that since there was obviously no express/implied promise of confidentiality by the photographer and no express indications of confidentiality by *Campbell*, the decision implicitly endorsed the radical view of confidence. However, this argument is not a strong one:[175] it could equally be the case that since the judges in the Court of Appeal decided that the information in the photographs in any event lacked the quality of confidence, they simply found it unnecessary to consider themselves whether an obligation of confidence could have been imposed had they made the converse finding.

---

[170] Ibid, at [23].

[171] This was because it was accepted that the press was entitled to expose the falsity of Campbell's previous public statements that she did not take drugs and was not a drug addict.

[172] On the basis of an express or implied promise of confidentiality (fellow patient) or relationship of trust and confidence (staff).

[173] Op cit, at [40](2).

[174] 'We think that this conclusion accords with the approach of the Judge to the photographs' (op cit, at 656).

[175] Contrary, on reflection to the author's previous view: Phillipson ('Transforming'), at 745–6.

Similarly, the judge in *Theakston v MGN*[176] was prepared to injunct any photographs of Theakston's encounter with the prostitutes, despite the absence of any circumstances imposing the obligation save the intimate nature of the events recorded, but, again the judge did not expressly consider how this could be done, making the finding an implicit one only.

There was therefore, some endorsement in the case law of the new view of confidence, though overall it was scarcely decisive, and none it was at appellate level. However, by far the most important decision prior to *Campbell* was that in *A v B plc*, in which the Court of Appeal dealt with the vexed issue of the requirement of an obligation of confidentiality with almost startling ease:

The need for the existence of a confidential relationship should not give rise to problems as to the law ... A duty of confidence will arise whenever the party subject to the duty is in a situation *where he either knows or ought to know that the other person can reasonably expect his privacy to be protected.*[177]

This passage, in making no stipulation as to the factors that can create the reasonable expectation of privacy, thus leaves open the possibility that it could arise simply on the basis of the obviously private nature of the information itself. It also quite openly fuses confidentiality and privacy into one cause of action—imposing a duty of confidentiality not on the basis of any of the traditional factors, but on the basis of a reasonable expectation of privacy. In such a case, the effect would be that the second requirement of the doctrine of confidence—that it was 'imparted in circumstances imposing an obligation of confidence'—would have been collapsed into the first—'the information itself must have the quality of confidence about it;' to put it another way, the second head would generally be satisfied when the first is.[178] In other words, the very requirement of the confidence action that distinguishes it from a pure privacy tort would virtually disappear. As the Court of Appeal put it in *Campbell*:

The development of the law of confidentiality since the Human Rights Act 1998 came into force has seen information described as 'confidential' not where it has been confided by one person to another, but where it relates to an aspect of an individual's private life which he does not choose to make public. We consider that the unjustifiable publication of such information would better be described as breach of privacy rather than breach of confidence.[179]

In other words, if the passage quoted from *A v B* above is put to its full potential use,

---

[176] Op cit. Theakston clearly had no pre-existing relationship with the surreptitious photographer and nor (on the evidence) did he make any express stipulation that the occasion was a confidential one. It is not likely that he would have done, in the circumstances.

[177] Op cit, at 551B.

[178] It should of course be noted that, save in the rare cases of a personal item, such as a diary, accidentally being left in a public place, a journalist wishing to obtain personal images or information without consent *will* often have to resort to surreptitious means or subterfuge, thus clearly satisfying the second head in any event.

[179] Op cit, at 663.

effectively a new action for breach of privacy would have come about, whether or not it is still termed 'breach of confidence.' Or as Keene LJ put it in *Douglas*:

Whether the resulting liability is described as being for breach of confidence or for breach of a right to privacy may be little more than deciding what label is to be attached to the cause of action.[180]

It should be noted that such a remodelled action would cover both surreptitious takings of information and instances in which the press obtain information about a person by interviewing those in whom they have confided. In such instances, an obligation of confidence could be imposed upon the newspapers directly, on the ground that the reasonable man would have realized that the information received should be kept confidential, due its clearly private character.[181] As just noted, a duty on the media was imposed directly in this way in *Venables and Thompson* albeit in drastic circumstances, and such a possibility was confirmed in *A v B plc*.[182]

What, then, was left for the House of Lords in *Campbell* to do, if the key transformation had already come about? The answer, we suggest, is two-fold. First, a point often missed at the time, the passage in *A v B* quoted above was strictly *obiter*: in the case actually before the court, the applicant *had* had a pre-existing relationship with the women who then sold the story of their relationship to the newspaper, so that the orthodox doctrine of confidence would have imposed an obligation of confidentiality in any event. Second, those parts of the judgment in which the court determines whether an obligation of confidentiality should be imposed in the particular case, present a very different picture: the radicalism inherent in the *obiter* comments above disappears, and the tendencies discussed above—the strong gravitational pull of orthodox notions of confidentiality upon the reasoning, overriding or displacing considerations deriving from Article 8—once again become apparent. Thus Woolf CJ observes:

In situations where the parties are not married (when they are, special considerations may arise) the fact that the confidence was a shared confidence which only one of the parties wishes to preserve does not extinguish the other party's right to have the confidence respected, but it does undermine that right . . . the more stable the relationship, the greater will be the significance which is attached to it.[183]

Thus the court found that there was a 'significant difference' between the confidentiality of stable relationships and transitory ones[184] and went on to quote with approval

---

[180] Op cit, at 1012.

[181] The successful use of this route would refute the view of the Law Commission (ibid, para 5.9) that cases such as *Fraser v Evans* ([1969] 1 QB 349) mean that the doctrine can give no remedy to the 'owner' of personal information where the promise of confidentiality is given to another, as where a newspaper promises a journalist that information he obtains on a celebrity will not be published in her lifetime, and then breaches that promise, leaving, so the Commission thought, the celebrity with no remedy. See also the doubts of Wacks on this point (*Privacy and Press Freedom*, London: Blackstones, 1995, 56).

[182] [2002] 3 WLR 542, para 11 (ix)–(x).   [183] Op cit, at 551H.   [184] Ibid, 560D–G.

Ouseley J's views in *Theakston* to like effect.[185] It concluded: 'The degree of confidentiality to which A was entitled, notwithstanding that [the two women] did not wish their relationships with A to be confidential, was very modest.'[186] Ouseley J's finding in *Theakston* was substantially identical.[187]

It was, however, very difficult to see why this followed, if the value to be protected in such cases is the right to control over personal information, or privacy. The issues of the duration of a relationship and the expectation of trust within it hark back to factors treated as determinative in the traditional doctrine of confidence discussed above,[188] *not* the strength of the privacy interest engaged. That interest, of course, relates to sexual life: its strength under Article 8 derives from the clear and repeated findings of principle at Strasbourg that sexuality,[189] and information relating to it,[190] engage a particularly intimate aspect of private life requiring special protection by the national authorities, in this case the court under section 6(1) HRA.[191] To this may be added the fact that the events in question had, in *A v B plc*, occurred in a clearly private setting—the bedroom—further increasing the expectation of privacy. The fact that the other party no longer wished to keep the information a secret should also not have been relevant, as previous English authority in fact indicates.[192] It may perhaps set up a conflict with the other party's right to freedom of expression, but that simply indicates that there is another principle against which the claim to privacy must be weighed, it does not go to the strength of the privacy claim itself.

On closer analysis, therefore, the reasoning of the court in both these cases was plagued by contradictions arising from the failure to resolve decisively the extent to which principles deriving from privacy substitute themselves for the traditional ingredients of the action in confidence. Traditionally confidentiality, as seen, was based upon *agreement* between two people to such a condition. Under such an approach, clearly, the fact that only one party ever wished to treat the information as so restricted was fatal to the applicants' claims. In contrast, if the court had genuinely been concerned with the individual's right to control personal information about themselves, flowing, as Sedley LJ said in *Douglas* 'from the fundamental value of personal autonomy',[193] then such a lack of agreement should have had very little to do with the matter. In short, while the Court in *A v B plc appeared* to sweep away the

---

[185] Ouseley J, op cit, at [59]: 'I consider it impossible however to invest with the protection of confidentiality all acts of physical intimacy regardless of circumstances.' His view was that, if the encounters with the prostitute imposed any obligation of confidentiality at all, which he doubted, this represented very much 'the outer limit of the laws' protection'.

[186] Op cit, at 561D–E.   [187] Op cit, at [61].   [188] See notes 143–146 above.

[189] *Dudgeon v UK* (1981) 4 EHRR 149, 165, at [52].

[190] *Lustig Prean v UK* (1999) 29 EHRR 548.

[191] Previous English authority is in fact to like effect. See *Stephens v Avery*, op cit, at 454F: 'To most people the details of their sexual lives are high on their list of those matters which they regard as confidential.'

[192] *Barrymore*, op cit, 602: 'Common sense dictates that when people enter into a [sexual] relationship of this nature, they do not do so for the purpose of it subsequently being published in *The Sun* or any other newspaper. The information about that relationship is for the relationship and not for a wider purpose.'

[193] Op cit, at 1001.

requirement of an obligation of confidentiality based on a pre-existing relationship, or agreement of confidentiality, the reasoning employed to resolve the actual case in front of it displayed a continuing attachment to just such notions.

The recent Court of Appeal decision in *D v L*,[194] which has so far attracted little or no comment, exemplified these tendencies even more strongly: in this instance, the court treated a case concerned, again, with very intimate personal information, entirely in orthodox confidentiality terms. The case concerned an application for an injunction to restrain the use of a tape-recording made secretly by the applicant's former partner, in which the applicant discussed details of his sexual proclivities. Clearly, in Strasbourg terms, there was, again, a weighty privacy issue involved, just as in *A v B* and *Theakston*. However, in this case, decided in 2003, Article 8 *is not even mentioned* in the judgment, let alone the Strasbourg jurisprudence on the importance of sexual life within Article 8. Instead, the reasoning is dominated by very traditional notions of equity, conscience and clean hands.[195] While there is extensive citation of dicta from *A v B*, there is no attempt to apply the new model of confidence outlined there, in which Article 8 is 'absorbed' into the action for confidence. Indeed, one could not even describe this case as disclosing an *equivocation* between the values of confidentiality and privacy; privacy does not enter the equation, and the judgment is dominated by considerations of confidentiality in the orthodox sense. The decision, in short, is a striking illustration of the manner in which the 'pro-confidentiality' aspects of *A v B* can be used to wipe Article 8 from judicial consideration, illustrating quite how hollow and ineffective can be the above-cited dicta in that judgment as to the 'absorption' of Article 8 into breach of confidence.

While *A v B* in particular thus radically opened up the *potential* for the transformation of confidence by the values of privacy, in many cases the actual decisions made were, as we have seen, rooted firmly *not* in such values, but in very traditional common law principles. More specifically, on the state of the law immediately prior to *Campbell*, whilst there were *dicta* suggesting that no traditional factors were needed to impose a duty of confidence, and at least one first instance decision which endorsed that view,[196] the courts had clearly not freed themselves from the shackles of traditional confidentiality values. The law stood in a state of uneasy ambivalence between its desire to protect privacy and the continuing pull of its roots in confidence. While the second limb of the action had seemingly been disposed of by *obiter dicta*, in practice it appeared to be in rude health. While Article 8 was said judicially to have reshaped the action, in practice its influence on decisions was negligible or non-existent. The maintenance in practice of confidentiality requirements meant that the courts' attempts to fulfil their duty to mould the common law into a remedy in order to fulfil their duty of acting compatibly with Article 8 were proving a failure. In

---

[194] [2004] EMLR 1.

[195] The fact that the applicant did not come to equity with clean hands—because he had written unpleasant letters to the applicant—was used as a major reason for denying him relief.

[196] *Venables and Thompson v News Group Newspapers* [2001] 1 All ER 908.

particular, it should be noted that in *Peck v UK*,[197] the Strasbourg court remarked that one reason for finding that the common law of confidentiality could not have afforded a remedy to Peck was its requirement that there be 'circumstances imposing an obligation of confidentiality', which the court found, would have been unlikely to have been fulfilled in the circumstances.[198]

This failing tendency on the part of the UK courts is illustrated further by comparing the outcome of the above decisions with that of the Strasbourg decision in *Campmany Y Diez de Revenga v Spain*.[199] A Spanish magazine and radio program had carried a story about what it described as 'a new sex scandal between an attractive aristocrat and a banker from this country', including pictures and details of their tryst. The Duchess involved brought a successful civil action against the applicant, for unlawful interference with her right to honour and to respect for her private life under Spanish law. Both damages and an order to print the full text of the judgment in print as large as that of the original story were given as remedies. The media bodies concerned applied to Strasbourg, alleging a breach of Article 10. The application was declared inadmissible as manifestly ill-founded, on the basis that the penalty imposed by the Spanish courts was a necessary and proportionate measure taken to protect the private life of the applicants. This is perhaps the closest case on the facts to decisions such as *A v B* and *Theakston* that Strasbourg has considered. The basic situation in all was sensational reportage upon illicit sexual behaviour. While there are differences on the facts, particularly in relation to *Theakston*,[200] the decision is at least a strong indicator that fleeting, and (in conventional terms) immoral sexual relationships attract the full protection of Article 8, contrary to the approach taken in the English cases, in which information relating to such relationships was seen as barely worth protection.

The impact of *Campbell*

In this area, it is suggested, *Campbell* has made a decisive contribution. The first, and crucial, point to make concerns the ratio of the judgment: a majority of the House of Lords found liability in confidence in respect of the publication of surreptitiously-taken photographs of the model outside Narcotics Anonymous, in the street. What, then, were the 'circumstances imposing an obligation of confidentiality'? There was clearly no pre-existing relationship between Campbell and the photographer; no communication between them; no express or implied promise by the photographer of confidentiality—quite the reverse. All these elements were therefore quite clearly disposed of. As Lord Nicholls put it: 'This cause of action has now firmly shaken off the limiting constraint of the need for an initial confidential relationship.'[201]

---

[197] (2003) 36 EHRR 41. The case is considered below, but in brief it arose from the complaint of Peck that he had no remedy in respect of the passing of footage of himself in a moment of private anguish following a suicide attempt, captured by CCTV cameras, from a local authority to various media outlets. The UK Government tried to argue that breach of confidence could have afforded him a remedy.

[198] Ibid, [111].   [199] (2000) no. 54224/00.

[200] For example, Theakston, as a TV presenter, was more of a public figure than the Duchess in *Campagny*.

[201] *Campbell v MGN Ltd* [2004] 2 AC 457 at [13–14].

But the ratio of this case goes much further: *unlike* in cases like *Shelley Films*, or, more recently *Douglas v Hello! Ltd*,[202] in which snatched photographs were injuncted on confidence grounds, there were no clear indications here that the scene was intended to be confidential, such as warning signs forbidding photography, or other external indications that the scene was confidential, such as the elaborate security precautions to prevent photography taken at the Douglas wedding. In fact, the only factor that could impose the obligation of confidence in relation to the photographs was the obviously private nature of the information itself—the fact that it concerned therapeutic treatment. This was then the first time that an English appellate court had imposed liability for use of personal information, in the absence of any circumstances imposing the obligation save for the nature of the information itself. And if it is the private nature of the information that can itself impose the obligation, then the second limb of confidence effectively ceases to exist: there has to be information of a private nature to fulfil the first limb in any event, so the second limb no longer has any independent content. It has disappeared.[203] 'Breach of confidence' simply becomes an action that protects against unauthorized publicity given to private facts.[204]

This then is clear, and unarguable, from the ratio of the case itself. But the Lords did not leave this implicit: it is made explicit in the clearest possible statements. Thus Lord Hope deliberately endorsed the expansive dicta of Lord Woolf cited above.[205] Lord Nicholls—one of the minority—said:

Now the law imposes a 'duty of confidence' whenever a person receives information he knows or ought to know is fairly and reasonably to be regarded as confidential.[206]

It may be noted that this formulation clearly omits the second limb of the confidence action.

Lord Hope went further, saying: 'If the information is obviously private, the situation will be one where the person to whom it relates can reasonably expect his privacy to be respected.'[207] These dicta precisely carry out the transformative step that the passage from *A v B* cited above[208] had opened the way to. It will be recalled that the dicta discussed above allowed for an obligation of confidentiality to be imposed where there was a reasonable expectation of privacy. Lord Hope now makes clear that the

---

[202] *Douglas v Hello! Ltd* [2003] 3 All ER 996; *Douglas v Hello! Ltd* [2005] 3 WLR 881. In that case, stringent security measures, including body searches of the guests, the sealing off of the part of the hotel used for the wedding had been put in place in an attempt to avoid unauthorized photography of the event.

[203] As acknowledged by Morgan: 'Privacy in the House of Lords—Again', op cit.

[204] It should be noted that whilst the photographs were found to attract liability only by the majority, the minority rejected this finding not on the basis that there was no obligation of confidence, but because of their finding that the photographs contained no information worthy of protection: i.e., that the first limb was not satisfied.

[205] Above, text to note 177.

[206] [2004] 2 AC 457 at [14]. Lady Hale also summarizes the essential requirement of the new-style action very clearly: 'The position we have reached is that [*prima facie* liability is made out] when the person publishing the information knows or ought to know that there is a reasonable expectation that the information in question will be kept confidential': ibid, [134].

[207] Ibid, [96].　　[208] Above text to note 177.

sole element required to give rise to that expectation is the fact that 'the information is obviously private'. This spells out in clear terms the demise of the second limb. Its removal gives us, in effect, a privacy tort, whatever the language used by the judiciary to describe it. As we shall see, the 2005 Court of Appeal judgment in *Douglas v Hello! Ltd*,[209] while emphatically affirming these developments, seems ready to take a further step in respect of terminology.

At this point, however, it is necessary to take a step backwards from our provincial excitement about developments in English law, seen in isolation. This chapter is comparing the right to privacy that Strasbourg has interpreted Article 8 as requiring, with that which English law has slowly developed from an old equitable action. As noted above, it was *essential* that English law take the step it now appears to have done, in ridding itself of the second limb of the *Coco* formulation. However, this step, although to be welcomed,[210] merely removes a negative—an element in breach of confidence that *prevented* it from becoming a real privacy remedy. What is of the most pressing concern, now this has seemingly been done, is what has happened to the first limb—in other words, what kinds of information are deemed capable and worthy of protection under the new action for breach of confidence.

WHAT KINDS OF PERSONAL INFORMATION CAN BE PROTECTED UNDER THE DOCTRINE OF CONFIDENCE?

The case law up to *Campbell*

Since most of the cases prior to the HRA had concerned commercial information, the courts had not, prior to that time, evolved any workable tests to decide what kinds of *personal* information would have this quality, save for the negative requirement that the information must not be 'in the public domain' and that it must not be mere trivia.

The post-HRA cases, apart from laying down a general test (considered below) have given substantial further guidance by way of example as to the kinds of information that may warrant protection, in terms of both substance and form. *A v B plc*[211] confirms previous findings in *Barrymore v News Group Newspapers Ltd*[212] and

---

[209] [2005] 3 WLR 881. This is the decision of the Court of Appeal on the appeal from the decision to award damages at final trial made by Lindsay J: [2003] 3 All ER 996 (*Douglas II*), the Court of Appeal having in 2001 declined to grant an injunction in the case: [2001] QB 967.

[210] Welcome, that is, if one takes the view, as the author has consistently done, that English judges will neither declare a general, free-standing tort of privacy (confirmed recently in *Wainwright v Home Office* ([2003] 3 WLR 1137, above at 711–12) nor interpret their duties under the HRA as requiring them to give direct effect to Article 8 in private law, as H.W.R. Wade and more recently others, such as Jonathan Morgan have argued, and that therefore development of breach of confidence is the only *realistic* means towards providing protection for privacy. It is not therefore suggested that breach of confidence provides the *ideal* privacy remedy, merely the only practically available one, given the actual views of the senior judiciary on these matters, and preferable to none. References are to H.W.R. Wade, 'Horizons of Horizontality' (2000) 116 *Law Quarterly Review*, 217 and J. Morgan, 'Privacy, Confidence, and Horizontal Effect: "Hello" Trouble' (2003) 62(2) *Cambridge Law Journal*, 444.

[211] Op cit.   [212] [1997] FSR 600.

Stephens v Avery,[213] that 'the law should afford the protection of confidentiality to facts concerning sexual relations [including those] outside marriage'.[214] To this, one can add the following classes of information meriting protection: a person's address;[215] photographs of the interior of a home;[216] details of domestic household arrangements;[217] of plastic surgery;[218] photographs of the nude[219] and semi-clothed[220] body and of a child's face used without permission in a local authority brochure.[221] It was also clear from the earlier decision in *X v Y* that it covered medical data.[222]

The courts are thus clearly minded to give a broad scope to the kinds of information warranting protection. They have also shown some sensitivity to the fact that, in cases concerning personal information, it is necessary to go beyond asking merely what information is being conveyed in factual terms, to enquiring also as to the impact of the *form* of the proposed publication. In *Douglas*[223]—which concerned the threatened publication of un-authorized photographs of the wedding of Catherine Zeta-Jones and Michael Douglas—it was argued that the disputed photos of the wedding fell into the category of mere tittle-tattle and that, in any event, 'the photographs did not convey any information which had the quality of confidence, because the guests were not prevented from imparting the same information subsequently, whether in words, by drawings based on recollection or any other means.' Both arguments were rejected 'without hesitation', as 'unsustainable'. As Keene LJ remarked: 'The photographs conveyed to the public information not otherwise truly obtainable, that is to say, what the event and its participants looked like.'[224] This indicates not only that physical appearance on a particular occasion can be protected under the law of confidence, but also that the law can distinguish between different *forms* of presenting the same information: the courts may attach liability to the publication of visual images of a particular occasion if it is felt that the images concerned convey something over and above a mere description. As Keene LJ put it, 'a picture paints a thousand words'.[225] This approach was confirmed in *Theakston*, in which the judge drew a distinction between a verbal description of Theakston's encounter, which was not protected, and photographs of the same events, which were.[226] Lord Hoffman, who found against Campbell, including on the matter of the photographs, conceded that, 'The publication of a photograph cannot necessarily be justified by saying that one would be entitled to publish a verbal description of the scene', approving *Douglas* on this point.[227] This recognition represented a significant development: instead of treating photographs merely as a set of 'facts'—as the traditional doctrine

---

[213] [1988] Ch 449.

[214] [2002] EMLR 7, at [56]. Though see below for the Court of Appeal's reservations on this point.

[215] *Mills v News Group Newspapers*, op cit.   [216] *Beckham v MGN*, op cit.

[217] *Blair v Associated Newspapers*, op cit.   [218] *Archer v Williams*, op cit.

[219] Unreported decision of *MacKay*, op cit; *Theakston*, op cit.

[220] *Holden v Express Newspapers Ltd*, op cit.

[221] *Jacqueline A v the London Borough of Newham LBC*, op cit.   [222] [1988] 2 All ER 650.

[223] [2001] QB 967, 997. The discussion in the text relates to the initial Court of Appeal decision on whether an injunction should be granted restraining publication.

[224] Op cit, at 1011.   [225] Ibid.   [226] Op cit, at [77]-[79].   [227] Op cit, at [72].

of confidence would do—the judges, putting on privacy spectacles, had started to look rather to the *impact*, including the emotional impact, of publication of a photographic record of the events in question. As we shall see below, the approach of the majority in *Campbell* decisively confirmed such an approach.

However, what, in the authors' view, remained problematic, prior to the Lords decision in *Campbell*, was the adoption of the test, taken from the Australian High Court decision in *Lenah Game Meats*, to the effect that information would be treated as deserving of protection if its disclosure 'would be highly offensive to a reasonable person of ordinary sensibilities.'[228] It was highly questionable whether the particular formulation chosen answered to the values of informational privacy discussed earlier in this chapter. No consideration had been given by the courts as to whether such a test was in harmony with such values, or the Article 8 jurisprudence, even though it was argued by the applicant in the Court of Appeal in *Campbell* that the test, by insisting on a 'high' level of offensiveness, understated the weight to be given to Article 8.[229] It is clear, of course, that if the law is seeking to protect control over '*personal* information,' it must have some way of deciding what kinds of information fall into that category. But if the courts are seeking to give effect to Article 8 in this area, then surely the easiest way of determining whether information is *prima facie* deserving of protection would be simply to enquire whether it is within the sphere of 'private life' under Article 8, as expounded in the Strasbourg jurisprudence,[230] rather than by thus borrowing a test from a jurisdiction governed by quite a different set of principles.[231]

In *Campbell v MGN*,[232] the Court of Appeal, reversing the first instance decision on point, found that the information in question—the fact that Campbell was receiving treatment for her drug addiction at Narcotics Anonymous and some details of that treatment—was too insignificant to warrant the court's intervention. The applicant had conceded that the Mirror was entitled to publish the vital fact that Campbell was a drug addict and was receiving treatment for her addiction.[233] Thus the finding was made on the basis that the additional information as to the details of the treatment was not something that a reasonable person would find 'highly offensive.[234] The Court also commented:

. . . the peripheral disclosure of Miss Campbell's attendance at Narcotics Anonymous was

---

[228] *Lenah Game Meats*, note 135 above, at [42]. The test was taken by the Australian High Court from the US tort. It was used by the Court of Appeal in *Campbell v MGN* (op cit, at 660) and impliedly approved in *A v B plc* (op cit, at 550G).

[229] Op cit, at 644.

[230] Again, it is now apparent that this point was put to the court in *Campbell*: ibid, at 643.

[231] The US, from which the test ultimately came, has no equivalent of Article 8 ECHR in its constitution. As Brooke LJ warned in *Douglas*: 'the courts in this country should be very cautious, now that the Human Rights Act 1998 is in force, when seeking to derive assistance from judgments in other jurisdictions founded on some different rights-based charter': op cit, 989.

[232] [2003] QB 633.

[233] This was because it was accepted that the press was entitled to expose the falsity of Campbell's previous public statements that she did not take drugs and was not a drug addict.

[234] Op cit, at 660–1.

[not], in its context, of sufficient significance to shock the conscience and justify the intervention of the court.[235]

Whether or not this disclosure 'shocked the conscience' was, however, arguably irrelevant. Unconscionability is the traditional language of breach of confidence;[236] offensiveness the language of the American privacy tort;[237] such tests are clearly not derived from Article 8, and 'unconscionability' at least, is certainly not a privacy value.[238] In fact, despite the court's finding that it must have regard to both Articles 8 and 10,[239] Phillips MR in this judgment[240] made no mention of Article 8 when making this key finding, let alone entering into any analysis of relevant Strasbourg jurisprudence. In *Z v Finland*,[241] for example, a case cited to the court in *Campbell*, the European Court observed that, 'the protection of . . . medical data is of *fundamental importance* to a person's enjoyment of his or her right to respect for private . . . life.' While the information disclosed about Campbell was not, in terms, 'medical data', in the sense of medical records, it was information relating to health and therapeutic treatment and such information is normally treated as axiomatically private in nature in this[242] and other jurisdictions.[243] Of particular importance is the fact that, as Morland J found at first instance in *Campbell*, such information falls under the definition of 'sensitive personal data' under the Data Protection Act, therefore attracting special protection against unauthorized processing.[244] For the Court thus to find that information that would be treated as of an especially private nature under a European Directive, and the Act of Parliament implementing it, is too trivial to merit protection at common law, seems incongruous, to say the very least. Thus we have the same tendency—to ignore Article 8 when making key findings—seen in *Theakston, A v B plc* and *D v L* on the protection of information relating to sexual life, in the context of the imposition of an obligation of confidentiality.[245]

The effect of the decision in *Campbell*

The decision of the House of Lords in *Campbell* has gone some way to remedying

---

235 Ibid, at 661.   236 See, e.g., *Francome v Mirror Group Newspapers* [1984] 1 WLR 892.

237 The US tort is defined as follows: 'One who gives publicity to a matter concerning the private life of another is subject to liability to the other . . . if the matter publicised is of a kind that (a) would be highly offensive to a reasonable person and (b) is not of legitimate concern to the public.' (Restatement (Second) of the Law of Torts, 625D).

238 In *LRT v Mayor of London* [2003] EMLR 4, at [57]–[58], Sedley LJ criticized the 'conscience' test in confidence cases, advocating the use of a proportionality exercise in its place.

239 Op cit, at [42].   240 That is, of the Court of Appeal, op cit.

241 25 EHRR 371, at [95] (emphasis added).

242 See *R v Dept of Health ex parte Source Informatics* [2001] QB 424: information on a prescription *prima facie* confidential.

243 See e.g. *Lenah Game Meats*, op cit, at [42]: information relating to, inter alia, 'health . . . easy to identify as private'.

244 Op cit, at [92]. Section 2 defines 'sensitive personal data'; such data must be processed in accordance with Schedule 3, under which the circumstances in which processing—including publication—may take place without explicit consent are very narrow.

245 Above, pp 735–8.

both these matters. The first key point is that the House recognized that the first port of call in determining whether there are facts worthy of protection should be the Article 8 case law. Second, they found that that the test of whether disclosure of the information would be highly offensive[246] was therefore *not* to be used as a threshold test, which had to be satisfied in all cases, but rather only as a tie-breaker, to determine marginal or doubtful cases and to be used to help determine the weight or seriousness of the privacy interest when balancing it against the competing interest in publication. The third notable feature of the case is that their Lordships also avoided the mistake of falling back upon orthodox confidence principles in deciding the case.

Firstly, as to the 'high offensiveness' test, it is worth setting out the relevant passage from *Lenah* in full:

Certain kinds of information about a person, such as information relating to health, personal relationships, or finances, may be easy to identify as private, as may certain kinds of activity which a reasonable person, applying contemporary standards of morals and behaviour, would understand to be meant to be unobserved. The requirement that disclosure or observation of information or conduct would be highly offensive to a reasonable person of ordinary sensibilities is in many circumstances a useful practical test of what is private.[247]

Essentially, the Court of Appeal, applying this test in the Campbell case, had asked itself the question, 'would a reasonable person of ordinary sensibilities, on reading that Miss Campbell was a drug addict have found it highly offensive, or even offensive, that the details as to her treatment and the photograph of her leaving the meeting were also published?'[248] It answered this question in the negative. In the House of Lords, Lord Hope found this approach to be wrong in law. In a strongly argued passage, his Lordship made two key findings. First, 'the test [of offensiveness] is not needed where the information can easily be identified as private:[249]

If the information is obviously private, the situation will be one where the person to whom it relates can reasonably expect his privacy to be respected. So there is normally no need to go on and ask whether it would be highly offensive for it to be published.[250]

This seems to be the correct reading of the passage just cited: where it is obvious that the information is private, the 'useful practical guide' of the offensiveness test will not be necessary. Second, his Lordship found that the information in question in the case was indeed clearly private in nature:

The private nature of these meetings [at NA] encourages addicts to attend them in the belief that they can do so anonymously. The assurance of privacy is an essential part of the exercise. The therapy is at risk of being damaged if the duty of confidence which the

---

[246] *Australian Broadcasting Corporation v Lenah Game Meats* (2001) 208 CLR 199 at [42]. The test was taken by the Australian High Court from the US tort. It was used by the Court of Appeal in *Campbell v MGN Ltd* [2003] QB 633 at 660 and impliedly approved in *A v B plc* [2002] 3 WLR 542, at 550G.
[247] *Lenah Game Meats* (ibid).   [248] *Campbell v MGN Ltd* [2003] QB 633, at [55].
[249] *Campbell v MGN Ltd* [2004] 2 AC 457, at [94].   [250] Ibid, at [96].

participants owe to each other is breached by making details of the therapy, such as where, when and how often it is being undertaken, public. I would hold that these details are obviously private.[251]

Ironically, of course, in *Lenah Game Meats* itself, Gleeson CJ had said that information relating to, inter alia 'health' was 'easy to identity as private'.[252] The UK Court of Appeal had thus misused the very test they had taken from Chief Justice Gleeson, not recognizing it as having two stages as follows: (a) is the information obviously private (e.g. related to health, sexual activity, finances etc)? (b) If *not*, then it may be useful to ask as an alternative, would its publication be highly offensive to a reasonable person? Since the information the court was concerned with was clearly 'related to health' (as it concerned therapeutic treatment for drug addiction) and therefore fell into part (a) of the test, there was no need to go onto the second part of the test. The 'highly offensive' limb should not have been applied. Lord Carswell confirmed this, stating, 'it is not necessary in this case to ask . . . whether disclosure of the information would be highly offensive to a reasonable person of ordinary sensibilities. It is sufficiently established by the nature of the material that it was private information.'[253] Lord Nicholls also expressed strong reservations about the test:

[The Gleeson] formulation should be used with care, for two reasons. First, the 'highly offensive' phrase is suggestive of a stricter test of private information than a reasonable expectation of privacy. Second, the 'highly offensive' formulation can all too easily bring into account, when deciding whether the disclosed information was private, considerations which go more properly to issues of proportionality; for instance, the degree of intrusion into private life, and the extent to which publication was a matter of proper public concern. This could be a recipe for confusion.[254]

Lady Hale similarly found: 'An objective reasonable expectation [of privacy] test is much simpler and clearer than the test sometimes quoted from the judgment of Gleeson CJ.'[255]

Lord Hope then went on to clarify that, when applying the offensiveness test, either in marginal cases, or to assess the degree of intrusion represented by the publication, two conditions applied. First, it should be asked not whether the reader of the material in question would find its publication offensive, as the Court of Appeal had seemingly suggested, but whether the individual to whom the information related— Campbell in this case—would so find it: 'The mind that has to be examined is that, not of the reader in general, but of the person who is affected by the publicity.'[256] Second, his Lordship clarified that the test is a mixed objective-subjective test:

Where the person is suffering from a condition that is in need of treatment, one has to try, in order to assess whether the disclosure would be objectionable, to put oneself into the shoes

---

[251] Ibid, at [95].
[252] *Australian Broadcasting Corporation v Lenah Game Meats* (2001) 208 CLR, at [41].
[253] *Campbell v MGN Ltd* [2004] 2 AC 457, at [166]. [254] Ibid, at [22]. [255] Ibid, at [135].
[256] Ibid, at [99].

of a reasonable person who is in need of that treatment. Otherwise the exercise is divorced from its context.[257]

In other words, the reasonable person is not endowed with the characteristics of the applicant, but is placed in the overall situation he or she is in, in order to assess his or her hypothetical response to publication. Lady Hale agreed: '[Gleeson CJ] was referring to the sensibilities of a reasonable person placed in the situation of the subject of the disclosure rather than to its recipient.'[258] Such an approach may be referred to as a 'situationally subjective' test, and it is worth noting that it was also put forward recently by the New Zealand High Court, in which Nicholson J remarked:

But [the test is] what a reasonable person of ordinary sensibilities would feel if they were in the same position, that is, in the context of the particular circumstances.[259]

Taking this approach, Lady Hale powerfully argued that the publication of the disputed extra details would be very likely to damage Campbell's therapy:

Revealing that she was attending Narcotics Anonymous enabled the paper to print the headline 'Naomi: I am a drug addict', not because she had said so to the paper but because it could assume that she had said this or something like it in a meeting. It also enabled the paper to talk about the meetings and how she was treated there, in a way which made it look as if the information came from someone who had been there with her, even if it simply came from general knowledge of how these meetings work. This all contributed to the sense of betrayal by someone close to her of which she spoke and which destroyed the value of Narcotics Anonymous as a safe haven for her.[260]

Lord Carswell substantially agreed.[261]

The treatment of the photographs in *Campbell*

A further point of significant interest is the manner in which the issue of the photographs accompanying the intrusive article was handled, a matter that is important in differentiating a privacy-based approach—essentially concerned with issues of intrusion and harm—from one based on confidentiality: one concerned with whether the information revealed by photographs can be said itself to be confidential. It should first of all be noted that their Lordships do not appear to find the fact the photographs were taken in the street to be problematic in terms of imposing liability given what they portrayed, a matter discussed further below.[262]

In terms of the treatment of the photographs specifically, for Lord Nicholls and Lord Hoffman, once it had been determined that publicizing the further details in

---

[257] Ibid, at [97–98].   [258] Ibid, at [136].   [259] *P v D* [2000] 2 NZLR 591 at [39].
[260] *Campbell v MGN Ltd* [2004] 2 AC 457 at [153].
[261] '[Publication of the extra details] intruded into what had some of the characteristics of medical treatment and it tended to deter her from continuing the treatment which was in her interest and also to inhibit other persons attending the course from staying with it, when they might be concerned that their participation might become public knowledge', ibid, at [165].
[262] See below at 759–62.

categories (3) and (4)[263] did not engage the applicant's private life, it followed as a matter of logic that the photographs, which merely conveyed the information in those categories (and did not portray Campbell in some embarrassing or undignified act or situation)[264] added nothing to the applicant's claim. Lord Nicholls was clear that the greater distress caused by the publication of the photographs was legally irrelevant:

The complaint regarding the photographs is of precisely the same character as the nature of the complaints regarding the text of the articles: the information conveyed by the photographs was private information. Thus the fact that the photographs were taken surreptitiously adds nothing to the only complaint being made.[265]

Their approach, then, was very much a formalistic one: the distress occasioned by the surreptitious photography is real, but, since the issue is purely to do with whether sufficiently sensitive private facts were revealed, that distress cannot be slotted into any of the limbs of the cause of action the court must consider. It must therefore be disregarded.

In contrast, Lord Hope found the effect of the photographs upon Campbell to be, not only relevant, but in fact the crucial factor that lead him to find against the newspaper.[266] This finding was based upon the likely impact of the publication of those photographs:

Any person in Miss Campbell's position, assuming her to be of ordinary sensibilities but assuming also that she had been photographed surreptitiously outside the place where she been receiving therapy for drug addiction, would have known what they were and would have been distressed on seeing the photographs. She would have seen their publication, in conjunction with the article which revealed what she had been doing when she was photographed and other details about her engagement in the therapy, as a gross interference with her right to respect for her private life.

Lady Hale similarly finds that the publication of the photographs 'added to the potential harm, by making Campbell think that she was being followed or betrayed, and deterring her from going back to the same place again'.[267]

Lord Hope and Lady Hale thus find a way in which the distressing impact of the photographs on someone in Campbell's situation can enter the legal equation: they do not go to the question of whether the facts are private are not, as the test from *Lenah* suggests; rather they go to the issue of how offensive and damaging the publicity given to those facts is, as a means of evaluating the overall weight of the privacy claim. Since the question of whether the publicity given to the relevant facts is offensive self-evidently includes the manner in which those facts are publicized (in this case by the use of surreptitiously taken photographs), then those photographs, by this route, become legally relevant once more. This more imaginative approach allows for the overall impact of the entire publication under consideration—including the

---

[263] Above, p 733.
[264] *Campbell v MGN Ltd* [2004] 2 AC 457 at [31] (per Lord Nicholls) and [76] (per Lord Hoffman).
[265] Ibid, at [30], emphasis added.   [266] Ibid, at [121].   [267] Ibid, at [155].

means used to acquire its contents—to be assessed. In this way, the 'offensiveness' test provides a means to a more holistic assessment of the impact on the applicant's private life and is thus to be welcomed. But this is quite a different manner from using it as a threshold test that must be used in every case.

The transformation of the common law: rhetoric and values

Finally, it should be noted that the House of Lords, in dealing with this limb of the action—traditionally, whether the information has the quality of confidence about it—decisively moved the terminology and the underlying concern of the law away from traditional notions of confidentiality towards a concern with privacy. As Lord Nicholls put it, 'Essentially the touchstone of private life is whether in respect of the disclosed facts the person in question had a reasonable expectation of privacy.'[268] Rather than speaking of whether the information is 'confidential', the question now seems to be whether 'the published information engaged Article 8 at all by being within the sphere of the complainant's private or family life'.[269] Article 8 therefore becomes the touchstone for the fulfilment of the first—now the only substantive—limb of the action. Whilst Lord Hope's speech has a heading, 'Was the information confidential?',[270] his Lordship goes on to state firmly: 'The underlying question in all cases where it is alleged that there has been a breach of the duty of confidence is whether the information that was disclosed was private and not public.'[271] Later in his speech, his Lordship referred to 'the right to privacy, which lies at the heart of the breach of confidence action.'[272] What is taking place here is an explicit reorientation of the underlying normative values of the action. Lord Nicholls declared: 'This tort, however labelled, affords respect for one aspect of an individual's privacy. That is the value underlying this cause of action.[273] Even more boldly he added:

the description of the information as 'confidential' is not altogether comfortable. Information about an individual's private life would not, in ordinary usage, be called 'confidential'. The more natural description today is that such information is private. The essence of the tort is better encapsulated now as misuse of private information.[274]

Lord Hoffman was even more explicit:

. . . the new approach takes a different view of the underlying value which the law protects. Instead of the cause of action being based upon the duty of good faith applicable to confidential personal information and trade secrets alike, it focuses upon the protection of human autonomy and dignity—the right to control the dissemination of information about one's private life and the right to the esteem and respect of other people.[275]

This is strong (albeit technically indirect)[276] horizontal effect: the dominant normative

---

[268] Ibid, at [21].   [269] Ibid, at [20] per Lord Nicholls.   [270] Ibid, at [88].
[271] Ibid, at [92].   [272] Ibid, at [105].   [273] Ibid, at [15]   [274] Ibid, at [14].
[275] Ibid, at [51].
[276] Because the applicant must still use an existing cause of action, rather than simply alleging breach of Article 8, without more, as their cause of action—which would be 'direct' horizontal effect, in the jargon.

values are taken from the right to private life, from Article 8, not from the action for confidence. It amounts to the adoption of the methodology described earlier, under which 'breach of confidence [is] treated simply as an empty shell into which Article 8 principles [are] poured.'[277] How far this process has gone may be seen in Lord Carswell's conclusion, which does not mention breach of confidence even formally:

> I would accordingly hold that the publication of the third, fourth and fifth elements in the article constituted an infringement of the appellant's right to privacy that cannot be justified and that she is entitled to a remedy.[278]

These dicta, then, represent the moment at which 'breach of confidence' becomes a label only: the values traditionally underpinning the action are explicitly and openly replaced with those deriving from the human right to privacy.

The Court of Appeal in its 2005 decision in *Douglas v Hello!*,[279] the only major case so far decided since *Campbell*, was presented, in a sense, with a choice as to how it 'read' or 'presented' the House of Lord's decision. While it is of course a subordinate court, it is not unknown for lower courts to 'read down' or 'expand' judgments of higher courts, thereby diminishing or enlarging their transformative effect. In this respect, the clear effect of *Douglas III* is to emphasize the more transformative aspects of the *Campbell* decision. Thus the radical dicta of their Lordships are highlighted; more conservative dicta or tendencies are not cited. Lord Nicholl's dicta as to the awkwardness of referring to confidentiality instead of privacy are foregrounded, as are the expansive dicta of Lord Hoffman that refer to the shift in the values underlying the action from 'the duty of good faith' to 'the protection of human autonomy and dignity.'[280] The Court accepts that the basis of the action is now the notion of a 'reasonable expectation of privacy', picking up on the congruence between Lords Hope and Hale in the majority as to the basic test for the action,[281] and its purpose— the protection of 'the individual's informational autonomy'.[282] Finally, the Court gives its own succinct summary of the development of this area of law:

> Megarry J in *Coco v A N Clark* identified two requirements for the creation of a duty of confidence. The first was that the information should be confidential in nature and the second was that it should have been imparted in circumstances importing a duty of confidence. As we have seen, it is now recognised that the second requirement is not necessary if it is plain that the information is confidential, and for the adjective 'confidential' one can substitute the word 'private'.[283]

In the result, the Court sums up the sole requirement now needed to make out a *prima facie* case:

> What the House was agreed upon was that the knowledge, actual or imputed, that

---

[277] Above, at 727.   [278] *Campbell*, at [171].

[279] [2005] 3 WLR 881 (Court of Appeal judgment on appeal from final trial); hereafter *Douglas III*.

[280] Ibid, at [51] of the HL judgment; cited at [79] of the CA judgment in *Douglas III*.

[281] *Douglas III* [2005] EWCA Civ 595 at [80].   [282] Ibid, at [81].   [283] Ibid, at [83].

information is private will normally impose on anyone publishing that information the duty to justify what, in the absence of justification, will be a wrongful invasion of privacy.[284]

It is now clear beyond doubt, then, that a person acquiring information can come under a legal duty not to publicize it simply by virtue of its obviously private character. Remarkably, and in this respect eschewing some of the coyness of the House of Lords in *Campbell*, the Court of Appeal was prepared quite openly to discard even the label of 'breach of confidence'. Thus, in a striking phrase, the court remarked:

> We conclude that, in so far as private information is concerned, we are required to adopt, as the vehicle for performing such duty as falls on the courts in relation to Convention rights, *the cause of action formerly described as breach of confidence*.[285]

The label, it appears, has disappeared now also: the courts have completed the transformation of breach of confidence into what may now be termed 'the tort of misuse of private information'.[286]

PUBLIC DOMAIN ISSUES

Introduction

Here we consider the issues arising when it is claimed that the information that the individual seeks to protect may lack the quality of confidence because it is already in the public domain. This is a crucial issue for an applicant seeking to make out an action in confidence, as the traditional (and linguistically natural) view was that information in the public domain *necessarily* lacked the quality of confidence. Section 12(4) HRA confirms that, when considering when to grant an injunction, the court must 'have regard to the extent to which the information has become, or is about to become, available to the public.' Two aspects of this issue arise in the cases: first, how much publicity must information which initially was not in the public domain receive before it loses the protection of the law; second, how will the courts treat information that may be considered public knowledge from the start because it was acquired in a 'public' situation or location. This second question in particular is of critical importance in relation to intrusive journalism. It is a situation beloved of law examiners—to quote Lord Goff[287]—but is also virtually the staple fare of large numbers of tabloid newspapers and other popular publications such as *Heat*: photographs of lovers kissing in a restaurant, or embracing in a park, of a topless celebrity sunbathing on a beach or by a swimming pool are nothing short of ubiquitous in English journalism.

Jurisprudence from other jurisdictions gives conflicting answers to the question

---

[284] Ibid, at [82].   [285] Ibid, at [53] (emphasis added).

[286] As Lord Nicholls says in *Campbell v MGN Ltd* [2004] 2 AC 457 at [14]: 'The essence of the tort is better encapsulated now as misuse of private information.' The question whether the action in fact falls to be treated as a tort or an equitable action is beyond the scope of this chapter, though it may be noted that the Court of Appeal took the latter view: *Douglas III* [2005] op cit, at [9].

[287] *Attorney General v Guardian Newspapers (No 2)* [1990] 1 AC 109, 281.

whether the publication of such pictures may be deemed an invasion of privacy. Under the American privacy tort, an absolutist view is taken, whereby what takes place in 'public' cannot by definition be 'private'.[288] As Prosser puts it: 'The decisions indicate that anything visible in a public place may be [given publicity], since this amounts to no more than giving publicity to what is already public and what any one present would be free to see',[289] an approach exemplified, for example in *Jaubert v Crowley Post-Signal Inc.*[290] Such approaches may be seen as straightforward 'location analysis'.[291] Thus in one case concerning publication of a photograph taken of a couple embracing in public, the Californian Supreme Court remarked that the publicity 'did not disclose anything that up to then had been private, but rather only extended knowledge of the particular incident to a somewhat larger public'.[292]

The advantages of this approach in terms of legal certainty and predictability are apparent; however, it relies, as a number of scholars have argued, on a simplistic and misleading attitude whereby privacy is treated is an all or nothing concept, rather than as a matter of degree.[293] Our everyday lives are in reality a constant trade-off between human interaction and social life on the one hand, and the maintenance of a reasonable degree—not an absolute state—of privacy on the other. The better approach is therefore more nuanced and recognizes that a degree of privacy may be retained in a semi-public environment, such as a restaurant,[294] or gymnasium.[295] Other jurisdictions, including Canada,[296] Germany,[297] and France,[298] take such a nuanced view of the matter, recognizing that, depending upon the circumstances, a degree of privacy may

[288] For a critique of this position, see H. Nissenbaum, 'Protecting Privacy in an Information Age: The Problem of Privacy in Public' (1998) 17 *Law and Philosophy* 559.

[289] D. Prosser, 'Privacy' (1960) 48 *California Law Review* 383, 394–5.

[290] 375 So 2d 1386 (L A 1979). Publication of a picture of the applicant's home in a newspaper was not actionable because the view of the home displayed was one which any passer-by would see.

[291] D. Zimmerman, 'Requiem for a Heavyweight: A Farewell to Warren and Brandeis's Privacy Tort' (1983), 68 *Cornell Law Review* 291, at 347.

[292] *Gill v Hearst Publishing Co.*, 253 P.2d 441 (1953) at 444–45.

[293] Gavison suggests that an individual 'enjoys perfect privacy when he is completely inaccessible to others' (op cit, at 428) without suggesting that this is anything other than an unrealistic and undesirable scenario; see also E. Paton-Simpson, 'Private Circles and Public Squares: Invasion of Privacy by the Publication of "Private Facts"' (1998) 61 *MLR* 318, 321–326; Feldman, 'Privacy Related Rights and their Social Value', op cit, at 39–49.

[294] See the decision of the German Supreme Court in the Princess Caroline case, discussed below.

[295] The location where photographs were taken of the former Princess in *HRH Princess of Wales* (1993), unreported.

[296] See the decision of the Canadian Supreme Court in *Les Editions Vice Versa Inc v Aubry* [1999] 5 BHRC 437, concerning the publication, without consent, of photographs of the plaintiff taken in the street.

[297] See BGH, 19 December 1995, BGHZ 131, 322–346; *Caroline III* NJW 1996 1128 (photographs of Princess Caroline of Monaco having dinner with her boyfriend in a garden restaurant, an intrusion into her private life). For discussion, see B. Markesenis and N. Nolte, 'Some Comparative Reflections on the Right of Privacy of Public Figures in Public Places', in R. Birks (ed.), *Privacy and Loyalty*, Oxford: Clarendon, 1997, 118 et seq. See also *Re C* (1999) 10 BHRC 131.

[298] E. Picard, 'The Right to Privacy in French Law', in, Markesenis (ed.) *Protecting Privacy*, Oxford: Clarendon, 1999, 91.

be retained in a public place. Particularly instructive on this point is a recent decision of the German Supreme Court[299] which provides a useful contrast to the American position. Princess Caroline of Monaco complained of photographs taken by the press of her having an intimate dinner with her boyfriend in a garden restaurant in France. The Court refused to follow the approach of the Appeal Court that privacy 'stopped at the doorstep' and found that the Princess had clearly 'retreated to a place of seclusion where [she wished] to be left alone' and that she was entitled to respect for that wish. She had 'transfer[ed] [her] private sphere of life to a place outside [her] home'. She had retired:

to a secluded place—away from the public eye (in eine örtliche Abgeschiedenheit)—where it was objectively clear to everyone that they wanted to be alone and where, confident of being away from prying eyes, they behaved in a given situation in a manner in which they would not behave in a public place. Unlawful interference with the protection of that privacy could therefore be made out if photos were published that had been taken secretly and/or by catching unawares a person who had retired to such a place. That was the position here, where the applicant and her boyfriend had withdrawn to the far end of a restaurant courtyard with the clear aim of being out of the public eye.[300]

While the presumption will be that events taking place in such places do not attract privacy protection, this may be rebutted if, as the court put it, it is clear by reference to 'objective criteria' that an individual wishes to be 'left alone' so that she can, 'relying on the seclusion of the place, behave in a manner which she would not have done if . . . in full view of the public'. Thus, identifying such places of seclusion is not to be done simplistically by reference solely to locality.[301]

A similar approach was taken in a recent decision of the Canadian Supreme Court;[302] the case concerned the publication, without consent, of a photograph of the applicant taken in public. The photograph did not show the applicant engaged in any private act, or partially unclothed, but it was held that the right to privacy included the right to control over ones' image. This is also the approach of the French courts: as one commentator summarizes the position: 'As a principle, acts pertaining to private life but performed in a public place deserve the protection of the law.' [303]

It will be seen that English law has moved from an initially inchoate view to a clear position that is significantly more protective of privacy in public than German law, but stops short of the French position, in which unauthorized photography *per se* amounts to an infringement of privacy rights.[304] The recent decision in *Von Hannover*

---

[299] BGH, 19 December 1995, BGHZ 131. We are indebted to the discussion of this decision in Markesenis and Nolte, 'Some Comparative Reflections', op cit, at 118 *et seq.*

[300] Op cit, at [23].

[301] Feldman expresses strong support for this view: 'Secrecy, Dignity or Autonomy', op cit, at 59–62 and 'Privacy-Related Rights', op cit, at 39–40.

[302] *Les Editions Vice Versa Inc v Aubry* [1999] 5 BHRC 437. The case concerned the publication, without consent, of photographs of the applicant taken in public.

[303] Picard, 'The Right to Privacy in French Law', in Markesenis (ed.) *Protecting Privacy*, op cit, at 91.

[304] Certain to subject exceptions; see ibid.

arguably affirms that English law is in compliance with the Convention, at least in terms of its treatment of *location* as an aspect of privacy protection.

Domestic cases on public domain prior to *Campbell*

It has been clear for some time that English courts have been happy to afford the protection of the law to information, whether captured in photographs or otherwise, that is known to quite large numbers of people, particularly where that information is of a personal nature. In *B v H Bauer Publishing Ltd*,[305] the judge noted with approval dicta in *AG v Guardian Newspapers (No 2)*,[306] to the effect that whether information is in the public domain will often be a matter of degree, so that prior disclosure to a limited group of people might not rob the information of its confidentiality and went on to suggest:

It may be more difficult to establish that confidentiality has gone for all purposes, in the context of personal information, by virtue of its having come to the attention of certain readers or categories of readers.

The other cases strongly confirm this impression. In *A v B plc*, at first instance,[307] the defendant submitted that the information in question—the claimant footballer's affair—could not be considered confidential, first because it was known to a number of people, up to 25, and second because the relationship had been partially conducted in public places, the couple having been seen kissing in night clubs and so on. The argument was robustly dismissed: the judge cited with approval *dicta* from *Stephens v Avery*, that 'information only ceases to be capable of protection as confidential when it is in fact known to a substantial number of people' and went on to conclude that the fact of the affair 'was known only to a very limited number of people. There is a world of difference between that and the disclosure of the details in a newspaper.'[308] This finding was not doubted on appeal. Similarly, in *Campbell*, there was no suggestion that the limited number of people who knew the details of the model's attendance at Narcotics Anonymous—in particular, her fellow patients—robbed the information of its confidential quality. The point was not even addressed in the speeches in the House of Lords decision. In *Mills v News Groups Newspapers*,[309] which concerned the threatened publication of the applicant's address in the *Sun*, a similar argument was again raised, and again dismissed, the judge remarking:

The fact that information may be known to a limited number of members of the public does not of itself prevent it having and retaining the character of confidentiality, or even that it has previously been very widely available.[310]

Similarly, in *Blair v Associated Newspapers*,[311] in which Cherie Blair was granted a series of injunctions against various parties to prevent the publication of details of her domestic arrangements, provided by a former nanny, even the fact that one print-run

---

[305] [2002] EMLR 8, at [26].   [306] [1990] 1 AC 109, 260.   [307] Op cit.
[308] These dicta are from the judgment of 30 April 2001.   [309] [2001] EMLR 41.
[310] Ibid, at [25].   [311] Case no. HQ0001236—a no of unreported decisions were delivered in 2001.

of the *Sunday Mail* carrying the offending article had already been distributed was held not to have robbed the information of its confidential quality. This decision in particular stretched the notion of the 'confidentiality' of information to a remarkable degree, since thousands must have read the offending article.

The decision in *Theakston v MGN*[312] is clearly out of line in this respect. In this case, a prostitute, with whom the television presenter had had an encounter in a brothel, sold an explicit and detailed description of it to a tabloid newspaper. Jamie Theakston sought to restrain publication in a breach of confidence action. One of the grounds on which he failed was precisely the 'public domain' point: Ouseley J doubted that the information relating to encounters with prostitutes in a brothel was capable of being confidential because, 'It is likely that other customers and a number of prostitutes will see who comes and goes.'[313] This conclusion, made without citation of any supporting authority, is open to serious doubt. It is clearly incompatible with the well-established principle cited above to the effect that knowledge by a small number of people of information does not prevent it from being confidential, especially given that in the case in question, only a handful of people could possibly have seen Theakston. Moreover, a brothel, a place in which intimate acts take place, would be generally considered to be a far more obviously 'private' place than, say a nightclub (as in *A v B*). The decision in *Peck v UK*,[314] discussed below, indicates that this decision is almost certainly out of line with Article 8 ECHR, as one would expect.

With the exception, however, of *Theakston*, such decisions indicate that the judges are quite happy to stretch the notion of the 'confidentiality' of information to perhaps a rather counter-intuitive degree. However, they also appear to rely upon inherently fuzzy judgments of degree: information remains confidential provided that is known only to 'limited' numbers of people (seemingly up to several thousand, at least in *Blair*), whereas it does not when it is known to 'substantial' numbers. Such an approach, as well as lacking a clear conceptual underpinning, is also conspicuously deficient in legal clarity, a serious problem given that privacy claims entail restrictions upon a Convention right—freedom of expression—and thus ought to be prescribed by law of reasonable clarity.[315] A perhaps more promising approach may be found in the recent decision in *Douglas II*, which concerned an application for damages in relation to the unauthorised publication of the wedding of Michael Douglas and Catherine Zeta-Jones, at which elaborate security measures had been taken to exclude the press,[316] unauthorised guests and any cameras, Lindsay J was confronted with the argument that the wedding could not be considered a confidential occasion because of the fact that, as Brooke LJ put it in the Court of Appeal: '[The couple] did not choose to have a private wedding attended by a few members of their family and a few friends in the normal sense of the words 'private wedding'.[317] Instead the guests

---

[312] Op cit.   [313] Ibid, at [62].   [314] (2003) no. 44647/98.
[315] See the well-known dicta in *Sunday Times v UK* A 30 (1979), at [52].
[316] Other than the representatives of *OK!* magazine, to which the couple had agreed to sell the rights to cover the wedding.
[317] Op cit, at 995, Brooke LJ.

numbered several hundred. Now the judge could have dealt with this submission purely on the basis of a question of degree: that though there were several hundred guests there, this was not a sufficiently substantial number to destroy the confidentiality of the information relating to the event. While glancing at this possibility, however, the judge founded also upon a more hard-edged answer:

To the extent that privacy consists of the inclusion only of the invited and the exclusion of all others, the wedding was as private as was possible consistent with its being a socially pleasant event.[318]

This approach may be seen to found on the basic principle of *control* over personal information, suggested above as the governing principle for this area of law. Rather than simply counting heads, and deciding at some inevitably arbitrary point that the attendance of 100 guests at an occasion does not destroy its confidentiality but that, say, 1000 does, the judge asks whether, regardless of numbers, there is a sense in which the subjects of the occasion sought to exert control and thus *choice* over who could observe the occasion. If such control is present, as with the Douglas wedding, then the occasion may be deemed private or confidential; if, however, the subjects allowed indiscriminate observation of the occasion, it may not.

Now this approach may be helpful where the court is considering a controlled occasion, such as a wedding or party. However, it would appear to suggest that privacy is *per se* lost if a private event takes place in an uncontrolled environment, such as a public space. If, say, a woman sunbathes topless, even on a quiet public beach, then the fact that she may be observed even by one or two persons over whom she can exercise no choice could be seen as destroying any claim she may make that any pictures taken of her in her unclothed state contained information of a private nature that should not be given mass publicity without her consent. But such a finding would be inconsistent with decisions in which information acquired in an 'uncontrolled' environment has nevertheless been treated as confidential. Examples include *A v B*, in which one of the locations was a nightclub, and *Holden v Express Newspapers Ltd*,[319] in which the actress and her husband obtained an interim injunction to prevent publication of photographs of themselves relaxing by the swimming pool of a hotel, taken from outside the hotel grounds using a long-range lens.

A different approach, then, is needed, but one that is still faithful to the foundational value that it has been suggested now underpins this area of law—control over personal information. This approach, instead of focusing upon control over the original participants or witnesses to the event in question instead treats as decisive the issue of what *use* the person in question reasonably foresaw being made of the information. Specifically, since those bringing confidence actions are invariably seeking to prevent publication in the *media* of personal information, this approach asks whether the

---

[318] Op cit, at [66].
[319] (QBD), 7 June 2001, Eady J, unrep. I am indebted to Tugendhat and Christie, *The Law of Privacy and the Media*, Oxford: OUP, 2002, at 218 for the description of this case.

person reasonably foresaw mass publicity being given to the event or information in question. In this respect, Professor Wacks has made the important point that 'any definition of "personal information" must . . . refer both to the quality of the information and to *the reasonable expectation of the individual concerning its use*';[320] that is, one cannot assess whether information is 'personal' or not, without looking at the use which the defendant has made or proposes to make of it. Interestingly, precisely this point was made by focus groups to researchers from the IPPR cited in their recent report on privacy and the media:[321] members of the public confirmed that they were happy to be caught on CCTV cameras in public spaces, *because there would be no open publication of the images*; conversely, one member objected to TV coverage of a football game which included 'his friend being shown in a lingering TV close-up, crying when his beloved Arsenal lost a game', something that was felt to be 'wrong'. The objection clearly is to the loss of anonymity: the exposure of a specific individual, without consent, to mass attention.

Some awareness of this indeed has been shown by the courts in the different context of the regulation of broadcasting. *R v BSC ex parte BBC*[322] concerned an application by the BBC to overturn a decision of the Broadcasting Standards Commission that the BBC had breached the BSC fairness and privacy code by secretly filming transactions in Dixons, in an attempt to reveal malpractice. Hale LJ observed: 'I also attach particular weight to the context, which is not only the secret filming without consent but also the potential use in the mass media without consent.' The Press Complaints Commission's Code of Practice (drawn up by the press itself), to which the courts will have to have regard,[323] similarly defines 'private places [as] public or private property where there is a reasonable expectation of privacy.'[324] A useful distinction has recently been offered in a report by the IPPR between 'restricted' and 'open' public space. The former would include spaces such as 'the office or workplace and as secluded beaches or sheltered picnic spots;' the latter included town centres, shopping malls and exposed beaches. In the latter, the authors argued, we self-monitor our behavior closely, because we are, as it were, 'front stage'; in the former, we are much less self-conscious, because we do not expect to be observed.[325]

Conversely, despite the terms of the Code that it polices, the Press Complaints Commission has shown its inability—or unwillingness—to grasp such nuanced factors in its ruling under the Press Code in the *Anna Ford* case.[326] The presenter

---

[320] *Personal Information: Privacy and the Law*, Oxford: Clarendon Press, 1980, at 24 (emphasis added).

[321] D. Tambini and C. Heyward, 'Regulating the trade in secrets: policy options', in Tambini and Heyward (eds), *Ruled by Recluses? Privacy, Journalism and the Media after the Human Rights Act*, London: IPPR, 2002.

[322] [2001] QB 885, 899.   [323] Under the HRA, s 12(4).

[324] The fact that an event takes place in a semi-public environment may, however, be a factor which can reasonably used in assessing the 'weight' of the privacy claim, when and if it is placed in the balance against any public interest in disclosure, including the interest in press freedom, a matter discussed in Chapters 13 and 15.

[325] D. Morrison and M. Svennevig, 'From "public interest" to "social importance": the public's view of the public interest' in Tambini and Heyward, op cit, at 69–70.

[326] Report 52, www.pcc.org.uk.

complained of a breach of the Code in respect of the publication of photographs surreptitiously taken of her and her family in swimwear relaxing on a beach. The PCC held that a publicly-accessible beach was *not* a place where the complainants could have had a reasonable expectation of privacy, even though it was clear that they had not consented to long-range photography and subsequent publication. The key factor that the PCC here missed is the appreciation that unauthorized broadcasts of such behaviour entails a loss of *choice* as to the audience who are the eventual recipients of the information. While the family would of course have foreseen that a small number of people on the beach may have seen them, they would not have been recognized and thus retained their anonymity. Exposing them to mass publicity, and simultaneously removing the anonymity that the family had sought, represented a violation of the principle of control over personal information and thus, *prima facie*, a breach of privacy.

The Strasbourg decision in *Peck v UK*

Now, however, the PCC and the courts, as public authorities under the HRA, will be *forced* to engage with this approach as a result of the decision of the Strasbourg court in *Peck v UK*,[327] which, rather than focusing upon the issue of control over the *original participants* or witnesses of the event in question, precisely treats as decisive the issue of control over the *use* made of the information by any observer. The applicant in *Peck* had been captured on Council CCTV cameras, wandering through the street carrying a knife, immediately after he had attempted to commit suicide by cutting his wrists. This footage was eventually passed by the local authority on to various local newspapers, which showed recognizable stills of the man, and to a news broadcast and the television programme, *Crime Beat*, both of which showed extracts from the CCTV footage, from which the man was recognizable, to an audience of hundreds of thousands. Peck, having failed on a judicial review of the Council's decision, took his case to Strasbourg, alleging a violation of Article 8 by the local authority through its action in passing the footage on without extracting adequate undertakings by the media bodies concerned as to the protection of Peck's privacy in its use. The UK Government's argument was that, 'the incident in question did not form part of [Peck's] private life given the substance of what was filmed and the location and circumstances of filming. The applicant's actions were already in the public domain.'[328] In other words, actions performed in a public place could not, by definition, be private: a straightforward invocation of the US approach.

The Court disagreed and found a breach of Article 8, reasoning as follows:

As a result [of the broadcasting of the footage], the relevant moment was viewed to an extent which far exceeded any exposure to a passer-by or to security observation . . . and to a degree surpassing that which the applicant could possibly have foreseen when he walked in Brentwood on 20 August 1995.[329]

---

[327] Op cit.   [328] Ibid, at [53].   [329] Ibid, at [62].

This is a passage of critical importance to this area of law, because it indicates that a public location *per se* cannot not rule out Article 8 protection: the critical question is whether the extent of publicity *subsequently* given to the events in question went beyond that which could have been foreseen at the time. Presumably, if the person in question *could* foresee and indeed expect such exposure, as, for example, where they take part in a filmed public demonstration, or give interviews to the media, there will be no invasion of private life, regardless of the nature of the information publicized. However, where there is *no* expectation either of being photographed or overheard, as where surreptitious photographs are taken of a person relaxing by a hotel pool,[330] on a beach,[331] or in a restaurant, *or where there is no expectation that any images recorded will be afforded mass publicity*—as in *Peck* itself—the fact that the location was a public or semi-public one will not prevent there being an invasion of private life.

It is clear that, if the test used in *Peck* is faithfully applied in domestic law,[332] it will radically extend the scope of privacy protection. In any case in which images of a private act were captured using hidden cameras or long range photography, the defendant newspaper would, as result, be unable to argue that the information was in the public domain, *regardless* of the location in which the act was performed, whether it was a street, restaurant or beach: the applicant would always be able to argue that, following *Peck*, publication of the images would result in the relevant moment being viewed to an extent 'surpassing' that which they could have foreseen. This would in principle remain the case, even if hundreds of people saw the original act took place. While such an approach might seem startlingly radical, it is worthy of note that it appears to be on all fours with the scheme of the Data Protection Act 1998, which gives effect to a directive specifically intended to protect privacy: the Act contains no provision whereby information ceases to be personal data under the Act simply because it was gathered or generated in a public location. Under the Act, the data controller has a defence in relation to processing of 'sensitive personal data' if that information has been made 'public as a result of steps deliberately taken by the data subject'.[333] However, it seems highly unlikely that merely performing an act such as sunbathing topless on a beach would be seen as deliberately making the information public. Presumably, this phrase implies an occasion where the applicant has herself, given sustained publicity to the occasion through, for example, media interviews so that the information concerned was voluntarily disclosed to the world at large.

It is noteworthy that if we apply this approach to the decision in *Theakston*, it

---

[330] As in *Holden v Express Newspapers* (QBD), 7 June 2001, Eady J, unrep.

[331] As in the case of Anna Ford's rejected complaint to the PCC: op cit.

[332] *Peck* of course concerned a challenge to interference in private life by the state: but, since the courts have accepted the application of Article 8 to cases involving interferences by private parties, it should in principle be applied in such situations. While, under s 2 HRA the duty on the court is only to 'take into account' relevant Strasbourg jurisprudence, Lord Slynn has said that, 'In the absence of some special circumstances . . . the court should follow any clear and constant jurisprudence of the European Court of Human Rights (*R v Secretary of State for the Environment, Transport and the Regions, ex parte Holding & Barnes Plc (Alconbury)* [2001] 2 WLR 1389, at [26]; see further Chapter 3 at note 230.

[333] Sch 3, at [5].

provides a clear finding that the answer arrived at in that that case as to the privacy of the occasion was wrong. Under the *Peck* approach, the fact that the sexual acts in question took place in a semi-public environment should have been irrelevant: it was the fact that there was no expectation by Theakston that mass publicity would be given to his encounters with the prostitutes that would determine the fact that the occasion should be regarded as a private one, despite its semi-public location.

However, it must be asked whether such a radical approach actually be given effect within the action for breach of confidence cases? At first blush, the answer would seem to be 'no': it would seem inapt to describe events taking place in the street, witnessed by numerous people as 'confidential'. This indeed is precisely the line taken by Morgan in a recent article:[334] his starting point is that confidentiality and privacy 'are radically different qualities, and, in particular, [that] much private information is not confidential.'[335] He cites the very fact that information 'in the public domain' cannot be protected under the law of confidence as evidence for this proposition, including specifically within the category of unprotectable information, photographs of an individual in a public space. However, it must be recalled that the formal, doctrinal test for whether information can be protected in breach of confidence cases is simply that it 'must have the necessary quality of confidence about it'.[336] This concept has no fixed meaning: it is readily open to the courts, in reliance upon their duty under sections 2 and 6 of the HRA, to re-interpret the notions of 'confidential information' and 'public domain' such that breach of confidence covers all information of a private character which the applicant did not intend or reasonably expect to be given mass publicity through the media. In such a way, the finding in *Peck* would be 'absorbed' into the action for breach of confidence. As the Court of Appeal in *A v B plc*[337] said: 'The court is able to [comply with s 6(1) HRA] by absorbing the rights which articles 8 and 10 protect into the long-established action for breach of confidence' The effect would be to allow the courts to, in effect, protect privacy rights, clothed in the barest fig-leaf of breach of confidence. The House of Lords' decision in *Campell v MGN*, we will now argue, does precisely this.

The treatment of 'public domain' in *Campbell*

It is tolerably clear that *Campbell* embraces the implications of *Peck*, sweeping aside the formalist objections given voice by Morgan. The minority, it is true, dismissed the appeal as regards the photographs, but this was because they had already decided that the information that Campbell was attending Narcotics Anonymous was not something that warranted the protection of the court, given Campbell's concession that the basic fact of her drug addiction and treatment for it could be published in the public interest. Thus Lord Nicholls remarked:

the pictorial information in the photographs added nothing of an essentially private

---

[334] J. Morgan, 'Privacy, confidence, and horizontal effect: "Hello" trouble' (2003) 62(2) *CLJ* 444.
[335] Ibid, at 452.   [336] See the definition from *Coco* above, op cit.   [337] Op cit, 546G.

nature. They showed nothing untoward. They conveyed no private information beyond that discussed in the article.[338]

Lord Hoffman agreed: remarking that photography without consent could not in itself give rise to liability, he thought that:

. . . the widespread publication of a photograph of someone which reveals him to be in a situation of humiliation or severe embarrassment, even if taken in a public place, may be an infringement of the privacy of his personal information.[339]

Lord Hoffman appeared to think that this followed from the decision in *Peck*—in which the footage released arguably did show the applicant in a situation of humiliation—but this, it is suggested, is questionable. What *Peck* establishes is that that one may engage in private actions or moments in public or semi-public spaces—that is, in actions which engage Article 8—and that the dissemination of pictures of such actions without consent is *prima facie* an infringement of that Article, subject of course, to a public interest/ Article 10 defence. There is no need—and no justification—for applying a special test of 'humiliation or severe embarrassment' to photographs, as Lord Hoffman here suggests.

The majority, by contrast, appear to accept *Peck* quite straightforwardly. As well as pointing out the *harm* that the photographs might cause[340] they do not appear to find the fact the photographs were taken in the street to be problematic in terms of imposing liability *given what they portrayed*. Lord Hope accepted that 'the *taking* of photographs in a public street must . . . be taken to be one of the ordinary incidents of living in a free community'[341], but then went on to draw an important distinction:

Miss Campbell could not have complained if the photographs had been taken to show the scene in the street by a passer-by and later published simply as street scenes. But these were not just pictures of a street scene where she happened to be when the photographs were taken. They were taken deliberately, in secret and with a view to their publication in conjunction with the article. The zoom lens was directed at the doorway of the place where the meeting had been taking place. The faces of others in the doorway were pixilated so as not to reveal their identity. Hers was not, the photographs were published and her privacy was invaded.[342]

Thus Lord Hope distinguishes between photographs of general street scenes, which simply *happen* to catch a particular individual, and those that are *intended* to capture a given individual, without their knowledge. It appears tolerably clear from the remainder of his speech, however, that the photographs in *Campbell* only attracted liability because they revealed a private fact—the treatment at NA—and because of their likely damaging impact on Campbell's therapy. Lady Hale makes this point somewhat clearer, in remarking that, '*The activity photographed must be private.*'[343] In the instant case, however, and like Lord Hope, she found that the photographs in

---

[338] Ibid, at [31].   [339] Ibid, at [75].
[340] See the speeches of Lord Hope at [121] and Lady Hale at [155].   [341] Ibid, at [122].
[342] Ibid, at [123].   [343] Ibid, at [154] (emphasis added).

question *did* convey private information. In short, then, the position in English law now seems clear: provided that the activity photographed is private, and particularly if that photography is surreptitious, then the mere fact that it took place in a public space will not prevent its being protected by the law. This result shows the willingness of the English courts, manipulating the extraordinary flexibility of the doctrine of confidence, to sweep aside its formal limitations. The House of Lords, in reliance on its duty to give effect to Article 8 ECHR in private law,[344] has simply reinterpreted the notions of 'confidential information' and 'public domain' such that breach of confidence covers all information of a private character which the applicant did not intend or reasonably expect to be given mass publicity through the media. The fact that the activity in question was performed in a public place does not become irrelevant—clearly, the most sensitive and intimate moments of human life[345] are not carried on in public: rather, this factor will go to the *weight* of the privacy claim when it is balanced against competing rights and interests; but it does not operate to exclude it *per se*.

It is worth noting that *Campbell*, remarkably, takes English law further even than the German courts have in terms of protecting privacy in public. As mentioned above, the German courts allowed for such protection, but only where it was clear that the applicant had, in some sense, sought seclusion. Thus, in relation to a complaint of Princess Caroline of Monaco that photographs taken by the press of her having an intimate dinner with her boyfriend in a garden restaurant in France violated her privacy, it was found that the Princess had clearly 'retreated to a place of seclusion where [she wished] to be left alone' and that she was entitled to respect for that wish. She had 'transfer[ed] [her] private sphere of life to a place outside [her] home'. While the presumption will be that events taking place in such places do *not* attract privacy protection, this may be rebutted if, as the Court put it, it is clear by reference to 'objective criteria' that an individual wishes to 'left alone' so that she can, 'relying on the seclusion of the place, behave in a manner which she would not have done if . . . in full view of the public.'[346] Thus Princess Monaco's complaints of invasion of privacy were upheld where she had retreated to a secluded corner of a garden restaurant, because in such a situation, objective indications of a desire to be let alone could be found.

Now it is clear, in contrast, that Naomi Campbell could point to no evidence of such a retreat into seclusion: the pictures taken of her simply recorded her in a public street. The cases are hard to compare, because the information revealed in the photographs of Campbell (details of her treatment of drug addiction) inherently engaged a stronger privacy interest than those of Princess Monaco, who was simply dining with a boyfriend, so that, in crude sense, the weightier privacy interest in *Campbell* could

[344] The majority appeared to accept (Lady Hale did so explicitly) such a duty.

[345] E.g. medical treatment, sexual activity, bodily functions, intimate conversations, etc.

[346] BGH, 19 December 1995, BGHZ 131, 322–346. For further discussion of this decision, see B. Markesenis and N. Nolte, 'Some Comparative Reflections on the Right of Privacy of Public Figures in Public Places', in R. Birks (ed.) *Privacy and Loyalty*, Oxford: Clarendon, 1997, at 118, *et seq.*

be seen as compensating for the more 'public' location. Nevertheless, under the doctrinal test formulated by the German courts, Campbell would quite clearly have failed to establish an enforceable privacy interest, just because there was no 'objective' retreat into seclusion. In this, formal sense, English law has gone further in protecting privacy than German law—a remarkable outcome for a common law jurisdiction that historically has lacked any right to privacy. It is noteworthy that the submission of the Association of Editors of German Magazines, intervening in the *Von Hannover* case, suggested that German law was 'halfway between French law and United Kingdom law,'[347] a striking example of how far *Campbell* has moved the latter.

It must be considered whether this new position in English law is compatible with *Von Hannover*. It had of course been clear for some time that Strasbourg jurisprudence does not require the narrow US approach.[348] *Friedl v Austria*[349] indicates, not surprisingly, that the taking and storage of photographs of a person voluntarily taking part in a public demonstration does not violate Article 8, given that they were stored for a narrow, specified purpose:[350] there can be no reasonable expectation of privacy in such a situation. However, in *PG and JH v UK*,[351] the Court found that the secret recording of the applicants' voices whilst they were being charged in a police station, and when in their police cell, did amount to an interference with their right to respect for private life. This was in spite of the fact that a police station could clearly be termed a semi-public environment. The finding in *Niemietz v Germany*,[352] that the search of person's office at work can engage Article 8 is to a similar effect: under a simple public/private distinction, such a location would be regarded as falling outside the private sphere. Thus Strasbourg's approach to Article 8 discloses avoidance of a simple public/private distinction based on location.

Von Hannover, however, broadens the scope of Article 8 still further—a matter discussed in detail in Chapter 13.[353] It is necessary here only to deal with the 'public domain' point. Quite simply, the judgment does not even accede to the possibility of presence in public space defeating a claim in privacy. By deliberately omitting to discuss the issue, the judgment implicitly dismisses outright any possibility of the straightforward US position. But it goes further: it explicitly rejects the German courts' suggestion that privacy in public places can arise only where the applicant has in some objective sense 'sought seclusion'. Clearly the Princess, in relation to the complained of pictures—depicting her engaged in everyday activities—had done no

---

[347] Op cit, at [46].

[348] The Commission in *X v United Kingdom* ((1973) 16 YBCHE, 328) found that photographs taken by police of a woman taking part in a demonstration disclosed no *prima facie* breach of Article 8, partly because of the 'public and voluntary' nature of her activities; however, Bygraves describes the decision as 'an outdated aberration' in Strasbourg case law ('Data Protection Pursuant to the Right to Privacy in Human Rights Treaties' [1999] 6(3) *IJLIT* 247, 265).

[349] (1995) 21 EHRR 83, esp 88–91.

[350] That is, to take a record of those who participated in a demonstration, for use in prosecutions in relation to public order offences.

[351] Application 44787/98, Judgment of 25 September 2001.   [352] A 251–B para 29 (1992).

[353] At 667–83.

such thing.[354] Nevertheless, the German courts' finding that no liability could attach to such photographs was found to violate Article 8. *Von Hannover*, on its face, therefore, leaves no room at all for a straightforward (locational) public domain defence. Indeed, the Court expressly rejected locational analysis as a tool 'the criterion of spatial isolation, although apposite in theory, is in reality too vague and difficult for the person concerned to determine in advance,'[355] although, presumably, the fact that activities are performed in public can, as suggested above, go to the *weight* of the privacy claim.

What is clear, in conclusion, is that despite inconsistencies between *Campbell* and *Von Hannover* as to the types of information or images that fall within Article 8, the two judgments are broadly in harmony in terms of their treatment of the 'public domain' issue. *Campbell* has orientated English privacy law decisively away from locational analysis towards a focus upon the nature of the acts publicized. The ratio of a House of Lords judgment now inescapably provides that events taking place in a public street can not only engage Article 8 but be protected by the common law of confidence. *Von Hannover* provides the most emphatic possible endorsement of this approach as regards Article 8.

DOES *CAMPBELL* PROVIDE THE LEVEL OF PROTECTION REQUIRED BY *VON HANNOVER?*

Before concluding this chapter, it is necessary to examine whether, radical as the decision in *Campbell* clearly is in terms of the developing English law of privacy, it answers to the requirements of the decision in *Von Hannover*. The latter was, of course, delivered *after* the House of Lords' decision in *Campbell*. In order to answer this question, it is necessary to recall for a moment what the new-style 'tort of misuse of private information' or 'new-style breach of confidence' now requires. As discussed above, the sole element that the applicant must now show in English law is that he or she had a 'reasonable expectation of privacy' in the information disclosed by the respondent. Once that threshold has been crossed, the courts will then turn to balancing the privacy interest against the expression interest of the applicant.[356] We know further that where the information concerned is 'obviously private', such a reasonable expectation will exist. If it is not, then the issue of whether its disclosure would be highly offensive to the applicant may be examined, presumably along with any other relevant factors, such as the location in which the applicant was when any photographs were taken, the means used to obtain them and the likely effects upon the applicant of publication.

The speeches of the majority in *Campbell* have been criticized for leaving the new test so unclear. As Moreham comments:

---

[354] See Chapter 13 at 677–8.   [355] Op cit, at [75].   [356] A matter considered in the next chapter.

Unfortunately, however, Lord Hope gave no indication of how a court might go about determining whether information is 'obviously private': he simply said that the fact that group therapy is widely recognised as effective treatment for drug addiction and that anonymity is an important part of that process meant that the requirement was satisfied in that instance. This seems problematic: one need only refer to the fact that two members of the House of Lords and a unanimous Court of Appeal held that what was 'obviously private' to Lord Hope was not private at all, to highlight the uncertainty such a requirement could create.[357]

This, however, is incorrect. The view of the Court of Appeal and the dissenters in the Lords was essentially that once it had been conceded that the information in the first two categories could be publicized, the remaining details were not significant enough to deserve protection. But *all* the judges involved in the case, and indeed, the *Mirror* itself, agreed that *all* of it was information that Campbell would have been entitled to keep private had she not told public lies about it.[358] In other words, all the judges in this case *did* recognize these details as 'obviously private.' Moreover, Moreham's broader point does not take account of the extensive citation of Article 8 case law: for example, the finding in *Z v Finland* that, 'the protection of . . . medical data is of *fundamental importance* to a person's enjoyment of his or her right to respect for private . . . life'[359] was quite evidently a major reason for the finding that the information was obviously private. Lord Nicholls, as noted above, spoke of determining whether the information fell within the remit of Article 8.[360] In other words, the test propounded—of a reasonable expectation of privacy, of whether the information is obviously private—is to be structured by reference to the Article 8 case law. Of course in this particular case, their Lordships took account of a variety of other factors: the duty of confidentiality lying upon those attending at NA, the harm that could be caused by its breach, and the fact that the case concerned therapeutic treatment, amongst others. But it is quite evident that their Lordships took the view that only certain classes of information would qualify as being 'obviously private'—as the citation of *Lenah Game Meats* itself indicates.

What then is the essential point of difference here between Strasbourg and English law? On its face, it is this: as discussed in the previous chapter,[361] on a literal reading, the Strasbourg decision takes the view that any publication of an unauthorized photograph specifically taken of a particular person[362] engaged in an everyday activity outside their official duties will involve a *prima facie* violation of Article 8. We referred to that reading of the case as 'the absolutist view'. In contrast, under English law, the

---

[357] N. Moreham, 'Recognising Privacy in England and New Zealand', (2005) 63(3) *CLJ* 555, at 556.

[358] See Lord Nicholls, *Campbell v MGN Ltd* [2004] 2 AC 457 at [24]: 'It was common ground between the parties that in the ordinary course the information in all five categories would attract the protection of article 8.' The Court of Appeal had made exactly the same finding: *Campbell v MGN Ltd* [2003] QB 633 at [38].

[359] 25 EHRR 371 at [95] (emphasis added).   [360] Above note 269 and accompanying text.

[361] See pp 667–83.

[362] The words 'specifically taken of a particular person' are used because this judgment would presumably not apply to photographs of normal street scenes in which individuals happen to be caught.

applicant must identify information that relates to a specific aspect of private life, as more narrowly understood, such as health, sexuality and the like. The difference is apparent at its starkest in the speech of Lady Hale:

We have not so far held that the mere fact of covert photography is sufficient to make the information contained in the photograph confidential. *The activity photographed must be private*. If this had been, and had been presented as, a picture of Naomi Campbell going about her business in a public street, there could have been no complaint . . . If . . . she pops out to the shops for a bottle of milk . . . there is nothing essentially private about that information nor can it be expected to damage her private life.[363]

Lord Hoffman appeared to agree:

In the present case, the pictures were taken without Ms Campbell's consent. That in my opinion is not enough to amount to a wrongful invasion of privacy. The famous and even the not so famous who go out in public must accept that they may be photographed without their consent, just as they may be observed by others without their consent.[364]

Lady Hale's comment that publications showing such pictures 'may not be a high order of freedom of speech but there is nothing to justify interfering with it'[365] is particularly significant. It can only be interpreted as meaning that in such a case, Article 8 would simply not be engaged, precisely the converse of the finding in *Von Hannover*.

Can the two decisions be reconciled? Of course, it should be recalled that whilst under the Human Rights Act, the UK courts are bound to act compatibly with 'the Convention rights' themselves,[366] they are not bound by the Strasbourg juris-prudence; it is something they must only take into account.[367] But assuming that the English courts will not wish flatly to disobey or disregard *Von Hannover*, it may be assumed that they will seek to reconcile the two decisions.[368] Interestingly, the Court of Appeal in *Douglas III*, the only major decision taken since the two judgments came out, did not even advert to the obvious differences between the two, let alone suggest how they could be resolved. To do so was not necessary in the case in hand, but at some point, the issue will arise. When it does, there will be two obvious courses of action.

One will be to interpret *Campbell* as simply holding that private facts are those falling within the scope of Article 8, as defined by the Strasbourg jurisprudence, now including *Von Hannover*. In other words, a person would have a reasonable expectation of privacy whenever they were engaged in activities that did not form part

---

[363] *Campbell v MGN Ltd* [2004] 2 AC 457 at [154] (emphasis added).   [364] Ibid, at [73].

[365] Ibid, at [154].

[366] S 6(1). In fact, of course, the decision in *Campbell* does not make it clear whether this is an absolute duty in the sphere of private common law: see Chapter 3 at 134–40.

[367] S 2(1).

[368] Lord Slynn has said that, 'In the absence of some special circumstances. . .the court should follow any clear and constant jurisprudence of the European Court of Human Rights' (*R v Secretary of State for the Environment, Transport and the Regions, ex parte Holding & Barnes Plc (Alconbury)* [2001] 2 WLR 1389, at [26]), a finding since affirmed in *R v Secretary of State for the Home Department ex parte Anderson* [2002] WL 31523285, per Lord Bingham, at [18].

of their official duties, however trivial. It would effectively convert the action for breach of confidence into a right to one's own image, subject to an 'official duties' defence.[369] This would have the effect of broadening enormously the reach of the common law; publishing a photograph of Naomi Campbell popping out for a pint of milk would become *prima facie* tortious. Given the historic caution of the English judges in relation to privacy, such a course seems most unlikely, and, we argued in the previous chapter, undesirable.[370] However, it should be noted that it is possible to find in *Campbell* some evidence that English law may be prepared to accept such an extension.

First of all, there is the almost teasing hint in Lady Hale's speech that the common law may not have exhausted its evolution in this respect: 'We have not *so far* held that the mere fact of covert photography is sufficient to make the information contained in the photograph confidential' (emphasis added).[371] Second, some little noticed *dicta* of Lord Hoffman add an important caveat to the notion that the act photographed 'must be private'. His Lordship comments:

Likewise, the publication of a photograph taken by intrusion into a private place (for example, by a long distance lens) may in itself by such an infringement, even if there is nothing embarrassing about the picture itself: *Hellewell v Chief Constable of Derbyshire* [1985] 1 WLR 804, 807.[372]

This in fact is either a simple mistake, or a judicial sleight of hand: for, whilst purporting simply to cite a principle established in *Hellewell*, these dicta actually *extend* that principle.[373] For in that case, Laws J referred to a photograph being taken of someone 'engaged in some private act'. As Lord Hoffman puts it, the requirement of some 'private act'—precisely what Lady Hale insisted upon in relation to photography in a public place—is seemingly dropped. Thus anyone photographed *in a private place*, regardless of the nature of what they are doing, can claim a *prima facie* infringement of private life. Lord Hoffman appears here to be suggesting a two-tier standard: in a public place, the applicant must show that the nature of the act was private (embarrassing or humiliating according to Lord Hoffman specifically); but if photographed in a private place, this is not necessary. In other words, privacy may be locational *or* action-based.

Finally, it should be noticed that Lord Hope was much more receptive, to put it at its lowest, to the position later taken by Strasbourg in *Von Hannover*:

The taking of photographs in a public street must . . . be taken to be one of the ordinary incidents of living in a free community. The real issue is whether publicising the content of the photographs would be offensive . . . A person who just happens to be in the street when the photograph was taken and appears in it only incidentally cannot as a general rule object to the publication of the photograph, for the reasons given by L'Heureux-Dubé and Bastarache JJ in *Aubry v Editions Vice-Versa Inc* [1998] 1 SCR 591, para 59. But the situation

---

[369] Or presumably that the particular person's image was only caught as part of a picture of a general street scene.

[370] See pp 682–3.   [371] *Campbell v MGN Ltd* [2004] 2 AC 457, at [154].   [372] Ibid, at [75].

[373] In fact, of course, *Hellewell* established no such principle: it merely contained *obiter* comments to this effect.

is different if the public nature of the place where a photograph is taken was simply used as background for one or more persons who constitute the true subject of the photograph. The question then arises, balancing the rights at issue, where the public's right to information can justify dissemination of a photograph taken without authorisation: *Aubry*, para 61. The European Court has recognised that a person who walks down a public street will inevitably be visible to any member of the public who is also present and, in the same way, to a security guard viewing the scene through closed circuit television: *PG v JH v United Kingdom*, para 57. But, as the court pointed out in the same paragraph, private life considerations may arise once any systematic or permanent record comes into existence of such material from the public domain.[374]

Here, in his apparent acceptance of the *Aubry* position that publication of a photograph taken without consent requires justification, in entering no qualification that the photograph taken without authorization must depict a private act of some sort, his Lordship appears to endorse the view that publishing deliberately-taken photographs of an individual without consent *does prima facie* engage the right to private life: thus the interest in private life will have to be balanced against 'the public's right to information'. But in this respect, Lord Hope was not supported by his brethren. As the Court of Appeal in *Douglas III* remarked, 'Baroness Hale was not prepared to go this far.'[375] It is apparent, therefore, that whilst the thrust of the speeches in *Campbell* are incompatible with the absolutist view of *Von Hannover*, there are also harbingers of further movement of the common law in the direction of the latter.

Despite these harbingers, one response to *Von Hannover* would be, not to develop the common law further than the point reached in Campbell, but for those who seek a remedy in respect of anodyne pictures to turn instead to the Data Protection Act. Whilst, as noted above,[376] the Act does not allow for the granting of interlocutory injunctions, it may be suggested that injunctions are primarily needed where the action relates to private information that is a secret—details of sexual life, of an affair, of medical or drug treatment, plastic surgery and so on. In such cases, the primary motivation is to prevent the publicizing of the information in question. But where the mischief is not the revelation of private facts, but the kind of systematic press harassment seen in *Von Hannover*, the need for an injunction is not so urgent, though it might, of course be considered desirable. Given that this is the case, the Data Protection Act, considered above,[377] appears well able to answer to the requirements of even the absolutist reading of *Von Hannover*. It will be recalled that the Act protects against the unfair processing of 'personal data', which is very broadly defined, and would plainly include photographs of the sort that were at issue in *Von Hannover*.[378] As discussed above, the Act, as interpreted, also provides that the surreptitious obtaining of photographs amount to 'unfair' obtaining of data, thus breaching the first Data Protection Principle. Thus, it would appear that where an applicant wanted to bring an action in relation to publication of unauthorized pictures, but the new privacy tort

---

[374] *Campbell v MGN Ltd* [2004] 2 AC 457, [122].   [375] op cit at [90].
[376] See p 721.   [377] See pp 717–21.   [378] See p 718.

could not be used because the pictures in question did not reveal any particularly sensitive information, such a person could instead use the DPA. Indeed, since the Act bites on 'processing' of data, rather than its disclosure or publication, an action could seemingly be brought *before* publication, simply in relation to the taking of pictures and the storage of them on the newspaper's database.[379] The newspaper would of course have a 'public interest defence',[380] but it would have to be interpreted and applied compatibly with both Articles 8 and 10,[381] and in the case of an anodyne picture published purely for gossip value, it seems most unlikely that the defence would be made out.[382] For those who find the common law falling short of the standard of protection attained in *Von Hannover*, the DPA may therefore be the remedy, provided an injunction is not required.[383] Furthermore, in cases where the complaint was persistent intrusion, door-stepping and photography, rather than pub-lication, then, as discussed above, a possible remedy exists under the Protection from Harassment Act 1997.[384]

Another possibility, in terms of bringing UK law into compliance with *Von Hannover* through the *common law* would be for English courts to 'read down' the decision in *Von Hannover* to bring it closer to the approach taken in *Campbell*. We suggested in Chapter 13 that there is a plausible reading of *Von Hannover*, (although one not without its difficulties) by which the decision is simply authority for the proposition that that the systematic and persistent pursuit and photographing of a person going about their everyday life and the publication of those photographs in mass circulation newspapers can give rise to a breach of Article 8. We suggested that what we actually have in *Von Hannover* is a judgment that combines two elements in coming to a finding that Article 8 is engaged: (a) the fact that the pictures related to the Princess's everyday life, not her official functions, *and* (b) the constant intrusion that the persist-ent photographing represented. If this reading of the case were adopted, the result in English law would be as follows. In determining whether a photograph of a person taken in a public or semi-public space[385] could amount to 'private information' for the purposes of the new privacy tort, the question would be *either* (a), whether the photo-graph taken of the person revealed or exposed some intimate aspect of their life (as in *Campbell* or *Peck*) *or* (b), whether the cumulative impact of the persistent taking and publishing of such photographs was such as to give rise to a level of intrusion sufficient to breach Article 8. Such a finding could be accommodated within the new law: while the information in the particular photograph might not be 'obviously private', the publication of the photograph in the context of such continuous harassment, could

---

[379] Though see above as to the restrictions on remedies: 721.

[380] Above, text to and notes 91 and 92.   [381] Per s 3(1) HRA.

[382] As discussed in the next chapter, the Court of Appeal in *Douglas III* found that there was no public interest in the publication of snatched photographs of a celebrity wedding: op cit, at [254].

[383] Above, text to and note 91.   [384] Above, at 716–17.

[385] As discussed above, it appears from *dicta* of Lord Hoffman, that photographs of someone on private property may be found to engage the new tort of invasion of privacy without the need to show that they reveal any particularly intimate or sensitive information.

satisfy the alternative test of being 'highly offensive to a reasonable person of ordinary sensibilities.'[386] Thus, if a case were brought in the English courts that concerned a one-off photograph of, e.g. a celebrity jogging in the park, the lack of persistent intrusion would clearly be a distinguishing factor that could lead the court to find that the *Von Hannover* principle was not engaged on the facts and that the information was neither obviously private, nor was its publication highly offensive.

This possible solution is not without its problems: for one thing, it would give rise to a fair degree of legal uncertainty as what level of pursuit or door-stepping would be considered enough to make publication of photographs so obtained 'highly offensive'; for another, given that the press harassment would, in most cases, consist of pursuit by journalists representing a number of different publications, it might seem unfair to single out one publication as 'highly offensive' when the real complaint was as to the cumulative impact of press attention. As to the latter, it may be said that the court would not be unreasonable in expecting journalists to have regard to the cumulative impact upon the applicant of mass media attention, of which they were a part, provided the defendants were aware of it. As to the former, it could be answered that the law routinely relies upon standards based on such vague and open-ended concepts as 'reasonableness', in, say, the law of negligence[387] and the law of harassment,[388] and that judicial decisions could fairly quickly start to clarify what types of conduct would tend to incur liability.[389] Examples could include: persisting in photography after being asked to stop on more than one occasion; the persistent use of surreptitious photography; intrusion into situations which, although not sensitive enough to amount to 'obviously private' occasions, yet had some element of intimacy, such as kissing a lover or playing with a child; persistent intrusion into semi-private locations, such as quiet restaurants, or secluded beaches. Whilst the press might well be alarmed at the thought of their liability being based upon such relatively open-ended principles, such a position would presumably be clearly preferable from a journalistic perspective to the imposition of the absolute *Von Hannover* standard.

CONCLUSION

The House of Lords decision in *Campbell* has given English law a privacy tort; more precisely a cause of action in respect of the misuse of personal information. Whether English judges continue to refer to it as 'breach of confidence' or more

---

[386] See above, pp 744–6.

[387] The notions of 'reasonable' forseeability of harm, and a reasonable level of care are central to the tort.

[388] See above at 716–17.

[389] For example, persisting in photography after being asked to stop on more than one occasion; the persistent use of surreptitious photography; intrusion into situations which, although not sensitive enough to amount to 'obviously private' occasions, yet had some element of intimacy, e.g. kissing a lover, playing with a child etc.

boldly, recognize that 'the law of confidence . . . like a mother swollen with the child of privacy . . . [has] given birth and the umbilical cord cut'[390] may be a matter of semantics only. The new tort consists of two elements: facts in relation to which there is a reasonable expectation of privacy, and unauthorized use of those facts. Once that threshold is crossed, the court moves directly to balancing the privacy interest with the competing expression rights of the press, an exercise driven by the Convention. Since the test of 'reasonable expectation of privacy' was that used very recently by the court in *Peck v UK*, it may in fact be said that, whilst we notionally have only indirect application of Article 8 through the common law action of confidence, the position arrived it as more or less the same as it would have been had Article 8 and its associated jurisprudence been directly applied by the courts. As commentators who have called for the radical development of breach of confidence to protect privacy, and for confidence to become merely a formal vessel through which Article 8 principles are given force, we warmly welcome this development. We believe that the goals in view in developing a privacy law—the protection of human dignity and autonomy, the movement away from the demeaning and debasing pursuit of certain figures and the destruction of their privacy in order to sell newspapers—are more than sufficient to encourage the judiciary to continue on the path that they have taken in developing a common law right to privacy.

Whether the newly-created English privacy tort goes as far as the decision in *Von Hannover* is, as discussed, highly debatable. As noted above, *Von Hannover appears* to require liability under Article 8 for the publication of any pictures taken without consent of people in everyday situations—precisely the 'popping out for a pint of milk' scenario that Lady Hale expressly stated would *not* incur liability under the common law. This chapter has discussed an interpretation of the latter that renders it considerably less absolutist in its demands on national privacy laws and it is to be anticipated that some such reading of *Von Hannover* will be adopted by the English courts as a means of reconciling that decision with *Campbell*. If not, as discussed above, the DPA appears well able to fill the gap between the two decisions. The following chapter considers defences available to the media in response to a claim for misuse of private information.

---

[390] These dicta are from the initial judgment of Jack J in *A v B*, 30 April 2001 (unreported), 16–17. For a very recent decision applying the 'reasonable expectation of privacy' test to a leak of Prince Charles' diaries, see *HRH Prince of Wales v Associated Newspapers* [2006] All ER CD 276 (Mar). See also *McKennit v Ash* [2005] EWHC 3003 (QB).

15

DEFENCES TO
PRIVACY ACTIONS
AND REMEDIES

'Exposure of the self to others in varying degrees is a concomitant of life in a civilised society. The risk of this exposure is an essential incident of life in a society which places a primary value upon freedom of speech and of the press'[1]

'The problem is whether the role, impact and obsessions of the media have now become a democratic liability'[2]

INTRODUCTION

As the previous chapter of this book made clear, English law now recognizes an effective privacy remedy against the misuse of personal information, even if doubts linger as to the precise parameters of that action. Any such remedy inevitably raises an acute apparent conflict with press freedom; moreover, it is controversial in relation to those who have themselves made use of the media to gain publicity for themselves, especially where such deliberately procured publicity has involved making disclosures about the person's private life. Therefore this chapter considers the 'defences' that the media may rely upon once a *prima facie* case of misuse of private information has been made out that answer to these concerns. We place the word 'defences' in inverted commas because, whilst the claim of waiver, or implied consent, discussed in a moment, *does* operate as a defence, in the sense that it is something that the media must prove, the claim that the applicant's case would place an unwarranted restriction upon media *freedom* is not, strictly, a defence as such: rather, once raised (as it invariably will be by the media), the court itself must ensure that it strikes a proper balance between the claims of private life and of expression.

---

[1] US Supreme Court: *Times Inc v Hill* U.S. 374 (1966).
[2] J. Seaton, 'Public, Private and the Media' (2003) *Political Quarterly*, 174.

These two issues of 'waiver' and the threat to press freedom are the most oft invoked by opponents and critics of any right to privacy and represent two of the most controversial issues this area of law raises. However, the introduction into UK law of a positive right to freedom of expression in the form of Article 10 of the Convention has answered the argument that the judiciary could not justifiably develop further potential curbs on expression, unless that value was itself correspondingly strengthened.[3] This chapter will argue, moreover, that the perception of inevitable conflict between speech and privacy is exaggerated and simplistic, and that an examination of the values underlying each reveals them to be in many respects mutually supportive, rather than invariably antagonistic. Our conclusion will be that the advent of the HRA has given the courts an opportunity to develop and re-balance the common law quite radically so as to provide proper protection for human dignity and autonomy, while carefully preserving the genuine and legitimate watchdog role of the press. Since the exemption for the press in the Data Protection Act[4] likewise requires a balancing act to be performed between the demands of privacy and the public interest in publicity, exactly the same principles should be applied to resolving this conflict, and the analysis below may be taken to apply equally to the DPA. However, we will also explain how the predominant approach of the courts prior to *Campbell*[5] failed to afford privacy the respect it deserves as a Convention right, while remaining uncritically receptive to the claims of what, in many cases, amounts to markedly 'low value' expression. In this area in particular, though, we will suggest that *Campbell* appears to provide a definitive correction to the problems thrown up by earlier decisions, if properly applied. The chapter concludes by looking briefly at the issue of remedies in privacy cases.

'IMPLIED CONSENT' OR 'WAIVER'

As suggested above, an argument often raised by the media in response to privacy cases is the claim that the applicant has sought publicity in the past and therefore in some way has consented, or should be deemed to have consented, to a current revelation to which he or she now objects. A recent work on privacy suggests referring to such a claim as one of 'waiver'.[6] Reported remarks of Lord Wakeham, Chair of the Press Complaints Commission, to the effect that the former Princess of Wales had made herself 'fair game' for public analysis of her private life by discussing it herself on television, exemplify this attitude.[7] The Commission he chaired has also consistently taken this line. As the IPPR remarked in a recent report:

---

[3] See, for example, R. Bagshaw, 'Obstacles on the Path to Privacy Torts' in R. Birks (ed.) *Privacy and Loyalty*, Oxford: Clarendon, 1997 at 143.

[4] See Chapter 14 at 721.   [5] [2004] 2 WLR 1232.

[6] Tugendhat and Christie, *The Law of Privacy and the Media*, Oxford: OUP, 2002, at 336.

[7] *The Times*, 2 May 1996.

The [PCC] has made clear on a number of occasions that it will take into account the extent to which similar matters have been discussed by the complainant or have been published before without complaint. [Its stance has been that]: 'Privacy is a right which can be compromised and those who talk about their private lives on their own terms must expect that there may be others who will do so, without their consent, in a less than agreeable way.'[8]

English judges in breach of confidence cases have in the past shown some receptivity to this claim, although there has been a tendency to conflate it with the different claim that the applicant's private life has *per se* lost its quality of confidentiality. In *Woodward v Hutchins*,[9] the Court of Appeal denied the applicants (pop singers) an injunction against a former employee in respect of newspaper articles giving detailed accounts of the singers' private lives. Bridge LJ reasoned that, 'those who seek and welcome publicity of every kind bearing upon their private lives so long as it shows them in a favourable light are in no position to complain of an invasion of their privacy by publicity which shows them in an unfavourable light'.[10] The decision is not clearly reasoned: the finding of the court, which was reached at great speed, may also have been directed towards the idea that, having sought publicity themselves, the group had effectively placed their private lives in the public domain; the decision also seems to have motivated by the idea that it was in the public interest to correct the false favourable impression that early publicity had given.[11] Lord Denning found: 'There is no doubt whatever that this pop group sought publicity ... [relating to] their private lives also.'[12] Nevertheless, a similar approach was taken in *Lennon v News Group Newspapers*[13] in which one party to a marriage was denied relief in respect of personal information concerning the relationship on the grounds that both had sought publicity about it on previous occasions. This attitude also prevails under the American tort: Elwood argues that celebrities[14] may be seen to have waived their right to privacy; thus he claims the defence to any privacy actions they may bring is implied consent.

Now a *realistic* doctrine of implied consent is clearly necessary, so that, for example, there would be no question of photographs of the Queen appearing on the balcony of Buckingham Palace engaging liability, since consent, although unspoken, would clearly be implicit.[15] Even where such consent may reasonably be assumed, the issue of the *extent* of that consent must be carefully established: as Tugendhat and Christie put

---

[8] D. Tambini and C. Heyward, 'Regulating the trade in secrets: policy options', in Tambini and Heyward (eds) *Ruled by Recluses? Privacy, Journalism and the Media after the Human Rights Act*, London: IPPR, 2002, at 85.

[9] [1977] WLR 760.

[10] Ibid, 765. See also Lord Denning at 763: 'There is no doubt that this ... group sought publicity ... [relating to] their private lives.'

[11] Ibid, at 764. [12] Ibid, at 763. [13] [1978] FSR 573.

[14] 'Outing, Privacy and the First Amendment' [1992] *Yale LJ* 747.

[15] See the comments of the Major Government in *Privacy and Media Intrusion: the Government's Response* Cm. 2918, para 3.14 and the rejoinder by Bingham LJ, 'Should there be a law to protect rights of personal privacy?' (1996) 5 *EHRLR* 450, 457.

it, 'The general rule is that is that consent will only be established where it is shown that the claimant agreed to the publication of substantially the same matter as was in fact published.'[16] In any event, in the typical privacy case, and particularly where the information has been obtained surreptitiously, it would be absurd for a newspaper to claim that the applicant would have given actual consent to publication if asked. Similarly, the claim that previous, voluntary revelations constitute some kind of generalized, all-purpose consent to future invasions of privacy is simply not plausible: no-one can realistically suppose that when for example a celebrity gives an interview to a newspaper about particular problems in a past or current marriage, she thereby gives *carte blanche* to the media to publish any information relating to her personal life which they can obtain in future. Such a notion is roundly rejected by the French courts, who only accept 'consent' defences if consent has been given to the actual publication in question or where a new publication merely repeats facts already published consensually:[17] Thus, as the quotation from *Woodward*[18] indicates, the 'consent' terminology is in reality merely a cloak for a purely normative contention: that since in the past the applicant has sought publicity for personal information, she *should not be allowed* to complain about this publication.

Clearly this doctrine could take two different forms. In what could be termed its 'blanket' form, courting of publicity for one area of private life would result in a loss of protection for all areas, an evidently unattractive proposition. Less drastic in effect is what could be called the 'differentiated' approach, whereby protection for private life is lost only where the applicant has courted publicity in relation to the same area of private life as that covered by the complained-of publication. Under this approach, it should also follow that, contrary to the PCC decision in *Carling*, a claim would still lie where the publication went further in terms of intimate detail than any disclosures voluntarily made by the claimant.

'WAIVER': THE POST-HRA CASE LAW

Decisions on this point since the HRA present a somewhat mixed picture, but any confusion has now, it is submitted, been decisively cleared up by the House of Lords' decision in *Campbell*. Brooke LJ in *Douglas*[19] was dismissive of the argument that the couple's admitted previous courting of publicity precluded protection for their privacy, remarking that he 'did not obtain any assistance' by citation of *Woodward v Hutchins*', a case which, he said, 'preceded modern developments in practice in relation to breach of confidence claims and which was concerned with the appropriateness of an injunction framed in astonishingly wide terms'. The court instead treated as relevant only the couple's approach to publicity *in relation to the information in*

---

[16] Op cit, at 334 and note 35.

[17] See Picard, 'The Right to Privacy in French Law', in Markesenis (ed.) *Protecting Privacy*, Oxford: Clarendon, 1999, at 91–2.

[18] Op cit, above.   [19] [2001] QB 967, 995.

dispute—namely the wedding itself.[20] Similarly in the Court of Appeal judgment in *Campbell v MGN*, it was found that Campbell 'has courted, rather than shunned publicity, [volunteering] . . . information about some aspects of her private life.'[21] But, as in *Douglas*, the only disclosures treated as relevant were those made in relation to the information in dispute—her voluntary statements that she did not take drugs and was not an addict. Had she not made these statements, she would, the court found, have been entitled to keep the fact of her treatment for drug addiction confidential,[22] despite her courting of publicity in other areas. In *Theakston*,[23] the judge accepted that the applicant's previous courting of favourable publicity in relation to his sexual life rendered it inapt for him to complain of the unfavourable publicity given to him now,—but that publicity of course related to the same area as he himself had publicized—his sexual life,[24]—a point echoed by Lindsay J in *Douglas II*.[25] However, the judge's finding in *Douglas II* was that that the couple's intention to sell photographs of their wedding did *not* rob it entirely of its private quality, the judge recognizing the value the couple attached to control over the images presented to the public.[26] Similarly in *Mills v News Group Newspapers*,[27] the judge 'took no account' of the argument that 'Ms Mills has for several years courted publicity.' Only in *A v B plc*[28] is there some confusion on this point. Woolf CJ remarked: 'If you have courted publicity then you have *less ground* to object to the intrusion which follows.' These dicta, though they do not make the point clear, presumably refer only to courting publicity *in relation to one's private life*, not, for example, to one's sporting prowess. His Lordship also failed to specify that only courting publicity in the same area as that now complained about can serve to weaken a privacy claim. However, the remarks above were in any event plainly *obiter*—the Court having approved Jack J's finding that the applicant had not in fact courted publicity—and it is apparent that the weight of authority from the other decisions is clearly hostile to the notion of a blanket waiver.

Any doubt on this matter has, in any event, now been laid to rest by the House of Lords. All their Lordships accepted that, as Lord Hoffman put it, '[Campbell] is a public figure who has had a long and symbiotic relationship with the media.'[29] Decisive rejection of the 'blanket waiver' approach, may, however, be seen in the fact that *none* of their Lordships appeared even to entertain the view that Campbell's publicity-seeking past could, *per se* destroy protection for her private life. The applicant herself had conceded that the Mirror was entitled to publish the fact that she was a drug addict and was receiving treatment for her addiction, because it was accepted that the press was entitled

---

[20] *Woodward* was also doubted at first instance in *Campbell v Frisbee* [2002] EMLR 10, at [40] and [41]: 'Lightman J may well be right to suggest that *Woodward v Hutchins* should no longer be applied . . .' [2003] EMCLR 3, at [34].

[21] [2003] QB 633, CA, 649.   [22] Ibid, at 657.   [23] *Theakston v MGN* [2002] EMLR 22.

[24] Ibid, at [89].

[25] 'I would accept that a claimant who has himself publicised a certain area of his private life (for example his sexual proclivities and activity) might well lose the protection otherwise available to him in that area *or, possibly, even more* generally: [2003] 3 All ER 996 at [226] (emphasis added).

[26] Ibid, at [217] and [224].   [27] [2001] EMLR 41, at [34].   [28] [2002] 3 WLR 542, at 552C.

[29] [2004] 2 WLR 1232, at [57].

to expose the falsity of her previous public statements that she did not take drugs and was not a drug addict. This, however, was on the basis that there was a public interest in preventing the public from being misled,[30] *not* on any notion that publicity-seeking *in itself* destroys an individual's reasonable expectation of privacy. The ratio of the judgment—that Campbell was entitled to privacy in respect of the details of her treatment for drug addiction—indicates not only that there can be no blanket waiver by prior publicity but that even publicity in relation to the area now complained of will defeat a complaint in privacy only in relation to those matters explicitly discussed by the applicant: Campbell's general statements that she was not a drug addict did not defeat her expectation of privacy in relation to the *details* of her treatment for drug addiction.

But the rejection of any notion of blanket waiver does not inhere only in the ratio of the judgment; it is expressed in the clearest possible terms in *dicta* of Lord Hoffman, significantly, one of the minority who found against Campbell:

[Campbell] is a public figure who has had a long and symbiotic relationship with the media. In my opinion, that would not in itself justify publication. A person may attract or even seek publicity about some aspects of his or her life without creating any public interest in the publication of personal information about other matters.[31]

Lord Hoffman suggested a more subtle version of waiver:

She and they have for many years both fed upon each other. She has given them stories to sell their papers and they have given her publicity to promote her career. This does not deprive Ms Campbell of the right to privacy in respect of areas of her life which she has not chosen to make public. But I think it means that when a newspaper publishes what is in substance a legitimate story, she cannot insist upon too great a nicety of judgment in the circumstantial detail with which the story is presented.[32]

In other words, waiver can operate so as to increase the latitude to the editor as to what details (perhaps including photographs) are needed to give the story colour and credibility.

Nevertheless, even the acceptance of the notion of a differentiated waiver is troubling in terms of the judicial attitude towards privacy. In none of these cases did the judges seek to enquire whether such a notion has any principled grounding in Article 8, though Lindsay J did remark in *Douglas II* that 'To hold that those who have sought any publicity lose all protection would be to repeal Article 8's application to very many of those who are likely most to need it.'[33] It was urged by the applicant before the Court of Appeal in *Campbell* that 'it is incompatible with Article 8 to say that a claimant who has welcomed publicity is in "no position to complain" of an invasion of privacy which shows him/her in an unfavourable light',[34] but no court has

---

[30] See, e.g., Lord Nicholls (ibid) at [24]: 'where a public figure chooses to present a false image and make untrue pronouncements about his or her life, the press will normally be entitled to put the record straight.' This approach was endorsed by Lord Hoffman at [58] and Lord Hope at [82].

[31] Ibid, at [57].   [32] Ibid, at [66].   [33] Op cit, at [226].

[34] Op cit, at 645. For a recent case, in which it was clearly accepted that waiver should be 'differential' but in which the doctrine had a disturbingly strong effect upon the decision, see *A v B* (2005) EMLR 36.

properly considered the point. There are, in fact, serious difficulties of principle with the notion of 'waiver', a matter to which we now turn.

WAIVER AND UNDERLYING PRIVACY VALUES

As we have argued previously,[35] the notion that a voluntary disclosure of private information prevents an individual from being able to complain about an *involuntary* disclosure is in fact wholly incompatible with the core privacy value of the individual's right to *control* over the release of personal information. All of us exercise this right to selective disclosure in our social lives: we may tell one friend an intimate secret and not another; at times be open, at others more reticent. No one denies our right to do this. A friend who is shown a personal letter on one occasion does not assume that he has thereby acquired the right to read, uninvited, all other such letters. In other words, to suggest that public figures should be treated as estopped from complaining about unwanted publicity because they had previously sought it would deny them the very *control* over personal information that is inherent in the notion of personal autonomy; previous disclosures amount not to an *abandonment* of the right to privacy, but an exercise of it.

It should be conceded, however, that, while this argument has considerable logical force, some unease may remain at the notion of completely disregarding an individual's own attitude to publicizing their private life, particularly where they have done so for gain. As Tugendhat and Christie put it:

[Celebrities] often court and gain from media coverage and the underlying concern in *Woodward* and *Lennon* surely was that celebrities might manipulate the media and the public by selective release of personal information for personal gain whilst exploiting the law of confidence to prevent unwanted revelations.[36]

There are, perhaps two points to be made in response to this concern: first, where such 'manipulation' amounted to a misleading of the public on a matter of importance, there would be a strong public interest defence to any privacy action.[37] Second, the concern could be answered through reasoning in the following way. A law of privacy cannot protect the right to selective disclosure in relation to any and all information relating to a person; only information that in some way relate to *private life*. There may be extreme situations in which the applicant has so thoroughly and repeatedly placed details about the same subject matter which it is now proposed to publish, that it may be inferred that the information in question is not any longer, to that person, truly private or personal.[38] Where the information has, as it were been sold 'for gain',

---

[35] Phillipson and Fenwick, 'Breach of Confidence as a Privacy Remedy in the Human Rights Act Era' (2000) 63 C 57 MLR, 660, 680.

[36] Op cit, at 344.   [37] This issue is discussed further below, at pp 800–5.

[38] Note that under the Data Protection Act 1998, the data controller has a defence in relation to processing of 'sensitive personal data' if that information has been made public as a result of steps deliberately taken by the data subject' (Sch 3, para 5).

as Tugendhat and Christie put it, this inference would be stronger: there is a clear difference between confiding a private fact to certain people in order to enhance one's relationship with them, and simply selling it. Thus in cases where a celebrity has, quite genuinely comodified an aspect of their personal life, it may be concluded that it has lost its private character. However, it is suggested that such an approach would be apposite only in fairly extreme cases. This appeared to be the approach adopted by Lord Nicholls in *Campbell*:

When talking to the media Miss Campbell went out of her way to say that, unlike many fashion models, she did not take drugs. By repeatedly making these assertions in public Miss Campbell could no longer have a reasonable expectation that this aspect of her life should be private. Public disclosure that, contrary to her assertions, she did in fact take drugs and had a serious drug problem for which she was being treated was not disclosure of private information.[39]

It will also be important to apply even this limited test with discernment. The US courts have not always done so: on some occasions they have drawn no distinction between voluntary and involuntary attainment of notoriety. Thus in *Metter v Los Angeles Examiner*[40] a person committed suicide by jumping from a high building and the court found that the victim had made herself a public figure 'for a brief period' through her own actions. However, the same result—denial of any right to privacy— was reached in *Kelly v Post Publishing Co.*,[41] where there was no element of voluntariness at all, the victim having died in a car accident. US courts have also been prone to finding that once someone has achieved notoriety in one area, whole other areas of their lives are opened up to close scrutiny as a result, as for example in *Ann-Margaret v High Society Magazine Inc*,[42] in which a well known actress was denied relief in respect of the publication of a nude photographs of her. This is clearly ethically inept. For example, a family might seek to launch a media campaign with a view to obtaining public support for a particular object, such as drawing attention to an injustice perpetrated on a family member by the criminal justice system, or in order to raise funds for the medical treatment of a child.[43] Once the object is attained, they may seek to retire from the public gaze. A sensitive application of this test would provide them with protection in so doing.

PRIVACY AND PRESS FREEDOM

INTRODUCTION

The most important concern relating to the development of a privacy remedy has always been the fear that the action will pose an unacceptable risk to freedom of the

---

[39] Op cit, at [24].   [40] 35 Cal. App. 2d 304 (1939).
[41] 327 Mass 275 (1951).   [42] 498 F Supp 401 (1980).
[43] The background to the decision in *R v Cambridge Health Authority, ex parte B* [1995] 1 WLR 898.

press. The main insurance against this possibility has always rested with the public interest defence, whereby disclosure of admittedly confidential information is permitted if this would serve the public interest,[44] now of course bolstered by Article 10 of the Convention. The guidance available from Strasbourg as to the correct approach to be taken in balancing the two Convention articles has been discussed in Chapter 13 and its application to the particular area we are concerned with here will be considered in a moment. But, given the lack of *detailed* consideration from Strasbourg of the issues at stake here, we suggest that if the balancing act is to produce consistent, principled and reasonably foreseeable resolutions of the conflicting interests at stake, rather than amounting merely to *ad hoc* exercises of judicial 'common sense', it is essential that it be approached with an awareness of the values underlying both freedom of the press and privacy itself, discussed in Chapters 1 and 13. As will be discussed below, it was precisely the failure to anchor the balancing exercise in the values underlying both speech and privacy that has led to a number of unsatisfactory outcomes and unconvincing reasoning in this area in a number of major decisions under the Act, though as in other areas, *Campbell* provides an encouraging example. Thus readers are referred to the discussion in Chapter 13 as an essential backdrop to the following analysis.

ASSESSING THE VALUE OF THE SPEECH CLAIM

It is well known that certain types of privacy interests are treated by Strasbourg as more weighty than others. Thus certain categories of material, such as those relating to health,[45] sexual orientation or activity[46] are regarded as 'particularly sensitive or intimate',[47] requiring compelling grounds to justify interference. An Article 8 interest can thus be weighted. However, as discussed in Chapter 13, one of the essential requirements for satisfactory judicial resolution of the conflict between privacy and speech in a particular cases is that the value of the speech claim, in Article 10 terms, is *also* considered. As we argue there, if this is not done, the courts will have weights for one side of the scales only; in other words, if they *assess* the weight of the privacy claim, but simply *assume* that of the speech argument, their approach will suffer from a structural imbalance that will preclude a fair resolution of the conflicting speech and privacy claims. *Von Hannover*[48] pre-dates the English case law this article

---

[44] While originally only allowing disclosure if it would reveal wrongdoing on the part of the applicant (*Gartside v Outram* [1856] 26 LJ Ch 113, 114 and in relation to copyright, *Glyn v Weston Feature Film Co.* [1916] 1 Ch 261) the strength of the public interest in question rather than the individual wrongdoing of the applicant is now the determining factor: see *Schering Chemicals v Falkman* [1981] 2 WLR 848, esp. 869, *X v Y, Attorney General v Jonathan Cape* [1976] 1 QB 752, *Lion Laboratories v Evans and Express Newspapers* [1984] 1 QB 530, *Hellewell; Attorney General v Guardian Newspapers (No 2)*, n 8 above, 282, per Lord Goff, and 268, per Lord Griffiths. See also *Fraser v Evans* [1969] 1 QB 349 and *W v Egdell* [1990] Ch 59.

[45] *Z v Finland* (1997) 25 EHRR 371.   [46] *Lustig-Prean v United Kingdom* (2000) 29 EHRR 493.

[47] Feldman, 'Information and Privacy', conference paper, Cambridge Centre for Public Law, *Freedom of Expression and Freedom of Information*, 19–20 February 2000.

[48] [2004] EMLR 21.

has discussed, including *Campbell,* but the point of general principle that it captures is readily explicable from previous case law,[49] but yet went wholly unappreciated in many of the relevant decisions. That point is the simple one that the weight of any claim under Article 10 should be assessed by reference to the contribution that the publication in question makes to a debate of serious public concern, and that where the speech makes no such contribution, it may very readily be overridden by counter-vailing Convention arguments, in this case, those deriving from Article 8. This point has been resoundingly missed in a number of recent English decisions. In particular, one notable tendency has been to treat the public interest in a story as separate from the issue of the application of Article 10, taking the view that the latter is fully engaged even where the former is wholly absent.[50] Thus in *A v B,* Lord Woolf held that Jack J at first instance had been wrong to assume that, since Flitcroft's right to private life was engaged, his case should prevail unless the newspaper could show that there was a public interest in what it wished to publish.[51] In *Theakston,* the judge said: 'I can see no public interest in the publication of the details of the [sexual] activity';[52] he nevertheless found that: 'the freedom of expression of the *Sunday People* and of the prostitute would be given greater weight than the extra degree of intrusion into the claimant's privacy'.[53] This was surely a perverse stance even before *Von Hannover,* given the European Court's repeated and clear invocations of the vital role of the press in informing the public on matters of serious public concern,[54] and previous decisions of the Court which had clearly indicated that privacy-invading speech cited is afforded a very low weight in the Convention system.[55]

A better approach, as clearly held in *Von Hannover*[56] — and now in *Campbell*— would be to treat considerations of public interest *not* as distinct from the issue of freedom of expression but as going to the *weight* of that claim, when it is balanced against privacy. Such an approach has indeed been approved of by *dicta* in *Douglas*— cited with approval in *A v B plc*—although we argue below that it was not *applied* in those decisions. In *Douglas,* Brooke LJ remarked:

In the absence of any public interest [in the story] the Court is especially bound to pay particular regard to the [Press Complaints Commission Code] and a newspaper which flouts the Code may have its claim to freedom of expression trumped by Article 10(2) considerations of privacy.[57]

Such an approach was applied in *Douglas II*: no public interest was claimed in the publication of the photographs and, given the obvious commercial cynicism of *Hello!*'s actions, the judge found that the clear breaches of the PCC Code through the

---

[49] See e.g. the discussion of the decisions in *N v Portugal* (App no. 20683/92, 20 February 1995) and *Tammer v Estonia* (App no. 41205/98, 6 February 2001) in Chapter 13 at 692–3.

[50] In *A v B plc,* Woolf CJ said: 'Any interference with the press has to be justified because it inevitably has some effect on the ability of the press to perform its role in society. This is the position *irrespective of whether a particular publication is desirable in the public interest*' (op cit, at 549E, emphasis added).

[51] Judgment of 30 April 2001.   [52] Op cit, at [75].   [53] Ibid, at [76].

[54] See e.g. *Thorgeir Thorgeirson v Iceland* (1992) A 239, at [50].   [55] See Chapter 13 at 692–3.

[56] See Chapter 13 at 694–5.   [57] Op cit, at 994; approved in *A v B plc,* op cit, at 554C.

use of surreptitious photography were such as to tip the balance against freedom of expression.[58] This, however, was something of an isolated example in the reported cases, at least before *Campbell*.[59]

In *Douglas*, the speech in question—details of a celebrity wedding—was surely a paradigmatic case of low value, non-political speech, satisfying nothing other than a desire for celebrity gossip. It clearly was of substantially less public interest than, say, the speech in question in *Tammer v Estonia*,[60] which concerned an allegation of an affair between the Prime Minister and a former political aide. The court in *Douglas*, however, seemingly paid no heed to the manifest weakness of the expression claim in Convention times, while at the same time making a shrewd analysis of the weakness of the privacy interests involved: as Sedley LJ put it, 'The first two claimants had sold most of the privacy they now seek to protect to the third claimant for a handsome sum.'[61]

The same phenomena appears in both *A v B plc* and *Theakston*. Both these decisions concerned low-value, non-political speech, closer to soft pornography[62] than serious journalism. Such 'speech', in holding up to public gaze intimate details of the sexual lives of its subjects, is arguably hostile to core values underlying freedom of expression: intrusive stories such as these directly attack the value of human development without outside interference from others,[63] and, through their possible deterrent effect in threatening the humiliating exposure of sexual irregularities, indirectly threaten substantive autonomy.[64] Again, however, the court, while showing no awareness of these clear weaknesses in the speech claim, went to some lengths to point out the relative poverty—as the judges saw it—of the privacy case. Indeed the court in *A v B* laid down guidance to the effect that it may not even be necessary to determine the *existence* of weaker privacy claims, so likely were they to be outweighed by the claims of freedom of expression:

... usually the answer to the question whether there exists a private interest worthy of protection will be obvious. In those cases in which the answer is not obvious, an answer will often be unnecessary. This is because the weaker the claim for privacy, the more likely that the claim for privacy will be outweighed by the claim based on freedom of expression.[65]

This reasoning is revealing: it shows no recognition of the proposition that whether the privacy interest is likely to be outweighed by the speech interest *depends upon the*

---

[58] Op cit, at [204]–[205].

[59] Expression rights did not succeed in the *Venables and Thompson* case [2001] 1 All ER 908; however, it is important to point out that in that case the boys' right to life was engaged.

[60] (2003) 37 EHRR 43; (2001) 10 BHRC 543. The case is discussed in Chapter 13 at 692–3, and Chapter 21 at 1067–8.

[61] Op cit, at 1006, *per* Sedley LJ.

[62] Sedley LJ has described it as 'mildly pornographic' material: *Cream Holdings*, [2003] Ch 650, above at [88].

[63] See Chapter 13 at 665–6.

[64] For the argument that freedom of expression can best be justified by an argument based on moral autonomy, see Chapter 1 at 13–14.

[65] Op cit, 550C.

nature of the speech in question. It thus neatly encapsulates the unbalanced approach to the two Convention rights described above.

The courts in both cases then went on to apply this approach, examining at some length the weaknesses of the privacy interest, while disregarding the nature of the speech. Given the transitory nature of the intimate relationships in question and the fact that the other parties to them did not wish to keep them private any longer, the Court in *A v B plc* concluded: 'In our view, to grant an injunction would be an unjustified interference with the freedom of the press.'[66] In *Theakston*, the conclusion, reached specifically on the right of the newspaper to convey intimate and prurient detail of the precise sexual acts that took place between Theakston and the prostitutes was even clearer:

> I do not consider that the confidentiality or privacy case in relation to the details of the sexual activity is *nearly strong enough* to warrant the degree of restriction involved.[67]

This despite the fact that the judge openly conceded that conveying such details to the public had no public interest value.[68] We would argue that the opposite was the case in both instances: the speech in question—conveying explicit details of the sexual activity of a celebrity—was surely of the lowest value in Convention terms; conversely, the invasion of privacy, entailing as it did a gross intrusion into one of the most intimate aspects of private life—sexuality—was surely of a very grave degree. Such cases therefore can quite straightforwardly be resolved in favour of the privacy interest at the level of principle.

Recognition—and *application*—of this approach was finally apparent in *Campbell*. For the first time in an English appellate privacy judgment we see an attempt to scrutinize not just the value of the *privacy* claim, but, as part and parcel of the 'parallel analysis' of proportionality,[69] of the *speech* claim as well. Thus Lord Hope remarked of the latter:

> Clayton and Tomlinson, *The Law of Human Rights* (2000), para 15.162, point out that the court has distinguished three kinds of expression: political expression, artistic expression and commercial expression, and that it consistently attaches great importance to political expression and applies rather less rigorous principles to expression which is artistic and commercial. According to the court's well-established case law, freedom of expression constitutes one of the essential foundations of a democratic society and one of the basic conditions for its progress and the self-fulfilment of each individual: *Tammer v Estonia* (2001) 37 EHRR 857, para 59. But there were no political or democratic values at stake here, nor has any pressing social need been identified.[70]

As Lord Nicholls acknowledged, 'The need to be free to disseminate information regarding Miss Campbell's drug addiction is of a lower order than the need for freedom to disseminate information on some other subjects such as political

---

[66] Ibid, at 561.   [67] Op cit, at [76] (emphasis added).
[68] 'I can see no public interest in the publication of the details of the [sexual] activity'; ibid, at [75].
[69] See Chapter 13 at 704–5.   [70] *Campbell v MGN Ltd* [2004] 2 AC 457 at [117].

information.'[71] Lady Hale also held that 'there are undoubtedly different types of speech' and that some of those 'are more deserving of protection in a democratic society than others', going on to recite the categories mentioned by Lord Hope:

This includes revealing information about public figures, especially those in elective office, which would otherwise be private but is relevant to their participation in public life. Intellectual and educational speech and expression are also important in a democracy, not least because they enable the development of individuals' potential to play a full part in society and in our democratic life. Artistic speech and expression is important for similar reasons, in fostering both individual originality and creativity and the free-thinking and dynamic society we so much value.[72]

Applying this approach to *Campbell*'s case, her Ladyship found that:

The political and social life of the community, and the intellectual, artistic or personal development of individuals, are not obviously assisted by poring over the intimate details of a fashion model's private life.[73]

Lord Hoffman similarly emphatically accepted the use of underlying values as a way of balancing the two interests:

Take the example . . . of the ordinary citizen whose attendance at NA is publicised in his local newspaper. The violation of the citizen's autonomy, dignity and self-esteem is plain and obvious. Do the civil and political values which underlie press freedom make it necessary to deny the citizen the right to protect such personal information? Not at all . . . there is no public interest whatever in publishing to the world the fact that the citizen has a drug dependency. The freedom to make such a statement weighs little in the balance against the privacy of personal information.[74]

These *dicta* indicate the long-overdue recognition by English courts in privacy cases that Article 10 does not engage a one-size-fits-all weight, opening the way to a principled resolution of clashes between expression interests and Article 8.

One note of caution should perhaps be entered, however: Anthony White QC has pointed out that Lord Hope's application of the notion that journalists must enjoy some margin of discretion in reporting stories arguably undermined the notion of presumptive equality:[75]

Had it not been for the publication of the photographs, and looking to the text only, I would have been inclined to regard the balance between these rights as about even. Such is the effect of the margin of appreciation that must, in a doubtful case, be given to the journalist. In that situation the proper conclusion to draw would have been that it had not been shown that the restriction on the article 10 right for which Miss Campbell argues was justified on grounds of proportionality.

As White puts it: 'Any suggestion that in the event of a draw Article 10 should prevail

---

[71] Ibid, at [29].   [72] Ibid, at [148].   [73] Ibid, at [148–9].   [74] Ibid, at [56].
[75] 'Confidentiality and the Emerging Law of Privacy' 2004 at [9]. Paper published on Matrix website.

inevitably awards [it] a degree of priority over Article 8'. This, then, is a troubling comment, but not one supported by any other aspect of the judgment.[76]

The level of intrusive detail as a proportionality issue

Prior to *Campbell*, in most of the decisions, the courts appeared to be concerned only with whether the interference with press freedom by the proposed privacy remedy could be justified. But when courts are conducting a 'parallel analysis', in which both parties are required to justify the interference they propose to make with the other's right, it is also necessary for judges to ask whether the complained-of publication went further than was necessary in vindicating the legitimate public interest in the story. In the past, courts, because they were concerned only with whether the interference with expression could be justified, tended to miss the point that stories which both revealed a private fact (e.g. of an affair, or sexual encounter)[77] *and* contained intimate details of it, should be scrutinized through a proportionality lens; such scrutiny asks whether the extra intrusion into private life represented by the detail could be justified by reference to the 'speech value' which those details added.[78] This then is the second difference in approach, discussed in Chapter 13,[79] which flows from conducting the dual exercise in proportionality, or 'parallel analysis.'

There was some occasional recognition of this point prior to *Campbell*. For example, in *Douglas*, the court showed a clear recognition of the notion that privacy claims may be more or less weighty depending upon the aspect of private life interfered with:

> ... any consideration of article 8 rights must reflect the Convention jurisprudence which acknowledges different degrees of privacy. The European Court of Human Rights ruled in *Dudgeon v United Kingdom* (1981) 4 EHRR 149 that the more intimate the aspect of private life which is being interfered with, the more serious must be the reasons for interference before the latter can be legitimate: see p 165, para 52.[80]

This was an issue that should have been considered in *A v B plc* in particular, precisely because it was clear that the complained-of publications went far further than simply reporting the *fact* of the footballer's affair (something which the court found did have a 'modicum of public interest).'[81] It was found as a fact that 'much of each [publication was] concerned with the salacious description of the sexual activity between the claimant and [two lap-dancers]. They are both intended for the prurient,'[82] in other words, designed to titillate. But the court expressly disclaimed any role for itself in looking at this matter of detail, referring to such matters merely as questions of taste:

---

[76] But see the discussion of *Re S* [2005] 1 AC 593 in Chapter 16 for another important decision in which the privacy interest was arguably marginalized in favour of a particular form of speech: reporting of criminal trials.

[77] As in *A v B plc* [2002] 3 WLR 542 and *Theakston v MGN* [2002] EMLR 22 respectively.

[78] See Chapter 13 at 683–90 for an examination of the 'speech value' of privacy-invading expression.

[79] See pp 704–5.   [80] [2001] QB 967, at 1012, *per* Kenne LJ.

[81] Op cit, at 561C.   [82] Ibid, 555F.

In drawing up a balance sheet between the respective interests of the parties courts should not act as censors or arbiters of taste. This is the task of others. If there is not a sufficient case for restraining publication, the fact that a more lurid approach will be adopted by the publication than the court would regard as acceptable is not relevant.[83]

And again, later:

Once it is accepted that the freedom of the press should prevail, then the form of reporting in the press is not a matter for the courts but for the Press Commission and the customers of the newspaper concerned.[84]

With respect, this is surely mistaken: the issue *is* a matter for the courts, precisely because it goes to the issue of proportionality. The more lurid and explicit the article, the greater the interference with Article 8, if it is published. A court taking Article 8 seriously would be bound to take the view that interferences with it should be the minimum necessary to satisfy the other, competing right. Once this is accepted, the detail about sexual activities would have to be shown to be justifiable in terms of the value it added under Article 10.

In the *Theakston* case, the judge did make some attempt to address this issue.[85] But he showed no recognition that what he was doing was part of a proportionality enquiry he was bound to undertake, and no real understanding of the argument that greater detail in reporting amounts to a graver intrusion into privacy which must be justified; he pointed to no value added by the detail that served to outweigh the graver violation of Article 8 it represented. Interesting, Lord Hoffman in *Campbell* later addressed, *obiter*, precisely this situation, speaking of:

cases in which (for example) there is a public interest in the disclosure of the existence of a sexual relationship (say, between a politician and someone whom she has appointed to public office) but the addition of salacious details or intimate photographs is disproportionate and unacceptable. The latter, even if accompanying a legitimate disclosure of the sexual relationship, would be too intrusive and demeaning.[86]

Campbell itself displays a clear application of the proportionality test to the competing speech and privacy interests, as the method of resolving the case. The value of the speech was assessed in Convention terms, as discussed above; but their Lordships accepted that it must further be asked whether the level of intrusive detail contained in the publication in question went further then was necessary in carrying out the press's legitimate function of informing the public. As Lord Hope put it, 'Decisions about the publication of material that is private to the individual raise issues that are not simply about presentation and editing.[87] Thus he found:

It is hard to see that there was any compelling need for the public to know the name of the organisation that she was attending for the therapy, or for the other details of it to be set out.[88]

This indeed was the whole basis for the finding in favour of Campbell by the majority:

---

[83] Ibid, 553C–D.   [84] Ibid, 561–562.   [85] Op cit, at [75]–[76].   [86] Op cit, at [60].
[87] Ibid, at [113].   [88] Ibid, at [118]

the publication was examined in terms of the five classes of information the articles represented[89] and the newspaper was, in effect, asked to justify the greater level of intrusion represented by the publication of the details of treatment and the photographs. The question as to whether that extra detail could be justified was put under the microscope: and it was found that there was no justification for it in terms of the public interest. *Both* sides therefore were forced to justify the intrusion into the rights of the others that they sought to make: it was found that Campbell could not justify imposing liability for publishing the basic facts because of the legitimate public interest in them—something she had indeed conceded; but equally it was found that the intrusive details—likely in themselves to cause greater damage to Campbell's attempts to rehabilitate herself than merely reporting her drug addiction—could not be justified. *Both* sides therefore had to give some ground; the case turned upon working out a way of ensuring the minimum impairment of each person's rights. A measure of both privacy *and* of free expression was retained, whereas in the Court of Appeal decision in *Campbell*, as well as in *A v B*, *Theakston* and in *D v L*,[90] expression was allowed full rein, with the result that the competing privacy rights were wholly overridden.

In short, the approach in *Campbell* amounted to a sensitive, contextual balancing exercise, resolved through examination of the value of the two claims and based upon the core Convention principle of proportionality. In this decision, English privacy law came of age as an effective remedy that pays full regard to freedom of expression as a qualified—not an absolute—value.[91]

HARD CASES CONCERNING 'THE PUBLIC INTEREST'

In the remainder of this chapter, we discuss difficult issues concerning the balancing of the public interest in publication against privacy rights that we have not yet considered. Whilst *Campbell* and *Von Hannover* have, as discussed, established the correct principles to be used both in the structural approach to weighing Articles 8 and 10 and as to the broad values that should be considered in assessing the weight of privacy and speech claims, as we have seen, much of that guidance is in general terms: the Court in *Von Hannover* held that courts are obliged to assess the weight of an Article 10 claim by reference to how far the publication in question contributes to debate on matters of legitimate or serious public concern. However, difficult issues arise in assessing just what *should* be seen as of 'legitimate' concern to the public. We know that speech concerning politicians or other holders of public office will generally be

---

[89] Namely: (1) the fact of Miss Campbell's drug addiction; (2) the fact that she was receiving treatment; (3) the fact that she was receiving treatment at Narcotics Anonymous; (4) the details of the treatment—how long she had been attending meetings, how often she went, how she was treated within the sessions themselves, the extent of her commitment, and the nature of her entrance on the specific occasion; and (5) the visual portrayal [through photographs] of her leaving a specific meeting with other addicts and being hugged before such a meeting by other members of the group receiving treatment. See the discussion in Chapter 14 at 732–3.

[90] [2004] EMLR 1.

[91] Although see *Re S*: as discussed fully in Chapter 16, in this case an extremely weighty privacy claim.

seen as of far more value, in Convention terms, than that relating to celebrities. But what about instances in which some section of the population takes the view that the way a politician behaves in her private life reflects upon her character and judgment and is something that therefore might affect their view of the government of which that person is a member? What of the view, held by many observers of contemporary culture, that for large sections of the public, the view and actions of celebrities have a much greater impact upon public discussion than those of politicians, who may be much less well known?[92] It is undoubtedly the case that much discussion of contemporary issues in the popular press, such as sexual behaviour, drug abuse, parenting and anorexia is, as a matter of fact, provoked by revelation and discussion of the choices made by celebrities and others in their private lives. Both the German courts[93] and as we shall see below, the US courts, have been at times heavily influenced by the difficulty in drawing a clear distinction between mere 'entertaining' expression, often in the form of celebrity reportage, and more serious reportage. They have accepted that there is a category of 'infotainment' in which celebrity stories may trigger discussion of legitimate issues such as those just mentioned, many of which (for example drug use and sexual behaviour) are of serious concern to governments.

As we saw, *all* the judges in the *Campbell* litigation were of the view that the press performed a legitimate function in the public interest in correcting the false impression Campbell had created as to her relationship with illegal drugs. Moreover, as is well known, much more flimsy public interest arguments than this one have been accepted by English courts as a reason for overriding privacy claims. These include, notoriously, the notion that the immoral sexual behaviour of football players[94] or television presenters[95] were of legitimate public concern, because they were 'role models' for young people, while the fact that the Chair of Britain's Olympic bid team had had an affair has also been judicially determined to be a matter of legitimate public concern,[96] as, most recently, have been the marital problems of David and Victoria Beckham.[97] In short, English judges seem wedded to the notion that information about the intimate private lives *not* only of politicians, but of various minor and major celebrities, may be of genuine public interest,[98] sufficient to override clearly

---

[92] There is a growing body of sociological research on the real impact on matters such as attitudes to fatherhood that truly iconic figures such as David Beckham may have (see, e.g. G. Whannel, 'David Beckham, Identity and Masculinity', (2002) 11(3) *Sociology Review*, 2–4; D. L. Andrews and S. J. Jackson (eds.) *Sports Stars: The Cultural Politics of Sporting Celebrity*, London: Routledge, 2001.

[93] As discussed in Chapter 13 at 693–4.   [94] *A v B plc* [2002] 3 WLR 542.

[95] *Theakston v MGN* [2002] EMLR 22.   [96] *Coe v Mirror Group Newspapers* (unrep) 29 May 2004.

[97] In a recent, unreported decision, the Beckhams were denied an injunction in relation to a story detailing problems within their marriage, including very intimate material, provided by their former nanny in clear breach of contract, apparently at least partly on the grounds of the 'public interest' of the story: see *The Guardian* 25 April 2005 http://media.guardian.co.uk/site/story/0,14173,1471125,00.html

[98] See B. Markesinis, C. O'Cinneide, J. Fedtke, and M. Hunter-Henin, 'Concerns and Ideas about the Developing English Law of Privacy (and How Knowledge of Foreign Law Might be of Help)' (2004) LII(1) *American Journal of Comparative Law* 133 at 158–160; G. Phillipson, 'Judicial Reasoning in Breach of Confidence Cases under the Human Rights Act: Not Taking Privacy Seriously?' [2003] *EHRLR* (*Privacy Special*) 53, 60–72.

weighty privacy claims. It seems tolerably clear from *Von Hannover* that the decisions in these cases take a view of the scope of the 'public interest' from which Strasbourg would strongly dissent. Clearer still are the indications from the decision of the court in *Campmany Y Diez de Revenga v Spain*[99], which concerned very similar facts to the cases just mentioned: sensational reportage of an affair between two persons of interest to the public, but who had no political or official role. In that case, the court found emphatically:

Like the Spanish courts, the Court considers that as they concentrated on the purely private aspects of the life of those concerned and even though those persons were known to the public, the reports in issue cannot be regarded as having contributed to a debate on a matter of general interest to society.[100]

In this instance, the Strasbourg court's view appears the more compelling; however, as the analysis of *Von Hannover* in Chapter 13 discloses,[101] the Strasbourg court's dismissal of reportage of private lives as a legitimate function of the press goes much, much further than this case. Arguably, Strasbourg takes an under-inclusive notion of the public interest, in which, seemingly, only the private lives of those who perform official duties can be of such legitimate concern, and then only exceptionally. Even then, the *Plon (Société)*[102] case indicates that a high degree of protection for privacy can be afforded even to those who held the highest political office,[103] whilst *Tammer v Estonia* indicates that the sexual life of former senior politicians can be wholly protected[104] from publicity. There does indeed appear to be a gulf in attitudes here, and little sign that English courts are heeding this aspect of the Strasbourg jurisprudence. In conclusion it may be said that English courts are too ready to accede to flimsy 'public interest' arguments in privacy cases, whilst Strasbourg arguably goes to the opposite extreme.

However, it was also argued in Chapter 13 that *Von Hannover*, perhaps because of the particular facts of the case, provides little in the way of concrete guidance on these difficult points (at pp 699–700). It is therefore issues such as these that the remainder of this part of the chapter will consider.

The relevance of the private lives of politicians

It is easy enough to think of instances in which revelations of the private lives of politicians in the media may be persuasively argued to be of legitimate concern to the public, even in Article 10 terms. An example often given is of a story concerning, say, the homosexual affairs of a politician who publicly advocated conservative 'family

---

[99] (2000) no. 54224/00. It concerned what was described in the Spanish media as 'a new sex scandal between an attractive aristocrat and a banker from this country', including pictures and details of their tryst.

[100] Ibid.   [101] See pp 694–6.   [102] No. 58148/00, 18 May 2004.

[103] In that the interim injunction in that case was found not to violate Article 10.

[104] (2001) 37 EHRR 857, [59]. In that case, the court found that penalties imposed by the national authorities upon the reporting of an affair between the former Prime Minister and a former political aide were not a violation of Article 10. The Minister had left office as Interior Minister only six months previously. See Chapter 21 at 1067–8.

values.' Such a story would contribute to political discussion, influence the standing of the political party in question, and reveal a public deception,[105] engaging the self-government and—to a lesser extent—the 'truth' justification quite strongly.[106] How, then, are these cases to be assessed?

In such 'fitness for office' cases, the *status* of the individual concerned would obviously be of some importance. English courts could build here on the US approach, which strives for a 'rough proportion[ality]', between the importance of the office the person holds and the range of ordinarily protected information that may be revealed'.[107] Not only does the public have a greater need to know about more powerful figures; such individuals must have foreseen the close scrutiny that their lives would come under through accepting the basic duty of democratic accountability when taking up office, a factor stressed both by domestic courts[108] and at Strasbourg.[109] Thus, where the applicant held elected position or was employed by the state to make decisions directly affecting the basic interests of the citizenry,[110] there would in general be a stronger argument for the press under the self-governance justification. However, the courts should be astute to recognize that certain persons, though formally only private citizens, may nevertheless wield what Lord Cooke recently described as 'great practical power over the lives of people or great influence in the formation of public opinion . . . [which] may indeed exceed that of most politicians.'[111] The most obvious examples would be the owners of newspaper and media companies, such as Rupert Murdoch. It should be recognized, however, that those who hold only *de facto* public power have accepted no duty of accountability to

---

[105] One of the defences to press intrusion in the Code of the PCC; see also *Woodward v Hutchins*, op cit, at 764); see also *Calcutt Committee on Privacy and Related Matters* (1990 Cmnd 1102), 12.23.

[106] It appears clear from a case Markesenis mentions (BGH May 5, 1964, BGHZ NJW 1964, 1471) that in Germany the interest in preventing a public figure from misleading the public may allow for the publication of otherwise protected information. In the case, an article which described the applicants' repeated adultery was found not to be actionable, as would normally be the case, since the applicant had in the past held himself out as a moralist (B. Markesenis and N. Nolte, 'Some Comparative Reflections on the Right of Privacy of Public Figures in Public Places', *Privacy and Loyalty*, Oxford: Clarendon, 1997, note 76).

[107] D. Prosser, 'Privacy' (1960) 48 *California Law Review* 383, 417. Thus he suggests that 'there is very little in the way of information about the President of the United States or any candidate for [that office] that is not a matter of legitimate concern'.

[108] See *Reynolds* ([1998] 3 WLR 862, 910, CA): '. . . those who engage in public life must expect and accept that their public conduct will be the subject of close scrutiny and robust criticism'. It should be noted that having regard to such a matter is *not* the same as the 'implied consent' argument earlier criticized. The foresight of risk of the person concerned becomes not a means of stripping away any *prima facie* claim to privacy that they may have, but rather as a means of adding weight to a speech argument *in competition* with an admitted privacy claim.

[109] See, e.g. *Lingens v Austria* (1986) 8 EHRR 407 at [42]: '. . . a politician . . . inevitably and knowingly lays himself open to close scrutiny of his every word and deed by both journalists and the public . . . and . . . must consequently display a greater degree of tolerance.'

[110] E.g., the Chairs of the Bank of England, the US Federal Reserve and the European Central Bank, Chief Constables of police, chairs of powerful quangos, etc.

[111] *Reynolds v Times Newspapers*, [1999] 4 All ER 609, 640. American courts have recognized this by developing a very broad, inclusive definition of the term 'public figures' for the purposes of the *Sullivan* test (376 US 254 (1964)) in defamation.

the public, the public have no control by means of the democratic process,[112] and nor are their salaries funded by the public. Consequently the public arguably has less right to know about them, although the fact that they engage directly in opinion formation, or have direct effects upon the polity[113] means that the public has a strong interest in any aspects of their lives which have a possible bearing on how they conduct their public activities. Lowest down the scale of importance come celebrities, who have no direct influence upon political events, but whose attitudes and behaviour may reasonably be guessed to have some effect upon the views of those who follow their lives. For that reason, but to a lesser extent, speech about celebrities *may* engage the self-governance rationale; to these three categories may be added two more: those who for a short time and for a particular reason only are thrust into the public gaze[114] and those who receive media attention simply because of their connection with the famous—the family of the late Princess Diana would be a good example.[115]

Some evaluation must also be made of the importance of the *subject matter* of the publication, a more difficult issue. Where it is claimed that it revealed matters 'relevant' to an assessment of an individual's fitness for office, an immediate problem arises: who is to decide whether a given piece of conduct is relevant to such an assessment? Suppose, for example, that an article revealed the extra-marital affair of a government Minister and the justification urged by the newspaper is the belief held by some that, 'If the Minister will lie to his wife about an affair, he will lie to the public about political matters.' If the court decided that this belief was nonsense, and that the affair was not relevant to the Minister's fitness for office, the judge would in effect be dictating to the public what it should and should not take into account in exercising its collective right to political self-determination.[116] But the exercise of this right surely involves not only the public judging a politician's fitness for office, but also being able to decide for themselves what criteria to employ in making that assessment. As Schauer has put it, 'in a democracy there appears to be a right to base one's voting decisions on criteria that other people take to be wrong.[117] And as Justice Powell said in *Gertz*,[118] such tests allow judges 'to determine, in the words of Mr Justice Marshall, "what information is relevant to self-government" '.

Real as this objection is, we suggest that it can be overcome. The alternative course

---

[112] For example, revelations about the private lives of various Conservative MPs in the early 1990s and about the former Welsh Secretary, Ron Davies, led directly to their falls from political life through the direct or indirect effect of public opinion. By contrast, even if the extensive and often adverse publicity given to the breakup of the marriage of Rupert Murdoch changed public opinion about him, no direct consequences could flow from this.

[113] As in the case, say, of chairpersons of powerful multi-national corporations, or trade unionists.

[114] The Lawrence family would be a good recent example.

[115] It is clear that the Earl and Countess Spencer only received such intensive—and intrusive—media attention because of their connection with the Princess. This is evident from the newspaper headlines accompanying the various stories.

[116] See *Gertz* 418 U.S. (1974) 323, 346.

[117] F. Schauer, 'Can Public Figures Have Private Lives?' in E. Paul, F. Miller, and J. Paul (eds) *The Right to Privacy*, Cambridge: CUP, 2000, at 297–306.

[118] 418 U.S. 323 (1974), at 346. This argument is also forcefully put by Professor Volokh: see note 130 below.

would require courts to allow publicity about virtually any aspects of a public figure's life, on the basis that it was not for the judiciary to say that such revelations could not be relevant to the views of *some* member of the public. The privacy of such figures could therefore be wholly destroyed, an outcome which must be wrong in principle under a system which, in accordance with the Convention, as confirmed by *Von Hannover*, is committed to a sensitive balancing of the two rights. In *Lingens* the Court remarked that the protection for reputation under Article 10(2) 'extends to politicians too, even when they are *not* acting in their private capacity'.[119] Thus, the right to privacy similarly must encompass politicians when they *are* acting in the private sphere, a conclusion clearly borne out by the decision in *Tammer v Estonia* and on which there seems to be something of a consensus in Europe.[120]

Moreover, a judge making some assessment of whether, say, a given piece of information was relevant to a Minister's fitness for office, would be making his judgement not out of contempt for the views of others, or paternalism, but simply because the rights of others demanded that a line be drawn somewhere. As Lord Nicholls has put it in the context of libel: '. . . an outside body, that is, some one other than the newspaper itself, [must] decides whether an occasion is privileged [that is, that publication is permissible]. This is bound to be so, if the decision of the press itself is not to be determinative of the propriety of publishing the particular material.[121] Finally, the courts could employ some relatively weak test whereby the press would have to show merely that in the view of a rational person the information could be of real relevance to an assessment of fitness for office. This would exclude bizarrely subjective claims of a need to know, such as the hypothetical example, cited by Timbini and Heyward, of the voter who insists on basing his decisions on the candidate's underwear.[122] The rational person should, however, be taken to be reasonably broad-minded and tolerant, in line with the view of the European Court that such values are essential in a democratic society:[123] such a person would not therefore require knowledge of matters which a tolerant person would disregard.

A more straightforward point arises out of 'fitness for office' cases: if the court decided that the basic facts conveyed should be protected under Article 10, it could go on to consider, under the parallel analysis, whether the *details* of the publication went further than necessary in informing the public. Thus it has been said that while the public may have a right to know about a Cabinet Minister's adulterous affair, they do *not* need to know 'the content of such a person's intimate conversations or the details

---

[119] Op cit, at [42] (emphasis added).

[120] The German Supreme Court has held that 'even politicians who are in the limelight are entitled to have their privacy respected' (BGHZ 72, 120, 122–123), an approach also taken in France and Italy (see Markesenis, (ed.) *Protecting Privacy*, Oxford: Clarendon, 1999).

[121] *Reynolds*, op cit, at 624

[122] D. Tambini and C. Heyward, 'Regulating the trade in secrets: policy options', in Tambini and Heyward (eds), *Ruled by Recluses? Privacy, Journalism and the Media after the Human Rights Act*, IPPR 2002, p 98.

[123] See, for example, *Otto Preminger* (1994) 19 EHRR 34, at [47].

of his or her sexual activity'.[124] As noted above, precisely this distinction was upheld, *obiter* in *Campbell*.[125] A court, then, might make some attempt to sift out those aspects of journalistic reportage which served some serious function from those which, under the mantle of promoting democratic accountability, merely peddled titillation or gossip.

Private facts stories that contribute more generally to public debate

In other cases, the justification for stories about an individual's private life will be, not that they are relevant to his or her fitness for office, but more generally, that they contribute to discussion of matters of general interest: as one American commentator puts it, '[The] media uses people's names, statements, experiences, and emotions to personalise otherwise impersonal accounts of trends or developments.'[126] Where such speech is not directly political, it will not lie at the core of the self-governance justification. But, to quote Lord Cooke, 'Matters other than those pertaining to government and politics may be just as important in the community'.[127] Such speech, which can 'inform the social, political, moral and philosophical positions of individual citizens'[128] could include revelations relating to matters as diverse as eating disorders, abortion, attitudes to sexuality, education and the like; it will often concern not politicians, but celebrities, their relatives and those who for a short time and for a particular reason only are thrust into the public gaze.

As the German Federal Court put it in the Princess Caroline case:

Nor can mere entertainment be denied any role in the formation of opinions. That would amount to unilaterally presuming that entertainment merely satisfies a desire for amusement, relaxation, escapism or diversion. Entertainment can also convey images of reality and propose subjects for debate that spark a process of discussion and assimilation relating to philosophies of life, values and behaviour models. In that respect it fulfils important social functions . . . When measured against the aim of protecting press freedom, entertainment in the press is neither negligible nor entirely worthless and therefore falls within the scope of application of fundamental rights . . .

The same is true of information about people. Personalization is an important journalistic means of attracting attention. Very often it is this which first arouses interest in a problem and stimulates a desire for factual information. Similarly, interest in a particular event or situation is usually stimulated by personalized accounts. Additionally, celebrities embody certain moral values and lifestyles. Many people base their choice of lifestyle on their example. They become points of crystallisation for adoption or rejection and act as examples or counter-examples. This is what explains the public interest in the various ups and downs occurring in their lives.[129]

---

[124] *Fourth Report of the National Heritage Select Committee on Privacy and Media Intrusion*, Appendix 24, HC 294–II (1993) at [5].

[125] See p 785.

[126] D. Anderson, 'The Failure of American Privacy Law' in B. Markesenis (ed.) *Protecting Privacy*, Oxford: Clarendon, 1999, at 142.

[127] *Reynolds*, op cit, at 640.   [128] Zimmerman, op cit, at 346.

[129] Quoted in *Von Hannover*. op cit, at [25].

One American commentator notes that it may be difficult to justify the social importance of a photograph of 'a celebrity entering a restaurant or vacationing on a beach',
but goes on: 'There is simply no easy way to distinguish between legitimate-news
gathering and the gathering of news that is purely sensational.'[130] The US Supreme
Court, in one of its most celebrated free speech cases, made the same point: 'The line
between the informing and the entertaining is too elusive for the protection of [the
free press].'[131]

It may be observed that such influence as celebrities have is merely a by-product of
their lives, is much more difficult to assess than the direct power of politicians, and
may relate solely to matters such as tastes in clothing, appearance and music, of
peripheral concern to public affairs; moreover, while they may frequently seek publicity they have generally not thrust themselves into direct influence upon political
life. The courts should therefore be slow to accept entirely impressionistic arguments
as to the influence such 'role models' have on issues relevant to the matters of serious
public concern, with which Article 10 is concerned. But there is also a more principled
objection to the use of a person's private life to provoke discussion, efficacious as
it may be. The example of 'outing' may be used: the argument in favour of such
revelations is that if the public comes to learn that a person they admire or respect is
homosexual, this may force them to re-examine their own prejudices against homosexuality.[132] The objection is that this justification is utilitarian to the point of
ruthlessness. It amounts in effect to forcing a person to provide highly personal
information for the purposes of fuelling public debate and therefore amounts to one
of the clearest breaches one could imagine of the Kantian imperative to treat persons
as ends in themselves. For example, the disputed article concerning the former child
prodigy in the American case of *Sidis*,[133] was 'a merciless . . . dissection' of Sidis' life,
which had a 'devastating effect' upon him, but was justified partly on the basis that it
provided 'helpful insights into the problems experienced by gifted children',[134] or as
the court said, it was 'instructive'.[135] It is apparent that such an approach would have
the effect, as in America, of virtually destroying the right to privacy, since almost all
pieces of personal information about a person in the public view could be seen as

---

[130] E. Volokh, 'Freedom of Speech and Information Privacy: The Troubling Implications of a Right to Stop
People from Speaking About You' (2000) 52 *Stan LR* 1049.

[131] *New York Times v Sullivan* 376 U.S. 254, 271–2 (1964). It should be noted that the Supreme Court has
in any event held that 'There is no doubt that entertainment, as well as news, enjoys First Amendment
protection', *Zaccchini v Sciprrs-Howard Broad Co.*, 433 U.S. 562, 578 (1978).

[132] For example, in the well-known US case of *Sipple v Chronicle Publishing Co.* (201 Cal Rpt 665 1984), an
ex-marine foiled an assassination attempt upon President Ford and thereafter attracted great media interest.
A Californian newspaper revealed that Sipple was homosexual, a matter which he had concealed from his
relatives, and which caused him great distress and embarrassment. The court rejected his claim for wrongful
disclosure of private facts partly on the basis that the information was already in the public domain but also
explicitly on the basis that 'the expose was motivated by the wish to combat the stereotyping of homosexuals
as "timid, weak and unheroic" and to discuss the possible homophobia of the President, who had been
somewhat backward in thanking Sipple'.

[133] *Sidis v F-R Publishing Corporation* (113 F.2d 806 (2d Cir. 1940)).

[134] Zimmerman, op cit, at note 336.   [135] Op cit, at 807.

relevant to *some* area of public debate.[136] Moreover, as argued in Chapter 13[137] one of the principal *justifications* for open discussion of different life-styles and the like is to promote autonomous choice and diversity: acts of intrusive journalism, likely to deter others from taking up controversial life styles, are in clear conflict with this aim.

Finally, in assessing the speech value of a given publication, the court should, as suggested above,[138] consider whether the restrictions which each party proposes to place upon the other are '*necessary* in a democratic society'. The applicant's concerns might in some cases be sufficiently answered, not by injuncting the publication but simply by requiring it to be anonymized. On the other hand, in relation to a publication which it was claimed contributed to public debate, it might be asked whether there was not another means of so contributing which would not have involved a violation of privacy.[139] Given that in our contemporary, confessional culture, there are a large number of people, ranging from private individuals to celebrities, who are prepared to reveal intimate aspects of their lives voluntarily, it might be difficult to maintain that the invasion of privacy involved in publishing wholly involuntary revelations was in any way *necessary* for that continuation of public debate which is admittedly valuable. The seeming inability of American courts to appreciate such considerations has led to some very disturbing decisions.[140]

In dealing with questions of the 'public interest', in particular disclosures, a number of decisions under the HRA are open to trenchant criticism. This applies in particular to some now notorious *dicta* in the judgment of Lord Woolf in *A v B*. In that case, the court, in seeking to define what kinds of disclosures will be found to attract a public interest found the issue to be related to the question of who can be treated as 'a public figure.' As a Council of Europe resolution quoted by Woolf CJ states:

6. . . . public figures must recognise that the special position they occupy in society—in many cases by choice—automatically entails increased pressure on their privacy.

7. Public figures are persons holding public office and/or using public resources and, more broadly speaking, all those who play a role in public life, whether in politics, the economy, the arts, the social sphere, sport or in any other domain.

8. It is often in the name of a one-sided interpretation of the right to freedom of expression, which is guaranteed in Article 10 of the European Convention on Human Rights, that the media invade people's privacy, claiming that their readers are entitled to know about public figures.

---

[136] See Anderson, op cit, at 141–3; cf. Zimmerman, op cit, at 353.   [137] At pp 686–7.

[138] Pp 784–6 above.

[139] Anderson (op cit, at 151–152) attacks the approach in such cases whereby it is asked only if the fact revealed is 'relevant' to a topic of genuine public interest.

[140] In *Florida Star v B.J.F.* (491 U.S. 524 (1989)) the Supreme Court held that a newspaper's revelation of a rape victim's name, resulting in her further terrorization by her assailant, was protected by the First Amendment, since 'the commission and investigation of [rape]' was 'a matter of paramount public import' (ibid, 536–537). It reached the same conclusion in *Cox Broadcasting Company v Cohn* (420 U.S. 469 (1975)) in relation to a TV broadcast giving details of a gang rape and the name of the 17 year old victim, in violation of state law; see Anderson, op cit, at 157–60.

9. Certain facts relating to the private lives of public figures, particularly politicians, may indeed be of interest to citizens, and it may therefore be legitimate for readers, who are also voters, to be informed of those facts.[141]

On one level, this resolution simply points up the unhelpfulness of using 'public figure' as an indicia of how much information one should be able to know about a given person. 'Public figures' we are told are 'all those who play a role in public life . . . in any domain.' Clearly, this simply transfers the definitional problem onto the notion of 'public life,' a concept no clearer than that of 'public figure'. In defining 'public figures', it also, troublingly, draws no distinction between Government Ministers, on the one hand, and well-known sportspersons on the other; however paragraph 9 makes clear that the public interest in knowing facts about such peoples' personal lives will be stronger where politicians are concerned, on the basis that citizens of a democracy may have a legitimate interest in knowing the private lives of politicians, because they are also voters.

What, however, does Lord Woolf make of this guidance? Starting with the welcome reassurance that 'A public figure is entitled to a private life', his Lordship then goes on:

Even trivial facts relating to a public figure can be of great interest to readers and other observers of the media. In many of these situations it would be overstating the position to say that there is a public interest in the information being published. It would be more accurate to say that the public have an understandable and so a legitimate interest in being told the information. If this is the situation then it can be appropriately taken into account by a court when deciding on which side of the line a case falls.[142]

What stands out here is the clear leap in this reasoning—one commentator refers to it as 'an extraordinary leap of logic':[143] Lord Woolf speaks of 'an understandable *and so a legitimate* interest in being told the information'. Now it is of course 'understandable' that members of the public may have an idle interest in knowing whether a particular footballer has been sleeping around or not; it is a trite observation that many people enjoy intrusive gossip. But the question is, what is the legal alchemy that converts this understandable *desire* to hear sexual gossip into a legitimate *public interest*, recognized and protected by law? (Note that this is a matter that 'can be appropriately taken into account by a court'). The answer is simple: the explanation surely required for the introduction of such a surprising and novel principle into judicial adjudication is entirely absent; thus the only justification offered here[144] for allowing the publication of such intrusive material, despite the gross violation of privacy that it may entail, is the fact that large amounts of people have a reliably-encountered desire to hear it.

Aside from the absence of justificatory reasoning on this point, a number of

---

[141] Resolution 1165 of 1998, cited at paragraph 11(xiii) of the judgment (note 5 above).

[142] Ibid, at 552.   [143] J. Rozenberg, *Privacy and the Press*, Oxford: OUP, 2004, p 53.

[144] Another is of course the press's freedom of expression under Article 10(1) EHCR (but as to this see above); the argument of the court here, however, was directed not to this point, but to the common law concept of public interest in publication.

positive objections may be made to the court's reasoning on this point. First these *dicta* take no heed of the fact, explored above, that Strasbourg, in a number of cases, even before *Von Hannover* has treated publications that invade private life as *lacking*, for that reason, a public interest, such that even very draconian penalties in relation to them have readily been found to be justified as a proportionate means of protecting private life under Article 8.[145] Second, they collapse the distinction, carefully maintained in successive previous judgments of the Court of Appeal, between 'the public interest' as a legal term of art on the one hand, and what is interesting to the public on the other. For example, in *Lion Laboratories v Evans*,[146] Stephenson LJ approved of precisely this distinction, referring to the like comments of Donaldson MR in *Francome*.[147] Much more recently, and in a case decided explicitly by reference to Article 10 ECHR, the Court of Appeal approved the following dicta of Sullivan J. at first instance:

One can think of many stories that are published in the newspapers in which the public are interested. But it would be difficult for a journalist to say with a straight face that there is a public interest in them being published.[148]

Woolf CJ offered no argument as to how the Court of Appeal, which of course is bound by its previous judgments,[149] could in this case legitimately lay down dicta that so clearly depart from this well-established distinction.[150]

It is also worth noting that his Lordship's judgment seems scarcely consonant with the definition of the public interest in the Code of Practice of the Press Complaints Commission,[151] to which the courts is directed under s 12 HRA to have regard in these cases.[152] The Code gives rather more concrete guidance as to the meaning of 'public interest', albeit in non-exhaustive form. It states:

1. The public interest includes:
    (i)   Detecting or exposing crime or a serious misdemeanour.
    (ii) Protecting public health and safety.
    (iii) Preventing the public from being misled by some statement or action of an individual or organisation.

---

[145] See Chapter 13 at 692–3, and Chapter 21 at 1067–8.

[146] [1985] QB 526, 537. See also *London Artists v Littler Ltd* [1969] 2 QB 375.

[147] [1984] 1 WLR 892, 898.

[148] *London Regional Transport v Mayor of London* [2003] EMLR 4, at [40]. In his judgment in the final trial of *Douglas v Hello*, Lindsay J robustly upheld this distinction: 'That the public would be interested is not to be confused with there being a public interest' (op cit, at [231]). He thus found that there was no public interest in the publication by *Hello!* of snatched photographs of the celebrity wedding.

[149] None of the limited exceptions to this rule applied in this instance.

[150] It is theoretically possible that the introduction of the ECHR into UK could furnish such a reason; however, no argument to this effect was offered and it is hard to see what it could be; as noted above, in the *London Transport case*, decided under the HRA, the Court of Appeal saw no reason why the inception of Article 10 should alter the long-established position in English law.

[151] HRA, s 12(4)(b) refers to 'any relevant privacy code'.

[152] per ss (1), s 12 applies whenever the court is considering granting any relief which would affect the Convention right to freedom of expression.

It may well be said that, following Lord Woolf's dicta in *A v B plc*, one could add:

(iv) Anything that some section of the public would like to hear about.

Evidently perceiving the weakness of the propositions on public interest put forward in the above passage, the Court of Appeal in *Campbell v MGN*[153] tried to rescue these dicta, which they thought might have been 'misunderstood by some', through a bold re-interpretation:

When Lord Woolf spoke of the public having 'an understandable and so a legitimate interest in being told' information, even including trivial facts, about a public figure, he was not speaking of private facts which a fair-minded person would consider it offensive to disclose. That is clear from his subsequent commendation of the guidance on striking a balance between Article 8 and Article 10 rights provided by the Council of Europe Resolution 1165 of 1998.[154]

With respect, this explanation is flatly implausible. Had Lord Woolf *not* been talking about the revelation of private facts, his comments would have been straight-forwardly irrelevant. No-one disputes that one may disclose of a public figure such non-sensitive facts as that she lives in London, or is a solicitor. There is no question of such disclosures attracting legal liability under a law of privacy or confidentiality; it would clearly therefore not be necessary for the Lord Chief Justice to remark, by the by, that the public might have a legitimate interest in hearing such facts. Thus his reference *must* have been to the disclosure of private facts. This is confirmed by the fact that the paragraph from which the contested dicta are drawn starts, 'Where an individual is a public figure he is entitled to have his *privacy* respected in appropriate circumstances'; the guidelines of which these dicta form part are said to be directed to first instance courts hearing claims arising from the publication of *private facts*. Finally, he states that the court may take into account such public interest 'in deciding on which side of the line a case falls.' Since a court would only be *involved* if the information disclosed arguably consisted of private facts, this makes it clear beyond argument that Lord Woolf *was* talking about the revelation of such facts, since it is only the revelation of such facts that may form the subject matter of a legal claim. Unequivocally, therefore, these *dicta* do suggest that there is a public interest in the revelation of private facts about a public figure if the public is interested in hearing them.

The Court of Appeal has however once again taken the opportunity to steer the judiciary strongly away from Lord Woolf's eccentric conception of the 'public interest'. In *Douglas III*,[155] the Court, speaking of the publication of snatched pictures of the couple's wedding, said:

In the present case, however, we find it difficult to see how it could be contended that the public interest (as opposed to public curiosity) could be involved over and above the general public interest in a free press. Particularly so, as it was clearly the intention

---

[153] [2003] 2 WLR 80.   [154] Ibid, at [40].   [155] [2005] 3 WLR 881.

of the Douglases and *OK!* to publish a large number of (much clearer) photographs of the same event.[156]

These dicta first of all clearly disavow any association between that which interests the public (public curiosity) and the public interest properly so called. But it is also noteworthy that, despite recognizing that there is such a 'general public interest' in a free press, the Court nevertheless finds that the Douglases would have had a 'virtually unanswerable case' to restrain publication.[157] Given that it is generally agreed that a wedding attended by 200 guests and which is about to be publicized to millions is not a particularly intimate or compelling privacy interest, these dicta amount to a clear indication that this 'general public interest' carries very little weight indeed with the judges.

Finally, a broader objection to the concept of the public interest advanced by Lord Woolf may be made: it is that the court at this point seems wholly to have lost sight of the fact that it is dealing with the circumstances in which *a human right*—the right to respect for private life[158]—may legitimately be invaded. Human rights are generally conceived of as *counter-majoritarian* principles; their *raison d'etre* is, at least in part, to act as protection against the tyranny even of the majority. Such is the essential difference between a polity based upon utilitarianism, or the satisfaction of the majority, and one founded upon some basic notion of human rights.[159] Effectively, if the interest that Lord Woolf describes can outweigh the right to privacy, then we have arrived at a point at which the fact that large amounts of people do not want you to be able to enjoy a particular right is a good reason for overriding it—in other words, the precise converse of the notion of human rights. The debasement of individual rights to the collective whim that this view appears to encapsulate brings to mind Schauer's caustic comment: 'Increases in knowledge that admittedly increase the pleasure of the knower are necessarily valuable only under a theory that treats pleasurable punchings of others as valuable . . .'[160]

This view, it is worth noting, is also one that takes us close to the view of some commentators upon the approach that should be taken by American courts in adjudicating upon the 'private facts' tort;[161] a defence will be made out if the newspaper can show that the publication is 'newsworthy'. The problem is, of course, that material appearing in the news media may by definition be accounted 'newsworthy' so that the

---

[156] Op cit, at [254].   [157] Ibid, at [253].

[158] The Court was clear that it was required to act compatibly with Article 8 in the case: 'Under section 6 of the [HRA], the court, as a public authority, is required not to act "in a way which is incompatible with a Convention right." The court is able to achieve this by absorbing the rights which articles 8 and 10 protect into the long-established action for breach of confidence.' ([2002] 3 WLR 542, at 546).

[159] For a very clear discussion on this point, see N. Simmonds, *Central Issues in Jurisprudence*, 2nd edn., London: Sweet and Maxwell, 2002, pp 143–51.

[160] F. Schauer, 'Reflections on the Value of Truth' (1991) 41 *Case Western Reserve Law Review* 699, 711.

[161] *The Restatement* (Second) of the Law of Torts, 625D defines the tort as follows: 'One who gives publicity to a matter concerning the private life of another is subject to liability to the other . . . if the matter publicised is of a kind that (a) would be highly offensive to a reasonable person and (b) is not of legitimate concern to the public.'

press *can* become judges in their own case. One commentator, Zimmerman, defends such a 'leave it to the press model', arguing that it 'may actually be the appropriate and principled response to the newsworthiness inquiry' because 'the economic survival of publishers and broadcasters depends upon their ability to provide a product that the public will buy.'[162] The problem with this view is that it renders the individual's privacy wholly dependent upon the standards of those who read a particular newspaper; the right to privacy is thus open to violation simply on the basis of public whim, legally recognized through the First Amendment. This view thus *precludes* any effective 'right' to privacy.[163] Hence the commentary on 'the failure of American privacy law;'[164] as one commentator puts it: 'The sweeping language of [this] law serves largely to mask the fact that the law provides almost no protection against privacy-invading disclosures.'[165] Or as Wacks puts it: 'It is widely acknowledged that the ... "newsworthiness" defence has effectively demolished the private-facts tort.'[166] This is the inevitable result of an approach that, in effect, denies the status of privacy as a human right. It may be defendable in the US, given the absolute terms of the First Amendment and the lack of any countervailing constitutional right to informational privacy: it is not so to a court which has found that, as a result of the HRA, it is bound to act compatibly with the ECHR,[167] since such an approach puts in jeopardy the presumptive equality of expression and speech rights, as discussed above.

The guidelines in *A v B* go on to add a further comment on the public interest test, which must have made the Court of Appeal the toast of the tabloid press:

The courts must not ignore the fact that if newspapers do not publish information which the public are interested in, there will be fewer newspapers published, which will not be in the public interest.[168]

A cruder definition of the public interest is hardly imaginable: the more newspapers sold the better; a sales figure of 100,000 copies of the *Sunday People* is, regardless of the content of that paper, a better outcome in the public interest than a figure of, say 50,000. This argument hardly needs to be stated for its extraordinarily unconvincing nature to be evident. Nevertheless, there are worrying echoes of it in *Campbell*. Lady Hale commented: 'One reason why press freedom is so important is that we need newspapers to sell in order to ensure that we still have newspapers at all',[169] while Lord Hoffman reminded us: 'We value the freedom of the press but the press is a commercial enterprise and can flourish only by selling newspapers.'[170]

---

[162] D. Zimmerman, 'Requiem for a Heavyweight: A Farewell to Warren and Brandeis's Privacy Tort' (1983) 68 *Cornell Law Review* 291, 353.

[163] Zimmerman defends this view on the basis that otherwise the judges must make class-based judgments about what kinds of desires for information are illegitimate (ibid, 354).

[164] This is indeed the title of D. Anderson's essay on the US 'private facts' tort in Markesenis (ed.) *Protecting Privacy*, Oxford: Clarendon, 1999.

[165] Ibid, at 140.   [166] *Privacy and Press Freedom*, London: Blackstones, 1995, p 113.

[167] See Chapter 3 at 134–43.   [168] Op cit, at 552.   [169] Lady Hale, op cit, at [162].

[170] Lord Hoffman, op cit, at [77].

Such statements do not advert to an obvious counter-argument on this point: that if the courts are able, through development of effective privacy rights, to *discourage* newspapers from publishing the kind of intimate gossip with which both these cases were concerned, then the result may well be a greater concentration in the media upon serious stories, including discussion of matters of real political and social importance. It is frequently remarked of countries which have effective privacy laws, such as France and Germany, that their media does not exhibit the 'gutter' quality associated with the UK tabloid press. In our fiercely competitive media market, the tendency of debased and lurid 'news' coverage in one newspaper to drive down the standards in another is very marked. The introduction of some legal protection for privacy might encourage a movement away from the prurient trivia which currently fills so many of our newspapers and, so far from threatening free speech in the press, could enhance it. In other words, given the physical limitations constraining news-papers in terms of space and frequency of publication, it may fairly be said that there is only so much available paper every day in the UK on which newsworthy speech is able to appear. If stories about the diets or clothes or sexual practices of celebrities squeeze out political speech, it can be said that low-value speech is stifling speech that is actually directed towards the maintenance of a truly democratic society. In itself this tendency runs counter to the Meiklejohnian argument for free speech from demo-cracy,[171] since it leads to the impoverishment of the diet of a very large number of newspaper readers and inhibits their ability to participate in an informed manner in a democracy. The development of a privacy law that was fully respectful of the press's *legitimate* role in a democracy would have at the least a *tendency* to arrest this debasement of standards, while at the same time it would be strongly in accordance with this key free speech justification. If one of the central aims of the Convention is, as the European Court has repeatedly stressed, the furtherance of a democratic soci-ety,[172] a tendency away from a preoccupation with lurid trivia and towards an interest in political coverage in the popular press could only be viewed as furthering that aim and thus as being wholly consonant with the values underlying Article 10.

Role models and the public's right 'not to be misled'[173]

It appears to now be widely accepted that, as Lord Nicholls put it in *Campbell*, in a statement of principle also endorsed by Lord Hope:[174]

. . . where a public figure chooses to present a false image and make untrue pronouncements about his or her life, the press will normally be entitled to put the record straight.[175]

---

[171] See above at pp 16–18.

[172] As noted above, the Court has repeatedly asserted that freedom of expression 'constitutes one of the essential foundations of a democratic society': see e.g., *Observer and Guardian v the United Kingdom* A 216 (1991).

[173] The argument addressed in the text is confined to the situation in which prior disclosures by a public figure have led to a *deception*, which it is in the public interest to correct. For discussion of the related but separate argument that such disclosures amount to a waiver of the person's privacy, see above, at 772–8.

[174] Op cit, at 82.   [175] Ibid, at [24]

As discussed above, this was the major reason why all the courts who heard the Campbell case accepted that, in Lord Hoffman's words,

the *Mirror* was entitled to publish the fact of Campbell's drug dependency and the fact that she was seeking treatment . . . [because] she had specifically given publicity to the very question of whether she took drugs and had falsely said that she did not. . . . This creates a sufficient public interest in the correction of the impression she had previously given.[176]

Lady Hale agreed that 'The press must be free to expose the truth and put the record straight.'[177]

This notion, while it appears in the PCC Code to which the courts must have regard, is it will be suggested, a troubling one, which requires further examination. In the *Campbell* decision, there were at least clear, public and untruthful statements by the applicant to be corrected, and the issue, drug addiction, was undeniably a matter of serious public concern. But this line of argument has also been used in cases with much more flimsy facts to support it. It was, for example, used in both *A v B* and *Theakston*; in each case it was said—and accepted by the court—that the figures in question, while not politicians, were role models of a sort and that it is important for the public not to be misled about such people. In these cases, this notion was pressed into action in these cases in a way that was thoroughly muddled. In the former case, the court laid down the general guideline that:

[A] public figure may hold a position where higher standards of conduct can be rightly expected by the public. [He] may be a role model whose conduct could well be emulated by others. He may set the fashion.[178]

Applying this to the facts before it, it found:

. . . it is not self-evident that how a well-known premiership football player chooses to spend his time off the football field does not have a modicum of public interest. Footballers are role models for young people and undesirable behaviour on their part can set an unfortunate example.[179]

In *Theakston* the argument was put with rather more conviction in a passage that is worth quoting in full:

I consider also that there is a real element of public interest in the publication at least of the first aspect of the proposed article with which I am currently concerned [i.e. the revelation of the bare facts, minus sexual detail]. The BBC employs [Theakston] and projects him through his role on 'Top of the Pops' to younger viewers, and also to listeners on his programmes as a suitable person, for them to respect and to receive via the television into their homes. Whilst he may not be presented as a role model, nonetheless the very nature of his job as a T.V. presenter of programmes for the younger viewer means that he will be seen as somebody whose lifestyle, publicised as it is, is one which does not attract moral opprobrium and would at least be generally harmless if followed . . . The activity in question here may make viewers or the parents of viewers react differently. It is insufficient in my

---

[176] Ibid, at [58].   [177] Ibid, at [151].   [178] Op cit, at [11] (xiii).   [179] Ibid, at [45].

judgment to overcome this point for Mr Tugendhat [Counsel for Theakston] to say that the newspaper could take its information to the BBC. The free press is not confined to the role of a confidential police force; it is entitled to communicate directly with the public for the public to reach its own conclusion. Indeed the more that Mr Tugendhat emphasised the potential degree of damage to the claimant's employment from the publication of the article the more it seemed to me that he was emphasising the public interest in its publication.[180]

The argument here is somewhat opaque, but the judge appears to suggest that Theakston has put about a false image of moral acceptability and that it is in the public interest for this misconception to be corrected. The suggestion also seems to be made that the publication of Theakston's escapades in the brothel additionally serves the function of showing that he is not living up to a part of his job contract. Now in general, conduct by an employee which falls short of what is expected of him by his employee is a private matter between the two of them: the public are not called upon to give a second opinion. But the judge dismisses the idea that this is perhaps something for the BBC alone: the public are entitled to form their own view on the matter.[181] In relation to both arguments—that the public are entitled to know that they have been deceived (in both cases), and, specifically, to form a view on Theakston's failure to live up to his image as a BBC presenter, as with that made in *A v B plc* that footballers are role models whose behaviour influences the young—three rejoinders may be made.

First of all, these arguments rely upon a factual *assumption* by the judges: that Theakston and Flitcroft, respectively, are persons whose conduct and example *will* influence the public: presumably in relation to their sexual conduct. But neither evidence nor substantial argument (any argument at all in *A v B*) is offered to support this assumption. A judge in the Australian High Court has recently remarked upon the dangers of such judicial 'fact-finding':

Judges sometimes make assumptions about current conditions and modern society as bases for their decisions. Great care is required when this is done. An assumption of such a kind may be unsafe because the judge making it is necessarily making an earlier assumption that he or she is sufficiently informed, or exposed to the subject matter in question, to enable an assumption to be made about it. That is why judges prefer to, and indeed are generally required to act on evidence actually adducted . . .[182]

---

[180] [2002] EMLR 22, at [69].

[181] This assertion also brushes aside an established line of case law, including Court of Appeal authorities, to the effect that, where a breach of confidence is argued to be necessary as revealing misconduct or fraud in relation to the performance of the person's official duties, notification to the competent authorities, rather than to the press, may often be the appropriate course of action: see *Francome v Mirror Group Newspapers* [1984] 1 WLR 892, CA; *Initial Services Ltd v Putterill* [1968] 1 QB 396, 405–6, *per* Lord Denning; *Imutran v Uncaged Campaigns Ltd* [2001] 2 All ER 385, paras 25–27, *per* Morritt VC; *Attorney-General v Guardian Newspapers (No 2)* [1990] 1 AC 109, 269, *per* Lord Griffiths; 282, *per* Lord Goff; 177, *per* Sir John Donaldson in the Court of Appeal. This may well be justifiable, given the stress laid by Strasbourg under Article 10 on the press's 'watchdog' role, but this could have been made explicit.

[182] *Australian Broadcasting Corporation v Lenah Game Meats* [2001] HCA 63, para 252, *per* J. Callinan, The case concerns confidentiality and privacy and was cited in *A v B plc.*

Here the essentially speculative assumptions about the attitudes of young people to figures such as Theakston and Flitcroft were made without any evidence, in a way that had an impact on the legal protection offered to another's right to privacy. Whether this is legitimate at all is seriously open to question.[183]

Second, even if one assumes that the assumptions made were correct—a major concession—the problem remains that both *Theakston* and *A v B plc* leave it wholly unclear what actual harm to the public interest is entailed by people having incorrect impressions about the private lives of people such as pop presenters and footballers.[184] If it is the case that those of the public who care about these things vaguely thinks that such and such a footballer is a faithful husband when he is not, that such and such a TV presenter would not ever visit a prostitute when in fact he has once done so, what is the clear public harm that can be identified? The notion that certain people are role models is generally advanced in order to argue that such people should in their public actions behave morally, so as to influence for good the behaviour of those who look up to, and are influenced by them. For example, David Beckham may legitimately be called upon to set an example to England fans and other footballers by conducting himself honourably and fairly as a footballer. But how does it follow that if certain people are in fact role models to some extent, *that itself* means that it is automatically harmful for those who look up to them to have incorrect information about some aspect not of their public persona, but their personal life?

There are of course certain figures in relation to which it can be argued with some force that it *does* matter if the public is mislead, even about their private lives. In the case of a moralizing politician, who places his or her conservative moral values into political argument, while concealing a flagrantly 'immoral' private life, there *is* a clear service to democracy if the latter is revealed: the politician has been relying on his private life as a way of persuading the public to support him and his political platform—he has sought to secure political advantage from the false image he has cultivated.[185] That information, that false impression matters, because it can affect the outcome of a political process: sway actual votes, perhaps; certainly affect the way in which the parties and their platforms are viewed by the public. But none of these considerations apply to the people with which the court was concerned in these two cases.

---

[183] The author is not suggesting that genuine 'role models' have *no* impact on societal attitudes; see the literature cited in note 92 above. The point made is that the assumption made here as to the *particular impact* (on sexual morality) of *relatively minor figures* was made without investigation or consideration of such research.

[184] It is possible that the judges may have had at the back of their minds Mill's argument in favour of free expression from its value in discovering the truth; however, this argument is thought to apply to discovering the truth in terms of *opinions* as to moral, political, social, and scientific propositions; it does not apply *per se* to the straightforward disclosure of private facts: see discussion above at pp 684–5.

[185] The example of John Major's affair with Edwina Currie, conducted at a time when the Prime Minister identified his party with conservative moral views on sexuality, and sacked certain ministers whose private lives did not conform to such a view, is, perhaps, apposite.

There is another, more philosophical point raised by the assumption that having false impressions about celebrities is in some way intrinsically harmful. The argument that *any* deception of the public entitles the media to put the record straight comes perilously close to destroying the very notion of the right to informational autonomy, or selective disclosure, which, as discussed in Chapter 13, many commentators see as lying at the heart of the right to privacy.[186] Such selective disclosure is something we all practice in our daily lives; arguably it is the only means of reconciling two fundamental human needs: to maintain some degree of privacy, and to communicate intimately about our lives with others in order to build and foster close relationships. Such selectivity in disclosure will, on occasions, *inevitably* lead to the creation of false assumptions about us in the minds of others. Indeed, this may be actively sought at times: for example someone who does not wish the fact that she is homosexual to be widely known outside her intimate circle of friends and family,[187] will inevitably be selective about whom she discloses this fact to.[188] She may further, under pressure, and if asked in a public environment, actively give a deceptive impression if asked about her sexuality, knowing that a refusal to answer will often be taken to give assent and thus effectively make the very revelation she objects to. Such a person has certainly 'misled the public', but it does not seem persuasive to argue that this *per se* entitle a journalist who discovers the truth to put the record straight. We cannot uphold—and ourselves practice—the right to selective disclosure and, consistently with that practice, insist that any and every misleading of the public is a wrong entitling the press to intrude into privacy to correct. Rather it should be asked whether that false impression actually matters in some way: for example, if the closet homosexual was an Anglican Bishop who supported exclusion of homosexuals from the priesthood, the revelation of his homosexuality would directly contribute to an important political debate as well as revealing a major piece of hypocrisy in the holder of a public office *that is related to that office*. By contrast, the revelation that a particular TV presenter has visited a brothel does not appear to do either.

The third argument relates to the confusion the judges appear to have fall into here as to whether it is the deception of the public that matters, or the moral 'damage' to those influenced by role models that may result if it transpires that such people do in fact behave in undesirable ways.[189] The difficulty is that, in the latter case, the harm

---

[186] See above, at p 662–4.

[187] The former actor Nigel Hawthorne is a good example. He concealed his private life for many years from the press, until the revelation of his homosexuality in 1995 caused a flurry of media focus on his personal life, causing him intense distress.

[188] It was noted above that Feldman argues that privacy protects what he identifies as the value in forming those spheres of social interaction and intimacy—work, friends, family, lovers—which are essential to human flourishing by protecting persons operating in a given sphere of existence from unjustified interference by those outside it: see D. Feldman, 'Secrecy, Dignity or Autonomy? Views of Privacy as a Civil Liberty' 47(2) CLP 42, 54.

[189] In other words, the fear is presumably that greater sexual 'immorality' may occur if role models are found to behave promiscuously.

that results flows from *publication*, not from the behaviour itself, and yet this 'moral harm' argument is used as an argument to *support* the very publication that causes the harm. Thus the only harm that the court could identify in *A v B plc* was that 'undesirable behaviour' by the footballer might set 'an unfortunate example;' yet giving publicity to this behaviour—i.e. doing the very thing that causes this harm—was somehow yet seen as *serving* the public interest. The same argument, though not clearly articulated, applies in the *Theakston* case: if Theakston were indeed a role model, whom viewers were expected to 'respect', then surely it is the *publicizing* of his morally abhorrent behaviour (as the judge saw it) that would have the effect of causing damage to the moral well-being of his young admirers about whom the judge is so concerned. Perversely, however, the court in both cases appeared to think that the damage flowing from giving publicity to such information was an argument that actually supported *allowing* that publicity. Lady Hale in *Campbell* appeared to be troubled by precisely this point, musing: 'It might be questioned why, if a role model has adopted a stance which all would agree is beneficial rather than detrimental to society, it is so important to reveal that she has feet of clay.'[190]

Clearly again, the case, say, of a politician who had been found out perpetrating a fraud with public money, is very different. In this case, it is the politician's dishonesty that *itself* renders him or her unfit for the job they have been elected to do. In contrast, in the case of Theakston, a presenter on a pop programme, his duty to the BBC is to present a morally acceptable *face* or *image* to the public, that is, ensure that any personal behaviour that might offend viewers was *kept private*. If, for example, Theakston enjoyed certain unusual sexual practices with his partners that some viewers might find distasteful or even morally repellent, then surely the duty he would owe to the BBC would be, not actually to abstain from such practices, but simply to ensure that they did not enter the public domain. Seen this way, it is the *newspaper* that is breaching the condition of Theakston's employment and any duty he has to the public. The judge appears to show some awareness of this when he talks of it being Theakston's lifestyle '*publicized as it is*' that may be seen as acceptable to follow. In other words, the (entirely speculative) danger to young people here arises from the publicity, not the lifestyle itself. The public interest in such cases, if there is any on either side, thus appears to lie in preventing the harmful *publicity*, not in the lifestyle itself. The only argument to be made against this view is that it is inherently beneficial for the public not to hold inaccurate views as to the morality or otherwise of the person's private conduct. But as discussed above, it is very hard to identify just what this benefit consists of.

---

190 Op cit, at [151].

REMEDIES[191]

Damages are available in confidence cases,[192] in addition to, or in substitution for, injunctive relief, and, it seems, regardless of whether the court could have ordered injunctive relief in the particular circumstances.[193] There is now authority for the proposition that damages for emotional distress may be awarded in 'private fact' cases. In *Campbell* damages were modestly assessed at a little over £14,000, including £1,000 for aggravated damages, in respect of the 'trashing' of Campbell's character in articles published after she commenced her action against the *Mirror*. In *Archer v Williams*[194] it was accepted that damages could be awarded for emotional distress, in this case caused by publication of details of plastic surgery: they were assessed at £2,500. Damages are also available under the Data Protection Act.[195] An account of profits may alternatively be ordered.[196] It will be immediately noted that these amounts are exceptionally modest and it may well be doubted whether, given the very substantial sums of money to be gained by publishing 'celebrity exclusives', these very low sums of money represent any form of deterrence to the media. Arguably, the awards of damages being made are simply insufficient to amount to any form of deterrent to actions—accepted to infringe the fundamental right to privacy—that are immensely profitable. The law, we would suggest, is in danger of relapsing into tokenism. However, the recent Court of Appeal judgment in *Douglas III* showed some welcome recognition of precisely this point: but left damages the same . . .

The sum [of damages awarded] is also small in the sense that it could not represent any real deterrent to a newspaper or magazine, with a large circulation, contemplating the publication of photographs which infringed an individual's privacy. Accordingly, particularly in the light of the state of competition in the newspaper and magazine industry, the refusal of an interlocutory injunction in a case such as this represents a strong potential disincentive to respect for aspects of private life, which the Convention intends should be respected.[197]

The obvious answer—aside from the granting of interim injunctions, when they can practically be obtained,[198] is the ordering of the remedy of an account of profits made

---

[191] Applicants will not be able to rely directly upon the Article 13 right to an 'effective remedy' which is not incorporated by the HRA (s 1(1)); reference to the relevant jurisprudence under s 2(1) *may* however be permissible: HL Deb vol 583 Col 477, 18 November 1997.

[192] Under Lord Cairns Act; damages were awarded in the decisions in *Douglas II* (affirmed in *Douglas III* and in *Campbell v MGN*).

[193] *Hooper v Rogers* [1975] 1 Ch 43, 48; *Race Relations Board v Applin* [1973] 1 QB 815; D. Capper, 'Damages for Breach of the Equitable Duty of Confidence' (1994) 14 LS 313; F. Gurry, *Breach of Confidence*, Oxford: Clarendon Press, 1984, Chapter 23.

[194] [2003] EMLR 38.   [195] See Chapter 14 at 720–1.   [196] Op cit, at [123].

[197] Op cit, at [225]–[257].

[198] Sometimes, of course, the person concerned will have no prior notice that an intrusive story is about to be published, and so will have no opportunity to apply for an injunction: this was, seemingly, the case in *Campbell*.

from the unlawful publication, based on the principle that no man shall profit from his wrong. As to this, the Court in *Douglas III* said:

If, however, *Hello!* had made a profit on the publication, we would have had no hesitation in accepting that the Douglases would have been entitled to seek an account of that profit. Such an approach may also serve to discourage any wrongful publication, at least where it is motivated by money. [199]

It is to be hoped that these dicta will encourage applicants to apply for, and courts to grant this remedy, which is likely substantially to outweigh the quanta of damages that have so far been awarded.

It should be noted in particular that this recent judgment of the Court of Appeal is likely to be of some importance in this area in relation to cases in which the applicant is complaining of the intrusion of unauthorized media into a situation in which an exclusive contract was awarded to one particular publication, as in *Douglas* itself. In that case, the Court of Appeal accepted that negotiating an exclusive contract with one media outlet was a legitimate way to control the press and protect the occasion's privacy. Both the High Court and the Court of Appeal accepted that there had been a breach of the couple's privacy by virtue of the publication of the unauthorized photographs, and awarded *circa* £14,000 damages. However, the Court of Appeal found that this interference with an exclusive contract gave no cause of action to *OK!*—the original beneficiaries of it. It therefore overturned the award of £1 million damages to *OK!*. The obvious problems is that the very meagre damages awarded, coupled with the enormous profits to be made by publishing such 'stolen' exclusives, provides in effect a financial incentive to invade privacy; accepting that a legal wrong will be done to the person whose occasion is intruded upon, but that the damages to be paid will be overwhelmingly outweighed by the profits. The Court of Appeal in *Douglas III* referred to the damages awarded as 'a very modest sum in the context of this litigation.'[200] In a sense, the very large award of damages originally awarded to *OK!*—over £1,000,000, had provided a powerful disincentive against such intrusive 'spoilers', a disincentive that has now been removed.[201]

However, the most important issue both for applicants and for the press is the basis on which the courts grant interim injunctions to restrain publication. From the applicant's perspective, obtaining such injunctions is vital in privacy cases, far more so than in defamation. This is because damage done to *reputation* by initial publication can be subsequently restored by a public finding that the allegation was false. By contrast, if private information is made public, the law can compensate for this harm at final trial by awarding damages, but it cannot in any way cure the invasion of privacy: it cannot erase the information revealed from peoples' memories. From the defendant's perspective, on the other hand, if the story is topical, even an interim injunction might kill it off completely. As Robertson and Nichol put it: 'In breach of confidence . . . the

---

[199] Ibid, at [249].   [200] Op cit, at [110].
[201] At the time of writing, the case is being appealed to the House of Lords.

critical stage is usually the application for an interim injunction . . . If the publisher is able to publish . . . the action will often evaporate . . . If the story is injuncted the publisher will often lose interest . . .'[202] Similarly, Leigh and Lustgarten comment: 'the interim stage is the critical one. It is effectively the disposition of the matter'.[203]

The test for injunctive relief in cases affecting freedom of expression is governed by section 12(3) HRA and applies generally to all such cases: it is considered in Chapter 3.[204] All that needs to be said here is that, in essence, in most cases, an injunction will be awarded only if the judge considers it more likely than not that the applicant will succeed at final trial.[205] Thus, if the scales appear to be evenly balanced between the parties, injunctive relief will be refused, as set out in *A v B*.[206] In terms of the Data Protection Act, its major drawback as a statutory privacy remedy is its bar on interim injunctions against the press.[207]

CONCLUSIONS

As this chapter has sought to demonstrate, the reconciliation of the clash between privacy and speech interests is one of the most difficult tasks that the courts have to tackle when confronted by privacy claims. In this respect, we welcome the decisive contribution that *Campbell* has made in putting to rights the previous structural emasculation of Article 8 by Article 10, and setting out clearly two key principles to be used when these rights collide: the minimum impairment of each right by the other, and a balancing exercise informed and directed by the values underpinning those rights in Strasbourg jurisprudence and legal philosophy, in particular the requirement of a genuine public interest to justify any publication that interferes with privacy rights. At present, however, there is something of a dissonance between English and Strasbourg conceptions as to what types of 'private fact' *can* make such a contribution. While English courts have been rightly criticized for swallowing flimsy press arguments of 'public interest', Strasbourg is in danger of adopting a rigid and artificial distinction between facts relating to politicians and those with official functions on the one hand and everyone else on the other,[208] thus taking insufficient account of the

---

[202] *Media Law*, 3rd edn., London: Penguin, 1992, 190.

[203] I. Leigh and L. Lustgarten, 'Making Rights Real: The Courts, Remedies, and the Human Rights Act' [1999] 55(3) *CLJ* 509, 533 (referring to the granting of interim injunctions generally); see also 551.

[204] See pp 153–7.

[205] As established by the House of Lords in *Cream Holdings Limited and others v Banerjee and others* [2004] 3 WLR 918: 'the general approach should be that courts will be exceedingly slow to make interim restraint orders where the applicant has not satisfied the court he will probably ("more likely than not") succeed at the trial' (*per* Lord Nicholls, at [22]).

[206] Op cit, at 240 ff.   [207] See Chapter 14 at 721.

[208] M. Sanderson, for example, argues that the *Von Hannover* decision wholly fails to recognize an intermediate category, *between* public officials and private citizens, of influential public figures: M. Sanderson, 'Is *Von Hannover v Germany* a Step Backward for the Substantive Analysis of Speech and Privacy Interests?' [2004] 6 *European Human Rights Law Review* 631, at 636–9.

enormous influence that nominally private actors can have on contemporary society. A compromise between the two positions is needed: one that is realistic in its appreciation of the importance of such influence and of the valuable role that 'infotainment' reportage *can* play in stimulating public debate, but rigorous in scrutinizing claims that reportage of private facts will have this effect and, on the particular facts of the case, is a necessary and proportionate means of doing so.

Whilst individual decisions remain of concern,[209] and it will take some time before it becomes clear whether *Campbell* will have the decisive influence on the law that one might expect, a cautiously optimistic conclusion is, we would argue, in order. We are within sight of the creation of a privacy law in the Human Rights Act era which is fully in harmony with the key aim of the Convention—to 'maintain and promote the ideals and values of a democratic society'.[210] It may now, perhaps, be recognized that a democratic society needs not only a vibrant and irreverent press to flourish; it is also one that must ensure a sphere of private space free from public accountability, for reflection, emotional release, experiments in living; for the development of family and other intimate relationships, for free association, and for free speech itself. It is to be hoped that the courts will now use the judgment in *Campbell* to decide cases in a way that allows the flourishing of individuals *and* the society in which they live, recognizing that free speech and privacy are crucial to both.

[209] For example, the wholly unreported decision to refuse the Beckhams an injunction in relation to a story as to problems within their marriage, including very intimate material, provided by their former nanny in clear breach of contract, apparently on the grounds of the 'public interest' of the story: see *The Guardian*, 25 April 2005, http://media.guardian.co.uk/site/story/0,14173,1471125,00.html

[210] *Kjeldsen v Denmark* (1976) 1 EHRR 711, 731.

16

RESTRICTIONS PROTECTING THE PRIVATE AND FAMILY LIFE OF CHILDREN

INTRODUCTION

This chapter concentrates on the conflict of rights between media free speech and the privacy of children, a conflict that forms a highly significant but neglected aspect of the post-HRA speech/privacy clash so very pertinent at the present time.[1] There are differences of emphasis between this clash of rights and that between the privacy of adults (in practice, usually celebrities) and media freedom, discussed in Chapters 14 and 15. In this instance the children in question have normally not courted publicity and could not be viewed as role models, although their situations do sometimes have a public interest dimension. They have normally come into the limelight due to unexpected misfortune. Thus arguments as to the extent to which they have exploited their private information are irrelevant and their privacy interests tend to relate to profound and life-changing experiences. Their privacy claims are not therefore contingent and precarious, as they can be in the case of celebrities, but strongly engage a range of private and family life-based values. So in this instance the clash between the rights can be particularly profound, but it might be anticipated that the courts would show particular sympathy towards the privacy claim. In fact the clash in question has in general elicited, it will be contended, a misguided response from the domestic courts[2] and there has been a tendency to minimize that claim.

The range of restrictions on what can be published about child welfare matters and

---

[1] This topic has been fairly extensively considered in relation to the privacy of adult celebrities, see Chapters 14 and 15; see also G. Phillipson, 'Transforming Breach of Confidence: Towards a Common Law Right of Privacy under the Human Rights Act' [2003] 66 *MLR* 726–758; H. Tomlinson, Q.C. and H. Rogers, 'Privacy and Expression: Convention Rights and Interim Injunctions' [2003] *EHRLR* (Special Issue: Privacy) 37.

[2] The pre-HRA academic consensus was also to the effect that the jurisprudence in this area was seriously flawed in relation to its failure to probe the limits of free speech in a principled fashion where it conflicts with minors' privacy claims. See: I. Cram, 'Minors' Privacy, Free Speech and the Courts' [1997] *PL*, 410–19; L. Woods, 'Freedom of Expression and the Protection of Minors' (2001) 13(2) *CFLQ*, 209–23.

disputes concerning children is at an unprecedented level.[3] Where restrictions cover the matter of upbringing they are enhanced by the 'paramountcy principle'—the principle deriving from s 1(1) Children Act 1989 (CA) that the child's welfare relating to upbringing automatically prevails over the rights of other parties.[4] Certain statutory restrictions leave virtually no leeway for consideration of the free speech claim. But in so far as the restrictions leave such leeway to the courts, the paramountcy principle stands in the way if it applies. In other words, it pre-empts a principled resolution of the conflict by ensuring that one side automatically wins out. In the terms of the European Convention on Human Rights, the Article 8 rights of the child to respect for private and family life[5] trump the Article 10[6] rights of the media,[7] where 'upbringing' is in issue so as to activate the principle. But judicial unease with this situation, especially in relation to the Human Rights Act, has failed to lead to debate as to what the welfare of the child genuinely requires where a conflict with reporting rights arises. Rather, it has manifested itself in a determination in the courts to avoid the issue by the use of exclusionary interpretations of the meaning of the term 'upbringing' so as to avoid an engagement with the conflict in question. It will be contended that the use of such interpretations has meant that media debate as to welfare is precluded or distorted—since issues relating to the central matter of upbringing are excluded from it—but that where the paramountcy principle can be found *not* to apply, the approach is almost equally flawed in taking a near-converse stance: the Article 8 rights of the child (as encapsulating aspects of the child's welfare) have in a number of instances figured merely as exceptions to be narrowly interpreted under Article 10(2). Even after that approach had been abandoned, formally speaking, it lingered on in the judicial stance taken to the child's private life claim.

[3] They are discussed below; for recent comment on their extent, see: M. Dodd, 'Children, the Press and a Missed Opportunity' [2002] *CFLQ*, 103–8 esp at 103; J. Dixon, 'Children and the Statutory Restraints on Publicity' [2001] Fam Law 757, esp 761.

[4] s 1(1) provides: 'When a court determines any question with respect to: upbringing of a child; or the administration of a child's property or the application of any income arising from it, the child's welfare shall be the court's paramount consideration.'

[5] Article 8 provides: '1. Everyone has the right to respect for his private and family life, his home and his correspondence. 2. There shall be no interference by a public authority with the exercise of this right except such as is in accordance with the law and is necessary in a democratic society in the interests of national security, public safety or the economic well being of the country, for the prevention of disorder or crime, for the protection of health or morals, or for the protection of the rights and freedoms of others.'

[6] Article 10 provides: '1. Everyone has the right to freedom of expression. This right shall include the freedom to hold opinions and receive and impart information and ideas without interference by public authority and regardless of frontiers . . . 2. The exercise of these freedoms, since it carries with it duties and responsibilities, may be subject to such formalities, conditions, restrictions or penalties as are prescribed by law and are necessary in a democratic society in the interests of national security, territorial integrity or public safety, for the prevention of disorder or crime, for the protection of health or morals, for the protection of the reputation or rights of others, for preventing the disclosure of information received in confidence or for maintaining the authority and impartiality of the judiciary.'

[7] There is a reluctance in the family law field to view the conflict in question as a matter of individual rights; see Butler Sloss LJ in *Re L (A Child) (Contact: Domestic Violence)* [2001] Fam 260 CA at para 294. The trump card metaphor is becoming common parlance, as indicated below: see *Re S (A Child)* [2003] 2 FCR 577, para 62, per Baroness Hale.

The inception of the Human Rights Act has called the judicial approaches to this conflict into question since the stance at the domestic and at the European levels differs. At the domestic level, where the paramountcy principle does not apply, media freedom of expression tends to win out unless a statutory restriction is imposed, while where it does apply, the Article 10 rights of the media hardly weigh in the scales at all. At the European level, however, the two rights are afforded a more equal weight. The emerging approach at Strasbourg to clashes between Articles 8 and 10 in general makes it clear that an automatic or near-automatic abrogation of one or the other right is unsustainable and entirely opposed to the values underlying the Convention. This chapter argues that therefore the established domestic approaches to this conflict of rights can no longer be sustained under the Human Rights Act. They are flawed since they depend on a refusal to afford *any* weight to an individual right when it comes into conflict with another such right, where the paramountcy principle applies. But where it does not apply a similar problem arises—there was, pre-HRA and in the very early post-HRA years, a refusal to accept that Articles 8 and 10 are of presumptively equal value, and the private and family life claim tended to be minimized. It will be argued that even at the present time there is a danger that lip service only will be paid to the presumptive equality of the two rights in this context. This was apparent, it will be argued in the recent leading case—*In Re S (a child)*.[8]

The comparison chosen—of clashes between Article 8 and Article 10 in this field—highlights the failure of the UK courts to adopt a consistent and theorized approach to the clashing rights issue. The key argument is that clashes of rights inevitably raise difficult moral questions and that therefore once the value of each individual right has been recognized, as it must be under a deontological document such as the European Convention on Human Rights, the issues of principle at stake should be identified in order to determine how far, if at all, the moral conflict is incommensurable and irreducible. Having sought to demonstrate that the domestic courts have strayed away from the approach espoused under the European Convention on Human Rights, despite the inception of the Human Rights Act, this chapter will move on to suggest a model under the HRA to be used for the resolution of the issue which engages with the underlying justificatory principles.

As discussed below, a range of restrictions on reporting related to children has incrementally accumulated. The current complex and chaotic web of restrictions relates strongly to the Article 8 rights of children to respect for private and family life, although certain restrictions also have the intention of protecting the administration of justice.[9] Below, the discussion covers the stance taken by the courts in adjudicating on such restrictions in relation to conflicts between the welfare of the child and the rights of the media in the pre-Human Rights Act era; it moves on to consider the changed stance under the HRA, arguing that misunderstandings of the Convention continued to bedevil the jurisprudence. Finally, a suggested model for the proper

---

[8] [2005] 1 AC 593; [2004] 4 All ER 683.

[9] A range of restrictions is discussed in Chapter 5 at 205–13.

resolution of such conflicts under the HRA is put forward which, it will be contended, is more firmly rooted in the Convention jurisprudence since it is fully premised on the presumptive equality of Articles 10 and 8.

DOMESTIC REPORTING RESTRICTIONS RELATING TO CHILDREN

The restrictions in question could be variously categorized. A certain group of them affect the reporting of proceedings held in private and a substantial proportion of such proceedings involve cases concerning children. The common law rule is that all courts, in the exercise of their inherent power to regulate their own proceedings in order to ensure that justice is done, have a discretion to sit in private, but due to the importance of the open justice principle the discretion is to be exercised only in exceptional circumstances.[10] Certain statutes expressly provide for hearings to be held in private in relation to matters involving children.[11] However, the mere fact that a hearing occurs in private does not automatically mean that *reporting* of the proceedings is restricted. Under s 12(1)(a) of the Administration of Justice Act 1960 it will be a *prima facie* contempt to report on proceedings held in private[12] where they relate to: wardship, adoption, guardianship, custody, upbringing of or access to an infant.[13] It has been found that the press cannot report any aspect of wardship proceedings,[14] but this is not an absolute restriction:[15] it has been found to cover 'statements of evidence, reports, accounts of interviews' and similar information.[16] In relation to other information linked to the proceedings the test is whether the information is 'within the mischief which the cloak of privacy in relation to the substance of the proceedings is designed to guard against'.[17]

Section 49 of the Children and Young Persons Act 1933 places restrictions on the identification of children or young persons convicted in the Youth Court, but the

---

[10] *Scott v Scott* [1913] AC 417.

[11] Adoption Act 1976 s 64; Magistrates Court Act 1980 s 69(2) as amended by the Children Act 1989 s 97. The Civil Procedure Rules 1998 Part 39 provide that a number of categories of hearing may take place in private; the decision whether to hold the hearing in private or in public is for the judge conducting it.

[12] Under the 1960 Act s 12(2), it is permissible to publish the text of all or part of an order made by a court sitting in private unless the court, having power to do so, expressly prohibits its publication.

[13] *Re F* [1977] Fam 58.

[14] See *Re X (A Minor) (Wardship: Injunction)* [1984] 1 WLR 1422 (the Mary Bell case).

[15] In *Pickering v Liverpool Daily Post and Echo Newspapers plc* [1991] 2 AC 370; [1991] 1 All ER 622, HL at 423 and 635, Lord Bridge observed: 'The essential privacy which is protected by each of the exemptions in paras (a)–(d) of s 12(1) attaches to the substance of the matters which the court has closed its doors to consider . . .'.

[16] *Re F (A Minor) (Publication of Information)* [1977] Fam105.

[17] *Pickering v Liverpool Daily Post and Echo Newspapers plc* [1991] 2 AC 370; [1991] 1 All ER 622 at 422–3 and 634.

restrictions can be lifted where a court is satisfied that this is in the public interest.[18] In relation to any proceedings in any court the court may make an order under s 39 of the 1933 Act prohibiting publication of particulars calculated to lead to the identification of any child concerned in the proceedings.[19] Section 39 orders are especially problematic for journalists since they frequently provide insufficient guidance as to what can safely be published.[20] Where s 12(1)(a) or s 39 do not apply, the High Court may nevertheless grant an injunction restraining reporting that might reveal a child's identity or other matters relating to a child as an aspect of its inherent jurisdiction to protect minors.[21] After the decision in *In Re X (A Minor) (Wardship: Jurisdiction)*[22] (the Mary Bell case), it can be seen that there was an increasing recourse to the court's asserted power to grant injunctions to restrain the publication of information about its wards or other children. The invention of this jurisdiction was described by Hoffmann LJ in *R v Central Independent Television*[23] in the following terms: 'the courts have, without any statutory or . . . other previous authority, assumed a power to create by injunction what is in effect a right of privacy for children'.

Finally, the action for breach of confidence could be utilized in some instances to protect information relating to a child from disclosure by the media.[24] However, due to the availability of the statutory restrictions discussed and the use of the courts' inherent jurisdiction, recourse to this action tends to be unnecessary in this context. Thus the identity of Mary Bell's daughter was protected until her 18th birthday by an injunction granted in the wardship proceedings instituted shortly after her birth.[25]

[18] Under the Crime Sentences 1997 s 45, which inserted s 49(4)(A) into the 1933 Act. The Youth Justice and Criminal Evidence Act 1999 s 44 creates an earlier starting point for the imposition of anonymity: protection against disclosure of identity for suspects, victims, witnesses now begins at the point of commencement of the criminal investigation. The Anti-Social Behaviour Act 2003 amends the Crime and Disorder Act 1998 s 1 to provide that s 49 does not apply to proceedings for orders under the 2003 Act, but that s 39 does apply.

[19] S 39 provides: 'In relation to any proceedings in any court the court may direct that—(a) no newspaper report of the proceedings shall reveal the name, address, or school, or include any particulars calculated to lead to the identification, of any child concerned in the proceedings, either as being the person by or against or in respect of whom the proceedings are taken, or as being a witness therein; (b) no picture shall be published in any newspaper as being or including a picture of any child or young person so concerned in the proceedings as aforesaid; except in sofar (if at all) as may be permitted by the direction of the court.' This section applies to sound and television broadcasts, and to cable programme services, as it applies to newspapers (Children and Young Persons Act 1963, s 57(4); Broadcasting Act 1990 Sched 20 para 3(2)).

[20] See *Briffett v DPP*; *Bradshaw v DPP* [2001] EWHC 841 (Admin) and commentary: M. Dodd, 'Children, the press—and a missed opportunity' [2002] 14(1) *CFLQ* 103–8.

[21] In *In Re M and N (Minors) (Wardship: Publication of Information)* [1990] Fam 211 Butler-Sloss L.J. found: 'The power of the courts to impose restrictions upon publication for the protection of children is derived from the inherent jurisdiction of the High Court exercising the powers of the Crown as *parens patriae*. It is not restricted to wardship . . .'. She relied on Lord Donaldson of Lymington M.R., who said in *In Re C. (A Minor) (Wardship: Medical Treatment) (No. 2)* [1990] Fam 39, 46 that wardship 'is the machinery for its exercise'. Ibid, 223.

[22] [1975] Fam 47.   [23] [1994] Fam 192, 204.

[24] See Chapter 14; see also the findings of the President of the Family Division in *Venables v MGN Ltd* [2001] 1 All ER 908 at 939; H. Fenwick and G. Phillipson, 'The Doctrine of Confidence as a Privacy Remedy in the Human Rights Act Era' [2000] 63 (5) *MLR* 660–93. See further J. Loughrey, 'Medical Information, Confidentiality and a child's right to privacy' [2003] 23(3) *LS* 510–535 esp at 511–13.

[25] *Re X (A Minor) (Wardship Proceedings Injunction)* [1984] 1 WLR 1422.

Once she was 18 an injunction was successfully sought protecting her identity on the ground of the action in confidence.[26] That injunction was sought on the basis of the invasion of privacy she would suffer if her identity became known, not on the ground that she might suffer physical attacks by vigilante groups—the basis for the grant of the injunction protecting the new identities of the child-killers of James Bulger, once they became 18.[27] The matter of consent can create difficulties in this context. If a *Gillick*-competent child has given consent to the publication of the information, although the adults around her consider that disclosure may be detrimental to her welfare,[28] the information can no longer be treated as confidential. So for a number of reasons reliance on the doctrine of confidence has not so far been very significant in respect of media disclosures of information relating to children.[29]

WEIGHING UP MEDIA FREEDOM AGAINST THE PRIVACY OF THE CHILD IN THE PRE-HRA ERA

Instances in which the High Court is exercising its inherent jurisdiction tend to create the most wide-ranging impact on media freedom to publish since the reporting is not necessarily linked to court proceedings. The decisions discussed below suggest that the conflict between free expression and privacy is most likely to occur where the inherent jurisdiction is being exercised (after *In Re S*, as discussed below, this term was replaced by the term 'the Convention jurisdiction'). But although the courts have more leeway in this context to consider solutions to this conflict, the arguments below as to the engagement of Articles 8 and 10 and the discussion of methods of resolving the conflict between them, would apply equally to the automatic reporting restrictions and to orders made under the other current powers. Reporting restrictions engage the 'privacy' of the child in the sense that the injunctions or orders are intended to protect the child's identity or other personal information. Thus in many instances her family

---

[26] *X, A Woman Formerly known as Mary Bell, Y v S O, News Group Newspapers Ltd, MGN Ltd* [2003] 2 FCR 686.

[27] See *Venables, Thompson v News Group Newspapers Ltd, Associated Newspapers Ltd, MGM Ltd.* [2001] 1 All ER 908. At the conclusion of their trial for murder, the judge granted comprehensive injunctions restricting publication of further information about the two boys, with no limit of time, based both under s 39 of the Children and Young Persons Act 1933 and the inherent jurisdiction of the High Court to deal with children. The claimants succeeded in obtaining injunctions once they reached 18 based on breach of confidence— injunctions principally designed to protect their new identities when they were released into the community. The court accepted that they would be at risk of physical harm if their true identities became known.

[28] See, for example, *Nottingham CC v October Films* [1999] 2 FLR 347; *Kelly v BBC* [2001] 1 FLR 197.

[29] However, the fact that the information in question has remained confidential may influence the courts' use of the inherent jurisdiction: see *In re Z (A Minor) (Identification: Restriction on Publication)* [1995] 4 All ER 96, 30.

life, her mental stability and her ability to form and develop relationships are also protected.[30]

In the pre-HRA era the courts sought to establish the boundaries between media freedom (recognized as an aspect of a common law right to freedom of expression)[31] and the privacy of the child in a series of decisions, culminating in the decision in *In re Z (A Minor) (Identification: Restrictions on Publication)*.[32] It was accepted that there was no need to strive to create a balance between media freedom and privacy once it was found that the matter at issue related to 'upbringing', and so the paramountcy principle[33] applied: where it did so it determined the issue without any doubt in favour of the child's 'welfare'.[34] However, where the reporting at issue could be viewed as unrelated directly to 'upbringing', some sort of balancing act had to be undertaken. The tendency was to allow freedom of publication to prevail due to the perceived strength of the value of freedom of expression under the common law. Where a court viewed a case as raising a genuine public interest, it was unlikely to restrain publication, or place only minimal restraints on it. In *Re W (A Minor) (Wardship: Freedom of Publication)*,[35] for instance, it was found that the placing of a ward who had previously suffered homosexual abuse, with a male homosexual couple as foster parents, raised public interest questions about the fostering policy of the local authority in question and therefore the newspaper in question had a right to raise such questions, despite the fact that it was accepted as quite possible that the identity of the ward would be disclosed.[36] The somewhat similar decision in *In Re W (A Minor) (Wardship: Restrictions on Publication)*[37] followed this prevailing approach. Four boys ranging in age from 15 to 10 were restrained from giving newspaper interviews concerning their determination to stay with their father, but on appeal it was found that the court had to balance the interests of the ward against the freedom of the press to publish and

---

[30] See *Bensaid v UK* [2001] 33 EHRR 10, para 47; *A and Byrne and Twenty-Twenty Television v United Kingdom* [1998] 25 EHRR CD 159.

[31] See: *ex parte Simms* [1999] 3WLR 328, *Reynolds v Times Newspapers* [1999] 4 All ER 609, *Derbyshire CC v Times Newspapers* [1993] AC 534.

[32] [1995] 4 All ER 961, CA.

[33] As indicated above (text to note 4), following s 1(1) of the Children Act 1989 (CA), the child's welfare is the court's paramount consideration when it determines any question with respect to the upbringing of the child. In *J v C* this was explained to mean: 'when all the relevant facts, relationships, claims and wishes of parents, risks, choices and other circumstances are taken into account and weighed, the course to be followed will be that which is most in the interests of the child's welfare.' [1970] AC 668, 710–11, per Lord McDermott.

[34] Freedom of publication can be viewed as a 'circumstance' which a responsible parent would take into account; see discussion of this point in *In re Z (A Minor) (Freedom of Publication)* [1995] 4 All ER 961.

[35] [1992] 1 All ER 794, CA.

[36] See also *In Re C (A Minor) (Wardship: Medical Treatment) (No. 2)* [1990] Fam 39, 46 in which a local newspaper was permitted, without identifying them, to publish a story concerning the removal of two children from their foster parents without proper consultation after a complaint of sexual abuse against the foster father.

[37] [1995] 2 FLR 466, CA. The case concerned children living with their father who had care and control under an order made in wardship. He allowed them to give interviews to a newspaper reporter, expressing their dislike of their mother and their dissatisfaction with their representation by the Official Solicitor.

comment about any legitimate matter; the order restraining publicity was amended so that it only prevented the sons' identification.

An outcome even more favourable to media freedom was reached in *R v Central Independent Television*.[38] A programme was made depicting a police investigation into a man subsequently convicted of offences of indecency. His wife, the plaintiff, did not wish her daughter, aged 5, who knew nothing of his convictions, to know what had occurred and therefore sought to have the programme altered so that it would not be possible to recognize her husband. The Court of Appeal refused the injunction, finding that the protection for the privacy of children under the inherent jurisdiction would not extend to covering publication of facts relating to those who were not carers of the child in question and which had occurred before the child was born. In other words, the limits of the protection for children's privacy were indicated: no overt balancing exercise between privacy and freedom of expression was necessary.

These decisions were clearly beginning to establish a spectrum of categories of case covering the balance to be struck between the privacy of the child and freedom of reporting. In the leading pre-HRA case, *In re Z (A Minor) (Identification: Restrictions on Publication)*,[39] these categories were made explicit. A first category of cases was recognized in which freedom of publication would always prevail over the welfare of the child. These were cases, it was found, which fall beyond the proper limit for the invocation of the wardship or inherent jurisdiction since upbringing is not in issue and the risk of harm to the child by invading her privacy may be viewed as incidental;[40] as Ward LJ put it: 'the freedom of the press is so fundamental that in this category it must triumph over welfare.[41] A further, second, category of cases was recognized—those in which the court does not have to determine an issue relating to upbringing but where the child's privacy is directly affected. In this category the child's interests are not paramount and a balancing exercise has to be performed between the child's privacy and media freedom.[42] The third category covered instances where a question of the child's upbringing or of the exercise of parental

[38] [1994] Fam 192.   [39] [1995] 4 All ER 961, CA.

[40] The court compared *In Re X (A Minor) (Wardship: Jurisdiction)* [1975] Fam 47 with *In Re X (A Minor) (Wardship: Injunction)* [1984] 1 WLR 1422. In the first case, concerning a book about X's father, the material was not a story about her or about the way she had been brought up, except indirectly since it revealed that her father was a philanderer. By contrast, the story in 1984 about X, Mary Bell's daughter, was directly about the fact that the authorities were permitting her to be brought up by a mother who was viewed by some as too evil to be entrusted with the care of a young child. See also *In Re M. and N. (Minors)(Wardship: Publication of Information)* [1990] Fam 211, at 231; *M v British Broadcasting Corpn* [1997] 1 FLR 51.

[41] He relied on an observation of Lord Shaw of Dunfermline in *Scott v Scott* [1913] AC 417, at 477: 'To remit the maintenance of constitutional [in this case one would say "fundamental human"] rights to the region of judicial discretion is to shift the foundations of freedom from the rock to the sand.' In this category a child is left to whatever remedies—most commonly the action for breach of confidence—an adult would have in the same circumstances.

[42] In *Re W (Freedom of Publication)* [1992] 1 All ER 794 the child's upbringing was a central focus of the publicity, although at the same time the court did not consider that it was determining a question relating to upbringing. Thus *Re W* was found to fall within this second category and therefore a balancing exercise had rightly occurred, whereas in *Central Television*—falling within the first—the privacy of the child was not found to weigh in the scales at all since the publicity did not concern the child directly or her upbringing.

responsibility *was* being determined, where the welfare of the child would be the para-mount consideration and her privacy interests would therefore trump competing free expression claims.[43]

In *In re Z* itself the issue before the court was found to relate to the upbringing of the child; a television company wished to make a film about Z (the daughter of Cecil Parkinson and Sarah Keays) and the treatment she was receiving for her particular educational needs at a specialized institution. It was envisaged that in demonstrating the methods and results of the institution Z would be identified and play an active part in the film. The court found that Z would be directly involved and that the proposed publicity would be harmful to her welfare. Therefore the instance was found to fall within the third category of cases since the paramountcy principle applied. The court did not therefore need to perform a balancing act and refused to vary the injunction that was already in place preventing commentary on her situation.[44]

CLASHES BETWEEN MEDIA FREE EXPRESSION CLAIMS UNDER ARTICLE 10 AND THE CHILD'S 'PRIVACY' UNDER ARTICLE 8 IN THE HRA ERA

Once the Human Rights Act came into force, a court in considering a clash between a restriction on publicity—deriving from statute or otherwise—and the privacy of a child, became bound to adhere to the Convention rights under s 6(1)[45] and had to take the Convention jurisprudence into account under s 2.[46] Under s 12(4) the court had to have 'particular regard' to Article 10. Thus the courts in exercising their inherent discretion to protect children also had to abide by all the Convention rights, in accordance with their duty under s 6(1). Where a restriction on publication was statutory the duty under s 6(1) continued to apply, but s 3(1)HRA also required its reinterpretation if necessary and if at all possible in order to ensure its compatibility

---

[43] This occurred in *Re C. (A Minor) (Wardship: Medical Treatment) (No. 2)* [1990] Fam 39 and in *In Re M. and N. (Minors) (Wardship: Termination of Access)* [1990] Fam 211. In this category the court is seen as exercising its 'custodial' jurisdiction.

[44] It may be noted that the decision in *Oxfordshire Council v L and F* [1997] 1 FLR 235 applied *In re Z*, but is out of accord with the line of authority considered since the privacy interest won out, possibly because no *media* body was involved. Publication by the parents of the story of their son's life, including his serious injury by a child-minder, was entirely disallowed. Even limited publication without identifying the parties, in order to further public discussion about supervision of child minders by the local authority, was prohibited. The restriction arose from s 12 of the Administration of Justice Act 1960, not the inherent jurisdiction of the court, since the matters in question had been the subject of care proceedings under the CA. Despite the fact that the paramountcy principle was not found to apply, the parents' free expression was outweighed by the need to preserve the welfare of the child-minder's children (although it is hard to see that it would have been threatened) and the confidentiality of care proceedings generally.

[45] Since courts are public authorities under s 6(3)(a).   [46] The jurisprudence is non-binding.

with the rights. The paramountcy principle itself as encapsulated in s 1(1) CA became theoretically subject to such reinterpretation under s 3(1)HRA.

In relation to the inherent jurisdiction, as the cases discussed from the pre-HRA era reveal, the courts had established a method of dealing with conflicts between the child's welfare and media freedom that largely excluded cases involving 'upbringing' from the battleground. It was only in respect of the second category of cases—where the child's privacy was at stake and at risk from media invasion—that the conflict had to be resolved, and in such instances, as indicated, it tended to be resolved in favour of the media, albeit with minimal restrictions on reporting. Doubtful distinctions were relied upon, as *In re Z* reveals, in pursuance of avoidance of the conflict. Once cases could be assigned to the 'upbringing' category on the one hand (the third grouping from *In re Z*) or the 'incidental' category on the other (the first grouping), conflict could be avoided. The general academic view was that adoption of these approaches had led to a failure to deal satisfactorily with the issues of both privacy and free speech at the level of principle.[47] It appeared to spring from the resistance of the courts, especially the Family Division, to the notion of individual rights as opposed to welfare.[48]

However, the somewhat simplistic or mechanistic analysis from *In re Z* was thrown into jeopardy by the inception of the Human Rights Act, since where the third category was applicable the Article 10 guarantee was almost automatically abrogated, while where the first or second applied, the Article 8 rights of the child were likely to be afforded no or insufficient weight. The pre-HRA treatment of both rights appeared therefore to become inconsistent with the courts' duty under s 6(1)HRA and also with the interpretative obligation under s 3(1): it might have been expected that s 3(1) would be used to reinterpret the paramountcy principle under s 1(1)CA so that Article 10 no longer suffered automatic abrogation where restrictions on publication related to upbringing. In what follows certain significant decisions are examined in which the *In re Z* categories were considered in the light of the HRA. However, by subtly manipulating the concept of 'upbringing', either under s 3(1)HRA or by using ordinary principles of interpretation, the courts have managed so far to avoid confronting the most difficult question of all—the compatibility of the paramountcy principle as currently conceived with Article 10. Instead the courts have succeeded in confining themselves to considering instances falling within the middle category from *In re Z*—wherein a balancing act between the two interests could be performed. But even in conducting that less difficult exercise, unsatisfactory reasoning processes were followed since there was, at least initially, a reluctance to accord Article 8 its status as a fully-fledged Convention right, once it came into conflict with Article 10.

---

[47] See: I. Cram, 'Minors' Privacy, Free Speech and the Courts' [1997] *PL* 410–419; L. Woods, 'Freedom of Expression and the protection of minors' (2001) 13(2) *CFLQ* 209–223.

[48] See Butler Sloss LJ in *Re L (A Child) (Contact: Domestic Violence)* [2001] Fam 260 CA, at para 294.

ARTICLE 8 RIGHTS OF CHILDREN AS EXCEPTIONS UNDER ARTICLE 10(2)?

The European Convention on Human Rights did not play a significant part in the decisions considered so far since, despite increasing reliance on the Convention in other areas of law pre-HRA,[49] the Family Division was content to balance media freedom against the child's welfare on the basis of common law understandings of those values. In *Kelly v BBC*,[50] however, the imminent inception of the Human Rights Act influenced the court to take Article 10 of the Convention fully into account. The case concerned a boy of 16, Kelly, who was made a ward of court after he disappeared from home to join a religious cult group. The BBC obtained an interview with him, but an order restraining publication of the detail of any report or interview with him or with members of the religious group was made, which the BBC challenged. It was accepted by both sides that the case was one in which the court did have jurisdiction to grant injunctive relief. The dispute between the parties was as to whether the case fell within the second or third of the three categories identified in *In re Z*. Clearly, if it was found to fall within the third, the paramountcy principle would apply and the interest in freedom of expression would be almost automatically overcome. Therefore it was crucial for counsel for the BBC to convince the court that the case fell within the second category and then to argue that the injunction could not be justified as necessary in a democratic society, under Article 10(2).

The court did not find it entirely easy to decide what distinguishes cases in the second category from those in the third. Clearly, this turned on the meaning assigned to the term 'upbringing'.[51] Munby J concluded: 'Upbringing . . . involves a process in which the parent, or other person in *loco parentis*, is the subject and of which the child is the object. . . . S 1(1)(a) CA therefore applies only to those processes or actions of which the child is the object, and not to those in which the child is the subject.' Munby J went on to find that *In re Z* had created a distinction between cases such as *In re W*, in which four boys without their father's involvement had given interviews to journalists, and cases in which the parent actively encourages or brings about the involvement of the child with the media. *In re Z*, he found, fell within the latter category in which the child is the object since, as he put it, referring to the words of Ward LJ, Z's mother wished to 'bring up her child as one who will play an active part in a television film'. The *In re W* case was viewed as similar to the instant one since Kelly had given the interview without the involvement of his grandmother or mother. The case was therefore viewed as one not involving upbringing and as a result as

---

[49] See e.g. the Court of Appeal decision in *Derbyshire CC v Times Newspapers* [1993] AC 534.

[50] [2001] 1 All ER 323; [2001] 2 WLR 253; [2001] Fam 59. The HRA came fully into force a few months after the case.

[51] In *In re Z* Ward LJ's conclusion was: 'a question of upbringing is determined whenever the central issue before the court is one which relates to how the child is being reared' (at 29). In the instant case, Munby J found that 'reared' carries the connotation of the 'bringing up, care for, treatment, education and instruction of the child throughout childhood by its parents or by those in *loco parentis*'.

within the second category; the paramountcy principle was inapplicable and therefore a 'so-called balancing exercise has to be performed'.[52]

In considering the claim of freedom of expression as compared with the need to safeguard the welfare of the child, Munby J pointed out that this exercise had in general been carried out in an unsatisfactory fashion in the Family Division due to its 'child-centred' approach: 'as Thorpe LJ [noted] in *In re G (Celebrities: Publicity)*[53] . . . Hoffmann LJ rightly said in his judgment in *R v Central Independent Television plc* there is an inevitable tendency for the Family Division judge at first instance to give too much weight to welfare and too little weight to freedom of speech'. Munby J found that the exceptions under Article 10(2) can only override the right when it is 'necessary in a democratic society' that they should do so. Therefore, he found, it is not a question of 'balancing' freedom of expression against one or more of the interests identified in paragraph 2 of Article 10. He found that those who seek to bring themselves within the protection of paragraph 2 must demonstrate convincingly that the protection applies. He went on to find that the arguments in favour of suppressing the interview were not sufficiently convincing.[54] Since the arguments were fairly evenly balanced, and he had already found that Article 10(2) places the burden on those seeking to make the case for interference with freedom of expression, he determined that injunctive relief could not be justified. No 'clear and identifiable harm' had been established so as to provide the necessary justification. He further found that the grant of an injunction framed as widely as the one he was being invited to make would have been wholly disproportionate to any aim that could legitimately be pursued on Kelly's behalf.

A similar instance arose in *In the matter of X (a child)*[55] in the sense that since the restraining order in question was not found to relate to the child's upbringing within the meaning of section 1(1) CA, the paramountcy principle was inapplicable. However, the significant difference was that in the few months since *Kelly* the HRA had come into force. It prompted the court to go even further than *Kelly* had done in accepting the primacy of media freedom once it was free to do so, having once again succeeded in excluding the instance from the third 'upbringing' category.[56] The court

---

[52] [2001] 1 All ER 323, 341. It was further found that a distinction arises where the court is concerned with the grant of an injunction *in rem* or *contra mundum*, as opposed to the grant of relief *in personam*: in the former cases the child's welfare will be paramount only if the court is determining a question with respect to the child's upbringing.

[53] [1999] 1 FLR 409, 418.

[54] It had been argued *inter alia* that Kelly would find it harder to reconcile himself with his family if the interview were broadcast. Munby J found that the argument that further publicity might be in his best interests was as plausible as the contrary argument put forward—that it would be opposed to them.

[55] [2001] 1 FCR 541.

[56] A newspaper publisher had applied for an order to vary an injunction granted to the local authority restraining foster parents from disclosing to the newspaper information concerning the local authority's policies in respect of trans-racial fostering. Relying on the analysis of Munby J in *Kelly*, Mrs Justice Bracewell found that in this instance the child should be viewed as the subject of the process of upbringing, not the object, since the issue before the court concerned restrictions on media reporting of issues alleged to be raised by the child's history. Therefore, since the reporting did not concern 'upbringing' as defined in *Kelly*, the case

proceeded to make the important finding, foreshadowed in *Kelly*, that while the exercise of its discretion had been referred to many times before October 2000 as a balancing exercise, such an exercise was no longer appropriate after the coming into force of the HRA. The court determined that it must rely on s 12(4) HRA and Article 10 in reaching its decision and went on to find: '[this] is not a balancing exercise in which the scales are evenly positioned at the commencement of the exercise. On the contrary, the scales are weighted at the beginning so that Article 10 prevails unless one of the defined derogations applies when given a narrow interpretation.' The application was granted on the basis that the injunction was too wide and it was varied accordingly. It was found that there was insufficient evidence to enable the court to find that the tests under Article 10(2) were satisfied in respect of one of the exceptions and there was a legitimate public interest in the disclosure of the information, in accordance with s 12(4)HRA. The same stance was taken in *Medway Council v BBC* [57] in an instance which once again was not found to involve a question of upbringing—the scales were weighted so that Art 10 prevailed, subject to an application of one of the derogations, narrowly defined.[58] Interestingly, a narrow construction under s 3(1)HRA of s 1(1)CA, allowing the case to be excluded from the 'upbringing' category, was found to accord with the demands of Art 10 and s 12(4)HRA.[59]

Although the recognition of the importance of media freedom in *Kelly, In the matter of X* and *Medway Council* is arguably welcome, the analysis in relation to Articles 8 and 10 in this line of authority is, it is contended, flawed. As the authors suggested in 2000 might occur under the HRA, this approach meant that Article 8 lost 'its Convention status as a fully-fledged right, becoming instead merely a narrowly interpreted exception to the right of freedom of expression.'[60] As discussed in Chapter 15,[61] this approach is clearly wrong since it demands that the protection of the right to privacy has to be justified as necessary in a democratic society, while media claims of free speech are simply assumed. But it is also hard to reconcile dicta in this line of authority with the Convention under the HRA since it assumes that where the paramountcy principle *is* found to apply, Article 10 can be almost automatically abrogated. However, some evidence of emerging judicial recognition of a need for a proper resolution of the conflict between Articles 8 and 10 in this context under the HRA where the principle does *not* apply was apparent in the most recent, and highly influential, decision to touch on the issues raised in *Kelly* and in *Re X*.

---

fell within the second category identified in *In re Z* where the court has jurisdiction but welfare is not paramount.

[57] [2002] 1 FLR 104.

[58] The case concerned the inherent jurisdiction of the court to restrain a broadcast of a consented-to interview with a boy of 13 who had been made one of the first subjects of an anti-social behaviour order. The local authority sought leave, under s 100(3) CA to prevent the broadcast of the interview; the application was refused. The boy, his mother and father supported the local authority's application.

[59] Para 29.   [60] Note 24 above, 686.   [61] See pp 779–82.

RE S: RECOGNITION OF THE 'DIFFICULT BALANCING EXERCISE' TO BE CONDUCTED

In *Re S (A Child)*[62] the Court of Appeal had to adjudicate on an appeal against an order made by Hedley J in the Family Division of the High Court.[63] The appeal raised a short but difficult point: 'can or should the court restrain the publication of the identity of a defendant and her victim in a murder trial to protect the privacy of her son who is the subject of care proceedings?' The victim was S's brother and there was psychiatric evidence to the effect that S, as an already vulnerable child, would suffer greater trauma and be at greater risk of later mental illness if he was subjected to bullying and teasing at school once the identity of his mother became known. Hedley J made an order based upon the standard form commonly used in the Family Division.[64] The order prohibited publication (a) of the name or address of the child and his school; (b) of any picture of the child or either of his parents; and (c) of any other information which might lead to the child's identification. The order expressly prevented any person 'publishing any particulars of or information relating to any part of the proceedings before any court which may or is calculated to lead to the identification of the said child'. The order was clearly designed to prohibit publication of the name of the mother and the deceased child in any report of the impending criminal trial. It was common ground that the order also prevented publication of any photographs of the mother or deceased child. The local paper applied ex parte for a modification of the order.[65] Hedley J changed the order to include in paragraph 8 the proviso that 'Nothing in this order shall of itself prevent any person (a) publishing any particulars of or information relating to any part of the proceedings before any court other than a court sitting in private . . .' However, paragraph 8 was stayed[66] so that the matter could be fully argued at an *inter partes* hearing.

At the hearing before Hedley J in chambers three national newspaper groups (the respondents) appeared on behalf of the press. The local newspaper withdrew to avoid the risk of being ordered to pay costs. The argument before Hedley J centred on the question whether the exception in paragraph 8(a) should remain in the order. The newspapers accepted that they should not refer to the child, S, but they wished to be able to publish the names and photographs of both parents and of S's dead brother. In particular, they wanted to publish photographs of S's brother with his mother. Since S was the same age as his brother was when he died, and they resembled each other, the photographs would indirectly identify S. The judge decided that the stay should be lifted and the exception in paragraph 8(a) should remain in the order. In other words, on the basis of his decision the newspapers were not prevented in reports of the

---

[62] [2003] 2 FCR 577; (2003) 147 SJLB 873. See also *Harris v Harris* [2001] 2 FLR 895 in which, while there was no detailed consideration of the balancing exercise between Article 10 (and 11), on the one hand, and Article 8 on the other, Munby J accepted (at para 384) that the approach adopted by Sedley LJ in *Douglas v Hello!* [2001] QB 967 should be followed in which Article 10 was *not* given presumptive priority.

[63] 19 February 2003.   [64] On 17 October 2002.

[65] 13 November 2002, *The Romford Recorder*.   [66] Until 13 December 2002.

criminal trial from publishing the identity of the defendant or her deceased son or photographs of them. Through his guardian the child appealed to the Court of Appeal against the inclusion of paragraph 8(a). The mother supported the appeal. (The criminal trial of the mother was due in November 2004.) Para 8(a) meant that S would be indirectly identified: the photos of his dead brother would aid in identifying him even for those who did not know his surname.

The Court of Appeal found, unanimously, that the question before them did *not* concern a matter of upbringing since, as Lady Justice Hale found: 'In deciding whether or not to make this order, the court is not exercising its jurisdiction over how S is to be brought up. That is being done in the care proceedings. Nor is it deciding how any aspect of parental responsibility should be met.'[67] Therefore, this was not an instance in which the paramountcy principle applied. Interestingly, the first instance judge had considered that even if the child's welfare *had* been the paramount consideration, he would have decided in the same way. The Court of Appeal disagreed, Lady Justice Hale finding that when the child's welfare *is* the paramount consideration, 'it rules on or determines the issue before the court. *It* is the trump card' (emphasis in the original).[68] It may be noted that the trump card metaphor was also used in *Medway Council*.[69]

It is contended that the finding regarding the concept of 'upbringing' is hard to reconcile with the findings from *In re Z* on that point. Following *In re Z* it may be asked whether *Re S* was not in fact concerned with upbringing. According to the evidence of an expert psychologist the child in question was more likely to suffer mental illness due to the results of the publicity and the father who was his main carer would have to deal with those effects: in what sense then was the publicity not linked strongly, but (partly) indirectly to upbringing? Further, if the child had to move school or home due to bullying after the publicity that would again affect his upbringing. Perhaps most pertinently of all, the placement of the child with the father was also likely to be affected by the publicity since the father was barely coping with the situation and might have failed to cope with further stress and trauma suffered by an already vulnerable child as a result of the publicity. S might have had to be taken into care. The publicity was likely to have both direct and indirect effects on S. S might have encountered it himself since he might have seen articles and pictures in the media about his dead brother and his mother. He was also likely to suffer harassment and teasing at school once the identity of his mother and further details of the crime became more widely known, during the period of the trial. That was also the period during which his own trauma and stress were likely to be at their height. In comparison, the child in *In re Z* was unlikely to suffer the first effect—her mother in fact considered that taking part in the documentary and viewing it would be beneficial for her. She was also unlikely to have her upbringing affected as an indirect effect of the

---

[67] As she put it 'Parents cannot prohibit press reporting of criminal proceedings in order to protect their children from harm, however much they might like to be able to do so' (para 22).
[68] *Per* Lady Justice Hale, para 62.   [69] Para 29.

broadcasting of the documentary, although possibly she might have become aware of secondary publicity as a result of it. Thus the only way in which the documentary could have been strongly linked to Z's upbringing would have been via the ultimate effects of the publicity. This was also the case in *In re S*.

It is argued therefore that the finding from *In re S* impliedly overturns the findings on 'upbringing' from *In re Z* and also means that it is very unlikely that the welfare principle will ever be found to apply in these instances of indirect effects on upbringing via media reporting. This is clearly the preferred course for the *courts* since it avoids a problematic conflict between s 1(1) CA and Article 10. But it might also mean that the courts are likely to be reluctant to focus too strongly on the effect of reporting on the family and private life of a child, since so doing appears to draw the effects on upbringing back into the equation. It creates tension in the decision since at one stage in the reasoning upbringing is excluded, but at a later stage it potentially re-enters the reasoning process when the private and family life claim is being considered. This is precisely what occurred, as discussed below, in the House of Lords decision in *In re S*. The better solution, as discussed below, is to reinterpret the welfare principle under s 3(1) HRA in order to avoid a conflict with Article 10 and to accept a broader definition of the term 'upbringing'. So doing might encourage the courts to focus strongly on the effects of reporting on upbringing, meaning that the significant issues truly at stake under the privacy claim manage to obtain a hearing.

THE 'ECHR JURISDICTION'

Having found that the welfare principle did not apply, the Court of Appeal went on to find that the case fell within the scope of the inherent jurisdiction of the High Court. Hale LJ (with the agreement of the other members of the court) observed:

Now that the Human Rights Act 1998 is in force, the relevance of the jurisdiction may simply be to provide the vehicle which enables the court to conduct the necessary balancing exercise between the competing rights of the child under Article 8 and the media under Article 10.[70]

But following the House of Lords decision in *Re S*[71] it is no longer necessary in these cases to show that the inherent jurisdiction applies. The House of Lords in *Re S* found unanimously that since the 1998 Act came into force, the earlier case law about the *existence* and scope of inherent jurisdiction did not have to be considered in the instant case or in 'similar' cases. Lord Steyn said: '*The foundation of the jurisdiction to restrain publicity in a case such as the present is now derived from convention rights under the ECHR*' (emphasis added).[72] In other words, the jurisdiction is not the 'vehicle' allowing for the balancing exercise to occur—the Convention rights themselves provide the vehicle. This looks at first sight like the creation of a form of direct

---

[70] At para [40].   [71] Note 8 above.   [72] At para [23].

horizontal effect since it would appear that in relation to assertions of a need for restraint to protect the privacy of the child there would be no need for the inherent jurisdiction even to *exist*. Further, the rights under the HRA would not be expected to deliver less than the existing cause of action which could have acted as the vehicle for their delivery. Possibly they could deliver *more* and that would then represent a form of direct horizontal effect since this would mean that there would not be an infusion of the right into the existing cause of action, but a replacement of that existing cause with an extended protection based only on the rights. In other words, Lord Steyn appeared to be stating that the technicalities of the inherent jurisdiction can be discarded and its place taken by the Convention rights. That would be direct horizontal effect as normally understood—the creation of a new cause of action allowing private parties to rely on the rights against each other. There would be no need to rely on an existing cause of action—as was thought to be the case in *Campbell*[73] in the context of adults' privacy. In other words, it might appear that adults could also rely on an 'ECHR jurisdiction' in asserting privacy claims.

On this point Lord Steyn said:

There are a number of specific consequences of the grant of an injunction as asked for in this case to be considered. First, while counsel for the child wanted to confine a ruling to the grant of an injunction restraining publication *to protect a child*, that will not do. *The jurisdiction under the ECHR could equally be invoked by an adult non-party faced with possible damaging publicity as a result of a trial of a parent, child or spouse* (emphasis added). Adult non-parties to a criminal trial must therefore be added to the prospective pool of applicants who could apply for such injunctions. This would confront newspapers with an ever wider spectrum of potentially costly proceedings and would seriously inhibit the freedom of the press to report criminal trials.[74]

Arguably, in his eagerness to close the floodgates on claims for restraint of reporting of criminal trials, Lord Steyn may, ironically, have opened them to actions seeking to enforce a right to respect for private life to be used against the press in a range of circumstances where the inherent jurisdiction (and the action for breach of confidence) might have been inapplicable. If an 'ECHR jurisdiction' is available, it would not be confined to invasions of privacy created by the reporting of criminal trials. The jurisdiction Lord Steyn envisages does not appear to be confined to instances in which the inherent jurisdiction would previously have been applicable—if it was so confined this finding would not make sense. Arguably, the 'ECHR jurisdiction' could extend to all instances in which Article 8 was engaged,[75] and adults would also be able to take advantage of it. This looks something like an acceptance of the doctrine of direct horizontal effect, or in any event direct effects, in the domestic courts. Clearly, Lord Steyn was seeking to explain why the 'ECHR jurisdiction' should not extend to

---

[73] [2004] 2 WLR 1232; see further Chapter 3 at 123–44, and Chapter 14 at 725–8.

[74] At para [32].

[75] This depends on what was meant by 'similar cases' in para 23. It already appears that the jurisdiction could extend to mentally disordered adults.

restraint on reporting of criminal trials, but the finding that such a jurisdiction exists means that new privacy actions might arise and create restraints on other forms of reporting.

Thus Lord Steyn appeared to consider that the jurisdiction under the ECHR could equally be invoked by an adult non-party faced with possible damaging publicity as a result of a trial of a parent, child or spouse.[76] This finding appears to confirm that direct horizontal effect is being created since it shows that causes of action can arise under Article 8 that could not have arisen under the inherent jurisdiction. 'The jurisdiction under the ECHR' appears to mean that adults and children can rely on the ECHR rights regardless—in the context he was considering—of the scope of the inherent jurisdiction. It appears to mean that they can merely rely on the rights in general. Possibly there would not be many instances in which an adult could use this cause of action where an action under the doctrine of breach of confidence would not also arise, but that possibility cannot be ruled out, and moreover there might be instances in which an adult would want to use this cause of action as an alternative to breach of confidence. Thus possibly there is some tension between this decision and that in *Campbell*—this decision could be viewed as marginalizing the doctrine of breach of confidence. At first sight the apparent creation of direct horizontal effect appears to mean that *Campbell* and *Re S* contradict each other on this point and that, since *Re S* is the later decision, such effect has been (probably inadvertently) created.

This part of Lord Steyn's judgment is highly problematic since it is ambiguously expressed and it will be interesting to see whether adults will seek to rely on it in instances in which the action for breach of confidence would not be available but where a Convention right—normally Article 8—applies. The obvious example would be in harassment cases where there are difficulties in relying on the Protection from Harassment Act 1978. This would be of interest if celebrities sought injunctions relying on the new jurisdiction to prevent media harassment. These issues take us outside the scope of this chapter,[77] but before leaving this topic it is suggested that the 'ECHR jurisdiction' is in fact very unlikely to be extended fully to adults and that Lord Steyn's remarks on that matter, which were, strictly speaking, *obiter*, will not be followed. The explanation for the creation of the new jurisdiction is, it is suggested, that the court is taking the place of the state in terms of protecting the child and that in this instance alone a form of direct horizontal effect has been created since there is little to be gained in seeking to distinguish the courts' duty under s 6 HRA from its duty under the inherent jurisdiction.

In any event, the simple question in this context appears now to be—is the child's Article 8 right engaged? If it is it must be balanced against the media's Article 10 right, on the *Campbell* model, as discussed below.

---

[76] At para [32].   [77] For further discussion see Chapter 14, esp at pp 714–21.

THE BALANCING ACT BETWEEN ARTICLES 8 AND 10

The Court of Appeal decision is of significance in relation to the balancing act and its findings that *in general* this balancing act should occur were not disputed in the Lords. Having found that the inherent jurisdiction applied, the Court then found, not without difficulty, that the case fell within the second category from *In re Z*. It was found that the 'information in the case lay somewhere in between that in *Re X* and *R v Central Television* and that in *Re M and N* or *Re W*.[78] The proposed publication did not relate directly to S's current upbringing. But equally it did not constitute 'the sort of remote and unconnected information about a deceased or long-absent parent' at issue in *Re X* and *R v Central Independent Television plc*. The reports related to recent events in his family life and therefore could be expected to have a real bearing on his future upbringing.

There was a further important aspect of the case—the information related to the identity of the defendant and her alleged victim in a murder trial. But it was concluded, relying on *ex parte Crook*,[79] that the important public interest in the identification of defendants, in particular those found guilty of serious crimes, can be outweighed in certain circumstances by the need to protect those affected by the crime from further harm. It was accepted that Article 6(1) would not be breached by the concealment of the defendant's identity: it was found that its importance lay in the relationship between the values it protects—the furtherance of the transparency of the administration of justice[80]—and the right to freedom of expression under Article 10(1). Unhampered media reports would play a part in safeguarding the public character of justice. Thus Article 6(1) provided an added dimension in the case.

In seeking to weigh up Articles 8 and 10 against each other the Court of Appeal found, in a highly significant break with the previous line of authority, that they must be considered as independent elements, on the basis, following *Douglas v Hello!*[81] and *A v B plc*,[82] that s 12(4)HRA does not give one pre-eminence over the other. The court relied on Lord Woolf's dictum in *A v B* to the effect that '[the court must] attach proper weight to the important rights which both articles are designed to protect. Each article is qualified expressly in a way which allows the interests under the other Article to be taken into account.' In the lower court it had been assumed that press freedom would be afforded primacy and that the Article 8 rights of the child would figure merely as exceptions under Article 10(2). It was accepted that this was clearly the wrong approach. The Court of Appeal then went on to consider the proportionality of the proposed interference with freedom of expression, and in so doing took into account not only the importance of press freedom in principle, but also the features of the case which made its exercise of especial importance. Such enhancing features were

---

[78] Para 37.
[79] [1995] 1 WLR 139. In that instance it was found that the likely harm to the surviving children of the defendants outweighed the effect on freedom of expression created by the restrictions on publication.
[80] *Diennet v France* [1995] 21 EHRR 554, at para 33, was referred to.
[81] [2001] QB 967, 1005, para 24.   [82] [2003] QB 195; [2003] 3 WLR 542, para 6.

found to include: the particular importance attached to the reporting of criminal trials; the right of the public to receive the information in question; the important issues raised regarding an unusual and controversial form of child abuse and about the conduct of the world famous children's hospital in which it was allegedly allowed to take place. Thus the public interest in allowing unrestricted reporting was found to be strong. However, that was not found to mean that it was impossible to justify any restriction, however limited, under Article 10(2). The court had to consider what restriction, if any, was needed to meet the legitimate aim of protecting the rights of S. If prohibiting publication of the family name and photographs was needed, the court had to consider how great an impact that would in fact have upon the freedom protected by Article 10, taking into account the greater public interest in knowing the names of persons convicted of serious crime rather than of those who are merely suspected or charged.

The court then went on to consider the matter from the perspective of S's Article 8 rights, media freedom figuring this time as an exception to them under Article 8(2). In considering the proportionality of the proposed interference with the right of S to respect for his private and family life, the judge had to take account of the magnitude of the interference proposed. Factors to be taken into account included: the extent to which the additional intrusion would add to the interference which had already taken place; the extent of any further harm that identifying publicity about the trial would do to the child's private and family life, in which his mental health was a 'crucial part'; the impact upon his father, other carers and his school, and the extent to which their task would be made harder by this kind of publicity, and the impact on his relationship with his mother in the short and the longer term. The nature of the publicity would be relevant in minimizing the interference: prolonged identifying publicity, with photographs, during the trial, would have a far greater impact than would publicity during the rather shorter period when the family might be identified if there was a conviction. In other words, Lady Justice Hale drew a distinction between the different periods of time during which publicity would occur, if unrestrained: the strength of the free expression claim (bolstered also by the values underlying the guarantee of open justice under Article 6(1)) would be at its greatest at the point at which the argument against publicity would be at its weakest.

Lady Justice Hale came to the conclusion that since the first instance judge had not considered each Article independently, and so had not conducted the difficult balancing exercise required by the Convention, the appeal should be allowed, in order that the exercise could be properly carried out by the first instance Family Division court. The two judges in the majority disagreed, finding that although the balancing exercise outlined by Lady Justice Hale should have been carried out, the result reached—that the restraining order should remain limited due to para 8(a)—would have been reached even if it had been properly carried out. They considered that the first instance judge had not carried out the exercise correctly, but had had factors relevant to the question of proportionality under Article 8 sufficiently in mind.

The House of Lords endorsed the parallel analysis from *Campbell* (which was of course based on the Court of Appeal judgment in *Re S*) in general, confirming that presumptive priority for speech *where it competes with another Convention right*, not a societal concern, has been decisively rejected. But Lord Steyn went on to find that the strong general rule allowing for the reporting of criminal trials normally created an exception to the 'ultimate balancing test' (the parallel analysis). The rule it was said could only be displaced by unusual or exceptional circumstances.[83] This point is pursued below. So Baroness Hale's balancing test *is* to be used in cases where the child's Art 8 right is engaged and clashes with the media's Art 10 right, *except*, it appears, in instances where the reporting relates to a criminal trial and the child would be indirectly identified. In that instance, on one reading of Lord Steyn's judgment, Article 8 appears to figure only as an exception to Article 10—in other words the House of Lords went back in this instance to the flawed reasoning adopted in the *Kelly* line of authority. Thus, although the Lords in *Re S* endorsed *Campbell*, there seemed to be no recognition of the fact that the decision departed from the fundamental approach of *Campbell*—that of presumptive equality.

However, a more satisfactory explanation of Lord Steyn's judgment in *Re S* was adopted in a significant subsequent case in the High Court in *Re W (Children)*.[84] In that instance the mother of two children (T, aged 3, and R, aged 6 months), who was HIV positive, had pleaded guilty to knowingly infecting the father of R with HIV; she was awaiting sentence under s 20 of the Offences Against the Person Act. It was apparent that the children were likely to suffer the hostility of the community if it was thought that they might be infected by the disease and their connection with the criminal trial of their mother was fully revealed. It seemed quite possible that their long term care placement would be jeopardized. The local council therefore sought an injunction to restrict publicity relating to the trial which might connect the children

---

[83] Lord Steyn: [18]. In oral argument it was accepted by both sides that the ordinary rule is that the press, as the watchdog of the public, may report everything that takes place in a criminal court. I would add that in European jurisprudence and in domestic practice this is a strong rule. It can only be displaced by unusual or exceptional circumstances. It is, however, not a mechanical rule. The duty of the court is to examine with care each application for a departure from the rule by reason of rights under Article 8.

Applying the rule in this instance: [37] In agreement with Hale LJ the majority of the Court of Appeal took the view that Hedley J had not analysed the case correctly in accordance with the provisions of the ECHR. Lord Steyn did not agree. He found that given the weight traditionally given to the importance of open reporting of criminal proceedings Article 10 would have presumptive priority and the question would be whether the right of the child under Article 8—in the particular instance—could outweigh the Article 10 interest. He made it reasonably clear that the Article 8 right of the child *would* outweigh the interest in open reporting of criminal proceedings where the paramountcy principle applied. In my view the judge analysed the case correctly under the ECHR. Given the weight traditionally given to the importance of open reporting of criminal proceedings it was in my view appropriate for him, in carrying out the balance required by the ECHR, to begin by acknowledging the force of the argument under Article 10 before considering whether the right of the child under Article 8 was sufficient to outweigh it. He went too far in saying that he would have come to the same conclusion even if he had been persuaded that this was a case where the child's welfare was indeed the paramount consideration under section 1(1) of the Children Act 1989. But that was not the shape of the case before him.

[84] *A Local Authority v (1) W (2) L (3) W (4) T & R (By The Children's Guardian)* [2005] EWHC 1564 (Fam).

to it. As in *Re S*, the injunction was intended to conceal the identity of the defendant and victim in the trial in order to protect the children, indirectly. Thus the facts of the two cases were very similar.

The problem faced by the President of the Family Division in *Re W* was to determine how to reconcile Lord Steyn's findings as to the presumptive equality of Arts 8 and 10 with his finding as to the strong general rule relating to the open justice principle. As indicated above, it appeared on one possible reading of Lord Steyn's findings that Art 10 was to be viewed as having presumptive priority where reporting relating to criminal trials was concerned. However, the President managed to find an explanation of Lord Steyn's findings that allowed Articles 8 and 10 to be balanced against each other on a basis of equality:

… the starting point is presumptive parity, in that neither article has precedence over or 'trumps' the other. The exercise of parallel analysis requires the court to examine the justification for interfering with each right and the issue of proportionality is to be considered in respect of each. It is not a mechanical exercise to be decided upon the basis of rival generalities. An intense focus on the comparative importance of the specific rights being claimed in the individual case is necessary before the ultimate balancing test in terms of proportionality is carried out. Having so stated, Lord Steyn strongly emphasised the interest in open justice as a factor to be accorded great weight in both the parallel analysis and the ultimate balancing test … However, nowhere did he indicate that the weight to be accorded to the right freely to report criminal proceedings would invariably be determinative of the outcome.[85]

In other words, the President interpreted Lord Steyn's findings as meaning that the interest in reporting criminal trials would always be a very weighty factor on the Article 10 side of the balancing act and very strong Article 8 arguments would have to arise in order for the Article 8 interest to prevail. The effect of these findings in relation to the balancing act that must occur under the HRA is considered below.

PROPER RESOLUTION OF THE CONFLICT UNDER THE HRA

Lady Justice Hale's judgment in *Re S* represents the closest approach yet, not only to a proper understanding of the method of resolving conflicts between Convention rights, but also to a partial acceptance of the need for the Family Division to confront fully the changes in judicial reasoning that the Human Rights Act necessitates. It demonstrates a complete break with the mistaken approach adopted in *Kelly*, *X* and *Medway Council* in which freedom of speech was given automatic priority once it was found that the paramountcy principle did not apply. However, highly significantly, by excluding the case on somewhat doubtful grounds from the upbringing category, the

---

[85] Op cit, note 8 at para 53.

Court backed away from a confrontation between that principle and Article 10 under the HRA. That principle, if it is to act as a 'trump card', is clearly incompatible with the Convention values. Below, the general question of the proper reconciliation of the conflict between Articles 8 and 10, even where upbringing *is* in issue, or where the child's privacy is only indirectly or inferentially affected, is considered in more detail in relation to all reporting restrictions designed to protect children. Since in *Re S* it was accepted in the House of Lords that the case fell outside the upbringing category there is still room for argument on this. The arguments below could also be used to attack the House of Lords' stance on something akin to presumptive priority for Article 10 where the rule on open justice reporting applies. But clearly that rule is now established, although there is no *automatic* abrogation of Article 8 rights.

The path forward does not involve, it is argued, continuing to refine the definition of upbringing almost out of existence in this context by the use of exclusionary interpretations under s 3(1)HRA so as to avoid invoking the paramountcy principle (as in *Re S* or *Medway Council*) in order to avoid the difficult questions raised in a conflict with Article 10. Instead it involves re-defining the paramountcy principle under s 3(1) so that even where it *is* in play, the conflict between Articles 8 and 10 can be properly resolved. At present resolution of the conflict is merely precluded since due to the effect of the absolutist presumption of the principle, the Article 8 right to respect for family life of the child[86] will—in effect—always win out where it clashes with Article 10, thereby denying Article 10's status as an individual right. It will be argued below that the Strasbourg approach to clashes between Articles 8 and 10 not only indicates that the paramountcy principle as currently conceived is incompatible with the demands of the HRA, but also confirms the Court of Appeal *Re S* approach—that Article 10 should not be afforded presumptive priority where the principle does not apply.

THE DEVELOPING STRASBOURG JURISPRUDENCE ON CLASHING RIGHTS

As discussed in Chapter 13, where a clash of rights occurs Strasbourg seeks to strike a fair balance between them under para 2 of the Article pleaded before the Court.[87] The reasoning process follows the structure demanded by the Article(s) invoked by the applicant at Strasbourg, but the other Convention right is given greater weight at the stage of determining the necessity of the interference in a democratic society than a societal interest would be.

The Article 8 'family' cases on clashes of rights—where the right of the parent to family life appears to clash with that of the child—have not in general been resolved

---

[86] It has been accepted in a number of the domestic cases that the welfare of the child can be viewed as an aspect of his or her Article 8 rights. See e.g. *Medway Council v BBC* [2002] 1 FLR 104, para 29.

[87] See pp 690–700. See also M. Tugendhat, QC and I. Christie, *The Law of Privacy and the Media*, Oxford: OUP, 2002, 420–1.

by reference to a principle of paramountcy—as that is understood domestically. Nor has it been assumed that the child's Article 8 rights can be viewed as exceptions to be narrowly construed. In *Elsholz v Germany*,[88] the applicant father claimed that his Article 8 rights had been breached by the refusal of the national court to allow him access to his child. The European Court of Human Rights, in finding that a violation of the father's Article 8 rights had occurred, reiterated the principle from *Johansen v Norway*[89] that a fair balance must be struck between the interests of the child and those of the parent. Similarly, in *Hansen v Turkey*,[90] a case in which the mother argued that failure to enforce contact had breached her Article 8 right to respect for family life, the Court found, citing *Hokkanen*[91] and *Ignaccolo-Zenide*[92]:

the rights and freedoms of all concerned must be taken into account, and more particularly the best interests of the child and his or her rights under Article 8 of the Convention. Where contacts with the parent might appear to threaten those interests or interfere with those rights, it is for the national authorities to strike a fair balance between them.

In other words, within the margin of appreciation of the member state, a fair balance must be struck between the Article 8 rights of the child and those of the parent, thereby ruling out the use of a presumption that precludes that balancing exercise, although the welfare of the child will be of especial significance.

As discussed in Chapter 13, the decisions in *Tammer v Estonia*,[93] *Peck v UK*[94] and *Von Hannover v Germany*[95] indicate that Strasbourg is readily able to find interferences with expression justified where a competing Convention right—Article 8—is at issue. *N v Portugal*[96] and *Barclay v United Kingdom*[97] also support this stance. Indeed, the Court has made clear that speech which is only concerned with publicizing private facts, with no relevance to serious public debate, will generally be afforded a particularly low weight under Article 10, such that interferences with it to uphold Article 8 rights will almost inevitably be justified.[98]

A and Byrne and Twenty-Twenty Television v United Kingdom[99] is of particular

---

[88] [2000] 2 FLR 486.   [89] (1996) 23 EHRR 33.

[90] (2004) 1 FLR 142, App no. 36141/97, para 98. Cf the previous decision in *Yousef v Netherlands* (2003) 1 FLR 210. It is argued that, bearing *Hansen* and the decision in *Hoppe v Germany* (2004) 38 EHRR 15 at para 44 in mind, *Yousef* is out of line with the Court's established and continuing line of reasoning on the interests of the child.

[91] (1994) A 299–A, 22.   [92] (2000) Reports of judgments and decisions 2000–I, 265.

[93] (2003) 37 EHRR 43; (2001) 10 BHRC 543.   [94] (2003) no. 44647/98.

[95] (2004) App no. 59320/00, judgment of 24 June 2004; see in particular paras 63,64,65,66.

[96] *N v Portugal*, App no. 20683/92, 20 February 1995. A magazine publisher's application complaining of a breach of Article 10 after being convicted of defamation and invasion of privacy in respect of the publication of photographs of a well-known businessman engaged in sexual activities was rejected as manifestly ill-founded. The Commission considered that the sanction was proportionate and necessary for the protection of the rights of others, one of which was clearly the right to protection from invasion of privacy through publication of true facts by other private individuals.

[97] (1999) App no. 35712/97 (admissibility only). The Court accepted that a lack of a remedy in respect of the filming of a private home, the island of Brecqhou, owned by the Barclay brothers, by reporters could in principle constitute a breach of Article 8, although on the facts no invasion of private life had occurred.

[98] See further Chapter 13 at pp 691–6.   [99] (1998) 25 EHRR CD 159.

significance in this line of authority. Decided prior to *Tammer* and *Peck*, it is neverthe-less in line with the findings in those decisions, and also reveals the stance taken at Strasbourg to the paramountcy principle where a clash with Article 10 arises. The clash of rights which occurred was resolved in favour of the Article 8 rights of the child (although the case was not argued in those terms), but it was also—most signifi-cantly—made clear that even in respect of a child's welfare, Article 8 does not take *automatic* priority over Article 10. The case concerned the restriction of freedom of expression represented by the refusal to vary the injunction in *In re Z*, discussed above.

The first applicant, the child (C)'s mother, argued that the Court's refusal to accept her decision that C should take part in the television programme had constituted a breach of her Article 8 right to respect for family life. The mother and the media applicants both complained of a breach of Article 10. The Commission took into account, in the context of Article 10, that the right to freedom of expression is one of the essential foundations of a democratic society and that prior restraints call for the 'most careful scrutiny'.[100] In addition, it found that, in considering the 'duties and responsibilities' of the applicants as persons exercising their freedom of expression through the making and production of a television programme, the potential impact of the programme on the public and consequently on C, had to be viewed as an important factor.[101] The Commission noted that by continuing the injunctions, the domestic courts prevented all the applicants from making a television programme featuring the education and development of C in an educational and behavioural institute; it found that the continuance of the injunction by the domestic courts constituted an interference with all three applicants' right to freedom of expression within the meaning of Article 10(1).

In relation to the question whether the interference could be considered 'necessary' under para 2 of both Articles 8 and 10, the Commission afforded a certain margin of appreciation in assessing whether the need existed. It conducted the examination of necessity under Article 8(2) but stated that the same principles and considerations would apply under Article 10(2). It took into account the purpose of the docu-mentary programme and the acceptance of the applicants' *bona fides* in this respect. The applicants submitted that the programme was of significant public interest in that it would inform the educational authorities in the United Kingdom, the families of those who suffer from the same problems as C, and those sufferers themselves about other educational and behavioural methods which could significantly improve the latter's potential. The first applicant (C's mother) submitted that since her decision to allow C to participate in the television programme was taken in good faith, for C's benefit and with the proper advice, the courts should have followed her decision unless they found it irrational or in bad faith.[102]

---

[100] *Observer and Guardian v United Kingdom*, (1991) 14 EHRR 153, paras 59–60.
[101] *Jersild v Denmark* (1995) 19 EHRR 1, para 31.
[102] She further submitted that the courts were not well placed to make the assessment they did; the judges were elderly males of an elite class unlikely to have had experience of raising children with handicaps like C

The Commission found that it was for the national authorities to strike a fair balance between the relevant competing interests: what would be decisive would be whether the national authorities had made such efforts 'as can be reasonably demanded under the special circumstances of the case' to accommodate the parents' rights.[103] The Commission took into account the fact that the applicant had jointly applied for the first of the injunctions under consideration with the express intention of protecting the privacy of C, and also the High Court's conclusion that the 'overwhelming probability' was that the transmission of the programme would attract extended secondary tabloid publicity largely because of C's parents' high profile. The High Court had taken the view that any short-term benefit for C deriving from the publicity was outweighed by the 'serious consequences' which transmission of the programme would entail for her. The Commission concluded that, in the circumstances of the present case and in view of the margin of appreciation accorded to states in this area, the imposition by the courts of their view as to the best interests of C was supported by 'relevant' as well as 'sufficient' reasons. The domestic courts had made such efforts as could be reasonably demanded to accommodate the first applicant's rights and the interference was accordingly proportionate to the legitimate aim pursued. The restriction was not therefore found to create a breach of Article 10 or—on the particular facts—of the Article 8 right to family life of the mother. The Commission added that the High Court considered that if it had had to carry out a balancing exercise (for the purposes of Article 10 of the Convention or otherwise) between the welfare of C and the public interest in the programme, it would have 'firmly seen the scales as coming down in favour of there being an order against the programme being made'. Importantly, the Commission did *not* find that where the UK courts had applied the paramountcy principle, the media's right should be narrowly interpreted or automatically abrogated so as to avoid an invasion of the child's interests (viewed as aspects of her Article 8 rights).

These decisions reveal the emerging stance at Strasbourg in relation to clashes of rights and particularly to conflicts between Articles 10 and 8. It can now be said to be clear that neither Article can be viewed as having presumptive priority where such conflicts occur. In such instances, the matter may be resolved by something close to a form of definitional balancing of the rights on the model offered by *Von Hannover*. In the application of the tests of necessity and proportionality, Strasbourg engages in something akin to a balancing exercise in which a broad margin of appreciation may be conceded to the national authorities. Since the protection of both rights is axiomatically necessary in a democratic society, the Court may be prepared to leave the national authorities with a wide discretion as to the precise balance to be struck in the member state between them.

---

and they could not possibly know how the transmission of the programme would affect C. She argued that the judges were wrong in considering that the transmission of the programme would adversely affect C.

[103] *Olsson v Sweden (No.2)*, (1994) 17 EHRR 134, para 90, and *Hokkanen v Finland* (1995) 19 EHRR 139, para 57.

PRESUMPTIVE PRIORITY FOR ARTICLE 10 UNDER THE HRA?

According presumptive priority to Article 10 would not be consonant with the approach of Strasbourg in the clashing rights cases discussed above: a careful examination of the competing claims of each right was undertaken on a basis of the equal value of the two rights.[104] As is apparent from the discussion in Chapter 13 of certain decisions prior to *Campbell*[105] and *Campbell* itself it can now be said with confidence that where the two rights collide, the notion of affording presumptive priority to Article 10 must be abandoned in favour of affording presumptive equality to the two rights[106] (and arguably this can also be said even where the open reporting of criminal proceedings is concerned, according to the analysis of *Re S* in *Re W*). This stance was clearly accepted domestically in the Court of Appeal decision in *Re S*, which set out the proper approach to speech/privacy claims (but only within cases in the second category from *In re Z*). That approach to such claims was then ratified by the House of Lords in their seminal decision in *Campbell v MGN*: Lord Hoffman said of balancing speech/privacy claims: 'There is in my view no question of automatic priority. Nor is there a presumption in favour of one rather than the other'.[107] Any other approach would probably have necessitated a declaration of the incompatibility of s 12(4) with Article 8. The sub-section can now be viewed therefore either merely as a (superfluous) reminder of the demands of Article 10, or as a means of drawing in the conflicting right under Article 8 since s 12(4) clearly covers Article 10(2) as well as Article 10(1).[108] Arguably, the former view accords more comfortably with the notion of presumptive equality.

The House of Lords in *Re S* endorsed the presumptive equality approach espoused in *Campbell* but then appeared to create an exception to it on the basis of the weight traditionally given to the importance of open reporting of criminal proceedings. Lord Steyn found that Hedley J's approach at first instance—of affording presumptive priority to Article 10 and then allowing Article 8 to figure only as an exception to it, was appropriate in this context. As discussed above, this approach could be viewed as

---

[104] See the views of Lord Steyn and Lord Cooke in *Reynolds v Times Newspapers* [1999] 4 All ER 609, 631 and 643.

[105] [2004] 2 WLR 1232; see further Chapter 13 at 703–5.

[106] As pointed out in *Campbell*, ibid, at para 138, this is consistent with Resolution 1165 (1998) of the Parliamentary Assembly of the Council of Europe, para 10, which affirms the equal value of the two rights.

[107] [2004] 2 WLR 1232; (2004) 154 *NLJ* 733; [2004] UKHL 22, at para 55. Baroness Hale of Richmond (at paras 138–141) made it clear that her own approach in *Re S* should be adopted in order to conduct the balancing exercise, and an exercise based on the presumptive equality of the two Articles was also adopted unanimously by the other Law Lords (see Lord Nicholls at paras 19 and 18, Lord Hope at paras 103–111, and Lord Carswell at para 167).

[108] See Sedley LJ in *Douglas v Hello!* [2001] QB 967, 1003 at para 137. S 12(4) is not needed to perform the task of drawing Article 8 into the frame since it is performed by s 6; however, Sedley LJ's interpretation accords with the impact of s 3 (which applies to s 12(4)) and refutes the notion that s 12(4) affords presumptive priority to Article 10. Lord Hope in *Campbell* approved of this approach to s 12(4): ibid at para 111.

denying Article 8's status as a fully fledged Convention right, where there is a clash between private life and the reporting of criminal proceedings. For the reasons given above, and rooted in the Convention clashing rights jurisprudence, it is suggested that this is the wrong approach and that even in relation to such reporting Articles 10 and 8 should have presumptive equality. Lord Steyn's judgment is confused on this point since at one point[109] it accepted that both Article 8(1) and 10(1) are engaged and yet then Hedley J's analysis is endorsed.[110] Hedley J had considered that Article 8 would figure only as an exception to Article 10—an implicit rejection of the parallel analysis model of reasoning. The creation of this exception is not rooted in the ECHR jurisprudence as Lord Steyn appeared to think. A number of Strasbourg cases were cited that supported the notion of the significance accorded to the open reporting of criminal proceedings[111] but those cases were not decided in the context of a clash with Article 8 rights. *Tammer v Estonia* demonstrates that even where a very significant form of expression is in issue, it may have to give way where a significant privacy interest arises. This could also be applied in relation to the form of expression in question in *Re S*. Thus the reading of Lord Steyn's judgment by the President of the Family Division in *Re W* is correct, although it was perhaps a rather strained interpretation. It is possible that in many—but not all—instances a clash such as that in *Re S* would result in an outcome favouring Art 10 due to the strength of the open justice principle, but the parallel analysis should still be fully conducted. In other words, the factor of the value of reporting of criminal trials would always tend to be a factor weighing heavily in the balance when conducting the parallel analysis. Thus the discussion will proceed on the basis that Lord Steyn's judgment need not be viewed as creating an exception to the principle of presumptive equality between Articles 8 and 10.

The adoption of presumptive equality means that there are also difficulties in reconciling the findings in the *first category of cases* from *In re Z* with the demands of Article 8 since in that category the privacy of the child is always unable to overcome the freedom of expression claim. *Central Independent Television plc*[112] is the leading authority establishing the boundaries of the inherent jurisdiction of the court in this context. In his judgment Hoffmann LJ expressed great reservations about any judge-made encroachments upon freedom of speech other than where there were restrictions sanctioned by common law or statute; the principle of a free press was, he found, more important than 'the misery of a five year old child'.[113] His point was not that freedom of expression inevitably overcomes other claims, but that where no legal restriction already applies, judges should not seek to create one due to the primacy of freedom of expression.[114] He was speaking in a pre-HRA context: since Article 8 has

---

[109] At paras [26] and [28].   [110] At para [37].   [111] At para [15].
[112] [1994] Fam 192.   [113] At 204.
[114] This was re-affirmed in *In re Z*. If this approach was followed under the HRA once an instance was assigned to the category of case in which the welfare of the child could be viewed as incidental to the reporting in question, the Article 8(1) right to respect for the home, for private and family life could not be vindicated

been given further effect in domestic law under the HRA, restrictions on freedom of expression inevitably arise from it; the judges are not being asked to create new exceptions, but merely to apply those that Parliament has chosen to introduce. It may now, however, be argued, post-HRA, that since the Court is a public authority under s 6(1) HRA, it must, in determining *both* the applicability of its inherent jurisdiction and the manner of its exercise, adhere to the demands of Article 8—demands, that is, that may now be viewed in part as aspects of an autonomous *domestic* human rights jurisprudence. As Lord Nicholls said in *Campbell*: 'The values embodied in articles 8 and 10 are as much applicable in disputes between individuals or between an individual and a non-governmental body such as a newspaper as they are in disputes between individuals and a public authority. In reaching this conclusion it is not necessary to pursue the controversial question whether the European Convention itself has this wider effect'.[115] The House of Lords' decision in *Re S* endorses this approach since it demands abandonment of the reliance on the inherent jurisdiction in favour of reliance on the Convention rights. Therefore if a child had an Article 8(1) claim to respect for his/her private life, even if previously the inherent jurisdiction would have been inapplicable, a cause of action appears to arise and the claim has to be tested against the competing Article 10 claim of the media. Clearly, since the Article 8 claim is likely to be weak, the Article 10 claim will probably prevail, but the two claims begin on a basis of presumptive equality.

DENYING THE PRIMACY OF ARTICLE 8; RECONFIGURING THE PARAMOUNTCY PRINCIPLE AND THE *IN RE Z* CATEGORIES

Ironically, although the theoretical underpinnings of the paramountcy principle and of Article 8 differ markedly,[116] the principle affords in effect automatic priority to the

---

since the inherent jurisdiction of the High Court would be viewed as inapplicable. However, it would not be possible to sustain such an argument in relation to every instance that might arise since it ignores the possibility that the impact on the child of the disclosure might be significant even where the connection was only inferential.

[115] [2004] 2 WLR 1232 at paras 17 and 18. (But see now the post-*Campbell* decision in *Von Hannover v Germany* (2004) App no. 59320/00, discussed above, which affirmed that the Convention does have this effect.) The model to be followed is that currently provided by breach of confidence decisions; see Baroness Hale on this point in *Campbell* at para 133. This model was relied upon in the line of authority stemming from *Douglas v Hello!* [2001] QB 967, including *A v B plc* [2002] EMLR 7 and *Campbell v MGN* [2002] EMLR 30. See further G. Phillipson [2003] note 1 above. On this argument, the inherent jurisdiction provides a power independent of the HRA or of any other statute, which then triggers the Court's duty in relation to the Convention rights under s 6(1)HRA, regardless of the fact that pre-HRA the instance might have failed to trigger the court's jurisdiction. This is clearly a crucial matter since the actions frequently concern two private parties and the instance that arises might be one in which no statutory power applies and a claim for breach of confidence would not lie since, for example, the child had consented to the disclosure. Thus, an arguable breach of the child's Article 8 rights might arise where no remedy was available, if the argument above was not accepted. If it was accepted that a *power* to restrain publicity was available, the two rights would then have to be considered on an equal footing although clearly, as discussed below, in most such instances the outcome would probably favour the media.

[116] There is general acceptance among family lawyers that s 1(1) CA, as it is currently interpreted, reflects a

child's Article 8 rights where matters of upbringing are found to be in issue: had it been found to apply in *Re S* it would have determined the matter automatically in favour of the Article 8 right. While the Court of Appeal accepted in *Re S* that the presumptive priority approach to Article 10 is flawed and that the two rights must be equally valued, it went on to create impliedly an exception to the principle of presumptive equality which in effect accorded automatic rather than presumptive priority to Article 8 through the operation of the paramountcy principle. The next step to be taken is to recognize the flaws in this approach and to undertake a reinterpretation of the principle in accordance with the demands of the HRA. Such an approach is supported by the domestic abandonment of presumptive priority for Article 10: if accordance of priority to Article 10 in relation to Article 8 is flawed, it would be inconsistent to continue to accept an un-balanced approach by affording priority to *Article 8* in conflicts with Article 10. A *fortiori* an approach affording *automatic* priority to Article 8 must be rejected.

Such a stance accords with the Strasbourg decisions discussed above and clearly calls into question the paramountcy principle itself and the *In re Z* categories. Although the categories were developed in the context of the exercise of the inherent jurisdiction of the courts, they have also been referred to as offering guidance in relation to other such restrictions.[117] The decision of the Commission in *Twenty-Twenty Television* gives important guidance under s 2HRA to domestic courts in situations in which a clash of rights arises, but the child's upbringing *is* in question. The decision, due largely to the margin of appreciation conceded to the domestic courts, fails to confront fully and directly the issue of paramountcy and the automatic abrogation of Article 10 rights envisaged in the Court of Appeal decision in *In re Z*. It takes the stance that since the same outcome would have been reached taking freedom of expression into account, the absolutist stance of the Court of Appeal, underpinned by the paramountcy principle, did not lead to a breach of Article 10. But, most significantly, the Commission made it clear that the restriction had to be justified within the tests under Article 10(2), thereby implicitly rejecting the paramountcy principle as interpreted domestically and the approach taken in the Court of Appeal in relation to the third category of cases that *In re Z* established. This is in accordance with the settled Strasbourg stance on this matter where clashes between Articles 8 and 10 arise. Where a settled stance can be discerned at Strasbourg the domestic courts are expected to follow the jurisprudence.[118]

In the post-HRA domestic cases considered the tests under Article 10(2) would not have been applicable had the paramountcy principle applied since it would have

---

predominantly utilitarian or consequentialist approach. See e.g. S. Harris-Short, in H. Fenwick, D. Bonner, and S. Harris-Short, 'Judicial Approaches to the HRA' [2003] 52 *ICLQ* 549–86 at 580: she speaks of the 'utilitarian welfare' approach of s 1(1).

[117] See *Oxfordshire CC* [1997] 1 FLR 235, note 44 above.

[118] Lord Slynn in *R (on the application of Alconbury Developments Ltd) v Secretary of State for the Environment* [2001] 2 WLR 1389 found: 'In the absence of some special circumstances it seems to me that the court should follow any clear and constant jurisprudence of the European Court of Human Rights.'

operated as a 'trump card': its impact on media freedom would not have had to be justified as necessary and proportionate to the aim pursued—protecting the child's privacy. It may be concluded that even where a child's upbringing as currently understood is in question, restrictions on reporting must be justified as necessary in a democratic society and as proportionate to the legitimate aim—of protecting the child's privacy—pursued (under the 'rights of others' rubric): a balancing exercise must be conducted. Since the paramountcy principle as currently understood and as applied in *In re Z*—creating the third category of cases—is not compatible with the application of those tests, a declaration of incompatibility under s 4HRA between s 1(1)CA and Article 10 could be made in a case impossible to exclude from that category, even where s 3(1)HRA was employed to narrow down the meaning of the term 'upbringing'. The case for such a declaration is even stronger than that arising in respect of incompatibility between s 12(4)HRA and Article 8 since the paramountcy principle has a greater abrogating effect on Article 10 than s 12(4) has on Article 8.

The better alternative would be to bring s 3(1) to bear on the principle itself rather than on the term 'upbringing'. The principle could be reconfigured under s 3(1) as an aspect of the child's Article 8 rights, and one that has a highly significant weight, but which is not *paramount*. Given the strength of the interpretative obligation under s 3(1), it is argued that the word 'paramount' can be interpreted as conveying the notion of *primacy*, rather than the meaning the courts have so far given it under the CA, whereby it has in reality meant 'sole'.[119] This re-interpretation of the term 'paramount' would be consistent with the requirements of Article 3(1) of the UN Convention on the Rights of the Child (CRC), under which the best interests of the child are a 'primary', not a paramount, consideration.[120] It follows from this argument that the Article 8 rights of the child would no longer need to be afforded, in effect, automatic priority where a matter of upbringing is at stake; they would be approached on a basis of presumptive equality with Article 10 claims. The term 'upbringing' would not need to be narrowed down or afforded obscure or distorted interpretations. It further follows that all three categories from *In re Z* should be merged. Moreover, the first no longer appears to be necessary at the jurisdictional stage of the argument.

Clearly, if the paramountcy principle is reconfigured under s 3(1)HRA, concerns might arise that media claims under Article 10 would tend to outweigh claims of privacy for the child under Article 8, even where her welfare was at stake. As indicated above, this occurred in a number of instances post-HRA where the principle was found *not* to apply. There might appear to be a danger that powerful media organizations would acquire an enhanced ability to exploit vulnerable children, sometimes for

---

[119] See S. Choudhry, 'The Adoption and Children Act 2002, the Welfare Principle and the HRA 1998—a Missed Opportunity' (2003) 15(2) *Child and Family Law Quarterly*, 119–138 at 138. She prefers the term 'pre-eminency'.

[120] The CRC has not been incorporated into domestic law, but UK judges are entitled to have regard to it in interpreting legislation on the assumption that Parliament would not have intended to legislate contrary to the UK's international legal obligations. The European Court of HR also uses the CRC as a guide to the interpretation of children's rights under Article 8 (see e.g. *Johansen v Norway* (1996) 23 EHRR 33).

largely commercial ends. It might have been thought that such fears would be allayed, now that the emerging judicial acceptance of the presumptive equality of Articles 8 and 10, rather than the presumptive priority of Article 10, has become firmly established, in *Campbell*. However, the decision of the Lords in *Re S* is disturbing in this respect. Not only does it on one reading appear to create an exception to the presumptive equality of the two Articles, it is also, more worryingly, indicative of a judicial tendency to minimize the Article 8 claim where free speech is also at stake.

THE *IN RE Z* CATEGORIES AFTER THE HOUSE OF LORDS' DECISION IN *RE S*

The *In re Z* categories still have a residual relevance after this decision since the decision did not attack the categories themselves as far as the conflict with Article 10 is concerned—indeed, it implicitly re-affirmed the second two. The notion of the protective and custodial jurisdictions appears however to have been subsumed in the question of the application of a child's Article 8 right to respect for private life. Assuming that that right is engaged in any particular instance—even arguably in instances in which the inherent jurisdiction would previously have been inexercisable, the position appears now to be as follows. There is a first (very large) category in which the paramountcy principle does not apply since upbringing is not in issue (in the sense that the concept can be interpreted narrowly in order to avoid dealing with the problem of a clash between the principle and Article 10), and the reporting relates to matters unrelated to criminal proceedings. In this category a balancing act between Articles 8 and 10 must be undertaken, on the *Campbell* model. This category now includes weak Article 8 claims which are likely to be readily overcome by the strength of the free expression principle. This new category covers the old first and second categories from *In re Z*. Depending on the reading adopted of the House of Lords' judgment in *Re S*, there may then be a second, new category in which the paramountcy principle does not apply since upbringing is not in issue, but the reporting *does* relate to criminal proceedings and a child's privacy would be indirectly affected. In this category it is less clear that a balancing act based on the presumptive equality of Articles 8 and 10 can occur, according to the House of Lords in *Re S*, and so, save for exceptional instances, the Article 10 claim of the media will win out. This category of case falls within the old second category from *In re Z* since in that category a balancing act of sorts was carried out, but on a basis of presumptive priority for Article 10—a flawed balancing act, now abandoned for cases within the new first category.

Obviously no declaration of incompatibility between Article 8 and this aspect of the ECHR jurisdiction would have to be made since no statutory provision is involved (assuming that s 12(4) HRA is not relied upon). Nevertheless, it is contended that a consciousness of the possible incompatibility will lead senior judges to seek to exclude cases from this category—to narrow down the field of application of Lord Steyn's *Re S* rule. This has already happened in *Re W*. Until Lord Steyn's rule is considered again by the House of Lords, it cannot be certain that the findings in *Re W* will be followed. However, for all the reasons given above, the findings in *Re W* are in accord with the Strasbourg jurisprudence and with the stance taken in *Campbell*. Therefore the better way of delineating this second category of case may merely be to view it as a sub-category of the first—one concerning criminal reporting in which the child's privacy right is highly likely to be displaced, but where presumptive equality is still the starting point for the balancing act.

Finally, there is a third (or second) category of cases based on the third category from *In re Z*. This category is unaffected by the decision in *Re S*. In this category the paramountcy principle applies and therefore, in effect, the Article 8 claim is enhanced—so that it automatically prevails *even if* the reporting relates to criminal proceedings. Lord Steyn made it clear that Hedley J had been wrong to say that even if the paramountcy principle had been applicable he would have decided in the same way—and allowed the reporting. Arguably, this comment was not however part of the ratio of the House of Lords decision. It is probable that the courts will continue to succeed in excluding cases from this category due to the possibility that a declaration of incompatibility under s 4 HRA between Article 10 and s 1(1)CA might have to be made if a case could not be so excluded. In other words, it may be that this category is almost certainly a merely notional one: in practice no case is likely to be found to fall within it.

However, a case might arise in which the facts are so analogous to those from *In re Z* that it is very difficult to avoid assigning it to the 'upbringing' category. If so, the courts might finally have to deal with the confrontation between s 1(1) CA and Article 10. Following the analysis above, the paramountcy principle would have to be recon-figured under s 3(1)HRA, leading to the abandonment of this category. If the Lords' decision in *Re S* is either read as in *Re W*, or marginalized and confined to its own facts—on the basis that it is out of line with the Strasbourg jurisprudence, and with the values espoused in *Campbell*, a far more persuasive decision—then the second category postulated here would become vestigial and virtually redundant. There would merely be a balancing act between Articles 8 and 10 in all these instances, where the child's private life was engaged. It is to the proper way to conduct that balancing act that this chapter now turns.

THE PARALLEL ANALYSIS

Once the equal value of the rights has been accepted, it follows that the courts should consider the grant of a prior restraint, in instances similar to those mentioned, from the perspectives of both Article 10 and Article 8,[121] although the welfare of the child

---

[121] Other Convention rights may also be relevant. If the *Re W* case ([1992] 1 All ER 794) had arisen after the HRA was in force it might have been possible to argue, under Article 14 read with Article 8, that there was also a discriminatory dimension to the findings: had the child been placed with a heterosexual couple after

will be highly significant where s 1(1)CA applies. In all instances in which a power to restrict publicity to protect a child arises, whether based on the ECHR jurisdiction of the court or otherwise, the court should seek to balance the two rights on the *Re S* model in accordance with the demands of the HRA. This process may be termed the 'parallel analysis':[122] the steps to be taken under it are considered in more detail below.

ARTICLES 8 AND 10: UNDERLYING RATIONALES

As discussed in Chapter 15, number of factors may be taken into account in conducting the parallel analysis in order to resolve clashes between the two guarantees. A starting point is to examine the extent to which the values accepted as underlying either Article are at stake in any particular instance. Where they are not fully at stake, an interference with the primary right is likely to be more readily justifiable. It is clear that claims of media freedom in this context do not necessarily partake fully in the classic justificatory rationales of free speech[123]—a point that is developed below.

As discussed in Chapters 2 and 15,[124] it is clear that both Strasbourg and the domestic courts have accepted a hierarchy of speech, with political speech attracting the most robust level of protection, artistic speech coming something of a poor second. These indications as to the established hierarchy of forms of speech at Strasbourg and domestically, and of the values underlying them, are of utility in seeking to identify underlying harmony between claims of media freedom and those of children to private and family life where they appear to be in competition. But it is also necessary to examine the values underlying Article 8 claims in general, and those relating to children in particular, although it is fair to say that a hierarchy of such values is not so readily apparent. Such claims may, especially in the case of children, be viewed as relating to both their private and their family life. As argued in Chapter 13, 'informational autonomy' is the key value underlying privacy in this area, although its protection can also afford indirect support to more substantive autonomy interests.[125]

But self-fulfilment may also be associated with privacy as a free-standing value in the sense that protection for the private life of the individual—which may take many forms—may provide the best conditions under which he or she may flourish. In *Bensaid v UK* the Court of Human Rights recognized the value of self-development, especially mental development, as an aspect of private life.[126] It is possible to identify

---

suffering heterosexual abuse the Court of Appeal might not have concluded so readily that public interest questions arose. The principle of open justice under Article 6(1) may add weight to the Article 10 argument.

[122] H. Tomlinson, QC and H. Rogers coined the term 'parallel analysis': 'Privacy and Expression: Convention Rights and Interim Injunctions' [2003] *EHRLR* (Special Issue: Privacy) 37, 50.

[123] See further E. Barendt, 'Press and Broadcasting Freedom: Does anyone have any rights to free speech?' (1991) 44 *CLP* 63, 65.

[124] Pp 50–72 and 792–800.   [125] See Chapter 13 at 662–6.

[126] 'Private life is a broad term not susceptible to exhaustive definition . . . Mental health must also be regarded as a crucial part of private life . . . Article 8 protects a right to identity . . . personal development, and . . . to develop relationships . . . The preservation of mental stability is in that context an indispensable precondition to effective enjoyment of the right to respect for private life' [2001] 33 EHRR 10, para 47.

further categories of material, in particular those relating to health[127] or sexual orientation or activity[128] that are regarded under Article 8 as 'particularly sensitive or intimate',[129] requiring especially compelling grounds to justify interference. These values may be particularly pertinent in relation to the privacy of children, as the primacy of the child's welfare, considered above in relation to certain of the 'family' cases under Article 8, indicates. The unauthorized disclosure of personal information relating to children is highly likely to have a greater impact on their personal development, including their ability to recover from traumatic events or sustain or develop beneficial relationships, than it would have on adults. Strasbourg recognized this possibility in the 'family cases' and in *Twenty-Twenty Television*; it has also been recognized domestically as indicated above.[130]

ARTICLES 8 AND 10 AS MUTUALLY SUPPORTIVE GUARANTEES

These findings should, it is argued, inform the parallel analysis. When examining instances in which the media wish to reveal private facts relating to children it becomes clear that the justificatory arguments underlying media freedom are quite frequently partially or largely inapplicable. In some instances speech that invades the privacy of children is likely to gain little, if any, support from the arguments from autonomy and self-development, so there will often be little or no justification at the level of principle for allowing it to override privacy. It may also be found that the rationales underlying *both* Articles 8 and 10 come down on the side of publicity or, conversely, secrecy. As the discussion in Chapter 13 indicates, the rights to freedom of speech and to privacy are in many respects, 'mutually supportive'[131] since the principles of autonomy and self-development underlie both Articles.

Millian justificatory arguments based on truth tend to have little application to the paradigmatic child privacy case, in which facts relating intimately to the child's private and family life are revealed. Reporting restraints attempting to prevent the publication of private facts only, and not general expressions of opinion, will pose little threat to that free and unhindered public debate about matters of importance which Mill's argument seeks to protect.[132] However, in certain of the cases considered, such as *In re Z* itself, this argument would support disclosure since the matters sought to be revealed would have formed part of a wider debate about the value of certain forms of education or upbringing.

---

[127] See *Z v Finland* (1998) 25 EHRR 371. See now the findings as to information relating to health matters in the House of Lords in *Campbell* note 105 above.

[128] See *Lustig-Prean v United Kingdom* (1999) 29 EHRR 548; 7 BHRC 65.

[129] D. Feldman, 'Information and privacy' in J. Beatson and Y. Cripps, *Freedom of Expression and Freedom of Information: Essays in Honour of Sir David Williams*, Oxford: OUP, 2000, chapter 19.

[130] See e.g. *In re Z* [1995] 4 All ER 961; *October Films* [1999] 2 FLR 347; Lady Justice Hale's judgment in *Re S* note 62 above.

[131] See pp 685–6. See also C. Emerson, 'The Right of Privacy and the Freedom of the Press' (1979) 14(2) *Harvard Civil Rights—Civil Liberties Law Review*, 329, 331.

[132] See E. Barendt, *Freedom of Speech*, Oxford: Clarendon, 1985, 191.

The justification for speech based on the argument from autonomy may also have an application in this area, depending on whether the child *herself* is seeking publicity as in *In re W (Wardship: Restrictions on Publication)* and *Kelly v BBC*. The value of autonomy underlying Article 8 could *also* speak in favour of publicity: where the child is *Gillick*-competent and seeks publicity, her informational autonomy is at stake in the sense that she is exercising a choice as to disclosure of aspects of her private life. Her informational autonomy would be invaded if disclosure was disallowed. Where a responsible and devoted parent or carer seeks publicity on behalf of the child, as in *Oxfordshire CC*[133] or *In re Z*, invocation of both Articles 8 and 10 could also point in the direction of disclosure. Indeed, in *Twenty Twenty Television v UK* the mother as applicant at Strasbourg sought to invoke both Articles in support of her claim for publicity on the ground that her freedom of expression and right to respect for her family life were both at stake. The child herself could have invoked her own Article 8 and 10 rights in support of publicity.

In such instances no real conflict between Articles 8 and 10 would arise except in so far as it was arguable under Article 8 that disclosure ran counter to the child's own welfare. Where publicity would clearly not further her best interests, a court, affording weight to her welfare in accordance with the stance of the Court of Human Rights discussed in relation to the family cases at Strasbourg and, where applicable, s 1(1)CA (encapsulating the new primacy principle), would uphold non-disclosure. Clearly, even a *Gillick*-competent child might fail to appreciate the harm that publicity could do and could be over-persuaded by reporters or by a parent/carer. In such instances the court would be expected to consider, not only the autonomy argument and the short-term benefits to the child in terms of, for example, enhanced self-esteem, but also the long-term detriment, including any impact on his development or ability to form or sustain relationships with his peers or others. However, where, as in the *Mary Bell* case,[134] or *Re S*, such arguments are not applicable, the child and her carers are opposed to publicity and there are also weighty welfare grounds for such opposition, it can be argued that disclosures could directly assault the informational autonomy of the child and those caring for her, and indirectly threaten their freedom of choice over substantive issues.[135] In such instances the speech in question, far from being bolstered by the autonomy rationale, is in direct conflict with it. But arguments based on the idea of uncertain and nebulous detriment to the child's welfare would hardly engage Article 8 and would be readily overcome where core values under both Articles 8 and 10 weighed on the other side of the balance. Where the speech was essential to inform a wider debate, the justificatory arguments under Article 10 would be strengthened.

Moreover, it is clearly apparent that the argument for speech from self development, since it seeks to facilitate human flourishing, far from inevitably opposing the

---

133 See note 44 above.   134 *Re X (A Minor) (Wardship Proceedings Injunction)* [1984] 1 WLR 1422.
135 Such matters could include choice of abode or of schools. See the discussion on this issue in Chapter 13 at 662–6.

right of the child to privacy, must support it to some extent since, as argued in Chapter 13, a reasonable degree of privacy is a requirement for individual self development, particularly the ability to form relationships, without which the capacity for individual growth would be severely curtailed. This argument, referred to in *Bensaid v UK*, clearly has an especially significant application in relation to the upbringing and welfare of the child. As indicated above, a version of the paramountcy principle—in which the child's welfare has primacy—is inevitably going to continue to obtain recognition on the basis of arguments based on the requirements for individual self development under Article 8. Where publicity threatens the welfare of the child, the argument that it should be suppressed would be readily to hand, not only under Article 8, but also under Article 10, on the basis that it would not further the fulfilment of the values underlying its free speech guarantee. This argument could readily have been used successfully in *Re S* to justify the restriction on reporting: the majority judges in the Court of Appeal and the Law Lords assumed too readily in that case, it is contended, that Articles 8 and 10 were entirely opposed in relation to the circumstances.

Conversely, where speech might *further* the welfare of the child, the values underlying both Articles speak in favour of publicity. Such instances arise where she might gain in self esteem through publicity (as the mother argued in *In re Z*) or where she desires publicity in order to reveal and express feelings of frustration or persecution (as in *In re W (Wardship: Restrictions on Publication)*) or, more controversially, where publication of true facts about the relationship with a parent, as a corrective to the parent's version already successfully placed in the public domain, could vindicate and ratify the child's own stance in respect of that relationship (*Harris v Harris*).[136]

Finally, the argument that prior restraints intended to safeguard the privacy of the child might inhibit journalistic debate on matters of significant public interest must be fully confronted. Clearly, political speech by its nature is unlikely in many instances to conflict with the Article 8 rights of children to private and family life. Such a conflict will not arise where political speech consists of the discussion of political ideas, institutions, and policies. The paradigm cases of journalistic invasions of privacy in this context tend to relate to criminal activity involving children or to the children of celebrities and may be driven merely by a desire for sensationalism for purely commercial considerations. Such publications hardly engage the press's right under Article 10 to impart 'information on matters of serious public concern'[137] or more general Convention values such as the furtherance of a democratic society.

---

[136] Munby J contended in that instance: 'Mr Harris has manipulated the press by feeding it tendentious accounts of these proceedings, enabled to do so because he has been able to . . . shelter behind the very privacy which hitherto has prevented anyone correcting his misrepresentations . . . the remedy for Mr Harris's antics . . . is publicity for the truth . . . the children's own best interests will be furthered by the public being told the truth . . .' [2001] 2 FLR 895 at paras 386–9, and see note 37 above.

[137] *Bladet Tromso and Stensaas v Norway* (2000) 29 EHRR 125, para 59.

However, far more so than in the typical 'celebrity privacy' cases,[138] political speech, broadly defined, does sometimes come into conflict with the Article 8 rights of children, as where it reveals failings or good practice of state representatives or within state institutions (*Re S, In re Z, Re C(A Minor), Re W(A Minor)(Restriction on Publication)), Re W(A Minor)(Freedom of Publication)), Oxfordshire Council v L and F)*, or opposes gendered concepts of parenting (*Re W(A Minor)(Restriction on Publication)*), or the techniques of cult groups (*Kelly*), or concerns criminal activity where there is an arguable public interest dimension (*Central Independent Television*).

Nevertheless, it is only in a fairly narrow category of cases that any genuine and serious conflict arises—those where a publication would reveal material furthering public knowledge or debate about matters of legitimate public concern *and* the privacy or autonomy or family life of the child would be adversely affected. Where a real conflict appeared to arise—as in *Re S* or *Re W*—the privacy interest could frequently be protected while invading the speech interest only minimally by means of a temporary order intended to conceal identity, so long as the order provided sufficient guidance to the media as to the material that could be published.[139] On this basis it is argued that the factual situations in both *Re S* and *Re W* supported restraint on the media: in *Re S* the revelation of the mother's identity was likely to affect S's ability to recover from the impact on him of his brother's death and mother's trial for the murder, and therefore it was especially crucial that her identity should not be revealed in the immediate aftermath of his brother's death. S was a victim in a very real sense of the alleged offence: he lost his mother (who was later imprisoned for the murder of his brother) and his brother, and his high risk of psychiatric harm was likely to be enhanced, according to expert evidence, depending on the level of publicity.[140] The suffering he was likely to undergo as a result of the publicity in terms of bullying and teasing was thought likely to have such an impact on him in terms of exacerbating the inevitable psychiatric harm he would suffer that the precarious placement with his father was thought to be likely to break down. In other words, the private and family life claims were very strong. The same was clearly true of the claim in *Re W*. But in contrast to Lord Steyn, the President examined the privacy claims of the children concerned in detail, finding that their Article 8 rights were very strongly engaged.

In contrast to the privacy claim in *Re S*, the speech claim was weak. The interest in open justice and the public interest in the issues surrounding the trial could have been served with relative efficacy at a later date, bearing in mind those compelling arguments for postponement. The speech interest engaged in publishing photographs of the mother with the dead boy and revealing the mother's name was minimal: discussion of the circumstances surrounding the murder could have occurred in the press on a basis of anonymity, at least during the mother's trial. The mother's name would clearly mean nothing to the vast majority of the readers of the newspapers in

---

138 Such as: *Douglas v Hello* [2001] QB 967; *Theakston* [2002] EMLR 22; *Campbell* [2002] EMLR 30, CA; [2004] UKHL 22, HL; *A v B plc* [2002] 3 WLR 542.

139 See note 20, above.   140 Hale LJ made these points at para [39] of the CA judgment.

question. Thus the public interest could have been served, since the case raised certain wider issues, while still protecting S. This was the stance taken towards the speech claim in *Re W*. In granting the injunction in order to protect the children, the President found:

... granting the injunction is [not] in fact likely to inhibit the press from reporting the case, nor should well-informed debate be significantly impaired simply because of the non-identification of the defendant or victim. It is said that the editor's principal wish is to be free to identify and publish a picture of the defendant *so as to report and convey an adequate understanding to the public*. I do not think the former is essential to the latter.[141]

THE STRUCTURE OF THE REASONING PROCESS AND THE MECHANICS OF THE HRA

In a case such as *In re Z*, arising under the HRA, the court could fulfil its duty under s 6(1) HRA and s 12(4) by adopting an approach which weighed up not only the strength of the Article 10 claim, but also took account under s 2 of the extent to which the values underlying Article 8 were at stake and in harmony with those under Article 10. Where a restriction on publicity was statutory s 3(1) would bite and would also demand that if possible a reinterpretation of it that took account of both Articles should be adopted. Where the restriction itself allowed no leeway for the parallel analysis in order to achieve compatibility with Article 10, a declaration of incompatibility should be issued under s 4.[142] Section 12(1) of the 1960 Act might be likely in future to attract such a declaration since it offers little leeway for media freedom.

In terms of the *structure* of the reasoning process, the court should begin by considering the issue from the perspectives of both Articles 8(1) and 10(1) in turn, on the Court of Appeal *Re S* model. In exceptional instances at the extremes the matter might be resolvable largely by reference to the scope of media rights under Article 10(1). Speech that invades the privacy of a child and which relates exclusively to her private life could be viewed as a form of expression that will inevitably be overcome by the strong Article 8 claim, requiring no justification under para 2 for its suppression.[143] Alternatively, and more satisfactorily, it could be viewed as a form of expression that only marginally deserves to fall within that term and therefore as very vulnerable to interference.[144] There is perhaps more scope for resolution of the conflict within Article 8(1). Where speech relating to an adult which has only the most incidental and

---

[141] Op cit, note 84 at para 63, emphasis in original.

[142] See further, I. Cram, 'Young Persons, Criminal Proceedings and Open Justice—A Comparative Perspective', *Yearbook of Copyright and Media Law*, Vol V (2000), 141–165.

[143] See *Von Hannover v Germany* note 95 above, at para 66. The findings in *Von Hannover* would clearly cover the children of celebrities or children who had attracted publicity due to their own or their parents' actions or situation, where the speech related purely to their private life. The term 'private life' was *not* found to cover especially intimate matters or secluded situations or activities, but the normal incidents of private life such as shopping expeditions (paras 49 and 61).

[144] See M. Tugendhat, QC and I. Christie, *The Law of Privacy and the Media*, Oxford: OUP, 2002, 420–1.

tenuous connection with the private or family life of a child is concerned, on factual bases even less compelling than that in *Central Television*, it might be argued that Article 8(1) is not engaged at all, in which case no conflict arises requiring resolution. Under s 6(1) HRA, as argued above, the inherent jurisdiction must be exercised in accordance with the Convention rights, thereby arguably extending its ambit via the doctrine of indirect horizontal effect. Following this argument, a power to restrict publication would *prima facie* be available where the child's claim had the *potential* to fall within Article 8(1); if on close examination it was found that the connection was too tenuous on the particular facts, the case could be resolved in favour of the Article 10 claim without recourse to Article 8(2).

But it is clear that 'definitional balancing' on the American model—that is, in this context, redefining the nature and content of the primary rights under either Article to create demarcations between those two rights—will only very rarely be possible, as will identifying and utilizing the underlying values at stake in order to avoid the conflict within para 1. In most instances, then, the extent to which the rationales discussed are at stake will be relevant, but this time in relation to the exercise of proportionality under para 2 of both Articles. The structure of the reasoning process would follow the contours laid down by Baroness Hale in *Re S* and by the Lords in *Campbell*, but the parallel analysis accepted as appropriate would also be used in cases involving upbringing. The court would consider the issue of any conflict between Articles 8 and 10 from at least two parallel perspectives.[145] The court would follow the standard Convention tests under Article 10(2), asking whether the interference with the primary guarantee proposed would be prescribed by law, necessary in a democratic society and proportionate to the legitimate aim of protecting the private and family life of the child—'the rights of others' protected under Article 8(1). The court should then consider freedom of expression as creating an exception to the right to respect for private and family life, under Article 8(2), again applying the tests of necessity and proportionality. But in each instance the application of the test of necessity would not require strict scrutiny in accordance with the findings deriving from the Strasbourg clashing rights cases such as *Tammer v Estonia*, since, as argued above, it is axiomatic that there is a pressing need to protect both rights in a democratic society. The test of proportionality would clearly be much more significant, as Sedley LJ indicated in a different context in *London Regional Transport v Mayor of London*,[146] since while it is clear that both privacy and speech must be protected, the particular restriction under consideration must be tailored towards satisfying this test under both Articles. Useful insights could be gleaned by asking, for example, both whether the publication in question was more intrusive than was necessary to further its legitimate aim of enabling and provoking discussion on matters of public interest, and, conversely, whether the remedy sought on behalf of the child would go further than necessary in order to protect the legitimate privacy interest.

---

[145] As pointed out above, other Convention Articles might be relevant.

[146] [2003] EMLR 4, para 49.

Factors strengthening either the privacy or the speech claim, including those indicated by Lady Justice Hale in *Re S*, could be taken into account in relation to the exercise of proportionality, as could any harmony that could be discerned between the underlying rationales of both Articles in respect of the factors relevant in the particular instance. Where the case would formerly have fallen within the 'upbringing' category in the domestic courts this would weigh heavily in the balance in terms of the child's interests under Article 8, but the factor of upbringing would not alone determine the outcome. For example, arguments under both Articles 8 and 10 might favour publicity as in *In re Z*, but there might be countervailing welfare arguments under Article 8 which could be answered to by allowing publication of the material in question but concealing the child's identity, thus allowing for a minimal invasion of the Article 10 guarantee. In terms of Article 10(2) the interference would then be proportionate to the legitimate aim pursued—that of protecting the child's welfare under Article 8(1), while taking into account the value of autonomy which would be served by allowing some publicity. A greater and more nuanced insight into the best interests of the child might be attained; the notion that publicity might in some circumstances serve those interests might begin to take hold. At the same time the claims of the media in this context would be subjected to greater scrutiny: dissonance between the values of free speech and the commercial interests of the media might be revealed. As Cram puts it in relation to minors' privacy claims: 'the courts [have failed] at times to probe free speech claims advanced by the media by reference to accepted free speech rationales.'[147]

CONCLUSIONS

This chapter has argued for a new approach to conflicts of rights in this context, taking as its starting point an equal weighting of Articles 8 and 10, and refusing thereafter to minimize the child's private and family life claim. As discussed above, there are a number of statutory restrictions on the reporting of the identity of children and it is hard to see how the parallel analysis can occur in imposing most of them since they leave little leeway for conducting it. Section 49 of the Children and Young Person's Act 1939, as amended, does leave room for conducting the parallel analysis since the restriction need not be imposed if it is not in the public interest to do so.[148] But certain restrictions, including s 39 of the 1939 Act and s 12(1)(a) of the Administration of Justice Act 1960, may eventually be the subject of a declaration of incompatibility with Art 10 under s 4 HRA since they leave too little, or no, room for

---

[147] See I. Cram, 'Minors' Privacy, Free Speech and the Courts' [1997] *PL* 410 at 419; see also 411–2; see further E. Barendt, 'Press and Broadcasting Freedom: Does anyone have any rights to free speech?' (1991) 44 *CLP* 63, 65.

[148] See note 18 above.

the balancing act.[149] The media may be understandably aggrieved at the far-reaching nature of a number of these restrictions, especially when the possibility of 'jigsaw' identification is taken into account.[150]

The restriction in this context flowing from the paramountcy principle is equally indefensible in free speech terms. In the Human Rights Act era a presumption—the principle—that throws a cloak of secrecy over the workings of the Family Division and over many aspects of decisions relating to the welfare of children has become increasingly problematic. The idea that publicity is almost always harmful is an outdated one that in itself may be inimical to welfare since it tends to stifle a debate that could otherwise flourish. The judicial determination post-HRA to narrow down the definition of 'upbringing' so as to avoid conflicts between child welfare and media freedom tends to lead to narrow and sterile definitions of the notion, to the detriment of debate in courts and in the media. But rather than artificially avoiding an engagement with the notion of 'upbringing' where restrictions on publication are in question so as to avoid a clash between Article 10 and the paramountcy principle, the courts could proceed to *expand* the concept (bringing cases such as Re S within it), since so doing would no longer lead to an automatic abrogation of speech rights. Such expansion could occur by re-defining the term 'upbringing' in s 1(1) CA under s 3 HRA by reference to the Article 8 concept of family life. Acceptance of the argument put forward here would render the courts freer to consider what upbringing involves in relation to the particular circumstances of a case, and would also allow the media greater freedom to engage in that debate. Greater insights could be obtained into the relationship between welfare and autonomy, a matter that has long bedevilled family law.[151] Debate as to the relationship between fatherhood and the welfare of the child[152] might become less constrained, leading thereby to a changed and more nuanced construction of 'the father'.[153] The quality of decision-making in the Family Division and in the courts in general in cases concerning children might be improved.

The change in judicial reasoning argued for here—which has significance in relation to other conflicts of rights—is partly a procedural one in the sense that it is seeking to open the door, under Articles 10(2) and 8(2), to a wider debate within the parallel exercise of proportionality as to what welfare is and as to the best methods of furthering it. It is substantive in the sense that it is arguing, in accordance with the deontological underpinnings of the Convention, for affording weight to media rights,

[149] See p 813 and note 19 above.　　[150] See note 20 above.

[151] Loughrey finds: 'the tension between the welfare interests and the autonomy rights of the child . . . is a recurring feature of child law' [2003] LS 510, 535.

[152] See R. Collier, 'In Search of the "Good" Father: Law, Family Practices and the Normative Reconstruction of Parenthood' in J. Dewar and S. Parker (eds) *Family Law: Processes, Practices and Pressures*, London: Kluwer, 2003.

[153] See further R. Deech, 'The Rights of Fathers: Social and Biological Concepts of Parenthood' in J. Eekelaar and P. Sarcevic (eds) *Parenthood in Modern Society*, London: Martinus Nijhof, 1993; J. Wallbank, 'The Campaign for Change of the Child Support Act 1991: Reconstituting the "Absent" Father' (1997) 6(2) *Social and Legal Studies*, 191–216 and J. Wallbank, 'Clause 106 of the Adoption and Children Bill: Legislation for the "Good" Father' (2002) 22(2) LS, 276–96, 277.

even where a conflict in relation to the child's upbringing appears to arise. It is clear that persuading the judges of the need to move from welfare to rights under the HRA will not be easy. Lady Hale's judgment in *Re S* demonstrates the contradictory nature of their response to the HRA in this field: on the one hand the decision reveals quite a sophisticated understanding of the value of individual rights under the Convention; on the other it illustrates the determination of the judges to resist the HRA where a particular strand of consequentialist thinking has become entrenched in a field of law. In fact the process of reasoning in the decision in the Court of Appeal in itself illustrates that movement towards a rights-based analysis may lead in the long run to a more sensitive, nuanced and subtle appreciation of welfare, to the benefit of children.

Most significantly, the changes argued for here would also address the strange legal oscillation currently occurring between over- and under-protection for the privacy of children. The anomalies caused by this oscillation have been exacerbated by the Lords' decision in *Re S*. Had the paramountcy principle applied, the decision would presumably have gone the other way despite the interest in open reporting. Since it did not the decision went almost automatically in favour of media freedom. Lip-service only was paid to the interests engaged by the private life claim. Use of the parallel analysis in all instances would lead to full scrutiny of the real basis of media free speech claims, with the result, in the wake of *Campbell* and *Von Hannover*, that in instances outside the 'upbringing' category the privacy of the child would nevertheless tend to prevail. This is probably the most significant point emerging from this chapter: the courts are more comfortable with free speech than with privacy claims and there are real dangers that the marginalization of the paramountcy principle that has occurred in these instances will enhance the probability that the privacy claim of the child will be minimized as it was in the House of Lords in *Re S*. That was a case tailor-made for the application of the Human Rights Act since real harm to a vulnerable child could have been averted. If the HRA is about anything it is about identifying the possibility of such harm and providing a new remedy where common law doctrine and Parliamentary endeavour had failed to do so. Clearly, the HRA's primary role is to protect the citizen against the arbitrary and oppressive use of state power. But the ability of large media corporations to invade privacy is equal to or even arguably surpasses that of the state, and therefore provision of such protection is equally necessary. It is a standing embarrassment to the members of the House of Lords, and in particular Lord Steyn, that that outcome was not achieved. The far more sensitive and sophisticated reasoning of the President of the Family Division in *Re W*, which succeeded in examining the real weight of both the speech and privacy claims put forward, may be indicative of the path that judicial reasoning is now likely to take in this context.

This chapter has sought to indicate that the provision for protecting the privacy of children has developed in a chaotic and unprincipled fashion. On the one hand there are various statutory restrictions on reporting that afford little or no room for the balancing act demanded by Articles 8 and 10. On the other, the inherent or 'ECHR jurisdiction' has developed in a distorted manner: in avoiding the absolutist effects of the paramountcy principle, it is falling into the trap of failing to provide privacy protection even where very strong claims for such protection arise. But this is not merely an argument for creating further restrictions on reporting, going well beyond the existing statutory ones: as has been indicated, harmony can be found between free speech and private life values even within an enhanced application of the ECHR jurisdiction.

17

REGULATION OF THE BROADCAST MEDIA AND THE PROTECTION OF PRIVACY

INTRODUCTION

This chapter will sketch the regulatory regime in relation to broadcasters for the protection of privacy. This will include consideration of an issue on which there appears to be no published academic commentary at all to date: the effect of the Communications Act 2003 on the protection of privacy.[1] One of the most significant aspects of the Act is the radical change it brings about in relation to the regulatory model for the BBC. However, it should be noted at the outset that in relation to this matter, the Act leaves much to be determined by the Agreement concluded between the BBC and the Government and that that Agreement may well be altered when the BBC's Charter is renewed in 2007.[2] Thus the effect of the Act in this area is subject to change when the new Agreement and Charter come into force on 1 January of that year.[3] However, a Deed of Amendment, dated 4 December 2003, made between the BBC and the Secretary of State for Culture, Media and Sport, has made significant changes consequential upon the 2003 Act. These, crucially, make the BBC subject, for the first time, to external regulation—by OFCOM—and to a system of sanctions for breach of the obligations now binding upon it, including the new, comprehensive Broadcasting Code.

This new Code was recently promulgated by OFCOM and came into force in July 2005.[4] Section 8 of the new Code deals with privacy, replacing the old Codes drawn up by the Independent Television Commission (ITC) and the Broadcasting Standards

---

[1] A literature search for this book uncovered no articles on the Communications Act 2003 and privacy; a useful summary of wider issues relating to the future governance and regulation of the BBC may be found in D. Sandelson and G. Smith, 'The Future Shape of the BBC: The Hutton Inquiry, Charter Review, and the Challenges Facing the BBC and the Government' (2004) 15(5) *Ent. L.R.* 2004, 137–46.

[2] The current Charter and Agreement expire on 31 December 2006.

[3] A Green Paper was published in 2005, with a White Paper expected thereafter.

[4] Specifically, 25 July 2005.

Commission (BSC). It is not the purpose of this chapter to give a detailed account of the regulatory structure represented by the Communications Act or to consider in exhaustive detail the new privacy code now policed by OFCOM. As discussed in the Introduction to this work, this book is a discussion of media law relating to free expression, not an exposition of media regulation. Moreover, complaints of invasions of privacy by the broadcast media are comparatively rare: the problem, on the whole, lies with the press, not broadcasters. For example, in 1995, of the 73 complaints adjudicated upon by the BSC under the fairness and privacy code, 'only seven involved purely privacy complaints'.[5] This chapter will therefore confine itself to an overview of the new arrangements and of the provisions of the Code, concentrating primarily upon the interface between Article 8 of the European Convention on Human Rights, the Human Rights Act and the regulatory regime.

Specifically, the principal concern of this chapter is to examine whether the new system for the protection of privacy put in place by the Communications Act and the HRA is in fact adequate, as assessed by the crucial decision of the European Court of Human Rights in *Peck v UK*.[6] *Peck* gives teeth to Article 8; the decision in *Von Hannover*,[7] discussed in detail in Chapter 13, strongly reinforces its demand for clear, effective privacy remedies. Specifically, *Peck* has something particular to tell us about the adequacy of regulatory regimes, such as the UK's, which place the emphasis not on individual remedies, but upon institutional guidance and after-the-fact sanctions. The key argument of this chapter is that the new system represented by the 2003 Act and the HRA together quite clearly and conspicuously fails to answer to the Court's decision in *Peck*. Indeed this seems to be an almost unprecedented instance in which the UK Government has made no attempt at all to comply with a Strasbourg judgment. However, as we will argue below, it may be that the recent decision of the House of Lords in *Campbell v MGN*[8] represents an instance of the common law riding to remedy the omission of the legislature, providing at least some of the protection that the Government and Parliament have failed to put in place.

PECK V UK: ARTICLE 8 AND THE BROADCAST MEDIA

Article 8 ECHR provides for a right to respect for private and family life.[9] There was, up until recently, very little jurisprudence by the Strasbourg court on the issue of whether insufficient remedies for *media*—as opposed to State—intrusion into privacy

---

[5] E. Barendt and L. Hitchens, *Media Law: Cases and Materials*, London: Pearson, 2000, at 415, note 23.
[6] (2003) 36 EHRR 41. See J. Welch, [2003] *EHRLR* (Privacy Special) 141 (*Peck v UK*—case comment).
[7] [2004] EMLR 21.   [8] [2004] 2 WLR 1232.
[9] The recent jurisprudence of the ECtHR in relation to media intrusion is discussed in detail in Chapter 13.

could breach Article 8. The recent, highly significant decision in *Peck v UK* now provides a clear framework in this area. The applicant had been captured on Council CCTV cameras on the high street in Brentwood, with a knife in his hand, immediately after he had attempted to commit suicide by cutting his wrists. This footage was passed by the local authority on to a local newspaper which showed stills of the moment, with no masking, to Anglia Television, which showed extracts in a news broadcast, and to the makers of a popular television programme, *Crime Beat*, which broadcast them—to an average audience of 9.2 million. Whilst attempts were made to mask Peck's identity in both broadcasts, it was later found by the regulators that the masking was inadequate, so that Peck was recognizable. He was in fact identified as the person in the broadcasts by both friends and neighbours.

Peck complained to the ITC, BSC and the PCC. The BSC upheld his complaint against the BBC, which had shown the *Crime Beat* programme, finding an unwarrantable infringement of his privacy; it directed the BBC to broadcast an apology. In relation to the complaint to the ITC, Anglia conceded that it had breached the ITC Code, a finding upheld by the ITC; Anglia had already apologized to Peck. The PCC rejected the complaint, on the basis that the events complained of had happened in the street, a public place. Peck also sought judicial review of the Council's decision to release the footage to the various media bodies. The court rejected his application:[10] as to illegality it found that there was explicit statutory authority for the use of CCTV cameras,[11] the purpose of which was to deter crime, (as well as assisting in solving particular crimes), and that publicizing the effectiveness of the cameras was incidental to that purpose, because it 'tended to increase the preventative effect of the [cameras]'; as such it fell within the scope of s 111 of the Local Government Act 1972.[12] In response to Peck's complaint that the decision had been *Wednesbury* unreasonable, the court found that it was not the fault of the Council, but of the television companies that his identity had been insufficiently masked, and that 'It was not unreasonable for the Council to conclude that the footage was a useful example of how a potentially dangerous situation can be avoided.'[13] There was, of course, as the judge noted, no general, enforceable right of privacy that Peck could rely upon, the events having taken place before the advent of the HRA; consequently, whilst the judge expressed sympathy for Peck's situation,[14] he could find no grounds for concluding that the Council had acted unlawfully.

Peck then applied to Strasbourg, alleging a violation of Article 8, and of Article 13—

---

[10] *R v Brentwood Council ex parte Peck* [1998] EMLR 697.

[11] s 163 Criminal Justice and Public Order Act 1994.

[12] s 111 of the Local Government Act 1972 allows Councils to do 'anything . . . which is calculated to facilitate, or is conducive or incidental to, the discharge of any of their functions. The Court found (per Harrison J) that: 'The making available to the media of footage from the CCTV film to show the effectiveness of the system can properly be said, in my judgment, to be incidental to and to facilitate the discharge of the Council's function under section 163 [of the 1994 Act, above] because it thereby increased, or tended to increase, the preventative effect of the equipment which they were providing for the purposes of the prevention of crime' (op cit, at 705).

[13] Ibid, at 707–8.   [14] Ibid, at 708.

the right to an effective remedy. The Court found a breach of Article 8: the local authority had not taken sufficient care in its agreements with the broadcasters to ensure that Peck's identity was not revealed. It could, the Court found, have sought his permission before releasing the material, or demanded written undertakings from the broadcasters that his identity would be properly protected, before releasing the material to them. The episode recorded—Peck's near suicide—clearly formed part of his private life, and the fact that it had been performed in a street did not preclude this, since Peck was not in the street to take part 'in any public event and he was not a public figure'.[15] The relevant point was that:

as a result [of the broadcasting of the footage], the relevant moment was viewed to an extent which far exceeded any exposure to a passer-by or to security observation . . . and to a degree surpassing that which the applicant could possibly have foreseen when he walked in Brentwood on 20 August 1995.[16]

On the facts, there was no sufficient public interest in the broadcasting of the episode to outweigh the intrusion into private life: whilst there were legitimate aims served— public safety, the prevention of disorder or crime—and publicizing the role that CCTV played in the prevention of crime was a strong state interest, it was unnecessary to reveal Peck's identity in so doing; ensuring his anonymity would have been a straightforward exercise.

Thus *Peck* establishes that for a public authority to release footage portraying private acts without consent to the broadcast media is *prima facie* a breach of Article 8 (subject of course to a freedom of expression defence). It can surely be extrapolated from this that if a broadcaster *which was itself* a public authority—such as (perhaps) the BBC[17]—had produced the film itself, using its own reporters and cameramen, and then broadcast it, there would have been a breach of Article 8 in that instance too. *Peck* does *not* make it clear whether Article 8 would have been breached had a private, commercial broadcaster, such as ITV or Channel 5, made and broadcast such a film, and the Court expressly declined to consider whether such bodies could be considered organs of the state. However, the decision in *Von Hannover*[18] now makes it plain beyond doubt that the state *is* responsible for instances in which private media bodies invade privacy and an insufficient, or no, remedy is provided by the state. The fact that there is no direct state involvement in the breach of privacy in question is irrelevant.[19] The breach of Article 8 in such a case arises from the failure of the state to afford victims a proper remedy against such bodies. This is readily supportable in principle: the drawing of a strict line between state broadcasters, such as the BBC, and private, but heavily regulated broadcasters, such as ITV would appear arbitrary: both have equal ability to invade privacy. In this case, the fact that

---

[15] *Peck v UK*, op cit, at [62].   [16] Ibid.

[17] See discussion in Chapter 3 as to whether the BBC is a hybrid (functional) public authority and as to those functions that are considered public functions: 114–22.

[18] (2004), Applic no. 59320/00.

[19] For detailed discussion of this decision and its implications, see Chapter 13 at 671–4 and 677–83.

the BBC is a state body should be irrelevant: its status as such does not add to its ability to intrude into privacy, while the state has clearly assumed responsibility for regulating the conduct of private broadcasters in relation to privacy. The following section of this chapter considers the new regulatory regime in the light of these decisions under Article 8.

THE REGULATORY REGIME: A SKETCH

When addressing the issue of media regulation in relation to privacy, it is necessary to consider not only the Communications Act 2003, but also the previous Broadcasting Act 1996; the Fairness and Privacy code published under s 107 of that Act and now revised and policed by Ofcom; the Human Rights Act 1998, and of course the case law of the Strasbourg Court just discussed. The 2003 Act may readily be seen as having improved—or at least simplified—the position in relation to protection for privacy. It sets up a single regulator for the broadcast media—Ofcom. Previously, the Broadcasting Standards Commission (BSC) regulated all the broadcast media, while the Independent Television Commission (ITC) regulated the independent television channels. Both the BSC and the ITC had drafted, and enforced, two codes each; one on taste and decency (covering, broadly, the portrayal of sex and violence) known as 'the standards code' and one on fairness and privacy, covering intrusion into privacy, misrepresentation, inaccuracy and so on. Under the position before the 2003 Act, the BSC code covered all the broadcasters, including the BBC, whereas the ITC code only covered the independent broadcasters. Thus the independent broadcasters were actually subject to two codes on privacy, and two Regulators—scarcely a satisfactory position.

The key difference between the two regimes prior to the 2003 Act was in terms of sanctions: the BSC could only require a broadcaster found to be in breach of its code to broadcast its findings and an apology if appropriate;[20] the ITC could, in addition to these sanctions, fine a broadcaster, and, in extreme cases, withdraw its licence.[21] Thus the BBC was under a much 'lighter' scheme of regulation. What then is the position under the new legislation?

The Government White Paper made it clear that the accent was on continuity with the old regime. In a brief paragraph dealing with privacy matters, the Government simply stated:

Traditionally, because of the invasive and powerful nature of broadcasting, people who believe they have had their privacy unjustifiably infringed or been unfairly presented have had the right to complain directly to an independent body which is able to make, and ensure the publication of, adjudications . . . The right to seek such redress from OFCOM will be retained as an important remedy for those directly affected by a programme.[22]

---

[20] Under s 119, Broadcasting Act 1996.   [21] Under various provisions of the Broadcasting Act 1990.
[22] A New Future for Communications, at [6.5], December 2000; www.communicationswhitepaper.gov.uk.

Essentially, therefore, Ofcom takes over the previous duties of the BSC[23] to draw up, revise, and hear complaints under the fairness and privacy code issued under section 107 of the Broadcasting Act 1996.[24] It also takes over the BSCs powers under section 119 of that Act[25] to force broadcasters to carry apologies and statements of findings following complaints. The substantive provisions of that Code, and the scanty case law relating to the interpretation of its predecessors—probably still a reliable guide to how the new Code will be interpreted—are considered below.

The crucial point is that the difference in the position between the BBC and the

[23] Schedule 1, para 14 of the 2003 Act provides:

'The following functions of the Broadcasting Standards Commission under Part 5 of the 1996 Act are transferred to OFCOM—
  (a) the Commission's function of drawing up and from time to time revising a code of practice under section 107 of that Act (codes of practice relation to fairness and privacy); and
  (b) their functions in relation to fairness complaints under that Part.

[24] Section 107 provides:

'(1) It shall be the duty of the BSC to draw up, and from time to time review; a code giving guidance as to principles to be observed, and practices to be followed, in connection with the avoidance of—
  (a) unjust or unfair treatment in programmes to which this section applies, or
  (b) unwarranted infringement of privacy in, or in connection with the obtaining of material included in, such programmes.
(2) It shall be the duty of each broadcasting or regulatory body, when drawing up or revising any code relating to principles and practice in connection with programmes, or in connection with the obtaining of material to be included in programmes, to reflect the general effect of so much of the code referred to in subsection (1) (as for the time being in force) as is relevant to the programmes in question.
(3) The BSC shall from time to time publish the code (as for the time being in force). (ss 4 relates to consultation and is omitted).
      Complaints can also be made directly to the BBC, to the Governors' Programme Complaints Committee, which is intended to function separately from the programme-making parts of the BBC. In this respect, the BBC retains a self-regulatory character, although now back-stopped by Ofcom.

[25] Section 119 provides:

(1) Where the BSC have—
  (a) considered and adjudicated upon a fairness complaint, or
  (b) considered and made their findings on a standards complaint,
  they may give directions of the kind specified in subsection (2).
(2) Those directions are—
  (a) where the relevant programme was broadcast by a broadcasting body, directions requiring that body to publish the matters mentioned in subsection (3) in such manner, and within such period, as may be specified in the directions, and;
  (b) where the relevant programme was included in a licensed service, directions requiring the appropriate regulatory body to direct the licence holder to publish those matters in such manner, and within such period, as may be so specified.
(3) Those matters are—
  (a) a summary of the complaint;
  (b) the BSC's findings on the complaint or a summary of them;
  (c) in the case of a standards complaint, any observations by the BSC on the complaint or a summary of any such observations.
(5) The form and content of any such summary as is mentioned in subsection (3)(a), (b) or (c) shall be such as may be approved by the BSC.
(6) A broadcasting or regulatory body shall comply with any directions given to them under this section.

independent broadcasters has been all but removed. This is because the 2003 Act opened the way for the BBC to be able, for the first time, to be fined by an independent regulator—Ofcom. The Act itself actually does not resolve the matter: section 198 simply gives power to Ofcom to regulate the BBC insofar as that is provided for in the BBC's Agreement with the Government.[26] In other words, it opened up the *possibility* of regulation by Ofcom on privacy matters, but left the decision as to whether that would actually come about to be made by the Secretary of State, who would bring about change by modifying the BBC Agreement. The amendments subsequently made in December 2003 to the BBC Agreement, mentioned above, are quite radical in effect. First, they insert the requirement to observe the fairness and privacy Code drawn up under the Broadcasting Act 1996 into the BBC Agreement for the first time. Previously, the BBC Agreement contained provisions requiring it to abide by the provisions of the standards code—on taste and decency—but had no provisions relating to invasion of privacy, a curious inconsistency perhaps explained by the fact that the last BBC Agreement came into force on 25th Jan 1996, before the Broadcasting Act 1996 was passed. Now, a new clause 5A states simply:

The Corporation shall secure the observance—

(a) in connection with the provisions of the Public Broadcasting Services, and

(b) in relation to the programmes included in the those services,

of the code for the time being in force under s 107 of the Broadcasting Act 1996 (the fairness [and privacy] code).

Thus the BBC's foundational agreement, for the first time, requires it to comply with that privacy code: it is in effect written into the BBC's Agreement and binding upon it. The second and even more radical change is that foreshadowed by section 198(3) of the 2003 Act, which allows for the imposition of penalties upon the BBC for breach of provisions in its Agreement and Charter.[27] The amended Agreement[28] provides for the

---

[26] Section 198 provides:

(1) It shall be a function of OFCOM, to the extent that provision for them to do so is contained in—
    (a) the BBC Charter and Agreement, and
    (b) the provisions of this Act and of Part 5 of the 1996 Act,
    to regulate the provision of the BBC's services and the carrying on by the BBC of other activities for purposes connected with the provision of those services.
(2) For the purposes of the carrying out of that function OFCOM—
    (a) are to have such powers and duties as may be conferred on them by or under the BBC Charter and Agreement; and
    (b) are entitled, to the extent that they are authorised to do so by the Secretary of State or under the terms of that Charter and Agreement, to act on his behalf in relation to that Charter and Agreement.

[27] s 198(3) provides:

The BBC must pay OFCOM such penalties in respect of contraventions by the BBC of provision made by or under—
(a) this Part, or
(b) the BBC Charter and Agreement,
as are imposed by OFCOM in exercise of powers conferred on them by that Charter and Agreement.

[28] Paragraph 13E.

imposition by Ofcom upon the BBC of financial penalties for breach of various enforceable requirements,[29] which[30] includes the fairness Code in clause 5A. Moreover, clause 13D provides that if Ofcom is satisfied that the BBC has breached an enforceable requirement, it may require the BBC to carry a correction or statement of Ofcom's findings upon its adjudication on any complaint.[31]

In contrast, the independent broadcasters are regulated by the 2003 Act directly. Section 326 provides that they too are bound by the fairness and privacy code;[32] they may be directed by Ofcom to carry statements of findings and corrections;[33] they can be fined for breach of the Code,[34] and, in extreme cases, licences may theoretically be revoked.[35] It should be noted however, that the ITC, which similarly had the power to impose fines, never once did so in relation to invasion of privacy so the imposition of either sanction is most unlikely in practice.

These provisions are bolstered by section 3(2) of the 2003 Act under which

---

[29] Clause 13E provides: '1. If OFCOM are satisfied that the Corporation has contravened a relevant enforceable requirement, they may serve on the Corporation a notice requiring it to pay them, within a specified period, a specified penalty.

13E.2 The amount of the penalty that may be imposed on any occasion under this clause shall not exceed the maximum specified for the time being in subsection 198(5) of the Communications Act 2003 [that is, £250,000].

[30] By virtue of clause 13F

[31] Clause 13D provides: '13D.1 This clause applies if OFCOM are satisfied—

(a) that the Corporation has, in relation to any of its services, contravened a relevant enforceable requirement; and

(b) that the contravention can be appropriately remedied by the inclusion in that service of a correction or a statement of findings (or both).

13D.2 OFCOM may from time to time direct the Corporation to include a correction or statement of findings (or both) in the service.

13D.3 A direction may require the correction or statement of findings to be in such form, and to be included in programmes at such times, as OFCOM may determine.'

Clause 13D applies to contravention of the fairness code by virtue of clause 13F.1.

[32] S 326 provides: 'The regulatory regime for every programme service licensed by a Broadcasting Act licence includes the conditions that OFCOM consider appropriate for securing observance—

(a) in connection with the provision of that service, and;

(b) in relation to the programmes included in that service,

of the code for the time being in force under section 107 of the 1996 Act (the fairness code).'

[33] Under section 236.

[34] S 237 provides:

If OFCOM are satisfied that the holder of a licence to provide a television licensable content service—

(a) has contravened a condition of the licence, or

(b) has failed to comply with a direction given by OFCOM under or by virtue of a provision of this Part, Part 1 of the 1990 Act or Part 5 of the 1996 Act, they may serve on him a notice requiring him to pay them, within a specified period, a specified penalty.

(2) The amount of the penalty under this section must not exceed the maximum penalty given by ss (3).

(3) The maximum penalty is whichever is the greater of—

(a) £250,000 and

(b) 5 per cent. of the qualifying revenue for the licence holder's last complete accounting period falling within the period for which his licence has been in force ('the relevant period').

[35] Under s 238.

Ofcom has the duty of ensuring the application of standards that provide adequate protection to members of the public and all other persons from what the Act calls 'unwarranted infringements of privacy', balanced of course against freedom of expression. Thus the BBC is now in the same position as the other broadcasters in relation to standards of privacy protection, correcting the anomalous position that existed previously. Nevertheless, the question remains as to whether this new scheme, which essentially amounts to a tidying up exercise, brings the UK regulatory regime into line with the requirements of the Convention as enunciated in *Peck v UK*, a question to which we now turn.

THE NEW REGULATORY REGIME, *PECK*, AND ARTICLE 8

Unfortunately, the answer to the above question appears to be clearly in the negative. Essentially, the problem lies in the fact that neither the Communications Act nor the Human Rights Act, even when taken together, provide adequate protection for privacy as required by the Convention *in all cases*. We will use the example of Peck himself, supposing that that he was today similarly aggrieved by a broadcast, to illustrate the point, though the discussion will not be confined to the particular facts of the *Peck* case, but will posit other examples. It would appear that a contemporary Peck would have three main options.

THE 'COMPLAINT AND ADJUDICATION' ROUTE

Peck could now complain to Ofcom; the new regulator would adjudicate on the complaint, under the privacy section of the new Broadcasting Code, and issue its adjudication. It could force the broadcaster to carry an apology, or correction, and, in extreme cases, impose a fine or even the revocation of its licence, although, as noted above, these latter two options are most unlikely in practice. As noted above, this would now be equally the case if it were the BBC[36] that had broadcast the offending programme. Are there satisfactory remedies for a broadcast that breaches Article 8, as well as the Code? The answer clearly seems to be: No. The European Court of Human Rights in *Peck*, having found a breach of Article 8, went on to consider whether there had been an 'effective remedy' available to Peck, as required by Article 13 of the Convention,[37] for that breach. It found that there had not been such a remedy, making the very clear finding that the potential to impose apologies or even fines on broadcasters did *not* satisfy the requirement of the Convention in this respect, essentially

---

[36] Aside from the theoretical possibility of licence revocation, which does not apply in relation to the BBC.

[37] Article 13, of course, is not incorporated by the HRA; nevertheless, it remains binding on the UK as a matter of international law.

because these did not provide any redress to the person aggrieved. It will be recalled that following Peck's complaint to it, the BSC had found a breach of the code and imposed the requirement that this finding be carried by the BBC. Nevertheless, the Court's finding was clear:

The Court finds that the lack of legal power of the commissions to award damages to the applicant means that those bodies could not provide an effective remedy to him. It notes that the ITC's power to impose a fine on the relevant television company does not amount to an award of damages to the applicant.[38]

It is here that the problem arises: for Ofcom, just like its predecessors, has no power to order broadcasters to pay damages to an aggrieved party. Nor can it *prevent* broadcasts: it acts only after the fact, in response to a complaint. It is in this sense that the Government appears to have ignored the decision in *Peck* in setting up the new regime under the 2003 Act. The BBC has been brought under much more stringent control by the regulators in relation to the protection of privacy. But precisely the problem identified in *Peck*—the inability of the regulatory bodies to award damages to complainants—has been left unchanged. Such a change could in principle have been made: since Ofcom can *fine* regulators, why not add to that the ability also to award damages? In deliberately failing to introduce such a power, the Government appears to have left itself wide open to a finding of a breach of Article 8, read with Article 13, were another situation like that in *Peck* to arise at the present.

Three possible reasons for the Government's reluctance to give Ofcom such a power come to mind. The first is a possible governmental fear that were such a power to have been given to Ofcom it might as a result have fallen within the remit of Article 6(1) ECHR as a tribunal determining civil rights and therefore have been bound to act fairly under the complex requirements of that Article; this might have obliged it to hold formal hearings, allow legal representation, formulate rules governing the admissibility of evidence and so on. In short, the effect might have been to turn Ofcom from a regulator into something more like a tribunal. However, since it has the power to fine broadcasters, it already exercises a punitive function: to give it a compensatory power as well would not seem a dramatic step. The second fear may have been that to give a power to award damages for breach of the privacy code might have encouraged complaints. The third was perhaps that to give Ofcom such a power might have increased the adversarial nature of the relationship between Ofcom and the broadcasters, when it is preferable for that relationship to be cooperative and educative. On the other hand, one might think that its power to award fines already places Ofcom at least potentially in such an adversarial stance; perhaps the distinction is that whereas fines are likely to be rarely or never imposed, if there were a power to award damages, there might be an expectation that they would be awarded whenever at least a non-trivial breach of the privacy Code was found. Whatever the reason, no such power exists. However, does the advent of the HRA remedy this apparent deficiency?

---

[38] *Peck*, op cit, at [109].

The HRA was not in force at the time of the *Peck* decision: can it fill the gap in protection we have identified, especially when the rapid recent development of the common law right to privacy is also taken into account? The answer would seem to be that it provides a partial, but not a complete remedy. In order to analyse the point, it is necessary to consider the two further avenues open to a current day Peck.[39]

JUDICIAL REVIEW OF OFCOM UNDER THE HRA

If Ofcom, after considering Peck's complaint of invasion of privacy, found against him, he could of course seek judicial review of Ofcom's decision. Ofcom is clearly a public authority under the Human Rights Act,[40] and therefore is itself bound to uphold Convention rights under section 6. But Peck could only be successful if he could convince the court that Ofcom had misinterpreted the Broadcasting Code, or its general statutory duties under the 1996 and 2003 Acts, including section 3, noted above. Now that Ofcom is a public authority under the HRA, and therefore bound by section 6, it must make sure that it interprets those provisions in accordance with Article 8—indeed that would follow in relation to section 3 of the 2003 by virtue of its express duty under s 3(1) HRA. So Ofcom must now not only interpret and apply the privacy code—it must do so in a way that upholds Article 8. This is now required by its duty under section 6 HRA of acting compatibly with the Convention rights. Moreover, if a modern day Peck were complaining of the release by a local authority of CCTV footage, the local authority making the decision would itself be bound by Article 8 under the HRA. This adds a layer of protection for Peck that was not there for him in the earlier decision: for in 1997, the local authority was not itself bound to respect his Article 8 rights, the HRA not then being in force.

The problem, however, is this: even if the court finds that Ofcom has failed in its section 6 duties, by interpreting the privacy code in a way that violates Article 8, this does not advance Pecks' case, because of the crucial issue of remedies. A finding by the court on judicial review that Ofcom had breached section 6 HRA cannot give Ofcom powers it does not have—the power to force the broadcaster to pay damages. And the court itself on such an action could be most unlikely to award damages itself. In theory, it would be possible for the court to award damages against Ofcom under s 8 HRA[41]

---

[39] We do not consider the possible use of s 3(1) HRA to 'interpret' the CA 2003 so as to insert into it a power for Ofcom to award damages in privacy cases. Such an intervention would amount to the plainest exercise of legislative, rather than a judicial function that may be imagined. It is clearly ruled out by the decision of the House of Lords, in a roughly analogous case, in *Re S and Re W (Care Orders)* [2002] 2 AC 291. See Chapter 3 at 161.

[40] As a government regulator it is clearly at the least a functional public authority in relation to all its regulatory functions. See Chapter 3 at 113.

[41] s 8(1) In relation to any act . . . of a public authority which the court finds is . . . unlawful, it may grant such relief or remedy, or make such order, within its powers as it considers just and appropriate.

(3) No award of damages is to be made unless, taking account of all the circumstances of the case, including
  (a) any other relief or remedy granted, or order made, in relation to the act in question (by that or any other court) . . .

for breach of Article 8. Since the action would be one for judicial review, however, it would seem extremely unlikely that the court would exercise this theoretical power: the most it would award, it seems, would be a declaration, or a quashing order, perhaps coupled with a mandatory order, requiring Ofcom to reconsider the case in the light of the court's findings on what Article 8 required. Even if the Court *were* minded to award damages, Ofcom would surely argue that, as a mere regulator, it *itself* had not caused the intrusion into privacy: that was done by the broadcaster. To award damages against Ofcom merely because of its failure to reach the right conclusion on the law in adjudicating upon Peck's complaint would surely be to make Ofcom pay for the sin of another party—the broadcaster itself.[42] It seems highly unlikely that the court would find that a mere misinterpretation by Ofcom of the privacy code had resulted in loss to Peck that required damages to be awarded in order to afford him 'just satisfaction'.[43] Such satisfaction would be achieved by remitting the case back to Ofcom to decide the case again on a proper interpretation of the Code. The resultant finding in Peck's favour by Ofcom would then give him 'just satisfaction'.

Moreover, a further problem would arise for Peck: previous decisions on applications for judicial review of adjudications of both the BSC and the earlier BCC point strongly to the supposition that that courts will be loath to disturb the findings of their successor, Ofcom. The courts, it seems clear, will take a markedly deferential approach to reviewing decisions of the regulator, being reluctant to interfere in the exercise of its expert judgment unless Ofcom has made a plain error of law, or abused its discretion. The leading decision in this area is *R v BSC ex parte BBC*;[44] essentially this case concerned an application by the BBC for judicial review of the BSC's findings that the privacy of a company, in this case Dixon's, had been invaded by secret recording in one of its stores by the BBC. Lord Woolf observed:

So long as the approach which [the Regulators] adopt is one to which, in their statutory context, the words 'infringement of privacy' are capable of applying then the courts should not interfere. It is only if an approach to 'infringement of privacy' by [them] goes beyond the area of tolerance that the courts can intervene. There will be situations which fall within the grey area where it will be very much a matter of judgment whether they fall within [their] ambit or not. In the latter situations, having regard to the role the legislation gives to [them], the answer to the scope of their remit is that it is something for [them] to determine, not the courts. The nature of their work and their membership are important when considering the role of the courts in relation to adjudications by [them]. What constitutes an infringement of privacy or bad taste or a failure to conform to proper standards of decency is very much a matter of personal judgment. This is not an area on which the courts are well equipped to adjudicate.[45]

---

the court is satisfied that the award is necessary to afford just satisfaction to the person in whose favour it is made.

[42] On the issue of remedies under the HRA, see, generally, Chapter 3 at 153–7 and Chapter 14 at 806–7.

[43] s 8(3)(a) above. This conclusion appears to be reinforced by the recent decision of the House of Lords in *R (Greenfield) v Secretary of State for the Home Department* [2005] UK HL 14; see esp [18]–[19].

[44] [2000] 3 WLR 1327, 1332.   [45] Ibid, at 1332.

Very much the same approach was taken in the earlier decision in *R v Broadcasting Complaints Commission, ex parte Granada Television Ltd*,[46] in which, on an application for judicial review of the then Commission's finding under a privacy code, Balcombe LJ said firmly:

It is a reasonable inference that another reason why Parliament did not provide a definition of privacy in the [Broadcasting Act 1990] is because it considered it more appropriate that the difficult questions of fact and degree and value judgment, which are raised by the concept of an infringement of privacy, are best left to a specialist body, such as the BCC, whose members have experience of broadcasting.[47]

He went on:

Unless on no interpretation of the word 'privacy' could the findings of the BCC be justified . . . there is no basis for the grant of judicial review . . . Whether in such a case there is an unwarranted infringement of privacy is a matter of fact and degree and as such for the decision of the BCC with which the court cannot interfere . . .[48]

As the above *dicta* make clear, the courts do not regard it as their task to decide, *de novo*, what the outcome should have been. Rather their role is to review the decisions of the regulators, affording them a very broad area of discretion, even where basic human rights, such as privacy, are in issue. This is partly on the basis that the primary determination has been entrusted to the regulators, not the courts, and partly a matter of institutional competence ('This is not an area on which the courts are well equipped to adjudicate').[49] It might immediately be objected that the reasoning behind this judgment, particularly as to institutional role, has been radically changed by the HRA, which, per section 6, now charges the courts with observing that Convention standards are observed, an argument considered in a moment. However, compelling as this argument seems, little comfort is given to it by two decisions on judicial review of media regulators handed down after the Human Rights Act came into force. In the first, the *Anna Ford* case,[50] which concerned an application for judicial review of the decision of the PCC on a complaint under its own privacy code, the judge observed:

English courts will continue to defer to the views of bodies like the [Press Complaints] Commission *even after the HRA came into force*. In summary, the type of balancing operation conducted by a specialist body such as the Commission is still regarded as a field of activity to which the courts should and will defer. The Commission is a body whose membership and expertise makes it much better equipped than the courts to resolve the difficult exercise of balancing the conflicting rights of Ms Ford and Mr Scott to privacy and of the newspapers to publish.[51]

The judge went on to say:

---

[46] [1995] EMLR 163.   [47] Ibid, at 167.   [48] Ibid, at 168.

[49] See the discussion in Chapter 3 on judicial reasoning on deference based on institutional role and competence: 151–3.

[50] *R (on the application of Ford) v Press Complaints Commission* [2002] EMLR 5.

[51] Ibid, at [28]—emphasis added.

My task is not to determine if Ms Ford's rights to privacy were infringed by the surreptitious taking of the photographs or their subsequent publication but to decide whether Ms Ford has an arguable case for exercising the limited supervisory powers of the Administrative Court.[52]

This latter pronouncement seems to ignore the obvious point that in this case, the two questions become one. Since both the PCC[53] and the court were public author-ities, determining if the former had acted within jurisdiction should precisely have involved determining whether it had correctly applied Article 8 in its interpretation and application of its Code. But, even aside from this point, the propositions made here are rather hard to swallow. Firstly, no evidence is offered in support of the judge's assertion as to the superior expertise of the PCC; second, it is, on its face, rather a counter-intuitive one: editors of newspapers (i.e. biased adjudicators) and others such as Lord Wakeham, a politician, and former accountant, are better placed than judges to decide upon the appropriate balance between *two legal rights*? If the judges are not best placed to adjudicate upon legal rights then it might well be wondered who is. Would the learned judge assert that a committee made up of lay persons and a strong minority of manufacturers[54] would be the best body to deter-mine the right balance between consumer protection in respect of injuries caused by defective products, and commercial freedom on the other? Deference may well be appropriate where there is a genuine expertise that the court does not possess, but not, surely in the field of balancing conflicting legal rights. Articles 8 and 10 of the Convention had by the time judgment was given in this case been introduced into UK law by the HRA; did not that serve to give them the 'high constitutional status' which Lord Hope said in *Kebilene*[55] would require that only a narrow or no area of discretion would be afforded to a decision concerning such rights? Something rather similar may be said of Lord Woolf's assertion that what is an invasion of privacy may be very much a matter of 'personal judgment'. Since the HRA now makes Article 8 binding upon both regulators and courts, this determination now becomes a matter of law—interpretation of Article 8—and thus one, surely that the courts *must* have the final word upon.

It may be pointed out that the *BSC* and *Granada* decisions were both made before the advent of the HRA, and the *Anna Ford* case decided only at High Court level; it could be suggested therefore that these decisions are not reliable guides to the likely conduct of higher courts under the HRA. Unfortunately, the decision of the House of Lords in *R (on the application of ProLife Alliance) v BBC*[56] gives strong endorsement at the highest level to the notion that a high degree of deference should be paid to

---

[52] Ibid, at [29].

[53] This appears to have been accepted as at the least a strongly arguable hypothesis by the court. It should be noted that the PCC has never formally accepted that it is a public authority under the HRA.

[54] The analogy is with the PCC: 7 out of 16 members are newspaper editors.

[55] *R v DPP ex parte Kebilene* [2002] 2 AC 326, 380–1.

[56] [2003] 2 WLR 1403.

media regulators.[57] The decision is considered in detail in Chapters 3[58] and 11,[59] but, it will be recalled that it concerned a refusal by the House of Lords to find unlawful the decision of the BBC and other, independent broadcasters to refuse to broadcast, uncut, a Party Election Broadcast by the ProLife party, which contained various shocking images of abortion. The House took a heavily deferential approach both to the particular decisions of the broadcasters not to air the PEB and to that of Parliament in deciding upon the particular 'taste and decency' regime. In short, nearly every judicial decision on media regulators indicates that even where fundamental rights are at stake, the courts are particularly reluctant to overturn the decisions of regulators exercising their statutory powers and duties.[60]

It should be noted however that there is a clear argument of principle for the adoption of a less deferential attitude to regulators in relation to issues of privacy, as opposed to those of taste and decency. As argued in Chapter 3,[61] part of the decision-making process involved in the latter cases consists of working out what exactly would be the likely (or actual) level of offence caused by a particular broadcast. This is a matter of fact, or more accurately, of expert opinion based upon experience: thus where a regulator makes a decision that a given part of a programme had caused (say) a high level of offence, that is a determination which, on the ground of deference based upon institutional competence,[62] should properly be deferred to by the courts. However, judicial review of decisions on *privacy* made by regulators essentially involve issues of normative evaluation. In a privacy case, there will generally be two issues: first, did the programme involve a *prima facie* intrusion into privacy; second, was that intrusion warranted?[63] It is suggested that both of these issues are legal-normative ones, given that the Code must be applied by Ofcom, as a public authority, in a way that is compatible with its own obligations under section 6(1) HRA to comply with the Convention rights. What constitutes an invasion of privacy, and whether such an invasion can be justified by reference to the public interest in the broadcast material are both now legal questions, which must be determined compatibly with Articles 8 and 10. They involve the interpretation of legal concepts and the balancing of legal principles against each other: this, contrary to what was said in the *Anna Ford* case,[64] is pre-eminently a judicial function. Of course, where the matter is a close one of judgment, and available legal materials (judgments of the domestic courts and of Strasbourg on the interpretation of Article 8 and how to balance it against Article 10) offer no clear-cut answer, the courts, given Ofcom's clear legal responsibility in this

---

[57] In this case the BBC Governors, in deciding not to broadcast a PEB as submitted by the ProLife Alliance Party.

[58] See pp 151–3.   [59] See pp 582–92.

[60] The exception, of course, is the decision of the Court of Appeal in the *ProLife* case, which robustly found the BBC's decision to be a wholly unjustifiable interference with the right to freedom of expression: [2002] 3 WLR 1080.

[61] At pp 152–3.

[62] See further J. Jowell, 'Judicial Deference: Servility, Civility or Institutional Capacity?' [2003] PL 592.

[63] See further below at 872–80 on the exact requirements of the new Broadcast Code.

[64] *R (on the application of Ford) v Press Complaints Commission* [2002] EMLR 5.

area under the terms of an Act of Parliament, may justifiably be slow to substitute their own opinion on matters of fine details for those of the regulator. But where there are persuasive arguments to the effect that Ofcom has interpreted the Code in a way that is *not* compatible with the requirements of Article 8, the Courts have a *duty* to so hold.

In short, an argument may be made that privacy cases demand a lesser degree of deference from the Courts than the mixed empirical/normative determinations made in relation to taste and decency decisions. Whether this argument will find any favour with the courts remains to be seen: it must be said that there appear to be little grounds for optimism in this respect, given the approach adopted in the cases just discussed.

USE OF THE HRA AGAINST THE BROADCASTER ITSELF

The third avenue open to our contemporary Peck, other than seeking judicial review of Ofcom's decision on his complaint, is to use the Human Rights Act, not against the regulator, but against the *broadcaster*, directly. But here again he finds a problem: the lack of the HRA's direct horizontal effect. Had it been the *BBC* that had invaded Peck's privacy, he could (perhaps) have invoked Article 8 directly against it, under s 6 of the HRA.[65] But if it is one of the *independent* broadcasters that he wishes to take action against, it is tolerably clear that he will be frustrated. Such a body is not 'a public authority' under the Human Rights Act and therefore not bound to respect his Convention rights. Thus, given that we now know from *Von Hannover* that the Court does require states to provide a remedy against private bodies for invasion of privacy, a significant gap still remains: if privacy is invaded by the BBC, the HRA *may* fill the gap identified in *Peck*—the lack of a legal remedy against the broadcaster—through the ability to bring proceedings for breach of Convention rights under s 7(1)(a).[66] But it is a *private* broadcaster which invades privacy, then that gap remains. Remarkably, therefore, the combination of the HRA and the 2003 Act together fails to answer to the requirements of the Convention.

The only possible way of filling that gap at present remains the common law. It is of course as possible to use the new-style breach of confidence action, discussed in Chapter 14, against a broadcaster as a newspaper; and that chapter explains just how broad and accommodating that action now is. It is of interest to note that the European Court in *Peck* was of the opinion that breach of confidence could *not* have been successfully used by the applicant: it considered that the information in question would have lacked the quality of confidence, since the events in question had taken place on a public street, and that Peck could not have shown the existence of 'circumstances importing an obligation of confidence'.[67] Following the decision in *Campbell v*

---

[65] See further on this, Chapter 3 at 114–22.
[66] *If* the Courts find the BBC to be a public authority.
[67] Op cit, at [111]. It should be noted that the domestic decision in *Peck* pre-dated even the first Court of Appeal decision in *Douglas v Hello* [2001] QB 967, 997.

MGN,[68] it is clear that the second problem has disappeared with the disappearance of that limb of the action: as Chapter 14 explains more fully, there were no 'circumstances imposing an obligation of confidence' in Campbell's case, in relation to the photographs taken of her in the street outside Narcotics Anonymous, but she succeeded in relation to them nonetheless. Moreover, the photographs in *Campbell* were taken in the street, just as were those in *Peck*, but were not for that reason found to lack the quality of confidence, a requirement that in any event appears to have modulated into one of 'reasonable expectation of privacy'. Thus in principle, our latter-day *Peck* could simply bring an action for confidence against the broadcaster, and, on the basis of *Campbell*, seemingly be likely to win.[69] It is possible therefore that, as suggested in the Introduction to this chapter, the common law has remedied the deficiencies left by Parliament. However, two caveats must be entered. First, it may be that the courts would find an action in confidence inapt against the broadcasters, on the basis that to allow such liability to be incurred at common law would clearly circumvent Parliament's decision to subject broadcasters to a regime *not* based on remedies but on regulation by Ofcom. In other words, deference to Parliament's decision and the regulator's special role—a motif that as seen above, figures heavily in all previous decisions concerning actions against media regulators—might lead the courts to decide that the use of a common law privacy action against a broadcaster would be inappropriate. Secondly, even if the courts did not make such a finding, it remains apparent, from *Wainwright v Home Office*[70] that there are situations involving a clear invasion of privacy, but *not* misuse of information, that breach of confidence, which still requires such misuse, simply *cannot* be stretched to cover. In cases in which the complaint was of simple harassment or intrusion by broadcast journalist therefore, without any broadcasting or other use of any information gained, the common law would be powerless to help, absent any physical trespass.[71] The new system, therefore still fails to provide comprehensive protection for the right to respect for private life protected under Article 8.

The Government, it seems, has been remarkably blind to the problem with remedies in this area from the outset. The White Paper setting out the principles underpinning what was to become the Communications Act 2003 was drafted well before the decision in *Peck* and could not have anticipated it. However, even so, it discloses clear evidence of muddled and insubstantial reasoning in relation to the remedies available for breach of privacy. As to the latter, it is notable that this whole issue is dealt with in a few brief paragraphs.[72] As to the former, it was noted above that the White Paper

---

[68] Op cit, HL.

[69] Subject of course to a defence based upon the broadcaster's freedom of expression under Article 10.

[70] [2003] 3 WLR 1137. Note that the decision of their Lordships was an appeal from a decision arising from a set of facts that pre-dated the coming into force of the HRA. Their Lordships were not therefore deciding whether the HRA required the introduction of a general tort.

[71] In extreme circumstances, a claim might lie under the Protection from Harassment Act 1997: see Chapter 14 at 716–17.

[72] *A New Future for Communications*, at [6.5], December 2000; www.communicationswhitepaper.gov.uk.

stressed the continuity of the proposed new scheme under Ofcom with the old one under the Broadcasting Act 1996. Having noted the principle of allowing complaint to an independent broadcaster, which can publish its adjudications, the White Paper states:

This approach is often the most effective means of redress for individuals or groups whose reputation may have been damaged, but who are unable or unwilling to pursue legal remedies.[73]

This is the only sentence in the White Paper dealing directly with the efficacy of the complaints procedure as a remedy for invasion of privacy—and it is a remarkable one. First of all, it is somewhat odd, to say the least, that in a section of the White Paper dealing with *privacy*, the Government addresses itself to the efficacy of the complaints procedure in relation to *reputation*. It gives the impression that the issue of such efficacy in relation to privacy complaints is being deliberately avoided. Second, the comparison (if that is what it is) with reputation is not only unhelpful but actively misleading. This is because damage done to *reputation* by initial publication can be subsequently restored by a public finding—such as one made by Ofcom—that the allegation made in the broadcast was false, provided the finding is sufficiently publicized. By contrast, if private information is wrongfully made public, an adjudication that a Code was breached in the process is very cold comfort indeed. Such a finding cannot in any way cure the invasion of privacy: it cannot erase the information revealed from peoples' memories, and nor does it provide, as an award of damages does, any form of redress for the harm done. Viewing an adjudication as an adequate means of redress indicates a view of privacy as a question only of regulatory policy: such an adjudication formally rebukes the broadcaster for its transgression, clarifies the interpretation of the provision in question, and presumably serves as a deterrent against future breaches. From a regulatory perspective, such a system looks like a sound one. But if one is looking *not* through a regulatory lens, but the prism of privacy as a human right, it is quite evident from the reasons given above that such a system is gravely deficient. The White Paper may have predated the specific finding in *Peck*, but it post-dated the Human Rights Act; nevertheless its approach—and that of the 2003 Act itself—indicates a clear failure to take privacy seriously as a legal and human right despite the introduction by the HRA of Article 8 into domestic law. It may be that further visits to Strasbourg will be the only way for complainants to force the Government to introduce such protection.

---

[73] Ibid.

PROTECTION THROUGH REGULATION: THE CONTENT OF THE PRIVACY CODE

THE CODE: GENERAL APPROACH

In this final part of this chapter, we turn to look briefly at the substantive provisions of the BSC privacy code now policed by Ofcom.[74] Until July 2005 Ofcom relied on the ITC Code and on the BSC Standards Code, pending its introduction of its own new Code. The new Code applied from July 2005 onwards to programmes, advertisements and text broadcast on all forms of television services and radio, including satellite and cable channels. While it is somewhat shorter than the old Code, and thus provides less detailed guidance, the principles it encapsulates are virtually identical, save for a couple of important changes, discussed below. It is clear that, as indicated above, the Code must now be interpreted and applied by Ofcom in accordance with both Articles 8 and 10, under its duty under section 6 HRA. Therefore its provisions should not, when so applied, give rise to any risk of violation of either Article; as will become apparent, the Code in any event appears to strike a sensitive and nuanced balance between these two rights.

It is important to stress that there are 'threshold' criteria that must be met before Ofcom will entertain a privacy complaint, similar in some ways to the requirements at the 'permission' stage of judicial review. They are summarized in Ofcom's Guidelines for the Handling of Fairness and Privacy Complaints, as follows:[75]

- the complainant must have a direct interest in the subject matter of the complaint;

- the matters complained of must not be the subject of legal proceedings in the UK or be more appropriately resolved by legal proceedings in the UK; and

- the complaint must not be frivolous.[76]

The first point is uncontroversial, as is the third. It is the second that it is worthy of note, since it precludes an individual from making a complaint if they have also launched legal proceedings (for example, for breach of confidence) in respect of the same matter. Since such proceedings may be launched immediately the applicant becomes aware of the intended broadcast, with the aim of securing an injunction preventing transmission, and then continued as an action for damages if the injunction is denied, this requirement could potentially rule out use of the complaints mechanism for a number of people.

As to the substantive provisions of the Code, two key points should be noted at the

---

[74] The Code is available from Ofcom's website, at http://www.ofcom.org.uk/tv/ifi/codes/bcode/?a=87101.

[75] Available http://www.ofcom.org.uk/tv/ifi/guidance/fairness/?a=87101.

[76] Guidelines, at [5].

outset. First, the Code, unlike the common law action for breach of confidence, covers publicity, intrusion *and* harassment. In other words, it covers not only the broadcasting of 'private facts', but also the means used to obtain the information. This appears fairly clear from the Code taken as a whole, though rather surprisingly, the clarity on this point in the old BSC Code has not been reproduced in Ofcom's new Code. The BSC Code stated unequivocally:

Privacy can be infringed during the obtaining of material for a programme, even if none of it is broadcast, as well as in the way in which material is used within the programme.[77]

No such provision appears in the new Code. The principle stated in the Code, upon which all the subsequent rules are based, is as follows: 'To ensure that broadcasters avoid any unwarranted infringement of privacy in programmes *and in connection with obtaining material* included in programmes'. This makes it clear that the Code covers not just the broadcasting of private information but the means used to obtain it. But the investigation in which those means were used, must, it seems, result in a programme that is actually broadcast. The Guidance on the Code published by Ofcom[78] states unequivocally that, 'Ofcom may only consider an infringement of privacy in the making of a programme if the programme is broadcast.' However, it appears that what is meant is simply that there must be a broadcast of the programme for there to be grounds for complaint. But if one was complaining about the methods used to obtain information (e.g. surreptitious recording), one would presumably not have to show that the specific information obtained was then broadcast, provided the recording took place to gather information for a programme that *was* then broadcast. Ofcom's consultation on the new Code, which highlights certain changes from the previous position,[79] makes no mention of any intention to make any change in this respect so presumably none was intended. That being said, it is to be regretted that the clarity on this point in the BSC Code is not to be found in the new Code.

A second key point is that the Code is fundamentally in tune with the approach of Strasbourg, and that of the House of Lords in *Campbell*, discussed in chapter 00, in two key respects. First it recognizes that neither freedom of expression nor privacy has any presumptive priority over the other. Second, it treats the contribution that a given programme makes to a matter of serious public interest as being the crucial matter to be taken into account in determining the correct balance to be struck between the two rights. Third, it explicitly uses the notion of proportionality in order to conduct the balancing exercise between the public interest and privacy, specifically stating, 'the means of obtaining material must be proportionate in all the circumstances and in particular to the subject matter of the programme'.[80] Rule 8.1 of the Code states:

Any infringement of privacy in programmes, or in connection with obtaining material

---

[77] At paragraph 15.

[78] http://www.ofcom.org.uk/tv/ifi/guidance/bguidance/guidacne8.pdf. The guidance is stated to be non-binding.

[79] Available at www.ofcom.org.uk/consult.   [80] Op cit, at [8.9].

included in programmes, must be warranted . . . In this section 'warranted' has a particular meaning. It means that where broadcasters wish to justify an infringement of privacy as warranted, they should be able to demonstrate why in the particular circumstances of the case, it is warranted. If the reason is that it is in the public interest, then the broadcaster should be able to demonstrate that the public interest outweighs the right to privacy. Examples of public interest would include revealing or detecting crime, protecting public health or safety, exposing misleading claims made by individuals or organisations or disclosing incompetence that affects the public.

One important point of change from the BSC Code should be noted. Ofcom made a deliberate decision to change the previous wording, which had stated that 'An infringement of privacy has to be justified by an overriding public interest in disclosure of the information.'[81] Under the new Code, the test is whether the infringement of privacy was 'unwarranted'—a broader term. Ofcom's consultation document[82] states that this change was made because the legislation 'does not specify that the public interest is the *only* way of warranting an infringement of privacy'. In other words, the new Code potentially allows for a larger class of reasons for intruding into privacy other than the public interest. Clearly the word 'unwarranted' will have to be applied compatibly with Article 8 ECHR. As we saw in Chapter 13, Strasbourg regards the public interest in the material published as being the crucial factor in determining whether an intrusion into privacy by the media is justified under paragraph 2 of Article 8. Thus if other grounds for such justification are offered by the media, Ofcom will have to scrutinize them with particular care to ensure that any such grounds are justifiable exceptions to the right to privacy under 8(2). An example of such a ground in fact appears in a case discussed further below, a judicial review of a decision of the Broadcasting Complaints Commission, (predecessor to the BSC).[83] A girl named Annette was abducted, raped, and murdered, and great publicity was given to the event. Two years later, Granada broadcast a programme, entitled, 'How safe are our children'; it included photos of Annette and footage of the search for her, as well as a voice-over explaining what happened to her. Her father saw the programme in a crowded pub, and became acutely upset. He complained to the BCC and his privacy complaint was upheld; Granada then challenged that finding on judicial review. The governing statute, the 1990 Broadcasting Act, used the term 'unwarranted invasion of privacy'. The Court of Appeal commented:

It was common ground before us that if the broadcasting of the programmes infringed the privacy of [the father] . . . it was open to the BCC to hold that the infringement was 'unwarranted' because of the absence of any warning to the complainants.[84]

In this case, therefore, the lack of justifiability in relation to the invasion of privacy lay in the fact that a simple step that could have been taken—to warn the family of the broadcast thus enabling the acute distress that occurred to have been avoided—was not taken. This rendered the invasion of privacy unwarranted. This presumably

---

[81] Op cit, at [14].   [82] Op cit, at [13].   [83] [1995] EMLR 163.   [84] Ibid, at 166.

constitutes an example of broader grounds than public interest of factors that could lead to a given intrusion into privacy being seen as warranted in a particular case. In fact, even with a warning to the family, Granada would still have had to justify the use of the Annette material on public interest grounds. In other words what this case indicated is that justifying factors could include but not be limited to the public interest in the material broadcast.

THE CODE: PARTICULAR ISSUES

An important matter that arose for judicial determination under the previous BSC Code was whether companies could maintain an action for breach of it. The BBC had secretly filmed transactions in Dixons' stores as part of an investigation into the selling of second hand goods as new. The filming did not reveal evidence of mal-practice, and therefore was not used in the 'Watchdog' programme. Dixons complained to the BSC, claiming that the filming was an unwarranted infringement of its privacy. The BSC upheld the complaint, and the BBC applied for judicial review of its decision. The first instance judgment found that a company could not complain of invasion of its privacy, but this was overturned by the Court of Appeal in *R v BSC ex parte BBC*.[85] The finding was based primarily upon the wording of the Broadcasting Act 1996, which, as noted above, remains the governing statute in relation to the privacy code. As Lord Woolf stressed:

What is important is that the BSC are not concerned with establishing legal rights, human or otherwise. All they are able to provide to those who wish to make a complaint is an avenue for doing so and, if the complaint is upheld, the right to such publicity (if any) of the fact that the complaint has been upheld as the BSC consider appropriate.[86]

In the light of this finding, little reliance was placed upon Article 8 ECHR, and the matter turned primarily upon the particular wording of the 1996 Act. As Lord Woolf observed: 'The context in which a word such as privacy is used can be important. I have sought to identify the context here, which is not the same as that under the Convention.'[87] In particular, reliance was placed upon s 111(1) of the Broadcasting Act, which provides that 'A fairness complaint may be made by an individual or a body of persons, *whether incorporated or not*' (emphasis added). The phrase 'a fairness complaint' includes, it should be noted, a privacy complaint. Lord Woolf's view was that:

If unfairness of this sort can be the subject of a complaint to the BSC by a company, I consider that this is a strong indication that a company can also make a complaint about the infringement of its privacy.[88]

Lady Hale was clearly also strongly influenced by this wording,[89] although she stated

---

85 [2000] 3 WLR 1327, 1332.   86 Ibid, at [13].   87 Ibid, at [17].
88 Ibid, at [32].   89 Ibid, at [41].

also that the case was concerned not with human rights 'but broadcasting stand-ards,'[90] something that could 'justify a wider view of the ambit of privacy than might be appropriate in some other contexts.' Nevertheless, despite all these caveats, the decision, we would suggest, was wrong in principle. Companies can clearly have rights to *confidentiality*, and to fair treatment; the latter notion could have been invoked—and used in future similar cases—without dragging in the notion of privacy. Aside from the conceptual incoherence of applying a notion intended to protect human dignity and autonomy to a legal construct, it is simply unnecessary to protect a company's privacy, as the case itself illustrates. If the persons filmed in the *Dixon's* case had been concerned about an intrusion into *their* privacy, then they could have complained as individuals. It would not, perhaps, be over cynical to suggest that Dixon's motive in bringing this action was not to protect its employees' privacy but to discourage the BBC from carrying out investigative journalism that might damage its reputation in future. Since the notion of confidentiality is itself rooted in notions of unconscionability, or unfairness, then clearly the fairness provisions of the code could provide the necessary protection where a company's confidentiality was invaded without adequate justification. Commercial entities that happen to have legal person-ality should not be able to make use of concepts designed to protect human rights.

Lord Woolf made it explicit that he was not making any finding as to what Article 8 would provide on this matter;[91] however, the recent decision in *Societe Colas Est v France*[92] at least partially opens the door to the application of Article 8 to companies. The applicant company had had its premises subject to sweeping search and seizure operations, without judicial authorization. The Court found the measures taken to be disproportionate to the aim pursued. For our purposes, the crucial part of the judgment is as follows:

The Court reiterates that the Convention is a living instrument which must be interpreted in the light of present-day conditions . . . As regards the rights secured to companies by the Convention, it should be pointed out that the Court has already recognised a company's right under Article 41 to compensation for non-pecuniary damage sustained as a result of a violation of Article 6 § 1 of the Convention (see *Comingersoll v Portugal* [GC], no. 35382/97, §§ 33–35, ECHR 2000–IV). Building on its dynamic interpretation of the Convention, the Court considers that the time has come to hold that in certain circumstances the rights guaranteed by Article 8 of the Convention may be construed as including the right to respect for a company's registered office, branches or other business premises (see, *mutatis mutandis, Niemietz v Germany*, A 251B, p 34, § 30).[93]

It should be noted that this judgment is restricted to the application of Article 8 to physical intrusion onto business premises, and that the finding was justified partly by the fact that in the French text of the Convention, in the phrase, 'Everyone has the right to respect for . . . his home' the word 'domicile' is used,—a broader term, as the

---

90 Ibid, at [44].   91 Ibid, at [34].   92 (2002) Application no. 37971/97.
93 Ibid, at [41].

Court observed, than the English translation of 'home'.[94] In other words, to say that unjustified physical intrusion into a company's *premises* falls within Article 8, is not to say that, for example, wrongful use of information held by, and relating to the company, would do so. Since the *Dixon's* case related to information and not physical intrusion, it may still be maintained, even following this decision, that Article 8 would not have applied to it.

A further matter that has arisen for determination is whether a person's privacy may be invaded, under the Code, by the re-publication of material once in the public domain. The point was considered in *R v BCC ex parte Granada*,[95] the facts of which appear above. One of the grounds upon which Granada sought judicial review of the BCC's decision that the broadcast represented an unwarranted invasion of privacy was the argument that there could be no legitimate complaint of invasion of privacy, since the material in question was already in the public domain. It was held that the issue to be determined was whether fresh revelations of material would cause fresh anguish, not whether the matter broadcast was technically in the public domain.

The BSC Code addressed this point expressly and similar provisions appear in the new Code, which provides:

Broadcasters should try to reduce the potential distress to victims and/or relatives when making or broadcasting programmes intended to examine past events that involve trauma to individuals (including crime) unless it is warranted to do otherwise. This applies to dramatic reconstructions and factual dramas, as well as factual programmes.

In particular, so far as is reasonably practicable, surviving victims, and/or the immediate families of those whose experience is to feature in a programme, should be informed of the plans for the programme and its intended broadcast, even if the events or material to be broadcast have been in the public domain in the past.[96]

Three further matters should be considered. The first relates to the issue of privacy in public places. Here, the Code takes a nuanced stance that seeks to leave the broadcast media the freedom to record and broadcast street scenes and genuinely public events, whilst recognizing that an element of privacy can be retained in public places. The relevant paragraph of the Code provides:

Legitimate expectations of privacy will vary according to the place and nature of the information, activity or condition in question, the extent to which it is in the public domain (if at all) and whether the individual concerned is already in the public eye. There may be circumstances where people can reasonably expect privacy even in a public place. Some activities and conditions may be of such a private nature that filming or recording, even in a public place, could involve an infringement of privacy.[97]

In relation to location, it specifically goes on to provide:

---

[94] 'The word "*domicile*" (in the French version of Article 8) has a broader connotation than the word "home" (ibid, at [40]).

[95] [1995] EMLR 163. [96] Op cit, at [8.19]. [97] Op cit, at [8.2].

When filming or recording in institutions, organisations or other agencies, permission should be obtained from the relevant authority or management, unless it is warranted to film or record without permission. Individual consent of employees or others whose appearance is incidental or where they are essentially anonymous members of the general public will not normally be required.

However, in potentially sensitive places such as ambulances, hospitals, schools, prisons or police stations, separate consent should normally be obtained before filming or recording and for broadcast from those in sensitive situations (unless not obtaining consent is warranted). If the individual will not be identifiable in the programme then separate consent for broadcast will not be required.[98]

It may be observed that these findings are clearly in line with the finding in *Peck*, considered above. A distinction is drawn between pictures that merely capture anonymous individuals incidentally and those that intrude into sensitive situations (as in *Peck* itself), in which case the invasion of privacy represented by broadcasting of the relevant images without consent[99] must be warranted in the particular circumstances, generally by a public interest consideration that outweighs the privacy interest at stake. The paragraphs dealing with intrusion into grief and distress[100] reinforce this distinction.

Second, the Code deals specifically with the use of hidden recording devices. It was noted in Chapter 13 that Strasbourg views surreptitious obtaining of personal data in this way with particular concern in the context of Article 8, and the Code answers to this. It provides:

Surreptitious filming or recording[101] should only be used where it is warranted. Normally, it will only be warranted if:

- there is *prima facie* evidence of a story in the public interest; and
- there are reasonable grounds to suspect that further material evidence could be obtained; and
- it is necessary to the credibility and authenticity of the programme.[102]

---

[98] Op cit, at 8.8.

[99] The Guidance adds to this, in wording that is clearly heavily influenced by *Peck*:

'Privacy is least likely to be infringed in a public place. Property that is privately owned, as are, for example, railway stations and shops, can be a public place if readily accessible to the public. However, there may be circumstances where people can reasonably expect a *degree* of privacy even in a public place. The degree will always be dependent on the circumstances.

Some activities and conditions may be of such a private nature that filming, even in a public place where there was normally no reasonable expectation of privacy, could involve an infringement of privacy. For example, a child in state of undress, someone with disfiguring medical condition or CCTV footage of suicide attempt.'

[100] Op cit, at [8.16]–[8.19].

[101] This is defined in the Code as follows: 'Surreptitious filming or recording includes the use of long lenses or recording devices, as well as leaving an unattended camera or recording device on private property without the full and informed consent of the occupiers or their agent. It may also include recording telephone conversations without the knowledge of the other party, or deliberately continuing a recording when the other party thinks that it has come to an end' (op cit, at [8.13]).

[102] Ibid. The Guidance makes clear that the same principles apply to material gained by others (e.g. by CCTV cameras).

The provisions for the recording of telephone conversations are governed by the same principles.[103]

Finally, the Code makes special provision for children:

8.20 Broadcasters should pay particular attention to the privacy of people under sixteen. They do not lose their rights to privacy because, for example, of the fame or notoriety of their parents or because of events in their schools.

8.21 Where a programme features an individual under sixteen or a vulnerable person in a way that infringes privacy, consent must be obtained from:

- a parent, guardian or other person of eighteen or over in loco parentis; and

- wherever possible, the individual concerned;

unless the subject matter is trivial or uncontroversial and the participation minor, or it is warranted to proceed without consent.

8.22 Persons under sixteen and vulnerable people should not be questioned about private matters without the consent of a parent, guardian or other person of eighteen or over in loco parentis (in the case of persons under sixteen), or a person with primary responsibility for their care (in the case of a vulnerable person), unless it is warranted to proceed without consent.

This is one area where the new Code appears less protective in its standards than the BSC provisions. The latter stated, 'Where consent has not been obtained or actually refused, any decision to go ahead can only be justified if the item is of overriding public interest and the child's appearance is *absolutely necessary*.'[104] It is to be regretted that this stricter standard is not applied in the new Code. However, the new Code's insistence that children do not lose their right to privacy merely because of the notoriety of their parents is to be welcomed.[105]

CONCLUSION

On the whole, the scheme for regulating the broadcasters in relation to invasion of privacy is a successful one. Complaints in relation to their invasions of privacy are, as noted above, rare, and the standards, as just discussed, strict and detailed, but allow always for an individualized balance to be struck between the public interest in a story and the privacy interests at stake. The crucial notion of 'public interest' is defined in a way that makes it clear that is in harmony with the Strasbourg notion of the press's

---

[103] Ibid, at [8.12].   [104] Op cit (emphasis added).

[105] Note the contrary—and disturbing—view on this matter taken by the New Zealand Court of Appeal in *Hoskings v Runtings* (2004) CA 101/03 at [124]: 'It is a matter of human nature that interest in the lives of public figures also extends to interest in the lives of their families. In such cases, the reasonable expectations of privacy in relation to at least some facts of the families' private lives may be diminished.'

watchdog role as the guardian of the public interest properly so called and of debate on matters of serious public concern.[106]

Nevertheless—and perhaps surprisingly, in view of the broadcasters' generally good record in this area—the Government, seemingly deliberately, has chosen to ignore Strasbourg's clear finding that a system of complaints and post-broadcast sanctions does *not* satisfy the requirements of Articles 8 and 13 of the Convention. The mere extension of that non-Convention-compliant scheme to the BBC by the 2003 Act and amendment of the Agreement is manifestly an unsatisfactory response to the finding that the UK had violated Articles 8 and 13 in *Peck v UK*. While, as Chapter 14 makes clear, the action for breach of confidence now *could* in principle cover situations like those in *Peck*, contrary to the views of the Court expressed at the time, it is equally clear that it could not cover cases of harassment or intrusion—that could themselves engage Article 8—where the material gained is not used. This in itself leaves a clear lacuna in the new scheme. Moreover, as discussed above, virtually every decision involving judicial review of the regulators has been heavily influenced by the notion of judicial deference to Parliament's choice in entrusting those regulators with the maintenance of standards in this area. It remains a possibility therefore, that the courts would refuse to allow such common law privacy actions against the broadcast media, viewing them as a means of undermining Parliament's intention in ruling out remedies in damages or injunctions against broadcasters. If that turns out to be the case, the gap in protection for privacy against the broadcast media could be wide indeed.

---

[106] In March 2006, the Government published its White Paper on the future of the BBC, entitled *A public service for all: the BBC in the digital age* Cm 6763; at the same time, a draft revised Royal Charter and Agreement, to start on 1 January 2007 was published: http://www.bbccharterreview.org.uk/have_your_say/white_paper/rchter_fwagreeement_mar06.pdf Clearly, it has not been possible for this chapter to take account of the developments these documents foreshadow. However, in terms of privacy regulation, the new regime appears to be very similar to the old. The BBC will continue to be bound by the Fairness Code in force under s 107 Broadcasting Act 1996, which, of course, includes the privacy code (see draft Agreement, at [45], replacing current clause 5A (above, p 860)). It will still be possible to make privacy complaints directly to the BBC, but these will now be made to the new Executive Board in the first instance. Ofcom will retain its power to fine the BBC (draft Agreement, at [92]) and to order remedial action (ibid at [91]) for breach of Relevant Enforceable Requirements, which, per new para 93, include the Fairness Code. (These provisions will replace paragraphs 13D-F of the Amended Agreement referred to in pp 860–2 above).

PART V

COPYRIGHT AND MEDIA FREEDOM

18

COPYRIGHT LAW, ARTICLE 10, AND MEDIA FREEDOM

INTRODUCTION

This chapter explores the relationship between copyright law and the right to freedom of expression. Once considered to have very little to do with one another, the potential conflict between these two rights has been the subject of considerable recent judicial[1] and scholarly[2] attention. The chapter begins with an outline of the variety of ways in which the exercise of a copyright interest can restrict expression and moves on to describe the safeguards for expression that exist within copyright law. It then considers the challenge presented to the traditional accommodation of speech interests within copyright law by the Human Rights Act 1998. While the Strasbourg case law on copyright is very limited,[3] Article 10 ought, in principle, to be relevant in many disputes concerning the use of copyright works.

Under the Human Rights Act, the Court of Appeal has had the opportunity to consider the relationship between Article 10 and the United Kingdom's copyright

---

[1] In the United Kingdom, see *Ashdown v Telegraph Group Ltd* [2002] Ch 149 (CA). In the United States, see *Eldred v Ashcroft* 537 US 186 (2003); *Universal City Studios Inc v Corley* 273 F 3d 429 (2nd Cir, 2001); *Sun Trust Bank v Houghton Mifflin Co* 252 F 3d 1165 (11th Cir, 2001). For discussion of cases in European civil law jurisdictions, see B. Hugenholtz, 'Copyright and Freedom of Expression in Europe', in N. Elkin-Koren and N.W. Netanel (eds), *The Commodification of Information*, Kluwer Law International, 2002, 239–63, and A. Strowel and F. Tulkens, 'Freedom of Expression and Copyright under Civil Law: Of Balance, Adaptation and Access' in J. Griffiths and U. Suthersanen (eds) *Copyright and Free Speech*, Oxford: Oxford University Press, 2005, 287–313.

[2] See F. Macmillan Patfield, 'Towards a Reconciliation of Free Speech and Copyright' 1996, *Yearbook of Copyright and Media Law*; J. Griffiths, 'Copyright Law and Censorship—The Impact of the Human Rights Act 1998', 1999, *Yearbook of Copyright and Media Law* 3; T. Pinto, 'The Influence of the ECHR on Intellectual Property Rights' 2002 EIPR 209; M. Birnhack, 'Acknowledging the Conflict between Copyright Law and Freedom of Expression under the Human Rights Act' 2003 *Ent LR* 24; M. Rushton, 'Copyright and Freedom of Expression: An Economic Analysis', in R. Towse, *Copyright in the Cultural Industries*, Cheltenham: Elgar Publishing, 2002, 51–62; J. Griffiths and U. Suthersanen (eds) *Copyright and Free Speech*, Oxford: Oxford University Press, 2005; P.L.C. Torremans, (ed.) *Copyright and Human Rights*, Kluwer Law International, 2004. In relation to the United States, see N.W. Netanel, 'Locating Copyright Within the First Amendment Skein' (2001) *Stanford L Rev* 1; J. Rubenfeld, 'The Freedom of Imagination: Copyright's Constitutionality' (2002) 112 *Yale LJ* 1; R. Tushnet, 'Copy This Essay: How Fair Use Doctrine Harms Free Speech and How Copying Serves it' (2004) 109 *Yale LJ* 101.

[3] See Section 4.1 below.

legislation, the Copyright Designs and Patents Act 1988 ('CDPA 1988'). It is argued here that the manner in which these competing interests were reconciled in *Ashdown v Telegraph Group Ltd*,[4] failed fully to take account of the media's interest in free communication and of the substantive demands of the right to freedom of expression. Following a critique of *Ashdown*, the chapter concludes by identifying situations, as yet unexplored by the courts in this jurisdiction, in which copyright and related laws present a current threat to the expression rights of users of copyright works.

HOW COPYRIGHT LAW RESTRICTS EXPRESSION

At one level, copyright serves a vital role in facilitating and encouraging freedom of expression. The Statute of Anne 1709, the first copyright enactment in the United Kingdom, had as its stated aim 'the Encouragement of Learning by vesting the Copies of printed Books in the Authors or Purchasers of such Copies, during the Times therein mentioned'.[5] Copyright was conceded to individual authors in return for the continued production and propagation of 'useful Books'. As an instrument of policy, the grant of a degree of time-limited enclosure from the intellectual commons was regarded as necessary in order to encourage the further development of that commons.[6] In the absence of some form of market protection, authors would have been forced either to abandon their profession or to seek patronage from wealthy sponsors or the State. This view, under which copyright law is regarded as the 'engine of free expression',[7] is compelling. However, the 'engine of free expression' argument is sometimes cited in support of a view that copyright law and free speech are necessarily complementary in all circumstances and, therefore, cannot be regarded as conflicting. This is unjustifiably optimistic. In reality, the argument serves only to support the existence of some form of copyright system and does not suggest that the most extensive powers possible ought to be granted to authors of copyright works in all possible situations.[8] As will be demonstrated below, there is no doubt that the powers

---

[4] [2002] Ch 149 (CA).   [5] 1709 Copyright Act ('Statute of Anne') 8 Anne c 19.

[6] Commentators differ as to the competing, and complementary, rationales underpinning the early modern copyright system. See for example: A. Birrell, *Copyright in Books*, Cassell & Co, 1899; B. Kaplan, *An Unhurried View of Copyright*, Columbia University Press, 1967; L.R. Patterson, *Copyright in Historical Perspective*, Vanderbilt University Press, 1968; J. Feather, *Publishing, Piracy and Politics: An Historical Study of Copyright in Britain*, Mansell, 1994; M. Rose, *Authors and Owners. The Invention of Copyright*, Harvard University Press, 1993; B. Sherman and L. Bently, *The Making of Modern Intellectual Property Law*, Cambridge University Press, 1999; J. Loewenstein, *The Author's Due: Printing and the Prehistory of Copyright*, University of Chicago Press, 2002; G. Davies, *Copyright and the Public Interest*, 2nd edn., London: Sweet & Maxwell, 2002; R. Deazley, *On the Origin of the Right to Copy: Charting the Movement of Copyright in Eighteenth Century Britain, 1695–1775*, Hart Publishing, 2004.

[7] See *Harper & Row Publishers v Nation Enterprises* 471 US 539 (1985) 558.

[8] See E. Barendt, 'Copyright and Free Speech Theory' in J. Griffiths and U. Suthersanen (eds) *Copyright and Free Speech*, Oxford University Press, 2005, 11–33.

granted under copyright law can be exercised in a manner that restricts the ability of other to express themselves freely.

First, however, in order fully to appreciate the relationship between copyright and freedom of expression, it is necessary to consider in greater detail the scope of the rights granted to copyright owners. Under the CDPA 1988:

... Copyright is a property right which subsists ... in the following descriptions of work—

(a) original literary, dramatic, musical or artistic works,

(b) sound recordings, films or broadcasts, and

(c) the typographical arrangement of published editions.

(CDPA 1988, s 1(1))

The individual categories of protected work themselves include a wide range of different forms of cultural product. Thus, for example, novels,[9] newspaper articles,[10] government memoranda,[11] trade directories,[12] business letters,[13] football pools,[14] and instructional leaflets[15] all constitute 'literary works'. The protected category of 'artistic works'[16] encompasses photographs,[17] technical drawings,[18] one-off sets of wrought iron gates,[19] and garden designs.[20] The category of 'film' includes not only feature films, but also amateur movies[21] and security videos.[22] In order to obtain protection under any of the categories listed in s 1(1)(a) CDPA 1988, copyright works must be 'original'. However, by contrast with other jurisdictions,[23] the standard of originality required by United Kingdom courts is notoriously low.[24] For example, a simple but accurate drawing of three concentric circles has been held to constitute a protected artistic work.[25] Furthermore, the expenditure of labour and skill in the creation of

---

[9] *Sweeney v Macmillan Publishers Ltd* [2002] RPC 651.   [10] *Byrne v Statist Co* [1914] 1 KB 622.

[11] *Commonwealth of Australia v John Fairfax & Sons Ltd* (1980) 32 ALR 485.

[12] *Kelly v Morris* (1866) LR 1 Eq 697.

[13] *British Oxygen Ltd v Liquid Air Ltd* [1925] 1 Ch 383.

[14] *Ladbroke (Football) Ltd v William Hill (Football) Ltd* [1964] 1 WLR 273 (HL).

[15] *Elanco Products Ltd v Mandops (Agrochemical Specialists) Ltd* [1980] RPC 213 (CA).

[16] CDPA 1988, s 4(1):

'In this Part "artistic work" means—

(a) a graphic work, photograph, sculpture or collage, irrespective of artistic quality,

(b) a work of architecture being a building or a model for a building, or

(c) a work of artistic craftsmanship.'

[17] *Bauman v Fussell* [1978] RPC 485 (CA).

[18] *British Leyland Motor Corp Ltd v Armstrong Patents Co Ltd* [1986] AC 577 (HL).

[19] *George Hensher Ltd v Restawile Upholstery (Lancs) Ltd* [1976] AC 64 (HL).

[20] *Vincent v Universal Housing Co Ltd* [1928–35] Mac CC 275.

[21] *Service Corp International Plc v Channel Four Television Corp* [1999] EMLR 83.

[22] *Hyde Park Residence Ltd v Yelland* [2001] Ch 143 (CA).

[23] For example, such as Germany and France. Even the United States has a higher requirement for originality, see *Feist Publications Inc v Rural Telephone Service Co Inc* 499 US 340 (1991).

[24] All that is required is that a work should originate from its author and should be the product of more than negligible or trivial effort or relevant skill in creation. See *Copinger and Skone James on Copyright*, K. Garnett, *et al.*, 15th edn. Sweet & Maxwell, 2005, 3–151.

[25] *Solar Thomson Engineering Co Ltd v Barton* [1977] RPC 537.

derivative works will also often be rewarded by the grant of a copyright interest. Thus, for example, translations, compilations, dramatizations, adaptations, and, in some instances, verbatim recordings[26] will all be protected by copyright. As a result of this liberal approach to copyright protection, the use of a very wide range of creative forms may only be possible if permission is obtained from a copyright owner. The potential impact upon the rights of others to express themselves freely is readily discernible.

The rights to control the use of a work are generally granted, in the first instance, to the work's author.[27] However, where he or she is employed at the time that a work is created in the course of employment, the employer will own the copyright interest in the work.[28] Once a work has been created, a copyright interest is freely transferable by its first owner. Following transfer, the transferee acquires the power to control the use of that work. It will not, therefore, always be the author of a work who is in a position to restrict its use. On death, copyright is transmissible as personal or moveable property.[29] In fact, some of the most notorious copyright disputes giving rise to issues of freedom of expression have concerned attempts by the estates of deceased creators to control the use of works.[30] At the end of the copyright term, a work falls into the public domain and is theoretically freely usable by all.[31] The term of copyright protection, however, is very long.[32] The copyright interest in an original literary, dramatic, musical, or artistic work written today, for example, will not expire until seventy years from the end of the year in which the author of that work dies.[33] In *Sweeney v Macmillan Publishers Ltd*,[34] James Joyce's estate relied successfully on its copyright interest in *Ulysses*, first published in 1922, in order to prevent publication of a 'Reader's Edition' of that work.

---

[26] *Walter v Lane* [1900] AC 539 (HL).   [27] CDPA 1988, s 11(1).
[28] CDPA 1988, s 11(2). Although s 11(2) only refers to literary, dramatic, musical, or artistic works and to films, ownership of the copyright in other forms of protected work (sound recordings, broadcasts, and typographical arrangements of published editions) are also likely to vest in an employer by virtue of the definition of the 'author' of such works contained in s 9 CDPA 1988. Where a work is created by an employee outside the course of his or her employment, but in breach of a fiduciary obligation owed to the employer, the employer may also own the copyright of that work in equity. See, for example, *Service Corp International Plc v Channel Four Television Corp* [1999] EMLR 83.
[29] CDPA 1988, s 90(1).
[30] See W. Chernaik and P. Parrinder (eds), *Sweeney v Macmillan Publishers Ltd* [2002] RPC 651; *Textual Monopolies: Literary Copyright and the Public Domain*, OHC Publications, 1997; M. Rimmer, 'Bloomsday: Copyright Estates and Cultural Festivals' (2005) 2:3 *SCRIPT-ed* 383; J. Griffiths, 'Copyright in English Literature: Denying the Public Domain' [2005] *EIPR* 150; *Godot*, TGI Paris (3rd Chamber), 15 October 1992, (1993) 155 *RIDA* 225.
[31] In exceptional circumstances, certain works created many years ago, but unpublished on the coming into force of the CDPA 1988, remain in copyright. See J. Griffiths, 'Copyright in English Literature: Denying the Public Domain' [2005] *EIPR* 150. See also, the 'publication right' for works in which copyright has lapsed (Copyright and Related Rights Regulations 1996, SI 1996/2967, reg 16).
[32] CDPA 1988, ss 12–15A. The term of copyright in the United Kingdom was extended in order to implement Directive 93/98 harmonizing the term of protection of copyright and certain related rights, [1993] OJ L 290/9. A comparable extension in the United States was unsuccessfully challenged for, amongst other things, violation of the First Amendment. See *Eldred v Ashcroft* 537 US 186 (2003), discussed in N.W. Netanel, 'Copyright and the First Amendment: What *Eldred* Misses and Portends' in J. Griffiths and U. Suthersanen (eds) *Copyright and Free Speech*, Oxford University Press, 2005, 127–52.
[33] CDPA 1988, s 12.   [34] [2002] RPC 651.

The scope of a copyright owner's right to control use of a work is set out in s 16 of the CDPA 1988:

[T]he owner of the copyright in a work has . . . the exclusive right to do the following acts in the United Kingdom—

   (a) to copy the work . . .;

   (b) to issue copies of the work to the public . . .;

   (ba) to rent or lend the work to the public . . .;

   (c) to perform, show or play the work in public . . .,

   (d) to communicate the work to the public . . .;

   (e) to make an adaptation of the work or do any of the above in relation to an adaptation . . .;

and those acts are referred to . . . as the 'acts restricted by the copyright'.

(CDPA 1988, s 16(1))

Thus, for example, the owner of copyright in a photograph is, *prima facie*, entitled to prevent the copying and publication of that photograph in a newspaper or book, its showing on a television programme, or its display on a website. Similarly, the owner of the copyright in a business letter may be entitled to object to the reading out of its contents in public, its reproduction in a newspaper or satirical magazine, its showing on television, and its retransmission via e-mail.

Furthermore, the powers of a copyright owner extend well beyond the ability to restrict complete and exact reproductions or performances of the whole of a copyright work. Under s 16(3) of the CDPA 1988:

References . . . to the doing of an act restricted by the copyright in a work are to the doing of it—

   . . . in relation to the work as a whole or any substantial part of it . . .

As a result, the owner of the copyright in the business letter described above will be able to prevent not only the reproduction of the *whole* letter, but also a reproduction of a portion of that letter, as long as the portion constitutes a 'substantial part' of the letter. In determining whether or not a 'substantial part' of a copyright work has been used, a court makes both a quantitative and a qualitative assessment.[35] Thus, for example, a part of a work that is quantitatively small may still constitute a 'substantial part' of that work. A 'substantial part' can also be made up of 'submerged' elements of that work, such as plot, characterization, or angle of viewpoint. Thus, for example, the owner of the copyright in a collection of letters may, for example, be entitled to object not only to the publication of a single letter from that collection, but also to the dramatization of incidents described in the letters. The owner of the copyright in a painting of a view may be entitled to prevent others from re-creating a version of the

---

[35] See, for example, *Ladbroke (Football) Ltd v William Hill (Football) Ltd* [1964] 1 WLR 273 (HL), 276; *Designers Guild Ltd v Russell Williams (Textiles) Ltd* [2001] 1 WLR 2416 (HL), 2422, 2425, 2431.

work by painting another picture from the same viewpoint.[36] Where the owner of a copyright interest successfully establishes that his or her property interest has been infringed, he or she may be entitled to a range of civil remedies, including an injunction, damages, or an account of profits and an order for delivery up. In certain circumstances, the copyright owner may be entitled to an award of 'additional damages'[37] and copyright infringement may constitute a criminal offence.[38]

In addition to the powers exercisable by the owner of a copyright interest, the *author*[39] of a copyright work has certain 'moral rights' related to the copyright work. These are not assignable and, therefore, remain with the author when the copyright interest is transferred. The relevant rights are (i) the right to be identified as the author of a work (the 'paternity right'),[40] (ii) the right to object to derogatory treatment of that work ('the integrity right'),[41] and (iii) the right to object to false attribution of a work.[42] These rights were first fully introduced into United Kingdom law under the CDPA 1988[43] and originate from civil law jurisdictions in which copyright (or 'author's right') has traditionally been much more protective of the non-economic, spiritual aspects of an author's work. As with the 'engine of free expression' argument discussed above, moral rights can be regarded, at one level, as creating a legal structure within which freedom of expression can flourish. In *Neo-Fascist Slant in Copyright Works*,[44] for example, a German court allowed an author to enforce his integrity right to prevent the publication of his musical works on a CD collection of works supporting neo-Nazi political aims. In such a case, the moral right functions as a form of 'right not to speak' by preventing the author from being associated with a context or viewpoint with which he disagrees.[45] Under instruments protecting fundamental freedoms, free speech rights generally encompass the right not to be forced to speak.[46]

Nevertheless, although moral rights can, at an abstract level, be regarded as rooted in free speech,[47] they also undoubtedly have the potential to restrict expression in particular instances. While the right to be identified as an author of a work presents little threat to expression rights because it imposes only a minimal obligation to acknowledge the author and title of a work, the potential effects of the integrity right and of the right to object to false attribution are greater. The right to object to derogatory treatment can be employed to foil the creation of derivative versions of a work of which an author disapproves.[48] Since its introduction in the CDPA 1988, very

---

[36] *Krisarts SA v Briarfine* [1977] FSR 557.   [37] CDPA 1988, s 97(2).

[38] CDPA 1988, ss 107–110.   [39] And also the director of a film.   [40] CDPA 1988, ss 77–79.

[41] CDPA 1988, ss 80–83.   [42] CDPA 1988, s 84.

[43] Although the right to object to false attribution of authorship had statutory predecessors. See, for example, Fine Arts Copyright Act 1862, s 7.

[44] [1996] ECC 375.   [45] A copyright interest can also be exercised for this purpose.

[46] See, for example, *West Virginia Board of Education v Barnette* 319 US 624 (1943).

[47] See Leslie Kim Treiger Bar-Am, 'The Moral Right of Integrity: A Freedom of Expression', Oxford Intellectual Property Research Centre, EJWP 08/04, http://www.oiprc.ox.ac.uk/EJWP0804.html.

[48] Under CDPA 1988, s 80:

few cases concerning this right have arisen[49] and those few that have been heard have largely been concerned with minor changes to creative works and, therefore, have not given rise to significant issues of freedom of expression.[50] However, jurisdictions in which moral rights have a longer pedigree provide examples of the way in which the integrity right can be employed in a manner that raises such issues. In *Godot*,[51] the representatives of the deceased dramatist, Samuel Beckett, succeeded in persuading a French court to prevent the staging of one of the dramatist's plays with female actors in roles that Beckett had wished to be played by men. It was held that the changes in the play would breach the author's right to 'respect' for his work. In *Turner Entertainment Company v Huston*, a film company's 'colourization' of John Huston's film *The Asphalt Jungle* breached the director's integrity right.[52] The potential of the right to object to false attribution to raise issues of free speech has already been demonstrated in this jurisdiction in *Clark v Associated Newspapers*.[53] In that case, the claimant, a prominent politician, relied successfully upon the right in proceedings against a newspaper group that had published a 'spoof' of the claimant's diaries. The parody was too subtle for many readers, who thought that it had actually been written by the claimant and the defendant was held liable for both false attribution of authorship and passing off.

In this section, we have sought briefly to explain of the way in which copyright law grants right-holders the capacity to restrict the ability of others to express themselves freely. In some instances, the exercise of this power need not concern us unduly. Many unlicensed uses of copyright works raise no free speech issues. As Barendt has pointed out, the argument that copyright infringements are *covered* by free speech guarantees is weak or non-existent in straightforward cases of commercial piracy, where the copier simply exploits the creative skill of others for financial gain.[54] However, in some

(1) The author of a copyright literary, dramatic, musical or artistic work, and the director of a copyright film, has the right in the circumstances mentioned in this section not to have his work subjected to derogatory treatment.

(2) for the purposes of this section—

    (a) 'treatment' of a work means any addition to, deletion from or alteration to or adaptation of the work, other than—

        (i) a translation of a literary or dramatic work, or

        (ii) an arrangement or transcription of a musical work involving no more than a change of key or register; and

    (b) the treatment of a work is derogatory if it amounts to distortion or mutilation of the work or is otherwise prejudicial to the honour or reputation of the author or director . . .

---

[49] *Morrison Leahy Music Limited v Lightbond Limited* [1993] EMLR 144; *Tidy v Trustees of the Natural History Museum* [1996] EIPR-D 86; *Pasterfield v Denham* [1999] FSR 168; *Confetti Records v Warner Music UK Ltd* [2003] EMLR 35.

[50] Although, in *Confetti Records*, the defendant made an unsuccessful attempt to persuade the court that Article 10 required it to 'read down' the right to object to derogatory treatment.

[51] *Godot*, TGI Paris (3rd Chamber), 15 October 1992, (1993) 155 *RIDA* 225.

[52] Cour Cass, 28 May 1991, (1991) 149 *RIDA* 197; CA Versailles, 10 December 1994, (1995) 164 *RIDA* 256.

[53] [1998] 1 All ER 959.

[54] E. Barendt, 'Copyright and Free Speech Theory' in J. Griffiths and U. Suthersanen (eds) *Copyright and Free Speech*, Oxford University Press, 2005, 18–19.

other situations, the exercise of a copyright interest raises very clear issues of free speech. Consider, for example, a defendant who has produced a parody or work of appropriation art using existing copyright works or an investigative journalist who wishes to bring a controversial security video or governmental memorandum to the attention of the public. In such circumstances, the right to freedom of expression is undoubtedly engaged.

PROTECTION FOR FREEDOM OF EXPRESSION WITHIN COPYRIGHT LAW

Even before the coming into force of an express statutory obligation to pay regard to the right to freedom of expression under the Human Rights Act, doctrines had been developed that served to mitigate the effects of copyright on freedom of expression.[55] The most important of these are outlined below.

COPYRIGHT LAW DOES NOT PERMIT A RIGHT-HOLDER TO CONTROL ALL USES OF A WORK

While it has been demonstrated that the range of activities to which a copyright owner is entitled to object is extensive, it is not all-encompassing. Uses that are not covered by the CDPA are beyond the control of the copyright owner. Thus, for example, a lawfully purchased work of art can be exhibited in a public place without the permission of the copyright owner,[56] a popular musical song can be sung by an individual in the privacy of his or her own bathroom, and a lawfully made reproduction of an artwork on the page of a magazine can be cut out, mounted on canvas, and sold.[57]

The range and significance of such unrestricted exploitations, however, is limited. Of more importance in protecting free speech is the fact that some uses of a copyright work will only be regarded as taking 'general ideas' or 'facts' from a work rather than a 'substantial part' of its expressive form. This principle is often described as the 'ideas/expression dichotomy'. Thus, for example, the Estate of James Joyce could not prevent a third party from writing a novel with a central protagonist set in Dublin over the course of a single day. However, if the third party were to take more detailed elements of plot, language, and characterization from *Ulysses*, he or she would be likely

---

[55] A number of doctrines originally developed by the judiciary have subsequently been granted statutory force. See, for example, the statutory defence of fair dealing under CDPA 1988, s 30 and the defence covering the making of subsequent works by an artist (CDPA 1988, s 64).

[56] The restricted act of 'performing, showing or playing a work in public' (CDPA 1988, s 19) does not apply in the case of artistic works (although cf ss 77 and 80).

[57] This is because the mounted picture is unlikely to be regarded as a reproduction. For recent Canadian consideration of this issue, see *Théberge v Galerie d'Art Petit Champlain Inc* [2002] SCR 336.

to be sued. This distinction between protected 'expression' and unprotected 'ideas' or 'facts' significantly reduces the likelihood that copyright will conflict with interests in freedom of expression.[58] For example, consider a situation in which a document revealing important information about the future policies of a political party is leaked to a national newspaper. The owner of the copyright in the document may be able to rely on that property interest to prevent *reproduction* of the document or of a substantial part of the document. However, that interest would not allow the copyright owner to prevent the newspaper from explaining the contents of the memorandum to its readership without reproducing it.

Nevertheless, the 'ideas/expression' dichotomy cannot, alone, prevent all conflict between copyright law and freedom of expression. First, there is, in many cases, no clear demarcation between 'ideas' and 'expression'.[59] Courts sometimes find copyright to have been infringed where a defendant has made significant changes to a work and where very little of the claimant's labour and skill remains in the defendant's work.[60] Secondly, there are situations where, in the interests of free speech, it is necessary to reproduce a work in its exact form. It is not, for example, possible to rephrase or describe a news photograph. Where there are potent reasons for permitting the publication of such a work, the 'ideas/expression dichotomy' will not adequately protect free speech interests.[61] This restriction does not only apply in the case of artistic works. In the case of the leaked political document described above, there may be good reasons for allowing a newspaper to publish the actual document rather than requiring it only to explain the contents of the document. If the document is of great significance, the newspaper's readers may have a justified interest in seeing its exact terms. As Netanel has observed, it will frequently be the case that 'speech will be grossly less convincing, moving, understandable, authentic, or believable if the speaker cannot copy the existing expression'.[62] The claim that the 'ideas/expression dichotomy' prevents all conflicts with the right to free speech is, as noted by Barendt, inconsistent with basic principles of free speech jurisprudence:

Freedom of speech means that the speaker determines the form in which propositions are put, as well as the intellectual content or subject matter of his or her discourse. The law improperly interferes with the exercise of that freedom if, for example, it proscribes the use of certain language on the ground that it is shocking or offensive. This fundamental principle is exemplified in cases which allow publishers the freedom to use indecent language or display sexually explicit images, provided (in most jurisdictions) that the expression does not amount to hard-core pornography (which is not covered by the freedom of speech/ expression clause at all). The European Court of Human Rights has developed a similar

---

[58] See M. Nimmer, 'Does Copyright Abridge the First Amendment Guarantees of Free Speech and Press?' (1970) 17 *UCLA L Rev* 1180.

[59] *L.B. (Plastics) Limited v Swish Products* [1979] FSR 145, 160 (per Lord Hailsham).

[60] *Elanco Products Ltd v Mandops (Agrochemical Specialists) Ltd* [1980] RPC 213 (CA).

[61] See discussion of the news photographs of the My Lai massacre in M. Nimmer, 'Does Copyright Abridge the First Amendment Guarantees of Free Speech and Press?' (1970) 17 *UCLA L Rev* 1180.

[62] N.W. Netanel, 'Locating Copyright within the First Amendment Skein', (2001) 54 *Stan L R* 1, 113.

principle in defamation cases, recognising that journalists have freedom under Article 10 of the ECHR to express their ideas in exaggerated or prejudiced terms, even though that may injure the self-esteem or standing of the persons criticised in their newspapers.[63]

PERMITTED ACTS UNDER THE COPYRIGHT DESIGNS AND PATENTS ACT 1988

The CDPA 1988 contains a lengthy list of 'permitted acts'. These provisions describe situations in which otherwise infringing acts will, in specific circumstances, be permitted without the consent of the copyright owner.[64] The various 'permitted acts' serve a wide range of social, cultural, and legal goals. A number of them can be regarded as, directly[65] or indirectly,[66] free speech-based. The most important of these is s 30, which permits use of a copyright work where such use constitutes fair dealing for the purpose of criticism or review (s 30(1))[67] or fair dealing for the purpose of reporting current events (s 30(2)).[68] Courts have confirmed that these provisions serve important free speech goals.[69]

Perhaps the most obvious example of a situation in which s 30(1) will apply is that of a literary critic who reproduces a 'substantial part' of a poem in the course of reviewing that poem or of other literary works. However, the provision permits not only criticism or review of the creative form of a work, but also criticism or review of whole genres of work,[70] of the ideas underlying works[71] and of actions taken in relation to a work.[72] Under s 30(2), a news broadcasting company may, for example, be entitled to use clips from copyright-protected films about events of current significance,[73] including major sporting events,[74] without obtaining permission from the owners of the copyright in those clips.

These defences promote informed and critical debate on political, social, and

---

[63] E. Barendt, 'Copyright and Free Speech Theory' in J. Griffiths and U. Suthersanen, (eds) *Copyright and Free Speech* (Oxford University Press, 2005) 2.21 (footnotes omitted).

[64] CDPA 1988, ss 28–76.   [65] See, for example, CDPA 1988, ss 31, 45, 57–60 and 62–64.

[66] See, for example, CDPA 1988, s 29, 36A–44A, 61 and 75.

[67] 'Fair dealing with a work for the purpose of criticism or review, of that or another work or of a performance of a work, does not infringe any copyright in the work provided that it is accompanied by a sufficient acknowledgement and provided that the work has been made available to the public.' (CDPA 1988, s 30(1)).

[68] 'Fair dealing with a work (other than a photograph) for the purpose of reporting current events does not infringe any copyright in the work provided that . . . it is accompanied by a sufficient acknowledgement.' (CDPA 1988, s 30(2)).

[69] See *Hubbard v Vosper* [1972] 2 QB 84; *British Broadcasting Corporation v British Satellite Broadcasting Ltd* [1991] All ER 833; *Time Warner Entertainment Company v Channel Four Television Corporation plc* [1994] EMLR 1; *PCR Limited v Dow Jones Telerate Limited* [1998] FSR 170 at 189; *Pro Sieben Media AG v Carlton UK Television* [1999] 1 WLR 605 (CA).

[70] *Pro Sieben Media AG v Carlton UK Television* [1999] 1 WLR 605 (CA).

[71] *Hubbard v Vosper* [1972] 2 QB 84.

[72] *Time Warner Entertainment Company v Channel Four Television Corporation plc* [1994] EMLR 1.

[73] *Pro Sieben Media AG v Carlton UK Television* [1999] 1 WLR 605 (CA).

[74] *Newspaper Licensing Agency Ltd v Marks and Spencer plc* [2001] Ch 257 (CA).

cultural affairs. However, they also are subject to a number of restrictions. First, there are limitations on the scope of the permitted statutory purposes. Some of these restrictions are apparent on the face of the provisions. Section 30(1), for example, does not permit criticism or review of a work where that work has not previously been made available to the public, and section 30(2) does not allow the use of *photographs* for the purpose of reporting current events. In addition, neither provision will apply in the absence of a 'sufficient acknowledgement' of the title and author of the work in question. Judicial interpretation has given rise to further restrictions on the scope of these defences to an action of infringement. For example, 'criticism or review' of a copyright work will not cover a situation in which a work is reproduced with only minor accompanying comment designed to place the work in its appropriate setting and to highlight its most important features,[75] and the concept of 'current events' is also relatively limited.[76]

A further important restriction upon the operation of s 30 is the fact that dealings with works will only be permitted where they are 'fair'. Courts have evolved a factor-based approach to fairness in this context. Under this approach, a defendant will have significant difficulties relying on s 30 where he or she uses an unpublished work,[77] where a work has been 'leaked',[78] where the use of a copyright work causes economic harm to the copyright owner,[79] or where a disproportionate amount of a work has been used.[80] This interpretation of the concept of fairness potentially conflicts with free speech interests. It may, for example, be particularly necessary for leaked, previously unseen, works to be published where they reveal matters of great public significance. Furthermore, a 'chilling' effect may be caused if a defendant is unable to predict in advance whether his or her dealing with a work is likely to be regarded as fair.

THE COMMON LAW 'PUBLIC INTEREST' PRINCIPLE

Courts have always assumed an ability to adjudicate upon the dissemination and protection of copyright material in a manner which functions outside the bounds of the statute, but falls within their inherent jurisdiction at common law. Typically, they have tended to exercise this inherent jurisdiction by refusing relief where the content of a claimant's work is obscene or sexually immoral, defamatory, blasphemous, or irreligious (and so, counter-intuitively, they have increased the opportunities for dissemination of the material).[81]

---

[75] *Commonwealth of Australia v John Fairfax & Sons Ltd* (1980) 32 ALR 485.

[76] *Distillers Co (Biochemicals) Ltd v Times Newspapers Ltd* [1975] QB 613; *Newspaper Licensing Agency Ltd v Marks and Spencer plc* [2001] Ch 257 (CA).

[77] *British Oxygen Co Ltd v Liquid Air Limited* [1925] Ch 383; *Hyde Park v Yelland* [2001] Ch 143 (CA).

[78] *Hyde Park v Yelland* [2001] Ch 143 (CA).

[79] *Ashdown v Telegraph Group Ltd* [2002] Ch 149 (CA).   [80] Ibid.

[81] For example, in *Glyn v Weston Feature Films*, Younger J refused to protect the claimant's work, observing that:

In addition to such situations in which the legal protection of the statute has been withheld on grounds of public policy, judges have, more recently, indicated that circumstances may exist in which the rights of a copyright owner must be qualified in accordance with a common law principle concerning the dissemination of information and material which the public has an interest in knowing. The decision laying down the modern, albeit somewhat tentative, foundations for this aspect of the common law public interest defence was that of the Court of Appeal in *Lion Laboratories v Evans*.[82] In that case, the defendants worked for the plaintiff company, which manufactured breathalysers that the police were using during a 'crackdown' on drink driving at Christmas 1983. The defendant employees removed a number of confidential documents casting doubt on the accuracy of the devices. The plaintiff company successfully relied upon both breach of confidence and infringement of copyright in seeking to prevent publication of the reports in the national press. In allowing the defendants' appeal, Stephenson LJ[83] observed that the established jurisprudence of the courts concerning the availability of a public interest defence in actions for breach of confidence[84] also applied in the case of copyright infringement.[85] However, this public interest principle was also held to be subject to limitations. Often, for example, it would only extend to disclosure to an appropriate recipient in authority and not to the public at large.[86] A distinction was also drawn between information that ought to be disclosed in the public interest and information which was simply 'interesting to the public',

---

'Stripped of its trappings [the work] is nothing more nor less than a sensual adulterous intrigue ... [I]t is clear that copyright cannot exist in a work of a tendency so grossly immoral as this, a work which, apart from its other objectionable features, advocates free love and justifies adultery where the marriage tie has become merely irksome' (*Glyn v Weston Feature Films* [1916] 1 Ch 261, 269).

See also *Murray v Benbow* (1822) Jacob 471; *Murray v Dugdale* (1823) *The Times* 22 July 1823; *Stockdale v Onwhyn* (1826) *The Times*, 11 January 1826. More recently in *AG v Guardian (No. 2)* [1990] 1 AC 109, the House of Lords held that Peter Wright would not be able to bring a copyright action preventing the infringement of his work, *Spycatcher*, within the UK because of the 'disgraceful circumstances' under which the book had been written. Not only did the House of Lords cite the *Glyn* decision with approval, but also seemed to extend the scope of the immorality exclusion to apply not only to the content of any particular work, but also to the circumstances in which the work was created. In general, see W.R. Cornish and D. Llewelyn, *Intellectual Property*, 5th edn., London: Sweet & Maxwell, 2003, 11–56, 448.

[82] *Lion Laboratories v Evans* [1985] QB 526. In relation to copyright and the public interest defence in general, see: J. Phillips, 'The Berne Convention and Public Interest' [1987] *EIPR* 108; G. Johnston, 'Copyright and Freedom of the Media: A Modest Proposal' [1996] *EIPR* 1996, 6; R. Burrell, 'Defending the Public Interest' [2000] *EIPR* 394.

[83] With whom O'Connor LJ agreed.

[84] See for example: *Initial Services v Putterill* [1968] 1 QB 396; *Fraser v Evans* [1969] 1 QB 349; *Hubbard v Vosper* [1972] 2 QB 84; *Woodward v Hutchins* [1977] 1 WLR 760; *British Steel Corporation v Granada Television Ltd* [1981] AC 1096.

[85] Stephenson LJ asserted that there was, in the context of a public interest defence 'no difference between confidence and copyright for the purposes of this case'; [1985] QB 526, 536. Griffiths LJ was slightly more equivocal, commenting: 'I am quite satisfied that the defence of public interest is now well established in actions for breach of confidence, and although there is less authority on the point, that it also extends to breach of copyright'; ibid, 550.

[86] *Lion Laboratories v Evans* [1985] QB 526 at 537 (per Stephenson LJ) and *A-G v Guardian Newspapers Ltd (No 2)* [1990] 1 AC 109 at 260 (per Lord Keith of Kinkel), at 279 (per Lord Griffiths) and at 282 (per Lord Goff).

disclosure of which was not permitted by the principle.[87] Further potential restrictions on the utility of the 'public interest' principle as a means of protecting freedom of expression arose as a result of subsequent judicial interpretation of its scope.

When the CDPA 1988 came into force, it contained a statutory concession stating that the rights granted under the Act did not affect 'any rule of law preventing or restricting the enforcement of copyright, *on grounds of public interest or otherwise*' (CDPA 1988, s 171(3)).[88] It seems clear that s 171(3) was intended to provide statutory recognition of the existence of the common law defence as applied in *Lion Laboratories*.[89] However, prior to the coming into force of the Human Rights Act, the availability of this defence in copyright cases was thrown into doubt by the decision of the Court of Appeal in *Hyde Park v Yelland*.[90] *Hyde Park* concerned *The Sun's* publication of images of Princess Diana and Dodi Fayed arriving at, and leaving, a Paris villa on the day before their death. The images were taken from a security video camera owned by a company controlled by Mohammed Al Fayed.[91] The company sued for infringement of copyright and applied for summary judgment. The defendants argued that use of the images was fair dealing for the purpose of reporting current events and also was covered by the 'public interest' principle described above. At first instance, Jacob J accepted both these arguments.[92] In relation to the public interest defence, he concluded that, while there had been no substantial basis in precedent for the decision of the Court of Appeal in *Lion Laboratories*,[93] the CDPA 1988 had provided statutory recognition of the existence of the defence.[94]

---

[87] *Lion Laboratories v Evans* [1985] QB 526, 537 (per Stephenson LJ). See also, *BSC v Granada TV Ltd* [1981] AC 1096 at 1169 (per Lord Wilberforce).

[88] CDPA 1988, s 171(3). During the passage of the CDPA 1988 through Parliament, Lord Morton of Shuna suggested introducing an express public interest defence into the legislation. The provision would have read simply: 'Copyright is not infringed by anything done in the public interest'. The need to introduce an explicit statutory defence on such terms was rejected at the time as unnecessary. Lord Beaverbrook, speaking for the government, commented that '[t]here is little point in codifying in statute what is already achieved by the courts'. He continued:

The amendment does not add to the principle already established by the courts in any way, and I am not aware of any pressing need . . . Consequently we feel it right to leave [the legislation] as it stands without this amendment . . . [the legislation] leaves in the hands of the courts the task of dealing with those exceptional cases where it is necessary to balance public interest criteria with the rights of copyright owners.

(Parliamentary Debates, Lords, vol 491, 75)

[89] For subsequent recognition of the existence of the principle, see, for example, the acknowledgement of the defence in *PCR v Dow Jones Telerate* [1998] FSR 170, *Service Corporation International plc v Channel 4* [1999] EMLR 83, and *Mars UK v Teknowledge* [2000] FSR 138.

[90] *Hyde Park v Yelland* [2001] Ch 143. For a critique of the Court of Appeal's decision see R. Burrell, 'Defending the Public Interest' [2000] *EIPR* 394.

[91] The security camera footage had been removed and sold to *The Sun* by the former head of security at the villa.

[92] *Hyde Park v Yelland* [1999] RPC 655.

[93] See, for example, the assessment of *Lion Laboratories* and the foundations of the public interest defence in the United Kingdom by Gummow J in *Collier Constructions v Foskett* (1990) 97 ALR 460 (referred to by Jacob J in *Hyde Park*).

[94] Jacob J himself observed: 'Once it is conceded, as it must be, that the courts in certain limited classes of case can refuse to recognise copyright altogether [for example, *Glyn*], the concession amounts to saying that

The Court of Appeal overturned Jacob J's decision on both grounds.[95] As to the public interest defence, Aldous LJ[96] drew a distinction between the application of such a defence in a breach of confidence action and its application in an allegation of copyright infringement. He held that, in copyright proceedings, the 'public interest' principle was limited to circumstances in which the court could exercise an 'inherent jurisdiction' to refuse to enforce a copyright interest. These circumstances were incapable of precise definition, but included situations where a work was (i) immoral, scandalous, or contrary to family life, (ii) injurious to public life, public health and safety, or the administration of justice, or (iii) when it incited or encouraged others to act in any manner referred to in (ii).[97]

DISCRETION TO AWARD AN INJUNCTION

Finally, in reviewing the 'internal' mechanisms within copyright law that serve to mitigate the conflict between that body of law and the right to freedom of expression, it is important not to overlook the fact that the grant of an injunction, either interim or final, falls within the discretion of the court. Even prior to the coming into force of the Human Rights Act 1998, the fact that a defendant's use of a copyright work could be justified as an exercise of his or her right to freedom of expression was sometimes considered to be a 'special factor' to be taken into account in deciding whether or not to grant an injunction.[98] For example, in *Secretary of State for the Home Department v Central Broadcasting Limited*,[99] the Home Secretary sought an injunction to prevent

none of the acts which Parliament has said are infringements are such. If the courts can do that then surely they can do the lesser thing of refusing to recognise a particular act as infringement when that act is in the public interest'; [1999] RPC 655, 667–8.

[95] As to the argument that the use of the work was fair dealing for the purpose of reporting current events, Aldous LJ, while accepting that the use may indeed have been to report current events, rejected the suggestion that the defendants' use was fair. The question of fairness was to be judged by an objective standard of whether a fair minded and honest person would have dealt with the copyright work in the way in which the defendants had. On this point Aldous LJ observed: 'I do not believe that a fair minded and honest person would pay for dishonestly taken driveway stills and publish them in a newspaper knowing that they had not been published or circulated when their only relevance was the fact that the Princess and Mr Dodi Al Fayed only stayed the 28 minutes at the Villa Windsor . . . To describe what *The Sun* did as fair dealing would be to give honour to dishonour'; [2001] Ch 143, 159.

[96] With whom Stuart-Smith LJ agreed.

[97] [2001] Ch 143, 168. Mance LJ was less categorical: 'I prefer to state no more in this case than that the circumstances in which the public interest may override copyright are probably not capable of precise categorisation or definition . . . it seems to me possible to conceive of situations where a copyright document itself appeared entirely innocuous, but its publication as a matter of fair dealing, or, in circumstances outside the scope of section 30, in the public interest—was justified by its significance in the context of other facts. *Hyde Park* [2001] Ch 143, 172.

[98] *American Cyanamid Co v Ethicon* [1975] AC 396, 409 (HL). For cases in which in which the courts have refused to exercise the discretion to award an injunction where free speech is at stake, see *Hubbard v Vosper* [1972] 2 QB 84 (CA); *Fraser v Evans* [1969] 1 QB 349; *Kennard v Lewis* [1983] FSR 343; *Service Corporation International plc v Channel Four Television Corporation* [1999] EMLR 83.

[99] [1993] EMLR 253.

the broadcasting of a filmed interview with the serial killer Dennis Nilsen. The parties were in dispute over the ownership of copyright in the film. The judge refused the plaintiff's application for an interim injunction and the Court of Appeal refused the defendant's appeal. Hirst LJ found that in this case:

The relative strength of the parties' claims on the merits is by no means clear in view of the fundamental conflict of evidence between the two sides which can only be reconciled at full trial. In these circumstances, in my judgment, we should not interfere with the defendant's freedom of speech, by which I mean their freedom to publish in full the programme, including the Nilsen interview.[100]

In practical terms, the flexibility allowed to courts in deciding whether or not to grant an injunction has provided a useful safeguard of freedom of expression. However, this mechanism is also subject to limitations. Judicial discretion has not always been exercised in favour of freedom of expression[101] and, even where it has, it does not insulate a defendant against an award of damages. While refusal to grant an injunction will allow a defendant's work to be published, the award of damages may have a significant 'chilling' impact on expression.[102]

COPYRIGHT LAW AND ARTICLE 10

Thus, before the coming into force of the Human Rights Act 1998, copyright law had already evolved a series of mechanisms designed to ensure that the potentially wide-reaching restraints on expression available to copyright owners do not interfere disproportionately with freedom of expression. However, as has been demonstrated, such mechanisms have significant limitations. In this section of the chapter, we consider the extent to which the introduction of an enforceable statutory right to freedom of expression under that Act affects this existing 'balance' of interests. In order to do this, we first consider both the limited Strasbourg jurisprudence on copyright and free speech and the manner in which the exercise of a copyright interest ought, as a matter of principle, to be analysed within the structure of Article 10. We then move on to set out, and to criticize, the way in which the Court of Appeal has handled the potential conflict of copyright and freedom of expression under the Human Rights Act.

---

[100] [1993] EMLR 253, 274.

[101] See, for example, *BBC v Precord*, unreported, 11 November 1991, discussed in M. Sayal, 'Copyright and Freedom of the Media: A Balancing Exercise?' [1995] *Entertainment LR* 263.

[102] See K. Garnett, 'The Impact of the Human Rights Act 1998 on United Kingdom Copyright Law' in J. Griffiths and U. Suthersanen, (eds) *Copyright and Free Speech*, Oxford University Press, 2005, 178–9.

The structure of, and jurisprudence on, Article 10 is analysed elsewhere in this volume.[103] However, at this point, it is necessary to explain how the exercise of a copyright interest ought to be regarded as a matter of principle under Article 10. There is no doubt that the exercise of a copyright interest to prevent another person from using a copyright work in the course of his or her own expression constitutes a *prima facie* interference with the right established under Article 10(1). That is, a claim for infringement of copyright is *covered* by Article 10(1), even where brought by a private party. However, under Article 10(2), a court may be justified in preventing or penalizing the exercise of a restricted act in relation to the copyright work. The rules established under CDPA 1988 seem likely to be held to be sufficiently foreseeable to be 'prescribed by law' within Article 10(2),[104] which permits interferences with freedom of expression for, *inter alia*, the purpose of 'the protection of . . . rights of others'. Such 'rights of others' include the property right held by a copyright owner.[105] However, vitally, under Article 10(2), interferences with freedom of expression, even where prescribed by law and established in pursuance of a legitimate aim, are only be permitted where 'necessary in a democratic society'; that is, where they constitute a proportionate response to a 'pressing social need'.

It could perhaps be argued that, in considering a case of copyright infringement within the structure established under Article 10, a court is not concerned with a conflict between two opposing, but equally fundamental rights and, therefore, that the analytical framework outlined in the paragraph above will be inappropriate. Such an argument could be based upon the fact that the interests of authors and owners of copyright interests are not only protected in positive law, but also under international human rights instruments. First, it could be argued that the right to free exercise of a property interest such as copyright is protected under Protocol 1, Art 1 of the ECHR[106] and other similar provisions in international instruments. Secondly, in some international human rights treaties, intellectual property rights themselves receive their own specific form of protection. Most notably, under Article 27 of the Universal Declaration of Human Rights, everyone has 'the right to the protection of moral and material interests resulting from any scientific, literary or artistic production of which he is the author'.[107]

---

[103] See Chapter 2 above.

[104] Although it could perhaps be argued that the question of fairness under the 'fair dealing' defences is so lacking in a predictable framework of principle as to fail this requirement. For an example of a recent case in which the concept of fairness was arguably interpreted in an unforeseeable manner, see *IPC Media Ltd v News Group Newspapers Ltd* [2005] EMLR 23.

[105] See *Chappell v United Kingdom* (1990) 12 EHRR 1.

[106] Cf *Smith Kline and French Laboratories v The Netherlands* 66 DR 70 (1990). See also, *School Book Case*, German Constitutional Court, 7 July 1971, GRUR, 1972, 481.

[107] For discussion, see P. Torremans, 'Copyright as a Human Right' in P. Torremans, (ed.) *Copyright and Human Rights*, Kluwer Law International, 2004, 1–20, and U. Suthersanen, 'Towards an International Public

Indeed, courts in the United Kingdom have sometimes referred to copyright's status as a property right, or as a right otherwise protected under international law, as a justification for censuring unlicensed use of a copyright work. However, the idea that courts are simply obliged to 'balance' two opposed, but equally weighted, rights in this context should be resisted. First, while the right to property is undoubtedly recognized internationally as a human right, states are typically accorded a wide margin of appreciation in regulating the right to property in order to advance the common good.[108] Furthermore, in permitting free uses of a copyright work, a court or legislature is not *taking away* a property right, but simply regulating the boundary between permissible and impermissible uses of the work. A copyright owner is never granted absolute dominion over his or her work. Secondly, the protection for intellectual property rights under international human rights instruments is imprecise and aspirational, rather than precise and justifiable. The obligations imposed by such provisions are quite different from the strong and detailed requirements of Article 10.

Thus, as a matter of principle, a copyright owner ought to have the burden of proving that the enforcement of his or her right is 'necessary in a democratic society'. In cases in which a copyright owner brings proceedings to protect its market position, or to ensure the integrity of its work against incompetent reproduction,[109] this condition will usually be satisfied very easily. However, where a copyright interest is exercised as a means of suppressing disclosure of information in a specific form[110] or as a means of preventing the publication of a version of the work of which the copyright owner disapproves, a court ought to consider more closely whether the interference is actually 'necessary in a democratic society'.[111] The answer to that enquiry ought to depend upon the respective strengths of the competing interests—the parties' motives, the nature of the claimant's work, the social value of the defendant's work, and other factors relating to the specific circumstances of the dispute. General principles deriving from the jurisprudence of the European Court of Human Rights on Article 10 will be highly relevant. A court ought, for example, to be obliged to be particularly vigilant where a copyright claim restricts public access to information on important aspects of public affairs[112] or has the effect of interfering with media freedom to report matters of public significance.[113] Less stringent review

Interest Rule? Human Rights and International Copyright Law' in J. Griffiths and U. Suthersanen, (eds) *Copyright and Free Speech*, Oxford University Press, 2005, 97–124.

108 See, for example, *Smith Kline and French Laboratories v The Netherlands* 66 DR 70 (1990). See also, *School Book Case*, German Constitutional Court, 7 July 1971, GRUR, 1972, 481.

109 See, for example, *Tidy v Trustees of the Natural History Museum* [1996] EIPR-D 86.

110 *Hyde Park Residence Ltd v Yelland* [2001] Ch 143 (CA); *Commonwealth of Australia v John Fairfax & Sons Ltd* (1980) 32 ALR 485; *Hubbard v Vosper* [1972] 2 QB 84.

111 For interesting US disputes concerning parodies, see *Campbell v Acuff-Rose Music* 510 US 569 (1994) and *Suntrust Bank v Houghton Mifflin Co.* 252 F 3d 1165 (11th Cir, 2001).

112 *Thorgeirson v Iceland* (1992) 14 EHRR 843.

113 *Jersild v Denmark* (1994) 19 EHRR 1, *Goodwin v United Kingdom* (1966) 22 EHRR 123.

may be required where the exercise of a copyright interest threatens to restrict the dissemination of derivative works of purely creative or artistic significance.[114]

The relationship between copyright law and Article 10 has never been considered directly by the Strasbourg Court. However, a small number of relevant cases were considered by the European Commission on Human Rights before its judicial role was assumed by the Court. *De Geillustererde Pers NV v The Netherlands*[115] concerned copyright in broadcast listings. A Dutch commercial magazine publisher complained that copyright restrictions on the publication of radio and television listings constituted an interference with its right to freedom of expression by a public authority. Dutch law at the time restricted the power to authorize publication of broadcasting listings to the broadcasting organizations themselves. Such a case raises connected issues of freedom of expression and freedom of information. The Commission held that Article 10 did not cover the right of *access* to the schedules.[116] In any event, the Commission concluded that there had been no violation of the complainant's rights under Article 10 because the information in question (the listings) was available from alternative sources (those listings authorized by the broadcasting authorities):

[T]here can be no question in the present case that the freedom of the press in general is threatened in the sense that the public is deprived of any specific information, i.e. in the present case, the programme data, by censorship or otherwise by reason of any undue state monopoly on news. On the contrary, every person in the Netherlands may inform himself about the forthcoming radio and television programmes through a variety of mass media representing various sections and tendencies of society.[117]

The issue was not even covered by Article 10(1) and, therefore, there was no question of the state having to justify its actions under Article 10(2).[118] In terms of authority, this decision is not weighty. However, it does indicate that, under Article 10, copyright restrictions that simply reduce the number of outlets for the dissemination of information to the public are to be treated differently from restrictions causing the public to be 'deprived of . . . specific information'.

The Commission decided a further complaint about the exercise of a copyright interest in *France 2 v France*.[119] The complaint in that case was brought by a French

---

[114] *Müller v Switzerland* (1991) 13 EHRR 212; *Otto Preminger Institute v Austria* (1995) 19 EHRR 34; *Wingrove v United Kingdom* (1997) 24 EHRR 1.

[115] No 5178/71; (1976) 8 DR 5; CM Res DH 77(1). The European Commission of Human Rights has also given a preliminary ruling on admissibility in a claim with similar facts in *NV Televizier v The Netherlands* (1966) YECHR 512, and for final settlement of the proceedings, (1968) 11 YECHR 782.

[116] For confirmation of this restriction on the scope of Article 10, see *Gaskin v United Kingdom* (1990) 12 EHRR 36.

[117] (1976) 8 DR 5, at para 86.

[118] For criticism of the European Commission's decision on this point, see E. Barendt, 'Copyright and Free Speech Theory' in J. Griffiths and U. Suthersanen, (eds) *Copyright and Free Speech*, Oxford University Press, 2005, 11, 23; B. Hugenholtz, 'Copyright and Freedom of Expression in Europe' in Dreyfuss *et al. Expanding the Boundaries of Intellectual Property*, Oxford University Press, 2001, 343, 359.

[119] B. Hugenholtz, ibid, 359–60.

television broadcasting company. In the course of a programme concerning the reopening of a renovated theatre, the camera focused a number of times on frescos painted by the artist Edouard Vuillard. In the national courts, a collecting society representing the owners of the copyright in the frescos successfully sought compensation for infringement of the author's rights by the broadcast company.[120] The broadcasting company brought a complaint against this decision to Strasbourg, arguing that it violated Article 10. The Commission held that copyright law was 'prescribed by law' for the purpose of protecting the 'rights of others' and that the restriction that it imposed upon the broadcasting company's freedom to express itself was acceptable because the decision of the French court did not prevent the broadcasters from reproducing the frescos, but only required them to pay royalties for having done so. As in *De Geillustererde Pers NV*, this decision focuses on the distinction between a restriction preventing the public from having access to a work and one that simply places obstacles in the way of access—in this instance, the obligation on the broadcasting company to pay to show the frescos. This solution represents a reasonably convenient compromise between the claims of the opposing parties. However, such a compromise may not be so acceptable where an award of damages is likely to have a greater 'chilling' effect on expression and where the expression in question concerns 'public affairs' rather than creative matters.

From a consideration of the general jurisprudence on Article 10, as well as the specific Commission decisions concerning copyright and freedom of expression, it is possible to discern a framework of principle within which courts in the United Kingdom ought to decide such disputes under the Human Rights Act. Under that Act, courts have an obligation to interpret the CDPA 1988 compatibly with Article 10 '[s]o far as it is possible to do so'.[121] This obligation applies whether a claimant is a public body or not. In addition, courts are also bound by section 12, which will, in certain respects, apply in copyright cases. In addition to the general guidance provided by section 12(4),[122] the procedural protection for freedom of expression granted under s 12(3) will be relevant in cases in which a claimant seeks an interim injunction in order to censor dissemination of copyright-protected material.[123]

---

[120] The Cour de Cassation had held that France 2's activities did not fall within the exception for 'brief quotation' in the French legislation.

[121] Human Rights Act 1998, s 3.

[122] 'The court must have particular regard to the importance of the Convention right to freedom of expression and, where the proceedings relate to material which the respondent claims, or which appears to the court, to be journalistic, literary or artistic material (or to conduct connected with such material), to—

(a) the extent to which—
   (i) the material has, or is about to, become available to the public; or
   (ii) it is, or would be, in the public interest for the material to be published;
(b) any relevant privacy code.'

[123] See *Cream Holdings Ltd v Banerjee* [2004] UKHL 44, discussed in K. Garnett, 'The Impact of the Human Rights Act 1998 on United Kingdom Copyright Law' in J. Griffiths and U. Suthersanen, (eds) *Copyright and Free Speech*, Oxford University Press, 2005, 171 at para 8.37.

ASHDOWN V TELEGRAPH GROUP LTD

In *Ashdown v Telegraph Group Ltd*, the United Kingdom courts had the opportunity to consider the impact of the Human Rights Act in copyright proceedings.[124] The case concerned a minute of a secret meeting attended by the claimant, Paddy Ashdown (then leader of the Liberal Democrat Party), and Tony Blair in the wake of Labour's election victory in 1997. The meeting concerned proposed co-operation between the Labour and Liberal Democrat parties. The nine-page minute was created by the claimant following the meeting and was shown to a very limited number of colleagues. In November 1999, when it had become known that the claimant was standing down from the leadership of the Liberal Democrats, Ashdown gave an interview to the BBC in which he referred to the possibility of publishing his political diaries, suggesting that they would contain material of a particularly sensitive nature. At about that time, the minute, amongst other material, was shown in strict confidence to a number of representatives of newspapers and publishing houses. Soon afterwards, the minute was leaked to the *Sunday Telegraph*. On 28 November 1999, the defendant, publisher of that newspaper, published three separate items about the minute and its revelations. One such item was a major story, incorporating about a fifth of the minute, either verbatim or in close paraphrase. Ashdown commenced proceedings against the defendants, claiming breach of confidence and copyright infringement. He applied for summary judgment in respect of the copyright claim only.

The defendant claimed that its publication of the minute was covered by the defences of fair dealing for the purpose of criticism or review under s 30(1) of the CDPA 1988, fair dealing for the purpose of reporting current events under s 30(2) of the CDPA 1988 and by the common law defence of public interest (as protected by s 171(3) CDPA 1988). The defendant also sought to argue that the court was now obliged to interpret s 30 and s 171(3) compatibly with Article 10 under the Human Rights Act. In support of these arguments, it claimed that the articles in question raised a matter of legitimate political controversy and promoted public knowledge and discussion of the actions of those responsible for governing the country. The information contained in the minute contradicted denials of proposals for a coalition Cabinet emanating from 10 Downing Street and referred to proposals that were highly controversial within the Labour Party.

In the High Court, Morritt VC awarded summary judgment to the claimant. The Vice-Chancellor accepted (rather reluctantly) that copyright constituted a restriction on the exercise of the right to freedom of expression:

Copyright does not protect ideas, only the material form in which they are expressed. It is therefore a restriction on the right of freedom of expression to inhibit another from copying the method of expression used by the copyright owner even though there may be open to him a host of other methods of expression of the same idea. It must follow that intellectual

---

[124] The discussion of *Ashdown* in this section of the chapter is based on J. Griffiths, 'Copyright Law after *Ashdown*: Time to Deal Fairly with the Public' [2002] *IPQ* 240.

property rights in general and copyright in particular constitute a restriction on the exercise of the right to freedom of expression.[125]

However, he rejected the suggestion that, as a result, courts were necessarily required to consider, on the facts of every individual case, first, whether the restrictions imposed by copyright law were necessary in a democratic society (in accordance with the requirements of Article 10(2)),[126] and, secondly, whether the copyright user was entitled to rely on additional defences over and above those set out in the legislation. In this regard, he did not consider that the implementation of the Human Rights Act had altered the existing nature of the balance between copyright owner and user as previously understood within the United Kingdom legal tradition. He gave two main reasons in support of this position. In the first place, he relied upon a 'floodgates' argument. If courts have to engage with arguments based upon Article 10 in every individual case, 'intellectual property litigation will burgeon out of control and the rights which the legislation apparently confers will be of no practical use except to those able and willing to litigate in all cases'.[127] Secondly, he considered that the CDPA 1988 itself recognized and confirmed the right to freedom of expression through the permitted acts defined within the legislation. That is, the copyright settlement encapsulated within the legislation sufficiently acknowledged and protected the claim that any individual might have to make use of another's copyright material in order to express themselves freely. In enacting 42 identifiable statutory defences '[t]he balance between the rights of the owner of the copyright and those of the public has been struck by the legislative organ of the democratic State itself'.[128] In Morritt VC's assessment, '[t]here is no room for any further defences outside the code which establishes the particular species of intellectual property in question'.[129]

On the facts of the case before him, the Vice-Chancellor found that the use was not for the purpose of criticism or review,[130] but accepted that it might be for the purpose of reporting current events. Even if it were, however, he rejected that the defendant's use of the material could be considered to be fair dealing. In this respect, he relied on

---

[125] [2001] Ch 685, para 12.

[126] It was accepted that the provisions of the CDPA were prescribed by law, and that the served the legitimate aim of protecting the rights of others, ibid, 693.

[127] Ibid.   [128] Ibid, para 13.

[129] Ibid, 696. Morritt VC also observed: 'I can see no reason why the court should travel outside the provisions of the 1988 Act and recognise on the facts of particular cases further or other exceptions to the restrictions on the exercise of the right to freedom of expression constituted by the 1988 Act', ibid, 694.

[130] On the grounds that the defendant's article sought neither to criticize nor review the minute in question, but instead sought to expose and criticize the actions of Blair and Ashdown in October 1997. Morritt VC commented: '[W]hat is required is that the copying shall take place as part of and for the purpose of criticising and reviewing the work' (at 669). Such a literal and narrow reading of the scope of s 30(1) is open to criticism, given previous decisions of the Court of Appeal in which it was held that, although the section makes reference to 'criticism or review, of that or another work or of a performance of the work', the statutory defence encompasses criticism of the ideas within a work as well as their social or moral implications (*Pro Sieben Media AG v Carlton UK Television Ltd* [1999] FSR 605, 610), and commentary upon the decision to withdraw a work from public circulation (*Time Warner v Channel Four TV* [1994] EMLR 3). See also the comments of Lord Denning in *Hubbard v Vosper* [1972] 2 QB 84.

three main factors in holding against the defendants: that the use was in commercial competition with the claimant, in that it substantially affected his ability to exploit the work commercially; that the material had not previously been published; and that the amount and importance of the material taken from the work was substantial both quantitatively and qualitatively.[131] On s 171(3), the Vice-Chancellor considered himself bound by the Court of Appeal's decision in *Hyde Park* and rejected the defendant's argument that its use of the material was in the public interest.

This decision, effectively holding that the CDPA 1988 was 'Human Rights Act-proof', exhibits unwarranted judicial conservatism.[132] Its acceptance that the statutory permitted acts adequately accommodate the demands of the ECHR in balancing the right to freedom of expression of copyright users against the property rights of the copyright owner can be criticized for a number of reasons. In the first place, it ignores the fact that that statutory balance is subject to a constant process of reconsideration and revision, whether driven by technological advance, national self-interest, attempts at regional harmonization, or by other forces. Even since the Vice-Chancellor's decision, the statutory balance has shifted, with the introduction of a new communication right and legislative protection for effective technological measures and a narrowing in the range of permitted acts available to the user of copyright material.[133] Of course, the fact that the legislative balance between copyright owner and user shifts in some manner does not necessarily mean that freedom of expression has been compromised unacceptably. However, to rule out judicial consideration of the matter *ab initio* would seem dangerous. Secondly, the approach is clearly inconsistent with the requirements of the European Convention. The view that the copyright legislation could, *as a whole*, satisfy the 'balance' of interests required by Article 10 is untenable. It is not open for a court to find that the *overall* legal framework secures compliance regardless of the application to the facts of a particular case. Such an approach cannot serve to protect individual rights. The Convention clearly requires a decision-making body to assess whether any interference with freedom of expression can be justified on an *individual* basis.[134]

---

[131] In this respect, Morritt VC was relying upon paragraph 20.16 in Laddie, Prescott, and Vitoria's *The Modern Law of Copyright and Designs*, 3rd edn., Butterworths, 2000, which reads: 'It is impossible to lay down any hard-and-fast definition of what is fair dealing, for it is a matter of fact, degree and impression. However, by far the most important factor is whether the alleged fair dealing is in fact commercially competing with the proprietor's exploitation of the copyright work . . . The second most important factor is whether is whether the work has already been published or exposed to the public . . . The third most important factor is the amount and importance of the work that has been taken.' See below for criticism of continued judicial reliance upon these criteria after the coming into force of the Human Rights Act.

[132] On the same day, the Vice-Chancellor handed down his decision in *Imutran v Uncaged Campaigns Ltd* [2001] 2 All ER 385. In that case, the claimant, a company specializing in xenotransplantation, sought an interlocutory injunction in breach of confidence and copyright to prevent the dissemination of numerous documents concerning its research. The Vice-Chancellor's judgment exhibited the same conservative approach to the effect of the Human Rights Act upon copyright law.

[133] See Conclusion below.

[134] See *Reynolds v Times Newspapers Ltd* [20000] EMLR 1 at 30 (per Lord Steyn); *Verein Gegen Tierfabriken v Switzerland* (2002) 34 EHRR 4.

THE COURT OF APPEAL'S ACCOMMODATION OF FREEDOM OF EXPRESSION IN *ASHDOWN*

The Telegraph Group appealed against the Vice-Chancellor's decision. The judgment of the Court of Appeal was given by Phillips MR, who observed that 'in most circumstances, the principle of freedom of expression will be sufficiently protected if there is a right to publish information and ideas set out in another's literary work, without copying the very words which that person has employed to convey the information or express the ideas'.[135] Nevertheless, emphasizing that the right to freedom of expression incorporates the right not only to impart but also to *receive* information, he continued:

There will be occasions when it is in the public interest not merely that information should be published, but that the public should be told the very words used by a person, notwithstanding that the author enjoys copyright in them. On occasions, indeed, it is the form and not the content of a document which is of interest.[136]

This being so, he conceded that 'rare circumstances' might arise where a defendant's right under Article 10 would conflict with the owner's rights, notwithstanding the exceptions contained in the CDPA 1988.[137] In such circumstances, under the Human Rights Act, a court would be bound to consider the circumstances of each individual case in order to ensure that the right to freedom of expression was being properly accommodated. Thus, by contrast with the judgment of the Vice-Chancellor, the precedence of the rights protected under the ECHR was acknowledged.

How then could the CDPA 1988 be interpreted in a manner that accommodated a right to use the copyright works in such circumstances? The most significant aspect of the Court of Appeal's judgment is the answer that it provides to this question. In many cases, it was suggested, a court could accommodate the requirements of Article 10 by simply refusing to exercise its discretion to award an injunction:

The first way in which it may be possible to do this is by declining the discretionary relief of an injunction. Usually, so it seems to us, such a step will be likely to be sufficient. If a newspaper considers it necessary to copy the exact words created by another, we can see no reason in principle why the newspaper should not indemnify the author for any loss caused to him, or alternatively account to him for any profit made as a result of copying his work. Freedom of expression should not normally carry with it the right to make free use of another's work.[138]

---

[135] [2002] Ch 149, 165. Earlier in his judgment Lord Phillips commented that: '[I]t is stretching the concept of freedom of expression to postulate that it extends to the freedom to convey ideas and information using the form of words devised by someone else', ibid, 163. His observations are similar to those of Justice Birch in the US case *Suntrust Bank v Houghton Mifflin Co.* 166 F 3d 65 (1999): 'Because of the First Amendment principles built into copyright law through the idea/expression dichotomy and the doctrine of fair use, courts often need not entertain related First Amendment arguments in a copyright case.'

[136] [2002] Ch 149, 166.

[137] Ibid, para 44. For discussion of situations in which such 'circumstances' may arise, see Section 4.3 below.

[138] Ibid, para 46.

However, it was conceded that even the grant of a financial remedy might sometimes infringe the right to freedom of expression.[139] In such cases, the Court of Appeal held that any incompatibility between Article 10 and the CDPA 1988 could be resolved through s 171(3)'s preservation of the common law 'public interest' defence.[140] In reconsidering the judgments of Stephenson LJ and Griffiths LJ in *Lion Laboratories*, Lord Phillips MR simply concluded that, in *Hyde Park v Yelland*, Aldous LJ had not been 'justified in circumscribing the public interest defence to breach of copyright as tightly as he did'. He preferred the dissenting opinion of Mance LJ, who had held that the circumstances in which the public interest was capable of overriding copyright were open-ended and incapable of precise categorization or definition.[141] While this reappraisal of the effect of s 171(3) and of the availability of the public interest defence was not contingent upon the enactment of the Human Rights Act, Phillips MR indicated that the common law defence provided the means for accommodating those 'rare circumstances' in which the user of a copyright work's right to freedom of expression come into apparent conflict with the property rights conferred by the CDPA.[142] This concession, however, came with a significant *caveat* from the bench: 'We do not see this leading to a flood of litigation.'[143] Despite this warning, the Court of Appeal in *Ashdown* succeeded in crafting an elegant structural solution to the challenge presented by the Human Rights Act. Whenever the right to freedom of expression demands that publication of a particular work should not be impeded, courts can, by employing a succession of legal mechanisms, ensure that publication will be allowed. This solution effectively insulates the judiciary from the obligation ever to issue a declaration of incompatibility under s 4 of the Human Rights Act in a copyright case.

However, as discussed above in relation to the decision of the High Court in *Ashdown*, the demands of Article 10 must be satisfied on the facts of each particular case. In this respect, the judgment of Phillips MR in *Ashdown* is much less satisfactory. On the facts, he found that this was not a case in which the court was required to consider the availability of the 'public interest' defence, declaring that 'the "fair dealing" defence under section 30 will normally afford the Court all the scope that it needs properly to reflect the public interest in freedom of expression and, in particular, the freedom of the press'.[144] In this context, he upheld the finding that the defendant's use of Ashdown's minute could not fall within s 30(1), because it had been engaged in criticism or review of a person or persons rather than 'of a work'. In respect of s 30(2),

---

[139] Ibid, para 47.   [140] Ibid, para 58.   [141] Ibid.

[142] Phillips MR commented in the following terms: 'Now that the Human Rights Act 1998 is in force, there is the clearest public interest in giving effect to the right to freedom of expression in those rare cases where this right trumps the rights conferred by the 1988 Act. In such circumstances we consider that s 171(3) of the Act permits the defence of public interest to be raised' (*Ashdown* [2002] Ch 149, 170).

[143] Ibid, 167. See also Phillips MR's comment that: 'We do not consider that this conclusion will lead to a flood of cases where freedom of expression is invoked as a defence to a claim for breach of copyright. It will be very rare for the public interest to justify the copying of the form of a work to which copyright attaches', ibid, 170.

[144] Ibid, 172.

he noted that this provision was 'clearly intended to protect the role of the media in informing the public about matters of current concern to the public'. On the facts, the content of the memo was 'arguably a matter of current interest to the public' because it could quite conceivably 'impinge upon the way in which the public would vote at the next general election'.[145] The central question, then, for the Court of Appeal was the same as that for the Vice-Chancellor; 'Was the defendant's use of the claimant's minute fair?' As the Vice-Chancellor had, the Court of Appeal considered this question primarily within the framework of the three most significant criteria identified in the case law by a leading text on copyright law—commercial competition; prior publication; and the amount and importance of the work taken (the 'Laddie factors').[146] On these factors, it concluded that 'without any additional regard to the effect of Article 10, there was no realistic prospect that a defence of fair dealing would be made out'.[147] The *Sunday Telegraph* article had competed with Ashdown's own intended exploitation of the minute in his autobiography and had reduced the value of the serialization rights for his memoirs.[148] In publishing the minute, the newspaper group had been motivated by commercial self-interest:

... [W]e are in no doubt that the extensive quotations of Mr Ashdown's own words added a flavour of the description of the events covered which made the article more attractive to read and will have been of significant commercial value in enabling the *Sunday Telegraph* to maintain, if not to enhance, the loyalty of its readership ...[149]

Furthermore, at the time of the newspaper's article, the minute had not previously been published. Finally, and vitally, a disproportionately large amount of the minute had been quoted. Having analysed the case within this traditional framework, Phillips MR paused to consider whether, under the Human Rights Act, the demands of Article 10 obliged him to resolve the question of 'fairness' differently. He asked whether 'the extensive reproduction of Mr Ashdown's own words was *necessary* in order to satisfy the reader that the account given of his meeting with Mr Blair was authoritative?'[150] The Court of Appeal did not consider that it had been necessary:

It appears to us that the minute was deliberately filleted in order to extract colourful passages that were most likely to add flavour to the article and thus to appeal to the readership of the newspaper. Mr Ashdown's work product was deployed in the way that it was for reasons that were essentially journalistic in furtherance of the commercial interests of the Telegraph Group. We do not consider it arguable that Article 10 requires that the Group should be able to profit from this use of Mr Ashdown's copyright without paying compensation.[151]

Thus, under the Human Rights Act, United Kingdom courts must generally seek to satisfy the requirements of Article 10 through existing mechanisms—the 'idea/

---

[145] Ibid.   [146] See n 131 above.   [147] Ibid, 175.   [148] Ibid, para 72.
[149] Ibid, paras 72, 82.   [150] Ibid. 175–76; emphasis added.   [151] Ibid. 176.

expression dichotomy', the discretion to refuse an injunction[152] or the statutory permitted acts—and these mechanisms are to be interpreted compatibly with Article 10
where necessary. Only where these are inadequate is the common law 'public interest'
principle to be employed to secure compatibility. Under which circumstances, then,
might a defendant be entitled to rely upon the public interest in making use of
another's copyright work? Clearly, courts will not permit the enforcement of a copyright interest in circumstances falling within the public policy grounds identified by
Aldous LJ in *Hyde Park*, for example, where reproduction is in the interests of the
administration of justice.[153] But in what other ways might the courts begin to develop
the common law defence should circumstances require them to do so?

Phillips MR suggested one such situation. In the context of s 30(2), he observed:
'[I]t is possible to conceive of information of the greatest public interest relating not
to a current event, but *to a document produced in the past.*'[154] Enabling use of copyright material properly to inform the public about *non-current events* of general
concern provides one example of a situation in which the common law principle may
be extended. The limits on permissible use set out in the CDPA 1988 also present
other circumstances in which the public interest might appropriately be invoked. For
example, Article 10 might also be relied upon in relation to the use of a *photographic
work* for the purpose of reporting current events or for the criticism or review
of a work that has not previously been made public. It is not difficult to envisage
circumstances in which it may be necessary for a media organization to reproduce
a controversial, or particularly revealing, photograph in the course of news reporting.[155] Equally, in order to safeguard the public's right to receive information under
Article 10, it may sometimes be necessary to permit criticism of material that has not
yet been made available to the public.

---

[152] Moreover, even should the defendant's use fall within this category, Phillips MR indicated that this may
not necessarily lead to the 'trumping' of the claimant's rights in their entirety. That is, he suggested that the
first way in which the courts might engage the public interest defence is by simply refusing the claimant
discretionary relief in the form of an injunction, but leaving him to any other remedy he might be entitled to
under the CDPA 1988. As Phillips MR observed '[f]reedom of expression should not normally carry with it
the right to make free use of another's work'; [2002] Ch 149, 167.

[153] On this type of use, Jacob J commented as follows at first instance in *Hyde Park v Yelland* [1999] RPC
655, 670: '[T]ake a case where a document, carefully researched and compiled by a team of bank robbers,
indicated the precise weaknesses of the security system of each of the branches of a major bank. Copyright is
normally accorded to carefully and skillfully compiled lists as being original works. But it can hardly be the
law that the police could not make copies of the list to give to the bank and its security advisors. Nor does it
make sense to say that the robbers could sue at least for nominal damages if the police did so. Or suppose
the police obtain from a security video a picture of a bank robber. Do they really have to get the permission of
the copyright owner (perhaps not readily identifiable in a hurry) before showing the picture of the robber on
television when seeking the help of the public to track him down? And if they do not do so, could the
copyright owner really sue for nominal damages? The questions only have to be asked to be answered.'

[154] [2002] Ch 149, 166. Alternatively, he suggested that 'the mere fact of publication, and any controversy
created by the disclosure' might, in any case, be sufficient to make the disclosure a 'current event' for the
purpose of falling within s 30(2). Often such a claim would be a 'bootstraps' argument of little merit, but on
other occasions (such as disclosure by the Public Record Office under the 30-year rule) it may have a more
solid basis (167).

[155] See note 61 above.

Consider, for example, the facts of *Hubbard v Vosper*.[156] In that case, Vosper had written a book that was heavily critical of the dangerous practices of the Church of Scientology, a religious sect founded by the claimant, L Ron Hubbard. Vosper had formerly been a member of the sect. In his book, he quoted extensively from bulletins and letters written by Hubbard that had been circulated only to certain initiates within the sect. In response to Hubbard's claim for infringement of copyright, Vosper argued that his use of the texts fell within the defence of fair dealing for the purpose of criticism or review. Hubbard disputed this, arguing that it could not be considered fair dealing to take substantial extracts from materials that had only been made available to a limited number of people and had not, therefore, been published to 'the world at large'.[157] Denning MR rejected the argument, observing:

> Although a literary work may not be published to the world at large, it may, however, be circulated to such a wide circle that it is 'fair dealing' to criticise it publicly in a newspaper, or elsewhere. This happens sometimes when a company sends a circular to the whole body of shareholders. It may be of such general interest that it is quite legitimate for a newspaper to make quotations from it, and to criticise them—or review them—without thereby being guilty of infringing copyright.[158]

Thus, the fact that the work had not been published was not fatal to the defendant's fair dealing defence so long as the work had been suitably widely circulated amongst certain members of the Church, despite the fact that, as a recipient of the information, Vosper had been required to sign a written undertaking to refrain from divulging the materials to anyone or to discuss them within the hearing of any persons.[159] Had Vosper been required to establish that the works in question had been 'made available to the public', as is now required under the provision, it seems less likely that a defence based upon s 30(1) would have succeeded.[160] However, given the controversial nature of the subject matter of the works and the importance of the defendant's aim in exposing the cult, if such a case were to occur today, it may well be one in which a court is required to apply the common law public interest principle in the defendant's favour.[161]

A further example of a situation in which the common law principle may need to be employed to ensure compatibility with Article 10 arises as a result of another restriction on the scope of s 30(1). As was demonstrated in *Ashdown*, the defence of

---

[156] *Hubbard v Vosper* [1972] 2 QB 84.

[157] Counsel for the claimant relied upon the dictum of Romer J in *British Oxygen Co Ltd v Liquid Air Ltd* [1925] Ch 383, 393 that 'it would be manifestly unfair that an unpublished literary work should, without the consent of the author, be the subject of public criticism, review or newspaper summary. Any such dealing with an unpublished literary work would not, therefore, in my opinion, be a "fair dealing" with the work'.

[158] [1972] 2 QB 84, 95.   [159] Ibid, 92.

[160] Laddie, Prescott, and Vitoria, for example, suggest that ' "the public" should be interpreted in the dictionary sense of "the community in general" and that a work is not "published" unless copies may be acquired, in principle, by any members of that community' *Modern Law of Copyright and Designs*, 3rd edn., Butterworths, 2000, para 5.38. See *HRH Prince of Wales v Associated Newspapers* [2006] EWHC 522.

[161] See also K. Garnett, 'The Impact of the Human Rights Act 1998 on United Kingdom Copyright Law' in J. Griffiths and U. Suthersanen, (eds) *Copyright and Free Speech*, Oxford University Press, 2005, 171, 196–7.

fair dealing for the purpose of criticism or review will not apply where a copyright work is used for the purpose of criticizing (or reviewing) something that is neither a work nor a performance of a work. An apposite example is that of political (or indeed any other forms of) satire or parody.[162] At present, the United Kingdom, unlike many other jurisdictions,[163] makes no express exception under the CDPA 1988 pertaining to the creation of works of parody based upon an existing copyright work, whether designed as a comment upon the source work in question, or intended to satirize or parody another work, or individual.[164] Therefore, where an individual draws upon an existing work to parody or satirize that work's author (perhaps the author of a set of political diaries), or indeed anyone else,[165] and where the satirist reproduces more than an insubstantial amount of the source work, he or she will have infringed the copyright in that work and will be unlikely to be entitled to shelter within the defence of fair dealing.[166] Given the effectiveness of parody as a form of criticism, especially within the political arena, the demands of Article 10 may lead courts to protect it by means of the common law public interest defence, even where it does not fall within the statutory defences. This, along with the other examples described above, provides some indication of the manner in which the public interest defence may be developed to safeguard freedom of expression.

THE SHORTCOMINGS OF THE APPROACH ADOPTED IN *ASHDOWN*

In accepting that freedom of expression considerations might require courts to develop the public interest principle at common law, the Court of Appeal accom-

---

[162] On copyright and parody in general, see: M. Spence, 'Intellectual Property and the Problem of Parody' [1998] *LQR* 594; E. Gredley and S. M. Maniatis, 'Parody: A Fatal Attraction? Part 1: The Nature of Parody and its Treatment in Copyright' [1997] *EIPR* 339; M. Rushton, 'Copyright and Freedom of Expression: an Economic Analysis' in R. Towse, *Copyright in the Cultural Industries*, Elgar Publishing, 2002, 51.

[163] Spain, Belgium and France all provide express legal exceptions for works of parody. In the US, works of parody will often be protected under a broader 'fair use' doctrine. See, for example, *Campbell v Acuff-Rose Music Inc.* 510 US 568 (1994).

[164] The Directive on Copyright and Related Rights in the Information Society expressly permits member states to include such an exception within their copyright legislation, see Directive 2001/29/EC, Art 5(3)(k).

[165] Think for example of a political cartoonist drawing inspiration from existing copyright materials to lampoon a politician of the moment.

[166] *Schweppes v Wellingtons* [1984] FSR 210. Given that the choice of source work is often central to the effective nature of the criticism or commentary being made, restricting the satirist to use of an insubstantial amount of a work only will more often than not simply render the reference to that source work redundant. That is, the less of the source work which is reproducible, the less likely it is that the source work will be identified. In addition, it should be noted that a parody may also be considered to have infringed the original author's moral rights in the source work (that is, that the work will have been subject to a derogatory treatment). See J. Griffiths, 'Not Such a "Timid Thing": The UK's Integrity Right and Freedom of Expression' in J. Griffiths and U. Suthersanen, (eds) *Copyright and Free Speech*, Oxford University Press, 2005, 211.

modated the demands of the Human Rights Act in a manner that, at first sight, appears to be considerably more sophisticated than the conservative approach to the European Convention adopted by the Vice-Chancellor. However, it may well be asked whether, in substance, his approach is any less conservative. While Phillips MR's judgment in *Ashdown* has all the trappings of a progressive accommodation of human rights principles within copyright jurisprudence, the decision suggests that, in reality, there may be little change from the pre-Human Rights Act position.

There are aspects of the Court of Appeal's general methodology that seem undesirable from the perspective of freedom of expression. First, it is an important aspect of the Court's accommodation of copyright law and Article 10 that the public interest principle should only be employed where none of the statutory defences are available:

Where part of a work is copied in the course of a report on current events, the 'fair dealing' defence under section 30 will normally afford the court all the scope that it needs properly to reflect the public interest in freedom of expression and, in particular, the freedom of the press. There will then be no need to give separate consideration to the availability of a public interest defence under section 171.[167]

This makes sense at a pragmatic level. However, such an approach seems highly suspect in principle. Arguments based upon fair dealing and the public interest are, and should remain, separate defences, governed by separate considerations, and, when advanced, should warrant the separate attentions of the court.[168] Secondly, it could also be argued that the method employed by the Court of Appeal in assessing whether or not the defendant had dealt fairly with the claimant's work in Ashdown is deeply flawed. The Court first considered whether the dealing would have been regarded as fair in a pre-Human Rights Act context, before proceeding to examine the relevance of Article 10. This hardly seems the most effective way of reading such legislation in a manner compatible with Convention rights. Indeed, it seems to approach the question of compatibility from the wrong perspective.

In any event, as noted previously, it was not sufficient for the Court of Appeal to devise a structure within which copyright law could be interpreted compatibly with the rights contained in the European Convention. On the facts of the particular case, it was necessary for it to achieve compatibility. It is in this respect that its decision seems least convincing. Indeed, it suggests that its primary aim was to ensure that the requirements of the Human Rights Act were formally recognized with as little substantive disruption to existing copyright norms as possible. In the following paragraphs, we consider a series of significant problems arising from the Court's decision to confirm the grant of summary judgment to Ashdown.

[167] Ibid, 252–3.
[168] In this respect, in *Beloff v Pressdram* [1973] FSR 33, 56, Ungoed-Thomas J observed that the two defences 'are governed by separate considerations. Fair dealing is a statutory defence limited to infringement of copyright only. But public interest is a defence outside and independent of statutes, is not limited to copyright cases, and is based upon a general principle of common law.'

In considering the 'fairness' of the defendant's dealing, the Court of Appeal considered that both economic injury to the claimant and the economic benefit derived by the defendant from use of the copyright work tended to demonstrate that the defendant was engaged in competition with the claimant and, presumptively, that the dealing was unfair. In this regard, the Court relied on a passage from *The Modern Law of Copyright and Designs* by Laddie *et al.*:

> By far the most important factor is whether the alleged fair dealing is in fact commercially competing with the proprietor's exploitation of the copyright work, a substitute for the probable purchase of unauthorized copies, and the like. If it is, the fair dealing defence will almost certainly fail . . .[169]

The ability to enforce copyright to secure a financial return lies at the core of the property right protected under Article 10(2). However, where there is a legitimate public interest in access to a copyright work, the claimant's financial loss cannot be conclusive. Claimants in defamation or privacy proceedings do not avoid the operation of defences such as qualified privilege and public interest by demonstrating the financial cost of a defendant's activities. There seems to be no legitimate reason why a copyright dispute should be treated any differently. Thus, under Article 10, the paramount significance placed upon a claimant's financial loss in the orthodox approach to fair dealing must be qualified where there is a legitimate public interest in access to a copyright work.

Even more questionable was the emphasis placed by the Court of Appeal on the defendant's financial gain from publication of the minute. The significance of this factor ought to have been considered more carefully in the light of Article 10, particularly as the defendant in *Ashdown* was a newspaper. There are justified concerns that media organizations will, if unrestrained, act abusively. However, the freedom of expression protected under Article 10 is an *instrumental* right. The media is strongly protected under that provision because it functions as the watchdog of the *public.*[170] Viewed in this light, the Court of Appeal's conclusion that the commercial motivation of the *Sunday Telegraph*'s publication rendered it presumptively unfair seems less than convincing. The fact that media organizations are motivated by profit has not in the past prevented them from relying upon their rights under Article 10 at Strasbourg. In the words of Jacob J in *Hyde Park Residence Ltd v Yelland*:

> [W]hen [the press] publish they will always expect to make money. They are not philanthropists. I do not think the fact that *The Sun* expected to make money derogates in any way from the 'fair dealing' (or any public interest) justification.[171]

In concentrating on the defendant's desire to profit from the use of Ashdown's

---

[169] *Ashdown v Telegraph Group Ltd* [2002] Ch 149 (CA), para 70.

[170] *Sunday Times v United Kingdom* (1979) 2 EHRR 243; *Lingens v Austria* (1986) 8 EHRR 407; *Bladet Tromso & Stenaas v Norway* (2000) 29 EHRR 125; *Goodwin v United Kingdom* (1996) 22 EHRR 123; *Castells v Spain* (1992) 14 EHRR 445.

[171] [1999] EMLR 654, 663. See also *Fraser-Woodward Ltd v BBC* [2005] EHLR 22, para 59.

minute, the Court of Appeal appears have been unduly concerned to remedy apparent unfairness between the parties to the proceedings. However, true accommodation of the demands of Article 10 requires fairness to be assessed by reference not only to the private interests of the parties but also by reference to the conflict between the rights of the *public* to receive information and the rights of the copyright owner to control use of a work.

In addition to this flawed approach to commercial competition, it is strongly arguable that the presumption operated by the Court of Appeal against fairness in the case of previously unpublished works does not do justice to the requirements of Article 10. In fact, where there is a public interest in the subject-matter of a copyright work, the public interest in disclosure of that work is likely to be greater where the work is unpublished than where the work has previously been published. Again, the assumption that dealings with an unpublished work, disclosed in breach of confidence, are presumptively unfair seems to derive from a concern for 'fairness' *inter partes*. However, investigative journalism provides a vital support for the interests protected under Article 10 and much valuable investigative journalism derives from 'leaks'.[172] The approach to fairness adopted by the Court of Appeal, under which the unpublished status of a work militates strongly against publication of a work unless such publication is held to be necessary in the public interest again inverts the structure of analysis required under Article 10.

A further significant criticism of the Court of Appeal's assessment of 'fairness' in *Ashdown* is to be levelled at its approach to the question of 'the amount and importance of the work taken'.[173] This factor was ultimately crucial in determining that the defendant's activities had been unfair, and thus fell outside s 30(2):

It is arguable that the Telegraph Group were justified in making limited quotation of Mr Ashdown's own words, in order to demonstrate that they were in a position to give an authentic account of the meeting . . . Can it be argued that the extensive reproduction of Mr Ashdown's own words was necessary in order to satisfy the reader that the account given of his meeting with Mr Blair was authoritative? We do not believe that it can. The statement by the Sunday Telegraph that they had obtained a copy of the minute coupled with one or two short extracts from it would have sufficed.[174]

This conclusion fails to pay adequate regard to the newspaper's right of freedom of expression. It is based upon an assumption that the use of a copyright owner's work must be *necessary* before pre-Human Rights Act considerations might be outweighed by the freedom of expression claim. Any adoption of a test of *necessity* in this context is problematic because it carries with it the danger of being resolved too readily in the claimant's favour and is symptomatic of the Court's over-optimistic assessment of the impact of the 'ideas/expression dichotomy'. Most importantly, however, the Court of

---

[172] *Goodwin v United Kingdom* (1966) 22 EHRR 123. For a recent example of a case in which the unpublished nature of a work favoured the claimant, see *HRH Prince of Wales v Associated Newspapers* [2006] EWHC 522.

[173] *Ashdown v Telegraph Group Ltd* [2002] Ch 149 (CA), paras 76–7.   [174] Ibid, para 81.

Appeal's conclusion exhibits a willingness to dictate the manner in which the *Sunday Telegraph* ought to have presented its article that is inconsistent with jurisprudence of the Court of Human Rights on Article 10. For example, in *Fressoz & Roire v France*, a case concerning prosecutions for the publication of leaked tax returns, the European Court of Human Rights stated that 'In essence, [Article 10] leaves it for journalists to decide whether or not it is necessary to reproduce such documents to ensure credibility'.[175] It is difficult to see how the Court of Appeal's bare assertion that the *Sunday Telegraph* ought to have explained that it had seen the claimant's minute and published 'one or two short extracts from it' can possibly be compatible with this principle.

A final criticism of the Court of Appeal's apparent solution to the conflict between copyright law and freedom of speech in *Ashdown* can be directed at its failure to pay adequate attention to the subject-matter of the defendant's article and to the nature of the claimant's work. The article within which the claimant's minute was reproduced contained matters of considerable political significance. The Court of Appeal itself noted that:

In a democratic society, information about a meeting between the Prime Minister and the opposition party leader during the then current Parliament to discuss possible close co-operation between the parties is very likely to be of legitimate and continuing public interest. It might impinge upon the way in which the public voted at the next election.[176]

Such information about matters of public importance is strongly protected under Article 10. Indeed, the single guiding principle of the jurisprudence of the European Court of Human Rights on that provision appears to be that interference with speech on matters of public importance requires a very high degree of justification.[177] In *Ashdown*, however, the Court of Appeal conceded only that the significance of the subject-matter of the newspaper's disclosure justified 'making limited quotation' from the minute.[178] This grudging approach does not do justice to the crucial significance of this factor in the Strasbourg case law.

At the same time, the Court failed to scrutinize the nature of the claimant's right in any detail at all. Not all copyright interests are of equal value. For example, entrepreneurial or related rights, such as broadcasts or sound recordings, are not as well protected as 'original' works.[179] Greater protection is granted to works exhibiting a higher degree of 'labour and skill' and relatively simple works receive a 'thinner' form of protection.[180] The more convincingly copyright protection can be justified in

[175] *Fressoz and Roire v France* (2001) 31 EHRR 28, paras 54–55. See also *Bergens Tidende v Norway* (2000) 31 EHRR 16, para 57.

[176] *Ashdown v Telegraph Group Ltd* [2002] Ch 149 (CA), para 64.

[177] *De Haes and Gijsels v Belgium* (1998) 25 EHRR 1, para 39; *Lingens v Austria* (1986) 8 EHRR 407; *Bowman v United Kingdom* (1998) 26 EHRR 1, *Fuentes Bobo v Spain* (2001) 31 EHRR 50; *Maronek v Slovakia* (2004) 38 EHRR 5; *Tammer v Estonia* (2003) 37 EHRR 43, cf *Janowski v Poland* (2000) 29 EHRR 705.

[178] *Ashdown v Telegraph Group Ltd* [2002] Ch 149 (CA), para 81. See also *HRH Prince of Wales v Associated Newspapers Ltd* [2006] EWHC 522.

[179] *Norowzian v Arks (No 1)* [1998] FSR 394; CDPA 1988 ss 12–15.

[180] *Kenrick & Co v Lawrence & Co* (1890) 25 QBD 99.

relation to a particular work, the stronger the powers granted to the copyright owner. In *Ashdown*, the claimant's right arguably deserved very little protection. The minute did not represent the culminating expression of extensive 'labour and skill'; it was simply a factual record of a meeting. Furthermore, the claimant was present at that meeting in his capacity as the leader of a national political party.[181] As such, his claim to be entitled to use copyright law to protect the fruits of this opportunity to secure personal financial advantage does not seem very strong. A proper analysis of the proportionality of copyright law's interference with the newspaper's right to freedom of expression ought to have been more searching than the rather complacent enquiry into the application of traditional fair dealing doctrine and the necessity of publication in the public interest conducted by the Court of Appeal.

CONCLUSION

In this chapter, we have sought to explain the way in which copyright law can restrict the right to freedom of expression and the partial protection for that right available as a result of mechanisms within traditional copyright doctrine. We have also considered the application of Article 10 to copyright law, both in principle and as determined by the United Kingdom courts under the Human Rights Act. It has been argued that the accommodation of these competing interests by the courts has been guided by a desire to maintain the traditional 'balance' of copyright law rather than by a wish to engage with the true demands of freedom of expression. This response is not an isolated one. In other jurisdictions, courts have also been reluctant to risk disruption to the status quo by acknowledging the supremacy of external norms such as free speech to the body of rules developed within copyright law[182] and by granting rights to users of copyright works.[183] It is possible that the status of copyright as *property*[184] and judges' fear of unbalancing the commercial structures based upon intellectual property law have resulted in this relative insulation of copyright law from free speech norms. In this respect, it differs significantly from neighbouring bodies of law such as defamation and privacy. It has been argued here, however, that such a conservative approach is unjustified. Copyright law presents very significant challenges to freedom of expression and these were not adequately acknowledged by the Court of Appeal in *Ashdown*.

This failure to provide a satisfactory restraint upon the exercise of copyright is particularly unfortunate in view of recent developments in copyright law. The scale of

---

[181] Under the ECHR, more extensive discussion of the activities of politicians is permitted than of private persons, see, for example, *Tammer v Estonia* (2001) 37 EHRR 857.

[182] See, for example, *Eldred v Ashcroft* 537 US 186 (2003)(US).

[183] See J. Waldron, 'From Authors to Copiers: Individual Rights and Social Values in Intellectual Property' (1993) 68 *Chicago-Kent L Rev* 840.

[184] See E. Barendt, 'Copyright and Free Speech Theory' in J. Griffiths and U. Suthersanen, (eds) *Copyright and Free Speech*, Oxford University Press, 2005, 2.30–2.35.

any potential conflict with the right to freedom of expression has already increased significantly since the decision in *Ashdown*. In response to rapid technological change and fear of piracy, a series of recent legislative developments have granted ever-stronger powers to copyright owners. In the United Kingdom, the most notable changes have been effected by the Copyright and Related Rights Regulations 2003, which implemented the provisions of the Directive on Copyright and Related Rights in the Information Society.[185] These Regulations increased the practical likelihood of copyright conflicting with freedom of expression by adding to the range of acts to which a copyright owner is entitled to object under the CDPA 1988.[186] While strengthening the position of copyright owners, the Regulations also circumscribed the availability of defences for users under the CDPA 1988.[187] In this concluding section of the chapter, we pause for a moment to note the particular threat presented by one aspect of this amended regime.

In a world of digital works delivered over networks, the 2003 Regulations have reinforced the power of copyright owners to exercise forms of self-help outside the traditional contours of copyright law—through the introduction of stronger legal protection for technological protection measures and through their failure to curtail contractual restraints on use superseding exceptions and limitations within the CDPA.[188] As more copyright owners incorporate technological protection measures controlling the manner in which users access and copy protected material, these measures will inevitably interfere more frequently with a user's ability to engage in

[185] Copyright and Related Rights Regulations 2003, SI 2498/2003, which came into force on the 31 October 2003 and implemented the European Directive on the harmonization of certain aspects of copyright and related rights in the information society, 2001/29/EC. For commentaries on the Directive see: D. Bainbridge, 'Implementing the Directive on Copyright in the Information Society' (2002) *IP&IT Law* 9; M. Hart, 'The Copyright in the Information Society Directive: An Overview' (2002) *EIPR* 58; T. Heide, 'The Approach to Innovation Under the Proposed Copyright Directive: Time for Mandatory Exceptions?' [2002] *IPQ* 215; M. Kretschmer, 'Digital Copyright: The End of an Era' (2003) *EIPR* 333; T. Vinje, 'Should We Begin Digging Copyright's Grave?' (2000) *EIPR* 551; H. Weise, 'The Justification of the Copyright System in the Digital Age' (2002) *EIPR* 387; T. Cook and L. Brazell, *The Copyright Directive: UK Implementation*, Jordans, 2004.

[186] For example, the regulations introduced a broad right to prevent the communication of a work to the public, whether by way of broadcast, or simply by making the work available to the public by electronic transmission in such a way that members of the public may access it from a place and at a time chosen by them (Copyright and Related Rights Regulations, reg 6, amending CDPA 1988, s 20).

[187] For example, concerning the permitted acts set out in the CDPA 1988, the Regulations affected the operation of s 29 (research and private study), s 30 (criticism, review and news reporting), s 32 (things done for the purposes of instruction or examination), s 35 (recordings by educational establishments of broadcasts), s 36 (reprographic copying by educational establishments), s 38–9 (copying by librarians), s 50 (observing, studying, and testing computer programs), s 61 (recordings of folksongs), s 63 (advertising artistic works for sale), s 67 (playing sound recordings for clubs, societies, etc.), s 70 (recording for the purpose of time-shifting), s 71 (photographs of broadcasts), s 72 (public showing or playing of broadcasts), s 73 (concerning the reception and retransmission of broadcasts), and s 74 (subtitling copies of broadcasts). It has even been suggested that United Kingdom courts may not be able legitimately to apply the 'public interest defence' under the Directive. The better view seems to be that, as a general principle of law, rather than a specific exception or limitation to copyright infringement, its operation is not curtailed. For discussion, see K. Garnett, 'The Impact of the Human Rights Act 1998 on United Kingdom Copyright Law' in J. Griffiths and U. Suthersanen, (eds) *Copyright and Free Speech*, Oxford University Press, 2005, 8.12.

[188] CDPA ss 296ZA–296ZF.

lawful reproduction from a copyright work in accordance with the statutory permitted acts. How, for example, do you make copies from a work, whether substantial or insubstantial, fair or unfair, when the work is copy-protected? Circumvention of such copy protection is, under the new legislative regime, likely to be unlawful.

The 2003 Regulations contain a half-hearted attempt to address the difficulty described above; providing that 'where the application of any effective technological measure . . . prevents a person from carrying out a permitted act in relation to that work', that person can issue a *notice of complaint* to the Secretary of State, who has available to him or her a number of possible courses of action to remedy the situation.[189] However, even ignoring the fact that, under this provision, the onus is placed upon the user of a copyright work to ensure that the owner is not using such technological protection measures to impinge upon otherwise lawful actions under the legislation,[190] and the very weak nature of the mechanism for addressing such complaints (with its emphasis on developing voluntary measures between owner and user), the right to complain to the Secretary of State does not apply to all the permitted acts under the CDPA 1988. In particular, it offers no protection for permitted acts designed to secure freedom of expression, such as those concerned with fair dealing for the purpose of criticism or review and fair dealing for the purpose of reporting current events. Moreover, the mechanism (such as it is) for ensuring that the use of effective technological measures does not interfere with the user's ability to engage in certain statutory permitted acts does not extend to copyright works 'made available to the public on agreed contractual terms in such a way that members of the public may access them from a place and at a time individually chosen by them'[191]—that is, copyright content delivered online on demand.[192] The relevance of this exclusion will of course increase significantly as more and more copyright-protected content is delivered online. The potential combined impact of technological protection measures and contractual use stipulations has led some commentators to call for the

---

[189] Copyright and Related Rights Regulations 2003, reg 24, implementing s 296ZE(2). The Secretary of State 'may give to the owner of that copyright work . . . such directions as appear to the Secretary of State to be requisite or expedient for the purpose of—(a) establishing whether any voluntary measure or agreement relevant to the copyright work the subject of the complaint subsists; or (b) (where it is established that there is no voluntary measure of agreement) ensuring that the owner . . . makes available to the complainant the means of carrying out the permitted act the subject of the complaint to the extent necessary to so benefit from that permitted act' (s 296ZE(3)).

[190] Parallels might be drawn with the complaints procedure for regulating the price of books set out in s 4 of the Statute of Anne 1709. Under this provision, the public could keep the activities of the book trade in check. The section never seems to have been invoked and was subsequently repealed in 1739.

[191] CDPA 1988, s 296ZE(9).

[192] For a discussion of the problems raised by these provisions, see: T. Heide, 'Copyright, Contract and the Legal Protection of Technological Measures—Not 'The Old Fashioned Way': Providing a Rational to the Copyright Exceptions Interface' (2003) *Journal of the Copyright Society of the USA* 315; N. Braun, 'The Interface between the Protection of Technological Measures and the Exercise of Exceptions to Copyright and Related Rights: Comparing the Situation in the United States and in the European Community' [2003] *EIPR* 496; S. Dusollier, 'Exceptions and Technological Measures in the European Copyright Directive of 2001—an Empty Promise' (2003) *IIC* 62; L. P. Loren, 'Technological Protections in Copyright Law: Is More Legal Protection Needed?' (2002) *International Review of Law Computers & Technology*, 133.

negotiation of much stronger users' rights than have been laid down in traditional copyright regimes.[193]

There is no doubt that, in some cases, the existence of such rights is mandated by the higher-order right to freedom of expression, such as that protected under Article 10. It would, for example, be odd if L Ron Hubbard's attempts to prevent quotation of his copyright works in critical literature were to succeed simply because those works were protected by technological protection measures and/or by contractual provisions prohibiting reproduction. However, cases in other jurisdictions,[194] and previous experience of the way in which courts have avoided confronting the conflict between copyright and freedom of expression in this jurisdiction, do not inspire confidence.[195] It seems likely that copyright law will remain relatively, and unjustifiably, immune from serious challenge from free speech norms until judges summon up the courage to depart more substantially from existing doctrine. If they do not do so, the conflict between the two rights will become more acute in future.

[193] See, ibid, Heide and Loren.

[194] See, for example, *Universal City Studios v Corley* F 3d 429 (2nd Cir, 2001).

[195] The mechanism for ensuring compatibility with Article 10 developed by the Court of Appeal in *Ashdown* may not be available in the case of statutory rights introduced after CDPA 1988. See *Mars UK Ltd v Tecknowledge* [2000] ECDR 99.

PART VI

MEDIA FREEDOM AND POLITICAL SPEECH

This Part begins in Chapter 19 by considering the law in this context, contained in the Official Secrets Act and in the common law action for breach of confidence. The chapter also examines rights to know in the Freedom of Information Act 2000. Chapter 20 moves on to consider freedom of political expression in broadcasting, examining the broadcasting ban on political advertising and the regulatory obligations of due impartiality and accuracy. Finally, this Part examines the relationship between defamation and political speech, in Chapter 21.

19

OFFICIAL SECRECY, ACCESS TO INFORMATION, AND THE MEDIA

INTRODUCTION[1]

This chapter is concerned with restraints upon the media created directly or indirectly by the law governing the release of sensitive government information, of 'official secrets'. It also considers the corollary—the positive rights to access to information held by public authorities now granted by the Freedom of Information Act 2000, which came into force on 1 January 2005. The latter Act is not strictly speaking part of 'media law', or the law of *media* freedom: the Act is only of concern to the media in that it is very likely that journalists, along with opposition politicians and campaigners, as well as concerned individuals, will make particular use of the Act, in order to obtain information. Moreover, since the Act gives positive rights to information, it does not, strictly, affect media *freedom*: it does not place restraints upon what the media may publish; rather it *assists* media bodies in their attempts to extract information from public authorities. Thus, quite properly, the freedom of information legislation is generally treated as an aspect of constitutional law, and taught as such.[2] Nevertheless, we offer a discussion here, taking account of developments since the Act came into force, simply because the Act is relevant to the overall position of the media as it seeks to hold government to account. For example, the law on disclosure of journalistic sources, discussed in Chapter 7, is difficult to assess without some knowledge of the means by which information about bodies such as hospitals, the police, and local authorities may be freely obtainable.

---

[1] General reading, see P. Birkinshaw, *Freedom of Information: The Law, the Practice and the Ideal*, 4th edn., London: Butterworths, 2005; Vincent, *The Culture of Secrecy, Britain 1832–1998*, Oxford: OUP, 1998; D. Feldman, *Civil Liberties and Human Rights in England and Wales*, 2nd edn., Oxford: OUP, 2002, Chapter 14; S.H. Bailey, D.J. Harris, and B.L. Jones, *Civil Liberties: Cases and Materials*, 5th edn., Oxford: OUP. 2001, Chapter 7; J.D. Baxter, *State Security, Privacy and Information*, London: Harvester Wheatsheaf, 1990; S. Shetreet, (ed.), *Free Speech and National Security*, London: Asper Publishers, 1991; P. Gill, *Policing Politics: Security, Intelligence and the Liberal Democratic State*, 1994; L. Lustgarten and I. Leigh, *In From the Cold: National Security and Parliamentary Democracy*, Oxford: Clarendon, 1994; N. Whitty, T. Murphy, and S. Livingstone, *Civil Liberties Law*, London: Butterworths, 2001, Chapter 7.

[2] See, for example, R. Austin, 'The Freedom of Information Act 2000:—A Sheep in Wolf's Clothing?', in J. Jowell and D. Oliver, *The Changing Constitution* (5th edn., Oxford: OUP, 2004).

In contrast, the law on official secrecy has some direct application to the media: there are indeed particular provisions of the Official Secrets Act that are aimed specifically at journalists,[3] while the restrictions the Act lays upon, for example, members of the security services, directly affects their ability to tell their stories through the media, as in the notorious David Shayler affair,[4] considered in detail below.

The overall concern of this chapter is with the degree to which a proper balance has been and is currently being struck between the interest of the individual in acquiring information and the interest of the State and public authorities in withholding it. Clearly, there are genuine public interests, including that of protecting national security, in keeping some information out of the public domain; the question is whether other interests that do not correspond with and may even be opposed to the interests of the public are also at work. Initially, it may be said that in the UK, the area of control over government information is one in which the State's supposed interest in keeping information secret has in general prevailed very readily over the individual interest in question. It has often been said that the UK is more obsessed with keeping government information secret than any other Western democracy.[5] It is clearly advantageous for the party in power to be able to control the flow of information in order to prevent public scrutiny of certain official decisions and in order to be able to release information selectively at convenient moments. The British Government has available a number of methods of keeping official information secret, including the deterrent effect of criminal sanctions under the Official Secrets Act 1989, the Civil Service Conduct Code,[6] around 80 statutory provisions engendering secrecy in various areas, and the civil action for breach of confidence. The situation of the civil servant in the UK who believes that disclosure as to a certain state of affairs is necessary in order to serve the public interest may therefore be contrasted with the situation of his or her counterpart in the US, where he or she would receive protection from detrimental action flowing from whistle-blowing[7] under the Civil Service Reform Act 1978. A weak form of a public interest defence might have been adopted under proposals in the government White Paper on freedom of information, published in July 1993.[8] It was proposed that the disclosure of information would not be penalized if the information was not 'genuinely confidential'. But when the Labour Government introduced the Public Interest Disclosure Act 1998, crown servants involved in security and intelligence activities, or those whose 'whistle-blowing' breaches the 1989 Act,

---

[3] See below at 934–6.

[4] For an overall look at the implications of that episode, see K. Best, 'The Control of Official Information: Implications of the Shayler Affair' (2000) 5(6) *Journal of Civil Liberties* 18.

[5] For example, G. Robertson, *Freedom, the Individual and the Law*, London: Penguin 1989, pp 129–31.

[6] See G. Drewry and T. Butcher, *The Civil Service Today*, London: Blackwell, 1991. It should be pointed out that the Civil Service Code, which came into force on 1 January 1996, contains a partial 'whistle-blowing' provision in paras 11–12.

[7] For discussion of the situation of UK and US civil servants and developments in the area, see Y. Cripps, 'Disclosure in the public interest: the predicament of the public sector employee' [1983] *PL* 600; Zellick, 'Whistle-blowing in US law' [1987] *PL* 311–13; Starke (1989) 63 *ALJ* 592–94.

[8] *Open Government*, 1993, HMSO. See below, pp 371–3, for discussion.

were expressly excluded from its ambit, leaving them unprotected from employment detriment.

The UK has traditionally resisted freedom of information legislation and, until 1989, criminalized the unauthorized disclosure of any official information at all, however trivial, under s 2 of the Official Secrets Act 1911, thereby creating a climate of secrecy in the Civil Service which greatly hampered the efforts of those who wished to obtain and publish information about the workings of government. The Freedom of Information Act 2000 signalled a break with the traditional culture of secrecy: 'the principle that communication was the privilege of the State rather than of the citizen was at last . . . reversed'.[9]

OFFICIAL SECRETS

SECTION 2 OF THE OFFICIAL SECRETS ACT 1911[10]

During the 19th century, as government departments grew larger and handled more official information, the problem of confidentiality grew more acute. Internal circulars such as the 1873 Treasury minute entitled *The Premature Disclosure of Official Information* urged secrecy on all members of government departments and threatened the dismissal of civil servants who disclosed any information; a Treasury minute issued in 1875 warned civil servants of the dangers of close links with the press.[11] The need for a further safeguard was emphasized in 1878 when one Marvin, who worked in the Foreign Office, gave details of a secret treaty negotiated between England and Russia to a particular newspaper. His motive appeared to be dissatisfaction with his job. He was prosecuted, but it was then discovered that no part of the criminal law covered the situation. He had memorized the information and thus had not stolen any document. He was not a spy and could not, therefore, be brought within the provisions of the Treason Act 1814. No conviction could be obtained and the Official Secrets Act 1889 was passed largely as a means of plugging the gap which had been discovered.

The 1889 Act made it an offence for a person wrongfully to communicate information obtained owing to his employment as a civil servant. However, the government grew dissatisfied with this measure; under its terms, the State had the burden of proving both *mens rea* and that the disclosure was not in the interests of the State. It was thought that a stronger measure was needed, and this led eventually to the passing of the Official Secrets Act 1911. It has often been suggested that the manner of its introduction into Parliament was disingenuous and misleading.[12] It was introduced

---

9 Vincent, *The Culture of Secrecy, Britain 1832–1998*, Oxford: OUP, 1998, p 321.
10 See D. Hooper, *Official Secrets*, London: Secker and Warburg, 1987, for history of the use of s 2.
11 See Robertson, op cit, at 53.
12 See *The Franks Report*, Cmnd 5104, 1972, para 50; Birkinshaw, op cit, at 76.

apparently in response to fears of espionage and by the Secretary of State for War, not by the Home Secretary, giving the impression that it was largely an anti-espionage measure. Section 1 did deal largely with espionage, but s 2 was aimed not at enemy agents, but at English civil servants and other crown employees. It was called, innocuously, 'an Act to re-enact the 1889 Act with amendments'. These disarming measures seem to have succeeded; it was passed in one afternoon and s 2 received no debate at all.

Section 2, which appeared to create a crime of strict liability, imposed a complete prohibition on the unauthorized dissemination of official information, however trivial. It is thought that the government clearly intended s 2 to have such a wide scope and had wanted such a provision for some time in order to prevent leaks of *any* kind of official information, whether or not connected with defence or national security.[13] It lacked any provision regarding the substance of the information disclosed so that technically it criminalized, for example, disclosure of the colour of the carpet in a minister's office. It criminalized the receiver of information as well as the communicator, although there did appear to be a requirement of *mens rea* as far as the receiver was concerned; he or she had to know that the disclosure had occurred in contravention of the Act. Thus, it afforded no recognition to the role of the press in informing the public.

There were surprisingly few prosecutions under s 2; it seems likely that it created an acceptance of secrecy in the civil service which tended to preclude disclosure. In one of the few cases which did come to court, *Fell*,[14] the Court of Appeal confirmed that liability was not dependent on the contents of the document in question or on whether the disclosure would have an effect prejudicial to the interests of the State. The eventual demise of s 2 came about owing to a number of factors, of which one appears to have been the realization that its draconian nature was perceived as unacceptable in a modern democracy and that, therefore, convictions under it could not be assured. Such a realization probably developed in response to the following three decisions, all of which reveal the direct interest the media has in official secrecy.

Aitken and Others[15] arose from the disclosure by a reporter, Aitken, that the UK Government had misled the British people as to the amount of aid the UK was giving Nigeria in its war against Biafra. The Government had suggested that it was supplying about 15 per cent of Nigeria's arms, whereas the figure should have been about 70 per cent. This figure derived from a Government document called the Scott Report, which Aitken disclosed to the press. Aitken was then prosecuted under s 2 for receiving and passing on information, but the judge at trial, Caulfield J, clearly had little sympathy with a case seemingly brought merely to assuage government embarrassment and which disclosed no national security interest. Furthermore, the facts obtained from the Scott Report were obtainable from other sources. The judge found that a requirement of *mens rea* was needed and, moreover, effectively directed the jury to acquit in a

---

[13] See ibid, at [50].   [14] [1963] Crim LR 207.
[15] Unreported. See J. Aitken, *Officially Secret*, London: Weidenfeld & Nicholson, 1971.

speech which placed weight on the freedom of the press and suggested that it should prevail given the lack of a significant competing interest. He considered that s 2 should be 'pensioned off'.

Tisdall[16] also created some adverse publicity for the government, owing to what was perceived as a very heavy-handed use of s 2. Sarah Tisdall worked in the Foreign Secretary's private office, and in the course of her duties she came across documents relating to the delivery of cruise missiles to the RAF base at Greenham Common. She discovered proposals to delay the announcement of their delivery until after it had occurred and to make the announcement in Parliament at the end of question time in order to avoid answering questions. She took the view that this political subterfuge was morally wrong and therefore leaked the documents to *The Guardian*. However, they were eventually traced back to her. She pleaded guilty to an offence under s 2 and received a prison sentence of six months—an outcome which was generally seen as harsh.[17]

A similar situation arose in *Ponting*,[18] the case which is usually credited with sounding the death knell of s 2. Clive Ponting, a senior civil servant in the Ministry of Defence, was responsible for policy on the operational activities of the Royal Navy at a time when opposition MPs, particularly Tam Dalyell, were pressing the government for information relating to the sinking of the *Belgrano* in the Falklands conflict. Michael Heseltine, then Secretary of State for Defence, decided to withhold such information from Parliament and therefore did not use a reply to parliamentary questions drafted by Ponting. He used instead a much briefer version of it and circulated a confidential minute indicating that answers on the rules of engagement in the Falklands conflict should not be given to questions put by the Parliamentary Select Committee on Foreign Affairs. Feeling that opposition MPs were being prevented from undertaking effective scrutiny of the workings of government, Ponting sent the unused reply and the minute anonymously to the Labour MP Tam Dalyell, who disclosed the documents to the press.

Ponting was charged with the offence of communicating information under s 2. The relevant sub-section reads:

... it is an offence for a person holding Crown office to communicate official information to any person other than a person he is authorised to communicate it to or a person to whom it is *in the interests of the State* his duty to communicate it. (emphasis added)

The defence relied on the phrase the 'interests of the State', arguing that the term 'the State' should be interpreted as 'the organized community' rather than the government. This interpretation seemed to be warranted by part of Lord Reid's judgment in *Chandler v DPP*.[19] Thus, it could be argued that it was in the interests of the nation as a whole that Parliament should not be misled and that there was a moral duty to

---

[16] (1984) *The Times*, 26 March.   [17] See Cripps, op cit.
[18] [1985] Crim LR 318; for comment, see G. Brewry, 'The *Ponting* case' [1985] *PL* 203, 212 and [1986] *Crim LR* 491.
[19] [1964] AC 763; [1962] 3 All ER 142, HL.

prevent this. The word 'duty' in s 2, it was claimed, therefore connoted a moral or public duty. However, the Crown relied upon other comments of Lord Reid in *Chandler* to the effect that where national security was a factor, the government would be the final arbiter of the State's interests. The judge, McCowan J, accepted this argument, finding that the 'interests of the State' were synonymous with those of the government of the day, and he therefore effectively directed the jury to convict. Despite this direction, they acquitted, presumably feeling that Ponting should have a defence if he was acting in the public interest in trying to prevent government suppression of matters of public interest. The prosecution and its outcome provoked considerable adverse publicity, the public perceiving it as an attempt at a cover-up which had failed, not because the judge showed integrity, but because the jury did.[20]

The decision in *Ponting* suggested that the very width of s 2 was undermining its credibility; its usefulness in instilling a culture of secrecy owing to its catch-all quality was seen as working against it. The outcome of the case may have influenced the decision not to prosecute Cathy Massiter, a former officer in the Security Service, in respect of her claims in a Channel 4 programme screened in March 1985 (*MI5's Official Secrets*) that MI5 had tapped the phones of trade union members and placed leading CND members under surveillance.[21] Section 2's lack of credibility may also have been a factor in the decision to bring civil as opposed to criminal proceedings against *The Guardian* and *The Observer* in respect of their disclosure of Peter Wright's allegations in *Spycatcher*: civil proceedings for breach of confidence were, in many ways, more convenient and certainly less risky than a s 2 prosecution. No jury would be involved and a temporary injunction could be obtained quickly in *ex parte* proceedings. However, the government did consider that the criminal rather than the civil law was, in general, a more appropriate weapon to use against people such as Ponting, and therefore thought it desirable that an effective criminal sanction should be available. When the government was eventually defeated in the *Spycatcher* litigation, the need for such a sanction became clearer.[22]

There had already been a long history of proposals for the reform of s 2. The Franks Committee, which was set up in response to Caulfield J's comments in *Aitken*, recommended[23] that s 2 should be replaced by narrower provisions which took into account the nature of the information disclosed. The Franks proposals formed the basis of the Government's White Paper on which the Official Secrets Act 1989 was

---

[20] For comment on the decision, see C. Ponting, *The Right to Know*, London: Sphere Books, 1985; Brewry, op cit.

[21] The Independent Broadcasting Association banned the programme pending the decision as to whether Massiter and the producers would be prosecuted. The decision not to prosecute was announced by Sir Michael Havers on 5 March 1985. An inquiry into telephone tapping by Lord Bridge reported on 6 March that all taps had been properly authorized. This, of course, did not address the allegation that some tapping had been carried out although unauthorized.

[22] *AG v Guardian (No 2)* [1990] 1 AC 109 (see below, at 950–3).

[23] *Report of the Committee on s 2 of the Official Secrets Act 1911*, Cmnd 5104, 1972; see W. Birtles, 'Big brother knows best: the Franks Report on section 2 of the Official Secrets Act' [1973] *PL* 100.

based. There had been various other attempts at reform; those put forward as Private Members' Bills were the more liberal. For example, Clement Freud MP put forward an Official Information Bill[24] which would have created a public right of access to official information, while the Protection of Official Information Bill,[25] put forward by Richard Shepherd MP in 1987, would have provided a public interest defence and a defence of prior disclosure.

THE OFFICIAL SECRETS ACT 1989[26]

Once the decision to reform the area of official secrecy had been taken, an opportunity was created for radical change, which could have included freedom of information legislation along the lines of the instruments in America and Canada. However, it was made clear from the outset that the legislation was unconcerned with freedom of information.[27] It decriminalizes disclosure of some official information, although an official who makes such disclosure may, of course, face an action for breach of confidence as well as disciplinary proceedings, but it makes no provision for allowing the release of any official documents into the public domain. Thus, claims made, for example, by Douglas Hurd (the then Home Secretary) that it is 'a great liberalising measure', clearly rest on other aspects of the Act. Aspects which are usually viewed as liberalizing features include the categorization of information covered which makes relevant the *substance* of the information, the introduction of tests for harm, the *mens rea* requirement of ss 5 and 6, the defences available and decriminalization of the receiver of information. In all these respects, the Act differs from its predecessor, but the nature of the changes has led commentators to question whether they will bring about any real liberalization.[28] Other aspects of the Act have also attracted criticism: it applies to persons other than Crown servants, including journalists; it contains no defences of public interest or of prior disclosure and no general requirement to prove *mens rea*. Thus, what is omitted from its provisions, including the failure to provide any right of access to information falling outside the protected categories, is arguably as significant as what is included. The Human Rights Act may provide a means of tempering the effects of the 1989 Act. There is obviously a tension between the two statutes, since the one binds public authorities—which includes government departments—under s 6 to observe the Convention rights, including the right to freedom of expression, while the other creates criminal liability for disclosure of information, whether or not the disclosure is in the public interest. Further, the 1989

---

[24] 1978–79, Bill 96.   [25] 1987–88, Bill 20.

[26] For comment on the 1989 Act see S. Palmer, 'The Government proposals for reforming s 2 of the Official Secrets Act 1911' [1988] *PL* 523; W. Hanbury, 'Illiberal reform of s 2' (1989) 133 *Sol Jo* 587; S. Palmer, 'Tightening secrecy law' [1990] *PL* 243; J. Griffith, 'The Official Secrets Act 1989' (1989) 16 *JLS* 273; D. Feldman, *Civil Liberties and Human Rights*, 1st edn, Oxford: OUP, 1993, Chapter 14.3.

[27] See the White Paper on s 2, Cmnd 7285, 1978; the Green Paper on *Freedom of Information*, Cmnd 7520, 1979; White Paper: *Reform of the Official Secrets Act 1911*, Cmnd 408, 1988.

[28] e.g., Ewing and Gearty, *Freedom under Thatcher*, Oxford: Clarendon, 1990, at 200.

Act must be interpreted under s 3 of the HRA so as to render it compatible with the Convention rights. The tension between the two was explored in the preliminary hearing in the *Shayler*[29] case (discussed below) in which it was argued unsuccessfully that s 1 of the 1989 Act is incompatible with Article 10. Below, the possible effects of Article 10 on the Official Secrets Act are indicated.

Criminal liability for disclosing information

The general prohibition on disclosing information under the Official Secrets Act 1911 was replaced by the more specific prohibitions under the Official Secrets Act 1989. Sections 1–4 of the 1989 Act (excepting the provisions of s 1(1)), which also determine the categorization of the information, all concern unauthorized disclosures by any present or former Crown servant or government contractor of information which has been acquired in the course of his or her employment. If a civil servant happened to acquire by other means information falling within one of the categories which he or she then disclosed, the provisions of s 5 would apply. Section 7 (below) governs the meaning of 'authorization', while ss 5 and 6 apply when *any* person—not only a Crown servant—discloses information falling within the protected categories. Security and intelligence information is covered by s 1. The category covers 'the work of or in support of, the security and intelligence services' and includes 'references to information held or transmitted by those services or by persons in support of . . . those services'.[30]

It is, therefore, a wide category and is not confined only to work done by members of the security and intelligence services. Section 1(1) is intended to prevent members or former members of the security services (and any person notified that he is subject to the provisions of the sub-section) disclosing anything at all relating or appearing to relate to[31] the operation of those services. All such members thus come under a lifelong duty to keep silent even though their information might reveal a serious abuse of power in the security services or some operational weakness. There is no need to show that any harm will or may flow from the disclosure, and so all information, however trivial, is covered. On its face, this blanket ban raises one of the most serious *prima facie* incompatibilities with Article 10. It is therefore worth examining briefly the Government arguments for such a ban. Essentially, four main reasons were put forward.[32]

First, it was argued that disclosures by agents or former agents carry particular credibility; however, this is presumably only relevant if the disclosure is in fact harmful. If the disclosure itself is anodyne, then its extra authority makes no difference. This therefore does not provide an argument for a blanket ban. Second, it was said that

---

[29] Preparatory hearing: (2001) *The Times*, 10 October, 98(40) LSG 40; CA.   [30] Section 1(9).

[31] Under s 1(2), misinformation falls within the information covered by s 1(1) as it includes 'making any statement which purports to be a disclosure of such information or which is intended to be taken as being such a disclosure'.

[32] They are summarized in the White Paper, op cit, at [40].

such disclosures reduce confidence of the public in the security services' ability and loyalty. This is (a) speculative and (b) not very convincing. If non-harmful revelations were made, it is unlikely that they would affect the publics' view. Moreover, it begs the question why the public should have an exaggeratedly positive view of the ability of the security services. Why is it especially important that the public at large have a positive view of the abilities of the security services, any more than, say, the armed forces or the Cabinet?

Third, it is said that disclosures by agents or former agents ought to be criminal because of the special duty of secrecy that the members of the security services accept. This is a circular argument: that special duty of secrecy is imposed by the law—of the OSA, and the law of confidence. This cannot be an argument for determining what the law should in fact be. Fourthly, it is said that because governments do not traditionally comment on assertions about the security services, a false report made by a former agent could be as damaging as a true one, because it would go undenied. Against this, it may be said that governments could simply make an exception to this general rule when a *former* agent is involved. Moreover, this argument again posits only a possible harm, that might come about in particular cases, not an invariable one. In fact, the Government did deny aspects of the claims made by former agent David Shayler: in particular his assertion that the SIS had planned for the assassination of Colonel Gadaffi was vigorously rebutted.[33] A further point to be noted about section 1(1) is that there is no defence that the material released was already in the public domain. This runs clearly counter to the finding both in *Attorney General v Guardian Newspapers Ltd (No 2)*[34] and in *Observer and Guardian v UK*[35] that the maintenance of a ban on the publication of information when it has entered the public domain is contrary to both common law and Article 10.[36]

Similar in nature to the blanket prohibition in section 1(1), and therefore considered here, is section 4(3), which covers information obtained by the use of intercept and security service warrants.[37] There is no harm test under this category. Thus, in so far as it covers the work of the security services, it creates a wide exception to the general need to show harm under s 1(3) when a Crown servant who is not a member of the security services makes a disclosure about the work of those services. The Government's defence of this blanket ban is as follows:

no information obtained by means of interception can be disclosed without assisting

---

[33] See Best, op cit, at 20.   [34] [1990] 1 AC 109.

[35] (1991) 14 EHRR 153; for comment see I. Leigh, 'Spycatcher in Strasbourg' [1992] PL 200–08.

[36] As was argued in the *Shayler* case: op cit.

[37] This applies to (a) any information obtained by reason of the interception of any communication in obedience to a warrant issued under s 2 of the Regulation of Investigatory Powers Act 2000, any information relating to the obtaining of information by reason of any such interception and any document or other article which is or has been used or held for use in or has been obtained by reason of any such interception; and (b) any information obtained by reason of action authorised by a warrant issued under s 3 of the Security Service Act 1989, any information relating to the obtaining of information by reason of any such action and any document or other article which is or has been used or held for use in or has been obtained by reason of any such action.

terrorism or crime, damaging national security or seriously breaching the privacy of private citizens.[38]

This is simply implausible. As for the privacy point, the *nature* of the information gained through phone tapping (e.g. details of a large drug transaction) may barely engage private life, although the mode of interception does, and there may be very strong public interest arguments on the other side sufficient to make the interference with private life proportionate. The fact that privacy is in question does not begin to justify a blanket ban on disclosure: to have such a ban does not allow for a balancing between Articles 10 and 8 but simply creates an abrogation of one at the expense of the other. It is not clear that the first part of the statement can be taken seriously: whether any damage would be caused by such revelations would plainly depend upon what was disclosed, and what information revealed thereby about the techniques of the security services.

The White Paper also addressed the argument that there should be a general public interest to which all the offences in the Act would be subject. It first of all deliberately mischaracterizes this argument—that there should be a defence of making revelations that were in the public interest, judged objectively—as being an argument that a defendant's good *motivation* should be a defence. The White Paper correctly states that the general rule is that motive is not relevant and that there are good grounds for sticking to this general rule.[39] This is true, but simply irrelevant: the argument about the public interest test does not revolve around motivation. The White Paper adds to this:

the proposals in this White Paper are designed to concentrate the protection of the criminal law on information which demonstrably requires its protection in the public interest. It cannot be acceptable that a person can lawfully disclose information which he knows may, for example, lead to loss of life simply because he conceives that he has a general reason of a public character for doing so.[40]

This is extraordinarily poor reasoning. The first sentence is simply question-begging: by including a blanket ban on *all* disclosures by members and former members of the security services, it clearly covers information that is *not* required to be protected in the public interest. The example given is simply a gross exaggeration. No-one is arguing for a defence for those who release information risking life; secondly, the wording 'because *he* conceives' implies that what is being argued for is a subjective test, rather than, of course, the actual objective public interest that is being proposed.

A more general, final concern about the White Paper is that it nowhere mentions Article 10 ECHR. As Lord Hope commented in *Shayler*, this 'leaves one with the uneasy feeling that . . . the problems which it raises were overlooked'.[41] The point is returned to below.

Section 1(3), which criminalizes disclosure of information relating to the security services by a former or present *Crown servant*, as opposed to a member of the security services, does include a test for harm under s 1(4), which provides that:

[38] Op cit, at [53].   [39] Op cit, at [59–60].   [40] Ibid, at [60].   [41] Op cit, at [41]

. . . a disclosure is damaging if:

(a) it causes damage to the work of or any part of, the security and intelligence services; or

(b) it is of information or a document or other article which is such that its un-authorised disclosure would be likely to cause such damage or which falls within a class or description of information, documents or articles the unauthorised disclosure of which would be likely to have that effect.

Taken at its lowest level, it is clear that this test may be very readily satisfied: it is not necessary to show that disclosure of the actual document in question has caused harm or would be likely to cause harm, merely that it belongs to a class of documents, disclosure of which would be *likely* to have that effect. Disclosure of a document containing insignificant information and incapable itself of causing the harm described under s 1(4)(a) can, therefore, be criminalized, suggesting that the importation of a harm test for Crown servants as opposed to members of the security services may not inevitably in practice create a very significant distinction between them. However, at the next level, harm must be likely to flow from disclosure of a specific document where, owing to its unique nature, it cannot be said to be one of a class of documents.

In such an instance, the ruling of the House of Lords in *Lord Advocate v Scotsman Publications Ltd*[42] suggests that the test for harm may be quite restrictively interpreted: it will be necessary to show quite a strong likelihood that harm will arise and the nature of the harm must be specified. The ruling was given in the context of civil proceedings for breach of confidence, but the House of Lords decided the case on the basis of the principles under the 1989 Act even though it was not then in force. The ruling concerned publication by a journalist of material relating to the work of the intelligence services. Thus, the test for harm had to be interpreted, according to s 5, in accordance with the test under s 1(3) as though the disclosure had been by a Crown servant. The Crown conceded that the information in question was innocuous, but argued that harm would be done because the publication would undermine confidence in the security services. The House of Lords, noting that there had already been a degree of prior publication, rejected this argument as unable alone to satisfy the test for harm. The case therefore gives some indication as to the interpretation the harm tests may receive. This ruling affords some protection for journalistic expression concerning the intelligence services which, under the HRA, would be in accordance with the high value Strasbourg has placed on expression critical of the workings of the State and State agents.[43]

Even taken at its highest level, the harm test is potentially very wide because of its open-textured wording. It states, in effect, that a disclosure of information in this category is damaging if it causes damage to the area of government operation covered

---

[42] [1990] 1 AC 812; [1989] 2 All ER 852, HL; for criticism of the ruling, see Walker [1990] *PL* 354.

[43] See *Thorgeirson v Iceland* (1992) 14 EHRR 843; *The Observer and the Guardian v UK* (1991) 14 EHRR 153. For discussion, see Chapter 2 at 50–5 and 61–8; Chapter 21 at 1056–64 (in the context of Article 10 deformation cases).

by the category. No clue is given as to what is meant by 'damage'; in many cases it would, therefore, be impossible for a Crown servant to determine beforehand whether or not a particular disclosure would be criminal. The only safe approach would be non-disclosure of almost all relevant information; the position of Crown servants under the 1989 Act in relation to information in this category is therefore only with some difficulty to be distinguished from that under the 1911 Act. However, the fact that there is a test for harm at all under s 1(3), however weak, affirms a distinction of perhaps symbolic importance between two groups of Crown servants because the first step in determining whether a disclosure may be criminalized is taken by reference to the *status* of the person making the disclosure rather than by the nature of the information, suggesting that s 1(1) is aimed at underpinning a culture of secrecy in the security services rather than at ensuring that no damaging disclosure is likely to be made.

Section 2 covers information relating to defence. What is meant by defence is set out in s 2(4):

(a) the size, shape, organisation, logistics, order of battle, deployment, operations, state of readiness and training of the armed forces of the Crown;

(b) the weapons, stores or other equipment of those forces and the invention, development, production and operation of such equipment and research relating to it;

(c) defence policy and strategy and military planning and intelligence;

(d) plans and measures for the maintenance of essential supplies and services that are or would be needed in time of war.

It must be shown that the disclosure in question is or would be likely to be damaging as defined under s 2(2):

(a) it damages the capability of, or of any part of, the armed forces of the Crown to carry out their tasks or leads to loss of life or injury to members of those forces or serious damage to the equipment or installations of those forces; or

(b) otherwise than as mentioned in para (a) above, it endangers the interests of the United Kingdom abroad, seriously obstructs the promotion or protection by the United Kingdom of those interests or endangers the safety of British citizens abroad; or

(c) it is of information or of a document or article which is such that its unauthorised disclosure would be likely to have any of those effects.

The first part of this test under (a), which is fairly specific and deals with quite serious harm, may be contrasted with (b), which is much wider. The opening words of (b) may mean that, although the *subject* of the harm may fall within (a), the level of harm can be considered within (b) since it does not fall within terms denoting harm used in (a). This could occur where, for example, there had been *damage* as opposed to 'serious damage' to installations abroad. Clearly, this interpretation would allow the harm test to be satisfied in a wider range of situations. On this interpretation, as far as disclosures concerning UK armed forces operating *abroad* are concerned, it would seem that (b) renders (a) largely redundant, so that (a) would tend to play a role only where the disclosure concerned operations within the UK. It may be noted that parts of this test are mere verbiage; it would be hard to draw a significant distinction between 'endangering' and 'seriously obstructing' the interests of the UK abroad. In fact, the overlapping of the harm tests within the categories and across the categories is a feature of this statute; the reasons why this may be so are considered below.

Information relating to international relations falls within s 3(1)(a). This category covers disclosure of 'any information, document or other article relating to international relations'. Clarification of this provision is undertaken by s 3(5), which creates a test to be used in order to determine whether information falls within it. First, it must concern the relations between States, between international organizations, or between an international organization and a State; secondly, it is said that this includes matter which is capable of affecting the relation between the UK and another State, or between the UK and an international organization. The harm test arises under s 3(2) and is identical to that arising under s 2(2)(b) and (c).

Section 3(1)(b) refers to confidential information emanating from other States or international organizations. This category covers 'any confidential information, document or other article which was obtained from a State other than the United Kingdom or an international organisation'. Clearly, the substance of this information might differ from that covered under s 3(1)(a), although some documents might fall within both categories. Under s 3(6), the information will be confidential if it is expressed to be so treated due to the terms under which it was obtained or if the circumstances in which it was obtained impute an obligation of confidence. The harm test under this category contained in s 3(3) is somewhat curious: the mere fact that the information is confidential or its nature or contents 'may' be sufficient to establish the likelihood that its disclosure would cause harm within the terms of s 3(2)(b) (which uses the terms of s 2(2)(b)). In other words, once the information is identified as falling within this category, a fiction is created that harm may automatically flow from its disclosure. This implies that there are circumstances (such as a particularly strong quality of confidentiality?) in which the only ingredient that the prosecution *must* prove is that the information falls within the category.

Given that s 3(3) uses the word 'may', thereby introducing uncertainty into the section, there is greater leeway for imposing a Convention-friendly interpretation on it. If the word 'may' is interpreted strictly, the circumstances in which it would be unnecessary to show harm would be greatly curtailed. It could then be argued that since harm or its likelihood must be shown, the harm test itself must be interpreted compatibly with Article 10. It would have to be shown that the interference in question answered to a pressing social need.[44] Depending on the circumstances, it could be argued that if, ultimately, the 'interests of the UK abroad' would be benefited by the disclosure, or on balance little affected, no pressing social need to interfere with the expression in question could be shown.

---

[44] *Sunday Times v UK* (1979) 2 EHRR 737. For discussion of the Article 10 requirements, see generally Chapter 2.

Section 4 is headed 'crime and special investigation powers'. Section 4(2) covers any information the disclosure of which:

(a) ... results in the commission of an offence; or facilitates an escape from legal custody or the doing of any other act prejudicial to the safekeeping of persons in legal custody; or impedes the prevention or detection of offences or the apprehension or prosecution of suspected offenders; or

(b) which is such that its unauthorised disclosure would be likely to have any of those effects.

'Legal custody' includes detention in pursuance of any enactment or any instrument made under an enactment (s 4(6)). In contrast to s 3(3), in which the test for harm may be satisfied once the information is identified as falling within the category, in s 4(2), once the test for harm has been satisfied, the information will necessarily be so identified. As with s 2, parts of this test could have been omitted, such as 'facilitates an escape', which would have been covered by the succeeding general words.

Section 5 is headed, 'information resulting from unauthorised disclosures or entrusted in confidence'. This is not a new category. Information will fall within s 5 if it falls within one or more of the previous categories and it has been disclosed to the defendant by a Crown servant, or falls within s 1 of the Official Secrets Act 1911. Section 5 is primarily aimed at journalists who receive information leaked to them by Crown servants, although it could of course cover anybody in that position. It is also aimed at the person to whom a document is entrusted by a Crown servant 'on terms requiring it to be held in confidence or in circumstances in which the Crown servant or government contractor could reasonably expect that it would be so held'.[45] The difference between entrusting and disclosing is significant in that, in the former instance, the document—but not the information it contains—will have been entrusted to the care of the person in question.[46]

These provisions are presumably aimed mainly at the journalist or other non-Crown servant who receives the information from another journalist who received it from the civil servant in question. However, this does not apply where the information has been *entrusted* to the defendant, but has never been *disclosed* to him or her; in that case, it must come directly from the civil servant, not from another person who had it entrusted to him or her.[47] The disclosure of the information or document by the person into whose possession it has come must not already be an offence under any of the six categories.

Since s 5 is aimed at journalists and potentially represents an interference with their role of informing the public, it requires a very strict interpretation under s 3 of the HRA, in accordance with Article 10, bearing in mind the emphasis placed by

[45] s 5(1)(ii)).
[46] If the Crown servant has disclosed or entrusted it to another who discloses it to the defendant, this will suffice (s 5(1)(a)(i) and (iii)).
[47] (s 5(1)(b)(ii)).

Strasbourg on the importance of that role.[48] In contrast to disclosure of information by a Crown servant under ss 1–4, s 5 does import a requirement of *mens rea* under s 5(2) which, as far as information falling within ss 1, 2, and 3 is concerned, consists of three elements. The defendant must disclose the information knowing or having reasonable cause to believe that it falls within one or more of the categories, that it has come into his possession as mentioned in sub-section (1) above and that it will be damaging.[49] As far as information falling within s 4 and probably s 3(1)(b) is concerned, only the first two of these elements will be relevant. Under s 5(6), only the first of these elements need be proved if the information came into the defendant's possession as a result of a contravention of s 1 of the Official Secrets Act 1911. Thus, as far as disclosure of such information is concerned, the *mens rea* requirement will be fulfilled even though the defendant believed that the disclosure would not be damaging and intended that it should not be. Indeed, since the *mens rea* includes an objective element, it may be satisfied under all the categories where the defendant did not in fact possess the belief in question, but had reasonable cause to possess it.

The requirement of *mens rea*, although not as strict as may at first appear, represents the only means of differentiating between journalists and Crown servants. The test for damage will be determined as it would be if the information was disclosed by a Crown servant in contravention of ss 1(3), 2(1), or 3(1) above. A court could afford recognition to the significance of the journalistic role, as required by Article 10, by placing a strong emphasis on the *mens rea* requirement. Where a journalist appeared to be acting in the public interest in making the disclosure, it would be possible for a court to interpret the *mens rea* requirement as disproved on the basis that it would be impossible to show that the defendant knew or should have known that the disclosure was damaging to the interest in question if on one view (even if mistaken) it could be seen as beneficial to it, and that was the view that the journalist took.

Section 4 is not mentioned, because the information will not be capable of falling within s 4(1) unless the harm test is satisfied. As already mentioned, there is no harm test under s 4(3). Thus, an interesting anomaly arises: if, for example, information relating to the work of MI5 is disclosed to a journalist by a security service agent, a distinction is drawn between disclosure by the agent and by the journalist: in general, it will not be assumed in the case of the latter that the disclosure will cause harm, but if the information relates to (say) telephone tapping, no such distinction is drawn. If the journalist is then charged with an offence falling within s 5 due to the disclosure of information under s (3), both he or she and the agent will be in an equally disadvantageous position as far as the harm test is concerned. The apparent recognition of journalistic duty effected by importing the harm test under s 1(3) into the situation where a security service member discloses information to a journalist, may therefore be circumvented where such information also falls within s 4(3).

---

[48] See, e.g., *Goodwin v UK* (1996) 22 EHRR 123. See also note 43 above. For discussion of s 3 HRA, see Chapter 3 at 157–63.
[49] (s 5(3)(b)).

Another apparent improvement which might tend to affect journalists more than others is the decriminalization of the receiver of information. If he or she refrains from publishing it, no liability will be incurred. Of course, this improvement might be said to be more theoretical than real, in that it was perhaps unlikely that the mere receiver would be prosecuted under the 1911 Act, even though that possibility did exist. The fact that journalists were included at all in the net of criminal liability under s 5 has been greatly criticized on the basis that some recognition should be given to the important role of the press in informing the public about government policy and actions.[50] In arguing for a restrictive interpretation of s 5 under s 3 of the HRA, a comparison could be drawn with the constitutional role of the press recognized in America by the *Pentagon Papers* case:[51] the Supreme Court determined that no restraining order on the press could be made so that the press would remain free to censure the government.

Section 6 covers the unauthorized publication abroad of information which falls into one of the other substantive categories apart from crime and special investigation powers. It covers the disclosure to a UK citizen of information which has been received in confidence from the UK by another State or international organization. Typically, the section might cover a leak of such information to a foreign journalist who then passed it on to a UK journalist. However, liability will not be incurred if the State or organization (or a member of the organization) authorizes the disclosure of the information to the public (s 6(3)). Again, since this section is aimed at journalists, a requirement of *mens rea* is imported: it must be shown under s 6(2) that the defendant made 'a damaging disclosure of [the information] knowing or having reasonable cause to believe that it is such as is mentioned in subsection (1) above and that its disclosure would be damaging'. However, it is important to note that under s 6(4), the test for harm under this section is to be determined 'as it would be in relation to a disclosure of the information, document or article in question by a Crown servant in contravention of s 1(3), 2(1) and 3(1) above'. Thus, although it appears that two tests must be satisfied in order to fulfil the *mens rea* requirement, the tests may in fact be conflated as far as s 3(1)(b) is concerned because proof that the defendant knew that the information fell within the relevant category may satisfy the requirement that he or she knew that the disclosure would be damaging. The requirement that *mens rea* be established is not, therefore, as favourable to the defendant as it appears to be because—as noted in respect of s 5—it may be satisfied even where the defendant believes that no damage will result. Once again, aside from this particular instance, this applies in all the categories due to the objective element in the *mens rea* arising from the words 'reasonable cause to believe'.

The requirement that the information, document or article is communicated in confidence will be satisfied as under s 3 if it is communicated in 'circumstances in which the person communicating it could reasonably expect that it would be so held' (s 6(5)). In other words, it need not be expressly designated 'confidential'.

A disclosure will not lead to liability under the Act if it is authorized, and so it is

---

[50] See, e.g., Ewing and Gearty, op cit, at 196–201.   [51] *New York Times Co v US* (1971) 403 US 713.

necessary to determine whether or not authorization has taken place. The meaning of 'authorised disclosures' is determined by s 7. A disclosure will be authorized if it is made in accordance with the official duty of the Crown servant or a person in whose case a notification for the purposes of s 1(1) is in force. As far as a government contractor is concerned, a disclosure will be authorized if made 'in accordance with an official authorisation' or 'for the purposes of the functions by virtue of which he is a government contractor and without contravening an official restriction'. A disclosure made by any other person will be authorized if it is made to a Crown servant for the purposes of his functions as such; or in accordance with an official authorization.

Defences

The defence available to Crown servants arises in each of the different categories and reads:

... it is a defence to prove that at the time of the alleged offence he did not know and had no reasonable cause to believe that the information, document or article in question was such as is mentioned (in the relevant subsection) or that its disclosure would be damaging within the meaning of that subsection.

Belief in authorization will also provide a defence under s 7. Thus, the Act appears to provide three defences for Crown servants: first, that the defendant did not know and had no reasonable cause to believe that the information fell into the category in question; secondly, that he or she did not know and had no reasonable cause to believe that the information would cause harm; and thirdly, that he or she believed that he or she had lawful authorization to make the disclosure *and* had no reasonable cause to believe otherwise. However, it is unclear whether there are three defences or only two; the Act may be read as requiring the defendant to prove that he or she did not know that the information fell into a particular category and that it was not realized that it would cause harm. This would arise if the word 'or' which links the first and second defences is expressed conjunctively: the defendant might be able to satisfy the second requirement but not the first, and therefore would find no protection from this defence.

The first two defences may be conflated in certain categories, largely because the second defence is intimately tied up with the harm tests and therefore, like them, operates on a number of levels. Where the harm test operates at its lowest level, only the first defence is available. Thus, a person falling under ss 1(1) or 4(3) has no opportunity at all of arguing that, for example, the triviality of the information or the fact that it was already in the public domain had given rise to an expectation that its disclosure would cause no harm at all. At the next level, under s 3(1)(b), because the test for harm may be satisfied merely by showing that the information falls within the sub-section, the second defence could be viewed as more apparent than real and could therefore be categorized along with the defence under s 1 as non-existent. However, following the argument regarding the interpretation of the harm test under this section above, this defence could be afforded some substance, under s 3 of the HRA. Under s 1(3), the second defence is extremely circumscribed. It would not necessarily avail the defendant to prove that for various reasons, it was believed on reasonable grounds before the disclosure took place that it would not cause harm. So long as the prosecution could prove a likelihood that harm would be caused from disclosure of documents falling into the same class, the harm test under the section would be satisfied and the defendant would be forced to prove that he or she had no reasonable cause to believe that disclosure of documents of that class would cause harm—a more difficult task than showing this in relation to the particular disclosure in question.

Generally, under all the other categories the harm test allows for argument under both the first and second defences, assuming that they are expressed disjunctively. However, under s 4(4), the second defence alone applies to information falling within the category under s 4(2)(a), while the first alone applies to information likely to have those effects under s 4(2)(b). This is anomalous, as it means that the disclosure of information which had had the effect of preventing an arrest could be met by the defence that it was not expected to have that effect, while information which had not yet had such an effect, but might have in future, would not necessarily be susceptible to such a defence. So long as the disclosure of the document was in fact likely to have the effect mentioned, it would be irrelevant that the defendant, while appreciating that it might in general have such effects, considered that they would not arise in the particular instance. Thus, a broader defence would be available in respect of the more significant disclosure, but not in respect of the less significant. This effect arises because, under s 4(2), the first defence is contained in the second owing to the use of the harm test as the means of identifying the information falling within the section.

Thus, it is clear that the Act is less generous towards the defendant in terms of the defences it makes available than it appears to be at first glance. Moreover, it is important to note that, although it is a general principle of criminal law that a defendant need have only an honest belief in the existence of facts which give rise to a defence, under the Act a defendant must have an honest and reasonable belief in such facts. However, as indicated, s 3 of the HRA could be used to broaden the defences in certain respects.

The Act contains no explicit public interest defence and it follows from the nature of the harm tests that one cannot be implied into it; on the face of it, any good flowing from disclosure of the information in question cannot be considered, merely any harm that might be caused. Thus, while it may be accepted that the Act at least allows argument as to a defendant's state of knowledge (albeit of very limited scope in certain instances) in making a disclosure to be led before a jury, it does not allow for argument as to the good intentions of the persons concerned, who may believe with reason that no other effective means of exposing iniquity exists. In particular, the information may concern corruption at such a high level that internal methods of addressing the problem would be ineffective. Clearly, good intentions are normally irrelevant in criminal trials: not many would argue that a robber should be able to adduce evidence that he intended to use the proceeds of his robbery to help the poor.

However, it is arguable that an exception to this rule should be made in respect of the Official Secrets Act in the form of an objectively assessed 'public interest' debate. A statute aimed specifically at those best placed to know of corruption or malpractice in government should, in a democracy, allow such a defence. The fact that it does not argues strongly against the likelihood that it will have a liberalizing impact. However, s 3 of the HRA could be used creatively, as indicated, to seek to introduce such a defence—in effect—through the back door.

The *Shayler* litigation

Whether or not such a use of the HRA is possible in respect of categories of information covered by a harm test, it appears that it is not possible in respect of s 1(1) and s 4(1). David Shayler, a former member of MI6, was charged with an offence under s 1(1) and s 4(1) in respect of his allegations that MI6 had been involved in a plot to assassinate Colonel Gadafy; further allegations exposed, Shayler claimed, serious illegality on the part of MI6, and were necessary to avert threats to life and limb and to personal property.[52] A preliminary hearing was held regarding the effect of the Human Rights Act on s 1(1). It was argued that since s 1(1) and s 4(1) are of an absolute nature, they are incompatible with Article 10 of the Convention, under the Human Rights Act, owing to the requirement that interference with expression should be proportionate to the legitimate aim pursued. In other words it was not possible, using s 3 of the HRA to harmonize these provisions of the 1989 Act with the requirements of the Convention would not be possible, since the two were plainly incompatible. Therefore a declaration of incompatibility should be granted, under s 4 of the Act. This argument was rejected in *Shayler*[53] Judge Moses found that there was no need to rely on s 3 HRA since no incompatibility between Article 10 and s 1(1) arose.[54] He reached the conclusion that s 3 could be ignored in reliance on the finding of the Lord Chief Justice in *Donoghue v Poplar Housing and Regeneration Community Assoc Ltd and the Secretary of State for the Environment*;[55] he said that 'unless legislation would otherwise be in breach of the Convention s 3 can be ignored; so courts should always first ascertain whether, absent s 3, there would be any breach of the Convention'.[56] The conclusion that ss 1(1) and 4(1) were not in breach of Article 10 was reached on the basis that Mr Shayler did have an avenue by which he could seek to make the disclosures in question. There were various persons to whom the disclosure could be made, including those identified in s 12. Further, significantly, under s 7(3) of the 1989 Act a disclosure can be made to others if authorized; those empowered to afford authorization are identified in s 12. Shayler could have sought authorization to make his disclosures from those identified under s 21 or from those prescribed as persons who can give authorizations. Such persons or bodies now include the new

---

[52] *R v Shayler* [2003] 1 AC 247.

[53] 16 May 2001; this judgment is not reported, but extracts are contained in the Court of Appeal judgment [2001] 1 WLR 2206.

[54] Paragraph 78 of the transcript of the judgment of Moses J.

[55] [2001] 3 WLR 183.   [56] Ibid, at [75].

Tribunal established under the Regulation of Investigatory Powers Act 2000 s 65[57] and a Minister of the Crown. Such persons could have authorized disclosure to other persons *not* identified in s 12 or prescribed.

Also, Mr Justice Moses found, a refusal of authorization would be subject, as the Crown accepted in the instant case, to judicial review. The refusal to grant authority would have to comply with Article 10 due to s 6 HRA; if it did not, the court in the judicial review proceedings would be expected to say so.[58] Mr Justice Moses went on to say 'It is not correct . . . to say that a restriction [under s 1(12) and 4(1)] is imposed irrespective of the public interest in disclosure. If there is a public interest it is . . . not unreasonable to expect at least one of the very large number of persons identified [by reference to s 12 and to the bodies prescribed] to recognize the public interest and to act upon it.'[59] He went on to call the suggestion that all those so identified would not authorize the disclosure in such circumstances far-fetched. But he thought that even if that possibility might arise 'it is a step too far to say that the proportionality of this legislation must be judged in the light of the possibility that the courts themselves [in judicial review proceedings in respect of a refusal of authorization] would countenance suppression of a disclosure which they considered necessary to avert injury to life, limb or serious damage to property even before October 2000.' Therefore, he found that no absolute ban on disclosure was imposed.

The Court of Appeal agreed that the interference with freedom of expression was in proportion to the legitimate aim pursued—that of protecting national security on the basis that the members of the security services, and those who pass information to them, must be able to be sure that the information will remain secret. The Court of Appeal also agreed that for the reasons given the absence of a 'public interest' defence in the 1989 Act does not breach the Convention. Mr Justice Moses had stated that had he found otherwise he would have considered the use of s 3 of the HRA but would have rejected the possibility put forward on behalf of Shayler, of inserting the word 'lawful' into s 1(9) so that s 1(1) would only cover the *lawful* work of the secret services. He also rejected the similar argument in respect of s 4. In so finding, he again relied on *Donoghue v Poplar Housing and Regeneration Community Assoc Ltd and the Secretary of State for the Environment*[60] in which Lord Woolf said that s 3 does not entitle the court to legislate.[61] This decision means that s 3 need not be used in relation to s 1(1) and s 4(1), and it is probable that the same arguments would apply if, in respect of disclosure of information falling within other categories, the defence sought to introduce a public interest defence.

The House of Lords' judgment in the case contains some encouraging signs, in terms of the influence of Article 10 ECHR upon the judgment, but is ultimately open

---

[57] The old tribunals set up under s 7 of the Interception of Communications Act, s 5 of the Security Services Act 1989, and s 9 of the Intelligence Services Act 1994 were prescribed for this purpose under the Official Secrets Act 1989(Prescription) Order 1990 SI 1990/200 as amended by SI 1993/847. That prescription now applies to the single Tribunal.

[58] Paragraphs 25 and 26 of the Transcript.   [59] Ibid, at [54].   [60] Ibid.

[61] Ibid, at [75] and [76].

to the same criticisms as the earlier judgments. Essentially, the House found that the OSA 1989 did need to be read compatibly with the requirements of proportionality under Article 10, but that the method of seeking permission to reveal information provided in the Act rendered the relevant provisions proportionate. The encouraging point that was stressed by their Lordships, especially Lord Hope, was that, upon any judicial review of a refusal to authorize release of information, a full Article 10 analysis would apply and be used. However, as argued below, this is likely to be a moot point. Looking at the decision more closely, the problem with it appears to lie not in the assessment of what Strasbourg case law on Article 10 demands, but upon the conclusions drawn from that case law as applied to the OSA. Thus Lord Bingham states:

The acid test is whether, in all the circumstances, the interference with the individual's Convention right prescribed by national law is greater than is required to meet the legitimate object which the state seeks to achieve.[62]

It was accepted generally that a truly blanket ban could not, by its nature, be proportionate. Lord Bingham conceded that such a ban 'permitting of no exception' would be inconsistent with 'the rigorous and particular scrutiny required to give effect to article 10(2)'.[63] Differences of approach were apparent between Lords Bingham and Hutton, on the one hand, who were quite readily convinced of the compatibility of the challenged provisions with Article 10, and the analysis of Lord Hope, which was both more sceptical on this point and gave more detailed consideration to the Strasbourg requirements. Thus Lord Bingham did not consider the proportionality test in any detail, or give much consideration to the type of expression in issue. Indeed, his Lordship appeared to assume that once it was shown that the ban was not technically a blanket one, proportionality was automatically satisfied.

There was no detailed examination as to whether such routes were likely to prove effective—indeed his Lordship's view on this matter appeared positively naïve—a point returned to below. Lord Hutton found that in the absence of any attempt by the applicant to lay his case before the authorities under the relevant provisions of the Act,[64] there was no evidence to show that these procedures would have been *ineffect-ive*. This essentially turns the proportionality exercise on its head. Under Article 10(2), the State has the burden of showing that the restrictions placed upon the right in question are justifiable; Lord Hutton's approach essentially asks the applicant to prove that the State's alternative means of protecting expression are *ineffective*, rather than requiring the State, by adducing 'relevant and sufficient reasons',[65] to show their effectiveness.

In contrast, Lord Hope did look at proportionality closely: identifying the second and third parts of the *Daly* case, he said:

The problem is that, if they are to be compatible with the Convention right, the nature of the restrictions [placed upon the right] must be sensitive to the facts of each case if they are to

---

[62] Op cit, at [26].   [63] Ibid, at 275.   [64] Under sections 7(3)(a) or (b).
[65] The standard often referred to under Article 10: see Chapter 2 at 93–5.

satisfy the second and third requirements of proportionality. The restrictions must be rational, fair and not arbitrary, and they must impair the fundamental right no more than is necessary. As I see it, the scheme of the Act is vulnerable to criticism on the ground that it lacks the necessary degree of sensitivity.[66]

But he then examined the fact that the authorization system would be subject to judicial review, which he thought would provide the necessary safeguard. Lord Hope did address the point that technically it would be impossible for an agent or former agent to bring judicial review, since the disclosure by him to his lawyer for the purposes of preparing the case of the information he wished to disclose would itself breach s 1 OSA. Therefore an implied right to legal advice was read into the scheme — a right, that is, to disclose the substance of the information covered by s 1(1) to a legal adviser, in order to prepare for a judicial review to challenge the refusal of the authorizer to give permission to disclose. As Lord Hope said:

I think that it follows that he has an implied right to legal assistance of his own choosing, especially if his dispute is with the state. Access to legal advice is one of the fundamental rights enjoyed by every citizen under the common law.[67]

Having granted this point, Lord Hope went on to hold that where permission to reveal information was sought and refused, the appropriate test on judicial review challenging that refusal would be as follows:

(1) What, with respect to that information, was the justification for the interference with the Convention right? (2) If the justification was that this was in the interests of national security, was there a pressing social need for that information not to be disclosed? And (3) if there was such a need, was the interference with the Convention right which was involved in withholding authorisation for the disclosure of that information no more than was necessary? This structured approach to judicial control of the question whether official authorisation should or should not be given will enable the court to give proper weight to the public interest considerations in favour of disclosure, while taking into account at the same time the informed view of the primary decision maker. By adopting this approach, the court will be giving effect to its duty under [s 6(1) HRA] to act in a way that is compatible with the Convention rights . . .[68]

Essentially therefore, the broad choice is between a legislative scheme in which the applicant makes disclosure and the court judges directly whether the disclosure should be permitted (whether under the OSA or under the breach of confidence doctrine) and the actual scheme of the Act, which rests on 'judicial review of decisions taken beforehand by administrators'[69] as to whether disclosure should be permitted. The first choice of course would require an Act which, *unlike* the OSA, subjects all the offences to a 'harm' test. Lord Hope came down in favour of the second system (judicial review) on a number of factors. First, the would-be discloser may not be in a position to appreciate all the harm that his or her disclosures might do; second,

---

[66] Op cit, at [69–70].   [67] Ibid, at [73].   [68] Ibid, at [79].   [69] Ibid, at [83].

gathering evidence of harm to bring a criminal prosecution could do more damage than the original disclosure.[70] This argument was constantly floated but no examples given; moreover, this argument ignores the point that on judicial review, the government would have to put forward evidence of harm to justify its prior refusal to authorize disclosure. Therefore this argument, although possibly true, does not help us to choose between the two choices of system, since it applies equally to each. Finally, Lord Hope makes the point that a successful prosecution would not in fact remedy the harm done by the original disclosure.[71]

The basic problem with the reliance placed by all the judges who heard this case upon the internal complaint route and judicial review is that the means they viewed as available to members or former members of the security services to expose iniquity are so unlikely to be used. It seems, to say the least, highly improbable that such a member would risk the employment detriment that might be likely to arise, especially if he or she then proceeded to seek judicial review of the decision. It would appear that it would place him or her in an impossible position in relation to colleagues and superiors. Of course, simply making the disclosure directly and then being prosecuted for it would also risk such detriment, even if the person was acquitted. However, the obvious route in such circumstances would be to make the disclosure anonymously. Former members of the services would not be subject to the same constraints in terms of employment detriment, but might be deterred from using the complaint route for the simple reason that they would probably view it as inefficacious. Lord Bingham cannot but sound naïve when he says:

If . . . the document or information revealed matters which, however, scandalous or embarrassing, would not damage any security or intelligence interest or impede the effective discharge by the service of its very important public functions, [a] decision [in favour of disclosure] might be appropriate.[72]

The Act has been in force for 16 years at the time of writing and no such member has ever successfully availed themselves of this route, although persons other than Shayler have made or sought to make disclosures to the public at large, as this chapter reveals.

Further, one crucial point that Lord Hope and the others wholly fail to recognize is that requiring a person wishing to speak to the media to take legal action *before* he can do so (seeking judicial review of the refusal to allow disclosure) is to place a very weighty fetter upon his freedom of expression. Effectively, such a system reverses the principle under Article 10(2) that the state must justify interference with freedom of expression. It places upon the would-be speaker the burden of forcing the State, through legal action, to *allow* him to speak. One would not normally think of human rights as being those which cannot be exercised without prior legal action. Moreover, one of the most important principles recognized at Strasbourg is that rights must be real, not tokenistic or illusory. It is argued that the right to freedom of expression— one of the central rights of the Convention—is rendered illusory by ss 1(1) and 4(1)

[70] Ibid, at [84].   [71] Ibid, at [85].   [72] Ibid, at [30].

of the OSA in relation to allegedly unlawful activities of the security services—a matter of great significance in a democracy.

One of the specific arguments heavily relied upon by their Lordships was one previously cited by the courts. Lord Hutton cited dicta of Lord Nicholls in *Attorney General v Blake*:[73]

It is of paramount importance that members of the service should have complete confidence in all their dealings with each other, and that those recruited as informers should have the like confidence. Undermining the willingness of prospective informers to co-operate with the services, or undermining the morale and trust between members of the services when engaged on secret and dangerous operations, would jeopardise the effectiveness of the service. An absolute rule against disclosure, visible to all, makes good sense.

The obvious rejoinder to this argument that members of the service and others must be able to trust each other to keep information secret is that such trust would surely be expected to extend only to information which did not reveal illegality. Otherwise, the policy of ss 1(1) and 4(1) of the OSA seems to be to promote criminal conspiracies among members of the services or between members and informants to conceal information revealing unlawful activities. Moreover, whilst it is common sense to believe that the willingness of informants to give information to the security services would be undermined if they feared that their identities might be later unmasked, this argument *cannot* support a blanket ban on *any* disclosures by members or former members of the services. It is highly doubtful that those considering giving information to the services are aware of the precise legal position under the OSA: a simple guarantee by the agent cultivating the source that their identity would always be kept secret would suffice.

As noted above, the impact of the OSA in terms of freedom of expression is further exacerbated, since no general defence of prior publication is provided; the only means of putting forward such argument would arise in one of the categories in which it was necessary to prove the likelihood that harm would flow from the disclosure; the prosecution might find it hard to establish such a likelihood where there had been a great deal of prior publication because no further harm could be caused. Obviously, once again, this will depend on the level at which the harm test operates. Where it operates at its lowest level, prior publication would be irrelevant. Thus, where a member of the security services repeated information falling within s 1 which had been published all over the world and in the UK, a conviction could still be obtained. This position is out of accord with Article 10: in such an instance, the imposition of criminal liability would be unable to preserve national security and, therefore, it would be disproportionate to the aim of so doing.

If such publication had occurred, but the information fell within s 1(3), the test for harm might be satisfied on the basis that, although no further harm could be caused by disclosure of the particular document, it nevertheless belonged to a class of

---

[73] [2001] 1 AC 268, 287.

documents the disclosure of which was likely to cause harm. However, where harm flowing from publication of a specific document is relied upon, *Lord Advocate v Scotsman Publications Ltd* suggests that a degree of prior publication may tend to defeat the argument that further publication can still cause harm. However, this suggestion must be treated with care, since the ruling was not given under the 1989 Act and the link between the Act and the civil law of confidence may not form part of its *ratio*.[74] It should also be noted that s 6 provides that information which has already been leaked abroad can still cause harm if disclosed in the UK. The only exception to this arises under s 6(3), which provides that no liability will arise if the disclosure was authorized by the State or international organization in question.

Conclusions

The claim that the Act is an improvement on its predecessor rests partly on the substance or significance of the information it covers. Such substance is made relevant first by the use of categorization; impliedly, trivial information relating to cups of tea or colours of carpets in government buildings is not covered (except in security services buildings) and, secondly, because even where information *does* fall within the category in question, its disclosure will not incur liability unless harm will or may flow from it (save in relation to ss 1(1) and 4 (3)). Thus, on the face of it, liability will not be incurred merely because the information disclosed covers a topic of significance such as defence. In other words, it does not seem to be assumed that because there is a public interest in keeping information of the particular type secret, it inevitably relates to any particular piece of information. However, in relation to many disclosures it is, in fact, misleading to speak of using a second method to narrow down further the amount of information covered because, as noted above, establishing that the information falls within the category in question is in fact (or may be; no guidance is given as to when this will be the case) synonymous with establishing that harm will occur in a number of instances.

Clearly, if only to avoid bringing the criminal law into disrepute, 'harm tests' which allow the substance of the information to be taken into account are to be preferred to the width of s 2 of the 1911 Act. However, although the 1989 Act embodies and emphasizes the notion of a test for harm in its reiteration of the term 'damaging', it is not necessary to show that harm has *actually occurred*. Bearing this important point in mind, it can be seen that the test for harm actually operates on four different levels:

(a) The lowest level arises in two categories, s 1(1) and s 4(3), where there is no explicit test for harm at all—impliedly, a disclosure is of its very nature harmful.

(b) In one category, s 3(1)(b), the test for harm is more apparent than real in that it may be identical to the test determining whether the information falls within the category at all.

---

[74] [1990] 1 AC 812; [1989] 2 All ER 852, HL. Only Lord Templeman clearly adverted to such a link.

(c) In s 1(3), there is a harm test, but the harm need not flow from or be likely to flow from disclosure of the specific document in question.

(d) In three categories, ss 2, 3 and 4, there is a harm test, but it is only necessary to prove that harm would be *likely* to occur due to the disclosure in question, whether it has occurred or not.

Even at the highest level, where it is necessary to show that the actual document in question would be likely to cause harm, the task of doing so is made easy due to the width of the tests themselves. Under s 2(2), for example, a disclosure of information relating to defence will be damaging if it is likely to seriously obstruct the interests of the UK abroad. Thus, the harm tests may be said to be concerned less with preventing damaging disclosures than with creating the *impression* that liability is confined to such disclosures.

These tests for harm are not made any more stringent in instances where a non-Crown servant—usually a journalist—discloses information since, under s 5, if anyone discloses information which falls into one of the categories covered, the test for harm will be determined by reference to that category. The journalist who publishes information and the Crown servant who discloses it to him or her are treated differently in terms of the test for harm only where the latter is a member of the security services disclosing information relating to those services.

One of the objections to the old s 2 of the 1911 Act was the failure to include a requirement to prove *mens rea*. The new Act includes such a requirement only as regards the leaking of information by non-Crown servants; in all other instances, it creates a 'reversed *mens rea*': the defence can attempt to prove that the defendant did not know (or have reasonable cause to know) of the nature of the information or that its disclosure would be damaging. We will return to this defence below. However, under ss 5 and 6, the prosecution must prove *mens rea*, which includes a requirement to show that the disclosure was made in the knowledge that it would be damaging. This is a step in the right direction and a clear improvement on the 1911 Act; nevertheless, the burden of proof on the prosecution would be very easy to discharge where the low-level harm tests of ss 1(3) and 3(1)(b) applied once it was shown that the defendant knew that the information fell within the category in question.

Under s 3 of the HRA it is strongly arguable that the Act needs to afford greater recognition to the important constitutional role of the journalist in order to bring it into line with the recognition afforded to that role at Strasbourg under Article 10. But unless s 3 is used creatively in order to create such recognition, a journalist who repeated allegations made by a future Peter Wright as to corruption or treachery in MI5 could be convicted if it could be shown, first, that he or she knew that the information related to the security services and, secondly, that disclosure of that *type* of information would be *likely* to cause damage to the work of the security services, regardless of whether the particular allegations would cause such damage. In the case of a journalist who repeated allegations made by a future Cathy Massiter (see p 926 above), it would only be necessary to show that the allegations related to telephone tapping and that the journalist knew that they did. Clearly, this would be a burden which would be readily discharged.

It may be argued—bearing in mind the scarcity of prosecutions under the 1911 Act—that the Official Secrets Acts were put in place mainly in order to create a deterrent effect and as a centrepiece in the general legal scheme engendering government secrecy, rather than with a view to their invocation. The 1989 Act may be effective as a means of creating greater government credibility in relation to official secrecy than its predecessor. It allows the claim of liberalization to be made and gives the impression that the anomalies in existence under the 1911 Act have been dealt with. It appears complex and wide-ranging partly due to overlapping between and within the categories and, therefore, will be likely to have a chilling effect because civil servants and others will not be certain as to the information covered except in very clear-cut cases. It may, therefore, prove more effective than the 1911 Act in deterring the press from publishing the revelations of a future Peter Wright in respect of the workings of the security services. Thus, it may rarely need to be invoked and, in fact, may have much greater symbolic than practical value.

In considering the impact of the Act, it must be borne in mind that many other criminal sanctions for the unauthorized disclosure of information exist and some of these clearly overlap with its provisions. Sections 1 and 4(3) work in conjunction with the provisions of the Security Services Act 1989 to prevent almost all media scrutiny of the operation of the security services. Even where a member of the public has a grievance concerning the operation of the services, it will probably not be possible to use a court action as a means of bringing such operations to the notice of the public: under s 5 of the Security Services Act, complaint can only be made to a tribunal and under s 5(4), the decisions of the tribunal are not questionable in any court of law. In a similar manner, s 4(3) of the Official Secrets Act, which prevents disclosure of information about telephone tapping, works in tandem with the Interception of Communications Act 1985. Under the 1985 Act, complaints can be made only to a tribunal whose decisions are not published, with no possibility of scrutiny by a court. Moreover, around 80 other statutory provisions provide sanctions to enforce secrecy on civil servants in the particular areas they cover. For example, s 11 of the Atomic Energy Act 1946 makes it an offence to communicate to an unauthorized person information relating to atomic energy plant. Further, s 1 of the Official Secrets Act 1911 is still available to punish spies. Thus, it is arguable that s 2 of the 1911 Act could merely have been repealed without being replaced.

A number of the provisions of the 1989 Act look increasingly anomalous in the Human Rights Act era. Although repeal of the Act is unlikely, the pressure to amend s 1(1), as the most pernicious section—in terms of its impact on State accountability—may eventually become irresistible, although the decision in *Shayler* now makes clear that it will not come from the judiciary.

Prosecutions under the Act are rare, and, where they attempt to punish a member of the security services for revealing illegality or abuse of power by the security services, are likely to expose the government to a huge amount of negative publicity, particularly if the matter to which the revelation relates is a sensitive one. The Katharine Gunn affair in 2003 illustrated these points powerfully. Ms Gunn was an employee at GCHQ, the government's listening installation. She discovered, through correspondence that crossed her desk, that the UK Government had been requested by the US Government to give assistance in spying on the diplomats of states who were temporary members of the UN Security Council, at UN Headquarters in New York, in order to gain information making it easier to convince such states to vote for the US-UK resolution in favour of military action. Such action would have plainly violated the Vienna Convention on diplomatic relations[75] and Gunn disclosed the request to the *Observer* newspaper, which, not surprisingly, splashed the story on its front cover on 2 March 2003. Gunn was arrested and a prosecution commenced for breach of section 1(1) of the OSA. However, the prosecution was abandoned in February 2004, when it emerged that the CPS would offer no evidence.[76] Gunn had stated her intention to plead a defence of necessity—the revelation of illegal conduct by the security services, and the avoidance of an illegal war, and thus the saving of lives; specifically, she had intimated that her lawyers would seek disclosure, as part of her defence, of the Attorney General's advice on the legality or otherwise of the Iraq war, before its inception, a matter of enormous political sensitivity to the Government. The case not only illustrated the undesirability from a government's point of view, of using the Act against a seemingly honest and concerned whistle-blower, but raised questions as to the real independence of the decision to drop the prosecution, given the intense embarrassment the case looked likely to cause the Government. The indefensible nature of section 1(1), leaving Gunn no ability to raise a public interest defence, even in an instance of such enormous public importance, was once more vividly illustrated.

BREACH OF CONFIDENCE

INTRODUCTION[77]

Breach of confidence is a civil remedy affording protection against the disclosure or use of information which is not generally known and which has been entrusted in circumstances imposing an obligation not to disclose it without authorization from the person who originally imparted it. This area of law developed as a means of

---

[75] As well, seemingly as the 1946 General Convention, Article 2(3), which provides the premises of the UN shall be immune from any form of search or interference.

[76] See the statement by Harriet Harman QC to the House of Commons: HC Deb, col 427 (26 Feb 2004).

[77] General reading: F. Gurry, *Breach of Confidence*, Oxford: Clarendon, 1985; Bailey, Harris, and Jones, op cit, at 435–52; G. Robertson and A.G.L. Nichol, *Media Law*, Chapter 4; R. Wacks, *Personal Information*, Oxford: Clarendon, 1989, Chapter 3; Feldman, op cit, at 648–8; the general development of the doctrine is discussed in Chapter 14 at 728–30.

protecting secret information belonging to individuals and organizations.[78] However, it can also be used by the government to prevent disclosure of sensitive information and is, in that sense, a back-up to the other measures available, including the Official Secrets Act 1989.[79] It is clear that governments are prepared to use actions for breach of confidence against civil servants and others in instances falling outside the protected categories—or within them. In some respects, breach of confidence actions may be more valuable than the criminal sanction provided by the 1989 Act. Their use may attract less publicity than a criminal trial, no jury will be involved, and they offer the possibility of quickly obtaining an interim injunction. The latter possibility is very valuable because, in many instances, the other party (usually a newspaper) will not pursue the case to a trial of the permanent injunction, since the secret will probably be stale news by that time. However, where the government, as opposed to a private individual, is concerned, the courts will not merely accept that it is in the public interest that the information should be kept confidential. It will have to be shown that the public interest in keeping the information confidential due to the harm its disclosure would cause is not outweighed by the public interest in disclosure.

Thus, in *AG v Jonathan Cape*,[80] when the Attorney General invoked the law of confidence to try to stop publication of Richard Crossman's memoirs on the ground that they concerned Cabinet discussions, the Lord Chief Justice accepted that such public secrets could be restrained, but only on the basis that the balance of the public interest came down in favour of suppression. As the discussions had taken place 10 years previously, it was not possible to show that harm would flow from their disclosure; the public interest in publication therefore prevailed.

The nature of the public interest defence—the interest in disclosure—was clarified in *Lion Laboratories v Evans and Express Newspapers*.[81] The Court of Appeal held that the defence extended beyond situations in which there had been serious wrongdoing by the plaintiff. Even where the plaintiff was blameless, publication would be excusable where it was possible to show a serious and legitimate interest in the revelation. Thus, the *Daily Express* was allowed to publish information extracted from the manufacturer of the intoximeter (a method of conducting breathalyser tests) even though it did not reveal iniquity on the part of the manufacturer. It did, however, reveal a matter of genuine public interest: that wrongful convictions might have been obtained in drink driving cases owing to possible deficiencies of the intoximeter.

Just as the Official Secrets Act creates a direct interference with political speech, the doctrine of confidence as employed by the government can do so too. Therefore, the use of the doctrine in such instances will require careful scrutiny, with Article 10 in

---

[78] See Chapter 14 at 728–30.

[79] For comment on its role in this respect see M.W. Bryan, 'The Crossman Diaries: developments in the law of breach of confidence' (1976) 92 *LQR* 180; D.G.T. Williams, 'The Crossman Diaries' (1976) *CLJ* 1; Lowe and Willmore, 'Secrets, media and the law' (1985) 48 *MLR* 592.

[80] [1976] QB 752.

[81] [1985] QB 526; [1984] 2 All ER 417, CA. See further Chapter 15 at 779, esp note 44.

mind. Since this is a common law doctrine, s 3 will not apply. But the courts have a duty under s 6 of the HRA to develop the doctrine compatibly with Article 10. Thus a court, as itself a public authority under s 6, is obliged to give effect to Article 10, among other provisions of the Convention, when considering the application of this doctrine. In so doing, the courts have more leeway than they do under s 3 of the HRA since no provision was included in the HRA allowing the common law to override the Convention rights. Since, in an action between the individual and the State, the vexed issue of horizontal effect does not arise,[82] this matter can be regarded as settled, since the State as employer is also presumably a public authority under s 6. Section 12(4) is also applicable where interference with the right to freedom of expression is in issue, as it inevitably will be in this context. Section 12(4) requires the Court to have particular regard to the right to freedom of expression under Article 10. Thus, s 12(4) provides added weight to the argument that in the instance in which the State seeks to suppress the expression of an individual using this doctrine, the court must consider the pressing social need to do so and the requirements of proportionality very carefully, interpreting those requirements strictly. In considering Article 10, the court should, under s 12(4)(a), take into account the extent to which the material is or is about to become available to the public and the public interest in publication. These two matters are central in breach of confidence actions. They imply that the State's task in obtaining an injunction where a small amount of prior publication has taken place—or is about to—has been made harder.

In breach of confidence actions the State, as indicated below, typically seeks an interim injunction and then, if it has obtained it, may proceed to the trial of the permanent injunction. However, s 12(3) of the HRA provides that prior restraint on expression should not be granted except where the court considers that the claimant is 'likely' to establish at trial that publication should not be allowed, which the House of Lords has found will generally mean 'more likely than not'.[83] Moreover, *ex parte* injunctions cannot be granted under s 12(2) unless there are compelling reasons why the respondent should not be notified or the applicant has taken all reasonable steps to notify the respondent. All these requirements under the HRA must now be taken into account in applying the doctrine of confidence. The result is likely to be that the doctrine will undergo quite a radical change from the interpretation afforded to it in the *Spycatcher* litigation, which is considered below.

THE *SPYCATCHER* LITIGATION

The leading case in this area is the House of Lords' decision in *AG v Guardian Newspapers Ltd (No 2)*,[84] which confirmed that the *Lion Laboratories Ltd v Evans* approach to the public interest defence is the correct one and also clarified certain other aspects of this area of the law. In 1985, the Attorney General commenced

---

[82] See Chapter 3 at 112 and 123–32.   [83] See Chapter 3 at 153–7.
[84] [1990] 1 AC 109; [1990] 3 WLR 776; [1988] 3 All ER 545, HL.

proceedings in New South Wales[85] in an attempt (which was ultimately unsuccessful)[86] to restrain publication of *Spycatcher* by Peter Wright. The book included allegations of illegal activity engaged in by MI5. In the UK, on 22 and 23 June 1986, *The Guardian* and *The Observer* published reports of the forthcoming hearing which included some *Spycatcher* material, and on 27 June the Attorney General obtained temporary *ex parte* injunctions preventing them from further disclosure of such material. *Inter partes* injunctions were granted against the newspapers on 11 July 1986. On 12 July 1987, *The Sunday Times* began publishing extracts from *Spycatcher* and the Attorney General obtained an injunction restraining publication on 16 July.

On 14 July 1987, the book was published in the US, and many copies were brought into the UK. On 30 July 1987, the House of Lords decided[87] (relying on *American Cyanamid Co v Ethicon Ltd*)[88] to continue the injunctions against the newspapers on the basis that the Attorney General still had an arguable case for permanent injunctions. In making this decision, the House of Lords were obviously influenced by the fact that publication of the information was an irreversible step. This is the usual approach at the interim stage: the court considers the balance of convenience between the two parties and will tend to come down on the side of the plaintiff because of the irrevocable nature of publication. However, since an interim injunction represents a prior restraint and is often the most crucial and, indeed, sometimes the *only* stage in the whole action, it may be argued that a presumption in favour of freedom of expression should be more readily allowed to tip the balance in favour of the defendant. This may especially be argued where publication from other sources has already occurred which will be likely to increase, and where the public interest in the information is very strong.

It is arguable that the House of Lords should have been able in July 1986 to break through the argument that once the confidentiality claim was set up, the only possible course was to transfix matters as at that point. The argument could have been broken through in the following way: the public interest in limiting the use of prior restraints could have been weighed against the interest in ensuring that everyone who sets up a legal claim has a right to have it heard free from interference. A prior restraint might be allowed even in respect of a matter of great public concern if the interest it protected was clearly made out, it did not go beyond what was needed to provide such protection and it was foreseeable that the restraint would achieve its objective. If it seemed probable that the restraint would not achieve its objective, it would cause an erosion of freedom of speech to no purpose. In the instant case, although the first of these conditions may have been satisfied, the other two, it is submitted, were not; the restraint should not, therefore, have been granted. Such reasoning would bring the law of confidence closer to adopting the principles used in defamation cases as regards

---

[85] [1987] 8 NSWLR 341.

[86] HC of Australia (1988) 165 CLR 30; for comment see F.A. Mann (1988) 104 *LQR* 497; M. Turnbull (1989) 105 *LQR* 382.

[87] *AG v Guardian Newspapers Ltd* [1987] 3 All ER 316; for comment, see S. Lee (1987) 103 *LQR* 506.

[88] [1975] AC 396; [1975] 1 All ER 504, HL.

the grant of interim injunctions.[89] If a case of this nature recurs now that the HRA is in force, such reasoning would be taken into account under s 12(4) and s 6; since, relying on either section the demands of Article 10 must be met, an injunction should not be granted where it is probable that it will not be able to serve the legitimate aim in question, owing to the probability that further publication abroad, or on the internet, will occur.

The judgment of the House of Lords did nothing to curb the use of 'gagging injunctions' in actions for breach of confidence where there had not been prior publication of the material. In any such action, even where the claim was of little merit, and the public interest in publication strong, it was possible to argue that its subject matter should be preserved intact until the merits of the claim could be considered. Even in an instance where the plaintiff (the State) then decided to drop the action before that point, publication of the material in question could be prevented for some substantial period of time. The House of Lords' decision was found to be in breach of Article 10 of the European Convention on Human Rights, as discussed below, but on the ground of prior publication, rather than public interest in the material.

In the trial of the permanent injunctions, *AG v Guardian (No 2)*,[90] the Crown argued that confidential information disclosed to third parties does not thereby lose its confidential character if the third parties know that the disclosure has been made in breach of a duty of confidence. A further reason for maintaining confidentiality in the particular instance was that the unauthorized disclosure of the information was thought likely to damage the trust which members of MI5 have in each other and might encourage others to follow suit. These factors, it was argued, established the public interest in keeping the information confidential.

On the other hand, it was argued on behalf of the newspapers that some of the information in *Spycatcher*, if true, disclosed that members of MI5 in their operations in England had committed serious breaches of domestic law in, for example, bugging foreign embassies or effecting unlawful entry into private premises. Most seriously, the book included the allegations that members of MI5 attempted to destabilize the administration of Mr Harold Wilson and that the Director General or Deputy Director General of MI5 was a spy. The defendants contended that the duty of non-disclosure to which newspapers coming into the unauthorized possession of confidential State secrets may be subject, does not extend to allegations of serious iniquity of this character.

It was determined at first instance and in the Court of Appeal that whether or not the newspapers would have had a duty to refrain from publishing *Spycatcher* material in June 1986 before its publication elsewhere, any such duty had now lapsed. The

---

[89] See *Bonnard v Perryman* [1891] 2 Ch 269; *Herbage v The Times Newspapers and Others* (1981) *The Times*, 1 May. For discussion, see Chapter 21 at 1098–1100.

[90] [1990] 1 AC 109; [1990] 3 WLR 776; [1988] 3 All ER 545, HL; in the Court of Appeal [1990] 1 AC 109; [1988] 3 All ER 545, p 594.

mere making of allegations of iniquity was insufficient, of itself, to justify overriding the duty of confidentiality, but the articles in question published in June 1986 had not contained information going beyond what the public was reasonably entitled to know and in so far as they went beyond what had been previously published, no detriment to national security had been shown which could outweigh the public interest in free speech, given the publication of Spycatcher that had already taken place. Thus, balancing the public interest in freedom of speech and the right to receive information against the countervailing interest of the Crown in national security, continuation of the injunctions was not necessary. The injunctions, however, continued until the House of Lords rejected the Attorney General's claim (AG v Guardian Newspapers Ltd (No 2))[91] on the basis that the interest in maintaining confidentiality was outweighed by the public interest in knowing of the allegations in Spycatcher. It was further determined that an injunction to restrain future publication of matters connected with the operations of the security services would amount to a comprehensive ban on publication and would undermine the operation of determining the balance of public interest in deciding whether such publication was to be prevented; accordingly, an injunction to prevent future publication which had not yet been threatened was not granted.

It appears likely that the permanent injunctions would have been granted but for the massive publication of Spycatcher abroad. That factor seems to have tipped the balance in favour of the newspapers. It is arguable that the operation of the public interest defence in this instance came too close to allowing for judicial value judgments rather than application of a clear legal rule. Without a Bill of Rights to protect freedom of speech, the Law Lords, it is suggested, showed a tendency to be swayed by establishment arguments. The judgment also made it clear that once the information has become available from other sources, even though the plaintiff played no part in its dissemination and indeed tried to prevent it, an injunction would be unlikely to be granted. This principle was affirmed in Lord Advocate v Scotsman Publications Ltd,[92] which concerned the publication of extracts from Inside Intelligence by Antony Cavendish. The interlocutory injunction sought by the Crown was refused by the House of Lords on the ground that there had been a small amount of prior publication and the possible damage to national security was very nebulous. The decision suggests that the degree of prior publication may be weighed against the significance of the disclosures in question: if less innocuous material had been in issue, an injunction might have been granted.

---

[91] [1990] 1 AC 109; [1990] 3 WLR 776; [1988] 3 All ER 545, p 638; for comment, see Williams (1989) 48 CLJ 1; Y. Cripps, 'Breach of copyright and confidence: the Spycatcher effect' [1989] PL 13; E. Barendt, 'Spycatcher and freedom of speech' [1989] PL 204; J. Michael, 'Spycatcher's end?' (1989) 52 MLR 389; B.J. Narain, (1988) 39 NILQ 73 and (1987) 137 NLJ 723 and 724; D. Burnett and R. Thomas (1989) 16 JLS 210; G. Jones, 'Breach of confidence—after Spycatcher' (1989) 42 CLP 49; D. Kingsford-Smith and D. Oliver, (eds), Economical With the Truth, 1990, chapters by Pannick and Austin; Ewing and Gearty, op cit, at 152–69; M. Turnbull, The Spycatcher Trial, Heinemann, 1988; Bailey, Harris, and Jones, op cit, at 435–50.

[92] [1990] 1 AC 812; [1989] 2 All ER 852, CA.

The Observer and *The Guardian* applied to the European Commission on Human Rights claiming, *inter alia*, that the grant of the temporary injunctions had breached Article 10 of the Convention, which guarantees freedom of expression. Having given its opinion that the temporary injunctions constituted such a breach, the Commission referred the case to the court. In *Observer and Guardian v UK*,[93] the Court found that the injunctions clearly constituted an interference with the newspapers' freedom of expression; the question was whether the interference fell within one of the exceptions provided for by para 2 of Article 10. The injunctions fell within two of the para 2 exceptions: maintaining the authority of the judiciary and protecting national security. However, those exceptions could be invoked only if the injunctions were necessary in a democratic society in the sense that they corresponded to a pressing social need and were proportionate to the aims pursued.

The court considered these questions with regard first to the period from 11 July 1986 to 30 July 1987. The injunctions had the aim of preventing publication of material which, according to evidence presented by the Attorney General, might have created a risk of detriment to MI5. The nature of the risk was uncertain as the exact contents of the book were not known at that time because it was still only available in manuscript form. Further, they ensured the preservation of the Attorney General's right to be granted a permanent injunction; if *Spycatcher* material had been published before that claim could be heard, the subject matter of the action would have been damaged or destroyed. In the court's view, these factors established the existence of a pressing social need. Were the actual restraints imposed proportionate to these aims? The injunctions did not prevent the papers pursuing a campaign for an inquiry into the operation of the security services and, though preventing publication for a long time—over a year—the material in question could not be classified as urgent news. Thus, it was found that the interference complained of was proportionate to the ends in view.

The court then considered the period from 30 July 1987 to 30 October 1988, after publication of *Spycatcher* had taken place in the US. That event changed the situation: in the court's view, the aims of the injunctions were no longer to keep secret information secret; it was to attempt to preserve the reputation of MI5 and to deter others who might be tempted to follow Peter Wright's example. It was uncertain whether the injunctions could achieve those aims and it was not clear that the newspapers who had not been concerned with the publication of *Spycatcher* should be enjoined as an example to others. Further, after 30 July, it was not possible to maintain the Attorney General's rights as a litigant because the substance of his claim had already been destroyed; had permanent injunctions been obtained against the newspapers, that would not have preserved the confidentiality of the material in question. Thus, the injunctions could no longer be said to be necessary either to protect national security or to maintain the authority of the judiciary. Maintenance of the injunctions after publication of the book in the US therefore constituted a violation of Article 10.

---

[93] (1991) 14 EHRR 153; for comment see I. Leigh, '*Spycatcher* in Strasbourg' [1992] *PL* 200–08.

This was a cautious judgment. It suggests that had the book been published in the US after the House of Lords' decision to uphold the temporary injunctions, no breach of Article 10 would have occurred, despite the fact that publication of extracts from the book had already occurred in the US[94] and the UK. The Court seems to have been readily persuaded by the Attorney General's argument that a widely framed injunction was needed in July 1986, but it is arguable that it was wider than it needed to be to prevent a risk to national security. It could have required the newspapers to refrain from publishing Wright material which had not been previously published by others until (if) the action to prevent publication of the book was lost. Such wording would have taken care of any national security interest; therefore, wording going beyond that was disproportionate to that aim.

Thus, although the newspapers 'won', the judgment is unlikely to have a significant liberalizing influence on the principles governing the grant of temporary injunctions on the grounds of breach of confidence. The minority judges in the court set themselves against the narrow view that the authority of the judiciary is best preserved by allowing a claim of confidentiality set up in the face of a strong competing public interest to found an infringement of freedom of speech for over a year. Judge Morenilla argued that prior restraint should be imposed in such circumstances only where disclosure would result in immediate, serious, and irreparable damage to the public interest.[95] It might be said that such a test would impair the authority of the judiciary in the sense that the rights of litigants would not be sufficiently protected. However, following the judgment of the Lords, the test at the interlocutory stage allowed a case based on a weak argument to prevail on the basis that the court could not weigh the evidence at that stage and therefore had to grant an injunction in order to preserve confidentiality until the case could be fully looked into. As noted above, this stance can mean that the other party does not pursue the case to the permanent stage and, therefore, freedom of speech is suppressed on very flimsy grounds. Thus, a greater burden to show the well-founded nature of the claim of danger to the public interest—even if not as heavy as that under the test proposed by Judge Morenilla—should be placed on the plaintiff, and such a burden would be, it is argued, more in accord with the duties of the court under ss 6 and 12 of the HRA.

The result of the ruling in the European Court of Human Rights appears to be that where there has been a substantial amount of prior publication, an interim injunction should not be granted, but that it can be when there is at least some evidence of a threat to national security posed by publication coupled with a lesser degree of prior publication. It meant that the action for breach of confidence was still of great value as part of the legal scheme bolstering government secrecy.

The position, however, has now been affected by the decision of the House of Lords

---

[94] The *Washington Post* published certain extracts in the US on 3 May 1987.

[95] He relied on the ruling to this effect of the US Supreme Court in *Nebraska Press Association v Stuart* (1976) 427 US 539.

in *Cream Holdings Limited and others v Banerjee.*[96] This decision gives the definitive interpretation of the meaning of section 12(3) HRA, which provides, *inter alia*, that no relief affecting the Convention right to freedom of expression '. . . is to be granted so as to restrain publication before trial unless the court is satisfied that the applicant is likely to establish that publication should not be allowed'. It is discussed in detail in Chapter 3 and it is not proposed to repeat that discussion here. The key point is that the effect of the decision of the House of Lords is that, in nearly all cases—absent the claim of immediate and serious danger to life, limb, or presumably national security—the party seeking the injunction, that is the government in these kinds of cases, must show not only an arguable case, as previously, but that it is 'more likely than not' that they will succeed at final trial.[97] This approach, assuming it is applied consistently to *Spycatcher*-type cases, should make it significantly harder for future governments to obtain gagging injunctions against the media. The post-HRA decision discussed below, although made before *Cream Holdings*, was taken under section 12(3) and appears to confirm this

Case law subsequent to *Spycatcher* and conclusions

The decision in *AG v Times*[98] suggest that Article 10 is having a greater impact in breach of confidence actions than it had at Strasbourg. Tomlinson, a former MI6 officer, wrote a book, *The Big Breach*, about his experiences in MI6[99] which *The Sunday Times* intended to serialize. There had been a small amount of publication of the material in Russia. The Attorney General sought an injunction to restrain publication. The key issue concerned the degree of prior publication required before it could be said that the material had lost its quality of confidentiality. The Attorney General proposed the formula: 'publication has come to the widespread attention of the public at large'.[100] This formula would have meant that injunctions could be obtained even after a high degree of prior publication and therefore it was unacceptable to *The Sunday Times*. However, the two parties agreed on a formula: that the material had already been published in any newspaper, magazine, or other publication whether within or outside the jurisdiction of the court, to such an extent that the information was in the public domain (other than in a case where the only such publication was made by or caused by the defendants). The Attorney General, however, contended that the defendants had to demonstrate that this was the case, which meant that they had to obtain clearance from the Attorney General before publishing.

In arguing against this contention at first instance, the newspaper invoked Article 10 and also relied on sections 12(3) and (4) of the HRA.[101] It was argued that the restriction proposed by the Attorney General would be disproportionate to the aim pursued and therefore could not be justified in a democratic society. The decision in

---

[96] [2004] 3 WLR 918. For comment see A.T.H. Smith [2005] 64(1) *CLJ* 4.

[97] See Chapter 3 at 153–7.   [98] [2001] EMLR 19.

[99] Tomlinson was charged with an offence under the Official Secrets Act, s 1, pleaded guilty and was imprisoned for six months.

[100] Op cit, at [2].   [101] See Chapter 3, note 1.

Bladet-Tromsø v Norway [102] was referred to, in which the Court said that it is incumbent on the media 'to impart information and ideas concerning matters of public interest. Not only does the press have the task of imparting such information and ideas, the public has the right to receive them.' [103] Taking these arguments into account, it was found at first instance that the Attorney General had to demonstrate why there was a public interest in restricting publication. No injunction was granted since it was found that he had not done so. On appeal, the same stance was taken. It was found that the requirement to seek clearance should not be imposed: the editor had to form his own judgment as to whether the material could be said to be already in the public domain. That position was, the Court found, most consonant with the requirements of Article 10 and s 12.

This decision suggests that, bearing in mind the requirements of the HRA, an injunction is unlikely to be granted where a small amount of prior publication has already taken place. It does not, however, decide the question of publication where no prior publication has taken place, but the material is of public interest (which could clearly have been said of the Wright material). Following *Bladet-Tromsø v Norway*, it is suggested that an injunction should not be granted where such material is likely, imminently, to come into the public domain, a position consistent with the demands of s 12(4), which refers to such a likelihood. Even where this cannot be said to be the case, it would be consonant with the requirements of Article 10 and s 12 to refuse to grant an injunction on the basis of the duty of newspapers to report on such material. The burden would be placed on the State to seek to establish that a countervailing pressing social need was present and that the injunction did not go further than necessary in order to serve the end in view. [104]

DEFENCE ADVISORY NOTICES[105]

The government and the media may avoid the head-on confrontation which occurred in the *Spycatcher* litigation by means of a curious institution known until 1992 as the 'D' (Defence) notice system. This system, which effectively means that the media censor themselves in respect of publication of official information, can obviate the need to seek injunctions to prevent publication. The 'D' Notice Committee was set up with the object of letting the press know which information could be printed and at what point: it was intended that if sensitive political information was covered by a 'D'

---

[102] (1999) 6 BHRC 599.   [103] Ibid, at [62].

[104] The manner in which the law of common law contempt may allow for the imposition of widespread restrictions upon the media on the back of an initial breach of confidence injunction is considered in detail in Chapter 6 at 289 et seq. For discussion of a further Strasbourg decision on injunctions to protect security services, see Chapter 2 at 55.

[105] On the system generally, see J. Jaconelli, 'The "D" Notice system' [1982] *PL* 39; D. Fairley (1990) 10 *OJLS* 430.

notice, an editor would decide against printing it. The system is entirely voluntary, and in theory the fact that a 'D' notice has not been issued does not mean that a prosecution under the Official Secrets Act 1989 is precluded, although in practice it is very unlikely. Further, guidance obtained from the Secretary to the Committee does not amount to a straightforward 'clearance'. Press representatives sit on the committee as well as civil servants and officers of the armed forces.

The value and purpose of the system was called into question due to the injunction obtained against the BBC in respect of *My Country Right or Wrong* as mentioned above. The programme concerned issues raised by the *Spycatcher* litigation; the BBC consulted the 'D' Notice Committee before broadcasting and were told that the programme did not affect national security. However, the Attorney General then obtained an injunction preventing transmission on the ground of breach of confidence, thereby disregarding the 'D' Notice Committee.

Some criticism has been levelled at the system: in the Third Report from the Defence Committee,[106] the 'D' notice system was examined and it was concluded that it was failing to fulfil its role. It was found that major newspapers did not consult their 'D' notices to see what was covered by them and that the wording of 'D' notices was so wide as to render them meaningless. The system conveyed an appearance of censorship which had provoked strong criticism. It was determined that the machinery for the administration of 'D' notices and the 'D' notices themselves needed revision. The review which followed this reduced the number of notices and confined them to specific areas. The system was reviewed again in 1992 (*The Defence Advisory Notices: A Review of the D Notice System*, MOD Open Government Document No 93/06), leading to a reduction in the number of notices to six. They were renamed Defence Advisory notices to reflect their voluntary nature.

FREEDOM OF INFORMATION: GENERAL PRINCIPLES AND THE POSITION PRIOR TO THE 2000 ACT

PRINCIPLES OF FREEDOM OF INFORMATION AND ARTICLE 10 ECHR

The citizen's 'right to know' is recognized in most democracies, including the US, Canada, Australia, New Zealand, Denmark, Sweden, Holland, Norway, Greece, and France. In such countries, the general principle of freedom of information is subject to exceptions where information falls into specific categories. In terms of principle, and in particular, as seen through the lens of Article 10 ECHR, an assertion of a right to access to information can be distinguished from an assertion of a free speech right,[107] although the two are clearly linked. This distinction receives support from

---

[106] (1979–80) HC 773, 640 i–v, *The 'D' Notice System.*
[107] *Leander v Sweden* (1987) A 116; *Guerra v Italy* (1998) 26 EHRR 357, esp at [53].

the wording of Article 10 itself, which speaks in terms of the freedom to 'receive and impart information', thus appearing to exclude from its provisions the right to demand information from the *un*willing speaker. Moreover, the phrase 'without interference from public authorities' does not suggest that governments should come under any duty to act in order to ensure that information is received.

There are at least three reasons why access to information is often treated as a distinct interest by commentators and constitutional courts. First, freedom of information can be justified by reference to values that go beyond those underlying freedom of speech. It is generally accepted that the quality of decision making will improve if access to official information allows citizens to scrutinize the workings of the government and public authorities generally. Moreover, the accountability of the government to the public is increased, since pressure can more readily be brought to bear on the government regarding the effects of its policies and citizens are able to make a more informed choice at election times, in accordance with the argument from democracy.

Secondly, information may be sought although it is not intended that it should be communicated to others. It is not clear that the free speech justifications considered in the Introduction to this book would apply to such a situation, and therefore it would tend to be considered purely as an access to information or privacy issue. Indeed, in such instances, the seeker of information might well be asserting a right not merely to gain access to the information, but also to have its confidential quality maintained. Access rights under the Data Protection Act 1998[108] often take account of both interests. Thus, it is clear that many demands for access to information are not based on an assertion of free speech interests. Rights of access to information overlap with certain privacy interests, since they may cover many situations in which a person might wish to receive information, apart from that of the individual who wishes to obtain and publicize government information. However, freedom of information is most readily associated with the demand for the receipt of information with a view to placing it in the public domain.

Thirdly, information intended to be placed in the public domain may be sought when there is no speaker willing to disclose it, or where the body which 'owns' the information is unwilling that it should be disclosed. Whether a demand for such communication should be regarded as an exercise of Article 10 rights or not,[109] it is clearly a necessary precondition for the production of speech and therefore can be treated as deserving of the same protection as 'speech', in that the result will be that the public will be informed and debate on issues of public interest will not be stifled.

---

[108] For brief discussion, see Chapter 14 at 717–21.

[109] The European Court of Human Rights takes the view that it should not. In the *Gaskin* case (1990) 12 EHRR 36, it viewed a demand for access to information which the body holding it did not wish to disclose as giving rise only to an Art 8 issue, not an Art 10 issue. The US Supreme Court has held that the First Amendment does not impose an affirmative duty on government to make information not in the public domain available to journalists (417 US 817). For discussion of this issue generally, see Barendt, *Freedom of Speech*, Oxford: OUP, 2nd edn., 2005, at 108–12.

The argument that such dissemination of information will render the government more readily accountable is strongly related to the justification for free speech discussed in the Introduction,[110] which argues that it is indispensable to democracy, since it enables informed participation by the citizenry.

However, freedom of speech guarantees, including Article 10, do not tend to encompass the imposition of positive obligations and, therefore, in general, are violated when a willing speaker is prevented from speaking rather than in the situation where information deriving ultimately from an unwilling speaker—usually the government—is sought, entailing the assertion of a positive right. Thus, a distinction should be drawn between gaining access to the information and then placing it in the public domain—the second situation giving rise to a free speech interest. However, these issues have tended to arise together within the legal scheme in the UK, which has traditionally protected a 'closed' system of government; it is therefore convenient to consider both within the same chapter.

As these remarks indicate, Article 10 of the Human Rights Act cannot be expected to have much impact on access to information, in the sense of using Article 10 to create an access right. The Freedom of Information (FoI) Act, introduced in 2000, provides for the first time a statutory right of access to official information. However, it is suggested that the basic *values* underlying Article 10, in particular the argument from democracy,[111] may be able to be relied upon in as a means of interpreting the provisions of the new FoI Act. Probably the most important value associated with freedom of information is the need for the citizen to understand as fully as possible the working of government, in order to render it accountable; the following discussion therefore places a strong emphasis on the choices that were made as to the release of information relating to public authorities—not only to central government—in the FoI Act 2000.

RIGHTS OF ACCESS TO INFORMATION PRIOR TO THE FREEDOM OF INFORMATION ACT[112]

The UK has traditionally resisted freedom of information legislation and, as seen above, until 1989, criminalized the unauthorized disclosure of any official information at all, however trivial, under s 2 of the Official Secrets Act 1911, thereby creating a climate of secrecy around government. The attitude to secrecy exemplified by US freedom of information legislation, which is founded on the presumption that information must be disclosed unless specifically exempted, may be contrasted with this traditional position in the UK. American freedom of information provision can, in particular, be contrasted with provision under the UK Public Records Act 1958,

---

[110] See pp 14–22.

[111] For discussion of the Court's 'privileging' of political speech, see Chapter 2 at 50–72.

[112] See, generally, Birkinshaw, op cit; *Reforming the Secret State*, 1990; 'The White Paper on open government' [1993] *PL* 557.

which is considered below. It provides a measure of access to official information, but only after 30 years or more have passed. Considering all the various and overlapping methods of preventing disclosure of official information in the UK, and bearing in mind the contrasting attitude to this issue evinced in other democracies, it is fair to say that that until 2000, the UK was being increasingly isolated in its stance as a resister of freedom of information legislation. Since virtually all other democracies had introduced such legislation, that stance was indefensible in a mature democracy. It was finally abandoned when the Freedom of Information Act 2000 was introduced.

However, even before that point, and before the Labour Government came to power in 1997, there had been certain developments under the Conservative Governments of 1989–97, especially under the Major Government, which suggested that a gradual movement towards more open government was taking place in the UK. The Data Protection Act 1984 allowed access to personal information held on computerized files. A very limited right to disclosure of information in the field of local government was created.[113] The Campaign for Freedom of Information had, from 1985 onwards, brought about acceptance of the principle of access rights in some areas of official action. It supported Private Members' Bills, which allowed for rights of access to information in certain limited areas. Disclosure of a range of information was decriminalized under the Official Secrets Act 1989, as indicated above.

After the 1992 general election, the Prime Minister promised a review of secrecy in Whitehall to be conducted by William Waldegrave, the minister with responsibility for the Citizen's Charter, which would concentrate on the large number of statutory instruments which prevent public disclosure of government information in various areas, with a view to removing those which did not appear to fulfil a pressing need. It was also promised that a list of secret Cabinet committees with their terms of reference and their ministerial membership would be published. It was proposed that reform of the Official Secrets Act 1989 would be undertaken, so that disclosure of a specific document would be criminalized as opposed to disclosure of a document belonging to a class of documents which might cause harm. In fact, this reform did not take place. A White Paper on Open Government (Cm 2290) was published in July 1993 and a Code of Practice on Access to Government Information was introduced in 1994. The Code has now been replaced by the Freedom of Information Act when the latter came into force on 1 January 2005. However, it is important to have a basic understanding of how the Code worked, and the scope of its exemptions, in order to decide how much of an advance the 2000 Act really is.

---

[113] Part VA of the Local Government Act 1972 (introduced by the Local Government (Access to Information) Act 1985. The right allowed members of the public to inspect local authority minutes, reports, and background papers and to take copies of them. However, a number of significant areas were exempt from the access right; also, council 'working parties' are exempt.

The Code provided that non-exempted government departments should publish 'facts and analysis of the facts which the government considers relevant and import- ant in framing major policy proposals and decisions',[114] 'explanatory material on departments' dealings with the public', and 'reasons for administrative decisions to those affected', and information in accordance with the Citizen's Charter on the operation of public services.[115] Such departments would also provide information on receipt of specific requests. A key limitation of the Code was that it afforded access only to information, as opposed to documents. As the Campaign for Freedom of Information has pointed out, this was: 'a potentially overwhelming defect: the opportunities for selective editing are obvious'.[116]

The Code was of course subject to exemptions. Particular exemptions are compared with those under the 2000 Act below, but it is useful to give a general indication of the scope and number of exemptions which existed under the Code. The exemptions could be divided into two groups: those subject to a harm test and those which were not. The key exemptions within the former group covered information relating to: defence, security and international relations, internal discussion and advice, law enforcement and legal proceedings, effective management of the economy and collec- tion of tax, effective management and operations of the public service, third parties' commercial confidence, immigration and nationality information, medical informa- tion given in confidence, information which was soon to be published or where disclosure would be premature, and research, statistics, and analysis where disclosure could be misleading. The latter group included information within the following categories: communications with the royal household, public employment, public appointments and honours, privacy of an individual, information given in confidence, information covered by statutory and other restrictions. Unreasonable, voluminous, and vexatious requests, or requests requiring an 'unreasonable diversion of resources', were also exempt.

The Act was 'enforced' by means of complaint to the Ombudsman. There were two main issues in relation to this method. First, members of the public could not complain directly to the public, but had to complain initially to an MP, who was then supposed to pass on the complaint to the Ombudsman. This was a widely criticized system.[117] Second, the Ombudsman, in keeping with the nature of his role, had no power to enforce his findings. His office worked by persuasion and there had been instances of refusals by Government departments to comply with recommendations for disclosure,[118] although these were rare instances. The Ombudsman's lack of powers to compel release of information merely highlighted the fact that the Code was ultimately a 'grace and favour' system, which gave no *right* to government information. The Freedom of Information Act 2000 thus signalled a break with the

---

[114] Paragraph 3(i).   [115] Paragraph 3(ii) and (iii).

[116] Appendices to the Minutes of Evidence taken before the Select Committee on the PCA, session 1993–94, HC 33 (1993–94), Vol II, p 258.

[117] See, e.g., the *Public Service Committee First Special Report*, HC 67 (1996–97), at [9].

[118] See below, note 180.

traditional culture of secrecy: 'the principle that communication was the privilege of the State rather than of the citizen was at last . . . reversed'.[119]

THE PUBLIC RECORDS ACTS

The UK Public Records Act 1958, as amended by the Public Records Act 1967, provides that public records will not be transferred to the Public Records Office in order to be made available for inspection until the expiration of 30 years, and longer periods can be prescribed for 'sensitive information'. Such information will include personal details about persons who are still living and papers affecting the security of the State. Some such information can be withheld for 100 years or for ever, and there is no means of challenging such decisions. For example, at the end of 1987, a great deal of information about the Windscale fire in 1957 was disclosed, although some items are still held back. Robertson argues that information is withheld to prevent embarrassment to bodies such as the police or civil servants rather than to descendants of persons mentioned in it; and in support of this he cites examples such as police reports on the NCCL (1935–41), flogging of vagrants (1919), and decisions against prosecuting James Joyce's *Ulysses* (1924) as instances of material which in January 1989 was listed as closed for a century.[120]

However, a somewhat less restrictive approach to the release of archives became apparent in 1994. In 1992–93, a review was conducted of methods of ensuring further openness in government and its results were published in a White Paper entitled *Open Government* (Cm 2290).[121] The White Paper, as well as proposing the Code of Practice on Access to Government Information already discussed, promised that there would be a reduction in the number of public records withheld from release beyond 30 years. A review group established by Lord Mackay in 1992 suggested that records should only be closed for more than 30 years where their disclosure would cause harm to defence, national security, international relations, and economic interests of the UK; information supplied in confidence; personal information which would cause substantial distress if disclosed. Under s 3(4) of the 1958 Act, records may still be retained within departments for 'administrative' reasons or for any other special reason.

The Freedom of Information (FoI) Act 2000, Part VI and Schedule 8 amends the 1958 Act. Part VI amends the exemptions of Part II of the 1958 Act in respect of historical records, with a view to enhancing the ease of access to them. Section 63(1) of the FoI Act reduces the number of exemptions that apply to such records. This is done in three tranches. First, exemptions are removed after 30 years in respect of a number of categories of information, including information prejudicial to the economic interests of the UK, information obtained with a view to prosecution, court

---

[119] D. Vincent, *The Culture of Secrecy, Britain 1832–1998*, Oxford: OUP, 1998, p 321.

[120] See G. Robertson, and Nicholl, op cit, 'Public Records' chapter.

[121] The White Paper proposals in relation to public records are considered by P. Birkinshaw, 'I only ask for information—the White Paper on open government' [1993] *PL* 557.

records, information prejudicial to public affairs and commercial interests. Secondly, one exemption is removed after 60 years—in respect of information concerning the conferring of honours. Thirdly, a large number of exemptions under s 31 relating to various investigations and the maintenance of law and order are removed after 100 years. These modest provisions are to be welcomed, as easing the task of historians, but their limited nature should be questioned; especially, it must be asked why any absolute exemptions, in particular those relating to intelligence information, remain.[122]

THE FREEDOM OF INFORMATION ACT 2000

INTRODUCTION

As suggested above, the position of the UK prior to the 2000 Act may be contrasted with the position in other democracies which have introduced freedom of information legislation[123] within the last 30 years. Canada introduced its Access to Information Act in 1982, while America has had such legislation since 1967. Its Freedom of Information Act 1967 applies to all parts of the Federal Government unless an exemption applies. Exempted categories include information concerning defence, law enforcement and foreign policy. The exemptions can be challenged in court and the onus of proof will be on the agency withholding the information to prove that disclosure could bring about the harm the exemption was intended to prevent. However, although the principle of freedom of information in America has attracted praise, its application in practice has often been criticized.[124] In particular, the American business community considers that the system is being abused by persons who have a particular financial interest in uncovering commercial information. A number of reforms have been suggested since 1980 and, in 1986, a major FoI Act reform was passed which extended the exemption available.

With the example set by other democracies in mind, commentators have been arguing for a number of years that the voluntary Code should be replaced by a broad statutory right of access to information, enforceable by another independent body or through the courts.[125] In particular, many commentators considered that one of the messages of the Scott Report, published in February 1996, was that the UK needed

---

[122] Cf the provision in respect of intelligence information held in the Public Record Office of Northern Ireland, which will no longer be subject to an absolute exemption, under FoI Act, s 64(2).

[123] See T. McBride, 'The Official Information Act 1982' (1984) 11 *NZULR* 82; L.J. Curtis, 'Freedom of information in Australia' (1983) 14 *Fed LR* 5; H.N. Janisch, 'The Canadian Access to Information Act' [1982] *PL* 534; for America, see M. Supperstone, *Brownlie's Law of Public Order and National Security*, London: Butterworths, 1982, pp 270–87; Birkinshaw, op cit, note 1, Chapter 2.

[124] For discussion of criticism in the US see Birkinshaw, op cit, at 39–40.

[125] See Birkinshaw, op cit; Tomkins, (*The Constitution After Scott: Government Unwrapped*, Oxford: Clarendon, 1998. Chapter 3, at 124–26.

an FoI Act, although it is impossible to know whether FoI could have prevented the Matrix Churchill affair.[126] The report tellingly revealed the lack of 'openness' in government: the system appeared to accept unquestioningly the need to tell Parliament and the public as little as possible about subjects which were seen as politically sensitive. It was apparent that the voluntary Code could not provide a sufficient response to the concerns which the report aroused. The Matrix Churchill affair, which led to the Scott Inquiry, would not, it seems, have come to the attention of the public but for the refusal of the judge in the *Matrix Churchill* trial to accept that the information covered by the PII certificates, relating to the change in the policy of selling arms to Iraq, could not be revealed. As the Select Committee on the PCA pointed out in its Second Report, an FoI Act would tend to change the culture of secrecy in government departments.

Nevertheless, the Conservative Governments of 1979–97 had no plans to enact FoI legislation. The Select Committee on the PCA recommended the introduction of an FoI Act,[127] but this proposal was rejected by the then Conservative Government.[128] In contrast, the Labour Government which came into office in 1997 had made a manifesto commitment to introduce an FoI Act. The White Paper, *Your Right to Know*,[129] was published on 11 December 1997. The White Paper stated: 'Unnecessary secrecy in government leads to arrogance in governance and defective decision-making . . . the climate of public opinion has changed: people expect much greater openness and accountability from government than they used to.'[130] A comprehensive statutory right of access to information was finally introduced with the inception of the Freedom of Information Act 2000.

The Act is the latest of the Labour Government's major measures of constitutional reform, receiving royal assent on 30 November 2000.[131] As will be indicated below, the White Paper proposed an FoI regime that would have had a radical impact.[132] Had it been implemented, not only would it have brought the UK into line with other democracies as regards its freedom of information provision, but also in a number of respects the legislation would have been more bold and radical than that in place in many other countries. When the Bill appeared, it was a grave disappointment,[133] but a number of improvements were made to it during the parliamentary process. The Act

---

[126] See P. Birkinshaw, 'Freedom of information' (1997) 50 *Parliamentary Affairs*, at 166; Tomkins, op cit, at 93, Chapter 3, at 123–6.

[127] Paragraph 126.   [128] HC 75, HC 67 (1996–97).   [129] Cm 3818.

[130] White Paper, *Your Right to Know*, Cm 3818, 1997.

[131] The best source of detailed critical analysis of the Bill may be found on the website of the Campaign for Freedom of Information (http://www.cfoi.org.uk), which contains numerous briefing notes and press releases. None of these is on the final text of the Act, but those prepared for the House of Lords' Committee, Report and Third Reading stages are extremely useful, provided they are read alongside the Act itself, and the following analysis has relied on those notes.

[132] See P. Birkinshaw, 'An "All singin' and all dancin'" affair: New Labour's proposals for FoI' (1998) *PL* 176.

[133] See P. Birkinshaw and N. Parry, 'Every trick in the book: the Freedom of Information Bill 1999' (1999) 4 *EHRLR* 373.

that has emerged cannot be termed radical—far from it—but it shows an adherence to the principle of openness which was absent in the Bill.

In what follows, the aim is to provide an overview of the key provisions of the Act and an indication of some of the main criticisms made of it during its passage through Parliament. It should be noted that initially that the Act does not extend to Scotland, which has introduced its own, somewhat tougher legislation, via the Scottish Parliament.[134]

FUNDAMENTALS OF FOI AND THE 2000 ACT[135]

Rodney Austin identifies a number of common features of FoI regimes, which, together, indicate in essence how FoI legislation differs from the approach taken by the UK up until the 2000 Act.[136] As indicated above, the historical approach of the UK has been to make no comprehensive statutory provision for disclosure of official information, except under the very limited provisions of the Public Records Act 1958; the starting point instead was the criminalization of disclosure in certain categories under the Official Secrets Acts and by virtue of numerous other statutory provisions. By contrast, the essence of FoI regimes, identified by Austin, are: the creation of public rights of access to official information; placing the determination and enforcement of those rights in the hands of an authority independent of government, whether the courts or an information commissioner; the extension of the basic right to information to cover 'all government records, at all levels of government and public authority, subject only to specific interests'.[137] The assumption lying behind FoI legislation is that the release of information is something which is desirable in general terms, the burden lying upon government to justify refusal to release in particular cases.

The 2000 Act may be said partially to share the bases of FoI legislation identified above; as will be explained below, it will give UK citizens, for the first time, a statutory right to official information, which will extend to all such information except that which the Act defines as exempt. In terms of enforcement, there is a mixed picture: as will appear below, the right to information given by the Act is enforceable by an independent Information Commissioner, who, in the final resort, can enforce her orders through invoking the courts' power to punish for contempt of court. However, the Commissioner's power to force government to disclose information will not apply to some of the information that may be released under the Act: her disclosure orders

---

[134] The Freedom of Information (Scotland) Act 2002, ASP 13.

[135] It should be noted that environmental information is covered separately by the Environment Information Regulations, which also came into force on 1 January 2005 and which cover '... information about pollution, energy, noise and radiation ... GMOs, air and water borne disease agents, food contamination, planning, road building and transport schemes'. The basic scheme of the Regulations is that of the 2000 Act, but 'The exemptions are fewer, all are subject to a public interest test and there is no upper cost limit for requests.' See 'Freedom of Information for Journalists'—CFOI website.

[136] 'The Freedom of Information Act 2000: A Sheep in Wolf's Clothing?', in J. Jowell and D. Oliver (eds), *The Changing Constitution*, 5th edn, Oxford: OUP, 2004, p 402.

[137] Ibid.

can in some cases be quashed by Ministerial veto. This is perhaps the first major concern about the Act. The second is the great number and width of the exemptions it contains and the fact that many of these amount to 'class exemptions' where, in order to refuse release of the information, it is not necessary to satisfy a 'harm test', that is, show that release of the particular information requested would prejudice a particular interest, but merely that the information falls into a specified class and is, for that reason alone, exempt.

THE SCOPE OF THE ACT

The Act covers 'public authorities'. Section 3 sets out the various ways in which a body can be a public authority. Instead of using the method adopted in the HRA, which, similarly, covers only 'public authorities' and which defines them by means of a very broad and general, non-exhaustive definition, the FoI Act takes the different route of listing a number of public authorities in Sched 1. The list is divided into two halves. First, Parts I–V list those bodies that are clearly public authorities; under s 6 of the HRA most, if not all, would be standard public authorities.[138] Second, Parts VI–VII list those bodies that are only public authorities so long as they continue to meet the conditions set out in s 4(2) and (3)—that they have been set up by government and their members appointed by central government. Such bodies would probably also be viewed as standard public authorities under the HRA. But the list is not exhaustive, since s 4(1) gives the Secretary of State the power to add bodies to the list in Parts VI–VII if they meet the conditions set out in ss 4(2) and (3), by Order. Further, s 5 provides the Secretary of State with a power to designate a body as a public authority even though it is not listed in Schedule 1, and does not meet the conditions set out in ss 4(2) and (3), but which appears to him to be exercising public functions. These bodies would probably be viewed as functional public authorities under s 6 of the HRA.[139] Under s 3(1)(b), a publicly owned company as defined in s 6 is automatically a public body; no formal designation is needed. Section 6 defines such bodies as those wholly owned by the Crown or any public authority listed in Schedule 1, other than government departments.

Some public authorities are covered only in respect of certain information they hold, in which case the Act only applies to that class of information (s 7(1)). Rather disturbingly, under s 7(3), the Secretary of State can amend Schedule 1 so that a particular public authority becomes one which is subject only to such limited coverage by the Act—in effect potentially drastically limiting the range of information which can be sought from that authority.

It is suggested that although the FoI follows the model of the HRA in differentiating between public authorities as indicated, and between private and public bodies, Schedule 1 read with ss 3–6 does *not* provide an exhaustive list of those bodies that are public authorities for the purposes of s 6 of the HRA, although these provisions

---

[138] See Chapter 3 at 112.   [139] See Chapter 3 at 112–19.

provide a useful guide. The security and intelligence services, which are presumably standard public authorities under s 6 of the HRA, are omitted from Schedule 1 and therefore they are completely excluded from the Act. They meet the conditions set out in ss 4(2) and (3), but are—it is readily apparent—unlikely to be added to Schedule 1, Parts VI–VII. The difference of approach between the two statutes is defensible; there may be cogent reasons why a body, such as the security service, should not provide information (although a *complete* exclusion is hard to defend), although it would be expected to observe the Convention rights in its operations.

Thus, the Act covers, in Schedule 1, all government departments, the House of Commons, the House of Lords, quangos, the NHS, administrative functions of courts and tribunals, police authorities and chief officers of police, the armed forces, local authorities, local public bodies, schools and other public educational institutions, public service broadcasters. Under s 5, private organizations may be designated as public authorities in so far as they carry out statutory functions, as may the privatized utilities and private bodies working on contracted-out functions. The coverage of the Act is therefore far greater than under the Code and it is notable that some private sector bodies may be covered, although the government made it clear in debate on the Bill that a distinction between private and public bodies in terms of their obligations under the FoI Act should be strictly maintained and that s 5 should be used only to designate bodies discharging public functions.[140] The FoI Act is clearly *not* to be extended into the realm of business. The Act has been praised for the very wide range of bodies which it covers; in comparison with FoI regimes abroad, the coverage is very generous. But it should be noted that its coverage of private bodies discharging public functions is subject to the exercise of a discretion by the Secretary of State.

THE BASIC RIGHTS GRANTED BY THE ACT

The Act begins with an apparently broad and generous statement of the rights it confers. The Act grants two basic rights. Section 1(1) states:

Any person making a request for information to a public authority is entitled—

(a) to be informed in writing by the public authority whether it holds information of the description specified in the request [this is referred to in the Act as 'the duty to confirm or deny']; and

(b) if that is the case, to have that information communicated to him.

It may be noted that the right conferred under s 1(1)(b) can cover original documents as well as 'information',[141] and in this respect the Act is clearly an improvement on the Code.

---

[140] HC Standing Committee B, 11 January 2000, Col 67.

[141] Section 84 defines information broadly to cover information 'recorded in any form', and in relation to matters covered by s 51(8) this includes unrecorded information. See also s 11(1), which provides that a public authority should allow an applicant to have copies or sight of the relevant document, or a summary of the information in it, according to the applicant's preferences, provided that satisfying the preferences expressed

Both these fundamental rights are subject to the numerous exemptions that the Act contains. In other words, broadly, where an authority is exempt from providing information under the Act, it is also entitled to refuse even to state whether it holds the information or not, although in some cases, it may only do this where stating whether it holds the information would have the effect of causing the prejudice that the exemption in question is designed to prevent. Such cases will be considered below.

EXEMPTIONS UNDER THE ACT

Under the White Paper, certain public bodies were to be completely excluded from the Act. One was Parliament, on the ground that, as stated in the White Paper, its deliberations are already open and on the public record. The security services, including GCHQ, were also excluded on the ground that they would not be able to carry out their duties effectively if subject to the legislation. Thus, the security services were to be subject to a blanket agency exemption. Apart from these exemptions, there were no exempt *categories* of information at all held by bodies subject to the Act. But seven specified interests were indicated in the White Paper, which took the place of the exemptions under the Code. The test for disclosure was based on an assessment of the harm that disclosure might cause and the need to safeguard the public interest. The test was: will this disclosure cause *substantial* harm to one of these interests? The first of these interests covered national security, defence, and international relations. Obviously, this interest covered a very wide range of information. A further five interests were: law enforcement, personal privacy, commercial confidentiality, the safety of the individual, the public, and the environment, and information supplied in confidence. Finally, there was an interest termed 'the integrity of decision-making and policy advice processes in government'. In this category, a different test was used: it was not necessary to show that disclosure of the information would cause substantial harm; a test of simple harm only was used. The reason for placing this information in a special category was, in the words of the White Paper: 'now more than ever, government needs space and time in which to assess arguments and conduct its own debates with a degree of privacy . . . [decision-making in government] can be damaged by random and premature disclosure of its deliberations under Freedom of Information legislation.' This exemption was possibly the most controversial, since it meant that the full background to a decision could remain undisclosed, tending to restrict debate and challenge to it.

Thus, the exemptions under the White Paper were relatively narrow and were subject to quite a strict harm test. They may be sharply contrasted with those that emerged under the Act which include a number of 'class' based exemptions. In certain respects, moreover, the Code was, on its face, more generous, as indicated at various

---

is 'reasonably practicable'. While Austin (op cit at 411 and 413) sees this as effectively reducing the rights granted to access to information only, not documents, this appears to us an unduly pessimistic reading of the Act.

points below. In particular, the total exemption under s 21 did not appear in the Code in as broad a form,[142] and the exemption under s 35 is broader than the equivalent exemption was under the Code—in para 2.

The exemptions under the Act rely on the key distinction between 'class' and 'harm-based' exemptions mentioned above. The harm-based exemptions under the Act are similar to those indicated in the White Paper: they require the public authority to show that the release of the information requested would, or would be likely to, cause prejudice to the interest specified in the exemption. However, it should be noted that even in relation to the 'harm-based' exemptions, the test used has been substantially watered down from that proposed in the White Paper. That document, as noted above, had used a 'substantial harm' test; the Act itself refers simply to 'prejudice'—a test that is evidently easier to satisfy. It may be noted that the equivalent Scottish Act uses the tougher test of 'substantial prejudice'. The Commissioner has issued a series of guidance notes on the interpretation and operation of the Act,[143] one of which deals with the 'prejudice' test.[144] Firstly, as to the meaning of prejudice, the Commissioner indicates how the term is to be interpreted, in general terms:

In legal terminology, prejudice is commonly understood to mean harm and the Information Commissioner regards them as being equivalent. So, when considering how disclosure of information would prejudice the subject of the exemption being claimed, the public authority may find it more helpful to consider issues of harm or damage. Although prejudice need not be substantial, the Commissioner expects that it be more than trivial. Strictly, the degree of prejudice is not specified, so any level of prejudice might be argued. However, public authorities should bear in mind that the less significant the prejudice is shown to be, the higher the chance of the public interest falling in favour of disclosure.

This indicates that, at the least, the Commissioner is not minded to countenance trivial claims of prejudice.

As noted above, the prejudice-based exemptions can be pleaded on the basis that prejudice would be 'likely' to be caused by the release of information; it is not necessary to show that it would definitely occur. As to this, the Commissioner has said:

The phrase 'likely to prejudice' has been considered by the courts in the case of *R (on the application of Alan Lord) and The Secretary of State for the Home Department*.[145] Although this case concerns the Data Protection Act, the Commissioner regards this interpretation as persuasive. The judgment reads:

'Likely connotes a degree of probability where there is a very significant and weighty chance of prejudice to the identified public interests. The degree of risk must be such that there "may very well" be prejudice to those interests, even if the risk falls short of being more probable than not.'

---

[142] Paragraph 8 of the Code refers to information obtainable under existing statutory rights. See p 974 for s 21 and pp 979–80 for s 35.

[143] Available on the Commissioner's website: see www.foi.gov.uk.

[144] *Freedom of Information Act Awareness Guidance No 20.*   [145] [2003] EWHC 2073.

In other words, the probability of prejudice occurring need not be 'more likely than not', but there should certainly be substantially more than a remote possibility. Once again, this approach will help to rule out flimsy or implausible claims of prejudice.

A number of exemptions are in any event class-based, meaning that in order to refuse the request, the authority only has to show that the information falls into the class of information covered by the exemption, not that its release would cause or be likely to cause harm or prejudice. It may be noted that the class exemptions can be further divided into two groups: those that are content-based, in the sense that no access to the information under the FoI or any other interest is available; and others, which relate not to the content of the information, but to the process of acquiring it. These distinctions are made clear below, in the first group of exemptions considered.

The Act complicates matters further by providing that, in relation to some, but not all, of the class exemptions, and almost all the 'harm exemptions', the authority, having decided that the information is *prima facie* exempt (either because the information falls into the requisite class exemption, or because the relevant harm test is satisfied, as the case may be), must still then go on to consider whether it should be released under the public interest test set out in s 2. This requires the authority to release the information unless 'in all the circumstances of the case, the public interest in maintaining the exemption outweighs the public interest in disclosing the information'. It should be noted that this provision was amended in the Lords so as to require release unless the interest in maintaining secrecy *'outweighs'* the interest in disclosure. This was thought to provide greater protection for freedom of information, since it must be demonstrated that the need for secrecy is the more compelling interest in the particular case.

The strengthening of the public interest test which took place in the Lords led some Liberal Democrat peers to claim that its application to class exemptions in effect transformed them into 'harm'-based exemptions. However, it should be noted that the Campaign for Freedom of Information (CFOI) emphatically rejected this view, on cogent grounds. While the application of a public interest test to the class exemptions does provide for the opportunity to balance the interest in disclosure against that in secrecy, the test is not the same as it would be if considering a harm test. As the CFOI notes, where information falls into a class exemption, and an authority objects to disclosure even under the public interest test, it will be able not only to argue that the specific disclosure would have harmful effects, *but also that the public interest would be harmed by any disclosure from within the relevant class of documents, regardless of the consequences of releasing the actual information in question.*[146] By contrast, under a prejudice test, the authority must be able to identify that harm would be caused by releasing the *specific information* requested.

---

[146] Freedom of Information Bill, House of Lords Third Reading, 21 November 2000 briefing notes, p 10.

In the result, the exemptions under the Act can actually be broken down into four different categories, starting with the most absolute exemptions and moving to the least. It is helpful to consider them in the order suggested by this categorization, because the Act does not set out the exemptions in any systematic way, but rather randomly, so that class exemptions are mixed in with 'harm-based' exemptions, and 'absolute exemptions' with both. It should be noted that the following categorization relates to categories of exemptions, not necessarily to categories of information, although the two may be synonymous. The four suggested categories are as follows, and are described in order of their illiberality.

(a) 'Total' exemptions: that is, class exemptions to which the public interest test in s 2 *does not apply*. Thus, the public authority concerned only has to show that information sought falls into the exempt class, not that its disclosure would cause any harm or prejudice; and, there is no duty to consider whether the public interest in maintaining the exemption outweighs the public interest in disclosing the information.

(b) Class exemptions to which the s 2 public interest test does apply. This is self-explanatory.

(c) Harm-based exemptions to which the s 2 public interest test does not apply. In these exemptions, the authority has to show that the release of the particular information concerned would cause or be likely to cause the relevant prejudice, but then need not go on to consider whether this prejudice outweighs the public interest in disclosure: once prejudice is established, that is the end of the matter.

(d) Harm-based exemptions to which the s 2 public interest test *does* apply. These are the exemptions under which it is hardest for the public authority concerned to resist the release of information. To do so, it must first demonstrate prejudice or likely prejudice from the release of the particular information request and then, even if prejudice is shown, go on to consider whether the public interest in forestalling that prejudice outweighs the public interest in disclosing the information under s 2.

These categories are important, not only in terms of the substantive legal tests which must be satisfied before information may be withheld: they also have crucial practical consequences in terms of time limits and enforcement. As explained below, the 20-day deadline for releasing information does not apply to information released only on public interest grounds. More importantly, the Commissioner's decision to order release on such grounds can, in relation to information held by certain governmental bodies, be vetoed by ministers (a matter discussed further below).

As to what 'the public interest' in the Act means, the Commissioner has again given guidance.[147] Defining 'the public interest' as 'simply something which serves the interests of the public, the Commissioner guidance asserts that therefore when applying the public interest test to a request for disclosure, 'the public authority is simply deciding whether in any particular case it serves the interests of the public better to withhold or to disclose information'. This, it has to be said, is not particularly helpful. However, the guidance goes on to make a number of rather more detailed points.

---

[147] Freedom of Information Act Awareness Guidance No 3.

It is important to bear in mind that the competing interests to be considered are the public interest favouring disclosure against the public (rather than private) interest favouring the withholding of information. There will often be a private interest in withholding information which would reveal incompetence on the part of or corruption within the public authority or which would simply cause embarrassment to the authority. However, the public interest will favour accountability and good administration and it is this interest that must be weighed against the public interest in not disclosing the information.[148]

This should be self-evident, but it is worth stating. More usefully perhaps, the Commissioner takes the view that 'There is a presumption running through the Act that openness is, in itself, to be regarded as something which is in the public interest.' The Guidance goes on to enumerate, non-exhaustively, some of the specific public-interest arguments in favour of disclosure generally:

- furthering the understanding of and participation in the public debate of issues of the day. This factor would come into play if disclosure would allow a more informed debate of issues under consideration by the Government or a local authority.

- promoting accountability and transparency by public authorities for decisions taken by them. Placing an obligation on authorities and officials to provide reasoned explanations for decisions made will improve the quality of decisions and administration.

- promoting accountability and transparency in the spending of public money. The public interest is likely to be served, for instance in the context of private sector delivery of public services, if the disclosure of information ensures greater competition and better value for money that is public. Disclosure of information as to gifts and expenses may also assure the public of the personal probity of elected leaders and officials.

- allowing individuals and companies to understand decisions made by public authorities affecting their lives and, in some cases, assisting individuals in challenging those decisions.

- bringing to light information affecting public health and public safety. The prompt disclosure of information by scientific and other experts may contribute not only to the prevention of accidents or outbreaks of disease but may also increase public confidence in official scientific advice.[149]

This is an encouraging statement of general principles. In particular, bearing in mind the sweeping exemptions relating to health and safety matters which might lead to an investigation, the last point made above is of great interest, as is the general weight placed upon the desirability of transparent decision-making and accountability.

We now turn to enumerating and commenting upon the numerous exemptions the Act contains, classifying them in accordance with the scheme outlined above.

---

[148] Ibid, at [C].   [149] Ibid, at [D].

Class exemptions not subject to the public interest test

First, there are the total exemptions—class exemptions that are not subject to the public interest test.

Most of these exemptions are fairly self-explanatory; therefore, explanation is given only where necessary. Section 21 covers information that is reasonably accessible to the applicant from other sources. It should be noted that this exemption applies even if the applicant would have to pay a higher fee than that provided by the Act to obtain the information (s 21(2)(a)) so long as the information can still be viewed as reasonably accessible. If the fee is excessive, this may no longer be the case. But, in order to be reasonably accessible, the information must be provided *as of right*. The duty to confirm or deny *does* apply, so an applicant would at least have to be told whether the authority to which he applied was holding the information. This is not an exemption in the usual sense of the word—as applied to freedom of information schemes—since it is not content-based and does not deprive the applicant of access to the information in general; it merely prevents him or her from obtaining it under the Act itself.

Section 23(1) covers information supplied by, or which relates to, the intelligence and security services, GCHQ, the special forces, and the various tribunals to which complaints may be made about their activities and about phone tapping. It should be noted that, as indicated above, the bodies mentioned in this exemption are not themselves covered by the Act at all. This exemption therefore applies to information which is held by *another public authority*, but which has been supplied by one of these bodies. Since it is a class exemption, it could apply to information which had no conceivable security implications, such as evidence of a massive overspend on MI5 or MI6's headquarters. The duty to confirm or deny does not apply to information in this category where complying with it would itself involve disclosure of information covered by this exemption. Bearing in mind the complete exclusion of the security and intelligence services from the Act, the use of this exemption unaccompanied by a harm test, and not subject to the public interest test, is likely to mean that sensitive matters of great political significance remain undisclosed, even if their disclosure would ultimately benefit those services or national security.

Section 32 covers information *which is only held* by virtue of being contained in a document or record served on a public authority in proceedings or made by a court or tribunal or party in any proceedings or contained in a document lodged with or created by a person conducting an inquiry or arbitration, for the purposes of the inquiry or arbitration. The duty to confirm or deny does not apply. Section 34 covers information where exemption from s 1(1)(b) is required for the purpose of avoiding an infringement of the privileges of either House of Parliament. The duty to confirm or deny does not apply to information in this category where compliance with it would entail a breach of parliamentary privilege.

The exemption under s 40(1) is a complex one, but essentially it covers two classes of data. The first is information which the inquirer would be able to obtain under the

Data Protection Act (DPA) 1998 because it is personal information which relates to him- or herself; the second covers personal information which relates to *others*, the disclosure of which would *contravene* one or more of the data protection principles or the right under the Act to prevent processing likely to cause damage or distress. The first part of this exemption is designed to ensure that the FoI Act does not give rights which overlap with those granted by the DPA; the second, to ensure that the FoI Act does not give rights which contravene the DPA.

There are a number of further total exemptions. Vexatious requests (s 14) and unduly costly requests (those where compliance would cost more than a reasonable amount, to be specified (s 12)), are exempt, but the duty to confirm or deny applies. Information the disclosure of which would contravene any other Act of Parliament (for example, the Official Secrets Act 1989) or would be incompatible with any EU obligation or constitute a contempt of court is exempt,[150] and the duty to confirm or deny does not apply to the extent that compliance with it would itself amount to a contravention of any of these provisions. This exemption ensures that the FoI Act cannot be seen impliedly to repeal the numerous provisions that criminalize the release of information, but rather preserves them all.

Information the disclosure of which would be an actionable breach of confidence (s 41) is exempt and the duty to confirm or deny does not apply if compliance with it would itself amount to a breach of confidence. This exemption requires some comment. While it is expressed as an absolute exemption, with no need to show that prejudice would be caused by release of the information, and no requirement to consider the public interest in disclosure, in fact the doctrine of confidence may contain the first of these requirements (that is, a need to show detriment—there are conflicting *dicta* on the matter)[151] and certainly contains the second—a need to consider any countervailing public interest in disclosure. This is clearly recognized by the relevant guidance.[152] The CFOI expressed concern at the time of the passage of the Act that while there is clearly some need to protect genuine confidences, governments could seek to protect all information supplied by third parties simply by agreeing with the third party at the time of the communication of the information that it would be treated in confidence. The information would then become confidential, provided that it was not already in the public domain, and subject to the public interest test and, possibly, to the need to show detriment. This potential problem—of 'contracting out' of the obligations under the Act—has however been recognized. The Access Code issued by the Lord Chancellor[153] takes a clear stance on this issue:

When entering into contracts public authorities should refuse to include contractual terms which purport to restrict the disclosure of information held by the authority and relating to the contract beyond the restrictions permitted by the Act. Public authorities cannot 'contract out' of their obligations under the Act. Unless an exemption provided for under the Act is applicable in relation to any particular information, a public authority

---

[150] S 44.   [151] See Chapter 14 at 728.
[152] Freedom of Information Act Awareness Guidance No 2.   [153] Under s 45 of the Act.

will be obliged to disclose that information in response to a request, regardless of the terms of any contract.[154]

What, however, remains of concern is that when adjudicating upon this exemption under the Act, the Commissioner reproduces as faithfully as possible the common law doctrine of confidence, which is now, of course, heavily influenced by Article 10 ECHR, meaning that the duty of confidence must also be tested against the requirements of that Article. In that respect, it is unfortunate that the Guidance published on this exemption does not mention this.

Class exemptions subject to the public interest test

The second category covers class exemptions subject to the public interest test. It will be recalled in relation to these exemptions that in practice, while the Commissioner will always have the last word on whether the information falls into the class in question, he or she will not always be able to enforce a finding that it should nevertheless be released on public interest grounds if the information is held by certain governmental bodies, since the ministerial veto may be used.

It is most convenient to quote the Act itself for the first of these exemptions. Under s 30(1):

Information held by a public authority is exempt information if it has at any time been held by the authority for the purposes of—

(a) any investigation which the public authority has a duty to conduct with a view to it being ascertained—
  (i) whether a person should be charged with an offence, or
  (ii) whether a person charged with an offence is guilty of it,
  (iii) any investigation which is conducted by the authority and in the circumstances may lead to a decision by the authority to institute criminal proceedings which the authority has power to conduct, or
(b) any criminal proceedings which the authority has power to conduct.

This exemption, together with that contained in s 35, is one of the most widely criticized provisions in the Act. It is a sweeping exemption, covering all information, whenever obtained, which relates to investigations that may lead to criminal proceedings. It represents a specific rejection of the recommendation of the MacPherson Report[155] that there should be no class exemption for information relating to police investigations. It also overlaps with the law enforcement of s 31, which does include a harm test. The exclusion of police operational matters and decisions echoes the approach under s 4 of the Official Secrets Act, but unlike s 4, no harm test is included. There are certain aspects of information relating to investigations which would appear to require disclosure in order to be in accord with the principle of openness

---

[154] Quoted in Freedom of Information Act Awareness Guidance No 2.

[155] The *MacPherson Report on the Stephen Lawrence Inquiry*, Cm 4262, 1999, proposed that all such matters should be covered by the FoI Act, subject only to a substantial harm test.

enshrined in the Act. For example, a citizen might suspect that his or her telephone had been tapped without authorization or that he or she had been unlawfully placed under surveillance by other means. Under the Act, no satisfactory method of discovering information relating to such a possibility will exist. It is therefore unfortunate that telephone tapping and electronic surveillance were not subjected to a substantial harm, or even a simple harm, test.

This exemption extends beyond protecting the police and the CPS. Other bodies will also be protected: it will cover all information obtained by safety agencies investigating accidents. Thus, it will cover bodies such as the Health and Safety Executive, the Railway Inspectorate, Nuclear Installations Inspectorate, Civil Aviation Authority, Marine and Coastguard Agency, environmental health officers, trading standards officers, and the Drinking Water Inspectorate. It will cover routine inspections as well as specific investigations, since both can lead to criminal prosecution. Thus, anything from an inspection of a section of railway track by the Railway Inspectorate, to a check upon hygiene in a restaurant by the Health and Safety Executive, could be covered. The duty to confirm or deny does not apply (s 30(3)). As the CFOI commented:

Reports into accidents involving dangerous cars, train crashes, unsafe domestic appliances, air disasters, chemical fires or nuclear incidents will go into a permanently secret filing cabinet. The same goes for reports into risks faced by workers or the public from industrial hazards. The results of safety inspections of the railways, nuclear plants and dangerous factories would be permanently exempt. This is the information that most people assume FoI legislation exists to provide.[156]

It is particularly hard to understand the need for such a sweeping class exemption when s 31 specifically exempts information which could prejudice the prevention or detection of crime, or legal proceedings brought by a public authority arising from various forms of investigation. That exemption will ensure that no information is released which could damage law enforcement and crime detection, while we have noted above that information which could amount to a contempt of court is also exempted. The CFOI noted that the recently retired director general of the Health and Safety Executive has said publicly that the work of the HSE does not require such sweeping protection.[157]

It should be noted that, where it has been decided that the information falls into the protected class, the authority must then go on to consider whether it should be released under the public interest test. Since most of the information above will not be held by a government department (see below), the Commissioner will be able to order disclosure if he or she thinks the information should be released under this provision, with no possibility of a ministerial veto. The Commissioner's own views on this exemption are therefore of particular importance.[158] One point the Commissioner

---

156 Freedom of Information Bill, House of Lords Committee Stage, 19 October 2000 briefing notes. Under the Act as passed, information under this exemption would not go into a 'permanently sealed filing cabinet': after 30 years it would become a historical record and the s 30 exemption would no longer apply.

157 Ibid.   158 See generally Freedom of Information Act Awareness Guidance No. 16.

makes in the relevant published guidance relates to timing and is of considerable importance:

As a general rule, the Commissioner recognises that the public interest in the disclosure of information is likely to be weaker whilst an investigation is being carried out. However once an investigation is completed, the public interest in understanding why an investigation reached a particular conclusion or in seeing that the investigation had been properly carried out is more likely to outweigh the public interest in maintaining the exemption. By the same token, there is likely to be a weaker public interest in disclosure of information about investigations which have been suspended but which may be reopened, than about those which have been concluded or abandoned.

If applied in a thorough-going way, this approach would lay to rest some of the more negative views as to the effect of this exemption, such as those of the CFOI, quoted above. The reports and safety records *will* be made public, under the public interest test, once completed or abandoned; the exemption will be seen as one designed to provide time-limited protection for sensitive ongoing investigations, rather than the very sweeping one that it first appears to be. Moreover, the Commissioner adds:

It should be noted that the presumption that information relating to ongoing investigations will not be released is not invariable. Much will depend upon the effect of disclosure with a stronger case for maintaining the exemption where the confidentiality of the information is critical to the success of the investigation.

This very strongly suggests that the exemption, although a class one, will be tested strongly against the public interest test: once into the balancing act, the public authority, to maintain the exemption, will have to produce real evidence of harm *in the particular case* to outweigh the public interest in disclosure.

One of the few decisions made by the Commissioner under the Act so far is of relevance here. It was made under section 31, not section 30, but, since the two categories cover such similar ground, it is a useful indicator in relation to both. The facts are scarcely dramatic:[159] an individual requested from Bridgend County Borough Council 'A copy of the last hygiene inspection report of the Heronston Hotel'; the Council refused the request,[160] arguing that to reveal it would prejudice the exercise of its function of 'ascertaining whether circumstances which would justify regulatory action in pursuance of any enactment exist or may arise'.[161] The enactment in question was the Food Safety Act 1990. The Council's argument was that:

. . . the release of inspection reports would undermine the way it carries out food hygiene inspections. It promotes an informal approach to the inspection of premises, where advice and practical assistance is given to businesses. . . . If information was publicly available, businesses would no longer be willing to have open discussions with inspectors. The Council would then be forced to adopt a formal inspection regime without the ability to protect the

---

[159] Decision Notice dated 9 December 2005; ref: FS50073296.
[160] Citing section 31(1)(g).   [161] A function listed in s 31(2)(c).

public by what it believes to be more effective means. This, it argues, would be prejudicial to the purpose at section 31(2)(c) of the Act.

The Commissioner rejected the Council's view. It is important that she did so without having to rely on the public interest test: she decided that the exemption itself was not fulfilled. This was because she took the view that 'that the release of this information would bring greater clarity to, and reinforce public confidence in, the inspection system'.[162] She also found that whilst release of the information might, as the Council argued, prejudice its informal inspections system, it would not affect the specific duties the Council had under the Food Safety Act, because it would still be obliged to carry out inspections and, if necessary, 'pursue formal regulatory action'. These points indicate a robust upholding of transparency as a good in itself and a sceptical attitude to the arguments of public authorities against it. More strikingly still, whilst the Commissioner did not formally have to consider the argument based on the public interest, since she did not find the exemption to apply at all, she did 'note that there is an overwhelming public interest in the disclosure of this category of information'. This is a significant statement, and indicates that robust policing by the Commissioner, who will not in this area be subject to the Ministerial veto, may lay to rest some of the fears generated by s 30, as to the transmission of information to the public about issues affecting health and safety.

The other major class exemption in this category, under s 35, has been just as criticized. It amounts to a sweeping exemption for virtually all information relating to the formation of government policy. Under s 35(1):

Information held by a government department or by the National Assembly for Wales is exempt information if it relates to—

(a) the formulation or development of government policy,

(b) Ministerial communications,

(c) the provision of advice by any of the Law Officers or any request for the provision of such advice, or

(d) the operation of any Ministerial private office.

The duty to confirm or deny does not apply.

This exemption is presumably intended to prevent government from having to decide policy in a goldfish bowl—to protect the freeness and frankness of Civil Service advice and of internal debate within government—but, once again, it appears to go far beyond what would sensibly be required to achieve this aim. Section 36 contains a harm-based exemption which covers almost exactly the same ground: it exempts government information which would, or would be likely to, inhibit (a) the free and frank provision of advice, or (b) the free and frank exchange of views for the purposes of deliberation, or (c) would otherwise prejudice, or would be likely otherwise to prejudice, the effective conduct of public affairs. Since this covers all information

---

[162] Statement of Reasons, op cit.

whose release might cause damage to the working of government—and is framed in very broad terms—it appears to be unnecessary to have a sweeping class exemption covering the same ground. Moreover, this exemption is not restricted to Civil Service advice; it covers also the background information used in preparing policy, including the underlying facts and their analysis. As the CFOI commented:

There would be no right to know about purely descriptive reports of existing practice, research reports, evidence on health hazards, assumptions about wage or inflation levels used in calculating costs, studies of overseas practice, consultants' findings or supporting data showing whether official assertions are realistic or not.[163]

The sole, and very limited, exception to this exemption appears in s 35(2); it applies only 'once a decision as to government policy has been taken', and covers 'any statistical information used to provide an informed background to the taking of the decision'. This was a concession made by the government fairly late in the Bill's passage through Parliament and it is very limited. First, unlike most other FoI regimes, by excluding only statistical information from the exemption, it allows the *analysis* of facts to be withheld. Secondly, it only applies once a decision has been taken. Thus, where the government gave consideration to introducing a new policy but then shelved the matter without a decision, statistics used during the consideration process would, bizarrely, remain exempt. However, the Commissioner's interpretation of the Act is again somewhat encouraging. As to the statistical exception, the published guidance firmly states:

Statistical information incorporates analyses, projections and meta-data, as well as the statistics themselves; numerical data which may take the form of a table or graph or simply be a sum total. Statistics must be derived from a recorded or repeatable methodology, and commentary on this is also statistical information.[164]

This suggests a somewhat broader reading of the phrase 'statistical information' than that given in the Act itself.

The Act is much more restrictive in this respect than the previous voluntary Code of Practice on Access to Government Information. The latter required both facts and the analysis of facts underlying policy decisions, including scientific analysis and expert appraisal, to be made available, once decisions were announced. Material relating to policy formation could only be withheld under a harm test—if disclosure would 'harm the frankness and candour of internal discussion'. The White Paper preceding the Bill proposed that there should be no class exemption for material in this area, but rather that, as under the Code, a harm test would have to be satisfied to prevent disclosure. However, the Commissioner has issued important guidance on this provision which all but changes it into a 'harm-based' test. In one of the strongest pronouncements made on the interpretation of the Act, the guidance states:

---

[163] Freedom of Information Bill, House of Lords Committee Stage, 19 October 2000 briefing notes, p 1.
[164] Freedom of Information Act Awareness Guidance No. 24.

The Information Commissioner's view is that there must be some clear, specific and credible evidence that the formulation or development of policy would be materially altered for the worse by the threat of disclosure under the Act.[165]

It will be immediately seen that this approach, by requiring 'specific . . . evidence' of a change 'for the worse', means that the Commissioner is in effect requiring prejudice to be shown: the whole point about a class exemption, in theory at least, is that it is unnecessary to show any such evidence; it is required only to show that the information in question falls within the exemption as defined. If carried through— and subject of course to use of the ministerial veto, this requirement would greatly ameliorate the negative effects of the section 35 exemption. The Commissioner adds specific factors to be taken into account in deciding whether the exemption is made out:

- In this particular case, would release of this information make civil servants less likely to provide full and frank advice or opinions on policy proposals? Would it, for example, prejudice working relationships by exposing dissenting views?

- Would the prospect of future release inhibit the debate and exploration of the full range of policy options that ought to be considered, even if on reflection some of them are seen as extreme?

- Would the prospect of release place civil servants in the position of having to defend everything that has been raised (and possibly later discounted) during deliberation?

- On the other hand, would the possibility of future release act as a deterrent against advice which is ill-considered, vague, poorly prepared or written in unnecessarily brusque or defamatory language? Would the prospect of release in fact enhance the quality of future advice?

- Is the main reason for exempting the information to spare a civil servant or a minister embarrassment? If so, then it is not appropriate to use this exemption.[166]

Two things are note-worthy about the above guidance: first of all, the whole thrust of it is that the effect of the release of the particular information under consideration is what is crucial: as just discussed, this comes very close to re-working this exemption into one based on harm or prejudice. Second, the guidance adverts to reasons why disclosure may actually *improve* the quality of advice and of policy deliberation. This runs directly against the notion of a class-based exemption, which of course is a legislative *presumption* that release will be harmful: by instructing public authorities, and being prepared itself to consider reasons why release may in fact be beneficial, this presumptive quality of the exemption is radically undermined.

The guidance on the application of the public interest test to this exemption is also positive. It emphasizes two distinct interests in disclosure—participation and accountability. In terms of the former, the Guidance notes that 'A key driver for FOI legislation is allowing people access to information that will allow informed participation in the development of government proposals or decisions which are of

<hr/>

165 Ibid, at [e].   166 Ibid.

concern to them',[167] and that participation 'cannot be meaningful' without access to information about how decisions are reached, including rejected policy options. These are powerful statements of principle in favour of disclosure. In terms of accountability, the Guidance specifically recognizes the role of FOI legislation in counterbalancing government control over the release of information by 'spin doctors', seeking to put the most favourable gloss upon it: release of information under the Act would, it asserts: 'better enable the public to make objective judgements on the facts'.[168] It also sets out two situations in which there will generally be a 'strong public interest in disclosure'. One is where the policy decision 'is going to lead to large amounts of public expenditure on a particular project'; the other is where there is a departure from 'routine procedures' or 'standard practices'. In other words, in cases where Ministers appear to be bending or breaking the rules, the public interest in finding out why will be heightened. Overall, the guidance given in relation to this section, if followed by government departments, or enforced upon them by the Commissioner, will have a notably liberalizing effect upon one of the most critical exemptions in the Act. It should, however, be recalled that, because, by definition, it will generally be information held by a government department, if the Commissioner orders disclosure on public interest grounds, the ministerial veto will be available to override him or her. It is too soon to tell what the governmental view on use of the veto will be.

Information intended for future publication where it is reasonable that it should be withheld until that future date is exempt (s 22), and the duty to confirm or deny does not apply to the extent that complying with it would itself entail disclosing such information. The problem with the class exemption under s 22 is its imprecision: it does not specify a period within which the information has to be intended for publication for this exemption to apply. The government repeatedly rejected amendments that would have provided that this exemption could only be relied upon if a date for publication within a short, specified period had already been fixed.

There are a number of further class exemptions. Information subject to legal privilege (s 42) is exempt. The duty to confirm or deny does not apply if compliance with it would itself breach legal privilege. Trade secrets (s 43(1)) are exempt, but the duty does apply. 'Communications with Her Majesty, with other members of the Royal Family or with the Royal Household' are exempt, as is information relating to 'the conferring by the Crown of any honour or dignity' (s 37), and the duty to confirm or deny does not apply. It is unclear why it is necessary to bestow a class exemption relating to the royal household and honours and dignities, although this follows the practice under the previous voluntary Code. A separate class exemption covers information obtained for the purposes of conducting criminal proceedings and a very wide variety of investigations (specified in s 31(2)) carried out under statute or the

---

[167] Ibid.   [168] Ibid, at [f].

prerogative, and which relate to the obtaining of information from confidential sources.

Harm-based exemptions not subject to the public interest test

This third category of exemptions has only one member. There is a general, harm-based exemption under s 36 for information the disclosure of which would be likely to prejudice the effective conduct of public affairs or inhibit free and frank discussion and advice. This exemption is subject to the general public interest test with one exception: for a reason that is not readily apparent, where the information in question is held by the Commons or Lords, the public interest test cannot be considered.

Harm-based exemptions which *are* subject to the public interest test

As harm-based exemptions, these are in one respect the least controversial aspect of the Act. But it should be noted that the Act departed from one of the most liberal and widely praised aspects of the White Paper, namely, the requirement that in order to make out such exemptions, the authority concerned would have to demonstrate 'substantial' harm. This has been changed to a test of simple prejudice, although government spokespersons attempted to deny that the change would make any difference in practice. In each case, the duty to confirm or deny does not apply if, or to the extent that, compliance with it would itself cause the prejudice which the exemption seeks to prevent.

These exemptions cover information the disclosure of which would prejudice or would be likely to prejudice: defence and the armed forces (s 26); international relations (s 27); the economy (s 29); the mental or physical health or safety of any individual (s 38); auditing functions of other public authorities (s 33); the prevention and detection of crime, legal proceedings brought by a public authority arising from an investigation conducted for any of the purposes specified in s 31(2) (above) and carried out under statute or prerogative; collection of tax; immigration controls; good order in prisons; the exercise by any public authority of its functions for any of the purposes specified in s 31(2) (above); relations between administrations in the UK (for example, between the Government and the Scottish Executive) (s 28). These exemptions are relatively straightforward, although they go beyond the information covered by the Official Secrets Act.

A number of these exemptions are more contentious. Section 24 covers information the disclosure of which would prejudice or would be likely to prejudice national security. The use of the national security exemption, albeit accompanied by the harm test, may mean that sensitive matters of great political significance remain undisclosed. In particular, the breadth and uncertainty of the term 'national security' may allow matters which fall only doubtfully within it to remain secret. Had the Act been in place at the time of the change in policy regarding arms sales to Iraq, the subject of the Scott Report, it is likely that information relating to it would not have been disclosed since it could have fallen within the exception clauses. The whole subject of arms sales will probably fall within the national security exception and possibly within other exceptions as well.[169]

Under s 43, information the disclosure of which would prejudice or would be likely to prejudice the commercial interests of any person (including the public authority holding it) is exempt. The CFOI commented that under this exemption, the prejudice referred to could be caused by consumers refusing to buy a dangerous product. Thus, they noted that the fact that a company had sold dangerous products, or behaved in some other improper manner, could be suppressed if disclosure would lead customers to buy alternative products or shareholders to sell their shares.[170] This is clearly correct; however, in the case of unsafe products, the public interest test would surely require disclosure. The Commissioner has indeed said specifically that:

> There would be strong public interest arguments in allowing access to information which would help protect the public from unsafe products or unscrupulous practices even though this might involve revealing a trade secret or other information whose disclosure might harm the commercial interests of a company.[171]

Section 36 covers information which, in the reasonable opinion of a qualified person, would prejudice or be likely to prejudice collective ministerial responsibility, or the work of the Executives of Northern Ireland and Wales, or which would be likely to inhibit the free and frank provision of advice, or the free and frank exchange of views for the purposes of deliberation, or would otherwise prejudice, or would be likely otherwise to prejudice, the effective conduct of public affairs. Two main criticisms of this exemption can be made. First, the test is not a wholly objective one, but is dependent upon 'the reasonable opinion of a qualified person'. The intention behind this provision is apparently to allow a person representing the department or body in question to make the primary determination of prejudice, with the Commissioner being able only to take issue with such a finding if it is irrational in the *Wednesbury* sense. The second main objection to this section is the 'catch-all' provision covering information the release of which could 'prejudice the effective conduct of public affairs', a phrase which is so vague and broad that it could mean almost anything.

Expiry of certain exemptions

As indicated above, the Act, through amendments to the Public Records Act, provides that some of the exemptions will cease to apply after a certain number of years, although these limitations are hardly generous. The following exemptions will cease to apply at all after 30 years (s 63(1)): s 28 (inter-UK relations); s 30(1) (information obtained during an investigation); s 32 (documents generated in litigation); s 33 (audit functions); s 35 (information relating to internal government discussion and advice); s 36 (information which could prejudice effective conduct of public affairs);

---

[169] See further the Minutes of Evidence before the Public Service Committee HC 313–1 of 1995–96 QQ 66 et seq.

[170] Freedom of Information Bill, House of Lords Committee Stage, 19 October 2000 briefing notes, p 1.

[171] Freedom of Information Act Awareness Guidance No 5, at [2].

s 37(1)(a) (communications with royal household); s 42 (legal professional privilege); and s 43 (trade secrets and information which could damage commercial interests). The exemptions under s 21 (information accessible by other means) and s 22 (information intended for future publication) will cease to apply after 30 years where the relevant document is held in a public record office (s 64(1)). Still less generously, information relating to the bestowing of honours and dignities (s 37(1)(b)) only ceases to be exempt after 60 years, while we will have to wait 100 years before the expiry of the exemption for information falling within s 31, that is, information which might prejudice law enforcement, the administration of justice, etc.

Additionally, one of the absolute exemptions—information provided by the security, intelligence, etc. services (s 23(1))—*will cease to be absolute* after 30 years, that is, the public interest in disclosure must be considered once 30 years have passed.

APPLYING FOR INFORMATION AND TIME LIMITS

Requests for information must be in writing (s 8) and, under s 9, a small fee may be charged. Information requested must generally be supplied within 20 days of the request (s 10(1)). However, there is an important exception to this: where an authority finds that information is *prima facie* exempt, either because it falls within a class exemption, or the requisite prejudice is thought to be present, but then goes on to consider whether the information should nevertheless be released under the public interest test, it does not have to make a decision within the normal 20-day deadline. Instead, it must release the information only within an unspecified 'reasonable period'.

Clearly, there may be practical problems in using the Act. The citizen may have difficulty in obtaining the document he or she requires. He or she might not be able to frame the request for information specifically enough in order to obtain the particular documents needed. The request might be met with the response that several hundred documents are available touching on the matter in question; the citizen might lack the expert knowledge needed to identify the particular document required. If so, under s 1(3), the authority arguably need not comply with the request and can continue to postpone its compliance until and if the requester succeeds in formulating the request more specifically. Section 1(3) does not allow the authority to postpone the request until it has had a chance to obtain further information, enabling it to deal with the request. However, the duty to provide advice and assistance so far as reasonable, provided for in section 16 of the Act,[172] would apply to an instance in which the authority was itself able to identify the requisite documents and did not genuinely require further information to do so. It would then come under a duty to assist the applicant in choosing the relevant documents. The Code of Practice published by

---

[172] S 16(1): It shall be the duty of a public authority to provide advice and assistance, so far as it would be reasonable to expect the authority to do so, to persons who propose to make, or have made, requests for information to it.

the Department for Constitutional Affairs[173] deals with the section 16 duty. In relation to the instant point, it states:

8. Authorities should, as far as reasonably practicable, provide assistance to the applicant to enable him or her to describe more clearly the information requested.

10. Appropriate assistance in this instance might include:

   •   providing an outline of the different kinds of information which might meet the terms of the request;

   •   providing access to detailed catalogues and indexes, where these are available, to help the applicant ascertain the nature and extent of the information held by the authority;

   •   providing a general response to the request setting out options for further information which could be provided on request.[174]

This is a helpful clarification that authorities cannot rely upon the applicant's ignorance as to the documents available, without seeking to provide a reasonable level of assistance in identifying the relevant documents.

In terms of time limits, early indications are that central government has a very mixed record on compliance with the Act's requirements within the limits set down.[175] In a press release, The Campaign for Freedom of Information said 'the government's figures showed that a "disturbing" level of requests were not being dealt with within the Act's time limits'.[176] Overall, more than a third (36 per cent) of Government departments failed to meet the deadline of 20 working days; 25 per cent failed even to tell the applicant that they needed extra time, as required by the Act. The Home Office had by far the worst record amongst government departments. In 60 per cent of all requests it failed either to respond to the request within 20 days, or even to inform the applicant that it needed more time within that period. The Campaign said this represented 'routine disregard for the Act's requirements'.[177] Other important Ministries did much better:

the Department for Transport and the Department for Constitutional Affairs both answered 83% of their requests within the basic 20 working day period. The Department for Work and Pensions met this time limit in 81% of cases and the Ministry of Defence, which received far more requests than any other department, met the 20 day limit for 71% of its requests.[178]

There was also disturbing variation in the extent to which the department concerned answered the requests put to it in full. The Department of Transport provided full answers in 76 per cent of cases, followed by the MOD, which managed 67 per cent.

---

[173] Under Section 45 of the Act. The Code is available at: http://www.dca.gov.uk/foi/codepafunc. htm#part1

[174] Op cit, at [8–10].

[175] See 'Freedom of Information Act 2000. Statistics on Implementation in Central Government.' Q1. January–March 2005; published on the website of the Department for Constitutional Affairs.

[176] Press Release, dated 23 June 2005, available on the Campaign's website: http://www.cfoi.org.uk.

[177] Ibid.   [178] Ibid.

However, 'at the other end of the scale the Department of Trade and Industry provided full answers in only 21 per cent of cases, the Home Office in 28 per cent and the Cabinet Office in 29 per cent of cases.' The Campaign said 'it's . . . clear that some parts of Whitehall are more committed to freedom of information than others.'

THE ENFORCEMENT MECHANISM

The basic mechanism

The enforcement review mechanism under the Act is far stronger than the mechanism established under the Code. The internal review of a decision to withhold information, established under the Code, was formalized under the Act and the role of the Ombudsman was taken over by that of the Information Commissioner. The Commissioner's powers are also much more extensive than those of the Ombudsman. As indicated below, he or she has the power to order disclosure of the information and can report a failure to disclose information to the courts, who can treat it in the same way as contempt of court. Under the White Paper, it was to be a criminal offence to destroy, alter, or withhold records relevant to an investigation of the Information Commissioner. It was also to become a criminal offence to shred documents requested by outsiders, including the media and the public. However, the two offences are omitted from the Act. No civil liability is incurred if a public authority does not comply with any duty imposed by the Act (s 56).

The rights granted under the Act are enforceable by the Data Protection Commissioner, now known as 'The Information Commissioner'. Importantly, the Commissioner has security of tenure, being dismissible only by the Crown following an address by both Houses of Parliament. An appeal lies from decisions of the Commissioner to the Information Tribunal, which is made up of experienced lawyers and 'persons to represent the interests' of those seeking information and of public authorities (Sched 2, Part II).

Under s 50: 'Any person (in this section referred to as "the complainant") may apply to the Commissioner for a decision whether, in any specified respect, a request for information made by the complainant to a public authority has been dealt with in accordance with [the Act].' The Commissioner must then make a decision unless the application has been made with 'undue delay', is frivolous or vexatious, or the complainant has not exhausted any complaints procedure provided by the public authority (s 50(1)). If the Commissioner decides that the authority concerned has failed to communicate information, or confirm or deny when required to do so by the Act, he or she must serve a 'decision notice' on the authority stating what it must do to satisfy the Act. He or she may also serve 'Information Notices' upon authorities, requiring the authority concerned to provide him or her with information about a particular application or its compliance with the Act generally.

The Commissioner may ultimately force a recalcitrant authority to act by serving upon it an enforcement notice, which (*per* s 52(1)) 'requir[es] the authority to take, within such time as may be specified in the notice, such steps as may be so specified for complying with those requirements'. If a public authority fails to comply with a Decision, Enforcement or Information Notice, the Commissioner can certify the failure in writing to the High Court, which, the Act provides (s 52(2)):

> may inquire into the matter and, after hearing any witness who may be produced against or on behalf of the public authority, and after hearing any statement that may be offered in defence, deal with the authority as if it had committed a contempt of court.

In other words, the Commissioner's decisions can, in the final analysis, be enforced just as can orders of the court. These powers are buttressed by powers of entry, search, and seizure to gain evidence of a failure by the authority to carry out its obligations under the Act, or comply with a Notice issued by the Commissioner (detailed in Schedule 3).

There does, however, appear to be a developing problem of overload. The Campaign for Freedom of Information reports that, as at November 2005, only 11 months after the Act came into force, there was a backlog of over 1,300 cases, and that some complaints had been with the Commissioner's office for more than 6 months without even being allocated to an investigating officer. This is of particular concern to the media, given that news stories may have a short shelf-life. Where a response is made to a public authorities for documents that would reveal some embarrassing failure or scandal, and media interest in the matter is temporarily intense, the authority may well be tempted just to refuse the request, in the knowledge that even though the Information Commissioner will almost certainly overturn its decision, by the time that is done, media interest in the story will have died down, and the interest generated by the eventual release of the documents will be minimal.

Appeals

The Commissioner's decisions are themselves subject to appeal to the Tribunal, and this power of appeal is exercisable upon the broadest possible grounds. The Act provides that either party may appeal to the Tribunal against a decision notice, and a public authority may appeal against an enforcement or information notice (s 57(2) and (3)), either on the basis that the notice is 'not in accordance with the law', or 'to the extent that the notice involved an exercise of discretion by the Commissioner, that he ought to have exercised his discretion differently' (s 58(1)). The Tribunal is also empowered to review 'any finding of fact on which the notice in question was based' and, as well as being empowered to quash decisions of the Commissioner, may 'substitute such other notice as could have been served by the Commissioner'. There is a further appeal from the Tribunal to the High Court, but on a 'point of law' only (s 59). In practice, this will probably be interpreted so as to allow review of the Tribunal's decisions, not just for error of law, but also on the other accepted heads of judicial review. Early indications are, however, that the Tribunal is in fact taking a more robust, pro-FOI stance than the Commissioner, which is a welcome development.[179]

---

[179] For details, see 'Information Tribunal's Early Decisions Lead to Greater Openness'—20 December 2005; available http://www.cfoi.org.uk/pdf/tribunalnote.pdf

THE MINISTERIAL VETO OF THE COMMISSIONER'S DECISIONS

The ministerial veto is another highly controversial aspect of the Act. The White Paper made no provision for such a power of veto, on the basis that to do so would undermine confidence in the regime. Such a veto clearly dilutes the basic FoI principle that a body independent from government should enforce the rights to information and since, in cases where the release of information could embarrass ministers, it constitutes them judge in their own cause, it is objectionable in principle.

For the veto to be exercisable, two conditions must be satisfied under s 53(1). First, the Notice which the veto will operate to quash must have been served on a government department, the Welsh Assembly, or 'any public authority designated for the purposes of this section by an order made by the Secretary of State'. Second, the Notice must order the release of information which is *prima facie* exempt but which the Commissioner has decided should nevertheless be released under the public interest test in s 2. (By *prima facie* exempt, it will be recalled, is meant information that either falls into a class exemption or, where prejudice is required to render it exempt, the Commissioner has adjudged the prejudice to be present.)

The veto is exercised by means of a certificate signed by the minister concerned, stating that he or she has 'on reasonable grounds formed the opinion that, in respect of the request or requests concerned, there was no failure' to comply with the Act. The decision must be made at a relatively senior level. If the information is sought from a department of the Northern Irish Executive or any NI public authority, it must be exercised by the First and Deputy Minister acting together; if sought from a Welsh department or any Welsh public authority, the Assembly First Secretary makes the decision; if it is sought from a UK Government department or any other public authority, the person responsible is a Cabinet minister. The reasons for the veto must be given to the complainant (s 56), unless doing so would reveal exempt information (s 57), and the certificate must be laid before Parliament or the Welsh/NI assembly as applicable. How much resort will be made to the veto, only time will tell. However, as the Campaign for FOI pointed out, a worrying precedent exists in that the Government has on several occasions refused to comply with rulings by the Ombudsman (PCA) under the previous Code of Practice on Access to Information. Examples include:[180] refusals to comply fully with a recommendation by the PCA as to the release information on Ministerial gifts; preventing the PCA from seeing papers of Cabinet committees which were dealing with the Human Rights Act; and the issuance of a certificate blocking disclosure of information about ministerial conflicts of interest on the grounds that it would be contrary to the public interest. These precedents are far from encouraging: it may be doubted that the additional safeguards built into the use of the veto in the Act will be enough to dissuade or deter Ministers from making use of it, although one may confidently predict an outcry in the media if and

---

[180] For the full report ((HC 951 (2002–03), see http://www.ombudsman.org.uk/pca/document/aoi03nj/index.htm.

when the veto is first used. The Phillis Committee on Government Communications, amongst other matters, called on the Government to publicly renounce the use of the veto.[181]

PUBLICATION SCHEMES

Under ss 19 and 20, public authorities must adopt 'publication schemes' relating to the publication of information by that authority, that is, schemes by which information is made generally available to the public, without a specific request having to be made. This is a significant aspect of the Act, since more citizens will thereby gain access to a wider range of information. The difficulty and expense of making a request will be avoided. The scheme can be devised by the authority or, under s 20, a model scheme devised by the Information Commissioner can be used. If a tailor-made scheme is used, it must be approved by the Commissioner (s 19(1)(a)). Therefore, authorities are likely to use the model schemes, thereby avoiding the need to submit the scheme for approval. Consistency between authorities is probably desirable as promoting transparency and thereby enhancing access to information. For early indications as to the schemes prepared by central government departments, see a report by the CFOI.[182]

CONCLUSIONS

Despite its weaknesses, the Act is a constitutional development whose significance can hardly be over-stated. The Act, enforceable by the Information Commissioner, is a clear improvement on the Code introduced by the Major Government. Rodney Austin described the draft Bill as 'a denial of democracy'.[183] It is suggested that the improvements made to the Bill during its passage through Parliament, while still leaving it a far weaker and more illiberal measure than the scheme proposed by the widely praised White Paper which preceded it, render this view no longer accurate. In particular, the public interest test has been strengthened, and applies to most of the exemptions in the Act, including, crucially, the key class exemptions relating to investigations and to the formation of Government policy; however, as the CFOI points out, it is misleading to view this as converting class exemptions into 'harm-based' ones, since the very existence of a class exemption is based upon a presumption, built into the Act, that such information is, as a class, of a type which generally

---

[181] See http://www.gcreview.gov.uk/news/FinalReport.pdf

[182] 'Central Government Publication Schemes: Good Practice', 0020http://www.cfoi.org.uk/pdf/ps_report.pdf

[183] R. Austin, 'Freedom of information: the constitutional impact', in J. Jowell and D. Oliver, op cit 4th edn., 2000, at 237. He describes the Act itself as 'a fraud on democratic accountability': 'A sheep in wolf's clothing' in Jowell and Oliver, op cit, 5th edn., 2004, at 415.

should not be released. Nevertheless, although it is still too early to tell, the attitude of the Information Commissioner as expressed in the published guidance indicates that, in reality, evidence of individual damage that would be done by publication will be required where a public authority seeks to resist the argument that publication should take place on public interest grounds.[184]

The Act does represent a turning point in British democracy in, for the first time in its history, removing the decision to release many classes of information from government and placing it in the hands of an independent agency, the Information Commissioner, and in giving a statutory 'right' to information, enforceable if necessary through the courts, to citizens. However, as seen, the Act fences round this basic right with so many restrictions that, depending upon its interpretation, much information of any conceivable interest could still be withheld. Whether this turns out to be the case in practice will depend primarily upon the robustness of the stance taken by the Commissioner, particularly in applying the public interest test to the class exemptions under the Act, where it will provide the only means of obtaining disclosure. Early signs in this respect are hopeful, but only the experience of several years will make clear what the Act has achieved.

[184] See above at 981–2.

20

FREEDOM OF POLITICAL EXPRESSION IN BROADCASTING

INTRODUCTION

Broadcasting, more than any other medium, is subject to content regulation on a range of grounds.[1] Most controversially, regulation of political content and curbs on political speech are a well established feature of the broadcast landscape in the UK. The main concern of this chapter is to analyse such interferences from the perspective of the relevant free speech rationales. The free speech rationale generally most pertinent in relation to the position of the mass media is the argument from democracy,[2] although the argument from truth may also be relevant.[3] But in order to provide a framework for the discussion something must be said about the relationship between such rationales and the broadcast media in the context of free political expression.

As discussed in Chapter 1, constitutional courts in a number of jurisdictions as well as international courts, appear to have accepted either that free speech claims of the mass media are indistinguishable from those of speakers generally,[4] or that if special protections for the mass communications media, over and above those for individuals, are to be recognized, they derive only from the argument from democracy, rather than from the special position of such media.[5] The European Court of Human Rights appears impliedly to have adopted the latter position in relation to public interest speech.[6] Under it, it follows that if the mass media are perceived as acting in opposition to such rationales, their protection can be diminished. Special privileges for the media are not viewed in deontological terms, but instrumentally—as a means of enhancing the expression of individuals.[7] This chapter will adopt a variant of that

---

[1] See Chapter 11 at 563–9.   [2] See Chapter 1 at 16–18.
[3] See Chapter 1 at 14–16.   [4] See Chapter 1 at 20–5.
[5] See pp 26–7; see further Barendt, E. M. *Freedom of Speech* 2nd ed OUP 2005 at 421.
[6] See e.g. *Goodwin v UK*, discussed Chapter 7 at 334–6. See further Chapter 2 at 69–71.
[7] See e.g. the European Court of HR: *Informationsverein Lentia and Others v Austria*, judgment of 24 November 1993, Series A no. 276, [38]: 'The Court has frequently stressed the fundamental role of freedom of expression in a democratic society, in particular where, through the press, it serves to impart information and ideas of general interest, which the public is moreover entitled to receive (see, for example, *mutatis mutandis,* the *Observer and Guardian v the United Kingdom* judgment of 26 November 1991, Series A no. 216,

position. It will argue that a perspective based on viewing media free speech as equivalent to that of individuals, but then extending special protection to the media in so far as it harmonizes with free speech arguments, is very valuable as a starting point, but is too limited a one to deal fully with certain of the special requirements placed on broadcasting that are discussed in this chapter. Such requirements can hardly be viewed as special privileges—they are certainly not universally welcomed by broadcasters.[8] This chapter is not concerned to consider special privileges for the media, but special obligations placed upon them, which would not necessarily be pertinent in relation to individual speakers, in particular the obligations to observe due impartiality. Such obligations are viewed as stemming from the privileged position of broadcasters, who can influence audiences of millions and are the subject of higher audience expectations than are the print media, especially in news reporting.

The result of imposing due impartiality requirements is that broadcast speech is *enhanced* in comparison with that of individual speakers who can merely express their own prejudices and unsubstantiated beliefs. In turn such speakers benefit since they have access to a trusted source of information. The BBC in particular is a trusted global brand. The availability of an accurate and trusted source of news is strongly supported by the argument from democracy since if citizens have no such source available to them, they may be unable to distinguish between inaccurate and accurate information in making political choices, or may become disaffected from the political process altogether. So it is argued that the special obligations or curbs placed upon broadcasting discussed in this chapter should be tested against the relevant free speech rationales, but that in considering whether the especially influential position of broadcasters justifies the obligations placed upon them, their position should not be viewed merely as equivalent to that of an individual speaker. Barendt argues: 'it is unsatisfactory simply to apply to modern mass communications media principles developed for individuals and the print media at the beginning of the century'.[9] Curbs that can be plausibly viewed as enhancing speech can be justified on that basis. This model is, it is argued, to be preferred to the US one in which the treatment of mass media speech as equivalent to that of individual speakers, and in particular the refusal to accept due impartiality obligations, has effects that, it is argued, run counter to the free speech rationales from democracy and truth.[10]

Government influence over political speech in broadcasting is clearly of enormous significance owing to the accepted value of such speech at Strasbourg and domestically,[11] and to the importance of broadcasting as the main means of informing the

pp 29–30, para 59). Such an undertaking cannot be successfully accomplished unless it is grounded in the principle of pluralism, of which the State is the ultimate guarantor. This observation is especially valid in relation to audio-visual media, whose programmes are often broadcast very widely'.

[8] See p 1011.

[9] See E. Barendt, chapter 3, p 47 'The First Amendment and the Media' in I. Loveland, (ed.) *Importing the First Amendment*, Oxford: Hart Publishing, 1998.

[10] See E. Barendt ibid. J. Weinberg, 'Broadcasting and Speech' (1993) 81 *California LR* 1103.

[11] See Chapter 2 at 50–5, Chapter 3 at 109, Chapter 7 at 580–2, Chapter 13 at 689–90.

public as to matters of public interest.[12] The openly partisan nature of the popular press means that broadcasting provides the only apparently impartial source of information for most people.[13] As Barendt puts it: 'the more recent evolution of broadcasting has meant that the public has different expectations of the audiovisual media than it has of newspapers or magazines. While it expects the print media to be biased or to adopt a selective coverage of issues of public interest, it has relied on radio and television to provide objective news . . .[14] However, although it might therefore appear that there is a *stronger* case on free speech grounds for protecting broadcasting as opposed to the press from direct state interference with content,[15] in terms of censorship or bans, this has not been accepted in Western constitutions. Broadcasting tends to receive less protection than the press.[16]

This chapter will acknowledge that it is hard to make a case based on the relevant speech rationales for accepting the *extent* to which there is greater state interference with broadcasting as opposed to the print media. Nevertheless, regulatory controls over broadcasting, but not the press, are generally more readily viewed as constitutionally acceptable.[17] This is true of the UK: as discussed in Chapter 11, far-reaching controls over broadcasting via statutory regulation are a well established feature of the mass communications landscape. It is also true of the US, where regulation of broadcasting has not been found to violate the First Amendment.[18] However, in the US content-based control over broadcasting on political grounds has been found to be unconstitutional.[19] The general rationale for broadcast regulation—scarcity of frequencies—is hardly pertinent today in the digital spectrum age, the age of spectrum plenty, but the notion that it is not inconsistent with free speech rationales to impose greater control on broadcasting than on the press remains pervasive.

In the UK control over broadcasting on grounds of both political content and standards of decency is an accepted feature of the regulatory regime for private and public sector broadcasting. The UK government currently exerts control over the presentation of political broadcasting by means of the statutory regime it has persuaded Parliament to put in place. This chapter begins by considering the rules designed to ensure impartiality in such broadcasting. It moves on to consider curbs

---

[12] See further B. Franklin, *Packaging Politics: Political Communications in Britain's Media Democracy*, Oxford: OUP, 2004.

[13] In a debate, 'Television impartiality', organized by the Campaign for Press and Broadcasting Freedom, 23 June 2003, Richard Tait, ITN's former editor-in-chief, cited a recent opinion poll which showed that 70 per cent of people trusted television news, whereas only 6 per cent trusted newspapers.

[14] See E. Barendt, *Freedom of Speech*, 2nd edn. Oxford: OUP, 2005, at 447.

[15] See Chapter 1 at 27–30.

[16] See E. Barendt, *Broadcasting Law*, Oxford: OUP, 1995, esp. chaps II and V.

[17] In the US see *Red Lion Broadcasting v FCC* 395 US 367 (1969); *Action for Children's Television v FCC* 58 F 3d 654 (DC Cir, 1995); in Germany see: Third Television case, 57 BVerfGE 295, 320 (1981); Fourth Television case, 73 BVerfGE 118, 152 (1986). It must be noted that the *Red Lion* case is regarded as anomalous in US speech jurisprudence, although it has not been over-ruled. Whether its general rationale for broadcast regulation—scarcity of frequencies—would be upheld today is doubtful.

[18] See Chapter 11 at 559.

[19] *FCC v League of Women Voters of California* (1984) 468 US 364. See also p 1009 below.

on political content of broadcasts since such legislation also exerts a more direct form of control by banning political advertising. Finally it considers the exceptional censorship powers the government has available to use in relation to private and public sector broadcasting.[20] Aside from the ban on political advertising, actual censorship has only occurred once in recent history and in an extreme situation. All these methods of affecting political broadcasting in independent television were features of the previous regulatory regime under the Broadcasting Act 1990, and they were all continued with little change under the Communications Act 2003. Similar curbs are imposed on the BBC via the BBC's Licence Agreement

This chapter seeks to set all these controls over broadcasting against the relevant free speech rationales in order to consider how far they are justified, especially when compared to the lack of comparable controls over the press. Its key argument is that while a strong case can be made on free speech grounds for controls answering directly to the argument for plurality and impartiality, despite the *prima facie* infringement of free expression they entail, the other interferences seem to have merely a historical basis and create over-broad constraints on broadcasting.

OBLIGATIONS OF DUE IMPARTIALITY AND ACCURACY

As discussed, the notion that regulation of broadcasting is consistent with free speech rationales is well established. Chapter 11 noted that this was the case in both Britain and the US in relation to matters of taste and decency.[21] Anomalously, the US appears to tolerate greater control of broadcasting on the ground of maintaining standards of decency, imposed by the Federal Communications Commission,[22] than Ofcom does in the UK. In contrast to the UK which accepts fairly far-reaching constraints on due impartiality grounds, they have been found in the US to be unconstitutional.[23] Thus while the US tolerates control on taste and decency grounds, it repudiates it on grounds of ensuring impartiality, an anomaly that appears to owe more to cultural norms and constraints than it does to general First Amendment jurisprudence.

The following discussion considers the imposition of rules in the UK seeking to impose due impartiality and accuracy in broadcasting. The rules place broadcasting in a special position since it is the only medium subject to such constraints. At the outset it may be pointed out that, although under the rules accuracy is viewed as an aspect of due impartiality, it can also be viewed as a separate objective. Accuracy is a necessary but not sufficient condition for impartiality. The converse does not apply, but it is

---

[20] In relation to non-BBC broadcasting the power arises under s 336(5) of the Communications Act 2003; there is an equivalent provision in the BBC's agreement. See p 1036 below.

[21] See pp 559–65.   [22] See Chapter 11 at 559–60.   [23] Note 19 above.

worth highlighting the value of accuracy as a separate enterprise since the value connoted by seeking to avoid partiality arguably does not draw sufficient attention to it. Of course what, precisely, is meant by 'impartiality' in today's pluralist society is a problematic matter. As Michael Grade, Chairman of the BBC, put it recently in a public lecture, *The Future of Impartiality*:

Broadcasters aspire to reflect society as it is in order to connect with their audiences. Today, that includes balancing the interests of people of many different faiths—and people of none. Many different value systems now co-exist and are accorded equal respect as long as they operate within the law. The BBC has to reflect that fact—and reflect it impartially. Things were different when the BBC was founded. In 1928, for example, the anonymous author of the BBC Handbook had no doubt about where the BBC's ethical centre of gravity lay. 'The BBC,' said the handbook, 'is doing its best to prevent any decay of Christianity in a nominally Christian country.'[24]

The imposition of due impartiality affecting broadcasting in independent television was a feature of the previous regulatory regime under the Broadcasting Act 1990; it was continued with little significant change under the Communications Act 2003. Similar curbs are imposed on the BBC via the BBC's Licence Agreement, as amended. But the highly important difference between the BBC and independent broadcasting in this context lies in the BBC's self-regulatory tradition. At present the BBC remains a largely self-regulatory body as regards controls on political grounds: it has greater autonomy in this respect than it has in relation to maintaining standards of offence-avoidance since Ofcom at present has no role in ensuring that due impartiality is observed in BBC broadcasting. The fall-out from the Gilligan incident in 2003 followed by the Hutton Report,[25] raised questions about the position of the Corporation in this respect, but its position is unlikely to change radically once its Charter is renewed from 2007 onwards.

THE SCHEME UNDER THE BROADCASTING ACT 1990

As indicated in Chapter 11, the Independent Broadcasting Authority (IBA) was, prior to the introduction of the Broadcasting Act 1990, charged with the regulation of independent television.[26] Before its abolition, it had acquired a reputation for determined resistance to government influence, largely due to its refusal to bow to political pressure in relation to Thames TV's investigation into the shooting of three IRA members on Gibraltar, *Death on the Rock*. An independent investigation into the making of the programme largely exonerated it of bias or of interference with the inquiry in Gibraltar.[27]

When the Broadcasting Act 1990 set up the ITC and the RA to replace the

---

[24] The Goodman Media Lecture: *The Future of Impartiality*, given at the Institute of Mechanical Engineers 11 May 2005.

[25] See pp 1004–6 below.   [26] See pp. 572–3.

[27] Windlesham/Rampton Report on *Death on the Rock*, (1989).

IBA, the 1990 Act imposed a detailed impartiality requirement on the ITC,[28] a controversial requirement that was clearly an interference with the freedom of expression of broadcasters—although arguably justifiable. The ITC was required, under the impartiality clause introduced by s 6(1)(c) of the 1990 Act, to set up a Code to require that politically sensitive programmes had to be balanced in order to ensure due impartiality. Such programmes could be balanced by means of a series of programmes (s 6(2)); it was not necessary that any one programme should be followed by another specific balancing programme. The ITC Programme Code cl 3.3(i) made it clear that a company could not be heard to argue that a programme which might be said to have an anti-government bias could be balanced by programmes broadcast by other companies: the company had to achieve impartiality in its own programming. The Code also indicated in cl 3.3 that it might sometimes be appropriate to ensure that opposing views were indicated in a single programme where it was unlikely that the subject would be considered again in the near future, or where the issues were of 'current or active controversy'. Further detailed guidance as to the requirements of due impartiality was provided by the Code when revised. It stated in its 'Objectives' in cl 3.1 that broadcasters do not have to be 'absolutely neutral on every controversial issue, but that they should deal even-handedly with opposing points of view in the arena of democratic debate'. Clause 3.2(i) explained that the term 'due' is significant, implying that the requirements of impartiality must be adequate to the nature of the subject and the type of programme.

The due impartiality requirement may have meant that some politically controversial programmes were not made: the expense and difficulty of setting up balancing programmes may have had a deterrent effect. In interpreting the Code, the companies may have acted cautiously and may have interpreted what is meant by 'bias' broadly. Thus, although the due impartiality provisions did seek to balance a need for impartiality against the need to protect freedom of expression, they may not have achieved that balance in practice.

THE CURRENT SCHEME—NON-BBC BROADCASTING

The due impartiality requirements are now contained in the Communications Act 2003, ss 319(c) and 320; they are reflected in s 5 of Ofcom's new Broadcasting Code which came into force in 2005. There are three key statutory requirements. First, under s 319(2)(c), news included in television and radio services must be presented with due impartiality. Second, under s 320(1)(a) the opinions of persons providing a programme service on matters of industrial or political controversy or current public policy must be excluded,[29] and, thirdly, under s 320(1)(b), all programming should

---

[28] The function of the Radio Authority (RA) was similar in that respect to that of the Independent Television Commission (ITC).

[29] s 320 (1) The requirements of this section are—(a) the exclusion, in the case of television and radio services (other than a restricted service within the meaning of section 245), from programmes included in

preserve due impartiality on those matters,[30] although this last requirement can be satisfied in relation to 'a series of programmes taken as a whole'.[31] The third require-ment, unlike the other two, represents something close to a form of 'must carry' requirement.[32] These provisions clearly create a sharp distinction between due impartiality in presentation of news and in other programmes. Due impartiality must be achieved in the reporting of news items, not over a series of programmes. The 2003 Act takes the stance that the objective of achieving due impartiality in independent television is the responsibility of Ofcom, just as it was of the ITC.

Ofcom now has the duty of ensuring that these impartiality requirements are met[33] and it can impose penalties if they are breached.[34] The due impartiality provisions are fleshed out in Ofcom's broadcasting Code, s 5.[35] The term 'due impartiality' is defined as follows in s 5:

'Due' is an important qualification to the concept of impartiality. Impartiality itself

---

any of those services of all expressions of the views or opinions of the person providing the service on any of the matters mentioned in subsection (2); (3) Subsection (1)(a) does not require—(a) the exclusion from television programmes of views or opinions relating to the provision of programme services; or (b) the exclusion from radio programmes of views or opinions relating to the provision of programme services.

[30] s 320 Special impartiality requirements

(1) The requirements of this section are . . .
   (b) the preservation, in the case of every television programme service, teletext service, national radio service and national digital sound programme service, of due impartiality, on the part of the person providing the service, as respects all of those matters;
   (c) the prevention, in the case of every local radio service, local digital sound programme service or radio licensable content service, of the giving of undue prominence in the programmes included in the service to the views and opinions of particular persons or bodies on any of those matters.
(2) Those matters are—
   (a) matters of political or industrial controversy; and
   (b) matters relating to current public policy. It may be noted that the requirement in s 320(1)(c) is less stringent than that in s 320(1)(b) since the requirement can be satisfied in all the programming of a service rather than in a specific series of programmes.

[31] s 320(4)(a).
[32] For other specific 'must carry' requirements, see Communications Act 2003, ss 296 and 309. The obligations are not imposed only on the public sector broadcasters. See Chapter 11 at 565.
[33] Under s 319(1) Ofcom has the duty of setting and reviewing standards in its new Code for the content of programmes in television and radio that they think are most likely to achieve this objective. Section 319(2) sets out the standards objectives; they include, in s 319(2)(c), the impartiality requirement regarding news reporting and the objective that the impartiality requirement of s 320 is met. Ofcom's regulatory regime must cover observance of due impartiality in licensed TV services: under s 325 (1) the regulatory regime for every programme service licensed by a Broadcasting Act licence includes conditions for securing—. . . (1) (a) that standards set under section 319 are observed in the provision of that service; and (b) procedures for the handling and resolution of complaints about the observance of those standards are established and main-tained. (2) It shall be the duty of OFCOM themselves to establish procedures for the handling and resolution of complaints about the observance of standards set under section 319.
[34] s 237 of the 2003 Act allows for the imposition of penalties, including financial penalties, for the contravention of licence conditions or of directions given by Ofcom. Under s 325(1)(b) procedures for the handling and resolution of complaints about the observance of those standards are established and main-tained. (2) It shall be the duty of OFCOM themselves to establish procedures for the handling and resolution of complaints about the observance of standards set under section 319.
[35] It came into force in 2005.

means not favouring one side over another. 'Due' means adequate or appropriate to the subject and nature of the programme. So 'due impartiality' does not mean an equal division of time has to be given to every view, or that every argument and every facet of every argument has to be represented. The approach to due impartiality may vary according to the nature of the subject, the type of programme and channel, the likely expectation of the audience as to content, and the extent to which the content and approach is signaled to the audience. Context, as defined in Section Two: Harm and Offence of the Code, is important.

It is of interest to note that the definition begins by stressing the qualifying effect of the term 'due'. Section 5 makes it clear that a degree of impartiality must be achieved, suitable to the context. It is clear that avoidance of bias is the key aim, but the means of achieving it do not need to be viewed in absolute terms. The new due impartiality requirement does not differ in essentials from the old one, although it is more detailed and lays greater emphasis on flexibility, especially in relation to the interpretation of the word 'due'. Under the ITC it was clear that the requirement was interpreted flexibly and that absolute neutrality in news programmes was not expected nor imposed.[36] The important factor appears to be to create a framework based on the principle of impartiality.

The Code begins in s 5.1 with an important statement of principle, reflecting the demand of s 319(2)(c):

News, in whatever form, must be reported with due accuracy and presented with due impartiality.

Other programmes must achieve due impartiality,[37] but the requirement is that programmes on matters of political or industrial controversy or current public policy may be balanced eventually by other programmes[38] so long as ultimately the service cannot be said to have adopted a one-sided view of a sensitive matter. The new impartiality regime is fairly prescriptive in requiring that there should be a reasonably clear linkage between the programmes and that this linkage should be made clear.[39]

---

[36] See pp 1000–1 regarding complaints of pro-war bias made against Fox News (a US news channel broadcasting to the UK via BSkyB). See below (note 47) for the view that the decision of the ITC was too far out of step with the principle of impartiality. See note 46 below regarding a complaint upheld by Ofcom against Fox News in 2004.

[37] Echoing the previous code requirement, Ofcom's Code indicates in s 5.5 that while due impartiality in programme services must be preserved on the matters specified in s 320(1)(b), it can be achieved in a series of programmes in a service taken as a whole. Note: Rules 5.5 to 5.12 apply to television programme services, teletext services, national radio and national digital sound programme services. Section 5.5: Due impartiality on matters of political or industrial controversy and matters relating to current public policy must be preserved on the part of any person providing a service (listed above). This may be achieved within a programme or over a series of programmes taken as a whole.

[38] The Code states in s 5.5 that this means: '. . . more than one programme in the same service, editorially linked, dealing with the same or related issues within an appropriate period and aimed at a like audience. A series can include, for example, a strand, or two programmes (such as a drama and a debate about the drama) or a "cluster" or "season" of programmes on the same subject'.

[39] This regime is as prescriptive as the old one in that, while it lays some emphasis on editorial freedom, it indicates that dates and times of 'balancing' programmes are normally required to be given in advance—as the old regime did. Section 5.6: The broadcast of editorially linked programmes dealing with the same subject

Where matters of 'major political and industrial controversy' are concerned, the linkage has to be clearer or, alternatively, impartiality must be achieved within one programme.[40] Further, 'an appropriately wide range of significant views must be included,'[41] while particular views must not be given 'undue prominence'.[42] Persons providing the service must not express opinions on 'matters of political and industrial controversy and matters relating to current public policy'[43] and accuracy must be observed.[44] The Code reflects the statutory provisions in more detail since news presenters are distinguished from presenters generally: the latter can express their own views but alternative viewpoints must also be represented.[45] This distinction allows for opinionated presenting, but not in relation to news coverage.

Ofcom took a fairly strict approach to the due impartiality rules prior to the introduction of its own Code. In particular it ruled in 2004 that a Fox News presenter had breached the previous ITC Programme Code rules on impartiality. The presenter had accused the BBC of anti-US bias on the day that the Hutton Report (see below) was published. The item was part of a 'personal view' slot, but Fox could not provide evidence to substantiate the claims made. In other words, Ofcom found that they were merely fabricated.[46] On the same facts Fox would probably be found to breach the

matter (as part of a 'series' in which the broadcaster aims to achieve due impartiality) should normally be made clear to the audience on air.

[40] s 5.11 In addition to the rules above, due impartiality must be preserved on matters of major political and industrial controversy and major matters relating to current public policy by the person providing a service (listed above) in each programme or in clearly linked and timely programmes.

[41] s 5.12 In dealing with matters of major political and industrial controversy and major matters relating to current public policy an appropriately wide range of significant views must be included and given due weight in each programme or in clearly linked and timely programmes. Views and facts must not be misrepresented.

[42] s 5.13 (only applying to radio services) Broadcasters should not give undue prominence to the views and opinions of particular persons or bodies on matters of political or industrial controversy and matters relating to current public policy in all the programmes included in any service taken as a whole.

[43] s 5.4 Programmes in the services (listed above) must exclude all expressions of the views and opinions of the person providing the service on matters of political and industrial controversy and matters relating to current public policy (unless that person is speaking in a legislative forum or in a court of law). Views and opinions relating to the provision of programme services are also excluded from this requirement. Section 5.8 Any personal interest of a reporter or presenter, which would call into question the due impartiality of the programme, must be made clear to the audience.

[44] s 5.7 Views and facts must not be misrepresented. Views must also be presented with due weight over appropriate timeframes.

[45] s 5.9 Presenters and reporters (with the exception of news presenters and reporters in news programmes), presenters of 'personal view' or 'authored' programmes or items, and chairs of discussion programmes may express their own views matters of political or industrial controversy or matters relating to current public policy. However, alternative viewpoints must be adequately represented either in the programme, or in a series of programmes taken as a whole. Additionally, presenters must not use the advantage of regular appearances to promote their views in a way that compromises the requirement for due impartiality. Presenter phone-ins must encourage and must not exclude alternative views.

[46] The broadcast complained about was on Fox News, 28 January 2004, 22:00; it was: *The Big Story: My Word*. Ofcom found: 'Fox News was unable to provide any substantial evidence to support the overall allegation that the BBC management had lied and the BBC had an anti-American obsession. It had also incorrectly attributed quotes to the reporter Andrew Gilligan. Even taking into account that this was a "personal view" item, the strength and number of allegations that John Gibson [the Fox presenter] made

current Code, 5.7 (accuracy) and 5.9 (provide balancing views). Ofcom's relatively non-compromising stance may be contrasted with the stance the ITC took in response to fairly similar allegations against Fox News (in this instance of pro-war bias) made in 2003.[47]

SELF-REGULATION IN THE BBC

Before embarking on discussion as to the specifics of the BBC's obligation to maintain impartiality, it is worth pointing out that impartiality must denote the ability to reflect a range of views, treating the government view as no more worthy than other legitimate views. The BBC's Charter is to be renewed with effect from 2007 until 2016, the intention being to create a 'strong and independent BBC'.[48] In this context the criticism made by the House of Lords Select Committee on BBC Charter Renewal that the *process* of renewal, which does not involve Parliament, but is entirely in the hands of the executive, may be highlighted.[49] Clearly, it is not a process that readily lends itself to the creation of a genuinely independent BBC, a matter that could be viewed as relevant to the issue of impartiality. The following discussion concentrates on the special position of the BBC at present, the extent to which it has successfully maintained due impartiality and accuracy, and the options for the future, post-Charter renewal from 2007.

against the BBC meant that Fox News should have offered the BBC an opportunity to respond. Fox News was therefore in breach of Sections 2.1 (respect for truth), 2.7 (opportunity to take part), and 3.5(b) (personal view programmes—opinions expressed must not rest upon false evidence) of the Programme Code' (standards ruling: 14.6.04; from Ofcom's website: ofcom.org.uk).

[47] Fox News is licensed to broadcast in Britain via BSkyB, and in June 2003 the Independent Television Commission cleared the pro-war News channel of partiality after British viewers complained about bias in its coverage of the conflict in Iraq. The ITC rejected nine complaints, finding that Fox News, which holds a British licence, had not breached the programme code on 'due impartiality' because the regulations did not require broadcasters to be 'absolutely neutral on every controversial issue.' Fox News was found by the ITC to met the due impartiality test because it is a 'rolling news channel'—unlike, e.g., a half-hour news programme— and included other points of view. The nine complaints about Fox's coverage were very specific, but generally did not take into account that, for example, a few minutes earlier or later, Fox had given coverage to a peace march. The network usually challenged any speaker, thus implying that there are other points of view. Richard Tait, ITN's former editor-in-chief, commented on this decision in a debate organized by the Campaign for Press and Broadcasting Freedom (note 85 below): 'The fact that the ITC cleared Fox News shows the way things are going but if the regulator says small channels can be judged by different criteria then we have sold the principle of impartiality.'

[48] Review of BBC's Royal Charter *A strong BBC, independent of government*, published May 2005. The White Paper is to be published in 2006.

[49] HL Paper 50–I, 15.3.05, introduction: We do not believe that the Government have seized this opportunity to secure a strong BBC which is truly independent of Government. The Government intend to continue to establish the BBC by Royal Charter through the Privy Council. The Government support this method because they control it. It is entirely up to the Government of the day to decide what goes into the Royal Charter and the associated Agreement between the BBC and the Secretary of State. We believe that the BBC's mandate and structure should be defined in statute rather than by Royal Charter. The passage of an Act through Parliament is more democratic, more independent and more transparent. It provides for all–party involvement and thus protects the BBC from the pressures exerted by any one political party.

The impartiality requirement under the 1990 Act only affected non-BBC broadcasting, although the BBC in its Agreement, Art 5, undertook to comply with similar duties. However, this undertaking was unenforceable, although the BBC generally complied. Cases of doubt would be referred up the Corporation management hierarchy: producers might refer to middle management, who might seek direction from departmental heads, who might then consult the Managing Director or even the Director General. Thus censorship was largely self-imposed; the government did not bring direct influence to bear via statutory constraints and a regulator.

However, the Board of Governors of the BBC is appointed by the government and, although they usually leave editorial matters to the Director General, they may occasionally intervene; they did so in 1985 in relation to a programme about an IRA sympathiser in Belfast, *Real Lives*, after condemnation of it by the Prime Minister—an incident which was perceived as damaging to the BBC's reputation for independence from the government.[50] On the other hand, certain incidents, such as coverage of the US bombing of Libya, led to expressions of concern in the 1980s from the Conservative Party about BBC 'bias' against the government, although this may have been partly mollified by the banning of a documentary on the Zircon spy satellite project in 1987 and of a documentary on the workings of Cabinet government. Both films were eventually shown with modification, the latter by Channel 4 in 1991.[51] Generally speaking, as Gibbons points out, the 'reference up' procedure tends to exclude the influence of the Governors, partly because thinking at the higher levels may be anticipated at the lower.[52]

The BBC remains at present self-regulatory in relation to due impartiality and accuracy, and it appears that this will essentially continue to be the case, albeit with some change as considered below, when the BBC's Charter is renewed at the end of 2006. At present the BBC Governors take the place of Ofcom; the BBC's internal governance document describes the Governors' role as, in a number of respects:

analogous to that of a regulator; ensuring that the BBC acts in accordance with the obligations placed on it by the Charter, by the Agreement and by Statute.[53]

Under the 2003 Act the BBC is drawn further into the external regulatory scheme *except* on the question of impartiality.[54] The due impartiality provision in s 5 of Ofcom's Code does *not* apply to the BBC, and so it remains unenforceable as far as the BBC is concerned. Ofcom can now impose penalties within the powers conferred by the Charter and Agreement if the BBC breaches the provisions of its Agreement or of

---

[50] G. Robertson and D. Nichol, *Media Law*, London: Penguin, 1992, p 484.

[51] See further P. Fiddich, 'Broadcasting: a catalogue of confrontation', in Buchan and Sumner (eds), *Glasnost in Britain: Against Censorship and in Defence of the Word*, London: Macmillan, 1989.

[52] T. Gibbons, *Regulating the Media*, 2nd edn., London: Sweet & Maxwell, 1998, p 141.

[53] BBC governance document entitled 'How the BBC's Board of Governors Fulfils its Responsibilities (the Board's Standing Orders)'. See www.bbc.co.uk/info/policies/governance/pdf/govso.pdf.

[54] As discussed in Chapter 11, the BBC Agreement, as amended, allows Ofcom to impose penalties, including financial ones, on the BBC if it contravenes a 'relevant enforceable requirement'. See pp 595–6.

Part 3 of the 2003 Act, but the Agreement as amended in 2003 excludes impartiality complaints from Ofcom's purview.[55] Thus a complaint regarding due impartiality can be made only to the BBC, not to Ofcom; in this respect due impartiality stands in contrast to the other matters of content regulation in which responsibility is shared.[56] Leaving the BBC outside the regulatory scheme under the 2003 reforms in relation to the due impartiality provisions of Ofcom's Code provides a significant means of maintaining the BBC's dwindling independence.

The key difference, then, between independent television and the BBC is that the BBC Governors still have the responsibility of ensuring due impartiality and accuracy. Thus if a complaint relates to the accuracy and impartiality of a programme, the BBC is finally responsible and, as discussed below, under current plans this will continue to be the case when the BBC Charter is renewed at the end of 2006, although under a new body—the BBC Trust. Complaints about harm and offence or fairness and privacy may be addressed by the BBC, by Ofcom or by both. Thus in relation to accuracy and impartiality in particular the Governors have to undertake a difficult dual role. On the one hand they have to determine the policy and direction of the Corporation in terms of serving the interests of the public. But on the other, they have a role almost equivalent to that of Ofcom in terms of regulation. Clearly, this dual role has the potential to create a conflict of interests. Ofcom is distant from determinations of policy in independent broadcasting in a way that the BBC Governors cannot be. Doubt may arise therefore as to whether they can show sufficient independence in ensuring impartiality. Ofcom has a number of roles in relation to maintaining impartiality—those of investigating, monitoring and enforcing. The BBC Governors in their regulatory mode would be expected to have the same roles.

There are superficial similarities between the schemes for independent and BBC broadcasting. The provisions of the BBC's Charter and Agreement governing impartiality are similar to those already discussed relating to independent television and policed by Ofcom.

The BBC's Agreement provides in relation to programme standards:

Art 5.1: The Corporation shall do all it can to secure that all programmes broadcast or transmitted by or on behalf of or under licence from the Corporation as part of the Home Services:—

(a) provide a properly balanced service consisting of a wide range of subject matter . . . (c) treat controversial subjects with due accuracy and impartiality, both in the Corporation's news services and in the more general field of programmes dealing with matters of public policy or of political or industrial controversy, and do not contain any material expressing

---

[55] s 198 Communications Act provides that Ofcom may impose penalties on the BBC within the powers conferred by the Charter and Agreement if it contravenes the provisions of Part 3 2003 Act or of its Charter and Agreement. Art 5B.3 of the Agreement as amended in 2003 omits s 319(c): 'For the purposes of this clause, 'Applicable Programme Code Standards' means—(a) those standards for the time being set under section 319 of the Communications Act 2003 which relate to the objectives set out in paragraphs (a), (b), (e), (f) and (l) of subsection (2) of that section . . .

[56] See Chapter 11 at 595 and Chapter 17 at 854 and 879 on this point.

the opinion of the Corporation on current affairs or matters of public policy other than broadcasting and matter contained in programmes which consist of proceedings in either House of Parliament or proceedings of a local authority or a committee of two or more local authorities . . .

The BBC's Agreement also allows for balance to be achieved over a series of programmes; it is somewhat more specific than Ofcom's Code as regards informing the audience about the balancing programmes,[57] but the principle that due impartiality—not absolute neutrality—should be secured, taking the context into account, is the same. As for independent broadcasting, it can be secured by a series as a whole.

But although the provisions are similar, it may be argued, as indicated, that there is an inherent weakness in the Governors' regulatory role. This was highlighted by the series of events that led up to the Hutton Report in 2004.[58] One of the conclusions of the Report was that the Governors had failed to discharge their watchdog or regulatory role adequately. The Report concerned a broadcast[59] of an unscripted interview with Andrew Gilligan, a reporter working for the programme. The interview was based on notes from a secret source, later revealed to be Dr David Kelly, a senior civil servant. Previously Gilligan had met up with Dr Kelly to discuss the government's dossier of intelligence justifying the Iraq war. Dr Kelly had indicated to Gilligan that the government had exaggerated the evidence in order to make a strong case and that some of the evidence which it had included in the dossier was—to its knowledge—unreliable. Gilligan in the broadcast relied on the notes he had made of the interview with Kelly in criticizing the government's policies prior to and during the Iraq war. He said that certain of the government's claims in its dossier justifying the war were based on unreliable evidence and that the government was deliberately exaggerating the evidence.

The government considered that the criticism in the broadcast was unfounded and accused the BBC of bias. In the period that followed, David Kelly's name was leaked to the press, meaning that he came under pressure and criticism. In the later Hutton inquiry it was found that the government had not deliberately leaked his name to the press, but had taken the stance that if a reporter discovered his name it would confirm it. However, Hutton did criticize the MOD, Kelly's employer, in that it delayed warning him that its press office had confirmed his name and did not offer him sufficient support at that point. After he found out that his name had been confirmed to

---

[57] Art 5.5(d): (i) that the dates and times of the other programmes comprised in the series should be announced at the time when the first programme so comprised is included in that service, or (ii) if that is not practicable, that advance notice should be given by other means of subsequent programmes so comprised which include material intended to secure, or assist in securing, that due impartiality is achieved in connection with the series as a whole; and those rules shall, in particular, indicate that due impartiality does not require absolute neutrality on every issue or detachment from fundamental democratic principles.

[58] Lord Hutton, Report of the Inquiry into the Circumstances Surrounding the Death of Dr David Kelly C.M.G. (hereafter 'the Hutton Report'). For comment on the Report see G. Smith and D. Sandelson, 'The Future Shape of the BBC—the Hutton Inquiry, Charter Review and the Challenges Facing the BBC and the Government' [2004] *Ent LR* 15(5) 137–146.

[59] The *Today* programme on BBC Radio 4 broadcast shortly after 6am, 29 May 2003.

the media he killed himself. The Hutton Inquiry was set up to examine the events surrounding his death.

In considering the broadcast and the government's complaints relating to it, Lord Hutton's report was highly critical of the BBC's management and of the Governors. It described the corporation's editorial system as 'defective' in that Mr Gilligan's allegations concerned a matter of the highest importance, but he was allowed to broadcast his report without first submitting it to the editors of the programme, meaning that they did not know what he would say and had not approved it.[60] It also found that the BBC management was at fault in a number of respects 'in failing to investigate properly the Government's complaints that the report in the broadcast made a false claim [regarding the government's knowledge of the intelligence justifying the war]'. He found that the investigation into the extent to which Gilligan's allegations were supported by his notes was insufficiently rigorous.[61] The fact that criticism of Gilligan and his relationship with the programme in question was not brought to the attention of the person investigating the complaint demonstrated, it was found, that there was a 'defect in the operation of the BBC's management system for consideration of complaints in respect of broadcasts'.[62] Almost immediately after the publication of the report, both the BBC's chairman, Gavyn Davies, and its director general, Greg Dyke, resigned.

Various conclusions could be drawn from this series of events and the Hutton findings. One possible one is that the government jeopardized the BBC's reputation for independence. It set out to attack the BBC over a matter in which it itself had an extremely strong interest. The broadcast constituted on its face political speech concerning a matter of the highest possible public interest. If the BBC was to broadcast material attacking the government's justification for the Iraq war, the reporters had to rely on anonymous sources. Such sources were always likely to be insiders and were clearly placed in a very difficult position. The government's position could be viewed as merely evincing a cynical determination to discredit anyone who sought to present a view to the public of the justification for the war that differed from the government one. Or it could be viewed as showing a determination to put the true facts before the public as to the government's stance on the intelligence information so that the public

---

[60] Ibid., Chapter 8, para.291(2). 'The allegations that Mr Gilligan was intending to broadcast in respect of the Government and the preparation of the dossier were very grave allegations in relation to a subject of great importance and I consider that the editorial system which the BBC permitted was defective in that Mr Gilligan was allowed to broadcast his report at 6.07am without editors having seen a script of what he was going to say and having considered whether it should be approved'.

[61] Before making the initial reply to the complaint, he found that the BBC management 'failed to make an examination of Mr Gilligan's notes on his personal organiser of his meeting with Dr Kelly to see if they supported the allegations which he had made in his broadcast'. After that point, when 'the BBC management did look at Mr Gilligan's notes after 27 June it failed to appreciate that the notes did not fully support the most serious of the allegations which he had reported in the 6.07am broadcast, and it therefore failed to draw the attention of the Governors to the lack of support in the notes for the most serious of the allegations.' ibid., Chapter 8, para 291(4).

[62] Ibid., Chapter 8, para 291(4). The criticism was in an email from Mr Kevin Marsh, the editor of the *Today* programme, on 27 June 2003 to Mr Stephen Mitchell, the Head of Radio News.

could make up its own mind as to that stance, based on accurate information. Hutton largely found that the government's dossier was not deliberately misleading.[63] The most reasonable conclusion appears to be that Gilligan made an error in his reporting, but that the government's complaints were out of proportion to that error—they stemmed from its overwhelming interest in the need to persuade the public of the reasonableness of its stance on the war.

If taken at face value, the findings of the Hutton Report constitute probably the most serious indictment of the BBC in its history since the Corporation was founded in 1927. The Hutton criticisms clearly go to the heart of the BBC's self-regulatory system. They reveal a significant defect in the BBC's mechanism for dealing with complaints relating to bias: the complaint is dealt with by the management of the BBC itself, in other words by the body that the complaint has been made against. It is not dealt with in terms of the investigation by the 'regulatory' body—the Governors. The Governors themselves did not investigate the government's complaints about the broadcast; they relied on the investigation by the management, which Hutton found to be defective. If one aspect of the Governors' role is analogous to that of a regulator, it appears that the Governors were not fully carrying it out. The Hutton findings can be viewed as calling into question the BBC's continued independence from the Ofcom system in relation to complaints of bias, or at the least as demonstrating that reform aimed at creating greater accountability under the Governors is required.

So the question arises whether, when the BBC's Charter is renewed in 2006, the Corporation should remain self-regulatory, as at present as regards due impartiality. A number of options arise for the government. The Corporation could be brought fully within the Ofcom system so that Ofcom takes over the Governors' regulatory role. (This could mean a shared role with Ofcom, as is already the case in relation to privacy and offence complaints, or it could mean giving Ofcom sole responsibility.) Or the role of the Governors could be over-hauled in an attempt to make them more effective as the regulatory body for the BBC, leaving the Corporation as a largely self-regulatory body. Unsurprisingly, as discussed below, this was the BBC's preferred option, and in the wake of Hutton internal reforms were undertaken with such an over-haul in mind.[64] The middle option is to create another body, charged with ensuring accountability, independent of the government and of Ofcom. This middle option represents the route that the government is taking, favouring creation of a BBC Trust. It was put forward in 2005 in the Green Paper reviewing the BBC's Royal Charter.[65] The Paper states:

---

[63] Ibid, Chapter 12 (3)(i).

[64] See: The BBC's Journalism After Hutton: *The Report of the Neil Review Team*, June 2004. The BBC commissioned and then implemented the Neil Report with a view to addressing the management failings identified by Hutton. A new Code of Practice was adopted from 1 February 2005; if a complainant is dissatisfied with the initial response, complaints can now go to the Independent Complaints Unit; if the complainant is still dissatisfied they can go to the Governors' Programme Complaints Committee (see bbc.co.uk/complaints).

[65] Review of BBC's Royal Charter *A Strong BBC, Independent of Government*, published May 2005. The White Paper, 'A Public Service for all: the BBC in the digital age', Cm 6763, was published in March 2006, and confirmed the 'white' aspects of the Green Paper.

The BBC governance system needs to be reformed and reconstituted, in order to provide clear structural separation between the functions of delivery and oversight . . . We propose the creation of a new body that we have called the BBC Trust to take on the oversight role . . . Responsibility for delivery would be delegated to a formally constituted Executive Board.[66]

It is important to note that although this is a Green Paper, the government stated expressly that parts of it were to be treated as 'White', including this part on governance and accountability.[67] In other words, although the 'White' aspects of the proposals could still be changed, it is unlikely that they will be.

There seems to be a degree of general agreement that BBC accountability requires reform. In oral evidence to the House of Lords Select Committee on BBC Charter Renewal, Michael Grade, Chairman of the BBC, said: 'The allegation that the governors of the BBC have historically been champions of management rather than champions of the BBC . . . is hard to refute'.[68] He also stated that in any event the BBC was undergoing a radical reform with a view to creating a separation between Governors and management.[69] However, the government made it clear in the Green Paper that such reform was viewed as insufficient. The BBC accepted the option of creating a BBC Trust in its Response to the Green Paper.[70] Clearly, it preferred that option to the more radical one of subjecting the BBC fully to the Ofcom regulatory system. Not only is Ofcom seen as a somewhat heavy-handed regulator by the broadcasters,[71] but the creation of a Trust preserves the BBC's unique position in broadcasting.

The remit of the new Trust includes:

. . . setting standards for quality of output, including safeguarding impartiality and accuracy; enforcing regulatory requirements; ensuring the highest standards of fairness and transparency in all complaints procedures, including ultimate responsibility for assessing questions of accuracy and impartiality in BBC output.

Thus the Trust will in future have the responsibility for dealing with complaints such as the one that arose in relation to the Gilligan broadcast. But the notion of creating a BBC Trust, rather than bringing the BBC fully within the Ofcom system regarding complaints as to accuracy and impartiality, has not met with universal approval, most notably from the House of Lords Select Committee on BBC Charter Renewal.[72] In its Report it found that change was necessary—that independent regulation of the BBC had become essential. However, it did not reach this conclusion on the basis that the regulatory system for the BBC—the Governors—had entirely broken down or had become wholly ineffective, despite the Hutton findings. It reached it on the basis of external changes in the broadcasting market and higher expectations of accountability:

---

66 Ibid, at p 10, para 3.1.   67 HL Paper 50–I, 15.3.05 at [47]. See note 65 on the White Paper.
68 HL Paper 50–II, Oral Evidence 15.3.05.   69 See note 64 above.
70 See Review of BBC's Royal Charter BBC's Response to *A Strong BBC, Independent of Government*, published May 2005. The document can be found online at bbc.co.uk/thefuture.
71 See G. Smith and D. Sandelson, 'The Future Shape of the BBC—the Hutton Inquiry, Charter Review and the Challenges Facing the BBC and the Government' [2004] *Ent LR* 15(5) 137–146, at 142.
72 *The Review of the Royal Charter*, Report of Session 1 05–06, HL Paper 50–I, 15.3.05.

Under the Governors the BBC developed into an internationally respected institution . . .
Lord Burns (previous Chair of the BBC) . . . believed change was necessary because the
world outside the BBC had changed not least in corporate governance and the shape of the
media industry (Q 240). We agree. The changing broadcasting market has put the BBC in an
increasingly complex and challenging market position that requires careful independent
regulation and distinct governance. In addition, the last decades have seen the emergence of
more rigorous systems of corporate governance in both the public and private sectors.[73]

But having found that reform was necessary, the Report then found that the BBC
Trust option represented a compromise that did not fully address concerns regarding
the separation of functions between governance and regulation. It found that although
the government proposals were intended to create a structure within which clear
separation of functions would be brought about, the possibility of confusion between
the functions had not been entirely obviated. The Report had sympathy with the
concern put forward in evidence to the Committee by BSkyB to the effect that:

By proposing a new BBC Trust to be responsible for 'oversight' (a term which encompasses
both governance and regulation) and a new Executive Board to be responsible for 'delivery',
the Green Paper seeks to clarify the distinction between the governance and management of
the BBC, rather than clarify the distinction between the governance and regulation of the
BBC . . . it does not address shortcomings in the current regulation of the BBC.[74]

The Report put forward its own proposed solution—that 'in order to secure clearly
independent regulation and clarity for complainants', Ofcom should take the 'final
responsibility' for BBC programme regulation: the BBC would deal with the complaint initially, but Ofcom would act as an appeals body.[75] If this proposal were to
be adopted, Ofcom's Content Board would then undertake the same regulatory
responsibilities for BBC content as it already has in relation to the other terrestrial
public service broadcasters. Its role would also be similar to the one it undertakes in
relation to commercial broadcasting, although since it would not be the first port of
call for complaints, but an appeals body, there would be a significant difference: the
BBC would continue to retain greater independence than the commercial broadcasters. Importantly, under this proposal, Ofcom would have the ultimate responsibility in relation to complaints about accuracy and impartiality, although ensuring the
accuracy of BBC reporting on a day to day basis would remain the responsibility of
the BBC. The Report viewed this division of responsibilities as a significant matter on
the basis that ensuring accuracy is in general a governance, not a regulatory issue. This
might also be said of commercial broadcasting, and in any event regulation, in creating a deterrent against inaccuracy and partiality, can also be viewed positively—as
encouraging accuracy and impartiality.

At present, however, the signs are that the government intends to implement its
proposal to create a BBC Trust which would take over the regulatory role of the BBC
Governors. Clearly, it may be argued that the criticism leveled at this proposal by the

[73] Ibid, at [51].   [74] Ibid, at [72].   [75] Ibid, at [106, 107].

Select Committee is cogent: there appears to be a danger that the regulatory and governance functions of the Trust might create a conflict of interests as they appeared to do in relation to the BBC Governors. The sharing of functions between Ofcom and the BBC is already complex, as Chapter 11 indicated,[76] in relation to complaints about offensive broadcasts. The creation of a different complaints mechanism for accuracy and impartiality complaints adds to the lack of clarity and transparency already apparent in the scheme. Perhaps most significantly, a system for creating accountability that does not depend ultimately on a fully independent body does not appear to satisfy the standards of accountability consumers have come to expect.

CONCLUSIONS

The due impartiality provisions may continue to mean that some politically controversial programmes are not made. In interpreting Ofcom's Code some companies may act cautiously and may decide to ignore some sensitive issues on political grounds. The due impartiality provisions create an infringement of freedom of expression in one sense since they interfere with the content of broadcasting. Section 320(b) of the 2003 Act can only affect a *positive* decision to broadcast a programme dealing with a sensitive issue; there is nothing in the arrangements for the franchising of independent television and radio to affect a decision to ignore some such issues on political grounds. The franchises go to the highest bidder once a 'quality control threshold' is satisfied. Nothing has been done to attempt to ensure that a political balance between franchise holders is achieved at that stage.

Nevertheless, the statutory impartiality rules also have some impact in *protecting* freedom of expression since they promote plurality and wider debate and seek to prevent the dominance of one set of views. The provisions protect the role of the broadcast media in informing the public since they deter broadcasters from providing exaggerated or deeply misleading portrayals of sensitive issues such as asylum-seeking, women's decisions on motherhood, or the work/family balance. A telling comparison may be made with the lack of such provisions in relation to the press. Comparison may also be made with the position in the US where interference on political grounds is viewed as unconstitutional with the result that certain presenters in US television make little or no attempt at impartiality.[77]

Provisions intended to ensure accuracy and impartiality clearly answer to the free speech justifications based on the arguments from democracy and truth, discussed in

---

[76] See pp 595–6.

[77] This, is it is argued, true of the Fox News Channel presenters (see M Grade's 2005 Public Lecture note 24 above). Richard Tait (note 85 below) 'feared what might happen in Britain if Channel 5 followed the example of Fox News which flew the US flag on screen and had sent a reporter to Iraq armed with a gun'. This strategy appears to win audiences and thereby it challenges the other broadcast companies. But obviously it means that US broadcast audiences do not have the same access to impartial news coverage as is available in the UK. Note the rejection by the ITC of nine complaints against Fox News in 2003 (note 47 above), but the upholding of complaints against Fox News by Ofcom in 2004 (note 46 above) on the grounds of bias and inaccuracy.

Chapter 1. But at the same time it is arguable that they do not create a level playing field in relation to criticism and attacks on government policy. The government has many means of conveying its message about policy to the public via the media. If broadcasts are to scrutinize or attack government policy they must often rely on unidentified insider sources, as discussed in Chapter 7.[78] But although 'leaking' is an endemic feature of UK political life, such sources may be in a very precarious position, as the Gilligan affair demonstrated. It may sometimes simply be too difficult to demonstrate that the information placed before the public is accurate. It may be the case that the information does in fact meet standards of accuracy, but it would not be possible to demonstrate that this is the case, either since there is a risk of revealing a source, or because the information cannot be obtained. Possibly in certain circumstances editorial risks, such as the one taken in relation to the Gilligan broadcast on the Iraq war, need to be taken since there is no other way of putting a view opposed to the government one before the public.

In this context an interesting comparison could be drawn between the Judith Miller affair in the US which also concerned the justification for the war in Iraq, discussed in Chapter 7,[79] and the Gilligan affair. In both instances anonymous insider sources were relied upon by the media in order to present a particular view of the justification relied upon by the governments in question to the public. In both instances allegations were made that the governments had sought to discredit insiders who had provided information that contradicted the government view of the need to go to war. But in the US the view put before the public by the reporters was favourable to the war; the information was leaked to the media directly from within the government to reporters generally viewed as right-wing Bush supporters. The US public may have received a generally inaccurate view of the justification for the war in Iraq, partly due to the efforts of a particular group of reporters. The press in the US, like the press in the UK, are subject to no externally imposed requirement to observe accuracy or impartiality. In the UK the information undermined the government justification for the war and was leaked to a reporter working for an organization— the BBC—that has traditionally taken a robustly independent stance. The resulting attack on the BBC by the government was viewed by the then Chairman of the BBC as part of an attempt to place improper pressure on the BBC regarding its reporting of the Iraq war.[80] The House of Lords Select Committee on BBC Charter Renewal considered that the Government's proposals in the Green Paper would not reduce the BBC's vulnerability to political pressure.[81] There is clearly a concern that the Corporation's ability to take a stance critical of government might be diminished under the new Charter.

But at the same time, retention of the principle of impartiality is supportable by reference to its value in enhancing the participation of citizens in a democracy. Clearly, some commercial broadcasters may find that the need to observe impartiality

---

[78] See pp 311–18 on this point.   [79] See pp 317–18.
[80] HL Paper 50–II, Oral Evidence 15.3.05.   [81] HL Paper 50–II, Oral Evidence 15.3.05.

is unduly restrictive in the new world of 'spectrum plenty'.[82] They may consider that the only driving force should be that of the market-place, and that opinionated news on the Fox News Channel[83] or *Daily Mail* model may be the way forward. However, there still appears to be quite a high level of support among broadcasters for the continuance of the impartiality rules, so long as they are interpreted with reasonable flexibility by Ofcom. In his recent lecture on *The Future of Impartiality* Michael Grade, Chairman of the BBC, concluded.'[84]

Now, when legitimate value systems compete, the BBC must act impartially. That applies to areas of cultural controversy, just as much as to the traditional areas of political and industrial debate as defined in the impartiality regulations. The claims and beliefs of religion are—or should be—open to debate, discussion, even satire, just as much as political or philosophical beliefs. Once a particular faith group is allowed to impose its vision of what is appropriate to broadcast, then the BBC's ability to reflect impartially the full breadth and scope of British society is diminished. In a digital universe . . . I would expect that there would still be an overwhelming demand for an impartial BBC, because much as people like opinions, they want—and need—the impartially reported version too.

In a recent debate organized by the Campaign for Press and Broadcasting Freedom,[85] Richard Tait, ITN's former editor-in-chief, found that the British tradition of fair and accurate television reporting had served the public well. He contended that those arguing for a relaxation of the rules on impartiality were ignoring the fact that Britain had a media-literate society: 'People buying a newspaper understand that their paper is taking a view . . . but it is the BBC and ITN, which are way ahead of the press, which the public trust. That is a public good and if you give it up, you must have a good rationale as to what you will get in return.'

A different view was put forward by Chris Shaw, Channel 5's controller of news and current affairs, who considered that opinionated news would create real diversity. He said:

Every news programme already comes with a ready-made set of prejudices . . . a middle class, essentially liberal and English, but not British, point of view. Young people and ethnic groups are alienated by this, so are the not so well educated, the C2s and Es. They are the people who switch off TV news because the agenda, treatment, and prejudices do not chime with their attitude of what is important in their world.

This argument appears to make a valid point in relation to connecting with certain audiences, although on an ungenerous interpretation it could be viewed as tantamount to a plea to pander to prejudice since it is more entertaining than impartiality. But it is contended that it is outweighed by the value of retaining one relatively

---

[82] Michael Grade lecture in 2005, note 24.   [83] See note 46 above, at [27].
[84] See note 46 above, at [32].
[85] The debate, 'Television impartiality', was organized by the Campaign for Press and Broadcasting Freedom and held at the headquarters of the National Union of Journalists on 23 June 2003.

impartial news source that the public can rely on[86]—especially at critical points in public life. Simply exposing news to the market place as though it was merely another media commodity would not create true diversity: the news market would be dominated by certain powerful players, as the broadcast entertainment market and the print media market is at present. Far from encountering a plurality of views, the broadcast audience would merely be exposed to more of the same—the opinionated news in the print media, dominated by the anti-liberal views associated with papers such as *The Sun* and *The Daily Mail*, would be replicated in the broadcast media.

THE BAN ON POLITICAL ADVERTISING

INTRODUCTION

Political advertising, sometimes referred to as 'advocacy advertising', refers to an advertising genre distinct from that covering the promotion of specific consumer products—consumer advertising—although the two verge into each other at the margins. Advocacy advertising covers a wide spectrum of forms of publicity, overlapping with consumer advertising at the one end and party political advertising at the other. It includes so-called 'cause-related' marketing—the promotion of a product by associating it with a particular social or political cause.[87] It covers at its heart issue-based advertising—the advertising of single issue interest groups seeking to sway public opinion towards a particular point of view, but it also covers the advertising of formal political parties and groupings.[88]

Parliament has made it clear in successive Acts of Parliament concerning broadcast regulation that political advertising should not be permitted on television or radio. This has been the case ever since commercial broadcasting began in the UK in the 1950s. Thus commercial advertising is permitted,[89] but advertising on behalf of pressure groups such as Amnesty continues to be forbidden. Under the statutory scheme

---

[86] A MORI survey for DCMS showed that 77per cent of the UK public believe the BBC to be independent and impartial, 80 per cent trust BBC News, and 82 per cent consider BBC News to be accurate. 84 per cent of people in the UK listen to or watch the BBC news each week. A recent YouGov poll commissioned by the Press Gazettee asked a representative sample of more than 2,000 members of the public to name one newspaper, magazine, broadcast news programme, or news website that they considered to be trustworthy. The BBC was mentioned five times more than its nearest rival (www.yougov.com).

[87] See S. Adkins, *Cause-related Marketing*, London: Butterworths, 2000. This form of advertising is especially associated with the companies Benetton and Monsanto.

[88] See for further discussion of the forms of advertising covered A. Scott, ' "A monstrous and unjustifiable infringement"? Political expression and the broadcasting ban on advocacy advertising' [2003] 66(2) *MLR* 224–44 at 225–6.

[89] It might be banned if it had mixed commercial and political objects. Scott (ibid, at 226) notes that when Monsanto launched an advertising campaign associating its products with a particular political message, it chose not to seek to place the advertisements with the broadcast media, placing them in the press instead.

governed by the Broadcasting Act 1990 the broadcasting of political advertising by a licensed service was prohibited.[90] The term 'political advertising' covered advertising by a body whose 'objects were wholly or mainly of a political nature'. The Independent Television Commission (ITC) and Radio Authority (RA) were under duties as regulatory bodies to ensure that this rule was complied with. Their powers to do so are described in Chapter 11.[91] In practice this ban meant that advertising from bodies of a political nature was automatically refused by the licensed services. The ban was continued with some modification, as discussed below, under the Communications Act 2003. Similar bans or stringent curbs are in force across most of Europe, although not in the US or Australia.[92]

The key rationale underlying such bans is the desirability of avoiding the undue influence of the public by powerful, well funded pressure groups.[93] The fear has been that such groups could exploit the powerful medium of broadcasting to subvert the democratic process, especially where they had succeeded in winning bidding wars for air-time. This rationale was one of the main ones put forward by the UK government when it recently decided to continue the ban, as discussed below.[94] As Scott puts it: 'The vision is that of democracy sold to the highest bidder . . . This argument aspires to dignify the prohibition as a bastion of democratic fairness . . . Its purported purpose is to deny wealthy groups a disproportionate access to such an important communications vehicle'.[95] This was the justification put forward by Tessa Jowell M.P., Secretary of State for Culture, Media and Sport, for continuing the ban under the 2003 broadcasting reforms: 'By denying powerful interests the chance to skew political debate, the current ban safeguards the public and democratic debate . . .'[96]

As discussed below, the ban appears to be incompatible with Art 10. It is possible under the particular constitutional balance created by the HRA to pass incompatible provisions in legislation.[97] That balance was intended to reflect the superior power of the democratically elected institution—Parliament, to legislate, as compared to the judicial power to *interpret* legislation. Thus the government used democratic means in order to suppress political speech, even though such speech appears to be underpinned by the argument from democracy.[98] Tessa Jowell's argument is to the effect that allowing political advertising would not further democracy and that therefore, as an instrumental argument, the rationale does not support the relaxation of the ban. If this argument could be shown to be incorrect, at least in relation to *some* speech caught by the ban, then such relaxation would be warranted in order to further democracy. The question is whether all speech covered by the ban ultimately subverts the

---

[90] Broadcasting Act 1990, ss 8(1)(a) and 92.   [91] At pp 572–4.

[92] See note 19 above. Australia regulates political advertising but does not ban it: see S. Miskin and R. Grant, Politics and Public Administration, Research Brief No 5 (04–05) *Political Advertising in Australia.* It may be noted that New Zealand has a ban similar to that in the UK.

[93] See the rationale put forward by the Swiss government, discussed below at pp 1021–2.

[94] See DTI/DCMS *A New Future for Communications* (the White Paper preceding the Communications Act 2003) Cm 5010 (2000), para 6.6.3.

[95] Ibid, at 236.   [96] Hansard, HC Vol. 395, col.788 (3 December 2002).

[97] See Chapter 3 at 150.   [98] See further Chapter 1 at 16–18.

democratic process, as Jowell claims, or whether the impact of the ban on the audience participation in the democracy outweighs that subverting effect, in relation to particular instances of political advertising. Exploration of the varying impacts of the ban in those terms will form a key focus of this section of this chapter.

Since the ban covers political advertising it has varying effects on the different groups and bodies affected by it. Mainstream political groups obtain air-time since their views and policies are rightly viewed by broadcasters as of the most central concern to the viewers. Mainstream politicians obtain air-time and can express their views in documentaries, discussions, interviews, and the like: thus they have many opportunities to speak directly to viewers via the most significant means of communication. Further, the main political parties can directly obtain air time, in the form of Party Broadcasts (PPBs) and Party Election Broadcasts (PEBs), transmitted free. Under ss 37 and 127 of the Political Parties, Elections and Referendums Act 2000 only registered parties and designated organizations are entitled to party political broadcasts or referendum campaign broadcasts. The rules governing PPBs and PEBs, discussed in Chapter 11,[99] make it very difficult for minority parties to qualify since they usually cannot put up enough candidates to do so. The saga behind the *ProLife Alliance* case in relation to the 2001 General Election, discussed in detail in Chapter 11, made this abundantly clear.[100]

This means that in the UK members of minor political parties are doubly marginalized compared to the three main parties in broadcast terms: they are much less likely to be interviewed or asked to appear on discussion shows, and their parties are also much less likely to be able to speak directly to the public via political advertising in the form of PPBs and PEBs. The position of pressure groups, such as Amnesty or Greenpeace who remain outside the party system, is even less favourable. They do not put up candidates for election and therefore have no chance of qualifying for a PPB and PEB, and at the same time they are unlikely to obtain air-time except within occasional documentaries. Not only does this mean that they have very limited opportunities of obtaining publicity within the powerful medium of broadcasting, they also have little control over the broadcast characterization of their own message.

Thus the ban on political advertising hits most hard at pressure groups and minority political parties expressing non-mainstream views—it has a far greater adverse effect on them than it has on the main political parties. The ban takes away the main opportunity for obtaining air-time that such groups would otherwise have had and reinforces their minority and marginalized status. Excluded from the airwaves and often (for different reasons) from the press, they have traditionally been able to seek expression for their message by means—such as direct action—which tend to alienate them further from the majority and re-emphasize their marginal status. The internet is changing this position, but the broadcast ban on political advertising still has great significance given the continuing and powerful influence of broadcasting.

In the other media, advertising, whether commercial or political, is covered by a

---

[99] See pp 577–9. See also note 105 below.   [100] See Chapter 11 at 577–86.

self-regulatory scheme operated by the Advertising Standards Authority (ASA).[101] It is only in broadcasting that political advertising is distinguished so sharply from commercial advertising. In broadcasting commercial advertising is also covered by a self-regulatory scheme operated by the ASA, although Ofcom also has an oversight role, as described in Chapter 11.[102]

THE CURRENT SCHEME

(i) The statutory prohibition

The statutory prohibition is now contained in the Communications Act 2003. The government took the decision, in introducing the 2003 reforms, not to relax or modify the ban,[103] despite the fact that, as discussed below, this meant that it considered that it could not issue a statement of the compatibility of the Act with the European Convention on Human Rights, and instead had to state that it nevertheless wanted to proceed with the Act, under s 19(b) HRA. The government was supported in this decision by the Parliamentary Committees that considered the matter prior to the introduction of the new Act.[104]

The use of the broadcast media for paid political advertising is now prohibited by ss 319 and 321 of the Communications Act 2003. Section 319(2)(g) imposes a duty on Ofcom to ensure that political advertising is not included in television or radio services. Section 321(2) provides that for the purposes of s 319(2)(g) an advertisement will contravene the prohibition on political advertising if it is—

(a) an advertisement which is inserted by or on behalf of a body whose objects are wholly or mainly of a political nature; (b) an advertisement which is directed towards a political end; or (c) an advertisement which has a connection with an industrial dispute

The ban appears to be even wider than these rules would warrant.[105] Section 321(3) provides a non-exhaustive definition of 'objects wholly or mainly of a political nature', which covers: influencing the outcome of elections, bringing about changes in the law, influencing political policy and influencing persons with public functions, including functions conferred via international agreements. These provisions make it clear that

---

[101] See Chapter 10 at 545–9.

[102] See pp 593–5. It may be noted that the advertising of religious bodies in broadcasting is regulated under s10 of the ASA Code.

[103] See note 90 above.

[104] See Joint Committee on the Draft Communications Bill, *The Draft Communications Bill* HL 169–I/HC876–I (2001–02) para 301; Committee on Standards in Public Life, *Fifth Report: The Funding of Political Parties in the UK* Cm 4057 (1998) recommendation 94.

[105] Rule 4 of the Television Advertising Standards Code of the Broadcast Committee of Advertising Practice (BCAP) reflects the ban; it prohibits commercials that: (a) may be inserted by or on behalf of any body whose objects are wholly or mainly of a political nature; (b) may be directed towards any political end; (c) may have any relation to any industrial dispute (with limited exceptions); or (d) may show partiality as respects matters of political or industrial controversy or relating to current public policy. It may be noted that the statute does not contain an equivalent to Rule 4(d) of the Television Advertising Standards Code; the Code is therefore wider than the statute and so creates a broader restriction.

this is an extremely broad and comprehensive prohibition. It may be noted that the objectives mentioned are not confined to the UK, but include influencing foreign governments and policy. This statutory definition of 'political advertising', for the purposes of the ban, is more detailed and explicit than in any previous legislation. In making a determination as to the question whether a body's objects are 'mainly political', it now clear, as discussed below,[106] that Ofcom will follow the decision in *R v Radio Authority ex parte Bull and Another*,[107] taken under the 1990 Broadcasting Act. Ofcom has now made it clear that it will take account of Lord Woolf's finding in that case that ancillary objectives that might be viewed as non-political in a different context can be viewed as political in the context of the body's objectives.[108] Thus Ofcom's stance, based on the *Bull* decision, appears to mean that the prohibition on political advertising is even wider than the statutory words, taken at face value, might be found to denote.

Given the breadth of the definition in s 321(3) it would be difficult for a group campaigning on issues relating to, for example, the environment or poverty, to argue that its objects were not political since it would clearly be open to the charge that it was seeking to influence the government rather than merely seeking to raise awareness on the subject. It would be open to such a group to argue that its objects were only *partly* of a 'political nature', but Ofcom's current stance on this matter does not suggest that it is especially receptive to this argument where a group has admitted that it is seeking to influence the government as an aspect of its objects. If a particular body managed to demonstrate that its objects were only partly political, its advertisement would still be prohibited if it could be viewed as 'directed towards a political end'.

The BBC does not carry paid advertising[109] and therefore the ban is of much less significance in relation to BBC broadcasting.[110] The general responsibility in relation to party political broadcasts is that of the Governors. It is made clear in the BBC's Licence Agreement, as amended in 2003, that the Governors can make decisions as to party political broadcasts within the parameters determined by sections 37 and 127 of the Political Parties, Elections and Referendums Act 2000.[111]

---

[106] For Ofcom's current stance in relation to this decision see p 1019 below.

[107] [1997] 3 WLR 1094.   [108] Note 122 below.   [109] See Article 10 of its Agreement.

[110] It could be enforced against the BBC by Ofcom if necessary. S 198 of the 2003 Act provides that Ofcom may impose financial penalties on the BBC within the powers conferred by the Charter and Agreement if it contravenes the provisions of Part 3 2003 Act or of its Charter and Agreement. See discussion in Chapter 11 at 595–6.

[111] Art 5E.1 The Corporation shall include, in some or all of the Public Broadcasting Services, party political broadcasts and referendum campaign broadcasts.

5E.2 The Governors shall determine from time to time—

(a) which of the Public Broadcasting Services shall include party political broadcasts and referendum campaign broadcasts; and

(b) the basis on which, and the terms and conditions subject to which, such broadcasts are to be so included.

5E.3 For the purposes of subclause 5E.2(b), the Governors may, in particular, determine, so far as they are permitted so to do by the provisions mentioned in subclause 5E.4,—

(a) the political parties on whose behalf party political broadcasts may be made; and

(b) the length and frequency of party political broadcasts and referendum campaign broadcasts.

Prima facie there do not appear to be any significant loop-holes in the Communications Act provisions that an interest group could exploit. They create thresholds that the advertiser and the advertisement, independently, have to cross. The two terms 'objects wholly or mainly of a political nature' and 'directed to a political end' create an important distinction between special interest groups: a group deemed *not* to be of a political nature can still advertise so long as its advertisements are not directed to a political end, whereas a group deemed 'mainly or wholly' political by Ofcom cannot advertise at all, however non-political a particular advertisement is. Thus some interest groups are entirely banned from the air-waves: they are not permitted to advertise on television or radio, regardless of the content of the advertisement.

Since this is an absolute ban it probably contravenes Article 10 of the European Convention on Human Rights, as discussed in detail below. The view taken by the government in introducing the Communications Bill was that the 2003 Act could not be declared to be compatible with the ECHR. The Communications Act is the only Act so far since the Human Rights Act came into force in 2000 not to be accompanied by a statement of compatibility. Section 19 HRA requires that Ministers responsible for government Bills either make a written statement that in their view the Bill is compatible with the Convention rights under s 19(1)(a), or that, even though they are unable to make such a statement, they wish the House to proceed with the Bill anyway, under s 19(1)(b). The Guidance given to Ministers is to the effect that for a s 19(1)(a) statement to be made it must be 'more likely than not that the provisions ... will stand up to challenge on Convention grounds'.[112] But if a s 19(1)(b) statement is made this does not have to be taken to mean that 'the provisions of the Bill are incompatible ... but that the Minister is unable to make a statement of compatibility'. The government took the view that ss 319 and 321 could not be declared to be compatible with Article 10 and so, in accordance with s 19(1)(b) Human Rights Act, no statement of compatibility was issued accompanying the Bill. The government was not prepared to modify the section by creating exceptions in order to seek to ensure compatibility, but the point was made in Parliament that the provisions need not be viewed as incompatible and that they would be defended if necessary.[113]

5E.4 The provisions mentioned in this subclause are sections 37 and 127 of the Political Parties, Elections and Referendums Act 2000 (only registered parties and designated organisations to be entitled to party political broadcasts or referendum campaign broadcasts.)

5E.5 Determinations made by the Governors for any of the purposes of this clause may make different provision for different cases.

5E.6 For the purposes of this clause, 'referendum campaign broadcast' has the meaning given by section 127 of the Political Parties, Elections and Referendums Act 2000.

[112] Department of Constitutional Affairs, Human Rights Act 1998 Guidance for Ministers (2nd edn.), www.dca.gov/hract/guidance.htm#how, para 36. See further D. Feldman, 'The Impact of Human Rights on the UK Legislative Process' (2004) 25(2) *Stat.L.R.* 91.

[113] See Hansard, HC Vol. 395, col. 789 (3 December 2002); Hansard, HL Vol. 646, cols 658–659 (25 March 2003).

(ii) Ofcom's role

Ofcom has the duty of ensuring that the ban is observed.[114] Section 319(1) of the 2003 Act requires Ofcom to set standards to ensure that the 'standards objectives' are met and those objectives include preventing the broadcasting of advertising that infringes the prohibition on political advertising in s 321(2). So the specific obligation to ensure that such advertising is not broadcast is placed on Ofcom and Ofcom has a number of sanctions at its command in meeting it.[115] Ofcom takes the stance that it will enforce the prohibition by making a ruling once it has received enquiries from broadcasters or post-transmission complaints. It cannot rule on the content of a broadcast pre-transmission. It may be concluded that unless the ban is successfully challenged, political advertising will not be broadcast on the BBC or on a licensed service. No instance of infringement of the ban occurred under the previous regime.

The early signs are that Ofcom is not seeking to interpret the statutory words restrictively. In September 2005 Ofcom decided that an advertisement by the campaigning group *Make Poverty History* (MPH) fell foul of the political advertising ban.[116] MPH is made up of a coalition of about 300 charities formed in 2004 to campaign against poverty in developing countries. The stance taken in this instance by Ofcom echoed that taken in 1997 by the ITC in relation to a somewhat similar television advertisement produced by Christian Aid about Third World Debt.[117] The advertisement for MPH[118] featured a number of celebrities stating: 'somebody dies avoidably through poverty every three seconds'.[119] A caption stated: 'Make Poverty History' and directed viewers to the MPH website which encouraged viewers to lobby the Prime Minister or government directly to make this a high priority on their political agenda. Ofcom first considered whether MPH was a body whose aims were wholly or mainly political, and as such was prohibited from advertising on television and radio,[120] and second whether the MPH advertisements, by directing viewers to the MPH website, were 'directed towards a political end' in breach of s 321(2)(b) of the Act,[121] in

---

[114] Section 2, Rule 15 of the BCAP Radio Advertising Standards Code (the Radio Code) is in similar terms to Rule 4(d) (note 105 above). The Broadcast Advertising Clearance Centre ('BACC') and Ofcom are both bound to ensure that Rule 4 is observed. The TV and Radio Codes are administered by the Advertising Standards Authority (ASA) and BCAP. Ofcom, however, remains responsible under the terms of a Memorandum of Understanding, between Ofcom and the ASA, for enforcing Section 4 of the TV Code and Section 2, Rule 15 of the Radio Code.

[115] The licensed services must abide by the ban on fear of penalty imposed by Ofcom since the s 319 conditions, which include the ban, must be covered under s 325 by the conditions included in Broadcasting Act licences, and s 237 allows for the imposition of penalties, including financial penalties, for the contravention of licence conditions.

[116] See Ofcom's website www.ofcom.org.uk; *The Guardian*, 13 September 2005; *The Church Times*, 16 September 2005.

[117] See report by C. Midgeley, *The Times*, 16 December 1997.

[118] In December 2004 the Broadcast Advertising Clearance Centre (BACC) had cleared the advertisement.

[119] In the advertisement, Brad Pitt, Kate Moss, and other celebrities clicked their fingers to mark the speed at which children were dieing in the Third World.

[120] Under sections 321(2) and (3) of the 2003 Act and Section 4(a) of the TV Code and Section 2 Rule 15(b) of the Radio Code.

[121] And Section 4(b) of the TV Code and Section 2 Rule 15 of the Radio Code.

that they sought to influence government policy and decision- making, contrary to s 321(3)(c) of the Act.

Ofcom found that it was clear from its website that MPH was lobbying the Government to change its policy and therefore it was clearly a body with political objects.[122] Ofcom noted that Lord Woolf in *R v Radio Authority ex parte Bull*[123] had stated that when a regulatory authority approaches the question: what is the nature of a body's activities, and in particular whether they are to be regarded as objects which are 'wholly or mainly political', he would expect the regulator to do 'no more than examine its [the organisation's] statement of its objects'. Ofcom considered that there was no doubt that the objects in MPH's manifesto were wholly or mainly political. Ofcom also noted Lord Woolf's statement that objectives ancillary to a principal political objective are also to be treated as political, and found: 'So, to promote, for instance, awareness of global poverty might not in itself be a political object, but where it is used to bring pressure upon a government so as to change its policy, the object of awareness-raising becomes political'. In its decision Ofcom concluded that MPH was a body whose objects are wholly or mainly of a political nature, and the inclusion in broadcast services of the MPH advertisements therefore breached the prohibition.[124] Thus MPH was entirely banned from advertising on the air-waves.

The main object of the advertisement was, Ofcom determined, to direct viewers to the website, rather than to, for example, raise money, and once at the website viewers would access the appeal to lobby the government. Therefore the advertisement itself was also directed towards a political end. This was an interesting aspect of the decision since it rested on the contents of a website—in itself beyond the reach of Ofcom. It raises questions about the ease of accessing the aspects of a website on which the 'political' material is made available, and about the strength of the link needed between the broadcast advertisement and the website before the former falls foul of the political advertising prohibition.

In taking this decision Ofcom departed from that of the television advertising regulatory body, BACC,[125] which had found that the activities of MPH were mainly charitable. The radio equivalent, the RACC, had also taken this stance. Ofcom also found that the due impartiality requirements, discussed above,[126] might well apply to other advertisements concerning the eradication of poverty, assuming that they did *not* fall foul of the political advertising prohibition. This decision was on its face, it is argued, in accordance with the requirements of s 321 as interpreted in s 321(3).

---

[122] Ofcom found that seeking to influence: 'policies relating to trade, debt and aid cannot in Ofcom's view be reasonably described as objectives which are not political in nature. There is, in our view, no escaping the fact that MPH has expressly characterized itself in its manifesto as an organization which seeks to achieve important changes to the policies of the UK government and those of other western governments. Furthermore, MPH's manifesto clearly urges, 'the UK government . . . [to]. . make laws . . .'.

[123] Note 107 above. See further J. Stevens and D. Feldman, 'Broadcasting Advertisements by Bodies with Political Objects, Judicial Review and the Influence of Charities Law' [1997] *PL* 615.

[124] Under the statute and under section 4(a) of the TV code.

[125] Note 114 above. See further Chapter 11 at 593–4 as to BACC.   [126] Pp 997–1001.

However, since Ofcom is a public authority under s 6(1) HRA, it has a duty to abide by Art 10 if it can. It is probable that it has been placed in the position of being forced to breach Art 10 due to the effect of primary legislation—s 321 of the 2003 Act.[127] However, as is discussed in detail below, it is not yet clear that the legislation is incompatible; thus in so far as it can, Ofcom should seek, within the parameters of that legislation, to abide by Art 10. It may be argued, therefore, that it should have sought to place a narrower interpretation on s 321 as it applied to MPH. The possibility of finding that MPH is a mainly charitable body, with some political objectives, was open to it. (It did not—and could not—have charitable status, but it did represent a large number of bodies which did have that status.)[128] That would have meant that the advertisement in question would have been banned, but that MPH could advertise on television and radio with the objective of raising awareness about world poverty or appealing for funds. Lord Woolf's interpretation of 'ancillary' objectives could have been departed from on the basis that otherwise the ban goes further than it needs to do to satisfy the relevant aim under Art 10(2). It was, it is argued, in this respect that Ofcom interpreted the statutory provisions too widely. Clearly, MPH had political objectives, but it was arguable that its charitable aims were more or equally significant.

CHALLENGES TO THE PROHIBITION UNDER THE HUMAN RIGHTS ACT

In the pre-HRA era the challenge of a sub-group of Amnesty International (a group campaigning on human rights abuses) to the ban under the 1990 Broadcasting Act in *R v Radio Authority ex parte Bull and Another*[129] was unsuccessful on the basis that a material proportion of the group's objects were political, although the way that the Radio Authority had reached its decision was criticized. The broadcast in question sought to draw attention to the genocide occurring in Rwanda. The challenge was based only on the narrow argument that the particular sub-group could be viewed as having a sufficient proportion of non-political objects. However, there is the strong probability of a successful challenge under the HRA in similar circumstances since the ban would be tested against the standards of Art 10, not merely those of reasonableness in applying the statutory words.

An interest group, such as MPH, might decide to mount a challenge to the ban under the HRA, relying on Art 10. The action would be likely to be brought in the form of judicial review of a decision of Ofcom's similar to the one it made in its findings regarding MPH. Two questions could arise, depending on the strategy adopted by the interest group's legal advisors: first, whether the ban based on

---

[127] See s 6(2)(a) and (b) HRA, discussed Chapter 3 and text to note 261, p 150.

[128] Organizations that are established to pursue political purposes. such as advocating changes in law or public policy, cannot have charitable status. Bodies that do have such a status are permitted to advertise—see s 10 of Ofcom's Broadcast Code (2005).

[129] [1997] 3 WLR 1094.

ss 319(2)(g) and 321 Communications Act 2003 combined is itself incompatible with
Art 10, and second whether Ofcom's particular decision on the facts was in accord
with the demands of Art 10. It may be noted that in the *ProLife Alliance* case,[130] on
somewhat similar facts, ProLife chose not to challenge the provisions in question
themselves, concentrating only on the second question. That course of action may
have been chosen because ProLife thought it possible that the only remedy they would
obtain would be a declaration of incompatibility, under s4 HRA. In this instance it is
more probable that the only remedy would be a declaration, and the emptiness of the
remedy is of course a deterrent to challengers. However, a campaigning group might
view a challenge in the form of a test case as worthwhile on the basis that it might
secure a change in the law for the future.

Thus, this discussion will begin with the first question. The fact that the 2003 Act
was not declared compatible with the Convention due to the prohibition in s321
indicates that the finding of such a breach, while not inevitable, would be probable.
But in order to make a determination on this matter it is necessary to consider what
Art 10 demands in this context, necessitating examination of the relevant Strasbourg
jurisprudence which would be taken into account under s 2 HRA.

(i) Strasbourg jurisprudence

In *VGT v Switzerland* a Commercial Television Company had refused to broadcast an
advertisement with an animal rights message on the basis that it was clearly political in
nature and therefore contravened the prohibition of political advertising in section
18(5) of the Swiss Radio and Television Act. The European Court of Human Rights
found that Article 10 was engaged even though both protagonists were private parties,
on the basis that domestic law, as interpreted domestically, had made lawful the treatment which the applicant association was complaining of.[131] In effect, the Court found,
political speech by the applicant association was prohibited. Therefore the Court found
that the responsibility of the respondent State within the meaning of Article 1 of the
Convention for any resultant breach of Article 10 was engaged on that basis.

It might have been thought that the interference did not answer to a legitimate aim
encapsulated within Art 10(2) of the Convention. The Swiss government submitted
that the refusal to broadcast the commercial at issue was 'aimed at enabling the
formation of public opinion protected from the pressures of powerful financial
groups, while at the same time promoting equal opportunities for the different components of society. The refusal also secured for the press a segment of the advertising
market, thus contributing towards its financial autonomy'. In the Government's opinion, therefore, the measure was justified 'for the protection of the . . . rights of others'
within the meaning of Article 10(2). The Court accepted this argument; it noted the
Federal Council's message to the Swiss Federal Parliament in which it explained that
the prohibition of political advertising served to prevent financially powerful groups

---

[130] [2004] 1 AC 185. See Chapter 11 at 578–92 for full discussion of the case.
[131] (2002) 34 EHRR 159, at [47].

from obtaining a competitive political advantage. Further, the Federal Court in its judgment had considered that the prohibition served, in addition, to 'ensure the independence of broadcasters, spare the political process from undue commercial influence, provide for a degree of equality of opportunity among the different forces of society and to support the press, which remained free to publish political advertisements'.

In assessing the necessity of the interference, the Court found that the Swiss authorities had a certain margin of appreciation in deciding whether there was a 'pressing social need' to refuse the broadcasting of the commercial. It noted that such a margin of appreciation is particularly essential in commercial matters, especially in an area 'as complex and fluctuating' as that of advertising.[132] However, the Court had already found that the applicant association's film fell outside the regular commercial context and in fact reflected controversial opinions relating to an ongoing debate in Western societies about the protection of animals. Clearly, the Swiss authorities themselves had regarded the content of the applicant association's commercial as being 'political' within the meaning of section 18(5) of the Federal Radio and Television Act. Therefore, since the advertisement represented political speech, the margin of appreciation afforded was much more circumscribed than it would have been in the context of purely commercial speech.[133] The Court therefore brought an intense focus—the closest form of scrutiny—to bear on the question whether the measure in question was proportionate to the aim pursued, and in so doing balanced the applicant association's freedom of expression with the reasons adduced by the Swiss authorities for the prohibition of political advertising. The Court found that the reasons adduced must be 'relevant' and 'sufficient' in respect of the *particular* interference with the rights under Article 10, not merely in relation to its general effect. The Court noted that the contested measure was applied only to radio and television broadcasts, and not to other media such as the press. The Court considered that a prohibition of political advertising which applies only to certain media, and not to others, is not of 'a particularly pressing nature'.

The Court was also unconvinced about the justifiability of applying the general prohibition to the applicant association. It had not been argued that the association itself constituted a powerful financial group which might endanger the independence of the broadcaster or influence public opinion unduly. Nor did it appear that the association was abusing a competitive advantage, since all it was seeking to do was engage in an ongoing general debate about animal protection and the rearing of animals. The Court said that it could not 'exclude that a prohibition of political advertising might be compatible with the requirements of Article 10 of the Convention in certain situations'.[134] However, it found that the domestic authorities had not

---

[132] At [69]. The Court relied on: *markt intern Verlag GmbH and Klaus Beermann v Germany*, judgment of 20 November 1989, Series A no. 165, pp 19–20, at 33, and *Jacubowski v Germany*, judgment of 23 June 1994, Series A no. 291-A, p 14, at 26.

[133] See Chapter 11 on this point.   [134] At [75].

demonstrated in a 'relevant and sufficient' manner why the grounds generally advanced in support of the prohibition of political advertising also served to justify the interference in the particular circumstances of the applicant association's case.[135]

The Government had pointed out that there were various other possibilities of broadcasting the information at issue, but the Court observed that the applicant association, aiming at reaching the entire Swiss public, had no other means than the national television programmes of the Swiss Radio and Television Company at its disposal, since these programmes were the only ones broadcast throughout the country. Private regional television channels and foreign television stations were not received nationwide. Thus a breach of Article 10 was found on the ground of lack of proportionality between the measure employed in order to achieve the aim in question.

The later decision of the European Court of Human Rights in *Murphy v Ireland*[136] also concerned a blanket broadcasting ban. Section 10(3) of Ireland's Radio and Television Act 1988 bans advertisements 'directed towards any religious or political end or which has any relation to an industrial dispute.' The applicant's advertisement began: 'What think ye of Christ?'; it was brief and largely intended to inform audiences regarding information sources about the historical basis of the resurrection.[137] It was banned by the Independent Radio and Television Commission and he took the case to Strasbourg, arguing that the s 10(3) ban breached his rights under Articles 9 and 10 ECHR.

The ECHR considered that the ban amounted to an interference with expression. It said: 'Article 10 protects not only the content and substance of information but also the means of dissemination since any restriction on the means necessarily interferes with the right to receive and impart information.'[138] However, the Court went on to find that the ban was justified as proportionate to the aim pursued. It reached this finding on the basis of according a much wider margin of appreciation to the state than it had in the *VGT* case on the basis that the ban in *Murphy* concerned 'intimate personal convictions within the sphere of morals or . . . religion'.[139] It said: 'it is this margin of appreciation which distinguishes the present case from the case of *Vgt Verein gegen Tierfabriken v Switzerland*. In the latter case, the Court considered that the advertisement prohibited concerned a matter of public interest to which a reduced margin of appreciation applied'.[140] This stance was in accord with a number of its previous decisions in the context of religious sensibilities.[141] This was the key distinction between the two cases—that the one dealt with religious, the other with political, expression.[142]

---

[135] At [75].   [136] (2004) 38 EHRR 13; [2003] ECHR 352 (10 July 2003).

[137] The text of the advert read: 'What think ye of Christ? Would you, like Peter, only say that he is the son of the living God? Have you ever exposed yourself to the historical facts about Christ? The Irish Faith Centre are presenting for Easter week an hour long video by Dr Jean Scott Phd on the evidence of the resurrection from Monday 10th—Saturday 15th April every night at 8.30 and Easter Sunday at 11.30am and also live by satellite at 7.30pm.'

[138] At [61].   [139] At [67].   [140] At [67].   [141] See Chapter 9 at 488–97.

[142] For criticism of the distinction created by the Court see 'You can't say "God" on the radio: Freedom of Expression, religious advertising and the broadcast media after *Murphy v Ireland*' A. Geddis [2004] 2 EHRLR 2004, 181–92.

In relation to the question of proportionality, the Court took into account the fact that, apart from advertisements in the broadcast media, the applicant's religious expression was not otherwise restricted. Other forms of broadcasting of religious matter were permitted and the print media could be utilized for advertisements. Those considerations provided, in the Court's view, highly 'relevant reasons' justifying the Irish State's prohibition of the broadcasting of religious advertisements.[143] The Court also took account of the need to provide a level playing field in relation to religious advertising in broadcasting.

Murphy v Ireland is in line with the previous admissibility decision in *United Christian Broadcasting*.[144] The applicant, a religious charity, complained that its application for a national radio licence had been rejected without any consideration being given to that application's merits. Under the Broadcasting Act 1990, political and religious bodies were not allowed to apply for national radio licences.[145] This was another blanket ban, without any exceptions. The applicant alleged a breach of Article 10 taken alone and in conjunction with Articles 9 and 14. The Government pointed out that the spectrum capacity for national radio services was very limited. It submitted that the restriction imposed on the applicant was designed to safeguard pluralism in the media and avoid discrimination between the many different religions practising throughout the United Kingdom. The ECtHR accepted the Government's submission and declared the application to be manifestly ill-founded. Although it was not expressly stated, it would seem that the ECtHR implicitly accepted the proposition that the Government's objectives could in practice only be achieved by the imposition of a blanket ban on religious bodies applying for national radio licences.

(ii) Applying the Strasbourg jurisprudence under the HRA

If these decisions are applied in the domestic context, under the HRA and Art 10, it is readily apparent that the ban would be viewed as representing an interference with expression under Art 10(1). In *VGT* the Court said on this point that the: 'refusal to broadcast . . . amounted to an interference by a public authority in the exercise of the rights guaranteed by Art 10',[146] and this finding also received support from *Murphy v Ireland*.[147] However, Lord Hoffmann, in the majority, found in *ProLife Alliance*[148] that the right under Art 10 in relation to access to broadcasting was not to be equated straightforwardly to a right to expression or receipt of information; it was a 'right to a fair consideration of being afforded the opportunity to do so; a right not to have one's access to public media denied on discriminatory, arbitrary or unreasonable grounds'.[149] This suggests that the tests for compatibility in relation to access to broadcasting set a lower standard than the test of proportionality under Art 10(2) in relation to political expression generally, a finding that does not sit easily with the determinations in the *VGT* case. It is suggested that the *ProLife* findings on this point

---

[143] At [75].   [144] Appl 44802/98 (2000) Admissibility only.
[145] See now s 350 and Sched 14 Communications Act 2003.   [146] At [48].   [147] At [61].
[148] [2004] 1 AC 185. See Chapter 11 at 578–92 for full discussion of the case.
[149] [2004] 1 AC 185 at [57]–[58]; see further Chapter 11 at 582–92.

are opposed to the settled jurisprudence of the ECHR.[150] In principle, the question should be whether the interference is proportionate to the aim pursued, not merely whether it is discriminatory, arbitrary or unreasonable. It is suggested that this is the better view, but the courts could depart from the interpretation of Art 10 from *VGT v Switzerland*,[151] bearing in mind that the courts are not bound by ECHR decisions under s2HRA. Further, it appears that the domestic courts do not need to follow ECHR case law if a post-HRA decision of the senior domestic courts is incompatible with it.[152] An activist court might succeed in distinguishing *ProLife* from an advertising ban case since *ProLife* did not concern an absolute ban. It might also take into account the fact that an application of ProLife's had already been found inadmissible at Strasbourg, whereas in this instance, the Strasbourg precedent most in point, *VGT*, had succeeded in showing a breach under Art 10. The discussion will proceed on the basis that the test of proportionality does need to be satisfied, but it will also consider the alternative possibility—that the ban would only be found to be incompatible with Art 10 if it was found to be discriminatory, arbitrary or unreasonable.

The interference would probably be viewed as having the legitimate aim of serving the 'rights of others' under Art 10(2), as in the *VGT* case. Although this would probably be the case, it should be noted that in *Chassagnou v France*[153] the Court said that when dealing with 'rights of others' that are not themselves competing Convention rights, 'only indisputable imperatives can justify interference with enjoyment of a Convention right.'[154] The rights at stake in this instance are clearly not Convention rights and so it might appear that they would have to be subjected to this test. *Chassagnou*, however, pre-dated *VGT* and therefore it can almost certainly be assumed that the rights at issue would pass this test. Chapter 9 gives an example of a case which indicates that this is not a consistent feature of the Court's jurisprudence—thus it cannot be viewed as applying the *Chassagnou* test with any degree of seriousness.[155]

A court would then consider whether the ban serves a 'pressing social need'. This is, as discussed in Chapter 2, a threshold test:[156] the question here would be—are the aims pursued by the ban sufficiently weighty and serious to justify the interference with speech, *in principle*? The aims are discussed above and include that of seeking to avoid the subversion of the democratic process by powerful interest groups. It is suggested that this test would be passed. A domestic court would then turn to the question of proportionality in considering whether the particular measure chosen—the absolute ban—is proportionate to the aims put forward. In other words, it would probably

---

[150] See Chapter 2 at 50–72 on this point.   [151] (2002) 34 EHRR 159.

[152] In *Price v Leeds CC* [2005] 1 WLR 1825 the Court of Appeal had to decide whether to follow the decision of the *House of Lords in Harrow LBC v Qazi* [2003] UKHL 43 or the subsequent decision of the ECHR in *Connors v UK* (2004) 40 EHRR 189 which it found was incompatible with *Qazi*. It declined to follow the decision in *Connors* and granted leave to appeal to the House of Lords. *ProLife* post-dated *VGT*, but there was no recognition in *ProLife* of incompatibility between the two decisions. It is reasonably clear that if a domestic court subsequently found that incompatibility between the two did arise it would follow the domestic decision. This follows *a fortiori* from *Price*. See further Chapter 1 at 10 on this point.

[153] (2000) 29 EHRR 615.   [154] At [113].   [155] At pp 494–7, 501, note 99.

[156] At pp 93–7.

accept that there is a pressing social need to regulate political advertising but might find that the ban is too far-reaching to be viewed as proportionate to the aim. In examining this question, since the ban concerns political, not religious or commercial speech, an intense focus should be brought to bear on the issues. *Murphy v Ireland* made it clear that the margin of appreciation conceded would be broader in the case of religious speech. As indicated above, that was the key distinction between *Murphy* and *VGT*. Therefore it is hard to see how *Murphy* or *United Christians* could be relied upon to support the use of deference in relation to a ban on *political* advertising, leaving aside the matter of the non-applicability of the margin of appreciation doctrine at the domestic level. The need for intense scrutiny is based on reliance on the *VGT* case, and on the general Strasbourg and domestic jurisprudence concerning media political speech.[157]

However, although the margin of appreciation doctrine is not available at the domestic level, the decision of the House of Lords in *ProLife Alliance* indicates that *even in the context of political speech*, the courts should be prepared to accord deference both to Parliament in deciding to continue the ban in the 2003 Act and to the expert regulator—in this instance, Ofcom. At this stage of the argument deference to Ofcom is irrelevant, although it will become relevant in relation to the second question which will be discussed below. At first glance there seems to be a clear conflict between *VGT* and *ProLife Alliance* as to the intensity of the scrutiny that should be brought to bear on the proportionality review. Of the two decisions, *VGT* is not binding under s 2 HRA but it is clearly the decision most closely in point since it concerned an outright ban of a very similar nature to the one under discussion. On the other hand, Lord Hoffman's remarks in *ProLife* as to deference to Parliament[158] appear to be apposite in this instance too, and *ProLife* is binding. Parliament did make a deliberate decision in relation to a post-HRA statute to pass provisions that were arguably in breach of Art 10, having been given notice under s 19(1)(b) HRA that this was possibly the case. Clearly, the courts do not have to accept that the provisions did in fact create such a breach,[159] but it may be argued at first glance that they should show some deference to Parliament's decision to pass them, a different issue.

But the question is—what does showing deference entail in this highly exceptional context? The courts have not so far tackled the question of deference in relation to provisions that Parliament itself has accepted are probably incompatible with a Convention Article. In this context deference appears to mean taking account of the probability that the provisions are indeed incompatible with Art 10 as the s 19(1)(b) HRA statement signalled. This is objectively evidenced on the face of the Bill in the statement—there is no difficulty in determining Parliament's intention. A finding by a court that the provisions are in fact incompatible would not therefore be out of line

---

[157] See Chapter 2 at 50–5, 61–72.   [158] See Chapter 11 at 584–6, 591–2, and see note 11 above.

[159] In *R v A* [2002] 1 AC 45 Lord Hope said, *obiter*, that s 19 statements are merely expressions of opinion by the Minister. He found that they are not binding on courts and do not have even persuasive authority (at [69]).

with the intention of Parliament—which on one rational reading of the debates, intended to pass incompatible provisions. The government's own position in the debates was, it is suggested, contradictory. It used the s 19(1)(b) HRA statement procedure but stated that it did not accept that the provisions were incompatible. Had it thought that the provisions could be viewed as compatible on a 'more likely than not' test then presumably it would have issued a statement under s 19(1)(a) HRA to that effect. Therefore Parliament must have considered that it was passing provisions that were probably incompatible with Article 10. Paying deference to that decision of Parliament does *not* appear to be incompatible with bringing an intense form of scrutiny to bear on the question of proportionality since Parliament has in a sense invited the courts to do just that.

Lewis argues that s 321 could be seen as 'merely an opening gambit' in a conversation between the organs of governance about the essence of rights whose content is 'essentially contestable'.[160] He cites in support Jack Straw's speech made during the passage of the Human Rights Bill to the effect that 'Parliament and the judiciary must engage in a serious dialogue about the operation and development of the rights in the Bill . . . this dialogue is the only way in which we can ensure the legislation is a living development that assists our citizens'.[161] This comment of Jack Straw's supports the argument that the government were opening a dialogue with the courts in making the s 19(1)(b) statement in the passage of the Communications Bill regarding the standard of scrutiny to be used. In general, courts may be prepared to defer to Parliament's view that provisions are compatible with the Convention rights. In this instance, the use of deference might be *more* likely to lead to a finding that the ban is *compatible* with Article 10. This would be a paradoxical result since Parliament considered that it was probably incompatible. Thus in this instance there would be no role for deference. On this argument the findings in *VGT* and *ProLife Alliance* as to the intensity of the scrutiny are not incompatible with each other since *ProLife*'s findings on the point appear to be inapplicable in this instance. The following discussion of proportionality will therefore proceed on the basis that the form of scrutiny adopted will be as intense as that used by the ECHR in *VGT*. It should be noted that even if this argument is wrong, it may be that it would make no difference to the outcome since it is arguable that even under a less intense form of scrutiny the very broad ban would not be found to satisfy the tests for proportionality.

Two key proportionality tests can be applied to the UK ban in order to determine whether it is proportionate to the aim pursued. In *VGT* the Court balanced the freedom of expression matters at stake against the reasons adduced by the Swiss authorities for the prohibition of political advertising—speech/harm balancing.[162] This would mean considering the value of the speech and the harm sought to be guarded against by the ban. As already indicated, the speech at issue is political

---

160   'Political Advertising and the Communications Act 2003' T. Lewis, [2005] 3 *EHRLR* 290–300 at 299.

161   Hansard, HC Vol. 314, col. 1141 (24 June 1998).

162   See Chapter 2 at 101–4 on this proportionality test.

communication and therefore it is accorded the highest value at Strasbourg. The fact that the expression right at issue is that of access to broadcasting time appeared to have little impact on the value accorded to it in the *VGT* case. The harm sought to be guarded against can be viewed as significant in a democracy since it concerns the need to avoid the undue swaying of public opinion by powerful interest groups or the 'selling of democracy to the highest bidder'. However, the Court of HR in *VGT* found that the value of the speech outweighed the potential harm caused by allowing the advertising. It considered that a prohibition applying only to certain media, and not to others, was not of 'a particularly pressing nature'. The application of the equivalent prohibition in the UK is of course also confined to certain media. The press in the UK are free to carry political advertising, as are other media, including cinemas. The opposing finding was reached in *Murphy*, but in the context of religious advertising only. So it appears that the ban would fail this proportionality test.

A second proportionality test concerns the need to choose 'the least intrusive' means of furthering the aim in question. The *de Freitas*[163] three stage test was discussed in Chapter 2;[164] the third *de Freitas* test concerns the need to choose the least intrusive measure—the measure that creates a minimal degree of harm to the primary right consistent with affording protection to the aim pursued. The seriousness of the interference has to be balanced against the importance of the aim sought to be pursued. This is means/end balancing—if there is another way of achieving the aim pursued that is less restrictive, it should be used. The ban could thus be found to be disproportionate to the aim pursued on the basis that it does not represent the least intrusive means of serving the end in question.[165] As discussed above, since the speech in question is political, this question should be considered under a strict standard of scrutiny. It should not be enough to find that although other measures could have been adopted instead of this blanket ban, it was not irrational to choose the ban as the measure to be adopted.

Two separate arguments could be put forward as to the breadth of the measure. First it could be noted that other means could have been adopted to serve the same end that would have created a more minimal impairment of the right. Under this argument it could readily be suggested that a more nuanced restriction should have been included in the 2003 Act, such as restricting the airtime allowed to any one group and/or imposing spending limits. Such measures would also have served the aim of preventing powerful groups from distorting the democratic agenda.

A further argument, which was the key one in the *VGT* case, could concern the *other* media outlets for advertising available to a group affected by the ban. If the ban leaves a range of outlets available it might be argued that it is proportionate to the aim pursued. But it is hard to see that the prohibition in *VGT* could be distinguished from the UK prohibition on political advertising in s 321 of the 2003 Act so as to find it to be

[163] From the decision of the Privy Council in *de Freitas v Permanent Secretary of Ministry of Agriculture, Fisheries, Lands and Housing* [1999] 1 AC 69, 80.
[164] See Chapter 2 at 91–3.   [165] See for discussion of this test, Chapter 2 at 98–101.

proportionate. Although there are a number of national television services in this country, they are all equally affected by the ban—apart from Satellite television. Satellite television reaches a relatively small audience and could hardly be viewed as an effective medium for carrying political advertising. Thus the prohibition means that, apart from PPBs and PEBs, political advertising cannot reach the whole nation via the broadcast media in a reasonably effective fashion. The position is therefore very similar to that in existence in Switzerland as indicated in the *VGT* case. The point was in fact made in that case that foreign stations could broadcast in Switzerland to the whole nation, but this was not found to be enough to displace the finding of disproportionality. The fact that PPBs and PEBs are available in the UK, but not in Switzerland, could also be used in defence of the UK ban. However, as discussed above, those means of obtaining publicity are in practice very rarely available to single issue interest groups since they do not normally field candidates in General Elections. ProLife Alliance was an exception, and even so it was still unable to qualify for a *nationwide* broadcast.[166] Thus the UK ban still has a severe impact on such groups. This argument might be used to defend the ban on grounds of proportionality in relation to a political party, but not in relation to a group such as MPH or Amnesty. So it appears that the ban also fails the means/end balancing test, on more than one argument.

On the face of it, then, if these tests for proportionality were applied, or one of them, a court would be likely to find that the ban is incompatible with Article 10 and would have to consider therefore making a declaration of the incompatibility under s 4 HRA. If a court considered only whether the ban is discriminatory, arbitrary or unreasonable, it might be found to be compatible with Article 10; it is not directly discriminatory since it applies to all groups equally. Possibly it could be viewed as creating indirectly discriminatory effects since it hits hardest at interest groups, as discussed above. But it might be viewed as having an objective justification[167] since it prevents the undermining of the PEB system: this is discussed further below. It could also be viewed as reasonable on the basis that it is very difficult, even if it had been confined to political parties, to avoid affecting electoral advertising by interest groups acting as a front for the main political parties and campaigning on issues central in party manifestos.

(iii) Using s 3(1) HRA?

On the assumption that incompatibility was found a judge would not make a declaration of it under s 4 HRA without first seeking to construe the words of s 321 compatibly with Article 10 if at all possible, under s 3(1) HRA. The mere fact that Parliamentary legal advisers considered that incompatibility had occurred would not preclude a fresh attempt to seek to achieve compatibility. Clearly, it is the function of the judiciary to have the final word on compatibility.[168]

The only option for a court seeking to avoid making a declaration of incompatibility would be to find that the prohibition can be rendered compatible with Article 10

---

[166] See Chapter 11 at 578–9.
[167] See discussion of this point in *ProLife Alliance*, Chapter 11 at 584–5.   [168] See note 159 above.

under s 3(1) HRA. There appear to be a number of possibilities under s 3. It is arguable that s 3(1) could be brought to bear on the following italicised words in s 312(2): 'objects . . . *mainly* of a *political* nature'; 'directed towards a *political* end'; an advertisement which has a *connection* with an industrial dispute.' The argument would be that these words should be interpreted narrowly in accordance with the doctrine of proportionality under Art 10(2). As discussed s 321 creates a ban that is disproportionate to the end in view since it is not the least intrusive method of achieving that end. Therefore it could be argued that as many groups as possible should be excluded from the coverage of the ban so as to narrow its ambit as much as it is possible to do without adopting an unacceptably distorted interpretation of the words. The provisions of s 321(3) would not make this task an easy one since they are so broad, although clearly s 3(1) could also be used to narrow down the meaning of the terms used in that section. If the relevant word in question was then afforded the narrowest possible interpretation, the group bringing the action in question might fall outside the ambit of the ban and therefore would be able to advertise. This might have occurred in the *ex p Bull* case had the HRA been in force at the time. Clearly, this route cannot be viewed as a non-problematic one: the necessity of narrowing down the definition—in effect—of political speech in order to circumvent the ban might well strike a human rights lawyer as very unfortunate.

Perhaps the most fruitful possibility following this argument would be to argue that where a group has mixed objects—some political, some non-political, the non-political objects need not be deemed political merely because they are arise in the context of the objective of influencing the government or political leaders. They could be viewed as stand-alone objects that the group would espouse even if it desisted from seeking to influence politicians. For example, the aim of raising public awareness on the issues of poverty or animal welfare could be linked either to fund-raising as a non-political objective or to bringing pressure to bear on the government. Where an aim had a mixed purpose in this sense it could be argued that the group could properly be viewed as having objects only partly of a political nature. Adoption of this stance would involve departure from the findings of Lord Woolf in the *ex p Bull* case. But s 2 HRA would appear to allow such departure in relation to domestic pre-HRA findings where support to do so can be found in the Strasbourg jurisprudence.[169] If the definition of a 'political' group was narrowed, so as to exclude groups such as MPH from its ambit, they could then advertise in broadcasting so long as the advertisement *itself* was not deemed political.

There appears to be little possibility of using s 3(1) to create broad exceptions to the prohibition itself without simply reversing the intention of Parliament. If the courts were to seek to adopt a proportionality test within the terms of ss 319 and 321, they would have to be prepared to depart from the literal meaning of the

[169] See Chapter 3 at 157–63 on the use of s 3(1)HRA to read words into statutory provisions or impose strained interpretations on them.

sections.[170] As Chapter 3 pointed out, courts are prepared to do this under s 3(1), but balk at using it where its effect would be to fundamentally undermine that intention as expressed through the provision in question—to go against the grain of the statute.[171] The addition of words such as 'subject to ensuring its compatibility with Article 10' would appear to do just that since on one view Parliament has deliberately decided to pass a provision that appears to breach Article 10.[172] The same could be said of reading in the word 'party' before the word 'political' in s 321. It could on the other hand be argued that the government did not admit in Parliament that the provisions are clearly incompatible with Article 10, and that Parliament passed them in the hope that they could be viewed as compatible or rendered compatible. This argument depends on the view a court might take of the intention of Parliament when faced with a statement under s 19(1)(b)HRA. But it is difficult to see the imposition of compatibility as according with the intention of Parliament. It is argued that the better view is that the courts should not strive to impose compatibility under s 3(1) on the provisions once it had been determined that they are indeed incompatible—unless quite significantly modified.

There are other reasons for taking a less proactive stance in relation to the use of s 3(1) in this context. The question of the precise wording of any exceptions is complex and a court might well consider that Parliament itself should engage in a wholescale reform, introducing carefully nuanced new rules on political advertising.[173] Difficult policy choices have to be made on what is essentially a political matter; courts would be likely to view it as falling outside the areas in which they have special expertise.[174] The amendments to the Act needed in order to give Ofcom sufficient guidance as to the groups who could advertise would probably be viewed as beyond the scope of the courts under s 3. All the instances in which the courts have taken an activist stance under s 3(1) but one have been in the criminal justice context where the courts have special competence and expertise.[175] In the one instance outside that context, *Ghaidan Mendoza*,[176] there were strong reasons for activism: the case concerned

---

[170] See *R v A* [2001] 2 Cr App R 21; [2002] 1 AC 45; for discussion see Chapter 3 at 158–9. A. Kavanagh's writings on s 3(1) have influenced this analysis. See in particular 'The elusive divide between interpretation and legislation under the HRA' (2004) 24(2) *OJLS* 259.

[171] In *R (on the application of Anderson) v Secretary of State for the Home Dept* [2003] 1 AC 837 in which the Secretary of State's role in sentencing was found to be incompatible with Art 6 since he could not be viewed as an independent and impartial tribunal. However, a declaration of incompatibility was made rather than seeking to use s 3(1) since the Secretary of State's role was such a fundamental feature of the statute as a whole—any other approach would have been against the grain of the statute. See further on this point Chapter 3 at 161–2.

[172] See further T. Lewis, 'Political Advertising and the Communications Act 2003' [2005] 3 EHRLR 290–300. Lewis takes the view that the courts would decline to use s 3 HRA in order to create compatibility with Article 10 since this would be opposed to the Parliamentary intention evinced in passing the 2003 Act.

[173] In this respect the precedents of *Bellinger* [2003] 2 AC 467 and of *Re S, Re W* [2002] 2 AC 291 could be followed—see Chapter 3 at 161–3.

[174] See *Bellinger* note 173 above.

[175] See *Lambert* [2001] 3 All ER 577; *Offen* [2001] 1 WLR 253; *R v A* [2002] 1 AC 45.

[176] [2004] 2 AC 557. See Chapter 3 at 162–3.

discrimination, a matter the courts would be likely to view as of higher constitutional importance than access to broadcasting. There seems to be a much stronger case for using s 4 HRA and making a declaration of the incompatibility,[177] and in making this point a court might well bear in mind the fact that the government made a promise to the Joint Committee on Human Rights to introduce remedial legislation if necessary.[178] There is a case for seeking to hold them to this promise.

(iv) Ofcom's application of the ban

The discussion now turns to the second question posed above—whether Ofcom's particular decision on the facts was in accord with the demands of Art 10. The question presupposes that Ofcom has already found that the ban applies to a particular group's advertisement. This question would arise under s 6 HRA, rather than s 3. Following *ProLife* the courts would tend to defer to the expertise of the regulator. The challenge might fail on the question of the proportion of a group's objects deemed political, although, as discussed above, Lord Woolf's interpretation in *Bull* could be departed from on this point. Assuming that the main objects of the group in question were so clearly political that this route was unavailable, a further possibility would be to find, in the case of the advertising of certain organizations, that no breach had occurred since the ban could be viewed as proportionate to the aim pursued in relation to that particular group. This might be the case where it could be said of a group that due to its particular nature it might endanger the independence of the broadcaster or influence public opinion unduly—the reasons likely to be adduced by the UK government for the continuance of the ban. But equally, as in *VGT*, the application of the ban might be found to breach Art 10, on the ground of disproportionality, where the group was merely trying to put across a cross-party political message. This could be said of MPH.

(v) Challenge at Strasbourg

There is also the possibility that a challenge will be mounted at Strasbourg. Possibly challengers would not have to exhaust domestic remedies, depending on the ground of challenge, since the only remedy available is not an effective one. From the point of view of the challenger, the group in question would continue to suffer a violation of its Art 10 rights even after obtaining a declaration of incompatibility, at least for a period of time, and possibly indefinitely. At present the government that decided to breach Art 10 in including this provision in the 2003 Act is still in power, and therefore there is

---

[177] This is the conclusion reached in the academic literature on s321. See A. Scott, ' "A monstrous and unjustifiable infringement"? Political expression and the broadcasting ban on advocacy advertising' [2003] 66(2) *MLR* 240–244 at 225–6 and T. Lewis, ibid, at 299–300. Barendt also takes this view: evidence to the Joint Committee on the Draft Communications Bill 17.6.02.

[178] Fourth Report, 2002–3, Scrutiny of Bills: Further Progress Report (HL Paper 50, HC 397), para 40. In *Bellinger* (note 173) the court took account of the fact that the government was about to introduce legislation on the subject at hand, as a reason for not using s 3. In this instance the government are not embarking on fresh legislation but the fact of the promise indicates a willingness to consider doing so.

little reason to expect that the relevant Minister would be responsive to a declaration, unless it has a change of policy. Further, there is at present no reason to expect that any future government would respond differently to a prohibition that has subsisted through a number of changes of government for fifty years. On the other hand the government, as discussed, has made a promise to introduce remedial measures. It is arguable, but not certain, that a challenge could be taken straight to Strasbourg if the challenge alleged a breach of Article 10, rather than seeking to establish that the group in question was not covered by the prohibition.

Although the government has (arguably) decided at the domestic level to continue to breach Article 10, there is no provision allowing it to do so at the international level unless it sought to enter a reservation to Article 10. It has not so far done so and therefore it may be assumed that a challenge would be likely to be successful at the international level, probably forcing the government to introduce an amendment to the 2003 Act into Parliament. The problem that the government would face if a group, such as Amnesty, mounted a challenge at Strasbourg would be that it would first have to argue that Amnesty's objects are primarily of a political nature—in order to justify the prohibition—but then, in order to avoid the most intense form of scrutiny under Article 10, it would have to argue that the speech in question was not political. That appears to represent an impossible task since such a position is so clearly logically flawed, as the Swiss government discovered in *VGT v Switzerland*.[179]

So until and if a successful challenge is mounted at Strasbourg, it may be likely that the UK will continue to breach Article 10: in this respect, freedom of expression does not extend to television and radio, and the ban continues to create discrimination against radio and television in favour of press, Internet, cinema, and billboard political advertising.

PROPOSALS FOR REFORM

As was demonstrated in the *VGT* case, commercial advertisers, who may well unduly influence the public, often in subliminal fashion and on issues that can be deemed political, can continue to dominate the public agenda. Any corrective to the predominance of commercial advertising, with its sanitizing of, for example, the impact of car and air travel on the environment in terms of global warming, cannot occur. Subtle messages about consumerism can be conveyed to the public through commercial advertising, while overtly political messages are banned. The extensive literature on the impact of advertising clearly indicates the dangers.[180] Clearly, relaxing the broadcasting ban would not address all the concerns thereby raised, but it would mean that messages opposed to consumerist ones could gain a hearing. They would be juxtaposed to the commercial message and might, as in the case of the

---

[179] (2002) 34 EHRR 159.

[180] See e.g. N. Klein, *No Logo*, London: Flamingo, 2000; W. Leiss, S. Kline, and S. Jhally, *Social Communication in Advertising*, London: Routledge, 1990; *Global and Multi-National Advertising*, B. Englis, (ed.) Croom-Helm, 1988.

MPH advertisements, throw it into relief.[181] Lewis offers a number of illustrative examples:

fast food corporations may target television advertisements at children, yet an organisation campaigning against child obesity may not; clothes and sports shoe companies may advertise their wares on television, yet groups wishing to publicise the plight of workers in developing countries employed by such corporations may not; supermarket chains may advertise the freshness of their 'out of season' cherry tomatoes and mange-tout peas, yet a group wishing to highlight the deleterious effects of the globalised economy which facilitates this consumption may not.[182]

Thus there is quite a strong case for reform. The problem with the ban in free speech terms is clearly its lack of proportionality. At the least the definition of 'objects of a mainly political nature' or 'political ends' could be narrowed so as to exclude semi-charitable groups such as *Make Poverty History*—groups that represent established charities. But a more wide-ranging possible reform would be to allow for political advertising by groups *other than* political parties—since they have an outlet through PPBs and PEBs.[183] The addition of the word 'party' before the word 'political' would achieve this aim. This amendment was put forward in relation to the Broadcasting Act 1996, but rejected by the government at the time.[184] Stringent curbs could then be placed upon such advertising by Ofcom, in particular that it would have to pass the tests indicated by the Court of Human Rights in the *VGT* case: that it did not unduly influence the public or abuse a competitive advantage. This would allow each advertisement to be considered by Ofcom on its own merits.

Thus this argument makes the case for some cautious relaxation of the political advertising prohibition, but accepts that the argument as to subversion of the democratic process by powerful interest groups is not without cogency. Moreover, allowing mainstream political parties to use paid political advertising would also run risks of distorting the political process. Continuance of the ban is supported by the Electoral Commission which has a duty to 'keep under review a range of electoral and political matters, including political advertising in the broadcast media.' In January 2003 the Commission published its Final report[185] in which it recommended that the ban on paid political advertising should remain, on the basis that Party political broadcasts offer political parties the most effective direct campaigning tools.[186] Significantly, the Commission's argument would appear to support a ban aimed at those who *can* take advantage of PEBs, but not otherwise.[187]

---

[181] See further Scott (note 177 above) on this point at 234.   [182] See Lewis (note 172 above) at 300.

[183] See the stance of the Electoral Commission, note 185 below.

[184] See HL Deb Vol 570 col. 482, 7.3.1996.

[185] Available from the Commission's website—www.electoralcommission.gov.uk.

[186] See further B. Franklin, *Packaging Politics: Political Communications in Britain's Media Democracy*, 2004.

[187] See also Scott (note 177 above, at 241–2) who concludes that broadcast electoral activity should remain proscribed, although special interest groups, not part of a political party, should be able to advertise. Lewis (note 172 above, at 294) finds: 'Even to have inserted the word "party" before the word "political" would have effected a more finely tailored approach and would have permitted a much wider range of groups to express their views whilst still meeting the legislative objective.'

A strict cap on the amount that individual groups could spend and on the air-time that they could command would be essential to avoid bidding wars and the dominance of the political agenda by powerful groups. Without such curbs powerful interest groups could create undue influence, especially in relation to general elections, particularly if political parties remained restricted to PEBs and PPBs. There would also be a danger that minorities, including sexual minorities, would be harassed or intimidated by such advertising. Advertisements of interest groups should also be subject to the due impartiality rules discussed below, as Ofcom found in its ruling in relation to MPH. The rule of most relevance would be s 5.7 of Ofcom's Broadcasting Code, requiring that facts should not be misrepresented. In the US, right-wing, religious extremist groups have used the airways to further their campaigns, making exaggerated and misleading claims[188] in so doing. The application of Ofcom's Code, as well as the air-time constraints discussed, could curb their advertising on channels available in the UK via satellite. Similar groups operating from within the UK would also be constrained in their use of broadcasting. Political advertising is not subject at present to the Code of the Advertising Standards Authority which covers misleading adverts,[189] and therefore the application of the due impartiality rules would be of particular significance if advocacy advertising was allowed in broadcasting.

This partial relaxation of the ban would at first glance adversely affect small or nascent political parties who find it hard or impossible to qualify for a PEB, but would still be unable to put forward their advertisements for broadcasting under the new rules. But in this context the example of ProLife Alliance, fully discussed in Chapter 11, is illustrative.[190] As indicated in that chapter, it was apparent that ProLife had gone to the expense of fielding candidates in the General Election, not because it seriously thought that any of them would be elected (and in the event all of them lost their deposits), but because it wanted to qualify for a PEB. Under the new rules a single issue group such as ProLife would not need to take this tortuous route in order to qualify for an advertisement—although, of course, it could still do so. It could merely de-register as a political party and present its campaign to the public as put forward by a single issue campaigning group rather than as by a political party. The problem of electoral advocacy remains—the possibility that interest groups might seek to sway elections by promoting candidates who appeared to support their views, thereby undermining the PEB system. But, as Scott points out, new legislation could seek to distinguish between 'electoral material' and issue-based material, on the precedent already set by Part IV of the Elections and Referendums Act 2000.[191]

Under these reforms minority political parties or independent candidates—as opposed to single issue interest groups—would continue to have to find the funds to field candidates in order to qualify for a PEB. It may be noted that the cost of

---

[188] See R. Hilliard and M. Keith, *Waves of Rancor: Tuning in the Radical Right*, esp. ch 3, London: ME Sharpe, 1999.

[189] See Chapter 10 at 545–9 and Chapter 11 at 593–5.   [190] See pp 578–9.

[191] Scott (note 177 above, at 242).

lost deposits in order to qualify for a free PEB is likely to be less than the cost of advertising on prime time television. Therefore it is not apparent that in terms of fairness their position would be significantly worsened under the new rules. The Electoral Commission's Report referred to above does not indicate that minority parties view the broadcasting ban as problematic.[192]

The instance of the US in which political advertising is highly prevalent in broadcasting, and arguably does have a subverting effect on the democratic process, indicates the dangers of relaxing the prohibition completely.[193] The case *in favour* of permitting political advertising is largely founded on the Meiklejohn argument from participation in a democracy.[194] Therefore if such advertising in practice subverts that participation the case for displacing curbs on it is undermined. So these proposals for reform do not advocate the complete abandonment of the prohibition.

EMERGENCY AND CENSORSHIP POWERS

The government had a direct power of censorship in relation to independent television under s 10(3) of the Broadcasting Act 1990.[195] Section 10(3) was repealed by the Communications Act 2003, but a very similar provision was included in the new Act in s 336(5) which provides:

The Secretary of State may, at any time, by notice require OFCOM to direct the holders of the Broadcasting Act licences specified in the notice to refrain from including in their licensed services any matter, or description of matter, specified in the notice.

This power places the government at one remove from the broadcasting organizations since it operates through Ofcom. The power under s 10(3) of the 1990 Act was of the widest possible nature since it allowed a ban on broadcasting 'any matter' or class of matter. Section 336(5) is equally wide; it uses the term 'description' rather than 'class' of matter, but this does not appear to be a significant difference—the term 'description' is possibly wider than the term 'class'. Under s 336(7) Ofcom must comply with a direction issued under s 336(5). The government also possesses such a power in relation to the BBC via Art 8.2 of the BBC's 1996 Licence Agreement, as amended.[196]

---

[192] Note 185 above.

[193] See G.W. Smith, *The Politics of Deceit: Saving Freedom and Democracy from Extinction*, Glenn W. Smith, 2004. The book contends: 'Today, Americans face a tyranny built upon contemporary political practices that devalue personal and communal responsibility as well as overall participation in the political process. Life-and-death political discussions and decisions are now limited to a virtual world of illusion and coercion. No politician has so cynically wielded these manipulative political practices as has George W. Bush.' See also F. Plasser and G. Plasser, *Global Political Campaigning*, Praeger Greenwood, 2002.

[194] See Chapter 1 at 16–18.

[195] Previously the power arose under the Broadcasting Act 1981, s 29(3).

[196] Under s 8.2 'The Secretary of State may from time to time by notice in writing require the Corporation to refrain at any specified time or at all times from broadcasting or transmitting any matter or matter of any class specified in such notice; and the Secretary of State may at any time or times vary or revoke any such notice.'

These powers are not expressed as emergency powers, but so far they have only been used to impose a ban in relation to national security. The Home Secretary also retains a further emergency power under s 133 of the 2003 Act of ordering that a particular licensed service should cease or restrict its broadcasting.[197] Emergency powers to take control over BBC broadcasting are contained in the BBC's Agreement.[198]

The power under s 10(3) has only been invoked once. It was invoked by the Secretary of State in 1988 in order to issue directives requiring the BBC and IBA to refrain from broadcasting words spoken by persons representing organizations proscribed under the Northern Ireland (Emergency Provisions) legislation and also Sinn Fein, Republican Sinn Fein and the Ulster Defence Association. The ban was challenged by the National Union of Journalists and others, but not by the broadcasting organizations themselves, in *Secretary of State for the Home Department ex p Brind and Others*.[199] The applicants submitted that the Home Secretary's discretionary powers were exercisable only in conformity with Art 10 of the European Convention; it

---

[197] S 132 (1) 'If the Secretary of State has reasonable grounds for believing that it is necessary to do so—

(a) to protect the public from any threat to public safety or public health, or

(b) in the interests of national security, he may, by a direction to OFCOM, require them to give a direction under subsection (3) to a person ("the relevant provider") who provides an electronic communications network or electronic communications service or who makes associated facilities available.

(2) OFCOM must comply with a requirement of the Secretary of State under subsection (1) by giving to the relevant provider such direction under subsection (3) as they consider necessary for the purpose of complying with the Secretary of State's direction.

(3) A direction under this section is—(a) a direction that the entitlement of the relevant provider to provide electronic communications networks or electronic communications services, or to make associated facilities available, is suspended (either generally or in relation to particular networks, services or facilities); or (b) a direction that that entitlement is restricted in the respects set out in the direction . . .

(7) Where OFCOM give a direction under subsection (3), they shall, as soon as practicable after doing so, provide that person with an opportunity of—(a) making representations about the effect of the direction; and (b) proposing steps for remedying the situation.'

Under s 133 (1) 'A person is guilty of an offence if he provides an electronic communications network or electronic communications service, or makes available any associated facility—

(a) while his entitlement to do so is suspended by a direction under section 132; or (b) in contravention of a restriction contained in such a direction.

(2) A person guilty of an offence under subsection (1) shall be liable—

(a) on summary conviction, to a fine not exceeding the statutory maximum;

(b) on conviction on indictment, to a fine.'

[198] S 8.3: If and whenever in the opinion of the Secretary of State an emergency shall have arisen in which it is expedient in the public interest that Her Majesty's Government in the United Kingdom shall have control over the broadcasting or transmission of any matter whatsoever by means of the stations or any of them, it shall be lawful for the Secretary of State to direct and cause the stations or any of them or any part thereof to be taken possession of in the name and on behalf of Her Majesty and to prevent the Corporation from using them, and also to cause the stations or any of them or any part thereof to be used for Her Majesty's service, or to take such other steps as he may think fit to secure control over the stations or any of them, and in that event any person authorised by the Secretary of State may enter upon the stations or any of them and the offices and works of the Corporation or any of them and take possession thereof and use the same as aforesaid.

[199] [1991] 1 AC 696; [1991] 1 All ER 720; [1991] 2 WLR 588, HL; [1990] 1 All ER 469, CA; for comment see Jowell [1990] *PL* 149 (on the Court of Appeal ruling).

was argued that the prohibition was disproportionate to the aim pursued, under Article 10(2).[200] The House of Lords found that the presumption regarding Article 10 would go far beyond the resolution of an ambiguity as it would assume that Parliament had intended to import the text of the Convention into domestic administrative law. As Parliament had chosen not to incorporate the Convention into domestic law this, it was found, was an unwarranted assumption. Clearly, the findings as to the Convention are no longer of significance due to the inception of the HRA. The Lords obviously did not have to make a final determination as to the question of proportionality, since they had already found that the discretion was not limited by the terms of Article 10. However, they indicated that the ban could be viewed as proportionate to the aim pursued since it did allow reporting of members of Sinn Fein so long as their voices were not heard.

It was further submitted that administrative action can be challenged by way of judicial review if it is disproportionate to the mischief at which it is aimed and that this particular exercise of power went further than was necessary to prevent terrorists increasing their standing. The House of Lords held that lack of proportionality was merely to be regarded as one aspect of *Wednesbury* unreasonableness, not as a separate head of challenge. The question to be asked was, therefore, whether the minister's decision was one which no reasonable minister could have made. Taking into account the fact that the directives did not restrict the reporting of information, but merely the manner of its presentation—direct speech—it was found that this ground of challenge had not been made out. The House of Lords indicated that the challenge might have succeeded had the interference been more wide ranging. These points are considered below in relation to the current provisions. Obviously those provisions, if used now, would be subject to full proportionality review rather than review based on *Wednesbury* reasonableness, under Article 10 and the HRA.

The ban meant that a Sinn Fein or IRA member could not be forced to justify their policies and therefore it caused offence to the principle that flawed or evil speech is most effectively combated by further speech.[201] Moreover, since it applied equally to historical programmes, it infringed the principle that the search for truth should override other interests except where a clear danger in allowing the speech may be shown. In its own terms, the ban may have been ineffective and self-defeating, not only because it did not appear to prevent the dubbing of the voices of Sinn Fein leaders and others by actors, but also because, ironically, it in itself publicized them,

---

[200] The applicants' argument was that Article 10 had to be taken into account on the basis that when legislation confers an administrative discretion on an authority which is capable of being exercised in a way which infringes human rights as protected by the Convention, it was presumed that the intention of the enabling legislation was that the discretion should be exercised within Convention limits. As the directives did not so conform, the minister had acted ultra vires since, it was argued, the prohibition was disproportionate to the aim pursued, under Article 10(2). The House of Lords agreed that the Convention could be used as a rule of statutory construction to resolve ambiguity in subsequent primary legislation, but disagreed with the submission that the issuing of the directives was therefore *ultra vires*, on the ground that it could not be presumed that discretionary powers were, by analogy, limited by the terms of the Convention.

[201] A principle that derives from Mill's argument from truth; see Chapter 1 at 14–16.

rather than denying them 'the oxygen of publicity'. For example, Gerry Adams, the leader of Sinn Fein, was able to publicize himself in America as the man whose voice could not be heard on UK air-waves. The ban remained in place until September 1994, when it was lifted after the IRA declared the cessation of violence. When the ceasefire broke down in 1996, the ban was not re-imposed.

Clearly, the inception of the HRA has had the effect of reversing the decision in *Brind* as regards the effect of the Convention on administrative powers. If the power of censorship is invoked again, under s 336(5), it will have to be used within Article 10 limits; therefore any ban would have to be proportionate to the aim pursued, under Article 10(2). The tests for proportionality from the *VGT* case[202] would apply to any future prohibition, although, depending on the context, the standard of scrutiny might not be as high as that adopted by the European Court of Human Rights in that instance. The Sinn Fein ban was upheld at Strasbourg in *Brind and McLaughlin v UK*.[203] The margin of appreciation conceded was wide, owing to the terrorist context, and the ban was found to be proportionate to the aims pursued since Sinn Fein's message could be broadcast, using dubbing, and its leaders could be viewed on television. Although obviously the margin of appreciation doctrine is not directly applicable in domestic courts, the standard of scrutiny adopted domestically varies according to the context, and—although this is not, it is argued, a legitimate stance— according to the extent to which the relevant Strasbourg jurisprudence has been affected by that doctrine.[204] If a ban was imposed in the context of national security, and if some reporting relating to the group in question was allowed, possibly using actors and dubbing, the ban might be viewed as proportionate to the aim pursued. However, the court would have to test the ban against the standards of Art 10. The *VGT* case would provide a starting point, since it concerned an absolute ban, although outside the context of national security.

In the current security context, related to a terrorist threat from extremist groups such as Al Qaeda, any prohibition similar to that imposed in *Brind*, would clearly be irrelevant since the groups in question are all already proscribed under the proscription provisions of the Terrorism Act 2000. Even a content-based prohibition on the broadcast of speech supporting the aims of such groups would be irrelevant since it is already an offence to demonstrate support for a proscribed group, under s 12(1) of the 2000 Act. Further similar but broader speech-based offences relating to the glorification of terrorism were introduced under the anti-terrorism legislation in 2006.[205] It is unclear therefore that the s 336(5) power has any relevance to the current security situation; the internet is the medium currently employed by persons expressing implied support for such groups.

---

[202] See above pp 1021–3. See also the tests from *Goodwin v UK* (1996) 22 EHRR 123. For discussion of those tests see Chapter 7 at 335–6.

[203] (1994) 18 EHRR CD 76.   [204] See Chapter 3 at 145–50.

[205] The Terrorism Act 2006, s 1. See Chapter 9 at 527–33 for discussion.

CONCLUSIONS

Clearly, the available and utilized forms of control over broadcasting freedom in the political sphere can be viewed very differently when they are examined with the relevant free speech rationales in mind. It has been found that the due impartiality controls are fully in tune with those rationales but the other interferences are opposed to them. Direct censorship in the form of the political advertising ban or under emergency powers constitutes a straightforward interference, while content-based controls, designed to ensure plurality, impartiality and diversity, are in accord with those free speech rationales since they enhance broadcast speech in comparison with that of individual speakers and also have instrumental value in enabling and enhancing the speech of such speakers. They allow the public to be informed on matters of strong public interest in an effective fashion. The general unquestioned acceptance of greater regulation for broadcasting appears to have allowed a number of anomalies to remain in place, even under the recent reforms under the Communications Act 2003 that were undertaken in the post-HRA era. The very fact that the due impartiality controls exist, renders the other curbs less justifiable. Once impartiality in broadcasting is safeguarded, it becomes, in terms of the speech rationales from truth and democracy, a more valuable means of mass communication than the print media, and therefore the application of a range of other controls, especially the political advertising ban, becomes more problematic since they are not applied to the press.

21

DEFAMATION AND 'POLITICAL SPEECH'

[the plaintiff] can get damages (swingeing damages!) for a statement made to others without showing that the statement was untrue, without showing that the statement did him the slightest harm, and without showing that the defendant was in any way wrong to make it (much less that the defendant owed him any duty of any kind). (Weir, *A Casebook on Tort*, 8th ed 1996, p 525).

INTRODUCTION

The preceding two chapters have examined direct state interference with free media expression in the political domain, through broadcasting and official secrets legislation. In closing this Part, we consider, by contrast, the interaction between political expression, and a second individual entitlement, recognized by ECHR and domestic law—to one's reputation—on the interface provided by domestic libel law.[1] This is an area which, in contrast to the protection of informational privacy, produces a much higher likelihood of a direct clash with important free speech interests. Whereas speech invading private life is likely, by its nature, not to be centrally concerned with issues of serious *public* concern, and is often trivial,[2] defamatory speech can be concerned with the character or competency of key political figures,[3] or with non-political but equally important speech of serious public concern.[4] Since, in other words, a person can be defamed equally in relation to their professional, public duties or their private life this area raises a more invariable and more serious clash between reputation and speech than that which occurs between privacy and speech. On the other hand, it might *prima facie* be thought that speech which is, in fact,

---

[1] See generally, P. Milmo, W. Rogers, C. Parkes, G. Walker, and G. Bussuttil, *Gatley on Libel and Slander*, London: Sweet & Maxwell, 1997; C. Duncan, R. Neill, and R. Rampton, *Duncan and Neill on Defamation*, London: Butterworths, 2000.

[2] As in the *Von Hannover* case [2004] EMLR 21.

[3] As in the key English and Strasbourg cases: *Reynolds v Times Newspapers Ltd* [1999] 3 WLR 1010 and *Lingens v Austria* (1986) 8 EHRR 407.

[4] *Bladet Tromsø and Stensaas v Norway* 29 EHRR 125.

untruthful[5] has less value than the truthful speech that is often complained of in 'private life' actions. Such a finding could be made primarily in reliance upon the audience's interest in receiving accurate political and public interest-related information. Receipt of such information can enhance the general capacity of persons to be active citizens, and also it may influence their participation in democracy more directly, where the allegations concern politicians. As we shall see below, the interest in allowing those defamed to clear their names through defamation law is often justified by the judges at least partly in terms of the interest of the audience in having false impressions corrected.

On the other hand, the task of reconciling speech and reputational interests was, at least until recently, conceptually more simple, as an intellectual task, than the complex process involved in balancing competing *Convention* rights, as in the privacy-speech sphere. However, as discussed at the conclusion of this chapter, the recent recognition of reputation as an aspect of Article 8 by both Strasbourg and, seemingly, the English courts, may result in a change of judicial approach to balancing the two interests. This is an area in which the judges, influenced by a canon of strong Strasbourg jurisprudence, have showed awareness since *Reynolds*[6] of the importance of media freedom in this area and, moreover, have based their reasoning quite explicitly on the values underpinning the speech in particular cases.

As Barendt observes, legal protection of individual reputation dates from Roman law, long predating recognition of free speech rights.[7] In the 20th century, however, with the emergence of international human rights norms, protection of reputation received a new explicit foundation in the value of human dignity.[8] Given the foundational role within the ECHR jurisprudence of free expression in pursuit of the circulation of ideas and checking abuse of power as an integral part of a healthy democracy, the treatment of political libel as a flashpoint between conflicting values serves as a further litmus test for the adequacy of the Convention's 'balancing' methodology under the HRA.

As discussed in the first section below, the traditional position in the common law world, including the UK, was that libel laws rendered protection for political speech injurious to individual reputation narrow and difficult to achieve.[9] The second part of this chapter considers the extensive body of Convention jurisprudence on the approach of the Strasbourg court to defamation as a limit upon freedom of expression. In the third part, we examine the decision in *Reynolds*, which represented the attempt by the House of Lords to bring English law into line with the Strasbourg

---

[5] The defence of qualified privilege discussed in this chapter is only required where the defendant cannot plead the defence of justification—that the allegations made were substantially true. See below at 1044.

[6] [1999] 3 WLR 1010.   [7] E. Barendt, *Freedom of Speech*, 2nd edn., OUP, 2005, at 198.

[8] With reference to German *Grundgesetz*—under German Basic Law (Art 79(3)), human dignity is a basic principle that 'may not be affected by any constitutional amendment': Barendt, op cit, p 198, note 2; also refers to Universal Declaration of Human Rights, Article 12 and International Covenant on Civil and Political Rights, Article 17.

[9] See generally E. Barendt, op cit, at 162–70.

jurisprudence, but also to produce a distinctively English stance on the balance to be struck. The fourth part traces developments in English law subsequent to *Reynolds* under the HRA. Across the common law would, the overall observed trend of recent decades has been to extend greater protection to free media expression, on matters of political or public interest, scaling back the traditional scope of actions in defamation. While there is some commonality in the approach of different common law jurisdictions to this problem, the exact parameters of protection for political communications, and the law's procedures for determining their applicability to the particular facts, have—despite in many cases common motivations—adopted quite different forms in different places. This chapter therefore undertakes comparisons between these various approaches, and assesses their respective merits.

POLITICAL DEFAMATION UNDER ENGLISH LAW: THE PRE-*REYNOLDS* POSITION

It has been suggested that the English common law tort of libel emerged from the practical need to provide legal means to vindicate wrongs to reputation leading to both civil actions and criminal penalties.[10] Accordingly, English libel law has concerned attacks on personal, moral, character (rather than, for example on dignity, or public office). A defamatory statement was described as one 'calculated to injure the reputation of another by exposing him to hatred, contempt, or ridicule'[11]; or, less restrictively, as words 'tend[ing] to lower the plaintiff in the estimation of right-thinking members of society generally.'[12] This principle extended in practice to statements impugning a person's 'competence in her chosen employment or occupation.'[13]

A plaintiff alleging libel was required only to prove that the publication was libellous (that is, tending to have the above effect) and that it referred to her; proof of particular damage was assumed as flowing from publication of the defamatory statement. Importantly, in light of recent developments in the UK, whether a statement was libellous was originally a matter for decision by the trial judge; only in the late 18th century did legislation transfer this decision to the jury.[14]

A word should be said as to damages. Primarily, libel damages are awarded for injury to reputation; as this is difficult, if not impossible, to quantify, the matter has usually been left to the jury.[15] Pecuniary loss may also be recoverable; aggravated damages may sound in relation to a defendant's conduct post-publication, including a

---

[10] I. Loveland, *Political Libels: A Comparative Study*, Oxford: Hart Publishing, 2000, p 3.

[11] *Parmiter v Coupland* (1840) 6 M & W 105 at 108.

[12] *Sim v Stretch, per* Lord Atkin, [1936] 2 All ER 1237 at 1240.

[13] Loveland, *Political Libels*, Oxford: Hart Publishing, 2000, at 4.

[14] In the Libel Act 1792: see Loveland, ibid, at 4. See further below at 1084–5 for discussion of *Reynolds'* impact in effectively retracting this issue from jury and reinstating it to the judge.

[15] Subject to statutory interventions discussed in the text.

failure to apologise, and the maintaining of justification at trial. Well before *Reynolds*, it was recognized that the sometimes massive sums awarded as damages in libel trials could have a disproportionately chilling effect on freedom of expression. *Rantzen v Mirror Group Newspapers*[16] considered a new provision under the Courts and Legal Services Act 1990,[17] which empowered the court to order a retrial where damages awarded in a tort action were 'excessive'; the Court of Appeal may alternatively substitute a different award of damages instead of ordering re-trial. In *Rantzen*, it was held that the court, in considering whether the award was necessary, should ask, 'could a reasonable jury have thought that this award was necessary to *compensate* the plaintiff and to re-establish his reputation?'

Guidance on this subject was given by the Strasbourg decision in *Tolstoy v UK*.[18] The Court found an award of £1.5 million awarded to a peer in defamation proceedings, stemming from a pamphlet accusing him of war crimes to be disproportionate, and thus a breach of Article 10. Tolstoy, the defendant in the libel proceedings, also argued that English law was excessively uncertain in governing the award of libel damages. However, the Court stressed the need for allowing flexibility in legal schemes for setting damages, given the range of libels that could be committed, suggesting that *Rantzen* was an adequate response to the Article 10 implications of excessive awards.

However, despite these reasonable restrictions eventually placed upon awards of damages, the law of defamation as so far described had a highly restrictive impact on free speech and the circulation of ideas. The law therefore developed various defences to actions in libel and slander. These now recognize that damage to an individual's reputation may, indeed be warranted; or, where this is not the case in the particular instance at hand, it should nevertheless be excused on grounds of the wider implications of imposing liability on the author of a libellous statement. Publication of true factual statements which damage reputation finds protection via the total defence of justification. This requires a defendant to prove, on the balance of probabilities, that defamatory allegations of fact were 'substantially true'.[19] Such an exemption clearly supports and is supported by Mill's market of ideas defence of free expression.[20]

Articulating the truth-sensitivity of free expression at common law, Lord Steyn in *Reynolds* cited Diplock J in *Silkin v Beaverbrook Newspapers Ltd*:[21]

In the first place, every man, whether he is in public life or not, is entitled not to have lies told about him; and by that is meant that one is not entitled to make statements of fact about a person which are untrue and which redound to his discredit, that is to say, tend to lower him in the estimation of right-thinking men.

---

[16] [1993] 4 All ER 975, *per* Neill LJ. See also *John v MGN* [1997] QB 586, CA.
[17] Per ss 8(1) & (2) and Rules of the Supreme Court, Order 59 rule 11(4).
[18] (1995) 20 EHRR 442.　　[19] *Edwards v Bell* (1824) 1 Bing 403, *Clarke v Taylor* (1836) 3 Scott 95.
[20] See discussion in Chapter 1 at 14–16.　　[21] [1958] 1 WLR 743 at 746.

The converse of this position provides one basis for the justification defence. Alternatively, its justification has been construed as being that a claimant cannot base a libel claim on statements conveying true facts because in this case she lacks the reputation on which the claim purports to be founded.[22] In any event, the principal limit of the justification defence has been the requirement placed on the defendant to prove the relevant facts. The difficulty for the defendant is that the relevant information usually lies in the claimant's hands. A notorious example[23] of a defence of justification that should plainly not have succeeded but did so, was an action by Aneurin Bevan and Richard Crossman against the *Spectator* magazine in 1957 in respect of an article alleging that they were both frequently drunk at an international conference. The pair were awarded £20,000 damages; it later emerged that both had lied on oath. Additionally, those with a reputation to lose may be in a powerful position, whereas those criticizing them may lack resources: the most vivid recent illustration of this was what became known as the 'David v Goliath' struggle between the McLibel Two, private citizens funded only by donations, and the global McDonalds corporation, a case considered further below.[24]

Justification is also, arguably, increasingly inadequate in the face of necessary public discussions of issues turning on complex, contested and scientific facts. Without additional shields against libel liability, and given the increasing role of private entities in public administration,[25] necessary and legitimate public discussion (of, for example, global warming, or of falsifiable stem cell research conducted in private labs) would be undermined.

In a further category of situations, it may be impossible to 'prove' truth. The need to safeguard expression in public of opinion, critique, and evaluation of facts explains the defence of honest comment on a matter of public interest. Subject to the condition that opinion must be based on true facts, protection has traditionally been wide:

[t]he question which the jury must consider is this: would any fair man, however prejudiced he may be, however exaggerated or obstinate his views, have said that which this criticism has said.[26]

The condition that comment should relate to 'public interest' information, to be covered by this defence, has also been widely construed: in this regard, Lord Denning, in *London Artists Ltd v Littler*[27] remarked:

Whenever a matter is such as to affect people at large, so that they may be legitimately interested in, or concerned at, what is going on; or what may happen to them or others; then it is a matter of public interest on which everyone is entitled to make fair comment.

---

[22] Loveland, *Political Libels*, at 7.   [23] Cited by Loveland, ibid, at 7–8.   [24] See p 1071.

[25] Public bodies, though not individual members of them, are prevented from bringing libel actions: *Derbyshire County Council v Times Newspapers* [1993] AC 534.

[26] *Per* Lord Esher in *Merivale v Carson* (1887) 20 QBD 275; see comments to like effect in *Reynolds*, op cit.

[27] [1969] 2 All ER 193, at 198, cited by Lord Nicholls in *Reynolds*, op cit, at 615a–b.

Justification and honest comment defences turn on the content of defamatory speech. The common law developed further defences, however, to protect speech made in particular situations. Firstly, absolute and statutory privilege safeguard statements made in particular fora (or the reporting, and therefore dissemination, thereof), free expression in which is regarded as a prerequisite to a functioning democracy. Primarily, absolute privilege affects court proceedings,[28] and proceedings in Parliament.[29] In *R v Wright*[30] absolute privilege was described thus:

though the publication of such proceedings may be to the disadvantage of the particular individual concerned, yet it is of vast importance to the public that the proceedings of courts of justice should be universally known. The general advantage to the public . . . more than counterbalances the inconvenience to private persons whose conduct may be the subject of such proceedings . . .

In other words, allowing libel claimants to sue on statements made in court or in Parliament would have a 'chilling effect' defeating the public interest: Parliament must be able freely and immediately to discuss emerging matters, debating and acting without waiting for proof, whereas it is the very objective of courts to establish truth. This justifies exceptionally allocating the risk of unearned damage to reputation to the individual. This may be seen as a clear example of the determination by 'audience rights' of the scope of protection for the individual speaker.[31]

Over time, the very limited 'situational' protection afforded to courts, Parliament, and the reporting thereof was extended by statute.[32] But, beyond protection for particular democratic institutions, what of journalistic statements, alleging or appearing to allege facts, which later turn out to be untrue? Such statements may address the same subject matter, or subjects of equally pressing public concern, as statements made, for example, inside Parliament. Protection for such statements, published in the general media, would appear, therefore, to be justifiable, in certain situations, by reference to the same principle as above, that is, of contributing to informed public debate. Only recently, however, has the common law protected such generally published defamatory misstatements of fact, through extension of the defence of qualified privilege.

Originally, this defence was founded on the existence of a special relationship between particular individuals—the maker, and recipient(s), of the statement in question—rather than on the qualities of the information published. This relationship

---

[28] *Curry v Walter* (1796) 1 Esp 456.   [29] *Wason v Walter* (1868) QB 73.   [30] (1799) 8 TR 292.
[31] See Chapter 1 at 27–8.
[32] E.g. Defamation Act 1996. See also s 7 and Schedule II Defamation Act 1952, which extends qualified privilege to: 'a fair and accurate report of the proceedings at any public meeting held in the United Kingdom, that is to say, a meeting bona fide and lawfully held for a lawful purpose and for the furtherance or discussion of any matter of public concern, whether the admission to the meeting is general or restricted.' The Defamation Act 1996 s 15 and Sched 1, paras 1–12 further established qualified privilege for a range of 'official' documents, subject to malice, and further conditions (relating to refusal to accede to a claimant's request for publication of explanations, and publications concerning matters not of public concern), e.g. worldwide legislatures, courts, public inquiries.

was seen as giving rise to a legal, moral or social duty on the part of the author to publish the information, combined with a corollary interest of the audience to receive the information.[33] Similarly, it was said that qualified privilege could pertain in circumstances where, in an exception to the presumptive protection of reputation, false defamatory statements had been:

. . . fairly made by a person in the discharge of some public or private duty, whether legal or moral, or in the conduct of his own affairs, in matters where his interest is concerned . . . [S]uch communications are protected for the common convenience and welfare of society; and the law has not restricted the right to make them within any narrow limits.[34]

Or again, on a privileged occasion, a person is so situated that, it 'becomes right in the interests of society' that he should tell certain facts to another.'[35] As Loveland puts it, 'Among the most oft-cited examples would be a father warning his daughter that her intended husband was a drunk or an adulterer, or a former employer writing a defamatory reference for an ex-employee to a new employer.'[36] This highlights the exceptional, relationship-based nature of traditional qualified privilege at common law.

Importantly, a second element of the defence of qualified privilege is the condition that defamatory factual misstatements must be honestly made: 'malicious' publication will attract liability. If a defendant succeeds in showing that publication was within the scope of qualified privilege, her good faith in doing so is presumed; it is then for the claimant to rebut qualified privilege, by proving 'express malice'. This requires proof that it is more likely than not that the defendant acted upon an improper motive (for example, a desire deliberately to injure the claimant) in publishing the statement; this will normally be assumed if it is shown that the defendant knew the statement to be false, or was reckless, as to its truth or falsity.[37]

In *Reynolds*, Lord Nicholls articulated the traditional basis of the defence as:

. . . [lying] in the law's recognition of the need, in the public interest, for a particular recipient to receive frank and uninhibited communication of particular information from a particular source.[38]

His Lordship continued:

There are occasions when the person to whom a statement is made has a *special interest* in

---

[33] *Adam v Ward* [1917] AC 309 at 334, per Lord Atkinson: '. . . a privileged occasion is . . . an occasion where the person who makes a communication has an interest or a duty, legal, social or moral, to make it to the person to whom it is made, and the person to whom it is so made has a corresponding interest or duty to receive it.'

[34] *Toogood v Spyring* (1834) 1 CR M & R 181; case concerned statement made, alleging faulty work, by defendant to plaintiff's employer.

[35] *Davies v Snead* (1870) LR 5 QB 608, per Blackburn J at 611, cited at 615g–h of *Reynolds*.

[36] I. Loveland, 'The Ongoing Evolution of *Reynolds* Privilege in Domestic Libel Law' (2003) 14(7) *Ent.LR* 178.

[37] With reference to *Horrocks v Lowe*, (1974) 1 All ER 662 per Lord Diplock; *Telnikoff v Matusevitch* [1991] 1 QB 102, 121; overruled on a different point [1992] 2 AC 343.

[38] *Per* Lord Nicholls, *Reynolds v Times Newspapers Ltd* [1999] 3 WLR 1010, 1017F–G.

learning the honestly held views of another person, even if those views are defamatory of someone else and cannot be proved to be true. When the interest is of sufficient importance to outweigh the need to protect reputation, the occasion is regarded as privileged.[39]

Taking account of this notion, Loveland suggests that decisions after *Toogood* required 'a considerable degree of personal or professional intimacy between the subject matter . . . disseminator, and its recipient'.[40] Thus, for example, allegations of criminal conduct made directly to police would be protected, whereas the same allegations published in a newspaper or other public forum would not.

The concomitant advantage of the basis of the defence in particularized relationships was the openness of its ambit: existing categories could not be exhaustive, and were applications of an 'underlying principle of public policy'.[41] Fair and accurate coverage of reports by certain public bodies were on this basis therefore gradually included. In time, qualified privilege thus turned on all the circumstances,[42] including the nature, status and source of the published material, and the circumstances of its publication. Nonetheless, qualified privilege still could not afford protection to statements on matters of general public interest made to the world at large, outside established categories. In *Blackshaw v Lord*,[43] for example, where a journalist had alleged that a former civil servant had been responsible for major incompetence in a government department, it was held that qualified privilege could not apply to statements published to the general public, there being in this case no foundation for any special duty to publish / receive.

As will appear below,[44] ultimately, in anticipation of the need to expand qualified privilege further in order to achieve compliance under the HRA with Article 10, Lord Nicholls in *Reynolds* effectively recast the rationale and basis of the original defence in finding qualified privilege applicable to media expression to a general mass audience. It is to the relevant Strasbourg jurisprudence under Article 10 encouraging that change that we turn below. However, in order to put that jurisprudence, and English law's response to it in context, it is convenient at this point to consider briefly approaches to this issue taken by other jurisdictions.

POLITICAL DEFAMATION: COMPARATIVE PERSPECTIVES

Many other jurisdictions have recognized the need to ameliorate in some way the normal rules of defamation when dealing with political, or public interest speech. Loveland gives a very clear explanation of this perceived need:

[39] *Reynolds*, op cit, at 615h (emphasis added).   [40] Loveland, *Political Libels*, at 9.
[41] *Reynolds*, op cit, at 616e, per Lord Nicholls.
[42] *London Association for the Protection of Trade v Greenlands Ltd* [1916] 2 AC 15, 23.
[43] [1984] QB 1.   [44] See pp 1076–83.

The justification for [some such] defence is purely instrumental. It is presumed to be better (or, to be more precise, less bad) that some false stories be published than that the fear of losing a libel action deters the press from running unproven stories which may turn out to be true. In the context of libellous stories about government bodies or politicians, this conclusion is based on the presumption that those people or bodies exercise such power over our lives that it is in our interest that we have as much 'true' information about them as possible. If the cost of maximising the output of true information is that some false stories are published, that is a price worth paying. It is the lesser of two competing constitutional evils.[45]

However, as appears below, different jurisdictions have arrived at very different answers to the question of where to find the best balance between these competing values.

THE US APPROACH

The landmark case in extending constitutional protection under the First Amendment to political libel was *Sullivan v New York Times*,[46] one of the major cases in US First Amendment jurisprudence. An Alabama City Commissioner had brought libel proceedings in response to an advert placed in the *New York Times* by a civil rights group. The advert had accused local authorities of harassing black activists, including Martin Luther King. In the Alabama courts, and though Sullivan himself was not named, the *Times*, and a number of individuals whose names had, unbeknownst to them, been mentioned in the advertisement, were held liable. The advertisement had contained a number of minor factual inaccuracies, and Alabama law allowed justification defence to succeed on condition of truth of all particulars. The jury at trial awarded $500,000 damages—a great financial blow to the sued activists.

On appeal, the US Supreme Court unanimously held that the Alabama state libel law breached the First Amendment's free speech requirement. There was no relevant category difference between criminal and civil law restraints imposed on free political speech—in both cases, restrictions should be minimal, because the free circulation of political information was crucial to the government's rule by 'informed consent'; nor were common law prohibitions more readily excusable than legislative ones. Importantly, furthermore, there was no clear boundary distinguishing the state from its officials: the former could not be allowed to pursue public criticism through the courts by proxy—the 'chilling' effect upon political discussion could be just the same.

---

[45] I. Loveland, 'Freedom of Political Expression: who needs the Human Rights Act?' (2001) *PL* 233 at 234.

[46] (1964) 376 US 254. For full background detail on the facts of the case, see I. Loveland, *Political Libels*, at 65, and on preceding US case law, Chapter 3, 'American Perspectives on Political Libels in the Early Democratic Era'. For further discussion, see also, R. A. Epstein, 'Was *New York Times v Sullivan* Wrong?' (1986) 53 *U Chi L Rev* 782, 787; I. Loveland, 'Privacy and Political Speech: An Agenda for the "Constitutionalisation" of the Law of Libel', in P. Birks, (ed.), *Privacy and Loyalty*, Oxford: Clarendon, 1997, 51–92; I. Leigh, 'Of Free Speech and Individual Reputation' in I. Loveland, (ed.), *Importing the First Amendment*, Oxford: Hart Publishing, 1998.

Consequently, it was found that Alabama state law's truth defence offered inadequate protection for free speech under the US Constitution. Requiring accuracy of every reported detail to avoid libel actions and damages was, in the political arena, likely to stymie publications of potential importance in discrediting executive authorities. Those in elected office, therefore, would now need to prove 'actual malice' where allegedly libellous speech addressed activities and qualities relevant to their public office. This test was to be set at the standard of 'knowing or reckless falsity' but, instead of proof on balance of probabilities, a new burden of 'convincing clarity' was introduced, further bolstering a defendant's position. Notably, in their partial dissent, Justices Black, Douglas and Goldberg would have prohibited any libel action challenging statements about public officials with respect to their official conduct, whether malicious or not, on grounds of the First Amendment's 'absolute, unconditional privilege to criticize official conduct despite the harm which may flow from excesses and abuses.'[47]

The major development in subsequent cases applying *Sullivan* has been the extension of the scope of protected subject matter, outwards from its original concern with elected office-holders, to a much more widely defined arena of public interest speech. In a privacy case, *Sullivan's* reasoning was amplified, and its actual malice test extended, to publications about newsworthy events and individuals involved in them—including their theatrical depiction.[48] The dissenting Justices of a split court, including Chief Justice Warren, however rejected a wider 'public interest' test, arguing that where information concerned private individuals, and there was no question of its instrumental value in informing electors' voting decisions, the additional protection established by *Sullivan* should not apply.

Further consideration of factors affecting an individual's public or private status was undertaken in *Curtis Publishing Co. v Butts*, and *Associated Press v Walker*.[49] In the former case, a university sports administrator was held to be a 'public figure', on grounds of public significance of his field of work; in the latter, an individual who had become involved in controversial civil rights activities, was also subject to the *Sullivan* test. On this footing, it was not surprising that alleged libels of electoral candidates should be included.[50] A winding back of *Hill* came in *Gertz v Robert Welch Inc.*,[51] where an individual lacked 'pervasive fame or notoriety', and had not courted publicity, state law should be permitted to protect her reputation against false criticism, by allowing compensation for damage to that reputation. *Gertz* also established that, under US law, fair comment was a total defence; more recently it has been held that, if facts are implied, a claimant must prove them false.[52] *Time Inc. v Firestone*[53] confirmed this, claiming a distinction between genuine 'public controversies' and matters merely attracting public attention; a high-profile divorce action could not be seen, either, as voluntarily courting publicity.

---

[47] (1964) 376 US 254 at 297.   [48] *Time Inc. v Hill* (1967) 385 US 374.   [49] 388 US 130 1967.
[50] *Monitor Patriot v Roy* (1971) 401 US 265.   [51] 418 US 323 (1974).
[52] *Milkovicth v Lorain Journal* 497 US 1 (1990).   [53] (1976) 424 US 448.

The US approach has been criticized for attaching too much weight to the status of a libel claimant, and too little, conversely, to whether the content of the speech itself is political.[54] Its negative consequences have also been pointed out. Barendt, for example, suggests that the US approach, of ' "definitional" balancing' may offer 'greater predictability'[55], but may only rarely allow 'deserving claimants, whether public figures or private individuals . . . [to] vindicate their reputation', speculating that the 'declining credibility of the press and the lower quality of public discourse' are consequences. On balance, Barendt argues, 'ad hoc balancing' is a preferable approach. In line with this view, both the 1975 Faulks Committee Review[56] and Supreme Court Committee on Defamation Practice and Procedure[57] rejected a *Sullivan*-style test for the UK.

AUSTRALIA

The law of political defamation adopted in Australia[58] has been described as a 'hybrid' between the US 'definitional' approach and the 'all factors considered' method emerging under the ECHR, in the UK, and also in Germany (see below). *Theophanous v Herald and Weekly Times Ltd*[59] gave first recognition, in light of the Australian Constitution, to an interest in the public at large in receiving political information.[60] The case was triggered by articles impugning an Australian politician's motives and conduct as Chair of a House of Representatives Committee on migration policy. The *Herald* sought to establish a new defence for false information pertaining to an MP's suitability for office where it was honestly believed to be true, and its publication took place during an election campaign.

The High Court[61] accepted that Australian libel law, in particular, the requirements of the common law defence of justification, unduly limited freedom of communication, protected by the Constitution, on political matters. Therefore, it granted new protection to the publication of material relevant to 'political discussion' by extending to it qualified privilege, on conditions that the defendant acted reasonably in all the circumstances, and that the information was not knowingly or recklessly false—in relation to which the defendant would bear the burden of proof. As to the definition of 'political discussion', potentially divergent descriptions were given. On one hand, the 'concept' was said to include '. . . discussion of the political views and public conduct of persons who are engaged in activities that have become the subject of

---

[54] *Freedom of Speech* at 209.

[55] Ibid, at 205, referring to article by M. B. Nimmer, 'The Right to Speak from Times to Time: First Amendment Theory applied to Libel and Misapplied to Privacy' (1968) 56 *California Law Rev* 935.

[56] Cmnd 5909 (1975) at [211]–[15].

[57] *Report on Practice and Procedure in Defamation*, July 1991, Chapter XIX.

[58] See I. Loveland, '*Sullivan v The New York Times* Goes Down Under' [1996] *PL* 126.

[59] (1994) 182 CLR 104, *per* Mason CJ, Toohey and Gaudron JJ; the case of *Stephens v West Australian Newspapers Ltd.* (1994) 182 CLR 211 was joined with *Theophanous*.

[60] Op cit, at 140.   [61] Australia's highest court.

political debate, for example. trade union leaders, Aboriginal political leaders, political and economic commentators.'[62] This, Barendt suggests, is a category wide enough to cover any matter of social concern, apart from commercial speech and scandal.[63] The option of a post-*Sullivan* 'public-figure' exemption was rejected.

Seen as an activist decision by the dissenting judges, an opportunity to review *Theophanus* arose before a newly constituted High Court in *Lange v Australian Broadcasting Corp.*[64] Lange, New Zealand's former Prime Minister, sued ABC following programmes questioning his conduct in office. The High Court founded a qualified privilege attaching to political subject matter, broadly defined, but perhaps giving greater emphasis to the political dimension than had *Theophanus*. The category would include issues of national and local government, and foreign politics and political bodies, as well as issues of immediate concern to voters' decisions in federal elections, because:

... each member of the Australian community has an interest in disseminating and receiving information, opinions and arguments concerning government and political matters that affect the people of Australia. The duty to disseminate such information is simply the correlative of the interest in receiving it.[65]

Carrying over the requirements of honest and reasonable publication, the latter would be required to be determined on all the facts of the case, including whether the defendant, '... took proper steps, so far as they were reasonably open, to verify the accuracy of the material ...', and a condition that she has 'sought a response from the person defamed and published the response made (if any)', subject to exception on grounds of practicability or necessity.[66] '[S]pite or ill-will' would exclude reasonableness of publication.[67]

The Australian approach is arguably preferable to that of the US in encouraging higher standards in journalism and reducing the risk of the casual destruction of reputation of (broadly defined) 'public figures' and the concomitant debasing of political discourse, but the scope of protected information is arguably too narrow. A very broad range of matters can go to make up a citizen's underlying political or philosophical outlook, while to many, issues outwith the scope of contemporary politics may be far more important than the range of current political debate.

NEW ZEALAND

Lange v Atkinson[68] gave qualified privilege a narrower scope than in Australia, although withdrawing the reasonableness requirement. With reference to a constitutional

---

[62] Op cit, at 118.   [63] With reference to *Theophanous*, op cit, at 123–4.
[64] *Lange v Australian Broadcasting Corp* (1997) 145 ALR 96; (1997) 189 CLR 520.   [65] Ibid, at 115.
[66] Op cit, at 118.
[67] Loveland suggests that in practice the test leaves little room for this exclusion, given Brennan J's assertion that desire to do 'political damage' will not amount to spite: ibid, at 150.
[68] [1998] 3 NZLR 424 affirming [1997] 2 NZLR 22.

commitment to open government, and the recent repeal of criminal libel laws, the New Zealand Court of Appeal found qualified privilege applicable to material relating to the conduct, or suitability for office, of individuals currently or formerly MPs, as well as electoral candidates. A public interest attached to communication about such groups that outweighed potential damage to reputation, irrespective of whether due care was exercised prior to its publication.[69]

This approach was considered, on appeal, by the Privy Council, in parallel with the House of Lords' deliberation in *Reynolds*.[70] On remission by the PC for reconsideration in light of *Reynolds*, the New Zealand Court of Appeal[71] declined to introduce a reasonableness requirement which could balance out a broader *scope* of qualified privilege, preferring its original narrow category of stronger protection. *Reynolds*, it argued, '. . . added to the uncertainty and chilling effect almost inevitably present in this area of the law'. Specifically, the Court was of the view that 'The blurring, perhaps even the removal, of the line between the occasion and its abuse in Lord Nicholls's non-exhaustive list must add significantly to [the] uncertainty [in both the principles of defamation law and their practical application].' It also opposed the adoption of *Reynolds* because 'it reduces the role of the jury in freedom of speech cases'.[72] The New Zealand Court of Appeal then redefined the concept of actual malice to provide a stronger safeguard against abuse, stating:

while carelessness will not of itself be sufficient to negate the defence, its existence may well support an assertion by the plaintiff of a lack of belief [in truth] or recklessness. In this way the concept of reasonable or responsible conduct on the part of a defendant in the particular circumstances becomes a legitimate consideration.[73]

Malice, of course, in New Zealand, as in English law, is an issue falling for determination by the jury.

Williams is strongly critical of the New Zealand approach, evaluating it as the 'least satisfactory'[74] of the three approaches of New Zealand, Australian and English law. While he concedes that it has 'the advantage of simplicity', in his view it takes an unjustifiably narrow view of the purpose of the public interest test, as doing nothing more than 'enable[ing] electors to make (informed) choices at the parliamentary ballot box'. In the result:

It permits damaging attacks on Members of Parliament (unless the claimant shows them to be malicious), while condemning all other defamatory attacks (unless the defendant shows them to be true). Picking out just one sort of domestic power-holder for special treatment in this way seems inappropriate. All the more so when a variety of individual and corporate, public and private, national and international players exercise diverse forms of influence that may broadly be regarded as politically significant.[75]

---

[69] See also *Lange v Atkinson and Australian Consolidated Press NZ Ltd.* [1998] 3 NZLR 424.

[70] *Lange v Atkinson (No 2)* [2000] 3 NZLR 385.   [71] *Lange v Atkinson* [2001] NZLR 257.

[72] Ibid, at 395.   [73] Ibid, at 400.

[74] K. Williams, 'Defaming Politicians: The Not So Common Law' (2000) 63 *MLR* 748, 753.

[75] Ibid, at 753–4.

This critique seems persuasive: it is very hard to conceive of MPs as a class having such significantly greater political power than other groups that special rules should be applied to them. In the UK, certainly, in which it is well accepted that media magnates, such as Rupert Murdoch exercise far greater political power than mere backbench MPs,[76] adoption of such an approach would seem simply blind to the realities of contemporary politics.

GERMANY

In Germany the right to reputation is protected under a number of Constitutional provisions: the Basic Law right to free expression is restricted with reference to 'right to inviolability of personal honour', and case law has held that reputation falls within the right to free development of personality, and the inviolable dignity of man, also providing justification for the criminal law of insult and civil defamation.[77] In this context, Constitutional Court decisions have adopted an approach giving detailed consideration to, and balancing, all relevant factors, rather than categorizing claimants or speech. As will appear below, and perhaps unsurprisingly, it is the German approach that is by far the closest to that developed by Strasbourg of the four surveyed above.

We will return below to consideration of these various approaches, in the context of evaluating both the Strasbourg case law and *Reynolds* privilege.

POLITICAL DEFAMATION: THE STRASBOURG JURISPRUDENCE

INTRODUCTION

As observed at the beginning of this chapter, libel law, which concerns conduct and legal relations between private individuals,[78] constitutes indirect state interference with both the right to free expression, and an individual's interest in the accuracy of her public reputation; both interests are acknowledged and protected by human rights norms in general and ECHR in particular. In terms of the ECHR-compliance of domestic libel laws, this entails two questions. First, in what situations and under what conditions is free expression injurious to reputation permitted? Secondly, and conversely, what restrictions does the ECHR *permit* on free speech exercised in the discussion of political matters and issues, on the grounds of unacceptable harm to the reputation of persons? A third issue relating to the restrictions, if any, on media

---

[76] See Chapter 1 at 21 for a brief discussion.
[77] See E. Barendt, *Freedom of Speech*, op cit, at 213–19.   [78] See Chapter 3 at 123–44.

publications that the Strasbourg Court may *demand* in order to safeguard reputation, is an issue of privacy.[79]

As seen in previous chapters of this work,[80] under the ECHR, in a manner reminiscent of the UK historical position (but in contrast to US, and now also other jurisdictions),[81] no explicit distinction is drawn between 'political' and other public interest expression more broadly. Nor does this wider category—although at the top of the hierarchy of speech under the ECHR—enjoy any specific special protection regime *vis a vis* other areas (artistic or commercial speech). However, as the following cases show, consistent with its general approach to the hierarchy of speech, outlined in Chapter 2, and in particular the importance of speech as a democratic safeguard,[82] the Strasbourg organs do demand greater latitude for expression with a public interest dimension, and afford a diminished protection for reputation within the public rather than the purely personal sphere.

It may, however, be suggested that an early phase can be discerned in Strasbourg case law, when the impact of libel laws on Art 10 was not properly scrutinized, and that it was the gradual appreciation of the impact of the US Supreme Court decision in *Sullivan*[83] that prompted applications challenging the compatibility of the criminal libel law of various states with Article 10, in the 1980s, followed by applications based on civil political libel only after 1990.[84] If true, this was in spite of the continuing expansion in the treatment of Art 10, including the landmark *Handyside v UK*[85] decision, discussed elsewhere.[86] In that decision, the Court referred to free expression as 'one of the essential foundations of democratic society, and a basic condition for its progress, and for each individual's self-fulfilment'; it identified 'pluralism, tolerance and broadmindedness' as essential characteristics of such a society, and as the basis on which to justify circulation of information and ideas which may 'offend, shock or disturb the State or any sector of the population.'[87] The Court also stressed, in accordance with Article 10(2), that

whoever exercises his freedom of expression undertakes 'duties and responsibilities', the scope of which depends on his situation and the technical means he uses. The Court cannot overlook such a person's 'duties' and 'responsibilities' when it enquires . . . whether 'restrictions' [are] . . . 'necessary' in a 'democratic society.'[88]

We turn now to consider the interplay of these principles in the leading cases. While we class the cases under various headings relating in most cases to the type of speech in issue, it should be noted that the theme of the care taken by the media body in question is one that cuts across these categories.

---

[79] See generally Chapter 13 and pp 1068–70.   [80] Chapter 2, Chapters 19 and 20.
[81] See above at 1051–4.   [82] See pp 50–5 and 61–72.   [83] 376 US 254 (1964).
[84] With reference to *Engel* Pub Ct B Vol 20, 82 (1974), a case following conviction for criminal libel for criticisms of government officials; and *X v Germany* App no. 6988/75, 3 D & R 159, Commission finding inadmissible application claiming German defamation laws breach of Article 10: Loveland, *Political Libels*, op cit, at 104–5, 108.
[85] *Handyside v UK* Series A No. 24, (1976) 1 EHRR 737.   [86] See Chapter 2 at 38, 61–3.
[87] Op cit, at [49].   [88] Ibid.

STRAIGHTFORWARD CASES OF 'POLITICAL SPEECH'

Lingens v Austria[89] is perhaps the most important decision of the Court in this area, and one of its most significant on Article 10. The applicant journalist challenged, as a breach of Article 10, his conviction—the outcome of a private prosecution for criminal libel raised by a former Austrian Chancellor, Bruno Kreisky. Lingens had published, in a political magazine, an article accusing Kreisky of political opportunism in forming a coalition with an extreme-right wing party, and of using his political office to avoid investigation of its leader in connection with Nazi atrocities. The Austrian Criminal Code established as an offence the publication of material accusing a person of 'possessing a contemptible character or attitude, or of behaviour contrary to honour or morality and of such a nature as . . . to lower him in public esteem'. Liability was subject to a defence of justification. Drawing a first important distinction, the Strasbourg Court found that the requirement, in criminal proceedings under the defence of justification, of proving the truth of opinions on the basis of undisputed facts, originating in political discussion, disproportionately interfered with Art 10(1): '[t]he existence of facts can be demonstrated, whereas the truth of value judgments is not susceptible to proof.'[90] Secondly, the Court, in a key passage, established the need, under the Convention, to distinguish between public criticism of a private citizen on the one hand and of a prominent politician on the other:

Freedom of the press . . . affords the public one of the best means of discovering and forming an opinion of the ideas and attitudes of political leaders. More generally, freedom of political debate is at the very core of the concept of a democratic society which prevails throughout the Convention. The limits of acceptable criticism are accordingly wider as regards a politician as such than as regards an individual. Unlike the latter, the former inevitably and knowingly lays himself open to close scrutiny of every word and deed by both journalists and the public at large, and he must consequently display a greater degree of tolerance.

No doubt Article 10(2) enables the reputation of others—that is to say, of all individuals—to be protected, and this protection extends to politicians too, even when they are not acting in their private capacity; but in such cases the requirements of such protection have to be weighed in relation to the interest of open discussion of political issues.[91]

Further, echoing the 'duty' aspect of English qualified privilege, and acknowledging that the evaluation of the human rights impact of libel laws must transcend the individual case, the Court commented:

Whilst the press must not overstep the bounds set, *inter alia*, for the protection of the reputation of others, it is nevertheless *incumbent on it* to impart information and ideas on political issues just as on those in other areas of public interest.[92]

---

[89] *Lingens v Austria* Series A No. 3 (1986) 8 EHRR 407.   [90] Ibid, at [46].

[91] Op cit, at [42]. See also *Incal v Turkey* judgment of 9 June 1998, at [54], for statement of converse principle, that limits of permissible criticism or other statements are narrower in relation to a private citizen than in relation to politicians or governments.

[92] Ibid, at [41] (emphasis added).

In consequence, the Court found that Art 10 required, in relation to misstatements of fact, that criminal libel provisions allocate to the *prosecution*, rather than the defendant, the burden of showing falsity and lack of reasonable grounds for belief in the truth of statements.

A cluster of other Strasbourg cases on clearly political speech disclose a similarly robust stance in its favour. In *Oberschlick v Austria*,[93] Oberschlick had published in a political journal, *Forum*, a draft of criminal charges he had sought to prosecute privately against the Secretary General of the Austrian Liberal Party, following his proposal to double family benefits to Austrian mothers, and halve them for 'immigrant mothers.' Oberschlick contended that these proposals were an advocacy of Nazism, a criminal offence under Austrian law. In response, the Secretary General, Grabher-Meyer, successfully prosecuted Oberschlick under the same criminal libel laws that had triggered the *Lingens* litigation. In finding a breach of Art 10, the Strasbourg Court decided that the publication had contributed to public debate on a matter of public importance, and it reiterated its statement in *Lingens* that, 'freedom of political debate is at the very core of the concept of a democratic society' under the Convention. It affirmed: 'Freedom of the press affords the public one of the best means of discovering and forming an opinion of the ideas and attitudes of political leaders.'[94] As in *Lingens*, the Court also reiterated the need for a distinction between the use of libel law to maintain politicians' political reputations, and those of private individuals:

the requirements of that protection [of reputation] have to be weighed against the interests of open discussion of political issues, since exceptions to freedom of expression must be interpreted narrowly.[95]

The Court found that Oberschlick's accusations of 'Nazism' were based on a comparison of public statements made by Grabher-Meyer with the 1920 Nazi manifesto;[96] they were therefore expressions of opinion clearly attached to stated sources and, as such, 'value judgments', rather than assertions of fact. Accordingly, since they were not amenable to proof, they ought not to have been the subject of a criminal prosecution. As to the article's provocative presentation of information, in the form of a mock-up of a criminal charge sheet, the Court found that, 'Article 10 protects not only the substance of the ideas and information expressed, but also the form in which they are conveyed.'[97]

Castells v Spain[98] is also well known as a defence of political speech against criminal libel. In 1979, a member of the Spanish Senate had, in newspaper articles, accused the Spanish 'government' of complicity in murders and violence against Basque activists. As a result, he was prosecuted, convicted and sentenced to a year's imprisonment. The relevant provisions, Article 161 of the Spanish Civil Code, made it an offence to 'seriously insult, falsely accuse or threaten the government'. Moreover, in the domestic

93 *Oberschlick v Austria* (1995) 19 EHRR 389.   94 Ibid, at [58]   95 Ibid, at [29].
96 Ibid, at [63].   97 Ibid, at [57].   98 *Castells v Spain* [1992] 14 EHRR 445.

proceedings, the Supreme Court had ruled inadmissible evidence of the truth of accusations made concerning political violence. Finding Castells' conviction in breach of Article 10, the Court held:

[T]he pre-eminent role of the press in a State governed by the rule of law must not be forgotten. Although it must not overstep various bounds set, *inter alia*, for the prevention of disorder and the protection of the reputation of others, it is nevertheless incumbent on it to impart information and ideas on political questions and on other matters of public interest . . . Freedom of the press affords the public one of the best means of discovering and forming an opinion on the ideas and attitudes of their political leaders . . . In a democratic system the actions or omissions of the government must be subject to the close scrutiny not only of the legislative and judicial authorities but also of the press and public opinion.[99]

The Court identified further distinctions, in addition to those two previously articulated between citizen and politician, and between a politician's personal and political reputation: 'the limits of permissible criticism *are wider with regard to the government* than in relation to a private citizen, or even a politician'.[100] It said, moreover, that 'while freedom of expression is for everybody, it is especially so for an elected representative of the people', who 'draws attention to their preoccupations and defends their interests',[101] so that restrictions on the speech of such representatives requires the 'closest scrutiny'. Neither could Castells lose his 'right to criticize the government'[102] by virtue of his choice to exercise it in a periodical, rather than in Parliament. The Court found that *some* measures might be necessary to protect government from defamatory, false or malicious accusations where public order is at stake, where, for example, accusations were 'devoid of foundation or formulated in bad faith.' However it held that a government's dominant position required the exercise of restraint, before criminal law could be used to censure free expression, particularly where less restrictive means were available to reply to unjustified attacks. It may be commented that the finding of a breach of Article 10 in *Castells* was more or less required by any court committed to adequate protection of political speech. A law criminalizing serious insult or criticism of *government*, with restrictions upon the ability of the applicant to prove the truth of what was said, strikes directly at the checking value of free speech and the pressing need to expose the government to sharp and robust criticism and accusation.

Oberschlick (No. 2)[103] concerned the applicant's conviction under a second provision of the Austrian Criminal Code which provided:

Anyone who, in public or in the presence of several others, insults, mocks, mistreats or threatens to mistreat a third person, shall be liable to imprisonment not exceeding three months or a fine.[104]

---

[99] Ibid, at [46].   [100] Ibid, emphasis added.   [101] Ibid, at [42].   [102] Ibid, at [43].
[103] (1997) 25 EHRR 357.   [104] Article 115 Austrian Criminal Code.

His prosecution this time arose from Oberschlick's response to a speech by Jorg Haider, then leader of Austria's far-right Freedom Party, and a regional governor, in an article, in which Haider was described as a 'Trottel' (idiot). The convicting court found that this term did not state an opinion; rather, it 'was nothing but an insult used to denigrate and disparage an individual in public';[105] it could not convey object-ive criticism. The Austrian Court of Appeal, upholding the decision below, found that, without reading the whole article, a reader would link the word to Haider's person, not to his reported speech; thus the word's use comprised an insult overstepping acceptable objective criticism.

Again adopting a contextual approach, the European Court of Human Rights assessed the use of the impugned word in relation to the article as a whole, took account of the situation of the article amongst other articles in the same issue of the journal, which had also addressed Haider's speech, and recognized the wider public debate and concerns providing the setting for the publication. Oberschlick's article had been published along with the text of the speech criticized and provided discern-ible objective reasons for the insulting word used. Rejecting the domestic authorities' view that the article had been a 'gratuitous personal attack', and recalling that Article 10 protects the form in which ideas are conveyed, not only their substance, the Court thus found that the words were used as part of a political discussion provoked by Haider's speech, and that the offence that might be caused by the use of the word 'trottel' was proportionate to the indignation provoked by Haider. Recalling its deci-sion in *Oberschlick (No 1)* and *Lingens*, the ECtHR reaffirmed that a greater degree of public criticism touching reputation is permissible against a politician than it would be against a private person; the former '. . . knowingly and inevitably lays himself open to close scrutiny of his every word and deed . . . and must display a greater degree of tolerance', 'since exceptions to freedom of expression must be interpreted narrowly'.

Schwabe v Austria[106] is a similar case on directly political speech. Schwabe was Chairman of the Young Austrian People's Party (OVP) and a Councillor. He had issued a press release suggesting that the Socialist head of regional government had no standing to call for the resignation of a second OVP politician, following a drink-driving incident, when his own Deputy had years earlier been convicted of a similar offence. As a result, Schwabe had been convicted of criminal libel (on grounds of an implied, inaccurate comparison between the precise nature of the two politicians' offences) and of reproaching an offender for a spent offence. The Strasbourg Court found that Schwabe's communication had been made in good faith, intended princi-pally to 'make a statement concerning political morality', as part of a 'general debate on political morals between . . . two rival parties'.[107] Clearly implying, again, a distinction between politicians and private individuals, it noted that,

A politician's previous criminal convictions of the kind at issue . . . together with his public

---

[105] Op cit, at [28].   [106] Application No. 00013704/88 (1992).   [107] Ibid, at [31–33].

conduct in other respects, may be relevant factors in assessing his fitness to exercise political functions. . . .[108]

The press release thus principally addressed a 'matter of public interest', to which its statement of details had been merely incidental. Moreover, the source of Schwabe's assertions of fact, on which his comparison had founded, was a court judgment.

Most of the above decisions may be seen as relatively straightforward.[109] What may be discerned in the following cases is the tendency of the Court (albeit sometimes hesitantly) to expand the zone of strongly-protected speech, beyond that directly concerned with attacks upon politicians. Some equivocation as to how far the judiciary should be considered as part of government in a broad sense, and thus as open to criticism, may be seen in two of the following, contrasting decisions.

EXPANDING PROTECTION FOR SPEECH BEYOND THE DIRECTLY 'POLITICAL': JUDGES, CIVIL SERVANTS, AND THE POLICE

The claimant in *Barfod v Denmark*[110] had accused two part-time lay judges of bias in a tax case, on the grounds that they were full-time employees of a government body party to the relevant proceedings. He was convicted under provisions of Danish criminal law prohibiting 'insulting acts or words' with the effect of degrading another person's 'honour'. The offence allowed for a justification defence, on the defendant's proof—although this did not extend to 'unduly insulting' remarks. Remarkably, the Strasbourg Court, in finding no breach of Article 10, suggested that this was a case of personal, rather than 'political' attack; the accusations were not 'part of political debate.' At the same time, however, the Court recognized the 'great importance of not discouraging members of the public, for fear of criminal or other sanctions, from voicing their opinions on issues of public concern';[111] but this was met, it found, by the fact that the journalist would have been free to criticize the judgment, rather than the judge. The decision appears inconsistent with Court's later reasoning, most significantly in relation to its narrow definition of highly regarded speech as 'political debate'; as appears below, in subsequent decisions, the Court took a much more expansive view of the contours of such speech.[112]

---

[108] Ibid, at [32].

[109] The same may be said of the decision in *Dalban v Romania* (2001) 31 EHRR 893, which concerned alleged fraud by the Chief Executive of a state-owned company and related misconduct by a politician, resulting in a conviction for criminal libel and a three-month prison sentence: a violation of Article 10 was found. *Sokolowski v Poland* (App no. 75955/01 (29 March 2005)) was a similarly straightforward case: it was found that Article 10 had been breached by the conviction for slander, punished by a fine, of an individual who had published a leaflet critical of local councillors. See also the recent decision in *Case of Ukrainian Media Group v Ukraine*, App no. 72713/01 (12 October 2005): the conviction of a private media company in proceedings launched by the leader of a Ukrainian political party, following publication of a critical article, at election time, for damage to her reputation as an MP, breached Article 10.

[110] *Barfod v Denmark* Series A No.149 (1989) 11 EHRR 493.   [111] Op cit, at [29].

[112] The case was not decided under the specific exception in paragraph 2 of Article 10 of 'upholding the authority of the judiciary'.

The Court's findings in *Barfod* may be contrasted with those in the later decision of *De Haes and Gijsel v Belgium*,[113] a decision which is perhaps more representative of the general tenor of the jurisprudence in this area. The applicant journalists had published articles criticizing certain Antwerp Appeal Court judges who had granted child custody to a father previously suspected of child abuse and incest; they had also suggested that the reason behind the decision was that the father happened also to be a member of the legal profession. The judges launched criminal defamation proceedings, relying on the offence under the Belgian Penal Code of insulting members of the judiciary; the offence was made out even where libellous remarks were based on facts. The journalists were convicted, and ordered to pay nominal damages. In contrast to *Barfod*, the ECtHR found that the convictions failed the test of 'necessity' and so were in breach of Art 10. Of first importance was that the articles addressed serious allegations concerning child welfare and the administration of justice, matters of clear public interest. The Court affirmed that: 'The courts . . . whose role is fundamental in a State based on the rule of law—must enjoy public confidence', and that accordingly judges must 'be protected from destructive attacks *that are unfounded*'.[114] Nevertheless, the Court highlighted the fact that overall the article was well researched, and factually correct; and that it contained 'a mass of detailed information' about relevant events, 'based on thorough research . . . and on the opinions of several experts.'[115] Any minor inaccuracies should be weighed, it was found, against the overall strength of the factual research.[116] Moreover, the article formed part of a genuine and serious debate in Belgium at the time concerning the criminal sexual abuse of children. While registering a caveat that no one should be exposed to defamatory criticism on grounds of the conduct of other members of her family, the Court furthermore rejected the judges' argument that discussion of their political sympathies comprised an attack on private honour. The view ventured on the underlying judicial motivation had, while based on reported facts, been a matter of opinion, in relation to which, the Court reaffirmed earlier statements that 'Article 10 protects not only the substance of the ideas and information expressed, but also the form in which they are conveyed';[117] thus, 'a degree of exaggeration, or even provocation', as well as insult and invective received protection under Article 10. Thus, although the writers had used polemical language, the Court would not hold this against them: the journalists could not 'be accused of having failed in their professional obligations by publishing what they had learned . . .'.[118] Barendt therefore cites this case for the proposition that the ECHR 'may not require [a defendant] to show more than a sufficient or some basis of fact to support . . . comment'—in addition to prohibiting a requirement on a defendant to 'justify a value judgment'.[119] The difference between *De Haes* and *Barfod*, assuming that they can be reconciled at all,[120] was perhaps that the allegations made in *De Haes*

---

[113] *De Haes Gijsels v Belgium* App. No. 19983/92 (1997); (1997) 25 EHRR 1.
[114] Ibid, at [37] (emphasis added).   [115] Ibid, at [39].   [116] Ibid, at [40].
[117] Ibid, at [48].   [118] Ibid, at [39].   [119] Barendt, *Freedom of Speech*, at 224.
[120] *Barfod* was not cited in the later decision.

appeared to be based much more solidly on proper research. Possibly, the context of the ongoing child abuse scandal in Belgium also contributed to the Court's seemingly much more generous assessment of the value of the speech in *De Haes*. Nevertheless, the *Barfod* decision remains anomalous in not attributing a high speech value to discussion of judicial bias.[121]

In the next cluster of decisions the Court grapples with the question as to how far speech not concerned with politicians or the judiciary, but plainly of genuine and serious public concern, should be afforded equal protection with more obviously 'political speech'. As we shall see, it is in this area that the Strasbourg court has diverged most significantly from the approaches taken in Australia and New Zealand.[122] The first three decisions discussed below concern the question how far the protection afforded to speech critical of politicians and judges should be extended to cover speech critical of civil servants.

In *Thoma v Luxembourg*[123] a radio journalist reported allegations, made in a newspaper, of corruption by officials in a particular government department, in a programme dedicated to the issue. Over 50 of the officials employed by the department launched a libel action against him. On the ground that he had failed to distinguish his own views from those in the allegations, he was found guilty and ordered to pay nominal damages. The Court, in a nuanced finding, determined that civil servants acting in their official capacity were legitimately subject to greater public criticism than private individuals, but also to a greater measure of protection than elected politicians. Finding that the topic, which was one of general public interest, was already being 'widely debated' in Luxembourg, the Court found that the conviction had been disproportionate. In particular, the approach of the domestic courts to the effect that, without formal distancing, journalists adopted all comments they reported, was found to place an undue restriction upon the press's role:

A general requirement for journalists systematically and formally to distance themselves from the content of a quotation . . . is not reconcilable with the press's role of providing information on current events, opinions and ideas.[124]

This was perhaps not a surprising decision, given that the case involved more or less pure reportage of an issue concerned directly with corruption in government.

It may be contrasted on the facts with *Pedersen & Baadsgaard v Denmark*,[125] in which no breach of Article 10 was found in relation to a successful libel action against TV journalists in respect of an allegation they had made of criminal conduct by a senior police officer during the course of a murder investigation which, their programme claimed, had led to a wrongful conviction. The Court found firstly that a police officer, as a civil servant, was susceptible to a lesser degree of criticism than a politician, confirming the stance taken in *Thoma v Luxembourg*.[126] But perhaps the

---

[121] As will appear further below.

[122] See above at 1051–2 for the discussion of *Lange v Australian Broadcasting Corporation* (1997) 189 CLR 520.

[123] (2003) 36 EHRR 21.   [124] Ibid, at [64].   [125] App no. 49017/99 (17 December 2004).

decisive finding in this case related to the apparent lack of proper journalistic stand-ards in reporting what was a serious allegation: no attempt had been made to verify the sole witness's evidence of the alleged criminal conduct, which was itself based on recollections of events taking place nine years ago. This case is significant therefore in finding that even in relation to the reporting of a matter of serious public concern, made on a prime time investigative TV programme on a national channel, journalistic responsibilities towards the reputation of others *must* be balanced against the import-ance of the speech in question. This appears to be an instance, like *Barfod*, in which the Court simply found a lack of an adequate factual matrix to justify the serious allegations made.

More significant in terms of the character of speech at issue is the decision in *Thorgeirson v Iceland*.[127] The application arose following the criminal conviction for defamation of a writer, who had published articles in a daily newspaper, referring to allegations, already in circulation locally, of police violence. Although a 'truth' defence was available, Thorgeirson had been unable to prove the allegations—which had not named individuals. He was found guilty of the criminal libel of a civil servant,[128] and fined. Perhaps the key point emerging from this case is the Court's response to a preliminary argument raised by the respondent government to the effect that *Barfod*[129] allowed wide restrictions on speech defamatory of the non-'political' reputation of public officials. Building upon its previous determination that political speech, under the Convention, is not restricted to matters of 'high politics',[130] the Court ruled decisively that, 'there is no warrant in its case law for distinguishing between political discussion and other matters of public concern.'[131] On this basis it found the issue of police brutality to be one of undoubted serious public concern; the speech was therefore worthy of a high level of protection. In terms of assessing how far the journalist had been culpable, the Court found relevant the following factors: that accounts reported in the articles had not been proved 'altogether untrue and merely invented';[132] that Thorgeirson had acted in good faith; that the aim of his communications had been, not merely to defame, but to encourage a public investiga-tion into complaints already made against the police, and that, in that context, although 'framed in particularly strong terms', the language used had not been excessive.[133] The Court also confirmed its previous findings that to require proof on matters of opinion in order to avoid conviction, was to fix a defendant with an 'unreasonable, if not impossible, task',[134] disproportionately interfering with Article 10.

A strikingly similar decision is *Nilsen and Johnsen v Norway*.[135] In the context of a

---

[126] Op cit.   [127] *Thorgeirson v Iceland* (1992) 14 EHRR 843.

[128] Under Article 108 Icelandic Penal Code, which provided: 'Whoever vituperates or otherwise insults a civil servant in words or actions or makes defamatory allegations against or about him when he is discharging his duty, shall be fined, detained or imprisoned for up to three years. An allegation, even if proven, may warrant a fine if made in an impudent manner.'

[129] Op cit.   [130] *Barfod v Denmark* (1991) 13 EHRR 493; *Barthold v Germany* (1985) 7 EHRR 383.

[131] *Thorgeirson*, op cit, at [64].   [132] Ibid, at [65].   [133] Ibid, at [67].   [134] Ibid, at [65].

[135] (1999) 30 EHRR 878.

lengthy controversy over police brutality in Bergen, which had resulted first, in an investigation of police misconduct, and then in an inquiry into misstatements by alleged victims, two police officers (also spokespersons of police professional associations) had publicly criticized a Government-appointed expert who had published a book that had been important in triggering the controversy. They were successfully sued for libel. The Court found, in line with its decision in *Thorgeirson*, that the defamatory speech 'bore on a matter of serious public concern',[136] and that there was thus 'little scope under Article 10(2) for restrictions' on it.[137] Further, counter-publications following initial allegations of police misconduct 'form[ed] part of the same debate', so that the former must also be subject to strict scrutiny.[138] In proceeding to evaluate the necessity of the intrusion into the officers' Article 10 rights, the Court moved on to consider the status of the impugned speech as fact or opinion, finding that the defamatory allegations imputing motives were matters of opinion, or value judgments,[139] rather than factual allegations, demonstrating that Strasbourg will not automatically adopt national authorities' categorization in this regard. Next, in performing its contextual assessment, the Court took account of the following factors: first, it suggested that, in the context of a heated and continuing debate of affairs of general concern, where professional reputations on both sides were at stake, a degree of exaggeration should be tolerated. Second, apparently extending the rationale of *Castells*, the Court held that a strict standard of scrutiny for restrictions on speech was required, especially where, as here, statements made by 'elected representatives of professional associations' were in issue. Finally, the Court had regard to the status and 'role of the injured party'. The 'admittedly harsh language in which the officers' allegations were expressed was not incommensurate with that used by the injured party who . . . had participated as a leading figure in the [public] debate'.[140]

SPEECH NOT RELATED TO GOVERNMENT BUT OF GENERAL PUBLIC INTEREST

Hertel v Switzerland[141] represents a further expansion of the zone of highly regarded speech. Hertel complained of a breach of Article 10 in respect of an injunction that had been issued by the Swiss courts to restrain him from making further publication of statements, based on his research, that microwave ovens were a risk to human health; a breach was punishable by criminal sanctions. Importantly, the Court classified his statements as of serious public concern. The wide margin of appreciation applicable in the commercial sphere was reduced when speech that might, in another setting, be merely commercial, in fact went beyond that sphere, and constituted 'participation in a debate affecting the public interest, for example, over public health'.[142] Further, the Court found it to be of little consequence that:

---

136 Ibid, at [46].   137 Ibid, at [43].   138 Ibid, at [44].   139 Ibid, at [50].
140 Ibid, at [53].   141 *Hertel v Switzerland* [1999] EHRLR 116.   142 Ibid, at [47].

[an] opinion is a minority one and may appear to be devoid of merit since, *in a sphere in which it is unlikely that any certainty exists*, it would be particularly unreasonable to restrict freedom of expression only to generally accepted ideas.[143]

This statement of principle is particularly important in stressing the need for debate on scientific matters, where knowledge is in a state of flux, as we suggested above.[144] It appears to flow particularly directly from classical Millian concerns over the importance for the discovery of truth of unhindered communication. In stressing the importance of the contribution of the article to a debate of general interest, the Court moved its jurisprudence on from the decisions in *Thorgeirson* and *Nilsen*, which had, it should be recalled, concerned allegations of abuse by state officials. As noted in Chapter 2,[145] while the Court was at pains in *Thorgeirson* to stress that a high level of Article 10 protection was not confined to 'political speech', many would regard the issue of police brutality or oppression as in fact a 'political' one. *Hertel* is thus a much clearer case in expanding the 'bubble' of protection from political to general public interest speech. This principle also found application in *Bergens Tidende v Norway*,[146] which concerned allegations of incompetence by a local cosmetic surgeon. The speech was found not to relate simply to one individual's competency, but to 'serious matters of public interest':[147] patient complaints of poor treatment were not 'private matters between the patient and surgeon', but 'matters in which the community at large has an interest'.[148]

This development in the scope of highly protected speech was confirmed by the decision in *Bladet Tromsø and Stensaas v Norway*.[149] A Norwegian inspector had compiled a report alleging animal cruelty by crew members on a seal-hunting boat. During a temporary embargo on the report by the Norwegian government, pending investigation of statutory offences, the applicant newspaper and editor had published the report's contents. In response, the crew had sued the newspaper, and editor personally, in libel. Once again, the Strasbourg court found itself required to account the 'overall background'. It thus considered it relevant that there was national controversy over seal hunting in Norway at relevant time.[150] More generally, it commented:

The most careful scrutiny . . . is called for when . . . the measures taken or sanctions imposed by the national authority are capable of discouraging the participation of the press in debates over matters of legitimate public concern.[151]

It also recognized that the articles in question were 'Part of an ongoing debate of evident concern to the local, national and international public, in which the views of a wide selection of interested actors were reported'. Further, the Court considered the

---

[143] Emphasis added.   [144] See above at 1045.   [145] See p 52.

[146] *Bergens Tidende v Norway* 31 EHRR 430, (2001) at [53] & [60].   [147] Ibid, at [51].

[148] A similar case is *Selisto v Finland*, App no. 56767/00 (16 November 2004), which concerned an allegation relating to a surgeon's intoxication during an operation, resulting in death.

[149] *Bladet Tromsø and Stensaas v Norway* 29 EHRR 125.   [150] Ibid, at [62]

[151] Ibid, at [64].

nature of the newspaper's coverage of salient issues. The crew members' views had been published in recent editions; articles taking varying stances on seal hunting had been published on an almost daily basis in a local newspaper, with a presumably stable readership.[152] Overall, reporting had been balanced. Importantly, the Court also considered the reliability of the *source* of the defamatory material reported. While the media's 'ordinary obligation' is 'to verify factual statements that [are] defamatory of private individuals':[153]

... the press should normally be entitled, when contributing to public debate on matters of legitimate concern, to rely on the contents of official reports without having to undertake independent research. Otherwise, the vital public watchdog role of the press may be undermined.[154]

In this regard and in general, however, Art 10's protection for journalists was subject to the *caveat* that 'they are acting in good faith in order to provide accurate and reliable information in accordance with the ethics of journalism'.[155] In this case, the journalists had met this standard. A further factor in determining whether to dispense with independent verification, the Court considered, was the 'nature and degree of the defamation'. Here, a 'number of factors limited the likely impact on reputation of the individual seal hunters concerned', in particular the fact that the article defamed neither the entire crew, nor named individuals. The Court stressed that both this factor, and the reliability of a source, should also be assessed with reference to knowledge and circumstances available at the time, not with the benefit of hindsight.

This decision thus confirms the extension of the area of strongly protected speech provided for by *Hertel*. In allowing the press some leeway in relying upon official reports, the Court also directly encouraged press debate of current, pressing issues. Its willingness to examine the effect of the newspaper's reportage as a whole exemplified its concern with the general role being played by the media body overall, rather than with what could be said about a single publication in isolation.

Much the same may be said of the decision in *Fressoz and Roire v France*,[156] which, while not a defamation case, is significant in confirming the broad reach of highly regarded speech under Article 10. The applicants in *Fressoz* were journalists. During a period of industrial unrest within the Peugeot motor car company, caused by the refusal of the management, led by M. Calvet, to award pay increases to the workforce, they published an article revealing the very large pay rises awarded during that period to M. Calvet himself. They proved the truth of this story by quoting figures from, and reproducing part of, M. Calvet's tax return, which had been sent to them anonymously. A criminal investigation relating to the theft of the tax returns by employees at the tax office was launched, but no-one there was charged. The applicants, however, were convicted of the offence of handling confidential

---

[152] Ibid, at [63].   [153] Ibid, at [66].   [154] Ibid, at [68].   [155] Ibid, at [65]
[156] (1999) 5 BHRC 654.

information obtained through a breach of professional confidence by an unidentified tax official and of handling stolen photocopies of M. Calvert's tax assessment and fined around £1,000 and £500 respectively. They applied to Strasbourg, alleging a breach of Article 10 ECHR.

The key issue under Article 10 was whether, as the applicants claimed, the article revealed matters of serious public interest. The Court found that it did:

> The article was published during an industrial dispute—widely reported in the press—at one of the major French car manufacturers ... The article showed that the company chairman had received large pay increases during the period under consideration while at the same time opposing his employees' claims for a rise. By making such a comparison against that background, the article ... was not intended to damage Mr Calvet's reputation but to contribute to the more general debate on a topic that interested the public (citing *Thorgeirson v Iceland* op cit).[157]

The Court found that the reproduction of part of the tax records in the publication fell within the media's discretion to choose the form, as well as the substance of the story being reported. It continued:

> Not only does the press have the task of imparting information and ideas on matters of public interest: the public also has a right to receive them ... That is particularly true in the instant case, as issues concerning employment and pay generally attract considerable attention. Consequently, an interference with the exercise of press freedom cannot be compatible with Article 10 of the Convention *unless it is justified by an overriding requirement in the public interest.*[158]

Both this decision and *Bladet Tromso* and *Hertel* thus display precisely the strong determination to protect the wide circulation of information and ideas relating to issues of serious public concern which, Chapter 2 suggested, is typical of the Court's Article 10 jurisprudence.[159]

DEFAMATORY SPEECH CONCERNING PRIVATE LIFE

We next consider a pair of cases in which the information in question related to the individual's private life. In *Tammer v Estonia*,[160] the editor of an Estonian daily newspaper had, in an interview with a second journalist, used words in Estonian that meant 'unfit and careless mother deserting her child' and 'person breaking up another's marriage', when referring to a woman who had, in previous years, been political counsellor to the former Prime Minister of Estonia and had had an affair with him, but who, by the time in question, was no longer active in government. She was, however, still in the public eye, and active in party politics. The editor was convicted for the criminal offence of insult and fined. Before a domestic court, which heard expert evidence on the issue, it was held the particular words used were abusive and

---

[157] Ibid, at [50].   [158] Ibid, at [52].   [159] See generally at 69–72.
[160] *Tammer v Estonia* (2003) 37 EHRR 43.

degrading; and that even public figures had the right to protection of their honour and dignity.

On this occasion, the Court found that Article 10 had *not* been breached. Recalling that Art 10(2)'s restriction implied the existence of a pressing social need, the Court again adopted an explicitly contextual view,[161] and found the particular words used excessive. First, although they 'amounted to value judgments', they were 'couched in offensive language, recourse to which was not necessary in order to express a "negative" opinion'. Second, even though the subject of the remarks had been in the public eye, and had been preparing to publish memoirs concerning her private life, it had not been shown that her 'private life was among the *issues that affected the public*' at the time of the article's publication, so that Tammer's remarks could 'scarcely be regarded as serving the public interest'; consequently, their use was not justified 'by considerations of public concern'—nor had they 'bor[n]e on a matter of general importance'.

This decision may be contrasted with *Karhuvaara & Iltalehti v Finland*,[162] in which an MP had proceeded in libel and privacy against a regional newspaper for publishing articles concerning her husband's criminal conviction for drunk and disorderly behaviour. The responsible journalist was convicted of libel and fined. The Court found a breach of Article 10. As in *Tammer*, the Court found that the stories printed about the MP's husband 'did not have any express bearing on political issues . . .', and 'did not pertain to any matter of *great* public interest.'[163] Nevertheless, the public still had 'the right to be informed, which is an essential right in a democratic society that, in certain special circumstances, may even extend to aspects of the private life of public figures, particularly where politicians are concerned.'[164] Noting the domestic court's opinion that 'conviction of the spouse of a politician could affect people's voting decisions', it therefore held that, 'at least to some degree, a matter of public interest was involved.' The distinction between the two cases is perhaps twofold. First, *Karhuvaara* concerned a person who was currently an MP, whereas *Tammer* was concerned with a former aide to a former Prime Minister. Voting intentions could be affected in the former case. Second, the information in question in *Tammer* concerned intimate aspects of private life—sexual behaviour and family relations. In *Karhuvaara*, in contrast, while the conduct revealed was that of the MP's spouse, not herself, drunk and disorderly behaviour is both a criminal offence and plainly anti-social conduct of a public nature. The claim of infringement of privacy was therefore much weaker in this case.

RECOGNITION OF REPUTATION GENERALLY AS AN ASPECT OF ARTICLE 8

Both the above cases raised fairly obvious issues concerning the protection of private and/or family life. However a trio of recent cases, all involving 'high value' speech,

---

[161] Ibid, at [61].   [162] App no. 53678/00 (2004).   [163] Emphasis added.
[164] Op cit, at [44]–[45], citing *Von Hanover v Germany* (App no. 59320/00).

disclose a development of potentially much greater significance in this area of law: the recognition of reputation as an aspect of Article 8. Although it is too early to say, the cases may also indicate a concomitantly stricter standard being applied to defamatory speech—as one would expect if such speech were seen to infringe, *prima facie*, another Convention right. In two out of three of these recent decisions, convictions for defamation were found justified, despite the fact that the speech was of the highest public interest; in the third, a breach was found in such circumstances only because of the draconian nature of the penalty.

Radio France v France[165] arose from a radio news bulletin based mainly on allegations contained in a magazine, concerning the activities of an active politician in the Vichy administration, as a result of which two radio journalists had been convicted of defaming a civil servant. Radio France was required to make civil reparation by repeatedly broadcasting an *erratum* message. For the first time in the context of libel, the ECtHR explicitly acknowledged that the right to protection of one's reputation lies within the scope of Article 8, as an 'element of the right to respect for private life.'[166] Secondly, in reaching a decision that Article 10 was not breached by the conviction, the Court found that the subject matter had been of the 'highest public interest', so that broadcasting about it was an 'integral part of the task allotted to the media in a democratic society', especially as relevant public debate was already alive at the time of broadcast. However, the journalists' insertion of a single false comment— that the defamed politician had admitted involvement in transporting Jews to death-camps—and adoption of a 'categorical tone', the force of which the original magazine article had lacked, alongside the bulletin being broadcast repeatedly all over France, meant that the need for 'utmost care and particular moderation' had not been met. The interference with the applicant's Article 10 rights was therefore justified.[167]

In *Chauvy & others v France*,[168] the applicants had published a book concerning allegations made about events leading to the discovery and arrest of French resistance leaders by Klaus Barbie in 1943, in which it was suggested that certain individuals may have been responsible. The Court observed that it was '. . . an integral part of freedom of expression to seek historical truth.'[169] In a significant passage, which departed from the notion of the state having to prove the 'necessity' of interferences with Article 10, the Court said that its function in Article 10 cases concerning libel is to:

verify whether the authorities struck a fair balance when protecting two values guaranteed by the Convention which may come into conflict in this type of case, namely . . . freedom of expression, protected by Art 10 and . . . the right of the persons attacked by the book to protect their reputation, a right which is protected by Art 8 of the Convention.[170]

---

165 App no. 53984/00 (30 March 2004).   166 Ibid, at [31].
167 It was also observed that criminal defamation is not, in view of the margin of appreciation, in itself a breach of Article 10: ibid, at [40].
168 App no. 64915/01 (29 September 2004) (2005) 41 EHRR 29.   169 Ibid, at [69].
170 Ibid, at [70], emphasis added.

In the instant case, it did not find a breach of Article 10: the conviction of the applicants for defamation followed a meticulous assessment by the domestic courts of the applicants' presentation of facts; convincing reasons had been offered for the finding that the author had 'failed to respect fundamental rules of historical method . . . and had made particularly grave insinuations.'[171] Also strongly significant for the finding was the fact that no orders had been made for the prohibition of publication, or the destruction, of the book. Rather, the fines and damages awarded had been modest, and the requirement to publish statements in five periodicals, and a warning in front of each copy of the book, was proportionate.

Conversely, in *Cumpana and Mazare v Romania*,[172] the severe penalties imposed founded a breach of Article 10, even though, apart from this, the ECtHR would have found the conviction 'necessary'. Notwithstanding the public interest of the subject matter (misappropriation of public funds), the convictions met a pressing social need because the relevant publications clearly asserted serious facts about named individuals, which had created an obligation, not met, on the journalists, to provide a sufficient factual basis.[173] The decision therefore indicates once again the prepared-ness of Strasbourg to insist upon relatively high journalistic standards, even in cases of 'high value' media expression, as well as the importance of the sanction in assessing the proportionality of interferences with Article 10 in this, as in other contexts.

While the Court's overall approach to investigating whether Article 10 had been breached in these cases did not show an obvious change, the recognition of reputation as an aspect of Article 8 is potentially of great significance. Rather than the burden being upon the state to justify interference with expression by reference to the familiar tests of necessity and proportionality, the approach would become one of 'fair bal-ance' between the two competing rights, rather than starting with the clear presump-tive priority of Article 10 over a competing, *non*-Convention interest in reputation. As just noted, the Court expressly adverted to such an approach in *Chauvy*. It is too early to say whether or not the Court's approach to Article 10 defamation cases will change substantively, in terms of offering greater protection for reputation than hitherto. But the formal acceptance of the engagement of Article 8 in such cases has clear potential consequences for domestic courts, as explored further below.[174]

PROCEDURAL ASPECTS OF DOMESTIC LIBEL LAW

Finally, two decisions concerning the UK raised questions about certain procedural aspects of English libel law, namely the unavailability of legal aid, and the requirement upon the defendant to prove the truth of defamatory allegations made. In *McVicar v UK*[175] a journalist had written an article alleging that athlete Linford Christie used prohibited performance-enhancing drugs. At trial in the ensuing libel proceedings,

---

[171] Ibid, at [77].   [172] App no. 33348/96 (17 December 2004).   [173] Ibid, at [101].
[174] See 1098–1102.   [175] (2002) 25 EHRR 22.

McVicar had conducted his own defence, due to the unavailability of legal aid for defendants to libel actions. The jury found McVicar's allegation substantially unproven; he was ordered to pay costs and not to repeat the libel. In response to arguments under Articles 6 and 10, the ECtHR held, *inter alia*, that the common law presumption of falsity—that is the requirement that a defendant, in libel, prove the substantial truth of her factual allegations, on balance of probabilities—did not breach Article 10. Further, with respect to the facts of this particular application, legal assistance was not required for a fair trial under Article 6: the relevant law was not sufficiently complex that McVicar, as an educated and experienced journalist, required legal assistance under Article 6(1).[176]

Steel & Morris v UK[177] arose from the London Greenpeace-McDonalds libel litigation. The applicants had been members of a small environmental group which, in the 1980s, launched a campaign against McDonalds, producing a leaflet alleging various and serious negative corporate practices. McDonalds brought libel proceedings. As legal aid was not, then, available for the defence of libel proceedings, the claimants conducted their own defence, over the course of a trial lasting years. McDonalds, by contrast, were represented by a team of experienced defamation lawyers. The trial judge found, overall, for McDonalds, although for the claimants on some issues; damages were awarded against the claimants which, though reduced, were still substantial in view of their limited resources.[178] As in *McVicar*, the Court stated that, whether Article 6 was breached through lack of legal aid depended on all the facts. In the instant case, in view of factors including the highly complex factual matrix, and severe personal financial consequences that ensued for the applicants, neither the measure of volunteer legal assistance they had received, nor judicial latitude afforded to them in the proceedings as litigants in person, could acceptably substitute for experienced professional representation. Inequality of arms, breaching Article 6, had therefore resulted, and in turn this lack of procedural fairness breached Article 10, as did the disproportionate award of damages. The Government's response to the judgment, it appears, is confined to pointing to the provisions of the Access to Justice Act 1999, under s 6(8), of which legal aid may be granted in defamation cases in 'exceptional circumstances'. See the 13th Report of the Joint Committee on Human Rights, 2005–2006, HL 133/HC 954, at [24]–[35] and Appendix 13.

THE STRASBOURG CASE LAW: CONCLUSIONS AND EVALUATION

Perhaps the most important overall comment to make is that Strasbourg plainly does not give to journalists the hunting licence that *Sullivan* grants to American journalists in pursuit of public figures, restrained only by the need to avoid acting maliciously. The Strasbourg Court quite plainly balances attempts made by the journalists to verify

---

[176] Citing *Airey v Ireland* (1979–80) 2 EHRR 305.

[177] *Steel & Morris v UK* App no. 68416/01 [2005] 41 EHRR 22; (2005) EMLR 15; the litigation arose out of the domestic libel trial in *McDonalds Corp v Steel* (unreported) 31 March 1999.

[178] They were never recovered, however.

allegations made against the value of the speech in question, having been prepared to find violations of Article 10 even in instances of high value speech, where inadequate attempts had been made to verify serious allegations. This tendency may have been strengthened by the recent finding that defamation engages an aspect of Article 8. We would suggest that the preceding discussion in fact discloses that there are seven organizing principles which the Court uses to determine whether the imposition of criminal or civil liability in respect of the publication of defamatory material is compatible with Article 10 in particular cases. We would summarize these principles as follows.

1. The significance, or weight, of the 'speech' at issue

This is perhaps the most obvious, and most important factor. As seen above, the jurisprudence discloses a progressive evolution in which the 'bubble' of highly regarded speech given enhanced protection has steadily expanded. Starting with directly political speech criticizing politicians and policies (*Castells v Spain*,[179] *Lingens v Austria*,[180] *Oberschlick v Austria*,[181] *Oberschlick (No. 2)*[182] and *Schwabe v Austria*),[183] protection has extended to encompass speech criticizing judges (*De Haes and Gijsel v Belgium*),[184] civil servants (*Thoma v Luxembourg*)[185] and the police (*Thorgeirson v Iceland*).[186] Significantly, it has thereafter grown to cover expression on matters of serious public concern which without such governmental overtones: *Hertel v Switzerland*[187] (safety of microwave ovens), *Fressoz v France*,[188] (alleged greed by management of nationalized company during industrial dispute), *Bladet Tromsø v Norway*[189] (allegations of cruelty during seal hunting), *Bergens Tidende v Norway*[190] (alleged incompetence by a local cosmetic surgeon) and *Selisto v Finland*,[191] (surgeon's alleged intoxication during an operation, resulting in death). In this respect, the finding in *Barfod v Denmark*[192] that criticism of alleged judicial bias did not form 'part of political debate' is plainly out of line. It is perhaps best explained as a case in which there was a failure in journalistic duty of care (the fifth criteria below).

One of Barendt's three overall conclusions on the Strasbourg case law is that it is concerned with the character and subject matter of the published material, rather than the formal status of the libel claimant.[193] Nevertheless, the Court has, in the above cases, set out a broad distinction between three classes of claimants. As seen above, it has found that politicians: '. . . knowingly and inevitably lay [themselves] open to close scrutiny of [their] every word and deed . . . and must display a greater degree of tolerance';[194] civil servants can expect a little more protection for reputation (*Thorgeirson v Iceland*), and private citizens the most of all: *Incal v Turkey*.[195] Thus,

---

[179] [1992] 14 EHRR 445.   [180] (1986) 8 EHRR 407.   [181] (1995) 19 EHRR 389.
[182] (1997) 25 EHRR 357.   [183] Application no. 00013704/88 (1992)   [184] (1997) 25 EHRR 1.
[185] (2003) 36 EHRR 21.   [186] (1992) 14 EHRR 843.   [187] [1999] EHRLR 116.
[188] (1999) 5 BHRC 654.   [189] (2000) 29 EHRR 125.   [190] (2001) 31 EHRR 430.
[191] App no. 56767/00 (16 November 2004).   [192] (1989) 11 EHRR 493.
[193] *Freedom of Speech*, op cit, at 223–5.   [194] *Lingen*, op cit, at [42].
[195] Judgment of 9 June 1998, at [54].

where speech is primarily concerned with a critique of someone's private life it will be seen as of decisively lower value, relatively easily outweighed by reputational or privacy interests: *Tammer v Estonia*,[196] *Von Hannover*.[197] Where the person concerned is a politician, however, the private lives of their spouses may be of sufficient public interest: *Karhuvaara & Iltalehti v Finland*[198] (publication of an article revealing the drink-driving conviction of an MP's spouse). Moreover, even politicians are entitled to some protection for their reputation, in performance of their public duties, as well, of course, as in relation to their private life: *Lingens*.

Finally, in relation to the nature of the speech in question, the Court has recognized that, 'Article 10 protects not only the substance of the ideas and information expressed, but also the form in which they are conveyed.'[199] Thus, 'A degree of exaggeration, or even provocation', as well as insult and invective receives protection under Art 10: *de Haes*.[200] Thus provocative media presentation such as the publication of a mock-up of a criminal charge sheet (*Oberschlick v Austria*) or the reproduction of tax records: (*Fressoz v France*) have therefore been found to be within the protective ambit of Article 10.

It is important to note, however, that the Court has not developed any form of categorical rule, in which particular classes of speech (e.g. that about politicians, or concerning political information) are *per se* protected in the absence of malice: the type of speech is but one factor, albeit probably the most important, to be assessed in combination with others, including the degree of journalistic care displayed, in order to determine whether Article 10 requires protection. This finding will be particularly important when we come to assess whether *Reynolds* privilege sufficiently answers to the requirements of the Strasbourg case law.

2. Whether burdens to prove allegations placed upon journalists by national law are excessive

In one of its clearest and most consistent findings of principle, the Strasbourg Court has held that requirements to prove the truth of comment (*Lingens, Oberschlick*), something said in *Thorgeirson* to be an 'unreasonable, if not impossible, task,'[201] breach Article 10. However, the Court has found that the English common law presumption of falsity—that is the requirement that a defendant, in libel, prove the substantial truth of her allegations, on the balance of probabilities, does not breach Article 10: *McVicar v UK*.[202]

3. Seriousness of the sanction imposed by the national courts

This is merely part of the ordinary proportionality assessment: criminal penalties and excessive liability in damages may cause a breach of Article 10 where otherwise there would not have been one: *Tolstoy v UK*,[203] *Cumpana and Mazare v Romania*.[204]

---

[196] (2003) 37 EHRR 43.   [197] [2004] EMLR 21.   [198] App no. 53678/00 (2004).
[199] Obershlick, op cit, at [57].   [200] Op cit, at 46.   [201] Op cit, at [65].
[202] (2002) 25 EHRR 22.   [203] (1995) 20 EHRR 442.
[204] App no. 33348/96 (17 December 2004).

Conversely, the relative moderation of the sanctions in *Chauvy v France*[205] was an important factor in preventing a breach of Article 10.

4. Was the media engaging in reportage as opposed to *adoption* of allegations?

It is an important part of the media's informational role for it to report upon allegations being made that legitimately concern the public. Therefore liability for simply reporting the facts of allegations made by others will tend to be excessive, *Thoma v Luxembourg*:[206]

A general requirement for journalists systematically and formally to distance themselves from the content of a quotation . . . is not reconcilable with the press' role of providing information on current events, opinions and ideas.[207]

In particular, journalists are entitled to repeat allegations made in official reports without attempts to verify them: *Bladet Tromsø and Stensaas v Norway*:[208]

. . . the press should normally be entitled, when contributing to public debate on matters of legitimate concern, to rely on the contents of official reports without having to undertake independent research. Otherwise, the vital public watchdog role of the press may be undermined.[209]

5. The 'duties and responsibilities' of journalists

The oft-repeated warning that 'the press must not overstep the bounds set, *inter alia*, for the protection of the reputation of others'[210] derives directly from the text of paragraph 2 of Article 10. Essentially, a conviction, or civil liability, may be found compatible with Article 10 where the allegations are serious and unsupported by an adequate factual matrix based upon reasonable attempts to investigate their reliability: *Pedersen & Baadsgaard v Denmark*,[211] *Barfod*, and *Radio France*.[212] In *Bladet Tromso* the Court said that the press should be protected providing 'they are acting in good faith in order to provide accurate and reliable information in accordance with the ethics of journalism'.[213] Part of this ethic means that the 'ordinary obligation' on the media is 'to verify factual statements that [are] defamatory of private individuals.'[214] In *De Haes* one factor that weighed strongly in the journalists' favour was that their articles criticizing judges contained 'a mass of detailed information' about relevant events, 'based on thorough research . . . and on the opinions of several experts.'[215] In this respect, the Court has stressed that the reliability of sources in particular should be assessed with reference to knowledge and circumstances available at the time, not with the benefit of hindsight: *Bladet Tromso*. Loveland sees the decision in *De Haes* decision as standing for the proposition that:

---

[205] App no. 64915/01 (29 September 2004) (2005) 41 EHRR 29.   [206] (2003) 36 EHRR 21.
[207] Ibid, at [64].   [208] 29 EHRR 125.   [209] Ibid, at [68].
[210] *Lingens*, op cit, at [41] (emphasis added).   [211] App no. 49017/99 (17 December 2004).
[212] App no. 53984/00 (30 March 2004). See above at 1089.   [213] Op cit, at [65].
[214] Ibid, at [66].   [215] Op cit, at [39].

a critical attack is unfounded only if its publishers have not exercised a reasonable level of journalistic care and scruple in satisfying themselves as to the truth of the underlying claim.

He comments that this test is broadly comparable with the position now adopted in Australia.[216]

6. Overall context

This is, of course, the broadest and most general factor. The Court will take into account the overall background to the debate in question: examples include the widespread public concern over the child abuse scandal in Belgium in *De Haes and Gijsel v Belgium*[217] and the public debate over government corruption in *Thoma v Luxembourg*.[218] Moreover, the Court does not necessarily assess a single publication in isolation: it may consider whether other reportage by the relevant media body has put the other side(s) of the matter. Thus, in *Bladet Tomso*[219] it had regard to the fact that the views of the defamed parties had been published in recent editions and that articles taking varying stances on seal hunting had been published on an almost daily basis in a local newspaper[220] in finding that, overall, reporting had been balanced. In *Nilsen and Johnsen v Norway*[221] the court took account of two further background, or contextual factors: first, it suggested that a degree of exaggeration in criticism should be tolerated,in the context of a heated and continuing debate of affairs of general concern, where professional reputations on both sides were at stake. Second, the Court had regard to the status and 'role of the injured party'. The 'admittedly harsh language in which the [police] officers' [defamatory] allegations were expressed was not incommensurate with that used by the injured party who . . . had participated as a leading figure in the [public] debate'.[222]

In *Hertel*, another contextual factor was considered: the fact that this was an instance in which an unpopular and only arguable proposition was being put forward on an issue surrounded by great uncertainty. It was said that it was important to disregard the fact that:

[an] opinion is a minority one and may appear to be devoid of merit since, *in a sphere in which it is unlikely that any certainty exists*, it would be particularly unreasonable to restrict freedom of expression only to generally accepted ideas.[223]

7. The applicability of Article 8

A very recent finding of the Court explored above is that reputation engages Article 8: *Radio France v France*.[224] As discussed above, the significance of this finding has not yet become clear, though it is possible that its consequence will be a closer scrutiny of the responsibility of media practice in reporting defamatory allegations. It would be

---

216 Loveland, 'A New Legal Landscape? Libel Law and Freedom of Political Expression in the United Kingdom' (2000) 5 *EHRLR* 476, at 480.
217 (1997) 25 EHRR 1.   218 (2003) 36 EHRR 21.   219 Op cit.   220 Ibid, at [63].
221 (1999) 30 EHRR 878. See above at 1063–4.   222 Op cit, at [53].   223 Emphasis added.
224 App no. 53984/00 (30 March 2004).

consistent with the Court's general Article 8 case law that the weight to be attached to the Article 8 claim engaged would vary significantly, depending upon the interests engaged.[225]

REYNOLDS V TIMES NEWSPAPERS: COMPLIANCE WITH ARTICLE 10?

As discussed in the first section of this chapter, until the late 1990s, English law did not provide any special protection from defamation law for misstatements of fact published to the general public by the media. The defence of qualified privilege was rather geared towards individuals in particular, proximate relationships with reciprocal duties and interests.[226] Our discussion of the relevant Strasbourg case law has shown that, by contrast, Strasbourg's treatment of libel laws, and their application, reaffirms the special status afforded under the Convention to media speech concerned with important public issues. Strasbourg's methodology, however, discloses certain similarities to the traditional common law approach, in taking account of all the circumstances of publication, rather than operating on the basis of categories or definitions, whether of individuals, or of content.

Before the entry into force of the HRA, it was therefore anticipated that an adjustment to UK domestic law would be necessary to achieve compliance with *Lingens*-type protection for public interest speech.[227] *Reynolds v Times Newspapers*[228] represented the House of Lords' attempt to achieve this outcome. In this section the decision is assessed, along with decisions articulating its subsequent evolution, with regard to Strasbourg standards, and in relation to the approaches of other common law jurisdictions.

In November 1994, the UK mainland edition of the *Sunday Times* published an article entitled 'Goodbye, Gombeen Man', concerning Albert Reynolds' resignation from the Irish Premiership and party leadership, which suggested that he had deliberately and dishonestly misled the *Dail* and members of his coalition government. The article had not recounted an explanation of relevant events offered by Reynolds in a statement made in the *Irish Dail* (Parliament). By contrast, the Irish edition of the *Sunday Times* of the same day had suggested that Reynolds had been unintentionally,

---

[225] See discussion in Chapter 13, note 103, and Chapter 15, note 80.

[226] As Loveland puts it, 'Among the most oft-cited examples would be a father warning his daughter that her intended husband was a drunk or an adulterer, or a former employer writing a defamatory reference for an ex-employee to a new employer.' ('The Ongoing Evolution of *Reynolds* Privilege in Domestic Libel Law' (2003) 14(7) *Ent.LR* 178.)

[227] Lord Diplock anticipated breach Article 10 in UK's criminal libel laws: *Gleaves v Deakin* [1979] 2 All ER 497: see Loveland, *Political Libels*, Oxford: Hart Publishing, 2000, p 106, note 81.

[228] *Reynolds v Times Newspapers Ltd. & others* [1999] 4 All ER 609, [2001] 2 AC 127, [1999] 3 WLR 1010; (2000) HRLR 134. Nicholls, Steyn, Cooke, Hope, Hobhouse LL. Subsequent references are to the AC report.

rather than wilfully, misleading. At a jury trial in the UK High Court in 1996,[229] the newspaper pleaded both justification and qualified privilege. The jury decided that the implication of dishonesty was unfounded; however, they also found that the defendants had not acted maliciously. The issue of qualified privilege was therefore determinative. The judge rejected the defendants' argument for a widened qualified privilege extending to 'political speech'. The defendants appealed, and Reynolds cross-appealed, on grounds of various alleged mis-directions to the jury. The Court of Appeal[230] ordered a retrial; it decided that, given the circumstances of publication, the article was not covered by qualified privilege. However, the Court granted leave to appeal on the point as an issue of public importance.

THE HOUSE OF LORDS—ARGUMENT AND DECISION

In the House of Lords, the *Sunday Times* argued for what, it suggested, would be an 'incremental development' of the common law, to create a new category of qualified privilege encompassing the publication, to the public at large, of 'political information', that is, information, opinion, and arguments concerning government and political matters affecting the people of the UK (a formulation apparently drawn from *Lange v Australian Broadcasting Corporation*,[231] an Australian decision).[232] It was argued that its effect should be that any defamatory statement made in political discussion, if published in good faith, would not found liability in libel; good faith would be present unless the writer 'knew the statement to be untrue or if he made the statement recklessly, not caring whether it was true or false, or if he was actuated by personal spite or some other improper motive.'[233] The *Sunday Times* further submitted that political information should be privileged '. . . regardless of the status and source of the material and the circumstances of the publication.'[234] The first benefit of this approach, it argued, was legal certainty, as against the unpredictability inherent in the approach whereby the courts would apply a public interest test to the facts in every case. Its second merit was in avoiding the appointment of judges to a 'position which in a free society ought to be occupied by the editor',[235] that of arbiter of public interest in publication. A public interest test, it suggested, effectively installed the court as a 'censor or licensing body'.[236] On Reynolds' behalf, it was argued that requiring proof of malice before public figures could establish libel would provide an inadequate restraint against publication of untrue defamatory statements.

In essence, the House of Lords' decision was to reject any move to category-based

---

[229] Decision of French J, of 25 November 1996.

[230] Lord Bingham CJ, Hirst, and Robert Walker LJJ [1998] 3 All ER 961, [1998] 3 WLR 862.

[231] (1997) 189 CLR 520.

[232] It was not argued that a 'public figure defence', along the lines suggested by *New York Times v Sullivan* (1964) 376 US 254 or the narrower definition in *Lange v Atkinson* [1998] 3 NZLR 424 should be introduced (for the introduction of a similar test in India, see *Rajagopal v State of Tamil Nadu* JT 1994 6 SC 524). For discussion of these tests see above at 1049–54.

[233] Op cit [2001] 2 AC 127, 191, per Lord Nicholls.   [234] Ibid, at 200.   [235] Ibid.

[236] Ibid.

special treatment for misstatements of fact by the media concerning political issues (whether defined by content or the status of the defamed subject) and, instead, to maintain the traditional common law methodology—imputation of an interest/duty, based on the particular facts of the case—while seeking to imbue this with respect for freedom of expression under the Convention. Two main justifications were offered for this outcome. First their Lordships felt that a category-based approach would offer inadequate protection for reputation. As Williams puts it:

Because the duty-interest test for privilege would be satisfied, virtually automatically, whenever the media turned to political questions, claimants would have to show malice, however wild the allegations. Since proving malice is notoriously difficult, requiring claim-ants to show a lack of honest belief against media defendants, who are not obliged to disclose their sources, would stack the cards unfairly. In this situation, a politician would have 'no means of clearing his name, and the public would have no means of knowing where the truth lay.[237]

Second, no principled distinction could be drawn between 'political' discussion and discussion of other matters of serious public concern. As Lord Cooke put it:

There are other public figures who exercise great practical power over the lives of people or great influence in the formation of public opinion or as role models. Such power or influ-ence may indeed exceed that of most politicians. The rights and interests of citizens in democracies are not restricted to the casting of votes. Matters other than those pertaining to government and politics may be just as important in the community; and they may have as strong a claim to be free of restraints on freedom of speech.[238]

Instead, it was found that the 'elasticity' of common law qualified privilege was capable of achieving the correct balance between individual reputation, and free media expression on all matters of public concern, by tailoring restrictions to the narrow limit set by 'necessity' on each occasion. 'This elasticity enables the court to give appropriate weight, in today's conditions, to the importance of freedom of expression by the media on all matters of public concern.'[239] Ten indicative factors were put forward as a suggested framework to assist courts in balancing these conflicting interests (discussed below).

In Lord Nicholls' speech, the issue before the court was said now to be characterized as one of conflicting rights.[240] Observing that, 'Historically the common law has set much store by protection of reputation',[241] his Lordship rearticulated this value in a clear attempt to render its terms more resonant with the Strasbourg framework:

Reputation is an integral and important part of the dignity of the individual',[242] which 'also forms the basis of many decisions in a democratic society which are fundamental to its well

---

[237] K. Williams, 'Defaming Politicians: The Not So Common Law' (2000) 63(5) *MLR* 748, 751, citing Lord Nicholls: (1999) 3 WLR 1010, at 1024.

[238] Op cit, at 220.   [239] Op cit, at 204.

[240] Op cit, at 190: 'this appeal concerns the interaction between two fundamental rights: freedom of expression and protection of reputation'.

[241] Op cit, at 192.   [242] Ibid, at 201.

being . . .; [when reputations were wrongly tainted by media] . . . society as well as the individual is the loser . . . Protection of reputation is conducive to the public good. It is in the public interest that the reputation of public figures should not be debased falsely. In the political field, in order to make an informed choice, the electorate needs to be able to identify the good as well as the bad.

His Lordship claimed that the common law had, 'long before the emergence of human rights conventions',[243] 'recognised the "chilling" effect of this rigorous reputation-protective principle'[244] on the 'basic right' and constitutional 'freedom to impart and receive information and ideas', and 'to disseminate and receive information on political matters [which] is essential to the proper functioning of the system of parliamentary democracy . . .'[245] This freedom '. . . enables those who elect representatives to Parliament to make an informed choice, regarding individuals as well as policies, and those elected to make informed decisions.' Therefore, equally, the common law had always acknowledged that:

There must be exceptions [to the right to reputation]. At times people must be able to speak and write freely, uninhibited by the prospect of being sued for damages should they be mistaken or misinformed. In the wider public interest, protection of reputation must then give way to a higher priority.[246]

However, Lord Nicholls' speech also acknowledged that to suggest that the common law had incorporated *effective* concern for free media expression[247] would be an act of 'wishful thinking'. In its traditional approach, publication to the world at large had been a 'special case', and as in *Blackshaw v Lord*,[248] rejection of a suggested new category of qualified privilege for 'fair information on a matter of public interest' had left public interest media speech without proper protection.

Nevertheless, Lord Nicholls maintained that a principled kernel was to be found in the common law reason for rejecting category-based protections for public interest speech, namely that 'A claim to privilege must be more precisely focused'.[249] Tying privilege to an evaluation of all the circumstances of publication was the key to an assessment, yielding, in every case, the correct answer to the question whether the information was 'of sufficient value to the public, so that, *in the public interest*, it should be protected by privilege'.[250] The US and Australian approaches were therefore rejected.

To guide assessment as to whether, in a particular case, publication of what turned out to be untruthful allegations should nevertheless be privileged, his Lordship enumerated a (non-exhaustive) list of ten criteria.

---

[243] Ibid, at 193.   [244] Ibid, at 192.

[245] Ibid, at 200. The House also cited *Campbell v Spottiswoode* 122 ER 288 at 291, per Crompton J: 'It is the right of all the Queen's subjects to discuss public matters. . .'

[246] Ibid, at 192 and 193.

[247] Citing e.g. the dictum of Cockburn CJ in *Cox v Feeney*, who had approved the view that 'a man has a right to publish, for the purpose of giving the public information, that which it is proper for the public to know': (1863) 4 F & F 13 at 19.

[248] [1983] 2 All ER 311.   [249] Op cit, at 196.   [250] Ibid, at 195.

i)   The seriousness of the allegation—'The more serious the charge, the more the public is misinformed and the individual harmed, if the allegation is not true.'[251]

ii)   The nature of the defamatory information, and the extent to which the relevant subject matter is of public concern.

iii) The source of the information: a source's lack of proximity to the events in question, or having an 'axe to grind', would tend to undermine her credibility; where a publication relied solely or mainly on such a source, it would consequently be less likely to deserve protection. Significantly, however, refusal to disclose identity of sources should not be a factor held against the media in any libel action.

iv)   Steps taken prior to publication to verify the defamatory information.

v)   The status of the information—for example, was the allegation already subject to an official investigation?

vi)   The urgency of the matter in question—its topicality.

vii) Whether comment had been sought from the plaintiff in advance of publication.

viii) Whether the article included the gist of the plaintiff's side of the story.

ix)   The article's tone. Where there was uncertainty, it would not be necessary to make assertions of fact—instead an article could 'raise queries or call for an investigation'.[252]

x)   The circumstances of the publication, including its timing.

In stressing that it was preferable to incorporate all relevant factors, the House thus rejected the Court of Appeal's articulation of a separate circumstantial test concerning the 'nature, status and source' of the material published,[253] to operate in addition to the traditional duty-interest / right-to-know test. Lord Nicholls stressed also that the weight to be given to the various factors would vary from case to case.

Lord Nicholls sought to bolster further the human rights value of these criteria by referring to section 12 HRA 1998,[254] and the press' vital investigative role. He also stressed that, in assessing the public's 'right to know', it was also to be accounted that the media act without the benefit and clarity of hindsight. In a strongly worded passage, he concluded:

Above all, the court should have particular regard to the importance of freedom of expression. The press discharges vital functions as a bloodhound as well as a watchdog. The court should be slow to conclude that a publication was not in the public interest and, therefore, the public had no right to know, especially when the information is in the field of political discussion. Any lingering doubts should be resolved in favour of publication.[255]

On the distinction between comment or opinion on the one hand and imputations of fact on the other, Lord Nicholls held that, in the former case, it would be adequate to

---

[251] Ibid, at 205.   [252] Ibid.

[253] In essence this had required an examination of whether there was an authoritative source from which the allegation was drawn; examples given included 'a government press release, or the report of a public company chairman, or the speech of a university vice-chancellor': [1998] 3 All ER 961 at 1004.

[254] See Chapter 2 at note 1.   [255] Op cit, at 205.

protect the individual against those defamatory statements that were malicious. In this case, the public could recognize an expression of opinion for being just that, and would decide for themselves whether it was persuasive. In the case of factual allegations, however, 'Those who read or hear such allegations are unlikely to have any means of knowing whether they are true or not'.[256] There was therefore a place for the additional hurdle imposed by the public 'right to know' test, before exempting factual assertions from liability. On past experience, his Lordship said, relying on the press themselves consistently to observe the professional ethics of journalism—a 'subjective' test, would *not* be an adequate alternative in this regard—despite the *Sunday Times'* urgings on this point. Court supervision, via the ten factors, was therefore essential.[257] As Lord Nicholls put it:

> The common law approach does mean that it is an outside body, that is, some one other than the newspaper itself, which decides whether an occasion is privileged. This is bound to be so, if the decision of the press itself is not to be determinative of the propriety of publishing the particular material. The court has the advantage of being impartial, independent of government, and accustomed to deciding disputed issues of fact and whether an occasion is privileged. No one has suggested that some other institution would be better suited for this task.[258]

Alluding to 'news media whose power and capacity to cause harm and distress are considerable',[259] his Lordship declared that the standard of responsible journalism could be equated with the duty of care owed by other professions to the public (for example, in negligence). In other words, his Lordship considered that the public has a right to know only where *responsible* journalism leads to publication of misstatement of fact in the political/public interest domain.

Turning to specific Article 10 arguments, his Lordship held first that, 'The common law approach accords with the present state of the human rights jurisprudence',[260] emphasizing that the Strasbourg jurisprudence clearly implies that there is a need for attention to the accuracy of the factual basis of journalistic reporting, even on matters of public concern. Such attention does not connote a requirement to prove or guarantee accuracy; rather it refers to the 'ethics of good journalism'[261] and to having a 'reasonable basis' for factual allegations.[262] Lord Nicholls also found that the

---

[256] Ibid, at 201.   [257] Ibid, at 202.   [258] Ibid, at 202–3.

[259] Ibid, at 202, citing *Lange v Atkinson* [1998] 3 NZLR 424 at 477, *per* Tipping J.

[260] Ibid, at 203. Lord Cooke also held that creating generic category 'would tend, in effect, to divert your Lordships from the European path'. And Lord Steyn stated that 'a test expressed in terms of a category of cases, such as political speech, is at variance with the jurisprudence of the European Court of Human Rights which in cases of competing rights and interests requires a balancing exercise in the light of the concrete facts of each case' (op cit (AC) at 210). In *McCartan Turkington Breen v Times Newspapers* [2001] 2 AC 277, 300, Lord Cooke reiterated that opinions in *Reynolds* intended to ensure that common law of England harmonized with human rights jurisprudence in general, ECHR in particular. Cf. *Berezovsky v Forbes (No. 2)* [2001] EMLR 45, para 11: CA refused to 'rest on the laurels of earlier judicial statements . . . that the English common law already conforms with Article 10.' See also *Branson v Bower* [2001] EMLR 800, at [6].

[261] Referring to *Fressoz v France* (1999) 5 BHRC 654.

[262] Referring to *Bladet Tromso v Norway* (unreported) (1999) 29 EHRR 125.

jurisprudence requires that no distinction be drawn as between political and other matters of public concern.[263]

Various arguments attempting to move the burden of proof onto the claimant in relation to the defence, for example, that it should be for the claimant, in relation to political defamation, to prove that the newspaper failed to exercise reasonable care or acted unreasonably in publishing,[264] were also rejected, on two grounds. First, it was found that such a shift would have far-reaching consequences, which had not been subject to full argument before the House. Second, if such a shift in the burden were to be extended only to *political* information, it would be incoherent in principle, given the House's broad rejection of a distinction between political information and information of serious public concern generally.

Applying the new principles to the case at hand, it was found that while the subject matter was 'undoubtedly of public concern', given that 'serious allegations' had been 'presented as statements of fact' and given the *Sunday Times*' failure to mention Reynolds' statement in the *Dail*, or otherwise to convey the gist of his response, there was no public right to know, and hence no qualified privilege.[265] Loveland explains why Reynolds rightly won on the particular facts:

> At the factual core of *Reynolds* is the point that *The Sunday Times* simultaneously ran two stories, each of which alleged quite different things. The longer, more thoroughly sourced story in the Irish edition cast Mr Reynolds as the hapless victim of circumstance. The condensed version run in the English edition portrayed him as a wilful liar. In that situation, the paper's claim that it did not know the London story was false, or was not recklessly indifferent to its truth, has minimal credibility.[266]

Lord Cooke, fully concurring, notably took the 'exception of malice' to be only 'a dubious safeguard', especially given the *Horrocks v Lowe*[267] direction, that is that 'mere carelessness, impulsiveness, vehemence of language and even gross and unreasoning prejudice' do not amount to malice—though recklessness to truth does. Lord Steyn similarly took objection to resting only on malice on related grounds, that in the UK, claimants lack US libel claimants' potential entitlement to important information touching on motive—and therefore malice—via pre-trial inquiry into sources and editorial decisions. Since, additionally, UK media bodies are not obliged to disclose sources, it would be too hard a task for even a political/public figure claimant to prove recklessness as to truth.[268] He also concurred in the contention that a separate category of political speech would not be consonant with the Strasbourg case law.

Lord Hobhouse, concurring, vehemently emphasized that:

> . . . it is the communication of *information not misinformation* which is the subject of this liberty. There is no human right to disseminate information that is not true. No public

---

[263] Citing *Thorgeirson*, (1992) 14 EHRR 843, at 863–4, 865.   [264] Op cit, at 203.

[265] Op cit, at 206.

[266] 'A New Legal Landscape? Libel Law and Freedom of Political Expression in the United Kingdom' (2000) 5 *EHRLR* 476, at 490.

[267] [1975] AC 135, 149.   [268] Op cit, at 219.

interest is served by publishing or communicating misinformation. The working of a democratic society depends on the members of that society being informed, not misinformed. Misleading people and the purveying as facts statements which are not true is destructive of the democratic society and should form no part of such a society. There is no duty to publish what is not true; there is no interest in being misinformed . . .[269]

These dicta perhaps underplay the fact that misstatements may be unintentional, and the deterrent effect of punishment in such cases upon political discussion generally. As Loveland puts it, 'that an easily satisfied cause of action in libel might deter the publication of "true" information is an argument which his Lordship does not entertain.'[270] But Lord Hobhouse's strength of feeling arguably leads him into further error. He goes on: 'The *publisher must show* that *the publication* was in the public interest and he does not do this by merely showing that the *subject matter* was of public interest.' But it seems arguable at least that the Strasbourg approach is rather concerned with the objective question of whether publication was in the public interest, rather than this being a question, proof of which is strictly allocated to the publisher.

REYNOLDS PRIVILEGE: EVALUATION

The House of Lords' decision in *Reynolds* received a cautious welcome from commentators generally, mixed with a fair amount of criticism. Williams,[271] for example, remarks that *Reynolds* 'represents a marked liberalisation, if not the full-blown "constitutionalisation" of libel that some commentators have called for.' However, he notes that 'little indication is given as to the weight to be attached to individual factors' and that terms such as 'public interest' are left largely un-explicated. He remarks that the *Reynolds*' defence 'may be dysfunctional if it makes libel litigation more likely, more protracted, and outcomes less predictable.'[272]

Loveland has put forward perhaps the strongest critique of *Reynolds*. He acknowledges it as 'a step forward in English law's protection of political expression', but goes on to assert that 'the judgment is—in terms both of its reasoning and result—a disappointment with potentially pervasive implications.'[273] His conclusion on *Reynolds* is that:

while . . . the 'surface language' of Lord Nicholls' judgment is all about the new constitutional frontier of the public's right of access to political information, its 'deep structure'[274] remains firmly embedded in English law's traditional approach to the political libel question as one requiring a balance to be struck between the reputation of defamed politicians and the liberty of the press.[275]

---

[269] Op cit, at 238.   [270] Loveland, op cit (*EHRLR*) at 489.

[271] K. Williams, 'Defaming Politicians: The Not So Common Law' (2000) 63 *MLR* 748, 754.

[272] Ibid, at 755.   [273] Op cit (*EHRLR*), at 491–2.

[274] The terminology in inverted commas is taken from what Loveland refers to as Joseph Weiler's 'seminal analysis of the ECJ's human rights jurisprudence': 'Eurocracy and Distrust' (1986) *Washington L.R.* 1103.

[275] Op cit (*EHRLR*), at 483–4.

Loveland notes the 'flexibility' inherent in *Reynolds* and comments:

A positive way of characterising such a legal principle would be to say that it offers the courts a very sensitive tool, which can be finely applied to construct ad hoc solutions to a myriad of divergent factual situations. Another way of spinning the principle would be to portray it as a recipe for chronic uncertainty: both for parties at the point of entry to litigation and—more significantly—for editors and journalists trying to decide whether a story should run. In a more abstract sense, this reading of *Reynolds* is deficient from a constitutional law perspective. *Reynolds'* lack of hard edges in respect both of its reach and its effect can be seen as undervaluing the significance of freedom of political expression within a democratic polity and denying that value the status of a fundamental constitutional principle.[276]

Elsewhere, he notes that some of the factors outlined by Lord Nicholls may be referred to as ' "culpability criteria", because they are concerned directly with how much care the publisher has taken to establish if factual claims are true', instancing:

3. The source of the information
4. The steps taken to verify the information
7. Whether comment was sought from the defendant.[277]

He comments,

In the USA, Australia and New Zealand such questions are matters to be considered when assessing whether the publisher has demonstrated 'malice' in the various senses that the term is used in those jurisdictions. Lord Nicholls suggests that the location of the test is irrelevant: 'there seem to be no significant practical difference between looking at all the circumstances to decide if a publication attracts privilege, and looking at all the circumstances to see if an acknowledged privilege is defeated'.[278]

But, Loveland suggests, the distinction *is* important: not only will the culpability factors decided by a judge, rather than a jury as they go to the issue of privilege, but:

More significantly, if, as in the USA, Australia and New Zealand, such factors fall within the second ('contents/effect') stage of the inquiry, they are being applied in a situation where the presumptive importance of the information has already been established. Under the Reynolds test, they go to the preliminary (reach) question of the importance of the information itself. This ordering devalues the substance of the information.[279]

Loveland is also critical of the retention of 'spite' as a factor that can negative privilege, even if the defendant honestly and reasonably believed the claim to be true:

The retention of spite as a ground of malice in political libel cases is not compatible with the 'informed electoral consent' principle that Lord Nicholls took as his starting point. Most, perhaps all, partisan political information is intended to 'damage' particular politicians either by influencing electors to vote against them or to vote in favour of other candidates.

---

[276] Loveland, op cit (*Ent LR*), at 182.   [277] Op cit (EHRLR) at 484.   [278] Ibid, at 484.
[279] Ibid.

From the audience's interest, spite is an irrelevance; it has no necessary bearing on the likelihood that the disseminated information is true.[280]

The point is well taken and, as will appear below, this point has now been addressed by the decision of the Court of Appeal in *Loutchansky*.[281]

Barendt, in contrast, is broadly supportive of the *Reynolds* case-by-case approach. He remarks:

While *comment* on public officials (and perhaps public figures) should be wholly free, it is not so clear that the free speech principle, even interpreted in the light of the argument from democracy, necessitates constitutional protection for false allegations of *fact* about such people.[282]

While we would broadly agree, it may be noted that *Reynolds* also amounts to a rejection of more imaginative possibilities, such as achieving an intermediate position between full defence and full liability in substantial damages. Obvious examples would include creating reverse burden of proof as to truth in certain classes of cases concerning 'political' information and/or creating a provision for a declaration of falsity where a defendant was found to have made false and defamatory statements but was saved by privilege.[283]

Our view would be that there is nothing about the *Reynolds* 10-point checklist that is incompatible on its face with the Strasbourg jurisprudence; the criteria enunciated therein, taken together with other principles of defamation law, broadly answer to the seven principles that we suggested animated the Convention case law above. English law does not require proof of value judgments (the defence of fair comment), and we have already seen that the burden of proof upon the defendant to prove the truth of factual allegations has been held to be compatible with Article 10 also.[284] While the rule that there is liability for each repetition of defamatory allegations might appear to fall foul of our suggested fourth Strasbourg principle on reportage, as opposed to adoption of allegations discussed above,[285] subsequent case law has, as we will see, answered to this requirement. The ninth *Reynolds* criteria, as to the tone of the article, should be explicitly glossed by domestic courts with reference to the fact that Article 10 permits journalists some degree of exaggeration and provocation in reporting matters of proper public concern.[286] These are relatively minor matters of interpretation of *Reynolds*, however. What is clear is that the Strasbourg jurisprudence does *not* require a *Sullivan*-type category based defence and, given its recent finding that Article 8 is engaged in defamation cases, such a defence might actually be held to be incompatible

---

[280] Ibid, at 485.

[281] *Loutchansky v Times Newspapers Ltd. and others (No 2)* [2002] 2 WLR 640 (5 December 2001).

[282] Barendt, *Freedom of Expression*, op cit, at 204. He cites Powell J, *Gertz v Robert Welch Inc* 419 US 323, 340 (1974) to the effect that. 'There is no constitutional value in false statements of fact.'

[283] New South Wales Law Reform Commission, *Report No 75, Defamation* (October 1995), at [6.2ff] — proposal for declaration of falsity procedure.

[284] See above at 1071.   [285] See p 1074.   [286] See above at p 1073.

with the Convention, as affording insufficient protection for reputation in particular cases. Moreover, we would agree with Barendt that an 'all factors considered' approach is preferable to the US or New Zealand stance, although it does carry the inevitable price of greater legal uncertainty. This does matter: even responsible media organizations may be unable to assess accurately in advance whether a defence of qualified privilege will be available, since in each case, it will require full investigation of the background to publication for a court to ascertain whether or not the public's 'right to know' was in play. The ECHR approach may of course also be criticized on this ground: Loveland refers to 'the (admittedly rather elusive) requirements of Article 10 . . .'[287] The particular difficulty with *Reynolds* lies in the fact that the ten-point checklist does not assign weight to the varying factors; therefore they can be manipulated by pro-reputation judges to produce distinctly media-unfriendly outcomes, while giving insufficient weight to the importance of the speech in appropriate cases. In short, whilst the *Reynolds* approach is perfectly *capable* of being compatible with that of Strasbourg, it would appear to be easy enough to apply it in a way that is not.

We turn now to the case law subsequent to *Reynolds* in order to establish whether this has indeed proved to be the case.

THE POST-*REYNOLDS* CASE LAW

SUCCESSFUL USES OF *REYNOLDS*

GKR Karate (UK) Ltd v Yorkshire Post Newspapers Ltd.[288] concerned allegations made in the *Leeds Weekly News* that the claimants, who ran karate schools, 'ripped people off', and generally ran a sub-standard organization. The article quoted, and drew authority from, the second defendant, who was part of an official English Karate governing body. Popplewell J in the High Court applied the test in *Reynolds* as follows. The allegations made were 'grave'. However, a journalist could 'responsibly' rely, without further inquiry, on information provided by the recognized spokesman for a sport's governing body; but making just one attempt to reach the subject of such allegations as made by paging service was inadequate, as was failing to mention relevant information that might tend to exonerate the subject of accusations made. A localized circulation heightened both the 'duty to receive' and to impart information, which can often be of more 'immediate concern' in such a context. There had been no urgency to publish the allegations, but accounting all the circumstances in the public interest, the free flow of information outweighed the slightly slapdash journalism

---

[287] Op cit (EHRLR), at 478.
[288] *GKR Karate (UK) Ltd v Yorkshire Post Newspapers Ltd and others* [2000] 2 All ER 931 *per* May LJ, Tuckey LJ concurring. The QBD is at (2001) 1 WLR 2571, (2000) EMLR 410.

behind the piece, which therefore attracted qualified privilege. Undoubtedly, the fact that the author was operating more or less alone, though subject to some editorial supervision, from her own telephone, for a 'community' style newspaper, influenced the result.

The decision, and its broad approach, were confirmed by the Court of Appeal, which additionally emphasized that, in assessing the 'circumstances of the publication' under *Reynolds* to decide whether qualified privilege existed, regard must be had to the circumstances as they appeared at the time of publication, not as subsequently revealed. Therefore a source's reliability is 'to be judged by how, objectively, it should have appeared to the defendant at the time', on the basis of her inquiries as to reliability. However, demonstrating the 'elasticity' of the *Reynolds* approach, it was reiterated that, 'There may be extreme cases where the urgency of communicating a warning is so great or the source of the information so reliable that publication of suspicion or speculation is justified.'[289] It is perhaps slightly surprising that the allegations in this case were afforded such importance—they hardly seem of the high constitutional value that the expansive dicta in *Reynolds* had in mind, as Loveland has remarked.[290] Nevertheless, given that there was, presumably, at least a possible risk of injury to those taking part in karate lessons without a properly skilled instructor, the case could be seen to come under the *Hertel v Switzerland*[291] principle, that information relating to public health is of high importance. What was perhaps decisive in the case was that the newspaper had relied upon information and opinion provided by the 'recognised spokesman for the governing body of the sport recognised by the Sports Council.'[292] This also brought them within the principle enunciated in *Bladet Tromsö and Stensaas v Norway*,[293] to the effect that '. . . the press should normally be entitled, when contributing to public debate on matters of legitimate concern, to rely on the contents of official reports without having to undertake independent research.'[294] Admittedly, the source relied upon here by the newspaper was not an 'official report', but it was akin to it, and this matter plainly was of considerable importance to the court. Broadly speaking, the decision seems sound.

In *Al-Fagih v H.H. Saudi Research & Marketing*[295] a newspaper with a daily circulation of about 1,500 in London, mainly to members of the Saudi community with particular interest in Saudi political affairs, reported libellous allegations made in the course of a political dispute between opponent members of a Saudi dissident organization, the Committee for Defence of Legitimate Rights. The High Court

---

[289] Stephenson LJ in *Blackshaw v Lord* QB, at 27.   [290] Op cit (*Ent. LR*), at 181.

[291] *Hertel v Switzerland* [1999] EHRLR 116 also *Bergens Tidende v Norway* (2001) 31 EHRR 430 and *Selisto v Finland* App no. 56767/00 (16 November 2004). See discussion above at 1064–5.

[292] Op cit (QB), at 413.

[293] *Bladet Tromsø and Stensaas v Norway* 29 EHRR 125. See discussion above at 1066.

[294] Ibid, at [68].

[295] *Al-Fagih v H.H. Saudi Research & Marketing (U.K.) Ltd* [2002] EMLR 13 Simon Brown, Mantell and Latham LJJ (*per* Simon Brown LJ, Mantell LJ dissenting; 5 November 2001).

rejected arguments for qualified privilege, on the basis that, absent any real attempt to verify the published allegation, which would have been easy to do, the defendant had failed to observe standards of responsible journalism. Additionally, Smith J had found that, over a series of articles, the newspaper had taken sides and implied the truth of allegations, and that the public interest in hearing an allegation, without knowing whether or not it was supposed to be true, was modest. Publication had not therefore been in the public interest.[296]

Before the Court of Appeal, the defendant publisher argued that, ' "Reportage" . . . certainly in the context of a political dispute such as arose here, should more readily attract qualified privilege than publications, as in *Reynolds* itself, by which the newspaper makes the allegation its own.'[297] In other words, this case, it was suggested, found the press in its 'watchdog' rather than its 'bloodhound' role. The majority held, applying *Reynolds*, that the report was protected by qualified privilege. While recalling that the repetition rule[298] applies to reporting of allegations made by others, a distinction, along Strasbourg lines, was accepted between repeating assertions as fact, and mere 'reportage' of the fact of them having been made. Applying this approach to the facts, it was found that the impugned articles had not suggested that the allegations were true.[299] Overall, with reference to *Lingens*,[300] in the context of a dispute being conducted publicly between political opponents, which was a 'matter of real interest and concern to the readership,'[301] qualified privilege was not forfeit merely because the newspaper had failed to verify the published allegations. On the issue of the personal criticisms repeated in the article, the Court declined to find that the fact that some of the allegations relating to a personal/sexual matter (that *Al-Fagih* had spread rumours about his opponent's alleged immoral behaviour) lacked 'obvious political importance'. According to Simon Brown LJ:

What *was* clear from these mutual allegations . . . [was] that one or other if not both of these leading Committee members were being shown to be disreputable, and that basic fact seems to be something which the [newspaper's] readership were entitled to be kept informed about.[302]

Similarly, according to Latham LJ, this was a story about a 'split in a political group which was clearly of significant interest to its readers', so that 'what is said by the one side in relation to the other is of itself of considerable interest. This is so whether what is said is of high political importance, or merely scurrilous gossip or personal

---

[296] 2 August 2000, per Smith J damages of £56,000 awarded.   [297] Op cit, at [6].

[298] As the Court succinctly described it: 'a report of a defamatory remark by A about B is not justified by proving merely that A said it: rather the substance of the charge must be proved. The jury cannot be invited to treat the allegation as reported as bearing any lesser defamatory meaning than the original allegation: see *Stern v Piper* [1997] QB 123': [2002] EMLR 13 at [35]. See also *Shah v Standard Chartered Bank* [1999] QB 241.

[299] Further, '. . . the interested reader would . . . have clearly understood that the allegation was likely to be met by refutation and/or counter-allegation': ibid, at [69].

[300] *Lingens v Austria*, op cit, at [42]; cited in *Al-Fagih*, op cit, at [30].   [301] Ibid.

[302] Ibid, at [49].

accusations.'[303] 'It is the fact that the allegation of a particular nature has been made which is in this context important, and not necessarily its truth or falsity.'[304]

On the verification issue, in light of the journalist's concession in evidence that 'he should at the very least have repeated Al-Fagih's general denial from the day before', their Lordships made some comments of interest. According to Latham LJ:

in the context of allegation, counter-allegation and refutation, where attribution is clear . . . verification is only likely to be of significance where the allegation is, for example, of criminality.[305]

Latham LJ also considered it relevant that the outcome of attempted verification would have been unknown. Simon Brown LJ was of like mind:

To my mind [the journalist] was entitled in this case to publish without attempting verification. Indeed in the present context verification could even be thought inconsistent with the objective reporting of the dispute.

At the same time, Simon Brown LJ cited *Reynolds* for the point that it could be, 'most unsatisfactory . . . to leave a newspaper open to publish a serious allegation which it had been wholly unable to verify.'[306] However, he went on to say that this would not be problematic:

Where . . . both sides to a political dispute are being fully, fairly and disinterestedly reported in their allegations and responses . . . [so that] the public is entitled to be informed of such a dispute without having to wait for the publisher, following an attempt at verification, to commit himself to one side or the other.[307]

It may be argued, however, that such an approach inadequately protects reputation. Where one party has given a provably false interview to a journalist, who has included detail of allegation in the article, it may be argued that the paper's duty is at least to take reasonable steps to find out which one is lying. But Simon Brown LJ expressly disapproved such a duty: 'In my judgment there was no need for the newspaper, at any rate at this early stage of mutual accusation, to commit itself to preferring and adopting the contentions of one side over the other.'[308] Mantell LJ, dissenting, considered that the journalist's 'failure to obtain Al-Fagil's response for publication at the same time as the defamatory statement coupled with the unnecessary haste with which the defendant rushed into printing this extremely damaging material,'[309] dictated that the judge below had correctly applied *Reynolds* to the facts before her. Plainly, the approach taken in the case is in harmony with one aspect of the Strasbourg case law—that merely reporting allegations engages a lesser responsibility placed on journalists than originating them, or adopting them: *Thoma v Luxembourg*.[310]

As to the general approach of *Reynolds*, regarding the relative priority of the rights and interests at stake, Simon Brown LJ found that the privilege:

---

[303] Ibid, at [65]. [304] Ibid. [305] Ibid, at [68]. [306] Ibid, at [51]. [307] Ibid, at [52].
[308] Ibid, at [49]. [309] Ibid, at [63]. [310] (2003) 36 EHRR 21. See above at 1074.

. . . is designed to enable a proper balance to be struck between on the one hand the cardinal importance of freedom of expression by the media on all matters of public concern, and on the other the right of an individual to his good reputation. Neither right is absolute, but the former, particularly in the field of political discussion, is of a higher order, a constitutional right of vital importance to the proper functioning of a democratic society.[311]

These dicta are something we must return to, in the context of the recent decision in *Greene v Associated Newspapers Ltd.*[312] Nevertheless, the *Reynolds* duty-interest test was also stated as properly:

. . . reflect[ing] on the one hand the importance of keeping the public informed and on the other *the need for responsible journalism* to guard against needless information.[313]

Barendt finds the decision acceptable; he agrees that the newspaper was 'reporting, not adopting' defamatory allegations, and that no requirement to check the story arose since it had, 'covered the claimant's version of events'.[314] Loveland comments that the decision 'seems to have picked up the *Reynolds* principle and used it to substantially weaken the impact of the repetition rule when public interest stories are in issue.'[315]

The above two decisions reveal that the *Reynolds* defence is working to protect reportage of general interest to the public, with a reasonably generous view of taken of what counts as journalistic due diligence in relation to verification. Both, however, have distinctive features: in *GKR Karate*, it appeared to be the fact that the newspaper had an authoritative foundation for the allegations from an expert source, which saved them from liability; in *Al-Fagih*, the fact that the newspaper was acting merely to report an exchange of allegations strongly influenced the court in its favour. *Armstrong v Times Newspapers Ltd*[316] also gives some comfort to the media, in holding that the failure to put allegations to a claimant should not necessarily be determinative of the defence of qualified privilege.

However, there are a cluster of decisions in which publishers have failed successfully to claim the privilege, due, essentially, to findings that they had taken insufficient care to verify allegations.

DENIAL OF *REYNOLDS* PRIVILEGE FOR FAILURE TO EXERCISE SUFFICIENT JOURNALIST CARE

Galloway v Telegraph Group Ltd[317] represents a direct contrast with *GKR Karate*, in finding essentially that the official source that the newspaper had tried to rely upon was unreliable. The case arose from articles in *The Telegraph* alleging that documents had been found in the Iraqi Foreign Ministry after the invasion of Iraq, showing that

---

[311] Ibid, at [26].
[312] [2005] QB 972, [2005] 1 All ER 30, [2004] EWCA Civ 1462, *per* Brooke, May and Dyson LJJ.
[313] Op cit, at [46] (emphasis added).   [314] *Freedom of Speech*, at 220.
[315] Op cit (*Ent LR*), at 180.
[316] [2005] EMLR 33 (29 July 2005); Brooke LJ (VP), Tuckey and Arden LJJ.
[317] [2004] EWCH 2786, (2005) EMLR 7 (2 December 2004) Eady J.

George Galloway MP had personally received funds diverted from Iraq's oil-for-food programme, that he had taken large sums of money from Saddam's regime and that his campaign for humanitarian assistance for Iraq was a front for his pursuit of personal financial advantage. When sued for libel by Galloway, the *Telegraph* pleaded qualified privilege. The Court found that the allegation made was of personal greed and that the *Telegraph* had indicated as its view that the evidence supporting this conclusion was overwhelming. Although it had offered Galloway an opportunity to respond to the allegations, and published his denials, the language used showed that in the newspaper's own view the denials were dishonest and unreliable and should be discounted by readers. Where the purpose of the article was to condemn an individual, the 'reportage exemption' from the repetition rule for neutral coverage of a political dispute could not, it was found, apply.[318]

Further applying the *Reynolds* test, it was found that serious allegations had been made, on a matter of public concern, which, if true, would be fatal to Galloway's reputation and political career; it was clear at the time of publication that the sources (as operatives within Saddam's regime) might well have had an axe to grind; no steps had been taken to verify information; there was no urgency in publication, other than the 'desire to secure a scoop'; some allegations were not put to Galloway; and the overall tone of the coverage was dramatic and condemnatory. Thus publication had not been in the public interest. Given the evident hostility of the newspaper in question to Galloway, the very serious nature of the allegations, the tone of the coverage, and the fact that the documents found could well have been forged, the outcome is not, perhaps, a surprising one. It was very recently upheld by the Court of Appeal.[319] Sir Anthony Clarke said that Eady J in the High Court had been 'plainly right to conclude that the newspaper was not neutral, but both embraced the allegations with relish and fervour and went on to embellish them'.[320]

James Gilbert Ltd and another v Mirror Group Newspapers Ltd,[321] in contrast, was an instance in which the newspaper was the originator of the allegations. The claimants were a manufacturer of sports balls. The *Sunday Mirror* had published an article alleging that an Indian sub-contractor was using child labour to manufacture JGL's products, but it had also reported a statement by the company to the effect that it did not use child labour, and the managing director's promise rapidly to launch an inquiry. Shortly afterwards, a further article, 'Slave balls firm breaks its promise', alleged that no investigation was in fact taking place. As it later emerged, the company had, by that time, indeed launched an investigation. In the resulting libel action, the *Mirror* therefore sought to rely on qualified privilege. Applying *Reynolds* in the High Court, Eady J held as follows. Accusing the managing director of lying was serious in itself, but assumed greater seriousness given the gravity of the original allegation

---

[318] Op cit, at [133].

[319] On 25 January 2006. See Chapter 7 at 312 and 317–18 on the issue of 'spin' in relation to journalistic sources.

[320] See '*Telegraph* loses Galloway libel appeal', *The Guardian*, 26 January 2006.

[321] *James Gilbert Ltd and another v Mirror Group Newspapers Ltd.* [2000] EMLR 680 (17 April 2000).

made, that of using child labour.[322] The issue was clearly one of public concern: 'it would indeed be a matter of legitimate public interest if a business conducted within this jurisdiction was obtaining its goods as a result of exploitation.'[323] However, the later, defamatory, article was of lesser public interest, the issues having been raised by the first a short time beforehand. As to source, the journalists had objective reason to question the reliability of their informant. The *Mirror* could easily have taken steps to verify the published information: this was 'an elementary omission'.[324] Lord Nicholls' criterion of the 'status of the information'—which referred, their Lordships considered, to official reports—in this instance had no role to play. Nor was there any compelling time factor: while it was clearly important to expedite the banning of child labour, with reference to the particular publication in question, 'The only compelling time factor . . . was the timing of the next edition of the *Sunday Mirror*'.[325] It was observed that newspapers should be careful to distinguish the public interest from their own commercial interest in relation to this factor; the relevant facts, indeed, 'could have been checked at somewhat greater leisure'.[326] Next, although the paper had approached the defamed subject for a pre-publication response, it had done so, '. . . without giving him an inkling of what was going to be alleged'. This 'was not in any sense giving him an adequate opportunity to comment'; it was found that the term 'adequate', 'means adequate for the purposes of giving rise to a duty to publish what turned out to be a false allegation'.[327] Further, the article did not contain the gist of the claimant's side, although this was in the defendants' hands well before publication, and its tone effectively adopted the statements of its source, instead of distancing itself from them. Thus, publication was not found to be in the public interest.[328]

Plainly, this was a case which turned not upon the nature of the speech, but on the level of care taken by the journalists. The complaint was as to a straightforward inaccuracy of fact: there was no question of the defendants being asked to prove the truth of an opinion, something which, as we have seen, tends in Strasbourg's eyes to place an undue burden on the media. The case may perhaps be comparable with *Pedersen & Baadsgaard v Denmark*,[329] *Baford*,[330] and *Radio France*,[331] in which Strasbourg found simply that the factual matrix was not adequate in terms of justifying the allegations made. It may be noted, however, that, as with the *GKR Karate* case, there was no citation of any Strasbourg case law. Reliance was placed purely upon *Reynolds* as an exhaustive statement of what is required to ensure that English libel law remains Article 10 compliant, a point we return to below. Moreover, the finding that there was a lesser public interest in the second article was, we suggest, highly doubtful. One of the legitimate roles of newspapers is to keep up the pressure for change on government and other bodies found to be acting reprehensibly; while the

---

[322] Ibid, at 700.   [323] Ibid.   [324] Ibid, at 701.   [325] Ibid, at 702.   [326] Ibid, at 702.
[327] Ibid.
[328] Eady described *Reynolds'* tenth factor as 'the general sweeping up point', ibid, at 703.
[329] App no. 49017/99 (17 December 2004): see above at 1074–5.   [330] Op cit.
[331] App no. 53984/00 (30 March 2004).

newspaper should have checked its facts more carefully, we do not think it right for a judge to find that a follow-up story is of lesser public interest than the initial coverage.

In *Grobbelaar v News Group Newspapers Ltd*[332] *the Sun* reported as fact allegations of match-fixing by Bruce Grobbelaar, goalkeeper for a prominent football club. While it appeared from evidence of recorded conversations between Grobbelaar and another that he had entered into such an agreement and accepted money in respect of it, there was no convincing evidence that he had in fact made deliberate errors to fix the outcome of games, as *The Sun* had suggested. The jury found for Grobbelar, and awarded him £85,000 in damages, a finding overturned as perverse by the Court of Appeal. The House of Lords reversed the judgment of the Court of Appeal, but reduced the damages awarded to a nominal sum of £1. Lord Hobhouse emphasized the linkage between likelihood of untruth, responsibility, and availability of the defence.

Article 10 is not a licence knowingly to publish untrue statements of fact about another on unprivileged occasions and the proper protection of the person defamed may require that repetitions of the untrue statements be restrained.[333] [Therefore] 'If [the journalistic author] thinks that he may be unable to prove its truth, he must make sure that he conducts himself responsibly so as to be able to rely upon qualified privilege. Few would quarrel with the proposition that newspapers which are publishing defamatory statements of fact which they may not be able to prove are true must behave responsibly if they wish to take advantage of the protection of the law of qualified privilege.

Barendt views this as an example of post-*Reynolds* cases in which, 'Sensational stories, in which allegations are presented as though they are statements of fact,' have been rightly denied qualified privilege.[334]

Jameel (Mohammed) v Wall Street Journal Europe[335] is a somewhat more significant decision, in that it appears to betray a serious misunderstanding by the High Court of the *Reynolds* test, and reveals the vulnerability of the ten-point checklist to an unduly pro-claimant interpretation. The Court held that, although the general subject matter of terrorism, its prevention and the tracing of those responsible for it, were clear matters of public interest, publication of the particular articles concerned was not so urgent as to justify denying the claimants the opportunity to comment meaningfully on the allegations, which had also failed to communicate the gist of the claimant's side of the story. In particular, Eady J found that the seriousness of the allegations both went to the potential damage to the claimant and the importance of the public being given truthful information. As Cram puts it:

This argued not only for putting the defendant under a greater burden to check the story before repeating it, but also for a greater need to give the subject of the story an opportunity to comment on the allegations. In practice, however, this interpretation may mean that both

---

[332] *Grobbelaar v News Group Newspapers Ltd. and another* [2002] UKHL 40; [2001] EWCA Civ 33; (2001) 2 All ER 437; (2001) EMLR 18.

[333] Ibid, at [63].   [334] Barendt, op cit, at 220.

[335] (2004) EMLR 11, 20 January 2004, *per* Eady J. The case concerned an allegation that the Jameel Group was named on a list of bank accounts to be monitored, in respect of suspicion of connection with terrorist funding.

seriousness and lack of seriousness will count against the existence of a privileged occasion, since in cases where a comparatively trivial allegation is made, the less pressing will be the need to air it without conducting thorough checks.[336]

Upholding, the Court of Appeal[337] reemphasized the importance of the content of the published material in determining whether publication is in the public interest: the observation of professional journalism standards, in itself, is not enough. Further, it was underlined that the 'public interest' is a more stringent test than that of whether the public would be 'interested' in receiving the relevant information. On these facts however, in any case, the responsible journalism test was not met, because the newspaper did not accede to a specific request from the claimant for more time to comment on the then proposed article. Interestingly, it was observed that one impact of *Reynolds* is that 'Issues of subjective belief which hitherto have only been relevant where malice is an issue now become relevant to the inquiry of whether responsible journalism has been exercised.'[338] Therefore, 'it may be necessary or at least admissible for a defendant to allege and prove subjective belief [in truth] in order to establish a defence of *Reynolds* privilege'.[339]

It was also argued for the defendants that it would not be proportionate, with regard to Arts 6 and 10 ECHR, to allow a corporation to recover damages for libel without proof of sustained pecuniary damage as a result; or, conversely, that, requiring a 'corporation to prove special damage in order to establish a cause of action in libel would produce a fairer balance between the freedom of the press and protection of individual reputation'.[340] However, given the difficulties of proving causative links between damage to reputation and pecuniary loss,[341] such a requirement, it was held, would preclude the necessary degree of protection for corporate reputations exposed to inaccurate reporting.[342]

Barendt's comment is that *Jameel* reflects 'a more conservative approach' in its requirement to give claimants a fair opportunity to put their side of the story.[343] Cram is highly critical of the High Court decision, which was not overturned by the Court of Appeal:

Echoing Lord Nicholls, Eady J. stated that there was no public interest in being misinformed as to the claimants' involvement/non-involvement with terrorist activity. Since any assessment of whether the public was being misinformed in a particular case may well require taking account of matters not known at the time of publication, this might be thought to fall into the error of letting the allegation be judged with the benefit of hindsight, something that was expressly discouraged by Lord Nicholls no less in Reynolds. The whole point about

---

[336] I. Cram, 'Reducing Uncertainty in Libel Law after *Reynolds v Times Newspapers? Jameel* and the Unfolding Defence of Qualified Privilege' (2004) 15(5) *Ent L.R.* 147, 148.

[337] *Jameel (Mohammed) v Wall Street Journal Europe SPRL* [2005] EWCA CIV 74 (3 February 2005, Lord Phillips MR, Sedley LJ, Jonathan Parker LJ).

[338] Op cit, at [17].   [339] Op cit, at [29].   [340] Op cit, at [110–111].

[341] As concluded by the 1975 Faulks Committee Report.   [342] Op cit, at [113].

[343] Barendt, *Freedom of Speech*, at 222.

the qualified privilege defence is that it exists to protect allegations the truth or falsity of which is not known.[344]

Such an approach—of finding that there is no public interest in being misinformed—comes very close to extinguishing the *Reynolds* privilege for information of public interest altogether, given that privilege is only ever pleaded when justification fails, and the publication has therefore been found to consist (to some extent), of mis-information. The whole point of the privilege is that it exists to protect discussion of matters of serious public concern *generally*. Therefore the issue to be looked at is whether the article in question relates to matter of such concern, not whether it was beneficial to the public to be *misled* by the article. It is therefore to be hoped that this mischaracterization of the role of the 'public interest' in defamatory stories will not be followed. It was in fact fairly clearly ruled out in the next case we consider, decided some time before *Jameel*.

LOUTCHANSKY: THE RE-CASTING OF *REYNOLDS*?

Loutchansky v Times Newspapers[345] is perhaps the most significant decision since *Reynolds*, not because of the outcome, but due to the general guidance the Court of Appeal offered on the test. The case comprised two consolidated libel actions against the publisher, editor and two *Times* journalists, concerning articles alleging that Loutchansky was the leader of a major Russian criminal organization involved in money laundering and smuggling nuclear weapons. It is important to note that the Court of Appeal's judgment did not in relation to the first action decide the question whether the publication was privileged: the finding was that Gray J in the High Court had applied the wrong test. The issue of privilege was therefore remitted back to trial for fresh consideration under the guidance the Court of Appeal laid down.[346] It was argued for the *Times*, in line with the New Zealand Court of Appeal's decision in *Lange v Atkinson*,[347] that *Reynolds* conflates what should be a two-part test and 'effect-ively pre-empts the jury's role in determining malice'[348] (because the judge will determine whether the journalist took adequate steps to verify the story, as part of the ten-point checklist). The Court of Appeal in this case returned to pre-*Reynolds* authorities, to show that in fact *Reynolds* represented a break with previous, more restrictive authorities. *Blackshaw v Lord*,[349] cited by Nicholls in *Reynolds* as having

---

[344] Op cit, at 148.

[345] *Loutchansky v Times Newspapers Ltd and others (No 2)* [2002] 2 WLR 640 (5 December 2001); Lord Phillips of Worth Matravers MR, Simon Brown, and Tuckey LJJ, *per* Lord Phillips MR for the court. For full discussion of facts, see *Loutchansky v Times Newspapers Ltd (No. 4)* [2001] EMLR 898.

[346] The second action concerned the fact that the defamatory material had been re-published on the newspaper's web-based archive. In that action, the Court dismissed the claim of qualified privilege, finding that: 'republication of the articles on the defendant's website was made in materially different circumstances from those obtaining at the time of the original newspaper publication; that the failure to attach any qualifications to the Internet articles published over the period of a year could not be described as responsible journalism.' (op cit, paragraph (2) of headnote).

[347] [2000] 3 NZLR 385.   [348] [2002] 2 WLR 640, at [26].   [349] [1984] QB 1.

'adopted substantially the right approach', had set a high hurdle for qualified privilege in relation to mass media publications:

There may be extreme cases where the urgency of communicating a warning is so great, or the source of the information so reliable, that publication of suspicion or speculation is justified; for example where there is a danger to the public from a suspected terrorist or the distribution of contaminated food or drugs . . .[350]

This, observed Lord Cooke in *McCartan Turkington Breen v Times*,[351] had been 'somewhat discouraging' for newspapers.[352] On this footing, the Court of Appeal admitted that it was, in reality, '. . . difficult to recognise in the approach to the defence conventionally adopted in the earlier jurisprudence the particular form of qualified privilege created . . . in *Reynolds*'. Indeed, the New Zealand Court of Appeal had correctly recognized *Reynolds* as a 'striking departure': 'although built upon an orthodox foundation, it is in reality *sui generis*'.[353]

Under *Reynolds* privilege, which attaches to the particular publication, rather than the traditional 'occasion of publication', it therefore needed to be understood that the 'interest' in receiving information, was 'that of the public in a modern democracy in free expression and, more particularly, in the promotion of a free and vigorous press to keep the public informed'.[354] In turn, the 'corresponding duty on the journalist (and equally on his editor) was to play his proper role in discharging that function' by behaving 'as a responsible journalist.' 'He can have no duty to publish unless he is acting responsibly any more than the public has an interest in reading whatever may be published irresponsibly'.[355] This was for the court, not the publisher, to decide. Elaborating responsible journalism further, the Court of Appeal suggested consideration of three factors:

i)   that qualified privilege will be likely to be a complete defence, since if it is made out, it is most unlikely that a claim of malice to defeat it would succeed;

ii)   setting too low a bar in terms of journalistic standards, 'would inevitably encourage too great a readiness to publish defamatory matter. Journalists should be rigorous, not lax, in their approach. It is in the interests of the public as well as the defamed individual that, wherever possible, truths and not untruths should be told';

iii)   conversely, too high a standard would 'deter newspapers from discharging their proper function of keeping the public informed'.[356]

As to i), the observation was that, if a newspaper has successfully argued *Reynolds* privilege, 'little scope remains for any subsequent finding of malice',[357] because the newspaper's conduct will already have been examined under the ten *Reynolds* factors. If its conduct passes those tests, it is very hard to see how it could, at a later stage in the analysis, also be found to have amounted to publishing material in wilful or reckless

---

[350] Stephenson LJ, ibid, at 27b, cited by the Court of Appeal in *Loutchansky*, op cit, at [31].
[351] [2001] 2 AC 277, at 301.   [352] Cited by the Court of Appeal, op cit, at [31].
[353] Ibid, at [32].   [354] Ibid, at [36].   [355] Ibid.   [356] Ibid, at [41].
[357] Ibid, at [33].

disregard for its truth. Significantly, the Court also doubted whether, if malice was pleaded on the basis of a spiteful motive, without evidence of disregard for the truth, this could override privilege accruing on objective grounds of public interest:

It may be doubted whether in truth there remains room for such a principle in a case of *Reynolds* privilege. Once the publication of a particular article is held to be in the public interest on the basis of the public's right to know, can the privilege really be lost because the journalist (or editor?) had the dominant motive of injuring the claimant rather than fulfilling his journalistic duty? It is a surprising thought.[358]

As Loveland puts it:

Putting the matter shortly, if Lord Nicholls' ten point plan requires—*inter alia*—that a paper prove it has not been reckless as to untruth in order to avail itself of the *Reynolds* privilege, it does not make much sense to assume that the privilege can be rebutted by the claimant proving the defendant was reckless . . . This seems a much clearer reading of the implications of *Reynolds* than was offered by the *Reynolds* court itself. Some observers might even feel inclined to say that *Loutchansky* takes clarification close to the point of overruling *Reynolds*.[359]

One final point regarding the judgment is worthy of note. The Court of Appeal rejected the proposed recasting of the *Reynolds* duty by Gray J in the High Court[360] so that it asked whether the publisher 'would have been open to legitimate criticism if it had failed to publish the article in question'. Lord Phillips M.R. said that this would be:

too stringent a test. There will undoubtedly be occasions when one newspaper would decide to publish and quite properly so, yet a second newspaper, no less properly would delay or abstain from publication. Not all journalism can be or should be expected to reach an identical view in every case. Responsible journalism will in certain circumstances permit equally of publication or of non-publication.[361]

A remarkable postscript to *Loutchansky*, in terms of this attempt to recast *Reynolds*, was that, as Cram points out, despite this firm dismissal of such a test by the Court of Appeal, it was used subsequently by Eady J in *Jameel*, who took as a useful cross-check, the question whether the publisher 'would have been open to legitimate criticism if it had failed to publish the article in question'.[362] This is simply a failure to attend to precedent: it is to be hoped that it will not be repeated.

  We would suggest that *Loutchansky* represents a useful clarification of *Reynolds* in a number of ways. It rules out creeping pro-claimant tendencies, such as the 'open to legitimate criticism' test and reminds lower courts that the 'public interest' element in *Reynolds* is there partly to protect a 'free and vigorous' (but responsible) press—a useful check to tendencies such as those in *Jameel* to brand stories that turn out to be inaccurate as *for that reason* lacking a public interest. It is probably sensible also, to

---

[358] Ibid, at [34].   [359] Op cit (*Ent LR*), at 180–1.   [360] [2001] EMLR 898.
[361] [2002] 1 All ER 652, at 670.   [362] Op cit, at 148.

rule out bad motive—without evidence of a failure to take steps to verify a story—as constituting 'malice' that can defeat qualified privilege. It is plain that the essence of *Reynolds* is an objective assessment of both the value of the story in public interest terms, and the care taken to check it: the personal motive of a particular journalist should not be allowed to enter the equation.

ACCEPTANCE OF ARTICLE 8 AND INTERLOCUTORY RELIEF

The final domestic decision we discuss here is *Greene v Associated Newspapers Ltd*,[363] a decision which is of interest in responding to an argument that the recognition by Strasbourg of reputation as engaging the protection of Article 8 should change the traditional approach of English defamation law, albeit in relation to remedies, rather than the substantive *Reynolds* test itself. The *Mail on Sunday* successfully resisted an application for an injunction in restraint of publication of various allegations that the claimant, Martha Greene, had had dealings with the convicted fraudster Peter Foster; the complained-of proposed article also revealed personal information about her attendance at Alcoholics Anonymous and treatment for breast cancer. The claimant had argued that the rule in *Bonnard v Perryman*,[364] that the claimant must show the alleged libel to be clearly untrue in order to obtain an interlocutory injunction restraining publication, required to be revisited in light of ss 6(1) and 12(3) HRA 1998.[365] Its inflexibility, it was complained, precluded the careful balancing on the facts of each case demanded by the ECHR approach. Instead, the claimant suggested, the judge should apply the 'threshold' test, of 'whether the claimant is able to demonstrate that she was *more likely than not* to be able to establish *at trial* that publication should not be allowed', following *Cream Holdings Ltd v Banerjee*,[366] the leading case on section 12(3), albeit one decided in the context of a claim in confidence, not defamation. Such an approach, it was claimed, was supported by Strasbourg's recognition, in the *Radio France* case,[367] that an individual's right to reputation was protected under Art 8. Fulford J determined the interim application in favour of publication, on the basis that the HRA 1998 had not affected the pre-existing rule in *Bonnard v Perryman*;[368] this, furthermore, remained practically workable.

The Court of Appeal agreed.[369] Using stronger terms, it stated that injunctions in restraint of publication would not be granted unless the claimant made it clear that *no defence* would succeed at trial. Brooke LJ opened judgment with these stirring words:

---

[363] [2005] QB 972, [2005] 1 All ER 30, [2004] EWCA Civ 1462, *per* Brooke, May and Dyson LJJ.

[364] [1891] 2 Ch 269.

[365] s 12 (3) HRA 1998: 'No such relief is to be granted so as to restrain publication before trial unless the court is satisfied that the applicant is likely to establish that publication should not be allowed.'

[366] (2005) 1 AC 253; (2004) 3 WLR 918; (2004) 4 All ER 617; (2005) EMLR 1; (2004) HRLR 39; (2004) UKHRR 1071. See discussion in Chapter 2 at 154–7.

[367] *Radio France v France*, App no. 53984/00 (30 March 2004): see above at 1068–70.

[368] [2004] EWHC 2322 (QB) *per* Fulford J.

[369] [2005] QB 972, [2005] 1 All ER 30, [2004] EWCA Civ 1462, *per* Brooke VP, May and Dyson LJJ.

In this country we have a free press. Our press is free to get things right and it is free to get things wrong. It is free to write after the manner of Milton, and it is free to write in a manner that would make Milton turn in his grave. Blackstone wrote in 1769 that the liberty of the press is essential in a free state, and this liberty consists in laying no previous restraints on publication. 'Every freeman', he said in his *Commentaries on the Laws of England*, vol IV, pp151–152, 'has an undoubted right to lay what sentiments he pleases before the public: to forbid this, is to destroy freedom of the press.'[370]

Brooke LJ emphasized the distinction made at common law between prior restraint and post-publication penalties, and the wholly exceptional nature of the former[371] (which may perhaps be seen as justifying the common law's pre *Reynolds* hesitance to extend special protection to the media: under English law, at least, minimal *actual* restraint on publication was permitted, despite the 'chilling' effect of post-publication damages). Significantly, the justification originally offered for imposing a very high threshold of certainty before an interim injunction would be granted, was that to do otherwise would wrongly situate in a judge's hands determination of what could be published, at a time when all the evidence in the case would not be in.[372]

The Court of Appeal thus found that *Bonnard v Perryman* was unaffected by section 12 HRA 1998, which had been intended to enhance, rather than undermine, protection for free expression at the interlocutory stage. The same was true of the court's own duty to act compatibly with Convention rights under s 6 HRA. Strasbourg had, in a UK case, recognized the need for strong caution in relation to the imposition of prior restraints against the media.[373] The House of Lords' decision in *Cream Holdings Ltd v Banerjee*[374] was distinguishable on the ground that it dealt with injunctions in restraint of breach of confidence—as 'Confidentiality, once breached, is lost forever.'[375] Defamation cases did not raise 'direct issues of privacy or confidentiality' and accordingly fell to be treated differently, particularly at the pre-trial stage.[376] Finally, the Court of Appeal made clear that, in its view, the *Radio France* decision, finding that the protection of reputation fell within Article 8, had not altered matters at all. The House of Lords, *In re S (A Child) Identification*[377] had held that a child's Art 8 rights 'paled into insignificance when compared with the importance to be attached to the freedom of the press to report a criminal trial.[378] 'Similarly', the Court said, 'the relevant Art 8 rights of the claimant in the present case cannot be accorded great weight (before the trial of this action takes place) when compared with the

---

[370] Op cit, at [1].

[371] With reference, in addition, to *Holley v Smyth* [1998] QB 726 *per* Auld LJ (on the arrival of jurisdiction to grant injunctions in libel); and *William Coulson & Sons v James Coulson & Co* [1998] 3 TLR 846.

[372] Op cit, at [57].   [373] *The Observer and The Guardian v UK* (1991) 14 EHRR 153.

[374] (2005) 1 AC 253; (2004) 3 WLR 918; (2004) 4 All ER 617; (2005) EMLR 1; (2004) HRLR 39; (2004) UKHRR 1071.

[375] Op cit, at [59], citing Lord Nicholls in *Reynolds*, [2005] 1 AC 253, at [18].

[376] *Greene*, op cit, at [81], with reference to House of Lords' judgment *In re S (a child) (Identification: Restriction on Publication)* [2005] 1 AC 593; and *Campbell v MGN Ltd* [2004] 2 AC 593.

[377] [2005] 1 AC 593. See further the discussion of the case in Chapter 16.

[378] *Per* Brooke LJ in *Greene*, at [81].

importance to be attached to the freedom of the press to report matters of public interest.'[379] While we find this approach somewhat crude, we would accept a basic distinction between the revelation of private facts (which cannot be wiped from public memory, once revealed) and damage to reputation—which can be restored by a successful action by the claimant.[380] In principle, therefore, the case for the granting of interim injunctions *is* much stronger in privacy cases. Moreover, there is merit in the Court of Appeal's observation that the interest in reputation receives strong protection in defamation *trials* via in particular the fact that the burden lies on the defendant to prove all defamatory allegations true. *Greene* plainly does not purport to alter the rule intended for pure 'privacy/confidentiality' claims established by *Cream Holdings*. It will involve claimants having to make the uncomfortable decision as to which facts it accepts as true and pleads therefore as misuse of private information/breach of confidence, and those which it rejects and wishes to plead as defamatory. That choice will then dictate the test to be applied if an injunction is sought. However, where a case raises an inextricable mixture of defamatory and private life issues, the rigidity of the *Bonnard v Perryman* rule may well require revisiting.

More importantly, the easy acceptance by the Court of Appeal in *Greene* of the applicability of Article 8 to libel cases is perhaps a little surprising. We find the notion that the right to respect for private life is engaged *per se* by libellous allegations somewhat counter-intuitive: where they relate purely to the manner in which a person carries out their official duties, for example, it seems somewhat perverse to find that issues of respect for private life arise. Plainly, the decision did nothing to address the issue of whether such acceptance will require any modification of the general *Reynolds* approach. Our tentative conclusion would be that such modification is probably not necessary (although we suggest below a gloss that should be added to two of Lord Nicholl's ten point checklist): the criteria themselves essentially seek to strike a fair balance between reputational and speech interests, and the real issue lies in how they are applied. The issue of the correct approach to balancing Articles 8 and 10 in general, both structurally and in terms of underlying normative argument, has been exhaustively canvassed in Chapters 13, 15 and 16, and we do not repeat that discussion here. It suffices to observe that it will be as essential in the area of defamation as it is in privacy to engage in a sensitive, contextual weighting of the two rights. In cases in which the burden of the defamatory statements relates to a person's discharge of their official duties, it would seem axiomatic that, while it may be accepted, following *Radio France*[381] that Article 8 is *engaged*, it should be afforded a relatively low *weight*, whilst, depending upon the facts, Article 10 might well figure strongly in such a case, if the claimant were a politician, or other important public figure. Conversely, where the allegations relate primarily to, for example, sexual misconduct, or other classically private-life issues, not only will the Article 8 claim be much stronger, but the Article 10 claim will be much weaker, as in *Tammer v Estonia*.[382] It may therefore be relatively

[379] Ibid.   [380] See Chapter 15, at 807–8.   [381] Op cit.

straightforward to arrive at an appropriate resolution of the competing Convention rights.

In terms of formal doctrinal change, perhaps all that is needed is that the first two of Lord Nicholls' ten criteria are approached in such a way as to allow Article 8 considerations to be taken into account. It will be recalled that the first two criteria are (1) the seriousness of the allegation, and (2) the nature of the defamatory information, and the extent to which the relevant subject matter is of public concern.[383] The latter in particular lends itself very well to an analysis of how far the allegations involve an intrusion into private life. Answering such a question will readily lead to a *prima facie* finding as to the relative strengths of the two Convention rights in the particular instance.

CONCLUSIONS

Reynolds has given the English courts a workable tool by which to apply Strasbourg principles in the area of political libel. Some of the decisions discussed above indicate that English courts will continue to insist upon quite high journalistic standards when they wish to plead qualified privilege. As Barendt observes, however:

The public has a free speech interest in the publication of fair, well-researched stories, not in those which are poorly put together and which gratuitously destroy the standing of people in public life. The House of Lords was, therefore, surely right to insist that the press and other media should be required to observe the standards of responsible journalism, which may often require publication to be delayed until sources have been corroborated and the claimant has been contacted to allow his version of events to be published with the allegations.[384]

We are inclined to agree. *Reynolds* took the crucial step of enunciating in principle a broad privilege for speech of serious public concern which turns out to be inaccurate and damaging to an individual's reputation. The press have a fair measure of protection in particular when they are merely reporting allegations made by others, provided that reportage, rather than *adoption* of allegations is the evident purpose of the article. *Reynolds* can, however, be criticized for its failure to assign weight to the various factors it sets out, as suggested above. In light of this, subsequent decisions can be criticised for exploiting that flexibility in a manner un-friendly to valuable media expression. As Barendt notes:

Despite . . . *Reynolds*, English courts are still inclined to ask whether there are good reasons for the freedom to prevail over reputation rights, rather than whether the need to protect the latter justifies infringement of freedom of expression [in contrast with the ECHR approach

---

[382] Op cit. See Chapter 13 at 692–3 for discussion of the case.   [383] See above at 1080.
[384] *Freedom of Speech*, at 222.

based on a] 'presumption in favour of freedom of expression which reflects the status of the freedom under the Convention'.[385]

The cure, we would suggest, is a close attention to the Strasbourg case law, which provides, as we have argued above, a more structured normative framework for resolving clashes between reputation and speech. As time passes since *Reynolds*, and its perhaps excessive flexibility becomes more and more apparent, it is to be hoped that the necessity of closer attention to the Strasbourg jurisprudence will become more apparent to the judiciary. Finally, we would argue that the acceptance in *Greene* of the engagement of Article 8 by reputation-based claims should not lead to a generic boosting of the interest in reputation: rather it should enhance the care with which courts go about balancing the competing interests by reference to the underlying values at stake in particular cases. In suitable cases, however, the presumption referred to by Barendt will now need to be abandoned.

[385] Ibid, at 225.

22

CONCLUSIONS

INTRODUCTION

This chapter does not seek to come to a definitive set of conclusions about the impact of the Human Rights Act on media freedom. The HRA has only been in force for just over five years, and in any event this subject of its very nature tends to be in a constant state of evolution. Thus any conclusions offered are interim and tentative. Instead, this chapter largely concentrates on identifying some of the main themes that have informed this book. Perhaps one of the main ones has concerned the *lack* of impact that the HRA is having on many aspects of media freedom. As discussed in Chapter 1, the HRA is not the equivalent of a domestic Bill of Rights and therefore was never likely to have a radical impact on media law. Nevertheless, not only has the HRA confirmed the status of freedom of expression as a positive right rather than a negative liberty, there are also signs that the theorizing of expression judgments is occurring, not only in the courts but also in the decisions of media regulators.[1] An ongoing constitutionalization of media freedom is apparent.

A further major theme has concerned an attempt at tracing an understanding of the differentiation between the values underpinning media freedom and freedom of expression generally, in judicial decisions at Strasbourg and domestically. We have sought to consider such decisions from the perspective of the theoretical model we set out in Chapter 1. We have scrutinized judicial approaches to media claims by considering the consonance between such claims and the free speech rationales considered in Chapter 1, rather than assuming an easy harmony between the two. As argued in Chapters 2, 7, 13, 15, and 16 in particular, the test for proportionality under Article 10(2), when properly applied, allows for an intense focus on the free speech values truly at stake.[2] Where a media claim is not, under such a scrutiny, instrumental in furthering audience rights by reference to the free speech rationales, it has been argued that it is significantly weakened and may therefore be overridden by competing claims of individuals or groups.

---

[1] A particular example relates to the decision of Ofcom in its adjudication upon complaints received relating to the decision by the BBC to screen *Jerry Springer: The Opera* in 2004: although these terms were not used, there was quite a rigorous application of the speech/harm proportionality test often used at Strasbourg; for discussion of the Ofcom decision, see Chapter 11 at 605–6.

[2] See Chapter 15 at 782–3.

EVOLUTIONARY CONVERGENCE

As Chapters 1 and 2 pointed out, it was always unlikely that the HRA would have a radical impact on media freedom, as has occurred in countries such as Canada that adopted a domestic Bill of Rights, because Article 10 of the Convention and common law free speech principles had already had a significant influence on media law. Moreover, judicial resistance to the idea that a 'foreign' import was needed in order to protect freedom of expression has led in a number of instances discussed in this book to a flawed and impoverished approach to the Convention. A number of devices have been adopted to avoid full engagement with the Convention. These have included: over-deference to Parliament or to expert regulators as in *ProLife Alliance*,[3] discussed mainly in Chapter 11, or in *R v Perrin*,[4] discussed in Chapters 8 and 12; assumptions that the balance required by the Convention has already been struck by legislation and therefore a strict proportionality analysis is not required, as in relation to copyright law in particular; misapplication of the Convention jurisprudence—failing to afford the same weight to free speech values as at Strasbourg, as in *Ashworth*[5] or *A-G v Punch*,[6] or leading to tokenistic assessments of the value of private life when it competes with media freedom, as in *Re S*.[7]

Thus, the enterprise of absorbing Article 10 into domestic law in a more direct and effective fashion, undertaken by the HRA, has been fraught with difficulties. There has often been an inconsistent, inadequate, or reluctant engagement with the Convention. The under-theorized nature of the Strasbourg jurisprudence and the influence of the margin of appreciation doctrine have aided and abetted this judicial stance. However, this book has traced an ongoing evolutionary convergence between Article 10, statute and common law. It has found that the HRA has accelerated the absorption of Article 10 into domestic law and raised judicial awareness of free expression issues. The decision in *Reynolds*,[8] for example, taken after the HRA was passed, but before it came into force, was a highly significant one, in enhancing protection for political speech; the House of Lords' decision in *Campbell*[9] showed a sophisticated grasp both of the values underlying Article 10, and of how it should be reconciled with the competing privacy interest.

After ranging over various media law fields in this book, a number of stages of development can be discerned in this ongoing convergence, albeit varying across different areas, and we propose to categorize them in five groupings as follows. First there are those areas where Article 10 had already had a significant substantive effect prior to the inception of the HRA, either as a result of decisions at Strasbourg, or due to the absorption of Article 10 into the common law or statutory interpretation. Thus

---

[3] [2003] 2 WLR 1403. See also Chapter 3 at 151–3.   [4] (2002) WL 347127.
[5] *Ashworth Hospital Authority v MGN Ltd* [2002] 1 WLR 2033. See Chapter 7.
[6] (2003) 1 AC 1046. See Chapter 6 at 291–301.   [7] [2004] UKHL 47. See Chapter 16.
[8] *Reynolds v Times Newspapers* [1999] 4 All ER 609. See Chapter 21.
[9] [2004] 2 AC 457.

the HRA was always unlikely to have a very significant impact on such aspects of media law. This is true, as Chapters 4, 5, and 6 on the fair trial/free speech balance pointed out, of much of statutory contempt law, due to the early influence of the seminal *Sunday Times* decision.[10] It can also be said of aspects of the *Reynolds* privilege discussed in Chapter 21. In such areas, as Chapter 6 in particular pointed out, the potential is there for the HRA to have an effect on the more minor or peripheral aspects of statutory interpretation,[11] but the judges tend to show a reluctance to engage in a close HRA analysis where they consider that Convention auditing has already occurred. The HRA could, even more pertinently, be used in relation to residual and anomalous aspects of the common law running alongside a statute that itself is broadly in conformity with the Convention. This has not so far occurred in this context, although the opportunity arose in the instance of *A-G v Punch*,[12] and that failure is considered below in relation to that grouping of decisions in which the Convention has been seriously misapplied.

Secondly, there are areas of media law in which the relevant Strasbourg jurisprudence is so weak, under-theorized, and impoverished that applying it would be likely to make little or no difference to a field of law. This grouping includes the areas of obscenity or indecency and blasphemy. As discussed in Part III, the Strasbourg explicit expression jurisprudence is heavily influenced by the margin of appreciation doctrine, and in general represents the weakest part of its free expression canon. It fails to provide a satisfactory guide for the judges to follow since it is notable both for its lack of adherence to the free speech rationales and for highly attenuated standards of proportionality review. This means that it provides no clear basis for the progressive reform of the archaic laws of obscenity, common law offences of conspiracy to corrupt public morals, outraging public decency, and blasphemy. It also means that there is no strong foundational free speech base to rely upon in order to challenge overly restrictive decisions of the broadcast regulator, Ofcom, or any of the other media regulators, as discussed in Chapters 10, 11, and 12. The free speech principle deriving from moral autonomy[13] has no clear point of entry into such decisions, via judicial review, since the vehicle that should be used for it, the Strasbourg jurisprudence, fails so signally to found upon the principle.

The classic statement of principle from *Handyside*[14] to the effect that freedom of expression extends to speech that offends, shocks, or disturbs, has no clear means of engagement with a content-based restraint founded upon offence avoidance and imposed upon the most significant medium—broadcasting. There are patchy signs of an untheorized acceptance of the speech-based moral autonomy principle in the domestic jurisprudence on explicit and offensive speech: they were evident in *R v Perrin*[15] and in *R v Video Appeals Committee of the BBFC ex parte BBFC*,[16] but the

---

[10] See Chapter 4 at 183–5.   [11] At pp 282–3.   [12] See note 6 above.
[13] See Chapter 1 at 13–14 and Chapter 8 at 413–22.
[14] *Handyside* v *UK* A 24 para 48 (1976). See Chapter 8 at 410–13.   [15] (2002) WL 347127.
[16] (2000) EMLR 850. See Chapter 12 at 632–4.

Strasbourg jurisprudence fails to provide a sound theoretical underpinning for such decisions. Indeed, the jurisprudence serves instead to legitimize repressive and unsatisfactory curbs on media freedom since it affords a misleading impression of human rights auditing to the laws in question.

In a third identifiable grouping of media fields, the HRA has had, in strong contrast, a substantial impact. The most obvious and striking example is in the area of privacy. In the most sophisticated and thoroughly reasoned post-HRA decision on media freedom, *Campbell v MGN*,[17] the House of Lords reaffirmed previous developments in this area, relying on Articles 8, 10, and s 6 HRA, and confirmed the movement that had already been occurring from the doctrine of breach of confidence to the tort of misuse of private information. *Campbell* was one of those decisions that can rank alongside the more striking and classic restatements of free speech principle from the US or Canadian Supreme Courts. Clearly, it is at first glimpse ironic that it concerned a development that was highly unwelcome to much of the UK media. However, it is a development that, as Chapters 1, 14, and 16 explained, was fully in accordance with free speech principle in terms of the model of that principle as it applies to the media relied upon in this book.

Campbell finally put to bed the mistaken notion that Article 10 had presumptive priority over Article 8 (and other Convention Articles): the reasoning was fundamentally based upon the principle of presumptive equality for the qualified Convention rights. An extremely significant flaw in common law free speech reasoning was thus finally addressed. As a consequential outgrowth, *Campbell* endorsed the 'parallel analysis'—the dual exercise in proportionality, or the 'ultimate balancing act'.[18] The 'parallel analysis' on its face should lead to a closer engagement with proportionality reasoning. The very fact of requiring a dual exercise to occur tends to foster an intense focus on the principles truly at stake. In particular, the extent to which the free speech rationales were truly engaged became more likely to occur, as indeed it did in *Campbell* itself.

In other words, the confusion between *media* claims and free speech ones that has bedevilled common law speech jurisprudence could be addressed. As discussed in Chapter 16, however, on reporting restrictions to protect children, the House of Lords decision in *Re S*[19] immediately demonstrated that this was not necessarily the case—that tokenistic approaches to values competing with free speech ones, a legacy of flawed previous free speech reasoning, still lingered on. However, the subsequent decision of the President of the Family Division post-*Re S*[20] demonstrated an understanding of the conflict between such reasoning and the Convention-based approach; such understanding suggests that the *Campbell* approach is likely to prevail. *Campbell* provides a model for the fusion of Convention values with common law ones under the HRA that is far more compelling than the model offered in *Re S*, and

---

[17] [2004] 2 AC 457.   [18] See Chapter 16 at 830.   [19] [2004] UKHL 47. See Chapter 16.
[20] *A Local Authority v (1) W (2) L (3) W (4) T & R (By The Children's Guardian)* [2005] EWHC 1564 (Fam), discussed Chapter 16 at 830–1.

therefore it is likely to direct the future development of the law, while *Re S* is quietly marginalized.

Similar, albeit less striking, developments can be discerned in the area of journalistic source protection, discussed in Chapter 7. The *Ashworth* case,[21] relying quite heavily on *Goodwin v UK*,[22] signalled a clear departure from the flawed reasoning in previous decisions. *Ashworth* took account of the strong weight placed upon the media's watchdog role by the Strasbourg Court in laying down a fundamental principle—that the value of source protection is constant and unvarying in free speech terms. This was a clear break with the previous reasoning, which reflected a common law principle of refusing to recognize a journalistic privilege of source protection. As Chapter 7 argued, source protection is a media privilege that is largely irrelevant to the ordinary speaker. It therefore requires justification, according to the free speech model advocated in this book, by reference to its instrumental value in terms of audience free speech rights. Although Chapter 7 did not advocate an unthinking acceptance of the value of source protection, viewing the US *Miller*[23] case as sounding a cautionary note, it concluded that this was an instance in which placing source protection at risk was far more dangerous to such audience speech rights, especially those from democracy and truth, than the opposing stance—the stance taken in *Goodwin* at Strasbourg. Chapter 7 did not put *Ashworth* forward as a model for post-HRA speech reasoning, but it did acknowledge the change of emphasis marked by the decision. If a fusion of the presumptive equality principle from *Campbell* with the stance taken in *Ashworth* as to the significance of source protection can occur in future, the failures of reasoning evident in *Ashworth* may not recur.

Fourthly, this book has identified a number of areas in which the Strasbourg jurisprudence could or should have an impact, but where it has so far failed to do so. This has occurred when the judiciary have misunderstood or misapplied the Strasbourg jurisprudence. They have done so, it was contended in Chapter 19, in relation to the near-absolute restrictions placed upon the media by a number of provisions under the Official Secrets Act 1989. *R v Shayler*[24] in the House of Lords failed to apply the Strasbourg speech jurisprudence in backing away from an adequate proportionality analysis.[25] The Lords precisely failed to adhere to the Strasbourg principle that Convention rights should not be upheld in a tokenistic or meaningless fashion. To a much lesser extent there was a misapplication of the jurisprudence in *Interbrew*,[26] as discussed in Chapter 7, since the courts, that chapter suggested, failed to give the weight to source protection given by Strasbourg in *Goodwin*.

---

[21] *Ashworth Hospital Authority v MGN Ltd* [2002] 1 WLR 2033. See Chapter 7 at 345–51.

[22] (1996) Reports 1996–II.

[23] *Judith Miller, Petitioner v US and M Cooper and Time inc, Petitioners v US*, Supreme Court (2005) No 04–1508; opinion of the court of appeals (Miller Pet. App. 1a–77a; Cooper Pet. App. 1a–85a) is reported at 397 F.3d 964. See Chapter 7 at 312.

[24] [2003] 1 AC 247   [25] See Chapter 19 at 940–4.

[26] [2002] EMLR 24. See Chapter 7 at 342–5.

The law of copyright is an area in which judicial resistance to any real application of the Convention to a well-settled legislative and common law scheme has been particularly marked, as discussed in Chapter 18. That chapter traced an evolution in judicial attitudes to Article 10 arguments against the enforcement of copyright from the outright refusal to acknowledge their legitimacy in the first instance decision in *Ashdown*,[27] to a half-hearted acceptance of them in the Court of Appeal decision in the same case.[28] While the Court of Appeal accepted in principle that such arguments could in rare cases affect the decisions made, their actual reasoning marginalized speech arguments in favour of a traditional application of the 'fair dealing' factors. The authors of that chapter conclude that, while the Court of Appeal judgment 'has all the trappings of a progressive accommodation of human rights principles within copyright jurisprudence, the decision suggests that, in reality, there may be little change from the pre-Human Rights Act position'.[29] This was in spite of the fact that the value of the speech in that case was of the highest order in Convention terms and the press were carrying out a classic 'watchdog' role in bringing the issues it raised to the public's attention. *Ashdown* must therefore rank with *Punch, ProLife Alliance*,[30] and *Shayler* as one of the more disappointing decisions for media freedom under the HRA so far.

A further obvious example of misapplication of the Convention arises in the context of common law contempt, as discussed in Chapter 6.[31] Such misapplication appears to arise in this context, not as a result of a misunderstanding of the jurisprudence, but as a result of a strong resistance to it, based on an entrenched common law stance. The *Tomlinson* decision[32] suggested that significant developments might occur, relying on s 6 HRA and Article 10, as did the Court of Appeal ruling in *A-G v Punch*. However, the House of Lords ruling in *Punch*, which exemplified some of the most impoverished and flawed judicial reasoning under the HRA,[33] and classically misapplied the Convention, has ensured that, for the time being, Article 10-friendly developments in that area have been stifled. *Punch* concerned political expression and a potential ban on the whole of the media in relation to an issue of great significance. In other words, the invasion of media freedom could not be characterized as minimal, or no more than necessary, and other less invasive alternatives were available. In terms of speech/harm balancing, the value of the speech was very high, while the harm that could be caused to national security by the revelations was doubtful and uncertain. Thus any reasonably rigorous proportionality analysis would have led to a finding of a breach of Article 10, and an extremely anomalous and unsatisfactory area of the common law could have been modified almost out of existence. Had the Court of Appeal ruling been followed, it would have become a virtual dead letter. Instead, the HRA was used in effect to legitimize a normative failing that has been endemic in common law speech reasoning: free expression

---

[27] [2001] Ch 685.   [28] [2002] Ch 149. See Chapter 18.   [29] See p 917.
[30] Discussed in Chapters 3, 11, and 17.   [31] See pp 291–302.
[32] [2001] EMLR 19. See Chapter 19 at 956–7.   [33] See note 6 above.

values should give way to national security claims, regardless of the spurious and uncertain nature of such claims. Such a strand of common law thinking can readily be discerned in the *Spycatcher* case[34]—*Punch*'s forerunner, providing the reasoning model it founded upon, and in *Guardian Newspapers*,[35] in which, as Chapter 7 pointed out, an extremely weak national security claim was allowed to prevail over the interest in protecting journalistic sources.

Resistance to the Convention and consequent misapplication of the jurisprudence has also occurred in the context of media regulation. *ProLife Alliance*[36] is one of the most disappointing of the group of post-HRA speech decisions in the House of Lords. As Chapter 11 on broadcast regulation argued, the judges misapplied both the Convention and the HRA itself. The weight attached to political expression at Strasbourg under Article 10 was not allowed to inform the domestic decision, while the obligations imposed on the judges by sections 3 and 6 HRA were largely disregarded.

Fifthly, and finally, there are a number of areas of media law where no suitable case has yet arisen. The obvious instance of this is the ban on political advertising in broadcasting, which has not yet been challenged in the courts. The HRA could have affected the Bill and Parliament's deliberations in passing the Communications Act 2003 which contains the ban, but, as Chapter 20 pointed out, the government took the deliberate decision to include the ban in provisions that probably breach Article 10. Although s 3 HRA could in theory be used in relation to the relevant provisions if a suitable case arises, it is more probable that the courts will take their lead from Parliament in declaring the incompatibility under section 4 HRA. Since the HRA reflects a particular constitutional balance in leaving the final word to Parliament, a breach of Article 10 may merely subsist until and if a case is brought to Strasbourg. The government made a decision to take full advantage of this attribute of the HRA—an interesting instance of the use of democratic means to suppress political speech, although it is to an extent very clearly underpinned by the argument from democracy.[37]

The other obvious example of a law that has not yet been tested under the HRA is, of course, the new law on incitement to religious hatred, discussed in Chapter 9. As argued in that chapter, the law is unlikely to be the subject of a section 4 declaration under the HRA. It will, however, require sensitive and principled reasoning by the judiciary, drawing on general Strasbourg principles, rather than the immediately applicable case law. In particular, the courts will be required to resolve a critical

---

[34] *A-G v Guardian Newspapers* [1987] 1 WLR 1248. See Chapter 12 at 950–6.

[35] [1984] 3 All ER 601; [1985] AC 339, 347, HL. See Chapter 7 at 329–31.

[36] [2003] 2 WLR 1403.

[37] See Chapter 20 for the argument that political advertising of non-party political groupings should be permitted in broadcasting on the ground that it constitutes a significant form of political expression—i.e. it facilitates participation in the democracy. The chapter argues that permitting *party* political speech would not further such participation, thereby defeating the argument based on that free speech rationale since it is an instrumental one.

question not satisfactorily resolved by Strasbourg: whether Article 9 ECHR provides a right to be free from outrage in relation to one's religious views. For the reasons canvassed in Chapter 9, it is to be hoped that the courts will resolve the tricky questions raised by the interpretation of the Convention case law in this area and make a strong finding *against* any such proposition.[38] If this is done, and the political character of any speech prosecuted under the new provisions given a proper weighting, depending upon its nature and the context in which it is uttered, the new provisions can be kept within manageable proportions as far as the media are concerned; they may even provide some assistance in tackling abuses of free speech that incite religious hatred, but masquerade as a critique of religious beliefs. Here, as in many other areas, much will depend upon the judiciary.

No suitable cases have yet arisen in relation to common law expression-based crimes, except in respect of common law contempt, in *A-G v Punch*. As discussed, that decision can hardly have encouraged the judges to use section 6 HRA and Article 10 to modify the highly unsatisfactory common law doctrines of conspiracy to corrupt public morals, outraging public decency, and blasphemy, if a suitable case arises. As indicated above, the Strasbourg explicit expression jurisprudence does not itself provide very much encouragement to modify these doctrines with the free speech rationales in mind. Oddly enough, the judges have been ready to overcome the difficulties presented by the doctrine of indirect horizontal effect in order to transform breach of confidence into a privacy tort, but when presented with a somewhat similar opportunity, with no such difficulties to be overcome, in *A-G v Punch*, they shied away.

Certain expression-based rights do not appear at all in the Convention and probably cannot be implied into it. The obvious one is that of access to information from an unwilling speaker. Access rights for journalists to particular forums—apart from courts—also probably cannot be implied into Article 10. Such claims either require special statutory provision—which is provided for access to information in the Freedom of Information Act 2000[39]—or appear simply to lack any domestic legal foundation. However, clearly, it would be possible to seek to persuade a domestic court to imply a right into Article 10 that had not yet been accepted at Strasbourg. That has already occurred successfully in the sphere of privacy rights under Article 8.[40]

This survey, ranging across the various fields of media law considered in this book, reveals that the HRA has had a far from uniform impact. It bears out the proposition

---

[38] See Chapter 9 at 488–99.

[39] See Chapter 19.

[40] As Lord Nicholls said in *Campbell*: 'The values embodied in articles 8 and 10 are as much applicable in disputes between individuals or between an individual and a non-governmental body such as a newspaper as they are in disputes between individuals and a public authority. In reaching this conclusion it is not necessary to pursue the controversial question whether the European Convention itself has this wider effect': [2004] 2 WLR 1232 at [17] and [18]. This finding pre-dated the post-*Campbell* decision in *Von Hannover v Germany* (2004) EMLR 21, discussed in Chapter 13, which affirmed that the Convention does have this effect.

put forward in Chapter 1 to the effect that the HRA cannot be viewed as a panacea for the ills of media freedom, despite its introduction of a modern free expression guarantee into UK law for the first time. The government and the judiciary have exploited or explored the gaps and inadequacies of both the Convention and the HRA in arriving at this position. Alternatively, at times they have merely disregarded fairly evident Convention demands. This is an unsurprising governmental stance. As far as the judiciary is concerned, it is possible to view the generally somewhat disappointing post-implementation Article 10 jurisprudence as something of a backlash against Strasbourg interference, as an early reaction to a demand to explore unfamiliar territory. As the judiciary familiarize themselves with the Convention jurisprudence, and develop their own more sophisticated domestic jurisprudence, the number of cases that fall within our fourth grouping is likely to diminish. There are early signs, explored particularly in Chapters 7, 15, and 16, of the emergence of a nascent, more theorized domestic media freedom jurisprudence under Article 10. Cases are also eventually likely to arise within our fifth grouping, offering the judges, especially in relation to explicit expression, the chance to take a stance more firmly rooted in the speech-based rationales than Strasbourg has.[41]

CONSTITUTIONALIZING THE POSITION OF THE MEDIA

This book has considered the changing position of the media in the UK's constitutional order. It has traced the process of change that has occurred by means of the development of common law free speech principles, the influence of Article 10 of the European Convention on Human Rights, and then of the Human Rights Act. As discussed, the effect of the HRA cannot be viewed as either dramatic or consistent. Is it possible to come to any firm conclusions as to the changed constitutional position of the media? The common law status of media freedom as merely a negative liberty was discarded some years ago, pre-HRA, although this was not a consistent development across all areas of media freedom. It could probably be said that the imminent inception of the HRA had a catalytic effect on the development of the common law right to free expression, as explored in Chapter 1. When the HRA came into force it confirmed the existence of such a right in formal terms. But as discussed in Chapter 1 the content ascribed to the right is uncertain: as this book has shown, it is not possible to see the application of the Strasbourg jurisprudence as a cure or a panacea for defects in the protection for media freedom in UK law. It cannot be said that a far more sophisticated recognition of distinctive media free speech rights has yet occurred. Indeed, application of the jurisprudence can legitimize interferences

---

[41] See generally Chapter 8 at 410–22.

with expression even where they are disproportionate. This was made clear in the discussion of the Strasbourg explicit expression jurisprudence in Chapters 8, 9, and 10. The government has been able to claim that various areas of media law are Convention-compliant and therefore have already been audited against human rights norms. The opposition by the Government to the repeal of the blasphemy laws when the Racial and Religious Hatred Bill was before Parliament in 2005–6 may have been partly bolstered by findings at Strasbourg that it was not in breach of Article 10.

The book has sought to reveal that the domestic judiciary are slowly and with difficulty building a post-HRA jurisprudential framework for the use of the HRA itself and for the acceptance of the Strasbourg jurisprudence into domestic law. *Ashworth* and *Campbell* provide good examples of this enterprise. The common law afforded a strong recognition to media freedom in certain contexts: in others, such as source protection or in relation to national security, the protection was very weak. The Convention provides a test—proportionality—that if applied in a rigorous fashion would expose some of these inadequacies. But the transition from established common law media freedom approaches to Convention-based ones is far from complete. This was illustrated in particular in Chapter 7.[42] Moreover, the domestic courts have failed to constitutionalize the free speech rationales in a coherent and consistent fashion, most notably in *ProLife Alliance*, in which the House of Lords failed to understand or apply the key free speech rationale relied upon at Strasbourg—the argument from democracy. This chapter turns finally to trace emerging signs of the development of central unifying free speech principles identified in this book as an aspect of the constitutionalism of media freedom.

RECOGNITION OF THE ENGAGEMENT OF THE MEDIA IN THE FREE SPEECH RATIONALES

In the introduction to this book, in Chapter 1, a number of models for the place of the media within the classic free speech rationales were put forward. It was pointed out that the domestic judiciary have traditionally tended to view free speech claims of the mass media as indistinguishable from those of speakers generally.[43] As discussed there, this model—the 'equivalence model'—holds benefits for the media since all the jurisprudence that has built up in a different age, with the powerless individual speaker in mind, can be adopted and relied upon in order to enhance the power of the mass communications media. Global media corporations can harness the power of free speech rhetoric. But this model is inherently unsympathetic to claims of special privileges for the media such as source protection or access to information. It still

---

[42] See in particular pp 342–55.   [43] See pp 4–5 and 20–1.

has quite a significant hold on judicial thinking, as Chapters 7, 16, and 19 in particular demonstrated.[44]

However, there is some evidence that a shift of emphasis is occurring. In Chapter 1 we argued that *all* media claims—not just claims for special privileges—should be rigorously assessed by reference to free speech interests, including those of the audience. If the exercise of free speech right by the media tends to oppose the attainment of the good represented by the arguments from democracy and truth by the audience, then the media claim could justifiably be denied. In making this point it should be noted that some parts of the 'media' *are* in a position equivalent to that of the individual speaker. Examples would include an artist publishing work in a small art gallery, as in *Gibson*,[45] or a 'blogger' posting fiction on the Internet, or a journalist writing an article for a newspaper. But the editorial and distribution processes of the newspaper would not have such equivalence. Nor would privileges, such as tax breaks, claimed by the Internet Service Provider. We argued for a 'variable geometry' of media protection based on the free speech rationales, encompassing both the variation in media claims based on speakers' rights, depending on the media body in question, and on the extent to which the exercise of such rights were in harmony, or opposed to, those of the audience. The 'variable geometry' model sought to follow the contours of media claims, taking account of such factors, without either under- or over-privileging them. At Strasbourg, in contrast to the common law stance, there is some recognition of the lack of equivalence between the media and the individual speaker, although at the same time there is a willingness to accord the media special privileges.

The acceptance of special privileges for the media was seen particularly in Chapter 7 in relation to *Goodwin v UK*.[46] But the Strasbourg Court strongly emphasized the point that such protection was predicated upon a harmony with audience rights. Where the media acted in its watchdog role it could hope for special privileges; if it failed to do so, in the sense that it put false or misleading information obtained from a source before the public, it might appear to be the case that there would still be a general interest in source protection, but that the value of the speech would be diminished since 'watchdog' values would no longer be engaged. Thus under the speech/harm balancing test from *Goodwin*, the other competing value would have more chance of overcoming the speech claim.

At the same time, Strasbourg does not appear to be fully prepared to treat the media merely as another rights-holder, on the equivalence model. This is especially apparent in its clashing rights jurisprudence, discussed in Chapters 13, 14, and 17.[47] In this context the domestic courts had tended to *over*-privilege the media since they were allowed to take advantage of previous powerful free speech arguments, enhancing their ability to invade the privacy of citizens.[48] Hence the common law doctrine of presumptive priority for speech, recently abandoned, as discussed above.

---

[44] See, e.g., pp 337–8.   [45] See Chapter 8 at 474–7.   [46] See pp 334–7.

[47] See, e.g., Chapter 13 at 680–2, in which the position of the media was strongly differentiated from that of an ordinary 'speaker'.

[48] See Chapters 13 and 15 at 703–5 and 779–82.

Strasbourg has either considered that no such priority should be accorded to speech, or, in its most recent decision in *Von Hannover*,[49] has taken full account of the *special* ability of the media to invade privacy—which is of course far greater than that of the individual rights-holder—and has been quick to be prepared to deny media free speech claims in this context. In other words, while it has espoused presumptive equality for the media claim as it confronts the private life one, it has shown an awareness of the trivial nature of such speech, combined with the privacy-invading potentiality of the media. *Von Hannover* may be usefully compared in this context with the domestic decision in *A v B plc*,[50] discussed in Chapter 15; the Court of Appeal in that decision revealed a signal failure to understand the extent to which it had been persuaded to over-privilege the media.

Thus Strasbourg has, it is suggested, shown a more sophisticated awareness of the hollowness of such media claims—of the extent to which they fail to engage the free speech rationales—and this is especially the case in much, although not all, of its clashing rights jurisprudence in the context of the privacy/speech conflict. The same could be said of its fair trial/free speech jurisprudence. As Chapters 4, 5, and 6 pointed out, the Court has not been prepared to allow the media to encroach too far on the fair trial right; this was explicitly stated in *Worm v Austria*.[51] In contrast, the domestic courts in the run up to the HRA in the late 1990s, began to move away from providing adequate protection for that right, most notably in *A-G v Guardian Newspapers*.[52] The argument is that this book has in general found the Strasbourg Court to be closer to the 'variable geometry' model espoused here than is common law principle.

We have identified some evidence of a domestic movement away from the 'equivalence' model towards the 'variable geometry' one, under the enhanced influence of the Convention driven by the Human Rights Act. The two key examples come from the areas of privacy and source protection. In *Campbell* the unsatisfactoriness of treating the media as simply another rights-holder was implicit in many passages in the speeches. Presumptive equality between speech and privacy rights was affirmed as the guiding principle. But clearly the equality is *presumptive* only: the kind of arguments as to the power of the media, and its use of needless intrusive detail, that later found favour in *Von Hannover*,[53] appeared to be present in the minds of the Law Lords also. Their stance was clearly driven by the recognition of the Strasbourg jurisprudential stance favouring presumptive equality in its clashing rights cases, such as *Peck*[54] or *Tammer v Estonia*.[55] Similarly, in *Ashworth* the strong stance taken in favour of source protection in *Goodwin* by the Strasbourg Court was highly influential; it was finally and clearly accepted that there had been a difference of emphasis between the common law stance and the Strasbourg one, and that the former had to be abandoned in favour of the latter. Special privileges for the media were accepted

---

[49] [2004] EMLR 21. See Chapter 13 at 680–2.   [50] [2002] 3 WLR 542, 550B. See pp 781–2.
[51] (1997) 25 EHRR 557. See Chapter 4 pp 00.   [52] [1999] EMLR 904. See Chapter 6 at 264–6.
[53] See Chapter 13 at 680–2.   [54] (2003) 36 EHRR 41; Chapter 13 at 692–3.
[55] (2003) 37 EHRR 43; (2001) 10 BHRC 543.

unreservedly. It must be noted that, even after *Goodwin*, judicial doubts had been expressed in *Camelot*[56] as to the existence of any real difference between the common law and the Strasbourg approach.

Thus, despite the weak and disappointing nature of some of the post-HRA media decisions, it is possible to see the emergent beginnings of a more sophisticated and theoretically informed media freedom jurisprudence in the post-HRA era—one that does not accept media free speech claims uncritically, but also one that is prepared to accept arguments for special media privileges where they are firmly situated in the free speech rationales. There are thus reasons to be optimistic about the Article 10 endeavour in English media law. The inception of the HRA has plainly forced judges to confront claims of media freedom, and the values underpinning them, much more directly than in previous cases. As Chapter 9 pointed out, decisions such as those in *Lemon*[57] on blasphemy, taken in the old common law tradition, indicate an almost complete lack of awareness that a serious interference with artistic expression was taking place. It would not be possible in such a case today for the judges to take this stance, given the existence of the HRA. Moreover, the judiciary are showing some readiness, when entering hitherto uncharted waters in assessing a particular area of media law directly against the free expression guarantee, to take account of arguments in academic literature, which can guide them in their novel tasks. Evidence of this is apparent, for example, in the development of a balanced right to privacy in *Campbell*.[58] There is also some preparedness to take account of speech jurisprudence from other jurisdictions with Bills or Charters of Rights.[59] Thus, the HRA inevitably brings with it the exposure of the judiciary to a wider range of arguments than hitherto as to the means of assessing the authenticity of media claims and balancing them against other individual and societal interests. It is hoped that this book will make a modest contribution to such arguments and hence to the realization of principled judicial reform of the law of media freedom under the Human Rights Act.

---

[56] [1998] EMLR 1; [1999] QB 124. See Chapter 7 at 337–8.
[57] [1979] AC 617; [1979] 2 WLR 281; [1979] 1 All ER 898, HL. See Chapter 9 at 482–5.
[58] See Chapter 15 at 782–6.   [59] See, e.g. the discussion of *Reynolds* in Chapter 21.

INDEX

9 780406 942890